LAW AND RELIGION

Aspen Select Series

LAW AND RELIGION: NATIONAL, INTERNATIONAL, AND COMPARATIVE PERSPECTIVES

Second Edition

W. Cole Durham, Jr.
Susa Young Gates University Professor of Law and
Founding Director, International Center for Law and Religion Studies
J. Reuben Clark Law School
Brigham Young University
Recurring Visiting Professor, Legal Studies
Central European University

Brett G. Scharffs
Rex E. Lee Chair and Professor of Law and
Director, International Center for Law and Religion Studies
J. Reuben Clark Law School
Brigham Young University
Recurring Visiting Professor, Legal Studies
Central European University

Wolters Kluwer

Published by Wolters Kluwer in New York.

Wolters Kluwer Legal & Regulatory U.S. serves customers worldwide with CCH, Aspen Publishers, and Kluwer Law International products. (www.WKLegaledu.com)

Cover images: Berthold Werner/CC; Andrew Shiva/Wikimedia; Max Pixel; pxhere; Erkethan/Wikimedia; Khalid Mahmood/CC; Maureen/flickr

To contact Customer Service, e-mail customer.service@wolterskluwer.com, call 1-800-234-1660, fax 1-800-901-9075, or mail correspondence to:

Wolters Kluwer
Attn: Order Department
PO Box 990
Frederick, MD 21705

Printed in the United States of America.

1 2 3 4 5 6 7 8 9 0

ISBN 978-1-5438-0603-8

Library of Congress Cataloging-in-Publication Data

Names: Durham, W. Cole, Jr., 1948- author. | Scharffs, Brett G., author.
Title: Law and religion : national, international, and comparative perspectives / W. Cole Durham, Jr., Susa Young Gates University Professor of Law and Founding Director, International Center for Law and Religion Studies, J. Reuben Clark Law School, Brigham Young University [and] Recurring Visiting Professor, Legal Studies, Central European University; Brett G. Scharffs, Rex E. Lee Chair and Professor of Law and Director, International Center for Law and Religion Studies, J. Reuben Clark Law School, Brigham Young University.
Description: Second edition. | New York : Wolters Kluwer, 2019. | Series: Aspen select series.
Identifiers: LCCN 2018052870 | ISBN 9781543806038
Subjects: LCSH: Freedom of religion. | Freedom of religion--United States. | LCGFT: Casebooks (Law)
Classification: LCC K3258 .D873 2019 | DDC 342.08/52--dc23 LC record available at https://lccn.loc.gov/2018052870

FSC
MIX
FSC® C103993

About Wolters Kluwer Legal & Regulatory U.S.

Wolters Kluwer Legal & Regulatory U.S. delivers expert content and solutions in the areas of law, corporate compliance, health compliance, reimbursement, and legal education. Its practical solutions help customers successfully navigate the demands of a changing environment to drive their daily activities, enhance decision quality and inspire confident outcomes.

Serving customers worldwide, its legal and regulatory portfolio includes products under the Aspen Publishers, CCH Incorporated, Kluwer Law International, ftwilliam.com and MediRegs names. They are regarded as exceptional and trusted resources for general legal and practice-specific knowledge, compliance and risk management, dynamic workflow solutions, and expert commentary.

To

Louise

and

Deirdre

with gratitude for love, patience, and support

INTERNATIONAL CONTRIBUTING EDITORS

Professor Juan Carlos Valderrama Adriansén, Emertitus Professor of Freedom of Religion Rights, Pontificia Universidad Católica del Peru, Lima, Peru; Past President, Instituto de Derecho Eclesiástico, Past President and Founde. Consorcio Latinoamericano de Libertad Religiosa

Professor Johan D. van der Vyver, I.T. Cohen Professor of International Law and Human Rights, Emory University School of Law, Atlanta, Georgia, USA; previously Professor of Law. University of the Witwatersrand, Johannesburg and Potchefstroom University for Christian Higher Education

Suzanne Sitthichai Disparte, Coordinating Editor (First Edition), Formerly International Center for Law and Religion Studies, J. Reuben Clark Law School, Brigham Young University, Provo, Utah, USA

Donlu DeWitt Thayer, Coordinating Editor (Second Edition), Publications Director, International Center for Law and Religion Studies, J. Reuben Clark Law School, Brigham Young University, Provo, Utah, USA

SUMMARY OF CONTENTS

CONTENTS

PREFACE TO THE FIRST EDITION

The guiding philosophy of this casebook is that less is more and more is more. We have attempted to cover the subject matter of law and religion in about half the pages of most law and religion casebooks: that's the less. We also address at least three times the subject matter, focusing a majority of the book on international and comparative law materials: that's the more, together with a voluminous Web Supplement that includes a broad array of US, international, and comparative law cases, commentary, and analysis.

In adopting this approach we have undertaken the rather audacious task of offering a new paradigm for studying law and religion. We hope it will be of interest to both US and international students of the law.

We believe this shift in focus to include international and comparative law materials is warranted by several tectonic shifts that have taken place in the last fifty years.

First, whether the world is flat, curved, or spiky, the forces of globalization are real: we live in a world that is smaller and more interconnected than ever before; travel and communication occur at speeds and with a frequency that were unimaginable even a generation ago. For many years, religion has been thought of as an archetypal "local" issue, but in recent years it has increasingly become a "global" concern. We believe the topic of law and religion can be addressed better by trying to locate local issues within a broader historical, political, and international context, and that even quintessentially local issues can be illuminated by viewing them from cross-cultural perspectives. This relates to a more fundamental reality: viewed globally, there is no majority religion, and believers and nonbelievers can all benefit from viewing ourselves as religious minorities.

A second reason for taking an international and comparative approach to the study of law and religion is that religion and religious commitment, rather than diminishing and becoming less important, as was widely expected by scholars and political leaders a generation ago, has increased. Indeed, today we are more likely to make the mistake of seeing religion as everywhere and dangerous, rather than viewing it as nothing and irrelevant. The tendency to view human affairs as presenting a titanic clash of civilizations has become something of the norm, albeit a disputed norm, as illustrated most powerfully by the challenges posed by (and the need to come to a deeper understanding and appreciation of) Islam, including Islam-inspired terrorism. We have endeavored to include a range of religious points of view in this book and have in particular taken seriously the opportunity to engage in a sustained way with Islam. Nearly every chapter includes materials on Islam and Muslim perspectives on a broad array of topics including the headscarf controversies in France and Turkey; the Danish cartoon controversy involving depictions of the Prophet Mohammed; female genital cutting (including the debate about whether this is or is not a Muslim issue); prohibitions on conversion, marriage, and family law issues; attempts to create Shari'a tribunals (e.g., within the framework of arbitration systems); and efforts to ground constitutional law on both Shari'a and human rights norms in Afghanistan and Iraq.

A third development is the groundbreaking work of the European Court of Human Rights. Beyond the awareness of most Americans, the ECtHR is an international court that gives over 900 million citizens of 47 countries a forum of last resort to bring cases claiming that their own governments have violated their human rights, including their religious freedom rights guaranteed by Article 9 of the European Convention for the Protection of Human Rights and Fundamental Freedoms. The Court's jurisprudence has become a powerful source of persuasive authority that is recognized around the world. Nearly every chapter includes cases from the European Court, often matched with US Supreme Court cases and comparative law materials from other countries on the same or similar issues. We also live in an era where in many circles the commitment to the rule of law and to the understanding of human rights as universal norms that apply to all countries at all times is being called into question from many quarters. Thus, we view with some urgency the need to think about issues involving law and religion from a human rights perspective, which is precisely what the European Court of Human Rights does.

Fourth, much of the most remarkable and nuanced work on religious freedom issues is being done by Constitutional and other courts in countries other than the United States. Viewing the landscape from a US perspective, it is important to recognize that these courts utilize, build upon, distinguish, and often take different paths from those followed by US courts. In an increasingly interconnected world, it is ever more untenable to proceed with blinders on, as if US courts are the only institutions that have grappled with the broad array of issues involving religious freedom. From an international vantage point, we hope this book will provide a useful resource for those working in other legal systems and that it will signal the growing interest and respect an increasing number of experts in the United States have for developments elsewhere. Due to the variety, not to mention sheer volume, of comparative law materials, we have had to be extremely selective in what is included in the book. Nevertheless, most chapters include representative samples of comparative law approaches, altogether representing approximately 20 different countries. We have not provided a comprehensive comparative study of any single country or region, opting instead to include cases from many different nations and areas of the world. The casebook's Web Supplement includes numerous additional cases from many countries, which should accommodate classes that want a more focused comparative study of particular jurisdictions.

A fifth reason for this new approach is that many of the distinctive features of the US system can be seen more clearly by engaging in comparative study. For example, the United States is almost unique in the world for not having a national government department devoted to religious affairs, which on balance is probably a good thing, but which works at least in part because our non-establishment clause minimizes the amount of cooperation and aid flowing to religious communities. In addition, registration and recognition of churches is a virtual non-issue in the United States, but it is one of the primary obstacles to religious freedom around the world. Another distinctive, although not unique, characteristic of the US system is that the First Amendment includes an Establishment Clause, prohibiting an establishment of religion, as well as a Free Exercise Clause, which aligns more closely with religious freedom provisions in international human rights instruments and most other constitutions. Nevertheless, other countries grapple with many of the issues that in the United States are categorized as Establishment Clause cases, so the US situation is not as unique as we (and others) sometimes imagine it to be. Comparative study also helps identify the strengths, weaknesses, and underlying assumptions of approaches taken by US courts. For example, focusing on how other legal systems have grappled with defining the permissible limitations on religious freedom sheds light on some of our own deepest challenges in determining when state interests are sufficiently great to justify overriding religious freedom claims.

By engaging in international and comparative law analysis, we can get a better view of the general legal topography, as well as a deeper understanding of the ways and places where legal systems get stuck or go off track in grappling with recurrent issues. We can see how similar situations are often viewed as raising very different types of legal questions, and how problems get addressed through different historical, cultural, and constitutional prisms.

***

A few words about case selection and editing may be helpful. We have had to be selective in cases we include and rather severe in the pruning we have conducted on them. Here we have been guided by several key principles.

First, we have focused on what we believe to be landmark cases, representing significant developments in legal doctrine. This means, for example, that we have omitted or relegated to notes and comments dozens of United States Establishment Clause cases involving the Supreme Court's tortured interpretation, application, and reinterpretation of the *Lemon* test in cases involving governmental aid to parochial schools and religious symbols on public property. We have done this partly out of mercy to students, but also because many of these cases have been overturned, distinguished, or disregarded by later cases.

Second, when there is a long line of cases on a subject, we have tried to include excerpts from early cases where doctrine is set, cases that illustrate different theoretical or doctrinal approaches, and the most recent cases, and have left out or summarized in notes and comments most of the intervening cases.

Third, we have looked for cases with interesting international and comparative law counterparts. To be sure, we have included cases that are distinctly American, including controversies over the Pledge of Allegiance, the study of creationism, and school prayer, but even in these areas there are often interesting comparative materials.

Fourth, in editing cases we have wielded an unforgiving scalpel. Cases that have generated dozens or even hundreds of pages of court opinion have been reduced to a few pages. We have undoubtedly cut out a fair amount of muscle as well as flab. In editing we have observed several guidelines. We have tried to give a fulsome account of the facts, have given the Court one and only one chance to explain the law, and have generally omitted the text of laws and quotations from other cases that are included elsewhere in the book. We have also omitted almost all footnotes, string citations, and even discussion of other cases. In order to enhance readability and save space, we have sometimes omitted ellipses or other indicia of editorial judgment. The casebook's Web Supplement includes the full text of the cases excerpted and most of the other materials that are either excerpted or described in notes and comments (to the extent copyright constraints on other sources have allowed). When a court or commentator's analysis seems perfunctory or incomplete, there is a good chance—although not an absolute certainty—that the fault lies with our editing, but the fault can be remedied by checking the Web Supplement.

Fifth, if a case is not interesting (at least to us), we omit it. There is plenty that is gripping, heartbreaking, and outrageous in the law of religious freedom. We haven't had to include anything that is not stimulating and important—unless you adhere to the rule of thumb invoked by one of our spouses to keep us humble: that anything we find interesting is by definition boring. Yet even she has conceded of late that the issues being addressed here have surpassed her most discerning interest threshold.

W. Cole Durham, Jr.
Brett G. Scharffs

December 2009

ACKNOWLEDGMENTS TO THE FIRST EDITION

Anyone who has worked at length in the law and religion field knows how vastly the relevant legal and historical materials exceed what can be distilled into any particular text, and how much one depends on experts from other jurisdictions and from other fields. Our indebtedness thus extends in countless directions, over many years, and we are conscious that there are many who have contributed significantly who must go unnamed. We hope they will understand the sincerity of our appreciation and respect.

Nonetheless, there are a number of people who deserve special mention. First, we owe a great debt of gratitude to students in our courses on religion-state issues for the past several years both at the J. Reuben Clark Law School of Brigham Young University and at Central European University in Budapest. The idea of writing this book emerged from our experience teaching these courses. For each of the past three years, students have gone the extra mile in wading through successive edits of the materials, giving us feedback, and often meeting on a weekly basis with us to identify additional materials and to hone the all-too-plentiful harvest of items suggested for inclusion. In addition, many of the summer research fellows who have worked at the International Center for Law and Religion Studies (ICLRS) over the past few summers have contributed to the process of gathering and editing materials. Special appreciation goes to Megan I. Grant, Nicole Davis, Michael Lewis, Blair Larsen, Matthew Baker, Taylor Turner, Valerie Paul, Erin Bradley, Jonghoon Han, Katie M. McIntosh, David N. Brown, George G. Nightingale, Scott W. Ellis, Alisa Rogers, Jeffrey A. Aird, and Samuel G. Brooks for going the extra mile in making contributions. We owe special thanks to our colleagues at ICLRS—Robert T. Smith, Elizabeth A. Clark Sewell, Gary B. Doxey, David M. Kirkham, Christine G. Scott, Holly M. S. Rasmussen and Deborah A. Wright—all of whom have contributed to the project of developing this book, either by unselfishly taking on added burdens so we could work on this project, or by contributing directly to assembling and editing materials. Many, many others at the J. Reuben Clark Law School, both on the faculty and the staff, have contributed in various ways to the emergence of this book. We are grateful for the support, comments, and suggestions from other faculty members. Frederick Mark Gedicks is always a generous colleague and has stimulated our thought and contributed to our understanding in many ways. We are also indebted to Lance B.

Wickman, William F. Atkin, Boyd J. Black, Scott E. Isaacson, and their colleagues working with the Office of General Council for The Church of Jesus Christ of Latter-day Saints, for their expertise on international legal matters affecting religious organizations and for their willingness to help identify and find relevant materials.

We also owe a particular debt of gratitude to our International Contributing Editors who are listed on a separate page. They have provided significant advice and help at various stages in planning the book.

Our only regret is that we have not been able to include more of what all of the foregoing have suggested. We are grateful for the opportunity the Web Supplement will provide for sharing more of the manifold contributions others have made.

We are particularly indebted to Suzanne Sitthichai Disparte, who was a key research assistant on this project already in her student days, and who has continued on for well over a year following graduation from law school to help see this project to conclusion. This book could not have emerged without her unflagging efforts, and her ability to keep things moving forward, even when travel schedules and conflicting assignments seemed to present constant obstacles and sources of delay.

The authors extend their appreciation to Aspen editor, John Devins, for his invaluable assistance, to the anonymous reviewers for their many helpful criticisms and suggestions, and especially to colleagues at other law schools—Mark Movsesian at Saint Johns University Law School and Robert Blitt at the University of Tennessee School of Law, who have used earlier versions of the materials that have been distilled into this book in courses they have taught, and who have been generous in sharing their recommendations for improvement of the book.

Finally, enough cannot be said for the patience and support from our wives and families. There have been countless hours when we have been missing in action because of the demands of working on this book. We will be indebted to them long into the future, and hope we can find ways to repay in small measure all they have endured and sacrificed to allow us to work on this book. Cole would like to thank his wife, Louise, for covering many bases while he has been absent as a result of this and related earlier initiatives. Brett would like to specifically thank his wife, Deirdre, and his children, Elliot, Sophelia, and Ella, for their support during this project.

In addition to the foregoing expressions of appreciation, the authors would like to thank the following copyright holders for permission to excerpt their materials:

Ahmed, Sahmeer, *Pluralism in British Islamic Reasoning: The Problem with Recognizing Islamic Law in the United Kingdom*. Used by permission of the Yale Journal of International Law.

Barker, Eileen, Why the Cults? "New Religious Movements and Freedom of Religion or Belief, in *Facilitating Freedom of Religion or Belief: A Deskbook* (Tore Lindholm, W. Cole Durham, Jr., and Bahia G. Tahzib-Lie, eds.). Copyright © 2004 by Koninklijke Brill NV. Reprinted by permission.

Bhutto, Benazir, *Reconciliation: Islam, Democracy, and the West*, pages 20–22, 27. Copyright © 2008 by Benazir Bhutto. Reprinted by permission of HarperCollins Publishers. For additional territory contact: Benazir Bhutto, c/o

The Wylie Agency, Inc. 250 West 57th Street, New York, NY 10107, Attn: Andrew Wylie.

Chan, Kim Kwong and Eric Carlson, *Religious Freedom in China: Policy, Administration, and Regulation: A Research Handbook.* Copyright © Kim Kwong Chang. Reprinted by permission.

Cheung, Anne S.Y., *In Search of a Theory of Cult and Freedom of Religion in China: The Case of Falun Gong.* Reprinted by permission of Pacific Rim Law & Policy Journal.

Dane, Perry, "The Varieties of Religious Autonomy," in Church Autonomy: A Comparative Survey (Gerhard Robbers, ed.). Used by permission of Peter Lang Publishing.

Durham Jr., W. Cole, Facilitating Freedom of Religion or Belief Through Religious Association Laws, in *Facilitating Freedom of Religion or Belief: A Deskbook* (Tore Lindholm, W. Cole Durham, Jr., and Bahia G. Tahzib-Lie, eds.). Copyright © 2004 by Koninklijke Brill NV. Reprinted by permission.

Durham Jr., W. Cole, Perspectives on Religious Liberty: A Comparative Framework, in *Religious Human Rights in Global Perspective.* Reprinted by permission of Koninklijke Brill NV.

Durham Jr., W. Cole and Christine G. Scott, Public Finance and the Religious Sector.

El Fadl, Khaled Abou, *The Place of Tolerance in Islam.* Copyright © 2002 by Joshua Cohen and Ian Lague. Reprinted by permission of Beacon Press, Boston.

Fautre, Willy, The Sect Issue in France and Belgium, in *International Perspectives on Freedom and Equality of Religious Belief.* Used by permission of the J.M. Dawson Instituted of Church-State Studies, Baylor University.

Federal Constitutional Court of the Federal Republic of Germany, Decisions of the Bundesverfassungsgericht, *Federal Constitutional Court, Federal Republic of Germany: The Law of Freedom of Faith and the Law of the Churches 1960–2003.* Copyright © by Nomos Verlagsgesellschaft. Used by permission.

Ferrari, Silvio, Religious Communities As Legal Persons: An Introduction to the National Reports, in *Churches and Other Organisations as Legal Persons: Proceedings of the 17th Meeting of the European Consortium for Church and State Research.* Copyright © by Uitgeverij Peeters. Used by permission.

Ferrari, Silvio, State and Church in Italy, in *State and Church in the European Union* (Gerhard Robbers, ed.). Used by permission of author, editor, and Nomos Publishing.

Glendon, Mary Ann, *A World Made New.* Copyright © 2001 by Mary Ann Glendon. Used by permission of Random House, Inc.

Grim, Brian J., Religious Freedom: Good for What Ails Us?. Reprinted by permission of *The Review of Faith & International Affairs*, www.RFIAonline.org.

Habeck, Mary, *Knowing the Enemy: Jihadist Ideology and the War on Terror.* Copyright © 2006 by Yale University. Reprinted by permission of Yale University Press.

Hoffman, Bruce, *Inside Terrorism.* Copyright © 1998 by Bruce Hoffman. Reprinted by permission of Columbia University Press.

Hussein, Gamil Muhammed, *Basic Guarantees in the Islamic Criminal Justice System, in Criminal Justice in Islam*. Copyright © Oxford Centre for Islamic Studies. Reprinted by permission.

Jaeger, David-Maria A., The Holy See's Understanding of Religious Freedom, in *Church and State: Towards Protection for Freedom of Religion*. Reprinted by permission of The Japanese Association of Comparative Constitutional Law.

King Jr., Martin Luther, Letter from Birmingham Jail. Copyright 1963 Dr. Martin Luther King Jr; copyright renewed 1991 Coretta Scott King. Reprinted by arrangement with The Heirs to the Estate of Martin Luther King Jr., c/o Writers House as agent for the proprietor New York, NY.

Kommers, Donald, Classroom Crucifix II Case and Lebach, in *The Constitutional Jurisprudence of the Federal Republic of Germany*, pp. 482–482 (excerpt). Copyright © 1997 by Duke University Press. All Rights Reserved. Used by permission of the publisher.

Lindholm, Tore, Philosophical and Religious Justifications of Freedom of Religion or Belief, in *Facilitating Freedom of Religion or Belief: A Deskbook* (Tore Lindholm, W. Cole Durham, Jr., and Bahia G. Tahzib-Lie, eds.). Copyright © 2004 by Koninklijke Brill NV. Reprinted by permission.

Mayer, Ann Elizabeth, *Islam and Human Rights: Tradition and Politics*. Copyright © 1999 by Westview Press, A Member of Perseus Books Group. Reprinted by permission of Westview Press, A Member of Perseus Books Group.

Meacham, Jon, *American Gospel*. Copyright © 2006 by Jon Meacham. Used by permission of Random House, Inc.

Nussbaum, Martha C., *Women and Human Development: The Capabilities Approach*. (Cambridge University Press 2000). Copyright © Martha C. Nussbaum 2000. Reprinted with the permission of Cambridge University Press.

Perry, Michael, *Love and Power: The Role of Religion and Morality in American Politics*. Copyright © 1991 by Oxford University Press. Reprinted by permission.

Peters, Edward, *Heresy and Authority in Medieval Europe*. (University of Pennsylvania Press 1980). Copyright © 1980 by Edward Peters. Reprinted with permission of the University of Pennsylvania Press.

Robert, Jacques, Religious Liberty and French Secularism. Reprinted with permission of the Brigham Young University Law Review.

Robbers, Gerhard, State and Church in Germany, in *State and Church in the European Union* (Gerhard Robbers, ed.). Used by permission of the author and Nomos Publishing.

Second Vatican Council, *Dignitatis Humanae*. Used by permission of the Libreria Editrice Vaticana.

Tabor, James D. and Eugene V. Gallagher, *Why Waco? Cults and the Battle for Religious Freedom in America*. Copyright © 1997 by James D. Tabor and Eugene V. Gallagher. Reprinted by permission of The University of California Press.

Tahzib-Lie, Bahia G., Dissenting Women, Religion or Belief, and the State: Contemporary Challenges that Require Attention in *Facilitating Freedom of Religion or Belief: A Deskbook* (Tore Lindholm, W. Cole Durham, Jr., and

Bahia G. Tahzib-Lie, eds.). Copyright © 2004 by Koninklijke Brill NV. Reprinted by permission.

Tierney, Brian, Religious Rights: A Historical Perspective, in *Religious Liberty in Western Thought* (Noel B. Reynolds & W. Cole Durham, Jr., eds.). Copyright © by Emory University. Reprinted by permission of Emory University.

Torfs, Rik, *Religion and State Relationships in Europe.* Reprinted by permission of Rik Torfs and the Institute for Global Engagement.

van der Vyver, Johan D., The Relationship of Freedom of Religion or Belief Norms to Other Human Rights, in *Facilitating Freedom of Religion or Belief: A Deskbook* (Tore Lindholm, W. Cole Durham, Jr., and Bahia G. Tahzib-Lie, eds.). Copyright © 2004 by Koninklijke Brill NV. Reprinted by permission.

Waldron, Jeremy, The War on Terror and the Image of God. Reprinted by permission of Jeremy Waldron and the Emory University Center for the Study of Law and Religion. A revised version of this chapter is included in John Witte, Jr. and Frank S. Alexander, eds., *Christianity and Human Rights: An Introduction* (Cambridge University Press, 2010).

PREFACE AND ACKNOWLEDGMENTS TO THE SECOND EDITION

The years during which we have been preparing revisions to this casebook have seen a great number of significant developments around the world in the dynamic field of law and religion. This second edition attempts to include the most important of these developments, current through mid-2018, without expanding too much the overall length of the book. In total, we have referenced some 100 new court cases, while eliminating discussion of about 20 cases that appeared in the first edition.[1] This has meant cutting or abbreviating some materials from the first edition, undertaking rather substantial editing of important cases from major courts and jurisdictions, and preparing short summaries of other important developments.

The following is a brief account of significant changes.

The four chapters of Part I (Frameworks) saw fewer changes than other chapters. In Chapter 1, which treats formative issues, users of the first edition will notice some enrichment to the section on the legacy of persecution. Most notable in the theoretical perspectives outlined in Chapter 2 is discussion concerning changing definitions of "religion" for purposes of claiming justifications for special legal protection. In Chapter 3, important changes to the discussion of international human rights perspectives include updates on the work and role of the European Court of Human Rights as well tracking of developments in the Islamic world, including legislation and court cases in various jurisdictions concerning head and face coverings in public space and of such endeavors as the 2015 Beirut Declaration on Religious Freedom, the 2016 Marrakesh Declaration on the Rights of Religious Minorities in Predominantly Muslim Communities, and the 2017 "Faith for Rights" initiative of the Office of the UN High Commissioner for Human Rights.

The five chapters of Part II (Freedom of Religion or Belief) have been substantially revised. Evolving international discussions of the legal implications of freedom of religious belief and expression (Chapter 5), of desirable or permissible limitations on religious actions and manifestations (Chapter 6), and of religious rights involving land use and of regulations in institutionalized settings such as prisons and the military (Chapter 7) have meant numerous changes, minor and major, to the material supporting these discussions. Not surprisingly, no chapters in the book have received more attention during revision than Chapter 8 (Responding to Religious Extremism) and Chapter 9 (Religious Conflict and

1. These cases continue to appear in the Web Supplement and its Case Table.

Tensions Between Religious Freedom and Other Rights). The sections in Chapter 8 dealing with new religious movements, sects, and cults have been reduced to make more space for issues surrounding religiously motivated terrorism. In Chapter 9, the discussion of genocide has been pared to make space for a great deal of new information, including a number of new cases from a variety of jurisdictions concerning religion in conflict with nondiscrimination norms, including those protecting women and minorities (both religious and sexual). Perhaps not surprisingly, the section on same-sex marriage has tripled in length. The *Masterpiece Cakeshop* decision was handed down just as the book was going to press, and more detailed treatment of that decision had to be left for the Web Supplement.

Part III treats the relationships between religious institutions and governments. Added to Chapter 10 is discussion of a number of important new cases from the United States and Europe concerning the autonomy of religious organizations and a new section treating access to sacred space in Spain, India, and Israel. Chapter 11 (association and legal personality) is reorganized and revised to include a registration case from Austria that formerly appeared in Chapter 12, discussion of new European Court of Human Rights cases involving Hungary and Turkey, and a new section on religious autonomy in China.

Changes to Chapter 12 involve updates on religion-state financial relationships in a number of European countries and in the United States, where changes in the "charitable choice" initiatives initiated and modified by two previous presidential administrations were undergoing further modification as we were making final changes to this book before press.

A significant addition to Chapter 13, which treats education, is discussion of the "Italian crucifix case" from the European Court of Human Rights, *Lautsi v. Italy*. A new section was added on religiously motivated homeschooling (primarily in Germany). Other additions track increasing tensions between non-discrimination norms and schools whose moral codes address sexual behavior. As this book went to press, pertinent legislation was pending in the United States (California), and a ruling in the very important Trinity Western University case had just been handed down by the Supreme Court of Canada and will also receive extensive and updating treatment in the Web Supplement.

Finally, changes to Chapter 14 (treating religion and public life) primarily involve new developments in the United States and Europe concerning displays of religious symbols and structures on public property.

In a project as complex as this one, with significant developments occurring continually, we are deeply grateful to our colleagues and to student researchers, too numerous at this point to mention individually, who have helped track, report, replace, delete, and report again over the years we have spent revising this book. Many of these changes have been tracked on the Web Supplement companion to the book, and some will remain there for reference, even though there is no space for them in the print volume.

We must mention one outstanding student, now colleague, Michael Worley, who has been with the project since 2014. Profound thanks to Michael for his patient and thorough contributions to research, writing, and analysis in this addition.

Last, but far, far from least, we owe an immense debt of gratitude to Donlu DeWitt Thayer, Publications Director at the International Center for Law and Religion Studies at BYU, who served as Coordinating Editor for the second edition. She has borne the tremendous burden of gathering updated materials, managing the flow of information from research assistants, editing contributions, regathering successive new batches of information, re-editing, re-writing, writing new material, and in general making countless additions, recommendations, and refinements that have made this a much better book. All of this has been done while carrying substantial additional burdens on many fronts in exemplary and unforgettable ways.

We also owe a significant debt of gratitude to colleagues and now deeply appreciated friends for work that is not immediately evident in this volume but has honored our work greatly. In particular we acknowledge those who have been and will continue to be involved in the translation of the book into several other languages. Translations supervised by Do Quang Hung (Vietnamese) and Liu Peng (Chinese) have been published. Translations personally undertaken or supervised by Fatih Öztürk (Turkish), Cekli Setya Pratiwi (Bahasa Indonesia), Seng Mai Aung (Burmese), Cristian Badillo (Spanish), Dmytro Vovk (Russian), Nehad Alhusban and Alaa Madanat (Arabic), and Nikos Maghioros (Greek) are in varying stages of development.

This second edition has been many years in preparation and has called upon the publication team at Wolters Kluwer for flexibility and cooperation. For their competence, efficiency, and extraordinary patience with the process of bringing this book to print, we especially are indebted to Sarah Hains and Kathy Langone of The Froebe Group.

Finally, copyright acknowledgments from the first edition are repeated here by reference. The editorial scalpel has meant that more and more material that has been included fits within the bounds of "fair use," but we want to thank all those working in the field, both those explicitly acknowledged and those we have cited throughout the book, for all the ideas and contributions from which we have so obviously and so deeply benefited.

W. Cole Durham, Jr.
Brett G. Scharffs

December 2018

ABBREVIATIONS INDEX

AU—African Union
CAN—Cult Awareness Network
CCPR—Covenant on Civil and Political Rights
CEDAW—Convention on the Elimination of All Forms of Discrimination against Women
CERD—Convention on the Elimination of All Forms of Racial Discrimination
CSCE—Conference on Security and Cooperation in Europe
ECHR—European Convention for the Protection of Human Rights and Fundamental Freedoms
ECommHR—European Commission of Human Rights
ECtHR—European Court of Humans Rights
FBO—Faith-based Organizations
ICCPR—International Covenant on Civil and Political Rights
ICESCR—International Covenant on Economic, Social, and Cultural Rights
ICJ—International Court of Justice
ILO—International Labor Organization
IRS—Internal Revenue Service
NRM—New Religious Movement
OAS—Organization of American States
OIC—Organization of the Islamic Conference (since 2011: Organization of Islamic Cooperation)
OSCE—Organization for Security and Cooperation in Europe
RFRA—Religious Freedom Restoration Act
RLUIPA—Religious Land Use and Institutionalized Persons Act
TEU—Treaty on the European Union
UDHR—Universal Declaration of Human Rights
UN—United Nations
UNESCO—United Nations Educational, Scientific and Cultural Organization
UNHRC—United Nations Human Rights Committee
USCIRF—United States Commission on International Religious Freedom
WHO—World Health Organization

INTRODUCTION

Congress shall make no law respecting an establishment of religion, or prohibiting the free exercise thereof.

—United States Constitution, First Amendment

Everyone has the right to freedom of thought, conscience and religion; this right includes freedom to change his religion or belief, and freedom, either alone or in community with others and in public or private, to manifest his religion or belief in teaching, practice, worship and observance.

—Universal Declaration of Human Rights, Article 18

Islam is the official religion of the State and it is a foundation source of legislation:

A. No law may be enacted that contradicts the established provisions of Islam.

B. No law may be enacted that contradicts the principles of democracy.

C. No law may be enacted that contradicts the rights and basic freedoms stipulated in this constitution.

—Constitution of Iraq, Section 1, Article 2

This book is an introduction to the study of law and religion. It adopts a thematic approach and endeavors to include not only materials that are commonly found in a US law school casebook on the Establishment and Free Exercise Clauses, but material that is international and comparative as well.

The book is divided into three parts: Frameworks, Freedom of Religion and Belief, and The Relationships Between Religious Institutions and the State.

Part I, Frameworks, is an introduction to various perspectives on freedom of religion or belief, with chapters focusing on history, theoretical and religious perspectives on religious freedom, international human rights, and comparative constitutional law.

Chapter 1 provides a brief history of the idea of religious freedom in Europe and the United States. Chapter 2 addresses various theoretical and religious perspectives on freedom of religion, including the issue of how to define what counts as a religion, and various justifications for defending the idea of freedom of conscience and belief. Chapter 2 also includes a brief introduction to religious perspectives on freedom of religion, including arguments from a variety of religious traditions defending both coercion and freedom in matters relating to religion. Chapter 3 introduces the international human rights approach to freedom of religion or belief, focusing on the key UN developments as well as the leading regional human rights regime: that established by the European Convention for the Protection of Human Rights and Fundamental Freedoms and implemented by the European Court of Human Rights. Chapter 4 gives a comparative overview of the variety of church-state configurations and the comparative constitutional arrangements that facilitate those relationships.

Part II, Freedom of Religion or Belief, addresses issues that in the United States typically arise under the Free Exercise Clause. Chapter 5 focuses on what we might think of as the core of religious freedom, the freedom of belief and the freedom of expression, including speech aimed at converting others and speech that is considered by some to be blasphemous or to result in "defamation of religion." Chapter 6 addresses several fundamental approaches to addressing the question of what limits may lawfully be applied to claims made in the name of religious freedom. Chapter 7 deals with religious rights in specialized regulatory contexts such as land use and in specialized institutional settings such as the military, prisons, and hospitals. Chapter 8 considers problems that arise in responding to extreme conduct undertaken in the name of religion, including religiously-motivated terrorism, as well as efforts to respond to dangerous sects and cults. Chapter 9 addresses some of the tensions that arise between religious freedom and other important rights, including women's rights and the rights of sexual minorities.

Part III, The Relationships Between Religious Institutions and the State, turns first to issues of institutional autonomy and to matters that straddle the free exercise/establishment divide in US law. Chapter 10 addresses issues relating to the autonomy of religious institutions, including disputes regarding church property, controversies that arise over hiring and firing church personnel, and issues involving who has the right to determine religious doctrine and teaching. Chapter 11 addresses the right of religious communities to acquire legal personality and related associational rights. Although this is to a large extent a non-issue in the United States, issues involving registration, recognition, and status for religious organizations constitute some of the most challenging legal issues confronting religious institutions in many parts of the world. Chapter 12 addresses financial relationships between religion and state, including religion-state models that involve direct state funding of (some) churches as well as systems such as that in the United States that permit significant, and growing, indirect forms of state aid to churches and church-affiliated non-profit enterprises. Chapter 13 addresses education, a sphere where many conflicts arise with respect to freedom of religion and non-establishment of religion. Finally, Chapter 14 addresses situations involving the role of religion in public life, including religious involvement in governmental activities, religious influence on law and public policy, the participation of religious organizations in the political process, and religious symbols on public property.

This casebook has been designed with the idea that supplemental online tools will be made available to expand coverage, allow greater depth in the exploration of issues, and track developing issues in the field. To this end we have created an extensive Web Supplement, access to which is available free of charge to all "qualified users" of the casebook (teachers of courses using the casebook as text or reference and their students, currently and previously enrolled).

The Web Supplement is organized chapter-by-chapter, keyed generally to material in the print volume, and includes full texts of many documents and all court cases summarized, referenced, or otherwise treated in the casebook, in so far as copyright regulations permit. In addition, cases referenced in the current edition or deleted from the previous edition, as well as relevant cases decided after publication of the current edition, are found in the Web Supplement as referenced in that online document's Case Table. Supplementary resources are indicated in the text body and in footnotes, and are frequently signaled by a box appearing at the end of a section or chapter, in the following form:

Additional Web Resources:	Additional cases as well as resources from the wider literature discussing religious freedom and proselytism

Among the resources of the Web Supplement are comparative legal materials from various jurisdictions. Because of space limitations, it has not been possible to include in the printed text the full range of cases and other legal materials relevant on any particular issue. Because the Web Supplement is continually being updated and expanded, we urge those using the casebook to check the Supplement periodically for developments.

The Web Supplement may be found at https://supplement.iclrs.org/2e. Additional materials are available (though not directly keyed to the text in the same way as the Web Supplement) in databases maintained by the International Center for Law and Religion Studies at www.iclrs.org.

PART

FRAMEWORKS

CHAPTER 1

FORMATIVE TENSIONS IN THE HISTORY OF RELIGIOUS FREEDOM

I. INTRODUCTION

Wherever there have been religiously diverse peoples occupying a common territory, tension has arisen between the demands of law and the provinces of religion. Governmental approaches to resolving such tension have ranged from the radically intolerant and coercive to the broad-minded and highly accommodating. Although it is difficult to make general pronouncements distinguishing one era or culture from another, as a general matter the Western world has followed a winding path from the early persecution of heretics and dissenting religions, through eras of forbearance and limited leniency toward nonconformists, to—finally, in the twentieth century—the widespread acknowledgment of religious liberty and freedom of thought, conscience, and belief as fundamental, nonderogable human rights.

This historical path has, of course, been fraught with obstacles and has not been without its ironies. As merely one well-known example, early Christians suffered dearly at the hands of the Roman emperors only to themselves assume the role of persecutor and prosecutor of religious unorthodoxies when the vagaries of history placed civil power in their hands. In the process, Christian thinkers managed to reconcile the burning of heretics with the admonition of their founder that they love their enemies. Nevertheless, this same admonition would later channel significant Christian contributions to the recognition of freedom of conscience and religion as a basic human right. Other religious traditions have followed similar crooked paths between persecution of and patience toward dissenters and minority religions, often depending upon whether they themselves enjoyed majority status in a given society.

Modern scholars have recognized that, over time,

> [f]or the most part, religious freedom has not been promoted as an end in itself, but as a technique for preserving stability, limiting conflict, or as a pretext for intervention. Through much of history, granting religious freedom has been used as means of avoiding conflict, whereas limiting its enjoyment has been a source of conflict. In general, there has been a shift away from the practice of attempting to ensure civil harmony by keeping people of different religions apart towards providing a common

institutional framework for facilitating peaceful coexistence. This is most evident in the modern regime of internationally codified universal human rights.[1]

Space constraints prevent an exploration of this vast history in any depth. Instead, this chapter highlights formative tensions in the development of law and philosophical inquiry regarding religious tolerance from the rise of the Roman Empire in the first century BCE through the rise of American free exercise jurisprudence and the creation of the European Court of Human Rights in the twentieth century.

Modern church-state law has its origins in Europe and was filtered primarily through British law and thinking on its way to the American colonies. Later the United States, in its own turn and through its constitutional provisions and contributions to international human rights documents, would have a significant influence on the development of relations between law and religion in the wider world. However, one cannot understand American church-state jurisprudence without understanding something of its European roots, and the history of Europe, in turn, "must be understood in terms of 'Christendom.' . . . Even after Rome fell, more and more of the peoples of Western Europe adopted Christianity, and the religion also became intertwined with the various [civil] authorities."[2]

The importance of European historical developments cannot be overstated in this regard. Here one sees the unfortunate and all-too-frequent pattern of the persecuted becoming persecutors. However, here also begins the story of the gradual separation over time of the law of the church and the law of the state. Shifting to America, one sees this trend continue with the development of laws that balance the competing concerns of protecting church from the state and state from the church. We see that freedom of religion is a foundational human right—historically, theoretically, and institutionally.

The chapter concludes with modern cases concerning religious speech that takes the form of proselytism. While the cases analyze issues using the latest constitutional and human rights ideas, they also represent the contemporary embodiment of age-old conflicts between rival religious communities. In that sense, they reflect in profound ways the current starting points for exploring some of the oldest of all human rights concerns.

II. THE LEGACY OF PERSECUTION

Religious persecution is as old as recorded history. It has taken forms ranging from social stigma to genocide, and believers, whether they have responded with fear or pride, patience or rebellion, have tended to have one thing in common: a belief that those who remain faithful will be rewarded, in this world, or in a better world to come.

To recount one ancient example, the Book of Daniel from the Hebrew *Ketuvim* and the Christian Old Testament tells the story of four young Israelite nobles—

1. Editors, with Nazila Ghanea, Introduction, in *Facilitating Freedom of Religion or Belief: A Deskbook* xxvii, xlvi (Tore Lindholm, W. Cole Durham, Jr., and Bahia G. Tahzib-Lie, eds., Martinus Nijhoff 2004).

2. Thomas C. Berg, *The State and Religion* 38 (West Group 2004) (1998).

Daniel ("God is my judge"), and his companions Hananiah ("beloved of the Lord"), Mishael ("who is as God"), and Azariah ("the Lord is my help")—who were taken from Israel to Babylon during the campaign of Nebuchadnezzar II to be trained in the king's service. In Babylon the young men were given new names: for Daniel, Belteshazzar ("Bel protects his life"), for the others, Shadrach, Meshach, and Abed-nego, all honoring local gods.

Their new names notwithstanding, the young men remained true to their heritage and traditions, and early on they gained the respect of the king by demonstrating their health and fitness after refusing to partake of food and drink prohibited by their religion. As they grew in favor and position, others envied them, and tried to undermine the positions they attained. When Shadrach, Meshach, and Abed-nego refused to obey the royal command to bow to a statue of the king, their enemies reported their behavior to the king, who sentenced them to death by burning. The young men faced their horrific sentence with confidence: "If it be so, our God whom we serve is able to deliver us from the burning fiery furnace, and he will deliver us out of thine hand, O king. But if not, be it known unto thee, O king, that we will not serve thy gods, nor worship the golden image which thou hast set up." The young men were bound and put into a "furnace exceeding hot." Those watching, however, saw "four men loose, walking in the midst of the fire" unharmed, and the "form of the fourth [was] like the Son of God." The king called the men out of the furnace, decreed that no one in his kingdom should "speak any thing amiss" of their God, and "promoted Shadrach, Meshach, and Abed-nego, in the province of Babylon." (From Daniel 3, KJV.)

Many years later, another totalitarian ruler, the benevolent Darius, had chosen Daniel to be one of three "presidents" over 120 princes of his Persian kingdom. Once again the Israelite's peers and subordinates were consumed with envy. Unable to find any "error or fault" in Daniel except "concerning the law of his God. . . . All the presidents of the kingdom, the governors, and the princes, the counsellors, and the captains . . . consulted together to establish a royal statute, and to make a firm decree, that whosoever shall ask a petition of any God or man for thirty days, save of . . . the king, he [should] be cast into the den of lions." The king was persuaded to sign the decree. Daniel was found praying to his God, and was delivered to the king for punishment. The king was "displeased with himself" and "set his heart on Daniel to deliver him," but he could not alter his own unalterable decree. He delivered Daniel to his punishment, though expressing his confidence that the God Daniel served continually would deliver him. Next morning, Darius was "exceeding glad" to find Daniel alive after a night shut up in a den of lions. Whereupon the king made another decree: "That in every dominion of my kingdom men tremble and fear before the God of Daniel: for he is the living God, and steadfast forever, and his kingdom that which shall not be destroyed, and his dominion shall be even unto the end." (From Daniel 6, KJV.)

These stories clearly illustrate the attitude of many religious individuals: although their beliefs may at times provoke anger and hatred, ultimately those who remain true will be protected from their enemies and be blessed far more than those who would fight against them.

A. FROM PERSECUTED TO PERSECUTOR

A flagrant flaw of human nature, which has been too often historically demonstrated, is the tendency of a majority group to abuse its power to the detriment and suffering of minority peoples. An unhappy irony occurs when these persecutors, emboldened by the strength of their numbers, have themselves previously suffered the pains of persecution. The history of the early Christians reflects this irony. In his famous history of the Roman Empire, Edward Gibbon notes:

> About fourscore years after the death of Christ, his innocent disciples were punished with death by the sentence of a proconsul of the most amiable and philosophic character, and according to the laws of an emperor distinguished by the wisdom and justice of his general administration. . . . [T]he Christians who obeyed the dictates and solicited the liberty of conscience, were alone, among all the subjects of the Roman Empire, excluded from the common benefits of their auspicious government.[3]

Gibbon goes on to reflect, however, that "from the time that Christianity was invested with the supreme power, the governors of the church have been no less diligently employed in displaying the cruelty, than in imitating the conduct, of their Pagan adversaries."[4]

The first recorded instance of Christian persecution by state authority occurred in the year 64, after a fire set Rome ablaze. To quell the rumor that he himself had started the fire, the Emperor Nero pointed to the Christians. As a result, Christians were executed in large numbers, thrown to wild animals, or burned as human torches in Nero's gardens. Early Christian writers asserted that the apostles Peter and Paul were martyred during this violent time. Christian persecution continued under Nero's successor, Domitian.

The earliest known official pronouncement on the treatment of Christians dates from the year 111. Pliny the Younger, governor of Bithynia, who was known as a just man, questioned the local policy of executing Christians who would not abjure and sacrifice to pagan gods. He wrote to the Emperor Trajan for guidance. Trajan approved Pliny's more tolerant approach and instructed that the state should not waste time hunting out the Christians. Of Christians who were brought before Pliny, those who denied Christianity and sacrificed to the gods must be released; only those who refused must be executed.[5]

With some variation among emperors, this approach in dealing with Christians became standard for Roman authority throughout the second century. Under the reign of Marcus Aurelius (161-180), however, public opinion turned increasingly against Christians, and for the next century-and-a-half their treatment by Roman authorities generally worsened, reaching a peak at the beginning of the fourth century. Not until the reign of Galerius Maximianus (305-311) would widespread persecution of Christians in the Roman Empire come to a halt. Upon the death of Galerius, the Empire was divided among four rulers. In his efforts to retake and

---

3. Edward Gibbon, *The History of the Decline and Fall of the Roman Empire: Volume I, the Turn of the Tide* 147–148 (Folio Society, Ltd. 1983) (1776).

4. *Id.*

5. Justo L. González, *The Story of Christianity: The Early Church to the Dawn of the Reformation* 40 (Harper & Row 1984).

reconsolidate the empire, Constantine took war to the other rulers. Two Christian historians personally acquainted with Constantine recorded that on the eve of battle he had a revelation instructing him to place a Christian symbol on his soldiers' shields. With the ensuing victory, Constantine ruled the entire western half of the Empire, and Christianity had found an imperial advocate.[6]

In 313 Constantine, still pursuing his campaign for supreme rule, met with his rival Licinius at Milan. There the two emperors concluded what is commonly known as the Edict of Milan, according to which they agreed to stop persecution of Christians and to restore all Christian properties. This edict marked the formal end of the Christian persecutions. Constantine ultimately achieved supreme rule of the Roman Empire and, perhaps because he attributed his victory on the Milvian Bridge to the vision he received of shields bearing Christian symbols, endowed Christianity with privileges, recognition, and respect previously known only to paganism.[7] In relatively short order, from the Edict of Milan to the Council of Nicea in 325 and the Edict of Theodisius in 380, Christianity was established as the state church, and heresies of every sort were outlawed.

Elaborate churches and liturgy emerged, creating in their wake a sort of clerical aristocracy and competitive clamoring for power and position. Non-Christian elements were introduced into the doctrines and practices of the church.[8] Protests over these developments marked the beginning of the monastic movement, with many expressing their displeasure with the new order by withdrawing to lives of ascetic solitude. Others, such as the Donatists in North Africa, declared outright that the church had become corrupted and that they alone remained the true church. These and other dissenters were often met with violence from the now-Christian state equal in ferocity to that perpetrated against Christians by the former Roman state. By the fifth century, the Theodosian Code contained more than 100 statutes actively penalizing heresy and heretics.

COMMENTS AND QUESTIONS

What accounts for the marked shift of Christians in the fourth century from being a persecuted to becoming a persecuting people? This seems to be a recurring historical phenomenon. What factors lead once-persecuted groups to become persecutors? What might prevent this from happening?

Additional Web Resources:	Materials on early history of church and state, including persecution of Christians and church-state structures after Christianity became dominant

6. *Id.* at 106–107.
7. *Id.* at 107–108. Paul Johnson, *A History of Christianity* 76 (Weidenfeld and Nicolson 1976).
8. Wallace K. Ferguson, Wallace Klippert, and Geoffrey Brunn, *A Survey of European Civilization* 88 (3d ed., Houghton Mifflin 1958).

B. PUNISHMENT OF HERESY

Once Christianity became entrenched, punishment of heresy became a recurrent practice. Today, the very idea of institutions such as the Inquisition and the image of heretics burning at the stake are repugnant. Brian Tierney describes the mindset that made such thinking possible:

> A decisive turning point in patristic thought came in the teaching of Augustine (354-430). In 395, when Augustine became bishop of Hippo in north Africa, he found the church in that region divided by a bitter schism between orthodox Catholics and a dissident group known as Donatists. Religious animosities gave rise to frequent civil disturbances, with riots and street fighting in the cities between the two factions. For years Augustine argued that only peaceful persuasion should be used to end the schism. Finally, however, he accepted the view of his fellow-bishops that the civil power should be called in to repress the dissidents.
>
> In some areas of political thought, medieval ideas were not so different from our own. Medieval people had quite well-developed concepts of representation and consent and government under law. But, when we turn to the idea of individual religious rights, their whole mindset was so alien to ours that it takes a considerable effort of historical imagination to enter into their world of thought. . . . The only bond of unity that held western Christian society together was the bond of a common religion. . . . Medieval people regarded heretics in much the same way [that we regard traitors to the state]; they held them guilty of treason to the church, and they treated them as traitors. When a common religion defined the whole way of life of a society, to reject it was to cut oneself off from the community, to become a sort of outlaw – and a dangerous outlaw from a medieval point of view.
>
> [Although Thomas Aquinas made a series of early arguments for toleration, he taught] heretics could be put to death. Sometimes the health of the whole body required that a diseased limb be cut away.
>
> Medieval people were so convinced of the truth of their religion that they could never see dissent from the accepted faith as arising simply from intellectual error, from a mistake in judgment. They thought that heresy must somehow stem from malice, from a perverted will that deliberately chose evil rather than good, Satan rather than God. Aquinas wrote, "Unfaithfulness is an act of the intellect, but moved by the will." This was the root cause of the medieval hatred of heresy. The heretics were seen, not only as traitors to the church, but as traitors to God. . . . Elementary justice and charity, it seemed, required that they be rooted out. The Inquisition that pursued this task with increasingly harsh and cruel measures, including the use of torture to extort confessions, was accepted as a necessary safeguard of Christian society.[9]

AN EARLY HERESY TRIAL: THE CASE OF JOHN HUS

Persecution of "heretics" gained momentum during medieval times and continued into the Reformation era. John Wycliffe, a scholar and theologian in Oxford, England, in the fourteenth century, published several treatises critical of the Roman Catholic Church. Among the practices he criticized were abuses by clergy of their position and influence, and he condemned the doctrine of transubstantiation. He also argued that the Bible should be translated into

---

9. Brian Tierney, Religious Rights: A Historical Perspective, in *Religious Liberty in Western Thought* 29, 33, 43–44, 45 (Noel B. Reynolds and W. Cole Durham, Jr., eds., Scholars Press for Emory Univ. 1996).

English.[10] One of the early full accounts of a trial for Christian heresy is the case of John Hus, a Bohemian priest tried in 1415 for supporting reform. Hus had been influenced by Wycliffe's writings, and he also spoke out against clerical abuses within the church. Eventually, he came to the attention of church authorities at the Council of Constance, which had been set up to unify the church and eradicate heresy. Although Hus contended that he did not espouse Wycliffe's ideas, the Council condemned him as a heretic on the basis of articles abstracted from his own writings and his refusal to condemn Wycliffe's writings. The following is an excerpt from the account of Hus's trial and punishment.[11]

> [On Friday, June 7,] they again brought [Hus] to a hearing in the said refectory, which was surrounded during each hearing by many city guards armed with swords, crossbows, axes, and spears. . . .
>
> [The Charge] stated that [Hus] in . . . 1410, at various times contrived, taught, and disputed about many errors and heresies both from the books of the late John Wyclif and from his own impudence and craftiness, defending them as far as he was able. . . .
>
> Further it is stated that the said John Hus obstinately preached and defended the erroneous articles of Wyclif in schools and in public sermons in the city of Prague. He replied that he had neither preached nor wished to follow the erroneous doctrine of Wyclif or of anyone else, as Wyclif was neither his father nor a Czech. And if Wyclif had disseminated some errors, let the English see to that.
>
> When they objected to him that he had resisted the condemnation of the forty-five articles of Wyclif, he replied that when the doctors had condemned his [Wyclif's] forty-five articles for the reason that none of them was Catholic, but that every one of them was either heretical, erroneous, or scandalous, he dared not consent to their condemnation because it was an offense to his conscience. . . .
>
> [. . . H]e declared specifically that he had not obstinately asserted any of those articles, but that he had resisted their condemnation along with other masters and had not consented to it, because he had wished to hear scriptural [proofs] or adequate reasons from those doctors which contended for the condemnation of the articles. . . .
>
> [Hus] replied that it was true that, twelve years ago, before his [Wyclif's] theological books had been [available] in Bohemia, and his books dealing with liberal arts had pleased [Hus] much, and he had known nothing but what was good of his life, he said: "I know not where the soul of that John W[yclif] is; but I hope that he is saved, but fear lest he be damned. Nevertheless, I would desire in hope that my soul were where the soul of John W[yclif] is!" And when he said that in the council, they laughed at him a great deal, shaking their heads. . . .
>
> Before he was led away, the cardinal of Cambrai said to him: "Master John, you said not long ago in the tower that you would wish humbly to submit to the judgment of the council. I counsel you, therefore, not to involve yourself in these errors, but to submit to the correction and instruction of the council; and the council will deal mercifully with you." . . .
>
> And he, Master John Hus, weeping, replied with humility: "Lord John, be sure that if I knew that I had written or preached anything erroneous against the law and against the holy mother Church, I would desire humbly to recant it – God is my witness! I have ever desired to be shown better and more relevant scripture than those

---

10. William Sime, *The Harbingers of the Reformation; or a Biographical Sketch of Wickliffe, Hus, and Jerome Boston* (Perkins & Marvin 1829).

11. Peter of Mladonovice, *The Examination and Execution of Hus*, reprinted in *Heresy and Authority in Medieval Europe: Documents in Translation* 289–297 (Edward Peters, ed., Univ. of Pennsylvania Press 1980).

that I have written and taught. And if they were shown me, I am ready most willingly to recant."

To those words one of the bishops present replied to Master John, "Do you wish to be wiser than the whole council?" The Master said to him, "I do not wish to be wiser than the whole council; but, I pray, give me the least one of the council who would instruct me by better and more relevant scripture, and I am ready instantly to recant!" To these words the bishops responded, "See, how obstinate he is in his heresy!" And with these words they ordered him to be taken back to the prison and went away. . . .

[The next day, July 6, Hus came before the Council for his final judgment and sentencing. The Council again read the articles containing the accusations. Hus was personally condemned for heresy, as were all the books he had written or translated, which were to be burned.]

. . . While the rest of the sentence was being read, [Hus] heard it kneeling and praying, looking up to heaven. When the sentence was concluded . . . in each of its particular points, Master John Hus again knelt and in a loud voice prayed for all his enemies and said: "Lord Jesus Christ, I implore Thee, forgive all my enemies for Thy great mercy's sake; and Thou knowest that they have falsely accused me and have produced false witnesses and have concocted false articles against me! Forgive them for Thy boundless mercy's sake!" And when he said this, many, especially the principal clergy, looked indignantly and jeered at him. . . .

[Before Hus was led out, a paper crown was placed upon his head, labeling him as a heretic. He was then taken to the place of execution, tied to a stake, and burned. Before he died, he again denied the charges against him, and prayed to God for mercy.]

COMMENTS AND QUESTIONS

1. Why did the members of the Council of Constance believe that condemning John Hus was justified? If the Council had recorded events surrounding the trial, how would the account differ from the story told by Hus's followers? Might it have described the case as more closely resembling treason?
2. Tierney argues that three factors ultimately led to the demise of punishment of heresy: (1) Skepticism rooted in Renaissance humanism questioned not the central doctrines of Christianity but many things about which Christians disagreed, such as predestination, free will, baptism, transubstantiation, and the Trinity. (2) Secular and economic interests in civil harmony should take priority over religious conformity. (3) The practice of persecution was contrary to the teaching of Jesus himself.[12] Which of these lines of argument seems most persuasive to you? Which do you think was most effective in ending punishment of heresy? Why?
3. Seventeenth-century Protestants often called for toleration of Jews and Turks, partially as a way of affirming a doctrine against forced conversion. Why would it be that they were much less willing to tolerate Catholics?[13]
4. Maruyama Masao was a Japanese historian and political theorist who became extremely influential in post-World War II Japan.[14] In a time when

12. Tierney, *supra* note 9, at 48–50.

13. *Id.* at 48.

14. Maruyama Masao, *International Dictionary of Intellectual Historians*, Ulrich Johannes Schneider and Donald R. Kelley, eds. (International Society for Intellectual History); Yoshikuni Igarashi, The Unfinished Business of Mourning: Maryama Masao and Postwar Japan's Struggle with the Wartime Past, *Positions: East Asia Cultures Critique*, 10 (1) (2002), 195-210.

many in his country were attempting to make sense of Japanese involvement in World War II, he published "The Logic and Psychology of Ultranationalism," an essay in which he put forward the theory of "transfer of oppression," a doctrine that has since gained considerable weight in the historical field. "In the absence of any free, subjective awareness," Maruyama wrote, "an individual's actions are not circumscribed by the dictates of conscience; instead, he is regulated by the existence of people in a higher class." In order to maintain the balance of the whole, the oppressed will exercise arbitrary power on those beneath them, especially sub-groups of themselves. "Just as Japan was subject to pressure from the Great Powers, so it would apply pressure to still weaker countries, a clear case of transfer psychology."[15]

Additional Web Resources:	Materials on medieval conceptions of heresy and apostasy; materials on the Inquisition and other heresy trials and witchcraft trials

III. THE EMERGENCE OF TOLERATION: THE ENGLISH EXPERIENCE

A. HISTORICAL DEVELOPMENT OF RELIGIOUS TOLERANCE IN ENGLAND

> If there were only one religion in England there would be danger of despotism, if there were two they would cut each other's throats, but there are thirty, and they live in peace and happiness.
>
> Voltaire, *Letters on England*, 1733[16]

The emergence of the idea of toleration can be traced in many settings, but the British experience has been particularly influential. The tension between religious and secular authorities was an important strand in English history, culminating with the break of the English church from the Pope in Rome during the reign of Henry VIII (1509-1547). However, this break with Rome did not signify a move toward individual liberty of conscience. There was still only one church in England, simply under a new head. Henry's jealousy of ecclesiastical power was evident in such legal provisions as the "Act for the Submission of the Clergy and Restraint of Appeals" (1534), in which the English clergy, upon threat of imprisonment and fine, were directed "that [neither] they nor any of them from henceforth shall presume to attempt, allege, claim, or put in ure [practice] any constitutions or ordinances, provincial or synodal, or any other canons; nor shall enact, promulge, or execute any such canons, constitutions, or ordinance

15. Maruyama Masao, *The Logic and Psychology of Ultrantionalism*, Alan Baumler, trans., adapted from Maruyama Masao, *Thought and Behavior in Modern Japanese Politics* (Oxford Univ. Press 1963), 16-18.

16. Voltaire, *Letters on England* 41 (Penguin Books 1980) (1733).

provincial, . . . unless the same clergy may have the king's most royal assent and licence. . . ."[17]

After the initial break from Rome, the religion of England followed the religion of the monarch. Queen Mary I (reigned 1553-1558) was quick to reverse Henry's perceived offenses against Rome in her "Statutes of Repeal" (1553 and 1555). The Second Statute of Repeal declared itself an act "repealing all statutes, articles, and provisions made against the see apostolic of Rome since the twentieth year of King Henry VIII. . . ."[18] The Parliament explained its rationale for enacting the statute by writing, "[S]ince the twentieth year of King Henry VIII of famous memory, . . . much false and erroneous doctrine hath been taught, preached, and written. . . ."[19]

The Parliament of Mary's successor, Elizabeth I (reigned 1558-1603), in its turn promulgated in 1559 "[a]n act restoring to the crown the ancient jurisdiction over the state ecclesiastical and spiritual and abolishing all foreign power [i.e., the papacy] repugnant to the same."[20]

As the Church of England became more permanently established, the mixing of secular and religious authority continued to be an issue of concern. During the contentious reign of Charles I (1625-1649), disputes between the Crown and Parliament, as well as the High Church and Puritans, culminated in the unprecedented execution of the monarch under the law. During Charles's reign, Parliament in 1641 completely barred clergy from holding public office. The Long Parliament's "Act Abolishing Temporal Power of the Clergy" declared "that no archbishop or bishop or other person that now is or hereafter shall be in holy orders, shall . . . have any seat or place, suffrage, or voice, or use, or execute any power or authority in the parliaments of this realm," nor sit in any other seat of civil government.[21]

How "graciously pleased" Charles really was about this act remains in question. In any event, Parliament, under his son and successor Charles II (reigned 1661-1685), readily repealed the act. About this same time, new developments in English law, while still asserting the supremacy of the Church of England and requiring various religious tests for those seeking public office,[22] the law (Charles's Royal Declaration of Indulgence of 1672), began to recognize the rights to worship of minority religions. However, these rights were by no means unlimited. The King's Declaration provided for the public assembly under

17. Act for the Submission of the Clergy and Restraint of Appeals (1534), reprinted in *1 Sources of English Constitutional History: A Selection of Documents from A.D. 600 to the Interregnum* 306 (Carl Stephenson and Frederick George Marcham, eds., trans., Harper & Row 1972) [hereinafter *1 Sources of English Constitutional History*].

18. *Id.* at 329.

19. *Id.*

20. Act of Supremacy (1559), reprinted in *1 Sources of English Constitutional History, supra* note 17 at 344.

21. Act Abolishing Temporal Power of the Clergy (1641), reprinted in *1 Sources of English Constitutional History*, supra note 17, at 486.

22. See Corporation Act (1661): "No person or persons shall forever hereafter be placed, elected, or chosen in or to any the offices or places aforesaid that shall not have within one year next before such election or choice taken the sacrament of the Lord's Supper according to the rites of the Church of England"; and First Test Act (1673): "This statute provides, inter alia, that all officers of the state shall receive the sacrament of the Lord's Supper according to the usage of the Church of England."

regulated circumstances of "all sorts of nonconformists and recusants, except the recusants of the Roman Catholic religion; to whom we shall no ways allow in public places of worship, but only indulge them their share in the common exemption from the executing the penal laws and the exercise of their worship in their private houses only."[23] The strong anti-Catholic sentiment prevalent in Britain under Charles II was further manifest in the Second Test Act (1678), "an act for the more effectual preserving the king's person and government, by disabling papists from sitting in either house of parliament."[24]

The English Bill of Rights (1689) and Act of Toleration (1689) continued to expand the rights of religious minorities. These exempted Church of England dissenters from many of the penalties previously imposed by law and granted Protestants considerable freedom in their worship practices and public/civic participation. Furthermore, when an oath of allegiance was required, loyalty to the Church of England was no longer required, but rather only renunciation of allegiance to the Pope. With few exceptions, freedom of religion for all Protestants had been realized. Catholics, however, would wait for another 140 years for the same privilege. Beginning in 1829, under the "Catholic Emancipation Act," Catholics would be permitted to hold any public office without having to deny their faith, upon the taking of an oath in which they denounced papist conspiracies to overthrow the monarchy and pledged their loyalty to the king.

COMMENTS AND QUESTIONS

1. While the Church in England recognized the Pope until the split during the English Reformation, for much of its history the Church of England was functionally independent of the Roman Church. Could this functional independence have helped the English justify the split with Rome and recognition of the king as the Church of England's head? What role might a notion of the "divine right of kings" play in justifying the king's appointing ecclesiastical leaders?
2. Much of the discrimination against Catholics was justified on the grounds that they would support the Pope in overthrowing the government and replacing it with a government loyal to the Pope. Was this a legitimate concern? To what extent was and is religious tolerance a foreign policy issue? Can similar concerns justify legal discrimination today? To what extent, for example, should (or do) foreign policy and national security considerations determine treatment of Muslims in countries in which they are immigrants or refugees?

B. JOHN LOCKE: A LETTER CONCERNING TOLERATION

The English philosopher John Locke is recognized as a key figure not only in the emergence of liberalism and social contract theory, but also in the framing of

---

23. Royal Declaration of Indulgence (1672), reprinted in *2 Sources of English Constitutional History: A Selection of Documents from the Interregnum to the Present* 559–560 (Carl Stephenson and Frederick George Marcham, eds., trans., Harper & Row 1972) [hereinafter *2 Sources of English Constitutional History*].

24. Second Test Act (1678), reprinted in *2 Sources of English Constitutional History,* 556.

modern conceptions of religious freedom. His work corresponds at the level of philosophy to the patterns of societal toleration emerging at the time. Many of his most fundamental arguments have become so axiomatic that their revolutionary nature is almost forgotten.[25] In fact, Locke's writings on the relationship between church and state represented a dramatic theoretical departure from previous thought on the subject. Throughout history, it was assumed that state implementation of religious belief was necessary for religious truth, and that religious and cultural homogeneity were necessary for political stability. The idea was that "an established homogeneous religion . . . could serve as a kind of social glue and ultimate motivation for loyalty and obedience to the regime."[26] In Europe, this impression was reinforced by the succession of religious wars that ravaged the continent.

In his *Letter Concerning Toleration*, first published in 1689, Locke rejected prevailing notions of church and state. He offered powerful arguments that state coercion is ineffectual in matters of religion, that the state can force no person to heaven. In fact, the best state religious coercion can gain is outward hypocrisy. Moreover, Locke contended that rather than destabilizing a regime, toleration and respect could have the opposite effect, creating within minority groups a source of social stability rather than social disintegration. Locke profoundly influenced many American thinkers, notably Thomas Jefferson and James Madison, who drew upon his work in building their cases for a broadened understanding of religious freedom. Locke's insights laid the foundations for most modern regimes of religious liberty.

The following passages express six of his key ideas:[27]

[Separation of Civil and Religious Spheres]

I esteem it above all things necessary to distinguish exactly the business of civil government from that of religion and to settle the just bounds that lie between the one and the other. If this be not done, there can be no end put to the controversies that will be always arising between those that have, or at least pretend to have, on the one side, a concernment for the interest of men's souls, and, on the other side, a care of the commonwealth.

The commonwealth seems to me to be a society of men constituted only for the procuring, preserving, and advancing their own civil interests. Civil interests I call life, liberty, health, and indolency of body; and the possession of outward things, such as money, lands, houses, furniture, and the like. It is the duty of the civil magistrate, by the impartial execution of equal laws, to secure unto all the people in general and to every one of his subjects in particular the just possession of these things belonging to this life.

[Civil Power Does Not Extend to the Religious Sphere]

Now that the whole jurisdiction of the magistrate reaches only to these civil concernments, and that all civil power, right and dominion, is bounded and confined to the only care of promoting these things; and that it neither can nor ought in any

---

25. Editors, Introduction, in *Religious Liberty in Western Thought* 9, 17 (Noel B. Reynolds and W. Cole Durham, Jr., eds., Scholars Press for Emory Univ. 1996).

26. W. Cole Durham, Jr., Perspectives on Religious Liberty: A Comparative Framework, in *Religious Human Rights in Global Perspective: Legal Perspectives* 1, 7 (Johan D. van der Vyver & John Witte Jr., eds., Martinus Nijhoff 1996).

27. John Locke, *A Letter Concerning Toleration* (William Popple, trans., Huddersfield 1796).

manner to be extended to the salvation of souls, these following considerations seem unto me abundantly to demonstrate.

First, because the care of souls is not committed to the civil magistrate, any more than to other men. It is not committed unto him, I say, by God; because it appears not that God has ever given any such authority to one man over another as to compel anyone to his religion. Nor can any such power be vested in the magistrate by the consent of the people, because no man can so far abandon the care of his own salvation as blindly to leave to the choice of any other, whether prince or subject, to prescribe to him what faith or worship he shall embrace.

[Second], the care of souls cannot belong to the civil magistrate, because his power consists only in outward force; but true and saving religion consists in the inward persuasion of the mind, without which nothing can be acceptable to God.

[Third], the care of the salvation of men's souls cannot belong to the magistrate; because, though the rigour of laws and the force of penalties were capable to convince and change men's minds, yet would not that help at all to the salvation of their souls. For there being but one truth, one way to heaven, what hope is there that more men would be led into it if they had no rule but the religion of the court and were put under the necessity to quit the light of their own reason, and oppose the dictates of their own consciences.

These considerations . . . seem unto me sufficient to conclude that all the power of civil government relates only to men's civil interests, is confined to the care of the things of this world, and hath nothing to do with the world to come.

[Religion Not Entitled to Assert Civil Power]

As the magistrate has no power to impose by his laws the use of any rites and ceremonies in any Church, so neither has he any power to forbid the use of such rites and ceremonies as are already received, approved, and practised by any Church; because, if he did so, he would destroy the Church itself. . . .

[L]et us inquire, in the next place: How far the duty of toleration extends, and what is required from everyone by it?

[F]irst, I hold that no church is bound, by the duty of toleration, to retain any such person in her bosom as, after admonition, continues obstinately to offend against the laws of the society. For, these being the condition of communion and the bond of the society, if the breach of them were permitted without any animadversion the society would immediately be thereby dissolved.

Secondly, no private person has any right in any manner to prejudice another person in his civil enjoyments because he is of another church or religion. These are not the business of religion. No violence nor injury is to be offered him, whether he be Christian or Pagan.

[C]hurches [also] stand, as it were, in the same relation to each other as private persons among themselves: nor has any one of them any manner of jurisdiction over any other; no, not even when the civil magistrate . . . comes to be of this or the other communion. For the civil government can give no new right to the church, nor the church to the civil government.

[Ecclesiastical authority] ought to be confined within the bounds of the Church, nor can it in any manner be extended to civil affairs, because the Church itself is a thing absolutely separate and distinct from the common-wealth. The boundaries on both sides are fixed and immovable.

[Incompetence of State to Ascertain Religious Truth]

[L]et us suppose two churches; the one of Arminians, the other of Calvinists; residing in the city of Constantinople. Will anyone say that either of these churches has right to deprive the members of the other of their estates and liberty (as we see practised elsewhere) because of their differing from it in some doctrines and ceremonies, whilst the Turks, in the meanwhile, silently stand by and laugh to see with what inhuman cruelty Christians thus rage against Christians? But if one of these churches hath this power of treating the other ill, I ask which of them it is to whom that power belongs, and by what right? It will be answered, undoubtedly, that it is the orthodox church which has the right of authority over the erroneous or heretical. This is, in great and specious words, to say just nothing at all. For every church is orthodox to itself; to others, erroneous or heretical. For whatsoever any church believes, it believes to be true and the contrary unto those things it pronounces to be error. So that the controversy between these churches about the truth of their doctrines and the purity of their worship is on both sides equal; nor is there any judge, either at Constantinople or elsewhere upon earth, by whose sentence it can be determined. The decision of that question belongs only to the Supreme judge of all men, to whom also alone belongs the punishment of the erroneous. In the meanwhile, let those men consider how heinously they sin, who, adding injustice, if not to their error, yet certainly to their pride, do rashly and arrogantly take upon them to misuse the servants of another master, who are not at all accountable to them.

[Plurality as a Source of Stability]

Let us therefore deal plainly. The magistrate is afraid of other Churches, but not of his own, because he is kind and favourable to the one, but severe and cruel to the other. These he cherishes and defends; those he continually scourges and oppresses. Let him turn the tables. Or let those dissenters enjoy but the same privileges in civils as his other subjects, and he will quickly find that these religious meetings will be no longer dangerous. Just and moderate governments are everywhere quiet, everywhere safe; but oppression raises ferments and makes men struggle to cast off an uneasy and tyrannical yoke. I know that seditions are very frequently raised upon pretence of religion, but it is as true that for religion subjects are frequently ill treated and live miserably. Believe me, the stirs that are made proceed not from any peculiar temper of this or that Church or religious society, but from the common disposition of all mankind, who when they groan under any heavy burthen endeavour naturally to shake off the yoke that galls their necks. There is only one thing which gathers people into seditious commotions, and that is oppression.

Now if that Church which agrees in religion with the prince be esteemed the chief support of any civil government, and that for no other reason (as has already been shown) than because the prince is kind and the laws are favourable to it, how much greater will be the security of government where all good subjects, of whatsoever Church they be, without any distinction upon account of religion, enjoying the same favour of the prince and the same benefit of the laws, shall become the common support and guard of it, and where none will have any occasion to fear the severity of the laws but those that do injuries to their neighbours and offend against the civil peace?

[No Obligation to Tolerate Intolerance]

Another more secret evil, but more dangerous to the commonwealth, is when men arrogate to themselves, and to those of their own sect, some peculiar prerogative covered over with a specious show of deceitful words, but in effect opposite to the civil right of the community. For example: we cannot find any sect that teaches, expressly and openly, that men are not obliged to keep their promise; that princes may be dethroned by those that differ from them in religion; or that the dominion of all things belongs only to themselves. For these things, proposed thus nakedly and plainly, would soon draw on them the eye and hand of the magistrate and awaken all the care of the commonwealth to a watchfulness against the spreading of so dangerous an evil. But, nevertheless, we find those that say the same things in other words. What else do they mean who teach that faith is not to be kept with heretics? Their meaning, forsooth, is that the privilege of breaking faith belongs unto themselves; for they declare all that are not of their communion to be heretics, or at least may declare them so whensoever they think fit. What can be the meaning of their asserting that kings excommunicated forfeit their crowns and kingdoms? It is evident that they thereby arrogate unto themselves the power of deposing kings, because they challenge the power of excommunication, as the peculiar right of their hierarchy. These, therefore, and the like, who attribute unto the faithful, religious, and orthodox, that is, in plain terms, unto themselves, any peculiar privilege or power above other mortals, in civil concernments; or who upon pretence of religion do challenge any manner of authority over such as are not associated with them in their ecclesiastical communion, I say these have no right to be tolerated by the magistrate; as neither those that will not own and teach the duty of tolerating all men in matters of mere religion.

COMMENTS AND QUESTIONS

1. Does Locke accurately depict the line between civil and religious authority? Is his delineation biased in favor of Catholicism or Protestantism?
2. Locke suggests that at least one of the reasons the civil magistrate should not intervene in religious matters is that authentic belief cannot be coerced; at best, a state can coerce only hypocritical, outward performance. Is this argument correct? Can state influence mold religious belief? If a state cannot compel belief, can it nonetheless block belief formation by preventing information dissemination?
3. Is Locke correct in claiming that the state is incompetent in matters of religion? Does this create a jurisdictional bar to state assessment of religion? Is the state competent to assess particularly dangerous forms of religion? What are the limits of state competence?
4. Locke argues that the intolerant need not be tolerated. Is this a workable principle for setting the outside limits of religious freedom? Of liberal theory in general? How wide a circle of protection does this principle draw? Various passages suggest that Locke thought Catholics, Muslims, and atheists should not be protected. Could Locke have had the right principle, but have applied it too narrowly?
5. Our historical experience suggests the notion that respect for difference can yield stability for a much more pluralistic society than Locke imagined. How pluralistic can a society get before it disintegrates? What holds pluralistic societies together?

Additional Web Resources:	Extended collection of passages from John Milton, John Locke, and other prominent thinkers associated with the rise of toleration

C. RELIGIOUS CONTRIBUTIONS TO RELIGIOUS FREEDOM

While it is often argued that "[t]olerance triumphed in the eighteenth century . . . because reason triumphed over faith," religious ideals actually contributed directly to the religious freedom clauses of the First Amendment of the US Constitution. In fact, Nicholas Miller has argued that the separation of church and state was originally a religious idea, promoted by "Biblically-conservative Christians." He further suggests that the liberal thinkers who promoted

Enlightenment thought, such as John Locke, were largely influenced by these Protestant religious ideas.[28]

Miller shows that toleration was in large measure the result of "the triumph of a particular strand of Protestant nonconformity" that taught "the right of private judgment in biblical interpretation." This Protestant principle played a major role in the Protestant revolution under the idea that all Christians have a duty to read the Bible and interpret its passages for themselves. It relates closely to Luther's doctrine that every Christian can pray directly to Christ themselves, interpret the Bible themselves, and question any aspect of the Church's teachings that are inconsistent with the Bible. This idea traces a respect for individual beliefs that propelled religious freedom in the teachings of "early Luther, the Anabaptists, Sebastian Castellio, the England Baptists, and John Milton."

While the right of private judgment played a major role in Enlightenment thought, it originated in Protestant theology and was only later borrowed by Enlightenment thinkers. Religiously orthodox leaders, such as Cotton Mather, were the first to invoke the idea in the American colonies. When the principle began to take an Enlightenment and secular tone, both religious leaders, including Mather and Josiah Smith, and Enlightenment thinkers, such as John Trenchard and Thomas Gordon, agreed that it originated from Protestant thought. Both groups identified the beliefs as coming from scripture. Only in the 1750s and 60s did the right become more often associated with Enlightenment thought.

However, theological and biblically conservative thinkers, especially Elisha Williams and Isaac Backus, continued to invoke the idea despite its secular branching promoted by thinkers such as Johnathan Mayhew. Williams and Backus were largely responsible for bringing the idea from the early eighteenth century to the American Revolution. In fact, Backus continued to be publicly active up to the writing of the Constitution, showing a strong Protestant influence through the Constitutional period.

In 1776, John Witherspoon and James Madison made their entrances into the public arena. Witherspoon was a pastor, professor, and college administrator who was responsible for the theological training that directly affected Madison's public thinking. Aside from William Penn, Witherspoon and Madison were probably the theological thinkers of the eighteenth century most responsible for applying the religious right of private judgment to actual governance. On 17 May 1776, Witherspoon gave a bold sermon entitled "The Dominion of Providence over the Affairs of Men" that was significant in relating religious freedom to the revolution. Witherspoon was directly involved in the passage of the Declaration of Independence, the Articles of Confederation, and the Constitution.

---

28. Nicholas Miller, *The Religious Roots of the First Amendment: Dissenting Protestants and the Separation of Church and State* (Oxford Univ. Press 2012).

IV. THE EMERGENCE OF RELIGIOUS LIBERTY RIGHTS: COMPETING APPROACHES

Many of America's first European settlers, especially in the northern British colonies, came to the western continent for religious reasons. The Puritans intended to establish at Massachusetts Bay "a city on a hill" that would stand as a model Christian society for all the world. Naturally, the law and cultural norms of these early colonies were imbued with religious content that held consequences for everyone, whether orthodox (as to the new or old orthodoxies), dissenters, passing merchants, or Native Americans. Despite regional differences, religious pluralism was a social reality throughout the colonies, and it created the experiential base for tolerance and religious liberty. In time the need for mutual understanding would be greatly magnified with the onset of the Revolutionary War (1775), was finally resolved through creation and enactment of the US Constitution (1789).

From an early period in American history, two broad approaches to the relation of religions and state institutions have emerged. The first, associated with Roger Williams, the founder of Rhode Island (1776), emphasized separation of religion from state to protect the "garden" of the church from the "wilderness" of the secular order. That is, the ideal of separation was advocated with the aim of protecting religion. The second, associated with Jefferson and drawing on French experience, defended separation with the aim of protecting state institutions from excessive religious influence. These contrasting rationales for religious freedom represent two key streams in the ongoing dialogue concerning the place of religion in American life. In a larger sense, they represent competing poles in the much wider global discourse concerning the secularity of state institutions and the way the state should interact with religious life.

These competing strands have played out in America against the background of surprisingly different church-state traditions, ranging from formally established "state" churches in early New England to more secular regimes elsewhere. Many Americans forget that when the First Amendment was framed, its pronouncement that "Congress shall make no law respecting an establishment of religion" was aimed at ensuring that the federal government would not interfere with established religions in several states. Here we focus on Massachusetts and Virginia, which yields models different yet representative of early American church-state relations. Their comparison gives some sense of how the competing approaches to church and state relations in America evolved.

A. SEPARATION FOR THE SAKE OF RELIGION

Roger Williams founded Rhode Island following his expulsion in 1635 from the Massachusetts Bay Colony. Interestingly, Williams's most famous written work was published in England during a return visit to his native country to seek a charter for his New World colony. *The Bloudy Tenent of Persecution* stands as a prominent and prescient early example of Anglo-American argument for religious liberty. The outline below is excerpted from the tract's introduction and lays out the basic principles of Williams's work. This is followed by a famous passage from a 1655 Letter to the Town of Providence that provides another slant on Williams's view of church and state.

The Bloudy Tenent of Persecution, for Cause of Conscience, Discussed, in a Conference betweene Truth and Peace (1644)

First, that the blood of so many hundred thousand souls of Protestants and Papists, spilt in the wars of present and former ages, for their respective consciences, is not required nor accepted by Jesus Christ the Prince of Peace.

Secondly, pregnant scriptures and arguments are throughout the work proposed against the doctrine of persecution for cause of conscience. . .

Fourthly, the doctrine of persecution for cause of conscience is proved guilty of all the blood of the souls crying for vengeance under the altar.

Fifthly, all civil states with their officers of justice in their respective constitutions and administrations are proved essentially civil, and therefore not judges, governors, or defenders of the spiritual or Christian state and worship.

Sixthly, it is the will and command of God that (since the coming of his Son the Lord Jesus) a permission of the most paganish, Jewish, Turkish, or anti-Christian consciences and worships, be granted to all men in all nations and countries; and they are only to be fought against with that sword which is only (in soul matters) able to conquer, to wit, the sword of God's Spirit, the Word of God. . .

Eighthly, God requireth not a uniformity of religion to be enacted and enforced in any civil state; which enforced uniformity (sooner or later) is the greatest occasion of civil war, ravishing of conscience, persecution of Christ Jesus in his servants, and of the hypocrisy and destruction of millions of souls. . . .

Eleventhly, the permission of other consciences and worships than a state professeth only can (according to God) procure a firm and lasting peace (good assurance being taken according to the wisdom of the civil state for uniformity of civil obedience from all sorts).

Twelfthly, lastly, true civility and Christianity may both flourish in a state or kingdom, notwithstanding the permission of divers and contrary con-sciences, either of Jew or Gentile. . . .

Letter to the Town of Providence (1655)

That ever I should speak or write a tittle, that tends to such an infinite liberty of conscience, is a mistake, and which I have ever disclaimed and abhorred. To prevent such mistakes, I shall at present only propose this case: There goes many a ship to sea, with many hundred souls in one ship, whose weal and woe is common, and is a true picture of a commonwealth, or a human combination or society. It hath fallen out sometimes, that both Papists and Protestants, Jews and Turks, may be embarked in one ship; upon which supposal I affirm, that all the liberty of conscience, that ever I pleaded for, turns upon these two hinges – that none of the Papists, Protestants, Jews or Turks, be forced to come to the ship's prayers or worship, nor compelled from their own particular prayers or worship, if they practice any. I further add, that I never denied, that notwithstanding this liberty, the commander of this ship ought to command the ship's course, yea, and also command that justice, peace and sobriety, be kept and practiced, both among the seamen and all the passengers. If any of the seamen refuse to perform their services, or passengers to pay their freight; if any refuse to help, in person or purse, toward the common charges or defence; if any refuse to obey the common laws and orders of the ship, concerning their common peace or preservation; if any shall mutiny and rise up against their commanders and officers; if any should preach or write that there ought to be no commanders or officers, because all are equal in Christ, therefore no masters nor officers, no laws nor orders, nor corrections nor punishments; – I say, I never denied, but in such cases, whatever is pre-tended, the commander or commanders may judge, resist, compel and punish such transgressors, according to their deserts and merits. This, if seriously and honestly minded, may, if it so please the Father of lights, let in some light to such as willingly shut not their eyes.

I remain studious of your common peace and liberty. . . .

B. SEPARATION FOR THE SAKE OF THE SECULAR STATE

Jefferson's Statute for Religious Freedom, drafted in 1777 and first submitted to Virginia's governing body in 1779, remains in many ways the classic Enlightenment affirmation of religious freedom. The version of the bill that was finally enacted in 1786 "outlawed any government compulsion to support religious worship or teaching and barred any civil penalties for individuals' religious opinions or belief."[29] Notably, Jefferson chose to include authorship of the statute as one of three accomplishments memorialized on his gravestone, ranking this with authorship of the Declaration of Independence and founding the University of Virginia. He did not even mention being president of the United States. Harvard historian Bernard Bailyn maintains that Jefferson's statute is "the most important document in US history, bar none."[30]

As you read the statute, ask yourself why it would merit such a lofty assessment.

VIRGINIA STATUTE FOR RELIGIOUS FREEDOM (1786)

Whereas, Almighty God hath created the mind free;

that all attempts to influence it by temporal punishment, or burdens, or by civil incapacitations, tend only to beget habits of hypocrisy and meanness, and are a departure from the plan of the Holy Author of our religion, who being Lord both of body and mind, yet chose not to propagate it by coercions on either, as was in his Almighty power to do;

that the impious presumption of legislators and rulers, civil as well as ecclesiastical, who, being themselves but fallible and uninspired men, have assumed dominion over the faith of others, setting up their own opinions and modes of thinking as the only true and infallible, and as such endeavoring to impose them on others, have established and maintained false religions over the greatest part of the world, and through all time;

---

29. W. Cole Durham, Jr., and Elizabeth A. Sewell, Virginia Founders and Birth of Religious Freedom, in *Lectures on Religion and the Founding of the American Republic*, 72 (John W. Welch and Stephen J. Fleming, eds., Brigham Young Univ. Press 2003).

30. Quoted in Garrett Ward Sheldon and Daniel L. Dreisbach, eds., *Religion and Political Culture in Jefferson's Virginia* 153 (Rowman and Littlefield 2000).

that to compel a man to furnish contributions of money for the propagation of opinions which he disbelieves, is sinful and tyrannical, and even the forcing him to support this or that teacher of his own religious persuasion, is depriving him of the comfortable liberty of giving his contributions to the particular pastor whose morals he would make his pattern, and whose powers he feels most persuasive to righteousness, and is withdrawing from ministry those temporary rewards which, proceeding from an approbation of their personal conduct, are an additional incitement to earnest and unremitting labors, for the instruction of mankind;

that our civil rights have no dependence on our religious opinions any more than our opinions in physics or geometry; that therefore the proscribing any citizen as unworthy the public confidence by laying upon him an incapacity of being called of offices of trust and emolument, unless he profess or renounce this or that religious opinion, is depriving him injuriously of those privileges and advantages to which, in common with his fellow citizens, he has a natural right; that it tends only to corrupt the principles of that religion it is meant to encourage, by bribing, with a monopoly of worldly honors and emoluments, those who will externally profess and conform to it;

that though, indeed, those are criminal who do not withstand such temptation, yet, neither are those innocent who lay the bait in their way; that to suffer the civil magistrate to intrude his powers into the field of opinion, and to restrain the profession or propagation of principles on supposition of their ill tendency, is a dangerous fallacy, which at once destroys all religious liberty, because he, being of course judge of that tendency, will make his opinions the rule of judgment, and approve or condemn the sentiments of others only as they shall square with or differ from his own; that it is time enough for the rightful purposes of civil government, for its officers to interfere, when principles break out into overt acts against peace and good order; and finally,

that truth is great and will prevail, if left to herself; that she is the proper and sufficient antagonist to error, and has nothing to fear from the conflict, unless by human interposition disarmed of her natural weapons, free argument and debate; errors ceasing to be dangerous when it is permitted freely to contradict them:

Be it enacted by the General Assembly, That no man shall be compelled to frequent or support any religious worship, place of ministry whatsoever, nor shall be enforced, restrained, molested, or burdened, in his body or goods, nor shall otherwise suffer on account of his religious opinions of belief; but that all men shall be free to profess, and by argument to maintain, their opinion in matters of religion, and that the same shall in no wise diminish, enlarge or affect their civil capacities.

And though we well know that this Assembly, elected by the people for the ordinary purposes of legislation only, have no power to restrain the acts of succeeding assemblies constituted with powers equal to our own, and that, therefore, to declare this act to be irrevocable would be of no effect in law; yet we are free to declare, and do declare, that the rights hereby asserted are of the natural rights of mankind; and that if any act shall be hereafter passed to repeal the present, or to narrow its operations, such act will be infringement of natural right.

COMMENTS AND QUESTIONS

While Williams and Jefferson represent two poles in American thought, their ideas are richer and more complex than simplified views of their positions might suggest. Thus, Williams was not concerned solely with protection of the church from the state any more than Jefferson was concerned only with protecting the state from religion. In what ways do their views overlap? To what extent are their differences mirrored in modern debates between religious believers and secularists? To what extent has the discussion changed?

Additional Web Resources:	Materials on Williams and Jefferson, including additional texts and biographical information, as well as materials on the two strands of American church-state theory they represent

C. THE MASSACHUSETTS EXPERIENCE

Having descended from those who settled their "city on a hill" and expelled Roger Williams (and other dissenters) from their community, the post-Revolutionary political leaders of Massachusetts were not willing to part with established laws and traditions favoring Congregationalists. Even the political ferment of the Revolutionary period, when the colonists worked in earnest to dismantle the trappings of English governance, did little to alter the situation in New England. Isaac Backus, a Baptist minister dedicated to advocating disestablishment of the Congregationalist church, attended the Continental Congress in 1775 to express frustration over and seek relief from establishment arrangements in Massachusetts. He later recalled the reaction of John Adams, who told him that the Baptists "might as well expect a change in the solar system."[31] At the same time, Congregationalists attempted to distinguish their favored status from the "evil" form of establishment instituted in England, where their Congregationalist forebears had been excluded and oppressed.

During the state constitutional convention in 1780, Baptist Noah Alden submitted a proposal drafted by Isaac Backus that would protect the right to voluntary worship.[32] The proposal was rejected and the convention finally resolved on the Article III of the Declaration of Rights. Article III allowed local governments, made up almost entirely of Congregationalists, "to make suitable provision . . . for the institution of public worship of GOD, and for the support and maintenance of public protestant teachers of piety, religion and

31. Isaac Backus, *A History of New England with Particular Reference to the Denomination of Christians Called Baptists* 201–202 (Arno Press 1969) (1871).

32. Carl H. Esbeck, Dissent and Disestablishment: The Church-State Settlement in the Early American Republic, 2004 *BYU L. Rev.* 1385, 1442 (2004).

morality."[33] The provision was justified in that "the happiness of a people, and the good order and preservation of civil government, essentially depend upon piety, religion and morality," which can only be spread through the community by religious institutions, and the government must be able "to promote" these values throughout the Commonwealth.[34]

Dissenters were able to win a few small concessions during the convention: church support might be "voluntary"; election of public teachers would be made by local governments and political bodies, as well as "religious societies"; and an individual's tax money would go "to the support of the public teacher or teachers of his own religious sect." However, in spite of these provisions and the concluding promise that "no subordination of any one sect or denomination to another shall ever be established by law,"[35] the practical effect of Article III was a continuation of the long-established system that favored the Congregationalists. Not surprisingly, the Baptists and other minority religious groups denounced Article III. They attacked it primarily as an improper interference of government in matters of conscience and religion. Moreover, they found its promise of equal protection hollow, given the fact that Congregationalists would control both administration and enforcement. Backus launched a pamphleteering campaign to try to prevent ratification. However, even though Article III as it stood only received 59 percent approval, falling short of the two-thirds majority required, the convention decided to count only those precincts that rejected it in full (as opposed to those who would have accepted it with modification) as votes against ratification.[36] Article III, therefore, became part of the Massachusetts Constitution.

The Massachusetts Constitution of 1780 further enmeshed church and state in two other provisions. First, it required state elected officials to swear two oaths of office: an oath of belief in "the christian religion" and an oath to renounce allegiance to foreign powers.[37] The latter oath was clearly aimed at excluding Catholics from public office, as evidenced by open admission of convention delegates.[38] Finally, this constitution allowed for legislative allocation of taxes to support the training of Congregationalist ministers at Harvard College.

Isaac Backus continued to advocate disestablishment in Massachusetts. However, these efforts held little promise in light of the establishment system's constitutional protection. Many dissatisfied Baptists exercised civil disobedience by refusing to pay the religious taxes required by law. Elijah Balkcom succeeded

---

33. A Declaration of the Rights of the Inhabitants of the Commonwealth of Massachusetts (1780), reprinted in *Journal of the Convention for Framing a Constitution for the State of Massachusetts Bay* 223–234 (A.H. Everett, comp., 1832) [hereinafter *Journal of the Convention*].

34. *Id.*

35. *Id.*

36. Esbeck, *supra* note 32, at 1443–1444.

37. Constitution of Massachusetts (1780), reprinted in *Journal of the Convention, supra* note 33, at 245–246.

38. An Address of the Convention to Their Constituents, reprinted in *Journal of the Convention, supra* note 33, at 220–221 ("Your Delegates did not conceive themselves to be vested with Power to set up one Denomination of Christians above another; . . . But we have nevertheless, found ourselves obliged by a Solemn Test, to provide for the exclusion of those from Offices who will not disclaim those Principles of Spiritual Jurisdiction which Roman Catholicks *in some Countries* have held, and which are subversive of a free Government established by the People.").

in suing the county assessors on the theory that the state Constitution was inconsistent in promising that no denomination would be subordinate to another but also requiring religious taxes to be paid to the support of the Congregationalist church if a person failed to direct them to his own church. Baptists encouraged by this judicial victory would, unfortunately, be disappointed again only two years later. In the case of Gershom Cutter, a similar scenario to Balkcom's, the Superior Court ruled that only churches incorporated by the state would be recognized by law. Since incorporating would mean submitting to the state legislature, the Baptists declined to follow this route.[39] Massachusetts would be the last American state to officially end the system of established religion. This was marked by two key developments. In 1821 the oath of office was changed by constitutional amendment to no longer require profession of belief in the Christian religion, and in 1833, religious taxation was ended by constitutional amendment.[40]

D. THE VIRGINIA EXPERIENCE

While political leaders in Massachusetts were reluctant to disestablish religion, prominent voices in Virginia took a decidedly different approach. As a result, perhaps nowhere more than in Virginia did the religious debate take on a form that would have such significant consequences for the American approach to church-state relations.

Virginia, the largest and most populous state in the new union, was also one of the states where the Church of England was most fully established, resulting in significant church-state controversies after the Revolution.[41] The debates over establishment of religion brought out Virginia's best talent. The views and writings of early Virginian leaders such as Thomas Jefferson, James Madison, Patrick Henry, and George Mason had a tremendous impact on the subsequent understanding and protection of religious freedom in the United States.

While Virginia was not the first state to end the establishment of religion, its decision and the documents arising in the course of developments there have had a particularly significant influence in the history of the United States, leading ultimately to the adoption of the First Amendment and eventually to the entire system of benevolent separation of church and state that has since emerged.

Concerning this period in Virginia, Jon Meacham has written:

> The road to religious freedom [in America] was not easy. In 1777, after a meeting at the Rising Sun Tavern in Fredericksburg, Virginia, Jefferson wrote a statute for religious freedom within the state. He drafted a bill, but it took almost a decade to become law. Opinion on both sides of the establishment question was strong – many believers saw no compelling reason to give up the flow of tax dollars – but the tide favored the more liberally minded.
>
> The events leading to the passage of the Virginia statute came to a head in 1784, when John Blair Smith, a Presbyterian clergyman and president of the private Hampden-Sydney College in Prince Edward County, petitioned the state legislature for public dollars on behalf of the Hanover Presbytery. Madison and Jefferson joined forces. "The legitimate powers of government extend to such acts only as are injurious

39. Esbeck, *supra* note 32, at 1444–1447.

40. *See* MGLA Const. Pt. 1, Art. 3; MGLA Const. Pt. 2, Ch. 6, Art. 1.

41. Thomas E. Buckley, *Church and State in Revolutionary Virginia (1776–1787)* 5 (Univ. Press of Virginia 1977).

to others," Jefferson, who was in Paris, once said. "But it does me no injury for my neighbor to say there are twenty gods, or no God. It neither picks my pocket nor breaks my leg." Madison, on the scene in Virginia, noted, "Whilst we assert for ourselves a freedom to embrace, to profess and to observe the religion which we believe to be of divine origin, we cannot deny an equal freedom to those whose minds have not yet yielded to the evidence which has convinced us."

Patrick Henry, then a lawmaker, disagreed. (By this time Jefferson and Madison had fallen out with Henry and opposed him on other issues. "What we have to do I think is devoutly to pray for his death," Jefferson wrote Madison of Henry at one point.) Henry's current proposal was to pay for "teachers of the Christian religion" with public money; Henry was the bill's chief sponsor, but he was elected governor in November 1784, a move that took him out of the legislature. With this opening, Madison struck in 1785, writing a "Memorial and Remonstrance" on the subject of state support for churches. When religious and civil power were intertwined, Madison said, "What have been its fruits? More or less in all places, pride and indolence in the clergy, ignorance and servility in the laity; in both, superstition, bigotry and persecution."

At one point the pro-Christian forces in Virginia tried to put Jesus in the middle of Jefferson's bill by including the phrase "Jesus Christ, the holy author of our religion," but the sectarians were beaten back, Jefferson said, "by a great majority," and his bill became law in January 1786. . . .

Despite the debates then and since, history has proven Madison and his colleagues largely right: in hindsight, a secular successor document to the Declaration of Independence made a great deal of sense, and there is no arguing with the Constitution's durability. In a way, the making of the Constitution and the subtle political and personal forces at work on Madison and the others foreshadowed how statesmen would have to balance God and government for years to come. Given the choice to tack toward the secular or the sectarian, they chose to practice what they had been preaching about severing church from state while creating a culture in which religion would rise or fall on its own merits.[42]

NOTE ON THE MEANING OF "ESTABLISHMENT"

The notion of an "establishment of religion" was clearly understood at the time of the founding to refer to official state religions such as those existing at the time in Europe. However, while establishment in Europe typically meant support for a single denomination, establishment in the colonies typically meant support of a variety of denominations on a nonpreferential basis.[43]

After the Revolution, only six states had state-established religions. Three of the six states—Massachusetts, Connecticut, and New Hampshire—"had a multiple, not a single, establishment under which Baptist, Episcopalian, Methodist, and Unitarian churches were publicly supported."[44] Massachusetts ended its establishment in 1833; Connecticut and New Hampshire ended theirs in 1818 and 1819, respectively.[45]

---

42. Jon Meacham, *American Gospel: God, the Founding Fathers, and the Making of a Nation* 84–87 (Random House, 2006).

43. Leonard W. Levy, *Establishment of Religion, in Encyclopedia of the American Constitution* 927, 928 (2d ed., Leonard W. Levy and Kenneth L. Karst, eds., Macmillan 2000).

44. *Id.*

45. *Id.*

Maryland and Georgia initially allowed what were in effect multiple establishments in that taxation for the support of Christian religions was permitted. South Carolina was similar, except that it allowed support only of Protestant religions.[46] Several states taxed their citizens for the support of religion but allowed each individual to choose which church his tax money would support. Establishment in the South had vanished by 1810.

COMMENTS AND QUESTIONS

Is the United States a "Christian nation"? This question gets considerable play in twenty-first century American culture and politics. Once again illustrating the notion of contrasting stands in American religious discourse, either answer to this question can find authoritative historical support. On the one hand is the 1797 *Treaty to Peace and Friendship between the United States and the Bey and Subjects of Tripoli, of Barbary*, which was unanimously approved by the Senate before being signed into law by President John Adams, and which clearly states that "the Government of the United States of America is not, in any sense, founded on the Christian religion." A hundred years later, in the 1892 case *Church of the Holy Trinity v. United States*, the Supreme Court referenced "a mass of organic utterances that this is a Christian nation" (143 US 457, 471). Might these two assertions, which seem clearly to contradict each other, be reconciled if their purpose and context in which they are made are considered?

Additional Web Resources:	Materials on religious freedom in North America, including background documents and debates leading up to the adoption of the First Amendment to the US Constitution, and relevant state constitutional provisions

V. RELIGIOUS CONFRONTATIONS IN THE MODERN ERA: CASES ON PROSELYTISM

A. POST-WORLD WAR II AMERICAN EXPERIENCE

The Free Exercise Clause began essentially as a limit on federal power. The original emphasis was on the limits placed on Congress. During the first 105 years of its existence, the Free Exercise Clause was not even applied to the states. The basic idea was that religious freedom was promoted sufficiently by constraining federal power per se.

In 1940 the United States Supreme Court addressed the applicability of the Free Exercise Clause to the states for the first time in *Cantwell v. Connecticut*, and held that this provision of the First Amendment did indeed apply to the states, through incorporation in the Fourteenth Amendment.

Cantwell marked the beginning of what has become modern American free exercise jurisprudence.

46. *Id.*

CANTWELL V. CONNECTICUT

Supreme Court of the United States, 310 U.S. 296 (1940)

Mr. Justice ROBERTS delivered the opinion of the Court.

[Three Jehovah's Witnesses, Newton Cantwell and his two sons, were convicted under an information that charged in its third count violation of §6294 of the General Statutes of Connecticut (which prohibited soliciting without receiving an administrative approval) and in its fifth count commission of the common law offense of inciting a breach of the peace. The convictions of all three were affirmed with respect to the third count, but only the conviction of Jesse Cantwell was affirmed on the fifth count.

With respect to the third count, the facts were that the appellants went from house to house in Cassius Street in New Haven with a bag of books, a portable phonograph, and set of records that, when played, described the books. The Cantwells would ask individuals they met for permission to play one of the records, and would attempt to sell a copy or to solicit a donation for the costs of publication. Cassius Street was a thickly populated neighborhood that was about 90 percent Roman Catholic. Section 6294 provided that "[n]o person shall solicit money, services, subscriptions or any valuable thing for any alleged religious, charitable or philanthropic cause from other than a member of the organization for whose benefit such person is soliciting . . . unless such cause shall have been approved by the secretary of the public welfare council. Upon application of any person in behalf of such cause, the secretary shall determine whether such cause is a religious one or is a bona fide object of charity . . . [and if so shall issue a certificate to that effect]."

The facts supporting the fifth count were that Jesse Cantwell stopped two men in the street, received permission to play a record that attacked the religion of the two men, who were Catholics. Both were incensed by the record and were tempted to strike Cantwell unless he went away. On being told to be on his way, he left their presence. There was no evidence that he was personally offensive or entered into any argument with those he interviewed.]

The [lower] court held that the charge was not assault or breach of the peace or threats on Cantwell's part, but invoking or inciting others to breach of the peace, and that the facts supported the conviction of that offense.

First. We hold that the statute, as construed and applied to the appellants, deprives them of their liberty without due process of law in contravention of the Fourteenth Amendment. The fundamental concept of liberty embodied in that Amendment embraces the liberties guaranteed by the First Amendment. The First Amendment declares that Congress shall make no law respecting an establishment of religion or prohibiting the free exercise thereof. The Fourteenth Amendment has rendered the legislatures of the states as incompetent as Congress to enact such laws. The constitutional inhibition of legislation on the subject of religion has a double aspect. On the one hand, it forestalls compulsion by law of the acceptance of any creed or the practice of any form of worship. Freedom of conscience and freedom to adhere to such religious organization or form of worship as the individual may choose cannot be restricted by law. On the other hand, it safeguards the free exercise of the chosen form of religion. Thus the Amendment embraces two concepts, – freedom to believe and freedom to act. The first is absolute but, in the nature of things, the second cannot be. Conduct remains subject to regulation for the protection of society. The freedom to act must have appropriate definition to preserve the enforcement of that protection. In every case the power to regulate must be so exercised as not, in attaining a permissible end, unduly to infringe the protected freedom. No one would contest the proposition that a state may not, by statute, wholly deny the right to preach or to disseminate religious views. Plainly such a previous and absolute restraint would violate the terms of the guarantee. It is equally clear that a state may by general and non-discriminatory legislation regulate the times, the places, and the manner of soliciting upon its streets, and of holding meetings thereon; and may in other respects safeguard the peace, good order and comfort of the community, without unconstitutionally invading the liberties protected by the Fourteenth Amendment. The appellants are right in their insistence that the Act in question is not such a regulation. If a certificate is procured, solicitation is permitted without restraint but, in the absence of a certificate, solicitation is altogether prohibited. . . .

The general regulation, in the public interest, of solicitation, which does not involve any religious test and does not unreasonably obstruct or delay the collection of funds, is not open to any constitutional objection, even though the collection be for a religious purpose. Such regulation would not constitute a prohibited previous restraint on the free exercise of religion or interpose an inadmissible obstacle to its exercise.

It will be noted, however, that the Act requires an application to the secretary of the public welfare council of the State; that he is empowered to determine whether the cause is a religious one, and that the issue of a certificate depends upon his affirmative action. If he finds that the cause is not that of religion, to solicit for it becomes a crime. He is not to issue a certificate as a matter of course. His decision to issue or refuse it involves appraisal of facts, the exercise of judgment, and the formation of an opinion. He is authorized to withhold his approval if he determines that the cause is not a religious one. Such a censorship of religion as the means of determining its right to survive is a denial of liberty protected by the First Amendment and included in the liberty which is within the protection of the Fourteenth.

Nothing we have said is intended even remotely to imply that, under the cloak of religion, persons may, with impunity, commit frauds upon the public. Certainly penal laws are available to punish such conduct. Even the exercise of religion may be at some slight inconvenience in order that the state may protect its citizens from injury. Without doubt a state may protect its citizens from fraudulent solicitation by requiring a stranger in the community, before permitting him publicly to solicit funds for any purpose, to establish his identity and his authority to act for the cause which he purports to represent. The state is likewise free to regulate the time and manner of solicitation generally, in the interest of public safety, peace, comfort or convenience. But to condition the solicitation of aid for the perpetuation of religious views or systems upon a license, the grant of which rests in the exercise of a determination by state authority as to what is a religious cause, is to lay a forbidden burden upon the exercise of liberty protected by the Constitution.

Second. We hold that, in the circumstances disclosed, the conviction of Jesse Cantwell on the fifth count must be set aside.

We find in the instant case no assault or threatening of bodily harm, no truculent bearing, no intentional discourtesy, no personal abuse. On the contrary, we find only an effort to persuade a willing listener to buy a book or to contribute money in the interest of what Cantwell, however misguided others may think him, conceived to be true religion.

In the realm of religious faith, and in that of political belief, sharp differences arise. In both fields the tenets of one man may seem the rankest error to his neighbor. To persuade others to his own point of view, the pleader, as we know, at times, resorts to exaggeration, to vilification of men who have been, or are, prominent in church or state, and even to false statement. But the people of this nation have ordained in the light of history, that, in spite of the probability of excesses and abuses, these liberties are, in the long view, essential to enlightened opinion and right conduct on the part of the citizens of a democracy.

The essential characteristic of these liberties is, that under their shield many types of life, character, opinion and belief can develop unmolested and unobstructed. Nowhere is this shield more necessary than in our own country for a people composed of many races and of many creeds. There are limits to the exercise of these liberties. The danger in these times from the coercive activities of those who in the delusion of racial or religious conceit would incite violence and breaches of the peace in order to deprive others of their equal right to the exercise of their liberties, is emphasized by events familiar to all. These and other transgressions of those limits the states appropriately may punish.

The judgment affirming the convictions on the third and fifth counts is reversed and the cause is remanded for further proceedings not inconsistent with this opinion. So ordered.

Reversed and remanded.

COMMENTS AND QUESTIONS

1. What is the standard set in *Cantwell* for determining whether a government provision that burdens religious freedom violates the Free Exercise Clause?
2. The behavior in which Cantwell was engaged could arguably have been protected under the Free Speech Clause of the First Amendment. Indeed, through American jurisprudence over the decades, much of religious activity has come to be protected by the Free Speech and Freedom of Assembly Clauses. Arguments have been made that, given this, the Free Exercise Clause is merely redundant. Can you see any merit in such a position?

B. THE EUROPEAN APPROACH

The European Convention and the European Court of Human Rights

The European Convention for the Protection of Human Rights and Fundamental Freedoms (European Convention on Human Rights—ECHR) was opened for signature by the Council of Europe on 4 September 1950, and went into force on 3 September 1953. It marked an affirmation of fundamental guarantees of dignity and human rights, and multiple and notorious violation of such rights during World War II.

The European Court of Humans Rights (ECtHR) was established pursuant to the ECHR. As of 2017, 47 states had joined the Council and ratified the ECHR. The ECtHR is composed of one judge from each contracting state. Upon joining the Court, each judge sits in his or her individual capacity and not as a representative of the state of his or her origin. Although the Court is sometimes criticized for being overly deferential to states, its broad jurisdiction over roughly 800,000,000 people living between Greenland and Vladivostok is all the more remarkable because of the number of states that have consented to its jurisdiction.

The first case decided by the European Court of Human Rights under Article 9 of the ECHR—the provision protecting freedom of religion or belief—was the 1993 case of *Kokkinakis v. Greece*, which was handed down almost 35 years after the Court was established. The European Commission of Human Rights, which served a screening function for the Court and was authorized to resolve many of its cases until the Commission's abolition in 1998, had previously handled a number of Article 9 cases, and the European Court itself had addressed a number of cases that involved religious issues but were decided under other provisions of the ECHR. Since 1993, there has been rapid growth in Article 9 case law. It is an interesting coincidence that the first US case holding the Free Exercise Clause applicable to the states and the case first applying Article 9 of the ECHR in Europe both involved evangelism.

KOKKINAKIS V. GREECE

European Court of Human Rights, App. No. 14307/88 (25 May 1993)

[The *Kokkinakis* case involved a Greek citizen, Minos Kokkinakis, who was convicted under a 1938 Greek statute that prohibited proselytizing. Mr. Kokkinakis was born Greek Orthodox but had converted to the Jehovah's Witness faith at the age of 17. By 1986 he had been arrested more than 60 times for proselytism and had been imprisoned more than once. On 2 March 1986, Mr. Kokkinakis and his wife were admitted by Mrs. Kyriakaki into her home, where they discussed Jehovah's Witness literature with her for 10 or 15 minutes. Mrs. Kyriakaki's husband was a cantor at a local Orthodox church, and when learned of the visit he called the police, who arrested Kokkinakis and his wife and incarcerated them at the local police station for the night.

The local Criminal Court found Mr. and Mrs. Kokkinakis guilty of unlawful proselytism, as defined in a 1939 amendment to the 1938 law:

> [Proselytism is] any direct or indirect attempt to intrude on the religious beliefs of a person of a different religious persuasion, with the aim of undermining those beliefs, either by any kind of inducement or promise of an inducement or moral support or material assistance, or by fraudulent means or by taking advantage of his inexperience, trust, need, low intellect or naïvety.

Since no material or moral inducements were involved, the applicable legal provisions required that the case be established by proving that Kokkinakis had intentionally taken advantage of the "inexperience, . . . low intellect or naïvety" of Mrs. Kyriakaki. Conviction of Mrs. Kokkinakis was quashed, but conviction of

Mr. Kokkinakis was upheld in the Crete Court of Appeal and Greek Court of Cassation. Mr. Kokkinakis appealed to the European Court of Human Rights, with the following result.]

A. General Principles

31. As enshrined in Article 9, freedom of thought, conscience and religion is one of the foundations of a "democratic society" within the meaning of the Convention. It is, in its religious dimension, one of the most vital elements that go to make up the identity of believers and their conception of life, but it is also a precious asset for atheists, agnostics, sceptics and the unconcerned. The pluralism indissociable from a democratic society, which has been dearly won over the centuries, depends on it.

While religious freedom is primarily a matter of individual conscience, it also implies, inter alia, freedom to "manifest [one's] religion". Bearing witness in words and deeds is bound up with the existence of religious convictions.

According to Article 9, freedom to manifest one's religion is not only exercisable in community with others, "in public" and within the circle of those whose faith one shares, but can also be asserted "alone" and "in private"; furthermore, it includes in principle the right to try to convince one's neighbour, for example through "teaching", failing which, moreover, "freedom to change [one's] religion or belief", enshrined in Article 9, would be likely to remain a dead letter.

32. The requirements of Article 9 are reflected in the Greek Constitution in so far as Article 13 of the latter declares that freedom of conscience in religious matters is inviolable and that there shall be freedom to practise any known religion. . . . Jehovah's Witnesses accordingly enjoy both the status of a "known religion" and the advantages flowing from that as regards observance. . . .

34. According to the Government, . . . restrictions [to Article 9, provided for in paragraph 2] were to be found in the Greek legal system. Article 13 of the 1975 Constitution forbade proselytism in respect of all religions without distinction; and section 4 of Law no. 1363/1938 . . . attached a criminal penalty to this prohibition. . . .

B. Application of the Principles

36. The sentence passed by the Lasithi Criminal Court and subsequently reduced by the Crete Court of Appeal . . . amounts to an interference with the exercise of Mr. Kokkinakis's right to "freedom to manifest [his] religion or belief". Such an interference is contrary to Article 9 unless it is "prescribed by law", directed at one or more of the legitimate aims in paragraph 2 and "necessary in a democratic society" for achieving them.

1. "Prescribed by Law"

40. . . . In this instance there existed a body of settled national case-law ... [that helped clarify the meaning of the provisions]. This case-law, which had been published and was accessible, supplemented the letter of section 4 and was such as to enable Mr. Kokkinakis to regulate his conduct in the matter.

41. The measure complained of was therefore "prescribed by law" within the meaning of Article 9 para. 2 of the Convention.

2. Legitimate Aim

42. The Government contended that a democratic State had to ensure the peaceful enjoyment of the personal freedoms of all those living on its territory. If, in particular, it was not vigilant to protect a person's religious beliefs and dignity from attempts to influence them by immoral and deceitful means, Article 9 para. 2 would in practice be rendered wholly nugatory.

43. In the applicant's submission, religion was part of the "constantly renewable flow of human thought" and it was impossible to conceive of its being excluded from public debate. A fair balance of personal rights made it necessary to accept that others' thought should be subject to a minimum of influence, otherwise the result would be a "strange society of silent animals that [would] think but . . . not express themselves, that [would] talk but . . . not communicate, and that [would] exist but . . . not coexist".

44. Having regard to the circumstances of the case and the actual terms of the relevant courts' decisions, the Court considers that the impugned measure was in pursuit of a legitimate aim under Article 9 para. 2, namely the protection of the rights and freedoms of others, relied on by the Government.

3. "Necessary in a Democratic Society"

45. Mr. Kokkinakis . . . was curious to know how a discourse delivered with conviction and based on holy books common to all Christians could infringe the rights of others. Mrs. Kyriakaki was an experienced adult woman with intellectual abilities; it was not possible, without flouting fundamental human rights, to make it a criminal offence for a Jehovah's Witness to have a conversation with a cantor's wife.

46. The Government maintained . . . [that] Mr. Kokkinakis's insistence on entering Mrs. Kyriakaki's home on a false pretext; the way in which he had approached her in order to gain her trust; and his "skilful" analysis of the Holy Scriptures calculated to "delude" the complainant, who did not possess any "adequate grounding in doctrine". . . . They pointed out that if the State remained indifferent to attacks on freedom of religious belief, major unrest would be caused that would probably disturb the social peace.

47. The Court has consistently held that a certain margin of appreciation is to be left to the Contracting States in assessing the existence and extent of the necessity of an interference, but this margin is subject to European supervision, embracing both the legislation and the decisions applying it, even those given by an independent court. The Court's task is to determine whether the measures taken at national level were justified in principle and proportionate. In order to rule on this latter point, the Court must weigh the requirements of the protection of the rights and liberties of others against the conduct of which the applicant stood accused.

48. First of all, a distinction has to be made between bearing Christian witness and improper proselytism. The former corresponds to true evangelism, which a report drawn up in 1956 under the auspices of the World Council of Churches describes as an essential mission and a responsibility of every Christian and every Church. The latter represents a corruption or deformation of it. It may, according to the same report, take the form of activities offering material or social advantages with a view to gaining new members for a Church or exerting improper pressure

on people in distress or in need; it may even entail the use of violence or brainwashing; more generally, it is not compatible with respect for the freedom of thought, conscience and religion of others. Scrutiny of section 4 of Law no. 1363/1938 shows that the relevant criteria adopted by the Greek legislature are reconcilable with the foregoing if and in so far as they are designed only to punish improper proselytism, which the Court does not have to define in the abstract in the present case.

49. The Court notes, however, that in their reasoning the Greek courts established the applicant's liability by merely reproducing the wording of section 4 and did not sufficiently specify in what way the accused had attempted to convince his neighbour by improper means. None of the facts they set out warrants that finding. That being so, it has not been shown that the applicant's conviction was justified in the circumstances of the case by a pressing social need. The contested measure therefore does not appear to have been proportionate to the legitimate aim pursued or, consequently, "necessary in a democratic society . . . for the protection of the rights and freedoms of others".

In conclusion, there has been a breach of Article 9 of the Convention. . . .

PARTLY CONCURRING OPINION OF JUDGE PETTITI

[Judge PETTITI distinguished himself from the majority by finding that the Greek criminal statute, with use of the expression "proselytism that is not respectable," itself violated Article 9.]

DISSENTING OPINION OF JUDGE VALTICOS

. . . My disagreement concerns both the scope of Article 9 and the assessment of the facts in this case. . . . As with all freedoms, everyone's freedom of religion must end where another person's begins. Freedom "either alone or in community with others and in public or private, to manifest [one's] religion", certainly means freedom to practise and manifest it, but not to attempt persistently to combat and alter the religion of others, to influence minds by active and often unreasonable propaganda. It is designed to ensure religious peace and tolerance, not to permit religious clashes and even wars, particularly at a time when many sects manage to entice simple, naïve souls by doubtful means. . . . In the case of this sect, what is involved is indeed a systematic attempt at conversion, and consequently an attack on the religious beliefs of others. That has nothing to do with Article 9, which is designed solely to protect the religion of individuals and not their right to attack that of others. . . .

Someone who proselytises seeks to convert others; he does not confine himself to affirming his faith but seeks to change that of others to his own. And the Petit Robert clarifies its explanation by giving the following quotation from Paul Valéry: "I consider it unworthy to want others to be of one's own opinion. Proselytism astonishes me." Whereas the term "proselytism" would, in my view, have sufficed to define the offence and to satisfy the principle that an offence must be defined in law, Greek criminal law, for the avoidance of any ambiguity, gives an illustration of it which, while intended as an explanation and an example (no doubt the commonest one), none the less constitutes a meaningful definition, and that is: "By 'proselytism' is meant, in particular, any direct or indirect attempt to intrude on the religious beliefs of a person of a different religious persuasion, with the aim of undermining those beliefs, either by any kind of inducement or promise of an inducement or moral support or material assistance, or by fraudulent means or by taking advantage of his inexperience, trust, need, low intellect or naïvety." This definition of, if one may so term it, rape of the beliefs of others cannot in any way be regarded as contrary to Article 9 of the Convention. On the contrary, it is such as to protect individuals' freedom of religious belief.

Let us look now at the facts of the case. On the one hand, we have a militant Jehovah's Witness, a hardbitten adept of proselytism, a specialist in conversion, a martyr of the criminal courts whose earlier convictions have served only to harden him in his militancy, and, on the other hand, the ideal victim, a naïve woman, the wife of a cantor in the Orthodox Church (if he manages to convert her, what a triumph!). He swoops on her, trumpets that he has good news for her (the play on words is obvious, but no doubt not to her), manages to get himself let in and, as an experienced commercial traveller and cunning purveyor of a faith he wants to spread, expounds to her his intellectual wares cunningly wrapped up in a mantle of universal peace and radiant happiness. Who, indeed, would not like peace and happiness? But is this the mere exposition of Mr. Kokkinakis's beliefs or is it not rather an attempt to beguile the simple soul of the cantor's wife? Does the Convention afford its protection to such undertakings? Certainly not. One further detail must be provided. The Greek Law does not in any way restrict the concept of proselytism to attempts at the intellectual corruption of Orthodox Christians but applies irrespective of the religion concerned. Admittedly, the Government's representative was not able to give concrete examples concerning other religions, but that is not surprising since the Orthodox religion is the religion of nearly the whole population and sects are going to fish for followers in the best-stocked waters. . . .

I should certainly be inclined to recommend the Government to give instructions that prosecutions should be avoided where harmless conversations are involved, but not in the case of systematic, persistent campaigns entailing actions bordering on unlawful entry. That having been said, I do not consider in any way that there has been a breach of the Convention.

PARTLY DISSENTING OPINION OF JUDGE MARTENS

[Judge MARTENS concluded that Article 9 does not allow member States to impose criminal penalties for attempts to induce one to change his or her religion. State interference in interactions between proselytisers and the proselytised is beyond the allowed reach of state power under Article 9. State inference in this exchange necessarily attributes "greater value to the freedom not to be proselytized than to the right to proselytize," thereby "protecting the former at the cost of the latter".]

COMMENTS AND QUESTIONS

1. Following the decision in *Kokkinakis*, both the applicant and the Greek state claimed victory. How could that be? In what sense did each side win?
2. What factors distinguish "bearing Christian witness" and "improper proselytism"? Twenty-one codes of conduct concerning religious persuasion are evaluated in the article "Voluntary Codes of Conduct for Religious

Persuasion: Effective Tools for Balancing Human Rights and Resolving Conflicts?"[47] The authors conclude that effective codes balance competing rights consistent with international law norms, respect multiple traditions, and address general audiences.

3. Most people would agree that using economic pressure to induce people to join a religion is inappropriate. Thus, offers of food or medical assistance to persons in extreme need on the condition that they convert seems unduly coercive. However, what if a religious community engages in outreach activities, makes no promises that economic advantages will flow from joining, but an individual believes that by joining, his life circumstances are likely to improve? What if this turns out to be true? What if an individual joins a religious community and receives financial aid from the religious community at a subsequent time when he or she falls on hard times? Is it permissible to teach prospective converts that if they join the community, they may receive rewards in heaven? How about temporal blessings?
4. Article 9 of the ECHR is almost identical to Article 18 of the Universal Declaration of Human Rights. (For further discussion of these provisions, see Chapter 3.) At the time Article 18 was adopted, some Muslims opposed the provision because it affirmed the right to change one's religion; some Muslim scholars hold that to convert from Islam to another religion is an offense that is sufficiently serious to warrant the death penalty. Though this point will be explored in greater detail later, for now it suffices to say that many took a different view at the time the Universal Declaration was debated. For example, Muhammad Zafrulla Khan, the foreign minister of Pakistan and member of the minority Ahmadi Muslim sect, promised the full support of his country for the Universal Declaration's article on religious freedom. He cited a passage from the Quran: "Let him who chooses to believe, believe, and him who chooses to disbelieve, disbelieve,"[48] noting that Islam itself is a proselytizing religion and expressing his view that faith cannot be obligatory and that the freedom to change one's religion is consistent with Islam.
5. What presuppositions lie behind the opposing views expressed in the previous comment? How do the competing views reflect the deeper tensions illustrated throughout this chapter? Is the idea of sharing religious beliefs, with the possibility that they may induce a change of views, a purely Western notion (consider Judge Valticos's quote of Valéry)? Is the idea that rejection of religious views is tantamount to treason and deserving of serious punishment a purely pre-modern idea? Is it permissible for one side to attempt to persuade the other on these issues?
6. In the so-called *Tobacco Atheist* case, the Federal Constitutional Court of Germany upheld denial of parole to a prison inmate who used tobacco and other

---

47. Voluntary Codes of Conduct for Religious Persuasion: Effective Tools for Balancing Human Rights and Resolving Conflicts? 6 *Religion and Human Rights* (2011), 151-183.

48. Mary Ann Glendon, *A World Made New* 168 (Random House 2001).

gifts to induce inmates to abandon their Christian beliefs.[49] The Court reasoned that

> [o]ne who violates limitations erected by the Basic Law's general order of values cannot claim freedom of belief. . . . The religiously neutral state cannot and should not define in detail the content of this freedom, because it is not allowed to evaluate its citizens' beliefs or nonbeliefs. Nevertheless, it must prevent misuse of this freedom. It follows from the Basic Law's order of values, especially from the dignity of the human being, that a misuse is especially apparent whenever the dignity of another person is violated. Recruiting for a belief and convincing someone to turn from another belief, normally legal activities, become misuses of the basic right if a person tries, directly or indirectly, to use a base or immoral instrument to lure other persons from their beliefs. . . . A person who exploits the special circumstances of penal servitude and promises and rewards someone with luxury goods in order to make him renounce his beliefs does not enjoy the benefit of the protection of Article 4 of the Basic Law. Article 4 of the Basic Law provides that "Freedom of faith and of conscience, and freedom to profess a religious or philosophical creed, shall be inviolable.

7. Would the *Kokkinakis* court agree with the decision in the *Tobacco Atheist* case? The German decision holds in effect that the freedom of belief being asserted by the *Tobacco Atheist* case amounts to a misuse of freedom because an affront to a higher value—dignity—is involved. Does the *Kokkinakis* case implicitly assess whether Mrs. Kyriakaki's dignity was violated by Mr. Kokkinakis, and then conclude that it was not, so that Mr. Kokkinakis's Article 9 right could be vindicated?

Additional Web Resources:	Cases as well as resources from the wider literature discussing religious freedom and proselytism

49. *Tobacco Atheist* case, Bundersverfassungsgericht [BVerfGE] [Federal Constitutional Court] 8 November 1960, 1 BvR 59/56, BVerfGE 12, 1 [FRG], in Donald P. Kommers, *The Constitutional Jurisprudence of the Federal Republic of Germany* 313 (Duke Univ. Press 1997).

CHAPTER 2

THEORETICAL AND RELGIOUS PERSPECTIVES ON FREEDOM OF RELIGION

I. INTRODUCTION

This chapter addresses two important threshold questions: how religion is defined and how freedom of religion can be justified. The first question is addressed in Section II. The second question is addressed in Sections III, IV, and V.

II. DEFINING RELIGION

The suggestion that religious freedom is a right deserving special protection would seem to presuppose that religion is a distinct and definable sphere of human affairs. But what precisely is the scope of what is being protected? How can or should the line be drawn separating what deserves protection as religion and what does not? To some extent, lawyers resist precise definitions lest those definitions limit their ability to maneuver as the world and experience changes.

Most of the time there is no doubt about whether a controversy involves religion. Potential borderline questions are further reduced in number with the recognition that the freedoms of thought, conscience, and belief, to use the international human rights formulation, should be broadly construed. As the United Nations Human Rights Committee has stated,

> Article 18 protects theistic, non-theistic and atheistic beliefs, as well as the right not to profess any religion or belief. The terms belief and religion are to be broadly construed. Article 18 is not limited in its application to traditional religions or to religions and beliefs with institutional characteristics or practices analogous to those of traditional religions. The Committee therefore views with concern any tendency to discriminate against any religion or belief for any reasons, including the fact that they are newly established, or represent religious minorities that may be the subject of hostility by a predominant religious community.[1]

1. UNHRC, General Comment 22, Article 18 (para. 2) (48th session, 1993).

While as a practical matter the problem of defining religion is not difficult in most cases, the theoretical challenges of delineating the precise boundaries of religion are daunting. In fact, many scholars consider the impossibility of defining religion "almost an article of methodological dogma."[2] Some reject the term as too vague and ambiguous.[3] Others point out that "religion" is a Western concept derived from European experience and argue that applying it to phenomena from other cultures necessarily misrepresents them.[4]

Still others criticize the notion that a religion should receive special protection or that it should be a preferred freedom.[5] But whatever the merits of such arguments, "virtually all legal systems . . . do in fact accord special respect to freedom of religion and belief,"[6] and where religious freedom exists as a separate right, some sort of definition of religion is necessary. Definitions are important for many reasons, including that in some countries the government requires a religion to have been present in the country for a (sometimes lengthy) period of time, before it is accorded legal status as a "religion." Such status often carries with it important legal and even financial benefits.

Creating a taxonomy of the approaches to defining religion is complex. Nevertheless, scholars have advocated and courts have utilized four primary approaches: first, "substantive" approaches, which seek to identify the essence or distinctive character of religious belief; second, "functional" approaches, which focus on the role that a set of beliefs plays in the life of a believer; third, "analogical" approaches, which look for sets of characteristics that are indicative of religious belief, although no particular characteristic will necessarily apply to everything that counts as religion; and fourth, "deferential" approaches, which focus on or defer to the self-understanding of the adherent as the baseline for defining what is and what is not religious.

In subsections B and C, we discuss each of these four approaches to defining religion, highlight examples of cases where courts have adopted particular types of analysis, and discuss scholarly debate surrounding these approaches. But first we address the challenges that face any attempt to define religion, and note some of the philosophical issues that lie beneath the surface of such attempts.

---

2. Brian C. Wilson, From the Lexical to the Polythetic: A Brief History of the Definition of Religion, in *What Is Religion? Origins, Definitions, and Explanations* 141 (Thomas A. Idinopulos and Brian C. Wilson, eds., Brill 1998).

3. *See, e.g.*, Nathaniel Stinnet, Note, Defining Away Religious Freedom in Europe: How Four Democracies Get Away with Discriminating Against Minority Religions, 28 *B.C. Int'l & Comp. L. Rev.* 429 (2005).

4. *See, e.g.*, Benson Saler, *Conceptualizing Religion: Immanent Anthropologists, Transcendent Natives, and Unbounded Categories* (Brill 1993).

5. *See, e.g.*, Steven G. Gey, Why Is Religion Special? Reconsidering the Accommodation of Religion Under the Religion Clauses of the First Amendment, 52 *U. Pitt. L. Rev.* 75 (1990); Steven D. Smith, The Rise and Fall of Religious Freedom in Constitutional Discourse, 140 *U. Pa. L. Rev.* 149 (1991).

6. W. Cole Durham, Jr., and Elizabeth A. Sewell, Definition of Religion, in *Religious Organizations in the United States: A Study of Identity, Liberty, and the Law* 3, 29–30 (James A. Serritella, ed., Carolina Academic Press 2006).

A. GENERAL ASPECTS OF THE DEFINITION PROBLEM

1. Problems of Over- and Under-Inclusive Definitions

Two primary problems confront any effort to identify groups as religious. One is the problem of over-inclusiveness: If our definition is too broad, then things that ought not be counted as religion will be. The other problem is under-inclusiveness: If our definition is too narrow, then things that ought to be counted as religion will not be. Over time, the tendency has been to move toward increasingly broader definitions of religion (and also to expand the scope of religious freedom protection to cover secular worldviews). Every definition seems to leave some belief system or another just "outside" the definition. Egalitarian pressures lead to broadening the definition to address the under-inclusiveness. However, stretching the definitions in this way can be like pulling taffy: The protections afforded get thinner as the range of protection is broadened.

2. Differentiating the Religious from the Non-Religious

One way to conceptualize this problem is to think of religion as being bounded by a circle, representing our favored definition. Emanating from the outer boundaries of that definitional circle is a series of spokes. The area between two spokes represents a field of activity related to religion but in some significant sense distinct. These other concepts might include things like politics, aesthetic experience, business or economic activity, mere personal belief, mental illness, and fraud.

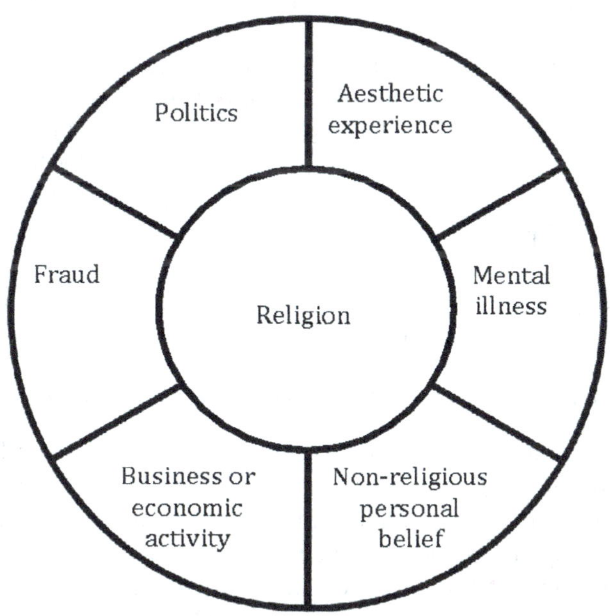

It becomes obvious quickly that drawing a line between religion and each of these other concepts or activities is more difficult that it might initially appear to be. For example, one person's heresy is another person's orthodoxy, so claims based on one person's religion may seem fraudulent to someone with a different belief system.

Similarly, the distinction between religion and non-religious personal belief can be problematic. Where is the line between protected religious belief and other, non-religious personal belief? For example, the US Supreme Court has held that a person has a religious freedom right to free exercise protection for a belief prohibiting Sabbath work. But, typically, someone who claimed a secular interest in staying home with her children on Saturdays cannot assert a religious freedom claim.

What about the distinction between religion and economic activity? When do the economic activities of a religious organization deserve religious freedom protection, and when should they be treated as ordinary business activities? Nearly all churches collect money from their members, most pay their clergy and staff, and many engage in economic activities, some related to but some seemingly quite far afield from their religious missions. Some teach that making donations to the church is a prerequisite of membership or good standing. Some churches charge what look like fees for services, which might make them look like quid pro quo economic exchanges. One common ground cited by governments for refusing to register an organization as a religion is that it is really a business.

The distinction between mental illness and religion is also unclear. If someone sees an angel who gives him or her directions, is that evidence that the person is a prophet, or that the person suffers from a mental illness?

How should we draw the line between religion and aesthetic experience? Many religious experiences, such as those involving music, poetry, and art, have a profound aesthetic dimension.

Perhaps most significant in today's world is the question of how one should draw the line between religion and politics. What if a religious organization advocates a political cause, takes a position on an important moral issue, endorses a political candidate, or sponsors a political party? Should religious communities be forbidden from engaging in some or all of these types of activities? What if a religious political party is committed to radically changing a secular democracy and implementing a vision of religious law for the state?

What might appear to be merely academic questions in reality have far-reaching real-world implications.

3. Nature of the Definition of Religion Problem

One significant challenge facing legal attempts to define religion is that the very definition of religion can be seen as a religious issue. The act of defining religion, particularly in legal contexts, is not neutral and scientific but partisan by nature, as it always presupposes some particular point of view with which not all religions will agree. Furthermore, the act of definition can have serious implications both for religious groups in particular and for society as a whole.

Determining how to define religion requires more than simply opening a dictionary or thinking about grammar. In many ways, defining religion is an intrinsically normative exercise, with the final outcome reflecting a particular worldview. A secular state, for example, may define religion in a dramatically different way than would a confessional state. Sorting, evaluating, and trying to reconcile various approaches is a very difficult process. To a significant extent, the power to define is the power to confer dignity and legitimacy.

States can use the power to define religion in a number of ways, resulting in endorsement or exclusion. For example, a state can define one form of religion as legitimate while criminalizing or discriminating against all others. This can occur when a state recognizes a single established religion or a prevailing religion while tolerating or marginalizing other religions. Another option is for a state to define religion to include "traditional religions" but exclude countercultural, new, or different groups. In contrast, modern constitutional democracies tend to define religion broadly to make room for a variety of belief systems. Even with inclusive definitions, states can employ carefully crafted limitations to prevent religion from being used as an excuse to trample other critical rights and interests.

4. Philosophical Conflicts Underlying Definitions of Religion

Beneath disputes about how to define religion lie layers of philosophical debate. Most of these debates are beyond the scope of our consideration, but it is helpful to have some sense of these because they can serve as signposts to help map the terrain of religious freedom. These include debates on the philosophy of language, philosophy of the social sciences, and even metaphysics. Each of these debates concerns basic assumptions that, although not directly implying one definition of religion or another, profoundly influence the manner in which definitions are pursued.

One ancient debate is metaphysical and is played out in controversies about the nature of language. The problem can be summarized roughly as a debate between the philosophical camps of "essentialism" and "nominalism." To simplify, the debate between essentialists and nominalists asks whether "religion" has an independent and intelligible essence or is merely an artificial linguistic category, constructed to aid human understanding of the world. According to the former view, defining the word depends on identifying religion's essence, its "unchanging and necessary qualities or properties . . . that by which it is what it is, including inherent developmental potentialities that can be realized or actualized in a world of change." In the latter view, defining religion means creating and describing a useful category, one that will serve a particular analytical or practical purpose while staying true to the everyday use of the term.

Another relevant debate comes from the philosophy of the social sciences, which asks whether the study of religion should focus on understanding it as much as possible from an insider perspective—that is, as it understands itself—or using an outsider perspective to achieve something resembling scientific objectivity. If religion is to be understood as believers themselves understand it, definitions will focus on the believers' doctrines and experiences. On the other hand, if religion is to be understood from an outside perspective, it will need to be defined in terms of the empirically observable—its effects on a person or group, the behavior it advocates, its cultural manifestations, and so forth. As we will see, some important disagreements between different approaches to definition hinge on this distinction.

Because attempts to find a legal definition of religion often borrow from various fields in academia, another difficulty arises: the different purposes for which such definitions are offered and the different criteria by which they should be judged. It may be that a valuable theological, sociological, or anthropological definition of religion may be nearly useless with respect to the law. A psychologist intending to study religion's effects on individuals' family relationships would likely base her definition of religion on different criteria than the Supreme Court would use in ruling on an Establishment Clause lawsuit.

The challenge of agreeing on the proper legal purpose for the definition of religion, however, is nearly as great as the challenge of agreeing on a definition. Differences in opinion about the scope of protection that should be afforded to religion by the law often coincide with differences in opinion about how religion should be defined.

COMMENTS AND QUESTIONS

1. In addition to determining whether a belief should be defined as being religious, other important preliminary issues are the sincerity and centrality of particular beliefs. In general, the state does not have an interest in protecting insincere or sham beliefs, those that are distant or tangential to fundamental beliefs, or those that might in fact reflect fraudulent, opportunistic, or other strategic behavior, or are even designed specifically to mock or satirize religion. There is always a risk that an individual may feign religious belief to gain the benefit of protection or exemption available to religious believers.
2. Does it ever make sense to provide protections to beliefs that might be insincere or that are not central to a system of belief?
3. Courts and government agencies in the twenty-first century in the United States and Europe have been confronted with asserted religious rights by such groups as pagans, Jedis, and Pastafarians and have reacted in inconsistent ways. The Church of the Flying Spaghetti Monster ("FSMism"), whose members call themselves Pastafarians, appeared in 2005 in response to the decision of the Kansas State Board of Education to permit teaching of Intelligent Design in science classes as an alternative to evolution. The FSM "deity" is described as an invisible and undetectable being resembling spaghetti and meatballs, who created the universe and continues to manifest by changing the results whenever a scientist carbon-dates an object. Pastafarians, essentially several thousand college students in North America and Europe, have moved from simply satirizing creationism to developing symbols, holidays, and literature, ordaining atheists to perform marriages, and making legal challenges to protect their rights to display images of their spaghetti god near public Nativity scenes and menorahs and to wear their religious regalia (pirate garb and headgear constructed of spaghetti strainers) in school and in identity photos. According to some observers, the "doctrine" of FSMism is at least as plausible as creationism, and in November 2015 the Registry of Motor Vehicles of Massachusetts, accepting the argument that FSMism is "a secular religion that uses parody to make its point," granted a Pastafarian woman a religious exception to the Registry rule prohibiting headcoverings in driver's license photos. In contrast, a US District Court in Nebraska, faced with the case of a

prisoner suing for access to Pastafarian literature and the right to wear the colander headgear in prison, ruled that FSMism was a satire rather than a religion that could be afforded First Amendment protections: "The FSM Gospel is plainly a work of satire, meant to entertain while making a pointed political statement. To read it as religious doctrine would be little different from grounding a 'religious exercise' on any other work of fiction."[7]

In December 2016 a Bulgarian court denied registration to the Church of the FSM on the grounds that Pastafarianism's history is one of deliberate antagonism to other religions, "with the movement potentially endangering inter-faith tolerance if its application was granted."[8] In August 2017, the Brandenburg State Court ruled that local authorities are within their rights in denying permits to the FSM to hang signs announcing its noodle masses along with Protestant and Catholic churches at town entrances. It does not depend, said the court, on whether the organization is a worldview or not. It cannot claim rights as a religious or a philosophical community, and the organization's criticism of other religions' beliefs is not a philosophy.[9]

B. APPROACHES THAT DEFINE RELIGION FROM A STANDPOINT EXTRINSIC TO RELIGIOUS COMMUNITIES

1. Essentialist Definitions

Early attempts to define religion often relied on a substantive or essentialist approach, distinguishing between religion and non-religion based on the content or character of a set of teachings or doctrines. This approach often identifies religion with a belief in a supreme being. For example, in 1890 the United States Supreme Court stated in *Davis v. Beason* that "[t]he term 'religion' has reference to one's views of his relations to his Creator, and to the obligations they impose of reverence for his being and character, and of obedience to his will."[10]

Such definitions are always under-inclusive, both because there are some religions that do not necessarily believe in a supreme being and because of the more general question about the extent to which religious freedom protections should extend to non-religious conscientious beliefs. Indeed, in the 1961 case *Torcaso v. Watkins*, the US Supreme Court implicitly overturned the definition it had used in *Beason*, recognizing in a footnote the existence of "religions in this country which do not teach what would generally be considered a belief in the existence of God" and including in this category "Buddhism, Taoism, Ethical Culture, Secular Humanism and others."[11]

---

7. *Cavanaugh v. Bartelt,* 178 F. Supp. 3d 819 (D. Neb. 2016) *affirmed no.* 16-2105 (8th Cir. 7 September 2016).

8. Bulgaria Denies Registration to Church of Flying Spaghetti Monster, *Novinite.com*, 28 December 2016.

9. Marivi Cabural, Flying Spaghetti Monster Church Cannot Advertise Noodle Masses [German court], *Vanguard*, 2 August 2017.

10. *Davis v. Beason*, 133 U.S. 333, 342 (1890). *See also United States v. MacIntosh*, 283 U.S. 605, 633–634 (Hughes, C.J., dissenting). ("The essence of religion is belief in a relation to God involving duties superior to those arising from any human relation.")

11. *Torcaso v. Watkins*, 367 U.S. 488, 495 n11 (1961).

More recently, two substantive criteria for recognizing a religion have been suggested by University of California Berkeley law professor Jesse Choper. First, he argues that religions teach belief in "[e]xtratemporal consequences"[12]—meaning eternal consequences for one's temporal decisions, particularly eternal rewards or punishment. Choper acknowledges, however, that this definition excludes many belief systems traditionally recognized as religious. He notes that in many Eastern and tribal religions, and even in orthodox Christianity, many believers reject the idea of postmortal rewards or punishments.

Recognizing these problems, Choper offers a second possible definition, pointing out that many of the religious beliefs his first definition excludes "share a common core with the extratemporal consequences precept."[13] This "common core" concerns a "transcendent reality" or "aspects of reality that are not observable in ordinary experience, but which are assumed to exist at another level. . . ."[14] Choper argues that "facts that are not observable in a conventional sense nor empirically verifiable, but are rather unknowable in the physical world, can only be experienced by the believer or taken on faith. No one, including government, can dictate or deny such experiences. Thus, it may be said that beliefs concerned with transcendent reality are outside the regulatory competence of the state."[15]

Still, Professor Choper acknowledges, the line between transcendent and purely rational causes of decision-making and behavior is often not easy to draw.[16] Stanley Ingber has pointed out that "Choper's proposal would force courts to explore these issues, immersing them deep in the intricacies of religious doctrine and the unique beliefs of individual claimants."[17] Inquiring into details of doctrine is a dubious role for a religiously neutral court.

Despite the difficulties associated with substantive approaches to defining religion, several countries continue to use them. While there is no common definition of religion under English law, various definitions, most often developed by courts or tribunals, have been applied for such reasons as determining the charitable status of an institution or registering a place of religious worship.[18] In 1999 the Charity Commissioners for England and Wales refused to register the Church of Scientology as a religious charity when, upon reviewing both English and foreign authorities, the Commissioners concluded that, for purposes of charity law, the necessary characteristics of religion included both belief in a supreme being and manifestation of that belief through worship.[19] This did not settle the matter, however, and the status of Scientology in the UK would be unclear for another dozen years. The Ministry of Defence confirmed that Scientology was a religion, while the UK Prison Service did not, although prisoners who were

---

12. Jesse H. Choper, Defining "Religion" in the First Amendment, 1982 *U. Ill. L. Rev.* 579, 597 (1982).

13. *Id.* at 602.

14. *Id.*

15. *Id.* at 603.

16. *Id.* at 603-604

17. Stanley Ingber, Religion or Ideology: A Needed Clarification of the Religion Clauses, 41 *Stan. L. Rev.* 233, 277.

18. Russell Sandberg, The Farce Awakens: Why the Charity Commission's decision on Jediism reveals a need to revisit the definition of religion, *Law & Religion UK*, 22 December 2016.

19. *Decision of the Charity Commission on Church of Scientology (England and Wales)*, 17 November 1999, 13–14.

registered Scientologists could "practice their religion and have access to a representative of the Church of Scientology if they wish[ed] to receive its ministry."[20]

In the Charities Act of 2011, however, the Commissioners expanded the definition of religion to include "(i) a religion which involves belief in more than one god, and (ii) a religion which does not involve belief in a god,"[21] and the UK Supreme Court cited this definition in December 2013 when issuing a unanimous judgment (*Hodkin*) in favor of a couple who desired to be married in the Scientologist chapel they regularly attended.[22] Scientology was a religion, said the Court, and their chapel was "a place of meeting for religious worship" meeting the legal requirement for "the solemnisation of marriage" (para. 65). In delivering the opinion Lord Toulson declared that "experience across the common law world over many years has shown the pitfalls of attempting to attach a narrowly circumscribed meaning to the word [religion]. . . . It is no good considering whether the members of the legislature over 150 years ago would have considered Scientology to be a religion because it did not exist" (para. 34). Therefore, "[u]nless there is some compelling contextual reason for holding otherwise religion should not be confined to religions which recognise a supreme deity. First and foremost, to do so would be a form of religious discrimination unacceptable in today's society. It would exclude Buddhism, along with other faiths such as Jainism, Taoism, Theosophy and part of Hinduism" (para. 51).

Lord Toulson then tried his own definition: "I would describe religion in summary as a spiritual or non-secular belief system, held by a group of adherents, which claims to explain mankind's place in the universe and relationship with the infinite, and to teach its adherents how they are to live their lives in conformity with the spiritual understanding associated with the belief system. . . . I emphasise that this is intended to be a description and not a definitive formula" (para. 57).

In December 2016 the Charity Commission rejected the application of The Temple of the Jedi Order (TOTJO) to be entered into the list of charities as it was "not satisfied that TOTJO is established for exclusively charitable purposes for the advancement of religion and/or the promotion of moral and ethical improvement for the benefit of the public."[23] Oddly enough, the decision was seen as important because this was the first reconsideration of the Commission's view of the meaning of religion in charity law in the light of the 2013 *Hodkin* opinion, though it provided "less clarity than might have been hoped."[24]

> Trying to define religion for charity law purposes is not easy. Any definition needs to be able to encompass all those world religions which would be expected to be accepted as religions in charity law, while not drawing in organisations which would not be expected to qualify. For example, the Church of the Flying Spaghetti Monster was

---

20. US Department of State, International Religious Freedom Report 2007: United Kingdom.

21. Charities Act 2011, section 3(2)(a) (up to date with all changes known to be in force on or before 17 July 2017).

22. *R (on the application of Hodkin and another) v. Registrar General of Births, Deaths and Marriages* [2013] UKSC 77 On appeal from [2012] EWHC 3635.

23. *Decision of the Charity Commission on The Temple of the Jedi Order*, 16 December 2016.

24. Nicola Evans, 11: Why Aren't Jedis Charitable?—The Meaning of Religion in Charity Law, *Brigham Dyson Bell Charity Law Blog*, 23 December 2016.

created as a satirical movement but has since been recognised legally as a religion in a number of jurisdictions.[25]

Given the fact that the Commission in *Jedi Order* considered "that that a religion/belief system should be characterised by a certain level of cogency, seriousness, cohesion and importance," it would be difficult to see why FSMism would be considered a religion and Jedism would not. In fact, as one legal scholar observed, "The understanding of the definition of religion for the purposes of charity and registration law is now hideously confused," leaving "a desperate need for the definition question to be revisited and for reform that increases clarity and inclusiveness."[26]

2. Functionalist Definitions

Rather than relying on the content of a set of beliefs, functional definitions focus on the role that beliefs or practices play in an individual's life. In this view, anything that plays the role of a religion is, by definition, a religion. The classical example of the functional approach is Paul Tillich's idea of faith as a person's "ultimate concern," which was invoked by the US Supreme Court in *United States v. Seeger,* 380 U.S. 163 (1965). The Court's use of this functional definition of religion as a person's "ultimate concern" led to a conclusion that a person objecting to the military draft was protected, even though his objections were not strictly religious, because his ethical belief took the functional place of a religious belief in his life.

How broadly the functional definition of *Seeger* could be interpreted became apparent a few years later in another conscientious objector case, *Welsh v. United States,* 398 U.S. 333 (1970). Welsh was denied exemption from the draft because there was no apparent religious basis for his objection to war. The government sought to distinguish Welsh's situation from Seeger's on the ground that Welsh "was far more insistent and explicit than Seeger in denying that his views were religious." For example, in filling out their conscientious objector applications, Seeger put quotation marks around the word "religious," but Welsh struck the word "religious" entirely and later characterized his beliefs as rooted in history and sociology. The Court rejected the government's argument, finding that "it places undue emphasis on the registrant's interpretation of his own beliefs."

Despite the criticisms it has engendered, the "ultimate concern" functional standard has much to recommend it. It avoids forcing judges to become theologians, simply ignoring questions of doctrine and ritual that make substantive definitions problematic. Under the "ultimate concern" definition, the government simply does not care what one believes or cares deeply about; it will protect the free exercise of whatever it most important to the believer. As critics have pointed out, however, this definition leaves the door open for nearly anything to be called religious belief.

Some courts deciding conscientious objection cases very similar to those of *Seeger* and *Welsh* have declined to follow a functionalist approach. For example, in the 1984 case *N. v. Sweden*, App. No. 10410/83, the European Commission of Human Rights confronted a case where a conscientious objector sought the same

25. *Id.*
26. Sandberg, The Farce Awakens, *supra* note 18.

type of protection that the Swedish government had extended to religious conscientious objectors such as Jehovah's Witnesses, although his objections were based upon "deepest personal conviction" rather than religion. The Commission ruled that "membership of such a religious sect as Jehovah's Witnesses is an objective fact which creates a high degree of probability that exemption is not granted to persons who simply wish to escape service, since it is unlikely that a person would join . . . only for the purpose of not having to perform military . . . service." Thus, the Swedish distinction between religious and non-religious claims was found to be reasonable and his claim was declared inadmissible.

Thirty years later, in 2014, the European Court of Human Rights, in *Buldu and Others v. Turkey*, App. No. 14017/08 identified an ECHR Article 9 right to conscientious objection:

> The refusal by the applicants, who are Jehovah's Witnesses, to perform military service for reasons of conscience certainly was a manifestation of their religious beliefs. The Court has no doubt that the repeated convictions of the applicants . . . as well as the risk of endless criminal prosecutions, . . . amount to an interference with their right to exercise the freedom to manifest their religion that is guaranteed by Article 9 of the Convention. (para. 84)

3. Analogical Definitions

Another approach, which Kent Greenawalt has labeled the analogical approach, seeks to distinguish between religion and non-religion by drawing analogies between the phenomena in question and phenomena that are clearly religious.[27] The analogical approach has been articulated by Judge Arlin M. Adams of the United States Third Circuit Court of Appeals in *Malnak v. Yogi*[28] and later in *Africa v. Commonwealth of Pennsylvania.*[29]

> First, a religion addresses fundamental and ultimate questions having to do with deep and imponderable matters. Second, a religion is comprehensive in nature; it consists of a belief-system as opposed to an isolated teaching. Third, a religion often can be recognized by the presence of certain formal and external signs . . . that may be analogized to accepted religions. Such signs might include formal services, ceremonial functions, the existence of clergy, structure and organization, efforts at propagation, observance of holidays and other similar manifestations associated with the traditional religions.[30]

Such indicia said, Adams "will be helpful, [but] they should not be thought of as a final 'test' for religion. Defining religion is a sensitive and important legal duty. Flexibility and careful consideration of each belief system are needed. Still, it is important to have some objective guidelines in order to avoid *ad hoc* justice."[31]

helpful indicia but not a final test.

27. Kent Greenawalt, Religion as a Concept in Constitutional Law, 72 *Cal. L. Rev.* 753, 767–768 (1984).

28. *Malnak v. Yogi*, 592 F.2d 197 (3d Cir. 1979) (holding that the teaching of a course in five New Jersey high schools called "the Science of Creative Intelligence Transcendental Meditation" constituted religious activity and violated the Establishment Clause).

29. *Africa v. Commonwealth of Pennsylvania*, 662 F.2d 1025 (3d Cir. 1981) (finding that MOVE, an organization alleged by a prisoner to be a religion in which he was a "naturalist minister," was not a religion and consequently holding that the state was not required to provide the prisoner with a special diet he claimed the religion mandated).

30. *Id.* at 1032, 1035.

31. *Malnak v. Yogi*, 592 F.2d at 210.

This approach differs from substantive definitions in that it does not tie the idea of religion inflexibly to any specific belief, or even to a particular function or set of functions. At the same time, it differs from functional definitions in that it can take such beliefs into account, arguing by analogy that because such beliefs are often seen in recognized religions, their presence in a group in question is evidence for its religiosity. Because of this, analogical definitions can have more content than functional definitions and provide more concrete boundaries for courts.

Anand Agneshwar has criticized the analogical approach, arguing that because these approaches depend on analogies with the "indisputably religious," they assume an uncontroversial set of "indisputably religious" phenomena from which they can draw comparisons. They therefore have no criteria for judging what is obviously religious and what is not, so their choice of any particular set of phenomena as an example of religion can appear arbitrary and ethnocentric.[32]

Agneshwar contends that allowing courts to use what is "indisputably religious" as a standard opens the door for judges to impose their own religious views and to manipulate the definition according to their own ideas about which belief systems deserve approval and which do not, violating the longstanding principle that the Supreme Court "should not punish what it perceives as false religious beliefs and reward what it sees as true beliefs."[33]

Sometimes it is not altogether clear what approach a court adopts. Consider the following example.

THE CHURCH OF THE NEW FAITH AND THE COMMISSIONER OF PAY-ROLL TAX

High Court of Australia [1983] HCA 40; 1983 154 CLR 120
On appeal from the Supreme Court of Victoria, 27 October 1983

Mason A.C.J. and Brennan J.

The corporation [The Church of the New Faith] was assessed under the Pay-roll Tax Act 1971 (Vict.). The wages assessed as liable to pay-roll tax under that Act were paid or payable during the period 1 July 1975 to 30 June 1977. The corporation objected to the assessment upon the ground that the wages were exempt under the provisions of s. 10(b). At the relevant time (the section was amended in 1979), s. 10(b) provided: "The wages liable to pay-roll tax under this Act do not include wages paid or payable – . . . (b) by a religious or public benevolent institution, or a public hospital." . . .

. . . Is Scientology a religion? . . . The question . . . is whether the beliefs, practices and observances which were established by the affidavits and oral evidence as the set of beliefs, practices and observances accepted by Scientologists are properly to be described as a religion. . . .

Freedom of religion, the paradigm freedom of conscience, is of the essence of a free society. The chief function in the law of a definition of religion is to mark

32. Anand Agneshwar, Note, Rediscovering God in the Constitution, 67 *N.Y.U. L. Rev.* 295, 316–317 (1992).

33. *Id.*

out an area within which a person subject to the law is free to believe and to act in accordance with his belief without legal restraint. . . .

An endeavour to define religion for legal purposes gives rise to peculiar difficulties. . . . A definition cannot be adopted merely because it would satisfy the majority of the community or because it corresponds with a concept currently accepted by that majority. The development of the law towards complete religious liberty and religious equality . . . would be subverted and the guarantees in s. 116 of the Constitution would lose their character as a bastion of freedom if religion were so defined as to exclude from its ambit minority religions out of the main streams of religious thought. . . .[34]

These considerations, tending against the adoption of a narrow definition, may suggest the rejection of any definition which would exclude from the category of religion the beliefs, practices and observances of any group who assert their beliefs, practices and observances to be religious. But such an assertion cannot be adopted as a legal criterion. The mantle of immunity would soon be in tatters if it were wrapped around beliefs, practices and observances of every kind whenever a group of adherents chose to call them a religion. . . . A more objective criterion is required.

That criterion must be found in the indicia exhibited by acknowledged religions, so that any set of beliefs, practices and observances which are accepted by a group of adherents and which exhibit that criterion will be held to be a religion. But what is the range of acknowledged religions from which the criterion is to be derived? The literature of comparative religion, modern means of communication and the diverse ethnic and cultural components of contemporary Australian society require that the search for religious indicia should not be confined to the Judaic group of religions – Judaism, Christianity, Islam – for the tenets of other acknowledged religions, including those which are not monotheistic or even theistic, are elements in the contemporary atmosphere of ideas. But the task of surveying the whole range of Judaic and other acknowledged religions is daunting. . . . The derivation of all the common indicia of religions is thus a task which a court cannot hope to perform by a detailed analysis of all acknowledged religions. Indeed, courts are not equipped to make such a study, and the acculturation of a judge in one religious environment would impede his understanding of others. But so broad a study is not required. The relevant inquiry is to ascertain what is meant by religion as an area of legal freedom or immunity, and that inquiry looks to those essential indicia of religion which attract that freedom or immunity. It is in truth an inquiry into legal policy. . . . Under our law, the State has no prophetic role in relation to religious belief; the State can neither declare supernatural truth nor determine the paths through which the human mind must search in a quest for supernatural truth. The courts are constrained to accord freedom to faith in the supernatural, for there are no means of finding upon evidence whether a postulated tenet of supernatural truth is erroneous or whether a supernatural revelation of truth has been made. . . .

---

34. Section 116 of Chapter V. The States, of the Commonwealth of Australia Constitution Act (9th July 1900) states in its entirety: "The Commonwealth shall not make any law for establishing any religion, or for imposing any religious observance, or for prohibiting the free exercise of any religion, and no religious test shall be required as a qualification for any office or public trust under the Commonwealth."

Religious belief is more than a cosmology; it is a belief in a supernatural Being, Thing or Principle. But religious belief is not by itself a religion. Religion is also concerned, at least to some extent, with a relationship between man and the supernatural order and with supernatural influence upon his life and conduct. . . .

What man feels constrained to do or to abstain from doing because of his faith in the supernatural is prima facie within the area of legal immunity, for his freedom to believe would be impaired by restriction upon conduct in which he engages in giving effect to that belief. The canons of conduct which he accepts as valid for himself in order to give effect to his belief in the supernatural are no less a part of his religion than the belief itself. Conversely, unless there be a real connexion between a person's belief in the supernatural and particular conduct in which that person engages, that conduct cannot itself be characterized as religious. . . . But the area of legal immunity marked out by the concept of religion cannot extend to all conduct in which a person may engage in giving effect to his faith in the supernatural. . . . Conduct in which a person engages in giving effect to his faith in the supernatural is religious, but it is excluded from the area of legal immunity marked out by the concept of religion if it offends against the ordinary laws, i.e., if it offends against laws which do not discriminate against religion generally or against particular religions or against conduct of a kind which is characteristic only of a religion.

We would therefore hold that, for the purposes of the law, the criteria of religion are twofold: first, belief in a supernatural Being, Thing or Principle; and second, the acceptance of canons of conduct in order to give effect to that belief, though canons of conduct which offend against the ordinary laws are outside the area of any immunity, privilege or right conferred on the grounds of religion. . . . [The trial judge found that Scientology's] predecessor in Australia was the Hubbard Association of Scientologists International ("H.A.S.I."), and that that Association had published, at some time not earlier than 1961, a magazine which unequivocally asserted "H.A.S.I. is non-religious – it does not demand any belief or faith nor is it in conflict with faith. People of all faiths use Scientology." His Honour investigated the subsequent history of the development of the cult, and found that a considerable transformation had ostensibly occurred. But his Honour thought that "the ecclesiastical appearance now assumed by the organization is no more than colourable in order to serve an ulterior purpose", namely, the purpose of acquiring the legal status of a religion so that the organization might have the fiscal and other benefits of that status in Australia and elsewhere and the purpose of avoiding the legal disabilities to which the organization was subject by reason of the Psychological Practices Act 1965 (Vict.). His Honour expressed his clear conviction that the purported transformation of Scientology to a religion was no more than a sham. . . .

Although the sincerity and integrity of the ordinary members of the Scientology movement were not in doubt, his Honour held that Scientology was "no less a sham because there are others prepared to accept and act upon such aims and beliefs as though they were credible when they cannot see them for what they are. Gullibility cannot convert something from what it is to something which it is not."

Yet charlatanism is a necessary price of religious freedom, and if a self-proclaimed teacher persuades others to believe in a religion which he propounds, lack of sincerity or integrity on his part is not incompatible with the religious character of the beliefs, practices and observances accepted by his followers. . . .

Belief in a Supreme Being is now a part of Scientology, but there is no tenet of Scientology which expresses a particular concept of a Supreme Being. The name of the Supreme Being is left as a matter of individual choice. Each adherent must make up his own mind what his God is. . . . The beliefs which . . . are accepted by members of the cult, satisfy the first criterion of a religion. But the second criterion is more troublesome. To satisfy the second criterion, the facts must show the acceptance of canons of conduct in order to give effect to a supernatural belief, not being canons of conduct which offend against the ordinary laws. . . .

The various codes of conduct are set out in The Creation of Human Ability – A Handbook for Scientologists. . . . However, we can perceive no relevant connexion between any canon of the codes of conduct and Scientologists' belief in the supernatural, unless auditing is itself a religious exercise satisfying the second indicium. . . .

Yet, . . . adherents, who number between 5,000 and 6,000 people in Victoria, accord blind reverence to what Mr. Hubbard has written and it may therefore be inferred that they perceive some unifying thread which makes the whole intelligible, or which assembles sufficient of a jigsaw to allow them to see themselves and what they do as part of a supernatural reality. We think an inference should be drawn – though the material to support it is not compelling – that the general group of adherents practice auditing and accept the other practices and observances of Scientology because, in doing what Mr. Hubbard bids or advises them to do, they perceive themselves to be giving effect to their supernatural beliefs. . . .

It follows that, whatever be the intentions of Mr. Hubbard and whatever be the motivation of the corporation, the state of the evidence in this case requires a finding that the general group of adherents have a religion. The question whether their beliefs, practices and observances are a religion must, in the state of that evidence, be answered affirmatively. That answer, according to the conventional basis adopted by the parties in fighting the case, must lead to a judgment for the corporation. . . .

We would grant special leave to appeal, allow the appeal and, pursuant to s. 33C of the Pay-roll Tax Act, reduce the assessment to pay-roll tax to nil. . . .

COMMENTS AND QUESTIONS

1. Which approach does the Australian court use in *The Church of the New Faith and the Commissioner of Pay-roll Tax*? Does this approach produce an effective definition for ascertaining "what is meant by religion as an area of legal freedom or immunity"?
2. The term *church* is found, but not specifically defined, in the Tax Code of the US Internal Revenue Service (IRS). In determining tax exemption for religious organizations, the IRS has considered a list of characteristics "generally attributed" to churches and "developed by the IRS and by court decisions."[35]

---

35. *See* "Churches" Defined, in Publication 1828, *Tax Guide for Churches and Religious Organizations.*

1. A distinct legal existence
2. A recognized creed and form of worship
3. A definite and distinct ecclesiastical government
4. A formal code of doctrine and discipline
5. A distinct religious history
6. A membership not associated with any other church or denomination
7. An organization of ordained ministers
8. Ordained ministers selected after completing prescribed courses of study
9. A literature of its own
10. Established places of worship
11. Regular congregations
12. Regular religious services
13. Sunday schools for the religious instruction of the young
14. Schools for the preparation of its members

The IRS acknowledges that in deciding whether an organization is a church for federal tax purposes, "[n]o single factor is controlling, although all fourteen may not be relevant to a given determination."[36] What are the advantages and disadvantages of an approach like this? How does a factor analysis approach such as this compare with an analogical approach?

3. In *Hernandez v. Commissioner*, 490 U.S. 680 (1989) the US Supreme Court ruled that payments made to branches of the Church of Scientology for "auditing and training services" received by members were not deductible charitable contributions because they represented a quid pro quo, a measurable, specific return for which the Church had "established and advertised prices." The plaintiffs had argued that the deduction should be allowed because the benefits were entirely religious. Justice O'Connor and Justice Scalia observed in a dissenting opinion that in no previous instance had IRS denied deductibility on a quid pro quo basis, even when the benefit was entirely spiritual or religious. As it was difficult to put monetary value on intangible religious benefits, the Government had always before chosen to ignore the quid pro quo argument. Why not in this case?[37] Why have Scientologists encountered such difficulty in so many places with gaining recognition as members of a church? Do you agree with the notion that self-definition should "count heavily in favor" of Scientologists in this matter? [38]
4. In defense of analogical definitions, George Freeman has argued that traditional attempts to define religion have been misguided.[39] According to Freeman, those who have tried to define religion have failed because they had an incorrect understanding of language and definition. They searched for a single "essence" of religion, one characteristic or a set of characteristics that would be both a necessary and a sufficient condition of a phenomenon's religiosity. Freeman

36. *American Guidance Foundation v. United States*, 490 F. Supp. 304 (D.D.C. 1980), citing Speech of Jerome Kurtz, IRS Commissioner, at PLI Seventh Biennial Conference on Tax Planning, 9 January 1978, reprinted in Fed. Taxes (P-H) P 54, 820 (1978).

37. In October 1993, after "decades of feuding," the IRS agreed to recognize the tax-exempt religious and charitable status of the Church of Scientology and more than 150 of its corporate entities.

38. *See* Durham and Sewell, *supra* note 6.

39. George C. Freeman III, The Misguided Search for the Constitutional Definition of "Religion," 71 *Geo. L.J.* 1519, 1520 (1983).

calls this essentialist approach misguided because, he reasons, religion has no single essence. How, then, should we go about distinguishing religion from non-religion? Freeman looks to Wittgenstein's "family resemblances" philosophy of language to see if similarities and relationships establish commonality instead of presuming that there must be something common to all.[40]

Freeman argues that the way we should go about recognizing religions is the same way we go about recognizing chairs. We start with the obvious case, the stereotypical chair, and then compare borderline cases with the obvious one to find similarities and differences. The number of similarities between an object and the standard chair may be sufficient to show that the object should be included within the class of chairs. In contrast, dissimilarities between an object and the standard chair may be too great, justifying exclusion from the general class.[41] What do you think of the use of Wittgenstein's "family resemblances" theory of language for legal definitions? Is it a useful way to deal with the ambiguities inherent in language, or does it add ambiguity and lead to subjective judgment?

5. Martin Riesebrodt wrote that "religion is based on communication with superhuman powers and is concerned with warding off misfortunes, coping with crises and laying the foundation for salvation."[42] What do you think of this definition? Are there religions which don't meet one or more of these criteria?

C. DEFERENTIAL APPROACHES TO DEFINING RELIGION

Another attempt to define religion centers, like the analogical approach, on an attempt to rephrase the question. Rather than merely changing how the courts go about deciding what is religion and what is non-religion, however, these deferential approaches start by shifting the focus of the inquiry and asking the extent to which courts and other state institutions should defer to the beliefs of communities themselves as to whether or not they are religious. The central insight of the deferential approach is that groups' self-definition as religious should be a relevant and often the deciding factor in courts' decisions as to whether they are religious. As Cole Durham and Elizabeth Clark Sewell have written, "[T]he fact that Scientology regards itself as a religion should count heavily in favor of its being regarded as such by others, whereas the fact that Marxism would be distressed by being labeled as a religion should count against its being so treated."[43]

The standard approach assumes that the problem of definition of religion poses a normal subsumption problem. That is, one needs to determine whether a certain set of facts (arguably religious belief or conduct) falls under a certain legal rule (one involving religious freedom). The state needs to know whether the belief or conduct is religious in order to determine whether the facts are properly subsumed. The difficulty is that here, subsumption is not a neutral process of legal

40. *Id.* at 1550; Ludwig Wittgenstein, *Philosophical Investigations* § 66 (G.E.M. Anscombe, trans., 1953).

41. Freeman, *supra* note 39, at 1551–1552.

42. Martin Riesebrodt, *The Promise of Salvation: A Theory of Religion* xii (Steven Rendall, trans., Univ. of Chicago Press 2010).

43. Durham and Sewell, *supra* note 6, at 38.

interpretation, but constitutes a case of the very problem the subsuming rule is intended to address. Full and limited deference approaches are designed to take this unique feature of the definition problem into account to varying degrees. Whereas a full deference approach would hold that a group's beliefs about whether it is religious or not are no more subject to state review than is the substantive content of religious doctrines, a limited deference view posits that the same standards of religious freedom that apply to ordinary conduct and beliefs also apply when the state tackles the subsumption problem posed by defining religion. Most would assume that the full deference approach would leave far too much room for strategic behavior; accordingly, in what follows, we focus on the limited deference approach.

This approach says that just as the government should allow people to practice their religious beliefs unless it has a compelling reason to interfere, it should accept people's description of their beliefs as religious unless it has a compelling reason not to. Proponents of this view maintain that this approach is the best way of doing justice to religious freedom:

> [I]f the state defines religion too narrowly, it violates religious freedom as surely as it would if it admitted a group was religious but then arbitrarily denied its justified religious freedom claim. Indeed, denial of a group's religious status constitutes an even deeper affront to religious freedom because it is not merely the denial of a particular claim, but an across-the-board denial of the right to assert any religious freedom claims.[44]

This observation is not entirely novel. Indeed, the Supreme Court's decision in *Seeger* said that the courts' assessment of beliefs' religiosity should hinge on the sincerity with which they are held and believers' own assessment as to whether they are religious.[45] However, *Seeger* did not work out the implications of this insight, instead including an "essentially objective" analogical standard: "Does the claimed belief occupy the same place in the life of the objector as an orthodox belief in God holds in the life of one clearly qualified for exemption?"[46] As we have seen, this was then defined using the "ultimate concern" functional definition borrowed from Paul Tillich.

Because the state's interest in defining religion would vary from issue to issue, this approach would require different definitions depending on what freedom of religion requires:

> It is vital to remember that the problem of definition takes on different contours in different contexts where different legal purposes are at play. Legal definitions are not merely abstract verbal signs for all seasons and settings; they serve a practical function in helping those who administer laws to make distinctions that are sensible and fair in various legal contexts. . . . In at least some contexts this tends to require differential strictness in definitions.[47]

Recognizing that the government will have to limit the concept of religion differently in different contexts, the deferential approach outlines the criteria based on which government can legitimately reject believers' self-definition as religious.

---

44. *Id.* at 37.
45. *United States v. Seeger,* 380 U.S. at 184
46. *Id.*
47. Durham and Sewell, *supra* note 6, at 39.

Durham and Sewell divide these into two categories: limitations implicit in the idea of religious freedom and those that give the state justification to override religious freedom.

The first limitation inherent to religious freedom is sincerity. Under the deferential approach, the person making a religious claim must show not only that she sincerely believes what she claims to believe but that she sincerely considers this belief to be religious. Just as there is no reason to grant free exercise protection based on beliefs the claimant does not actually hold, there is no reason to give deference to a believer's definition of her beliefs as religious if she herself does not in fact consider them religious. The second limitation inherent to religious freedom is the reverse side of the first, namely that claims of religiosity made for fraudulent or strategic reasons deserve no deference or protection.

Though the Supreme Court has recognized that determinations of sincerity are permissible in freedom of religion cases—since, after all, it makes little sense to extend protection to beliefs not actually held—such determinations can be a challenge. Durham and Sewell argue that the burden should be on the claimant to provide evidence that she does in fact believe the things she claims to hold; evidence would vary depending on the content of the claimed belief. In any case, courts must not let their own estimations of beliefs' plausibility influence their determination of whether claimants actually believe them, since many religions proclaim beliefs that seem strange and incredible to outsiders. Being a member of a group that teaches those beliefs and claims to be religious is helpful.[48]

Even when courts determine that a claimant does sincerely believe what she claims to believe and does sincerely consider her beliefs to be religious, courts may find compelling reasons to not accept the believer's own classification. One should note that this is a different question from whether the state has a compelling interest not to accommodate legitimate religious claims that have been recognized as genuinely religious. The question here is not whether the government has a compelling interest to deny a particular claim but rather a much stricter standard: "whether there is some overriding reason to impose a total ban on the right of the group or its members to bring their individualized claims [in a particular context], bearing in mind the considerable likelihood that a determination of religiousness in one context will spill over into others."[49] This would likely prove easier in cases where merely individual beliefs, rather than the claims of whole religious groups, would be at stake. In such circumstances, courts would "simply assume religiousness (or non-religiousness) for purposes of analysis, and show why overriding state interests would in any event dictate an outcome adverse to the claimant."[50]

COMMENTS AND QUESTIONS

Tax regulations in the United States allow an inquiry into a church's tax liability only if a high level Treasury official "reasonably believes, on the basis of

---

48. *See N. v. Sweden*, App. No. 10410/83 (ECmHR Admissibility Decision, 11 October 1984), 208 (noting that church membership creates a "high degree of probability that exemption is not granted to persons who simply wish to escape service").

49. Durham and Sewell at 55.

50. *Id.* at 56.

facts and circumstances recorded in writing, that the organization (1) may not qualify for tax exemption as a church; (2) may be carrying on unrelated trade or business . . . [as defined in the Internal Revenue Code]; or (3) may be otherwise engaged in activities subject to tax." *See* 26 C.F.R. 301.7611-1. To determine whether an organization constitutes a "church" within these rules concerning church tax inquiries, the applicable Internal Revenue Service regulation provides that "[s]olely for purposes of applying the procedures of section 7611 . . . the term 'church' includes any organization claiming to be a church and any convention or association of churches." Is there a reason that this type of deferential standard is more vital in the context of tax audits and other inquiries? Could this type of deferential definition be extended more generally or is it necessary to fall back on an analogical or functional type definition in other contexts?

D. ISLAM AND THE DEFINITION OF RELIGION

The common distinction in Christianity between the religious and secular, or the sacred and the profane, is not similarly relevant in Islam. Professor Seyyed Hossein Nasr explains:

> In the unitary perspective of Islam, all aspects of life, as well as all degrees of cosmic manifestation, are governed by a single principle and are unified by a common centre... In essence, therefore, everything is sacred and nothing profane because everything bears within itself the fragrance of the divine.
>
> In such a perspective, the meaning of religion and secularism appears in a new light. Religion becomes the revelation sent by God to man to guide him towards Unity and to help him become what he always 'was' but has forgotten; that is, to make him remember and regain the celestial beatitude which he once enjoyed before falling into the prison of the senses. Religion may be considered ultimately as the Divine guide by the help of which mean can overcome the ontological barrier separating him from his Divine Origin, although in essence he has never been separated from it. Moreover, religion becomes not a single instance of Divine guidance but all the revelations sent through the 124,000 prophets mentioned in traditional Islamic sources to the people of all ages and nations, of which the last in the present cycle of humanity is Muhammad – upon whom be blessings and peace. So it is that the Prophet claimed not to have brought anything new but to have re-stated the Truth claimed by all the previous prophets and to have re-established the primordial tradition (*al-din al-hanif*) which is the truth lying within the nature of things.[51]

COMMENTS AND QUESTIONS

Given Professor Nasr's explanation of the "unitary perspective" of Islam, what do you think of the following passage from Professor Abdullahi Ahmed An-Na'im?

> In order to be a Muslim by conviction and free choice, which is the only way one can be a Muslim, I need a secular state. By a secular state I mean one that is neutral regarding religious doctrine, one that does not claim or pretend to enforce Shari'a—the religious law of Islam—simply because compliance with Shari'a cannot be coerced by fear of state institutions or faked to appease their officials. . . . My call for the state, and not society, to be secular is intended to enhance and protect genuine religious

51. Seyyed Hossein Nasr, *Islamic Life and Thought* 708 (State Univ. of New York Press 1981).

> observance, to affirm, nurture, and regulate the role of Islam in the public life of the community. Conversely, I . . . argue that the claim of a so-called Islamic state to coercively enforce Shari'a repudiates the foundational role of Islam in the socialization of children and the sanctification of social institutions and relationships. . . . When observed voluntarily, Shari'a plays a fundamental role in the shaping and developing of ethical norms and values that can be reflected in general legislation and public policy through the democratic political process. But I [argue] that Shari'a principles cannot be enacted and enforced by the state as public law and public policy solely on the grounds that they are believed to be part of Shari'a. If such enactment and enforcement is attempted, the outcome will necessarily be the political will of the state and not the religious law of Islam.[52]

III. GENERAL JUSTIFICATIONS FOR FREEDOM OF RELIGION AND BELIEF

We now shift our attention from the question of how to define religion to the question of why it deserves protection. The justifications for religious freedom are many, varied, often complimentary, and occasionally contradictory. There are also concerns about some negative features of religion that may argue for curtailing religious freedom. In a large sense, the justifications for freedom of religion or belief, as well as the arguments for setting some limitations, run through virtually all the cases in this book. In this chapter, we are only able to touch on a few of the major arguments. Many of these arguments tend to be made when constitutional provisions are adopted, and are simply assumed in the context of adjudicating constitutional cases. Our hope is that the remainder of this chapter will set the stage for many of the cases and controversies considered later in the book.

A. CLASSIC ARGUMENTS FOR RELIGIOUS FREEDOM

Many of the key, foundational arguments for religious freedom derive from Lockean thought, which was studied in Chapter 1. We now examine some of the arguments championed by early American founders. As you read the passages that follow, you may want to ask yourself how the American arguments relate to the Lockean position. To what extent are the American arguments new and innovative, and to what extent do they draw on Lockean or more general British background?

1. Early American Arguments

As noted in Chapter 1, eighteenth-century Virginia was a honing ground for early American arguments justifying or curtailing various dimensions of religious freedom. In particular, Patrick Henry's assessment bill, James Madison's Memorial and Remonstrance, and Thomas Jefferson's religious liberty statute are three of the most significant documents leading up to the adoption of the First Amendment.

Following the Revolutionary War, prior to the assessment bill, many Americans feared that their newly founded society was degenerating, resulting in a decline in public virtue, which many regarded as critical to the success of the

52. Abdullahi Ahmed An-Na'im, *Islam and the Secular State* 1 (Harvard Univ. Press 2008).

republican government. Some pointed to the decreasing influence of religion as one of the primary problems. One idea that quickly gained momentum was to strengthen the impact of religion through state support, thereby helping to cultivate a more virtuous citizenry. As mentioned in Chapter 1, Patrick Henry, one of the state's most powerful politicians, joined this movement, proposing that the state legislature adopt a general assessment to support churches in Virginia, with taxpayers free to select the specific church that would receive their funds.[53]

After Patrick Henry presented the assessment bill, opponents delayed the final vote on the measure, so they could have time to mount a public attack. James Madison, one of the most prominent challengers, began working on a petition to rally public opposition. The result, Madison's *Memorial and Remonstrance*, was circulated throughout the state, contributing to the bill's demise and paving the way for the passage of Jefferson's Virginia Statute for Religious Freedom. This critical document outlines some of the most forceful arguments in support of church-state separation, many of which remain highly relevant and persuasive today.[54]

JAMES MADISON, MEMORIAL AND REMONSTRANCE AGAINST RELIGIOUS ASSESSMENTS (1785)

We, the subscribers, citizens of the said Commonwealth, having taken into serious consideration, a Bill printed by order of the last Session of General Assembly, entitled "A Bill establishing a provision for Teachers of the Christian Religion," and conceiving that the same, if finally armed with the sanctions of a law, will be a dangerous abuse of power, are bound as faithful members of a free State, to remonstrate against it, and to declare the reasons by which we are determined. We remonstrate against the said Bill,

1. Because we hold it for a fundamental and undeniable truth, "that religion, or the duty which we owe to our Creator, and the manner of discharging it, can be directed only by reason and conviction, not by force or violence." The Religion then of every man must be left to the conviction and conscience of every man; and it is the right of every man to exercise it as these may dictate. This right is in its nature an unalienable right. It is unalienable; because the opinions of men, depending only on the evidence contemplated by their own minds, cannot follow the dictates of other men: It is unalienable also; because what is here a right towards men, is a duty towards the Creator. It is the duty of every man to render to the Creator such homage, and such only, as he believes to be acceptable to him. This duty is precedent both in order of time and in degree of obligation, to the claims of Civil Society. Before any man can be considered as a member of Civil Society, he must be considered as a subject of the Governor of the Universe: And if a member of Civil Society, do it with a saving of his allegiance to the Universal Sovereign. We maintain therefore that in matters of Religion, no man's right is abridged by the institution of Civil Society, and that Religion is wholly exempt from its cognizance. True it is, that no other rule exists, by which any question

53. *See* W. Cole Durham, Jr., and Elizabeth A. Sewell, Virginia Founders and the Birth of Religious Freedom, in *Lectures on Religion and the Founding of the American Republic,* 70–71 (John W. Welch and Stephen J. Fleming, eds., Brigham Young Univ. Press 2003).

54. *Id.* at 71.

which may divide a Society, can be ultimately determined, but the will of the majority; but it is also true, that the majority may trespass on the rights of the minority.

2. Because if Religion be exempt from the authority of the Society at large, still less can it be subject to that of the Legislative Body. The latter are but the creatures and vicegerents of the former. Their jurisdiction is both derivative and limited: it is limited with regard to the co-ordinate departments, more necessarily is it limited with regard to the constituents. The preservation of a free government requires not merely, that the metes and bounds which separate each department of power be invariably maintained; but more especially, that neither of them be suffered to overleap the great Barrier which defends the rights of the people. The Rulers who are guilty of such an encroachment, exceed the commission from which they derive their authority, and are Tyrants. The People who submit to it are governed by laws made neither by themselves, nor by an authority derived from them, and are slaves.

3. Because, it is proper to take alarm at the first experiment on our liberties. We hold this prudent jealousy to be the first duty of citizens, and one of [the] noblest characteristics of the late Revolution. The freemen of America did not wait till usurped power had strengthened itself by exercise, and entangled the question in precedents. They saw all the consequences in the principle, and they avoided the consequences by denying the principle. . . .

4. Because, the bill violates the equality which ought to be the basis of every law, and which is more indispensable, in proportion as the validity or expediency of any law is more liable to be impeached. If "all men are by nature equally free and independent," all men are to be considered as entering into Society on equal conditions; as relinquishing no more, and therefore retaining no less, one than another, of their natural rights. Above all are they to be considered as retaining an "equal title to the free exercise of Religion according to the dictates of Conscience." Whilst we assert for ourselves a freedom to embrace, to profess and to observe the Religion which we believe to be of divine origin, we cannot deny an equal freedom to those whose minds have not yet yielded to the evidence which has convinced us. If this freedom be abused, it is an offence against God, not against man: To God, therefore, not to men, must an account of it be rendered. . . .

5. Because the Bill implies either that the Civil Magistrate is a competent Judge of Religious truth; or that he may employ Religion as an engine of Civil policy. The first is an arrogant pretension falsified by the contradictory opinions of Rulers in all ages, and throughout the world: The second an unhallowed perversion of the means of salvation.

6. Because the establishment proposed by the Bill is not requisite for the support of the Christian Religion. To say that it is, is a contradiction to the Christian Religion itself; for every page of it disavows a dependence on the powers of this world: it is a contradiction to fact; for it is known that this Religion both existed and flourished, not only without the support of human laws, but in spite of every opposition from them; and not only during the period of miraculous aid, but long after it had been left to its own evidence, and the ordinary care of Providence. . . .

7. Because experience witnesseth that ecclesiastical establishments, instead of maintaining the purity and efficacy of Religion, have had a contrary operation. During almost fifteen centuries, has the legal establishment of Christianity been on

trial. What have been its fruits? More or less in all places, pride and indolence in the Clergy; ignorance and servility in the laity; in both, superstition, bigotry and persecution. . . .

8. Because the establishment in question is not necessary for the support of Civil Government. If it be urged as necessary for the support of Civil Government only as it is a means of supporting Religion, and it be not necessary for the latter purpose, it cannot be necessary for the former. If Religion be not within [the] cognizance of Civil Government, how can its legal establishment be necessary to civil Government? What influence in fact have ecclesiastical establishments had on Civil Society? In some instances they have been seen to erect a spiritual tyranny on the ruins of the Civil authority; in many instances they have been seen upholding the thrones of political tyranny; in no instance have they been seen the guardians of the liberties of the people. Rulers who wished to subvert the public liberty, may have found an established clergy convenient auxiliaries. A just government, instituted to secure & perpetuate it, needs them not. Such a government will be best supported by protecting every citizen in the enjoyment of his Religion with the same equal hand which protects his person and his property; by neither invading the equal rights by any Sect, nor suffering any Sect to invade those of another.

9. Because the proposed establishment is a departure from the generous policy, which, offering an asylum to the persecuted and oppressed of every Nation and Religion, promised a lustre to our country, and an accession to the number of its citizens. . . . Distant as it may be, in its present form, from the Inquisition it differs from it only in degree. The one is the first step, the other the last in the career of intolerance. The magnanimous sufferer under this cruel scourge in foreign Regions, must view the Bill as a Beacon on our Coast, warning him to seek some other haven, where liberty and philanthropy in their due extent may offer a more certain repose from his troubles.

10. Because, it will have a like tendency to banish our Citizens. The allurements presented by other situations are every day thinning their number. To superadd a fresh motive to emigration, by revoking the liberty which they now enjoy, would be the same species of folly which has dishonoured and depopulated flourishing kingdoms.

11. Because, it will destroy that moderation and harmony which the forbearance of our laws to intermeddle with Religion, has produced among its several sects. Torrents of blood have been spilt in the old world, by vain attempts of the secular arm to extinguish Religious discord, by proscribing all difference in Religious opinions. Time has at length revealed the true remedy. Every relaxation of narrow and rigorous policy, wherever it has been tried, has been found to assuage the disease. . . .

12. Because, the policy of the bill is adverse to the diffusion of the light of Christianity. The first wish of those who enjoy this precious gift, ought to be that it may be imparted to the whole race of mankind. Compare the number of those who have as yet received it with the number still remaining under the dominion of false Religions; and how small is the former! Does the policy of the Bill tend to lessen the disproportion? No; it at once discourages those who are strangers to the light of [revelation] from coming into the Region of it; and countenances, by example the nations who continue in darkness, in shutting out those who might

convey it to them. Instead of leveling as far as possible, every obstacle to the victorious progress of truth, the Bill with an ignoble and unchristian timidity would circumscribe it, with a wall of defence, against the encroachments of error.

13. Because attempts to enforce by legal sanctions, acts obnoxious to so great a proportion of Citizens, tend to enervate the laws in general, and to slacken the bands of Society. If it be difficult to execute any law which is not generally deemed necessary or salutary, what must be the case where it is deemed invalid and dangerous? and what may be the effect of so striking an example of impotency in the Government, on its general authority?

14. Because a measure of such singular magnitude and delicacy ought not to be imposed, without the clearest evidence that it is called for by a majority of citizens: and no satisfactory method is yet proposed by which the voice of the majority in this case may be determined, or its influence secured. . . .

15. Because, finally, "the equal right of every citizen to the free exercise of his Religion according to the dictates of conscience" is held by the same tenure with all our other rights. If we recur to its origin, it is equally the gift of nature; if we weigh its importance, it cannot be less dear to us; if we consult the Declaration of those rights which pertain to the good people of Virginia, as the "basis and foundation of Government," it is enumerated with equal solemnity, or rather studied emphasis. Either then, we must say, that the will of the Legislature is the only measure of their authority; and that in the plenitude of this authority, they may sweep away all our fundamental rights; or, that they are bound to leave this particular right untouched and sacred: Either we must say, that they may controul the freedom of the press, may abolish the trial by jury, may swallow up the Executive and Judiciary Powers of the State; nay that they may despoil us of our very right of suffrage, and erect themselves into an independent and hereditary assembly: or we must say, that they have no authority to enact into law the Bill under consideration.

We the subscribers say, that the General Assembly of this Commonwealth have no such authority: And that no effort may be omitted on our part against so dangerous an usurpation, we oppose to it, this remonstrance; earnestly praying, as we are in duty bound, that the Supreme Lawgiver of the Universe, by illuminating those to whom it is addressed, may on the one hand, turn their Councils from every act which would affront his holy prerogative, or violate the trust committed to them: and on the other, guide them into every measure which may be worthy of his [blessing, may re]dound to their own praise, and may establish more firmly the liberties, the prosperity, and the Happiness of the Commonwealth.

COMMENTS AND QUESTIONS

1. Madison draws upon a line of thought going back to arguments in Locke's *A Letter Concerning Toleration* to explain that, contrary to the common assumption that endorsing or supporting religion would give added stability to a country, a broad understanding of religious freedom that treats all citizens equally gives greater legitimacy and stability to a nation. Not only does such a nation gain a "lustre to [the] country" by taking in religious refugees, but the "moderation and harmony" gained will increase support for a government, promote health and prosperity, and prevent animosities and jealousies over

government preference and support.[55] What other Lockean views does Madison allude to? How do arguments in the Memorial and Remonstrance relate to Locke's social contract theory?

2. Over the last century, American courts have often turned to the Memorial and Remonstrance to try to decipher how the Founders understood concepts of church-state separation and establishment. In *Everson v. Board of Education*, 330 US 1 (1947) a foundational Establishment Clause case, Justice Rutledge wrote in his dissenting opinion that because Madison's Remonstrance "[r]eflect[s] not only the many legislative conflicts over the Assessment Bill and the Bill for Establishing Religious Freedom but also, for example, the struggles for religious incorporations and the continued maintenance of the glebes" that the document "is at once the most concise and the most accurate statement of the views of the First Amendment's author concerning what is 'an establishment of religion'" (37-38). How could arguments from the Remonstrance be used in debating for or against contested measures such as school prayer, parochial school vouchers, and public monuments associated with religion?

2. Contemporary Empirical Justification

Recent studies of data on religious freedoms internationally challenge the thesis that a homogeneous religious society is ideal. The studies now make it clear that the existence of cultural and religious difference is not the best predictor of religious violence in a given area. The more powerful predictor is a government's level of restrictions on religion, which also shows significant positive associations with other important civil liberties.[56] Where religious freedoms are, it appears, freedoms of the press and speech are also. The significant positive statistical relationships between religious liberty and other social goods do not end with political freedoms, however. Analysis of recent data suggests that overall levels of well-being are closely linked with religious freedoms.

Brian J. Grim and Roger Finke demonstrated—based on a study of nearly 200 countries—that government restriction of religious freedom is a powerful predictor of violent religious persecution.[57] Low levels of religious violence coincide with low levels of government restriction on religious liberty. Contrary to those who see cultural and religious differences as the seed of national and international discord, Grim and Finke claim that it is the fact of restrictions on religious liberty rather than the fact of religious plurality that catalyzes religious violence and persecution. In order to defuse the explosive power of religious diversity, they argue, governments should first look to their protection of religious freedoms. Rather than attempt to promote civic peace and social order by burdening minority religious groups with restrictions as the governments of some countries do, governments should promote religious freedoms. Grim and Finke's case studies

55. James Madison, *The Papers of James Madison* 8:302 (William T. Hutchinson and William M.E. Rachal, eds., Univ. of Chicago Press 1962).

56. Brian J. Grim & Roger Finke, *The Price of Freedom Denied: Religious Persecution and Conflict in the Twenty-First Century* 68 (Cambridge Univ. Press 2011).

57. *Id.* at 79–80.

reveal a bitter irony: Restrictions on religious freedoms aimed at promoting order and peace have often led to increased religious violence.[58]

Grim and Finke also considered the strong positive relationships between religious freedoms and other essential social goods, especially the powerful connections religious freedoms have with other civil liberties, press freedoms, and political freedoms.[59] They note that the evidence is growing that religious freedom is a crucial part of what Nobel Prize winning economist Amartya Sen describes as a "bundled commodity" of human freedoms, which include freedoms of the press, civil liberties, and other political freedoms.[60] Yet while the strong links between these freedoms and basic social goods are well demonstrated, the causal relationships among them are yet to be understood. Grim and Finke conclude that enforcing religious liberty comes with a price, but the price of denying religious freedom may be a far higher price.[61]

B. NATURAL LAW, NATURAL RIGHTS, AND RELIGIOUS FREEDOM

Another major strand of reasoning in support of religious freedom flows from the tradition of natural law and natural rights. These ideas rest on the belief that certain values, rights, and principles of morality are universally applicable and can be identified through human reason. The classic example of such thought is found in the opening lines of the American Declaration of Independence:

> When in the Course of human events it becomes necessary for one people to dissolve the political bands which have connected them with another and to assume among the powers of the earth, the separate and equal station to which the Laws of Nature and of Nature's God entitle them, a decent respect to the opinions of mankind requires that they should declare the causes which impel them to the separation.
>
> We hold these truths to be self-evident, that all men are created equal, that they are endowed by their Creator with certain unalienable Rights, that among these are Life, Liberty and the pursuit of Happiness.

The assertion that "the Laws of Nature and of Nature's God" and "certain unalienable Rights" are "self-evident" truths reflects the belief in the natural right foundation of religious freedom, as well as of many other rights.

James Madison, as a legislator and polemicist, contributed writings that reflect his deep-seated belief that religious liberty is a natural right. When the Virginia Declaration of Rights was first drafted by George Mason, Madison revised the promise of religious tolerance by government to employ language that more powerfully enshrined religious liberty as a natural and absolute right: "all men are equally entitled to the free exercise of religion." Ultimately, on the strength and conviction of Madison's arguments during the founding period,

> [t]he axiom emerged (shall we say) that liberty of conscience stands above and apart from the power of the state to legislate as a God-given, inalienable natural right of every individual person. It is antecedent to citizenship and independent of it, woven into human nature as inseparable from man's very being or specific essence. This is

58. *See, e.g. Id.* at 88–119 (comparing Japan, India, and Nigeria).
59. *Id.* at 205, 206 fig. 7.2.
60. *Id.* at 206.
61. *Id.* at 213.

the high ground theoretically claimed and politically won in the struggle for religious liberty, as the victory was conceived by Madison, his supporters, and associates.[62]

Though philosophical and political liberalism have largely moved on to other justifications of religious freedom, the idea of a natural right to religious liberty remains part of today's philosophical debate. For example, Robert George argues for religious freedom based on the intrinsic value of religion, a value that by its very nature cannot be achieved coercively:

> [T]he right to religious freedom is grounded precisely in the value of religion, considered as an ultimate intelligible reason for action, a basic human good. Is religion a value? . . . Irrespective of whether unaided reason can conclude on the basis of a valid argument that God exists—indeed, even if it turns out that God does not exist—there is an important sense in which religion is a basic human good, an intrinsic and irreducible aspect of the well-being and flourishing of human persons. Religion is a basic human good if it provides an ultimate intelligible reason for action. But agnostics and even atheists can easily grasp the intelligible point of considering whether there is some ultimate, more-than-human source of meaning and value, of enquiring as best one can into the truth of the matter, and of ordering one's life on the basis of one's best judgment. Doing that is participating in the good of religion. . . .
>
> For the sake of religion, then, considered as a value that practical reason can identify as an intrinsic aspect of the integral good of all human beings, government may never legitimately coerce religious belief; nor may it require religious observance or practice; nor may it forbid them for religious reasons. (To that extent, freedom of religion is absolute.) Moreover, government, for the sake of the good of religion, should protect individuals and religious communities from others who would try to coerce them in religious matters on the basis of theological objections to their beliefs and practices.[63]

COMMENTS AND QUESTIONS

1. What grounds can you see for the Declaration's assertion of self-evident rights? Do you consider them definitively self-evident, or is it possible for reasonable people to disagree about them?
2. Do you accept George's argument that religion is intrinsic to human well-being and flourishing? How might a religious freedom regime based on George's arguments differ from one based merely on concerns about enhancing social cohesion?
3. Natural law arguments have lost traction in many settings. Do they have greater plausibility in the international human rights arena? Many human rights activists would continue to assert that the rights they defend are universally valid. Is this the contemporary version of a natural rights claim? Or are claims that human rights lack genuine universality more persuasive, thereby providing a refutation at the international level of the validity of natural law claims?

---

62. Ellis Sandoz, Religious Liberty and Religion in the American Founding Revisited, in *Religious Liberty in Western Thought* 245, 275 (Noel B. Reynolds and W. Cole Durham, Jr., eds., Scholars Press 1996).

63. Robert P. George, *Making Men Moral: Civil Liberties and Public Morality* 221–222 (Oxford Univ. Press 1993).

C. HUMAN DIGNITY

We next consider "the remarkably thoughtful justification put forward by the founding mothers and fathers of modern human rights: the drafters of the Universal Declaration of Human Rights 1947-1948," as explained by Norwegian scholar Tore Lindholm.

Pointing to Articles 1 and 29 as well as the Preamble of the Universal Declaration of Human Rights, Lindholm asserts two basic premises.

> [First], Every human being is born free and equal in dignity; human beings are, furthermore, presumed to be sufficiently reasonable and conscientious to observe a decent public order defined in terms of human rights. [Second], If peoples organized as sovereign states, under such global circumstances for human freedom and dignity as prevail in the world now and in the foreseeable future, are not to disregard their moral commitment proclaimed in [the first premise], they are obliged to seek to agree on and establish an international regime for the domestic protection of people's dignity and freedom, by means of legally and politically codified rights, to be called "human rights".[64]

Lindholm goes on to pose the question "[H]ow are human rights 'derived' from human dignity?" His own response is that

> A good beginning to an answer is . . . to make the notion of inherent human dignity operational for human rights as it were, by saying that if all humans have inherent dignity, then *there is something about each and every human being* such that certain things ought not to be done to her and certain other things ought to be done for her. . . . [However,] we are still several steps away from justifying *human rights*, that is, justifying universally applicable entitlements that trump other political and moral interests.
>
> The first step is to be clear about "the circumstances of rights." It is not a self-evident universal truth that people have rights in virtue of their inherent dignity. In a flourishing closed, small, prosperous, and morally harmonious society where people are oblivious of rights and lead fulfilling lives without rights, the very introduction of rights could bring moral decline, perhaps by aggravating interpersonal conflicts. The costs of rights are not just financial, but possibly moral. Nozick's proposition, "Individuals have rights and there are things no person or group may do to them (without violating their rights)"[65] is an important truth in any modern, complex, and plural society. It is not a universal moral truth, not true in all social worlds. A social world in which Nozick's proposition is true is one in which the circumstances of rights obtain.
>
> A next step is to elucidate what goods and benefits people shall have secure access to by means of rights. The interest or values to be protected by a right must, for a morally justified human right to exist, be of great importance to people either generally or in significant cases and be significantly linked with people's chance to lead lives answering to human dignity. Moreover, a good or benefit, even if deemed very important for a dignified human life, should not by right be protected as a human right unless general and minimally effective and even-handed protection is, or can be made, socially feasible. Hence, to be dearly loved; to avoid early sudden death or severe conflicts; or to have a happy family life are some very cherished goods that are unsuitable for protection by rights. Jefferson in the Declaration of Independence, when enumerating the most important goods to be protected by natural rights, included "life,

---

64. Tore Lindholm, Philosophical and Religious Justifications of Freedom of Religion or Belief, in *Facilitating Freedom of Religion or Belief: A Deskbook* 47 (Tore Lindholm, W. Cole Durham, Jr., and Bahia G. Tahzib-Lie, eds., Martinus Nijhoff 2004).

65. Robert Nozick, *Anarchy, State, and Utopia* ix (Basic Books 1974).

> liberty and the pursuit of happiness." It would have been improper to proclaim a natural right to happiness since happiness whether as a full-fledged morally successful life or as a felicitous feeling cannot properly be safe-guarded by means of rights.
>
> A reasonable counterargument to a proposal for something to be [a] human rights-protected good would be to show that there are alternative ways of protecting the good in question that are more suitable for the purpose, or less costly, or more efficient, than rights.
>
> Finally, in this rudimentary checklist of considerations pertaining to "the derivation of human rights from human dignity," I mention that the addressees of modern human rights, saddled by internationally binding law with the burden of implementing human rights protection for all human beings everywhere in the world, had to be modern territorial states, each state catering to people under their respective jurisdictions. In our world only states could have the requisite legitimacy, power, coercive apparatus, and other resources it takes. But for that reason, only norms and mechanisms that can attract reasonably broad international support can attain human rights status. [66]

Lindholm considers human dignity to be a justification for religious freedom both basic and broad enough to encompass many and perhaps all different justifications of religious freedoms. Working out the implications of human dignity is therefore not a purely logical or philosophical exercise, then, but a political one, involving debate and compromise between all parties involved that will leave many important differences unsettled while still leading to a stable consensus in favor of religious freedom. This process will be discussed in more depth below as a possible solution to the problem of multiple incompatible justifications.

COMMENTS AND QUESTIONS

The meaning and grounds of human dignity is one of the recurrent themes that we will see again and again. Consider what you think might be the basis for and implications of the idea that everyone possesses an inherent human dignity.

IV. RELIGIOUS ARGUMENTS FOR FREEDOM, TOLERANCE, AND MUTUAL RESPECT

Religious believers often view their own faith traditions as being rooted in love, respect, and persuasion. However, nearly every religious tradition of which we are aware, certainly those with a long history, has a mixed record with respect to religious freedom. Most religious traditions are complex and have multiple sources of what is regarded as authoritative or sacred. Most religious traditions have been utilized by adherents to justify coercion as well as freedom. This takes a variety of forms, including forcing people to convert, often in the name of saving their souls, or establishing or preserving national identity, solidarity, and stability. It has also involved various aggressive forms of proselytism and cultural hegemony.

For example, the doctrine of the Catholic Church describes sins involving the changing of religion. In particular, there are three sins against the faith: heresy, apostasy, and schism. Under some interpretations of Catholic doctrine, the penalty

---

66. Lindholm, *supra* note 64, at 48–49.

for each of the three sins is the same—excommunication. However, each sin constitutes a different particular act.

According to the *Catechism of the Catholic Church,* heresy is "the obstinate post-baptismal denial of some truth which must be believed with divine and Catholic faith, or it is likewise an obstinate doubt concerning the same."[67] Apostasy is "the total repudiation of the Christian faith." Schism is defined as "the refusal of submission to the Roman Pontiff or of communion with the members of the Church subject to him." Thus, the changing of religious theology is viewed in varying ways as a sin by the Catholic Church.[68]

Others who are critical of religion see faith as one, if not the dominant, source of evil and wrongdoing in the world. These views, too, are an oversimplification and tend to exaggerate and distort the role that religion has played in political and economic events.

At the same time, it is a tenet of almost all religions that each person should treat others with love and respect. Almost all religions have passages in holy texts or writings by leaders that promote this ethic of reciprocity. The Golden Rule of Christianity, for example, is often expressed as "Do unto others as you would have them do unto you." The Golden Rule thus provides a basis for recognition of and respect for religious freedom within religions. Within Buddhism a similar sentiment is recorded this reflection of the Buddha: "For a state that is not pleasant or delightful to me must be so to him also; and a state that is not pleasing or delightful to me, how could I inflict that upon another?"[69]

Since World War II, a number of organizations (including both religious and non-religious groups) have adopted policy statements that express support for religious freedom. These include the Baptist World Alliance,[70] the World Council of Churches,[71] and many others. A particularly significant example is the Catholic Church's Second Vatican Council Declaration on Religious Freedom, *Dignitatis Humanae*, adopted in 1965. Consider the following passages from that Declaration:

> This Vatican Council declares that the human person has a right to religious freedom. This freedom means that all men are to be immune from coercion on the part of individuals or of social groups and of any human power, in such wise that no one is to be forced to act in a manner contrary to his own beliefs.
>
> The council further declares that the right to religious freedom has its foundation in the very dignity of the human person as this dignity is known through the revealed word of God and by reason itself. This right of the human person to religious freedom

---

67. Catechism of the Catholic Church para. 2089 (US Catholic Conference, Inc. trans., 1994).

68. Interestingly, the Catholic Church's view of church-state relationships (and thus, of religious freedom) has appeared to evolve over the centuries. *See, e.g.* Pope St. Pius X, Vehementer Nos § 3. February 1906, available in English at *Papal Encyclicals Online,* http://www.papalencyclicals.net/pius10/p10law.htm. ("That the State must be separated from the Church is a thesis absolutely false, a most pernicious error.")

69. *Samyutta Nikaya* v. 353–354, *see, e.g.,* in Peter Harvey, *An Introduction to Buddhist Ethics: Foundations, Values and Issues (Introduction to Religion)* 33 (Cambridge Univ. Press 2000).

70. *See* Centennial Statement, Baptist World Alliance Centenary Congress, Birmingham, United Kingdom, July 2005.

71. *See, e.g.*, Statement on the Politicization of Religion and Rights of Religious Minorities, World Council of Churches 10th Assembly, 20 October to 8 November 2013, Busan, Republic of Korea, Document PIC 02.1.

> is to be recognized in the constitutional law whereby society is governed and thus it is to become a civil right.
>
> It is in accordance with their dignity as persons—that is, beings endowed with reason and free will and therefore privileged to bear personal responsibility—that all men should be at once impelled by nature and also bound by a moral obligation to seek the truth, especially religious truth. However, men cannot discharge these obligations in a manner in keeping with their own nature unless they enjoy immunity from external coercion as well as psychological freedom. [T]he right to this immunity continues to exist even in those who do not live up to their obligation of seeking the truth and adhering to it and the exercise of this right is not to be impeded, provided that just public order be observed. . . .
>
> The declaration of this Vatican Council on the right of man to religious freedom has its foundation in the dignity of the person, whose exigencies have come to be more fully known to human reason through centuries of experience. What is more, this doctrine of freedom has roots in divine revelation, and for this reason Christians are bound to respect it all the more conscientiously. Revelation disclose[s] the dignity of the human person in its full dimensions. It gives evidence of the respect which Christ showed toward the freedom with which man is to fulfill his duty of belief in the word of God and it gives us lessons in the spirit which disciples of such a Master ought to adopt and continually follow.

Professor of Canon Law, Reverend Father David-Maria Jaeger has explained the significance of this Declaration by the Catholic Church.[72]

> The Catholic religion is a "universal religion," in the sense that the belief is essential to it that it is meant for all human beings, everywhere, that it—and it alone—is the true religion; that it … alone—represents the direct revelation of God; that it—and it alone—represents . . . the definitive revelation of God . . . .
>
> This is a bold statement to make, and today's exigencies of "political correctness," so to speak, mean that it is not often made in this stark manner by "responsible" speakers. Yet it is a statement that does go to the heart of the matter, and that is necessary to explain the Catholic Church's understanding of religious freedom. What it means then, for the present purpose, is that however the Catholic understanding of religious freedom may be expounded, it cannot possibly rest on any kind of atheism, religious relativism or indifferentism. It cannot be referred to a conviction that there is no God. It cannot be due to an assumption that "one religion is as good as another," and that, "non-religion is as good as this or any religion," or that, "any religion would be pleasing to God." It cannot be based on a conviction that, "religion does not matter to persons or societies," or else that, "it is impossible, or it may well be impossible, for human beings to know the truth about God, to know which is the true religion." Finally, the Catholic understanding of religious freedom cannot be based on the theory that religion is a purely private matter, to be confined within the sphere of individual and family life, or at most within circumscribed communities of believers, and that religion does not give rise to obligations binding upon civil government.

Yet the *Dignitatis Humanae* describes freedom of religion as having "roots in divine revelation" and having its foundation in "the very dignity of the human person." Father Jaeger poses the question "Is there not an antithesis between the religious conviction concerning the one true religion, and the similarly religious conviction concerning the moral—not just the physical—inviolability of the human

---

72. David-Maria A. Jaeger, The Holy See's Understanding of Religious Freedom, in *Church and State: Towards Protection for Freedom of Religion,* International Conference on Comparative Constitutional Law 449, 451–452 (Japanese Association of Comparative Constitutional Law 2005).

person and therefore of the rights inherent in human personality?" In answering this question, Father Jaeger points out that

> [t]he Declaration goes on to give a seemingly complex, very subtle, and progressively developing rationale, which . . . might be described as resting on twin pillars, as it were: There is the inviolability of the human conscience, with which none may interfere. This constitutes an absolute barrier to any pretension by any human power. Any pretension to control a human being can never go beyond the line that demarcates this absolutely inviolable and morally and legally impenetrable sphere. But—and this is the second pillar—matters do not stop here. Respect for the freedom of conscience is essential to the divine purpose to draw human beings to an intelligent and free recognition of revealed divine Truth. Because of the very nature of faith, according to the Catholic religion itself, there would be little point to embracing it except it be a truly human choice, a choice made by the human being as God created him, namely as a free acting subject, employing the uniquely and specifically human faculties of intellect and will and governed by his conscience alone. Human beings as created by God have the capacity and the moral duty to seek the true religion—which is objectively one—and once found to embrace it and follow where it leads. However, this capacity and the value of actualising it properly are intrinsically fatally damaged by any kind of coercion.[73]

Professor Khaled Abou El Fadl, one of the leading authorities in Islamic Law in the United States and Europe, offers insight into the perception of religious freedom within the Islamic tradition.

> At the most rudimentary level, the Qur'an itself is explicit in prohibiting any form of coerced conversions to Islam. It contends that truth and falsity are clear and distinct, and so whomever wishes to believe may do so, but no duress is permitted in religion: "There is no compulsion in matters of faith." Of course . . . this response is incomplete —even if forced conversions to Islam are prohibited, aggressive warfare to spread Islamic power over non-believers might still be allowed. Does the Qur'an condone such expansionist wars?
>
> Interestingly, Islamic tradition does not have a notion of holy war. Jihad simply means to strive hard or struggle in pursuit of a just cause, and according to the Prophet of Islam, the highest form of jihad is the struggle waged to cleanse oneself from the vices of the heart. Holy war (al-harb al-muqaddasah) is not an expression used by the Qur'anic text or Muslim theologians. . . . The Qur'anic text does not recognize the idea of unlimited warfare, and does not consider the simple fact of the belligerent's Muslim identity to be sufficient to establish the justness of his cause. In other words, the Qur'an entertains the possibility that the Muslim combatant might be the unjust party in a conflict. . . .
>
> Ultimately, the Qur'an, or any text, speaks through its reader. . . . Consequently the meaning of the text is often only as moral as its reader. If the reader is intolerant, hateful, or oppressive, so will be the interpretation of the text.
>
> It would be disingenuous to deny that the Qur'an and other Islamic sources offer possibilities of intolerant interpretation. Clearly these possibilities are exploited by the contemporary puritans and supremacists. But the text does not command such intolerant readings.[74]

There are also arguments supporting the social origin of legal and ethical obligations. For example, Ubuntu, a sub-Saharan African philosophy, defines the human experience as a communal one. While no single translation encompasses

73. *Id.* at 456.

74. Khaled Abou El Fadl, *The Place of Tolerance in Islam* 18–19, 22–23 (Joshua Cohen and Ian Lague, eds., Beacon Press 2002).

all of Ubuntu's meaning, the most common explanation is that "a person is a person through other persons." This perspective includes both an individual standard of moral conduct, and a "phenomenon" connecting all of humanity. While Ubuntu seems to lack a prime facie religious connotation, its traditional meaning is "deeply religious." Because one cannot exist without one's ancestors, Ubuntu prescribes reverence to one's forbearers.

Ubuntu's impact on the law, particularly in South Africa, emphasizes reconciliation rather than retributive justice. The South African Constitutional Court, for example, prohibited capital punishment on the reasoning that its retributive nature conflicted with Ubuntu's direction to find reconciliation in the pursuit of justice. Reconciliation rather than punishment drives South Africa's efforts to address its apartheid-era past as well, largely due to Ubuntu's influence.

Lithuanian/French philosopher Emmanuel Levinas also presents a communal approach to the human experience. According to Levinas, a life in isolation is fundamentally egoist and driven by consumption. Ethics exist only when two or more people are present. By herself, a person encounters her environment with the intent to enjoy, or consume what she finds. When a "face-to-face" encounter with another occurs, the other person resists consumption. The "other" says "I am not yours to be enjoyed: I am absolutely other." This resistance is unexpected, and it obligates the first person to respond, giving her responsibility to the "other." For Levinas, the other "orders and ordains" us, and calls us into giving to and serving the other. Such proximity demonstrates humanity's innate social orientation. When a person has responsibility to another, she is "made to stand in the place of the other." This interaction occurs as a natural consequence of meeting another. Levinas argues that such substitution shows that the meaning of being a social subject is primarily to be for the other person.[75]

COMMENTS AND QUESTIONS

1. Some of the foregoing justifications for religious freedom and tolerance have secular sources; others are rooted in religious traditions. Which are likely to be more persuasive? Which justifications seem most appropriate in judicial settings? In legislative settings? In private settings? To what extent can individuals in one tradition understand and appreciate the justifications advanced in another?
2. Supposing one faith happened to be unambiguously correct, what would be the value of forcing people to live that way?
3. The African concept "ubuntu" seems to have a lot in common with other ideas, such as the Confucian ideal of "ren" or two-man-mindedness that is discussed in Chapter 3. Are you familiar with similar ideas in other traditions?

Additional Web Resources:	Declarations, policy statements, and teachings in support of religious freedom drawn from various religious traditions

75. *See, e.g.*, Emmanuel Levinas, *Totality and Infinity: An Essay on Exteriority*, trans. Alphonso Lingis (Duquesne Univ. Press 1969); Ethics *and Infinity: Conversations with Phillippe Nemo* (Richard A. Cohen, trans., Duquesne Univ. Press 1985); *Time and the Other* (Richard A. Cohen, trans., Duquesne Univ. Press 1987).

V. THE VALUE OF MULTIPLE JUSTIFICATIONS

Plurality is the practical reality of life in modern states. There are no functioning states without religious minorities and the presence of at least some religious diversity. This is not surprising when one considers that even within most families there is at least some degree of difference in religious or non- religious attitudes. This means that deeply rooted difference is something that every state must be able to address. The difficulty is that not only do the basic belief systems differ; the conceptions of the types of political structures needed to address difference and the justification of rights within these systems differ as well. Faced with such theoretical divergence, how is social stability to be achieved?

A. OVERLAPPING CONSENSUS

In his work *Political Liberalism*, John Rawls argues that, in a society where there exists a plurality of reasonable comprehensive doctrines, there is no comprehensive doctrine sufficient to provide social unity. In such a society, "[s]ocial unity is based on a consensus on the political conception; and stability is possible when the doctrines making up the consensus are affirmed by society's politically active citizens and [are reasonably consistent with] the requirements of justice."[76] In essence, the theory is that for political liberalism to be possible, individuals must not insist on the enforcement of their own comprehensive doctrine, no matter how true they believe it to be, but rather should separate political values upon which all can agree from nonpolitical values upon which several groups may reasonably disagree.

According to Rawls, political liberalism is possible only if fundamental questions of justice and constitutional essentials are settled by political values and those values are sufficient "to override all other values that may come in conflict with them."[77] In other words, since it is a permanent fact that, in a pluralistic society, individuals will reasonably disagree without compromise on certain values, such as religion, the political power, or power of the collective body, should not be used to enforce the nonpolitical values of only one group. This is possible as long as political values, as distinguished from nonpolitical values, are sufficient to answer the fundamental questions "in ways that all citizens can reasonably be expected to endorse in light of their common human reason," [78] and as long as there are ways for people to hold reasonable nonpolitical values in concert with the political values espoused by the citizenry as a whole. Rawls concludes that history shows that this arrangement is indeed possible.

A major problem with Rawls's conception of overlapping consensus is that it is difficult to distinguish genuine consensus from a mere modus vivendi—that is, a state of affairs that appears to be stable, but in reality is contingent on circumstances that make the arrangement beneficial to the interests of all involved. Once the circumstances change, the apparent stability disappears. Rawls argues that overlapping consensus is more than a modus vivendi because of three inherent features:

---

76. John Rawls, *Political Liberalism* 134 (Columbia Univ. Press 1993).

77. *Id.* at 138.

78. *Id.* at 140.

> [F]irst, the object of consensus, the political conception of justice, is itself a moral conception. And second, it is affirmed on moral grounds. . . . An overlapping consensus, therefore, is not merely a consensus on accepting certain authorities, or on complying with certain institutional arrangements, founded on a convergence of self- or group interests. All those who affirm the political conception start from within their own comprehensive view and draw on the religious, philosophical, and moral grounds it provides.[79]

The third feature is that the consensus, unlike a modus vivendi, will be stable. Since the principles contained in the overlapping consensus are included in all of the reasonable comprehensive doctrines represented, they will not be abandoned even if one comprehensive view becomes dominant.

> [T]he political conception will still be supported regardless of shifts in the distribution of political power. Each view supports the political conception for its own sake, or on its own merits. The test for this is whether the consensus is stable with respect to changes in the distribution of power among views. This feature of stability highlights a basic contrast between an overlapping consensus and a modus vivendi, the stability of which does depend on happenstance and a balance of relative forces.[80]

In many respects, the idea of religious freedom provides a model of how Rawlsian overlapping consensus might work. Differing comprehensive religious views might vary in their beliefs about the nature of deity, man's place in the world, ethical obligations, and so forth, but have a shared conception of how the political order should be structured. (Among other things, the constitutional protections would likely include a commitment to freedom of religion or belief, and would be attractive to religious groups in part for that reason.) This set of political beliefs would be affirmed on moral and/or religious grounds. The overlapping consensus would be stable because commitment to the political conception would rest on principle, and not merely on the interests of religious groups.

B. OVERLAPPING JUSTIFICATION

If freedom of religion really entails freedom to believe whatever one wants about important questions of life, it certainly must entail freedom to believe in whichever justification for religious freedom one finds most convincing or most compatible with one's religious beliefs. As Norwegian philosopher Tore Lindholm points out, however, this raises two dilemmas. The first can be stated briefly: "How can I reasonably respect proponents of doctrines and practices that contradict my own serious commitments without, somehow, renouncing those commitments?"[81] The second is more complex:

> The dilemma is this: A plurality of sets of incompatible premises, each of which may constitute internally well-grounded support for freedom of religion or belief, appears as a whole to be incoherent and hence not a reasonable public grounding. [This] dilemma calls attention to the stability hazards of plural societies that have failed to

79. *Id.* at 147.

80. *Id.* at 148.

81. Tore Lindholm, Philosophical and Religious Justifications of Freedom of Religion or Belief, in *Facilitating Freedom of Religion or Belief: A Deskbook* 23 (Tore Lindholm, W. Cole Durham, Jr., and Bahia Tahzib-Lie, eds., Martinus Nijhoff 2004).

> spell out and entrench a shared public understanding of the basis for moral solidarity across religious and life-stance divides.[82]

To address these dilemmas, Lindholm develops a theory of "overlapping justification" of freedom of religion or belief. In his view, human rights derive

> from the public global commitment to heed the inherent dignity of every human being but only by way of complex processes of deliberation and negotiation with moral, religious, cultural, political, economic, diplomatic, and other inputs. Human rights are not deduced by philosophy professors and theological doctors. They are generated in complex international and transnational processes of argument, bargaining, and compromise—processes to which philosophers and clerics have made significant but not always decisive contributions.
>
> The public moral legitimacy of modern human rights may be expressed by saying they have survived and are reasonably expected to survive unobstructed and informed public discussion. Though much disputed and criticized, the framework of modern human rights has so far proven its mettle under open public scrutiny. . . .
>
> Justification of a problematic moral norm, at the level of the individual, does not require that the norm be deduced from unproblematic (or "certain" or "self-evident") higher principles. This ideal of justification is beautifully neat, but hardly ever reasonably practicable. We surely have moral principles that we are not willing to compromise, but their reasoned acceptance is often dependent on the wealth of moral implication we draw from them in the light of the totality of other values and beliefs we hold to, and they are often entrenched in the moral or religious traditions to which we belong. Reasonable justification has to be holistic and fallibilist: we have good reason to accept only what "best" fits into the totality of our knowledge, values, commitments, and beliefs (remembering that among our cherished commitments we may include open-mindedness, taking arguments seriously, and respect for fellow human beings and their plights).[83]

Assuming that human beings will continue for the foreseeable future to be divided by deep difference, he maintains that the question is how we can

> reasonably secure both principled solidarity based on mutual respect across religious and life-stance divides and unflinching doctrinal integrity of, and commitment to, our differing normative traditions. Reasoning in a virtuous circle [Lindholm's] answer draws on the established modern tradition of internationally recognized human rights, rooted in an emerging worldwide public commitment to heed as inviolable the inherent dignity of every human being.[84]

What is needed is not a "fully realized" version of an overlapping justification for freedom of religion or belief, in which "competent and serious adherents of each set of rival religious or life-stance traditions reasonably hold this universally applicable human right to be well-supported by each of the separate normative traditions" at issue. Rather, all that is needed is that "each party ha[ve] knowledge and understanding of the internal grounding of his or her own belief system" and that "he or she have reasonable trust in the cogency of the other party's espousal of the right."[85]

Where such "overlapping justification" is present, mutual respect and solidarity is doctrinally secure for the following reason:

---

82. *Id.* at 23–24.
83. *Id.* at 49–50.
84. *Id.* at 51.
85. *Id.*

> If my faith requires me to respect and stand up for your religious freedom and I know yours requires the same from you, and you and I know that we share this knowledge, then you and I stand in a relation of friendship to one another. Of course, our comprehensive religious doctrines clash, and we know this well. . . . [There may be reason for] serious interreligious argument. [But good], civil and candid polemics are not off limits between people who know they are friends.[86]

C. INCOMPLETELY THEORIZED AGREEMENTS

Lindholm's "overlapping justification" solution is similar to what Cass Sunstein calls "incompletely theorized agreements"—agreements between people of differing views that leave room for a substantial amount of disagreement while still providing some common basis for government and society. Consider the following excerpt:

> Incompletely theorized agreements play a pervasive role in law and society. It is rare for a person, and especially for a group, to theorize any subject completely—that is, to accept both a highly abstract theory and a series of steps that relate the theory to a concrete conclusion. In fact, people often reach incompletely theorized agreements on a general principle. Such agreements are incompletely theorized in the sense that people who accept the principle need not agree on what it entails in particular cases. People know that murder is wrong, but they disagree about abortion. They favor racial equality, but they are divided on affirmative action. Hence there is a familiar phenomenon of a comfortable and even emphatic agreement on a general principle, accompanied by sharp disagreement about particular cases.
>
> This sort of agreement is incompletely theorized in the sense that it is incompletely specified—a familiar phenomenon with constitutional provisions and regulatory standards in administrative law. Incompletely specified agreements have distinctive social uses. They may permit acceptance of a general aspiration when people are unclear about what the aspiration means, and in this sense, they can maintain a measure of both stability and flexibility over time. At the same time, they can conceal the fact of large-scale social disagreement about particular cases. . . .
>
> My special interest here is in a third kind of phenomenon—incompletely theorized agreements on particular outcomes, accompanied by agreements on the low-level principles that account for them. These terms contain some ambiguities. There is no algorithm by which to distinguish between a high-level theory and one that operates at an intermediate or low level. We might consider Kantianism and utilitarianism as conspicuous examples of high-level theories and see legal illustrations in the many (academic) efforts to understand such areas as tort law, contract law, free speech, and the law of equality to be undergirded by highly abstract theories of the right or the good. By contrast, we might think of low-level principles as including most of the ordinary material of legal doctrine—the general class of principles and justifications that are not said to derive from any particular large theories of the right or the good, that have ambiguous relations to large theories, and that are compatible with more than one such theory.[87]

Basing religious freedom on such understandings of agreement—on overlapping justifications or on incompletely theorized agreements—protects both religious freedom rights in practice and the very important theoretical right for believers to choose that justification of religious freedom that best fits their religion. By doing so,

---

86. *Id.* at 53.

87. Cass Sunstein, Incompletely Theorized Agreements, 108 *Harv. L. Rev.* 1733, 1739–1740 (1995) (footnotes omitted).

they accomplish a difficult but all-important task: fulfilling the secular purposes of religious freedom (e.g., autonomy and social cohesion) while not requiring believers to subordinate their beliefs to those purposes. With such a solution, religious believers can continue to affirm their beliefs as the most important part of their lives while living and participating in society, tolerating others, and obeying the laws of the land.

COMMENTS AND QUESTIONS

1. To what extent must those holding different views agree in order to achieve a stable and peaceful society? In this regard, what differences do you see between Rawls's overlapping consensus, Lindholm's overlapping justifications, and Sunstein's incompletely theorized agreements?
2. In Rawls's view, political liberalism can be achieved as a stable order only if fundamental questions of justice and constitutional essentials are settled by political values and those values are sufficient "to override all other values that may come in conflict with them."[88] What if religious doctrines on certain issues are inconsistent with what others hold to be "constitutional essentials and matters of basic justice"[89]? This might be the case if religious doctrine required establishment of a particular (and non-liberal) political order. But it might also be the case if there were a certain, relatively small number of issues on which the religious community had very strong views. (Consider abortion, military service, same-sex marriage, willingness to take blood transfusions, etc.). Does the fact that religious communities cannot compromise on some of these issues preclude their consenting to a liberal regime? How strong must the religious freedom protections be to secure their support?
3. In recent years, one of the major debates about international human rights is whether they are indeed universal, as explicitly claimed in the "Universal Declaration of Human Rights," or whether they are infected with a Western bias, and may even constitute a form of neo-imperialism. We will turn to the history and content of modern human rights thinking in Chapter 3. How might ideas such as overlapping consensus, overlapping justifications, and incompletely theorized agreements relate to thinking about human rights?

Additional Web Resources:	A variety of sources addressing the debate on the universality of human rights

88. Rawls, *supra* note 76, at 138.
89. *Id.* at 137–138.

CHAPTER 3

INTERNATIONAL HUMAN RIGHTS PERSPECTIVES ON FREEDOM OF RELIGION OR BELIEF

I. INTRODUCTION

This chapter outlines the emergence of the international norms and institutions that protect freedom of religion and belief. Because of space constraints, only key provisions of the main international law documents are included in the text. More extensive materials are available on the Web Supplement. In Section II we discuss the historical development of religious freedom as a protected right in international law. Sections III and IV focus on the role of the United Nations (UN) in the post–World War II period. These Sections discuss the primary international human rights instruments promulgated by the United Nations, including the Universal Declaration of Human Rights (UDHR) and the International Covenant on Civil and Political Rights (ICCPR). Section V addresses the evolving role of various UN organizations that monitor and promote human rights, such as the Commission on Human Rights and the Human Rights Committee. This introduction will only sketch these materials and institutions in broad strokes, and we will return to many of them throughout the book.

Section VI introduces regional efforts to promote human rights. The most significant of the regional institutions is the European Court of Human Rights (ECtHR), a supranational court that gives individual citizens in numerous European and former Soviet sphere countries a forum of last resort to assert claims that their own governments are in violation of the human rights protected by the European Convention for the Protection of Human Rights and Fundamental Freedoms, commonly known as the European Convention on Human Rights (ECHR or "the Convention"). Since this book will cover numerous cases involving religious freedom decided by the ECtHR and its precursor institution, the European Commission of Human Rights (ECmHR), this section will present some background information about the history and operation of this remarkable institution.

Section VII is a brief discussion of how the international human rights norms and instruments are implemented in the domestic law of individual states.

II. THE EVOLUTION OF INTERNATIONAL PROTECTION OF FREEDOM OF RELIGION OR BELIEF

Religion has always played a role in international affairs. It has often been a factor in international disputes, in the administration of international empires, and in the practical administration of domestic governmental affairs. Freedom of religion is the oldest of the internationally recognized human rights, although its earliest incarnations were far different from and much more restrictive than current protections.

Three broad stages can be discerned in the evolution of religious freedom protections. The first is associated with resolution of the religious wars in Europe in the sixteenth and seventeenth centuries. The first landmark from this period was the Peace of Augsburg in 1555, which recognized that Catholic and Lutheran rulers would have equal stakes in the Holy Roman Empire, and permitted the lay (but not ecclesiastical) rulers to determine which religion would be established in their domains. The Peace of Augsburg is the source of the famous principle of *cuius regio, eius religio* (whose realm, his religion), which shaped the religious landscape of Europe for centuries. This basic principle was reinforced and clarified by the Peace of Westphalia, concluded in the treaties of Osnabrück and Münster in 1648. The Westphalia accords accepted the Reformed (Calvinist) tradition as well as the Lutheran and Catholic religions. Christians living in countries in which theirs was not the established religion could practice their religion in private and during appointed hours in public. In general, the focus of this first phase was on freedom of religion for rulers and states, and the provision for individuals remained quite restrictive. This stage was marked by the emergence of a secular international order that served for years to come as a technique for achieving religious peace.

The second stage sought to protect religious freedom with the use of treaties dealing with minorities. These had antecedents in "capitulations" allowing Christians to establish autonomous communities that ultimately were protected by major European powers. The 1878 Treaty of Berlin provided that "difference of religious creeds and confessions shall not be alleged against any person as a ground for exclusion or incapacity. . . ." This set a significant precedent for prohibiting discrimination against minorities. Following World War I, this became a matter of particular concern with respect to the treatment of Jewish minorities. Minority protections aimed at providing more effective protection were introduced in the Polish Minorities Treaty, and this became the model for a series of minorities treaties that were imposed on the newly created states of Poland, Yugoslavia, and Czechoslovakia at the time of their recognition, and on Romania and Greece when they received territorial gains under the peace treaties. The key provision (Article 2) of the various treaties provided that the state in question

> undertakes to assure full and complete protection of life and liberty to all inhabitants of [the country] without distinction of birth, nationality, language, race, or religion.

> All inhabitants [of the country] shall be entitled to the free exercise, whether public or private, of any creed, religion, or belief, whose practices are not inconsistent with public order or public morals.

In the end, however, the minorities treaties proved to be a failure, as demonstrated by the tragedy of the Holocaust.

The third stage was marked by the emergence of freedom of religion or belief as a fundamental human right protected by international human rights law following World War II. Following the creation of the United Nations, the international community shifted its focus from minority and group rights to the protection of individual rights that were ultimately articulated in what has come to be known as the International Bill of Rights, consisting of the Universal Declaration of Human Rights (UDHR, 1948); the International Covenant on Economic, Social and Cultural Rights (ICESCR, adopted 1966, in force 1976); and the International Covenant on Civil and Political Rights (ICCPR, adopted 1966, in force 1976). The Universal Declaration, as its name suggests, was a declaration formally adopted by the General Assembly of the United Nations, but it did not have formal treaty status. With recognition of the need to develop legally binding international norms, efforts moved forward to develop formal treaty language that would incorporate the norms recognized by the Universal Declaration. The hallmark of the third stage is recognition of individual human rights, with the right to freedom of religion or belief standing as one of the preeminent fundamental rights.

III. FREEDOM OF RELIGION AND THE UNIVERSAL DECLARATION OF HUMAN RIGHTS

The key language respecting freedom of religion or belief in the Universal Declaration of Human Rights (UDHR) is found in the following articles:

> **Article 1.** All human beings are born free and equal in dignity and rights. They are endowed with reason and conscience and should act towards one another in a spirit of brotherhood.
>
> **Article 2.** Everyone is entitled to all the rights and freedoms set forth in this Declaration, without distinction of any kind, such as race, colour, sex, language, religion, political or other opinion, national or social origin, property, birth or other status. Furthermore, no distinction shall be made on the basis of the political, jurisdictional or international status of the country or territory to which a person belongs, whether it be independent, trust, non-self-governing or under any other limitation of sovereignty.
>
> **Article 18.** Everyone has the right to freedom of thought, conscience and religion; this right includes freedom to change his religion or belief, and freedom, either alone or in community with others and in public or private, to manifest his religion or belief in teaching, practice, worship and observance.

These articles do not include a limitation clause, but they are subject to the UDHR's general limitations clause:

> **Article 29.**
>
> 1. Everyone has duties to the community in which alone the free and full development of his personality is possible.

> 2. In the exercise of his rights and freedoms, everyone shall be subject only to such limitations as are determined by law solely for the purpose of securing due recognition and respect for the rights and freedoms of others and of meeting the just requirements of morality, public order and the general welfare in a democratic society.
>
> 3. These rights and freedoms may in no case be exercised contrary to the purposes and principles of the United Nations.

The drafting process that led to the adoption of the UDHR was lengthy and subject to the scrutiny of many potentially disapproving views. There was intense and focused debate between member states over the meaning and inclusion of nearly every word. The process of drafting the Declaration was not high theory but was an exercise in identifying the practices and norms in existence in most nations, and an effort to build on common understanding. In fact, a group of philosophers involved in the preparatory work for the Declaration began "by sending a questionnaire to statesmen and scholars around the world . . . soliciting their views on the idea of a universal declaration of human rights."[1] John Humphrey of Canada directed his staff to study every existing constitution and rights instrument in the world to discover the principles most widely shared among nations. Drafters structured the language of the UDHR to be a composite reflection of the existing norms, rather than resting on a single, unifying theory. Focusing on practices and actions, rather than theory and motivations, allowed drafters to achieve consensus despite the complicated issues addressed in the Declaration.[2] French Catholic philosopher Jacques Maritain wrote in his introduction to the collective response by the UNESCO National Commission that at one of the Commission meetings where human rights were being discussed, "someone expressed astonishment that certain champions of violently opposed ideologies had agreed on a list of those rights. 'Yes,' they said, 'we agree about the rights, but on condition no one asks us why.' That 'why' is where the argument begins."[3]

One of the most difficult issues to arise in framing the UDHR was religious freedom. On this issue, the Declaration's provision underwent considerable revision during the drafting process. The original draft, created by John Humphrey, provided simply that "there shall be freedom of conscience and belief and of private and public religious worship."[4] The Human Rights Commission draft of June 1947 modified the provision to state that "individual freedom of thought and conscience, to hold or change beliefs, is an absolute and sacred right. The practice of a private or public worship, religious observances, and manifestations of differing convictions can be subject only to such limitations as are necessary to protect public order, morals and the rights and freedoms of others."[5] The Third Committee Draft read, "Everyone has the right to freedom of thought, conscience and religion; this right includes freedom to change his religion or belief, and freedom either alone or in community with others and in public or private, to manifest his religion or belief in teaching, practice, worship and observance."[6]

---

1. Mary Ann Glendon, *A World Made New* 51 (Random House 2001).
2. *Id.* at 77.
3. Jacques Maritain, *Human Rights: Comments and Interpretations*, UN Doc. UNESCO/PHS/3 (rev), Introduction (1948).
4. Glendon, *supra* note 1, at 272.
5. *Id.* at 285.
6. *Id.* at 205.

This language became Article 18 of the Declaration as it is today. The UDHR was ultimately adopted by a vote of 48 in favor and with 8 abstentions, including the Soviet bloc, South Africa, and Saudi Arabia. None opposed.[7]

Harvard law professor Mary Ann Glendon described the impact of the UDHR as follows:

> In the years that followed [the passage of the Declaration], to the astonishment of many, human rights would become a political factor that not even the most hard-shelled realist could ignore. The Universal Declaration would become an instrument, as well as the most prominent symbol, of changes that would amplify the voices of the weak in the corridors of power. It challenged the long-standing view that a sovereign state's treatment of its own citizens was that nation's business and no one else's. It gave expression to diffuse, deep-seated longings and lent wings to movements that would soon bring down colonial empires. Its thirty concise articles inspired or influenced scores of postwar and postcolonial constitutions and treaties, including the new constitutions of Germany, Japan, and Italy. It became the polestar of an army of international human rights activists, who pressure governments to live up to their pledges and train the searchlight of publicity on abuses that would have remained hidden in former times. Confirming the worst fears held in 1948 by the Soviet Union and South Africa, the Declaration provided a rallying point for the freedom movements that spurred the collapse of totalitarian regimes in Eastern Europe and the demise of apartheid. It is the parent document, the primary inspiration, for most rights instruments in the world today. . . . Today, the Declaration is the single most important reference point for cross-national discussions of how to order our future together on our increasingly conflict-ridden and interdependent planet.[8]

COMMENTS AND QUESTIONS

1. Early drafts of Article 1 did not contain references to reason or conscience as basic human attributes. When the Committee decided to add the reference to reason, P.C. Chang, the Human Rights Committee delegate from China, suggested that the Preamble also include the Chinese word *ren* (仁) as a guiding principle.[9] This character is a composite of the characters for man (人) and two (二); thus its literal translation is "two-man mindedness." There is no direct translation in English, but the concept is often translated as "benevolence," "empathy," or "compassion." In the UDHR it was translated as "conscience," a translation that perhaps does not do justice to the concept. Ren is one of the essential concepts of Confucianism. It is the duty that superiors owe to their subordinates. Ren's focus on the dignity of others and one's responsibility toward them, as opposed to the internal focus of conscience as a guide to one's actions, may have suggested that rights should be balanced by responsibilities. By using "conscience" as the translation, did the drafters forgo an opportunity to frame the UDHR in a way that would call attention to responsibilities as well as to rights? Is the idea of "ren" better captured in the Article 1 injunction that all persons should treat each other with a spirit of brotherhood? Does that quite capture the idea of "ren"?
2. At the time the UDHR was being debated, Jamil Baroody of Saudi Arabia argued that the draft's provisions for religious freedom were Western in

7. *Id.* at 170.
8. *Id.* at xvi–xvii.
9. *Id.* at 67.

concept. Dr. Chang, from China, pleaded with the delegates to try to see things from a broader perspective, reminding them that the Declaration was "meant for all men everywhere,"[10] which would require some openness toward each culture's contributions. Which seems the more accurate view? Which approach is preferable? Or are they compatible?

3. How might a concept such as the African idea "ubuntu" (discussed in Chapter 2), which suggests that "a person is a person through other persons" contribute to discussions concerning a truly universal human rights regime?

IV. THE INTERNATIONAL COVENANTS

The UN Human Rights Commission planned to follow up the non-binding Universal Declaration of Human Rights immediately with a binding, universal convention.[11] However, ideological differences between the Western states and the Soviet bloc prevented progress on a single covenant. Eastern states insisted that the covenant should provide for economic, social, and cultural rights, in addition to civil and political rights, while Western states refused to commit to a framework with economic and social standards bearing the same legal force as the human rights standards.[12] In 1951, the Commission decided to adopt the two-covenant approach championed by the Western states and resumed drafting work.

The process of hammering out the two conventions took an additional 15 years. The resulting covenants were titled the International Covenant on Civil and Political Rights (ICCPR) and the International Covenant on Economic, Social, and Cultural Rights (ICESCR). Surprisingly, despite the sharp divide in opinion over the content of the covenants, both were adopted unanimously (along with the first Optional Protocol) by the General Assembly in December 1966 and entered into force in 1976.

While the UDHR carries moral force and is often viewed as having the force of customary international law, the two covenants are binding, positive law. Compliance with the terms of the covenants is required by the Vienna Convention on the Law of Treaties. Further, whereas states can derogate from some duties acquired through treaties, human rights obligations that are "fundamental" are nonderogable and cannot be avoided by reservation, objection, or declarations by states parties to the covenants.[13] As a legally binding treaty, the ICCPR includes various enforcement mechanisms. The Covenant creates the Human Rights Committee, which administers the reporting system also established by the Covenant.

As of November 2018, 165 states were party to the ICESCR,[14] and 172 states

---

10. *Id.* at 142.

11. *See* Richard B. Lillich, Hurst Hannum, S. James Anaya & Dinah L. Shelton, *International Human Rights: Problems of Law, Policy, and Practice* 85–86 (4th ed., Aspen 2006).

12. *Id.*

13. *See e.g.*, General Comment No. 29, UN Doc. CCPR/CR/21/Add. 11 (2001).

14. *See* International Covenant on Economic, Social and Cultural Rights (entered into force 3 January 1976).

were party to the ICCPR.[15] The United States had signed but not ratified the ICESCR, but had ratified (in 1992) the ICCPR, albeit with significant reservations (particularly with regard to freedom of expression, but interestingly, not with respect to freedom of religion), while China had signed but not ratified the ICCPR and had ratified the ICESCR. Iran and Iraq have ratified both covenants. Cuba signed both covenants in 2008 but as of November 2018 had not ratified either. Malaysia, Myanmar, and Saudi Arabia are among the nations that have declined either to sign or to ratify either covenant.

A. THE INTERNATIONAL COVENANT ON CIVIL AND POLITICAL RIGHTS AND THE OPTIONAL PROTOCOL

The major provisions relevant to freedom of religion or belief are contained in the ICCPR, and include the following:

Article 18.

1. Everyone shall have the right to freedom of thought, conscience and religion. This right shall include freedom to have or to adopt a religion or belief of his choice, and freedom, either individually or in community with others and in public or private, to manifest his religion or belief in worship, observance, practice and teaching.

2. No one shall be subject to coercion which would impair his freedom to have or to adopt a religion or belief of his choice.

3. Freedom to manifest one's religion or beliefs may be subject only to such limitations as are prescribed by law and are necessary to protect public safety, order, health, or morals or the fundamental rights and freedoms of others.

4. The States Parties to the present Covenant undertake to have respect for the liberty of parents and, when applicable, legal guardians to ensure the religious and moral education of their children in conformity with their own convictions.

Article 19.

1. Everyone shall have the right to hold opinions without interference.

2. Everyone shall have the right to freedom of expression; this right shall include freedom to seek, receive and impart information and ideas of all kinds, regardless of frontiers, either orally, in writing or in print, in the form of art, or through any other media of his choice.

3. The exercise of the rights provided for in paragraph 2 of this article carries with it special duties and responsibilities. It may therefore be subject to certain restrictions, but these shall only be such as are provided by law and are necessary:

(a) For respect of the rights or reputations of others;

(b) For the protection of national security or of public order (*ordre public*), or of public health or morals.

Article 20.

1. [omitted]

2. Any advocacy of national, racial or religious hatred that constitutes incitement to discrimination, hostility or violence shall be prohibited by law.

Article 21.

The right of peaceful assembly shall be recognized. No restrictions may be placed on the exercise of this right other than those imposed in conformity with the law and which are necessary in a democratic society in the interests of national security or public safety, public order (*ordre public*), the protection of public health or morals or the protection of the rights and freedoms of others.

---

15. *See* International Covenant on Civil and Political Rights (entered into force 23 March 1979).

> **Article 27.**
> In those States in which ethnic, religious or linguistic minorities exist, persons belonging to such minorities shall not be denied the right, in community with the other members of their group, to enjoy their own culture, to profess and practise their own religion, or to use their own language.

The Optional Protocol to the ICCPR also has significant implications for freedom of religion. Article 1 of the Optional Protocol provides:

> A State Party to the Covenant that becomes a Party to the present Protocol recognizes the competence of the Committee to receive and consider communications from individuals subject to its jurisdiction who claim to be victims of a violation by that State Party of any of the rights set forth in the Covenant.

Subject to the requirements that the communication concerns a state party to the Covenant, that domestic remedies have been exhausted, and that the communication is not anonymous or abusive, the Committee will bring the communications to the attention of the state party, which shall have time to prepare a written response, clarifying the matter and any remedies that have been taken by the state. The Human Rights Committee also is instructed to prepare annual reports of its activities under the Protocol.

B. THE 1981 DECLARATION ON THE ELIMINATION OF ALL FORMS OF INTOLERANCE AND DISCRIMINATION BASED ON RELIGION OR BELIEF

While work was underway to finalize the international covenants, efforts moved forward to adopt conventions on the elimination of racial discrimination and elimination of religious intolerance and discrimination. This led relatively rapidly to the adoption in 1965 of the Convention on the Elimination of All Forms of Racial Discrimination (CERD), which entered into force in 1969. However, because of international politics and a greater complexity of issues, consensus sufficient to create a legally binding treaty concerning religion has never happened. The decision to adopt a Declaration instead resulted in the United Nations General Assembly adopting in 1981 its Declaration on the Elimination of All Forms of Intolerance and Discrimination Based on Religion or Belief ("the 1981 Declaration").

The 1981 Declaration has eight articles, and the first five repeat virtually verbatim language that was already included in other binding documents, such as the ICCPR and the Convention on the Rights of the Child. Article 7 repeats the requirements of Article 2(2) of the ICCPR that legal remedies be made available to give practical effect to the recognized rights. Thus the 1981 Declaration goes beyond typical UN resolutions in that it incorporates treaty language that is legally binding for the great majority of countries.

Article 8 has additional importance. It affirms that "[n]othing in the present Declaration shall be construed as restricting or derogating from any right defined in the Universal Declaration of Human Rights and the International Covenants on Human Rights." Thus, although Article 1 speaks only of the "freedom to have a religion or whatever belief of his choice," this should not be interpreted as impugning the "freedom to change his religion or belief."[16] Guaranteed in the UDHR is the right to "have or adopt a religion of one's choice" under the ICCPR.[17] The pressure to omit the words "change" and "adopt" came from Muslim countries, based upon interpretations of the Koran that forbid a Muslim to change religion.[18] The inclusion of Article 8 reaffirmed the right to "change" or "adopt" by emphasizing the continued force of earlier documents.[19]

The only portion of the 1981 Declaration not already embodied in other internationally binding documents is Article 6, which describes in greater detail the concrete requirements of the right to freedom of religion or belief as follows:

> **Article 6.**
> In accordance with article 1 of the present Declaration, and subject to the provisions of article 1, paragraph 3, the right to freedom of thought, conscience, religion or belief shall include, inter alia, the following freedoms:
> (a) To worship or assemble in connexion with a religion or belief, and to establish and maintain places for these purposes;
> (b) To establish and maintain appropriate charitable or humanitarian institutions;
> (c) To make, acquire and use to an adequate extent the necessary articles and materials related to the rites or customs of a religion or belief;
> (d) To write, issue and disseminate relevant publications in these areas;
> (e) To teach a religion or belief in places suitable for these purposes;
> (f) To solicit and receive voluntary financial and other contributions from individuals and institutions;
> (g) To train, appoint, elect or designate by succession appropriate leaders called for by the requirements and standards of any religion or belief;
> (h) To observe days of rest and to celebrate holidays and ceremonies in accordance with the precepts of one's religion or belief;
> (i) To establish and maintain communications with individuals and communities in matters of religion and belief at the national and international levels.

COMMENTS AND QUESTIONS

1. Many have argued that the provisions of the 1981 Declaration constitute customary international law. In view of the fact that most of the provisions are either recodifications of previously adopted multilateral treaties or, in the case of Article 6, rather uncontroversial statements of the concrete implications of abstract but binding norms spelled out in other treaties, could one make the stronger claim that the 1981 Declaration actually has the status of binding international law?
2. Are there key features of the right to freedom of religion or belief that are not adequately addressed in the 1981 Declaration? Would you recommend pressing forward to develop a binding convention on freedom of religion or belief? Why or why not?

---

16. Universal Declaration of Human Rights, GA Res. 217(III), UN GAOR, 3d Sess., Supp. No. 13, UN Doc. A 810 (1948), at art. 18.

17. International Covenant on Civil and Political Rights, GA Res. 2200A (XXI), UN Doc A/RES/2200A(XXI) (1966), at art. 18.

18. Paul M. Taylor, *Freedom of Religion: UN and European Human Rights Law and* Practice 35-36 (Cambridge Univ. Press 2005).

19. Declaration on the Elimination of All Forms of Intolerance and of Discrimination based on Religion or Belief, GA Res. 36/55, UN Doc A/RES/36/55 (1981), at art. 8.

V. UNITED NATIONS MONITORING INSTITUTIONS

Over the years, the United Nations has set up various institutions to monitor and promote state compliance with human rights commitments, including the right of freedom of religion or belief. We focus here on the United Nations Commission on Human Rights and its 2006 replacement, the United Nations Human Rights Council (UNHRC), and on the UN Human Rights Committee (CCPR),[20] the treaty body charged with monitoring compliance with the ICCPR. A number of other UN institutions have a significant impact on the implementation of freedom of religion or belief, including the United Nations Educational, Scientific and Cultural Organization (UNESCO), the International Labour Organization (ILO), and the World Health Organization (WHO). One of the ongoing challenges is to find institutional structures that can facilitate optimal implementation of norms governing freedom of religion or belief.

A. THE ROLE AND SIGNIFICANCE OF THE UN COMMISSION ON HUMAN RIGHTS AND THE UN HUMAN RIGHTS COUNCIL

As the first human rights body established by the United Nations, the Commission on Human Rights had a profound impact on thinking about religious freedom in international law.[21] Commenting on the development of the Commission, Theo van Boven notes that "[s]ince its establishment in 1946, pursuant to Article 68 of the United Nations Charter, the Commission has been actively involved in efforts to define, promote, and protect freedom of religion or belief as one of the most basic human rights and fundamental freedoms."[22]

The Commission's religious freedom work can be divided into three stages. During the first stage (1946–1955), the Commission played a key role in drafting what have become the key international human rights instruments outlining the freedom of religion or belief. The second stage (1960–1981) culminated, after extended "ideological and political arm wrestling," [23] in the 1981 Declaration. While additional human rights instruments have emerged in the years since, much of the Commission's work since 1981 has focused on the monitoring and implementation. The Commission appointed a Special Rapporteur, originally designated the Special Rapporteur on Religious Intolerance, now known as the Special Rapporteur on Freedom of Religion or Belief, in 1986. Under the mandate of this office successive Rapporteurs have conducted site visits, responded to reports of violations, organized conferences on relevant issues, recommended remedial measures regarding state action inconsistent with religious freedom standards, and submitted annual reports.

---

20. The Human Rights Council and the Human Rights Committee are both sometimes identified as UNHRC or HRC. To avoid confusion, the Committee is properly designated CCPR, a shortened form of the treaty (ICCPR) that it monitors.

21. *See* Theo van Boven, The United Nations Commission on Human Rights and Freedom of Religion or Belief, in *Facilitating Freedom of Religion or Belief: A Deskbook* 173–188 (Tore Lindholm, W. Cole Durham, Jr., and Bahia G. Tahzib-Lie, eds., Martinus Nijhoff 2004).

22. *Id.* at 173.

23. *Id.*

In its final stages, the Commission faced major criticisms. Many of its members were representatives of countries that were among the worst human rights offenders and used their positions to deflect rather than enhance efforts to strengthen human rights compliance. This and a number of other factors ultimately sparked reform measures that resulted on 15 March 2006 in the replacement of the Human Rights Commission with a significantly restructured body created by the UN General Assembly—the Human Rights Council (HRC), "an intergovernmental body within the UN system made up of 47 States" that is "responsible for strengthening the promotion and protection of human rights around the globe," with the main purpose of "addressing situations of human rights violations and mak[ing] recommendations on them."[24]

One of the most significant procedural developments associated with the Human Rights Council is the Universal Periodic Review (UPR), a State-driven process based on equal treatment for all countries and involving a review of the human rights records of all 193 UN member states once every four years.[25] According to a resolution passed in 2011, the second and subsequent cycles were extended to four and a half years, divided into 14 "sessions."

Reviews are conducted by the UPR Working Group, which consists of 47 members of the HRC. The first two rounds of reviews were completed in 2012 and 2017. Fourteen countries are reviewed in most sessions, during a three-and-a-half hour meeting in which each review country is assisted by a "troika" of three other countries, who serve as rapporteurs to assist in the preparation of "outcome reports" detailing the extent to which States respect their human rights obligations set out in: (1) the UN Charter; (2) the UDHR; (3) human rights instruments to which the State is party; (4) voluntary pledges and commitments made by the State; and (5) applicable international humanitarian law. The "ultimate goal of UPR is the improvement of the human rights situation in every country."[26]

The reports and reporting sessions are relatively brief given the range of issues involved. Nonetheless, particularly when coupled with NGO input and wide publicizing of the results, the process has significant potential for fostering enhanced implementation. The review process allows states and other stakeholders to ask questions of other states about their human rights performance. In the early rounds of review, only 2.9 percent of all questions related to religious freedom issues, with most of these questions being posed by the United Kingdom, Canada, the United States, and the Holy See.[27] The percentage is perhaps not surprising given the range of other human rights issues involved. Significantly, such issues have received considerable attention when raised, but tend to be viewed as sensitive, and have led to recommendations later in the process less often.[28] As States and NGOs become more adept at working with the process, stronger impact can be expected.

---

24. *See* UN Office of High Commissioner for Human Rights, *Welcome to the Human Rights Council.*

25. *See* UN Office of High Commissioner for Human Rights, *Universal Periodic Review.*

26. *See* UN Office of High Commissioner for Human Rights, *Basic Facts about the UPR.*

27. George Jarvis, Kathryn Jarvis, and Marie Kulbeth, *Just What Happened to Freedom of Religion at the Recent Universal Periodic Review*, paper presented at the NGO Committee on Freedom of Religion or Belief (5 June 2008).

28. *Id.*

B. THE UNITED NATIONS HUMAN RIGHTS COMMITTEE

Another major body established by the United Nations that deals with religious freedom issues is the Human Rights Committee (HRC, or CCPR), which is a "treaty body" created pursuant to the International Covenant on Civil and Political Rights (ICCPR) to oversee state compliance with that instrument. Committee members are prominent global human rights experts who serve in their personal capacities. The Committee is thus an independent expert organ responsible for interpreting ICCPR provisions.[29]

The Human Rights Committee has three primary functions: (1) reviewing periodic reports that states are required to submit, which often allows assessment of state compliance with the Covenant; (2) producing general comments that interpret specific Covenant provisions or address general procedural and substantive issues; and (3) reviewing individual complaints arising from individuals in states that have ratified the Optional Protocol that allow such individual communications.[30]

The Human Rights Committee has produced a number of general comments germane to freedom of religion or belief. The most important of these is its General Comment No. 22 on Article 18, which fleshes out the meaning of freedom of religion or belief in significant ways, stressing the importance of a broad understanding of the scope of those entitled to protection, stating that internal forum matters are protected absolutely, emphasizing the narrowness of the circumstances under which religious freedom may be limited, and so forth.[31] General Comment No. 34 on Article 19, addressing freedom of expression, is also noteworthy in its provision that "[p]rohibition of displays of lack of respect for a religion or other belief system, including blasphemy laws, are incompatible with the Covenant [ICCPR] except in the specific circumstances envisioned by Article 20, paragraph 2, of the Covenant."[32]

With respect to the individual complaints, the Committee functions somewhat differently than a court, working solely with written submissions and issuing final views that as a technical matter are not formally binding, although they are more than mere recommendations in that they constitute "legal interpretations issued by the independent international expert body established by the Covenant for the purpose of interpreting the Covenant."[33] The following is an example of such a complaint and Committee finding.

---

29. *See* Martin Scheinin, The Human Rights Committee and Freedom of Religion or Belief, in *Facilitating Freedom of Religion or Belief: A Deskbook* 189–202 (Tore Lindholm, W. Cole Durham, Jr., and Bahia G. Tahzib-Lie, eds., Martinus Nijhoff 2004). [Footnotes generally omitted.]

30. *Id.* at 190-193.

31. UN Human Rights Committee, General Comment No. 22 on Article 18 (Freedom of Thought, Conscience or Religion) of the International Covenant on Civil and Political Rights, CCPR/C/21/Rev.1/Add.4 (30 July 1993).

32. UN Human Rights Committee, General Comment No. 34 on Article 19 (Freedoms of Opinion and Expression) of the International Covenant on Civil and Political Rights, CCPR/C/GC/34 (12 September 2011), at para. 48.

33. Scheinin, *supra* note 29, at 192.

RAIHON HUDOYBERGANOVA V. UZBEKISTAN

UN Human Rights Committee, Communication No. 931/2000, UNHRC (2004)

[Ms. Hudoyberganova was a student at the Farsi Department at the Faculty of languages of the Tashkent State Institute for Eastern Language. In 1998, a regulation prohibiting the wearing of religious clothing was adopted, resulting in the expulsion of those students who continued to wear the headscarf. Hudoyberganova claims that her exclusion from University because she worse a headscarf for religious reasons violated articles 18 and 19 of the Covenant.]

Examination of the Merits

. . . The Committee considers that the freedom to manifest one's religion encompasses the right to wear clothes or attire in public which is in conformity with the individual's faith or religion. Furthermore, it considers that to prevent a person from wearing religious clothing in public or private may constitute a violation of article 18, paragraph 2, which prohibits any coercion that would impair the individual's freedom to have or adopt a religion. As reflected in the Committee's General Comment No. 22 (para. 5), policies or practices that have the same intention or effect as direct coercion, such as those restricting access to education, are inconsistent with article 18, paragraph 2. It recalls, however, that the freedom to manifest one's religion or beliefs is not absolute and may be subject to limitations, which are prescribed by law and are necessary to protect public safety, order, health, or morals, or the fundamental rights and freedoms of others (article 18, paragraph 3, of the Covenant). In the present case, the author's exclusion took place on 15 March 1998, and was based on the provisions of the Institute's new regulations. The Committee notes that the State party has not invoked any specific ground for which the restriction imposed on the author would in its view be necessary in the meaning of article 18, paragraph 3. Instead, the State party has sought to justify the expulsion of the author from University because of her refusal to comply with the ban. . . . In the particular circumstances of the present case, and without either prejudging the right of a State party to limit expressions of religion and belief in the context of article 18 of the Covenant and duly taking into account the specifics of the context, or prejudging the right of academic institutions to adopt specific regulations relating to their own functioning, the Committee is led to conclude, in the absence of any justification provided by the State party, that there has been a violation of article 18, paragraph 2.

In accordance with article 2, paragraph 3(a), of the Covenant, the State party is under an obligation to provide Ms. Hudoyberganova with an effective remedy. The State party is under an obligation to take measures to prevent similar violations in the future.

Bearing in mind that, by becoming a party to the Optional Protocol, the State party has recognized the competence of the Committee to determine whether there has been a violation of the Covenant or not and that, pursuant to article 2 of the Covenant, the State party has undertaken to ensure to all individuals within its territory or subject to its jurisdiction the rights recognized in the Covenant and to provide an effective and enforceable remedy in case a violation has been established, the Committee wishes to receive from the State party, within 90 days, information about the measures taken to give effect to the Committee's Views.

* * *

Following the ruling, the US State Department reported that "there were no reports of women feeling uncomfortable about [wearing the hijab] during the reporting period. Nevertheless, there were credible reports that some students were prohibited from wearing headscarves at schools."[34]

Additional Web Resources:	**Other institutions:** Information about additional international institutions that address aspects of religious freedom issues, including UNESCO, the International Labor Organization, World Health Organization, World Intellectual Property Organization, and the Office of the High Commissioner for Human Rights **Other international instruments:** Global human rights and related instruments are discussed more fully on the Web Supplement

NOTE ON THE ROLE OF NONGOVERNMENTAL ORGANIZATIONS IN PROMOTING FREEDOM OF RELIGION AND BELIEF

Nongovernmental organizations (NGOs) play a significant role in promoting freedom of religion or belief and other human rights worldwide.[35] NGOs that endorse religious freedom are "typically established as nonprofit organizations and receive funding from membership dues, grants from foundations, and private donations from individuals, corporations, religious communities, governments, or intergovernmental or interchurch organizations."[36] Another approach is for individual religious groups, which also qualify as NGOs, to promote religious freedom directly. Religious groups may also form broader organizations, coalitions, or fellowships, such as the World Council of Churches or the Council of European Churches.

NGOs use a number of methods to further religious freedom. These methods include "standard setting, violation reporting, providing technical advice, lobbying and agenda setting, conflict resolution, networking, facilitating interfaith cooperation, and education."[37] In monitoring compliance with religious freedom standards and calling attention to violations, NGOs significantly supplement or perhaps even surpass the work of the state. In some instances, NGOs contribute to state and international reports, such as those issued by the UN Special Rapporteur on Freedom of Religion or Belief and the US Commission on

---

34. US Department of State, International Religious Freedom Report 2006: Uzbekistan.

35. *See generally* Elizabeth A. Sewell, Facilitating Freedom of Religion or Belief through NGOs, in *Facilitating Freedom of Religion or Belief: A Deskbook* 819–842 (Tore Lindholm, W. Cole Durham, Jr., and Bahia G. Tahzib-Lie, eds., Martinus Nijhoff 2004).

36. *Id.* at 827.

37. *Id.* at 828.

International Religious Freedom (USCIRF). In addition, NGOs often circulate their own reports on the status of religious freedom and problematic cases.[38]

Elizabeth Clark Sewell notes that

> NGOs have vast potential to promote freedom of religious belief. . . . Success in promoting socialization of human rights norms requires a combination of compliance monitoring, shaming, moral persuasion, use of leverage, academic research, policy-making efforts, and many other activities. While a view of the spectrum of human rights NGOs seems to reveal a multiplicity of organizations and perhaps mere chaos, the natural disorderliness inherent in the independent ordering of NGOs can prove to be extremely effective when they work together.[39]

Additional Web Resources:	Information on relevant NGOs

VI. REGIONAL HUMAN RIGHTS REGIMES

Since the creation of the United Nations and the adoption of the Universal Declaration of Human Rights, a number of regional multinational organizations have been created that have among their purposes the fostering of human rights, including the right to freedom of religion or belief. In this section we focus primarily on institutions that include the nations of Europe, because they have been particularly significant and effective. In addition to the institutions of the Council of Europe and the European Union, there are a number of regional organizations that focus on human rights issues and are important for freedom of religion or belief. These include the Organization for Security and Co-operation in Europe (OSCE), the Organization of American States (OAS), the African Union (AU), and the Organization of Islamic Cooperation (OIC).

A. THE COUNCIL OF EUROPE INSTITUTIONS

From a human rights perspective, the most effective of the regional organizations has been the Council of Europe (CoE). Founded by ten European countries on 5 May 1949, the Council now (2017) comprises 47 member states, including all of the countries of Europe (including Turkey and Russia), except Belarus and Vatican City. The primary policy- and decision-making bodies of the CoE are the Committee of Ministers, comprising the Ministers of Foreign Affairs of the various member states, and the Parliamentary Assembly (PACE), which has 630 members. The European Convention for the Protection of Human Rights and Fundamental Freedoms (commonly referred to as the European Convention on Human Rights [ECHR] or "the Convention") was drafted under the auspices of the CoE and signed in Rome on 4 November 1950. Entering into force on 3 September 1953, the ECHR specifies the fundamental substantive rights to be protected for

38. *See, e.g.,* Amnesty International, Council of European Churches, Forum 18 New Service, Freedom House, Human Rights Without Frontiers International, World Council of Churches. See the Web Supplement for a more complete and updating list.

39. Sewell, *supra* note 35, at 841–842.

citizens of CoE member states and establishes mechanisms for enforcing those rights. Three institutions have been entrusted with enforcement responsibilities: the European Commission of Human Rights (ECmHR, set up in 1954) and its successor institution, the European Court of Human Rights (ECtHR[40]), set up in 1959), along with the Committee of Ministers of the Council of Europe.

1. The European Court of Human Rights

In view of the importance of the European Court of Human Rights and the decisions it renders, it is helpful to understand its structure and procedures, and to know something about how those procedures have been modified in response to changing needs. The Court and its procedures are established by ECHR Articles 19-51 and several subsequent protocols. The Convention provides for two types of applications to the Court: those dealing with interstate matters, which have been relatively rare, and those involving claims by individuals against a State.

The right of individuals to file complaints was a major innovation, especially given the strength of the interest of nation states in protecting national sovereignty.[41] Initially, states were permitted to choose whether they would allow complaints to be filed against them, and at the outset only three of the original ten High Contracting States recognized this right. However, by 1990 all Contracting States (22 at the time) had recognized the right, and by the time Protocol No. 11 took effect in 1998, recognition of the right to individual petition had become mandatory for Member States.[42]

The 47 judges of the Court, one from each Member State, serving in their individual capacities and not as representatives of states, are elected by the Parliamentary Assembly of the Council of Europe from a list of three candidates submitted by each state. Judges are assigned to one of five geographically and gender balanced Sections, whose composition takes into account the different legal systems of the Contracting States and is varied every three years. From 1998 until 2010 they were elected for renewable terms of six years, but judges now serve one non-renewable term of nine years, to conclude before they reach age 70.

a. Procedures

The procedure before the Court is "adversarial and public". It is largely a written procedure. Hearings are held in only a very small minority of cases and are almost always public. Court documents are, in principle, accessible to the public.[43]

It is common for individual applicants to present their own case before the Court. Once an application is found admissible and has been communicated to the respondent state, applicants should be legally represented.[44] Article 6(1) of the ECHR guarantees the right to legal assistance in civil proceedings, subject to a

---

40. Though the Court is often abbreviated ECHR, ECtHR usefully distinguishes Court from the Convention.

41. Philip Leach, *Taking a Case to the European Court of Human Rights* 6 (2d ed., Oxford Univ. Press 2005).

42. See Ed Bates, *The Evolution of the European Convention on Human Rights: From Its Inception to the Creation of a Permanent Court of Human Rights* 134 ff (Oxford Univ. Press 2011).

43. *European Court of Human Rights Annual Report 2011* (Registry of the European Court of Human Rights, Strasbourg 2012), para. 20.

44. Annual Report 2011 at para. 21.

financial means test.[45] Applicants needing financial assistance should apply for legal aid at the beginning of the process. Aid, if granted, is awarded later.[46]

All new applications are initially sifted by the lawyers of the Court's Registry (staff), who refer applications for a decision of admissibility to the appropriate judicial formation,[47] meaning to a seven-judge Chamber or (since 1998) to a Committee of three judges, composed within a Chamber or (since 2010) to a single judge, who may hear and dismiss applications that are "manifestly inadmissible." Committees may, by unanimous vote, not only render admissibility decisions, but may in cases already covered by well-established case law, issue judgment on the merits.[48]

The great majority of judgments are given by Chambers formed within the Sections, comprising the President of the Section, the "national judge" (the judge elected in respect of the state against which the application was lodged), and five other judges designated by the Section President in rotation.[49] If the judge elected in respect of the respondent is not a member of the Section, the national judge (from another Section) sits as an ex officio member of the Chamber.[50] Chambers may rule simultaneously on the admissibility and the merits of the case and at the same time order just satisfaction.

Grand Chambers of the Court composed of 17 judges, including the President, Vice-Presidents, and Section Presidents, and others drawn by lot, deal with cases that raise serious questions of interpretation or application of the Convention, or a serious issue of general importance. A Chamber may relinquish jurisdiction in a case to the Grand Chamber at any stage in the procedure before judgment, as long as both parties consent. Where judgment has been delivered in a case, either party may, within a period of three months, request referral of the case to the Grand Chamber. If the request is not granted, the judgment in the case becomes final. In the rare case that a request is granted, the whole case is reheard (de novo).[51]

The Commission Era (1954-1998)

Protocol No. 11, which took force in 1998, fundamentally changed the machinery of the Court. It is nevertheless important to understand how the prior procedure worked, because many of the cases foundational to subsequent ECtHR judgments were decided under the earlier system.

Until 1998, the Commission examined the admissibility of applicants' complaints and explored the possibility of reaching a friendly settlement for those found admissible. If there was no settlement, the Commission transmitted a non-binding report of its opinion on the merits to the Committee of Ministers. If the relevant state had accepted the compulsory jurisdiction of the Court, the Commission and/or the state had three months following transmission of the report

45. *See* Legal Aid, in *Handbook on European Law Relating to Access to Justice*, ch. 3 (European Union Agency for Fundamental Rights and Council of Europe, 2016).

46. *See Preparing a Case for the European Court of Human Rights* (HG.org Legal Resources).

47. *Id.* at para. 23.

48. *The ECHR in 50 Questions* (Public Relations Unit, European Court of Human Rights, February 2014).

49. *Id.*

50. *See Rules of Court* (Registry of the European Court of Human Rights, November 2016).

51. *The EHCR in 50 Questions.*

to bring the case before the Court for a final binding adjudication. If the case was not referred to the Court, the Committee of Ministers decided whether there had been a violation and, if appropriate, awarded "just satisfaction" to the claimant. The Committee of Ministers was also responsible for executing the Court's judgments.

Individuals were not entitled to bring their cases before the Court on their own initiative until 1994, when Protocol 9 amended the Convention to allow applicants to submit a case to a screening panel of three judges, who could decide, by unanimous vote, that a case which did not "raise a serious question affecting the interpretation or application of the Convention" and did not "for any other reason warrant consideration by the Court" would not be heard by the Court. This decision would then be reviewed by the Committee of Ministers, who would decide whether a violation had occurred.[52]

In the background, these procedural arrangements were being wrenched by the expansion of the Council of Europe and the exponential growth of complaints. The Court grew from ten cases a decade in the 1960s to more than 50 judgments a year in the 1990s. Faced with an increasing caseload, the Council of Europe adopted Protocol No. 11 to the ECHR in 1998.[53]

After Protocol No. 11 (1998)

Protocol No. 11 eliminated the role of the European Commission of Human Rights. Under the new procedures, the screening function previously entrusted to the Commission was assigned to the Court itself, and the Committee of Ministers' adjudicative function was abolished. Applicants could now bring their cases directly before the court.

The formation of the three-judge Committees within the Sections was created to streamline the Court's work by rejecting applications that are clearly inadmissible, that have less chance of succeeding, as well as "repetitive" cases, those that are broadly similar to cases brought previously against the same Member State. Such cases, by unanimous vote of the Committee, without a Chamber hearing, and with no possibility of appeal, could be found inadmissible.

Between 1959 and 1998, the Court had seen about 45,000 completed case files, an average of some 40 applications per year. The caseload increased dramatically after the implementation of Protocol No. 11. In 1999 alone, 8,400 applications were received, and the number continued to grow exponentially, with applications reaching 28,200 in 2002. Protocol No. 14 was developed against this backdrop.

After Protocol No. 14 (2010)[54]

Protocol No. 14 was opened for signature in 2004 but entered into force only in 2010, after ratification by Russia. Applications allocated by the Court to judicial formation soared from 32,500 in 2004 to 61,100 in 2010. The changes in judicial formation of Protocol No. 14 were crucial to the Court's attempts to deal with this

52. Protocol No. 9 to the Convention for the Protection of Human Rights and Fundamental Freedoms (ETS No. 140), Rome, 6.XI.1990. Repealed by Protocol No. 11.

53. Protocol No. 11 to the Convention for the Protection of Human Rights and Fundamental Freedoms, Restructuring the Control Machinery Established Thereby (European Court of Human Rights, Strasbourg.II.V.1994).

54. Protocol No. 14 to the Convention for the Protection of Human Rights and Fundamental Freedoms, Amending the Control System of the Convention (CETS 194, 13.V.2004)

volume. Essential to this process was the "single-judge formation" by which judges appointed by the President of the Court for a period of 12 months could individually declare inadmissible or strike out of the Court's list of cases an application where such a decision could be taken without further reexamination.[55] The change in the competence of the three-judge committees to enable them to render judgment on the merits further streamlined the procedure, as did a new provision that cases in which the applicant has not suffered a "significant disadvantage" may be found inadmissible. Further, under a new mechanism introduced to assist enforcement of judgments, the Committee of Ministers can ask the Court for an interpretation of a judgment and can even bring a Member State before the Court for non-compliance of a previous judgment against that State.

Protocol 14 also allows for European Union accession to the Convention, as called for in Article 6 of the Treaty of Lisbon, making the EU the 48th Contracting Party to the ECHR. However, although seen by the Council of Europe as "destined to be a landmark in European legal history because it will make it possible, at last, for individuals and undertakings to apply to the European Court of Human Rights for review of the acts of EU institutions,"[56] the accession was blocked by a judgment of the Court of Justice of the European Union (CJEU) in December 2014[57], and though the matter continues to be the subject of hearings by the EU Parliament, as of the end of 2018 the accession had not taken place.[58]

Protocol Nos. 15 and 16

Since 2010, five high-level conferences on the future of the Court have been organized to identify methods of guaranteeing the long-term effectiveness of the Convention system.[59] As a result, two additional protocols were developed, and adopted in 2013. Protocol 15 requires ratification of all Member States, and as of November 2018 still lacked approval of Bosnia and Herzegovina and Italy. If implemented, this provision would reduce from six to four months the time within which an application must be lodged with the Court after a final national decision and would insert references to the principle of subsidiarity and the doctrine of the margin of appreciation into the Convention's preamble. Meantime, requiring approval by only ten Member States, the companion Protocol 16 took effect in

55. *Rules of the Court* (Registry of the Court, Strasbourg, 14 November 2016).

56. European Court of Human Rights, *What Is EU Accession? Accession of the European Union*, Official Texts, http://www.echr.coe.int/Pages/home.aspx?p=basictexts/accessionEU&c=.

57. Court of Justice of the European Union, *Accession of the European Union to the European Convention for the Protection of Human Rights and Fundamental Freedoms – Compatibility of the draft agreement with the EU and FEU Treaties*, Case Opinion 2/13, 18 December 2014. The CJEU found the Draft Agreement for EU accession to ECHR to be incompatible with TEU article 6(2) because it (a) undermined CJEU autonomy (b) allowed for a second dispute resolution mechanism among member states, against the treaties (c) allowed the EU and a member state to be sued together and allowed the ECtHR to illegitimately interpret EU law and allocate responsibility between the EU and member states, (d) did not allow the CJEU to decide if an issue of law was already dealt with, before the ECtHR heard a case, and (e) the ECtHR was illegitimately being given power of judicial review over Common Foreign and Security Policy.

58. *See, e. g.*, European Parliament, *Accession to the European Convention on Human Rights (ECHR): Stocktaking after the ECJ's opinion and way forward*, Hearing 20 April 2016, and Completion of EU Accession to the ECHR: Legislative Timetable.

59. In Interlaken (2010), Izmir (2011), Brighton (2012), Oslo (2014), and Copenhagen (2018). Follow history and development of these events on the website of the European Court of Human Rights / Official texts / Reform of the Court / History of the Court's Reforms.

August 2018. This "dialogue protocol" allows Member States' highest tribunals to request advisory opinions of the Court on questions of principle relating to the interpretation or application of the rights and freedoms defined in the Convention, effectively "rebalancing" the Convention system and enhancing the position of States Parties."[60] Implementation of Protocol 16, noted Court President Guido Raimondi, was a milestone in the history of the Convention, and "a major step forward in human rights protection in Europe, as well as being a fresh challenge for our Court."[61]

b. Caseload and Distribution of Cases

More than 750,000 applications were allocated to judicial formation between 1959 and 2018, resulting in some 21,000 judgments over the Court's 57-year history, approximately 95 percent of these occurring since 1999. Following the entry into force of Protocol 14, the number of applications continued to increase, but the number of judgments rendered began to drop, from a high of 1,625 in 2009 to under 1000 per year between 2013 and 2016.[62] During 2017, applications allocated showed a 20 percent increase over 2016. However, during this period the number of decisions increased by 123 percent, with a remarkable 709 percent increase in judgments and a 92 percent increase in applications found inadmissible or otherwise stricken out.[63] The process of the single-judge formation has been particularly helpful in this process of reducing the backlog of cases.

In spite of such successes, however, Judge Raimondi noted at the beginning of 2018 that the situation remained fragile. The dramatic drop in pending applications by that time to 56,250 cases, compared to 79,750 at the beginning of 2017, was in some respects an "illusory" improvement, since the remaining cases constituted the "hard core" of the judicial backlog, raising serious issues that needed careful attention.[64] Moreover, part of this dramatic reduction was the result of implementing the "pilot judgment" procedure, whereby cases raising an issue previously decided by the Court can be transmitted to the Committee of Ministers to work with the respondent government to ensure enforcement of the terms of previously decided cases addressing the same issues as the new applications. Under this procedure, more than 12,000 applications were stricken from the Court's roster in the single Grand Chamber case, *Burmych and Others v. Ukraine* (App. Nos. 46852/13 et al., 12 October 2017), since the same issues had been ruled on in the pilot judgment *Ivanov v. Ukraine* (App. No. 40450/04, 15 October 2009).

---

60. Sarah Lambrecht, Undue political pressure is not dialogue: The draft Copenhagen Declaration and its potential repercussions on the Court's independence, *Strasbourg Observers*, 2 March 2018. *See also* European Court of Human Rights, *Opinion on the draft Copenhagen Document, Adopted by the Bureau in light of the discussion in the Plenary Court on 19 February 2018*. A compilation of materials, including debates about the principles involved, appears on the Web Supplement and at http://bit.ly/2tc1Mpt.

61. Registrar of the European Court of Human Rights, *France ratifies Protocol No. 16 to the European Convention on Human Rights, triggering its entry into force*, ECHR 143 (2018), 12 April 2018.

62. By way of comparison, the United States Supreme Court (with 9 instead of 47 judges) has some 6,000–7,000 cases on its docket each year and typically delivers formal written opinions in 70–80 of those cases.

63. *Annual Report European Court of Human Rights 2017* (Provisional).

64. *Id.*

At the heart of the *Burmych* judgment, notes Judge Raimondi, lie the principles of subsidiarity and shared responsibility. "Each of the stakeholders in the European human rights protection mechanism—the Court, the Committee of Ministers and the State concerned—must fulfil its obligations." At the same time Member States must introduce both preventive and compensatory measures that must be exercised by would-be applicants before they turn to Strasbourg. For this reason the Court dismissed, on grounds of failure to exhaust domestic remedies, some 27,000 applications related to measures taken following the attempted coup d'état in Turkey or 6,000 cases concerning prison overcrowding in Hungary.[65]

There is "no magic formula", says Judge Raimondi, for dealing with the large number of applications resulting from systemic problems in a few countries, or with crises occurring in Europe. However, 60 Factsheets on the Court's case law, training videos relating to asylum and terrorism, the launch of a fifth *European Law Handbook*, the end of a four-year project to translate key case law into select languages … all contribute to a positive outlook.[66]

The Court's caseload has focused heavily on criminal and procedural matter. In 84 percent of judgments issued between 1959 and 2017, the Court found at least one violation of the Convention by the respondent state, with 40 percent of violations involving Article 6 (fair trial), 13 percent Article 5 (right to liberty and security), 12 percent involving Article 1 of Protocol No. 1 (property), 11 percent Article 3 (prohibition on inhuman and degrading treatment), 8 percent Article 13 (right to an effective remedy), 4.7 percent Article 8 (right to respect for private and family life, home and correspondence), 4.6 percent Article 2 (right to life).[67]

This means that fewer than 6 percent of the Court's judgments deal with freedom of religion, freedom of expression, and a variety of other claims. Nevertheless, the impact of Article 9 cases, all of which have been decided since 1993, has been disproportionately high. The important Article 9 issues discussed by the Court include the wearing of religious symbols or clothing in public places, the process of registration and receiving recognition as a religious group, religious association where employment in religious organizations might depend on a person's religious qualifications, proselytism, hate speech, and defamation of religion.[68]

c. Admissibility

A key threshold determination in every case is whether it is admissible. Under Article 35 of the ECHR, the Court "may only deal with the matter after all domestic remedies have been exhausted." Further, it may not deal with any application that is anonymous, is substantially the same as a matter already examined by the court or another international tribunal, or is "incompatible with the provisions of the Convention or the protocols thereto, manifestly ill-founded, or an abuse of the right of application." For the most part, inadmissibility decisions

65. *Id.*

66. Annual Report European Court of Human Rights 2016.

67. *ECHR Overview 1959-2017* (Public Relations Unit, European Court of Human Rights, March 2018), https://www.echr.coe.int/Documents/Overview_19592017_ENG.pdf.

68. Brett Scharffs, Symposium Introduction: The Freedom of Religion and Belief Jurisprudence of the European Court of Human Rights: Legal, Moral, Political, and Religious Perspectives, 26 *J. L. & Religion* 249 (2010).

shed little light on the contours of substantive rights such as the right to freedom of religion or belief. In some cases, however, such as those found inadmissible because they are manifestly ill-founded, the substance of rights may come into play. One of the hazards is that summary determinations of inadmissibility are sometimes used to avoid full analysis of the issues precisely because freedom of religion decisions are often difficult and sensitive.

d. Standing

A threshold issue bearing on admissibility that has particular relevance to freedom of religion or belief is standing. Article 34 of the ECHR defines who may bring individual applications as follows: "The Court may receive applications from any person, non-governmental organization, or group of individuals claiming to be the victim of a violation by one of the High Contracting Parties of the rights set forth in the Convention or the protocols thereto." Two issues have been of particular significance for religious communities in this regard. First, can they assert claims in their own right? And second, at what point does state action become sufficiently concrete that a religious community counts as a "victim of a violation"?

The Commission initially addressed the first of these issues in *Church of X v. United Kingdom.*[69] The case involved an application brought by a corporation that had been formed to incorporate the Church of Scientology. The church had operated for some time in the United Kingdom, but following submission of a written answer to a parliamentary question by the Minister of Health describing "scientology as being a pseudo-philosophical cult the practice of which was potentially harmful to its adherents," the government undertook a variety of measures aimed at restricting the growth of the organization. The church, acting as a corporate entity, asserted the "violation of its own rights and/or of the collective rights of its members" to manifest their religion and to do so without being discriminated against. However, no natural person was named as a party. The Commission accepted that the case was brought by and on behalf of the corporation itself and its individual members. However, it held that "a corporation being a legal and not a natural person, is incapable of having or exercising the rights mentioned in Article 9, paragraph (1) of the Convention . . . ," and thus the claims of the corporation were found inadmissible.

Subsequently, the Commission revised its position on this point. In *X and the Church of Scientology v. Sweden,*[70] claims were brought by both a minister of the Church and the Church as a representative of its members. Expressly revising its earlier decision, the Commission held it was now of the opinion that the

> distinction between the Church and its members under Article 9(1) is essentially artificial. When a Church body lodges an application under the Convention, it does so in reality, on behalf of its members. It should therefore be accepted that a church body is capable of possessing and exercising the rights contained in Article 9(1) in its own capacity as representative of its members.

The Commission has further indicated that either "a church body or . . . an association with religious and philosophical objects, is capable of possessing and

69. *Church of X v. United Kingdom*, App. No. 3798/68 (ECmHR, 17 December 1968).
70. In *X and the Church of Scientology v. Sweden,* App. No. 7805/77 (ECmHR Admissibility Decision, 5 May 1979).

exercising the rights contained in Article 9(1) in its own capacity as a representative of its members. . . ."[71] The Commission continued to assume, however, that the rights of a religious community are derivative from the rights of its members. As a functional matter, so long as there is a concurrence of views between those controlling the corporation and at least some members, there is not likely to be a difference between a corporation's ability to assert its own rights and to assert the rights of its members. In any event, the approach taken by the Commission appears more sensible, because "in many of these cases the nomination of a person or persons as the applicant is essentially artificial and the Church is the most appropriate body to bring a claim."[72] This approach makes it easier for religious groups to claim "widespread discrimination or government persecution of a religious group."[73]

The Court addressed the second issue (what counts as being a "victim of a violation") in *Religionsgemeinschaft der Zeugen Jehovas v. Austria*.[74] In that case, Austria had imposed substantial delays on the granting of recognized status to the Jehovah's Witnesses and had discriminated against them as a result. In the course of sustaining the discrimination claim, the Court elaborated the "victim" requirement as follows:

> [I]n proceedings originating in an application lodged under Article 34 of the Convention [the Court] has to confine itself, as far as possible, to the examination of the concrete case before it. Its task is not to review domestic law and practice *in abstracto* and to express a view as to the compatibility of the provisions of legislation with the Convention, but to determine whether the manner in which they were applied to or affected the applicant gave rise to a violation of the Convention. . . . Accordingly, by the term "victim", Article 34 .. . . means the person directly affected by the act or omission which is in issue. Article 34 of the Convention may not be used to found an action in the nature of an *actio popularis*. It may only exceptionally entitle individuals to contend that a law violates their rights by itself, in the absence of an individual measure of implementation, if they run the risk of being directly affected by it.[75]

A dissenting judge took the position that the applicants in the case (a religious community and four individual members) were not victims, because the delay in granting recognized status had not "prevented them from manifesting their belief in worship, teaching, practice and observance," nor did they "complain of any measures of interference with the [community's] internal organization."[76] Among other things, they may have been able to acquire a lower level of entity status, which would have allowed them to carry out their religious affairs. The majority, in contrast, held that there was sufficient unwarranted unequal treatment to accept the applicants' claims that they were "[victims] of a violation."

---

71. *Omkarananda and the Divine Light Zentrum v. Switzerland*, App. No. 8118/77 (ECmHR Admissibility Decision, 19 March 1981).

72. Carolyn Evans, *Freedom of Religion under the European Convention on Human Rights* 14 (Oxford Univ. Press 2001).

73. *Id.* at 15.

74. *Religionsgemeinschaft der Zeugen Jehovas v. Austria*, App. No. 40825/98 (ECtHR, 31 July 2008).

75. *Id.* at § 90.

76. *Id.* (Steiner, J., dissenting in part).

2. Key Religion Provisions of the European Convention on Human Rights

The most important article in the Convention dealing with freedom of religion or belief is Article 9, which states:

> Everyone has the right to freedom of thought, conscience and religion; this right includes freedom to change his religion or belief, and freedom, either alone or in community with others and in public or private, to manifest his religion or belief, in worship, teaching, practice and observance.
>
> Freedom to manifest one's religion or beliefs shall be subject only to such limitations as are prescribed by law and are necessary in a democratic society in the interests of public safety, for the protection of public order, health or morals, or for the protection of the rights and freedoms of others.

Article 14 is also important, as it guards against discrimination in the extent to which other Convention rights, including those of Article 9, are protected:

> The enjoyment of the rights and freedoms set out in this Convention shall be secured without discrimination on any grounds such as sex, race, colour, language, religion, political or other opinion, national or social origin, association with a minority, property, birth or other status.

Article 2 of the First Protocol to the Convention also serves to protect religious freedom:

> No person shall be denied the right to an education. In the exercise of any functions which it assumes in relation to education and teaching, the State shall respect the rights of parents to ensure such education and teaching in conformity with their own religious and philosophical convictions.

This article was one of the most controversial in the Convention and had to be included in a separate protocol because agreement on its wording could not be reached in time for the signing of the main instrument.

As discussed in Chapter 1, the first ECtHR case decided under Article 9 was *Kokkinakis v. Greece* in 1993. Much earlier, however, an applicant from the United Kingdom had complained to the Court about a violation of her Article 9 rights to manifest her beliefs.

ARROWSMITH V. UNITED KINGDOM

European Commission of Human Rights, App. No. 7050/75 (12 October 1978)

[The applicant, Miss Pat Arrowsmith, is a citizen of the United Kingdom. On 20 May 1974 she was convicted under the Incitement to Disaffection Act of 1934, mainly on the ground that she had distributed leaflets to troops stationed at an army camp aimed at seducing them from their duty or allegiance in relation to service in Northern Ireland. She was sentenced to 18 months imprisonment, and the conviction was duly affirmed. In her application to the European Court of Human Rights, she claimed, among other things, that her conviction interfered with her right to manifest her pacifist belief as guaranteed by Article 9 (1) of the Convention.]

IV. Opinion of the Commission
(2) As to Article 9 of the Convention

The applicant is undisputedly a convinced pacifist. The respondent Government have accepted her definition of pacifism as being: The commitment, in both theory and practice, to the philosophy of securing one's political or other objectives without resort to the threat or use of force against another human being under any circumstances, even in response to the threat of or use of force.

The Commission is of the opinion that pacifism as a philosophy and, in particular, as defined above, falls within the ambit of the right to freedom of thought and conscience. The attitude of pacifism may therefore be seen as a belief ('conviction') protected by Article 9(1). It remains to be determined whether or not the distribution by the applicant of the leaflets here in question was also protected by Article 9(1) as being the manifestation of her pacifist belief.

Article 9(1) enumerates possible forms of the manifestation of a religion or a belief, namely, worship, teaching, practice and observance, and the applicant submits that by distributing the leaflets she 'practised' her belief.

The Commission considers that the term 'practice' as employed in Article 9(1) does not cover each act which is motivated or influenced by a religion or a belief. It is true that public declarations proclaiming generally the idea of pacifism and urging the acceptance of a commitment to non-violence may be considered as a normal and recognised manifestation of pacifist belief. However, when the actions of individuals do not actually express the belief concerned they cannot be considered to be as such protected by Article 9(1), even when they are motivated or influenced by it.

The leaflet here in question starts with the citation of the statements of two ex-soldiers one of whom says:

> I'm not against being a soldier. I would be willing to fight to defend this country against an invader – I'd be willing to fight for a cause I could believe in. But what is happening in Ireland is all wrong.

Although this is an individual opinion of a person who is not necessarily linked to the organisation which edited the leaflet its citation nevertheless indicates that the authors consider it recommendable. It can therefore not be found that the leaflet conveys the idea that one should under no circumstances, even not in response to the threat of or the use of force, secure one's political or other objectives by violent means. It only follows from the contents of the leaflet that its authors were opposed to British policy in Northern Ireland.

This view is not only expressed in the statement of the ex-soldier but also by the authors of the leaflet who comment the citation as follows:

> We are aware that there are British soldiers who are leaving the army, or who want to, because of British policy in Northern Ireland. We are glad about this and hope many more will do so.

And under the heading: 'Open refusal to be posted to Northern Ireland' the following passages:

> A soldier who publicly stated that he refused to serve in Northern Ireland . . . would be setting an example to other soldiers: strengthening their resolve to resist the Government's disastrous policy.

> But soldiers who believe, as we do, that it is wrong for British troops to be in Northern Ireland are asked to consider whether it is better to be killed for a cause you do not believe in or to be imprisoned for refusing to take part in the conflict.

The leaflets were not addressed and distributed to the public in general but to specific soldiers who might shortly be posted to Northern Ireland. The soldiers were, according to the contents of the leaflet, given the advice to go absent without leave, or openly to refuse to be posted to Northern Ireland. This advice was not clearly given in order to further pacifist ideas.

The Commission finds that the leaflets did not express pacifist views. The Commission considers, therefore, that the applicant, by distributing the leaflets, did not manifest her belief in the sense of Article 9(1). It follows that her conviction and sentence for the distribution of these leaflets did not in any way interfere with the exercise of her rights under this provision.

COMMENTS AND QUESTIONS

1. If the Commission determined that pacifism is a form of protected belief, why did Arrowsmith's "exercise" of this religious belief not fall within the protection of Article 9? What acts "motivated or influenced by a religion or a belief" should the term "practice" as employed in Article 9(1) cover?
2. The European Court, as opposed to the Commission, "has not placed such extensive, repetitive reliance on *Arrowsmith* principles . . . ."[77] Did the Commission impose excessive constraints on "manifestation of religion"? Shouldn't some actions that are "motivated by religion" count as "manifestations" even though they don't directly express the belief?

LEYLA ŞAHIN V. TURKEY

European Court of Human Rights, App. No. 44774/98, Grand Chamber (2005)

15. On 26 August 1997 the applicant enrolled at the Cerrahpas¸a Faculty of Medicine at Istanbul University.

16. On 23 February 1998 the Vice Chancellor of Istanbul University issued a circular, the relevant part of which provides:

> By virtue of the Constitution, the law and regulations, and in accordance with the case-law of the Supreme Administrative Court and the European Commission of Human Rights and the resolutions adopted by the university administrative boards, students whose 'heads are covered' (who wear the Islamic headscarf) and students with beards must not be admitted to lectures, courses or tutorials. Consequently, the name and number of any student with a beard or wearing the Islamic headscarf must not be added to the lists of registered students . . .

[The applicant was denied access to a written examination on 12 March 1998 and then suspended from the university for a semester on 13 April 1999, pursuant to the Students Disciplinary Procedure Rules, for wearing the Islamic headscarf.]

70. The applicant submitted that the ban on wearing the Islamic headscarf in institutions of higher education constituted an unjustified interference with her

77. Paul M. Taylor, *Freedom of Religion: UN and European Human Rights Law and Practice* 216 (Cambridge Univ. Press 2005).

right to freedom of religion, in particular, her right to manifest her religion. She relied on Article 9 of the Convention [for her assertions.]

The Court's Assessment

78. The applicant said that, by wearing the headscarf, she was obeying a religious precept and thereby manifesting her desire to comply strictly with the duties imposed by the Islamic faith. The Court proceeds on the assumption that the regulations in issue, which placed restrictions of place and manner on the right to wear the Islamic headscarf in universities, constituted an interference with the applicant's right to manifest her religion.

89. As the Constitutional Court noted in its judgment of 9 April 1991, the wording of [the relevant section of Turkish law] shows that freedom of dress in institutions of higher education is not absolute. Under the terms of that provision, students are free to dress as they wish "provided that [their choice] does not contravene the laws in force."

[The meaning of the words "laws in force" is therefore paramount to the discussion. The wearing of the Islamic headscarf in universities contrary to the Constitution, which is clearly included under the "laws in force."]

93. In addition, the Supreme Administrative Court had by then consistently held for a number of years that wearing the Islamic headscarf at university was not compatible with the fundamental principles of the Republic, since the headscarf was in the process of becoming the symbol of a vision that was contrary to the freedoms of women and those fundamental principles.

[The Court finds that there was a legal basis for interference in Turkish law because the law was accessible and sufficiently precise to be foreseeable. A rule does not have to be applied rigorously in all cases in order to be foreseeable. Furthermore, the applicant was well aware of the regulation before she enrolled, which existed at Istanbul University since before 1994.]

"Necessary in a Democratic Society"

105. While religious freedom is primarily a matter of individual conscience, it also implies, *inter alia*, freedom to manifest one's religion, alone and in private, or in community with others, in public and within the circle of those whose faith one shares. Article 9 lists the various forms which manifestation of one's religion or belief may take, namely worship, teaching, practice and observance [but] does not protect every act motivated or inspired by a religion or belief (*Arrowsmith* . . .).

106. In democratic societies, in which several religions coexist within one and the same population, it may be necessary to place restrictions on freedom to manifest one's religion or belief in order to reconcile the interests of the various groups and ensure that everyone's beliefs are respected (*Kokkinakis*, p. 18, §33). This follows both from paragraph 2 of Article 9 and the State's positive obligation under Article 1 of the Convention to secure to everyone within its jurisdiction the rights and freedoms defined [in the Convention]. Where questions concerning the relationship between State and religions are at stake, on which opinion in a democratic society may reasonably differ widely, the role of the national decision-making body must be given special importance. . . . This will notably be the case when it comes to regulating the wearing of religious symbols in educational institutions, especially in view of the diversity of the approaches taken by national

authorities on the issue. It is not possible to discern throughout Europe a uniform conception of the significance of religion in society *(Otto-Preminger-Institut v. Austria*) and the meaning or impact of the public expression of a religious belief will differ according to time and context (see *Dahlab v. Switzerland*).

110. This margin of appreciation goes hand in hand with a European supervision embracing both the law and the decisions applying it. The Court's task is to determine whether the measures taken at national level were justified in principle and proportionate. In delimiting the extent of the margin of appreciation in the present case the Court must have regard to what is at stake, namely the need to protect the rights and freedoms of others, to preserve public order and to secure civil peace and true religious pluralism, which is vital to the survival of a democratic society. . . .

111. The Court also notes that in the decisions of *Karaduman v. Turkey* and *Dahlab v. Switzerland* the Convention institutions found that in a democratic society the State was entitled to place restrictions on the wearing of the Islamic headscarf if it was incompatible with the pursued aim of protecting the rights and freedoms of others, public order and public safety. In the *Karaduman* case, measures taken in universities to prevent certain fundamentalist religious movements from exerting pressure on students who did not practise their religion or who belonged to another religion were found to be justified under Article 9 §2 of the Convention. Consequently, it is established that institutions of higher education may regulate the manifestation of the rites and symbols of a religion by imposing restrictions as to the place and manner of such manifestation with the aim of ensuring peaceful co-existence between students of various faiths and thus protecting public order and the beliefs of others. In the *Dahlab* case, which concerned the teacher of a class of small children, the Court stressed among other matters the "powerful external symbol" which her wearing a headscarf represented and questioned whether it might have some kind of proselytising effect, seeing that it appeared to be imposed on women by a religious precept that was hard to reconcile with the principle of gender equality. It also noted that wearing the Islamic headscarf could not easily be reconciled with the message of tolerance, respect for others and, above all, equality and non-discrimination that all teachers in a democratic society should convey to their pupils. …

(ii) Application of the Foregoing Principles to the Present Case

114. As the Chamber rightly stated (see paragraph 106 of its judgment), the Court considers this notion of secularism to be consistent with the values underpinning the Convention. It finds that upholding that principle, which is undoubtedly one of the fundamental principles of the Turkish State which are in harmony with the rule of law and respect for human rights, may be considered necessary to protect the democratic system in Turkey. An attitude which fails to respect that principle will not necessarily be accepted as being covered by the freedom to manifest one's religion and will not enjoy the protection of Article 9 of the Convention (see *Refah Partisi (the Welfare Party) and Others*, § 93).

115. After examining the parties' arguments, the Grand Chamber sees no good reason to depart from the approach taken by the Chamber as follows:

> The Court . . . notes the emphasis placed in the Turkish constitutional system on the protection of the rights of women. . . . Gender equality—recognised by the European

Court as one of the key principles underlying the Convention and a goal to be achieved by member States of the Council of Europe—was also found by the Turkish Constitutional Court to be a principle implicit in the values underlying the Constitution. . . . In addition, like the Constitutional Court . . . , the Court considers that, when examining the question of the Islamic headscarf in the Turkish context, there must be borne in mind the impact which wearing such a symbol, which is presented or perceived as a compulsory religious duty, may have on those who choose not to wear it. As has already been noted (see *Karaduman* and *Refah Partisi and Others*), the issues at stake include the protection of the "rights and freedoms of others" and the "maintenance of public order" in a country in which the majority of the population, while professing a strong attachment to the rights of women and a secular way of life, adhere to the Islamic faith.

116. Having regard to the above background, it is the principle of secularism, as elucidated by the Constitutional Court, which is the paramount consideration underlying the ban on the wearing of religious symbols in universities. In such a context, where the values of pluralism, respect for the rights of others and, in particular, equality before the law of men and women are being taught and applied in practice, it is understandable that the relevant authorities should wish to preserve the secular nature of the institution concerned and so consider it contrary to such values to allow religious attire, including, as in the present case, the Islamic headscarf, to be worn.

117. The Court must now determine whether in the instant case there was a reasonable relationship of proportionality between the means employed and the legitimate objectives pursued by the interference.

118. Like the Chamber, the Grand Chamber notes at the outset that it is common ground that practising Muslim students in Turkish universities are free, within the limits imposed by educational organisational constraints, to manifest their religion in accordance with habitual forms of Muslim observance. In addition, the resolution adopted by Istanbul University on 9 July 1998 shows that various other forms of religious attire are also forbidden on the university premises.

122. In the light of the foregoing and having regard to the Contracting States' margin of appreciation in this sphere, the Court finds that the interference in issue was justified in principle and proportionate to the aim pursued. Consequently, there has been no breach of Article 9 of the Convention.

* * *

Turkey's parliament voted in early February 2008 to end the ban on wearing headscarves in public universities by passing a constitutional reform package. In June 2008 the Constitutional Court overturned these reforms and reinstated the ban on constitutional grounds of the secularity of the State. In 2010, the head of the Turkish Higher Educational council, Yusuf Ziya Özcan, announced that university instructors may not take action against students wearing the headscarf. While this goes against the Constitutional Court ruling, wearing headscarves is now (2017) unofficially tolerated; all universities permit students to wear the headscarf on campus.

COMMENTS AND QUESTIONS

1. In 2008 the European Court of Human Rights found inadmissible the case of Mr. Shingara Mann Singh, a Sikh who was a naturalized French citizen, who filed suit against France for refusing him a driver's license because he would not remove his turban, which he wore out of religious duty, for his photograph. The ECtHR agreed with France that this limitation on religious freedom as protected by Article 9 ECHR was justified in the interest of public safety and justifiable fraud prevention. Mr. Mann Singh tried again in 2013, this time with the UN Human Rights Committee over the issue of his passport photo. The Committee, applying ICCPR Article 18, held that Mr. Mann Singh's "wearing of a turban was not only regarded as a religious duty, but was also tied in with [his] identity," and France had not shown that such an interference was necessary. "Furthermore, even if the obligation to remove the turban for the identity photograph might be described as a one-time requirement, it would potentially interfere with the claimant's freedom of religion on a continuing basis because he would always appear without his religious head covering in the identity photograph and could thus be compelled to remove his turban during identity checks."[78]
2. A ban on face coverings in public, which may be promoted by an appeal to safety concerns, but which effectively targets Muslim women who wear the niqab (covering the face except for the eyes) or burqa (complete body covering with a semi-transparent covering over the eyes), has been sustained in several Western countries and in some African nations. France was the first European country to pass such a ban, with a law that took effect in April 2011, prohibiting all face coverings in public "unless the covering is legally required, work-related, on health grounds, to practice sport or during artistic and 'traditional' events."[79] A major stated reason for the ban is a preservation of French identity and the French idea of laïcité, "a comprehensive ideal whose purpose is to symbolize, promote, and preserve the French Republic's founding principles of liberty, equality, and fraternity." Supporters also believe the ban helps preserve French culture, facilitates face-to-face interaction in open societies, condemns Islamic oppression of women and promote gender equality, and counters what they consider to be separatist tendencies among Muslims.
3. 1 July 2014 the Grand Chamber of the European Court of Human Rights issued judgment in *S.A.S. v. France* (App. No. 43835/11), a case brought by a young Muslim woman in a challenge to the French Law "prohibiting the concealment of one's face in public places." In upholding the law, the Court accepted France's proposal that this law, which was neutral on its face but obviously targeted Muslim women, pursued two "legitimate aims": preserving public safety and "respect for the minimum set of values of an open and democratic society" (paras. 114-122). The Court found, however, that France did not demonstrate that a blanket ban on facial coverings in public places was

---

78. *See Mann Singh v. France*, App No. 24479/07 (ECtHR, 13 November 2008); *Mann Singh v. France*, CCPR/C/108/D/1928/2010, 26 September 2013; Donlu Thayer, Case Note, Mann Singh v. France, *Oxford J. L. & Relig.* (2014) 3 (1), 178-179.

79. Article 2, Loi interdisant la dissimulation du visage dans l'espace public.

necessary for the promotion of public safety under the ECHR. What the Court found more convincing was a concept not specifically articulated in the Convention: the concept of "living together," which could be connected to the legitimate aim and explicitly listed "protection of the rights and freedoms of others" articulated in ECHR articles 8 and 9. In a democratic society with diverse religious beliefs, said the Court, "it may be necessary to place limitations on freedom to manifest one's religion or beliefs in order to reconcile the interests of the various groups and ensure that everyone's beliefs are respected" (para. 26). France is in a better position than the Court to make the judgment call in this area for its own society. Granted the "margin of appreciation" typically granted by the Court to Member States, "It indeed falls within the powers of the State to secure the conditions whereby individuals can live together in their diversity" (para. 142).[80] This view was reiterated in July 2017 when the Court's holdings in *Belcacemi and Oussar v. Belgium* (App. No. 37798/13) and *Dakir v. Belgium* (App. No. 4619/12) affirmed that "the question whether or not it should be permitted to wear the full-face veil in public places in Belgium constituted a choice of society," and such a choice did not violate the Article 9 rights of women native to or residing in Belgium who desired to wear face-coverings in public.

4. In March 2015, the Federal Constitutional Court of Germany ruled that a flat ban on headscarves worn by public school teachers is unconstitutional, explicitly stating that the freedom of religion or belief granted by the German Basic Law allowed women in state schools to conform with a dress code stipulated by religion. Forbidding women to wear the headscarf effectively excludes them from teaching and thus violates the constitutional requirement not to discriminate against women.
5. In a judgment of 26 November 2015, the ECtHR once again ruled for France and against a veiled Muslim woman, in this case a social worker in the psychiatric department of a public health establishment in Paris whose contract was not renewed when she refused to stop wearing her veil upon complaints by patients. In *Ebrahimian v. France* (App. No. 64846/11), a unanimous Court found no violation of the woman's Article 9 rights, "as wearing the Muslim veil had been considered by the authorities as an ostentatious manifestation of religion that was incompatible with the requirement of neutrality incumbent on public officials in discharging their functions."

> The applicant had been ordered to observe the principle of secularism within the meaning of Article 1 of the French Constitution and the requirement of neutrality deriving from that principle. According to the national courts, it had been necessary to uphold the secular character of the State and thus protect the hospital patients from any risk of partiality in the name of their right to their own freedom of conscience. The necessity of protecting the rights and liberties of others—that is, respect of everyone's freedom of religion—had formed the basis of the decision in questions.[81]

80. For further discussion of this case, *see* Chapter 4, IV D. The French Model of Separation.

81. *Non-renewal of contract, in a public establishment, of a social assistant refusing to remove her veil was not contrary to the European Convention on Human Rights*, Press Release issued by the European Court of Human Rights, No. 370, Registrar of the Court, 16 November 2015.

6. To many observers *Ebrahimian* was an unfortunate decision.[82] To such thinkers, the Court "finally got it right" in its 18 September 2018 judgment in *Lachiri v. Belgium* (App. No. 3413/09), where it found by six votes to one that excluding a Muslim woman from the courtroom for refusing to remove her hijab violated her Article 9 rights. Would the fact that Ms. Lachiri was "an ordinary citizen, not representing the State" be sufficient to account for such a difference in the Court's ruling?
7. On 14 March 2017, the Grand Chamber of the Court of Justice of the European Union (CJEU) also issued preliminary rulings on the wearing of the Muslim headscarf in the workplace. Following upon the contrary opinions of two Advocates General—in *Achbita v. G4S Secure Solutions*, C-157/15 (from Belgium) and *Bougnaoui v. Micropole SA*, C-188/15 (from France)[83]—the Court "found that under the right circumstances a company might be entitled to have a policy [which disallowed all religious, political or philosophical signs in the workplace]. One condition was that the policy must be in writing—in the interests of certainty and clarity. Another condition was that it must apply without distinction to all beliefs."[84]
8. Religious attire cases come of course in varieties other than the Islamic head and body coverings. One US case, *Fraternal Order of Police v. City of Newark*, 170 F.3d 359 (3d Cir. 1999), is noteworthy in part because the author, Judge Samuel Alito, is since 2006 on the US Supreme Court. He wrote:

> This appeal presents the question whether the policy of the Newark (NJ) Police Department regarding the wearing of beards by officers violates the Free Exercise Clause of the First Amendment. Under that policy, which the District Court held to be unconstitutional, exemptions are made for medical reasons (typically because of a skin condition called pseudo folliculitis barbae), but the Department refuses to make exemptions for officers whose religious beliefs prohibit them from shaving their beards. Officers Faruq Abdul-Aziz and Shakoor Mustafa are both devout Sunni Muslims who assert that they believe that they are under a religious obligation to grow their beards. The Sunnah says . . . the refusal by a Sunni Muslim male who can grow a beard, to wear one is a major sin. Because the Department makes exemptions from its policy for secular reasons and has not offered any substantial justification for refusing to provide similar treatment for officers who are required to wear beards for religious reasons, we conclude that the Department's policy violates the First Amendment. Accordingly, we affirm the District Court's order permanently enjoining the Department from disciplining two Islamic officers who have refused to shave their beards for religious reasons.

9. In your opinion, is the European approach in *Şahin* or the US approach in *Fraternal Order of Police* more respectful of religion and conscience? Is either approach superior in addressing the concern that every man will become a law unto themselves if exceptions are created for religious belief?

---

82. Readers of the academic blog *Stragbourg Observers* voted *Ebrahimian* the Court's worst decision of 2015.

83. See the Web Supplement for links to the Opinions of Advocate General *Kokott* in *Achbita* and Advocate General Sharpston in *Bougnaoui*, the Judgments of the Court in the twin cases, and the full text of the Court's press release: *An internal rule of an undertaking which prohibits the visible wearing of any political, philosophical or religious sign does not constitute direct discrimination*, Press Release No. 30/17 of the Court of Justice for the European Union, 14 March 2017.

84. Gareth David, Achbita v G4S: Religious Equality Squeezed between Profit and Prejudice, *European Law Blog*, 6 April 2017.

10. Under what circumstances should the manifestation of sincerely held religious beliefs be curtailed in the public interest? A number of European countries have banned the wearing of any overtly religious symbol in public schools and universities. The laws generally ban all ostentatious religious symbols, including Muslim head coverings, Jewish yarmulkes, sheikh turbans, and large Christian crosses. Generally not prohibited are small, unobtrusive symbols, including a Muslim crescent, a Christian cross, or a Jewish Star of David. The major reason offered for these bans is to keep religion out of the classroom and protect the secularity of the particular state. [See discussions of *Eweida and Others v. UK*, App. No. 48420/10 (ECtHR Grand Chamber, 15 January 2013) in Chapter 9 and *Lautsi v. Italy*, App. No. 30814/16 (ECtHR Grand Chamber, 18 March 2011), in Chapter 13.]
11. In Canada, the United Kingdom, and the United States, courts have struggled to balance the court's interests in the proceedings of a fair trial with a Muslim woman's religious freedom right to veil her face in public. Beginning in 2011 the government of Canada placed a ban on face coverings when swearing the oath of citizenship. In February 2015, the Federal Court of Canada ruled that such a ban was a breach of the Canadian Charter, a court ruling "unusual because the decision was based on the finding that the ban mandated by the immigration minister violated the government's own immigration laws."
12. What do you think about the more recent rulings of the European Court of Human Rights concerning limitations placed on rights to manifest religion in dress, justified by the interest of others in a secular society, as judged by a "margin of appreciation" granted to the State? Who was right in the Mann Singh case, the ECtHR or the UN Human Rights Committee?
13. The ECtHR in *S.A.S. v. France* found the "living together" argument to be a more compelling reason for limiting religious expression than the public safety argument. A few months after this judgment was rendered in Strasbourg, the African country of Chad, following suicide-bombing attacks carried out by burqa-clad perpetrators, banned the "camouflage" garment, with threats that security forces would seize existing garments from markets and burn them, and those found wearing them would be "arrested, tried and sentenced after summary proceedings."[85] Cameroon, Niger, and Congo-Brazzaville followed with similar, more localized bans, which Nigeria and Senegal also contemplated.[86] Would such actual rather than theoretical evidence of threats to public safety change the calculus in the ECtHR reasoning? Chad is, by a small margin, a Muslim-majority country, whose constitution declares it a secular state with protections for religious freedom that can be restricted, in the terms of Article 5 of the Universal Declaration of Human Rights to which Chad is signatory, "by respect for the freedoms and rights of others and the obligation to safeguard the public order and good morals."[87] Does the action of the government in banning burqas seem like a limitation on religious freedom for the sake of public order and morals, or could it be seen as essentially a ban on a dangerous object?

---

85. *See* The Veil in West Africa: Banning the Burqa, *Economist*, 13 February 2016. *See also* Chapter 6 of this title for a full discussion of Limitations on Freedom of Religion or Belief.

86. *Id.*

87. Article 5, Universal Declaration of Human Rights.

B. THE EUROPEAN UNION

1. Treaties Establishing the European Union

In an effort to bring about a peaceful, united, and prosperous union that could forestall such divisions as those that had caused two bloody world wars on the continent, European leaders in the years following World War II established a series of international agreements to form a European Union (EU), in which member states would agree to accept the imposition of laws created by EU institutions, and thereby agree to share part of their sovereignty with the Union. The process began with the Treaty of Rome, officially the Treaty establishing the European Economic Community (EEC), which took effect on 1 January 1958. By provision of the Treaty on the European Union (TEU), signed in Maastricht in 1992, the EEC, renamed the European Community, became one of the three "foundational pillars" of the European Union, along with common policy in security and foreign affairs and cooperation of judicial and police authorities in criminal matters. These two treaties formed the constitutional basis of the European Union.

The TEU has been amended several times, most notably by the Treaty of Amsterdam (1999), which placed greater emphasis on citizenship and the rights of individuals, the Treaty of Nice (2001), which reformed the Union's institutional structure, and the Treaty of Lisbon (2009), or Reform Treaty, which eliminated the pillar system and renamed the Treaty of Rome as the Treaty on the Functioning of the European Union (TFEU).

In 2004, representatives of the then-existing 25 EU member states signed a Treaty establishing a Constitution for Europe (TCE), which would have replaced the existing treaties and given legal force to the Charter of Fundamental Rights of the European Union (CFR), which had been proclaimed by the European Parliament, Council, and Commission in 2000. The TCE, however, was ratified by only 18 states, and when French and Dutch voters rejected it in 2005, the move towards a European Constitution stopped. Instead, the CFR became legally binding on the EU under the provisions of Article 6 of the Treaty of Lisbon, which also provided for EU accession to the European Convention, and by Article 6(3), "Fundamental rights, as guaranteed by the European Convention ... and as they result from the constitutional traditions common to the Member States, shall constitute general principles of the Union's law."

The CFR, under six titles: Dignity, Freedoms, Equality, Solidarity, Citizens' Rights, and Justice, brings together in a single document the fundamental rights protected in the EU. In May 2010, members of the EU College of Commissioners for the first time swore a solemn declaration to uphold the Charter, as well as the European treaties under its competence.[88]

CFR Article 10 provides: "Everyone has the right to freedom of thought, conscience and religion. This right includes freedom to change religion or belief and freedom, either alone or in community with others and in public or private, to manifest religion or belief, in worship, teaching, practice and observance." Article 10 also recognizes the right to conscientious objection, "in accordance with the

88. *See* Charter of Fundamental Rights of the European Union.

national laws governing the exercise of this right." The issue of permissible limitations is addressed in Article 52, which provides, "Any limitation on the exercise of the rights and freedoms recognized by this Charter must be provided for by law and respect the essence of those rights and freedoms. Subject to the principle of proportionality, limitations may be made only if they are necessary and genuinely meet objectives of general interest recognized by the Union or the need to protect the rights and freedoms of others." Although on its face this provision might seem to contemplate a permissive interpretation of acceptable limitations, Article 52 also states, "Insofar as this Charter contains rights which correspond to rights guaranteed by the Convention for the Protection of Human Rights and Fundamental Freedoms, the meaning and scope of those rights shall be the same as those laid down by the said Convention. This provision shall not prevent Union law providing more extensive protection." In addition, Article 53 states, "Nothing in this Charter shall be interpreted as restricting or adversely affecting human rights and fundamental freedoms" as recognized in other human rights instruments, including the European Convention.

2. Declaration on the Status of Churches and Non-Confessional Organizations (1997)

The Declaration on the Status of Churches and Non-confessional Organizations was included as part of the Treaty of Amsterdam and became therefore a declaration of European Union law with respect to religious and non-confessional organizations. The declaration protects both specifically religious organizations—churches—and organizations that are not linked with a particular religion but provide a forum for expression of certain beliefs and/or philosophies—non-confessional organizations. Article 11 states, "The European Union respects and does not prejudice the status under national law of churches and religious associations or communities in the Member States. The European Union equally respects the status of philosophical and non-confessional organisations."

This provision was extended into Article 17 of the TFEU: "1. The Union respects and does not prejudice the status under national law of churches and religious associations or communities in the Member States. 2. The Union equally respects the status under national law of philosophical and nonconfessional organisations. 3. Recognising their identity and their specific contribution, the Union shall maintain an open, transparent and regular dialogue with these churches and organisations."

C. THE ORGANIZATION OF (FORMERLY CONFERENCE ON) SECURITY AND CO-OPERATION IN EUROPE

The Conference on Security and Co-operation in Europe (CSCE) was born out of a conference involving 35 European countries and the United States and Canada, held in Helsinki, Finland, from November 1972 until July 1975. Those 35 European states signed the concluding document of the conference: the Final Act of the Conference on Security and Co-operation in Europe (also known as the Helsinki Accords or the Final Act, excerpted below). The Final Act is not classified as a treaty and is not legally binding, but is a politically binding agreement seeking to increase security and cooperation among CSCE member states. The Final Act suggested that regular follow-up meetings to the Helsinki conference be held. Many significant documents have been produced from these follow-up meetings, adding significant detail and concreteness to commitments regarding freedom of religion or belief. In 1990, with the Charter of Paris for a New Europe, the CSCE's role expanded from a mere forum for discussion to an active security organization as well. In January 1995, Partnership the Budapest Document toward a Genuine Partnership officially changed the CSCE's name to the Organization for Security and Co-operation in Europe (OSCE) in a New Era (1994).

The OSCE has since grown from its original 35 to 57 participating states. Members of the OSCE include the countries in Western and Eastern Europe, countries in central Asia, Russia, the United States, and Canada. The organization pursues both standard-setting measures and conflict-preventive measures to further the security of its member states. Standard setting takes place in the diverse areas of military security, economic and environmental cooperation, and human rights. The OSCE views protection of human rights as not only a means of improving human life, but also as a means of increasing security.

One of the virtues of the OSCE commitments—perhaps made possible because they are politically but not legally binding—is that they are much more concrete than classic international human rights instruments such as the ICCPR. Starting with Principle VII of the Helsinki Final Act, which affirmed "respect for human rights and fundamental freedoms, including the freedom of thought, conscience, religion or belief," OSCE commitments on human rights matters now fill lengthy volumes[89] and constitute important "soft law" on virtually all human rights topics, including freedom of religion or belief

Urban Gibson and Karen S. Lord, Advancements in Standard Setting: Religious Liberty and OSCE Commitments

In *Facilitating Freedom of Religion or Belief: A Deskbook* 239–254 (Tore Lindholm, W. Cole Durham, Jr., and Bahia G. Tahzib-Lie, eds., Martinus Nijhoff 2004)

Religious liberty has been an integral part of the OSCE process. From the Helsinki Final Act to the Vienna and Copenhagen Concluding Documents, the OSCE participating States have affirmed time and time again that religious liberty is a fundamental human right. The freedom to profess and practice a religion alone or in community, the freedom to meet with and exchange information with co-religionists regardless of frontiers, the freedom to freely present to others and discuss one's religious views, and the freedom to change one's religion have all been enshrined in the OSCE documents. Participating States have also committed to eliminating and preventing discrimination based on religious grounds in all fields of civil, political, economic, social, and cultural life. Noninterference in the affairs of religious communities, such as selection of personnel, is also central to the OSCE understanding of religious liberty. Religious

---

89. For useful compilations of OSCE human rights commitments, see *OSCE Human Dimension Commitments: Volume 1, Thematic Compilation* (3d ed. 2012) and *OSCE Human Dimension Commitments, Volume 2, Chronological Compilation* (3d ed. 2012).

education in any language is protected along with the right for parents to ensure religious education of their children in line with their own convictions. Participating States have also pledged to allow the training of religious personnel in appropriate institutions. The Helsinki commitments are by far the clearest delineation of religious liberty commitments in the international arena.

D. ORGANIZATION OF ISLAMIC COOPERATION

The Organization of the Islamic Conference (OIC) was formed by the adoption of the Charter of the Islamic Conference at the Third Islamic Conference of Foreign Ministers on 4 March 1972. In June 2011, the OIC changed its name to the Organization of Islamic Cooperation, by consensus of the member states at the Thirty-eighth Session of the Council of Foreign Ministers, meeting in Astana, Kazakhstan. The OIC is the world's second largest inter-governmental organization after the United Nations. Membership is open to "every Muslim state." Currently (2018) there are 57 Member States, which include those states where Islam is the official state religion as well as other states where the majority or significant portion of the population is Muslim. "The Organization is the collective voice of the Muslim world," working to "safeguard and protect the interests of the Muslim world in the spirit of promoting international peace and harmony".[90]

The present Charter, adopted by the Eleventh Islamic Summit held in Dakar in March 2008, laid down the objectives and principles of the organization, whose fundamental purpose is to strengthen the solidarity and cooperation among the member states.

The OIC has established a variety of specialized agencies in the fields of economic development, education, trade, technology, culture, and information. In the field of law, the OIC has sought to establish an International Islamic Court of Justice and an Islamic Commission of International Law. These institutions, along with the Cairo Declaration of Human Rights in Islam, apparently reflect the desire to develop a distinctively Islamic conceptualization of international law.[91]

Resolutions on Political Affairs Adopted by the Thirty-Eighth Session of the Council of Foreign Ministers

Astana, Republic of Kazakhstan (28-30 June 2011)

The OIC discussed current concerns of the Islamic world in its 2011 Conference of Foreign Ministers, including the conflicts in Iraq, Afghanistan, and Syria. However, a major issue of concern for the OIC was the defamation of religion in response to UN Human Rights Committee 2011 resolution combating intolerance of religion. In the new resolution the term "defamation" is not used, nor is there any direct reference to Islam. Furthermore, the previous defamation resolution sought to criminalize the defamation of Islam, where the new resolution calls for criminalization only where there is the incitement of imminent violence.

---

90. *See* OIC website, About/History.

91. *Religion and Human Rights: Basic Documents* 184 (Tad Stahnke and J. Paul Martin, eds., Center for the Study of Human Rights, Columbia Univ. 1998).

The OIC has stressed that the previous Human Rights Committee defamation of religion resolutions remain valid and necessary. In Resolution No. 34/38-POL on Combating Islamophobia and Eliminating Hatred and Prejudice Against Islam from its recent Conference, the OIC reaffirm "all OIC resolutions on the subject, which stress, inter alia, the need for effectively combating defamation of Islam and incitement to religious hatred, hostility, violence and discrimination against Islam and Muslims, as well as the growing trend of Islamophobia."

The OIC stressed the importance of prohibiting the defamation of Islam in a post September 11, 2001 world. The OIC expressed its deep concern for stereotyping, discrimination, and acts of violence against Muslims as well as condemned Switzerland's ban of the construction of minarets and the burning of the Holy Quran in the United States. The OIC called "upon all States to prevent any advocacy of religious discrimination, hostility or violence and defamation of Islam by incorporating legal and administrative measures which render defamation illegal and punishable by law." Furthermore in Resolution No. 35/38-Pol on Combating Defamation of Religions, the OIC emphasized that according to Article 29 of the Universal Declaration of Human Rights, the freedom of expression may be subject to limitations that are provided for by law and are "necessary for respect of the rights or reputations of others, protection of national security or of public order, public health or morals and general welfare." [92]

THE CAIRO DECLARATION ON HUMAN RIGHTS IN ISLAM (1990)

Wishing to contribute to the efforts of mankind to assert human rights, to protect man from exploitation and persecution, and to affirm his freedom and right to a dignified life in accordance with the Islamic Shari'a;

Believing that fundamental rights and universal freedoms in Islam are an integral part of the Islamic religion and that no one as a matter of principle has the right to suspend them in whole or in part or violate or ignore them in as much as they are binding divine commandments, which are contained in the Revealed Books of God and were sent through the last of His Prophets to complete the preceding divine messages thereby making their observance an act of worship and their neglect or violation an abominable sin, and accordingly every person is individually responsible—and the Ummah collectively responsible—for their safeguard.

Proceeding from the above-mentioned principles, declare the following:

Article 1

(a) All human beings form one family whose members are united by submission to God and descent from Adam. All men are equal in terms of basic human dignity and basic obligations and responsibilities, without any discrimination on the grounds of race, colour, language, sex, religious belief, political affiliation, social

92. OIC, *On Combating Defamation of Religions*, Res. No. 35/38-POL, compiled in Resolutions on Political Affairs, OIC Doc. OIC/CFM-38/2011/POL/FINAL (June 28–30, 2011). *See* Robert C. Blitt, Defamation of Religion: Rumors of Its Death Are Greatly Exaggerated, 62 *Case W. Res. L. Rev.* 347–397 (2011) and Brett G. Scharffs, International Law and the Defamation of Religion Conundrum, 11 *Rev. Faith & Int'l Affairs* 66-75 (2013).

status or other considerations. True faith is the guarantee for enhancing such dignity along the path to human perfection. . . .

Article 6

(a) Woman is equal to man in human dignity, and has rights to enjoy as well as duties to perform; she has her own civil entity and financial independence, and the right to retain her name and lineage.

(b) The husband is responsible for the support and welfare of the family.

Article 9

(a) [omitted]

(b) Every human being has the right to receive both religious and worldly education from . . . institutions of education and guidance, including the family, the school, the university, the media, etc., and in such an integrated and balanced manner as to develop his personality, strengthen his faith in God and promote his respect for and defence of both rights and obligations.

Article 10

Islam is the religion of unspoiled nature. It is prohibited to exercise any form of compulsion on man or to exploit his poverty or ignorance in order to convert him to another religion or to atheism.

Article 18

(a) Everyone shall have the right to live in security for himself, his religion, his dependents, his honour and his property. . . .

Article 19

(a) All individuals are equal before the law, without distinction between the ruler and the ruled.

(b) The right to resort to justice is guaranteed to everyone.

(c) Liability is in essence personal.

(d) There shall be no crime or punishment except as provided for in the Shari'a.

(e) A defendant is innocent until his guilt is proven in a fair trial in which he shall be given all the guarantees of defence.

Article 24

All the rights and freedoms stipulated in this Declaration are subject to the Islamic Shari'a.

COMMENTS AND QUESTIONS

1. How do the other regional human rights regimes compare with the European Court of Human Rights?
2. Is the Cairo Declaration on Human Rights in Islam likely to facilitate or terminate a human rights dialogue?
3. There is no provision for equality in the Cairo Declaration. It is unclear whether it would afford protection to religious minorities or women, particularly in a system like the one it envisages, in which all rights and freedoms are subject to the Shari'a.
4. In June 2015, Makassed, a Sunni philanthropic association in Lebanon, issued a statement, the "Beirut Declaration on Religious Freedom," reiterating "Islam's desire to live alongside Christians, noting that no one can be forced to convert or be persecuted for holding beliefs different from one's own." For this group, "Islam bans war against those who are different, and forbids expelling them from their land or limiting their freedom in the name of religion. Such a pronouncement is meant to stake out a clear position for Lebanon's Muslims against the violence carried out in the name of their

religion. In it, the basic teachings of Islam are laid out against those who hold the faith hostage for the sake of power."[93]

5. In January, 2016, the Marrakesh Declaration on the Rights of Religious Minorities in Predominantly Muslim Majority Communities was adopted at a conference marking the 1400th anniversary of the Charter of Medina. It called upon Muslim scholars and intellectuals to develop a "jurisprudence of the concept of 'citizenship' which is inclusive of diverse groups and rooted in Islamic tradition. It further called for establishment of a "broad movement for the just treatment of religious minorities in Muslim countries," and affirmed that "it is unconscionable to employ religion for the purpose of aggressing upon the rights of religious minorities in Muslim countries."[94]
6. In March of 2017, the Office of the UN High Commissioner for Human Rights (OHCHR) launched an initiative on "Faith for Rights" aimed at exploring the mutually enriching connections between religions and human rights. An OHCHR workshop convened at the time adopted the "Beirut Declaration and its 18 Commitments on Faith for Rights," a 46-page document in English, French and Arabic that emphasizes many ways in which "religious or belief convictions are one of the fundamental sources of protection for human dignity and freedoms of all individuals and communities" and identifies many ways that religious groups can work together to achieve better implementation of ideals of freedom of religion or belief.[95] What differences do you see in the fundamental approaches of the Cairo Declaration, the Marrakesh Declaration, and the two (non-related) Beirut Declarations?

VII. THE IMPLEMENTATION OF INTERNATIONAL NORMS IN NATIONAL LEGAL SYSTEMS

A. TREATIES

The existence of international instruments and norms is, of course, not the final indicator of how the rights and laws embodied in those instruments will be treated by individual governments. To understand the realistic effect of the principal international human rights treaties in a particular state, we must first know whether they have been ratified by that state. The Office of the United Nations High Commissioner for Human Rights provides up-to-date information on the status of ratifications of human rights treaties on its website.[96]

Even if a state has ratified a treaty, we must still ascertain whether the state entered any reservations to that treaty or declarations of interpretation, either of which may potentially alter that state's application of the rights and norms set forth by the treaty. For example, when France ratified the International Covenant of

93. *The Beirut Declaration on Religious Freedom* (Makassed Association, 20 June 2015).

94. *Executive Summary of the Marrakesh Declaration on the Rights of Religious Minorities in Predominantly Muslim Majority Communities*, 25–27 January 2016.

95. United Nations Human Rights Office of the High Commissioner (OHCHR), *The Beirut Declaration and ts 18 Commitments on Faith for Rights: Report and Outlook*, 4th ed., September 2018, https://www.ohchr.org/Documents/Press/Faith4Rights.pdf.

96. *See* OHCHR Status of Ratification Interactive Dashboard.

Civil and Political Rights in 1980, it entered reservations to several of the Covenant's articles. One reservation stated, "In the light of article 2 of the Constitution of the French Republic, the French Government declares that article 27 is not applicable so far as the Republic is concerned."[97] Article 2 of the French Constitution provides that the language of the Republic shall be French, while Article 27 of the ICCPR provides, "In those States in which ethnic, religious or linguistic minorities exist, persons belonging to such minorities shall not be denied the right, in community with the other members of their group, to enjoy their own culture, to profess and practise their own religion, or to use their own language." Since 1993 the UN International Law Commission has developed and clarified existing provisions concerning reservations to treaties to create a guide to state practice. This guide addresses important issues such as the validity of reservations (the conditions for the lawfulness of reservations and their applicability to another State) and objections to reservations (in particular, the admissibility and scope of objections to a reservation which is neither prohibited by the treaty nor contrary to its object and purpose).[98]

Still another question in the human rights domain is whether the treaty in question grants standing to individuals to enforce a treaty. Traditionally, individual enforcement rights were rare; treaties were thought of as agreements between nations, and only the nations had standing to seek enforcement.

Once we know whether a state has ratified a treaty and whether it entered any reservations that affect the state's recognition of rights provided for in the treaty, we need to know whether that treaty is actually incorporated into the domestic law of the country.[99] Application is not always automatic upon ratification. The procedure for "transforming" international law into national law varies from country to country. This procedure is often spelled out in the country's constitution, legislation, or judicial decisions. In so-called monist jurisdictions, treaties become an operative part of the country's law immediately upon ratification.[100] In "dualist" states, in contrast, treaties are regarded as a separate (hence dual) legal system, and become part of the normal legal system only as the result of an "act of transformation."[101] In these states, no treaty is to be considered binding domestic law until it is incorporated by legislative action.[102] The United States falls somewhere in between: "while treaties may comprise international commitments . . . they are not domestic law unless Congress has either enacted

97. *Id.* at France/Declarations/ICCPR/(8).

98. UN Office of Legal Affairs, *Guide to Practice on Reservations to Treaties 2011*.

99. For an overview of the issues involved, *see* John H. Jackson, Status of Treaties in Domestic Legal Systems, 86 *Am. J. Int'l L.* 310, 313–315 (1992); *Brownlie's Principles of Public International Law* (8th ed., Oxford Univ. Press 2013); McDougal, The Impact of International Law upon National Law: A Policy-Oriented Perspective, 4 *South Dakota. L. Rev.* 25 (1959).

100. *See, e.g.*, Article 132 of the Constitution of Niger, providing that "[t]reaties or agreements which have been duly ratified shall, upon their publication, have a higher authority than the laws, provided that each agreement or treaty is applied by the other party."

101. Jackson, *supra* note 86, at 313–315.

102. *See, e.g.*, Article 111(b) of the Constitution of Zimbabwe, which provides, "Except as otherwise provided by this Constitution or by or under an Act of Parliament, any convention, treaty or agreement acceded to, concluded or executed by or under the authority of the President with one or more foreign states or governments or international organizations . . . shall not form part of the law of Zimbabwe unless it has been incorporated into the law by or under an Act of Parliament."

implementing statutes or the treaty itself conveys an intention that it be 'self-executing' and is ratified on these terms."[103]

Finally, even if we know whether a state has ratified a treaty, whether there are any applicable reservations, and whether the treaty has been incorporated into the domestic law of the state, there remains the question of whether the state truly implements the treaty's provisions in practice.

B. CONSTITUTIONS

Of the 177 existing constitutions of the world's UN-recognized countries, partially recognized countries, and dependent territories, all but 21 of them promulgated since 1948, including virtually every European constitution and the constitution of every independent country in the Western Hemisphere, contain provisions affirming the right to freedom of religion or belief.[104]

C. OTHER IMPLEMENTATION MECHANISMS

National Human Rights Institutions (NHRIs) are State bodies with a constitutional and/or legislative mandate to protect and promote human rights. Though these are part of the State apparatus and are funded by the State, establishing and strengthening NHRIs has been a priority for UN Office of the High Commissioner for Human Rights (OHCHR) and for other parts of the United Nations system, such as the United Nations Development Programme (UNDP). The number of NHRIs has surged in recent decades, bringing substantive and operational challenges, due to institutional and thematic diversity, a need for minimum standards, and the establishment of core protection activities, especially in countries where there are serious human rights issues.[105]

For more about NRHIs see the website of the OHCHR (OHCHR and NHRIs), and the Web Supplement.

Additional Web Resources:	Information concerning efforts by the United States pursuant to the International Religious Freedom Act to encourage compliance with international commitments regarding freedom of religion or belief List of freedom of religion or belief provisions of world constitutions

103. *Medellin v. Texas*, 128 S.Ct. 1346, 1356 (2008).

104. *See* W. Cole Durham, Jr., and Robert T. Smith, Appendix: Comparative Provisions on Religion and Religious Freedom around the World § 37:20, in *Religious Organizations and the Law* Vol. 4 (Thomson Reuters, 2nd ed. 2017).

105. *National Human Rights Institutions: History, Principles, Roles and Responsibilities* (United Nations Professional Training Series No. 4, 2010).

CHAPTER 4

COMPARATIVE CONSTITUTIONAL PERSPECTIVES ON RELIGION-STATE RELATIONSHIPS

I. INTRODUCTION

This chapter provides an introductory framework for thinking about the range of possible religion-state relationships. While it is necessary to describe the differing approaches in terms of distinctive types or models, it is important to bear in mind that no system is static, and most share features of multiple models. Nevertheless, the typology we describe provides a useful conceptual framework of the major types of regimes that exist in the world today.

One of the principal theses of this chapter is that religious freedom can exist in a variety of forms, though some institutional arrangements are less likely to promote religious freedom than others, and of course, some are totally incompatible with it. The aim here is to provide a framework for comparing different regimes, not only to facilitate analysis of strengths and weaknesses but also, perhaps even more importantly, to allow deeper exploration of the ideas and commitments that varying configurations reflect.

We speak of "religion-state" rather than "church-state" relationships. Christian denominations typically have churches; other religious traditions have synagogues, mosques, temples, or other institutions. Not only do the structures used for worship differ, but overall ways of conceptualizing and organizing the relationship of religious and state institutions may be quite different. When we do lapse into the "church-state" vocabulary long standard in the West, we intend the term "church" to be understood broadly and inclusively to mean the institutional manifestation or organization of a religion, which may have local, regional, national, and international dimensions.

II. THE RANGE OF POSSIBLE RELIGION-STATE STRUCTURES

A. A COMPARATIVE FRAMEWORK FOR CONCEPTUALIZING RELIGION-STATE RELATIONSHIPS[1]

The degree of religious liberty in a particular society may be assessed along two dimensions—one involving the degree to which state action burdens religious belief and conduct (what we describe as the religious freedom continuum), and another involving the degree of identification between governmental and religious institutions (the religion-state identification continuum). In the United States, because of the wording, structure, and Supreme Court interpretation of the religion clause of the First Amendment, these two dimensions are thought of respectively as the "free exercise" and "establishment" aspects of religious liberty. But for comparative purposes, it is useful to think more broadly in terms of varying degrees of religious freedom and religion-state identification.

There is a tendency to assume a straightforward linear correlation between these two values that is represented in Figure 4.1. This diagram suggests that a high degree of religious freedom correlates with a low degree of religion-state identification and that a low degree of religious freedom correlates with a high degree of religion-state identification. While this may capture a certain intuition about the relationship of religious freedom and church-state identification, it is an oversimplification, and in fact a misleading one. When one reviews the world's legal systems, one quickly realizes that while there are many systems for which the correlation holds true (e.g., those of France and the United States), there are many others for which the correlation does not hold. For example, there are regimes with established churches that have high degrees of religious freedom (e.g., the United Kingdom and Finland) and regimes with strong separation of religion and state that rank low in religious freedom (e.g., Soviet-era Russia and Albania).

Figure 4.1

But this lack of correlation is puzzling. After all, a major reason in most countries that constitutional arrangements address the configuration of religious

1. This section is adapted from W. Cole Durham, Jr., A Comparative Framework for Analyzing Religious Liberty, in *Religious Human Rights in Global Perspective: Legal Perspectives* 7 (Johan D. van der Vyver & John Witte Jr., eds., Kluwer Law International 1996).

and state institutions is that there is an assumed correlation between institutional configurations and optimal conditions for religious life. The answer to this seeming paradox lies in reconceptualizing the religion-state identification continuum in two respects. First, it is important to recognize that the range of possible relationships runs not merely from complete identification to non-identification. In fact, the possibilities run from complete (and positive) identification through non-identification to outright hostility and persecution (i.e., negative identification). Second, in order for the correlations between institutional configurations and the religious freedom continuum to become clear, the identification continuum needs to be laid out as a loop, as shown in Figure 4.2.

Figure 4.2

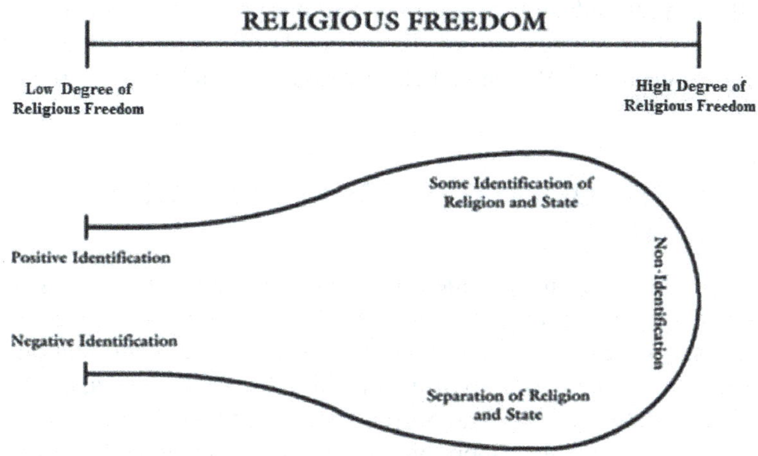

What this schematization suggests is that lack of religious freedom correlates with a high degree of *either* positive *or* negative identification of the state with religion. It is fairly obvious why negative identification correlates with lack of religious freedom: State hostility toward religion and outright persecution by the state clearly results in a diminution of religious freedom. Moreover, it is fairly clear how positive identification with one religion will lead to diminished freedom for other religions (and also for dissenters from the dominant religion).

Less obvious is that the majority religion, because it is likely to become a captive of state apparatus, might also experience a considerable reduction of its liberty. This is a major reason why the disestablishment process, which culminated in 2000 in the disestablishment of the Swedish state church, was supported by the state church itself. A similar process, also supported by the state church, took place in Norway in 2012, after which it was no longer required that half of the government ministers be members of the Lutheran Church of Norway, now renamed The People's Church, nor would the government participate in the appointment of bishops and deans.

Further, this schematization clarifies that we cannot simply assume that the more rigorously one separates church and state, the more religious liberty will be enhanced. At some point, as the position of systems moves along the continuum, aggressive separationism will lead to the exhibition of hostility toward religion. Mechanical insistence on separation at all costs may push a system toward inadvertent insensitivity and ultimately intentional persecution.

The model also captures a related but less obvious reality. Changes in political regimes often move back and forth between extreme positions near the ends of the identification gradient, skipping more moderate intermediate positions. For example, the history of church-state experience in Spain over much of the past two centuries reflects dramatic shifts back and forth from regimes strongly supportive of an established church to secularist, anti-clerical regimes. In Australia and perhaps the United Kingdom, there is vacillation between cooperation and a reasonably robust secularism. In other settings, fundamentalist regimes may be replaced by radically secularist regimes, and vice versa. Secular control regimes (such as China) share many characteristics of systems with an established or preferred set of religious groups. What the diagram suggests is that such shifts back and forth between radically contrasting religious and secular ideologies may not be wide pendulum swings but vacillating shifts of control between highly polarized political groupings that in fact closely resemble each other in their drive for power.

B. THE RANGE OF INSTITUTIONAL RELIGION-STATE RELATIONSHIPS

Focusing on the religion-state identification continuum, we can identify a number of recurring types of religion-state relationships. Figure 4.3 depicts a range of historical types of religion-state configurations along the identification loop. These are listed along the outer loop of the diagram: theocratic states, established religions, religious status systems, and others. Various attitudes of the state toward religion are listed along the inner loop: monopoly, toleration, equal treatment, and so on. The various "types" will be described next.

At the outset, we reiterate that the categories in Figure 4.3 are abstract or analytical types, and actual historical configurations are more complex and more varied. Also, we believe the outer and inner loops are elastic in the sense that various types and attitudes may "slip around" the basic religion-state identification continuum. That is, for some societies accommodation may be the type of religion-state configuration that optimizes religious freedom; for others stricter separation may be preferred. At the same time, the outer loop is not infinitely elastic: It is difficult to imagine that religious status systems (upper loop) or religious control systems (lower loop) could be "pulled" around the identification continuum to be positioned at a point that correlates with optimal religious freedom.

The inner loop is elastic in a different way. Attitudes such as toleration and equal treatment may be exemplified in a range of different types of regimes, and thus they may overlap. For example, accommodationist regimes are tolerant, protect substantive equality among differing religious groups, and constitute a form of secularity.

In analyzing the various types, we start at the positive end of the continuum, because in most parts of the world, the evolution has been from positive identification (i.e., official religions) to more open and often more secular systems. The question is: Where along the continuum does each country and culture find the optimal configuration, and at what points at the positive and negative ends do systems move out of the domain of liberty into the zone of violation of the rights to freedom of religion or belief?

Figure 4.3

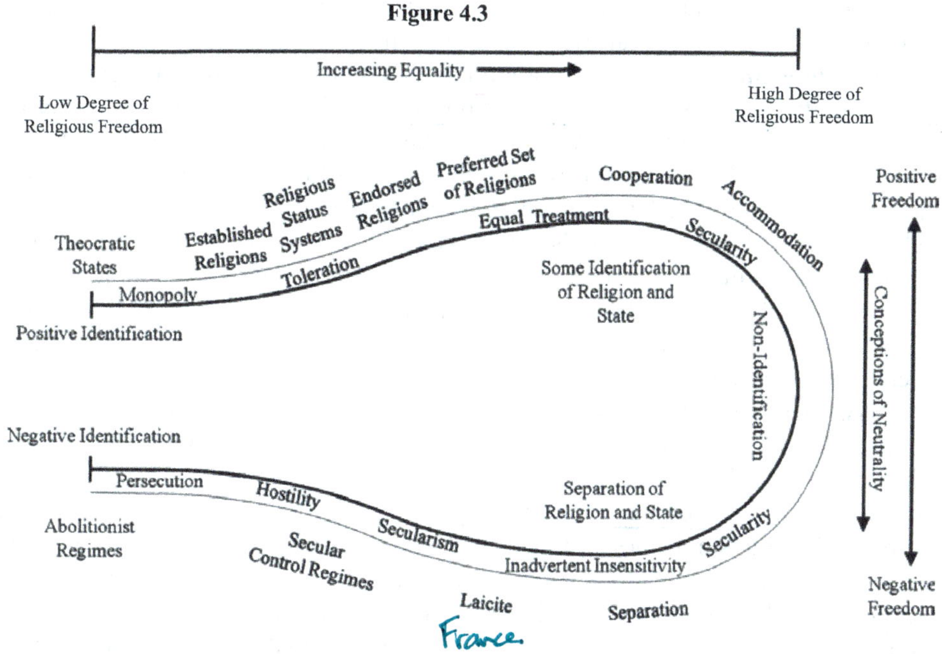

Absolute Theocracy. Beginning at the positive identification end of the continuum, one first encounters *absolute theocracies* of the type associated with stereotypical views of Islamic fundamentalism. In fact, a range of regimes are possible in Muslim theory and practice, depending on the scope given to Muslim beliefs about toleration and depending on the extent to which flexible interpretation of Islamic law (Shari'a) leaves open normative space for adherents of other belief systems, and whether Shari'a is directly applicable as part of Constitutional or customary law, or whether it must be enacted by the legislature. What is significant about the absolutist positions is their claim to monopolize religious space. Certain historical forms of Christian, Hindu, and Buddhist beliefs, among others, have asserted monopolistic positions in various societies over time.

Established Churches. The next step along the church-state identification continuum would be an established or official state church. The notion of an "established church" is vague and can in fact cover a range of possible church-state configurations with very different implications for the religious freedom of dissenters and minority groups. At one extreme, a regime with an established church that is granted a strictly enforced monopoly in religious affairs may closely resemble theocratic rule. Spain, England, and many other European countries following the Peace of Westphalia in 1648 had such systems, as have countless systems in other parts of the world. Sometimes, such as in the US Colonial era, establishment may involve state support of several preferred religious groups. Some countries that have an established religion nevertheless tolerate a restricted set of divergent beliefs. In fact, the historical pattern has been for established religions to become more tolerant over time. A country in which Islam is the official religion but that tolerates "people of the Book" is another example. A country with an established Christian church that tolerates a number of major faiths but disparages others is another. Another position is a country that maintains an established church but guarantees equal treatment for all other religious beliefs. Contemporary Great Britain is a prominent example.

Religious Status Systems. In a number of countries, multiple religions have official status in the sense that at least portions of the religious law of differing traditions are binding on those belonging to those traditions. For example, in Israel, India, and a number of countries with substantial Muslim populations, personal law (typically including laws governing marriage, family, divorce, succession, and related fields) depends on one's religious status. If one is Jewish, Jewish law applies; if Muslim, Shari'a applies; and so forth. These religiously plural systems tend to treat religious identity as more a matter of birth and status than choice, and may be more or less flexible in recognizing rights of exit from the officially recognized religious group.

Historically Favored and Endorsed Churches. The next category consists of regimes that fall short of formally affirming that one particular church is the official church of the nation but acknowledge that a particular church has a special place in the country's history and traditions. This is quite typical in countries where Roman Catholicism is predominant and a new constitution has been adopted relatively recently (typically since Vatican II). The endorsed church is specially acknowledged though not made the official religion, and the country's constitution asserts that other groups are entitled to equal protection. Sometimes the endorsement is relatively innocuous and remains strictly limited to recognition that a particular religious tradition has played an important role in a country's history and culture. In other cases, endorsement operates as a thinly disguised method of preserving the prerogatives of establishment and channeling significant state aid to the favored church (or perhaps churches) while maintaining the formal appearance of a more liberal regime.

Preferred Set of Religions. A number of regimes suggest in various ways that a certain set of religions deserve preference. Sometimes this is done by distinguishing traditional religions and giving them special status or privilege. This may also be implicit in "multi-tier" regimes that give different groups different levels of recognition. Theoretically, these multi-tier systems set out ostensibly objective criteria for differential treatment, but generally the result is the same as explicitly giving favored treatment to traditional groups.

Cooperationist Regimes. The next category of regime grants no special status to dominant churches, but the state continues to cooperate closely with churches in a variety of ways. Germany provides the prototypical example of this type of regime, though it is certainly not alone in this regard. Most European religion-state systems are cooperationist. The cooperationist state may provide significant funding to various church-related activities, such as religious education or maintenance of churches, payment of clergy, and so forth. Very often in such regimes, relations with churches are managed through special agreements such as concordats. Spain, Italy, and Poland as well as several Latin American countries follow this pattern. The state may also cooperate in helping with the gathering of contributions (e.g., the withholding of "church tax" in Germany).

Cooperationist countries frequently have patterns of aid or assistance that benefit larger denominations in particular. However, they do not specifically endorse any religion, and they are committed to affording equal treatment (as they understand equality) to all religious organizations. Equal treatment, it is often said, does not entail identical treatment. Since different religious communities have different needs, cooperationist programs can raise more complex interdenominational problems of equal treatment. It is all too easy to slip from cooperation into patterns of state preference. Also, in comparison with more separationist regimes, more complex questions of protecting the self-determination and internal autonomy of religious organizations arise.

Accommodationist Regimes. A regime may incline toward separation of religion and state, yet retain a posture of benevolent neutrality toward religion. Accommodationism might be thought of as cooperationism without the provision of any direct financial subsidies to religion or religious education. An accommodationist regime would have no qualms about recognizing the importance of religion as part of national or local culture; accommodating religious symbols in public settings; allowing tax, dietary, holiday, Sabbath, and other kinds of exemptions; and so forth. Note that the growth of the state intensifies the need for accommodation. As state influence becomes more pervasive and regulatory burdens expand, refusal to make religious exemptions or accommodations shades into state hostility toward religion.

Separationist Regimes. The slogan "separation of church and state" can be used to cover a fairly broad and diverse range of regimes. At the benign end, separationism differs relatively little from accommodationism. The major difference is that separationism, as its name suggests, insists on more rigid sequestration of religion and state. Any suggestion of public support for religion is deemed inappropriate. Religious symbols in public displays are not allowed. Granting religion-based exemptions from general public laws may be viewed as impermissible favoritism toward religion. The mere reliance on religious premises in public argument may be deemed to run afoul of the church-state separation principle. Members of the clergy are sometimes prohibited from holding public office.

Less benign forms of separationism make stronger attempts to cordon off religion from public life. In many contexts, the practical problems arise from inadvertent insensitivity. Regulations as initially formulated often lack anti-religious animus; those drafting the regulations were simply unaware of the religious implications of their regulations. At some point, those afflicted by the unintended burden bring the problem to the attention of government officials. The question then becomes whether reasonable accommodations can be worked out; if so there is a shift toward an accommodationist system, or officials may believe they lack authority to make such accommodations. Inadvertent insensitivity is the flip side of the subtle or not-so-subtle privileging of groups in cooperationist regimes.

One of the questions posed by separationist regimes is the extent to which religion should have a public role. Note that even if religious communities do not have an official or endorsed role in the state sphere, they could still have a significant public role, assuming that the public sphere is broader than the sphere of the state. Recent years have witnessed a significant resurgence of religion in public life, and there are significant issues about what is permissible and appropriate, and indeed, when discrimination or deprivation of rights occurs if some public role is not allowed.

On the other hand, if the aim is to separate public and private life into non-overlapping spheres, and to limit religion to the private sphere, then as the public sphere of the welfare state expands, the space available for religion can shrink substantially. One form this can take is a tightening of the state monopoly on charitable, educational, social, and other welfare services. "Separation" in its most objectionable guise demands that religion retreat from any domain that the state desires to occupy, but is untroubled by intrusive state regulation and intervention in religious affairs.

Secular Control Regimes. A control regime shares some surface similarities with established and historically favored religions and cooperationist regimes. Although there is often substantial state financial aid to select religious groups, state authorities exercise considerable influence over the selection of church leadership and even doctrine and practice. The goal is more explicitly to use religion for the state's own ends, or to emphasize freedom *from* religion for ideological reasons, or to try to limit the possibility that churches will become a threat to the ruling coalition or a competing source of popular legitimacy within the society. Established church regimes can also be a type of control regime, but in recent years, secular control regimes have been particularly problematic.

Abolitionist States. At the negative end of the identification continuum are regimes that have the overt goal of eliminating religion as a social factor. Albania during the Soviet era is perhaps the foremost example of this approach. Historically, a more common pattern has been to subject predominant religions to control while seeking to eliminate or drive minority groups from the country. The Holocaust is the most horrendous example. Less extreme are situations involving overt persecution, hostility, or discrimination.

Other Implications. Besides identifying and plotting a range of different types of religion-state regimes, the schematization in Figure 4.3 is helpful in bringing out a number of other points about religion-state relations. First, while there are important differences between religious freedom and religious equality (e.g., one can imagine a society in which everyone is treated equally in that all are allowed no religious freedom), the general pattern is that increasing equality and increasing freedom of religion go together. For the most part, equal treatment fosters greater religious freedom.

Second, as suggested by the arrow at the far right of the diagram, differing types of free regimes may reflect differing conceptions of freedom. Utilizing Isaiah Berlin's terminology, cooperationist regimes reflect a positive conception of freedom, in that they assume that the state should help actualize the conditions of freedom, such as by providing funding.

Separationist regimes, in contrast, tend to reply upon a negative conception of freedom according to which religious freedom is maximized by minimizing state intervention. Systems on the top half of the loop seem to exhibit a preference for positive conceptions of liberty, and systems on the bottom half of the loop seem to incline towards negative liberty.

Third, different regime types reflect differing assumptions about the neutrality of the state. One model of neutrality is state inaction. A second model is neutrality as the impartiality of an unbiased umpire. As applied to religious matters, this model requires that the state act in formally neutral and religion-blind ways. A third model views the state as the monitor of an open forum. The state in this model can impose time, place, and manner restrictions on the marketplace of ideas, and can impose certain constraints to avoid violence and fraud; but otherwise the state plays a minimalist role.

The first three models support varying versions of separationism. A fourth model of neutrality calls for substantive equal treatment. That is, the basic principle is that similarly situated individuals should be treated equally, but substantive differences of position should be taken into account, and conscientious beliefs are relevant differences that should be accommodated. This model of neutrality correlates with the principles of an accommodationist regime. A fifth model is a "second generation rights" version of the fourth. That is, it views actualization of substantive rights as an affirmative or positive obligation of the state, and thus supports cooperationist regimes. Most credible religion-state regimes that are sensitive to human rights concerns inhabit a range somewhere in the neutralist zone, as defined by at least one of the foregoing conceptions of neutrality.

Fourth, a word should be said about the contrast between secularism and secularity. Both ideas are linked to the general historical process of secularization, but as we use the terms, they have significantly different meanings and practical implications. By "secularism" we mean an ideological position that is committed to promoting a secular order. By "secularity," in contrast, we mean an approach to religion-state relations that avoids identification of the state with any particular religion or ideology (including secularism itself) and that provides a neutral framework capable of accommodating a broad range of religions and beliefs. In fact, in most modern legal systems, there are proponents of both types of views. Constitutional and other legal texts addressing religion-state issues can often be interpreted as supporting one or the other of these views, and in fact, some of the key debates turn on the difference between these two approaches. Historically, French *laïcité* is closer to secularism, while American separation of church and state is closer to secularity. But there are debates in both societies about how strictly secular the state (and the public realm) should be. This tension between two conceptions of the secular runs through much of religion-state theory in contemporary settings.

COMMENTS AND QUESTIONS

1. What category or group of categories most accurately describes the situation in your home country or in countries with which you are familiar?
2. How might perceptions of whether a given system has a high degree of religious freedom vary if you are part of a religious majority as opposed to a religious minority? What if you are a non-believer, or someone whose identification with a particular religious tradition is primarily cultural rather than a matter of faith? What if you are halfhearted, uncommitted, or uncertain about your religious commitments? For example, if you are live in a cooperationist regime, how might your views about the value of cooperation vary if you belong or don't belong to a favored group? Should our preference

be the same regardless of our own personal commitments to, about, or against religion? Or does where we stand inevitably depend upon where we sit?

3. Majority religious groups often argue that they should receive special treatment or recognition, based on their historical or contemporary contributions to a society. Sometimes these arguments for special treatment look a lot like the arguments that industrial monopolists make in favor of protecting their monopolies. Do they seem valid or merely self-serving? Is it dominant majorities who need special treatment or minorities? Or should special accommodations be made for both?

Additional Web Resources:	More extensive materials relating to each type of religion-state regime

III. POSITIVE IDENTIFICATION REGIMES

Given the space constraints of this volume, it is not possible to explore each type of religion-state relation in detail. In what follows, we focus primarily on the portion of the religion-identification continuum lying between cooperation and laïcité inasmuch as most major democratic systems fall in this range. Some attention is paid to alternative regimes in extended notes as a reminder of the conditions that can arise as a state moves too far away from non-identification.

Professor Silvio Ferrari has explained that cooperationist regimes are the dominant pattern in Europe. In his view, these systems have the following features: "substantial respect of individual religious freedom, guarantee of the autonomy and, in particular, the self-administration of the religious denominations, and selective collaboration of the states with the churches."[2] European countries have become so tolerant and equalitarian that that they have become difficult to distinguish from cooperationist regimes, with the exception that as a formal matter they still privilege one (or more) religion(s).

Thus, even before the disestablishment of the Lutheran Church in Norway, other denominations that wished to receive state support could do so in proportion to their membership, and the humanists receive a comparable share. At the other extreme, even laicist France allows substantial funding to cover maintenance of churches with historical value and to support teaching of secular subjects in private religiously affiliated schools. An interesting question is whether even the United States, with the recent loosening of Establishment Clause barriers to various types of state funding of religious education and social activities, is converging to some extent with cooperationist models.

2. Silvio Ferrari, Conclusion: Church and State in Post-Communist Europe 421, in *Law and Religion in Post-Communist Europe* (Silvio Ferrari and W. Cole Durham, Jr., eds., Peeters 2003).

A. THE SPANISH EXPERIENCE

Spain provides a particularly interesting case because it has made the transition successfully from being a clear example of a regime with a very strong and exclusive established church linked to an authoritarian regime to a cooperationist system situated in a democratic setting (with some residual "endorsed church" characteristics).

Through much of its history, Spain was the classic example of a regime with an established church. Starting in the late fifteenth century with the creation of the modern Spanish state, nationality was fused with religious affiliation. To be Spanish was to be Catholic. Persecution of religious minorities was a state-supported activity, and, as a consequence, religious minorities were almost unknown until early in the twentieth century, with the exception of small Muslim and Jewish communities that survived the Reconquista but remained largely hidden away from the public view. Beginning with the French Revolution and its spillover effects in Spain, and continuing through the nineteenth and twentieth centuries, Spanish politics vacillated wildly between pro-Church and anti-Church laicist regimes. The transition to a modern democratic regime began even before Franco's death. With the change in Church attitude signaled by the Second Vatican Council on church-state issues, the Spanish bishops and the Holy See began to pressure the Franco regime for more religious freedom, leading to a 1967 law granting real freedom for religious minorities despite a reluctant Franco.

After Franco's death the Church continued to lobby for greater religious freedom, but at the same time sought to protect some aspects of its traditional position by a concordat entered into on 28 July 1976. This was supplanted by another concordat that was negotiated essentially in tandem with the drafting of the 1978 Spanish Constitution and was signed 3 January 1979, just one week after promulgation of the Constitution. A year and a half later, the Spanish Parliament adopted the 1980 Organic Law on Religious Freedom (Ley Orgánica de Libertad Religiosa, or LOLR), which laid the foundation for cooperation agreements modeled to some degree on the 1979 concordat. Based on the LOLR, agreements between the Spanish state and three federations of religious communities (Protestant, Jewish, and Islamic) were entered into in 1992. The theory of the LOLR is that the Spanish church-state system has four fundamental "informing principles" (principios informadorcs): (1) religious freedom, (2) equality, (3) state neutrality, and (4) state cooperation with churches and religious communities. Thus, within a relatively few years, Spain successfully made the transition from an authoritarian state-church system to a democratic cooperationist regime. The aim of the transition, which has brought major benefits to most religious groups, was to bring others "up to" the level of the Roman Catholic Church. The difficulty in Spain (and other cooperationist regimes) is that the intended upward equalization does not always trickle down to the full range of smaller religious groups. One arena in which this is often visible is the tax system, as suggested by the following European Commission case.

ORTEGA MORATILLA V. SPAIN

European Commission of Human Rights, App. No. 17522/90 (11 January 1992)

[In June 1985, the applicants, an evangelical Protestant church and minister, requested an exemption from property tax in respect of their place of worship in Valencia, arguing in particular that the Catholic Church enjoyed such exemption. The tax office refused this request on the ground that the exemption enjoyed by the Catholic Church was provided for in the concordat between Spain and the Holy See signed in 1979, whereas there was no legal basis for granting the applicants such exemption. The applicants then appealed this decision, losing at all levels in the domestic legal system. After thus exhausting domestic remedies, they applied for relief to the European Commission of Human Rights.

The Law

1. The applicants complain in the first place that levying property tax in respect of the premises they use for worship infringes their right to freedom of religion set forth in Article 9 of the Convention. . . .

The Commission notes that under the terms of this provision the right to freedom of religion includes the right to manifest one's religion, in public or in private, in worship or observance. The possibility of possessing premises open to adherents and used for the above purposes is clearly one of the means of exercising this right. However, the Commission fails to see how a right to exemption of places of worship from all forms of taxation can be derived from Article 9 of the Convention. It considers that the right to freedom of religion by no means implies that churches or their adherents must be granted a different tax status from that of other taxpayers . . . . It follows that in this respect the application is manifestly ill founded and must be rejected pursuant to Article 27 para. 3 of the Convention.

2. The applicants further allege that, as the Catholic Church in Spain enjoys exemption from property tax in respect of places of worship, the refusal of their request to be treated in the same way for tax purposes infringes Article 14 of the Convention in conjunction with Article 9.

Article 14 of the Convention reads as follows:

> The enjoyment of the rights and freedoms set forth in this Convention shall be secured without discrimination on any ground such as sex. race, colour, language, religion, political or other opinion, national or social origin, association with a national minority, property, birth or other status.

However, the Commission recalls that this provision does not prohibit all differences in treatment in the exercise of the rights and freedoms recognised, equality of treatment being violated only where the difference in treatment has no objective and reasonable justification. . . .

The Commission notes that the Freedom of Religion Act (Institutional Act No. 7/1980) [LOLR] authorises agreements between the State and the various churches or religious associations according to the number of their adherents and the beliefs of the majority of Spanish citizens. It observes that the tax exemptions enjoyed by the Catholic Church in Spain are provided for by the agreements concluded on 3 January 1979 between Spain and the Holy See, which place reciprocal obligations on the two parties. For example, the Catholic Church has undertaken to place its historical, artistic and documentary heritage at the service of the Spanish people (Agreement on education and cultural affairs, Article XV). On the other hand, its places of worship enjoy tax exemption (Agreement on economic affairs, Article IV).

However, the applicant church has not concluded such a concordat with the Spanish State, and it does not appear from the file that it has sought to do so. Consequently, it does not have the same obligations to fulfil vis-à-vis the State.

It follows that this complaint must be rejected as being manifestly ill founded within the meaning of Article 27 para. 2 of the Convention.[3]

COMMENTS AND QUESTIONS

1. The Commission's analysis appears to be a simple application of the maxim that it is not discriminatory for dissimilar situations to be treated differently. Is this a fair characterization of the situation here? Does it make sense to afford special privileges in exchange for special obligations? Why are the Catholic Church and the petitioner not similarly situated?
2. Not long after decision of the foregoing case, many Protestant churches formed a federation that entered into an agreement with the government, authorizing tax exemptions for religious property. Suppose another non-Catholic religious group, one that is denied membership in this federation, brings a claim for an exemption from property tax. Would such a group have a stronger Article 14 claim?
3. What factors would constitute "objective and reasonable justifications" for differential treatment in such circumstances?

B. GERMAN EXPERIENCE: ISSUES SURROUNDING "CHURCH TAX"

A prominent example of cooperationism in the German system is the so-called church tax. The church tax was instituted at the beginning of the 19th century in order to relieve the national budget of its obligations to the churches, which were in turn based on the secularization of church property. Those desiring to be free of the tax may achieve that result by leaving the church. Withdrawal from the church is effected by de-registering with the proper State officials and simply means that one has, according to the State classification, officially ended one's membership of the particular church in question. However, most Protestant churches see the withdrawal as a withdrawal from their particular church as well. The Catholic Church, as a general rule, views the withdrawal as a serious violation of the person's obligations to the church, without bringing into question the theological dimension of church membership.[4]

This "tax" is often misunderstood; to the normal taxpayer, it looks like an amount withheld from earnings along with other taxes that are collected as part of the state tax system. The legal reality is somewhat different. Many churches have

3. For a fuller account of Spanish developments, see Javier Martínez-Torrón, *Religion and Law in Spain* (Wolters Kluwer L. & Bus. 2014).

4. Paraphrase from Gerhard Robbers, State and Church in Germany, in *State and Church in the European Union* 89–90 (2d ed., Gerhard Robbers, ed., Nomos 2005).

the status of "corporations under public law." Churches with this status are eligible to, among other things, levy the church tax on their members. As Professor Gerhard Robbers has described it,

> This tax functions like a membership fee. Those churches that do tax their members usually levy a tax of eight or nine percent of what the member pays in state income taxes. Some of the taxing churches use the state's taxation system, i.e., the state machinery collects the church tax. For this service, a church pays four to five percent of its tax revenue to the state. Indeed, the church tax system was introduced to de-establish former state churches in the nineteenth century and to force them to depend on their own income. The institution of church taxes is thus a consequence of state neutrality.[5]

Significantly, it is now well established as a result of constitutional court decisions that an individual who resigns his or her membership in a church may no longer be compelled to pay the church tax. Such resignations are most common around the time when taxes are due, although the numbers are not overwhelming. Most Germans continue to pay the church tax. Note that the tax is channeled to the church with which the individual is affiliated. The tax system is not used to coerce an adherent of one belief system to support the beliefs of some other group or groups. Many smaller religious communities have the status of a "corporation under public law." While they are theoretically entitled to participate in the church tax system, few do so. The decision not to take the funds is often a matter of religious principle. Despite these basic protections, problems occur, as suggested by the following cases.

MIXED-MARRIAGE CHURCH TAX CASE

German Federal Constitutional Court, 19 BVerfGE 226 (1965)

[Baden-Württemberg's Church Tax Act provided that all employees are subject to a church tax on wages if they or their spouses belong to a religious association authorized to tax. The result was that in mixed-faith marriages, one of the spouses who was not a member of the relevant church might end up paying taxes to that church. The First Senate of the Federal Constitutional Court decided as follows:]

Section 6(2) of the Church Tax Act violates the fundamental right of an employee who is not a member of a religious association as derived from Article 2(1) of the Basic Law [which provides that "[e]veryone shall have the right to the free development of his personality insofar as he does not violate the rights of others or offend against the constitutional order or the moral code."] . . . [Under the Tax Act, an] employee is required to pay the church tax simply because his spouse is a church member. Thus, because of the state law, the employee must pay the church tax although he does not belong to a church authorized to tax him.

As this court has said, a law may not be viewed as part of the constitutional order if it obligates a person to pay financial benefits to a religious association of which he or she is not a member. Because the nonmember employee has no legal way of avoiding this tax liability, the Church Tax Act impermissibly interferes with his right to personality under Article 2(1) of the Basic Law. . . .

---

5. Gerhard Robbers, Religious Freedom in Germany, 2001 *BYU L. Rev.* 643, 661.

The argument is erroneous that subjecting the nonmember spouse to the church tax may be justified because of the nature of marriage as a permanent union of the partners into a complete community of all aspects of life.

In a mixed-faith marriage, no community exists in the exact areas being considered—i.e., religious convictions and beliefs. The marital community is not based upon mutual recognition of religious articles of faith, values, and obligations. Consequently, it would be unreasonable and would contradict the libertarian constitutional system of the Basic Law if one wished to force the nonmember spouse to establish direct relations—even if only financial ones—to a religious community by imposing unavoidable legal sanctions. If, as the Federal Constitutional Court and the Federal High Court of Justice have said, each partner may believe what he chooses and may even convert to another religious belief without being guilty of a marital transgression, then one partner's connection with a church does not obligate the other partner. Hence it is impermissible to argue that because the nonmember spouse made the decision to marry his spouse he should not assert a violation of his religious freedom when he is forced to pay his spouse's church tax obligation. Each partner must decide if he wants and is able to make concessions in religious and ideological matters. The tolerance that married persons of different faiths owe one another may not lead to the creation of legal ties to third parties, especially not to churches and other religious associations.[6]

COMMENTS AND QUESTIONS

The German church tax decisions take great care to ensure that church tax liabilities will not be imposed on those who have resigned church membership. Is the system as circumspect in avoiding the imposition of more subtle pressures to conform and accept the obligations? That is, does the willingness to cooperate depend on coercive pressures? Does the system treat fairly a spouse whose work takes place within the home but is not compensated?

C. PROVISIONS OF THE 2005 IRAQI CONSTITUTION

A variety of countries have majority Muslim populations. The legal systems in those countries, and the extent to which and ways in which they incorporate Islamic law into their legal systems, vary widely. Here we consider only Iraq, an unusual case because it adopted a new constitution while under foreign occupation, but one that nonetheless presented in stark form issues faced in several other Muslim countries.

Within the Iraqi Constitution adopted in 2005, the key provision on the relation of religion and the state is found in Article 2, which provides as follows:

Article 2. First
Islam is the official religion of the State and is a foundation source of legislation:

A. No law may be enacted that contradicts the established provisions of Islam.
B. No law may be enacted that contradicts the principles of democracy.
C. No law may be enacted that contradicts the rights and basic freedoms stipulated in this Constitution.

---

6. Translation from Donald P. Kommers, *The Constitutional Jurisprudence of the Federal Republic of Germany* 487–488 (2d. ed., Duke Univ. Press 1997).

Second
This Constitution guarantees the Islamic identity of the majority of the Iraqi people and guarantees the full religious rights of all individuals to freedom of religious belief and practice such as Christians, Yazedis, and Mandean Sabeans.

Religious rights are addressed in depth in Section Two: Rights and Freedoms. Articles 14 and 29 address the part religion should play as a civil right. Articles 41, 42, and 43 deal with issues relating to freedom of religion or belief.

Article 14
Iraqis are equal before the law without discrimination based on gender, race, ethnicity, nationality, origin, color, religion, sect, belief or opinion, or economic or social status.

Article 29
First

A. The family is the foundation of society; the State preserves its entity and its religious, moral and patriotic values.

Article 41
Iraqis are free in their commitment to their personal status according to their religions, sects, beliefs, or choices, and this shall be regulated by law.

Article 42
Each individual shall have the freedom of thought, conscience, and belief.

Article 43
First
The followers of all religions and sects are free in the:

A. Practice of religious rites, including the Husseini ceremonies (Shiite religious ceremonies).
B. Management of the endowments, its affairs and its religious institutions. The law shall regulate this.

Second
The state guarantees freedom of worship and the protection of the places of worship.

At the end of the Rights and Freedoms Section, Article 46 stands as a type of "limitations clause" that could have significant implications for the legislature and the judiciary as they attempt to interpret the articles dealing with religious freedom.

Article 46
There may not be a restriction or limit on the practice of any rights or liberties stipulated in this constitution, except by law or on the basis of it, and insofar as that limitation or restriction does not violate the essence of the right or freedom.

COMMENTS AND QUESTIONS

Is Article 2 coherent? At the time of its adoption, some observers criticized this framework as providing something for everyone, including Islamists who would enforce a strict version of Shari'a and those concerned with human rights. Others praised the framework as a remarkable example of politics being the art of the possible, skillfully leaving certain conflicts for a later day and providing a framework for liberalizing trends. What do you think? Now that more than fifteen years have passed since the adoption of the Iraqi Constitution, what do you think of these predictions?

Additional Web Resources:	Condordats, the LOLR, and the agreements with Protestant, Jewish, and Islamic groups in Spain Constitutional provisions dealing with freedom of religion or belief in countries with Muslim majorities

D. EMERGING POSITIVE IDENTIFICATION REGIMES IN THE MUSLIM WORLD

Beginning in December 2010, Northern Africa and the Middle East experienced widespread demonstrations and protests, an era that quickly became known as the Arab Spring. Uprisings resulted in revolutions with varied initial outcomes—some successfully overthrew the existing governments, some resulted in political change in the existing government, and some failed to cause any meaningful change. The secular regimes of Zine Al Abidine Ben Ali in Tunisia, Hosni Mubarak in Egypt, Muamar Gaddafi in Libya, and Ali Abdullah Saleh in Yemen were all removed from power. These regimes tried to channel and control religion, but they were replaced by even more religious regimes, some of which tried to increase the degree of cooperation or even identification between religion and the state. In the words of a US-based religious-freedom watchdog, the United States Commission on International Religious Freedom, "In times of transition, the situation of religious minorities in these societies comes to the forefront . . . . Some members of society who have long been oppressed seek greater freedom and respect for their rights while others fear change. Those differing aspirations can exacerbate existing tension."[7]

The effects of the Arab Spring uprisings in Egypt illustrate this cycle. Initially, with the election of Mohamed Morsi from the Muslim Brotherhood, the country appeared to shift towards a religious regime.[8] Concerns regarding the vulnerability of religious minorities increased.[9] In response to these concerns, the government did little either to prevent or punish violence against Christians, particularly Coptic Christians. Fresh protests culminated in a military coup in July 2013.

Morsi was deposed, and an interim government supported by Egyptian security forces was established. The new government instituted a crackdown on the Muslim Brotherhood, culminating in legal prohibitions against the party. The constitution supported by the new government declares Islam the state religion and recognizes the influence of Shari'a law on the legislative process, but it also guarantees religious liberty for religious minorities. However, since the initial Arab Spring uprisings the government has prosecuted a number of individuals for blasphemy.

The Tunisian constitution attempts to strike a similar balance between maintaining an Islamic state and guaranteeing religious freedom. Though Islam is the declared state religion, the constitution names the state "the guardian of

7. Annual Report of the United States Commission on International Religious Freedom (USCIRF), March 2012.

8. Amir K. Bagherpour, Religion and the Evolution of Democracy: A Revised Selectorate Model for the Arab Spring, *CGU Theses & Dissertations*, Paper 53 (2012). http://scholarship.claremont. edu/cgu_etd/53.

9. USCIRF Report 2012, *supra* note 7.

religion" and broadly guarantees religious freedom and free exercise rights. There is no provision adopting Shari'a. However, the same article expresses the state's obligation to the "protection of the sacred, and the prohibition of all violations thereof." This language has been used to justify blasphemy cases, similar to those in Egypt.[10]

Other Islamic countries have, without qualifications like those used by Egypt and Tunisia, adopted Shari'a as the source of legislation. The Libyan constitution, ratified in February 2011, declared Shari'a to be the primary source of legislation. In May 2014, Brunei began implementing a Shari'a-based penal code, the first East Asian nation to do so.

In the summer of 2014, the violent Sunni fundamentalist group variously known as the Islamic State of Iraq and Greater Syria/al-Sham (ISIS), the Islamic State of Iraq and the Levant (ISIL), or by the Arabic acronym "Daesh," led an insurgency in northern Iraq and Syria. Capitalizing on the Syrian civil war and tensions between Iraqi Sunnis and the Shia-backed government, the group quickly captured a broad region stretching from Aleppo, Syria to the outskirts of Baghdad, Iraq. As part of its fundamentalist ideology, the group imposed strict Shari'a law in the occupied regions. Then, in June 2014, the group announced the formation of the "Islamic State," or "Caliphate," with its leader Abu Bakr al-Baghdadi, "the Caliph," and "leader for Muslims everywhere." Even among other extremist groups, this group's creation of the Caliphate was seen as an extreme and potentially alienating act. By mid 2017, only three years since it was announced, most ISIS strongholds had been destroyed or retaken, its forces had been scattered, in-fighting was reported, and al-Baghdadi was rumored to be dead.

IV. NON-IDENTIFICATION: THE TENSION BETWEEN ACCOMMODATION AND SEPARATION, AND BETWEEN COOPERATING AND SECULARISM

A. THE ACCOMMODATION/SEPARATION DEBATE IN THE UNITED STATES

The United States' system of government has been characterized from the beginning of its constitutional history by freedom of religion and institutional separation of state and religious institutions, at least on the national level. The situation in the United States is somewhat distinctive in that there are two constitutional provisions relating to religion: the Establishment Clause, which states, "Congress shall make no law respecting an establishment of religion," and the Free Exercise Clause, which states that Congress shall make no law "prohibiting the free exercise" of religion. In contrast, international norms protecting freedom of religion or belief lack a requirement of institutional separation of religion and state, and provide only "free exercise"–type protections,

10. Katrina Lantos Swett and M. Zuhdi Jasser, Blasphemy bans threaten "Arab Spring," religious freedom, *The Hill*, 16 May 2012; Tunisia: Prison, Fines for Offending "Sacred Values," *Human Rights Watch*, 3 August 2012; Robert C. Blitt, Tunisia: Springtime for Defamation of Religion, *Jurist–Forum*, 13 August 2012.

presumably because many of the world's legal systems do not insist on institutional separation of church and state.

But the United States' system is not as distinctive as it initially might seem. First, a number of other countries, including Australia, Japan, and the Philippines, have provisions modeled after the Establishment Clause. Second, many jurisdictions have provisions that emphasize the secular character of the state. This is common in both the Francophone and formerly Communist parts of the world, even where the prevailing religion is Islam. Third, virtually all modern constitutions protect equality rights. These may, of course, be interpreted in very different ways, but one of the common functional effects is to limit discrimination against individuals and groups on the basis of religion, and this will often operate to reduce the privileging of favored or established religious groups. Fourth, religious freedom rights are generally understood to include rights of religious groups to autonomy in their own affairs. This necessarily implies some measure of institutional separation and non-entanglement, which amounts functionally to non-establishment. Finally, many countries have constitutional provisions calling for separation of religious and state institutions with differing degrees of harshness, from relatively benign provisions to those evincing hostility or persecution, such as those of many of the formerly Communist regimes.

To a significant extent, the history of church-state relations in the United States has been dominated by an ongoing dialectic between two streams of thought about what the Establishment Clause means. On one side is a separationist stream, symbolized by Thomas Jefferson's "wall of separation between Church & State." On the other side is an accommodationist stream, illustrated by such texts as early presidential proclamations regarding Thanksgiving holidays, a generally friendly posture toward religion, and the willingness to grant exemptions to account for religious difference.

While the Establishment Clause dates back to the adoption of the Bill of Rights in 1791, virtually all of the case law under the Establishment Clause has been decided since 1947, when the Supreme Court handed down *Everson v. Board of Education*, 330 U.S. 1 (1947), and held for the first time that the federal Establishment Clause was applicable to the states. The tension between the separationist and accommodationist paradigms that has occupied much of the subsequent Establishment Clause litigation is prefigured in *Everson*. The question in the case was whether a school board could subsidize school bus transportation for children attending private religious schools.

This case provides an important illustration of the complicated nature of the separation versus accommodation debate. The first half of Justice Black's majority opinion sounds very separationist, but somewhere in the middle of the opinion he changes direction, and the second half is accommodationist. As you read the opinion, pay careful attention to the rhetoric that Justice Black uses in each part of the decision. Remarkably, Black's opinion contains the seeds of nearly all the arguments that would be made in the subsequent 50-year struggle over separationist and accommodationist readings of the Establishment Clause.

EVERSON V. BOARD OF EDUCATION

Supreme Court of the United States, 330 U.S. 1 (1947)

Mr. Justice BLACK delivered the opinion of the Court.

A New Jersey statute authorizes its local school districts to make rules and contracts for the transportation of children to and from schools. The appellee, a township board of education, acting pursuant to this statute authorized reimbursement to parents of money expended by them for the bus transportation of their children on regular busses operated by the public transportation system. Part of this money was for the payment of transportation of some children in the community to Catholic parochial schools. These church schools give their students, in addition to secular education, regular religious instruction conforming to the religious tenets and modes of worship of the Catholic Faith. . . .

The appellant contends that the statute and the resolution forced inhabitants to pay taxes to help support and maintain schools which are dedicated to, and which regularly teach, the Catholic Faith. This is alleged to be a use of State power to support church schools contrary to the prohibition of the First Amendment which the Fourteenth Amendment made applicable to the states.

The New Jersey statute is challenged as a "law respecting an establishment of religion." The First Amendment, as made applicable to the states by the Fourteenth Amendment, commands that a state "shall make no law respecting an establishment of religion, or prohibiting the free exercise thereof." These words of the First Amendment reflected in the minds of early Americans a vivid mental picture of conditions and practices which they fervently wished to stamp out in order to preserve liberty for themselves and for their posterity. Whether this New Jersey law is one respecting the "establishment of religion" requires an understanding of the meaning of that language, particularly with respect to the imposition of taxes. . . . Once again, therefore, it is not inappropriate briefly to review the background and environment of the period in which that constitutional language was fashioned and adopted.

A large proportion of the early settlers of this country came here from Europe to escape the bondage of laws which compelled them to support and attend government favored churches. The centuries immediately before and contemporaneous with the colonization of America had been filled with turmoil, civil strife, and persecutions, generated in large part by established sects determined to maintain their absolute political and religious supremacy. With the power of government supporting them, at various times and places, Catholics had persecuted Protestants, Protestants had persecuted Catholics, Protestant sects had persecuted other Protestant sects, Catholics of one shade of belief had persecuted Catholics of another shade of belief, and all of these had from time to time persecuted Jews. In efforts to force loyalty to whatever religious group happened to be on top and in league with the government of a particular time and place, men and women had been fined, cast in jail, cruelly tortured, and killed. Among the offenses for which these punishments had been inflicted were such things as speaking disrespectfully of the views of ministers of government-established churches, nonattendance at those churches, expressions of non-belief in their doctrines, and failure to pay taxes and tithes to support them.

These practices of the old world were transplanted to and began to thrive in the soil of the new America. The very charters granted by the English Crown . . . authorized individuals and companies to erect religious establishments which all, whether believers or non-believers, would be required to support and attend. An exercise of this authority was accompanied by a repetition of many of the old world practices and persecutions. . . .

These practices became so commonplace as to shock the freedom-loving colonials into a feeling of abhorrence. The imposition of taxes to pay ministers' salaries and to build and maintain churches and church property aroused their indignation. It was these feelings which found expression in the First Amendment. . . . Virginia, where the established church had achieved a dominant influence in political affairs and where many excesses attracted wide public attention, provided a great stimulus and able leadership for the moment. The people there, as elsewhere, reached the conviction that individual religious liberty could be achieved best under a government which was stripped of all power to tax, to support, or otherwise to assist any or all religions, or to interfere with the beliefs of any religious individual or group.

The movement toward this end reached its dramatic climax in Virginia in 1785-86 when the Virginia legislative body was about to renew Virginia's tax levy for the support of the established church. Thomas Jefferson and James Madison led the fight against this tax. Madison wrote his great Memorial and Remonstrance against the law. In it, he eloquently argued that a true religion did not need the support of law; that no person, either believer or non-believer, should be taxed to support a religious institution of any kind; that the best interest of a society required that the minds of men always be wholly free; and that cruel persecutions were the inevitable result of government-established religions. Madison's Remonstrance received strong support throughout Virginia, and the Assembly postponed consideration of the proposed tax measure until its next session. When the proposal came up for consideration at that session, it not only died in committee, but the Assembly enacted the famous "Virginia Bill for Religious Liberty" originally written by Thomas Jefferson.

The preamble to that Bill stated among other things that ". . . to compel a man to furnish contributions of money for the propagation of opinions which he disbelieves, is sinful and tyrannical; that even the forcing him to support this or that teacher of his own religious persuasion, is depriving him of the comfortable liberty of giving his contributions to the particular pastor, whose morals he would make his pattern."

And the statute itself enacted

> That no man shall be compelled to frequent or support any religious worship, place, or ministry whatsoever, nor shall be enforced, restrained, molested, or burthened, in his body or goods, nor shall otherwise suffer on account of his religious opinions or belief. . . .

This Court has previously recognized that the provisions of the First Amendment, in the drafting and adoption of which Madison and Jefferson played such leading roles, had the same objective and were intended to provide the same protection against governmental intrusion on religious liberty as the Virginia statute. Prior to the adoption of the Fourteenth Amendment, the First Amendment did not apply as a restraint against the states. Most of them did soon provide similar constitutional protections for religious liberty. But some states persisted for about half a century in imposing restraints upon the free exercise of religion and in discriminating against particular religious groups. . . . [Nonetheless, there] is every reason to give . . . broad interpretation to the "establishment of religion" clause.

The "establishment of religion" clause of the First Amendment means at least this: Neither a state nor the Federal Government can set up a church. Neither can pass laws which aid one religion, aid all religions, or prefer one religion over another. Neither can force nor influence a person to go to or to remain away from church against his will or force him to profess a belief or disbelief in any religion. No person can be punished for entertaining or professing religious beliefs or disbeliefs, for church attendance or non-attendance. No tax in any amount, large or small, can be levied to support any religious activities or institutions, whatever they may be called, or whatever from they may adopt to teach or practice religion. Neither a state nor the Federal Government can, openly or secretly, participate in the affairs of any religious organizations or groups and vice versa. In the words of Jefferson, the clause against establishment of religion by law was intended to erect "a wall of separation between Church and State."

We must consider the New Jersey statute in accordance with the foregoing limitations imposed by the First Amendment. But we must not strike that state statute down if it is within the state's constitutional power even though it approaches the verge of that power. New Jersey cannot consistently with the "establishment of religion" clause of the First Amendment contribute tax-raised funds to the support of an institution which teaches the tenets and faith of any church. On the other hand, other language of the amendment commands that New Jersey cannot hamper its citizens in the free exercise of their own religion. Consequently, it cannot exclude individual [members of any faith], because of their faith, or lack of it, from receiving the benefits of public welfare legislation. While we do not mean to intimate that a state could not provide transportation only to children attending public schools, we must be careful, in protecting the citizens of New Jersey against state-established churches, to be sure that we do not inadvertently prohibit New Jersey from extending its general State law benefits to all its citizens without regard to their religious belief.

Measured by these standards, we cannot say that the First Amendment prohibits New Jersey from spending tax-raised funds to pay the bus fares of parochial school pupils as a part of a general program under which it pays the fares of pupils attending public and other schools. It is undoubtedly true that children are helped to get to church schools. There is even a possibility that some of the children might not be sent to the church schools if the parents were compelled to pay their children's bus fares out of their own pockets when transportation to a public school would have been paid for by the State. . . . Similarly, parents might be reluctant to permit their children to attend schools which the state had cut off from such general government services as ordinary police and fire protection, connections for sewage disposal, public highways and sidewalks. Of course, cutting off church schools from these services, so separate and so indisputably marked off from the religious function, would make it far more difficult for the schools to operate. But such is obviously not the purpose of the First Amendment. That Amendment requires the state to be a neutral in its relations with groups of religious believers and non-believers; it does not require the state to be their adversary. State power is no more to be used so as to handicap religions, than it is to favor them.

This Court has said that parents may, in the discharge of their duty under state compulsory education laws, send their children to a religious rather than a public school if the school meets the secular educational requirements which the state has power to impose. It appears that these parochial schools meet New Jersey's requirements. The State contributes no money to the schools. It does not support them. Its legislation, as applied, does no more than provide a general program to help parents get their children, regardless of their religion, safely and expeditiously to and from accredited schools.

The First Amendment has erected a wall between church and state. That wall must be kept high and impregnable. We could not approve the slightest breach. New Jersey has not breached it here.

Affirmed.

[Separate dissent by Justice JACKSON has been omitted.]

Mr. Justice RUTLEDGE, with whom Mr. Justice FRANKFURTER, Mr. Justice JACKSON and Mr. Justice BURTON agree, dissenting.

I cannot believe that [Jefferson] . . . could have joined in this decision. Neither so high nor so impregnable today as yesterday is the wall raised between church and state by Virginia's great statute of religious freedom and the First Amendment, now made applicable to all the states by the Fourteenth. . . .

This case forces us to determine squarely for the first time what was "an establishment of religion" in the First Amendment's conception; and by that measure to decide whether New Jersey's action violates its command.

Not simply an established church, but any law respecting an establishment of religion is forbidden. The Amendment was broadly but not loosely phrased. The Amendment's purpose was not to strike merely at the official establishment of a single sect, creed or religion, outlawing only a formal relation such as had prevailed in England and some of the colonies. Necessarily it was to uproot all such relationships. But the object was broader than separating church and state in this narrow sense. It was to create a complete and permanent separation of the spheres of religious activity and civil authority by comprehensively forbidding every form of public aid or support for religion. In proof the Amendment's wording and history unite with this Court's consistent utterances whenever attention has been fixed directly upon the question. . . .

"Religion" appears only once in the Amendment. But the word governs two prohibitions and governs them alike. It does not have two meanings, one narrow to forbid "an establishment" and another, much broader, for securing "the free exercise thereof." "Thereof" brings down "religion" with its entire and exact content, no more and no less, from the first into the second guaranty, so that Congress and now the states are as broadly restricted concerning the one as they are regarding the other.

The prohibition broadly forbids state support, financial or other, of religion in any guise, form or degree. It outlaws all use of public funds for religious purposes.

. . .

The climactic period of the Virginia struggle covers the decade 1776-1786, from adoption of the Declaration of Rights to enactment of the Statute for Religious Freedom. The climax came in the legislative struggle of 1784-1785 over the Assessment Bill. This was nothing more nor less than a taxing measure for the support of religion, designed to revive the payment of tithes suspended since 1777. So long as it singled out a particular sect for preference it incurred the active and general hostility of dissentient groups. It was broadened to include them, with the result that some subsided temporarily in their opposition. As altered, the bill gave to each taxpayer the privilege of designating which church should receive his share of the tax. In default of designation the legislature applied it to pious uses. But what is of the utmost significance here, in its final form the bill left the taxpayer the option of giving his tax to education.

Madison was unyielding at all times, opposing with all his vigor the general and nondiscriminatory as he had the earlier particular and discriminatory assessments proposed.

As [Madison's historic Memorial and] Remonstrance discloses throughout, Madison opposed every form and degree of official relation between religion and civil authority. For him religion was a wholly private matter beyond the scope of civil power either to restrain or to support. Denial or abridgment of religious freedom was a violation of rights both of conscience and of natural equality. State aid was no less obnoxious or destructive to freedom and to religion itself than other forms of state interference. "Establishment" and "free exercise" were correlative and coextensive ideas, representing only different facets of the single great and fundamental freedom. In no phase was he more unrelentingly absolute than in opposing state support or aid by taxation.

In view of this history no further proof is needed that the Amendment forbids any appropriation, large or small, from public funds to aid or support any and all religious exercises. . . .

This is not therefore just a little case over bus fares. In paraphrase of Madison, distant as it may be in its present form from a complete establishment of religion, it differs from it only in degree; and is the first step in that direction.

The problem then cannot be cast in terms of legal discrimination or its absence. This would be true, even though the state in giving aid should treat all religious instruction alike. Thus, if the present statute and its application were shown to apply equally to all religious schools of whatever faith, yet in the light of our tradition it could not stand. . . . The person who embraces no creed also would be forced to pay for teaching what he does not believe. Again, it was the furnishing of "contributions of money for the propagation of opinions which he disbelieves" that the fathers outlawed. That consequence and effect are not removed by multiplying to all-inclusiveness the sects for which support is exacted. The Constitution requires, not comprehensive identification of state with religion, but complete separation. . . .

The matter is not one of quantity, to be measured by the amount of money expended. Now as in Madison's day it is one of principle, to keep separate the separate spheres as the First Amendment drew them; to prevent the first experiment upon our liberties; and to keep the question from becoming entangled in corrosive precedents. We should not be less strict to keep strong and untarnished the one side of the shield of religious freedom than we have been of the other.

The judgment should be reversed.

COMMENTS AND QUESTIONS

1. Nearly every argument found in Establishment Clause jurisprudence over the subsequent half century is prefigured in the majority and dissenting opinions in *Everson v. Board of Education*. Indeed, many of these opposing arguments are present in Justice Black's majority opinion, which seems to be at war with itself. Can you identify the key strands of the separationist interpretation of the Establishment Clause present in the case? What are the key strands of the accommodationist interpretation of the Establishment Clause that are evident?
2. *Everson* reflects the debate between the fundamental ideas of the American creed: liberty and equality. One fascinating aspect of Justice Black's majority opinion in *Everson* is that the first half focuses on the need for liberty to choose religious beliefs without government interference, coercion, or support and consequently emphasizes separationist arguments (e.g., arguments about early settlers who came to escape the bondage of religious laws, the Memorial and Remonstrance against taxes levied for religious purposes, the meaning of the First Amendment, the Wall of Separation). The second half of the opinion reflects the need for equality and makes accommodationist arguments, which involve government neutrality toward religious groups through the distribution of benefits to all individuals regardless of religion. Can you identify the point of the shift between the concern for liberty (with its separationist implications) and the concern for equality (with its accommodationist implications)? Can you imagine an accommodationist position that fosters liberty more than equality?

B. THE AUSTRALIAN APPROACH

With language similar to that of the United States Constitution, Section 116 of the Australian Constitution provides that "[t]he Commonwealth shall not make any law for establishing any religion, or for imposing any religious observance, or for prohibiting the free exercise of any religion, and no religious test shall be required as a qualification for any office or public trust under the Commonwealth." Unlike the force and effect of the religion clauses in the United States, however, these prohibitions have been interpreted narrowly and do not extend to state legislative powers in Australia. Justice Keith Mason noted that Section 116 "does not preclude government aid to religious institutions and it does not prevent religious displays in the public arena" and that although Australia's "constitutionally laid back polity is free to debate prayers in Parliament and Christmas trees in public schools and public places . . . the debate does not take place in the High Court of Australia."

Australian Parliaments have also stayed away from legislating in matters of religion even though they have the power to do so. Justice Mason remarked, "The practical consequence of keeping religious issues out of our Parliaments and

Courts has been that, unlike our colleagues in the United States, judges in this country have not been embroiled in the often evanescent culture wars of the day."[11]

A primary example of this philosophy in Australian jurisprudence concerning the religion clauses of Section 116 can be seen the 1981 case *Black v. Commonwealth*, the High Court's first and only Establishment Clause decision. The case concerned a challenge to federal legislation that allowed for state aid to private schools, which were largely religious and predominantly Catholic. The Court interpreted the Establishment Clause as controlling only the purposes of government legislation, not necessarily the effects. Under this premise, the Court's majority held that the law providing for state aid did not violate Section 116 and that only a law deliberately intending to establish a national church would be prohibited by that section. This narrow interpretation of the Establishment Clause has also been adopted in application of the other religion clauses in the Australia Constitution.

C. VARIETIES OF SEPARATION: BENIGN NEUTRALITY OR HOSTILITY TOWARD RELIGION

The term "separationist" can be used to cover a diverse range of regimes. This section first examines a series of positions the US Supreme Court has taken that articulate divergent tests for assessing religion-state separation required by the First Amendment's Establishment Clause jurisprudence. The following section turns to varying models of the idea of a secular or lay state. What becomes evident is that a secular state may be respectful and supportive of religion and belief or may be oppressive and detrimental. In either case, the defining characteristic of a separationist state often seems to be a sequestration of the "public sphere" from the "private sphere," with religion compartmentalized in the private realm, where it may not intrude in public life and state affairs. But much depends on how the two spheres are conceptualized. Is it necessarily the case that the line separating religion and state always coincides with the public/private divide? Perhaps there is a conception of separation of religion and state in which both can find legitimate but independent public spheres.

1. The Three-Prong Test of *Lemon v. Kurtzman*

The 1971 US Supreme Court case *Lemon v. Kurtzman*, 403 U.S. 602, is remembered for its three-prong test, which has guided much subsequent Establishment Clause analysis. Over time, the *Lemon* test became not only the primary mechanism used by the Court in establishment cases, but one of the most controversial doctrines in the history of constitutional adjudication. Writing in 1985 Justice Powell defended the test: "In a word, it has been the law. Respect for stare decisis should require us to follow *Lemon*." [12] In dissent in the same case Justice Rehnquist asserted that the *Lemon* test "has produced only consistent unpredictability" and "has simply not provided adequate standards for deciding

---

11. Justice Keith Mason, Law and Religion in Australia, National Forum on Australia's Christian Heritage, (Speech delivered at National Forum on Australia's Christian Heritage, Canberra, 7 August 2006).

12. *Wallace v. Jaffree*, 472 U.S. 38, 63 (1985) (Powell, J., concurrring).

Establishment Clause cases. [Even worse it] has caused this Court to fracture into unworkable plurality opinions."[13] In 1993 Justice Scalia famously referred to the *Lemon* test as a "ghoul in a late-night horror movie that repeatedly sits up in its grave and shuffles abroad, after being repeatedly killed and buried. . . . Over the years . . . no fewer than five of the currently sitting Justices have, in their own opinions, personally driven pencils through the creature's heart . . . , and a sixth has joined an opinion doing so."[14] For all the criticism it has received, the *Lemon* test has never been formally repudiated by the Court.

LEMON V. KURTZMAN

Supreme Court of the United States, 403 U.S. 602 (1971)

[The Court's Syllabus:] Rhode Island's 1969 Salary Supplement Act provides for a 15% salary supplement to be paid to teachers in nonpublic schools at which the average per-pupil expenditure on secular education is below the average in public schools. Eligible teachers must teach only courses offered in the public schools, using only materials used in the public schools, and must agree not to teach courses in religion. . . . Pennsylvania's Nonpublic Elementary and Secondary Education Act ... authorizes the state Superintendent of Public Instruction to "purchase" certain "secular educational services" from nonpublic schools, directly reimbursing those schools solely for teachers' salaries, textbooks, and instructional materials. Reimbursement is restricted to courses in specific secular subjects, the textbooks and materials must be approved by the Superintendent, and no payment is to be made for any course containing "any subject matter expressing religious teaching, or the morals or forms of worship of any sect." Contracts were made with schools that have more than 20% of all the students in the State, most of which were affiliated with the Roman Catholic Church.

Mr. CHIEF JUSTICE BURGER delivered the opinion of the Court.

These two appeals raise questions as to [similar] Pennsylvania and Rhode Island statutes providing state aid to church-related elementary and secondary schools. . . . We hold that both statutes are unconstitutional. . . .

The language of the Religion Clauses of the First Amendment is at best opaque, particularly when compared with other portions of the Amendment. Its authors did not simply prohibit the establishment of a state church or a state religion, an area history shows they regarded as very important and fraught with great dangers. Instead they commanded that there should be "no law *respecting* an establishment of religion." A given law might not *establish* a state religion but nevertheless be one "respecting" that end in the sense of being a step that could lead to such establishment and hence offend the First Amendment.

Every analysis in this area must begin with consideration of the cumulative criteria developed by the Court over many years. Three such tests may be gleaned from our cases. First, the statute must have a secular legislative purpose; second, its principal or primary effect must be one that neither advances nor inhibits religion . . . ; finally, the statute must not foster "an excessive government entanglement with religion." . . .

13. *Id.* at 110, 112 (Rehnquist, J., dissenting).

14. *Lamb's Chapel v. Center Moriches Union Free School Dist.*, 508 U.S. 384, 398 (1993) (Scalia, J., dissenting).

[The Court found no basis for a conclusion that the legislative intent was to advance religion, and also found it unnecessary to address the second of the three tests, finding that the excessive entanglement test produced the necessary holding.]

. . . Our prior holdings do not call for total separation between church and state; total separation is not possible in an absolute sense. Some relationship between government and religious organizations is inevitable. In order to determine whether the government entanglement with religion is excessive, we must examine the character and purposes of the institutions that are benefited, the nature of the aid that the State provides, and the resulting relationship between the government and the religious authority. . . . Here we find that both statutes foster an impermissible degree of entanglement.

The District Court made extensive findings on the grave potential for excessive entanglement that inheres in the religious character and purpose of the Roman Catholic elementary schools of Rhode Island, to date the sole beneficiaries of the Rhode Island Salary Supplement Act.

The church schools involved in the program are located close to parish churches. This understandably permits convenient access for religious exercises since instruction in faith and morals is part of the total educational process. The school buildings contain identifying religious symbols such as crosses on the exterior and crucifixes, and religious paintings and statues either in the classrooms or hallways. Although only approximately 30 minutes a day are devoted to direct religious instruction, there are religiously oriented extracurricular activities. Approximately two-thirds of the teachers in these schools are nuns of various religious orders. Their dedicated efforts provide an atmosphere in which religious instruction and religious vocations are natural and proper parts of life in such schools. Indeed, as the District Court found, the role of teaching nuns in enhancing the religious atmosphere has led the parochial school authorities to attempt to maintain a one-to-one ratio between nuns and lay teachers in all schools rather than to permit some to be staffed almost entirely by lay teachers.

On the basis of these findings the District Court concluded that . . . parochial schools involve substantial religious activity and purpose. The substantial religious character of these church-related schools gives rise to entangling church-state relationships of the kind the Religion Clauses sought to avoid. [T]he considerable religious activities of these schools led the legislature to provide for careful governmental controls and surveillance by state authorities in order to ensure that state aid supports only secular education.

The dangers and corresponding entanglements are enhanced by the particular form of aid that the Rhode Island Act provides. . . . We cannot ignore the danger that a teacher under religious control and discipline poses to the separation of the religious from the purely secular aspects of pre-college education. In our view the record shows these dangers are present to a substantial degree. Religious authority necessarily pervades the school system. . . .

We need not and do not assume that teachers in parochial schools will be guilty of bad faith or any conscious design to evade the limitations imposed by the statute and the First Amendment. We simply recognize that a dedicated religious person, teaching in a school affiliated with his or her faith and operated to inculcate its tenets, will inevitably experience great difficulty in remaining religiously neutral.

The Rhode Island Legislature has not, and could not, provide state aid on the basis of a mere assumption that secular teachers under religious discipline can avoid conflicts. The State must be certain, given the Religion Clauses, that subsidized teachers do not inculcate religion. . . . A comprehensive, discriminating, and continuing state surveillance will inevitably be required to ensure that these restrictions are obeyed and the First Amendment otherwise respected. Unlike a book, a teacher cannot be inspected once so as to determine the extent and intent of his or her personal beliefs and subjective acceptance of the limitations imposed by the First Amendment. These prophylactic contacts will involve excessive and enduring entanglement between state and church. . . .

A certain momentum develops in constitutional theory and it can be a "downhill thrust" easily set in motion but difficult to retard or stop. Development by momentum is not invariably bad; indeed, it is the way the common law has grown, but it is a force to be recognized and reckoned with. The dangers are increased by the difficulty of perceiving in advance exactly where the "verge" of the precipice lies. As well as constituting an independent evil against which the Religion Clauses were intended to protect, involvement or entanglement between government and religion serves as a warning signal.

Finally, nothing we have said can be construed to disparage the role of church-related elementary and secondary schools in our national life. The merit and benefits of these schools, however, are not the issue before us in these cases. The sole question is whether state aid to these schools can be squared with the dictates of the Religion Clauses. Under our system the choice has been made that government is to be entirely excluded from the area of religious instruction and churches excluded from the affairs of government. The Constitution decrees that religion must be a private matter for the individual, the family, and the institutions of private choice, and that while some involvement and entanglement are inevitable, lines must be drawn. . . .

COMMENTS AND QUESTIONS

1. Does the three-prong *Lemon* test seem likely to generate separationist or accommodationist outcomes in Establishment Clause cases? Which elements of the test are likely to be most significant in deciding cases?
2. Is there any irony in Justice Berger's "downhill thrust" argument? Within 20 years, in *Employment Div. v. Smith*, 494 U.S. 872 (1990), the Supreme Court abrogated the level of scrutiny given to laws allegedly infringing on the Free Exercise Clause. Could the Court's decision in *Lemon* be seen as the impetus of a "downhill thrust" leading to a more separationist approach to religion?

2. History and Tradition

In *Town of Greece v. Galloway*, a 2014 case about the constitutionality of a town's permitting volunteer chaplains to open its monthly town council meetings with prayer, the Court did not mention the *Lemon* test, in spite of the apparent Establishment Clause implications. The Court instead invoked the 1993 case *Marsh v. Chambers*, and focused on historical practice in assessing whether or not the practice violated the Establishment Clause.

TOWN OF GREECE V. GALLOWAY

Supreme Court of the United States, 134 S.Ct. 1811 (2014)

Justice KENNEDY delivered the opinion of the Court, except as to Part II-B[*]

The Court must decide whether the town of Greece, New York, imposes an impermissible establishment of religion by opening its monthly board meetings with a prayer. It must be concluded, consistent with the Court's opinion in *Marsh v. Chambers*, 463 U.S. 783 (1983), that no violation of the Constitution has been shown.

Greece, a town with a population of 94,000, is in upstate New York. For some years, it began its monthly town board meetings with a moment of silence. In 1999, the newly elected town supervisor, John Auberger, decided to replicate the prayer practice he had found meaningful while serving in the county legislature. Following the roll call and recitation of the Pledge of Allegiance, Auberger would invite a local clergyman to the front of the room to deliver an invocation. After the prayer, Auberger would thank the minister for serving as the board's "chaplain for the month" and present him with a commemorative plaque. The prayer was intended to place town board members in a solemn and deliberative frame of mind, invoke divine guidance in town affairs, and follow a tradition practiced by Congress and dozens of state legislatures.

The town followed an informal method for selecting prayer givers, all of whom were unpaid volunteers. A town employee would call the congregations listed in a local directory until she found a minister available for that month's meeting. The town eventually compiled a list of willing "board chaplains" who had accepted invitations and agreed to return in the future. The town at no point excluded or denied an opportunity to a would-be prayer giver. Its leaders maintained that a minister or layperson of any persuasion, including an atheist, could give the invocation. But nearly all of the congregations in town were Christian; and from 1999 to 2007, all of the participating ministers were too.

Greece neither reviewed the prayers in advance of the meetings nor provided guidance as to their tone or content, in the belief that exercising any degree of control over the prayers would infringe both the free exercise and speech rights of the ministers. The town instead left the guest clergy free to compose their own devotions. The resulting prayers often sounded both civic and religious themes. Typical were invocations that asked the divinity to abide at the meeting and bestow blessings on the community . . . .

Some of the ministers spoke in a distinctly Christian idiom; and a minority invoked religious holidays, scripture, or doctrine . . . .

Respondents Susan Galloway and Linda Stephens attended town board meetings to speak about issues of local concern, and they objected that the prayers violated their religious or philosophical views. . . .

Galloway and Stephens brought suit [alleging] that the town violated the First Amendment's Establishment Clause by preferring Christians over other prayer givers and by sponsoring sectarian prayers, such as those given "in Jesus' name", [and sought] an injunction that would limit the town to "inclusive and ecumenical" prayers that referred only to a "generic God" and would not associate the government with any one faith or belief.

The District Court on summary judgment upheld the prayer practice as consistent with the First Amendment. It found no impermissible preference for Christianity, noting that the town had opened the prayer program to all creeds and excluded none. Although most of the prayer givers were Christian, this fact reflected only the predominantly Christian identity of the town's congregations, rather than an official policy or practice of discriminating against minority faiths. . . .

The District Court also rejected the theory that legislative prayer must be nonsectarian. ...With respect to the prayer in Greece, the District Court concluded that references to Jesus, and the occasional request that the audience stand for the prayer, did not amount to impermissible proselytizing. It located in *Marsh* no additional requirement that the prayers be purged of sectarian content. In this regard the court quoted recent invocations offered in the U.S. House of Representatives "in the name of our Lord Jesus Christ," and situated prayer in this context as part a long tradition. . . .

The Court of Appeals for the Second Circuit reversed. It held that some aspects of the prayer program, viewed in their totality by a reasonable observer, conveyed the message that Greece was endorsing Christianity. The town's failure to promote the prayer opportunity to the public, or to invite ministers from congregations outside the town limits, all but "ensured a Christian viewpoint." Although the court found no inherent problem in the sectarian content of the prayers, it concluded that the "steady drumbeat" of Christian prayer, unbroken by invocations from other faith traditions, tended to affiliate the town with Christianity. Finally, the court found it relevant that guest clergy sometimes spoke on behalf of all present at the meeting, as by saying "let us pray," or by asking audience members to stand and bow their heads: "The invitation . . . to participate in the prayer . . . placed audience members who are nonreligious or adherents of non-Christian religion in the awkward position of either participating in prayers invoking beliefs they did not share or appearing to show disrespect for the invocation." That board members bowed their heads or made the sign of the cross further conveyed the message that the town endorsed Christianity. The Court of Appeals emphasized that it was the "interaction of the facts present in this case," rather than any single element, that rendered the prayer unconstitutional. . . .

In *Marsh v. Chambers*, the Court found no First Amendment violation in the Nebraska Legislature's practice of opening its sessions with a prayer delivered by a chaplain paid from state funds. The decision concluded that legislative prayer, while religious in nature, has long been understood as compatible with the Establishment Clause. As practiced by Congress since the framing of the Constitution, legislative prayer lends gravity to public business, reminds lawmakers to transcend petty differences in pursuit of a higher purpose, and expresses a common aspiration to a just and peaceful society. ... The Court has considered this symbolic expression to be a "tolerable acknowledgement of beliefs widely held," rather than a first, treacherous step towards establishment of a state church.

Marsh is sometimes described as "carving out an exception" to the Court's Establishment Clause jurisprudence, because it sustained legislative prayer without subjecting the practice to "any of the formal `tests' that have traditionally structured" this inquiry. [citation omitted]. The Court in *Marsh* found those tests unnecessary because history supported the conclusion that legislative invocations are compatible with the Establishment Clause. The First Congress made it an early item of business to appoint and pay official chaplains, and both the House and Senate have maintained the office virtually uninterrupted since that time. . . .

An insistence on nonsectarian or ecumenical prayer as a single, fixed standard is not consistent with the tradition of legislative prayer outlined in the Court's cases. . . .

To hold that invocations must be nonsectarian would force the legislatures that sponsor prayers and the courts that are asked to decide these cases to act as supervisors and censors of religious speech, a rule that would involve government in religious matters to a far greater degree than is the case under the town's current practice of neither editing or approving prayers in advance nor criticizing their content after the fact. . . . Government may not mandate a civic religion that stifles any but the most generic reference to the sacred any more than it may prescribe a religious orthodoxy. . . .

Because it is unlikely that prayer will be inclusive beyond dispute, it would be unwise to adopt what respondents think is the next-best option: permitting those religious words, and only those words, that are acceptable to the majority, even if they will exclude some. *Torcaso v. Watkins*, 367 U.S. 488 (1961). The First Amendment is not a majority rule, and government may not seek to define permissible categories of religious speech. Once it invites prayer into the public sphere, government must permit a prayer giver to address his or her own God or gods as conscience dictates, unfettered by what an administrator or judge considers to be nonsectarian. . . .

This case can be distinguished from the conclusions and holding of *Lee v. Weisman*, 505 U.S. 577 (1992). There the Court found that, in the context of a graduation where school authorities maintained close supervision over the conduct of the students and the substance of the ceremony, a religious invocation was coercive as to an objecting student. Four Justices dissented in Lee, but the circumstances the Court confronted there are not present in this case and do not control its outcome. Nothing in the record suggests that members of the public are dissuaded from leaving the meeting room during the prayer, arriving late, or even, as happened here, making a later protest. . . .

Ceremonial prayer is but a recognition that, since this Nation was founded and until the present day, many Americans deem that their own existence must be understood by precepts far beyond the authority of government to alter or define and that willing participation in civic affairs can be consistent with a brief acknowledgment of their belief in a higher power, always with due respect for those who adhere to other beliefs. The prayer in this case has a permissible ceremonial purpose. It is not an unconstitutional establishment of religion. …

The town of Greece does not violate the First Amendment by opening its meetings with prayer that comports with our tradition and does not coerce participation by nonadherents. The judgment of the US Court of Appeals for the Second Circuit is *reversed.*

Mr. Justice BREYER, dissenting.

As we all recognize, this is a "fact-sensitive" case. The Court of Appeals did not believe that the Constitution forbids legislative prayers that incorporate content associated with a particular denomination.

In essence, the Court of Appeals merely held that the town must do more than it had previously done to try to make its prayer practices inclusive of other faiths. And it did not prescribe a single constitutionally required method for doing so.

In my view, the Court of Appeals' conclusion and its reasoning are convincing. . . . I also here emphasize several factors that I believe underlie the conclusion that, on the particular facts of this case, the town's prayer practice violated the Establishment Clause.

First, Greece is a predominantly Christian town, but it is not exclusively so. [There is] a Buddhist temple within the town and several Jewish synagogues just outside its borders . . . . Yet during the more than 120 monthly meetings at which prayers were delivered during the record period (from 1999 to 2010), only four prayers were delivered by non-Christians. And all of these occurred in 2008, shortly after the plaintiffs began complaining about the town's Christian prayer practice and nearly a decade after that practice had commenced. . . . To be precise: During 2008 two prayers were delivered by a Jewish layman, one by the chairman of a Baha'i congregation, and one by a Wiccan priestess.

Second, the town made no significant effort to inform the area's non-Christian houses of worship about the possibility of delivering an opening prayer. . . .

The plaintiffs do not argue that the town intentionally discriminated against non-Christians when choosing whom to invite, and the town claims, plausibly, that it would have allowed anyone who asked to give an invocation to do so. Rather, the evident reasons why the town consistently chose Christian prayer givers are that the Buddhist and Jewish temples mentioned above were not listed in the Community Guide or the Greece Post and that the town limited its list of clergy almost exclusively to representatives of houses of worship situated within Greece's town limits . . . .

Third, in this context, the fact that nearly all of the prayers given reflected a single denomination takes on significance. That significance would have been the same had all the prayers been Jewish, or Hindu, or Buddhist, or of any other denomination. The significance is that, in a context where religious minorities exist and where more could easily have been done to include their participation, the town chose to do nothing. It could, for example, have posted its policy of permitting anyone to give an invocation on its website, greeceny.gov, which provides dates and times of upcoming town board meetings along with minutes of prior meetings. It could have announced inclusive policies at the beginning of its board meetings, just before introducing the month's prayer giver. It could have provided information to those houses of worship of all faiths that lie just outside its borders and include citizens of Greece among their members. Given that the town could easily have made these or similar efforts but chose not to, the fact that all of the prayers (aside from the 2008 outliers) were given by adherents of a single religion reflects a lack of effort to include others. . . .

Fourth, the fact that the board meeting audience included citizens with business to conduct also contributes to the importance of making more of an effort to include members of other denominations. It does not, however, automatically change the nature of the meeting from one where an opening prayer is permissible under the Establishment Clause to one where it is not.

Fifth, it is not normally government's place to rewrite, to parse, or to critique the language of particular prayers. And it is always possible that members of one religious group will find that prayers of other groups (or perhaps even a moment of silence) are not compatible with their faith. Despite this risk, the Constitution does not forbid opening prayers. But neither does the Constitution forbid efforts to explain to those who give the prayers the nature of the occasion and the audience.

. . . Under these circumstances, I would affirm the judgment of the Court of Appeals that Greece's prayer practice violated the Establishment Clause.

COMMENTS AND QUESTIONS

1. What do you think the outcome of the case would have been if the Court had applied the *Lemon* test?
2. Who gives better practical guidance for a political body wanting to engage in an inclusive and sensitive prayer practice, the majority opinion, or Justice Breyer's dissent? If a legislature or town council is committed to a pluralistic and inclusive approach, what guidelines might it follow?
3. Can action by a private citizen create an Establishment Clause violation?
4. Consider what might happen if a minister stood and prayed, "O God, we thank thee that thou hast chosen the members of my faith to be saved, and are saddened that all others will burn in Hell. We hope the listeners and the Town Council will come unto thee through my faith."
5. Would there be a great or lesser chance of an Establishment Clause violation if the Town of Greece insisted that all prayers be "ecumenical" in character and eliminate all references, for example, to Jesus Christ?
6. In its April 2015 decision in *Mouvement laïque québécois v. Saguenay (City),* 2015 SCC 16 ([2015] 2 SCR 3), the Supreme Court of Canada held that a "non-denominational and fundamentally inclusive" prayer prescribed by municipal by-law to be recited by the mayor at the start of municipal council meetings of the City of Saguenay in Quebec violated the duty of religious neutrality imposed by the Quebec Charter of Human Rights and Freedoms and the Canadian Charter of Rights and Freedoms. Before and after reciting the prayer, the mayor and other members of the municipal council would cross themselves. As explained by the Court:

> In one of the council chambers, there was a Sacred Heart statue fitted with a red electric votive light. In another, there was a crucifix hanging on the wall. S, who considers himself an atheist, felt uncomfortable with this display, which he considered religious, and asked the mayor to stop the practice. When the mayor refused, S complained to the Commission des droits de la personne et des droits de la jeunesse. He argued that his freedom of conscience and religion was being infringed, contrary to ss. 3 and 10 of the Quebec Charter, and asked that the recitation of the prayer cease and that all religious symbols be removed from council chambers.

In its ruling the Court observed:

> Neither the Quebec Charter nor the Canadian Charter expressly imposes a duty of religious neutrality on the state. This duty results from an evolving interpretation of freedom of conscience and religion. . . .
>
> By expressing no preference, the state ensures that it preserves a neutral public space that is free of discrimination and in which true freedom to believe or

> not to believe is enjoyed by everyone equally, given that everyone is valued equally. I note that a neutral public space does not mean the homogenization of private players in that space. Neutrality is required of institutions and the state, not individuals. . . . On the contrary, a neutral public space free from coercion, pressure and judgment on the part of public authorities in matters of spirituality is intended to protect every person's freedom and dignity. The neutrality of the public space therefore helps preserve and promote the multicultural nature of Canadian society enshrined in s. 27 of the Canadian Charter. (paras 71, 74)

How does the Canadian concept of state neutrality compare to or contrast with the US notion of a "wall of separation" between church and state? How might the Court that decided *Town of Greece* have decided *Saguenay*?

3. Endorsement

In *Lynch v. Donnelly*, the Court addressed the question of whether a city's Christmas display that included a crèche violated the Establishment Clause. Chief Justice Burger concluded that it did not, but the standard for evaluating such displays was unclear. Justice O'Connor's concurring opinion provided the opportunity for the introduction of a test based on whether the state's action constituted an endorsement of religion or a particular religion.

LYNCH V. DONNELLY

Supreme Court of the United States, 465 U.S. 668 (1984)

Chief Justice BURGER delivered the opinion of the Court.

We granted certiorari to decide whether the Establishment Clause of the First Amendment prohibits a municipality from including a crèche, or Nativity scene, in its annual Christmas display.

Each year, in cooperation with the downtown retail merchants' association, the city of Pawtucket, R.I., erects a Christmas display as part of its observance of the Christmas holiday season. The display is situated in a park owned by a nonprofit organization and located in the heart of the shopping district. The Pawtucket display comprises many of the figures and decorations traditionally associated with Christmas, including, among other things, a Santa Claus house, reindeer pulling Santa's sleigh, candy-striped poles, a Christmas tree, carolers, cutout figures representing such characters as a clown, an elephant, and a teddy bear, hundreds of colored lights, a large banner that reads "SEASONS GREETINGS," and the crèche at issue here. All components of this display are owned by the city.

The crèche, which has been included in the display for 40 or more years, consists of the traditional figures, including the Infant Jesus, Mary and Joseph, angels, shepherds, kings, and animals, all ranging in height from 5" to 5'. In 1973, when the present crèche was acquired, it cost the city $1,365; it now is valued at $200. The erection and dismantling of the crèche costs the city about $20 per year; nominal expenses are incurred in lighting the crèche. No money has been expended on its maintenance for the past 10 years.

Respondents, Pawtucket residents and individual members of the Rhode Island affiliate of the American Civil Liberties Union, and the affiliate itself, brought this action in the United States District Court for Rhode Island, challenging the city's inclusion of the crèche in the annual display. [The District Court and the First Circuit held that the display violated the Establishment Clause.]

We reverse. . . .

III.

. . . Entanglement is a question of kind and degree. In this case, however, there is no reason to disturb the District Court's finding on the absence of administrative entanglement. There is no evidence of contact with church authorities concerning the content or design of the exhibit prior to or since Pawtucket's purchase of the crèche. No expenditures for maintenance of the crèche have been necessary; and since the city owns the crèche, now valued at $200, the tangible material it contributes is *de minimis*. There is nothing here, of course, like the "comprehensive, discriminating, and continuing state surveillance" or the "enduring entanglement" present in *Lemon* . . . .

Of course the crèche is identified with one religious faith but no more so than the examples we have set out from prior cases in which we found no conflict with the Establishment Clause. To forbid the use of this one passive symbol – the crèche – at the very time people are taking note of the season with Christmas hymns and carols in public schools and other public places, and while the Congress and legislatures open sessions with prayers by paid chaplains, would be a stilted overreaction contrary to our history and to our holdings. If the presence of the crèche in this display violates the Establishment Clause, a host of other forms of taking official note of Christmas, and of our religious heritage, are equally offensive to the Constitution. . . .

We hold that, notwithstanding the religious significance of the crèche, the city of Pawtucket has not violated the Establishment Clause of the First Amendment. Accordingly, the judgment of the Court of Appeals is reversed. *It is so ordered.*

Justice O'CONNOR, concurring.

. . . I write separately to suggest a clarification of our Establishment Clause doctrine. The suggested approach leads to the same result in this case as that taken by the Court, and the Court's opinion, as I read it, is consistent with my analysis. . . .

The Establishment Clause prohibits government from making adherence to a religion relevant in any way to a person's standing in the political community. Government can run afoul of that prohibition in two principal ways.

One is excessive entanglement with religious institutions, which may interfere with the independence of the institutions, give the institutions access to government or governmental powers not fully shared by nonadherents of the religion, and foster the creation of political constituencies defined along religious lines. The second and more direct infringement is government endorsement or disapproval of religion. Endorsement sends a message to non-adherents that they are outsiders, not full members of the political community, and an accompanying message to adherents that they are insiders, favored members of the political community. Disapproval sends the opposite message.

Our prior cases have used the three-part test articulated in *Lemon v. Kurtzman* as a guide to detecting these two forms of unconstitutional government action. It has never been entirely clear, however, how the three parts of the test relate to the principles enshrined in the Establishment Clause. Focusing on institutional entanglement and on endorsement or disapproval of religion clarifies the *Lemon* test as an analytical device. . . .

The central issue in this case is whether Pawtucket has endorsed Christianity by its display of the crèche. To answer that question, we must examine both what Pawtucket intended to communicate in displaying the crèche and what message the city's display actually conveyed. The purpose and effect prongs of the *Lemon* test represent these two aspects of the meaning of the city's action.

The meaning of a statement to its audience depends both on the intention of the speaker and on the "objective" meaning of the statement in the community. Some listeners need not rely solely on the words themselves in discerning the speaker's intent: they can judge the intent by, for example, examining the context of the statement or asking questions of the speaker. Other listeners do not have or will not seek access to such evidence of intent. They will rely instead on the words themselves; for them the message actually conveyed may be something not actually intended. If the audience is large, as it always is when government "speaks" by word or deed, some portion of the audience will inevitably receive a message determined by the "objective" content of the statement, and some portion will inevitably receive the intended message. Examination of both the subjective and the objective components of the message communicated by a government action is therefore necessary to determine whether the action carries a forbidden meaning.

The purpose prong of the *Lemon* test asks whether government's actual purpose is to endorse or disapprove of religion. The effect prong asks whether, irrespective of government's actual purpose, the practice under review in fact conveys a message of endorsement or disapproval. An affirmative answer to either question should render the challenged practice invalid.

The purpose prong of the *Lemon* test requires that a government activity have a secular purpose. That requirement is not satisfied, however, by the mere existence of some secular purpose, however dominated by religious purposes. . . . The proper inquiry under the purpose prong of *Lemon*, I submit, is whether the government intends to convey a message of endorsement or disapproval of religion.

Applying that formulation to this case, I would find that Pawtucket did not intend to convey any message of endorsement of Christianity or disapproval of non-Christian religions. The evident purpose of including the crèche in the display was not promotion of the religious content of the crèche but celebration of the public holiday through its traditional symbols. Celebration of public holidays, which have cultural significance even if they also have religious aspects, is a legitimate secular purpose. . . .

Focusing on the evil of government endorsement or disapproval of religion makes clear that the effect prong of the *Lemon* test is properly interpreted not to require invalidation of a government practice merely because it in fact causes, even as a primary effect, advancement or inhibition of religion. . . . What is crucial is that a government practice not have the effect of communicating a message of government endorsement or disapproval of religion. It is only practices having that effect, whether intentionally or unintentionally, that make religion relevant, in reality or public perception, to status in the political community.

Pawtucket's display of its crèche, I believe, does not communicate a message that the government intends to endorse the Christian beliefs represented by the crèche. Although the religious and indeed sectarian significance of the crèche, as the District Court found, is not neutralized by the setting, the overall holiday setting changes what viewers may fairly understand to be the purpose of the display—as a typical museum setting, though not neutralizing the religious content of a religious painting, negates any message of endorsement of that content. The display celebrates a public holiday, and no one contends that declaration of that holiday is understood to be an endorsement of religion. The holiday itself has very strong secular components and traditions. Government celebration of the holiday, which is extremely common, generally is not understood to endorse the religious content of the holiday, just as government celebration of Thanksgiving is not so understood. The crèche is a traditional symbol of the holiday that is very commonly displayed along with purely secular symbols, as it was in Pawtucket.

These features combine to make the government's display of the crèche in this particular physical setting no more an endorsement of religion than such governmental "acknowledgments" of religion as legislative prayers of the type approved in *Marsh*, government declaration of Thanksgiving as a public holiday, printing of "In God We Trust" on coins, and opening court sessions with "God save the United States and this honorable court." Those government acknowledgments of religion serve, in the only ways reasonably possible in our culture, the legitimate secular purposes of solemnizing public occasions, expressing confidence in the future, and encouraging the recognition of what is worthy of appreciation in society. For that reason, and because of their history and ubiquity, those practices are not understood as conveying government approval of particular religious beliefs. The display of the crèche likewise serves a secular purpose – celebration of a public holiday with traditional symbols. It cannot fairly be understood to convey a message of government endorsement of religion. . . .

I agree with the Court that the judgment below must be reversed.

COMMENTS AND QUESTIONS

1. Would it make a difference if the crèche was the only element of the public display? A primary element? Does insistence on deemphasizing the religious elements endorse a commercial, secular or anti-religious message? From a religious standpoint, is preserving the crèche at the cost of required commercialization really a victory?
2. Is "endorsement" an improvement over "advancing" religion as an analytical focus in Establishment Clause cases?
3. What does Justice O'Connor mean by the "objective" meaning of religious symbols? Does such an idea make sense?

4. Neutrality

In 1985, in *Aguilar v. Felton*, the Supreme Court held that the Establishment Clause barred the New York City Board of Education from sending public school teachers into parochial schools to provide remedial education to disadvantaged children pursuant to a program mandated by Title I of the Elementary and Secondary Education Act. Twelve years later, in *Agostini v. Felton*, the Court reversed course, finding *Aguilar* not consistent with the Court's subsequent Establishment Clause decisions. In this case the emphasis was on whether the program in question was neutral in its application between religious and non-religious beneficiaries.

AGOSTINI V. FELTON

Supreme Court of the United States, 521 U.S. 203 (1997)

Justice O'CONNOR delivered the opinion of the Court.

. . . . As we have repeatedly recognized, government inculcation of religious beliefs has the impermissible effect of advancing religion. Our cases subsequent to *Aguilar* have, however, modified in two significant respects the approach we use to assess indoctrination. First, we have abandoned the presumption erected in *Meek* and *Ball* that the placement of public employees on parochial school grounds inevitably results in the impermissible effect of state-sponsored indoctrination or constitutes a symbolic union between government and religion. . . . Second, we have departed from the rule relied on in *Ball* that all government aid that directly assists the educational function of religious schools is invalid. . . .

A number of our Establishment Clause cases have found that the criteria used for identifying beneficiaries . . . might themselves have the effect of advancing religion by creating a financial incentive to undertake religious indoctrination. This incentive is not present, however, where the aid is allocated on the basis of neutral, secular criteria that neither favor nor disfavor religion, and is made available to both religious and secular beneficiaries on a nondiscriminatory basis. Under such circumstances, the aid is less likely to have the effect of advancing religion. . . .

Applying this reasoning to New York City's Title I program, it is clear that Title I services are allocated on the basis of criteria that neither favor nor disfavor religion. The services are available to all children who meet the Act's eligibility requirements, no matter what their religious beliefs or where they go to school.

The Board's program does not, therefore, give aid recipients any incentive to modify their religious beliefs or practices in order to obtain those services. . . .

We turn now to *Aguilar*'s conclusion that New York City's Title I program resulted in an excessive entanglement between church and state. Whether a government aid program results in such an entanglement has consistently been an aspect of our Establishment Clause analysis. We have considered entanglement both in the course of assessing whether an aid program has an impermissible effect of advancing religion, *Walz*, and as a factor separate and apart from "effect," *Lemon*. Regardless of how we have characterized the issue, however, the factors we use to assess whether an entanglement is "excessive" are similar to the factors we use to examine "effect." That is, to assess entanglement, we have looked to "the character and purposes of the institutions that are benefited, the nature of the aid that the State provides, and the resulting relationship between the government and religious authority." Similarly, we have assessed a law's "effect" by examining the character of the institutions benefited (*e.g.*, whether the religious institutions were "predominantly religious"), see *Meek*. Indeed, in *Lemon* itself, the entanglement that the Court found "independently" to necessitate the program's invalidation also was found to have the effect of inhibiting religion.

Not all entanglements, of course, have the effect of advancing or inhibiting religion. Interaction between church and state is inevitable, and we have always tolerated some level of involvement between the two. Entanglement must be "excessive" before it runs afoul of the Establishment Clause. . . .

To summarize, New York City's Title I program does not run afoul of any of three primary criteria we currently use to evaluate whether government aid has the effect of advancing religion: It does not result in governmental indoctrination; define its recipients by reference to religion; or create an excessive entanglement. We therefore hold that a federally funded program providing supplemental, remedial instruction to disadvantaged children on a neutral basis is not invalid under the Establishment Clause when such instruction is given on the premises of sectarian schools by government employees pursuant to a program containing safeguards such as those present here. The same considerations that justify this holding require us to conclude that this carefully constrained program also cannot reasonably be viewed as an endorsement of religion. Accordingly, we must acknowledge that *Aguilar*, as well as the portion of [*Grand Rapids School District v.*] *Ball* addressing Grand Rapids' Shared Time program, are no longer good law.

COMMENTS AND QUESTIONS

1. *Agostini v. Felton* signals a significant shift in the interpretation of the Establishment Clause, from an approach that focuses on freedom to an approach that focuses on equality. How is this shift evident? Is this a step in the right direction?
2. How would you describe the tests applied by the Supreme Court in the four cases summarized here? What is the relationship between the *Lemon* test, an approach that focuses on history and tradition, an approach that considers whether an action has the purpose or effect of endorsing a particular religious point of view, and an approach that focuses on neutrality and nondiscrimination? Which, if any, of these approaches seems to capture the underlying purpose and intent that motivated the adoption of the Establishment Clause?

D. THE FRENCH MODEL OF SEPARATION (LAÏCITÉ)

The French ideal of laïcité refers to a distinctively French conception of the secular state. As the French Professor Elisabeth Zoller has stated:

> Laïcité is often presented as a "French exception," an apt designation, at least linguistically. The term cannot truly be translated into non-Romance languages. In law, laïcité is always defined as the separation of church and state. When the First Article of France's 1958 Constitution defined France as a "secular Republic," it meant neither more nor less than that the French Republic is founded on the principle of separation of state and religion; it is no longer, as was the case in 1789, based on the ecclesiastical foundation of the state. Laïcité excludes religion and religions of the

state; it prohibits the state from collaborating or cooperating with one religion, either in directing its organization or its functioning, or in allowing its clerics to meddle in public affairs.[15]

Laïcité is a term that can be understood in two ways. On one level, laïcité signifies the separation of church and state, or of religion and politics. On another level, laïcité as it is more or less understood in France, recalls the collection of civil, civic, and political values that come from the Declaration of the Rights of Man of 1789, the preamble to the Constitution of 1946, and the fundamental principles recognized by the laws of the Republic. These values form the moral conscience of the Republic and are the civil religion of the state.[16]

No short excerpt can hope to capture the French notion of laïcité in all its historical complexity and resonance. In what follows, we first note the constitutional starting points in the French legal tradition on this point, and then turn to an explication of contrasting French and US conceptions of laïcité and religious freedom in the context of the Islamic headscarf controversy.

THE FRENCH CONSTITUTIONAL FRAMEWORK

The October 4, 1958 Constitution of France establishes France as a secular republic:

> Article 1: France shall be an indivisible, secular, democratic and social Republic. It shall ensure the equality of all citizens before the law, without distinction of origin, race or religion. It shall respect all beliefs.

Articles 1 and 2 of the French Law of 1905 provide a description of what being a "secular republic" means in France:[17]

> Article 1: The Republic ensures the liberty of conscience. It guarantees the free exercise of religion, under restrictions prescribed by the interest in public order.
> Article 2: The Republic does not recognize, remunerate, or subsidize any religious denomination.[18]

Reaching back over a century earlier, the French Declaration of the Rights of Man in 1789 defined the limits of religious liberty: "No one shall be disquieted on account of his opinions, including his religious views, provided their manifestation does not disturb the public order established by the law."

T. Jeremy Gunn, Under God but not the Scarf: The Founding Myths of Religious Freedom in the United States and Laïcité in France

46 *J. Church & State* 7 (2004)

March 2004, the French parliament adopted a law that prohibits public school students from wearing clothing and insignia that "conspicuously manifest a religious affiliation." The law was approved by an overwhelming vote of 494-36 in the National Assembly, 276-20 in the Senate, and was strongly supported by

15. Elisabeth Zoller, Laïcité in the United States or The Separation of Church and State in Pluralist Society, 13 *Ind. J. Global Legal Studies* (2), 561–562 (2006).

16. *Id.* at 591–592.

17. Jacques Robert, Religious Liberty and French Secularism, 2003 *BYU L. Rev.* 639.

18. *See* Law of Dec. 9, 1905, arts. 1-2, J.O., Dec. 11, 1905, p. 7205 [hereinafter Law of 1905].

popular opinion throughout France. The momentum for adopting such a law began in March 2003, when Prime Minister Jean-Pierre Raffarin of the governing conservative party UMP (Union pour un Mouvement Populaire) said in a radio interview that Muslim headscarves should "absolutely" be prohibited in public schools. A string of endorsements for such a law followed during the next few months, culminating in a December 2003 speech by President Jacques Chirac, also of the UMP, in which he similarly proposed that a law be adopted. Although the highest French administrative court (the Conseil d'État) had ruled as early as 1989 that French children have the constitutional right to wear religious insignia to school, and although many scholars of religion and law believed the law would be a bad idea, the Socialist Party joined arms with the conservatives in the cause that had the support of a majority of the French population. . . .

France and the United States have some obvious underlying similarities. Their respective constitutions include the world's two oldest human rights texts that are currently in force: the French Declaration of the Rights of Man and Citizen and the American Bill of Rights. They were drafted within a few weeks of each other in the latter part of 1789. The human rights assumptions underlying these two documents are now the recognized (if not always respected) norm in virtually every written constitution in the world as well as in all of the basic international human rights instruments.

With regard to freedom of conscience and religion, however, the two countries certainly have different linguistic starting points. Whereas in the United States the guiding principle is "religious freedom," the French use laïcité. Although laïcité is often translated as "secular" or "secularism," the English words do not evoke the important connotations of the French. *Laïcité*, which was first coined in late nineteenth-century France, describes a particular attitude about the proper relationship between church and state. It derives from *laïc* or *laïque*, words originally used to signify monastic orders whose members were not ordained to the clergy, thus corresponding very closely to the English "lay" and even "secular" in the original sense of people who had taken vows to live celibate religious lives but who were not ordained into the clergy. From the late eighteenth to the early twentieth century, the terms laïc and then laïcité came to refer to policies designed to restrict (or even eliminate) clerical and religious influence over the state. Ironically, the word laïc thus evolved from having a distinctly religious meaning, to later becoming anti-clerical, and ultimately meaning, at least for some, "anti-religion." (Many Americans similarly believe that "secular" means "anti-religious" rather than "non-religious.") Unlike France, where laïcité might have the connotation of the state protecting itself from the excesses of religion, the term "religious freedom" in the United States would be more likely to have the connotation of religion being protected from the excesses of the state. Thus Americans are more likely to be predisposed to have suspicions about state laws regulating religion while the French are more likely to be suspicious of an absence of regulation of religious activity. At least this is the theory.

The popular rhetoric in each country transforms the basic attitudes about *laïcité* and religious freedom into what can be called "founding myths." These myths are often described as embodying the unifying values of freedom, neutrality, and equality on which the respective republics were founded, but also as constituting an essential dimension of their unique identities. The French identity, as imagined, includes the comforting belief that the state protects its citizens from religious excesses. The American identity, as imagined, is that "we are a religious people." Thus *laïcité* and religious freedom, although defined as embodying neutrality, tolerance, equality, and freedom of conscience, are at risk of being applied in ways that divide citizens on the basis of their beliefs and convictions.

Two controversies in France and the United States involving religion in the public schools illustrate the parallel uses of the myths of *laïcité* and "religious freedom" to reinforce popular notions of national identity. In the name of *laïcité*, the French National Assembly has now adopted (with the support of the majority of the population), a law prohibiting children from wearing conspicuous religious clothing and insignia at public schools, including Islamic headscarves (*voiles*), Jewish skullcaps (kippas), and Christian crosses. Similarly, in the name of "religious freedom," the American political establishment and much of the judiciary (with widespread popular support), insists that public school officials should lead children in reciting a pledge of allegiance declaring that the United States is "one Nation under God" and that this practice should be defended against a constitutional challenge. "Neutrality" and "equality" are used in France to prevent religious expression in schools; "neutrality" and "equality" are used in the United States to propagate state-sponsored theological declarations in schools.

French and American observers are likely to see the state actions on the opposite side of the Atlantic—banning religious clothing and promoting state-sponsored declarations about God—as violating the very principles of neutrality, tolerance, freedom of conscience, and human rights that their own countries scrupulously respect. Easily spotting the speck in the other's eye, they are blind to obstacles in their own. . . .

French public rhetoric treats laïcité as a unifying and founding principle of the French Republic. (It is a constitutional principle appearing in article 1 of the 1958 Constitution.) One particularly striking, though not altogether unusual example of the homage to laïcité, was provided in a December 2003 speech by President Chirac. In it, he identified laïcité as the "cornerstone" (pierre angulaire) of the Republic. It is "inscribed in our traditions. It is at the heart of our republican identity." . . . It is a doctrine that protects the basic rights of belief. "Laïcité guarantees the freedom of conscience. It protects the freedom to believe or not to believe. It assures all of the possibility to express and practice their faith peaceably, freely, but without threatening others with one's own convictions or beliefs." . . .

Americans might be amused to hear such effusive praise for a seemingly vague doctrine. But perhaps they might first consider some rhetoric emanating from their own country. In January 2002, President George Bush declared that "Religious freedom is a cornerstone of our Republic, a core principle of our Constitution, and a fundamental human right. Many of those who first settled in America, such as Pilgrims, came for the freedom of worship and belief that this new land promised." . . .

Quotations like those cited above fill the airwaves, newspapers, magazines, and speeches in both countries. The doctrines of laïcité and religious freedom are treated as founding pillars of the countries, as principles that have been respected through history, as beliefs that unite citizens, and as shared values that help create the treasured and unique identities of the two countries. . . .

The French and American founding myths of laïcité and religious freedom thus have several characteristics in common: they are revered as foundational cornerstones; they are described as having emerged gloriously from the historical past; they are described as explaining the essence of the nation's values; and they are offered as principles that unite all citizens of the republic. But they also have a darker underside. Although they profess to be unifying, their legacy also has been one of dividing and ostracizing those whose beliefs are found to be different from the accepted norm. The two cornerstone doctrines were not established by a founding generation and then passed on to subsequent generations as a doctrine that unites all citizens; rather, they developed in fits and starts and frequently were used to divide citizens from each other. [The French headscarf controversy gives us] a contemporary window into the [French use of its] founding myths.

In July 2003, after several of the leading politicians in France had recommended the adoption of a law to ban religious attire from public schools, President Chirac appointed a group of prominent French scholars and officials to make its own recommendations. Known as the "Stasi Commission" (after its chairman, Bernard Stasi), it issued its report in early December 2003. The Commission made several recommendations, including improving living standards in some economically depressed communities and improving education about religion and *laïcité*. The media, however, focused almost exclusively on only one of the Commission's recommendations: prohibiting public school students from wearing "clothing and insignia signifying a religious or political affiliation." Although phrased in the neutral words of "clothing" and "insignia," the media immediately interpreted it to be a recommendation to prevent Muslim girls from wearing headscarves in schools.

The Stasi Commission's report began with a lengthy praise of the doctrine of laïcité. Although the encomiums were somewhat less flowery than those of President Chirac, the admiration was unmistakable. Among the admired aspects of laïcité were its respect for neutrality and equality. The Commission of course recognized that its function was not simply to praise laïcité, nor even to discuss religious clothing generally, but to address specifically the Islamic headscarf, which it characterized as the "explosive" issue. When we focus specifically on the Commission's treatment of the issue that prompted its creation and that served as the basis of its most prominent recommendation, it is disappointing to see just how shallow the Commission's analysis was. Though its report was seventy-eight pages in length, only a few short pages even discussed the core issue of headscarves or other religious clothing. And here the Commission's analysis is surprising both for what it says and what it does not say.

First, the Commission does not assert that the wearing of headscarves (or other religious attire) is becoming increasingly disruptive in schools. In fact, the Commission makes no attempt at all to quantify the alleged problem or to identify trends—a rather striking omission for a group with such serious scholars among its members. The Commission failed even to note that the responsible official from the Ministry of Education—who was herself a Member of the Commission—had reported earlier in the year that the number of problematic cases had been sharply reduced.

Second, the Commission did not analyze or consider any reasons or religious motivations for why children might want to wear religious clothing or insignia to school. The Commission did not consider whether the wearing of headcoverings by Jewish boys or Muslim girls was prompted by religious piety, personal modesty, or cultural identification. The Commission's report never even considered the rights of religion or belief that might be infringed if its recommendation to ban religious clothing were adopted or why its analysis should supersede that of the Conseil d'État that had held children have a constitutional right to wear such clothing. This is probably the most striking omission and failure in the report.

Third, the Commission responded to the allegation that some families and communities coerce (and even threaten) Muslim girls into wearing the headscarf. The Commission was deeply disturbed about such undue pressure on the girls and asserted that the French state has an obligation to protect these vulnerable children. It also feared that community pressure on the girls was contributing to sex segregation and an inferior status for Muslim girls and women. While the Commission was certainly correct to identify these serious issues, its analysis as a whole suggests that it had a rather erratic concern about coercion. Whereas it condemned coercion to wear the headscarf, it revealed no comparable interest in coercion not to wear the headscarf. Although there is in France strong media, school, popular, and political antagonism directed at the wearing of the headscarf, the Stasi Commission failed to criticize this coercion. Its selective concern with coercion was further revealed in its discussion of Jewish boys who are ridiculed and threatened when they wear the skullcap.

Whereas the Commission had argued that the state has a responsibility to protect girls who do not want to wear the headscarf, it did not see any responsibility of the state to ensure that boys who wish to wear the skullcap are protected in this choice against coercion and harassment. . . .

Finally, the Commission offered no analysis to show that its recommendation—banning religious clothing—would ameliorate the problems that it identified: coercion and sexual discrimination. Indeed, even if we accepted the Commission's explanation of why girls wear the headscarf (community harassment if they do not comply), we are offered no analysis to show why banning the headscarf at schools would solve the problem. In fact, if the Commission's underlying analysis about coercion is true, we can well imagine the possibility that community threats on the unfortunate girls will increase if they are forced to unveil themselves in schools. We also can imagine, again assuming that the Commission's explanation is correct, that girls suffering from coercion might withdraw from state schools and be placed in private religious schools, thereby exacerbating the sex segregation that the Commission professedly deplores.

If we step back for a moment and look globally at what the Commission did, there are two important observations. First, it did not take seriously the rights of conscience and belief of the children. Second, the solution offered—banning religious attire in public schools—is not shown to solve the problem the Commission identified and it may well be counterproductive. Thus it appears that the Commission was perhaps less interested in eliminating coercion and sex segregation than it was in recommending that schools have the appearance of laïcité. The Commission could have said that "what unites us as French citizens is our respect for the choices of individuals to believe or not to believe as their consciences dictate." Unfortunately, the Commission essentially said that "what unites us as French citizens is a particular notion of laïcité that abhors the appearance of religious differences in schools." The Commission's application of neutrality and equality means that everyone has the equal right not to wear religious clothing. . . .

Though laïcité and religious freedom were not the founding principles of tolerance and neutrality as the rhetoric sometimes suggests, it is important to recognize that they have made some important and positive contributions. One of the principal values of laïcité is the official respect it accords for beliefs that are not religious, and for recognizing the human dignity of the many people who do not find strength or value in religion. Whether such nonbelievers are scientists, philosophers, doctors, political leaders, or day laborers, they are officially respected by a laïc state for their profound contributions to society, and they are valued as people who are fully entitled to participate in the political world and in public discourse.

With regard to the United States, there has emerged—albeit more recently than the myth implies—a very healthy presumption that people of widely divergent religious beliefs should be protected by the state and that respecting religious freedom positively aids the health and strength of the state. Such policies and attitudes are not only fully consistent with international human rights standards that protect freedom of religion, they are also deeply respectful of human dignity and individual choice to devote all or part of one's life to religion. While much of the world becomes increasingly secular and skeptical, and while other parts of the world seem to be increasingly religious, it is no small accomplishment for the United States to be in the vanguard of stimulating scientific discovery and protecting freedom of religion.

At the moment, unfortunately, it appears that many proponents of French laïcité and American religiosity are wrapping themselves in their myths rather than embracing the essence of their teachers' deepest principles: tolerance (rather than uniformity) and personal piety (rather than formulaic public pronouncements). We should hope that those who have devout beliefs in God and those who respect human rights would understand that decisions about religion and faith should be made by individuals, their families, and their faith and belief communities—and not by states legislating religious dress codes or professions of faith. Whereas the myths might not support such a solution, the principles of tolerance, equality, and neutrality certainly should.

COMMENTS AND QUESTIONS

1. The *Şahin* decision excerpted in Chapter 3 was pending before the European Court of Human Rights at the time of the Stasi Commission hearings and the adoption of the law banning clothing and insignia that "conspicuously manifest a religious affiliation." The initial judgment from the European Court was handed down on 29 June 2004, less than four months after the French law was adopted. The Grand Chamber decision followed on 10 November 2005. *Şahin* technically involved Turkey, but the Court was of course not oblivious to the parallel issues in France. Could a French applicant challenging the French anti-headscarf law distinguish the French and Turkish situations?

2. One of the worries behind the *Şahin* decision in Turkey is that those wearing headscarves represent political pressure to move toward a more Islamic state. A classic Islamic model is one in which various religious communities are each allowed to coexist in the country with their own religiously based legal systems. In a sense, the model of laïcité or Turkish secularism could be understood as a response to the possibility of this type of legal pluralism and the religious status systems that result.[19] At what point does the risk of transformation into a radically different type of system justify stronger intervention in religious affairs and stronger control of religious expression and symbols in public settings?
3. Gunn suggests that religious liberty in the United States and laïcité in France have taken on the aura of "founding myths." Would you agree? Do the myths blind us to some of the underlying realities, both in terms of what happened historically and in terms of how we apply the concepts today? Often a myth, particularly a founding myth, contains a deep core of cultural truth. Taken in that sense, what do the competing ideals of religious liberty and laïcité ′ reveal about the US and French cultures?
4. Secularity and secularism are two related but distinctive ideological frameworks for creating a separation of religion and state.[20] Secularity posits that the state should avoid identifying itself with any particular religion; the state avoids showing favoritism toward any particular denomination so that all are equally free to exercise any religion that they so choose. Secularity is typified by the United States' concept of freedom of religion, which is that religions organizations should be protected from state control. On the other hand, secularism posits that the state should actively promote a secular order in order to preempt religious encroachment into the state sphere. Secularism is exemplified by the French concept of laicité, which aims to protect the state from the excesses of religion.
5. This distinction has important implications for democratic secular constitutional liberalism. First, secularity and secularism each drive the state's pursuit of liberty differently. Secularity concerns itself with protecting the freedom to be one's own master, and thus advances policies of self-direction and religious autonomy, whereas secularism "is willing to marshal the coercive means of the state to help citizens along to becoming genuinely rational and virtuous, as the ideal defines and envisions those terms,"[21] because it protects freedom from interference with one's religious beliefs. Second, secularity advances policies that avoid making any value judgments about beliefs whereas secularism tends to impose secular beliefs on everyone. Third, secularity advances "thin theories of the good"—meaning it concerns itself with fundamental rights for a broad range of people—while secularism is concerned with "thick theories," or protecting the state's own complex secular belief system.[22]

---

19. *See, e.g.*, Fatih Öztürk, *Ottoman and Turkish Law* (iUniverse 2014).

20. The material in this comment is taken from Brett G. Scharffs, Four Views of the Citadel: The Consequential Distinction between Secularity and Secularism, 16 *Rel. & Hum. Rts*. 109–126 (2011).

21. *Id.* at 114.

22. *Id.* at 118–21, citing John Rawls, *A Theory of Justice* 395 (Harvard University Press 1971).

6. In October 2010, France passed a more general law "prohibiting the concealment of one's face in public places." Similar bans have passed in or are being contemplated in a number of European countries, including Belgium. Why do you think these new laws, though popularly termed "burqa bans," do not specifically reference religious attire? What differences might this make?
7. To answer the question just posed, consider the following: The 2010 French law, like the 2004 anti-headscarf law, was preceded by study and recommendations by a parliamentary commission, which issued a report including the assertion that the wearing of the full-face veil "existed before the advent of Islam and did not have the nature of a religious precept, but stemmed from a radical affirmation of individuals in search of identity in society and from the action of extremist fundamentalist movements." It was thus necessary to "release women from the subservience of the full-face veil" (paras. 16-17).[23] In response, a French National Advisory Commission took the view that "the principle of secularism alone could not serve as a basis for such a general measure, since it was not for the State to determine whether or not a given matter fell within the realm of religion, and that public order could justify a prohibition only if it were limited in space and time. The opinion also emphasized the risk of stigmatizing Muslims and pointed out that a general prohibition could be detrimental to women, because those who were made to wear the full-face veil would additionally become deprived of access to public areas" (para. 18). The Conseil d'État "found it impossible to recommend a ban on the full veil alone, as a garment representing values that were incompatible with those of the Republic, in that such a ban would be legally weak and difficult to apply in practice" (para. 22). Nevertheless, the ban was passed unanimously by the French National Assembly.
8. The 2010 French law was challenged by a devout French Muslim woman in the ECtHR case *S.A.S. v. France*, App. No. 43835/11 (1 July 2014), summarized in Chapter 3. In some ways the judgment in this case, representing a large margin (15-2) of a Grand Chamber of the Court, shows a "balanced and careful reasoning concerning the right to manifest a religion" that departs from its "highly criticized stance towards the practice of wearing religious garments by Muslim women [in *Dahlab* and *Şahin*]."[24] However, part of the French government's justification for the 2010 ban was respect for the principle of fraternité, a value of an open and democratic society that includes respect and comprehends the concept of "living together." Though not recognized as a ground of limitation in the ECHR, the Court accepted this as part of the "protection of the rights and freedoms of others" (para. 121). Unlike its gender equality and human dignity companions, the "living together" claim survives as a legitimate aim, which helped the Court find that the 2010 law was within the government's "margin of appreciation" for regulating its own. It has been suggested that the "addition of 'living together' to secularism, gender equality, public safety and the protection of children as permissible grounds of

---

23. Citations in this paragraph are to the *S.A.S. v. France* (App. No. 43835/11, ECtHR Grand Chamber, 1 July 2014).

24. *See* Saïla Ouald Chaib, S.A.S. v. France: Missed Opportunity to Do Full Justice to Women Wearing a Face Veil, *Strasbourg Observers*, 3 July 2014.

limitation" in such cases is an erosion of "what little remain[s] of right to manifest religion . . . ."[25] Do you agree?

Additional Web Resources:	Substantial additional materials are available regarding religious status systems, including materials on the Iraqi constitution, extremist groups, Israel, and on millet systems in a number of Islamic countries

V. HAZARDS OF EXCESSIVE POSITIVE OR NEGATIVE IDENTIFICATION

A. POSITIVE IDENTIFICATION: IRAN AND SAUDI ARABIA

Iran and Saudi Arabia are two examples of extreme "positive" religious identification, countries that identify themselves by their religion. In each country the religion is Islam. However, in each, total identification with one of the two major divisions in Islam—the Sunni and the Shia—leaves the countries at perpetual, sometimes violent, odds, as is shown in these passages from the US State Department's International Religious Freedom Report for 2015.

1. Iran

The constitution declares the country to be an Islamic Republic, and Ja'afari Shia Islam to be the official state religion. It states all laws and regulations must be based on "Islamic criteria" and official interpretation of Shari'a. The constitution states citizens shall enjoy human, political, economic, and other rights, "in conformity with Islamic criteria." The penal code specifies the death sentence for proselytizing and attempts by non-Muslims to convert Muslims, as well as for moharebeh ("enmity against God") and sabb al-nabi ("insulting the prophets"). The constitution stipulates the five major Sunni schools be "accorded full respect" and enjoy official status in matters of religious education and certain personal affairs. "Within the limits of the law," the constitution states Zoroastrians, Jews, and Christians are the only recognized religious minorities permitted to worship freely and to form religious societies, although proselytizing is prohibited. The government executed at least 20 individuals on charges of moharebeh, among them a number of Sunni Kurds. A number of other prisoners, including several Sunni preachers, remained in custody awaiting a government decision to carry out their death sentences. According to the Iran Human Rights Documentation Center database, at least 250 members of minority religious groups remained imprisoned, including Sunnis, Bahais, Christian converts, Sufis, Yarsanis, and Zoroastrians. Shia religious leaders who did not support government policies reportedly continued to faced intimidation and arrest. The government continued to harass Bahais, and regulated Christian religious practices closely to enforce the

25. Stephanie Berry, SAS v France: Does Anything Remain of the Right to Manifest Religion?, *EJIL: Talk!*

prohibition on proselytizing. Security officials continued to raid prayer sites belonging to Sunnis. Government-sponsored public denunciations of the Bahai faith increased. Antisemitic rhetoric also continued to appear in official statements. There were reports of authorities placing restrictions on Bahai businesses or forcing them to shut down.

Non-Muslims and non-Shia reportedly continued to face societal discrimination, especially the Bahai community, which reported continuing problems at different levels of society, including personal harassment. There were reports of non-Bahais being pressured to refuse employment to Bahais or dismissing Bahais from their private sector jobs. Shia clerics and prayer leaders reportedly continued to denounce Sufism and the activities of Sufis in both sermons and public statements.[26]

2. Saudi Arabia

Sunni Islam is the official religion, and the country's constitution is the Quran and the Sunna, or traditions of the Prophet Muhammad. The legal system is based on the Hanbali School of Sunni Islamic jurisprudence, and freedom of religion is not addressed in the law. The law criminalizes "calling for atheist thought," "calling into question the Islamic religion," and "sowing discord in society." One citizen was publicly lashed 50 times in accordance with a sentence based on his 2013 conviction for violating Islamic values, violating Shari'a, committing blasphemy, and mocking religious symbols on the internet. The government imprisoned individuals accused of apostasy and blasphemy, violating Islamic values, insulting Islam, black magic, sorcery, and "immoral activity." The government sentenced at least two individuals to death for apostasy and blasphemy, and both sentences were pending appeal at year's end. Citing rules on activities such as gender mixing, noise disturbances, and immigration violations, the government harassed, detained, arrested, and occasionally deported some foreign residents who participated in private non-Islamic religious activities. Instances of prejudice and discrimination against Shia Muslims continued to occur with respect to access to public services and equitable representation in government, educational and public-sector employment opportunities, and judicial matters. Shia clerics and activists who advocated for equal treatment of Shia Muslims were arrested, and at least one Shia cleric awaited execution after being convicted on charges of "violent opposition" to the government. The government continued to censor or block media content it deemed objectionable, and employed religious police to enforce public morality. The government did not recognize the freedom to practice publicly any non-Muslim religions. The Commission for the Promotion of Virtue and Prevention of Vice (CPVPV) continued to receive criticism in both traditional and social media for aggressive policing. The government did not complete its project with the stated aim of removing content disparaging religions other than Islam from textbooks, although it continued to phase in a newly revised curriculum.

Instances of societal prejudice and discrimination against Shia Muslims continued regarding private-sector employment. Social media provided an outlet to discuss current events and religious issues, which sometimes included making

26. US Department of State, International Religious Freedom Report for 2015: Iran.

disparaging remarks about members of religious groups. Editorial cartoons exhibited antisemitism characterized by the use of stereotypical images of Jews along with Jewish symbols, particularly at times of heightened political tension with Israel.[27]

B. NEGATIVE IDENTIFICATION: MILITANT SECULARISM IN COMMUNIST ALBANIA

With the swift rise of Communism in Albania following World War II came the near complete extinction of religious liberty. Enver Hoxha, the head of the Communist Party, considered religion anti-socialist and divisive, and actively sought the eradication of religious institutions. Most property owned by religious institutions was nationalized; many clergy and believers were put on trial, tortured, and killed; and foreign priests were expelled. Although the Communist constitution guaranteed religious freedom in theory, the government imposed extreme burdens on religious institutions in practice. For example, the Decree on Religious Communities, passed in January 1949, severely sanctioned religious communities, requiring government approval for all appointments and practices, terminating the activities of those with foreign headquarters, forbidding them from educating the young, and denying them the right to own land and operate charitable institutions.

The United States Library of Congress provides the following description of Hoxha's anti-religious campaign:[28]

> Although there were tactical variations in Hoxha's approach to each of the major denominations, his overarching objective was the eventual destruction of all organized religion in Albania. In the late 1940s and 1950s, the regime achieved control over the Muslim faith by formalizing the split between the Sunni and Bektashi sects, eliminating all leaders who opposed Hoxha's policies, and exploiting those who were more tractable. Steps were also taken to purge all Orthodox clergy who did not yield to the demands of the regime, and to use the church as a means of mobilizing the Orthodox population behind government policies. The Roman Catholic Church, chiefly because it maintained close relations with the Vatican and was more highly organized than the Muslim and Orthodox faiths, became the principal target of persecution. Between 1945 and 1953, the number of priests was reduced drastically and the number of Roman Catholic churches was decreased from 253 to 100. All Catholics were stigmatized as fascists, although only a minority had collaborated with the Italian occupation authorities during World War II.
>
> The campaign against religion peaked in the 1960s. Inspired by China's Cultural Revolution, Hoxha called for an aggressive cultural-educational struggle against "religious superstition" and assigned the antireligious mission to Albania's students. By May 1967, religious institutions had been forced to relinquish all 2,169 churches, mosques, cloisters, and shrines in Albania, many of which were converted into cultural centers for young people. As the literary monthly Nendori reported the event, the youth had thus "created the first atheist nation in the world."
>
> The clergy were publicly vilified and humiliated, their vestments taken and desecrated. Many Muslim mullahs and Orthodox priests buckled under and renounced their "parasitic" past. More than 200 clerics of various faiths were imprisoned, others were forced to seek work in either industry or agriculture, and some were executed or

27. US Department of State, International Religious Freedom Report for 2015: Saudi Arabia.

28. Library of Congress, Albania: A Country Study, in *Religion: Hoxha's Antireligious Campaign* (Raymond Zickel & Walter R. Iwaskiw, eds., 1994).

> starved to death. The cloister of the Franciscan order in Shkodër was set on fire, which resulted in the death of four elderly monks. . . .
>
> Hoxha's brutal antireligious campaign succeeded in eradicating formal worship, but some Albanians continued to practice their faith clandestinely, risking severe punishment. Individuals caught with Bibles, icons, or other religious objects faced long prison sentences. Parents were afraid to pass on their faith, for fear that their children would tell others. Officials tried to entrap practicing Christians and Muslims during religious fasts, such as Lent and Ramadan, by distributing dairy products and other forbidden foods in school and at work, and then publicly denouncing those who refused the food. Clergy who conducted secret services were incarcerated; in 1980, a Jesuit priest was sentenced to "life until death" for baptizing his nephew's newborn twins.

In 1967, the government officially outlawed religion and announced that all previous decrees establishing organized religious institutions were null and void. Nearly a decade later,

> [t]he culmination of this so-called revolution was reached with the Constitution of 1976. The preamble of this Constitution declared that the bases of religious obscurantism were destroyed. Further, the 1976 Constitution provided that the Albanian state did not recognize any religion and carried out atheist propaganda in order to introduce new scientific materialistic ideas.
>
> Also, the Constitution prohibited the establishment of any religious organizations and equated them with organizations of fascist, anti-democratic, and antisocialist character. The Albania state considered itself the first atheist state in the world.[29]

With the fall of Communism in 1990 came the rebirth of religious freedom in Albania. In 1991, while laying the groundwork for a new constitution, the People's Assembly adopted the Law on the Main Constitutional Provisions, which reflected principles of religious freedom from the pre-Communist era, such as the secular status of the government and its responsibility to protect freedom of religious belief and create an environment in which that belief can be safely expressed. The bill of rights declared the inviolability of freedom of thought, conscience, and religion. Finally, the law guaranteed the freedom to change religion or manifest, publicly or privately, religious beliefs.

In November 1998, the Albanian government approved its post-Communist constitution, which has been found to meet international standards for the protection of religious rights and freedoms.[30] Since that time there has been a significant improvement in the protection of religious freedom in Albania. According to a US State Department report issued in 2013, "There were no reports of societal abuses or discrimination based on religious affiliation, belief, or practice, although ethnicity and religion were often closely linked, particularly within the Greek minority, making it difficult to categorize some incidents as either ethnically or religiously motivated."[31]

---

29. Evis Karandrea, Church and State in Albania, in *Law and Religion in Post-Communist Europe* 26-27 (Silvio Ferrari, W. Cole Durham, Jr., & Elizabeth A. Sewell, eds., Peeters 2003).

30. *Id.*

31. US Department of State, International Religious Freedom Report for 2013: Albania.

COMMENTS AND QUESTIONS

1. The Albanian case is one of the extreme cases of religious persecution in history. What are the social and political dynamics that can lead to the transformation of a regime located between cooperation and secularism on the religion-state identification continuum into a control or abolitionist regime?
2. What is the more likely precursor of an abolitionist or strong control regime: an established religion or a laïcist regime?
3. After 1990, many formerly Communist regimes went through a process of transition toward more democratic regimes. As a regime tries to move out of the strong "negative identification" position, what are the best options for adjusting the religion-state system to optimize religious freedom? In many of these countries, a major issue has been restitution of property to religious communities that had been expropriated by the former Communist regime. This obviously involves massive transfers of property to the historically dominant religion or religions in the country. Should this be regarded as a violation of separation principles? Many of the indigenous religions had suffered crippling blows from persecution during the Communist era. Should this justify intensified "cooperation" in the form of financial aid to various religious communities? Should the state raise "barriers to entrance" against other religious groups while the indigenous communities rebuild? Should different principles of freedom of religion apply during periods of transition that allow states greater flexibility to aid or inhibit religion? Or do periods of transition provide opportunities to make major leaps forward in strengthening human rights protections?
4. Compare and contrast the methods used by Albania to forbid religion with those used by Saudi Arabia and Iran to enforce religion.

Additional Web Resources:	Substantial additional materials are available regarding control and abolitionist regimes. In particular, there are substantial sets of materials on China (as an example of a control regime), and on Russia and other Central and Eastern European countries as examples of control regimes in various stages of transition toward democracy. Other materials explain the history of the Sunni/Shia schism in Islam

VI. CONCLUSION

While it cannot be said that any one type of church-state relationship automatically yields "ideal" or "optimal" results across all legal systems, in that it maximizes freedom for believers, non-believers, and the unconcerned, the institutional relationships between religion and the state do tend to raise predictable sets of challenges for freedom. Some systems appear to be more conducive to broad protection of freedom of religion or belief, and others appear more prone to lapse into excessive positive or negative identification with religion. As we proceed through the remaining chapters of the book, we hope the comparative framework developed here will lend depth to analysis of the recurrent types of problems regimes face in dealing with the interface of religion, the state, and society.

PART II

FREEDOM OF RELIGION OR BELIEF

Part I of this book provided an overview of the broad frameworks within which rights to freedom of religion and belief are situated and justified in modern states: the historical and philosophical background, international human rights standards, and comparative constitutional perspectives on the institutional relationships between religion and the state.

In this part we turn to what are generally regarded as the core issues of religious liberty. Chapter 5 addresses freedom of conscience and internal belief, the right to be free from coercion in the expression (or non-expression) of beliefs, the right to engage in efforts aimed at religious persuasion, and analysis of where the legal limits lie in dealing with offensive speech that is either motivated by religious beliefs or targets religious sensitivities.

That discussion helps pave the way for the analysis in Chapter 6 of permissible limitations on religious freedom or, stated differently, the extent to which religious freedom claims warrant exceptions from or adaptation of neutral and general laws that would typically apply. As a functional matter, the scope of religious freedom is in fact defined by the limits or degree of accommodation established by legislators, courts and other administrative bodies with respect to religious freedom claims. Different legal systems have developed different techniques for setting these boundaries, and Chapter 6 explores various constitutional and international human rights approaches.

Chapters 7 through 9 are variations on the limitations theme of Chapter 6. Chapter 7 examines limits on freedom of religion or belief in distinctive institutional contexts. The two broad areas examined—land use issues and rights in particular institutional settings (for example prisons, the military, and health institutions)—correspond to the areas that have been the focus of the Religious Land Use and Institutionalized Persons Act (RLUIPA) in the United States. In fact, these are recurring areas of practical concern in every legal system, hence we explore them in detail. Cases in these areas not only account for a large volume of disagreement and litigation, they are representative of a broader range of bureaucratic encounters with religious claims in modern welfare states. The cases highlight, among other things, the risks of delegating state power to religious groups, the difficulties of maintaining state neutrality, and the challenge of defining legal standards in ways that effectively limit abuse of administrative discretion.

Chapter 8 looks at limitations from the perspective of growing concern about various types of religious extremism. The chapter addresses new religious movements and religiously motivated acts of violence and terror. It raises questions about how we can avoid negative stereotyping of unfamiliar groups without discounting the genuine threats some groups pose to public safety, health, and order. Finally, Chapter 9 looks at a number of fundamental collisions between religious freedom claims and other fundamental rights. Although religious freedom and other rights usually interact in synergistic ways, there are occasional situations in which collisions occur. Among the most controversial current issues is how religious freedom rights should be balanced against non-discrimination norms in other areas such as race, gender, and especially sexual orientation and gender identity.

In general, then, the movement in this part of the book is from the inner domain of conscience to the external sphere of religious conduct and an examination of countervailing social concerns of increasing legal and constitutional magnitude. Because the law tends to focus on the problematic cases, there is a danger that those studying the field can lose sight of the values protected by freedom of religion and belief. This involves more than the typical skew of legal studies toward hard cases; it represents a risk that those studying the borderline cases of religious freedom may forget why the core protections are so important. We hope that the grounding of religious freedom addressed in various ways in Part I will contribute to a depth of thought about the appropriate balances that need to be struck and help to counter the possibility of over estimating the problems associated with freedom of religion and belief that might arise from focusing on difficult borderline cases.

CHAPTER 5

FREEDOM OF RELIGIOUS BELIEF AND EXPRESSION

I. INTRODUCTION

This chapter considers the core of religious freedom: belief and expression. It addresses those aspects that lie in the "*forum internum*"—that sphere of religious freedom that has long been accorded absolute protection and that has a particular place in the jurisprudence of the European Court of Human Rights.[1] In the words of the United States Supreme Court, free exercise of religion "embraces two concepts—freedom to believe and freedom to act. The first is absolute but, in the nature of things, the second cannot be."[2] Key international instruments take essentially the same position by providing that only "manifestations" of religion or belief may be limited, thus defining as inviolate the inner sanctum of conscience.[3] Expression extends outward beyond inner belief and involves communicating internal beliefs to the external world. It is at least in part because of the close linkage of expression to the inner domain of "thought, conscience and religion," and thereby to the core of human dignity, that freedom of expression is so important to the related right of freedom of religion and belief in the constellation of constitutional and human rights.

Our purpose here is to consider the contexts in which freedom of religion and freedom of expression overlap. Section II looks at issues that test the boundaries of the absolutely protected domain of the *forum internum*. Are there actual cases where the "absolute" dimension of religious freedom receives practical protection? Does punishment of certain omissions (failure to report information gleaned from a confession) or coercion of certain expressions (compelled flag salutes) transgress these boundaries? The main emphasis here is on compelled patriotic observances that run counter to religious belief, but related questions about oath taking and confidential religious communications are also raised. The deeper issue is how fully inner conscientious objection to state-mandated conduct *should* be protected. Is it only prohibition of state-coerced expression that receives absolute protection?

---

1. *See* Jim Murdoch, Protecting the right to freedom of thought, conscience and religion under the European Convention on Human Rights 18–24 (Council of Europe 2012).

2. *Cantwell v. Connecticut*, 310 U.S. 296, 303–304 (1940).

3. *See, e.g.*, ICCPR art. 18(3); ECHR art. 9(2).

Section III addresses religious speech itself. Many countries, including the United States, have separate provisions regarding freedom of speech that protect all speakers, including religious persons. Building on cases involving religious persuasion and proselytism from Chapter 1, this section examines issues at the threshold of the internal forum. Whether or not efforts to convert constitute conduct, they clearly involve speech. Is there any reason to think that religious speech is entitled to less protection than other forms of speech? Moreover, regardless of what one thinks of the right of the missionary or religious teacher, what about the recipient of such communications? Should the right to "change" one's religion be absolutely protected? Or may state paternalism intrude into the internal forum? This has always been a sensitive issue and has been contested in the modern human rights context since the adoption of the Universal Declaration of Human Rights in 1948. A variety of types of laws that seek to place limits on religious expression are addressed: anti-conversion laws, laws placing limits on religiously motivated speech that offends or harms others, hate speech, and others.

Section IV addresses conflicts between freedom of religion and freedom of expression that arise when religious or religiously motivated speech offends others or when speech is critical or contemptuous of religion. This involves issues of blasphemy, hate speech, and other sorts of expression that offend religious sensitivities. Note that to some extent, limitations on the display or wearing of religious symbols or other limitations on public religious expression advanced in the interest of separation of religion and state (issues addressed in Chapter 14) may also be designed to avoid religiously grounded offense—the offense of messages of exclusion or discrimination.

Finally, Section V provides a brief comment on the relationship of freedom of religion and freedom of expression from a different perspective, addressing the question of whether freedom of religion is redundant? That is, could freedom of religion be adequately protected by a sufficiently expansive version of freedom of expression, association, and assembly?

II. PROTECTION OF THE CORE DOMAIN OF CONSCIENCE: RELIGIOUS BELIEF AND THE INTERNAL FORUM

One might think that the real test for "mere belief" or "internal forum" status is that the belief is "totally internal" in the sense that it is not accessible to other minds, and thus by definition cannot have social impact. In many ways, the American belief/action distinction appears to have proceeded on this assumption. Despite the lip service it receives, it has never had real doctrinal bite—perhaps because there appear to be no legally relevant situations to which the absolute protections for mere belief would apply.

However, there are a number of settings in which internal forum claims do pose practical issues. For example, what Germans would call "negative confessional freedom"—the freedom not to disclose one's beliefs—becomes a practical issue when states require that one's religion be disclosed on identity cards, in census data, and in other settings. A similar notion might be at play in long-standing rules that forbid mandatory patriotic observances.

Conduct is involved in these settings, to be sure, but what is troubling about these cases is the coercive intrusion into the internal forum: a sense that the state has exceeded its legitimate jurisdiction.

The following materials focus on coerced patriotic observances, but similar questions arise in cases involving mandatory oaths or the protection of confidential communications such as confessions in religious settings.

These issues are significant not only in their own right but also because they may call for deeper thinking about basic analytic structures that courts use to decide constitutional and human rights cases. State power can impact the inner domain of conscience. But because internal forum questions arise relatively rarely, there is a tendency to think that all religious freedom cases are decided using tests designed for external forum settings. This ignores the idea that the internal forum protections are absolute and deserve heightened protections. In part, the "absoluteness" of the internal forum domain might merely be a statement of factual limits on state power, suggesting that the absoluteness will collapse whenever state power can effectively assert itself. Something more than the act/omission or internal-mind/external-world distinctions are at play. It is not merely because the conscientious actor wants to remain within the internal domain by refraining from coming out into the external world that we think it is inappropriate for the state to intrude in this domain. Potential violations of human dignity are at stake. Moreover, as some of the examples suggest, there is something jurisdictional involved as well. Even the most compelling state interests do not seem to justify incursions into the core domain of conscience; or if some type of balancing remains appropriate, the stakes are significantly different, and the scale would seem to weigh heavily in favor of conscience.

At a time when protections for religious freedom seem to be eroding, it is worth rethinking internal forum protections. Do they suggest areas within the general domain of religious freedom where heightened (and indeed, absolute) protections should be available? If compelling state interest analysis in the United States or "necessity" analysis in international and European settings recede and no longer cover such areas, would direct appeal to internal forum standards at least sometimes provide replacement protections?

One of the reasons to recognize internal forum concerns is precisely to remind us that the typical tools that have been developed by legal systems to analyze the outer boundaries of religious freedom in the external social and political world may not apply to internal forum questions or, for that matter, to areas closely tied to this fundamental domain of human dignity.

A. COMPELLED PATRIOTIC OBSERVANCES IN THE UNITED STATES

Note on *Minersville School District v. Gobitis*

Supreme Court of the United States, 310 U.S. 386 (1940)

In the 1940 case *Minersville School District v. Gobitis*, 310 U.S. 386 (1940), the Supreme Court, focusing on the state's right to determine appropriate means to inculcate patriotism in children, held that a state statute that compelled flag salutes in public schools—with no exemption for religious objectors—was constitutional.

The values of uniformity, patriotism, and equality were used to justify compelling students to participate in reciting the Pledge of Allegiance. By an 8–1 margin, the Supreme Court decided against the dissenting Jehovah's Witness children and for the School District.

After lobbying Chief Justice Hughes for the assignment, Justice Felix Frankfurter wrote the majority opinion for the Court.[4] He focused on two principal arguments: free exercise and due process. Citing the "secular regulation" rule, Justice Frankfurter wrote:

> Conscientious scruples have not, in the course of the long struggle for religious toleration, relieved the individual from obedience to a general law not aimed at the promotion or restriction of religious beliefs. The mere possession of religious convictions which contradict the relevant concerns of a political society does not relieve the citizen from the discharge of political responsibilities. The necessity for this adjustment has again and again been recognized.[5]

In response to the due process argument, Frankfurter wheeled out the heavy artillery, quoting Abraham Lincoln's famous question, "Must a government of necessity be too strong for the liberties of its people, or too weak to maintain its own existence?"[6] Having thus raised the stakes to the very existence of the government, Frankfurter said,

> The ultimate foundation of a free society is the binding tie of cohesive sentiment. Such a sentiment is fostered by all those agencies of the mind and spirit which may serve to gather up the traditions of a people. . . . The flag is the symbol of our national unity, transcending all internal differences.[7]

Frankfurter bolstered this argument about the symbolic significance of the flag to national unity with an appeal to judicial restraint and respect for the political judgments of those who enacted the Minersville regulation. As Noah Feldman has explained, "Frankfurter was proud of his opinion. He believed he had shown how liberal constitutional theory worked in practice. It respected civil liberties without interfering in legislative judgments. And it was able to recognize important political values, like the need to promote national unity."[8] Deferring to the political judgment of the Pennsylvania school officials was an exercise of judicial restraint, one of the lodestars in Frankfurter's constitutional galaxy.[9]

---

4. According to Noah Feldman, Frankfurter "had multiple reasons to be engaged with the undertaking. As Frankfurter framed the issues, the case was an opportunity to expound the constitutional theory [of judicial restraint] he had developed. Just as important, Frankfurter was a careful student of international affairs and a Europe watcher who had identified Hitler's threat early, and so was staunchly pro-war." Noah Feldman, *Scorpions: The Battles and Triumphs of FDR's Great Supreme Court Justices* 181 (Twelve 2010).

5. *Gobitis*, 310 U.S. at 594–95.

6. 310 U.S. at 596.

7. *Id.*

8. Feldman, *supra* note 4, at 182.

9. Indeed, Frankfurter, who had been a member of the national committee of the American Civil Liberties Union before joining the court, desired to have it both ways. Frankfurter viewed himself as a civil libertarian, and the ACLU had filed a brief in the case on behalf of the Gobitises. Frankfurter said that, in his view, the best way to promote national unity was not by forcing everyone to salute the flag—rather he favored tolerating such "crotchety" beliefs. *Id.* "But, Frankfurter went on to explain, the job of the Court was not to decide whether the school board had followed the best course of action. It was, instead, to ascertain whether the school board had made a reasonable choice in requiring the children to salute."

Perhaps most significantly, Justice Frankfurter cited the importance of the values weighing against the Gobitis children's free exercise and due process rights: "We are dealing with an interest inferior to none in the hierarchy of legal values. National unity is the basis of national security."[10]

Justices Black, Reed, Douglas, and Murphy (who were, like Justice Frankfurter, Roosevelt appointees to the Supreme Court), along with Justices Roberts and Hughes (Hoover appointees), wholeheartedly joined Frankfurter's opinion. Justice Douglas, for example, demonstrated the high level of enthusiasm among the members of the majority when he called the draft "historic" and "truly statesmanlike."[11]

Thereafter followed the greatest outbreak of religious intolerance in twentieth-century America. At least 31 states took legal steps to expel children who refused to salute the flag in schools. Numerous instances of vigilantism against Jehovah's Witnesses who refused to salute the flag were reported. These included mob beatings, burning of Jehovah's Witnesses Kingdom Halls, and attacks on houses where Jehovah's Witnesses were believed to live. One of the most common occurrences of vigilantism was the arbitrary imprisonment of Jehovah's Witnesses. Sometimes this imprisonment was ostensibly for the purpose of protecting the Jehovah's Witnesses from mobs, but more often it was participation by authorities in the persecution of Jehovah's Witnesses after *Gobitis.*[12]

Things gradually improved after the *Barnette* case, which took the unusual step of reversing *Gobitis*, a recent near unanimous decision.

West Virginia State Board of Education v. Barnette

Supreme Court of the United States, 319 U.S. 624 (1943)

Mr. Justice Jackson delivered the opinion of the Court.

Following the decision by this Court on June 3, 1940, in *Minersville School District v. Gobitis*, 310 U.S. 586, the West Virginia legislature . . . adopted a resolution ordering that the salute to the flag become "a regular part of the program of activities in the public schools," that all teachers and pupils "shall be required to participate in the salute honoring the Nation represented by the Flag; provided, however, that refusal to salute the Flag be regarded as an act of insubordination."

The resolution originally required the "commonly accepted salute to the Flag" which it defined. Objections to the salute as "being too much like Hitler's" were raised by the Parent and Teachers Association, the Boy and Girl Scouts, the Red Cross, and the Federation of Women's Clubs. Some modification appears to have been made in deference to these objections, but no concession was made to Jehovah's Witnesses. What is now required is the "stiff-arm" salute, the saluter to

10. 310 U.S. at 595. As Feldman explains, in Frankfurter's view patriotism "was the glue that held the nation together: 'The flag is a symbol of our national unity, transcending all internal differences, however large, within the framework of the Constitution.'" *supra* note 4, at 181. To put an exclamation point on this view, Frankfurter quoted Oliver Wendell Holmes: "We live by symbols." 310 U.S. at 596, quoted in Feldman, *supra* note 4, at 181 n.9.

11. Feldman, *supra* note 4, at 182.

12. For a comprehensive discussion of the treatment of Jehovah's Witnesses after *Gobitis*, *see* David R. Manwaring, *Render Unto Caesar: The Flag Salute Controversy* 163–167 (Univ. of Chicago Press 1962). *See also* Brett G. Scharffs, Echoes from the Past: What We Can Learn About Unity, Belonging and Respecting Differences from the Flag Salute Cases, 25 *BYU J. Pub. L.* 361 (2011).

keep the right hand raised with palm turned up while the following is repeated: "I pledge allegiance to the Flag of the United States of America and to the Republic for which it stands; one Nation, indivisible, with liberty and justice for all."

Failure to conform is "insubordination" dealt with by expulsion. Readmission is denied by statute until compliance. Meanwhile the expelled child is "unlawfully absent" and may be proceeded against as a delinquent. His parents or guardians are liable to prosecution, and if convicted are subject to fine not exceeding $50 and jail term not exceeding thirty days.

Appellees, citizens of the United States and of West Virginia, brought suit in the United States District Court for themselves and others similarly situated asking its injunction to restrain enforcement of these laws and regulations against Jehovah's Witnesses. The Witnesses' . . . beliefs include a literal version of Exodus, Chapter 20, verses 4 and 5, which says: "Thou shalt not make unto thee any graven image. . . ." They consider that the flag is an "image" within this command. For this reason they refuse to salute it. . . .

The very purpose of a Bill of Rights was to withdraw certain subjects from the vicissitudes of political controversy, to place them beyond the reach of majorities and officials and to establish them as legal principles to be applied by the courts. One's right to life, liberty, and property, to free speech, a free press, freedom of worship and assembly, and other fundamental rights may not be submitted to vote; they depend on the outcome of no elections. . . .

[At] the very heart of the *Gobitis* opinion [is its reasoning] that "National unity is the basis of national security," that the authorities have "the right to select appropriate means for its attainment," and hence reaches the conclusion that such compulsory measures toward "national unity" are constitutional. Upon the verity of this assumption depends our answer in this case.

National unity as an end which officials may foster by persuasion and example is not in question. The problem is whether under our Constitution compulsion as here employed is a permissible means for its achievement.

Struggles to coerce uniformity of sentiment in support of some end thought essential to their time and country have been waged by many good as well as by evil men. Nationalism is a relatively recent phenomenon but at other times and places the ends have been racial or territorial security, support of a dynasty or regime, and particular plans for saving souls. As first and moderate methods to attain unity have failed, those bent on its accomplishment must resort to an ever-increasing severity. As governmental pressure toward unity becomes greater, so strife becomes more bitter as to whose unity it shall be. . . . Ultimate futility of such attempts to compel coherence is the lesson of every such effort from the Roman drive to stamp out Christianity as a disturber of its pagan unity, the Inquisition as a means to religious and dynastic unity, the Siberian exiles as a means to Russian unity, down to the fast failing efforts of our present totalitarian enemies. Those who begin coercive elimination of dissent soon find themselves exterminating dissenters. Compulsory unification of opinion achieves only the unanimity of the graveyard.

The First Amendment to our Constitution was designed to avoid these ends by avoiding these beginnings. There is no mysticism in the American concept of the State or of the nature or origin of its authority. We set up government by consent of the governed, and the Bill of Rights denies those in power any legal opportunity to coerce that consent.

The case is made difficult not because the principles of its decision are obscure but because the flag involved is our own. Nevertheless, we apply the limitations of the Constitution with no fear that freedom to be intellectually and spiritually diverse or even contrary will disintegrate the social organization. To believe that patriotism will not flourish if patriotic ceremonies are voluntary and spontaneous instead of a compulsory routine is to make an unflattering estimate of the appeal of our institutions to free minds. We can have intellectual individualism and the rich cultural diversities that we owe to exceptional minds only at the price of occasional eccentricity and abnormal attitudes. When they are so harmless to others or to the State as those we deal with here, the price is not too great. But freedom to differ is not limited to things that do not matter much. That would be a mere shadow of freedom. The test of its substance is the right to differ as to things that touch the heart of the existing order.

If there is any fixed star in our constitutional constellation, it is that no official, high or petty, can prescribe what shall be orthodox in politics, nationalism, religion, or other matters of opinion or force citizens to confess by word or act their faith therein.

We think the action of the local authorities in compelling the flag salute and pledge transcends constitutional limitations on their power and invades the sphere of intellect and spirit which it is the purpose of the First Amendment to our Constitution to reserve from all official control.

The decision of this Court in *Minersville School District v. Gobitis* and the holdings of those few *per curiam* decisions which preceded and foreshadowed it are overruled, and the judgment enjoining enforcement of the West Virginia Regulation is affirmed.

Affirmed.

[In his dissent, Justice Frankfurter saw this case turning on the role of the judiciary in the legislative process. He argued reasonable men could differ as to the necessity of a compulsory flag salute as a way of promoting good citizenship, and he argued it is not the role of the judiciary to deem a law unconstitutional when the legislature could have had a reasonable basis for passing it. He would have given deference to the state legislature in this case. He reasoned that legislative actions could only override religious liberty concerns in major concerns of the state, and that it should be up to each state to decide what major concerns in their area were. It is important to note that Justice Frankfurter did not take his decision lightly. He began his opinion by recognizing that, as a Jew, he is part of a group that is often the victim of religious discrimination. However, he indicated that the wants of the majority, when encapsulated in a law not aimed at religion, should override the religious rights of the minority in this case.]

COMMENTS AND QUESTIONS

1. In 1940, when *Gobitis* was decided, America had not yet entered World War II but was growing more concerned with reports of Hitler's activities. Nationalism and isolationism were powerful forces at the time in US culture and politics. National unity was also a big issue. There were great fears of divisive foreign

influences. Relevant laws and regulations were enacted, including Executive Order 9066, which mandated the forced removal of thousands of Japanese Americans from their homes to detention camps for the duration of the war. However, by the time *Barnette* was decided in 1943, America had entered World War II and was more unified than it had been three years previously.

2. How could the changing political climate have influenced how the Supreme Court viewed the issue of allowing exemptions from flag salute laws? What would be some of the implications for religious freedom if Justice Frankfurter's approach had represented the majority opinion in *Barnette*?
3. Does Justice Jackson use a balancing approach, or does his opinion reflect a more absolute commitment to protect the rights of inner conscience that were infringed?

B. EUROPE

NOTE ON *EFSTRATIOU v. GREECE*

European Court of Human Rights, App. No. 24095/94 (18 December1996)

The European Court of Human Rights found no Article 9 violation in the Greek government's decision to suspend Sophia Efstratiou from school after she refused to participate in parades commemorating the outbreak of war between Greece and Fascist Italy. Efstratiou, a Jehovah's Witness, had been excused from religious instruction and Orthodox Mass at her school. However, despite her assertion that her beliefs obligated her to express her pacifism by avoiding all events associated with the military, she was not excused from participating in the 1993 National Day military parade and was suspended for two days. She was again suspended, for one day, for not participating in the 1994 National Day school parade. Sophia and her parents appealed to the Court under Article 9 of the Convention, defining their pacifism as a religious belief and claiming religious discrimination. The freedom to exercise religion, they argued, also worked negatively: They should also have the right to refrain from activities inconsistent with their beliefs. The Court held that in exempting her from religious instruction and Orthodox Mass, Sophia's school had already demonstrated sensitivity to her religious beliefs; moreover, in the court's view the parade was not offensive enough to wound Sophia's parents' beliefs and, therefore, requiring her to participate did not constitute a violation of Article 9.

COMMENTS AND QUESTIONS

1. What about the payment of taxes and other civil support: Does paying taxes to a political entity equate to a patriotic observance? *See United States v. Lee*, 455 U.S. 252 (1982) (holding that religious beliefs do not entitle Amish workers to an exemption from the requirement to pay Social Security tax). In *Employment Division v. Smith,* 494 U.S. 872 (1990), the United States Supreme Court cited *Gobitis* as if it had not been reversed, and held that neutral and general laws could override free exercise claims. Does *Smith* un-reverse *Gobitis*? Is coerced patriotic observance in *Barnette* distinguishable from coerced compliance with drug laws (through denial of unemployment benefits

following dismissal for drug use)?

2. Could jury duty or other civic duties amount to a ritual that is alien or contrary to one's religious tenets? Should exemption from these civic duties be allowed?
3. Consider a Catholic priest who lives in a state that has adopted legislation requiring any adult who becomes aware of child abuse to report it to state authorities. The priest learns of a child abuse situation as a result of a confession by one of his parishioners. Under Catholic canon, breaking the seal of the confessional is a grave sin. Should the priest be exempted from the law? Should he be sent to jail for refusal to comply? Note that the state clearly has a compelling state interest in preventing child abuse. Are there any conscientious claims that should not give way to a compelling state interest?

III. RELIGIOUS SPEECH

A. RELIGIOUS PERSUASION

1. The United States

In a series of cases decided in the 1940s, *Cantwell v. Connecticut*, *Murdock v. Pennsylvania*, and *Follett v. McCormick*, the Supreme Court struck down license and occupation taxes imposed on Jehovah's Witnesses who sold religious reading materials through door-to-door proselytizing. In *Murdock*, the Court noted that

> missionary evangelism—as old as the history of printing presses. It has been a potent force in various religious movements down through the years. . . This form of religious activity occupies the same high estate under the First Amendment as do worship in the churches and preaching from the pulpits. It has the same claim to protection as the more orthodox and conventional exercises of religion. It also has the same claim as the others to the guarantees of freedom of speech and freedom of the press.[13]

In *Watchtower Bible & Tract Society v. Village of Stratton*, 536 U.S. 150 (2002), another case involving the Jehovah's Witnesses, the Supreme Court held that a city regulation requiring uninvited religious door-to-door solicitors to obtain a state license violated their free speech rights.

2. Europe

NOTE ON *LARISSIS AND OTHERS v. GREECE*

ECtHR, App. Nos. 23372/94 and two others (24 February 1998)

In addition to the *Kokkinakis* case, discussed in Chapter 1, the European Court of Human Rights addressed the issue of improper proselytizing in *Larissis and Others v. Greece*. The Court held in that case that an effort by a military officer to convert a subordinate constituted impermissible proselytizing, because of the inherent coercive pressure in this type of hierarchical situation. On the other hand,

---

13. *Cantwell v. Connecticut*, 310 U.S. 296 (1940); *Murdock v. Pennsylvania*, 319 U.S. 105, 108–109 (1943); *Follett v. McCormick*, 321 U.S. 573 (1944).

the attempt by someone in the military to convert an ordinary citizen was not similarly tainted with impermissible pressure.

The applicants in *Larissis* were three officers of the Greek air force, charged with impermissible proselytizing of airmen under their command, and convicted in Greek Courts. The officers appealed to the European Court of Human Rights, claiming that their convictions constituted a violation of their right to manifest their religion or belief under Article 9 of the European Convention on Human Rights. The Court acknowledged that the officers' Article 9 rights had been interfered with, and proceeded to determine "whether such interference was 'prescribed by law,' pursued a legitimate aim and was 'necessary in a democratic society' within the meaning of Article 9 §2."

In its analysis of whether the interference was necessary in a democratic society, the Court stated in part:

> . . . while religious freedom is primarily a matter of individual conscience, it also implies, inter alia, freedom to "manifest [one's] religion", including the right to try to convince one's neighbour, for example through "teaching". . . .
>
> Article 9 does not, however, protect every act motivated or inspired by a religion or belief. It does not, for example, protect improper proselytism, such as the offering of material or social advantage or the application of improper pressure with a view to gaining new members for a Church. ...
>
> The Court's task is to determine whether the measures taken against the applicants were justified in principle and proportionate. In order to do this, it must weigh the requirements of the protection of the rights and liberties of others against the conduct of the applicants. (paras. 45-46)

Noting that "different factors come into the balance in relation to the proselytizing of the airmen and that of the civilians," the Court proceeded to assess the two matters separately.

> [T]he hierarchical structures which are a feature of life in the armed forces may colour every aspect of the relations between military and personnel, making it difficult for a subordinate to rebuff the approaches of an individual of superior rank or to withdraw from a conversation initiated by him. Thus, what would in the civilian world be seen as an innocuous exchange of ideas which the recipient is free to accept or object, may, within the confines of military life, be viewed as a form of harassment or the application of undue pressure in abuse of power. (para. 51)

Accordingly, the Court concluded that the measures taken against the officers for proselytizing the airmen were justified because the airmen felt they were under pressure to listen to and participate in the religious conversation. The measures taken in relation to proselytizing civilians, on the other hand, were not justified because there was no such pressure.

COMMENTS AND QUESTIONS

1. A 2010 United States Air Force Academy survey revealed that 41 percent of non-Christian cadets and 19 percent of all cadets were subjected to unwanted proselytizing.[14] Does it make sense for rules about religious persuasion to be different in the military? What about efforts to engage in religious persuasion

14. Dan Elliott, 41% of Non-Christian AF Cadets Cite Proselytizing, *Associated Press,* 29 October 2010.

in a state university setting? What if witnessing activity is done by a faculty sponsor at a meeting of a campus religious organization (assuming that participation in the organization is voluntary and none of the students are taking classes from the faculty sponsor)?

2. In 2005, Michael ("Mikey") Weinstein and other graduates of the United States Air Force Academy brought suit charging that a pattern and practice had developed at the Academy of supporting evangelical Christianity. Weinstein cited pressures to participate in worship services and a chaplain's encouraging other cadets to proselytize their non-Christian peers. He also cited an incident where the Deputy Chief of Chaplains of the US Air Force allegedly said, "We will not proselytize, but we reserve the right to evangelize the unchurched." Despite airmen's requests, this policy was not repudiated. The case was dismissed for lack of standing to challenge future Air Force policies. *See Weinstein v. U.S. Air Force*, 468 F. Supp. 2d 1366, 1370–1373 (D.N.M. 2006). If such a case were brought by current cadets with standing, it would likely arise as an Establishment Clause case in the United States. But to what extent would Air Force Academy administrators, professors, chaplains, and students have free exercise rights to engage in such persuasive activities?
3. Weinstein is the founder of the Military Religious Freedom Foundation (MRFF), whose stated goals are to ensure that members of the US Armed Forces receive the constitutional guarantee of religious freedom to which they are entitled. In February 2011 MRFF litigation sparked by a prayer luncheon hosted by the Air Force Academy's chaplain service, where a fundamentalist retired Marine Corps Lieutenant was the keynote speaker, was reviewed by a federal judge, who ruled plaintiffs lacked sufficient legal standing to challenge the event. Later in 2011, however, MRFF noted a "significant victory" when the Air Force revised the ethical indoctrination course material, removing Biblical verses and other Christian religious teachings, to which nuclear missile launch officers were exposed as a standard component of their training.
4. In June of 2014 the US Navy, in response to a letter from the Freedom from Religion Foundation (FFRF), issued a directive to remove all Bibles, which are provided free of charge by Nashville-based Gideons International, from all International Navy Lodges' rooms. FFRF claimed that Gideon Bibles were common but that other religious materials such as the Book of Mormon and Koran were not present, which they said raised "constitutional concerns." Christian groups responded in opposition to the directive. In August of 2014 the Navy reported that the decision to remove the Bibles was being reviewed by senior Navy leadership, and in the meantime the Bibles would be returned to the Lodges' rooms. Do you see any potential "constitutional concerns" with Gideon Bibles in Navy Lodges' rooms? Can the mere presence of Bibles in lodges be considered a proselytizing effort? Would the constitutional issue change if other religious books were also present?

3. Malaysia

As will be discussed further below, some widespread interpretations of Islamic beliefs hold that renunciation of Islam for another religion is forbidden. While some Islamic countries go so far as to completely forbid conversion from Islam, others simply restrict proselytism, which would have the effect of at least reducing the number of conversions. In Malaysia, Article 11 of the Federal Constitution provides:

> 1. Every person has the right to profess and practice his religion and, subject to Clause (4), to propagate it. . . .
>
> 4. State law and in respect of the Federal Territories of Kuala Lumpur and Labuan, federal law may control or restrict the propagation of any religious doctrine or belief among persons professing the religion of Islam.

In 1989, as recorded in the report of the UN Special Rapporteur on Religious Intolerance,[15] the Malaysian government responded to criticism of this article by arguing that the "scope of the enactments is limited to only 'control and restrict the propagation of non-Islamic religious doctrines and beliefs among persons professing the religion of Islam'" and therefore "could not in any way diminish the enjoyment by non-Muslims of freedom of thought, conscience and religion." The government further explained that the laws were not intended to control Muslims "in the matter of their thought, conscience or religion," but merely protected "Muslims from being subjected to attempts to convert them to another religion." In fact, the government explained that any Muslim could "seek knowledge about another religion or even profess another religion" and that the laws are "not capable of deterring him."

In spite of the Malaysian government's assurance that the laws regulating proselytism "are not capable of deterring" Muslims who wish to profess another religion, Muslims who do wish to change religion may find it difficult to do so. In 1998 an ethnic Malay woman from Kuala Lumpur named Azlina Jailani was baptized a Christian.[16] In 1999, Jailani had her name changed to Lina Joy, but she was not allowed to have the religion indicated on her state-issued identification card changed from Islam to Christian. This, in turn, has prevented her from marrying her Christian fiancé, since Islamic law does not allow women to marry outside the faith. On appeal in 2007, Malaysia's High Court ruled that it had no jurisdiction on the matter and that the issue of whether Joy had apostatized was to be left to the Malaysian Shari'a Courts. With success apparently unlikely, Lina Joy left the country rather than appeal to the Shari'a Court.[17]

The case of Revathi Masoosai, a Muslim-born woman who had married a Hindu man, illustrates the problems of litigation in the Shari'a Court. In that case, the Shari'a Court forcibly separated Revathi from her husband and ordered her confined in a "rehabilitation" center for 180 days. The court also placed Revathi's daughter with Revathi's Muslim parents. After completing her sentence, Revathi was placed in the custody of her parents and banned from living with her husband.

COMMENTS AND QUESTIONS

The final verses of the Gospel of Matthew in the New Testament contain what is known as the "Great Commission." In these verses, the risen Jesus addresses his

---

15. Report of the UN Special Rapporteur on Religious Intolerance, Angelo Vidal d'Alemida Ribeiro, UN Doc E/CN.4/1990.46, 22 January 1990.

16. Malaysia: Lina Joy's Despair, *The Economist*, 31 May 2007. Imran Imtiaz Shah Yacob, Doing the Impossible: Quitting Islam in Malaysia, *Asia Sentinel*, 27 April 2007.

17. US Department of State, International Religious Freedom Report 2008: Malaysia.

disciples, saying: "Go ye therefore, and teach all nations, baptizing them in the name of the Father, and of the Son, and of the Holy Ghost: Teaching them to observe all things whatsoever I have commanded you. . . ." (Matt. 28:19–20). For Christians who believe that these verses require missionary activities, is it true to say, as the Malaysian response to criticism from the UN Special Rapporteur on Intolerance does, that "laws [restricting missionary work among Muslims] are not capable in any way of diminishing the enjoyment by non-Muslims of freedom of thought, conscience and religion"? Does the right to freedom of religion or belief extend beyond holding the beliefs internally and engaging in joint rituals or practices with fellow believers? Should differences in current religious affiliation (Christian, Muslim, Jewish, Hindu, etc.) justify differing treatments of missionary work as a matter of international law?

4. Israel

Missionary work in Israel is not illegal per se. However, proselytism is restricted by Sections 174 and 368 of the Criminal Law. Section 174 prohibits conversion or attempted conversion of minors, and Section 368 prohibits the offering of material benefits in connection with conversion. While a number of complaints are filed each year alleging violation of these two laws, most are dismissed for lack of evidence, and none has ever resulted in a conviction. More fundamentally, those of the Jewish faith generally oppose proselytization of their own faith and are sensitive about the efforts of others to proselytize Jews.

While Israel does not have a written constitution, a complete ban on proselytism seems to conflict with Israel's "Basic Law" on Human Dignity and Liberty. (The Basic Laws do not form a constitution, but they do take precedence over other laws when there is a conflict.) This Basic Law guarantees the protection of fundamental human rights. While it does not specifically identify freedom of religion as a fundamental human right, it states that rights are to be "upheld in the spirit of the principles set forth in the Declaration of the Establishment of the State of Israel." The Declaration promises that Israel "will ensure complete equality of social and political rights to all its inhabitants irrespective of religion, race or sex; it will guarantee freedom of religion, conscience, language, education and culture; it will safeguard the Holy Places of all religions; and it will be faithful to the principles of the Charter of the United Nations."[18]

COMMENTS AND QUESTIONS

1. At what point does discussing or sharing religious beliefs, or affirmative witnessing of beliefs become "improper proselytism"? If an individual engages in comparable sharing of political beliefs or attempts to persuade others of political viewpoints, would the speech be the subject of legitimate state regulation?
2. Moshe Hirsch contends that the shift from international documents such as the 1948 Universal Declaration of Human Rights, which spoke of the right to "change" one's religion, to formulations such as that in the 1996 International Covenant on Civil and Political Rights, which protects the right "to have or

18. Declaration of the Establishment of the State of Israel, 14 May 1948.

adopt a religion or belief," reflects a shift in the balance between two rights that are in tension when religious persuasion is involved: the freedom to engage in proselytism and the individual's freedom to maintain a religion without interference. He contends that the appropriate balance between these two rights is best struck by recognizing that some regulation of proselytism should be allowed in what he calls the "semi-private religious domain." The idea behind this semi-private domain is that "persons should not be asked to reveal or discuss their religious preference, either explicitly or implicitly through a request to participate in a religious activity, unless they have previously expressed a desire to do so."[19] In his view, "actively approaching other persons in order to persuade them to indicate or discuss their religious beliefs . . . could be prohibited,"[20] whereas "operating a religious center that provides religious articles or services to persons who indicate their will to receive them is permitted under this principle."[21] Hirsch also maintains that "the operation of religious television and radio channels, as well as mailing various documents, is permissible under this principle."[22] Does this view proscribe activity such as that of Kokkinakis (discussed in Chapter 1)? How does this view effect street contacts, billboards, and personal/business signage? Should we be more concerned about a street or internet evangelist enquiring about someone's religious beliefs or affiliation, or of the government doing so? Why?

B. ANTI-CONVERSION LAWS

1. India

Religious conversion has long been an issue of great concern in India. Even during the period of British control, several of the Princely States passed laws banning conversion. The earliest legislation to ban religious conversion was the Raigarh State Conversion Act 1936. After obtaining independence, India adopted a constitution in 1949 that included protection for freedom of religion. While a significant faction argued for inclusion of a provision banning coercive conversion, the drafters settled on Article 25, which provides, "(1) Subject to public order, morality and health and to the other provisions of this Part, all persons are equally entitled to freedom of conscience and the right freely to profess, practice and *propagate* religion" (emphasis added).

Despite this explicit guarantee of freedom to propagate religion, there are (as of early 2018) laws restricting religious conversion in seven of India's 29 states[23] and proposed in at least two more. Ironically, most of these laws carry the title "Freedom of Religion Act." Most contain provisions prohibiting conversion by "force," "allurement," or "fraudulent means," though definitions for these terms

19. Moshe Hirsch, The Freedom of Proselytism under the Fundamental Agreement and International Law, in *The Vatican-Israel Accords: Political, Legal and Theological Contexts* 183, 189–191 (Marshall J. Breger, ed., Univ. of Notre Dame Press 2004).

20. *Id.* at 190–191.

21. *Id.* at 191.

22. *Id.* at 201 n. 58.

23. US Department of State, International Religious Freedom Report 2016: India.

are fairly loose. Many also require those who wish to convert either to inform the district magistrate of their intention or to obtain permission from the magistrate to perform the conversion ceremony. While the earlier laws generally prohibited all "forced" conversions, many now include an exemption for conversion or reconversion to Hinduism.

While many see a straightforward conflict between these laws' restrictions on religious conversion and the constitutional guarantee of freedom to propagate religion, the Supreme Court of India upheld the constitutionality of these laws in the following case.

REV. STANILAUS V. MADHYA PRADESH & OTHERS

Supreme Court of India, 1977 AIR 908 (17 January 1977)

[Reverend Stanislaus had been prosecuted under Madhya Pradesh's anti-conversion law after he refused to register conversions. Stanislaus raised a preliminary objection to the law, which was eventually appealed via the Madhya Pradesh High Court to the India Supreme Court. A similar challenge had been made to the anti-conversion law in Orissa, with the opposite outcome in the High Court there, so the Supreme Court consolidated the cases. However, the Court considered only the facts of Stanislaus's case because they were dispositive of the issue.]

RAY, C.J.

The common questions which have been raised for our consideration are whether the two Acts were violative of the fundamental right guaranteed under Article 25(1) of the Constitution, and (2) whether the State Legislatures were competent to enact them.

Counsel for the appellant has argued that the right to "propagate" one's religion means the right to convert a person to one's own religion. On that basis, counsel has argued further that the right to convert a person to one's own religion is a fundamental right guaranteed by Article 25 (1) of the Constitution. The expression "propagate" has been defined in the Shorter Oxford Dictionary to mean "to spread from person to person, or from place to place, to disseminate, diffuse (a statement, belief, practice, etc.)". According to the Century Dictionary (which is an Encylopaedic Lexicon of the English Language) Vol. VI, "propagate" means as follows: "To transmit or spread from person to person or from place to place; carry forward or onward; diffuse; extend; as to propagate a report; to propagate the Christian religion."

We have no doubt that it is in this sense that the word "propagate" has been used in Article 25(1), for what the Article grants is not the right to convert another person to one's own religion, but to transmit or spread one's religion by an exposition of its tenets. It has to be remembered that Article 25(1) guarantees "freedom of conscience" to every citizen, and not merely to the followers of one particular religion, and that, in turn, postulates that there is no fundamental right to convert another person to one's own religion because if a person purposely undertakes the conversion of another person to his religion, as distinguished from his effort to transmit or spread the tenets of his religion, that would impinge on the "freedom of conscience" guaranteed to all the citizens of the country alike. . .

This Court has given the correct meaning of the Article, and we find no justification for the view that it grants a fundamental right to convert persons to one's own religion. It has to be appreciated that the freedom of religion enshrined in the Article is not guaranteed in respect of one religion only, but covers all religions alike, and it can be properly enjoyed by a person if he exercises his right in a manner commensurate with the like freedom of persons following the other religions. What is freedom for one, is freedom for the other, in equal measure, and there can therefore be no such thing as a fundamental right to convert any person to one's own religion.

It is not in controversy that the Madhya Pradesh Act provides for the prohibition of conversion from one religion to another by use of force or allurement, or by fraudulent means, and matters incidental thereto. The expressions "allurement" and "fraud" have been defined by the Act. The Acts therefore clearly provide for the maintenance of public order for, if forcible conversion had not been prohibited, that would have created public disorder in the States.

The expression "public order" is of wide connotation. It has been held by this Court in *Ramesh Thapper v. The State of Madras* that "'public order' is an expression of wide connotation and signifies state of tranquility which prevails among the members of a political society as a result of internal regulations enforced by the Government which they have established". . . Thus if an attempt is made to raise communal passions, e.g., on the ground that someone has been "forcibly" converted to another religion, it would, in all probability, give rise to an apprehension of a breach of the public order, affecting the community at large. The impugned Acts therefore fall within [the purview of state power to regulate in the interest of public order].

COMMENTS AND QUESTIONS

1. Does it make a difference whether an anti-conversion law criminalizes the activity of the missionary or the convert? Is the Court's notion that a right to convert would violate the religious freedom of the convert credible? It seems doubtful that a missionary would claim anything but a right to propagate, with the ultimate decision being left to the potential convert.
2. How broadly should "public order" be construed? Is a reduction in tranquility reflected in the fact that members of other religious communities are offended by the mere fact of proselytizing (though not otherwise motivated to action) sufficient to justify regulation? If missionary efforts threaten to bring about communal violence, does that justify imposing constraints on missionary work? What if the threatened violence is only an assault on the missionary? How great and how imminent must the risk of violence be to justify state action deterring or enjoining missionary speech?
3. Article 20(2) of the ICCPR provides: "Any advocacy of national, racial or religious hatred that constitutes incitement to discrimination, hostility or violence shall be prohibited by law." Could constraints on the missionary work of *Kokkinakis v. Greece* (see Chapter 1) be justified by this provision? Of *Cantwell v. Connecticut* (see Chapter 1)?

2. Islam

Gamil Muhammed Hussein, Basic Guarantees in the Islamic Criminal Justice System

In *Criminal Justice in Islam* 37, 42–43 (Muhammad Abdel Haleem, Adel Omar Sherif, and Kate Daniels, eds., Oxford Univ. Press 2003)

Hudud offences under Islamic Shari'a are crimes against God or against the essential system and basic foundations of the Islamic state, or against the interests of society as a whole. Punishments for such crimes are determined by God in the Qur'an or by the Prophet in the *sunna*. *Hudud* crimes, once proven before the judge, are not and cannot be subject to forgiveness or pardon; punishment must be imposed upon criminals who are proven guilty of committing such crimes. [Description of the *hudud* crime of *ridda* (turning back from the Muslim faith) follows:]

Turning back from the Muslim faith (*ridda*) is discussed in the Qur'an: "And if any of you turn back from their faith and die in unbelief, their works will bear no fruit in this life and in the Hereafter; they will be companions of the Fire and will abide therein." (Q.2:217) Equally, the Prophet proclaimed: "Kill whoever turns back from his faith."

In order for this crime to exist, however, a person must knowingly and willfully commit an act, abstain from committing an act, or make a pronouncement which has the effect of making him/her turn back from the Islamic faith. . . .

The punishment for this crime, in this life, is death. The purposes behind this severe punishment for those who change their Islamic faith or turn back from their faith are to protect the Muslim *umma* from discord, spying, disrespect and mockery. Under the Shari'a, Islam is a religion, a nationality and a state; adherents of Islam are members of the Islamic State and the Muslim *umma*, and enjoy Muslim 'nationality'. Thus, to turn back from the Islamic faith in an open way is tantamount to waging war against God, the Apostle, and the Muslim state or *umma*. Therefore, severe punishment is required to defend the *umma* against this serious crime.

COMMENTS AND QUESTIONS

1. While the foregoing reflects the views of classical Islamic jurists, there is a significant group of Muslim scholars who take the view that the passages on which the harsh sanctions for apostasy are based really refer to desertion and treason at the time of Mohammed and do not necessarily apply today.[24] This view is supported by the fact that, while the Qur'an addresses the very serious sin of apostasy on several occasions, it never pronounces an earthly sanction.

24. Nazila Ghanea, Apostasy and Freedom to Change Religion or Belief, in *Facilitating Freedom of Religion or Belief: A Deskbook* 681–685 (Tore Lindholm, W. Cole Durham, Jr., and Bahia G. Tahzib-Lie, eds., Martinus Nijhoff 2004). *See also* Heiner Bielefeldt, Nazila Ghanea, and Michael Wiener, Freedom to Adopt, Change, or Renounce a Religion or Belief, in *Freedom of Religion or Belief: An International Law Commentary* 55-74 (Oxford Univ. Press 2016).

2. The Qur'an contains several passages that appear consistent with religious freedom: "Unto you your religion, and unto me my religion" [Qur'an 109:6], "Whosoever will, let him believe, and whosoever will, let him disbelieve" [Qur'an 18:29], and "There is no compulsion in religion. The right direction is distinct from error" [Qur'an 2:256]. Scholars who argue that apostasy should not be punishable find it strange that the Qur'an would outline punishments for lesser crimes such as theft or adultery, but remain silent on the punishment of the only crime that is thought to carry a mandatory death sentence, leaving such a detail to a less certain *hadith.*[25] At a minimum, there are a diversity of views on this controversial notion.[26]

ANN ELIZABETH MAYER, ISLAM AND HUMAN RIGHTS: TRADITION AND POLITICS

From Ann Elizabeth Mayer, 170–171 (Westview Press, 5th ed. 2012)

Freedom of religion is a topic where Islamic human rights schemes clash directly with international human rights law. ... [Such schemes] are written to accommodate the premodern jurists' rule that bars conversion from Islam, and they accommodate states' prerogative to decree that any people they wish to so designate are apostates. ... Many Muslims question the rules and punishing conversion from Islam set forth by the premodern jurists. The latter tended to say that apostates were to be given an opportunity to repent and return to Islam, but if they refused, they were to be executed if they were men or imprisoned until they changed their minds if they were women. Premodern *shari'a* rules also provided that apostasy constituted civil death, meaning, among other things, that the apostate's marriage would be dissolved, and the apostate would become incapable of inheriting. Naturally, the *shari'a* imposed no penalty on conversion to Islam from other faiths.

Progressive thinkers have stressed that there are plausible interpretations of the Islamic sources that accommodate religious freedom. Muslims who oppose criminalizing apostasy point out that the death penalty for apostasy is not called for in the Qur'an. Indeed, in the Qur'an 2:256, one reads a specific admonition that there must be no compulsion in religion, and various passages speak as if belief or unbelief is a personal choice. . . .

Contemporary scholars often observe that the premodern jurists' rules on apostasy were extrapolated from incidents from the Prophet's life and from historical events after his death that are open to a variety of constructions and that do not necessarily provide justification for executing apostates, as in cases where the penalty was actually for treason. The Lebanese scholar Subhi Mahmassani asserts that the circumstances in which the penalty was meant to apply were intended to be narrow ones. He points out that the Prophet never killed anyone merely for apostasy ant that the death penalty was applied when the act of apostasy from Islam was linked to an act of political betrayal of the community. This being

---

25. *Id.*

26. *See generally* Donna E. Arzt, The Treatment of Religious Dissidents Under Classic and Contemporary Islamic Law, in *Religious Human Rights in Global Perspective* 387–453 (John Witte Jr., and Johan D. van der Vyver, eds., Martinus Nijhoff 1996).

the case, Mahmassani argues that the death penalty was not meant to apply to a simple change of faith but to punish acts such as treason, joining forces with the enemy, and sedition. [notes omitted]

The enforcement of the death penalty for apostasy varies among Islamic states. Some states have enacted laws that explicitly pronounce death for apostasy. Others have effected the same result by incorporating Islamic jurisprudence into the state law. Some states, such as Malaysia, still view apostasy as a crime but inflict a lesser punishment—such as imprisonment. The penalties may also differ depending on the sex of the apostate and whether the person was born a Muslim or converted to Islam.

In 1989, the United Nations Special Rapporteur for the Implementation of the Declaration on the Elimination of All Forms of Intolerance and of Discrimination Based on Religion or Belief requested that the government of Mauritania respond to information that Section 306 of its Penal Code authorized the death sentence for Muslims who abandon their faith. The government responded by claiming that "Mauritanian law does not encourage intolerance or discrimination based on belief," but that certain limitations to freedom of religion were necessary to "safeguard security, public order and morality."[27] It justified its punishment for apostasy by explaining that its residents were free to embrace whatever beliefs they desired, but that "any person who embraces [Islam] of his own free will must be assumed to have accepted all its teachings, including the rules governing apostasy. Apostasy from this religion, which guarantees so many freedoms and so much security, stability and social justice, is regarded as high treason and everyone is aware of the penalties that States impose for this type of offence, which threatens their stability and their very existence."[28] Whether or not this argument is persuasive in relation to converts is questionable enough. However, it seems nearly impossible to defend with respect to those who are born into Islam and are not necessarily in a position to make a fully informed choice "of [their] own free will" in accepting Islam.

3. Report of the UN Special Rapporteur on Freedom of Religion or Belief

In his Interim Report to the Sixty-Seventh Session of the UN General Assembly on 13 August 2012, the UN Special Rapporteur on freedom of religion or belief, Heiner Bielefeldt, included a systematic assessment of the right to conversion. The passages that follow are quoted or paraphrased from that assessment.[29]

III. Right to conversion as part of freedom of religion or belief (paraphrase)

Both the right to change one's own religion or belief and the right not to be forced to convert "have the rank of an absolutely protected right" because they "fall within the ambit

---

27. Special Rapporteur for the Implementation of the Declaration on the Elimination of All Forms of Intolerance and of Discrimination Based on Religion or Belief, Report submitted by Mr. Angelo Vidal d'Almeida Ribeiro, at 109, UN Doc. E/CN.4/1991/56 (18 January 1991).

28. *Id.*

29. From Heiner Bielefeldt, UN Special Rapporteur for Freedom of Religion or Belief, UN GAOR, 67th Sess., UN Doc. A/67/303, 13 August 2012.

of the *forum internum*, which has the status of absolute protection." Various countries have nonetheless restricted these rights by imposing criminal sanctions regarding conversion, excluding individuals from important societal sectors such as educational institutions, terrorizing converts, and creating obstacles to interreligious marriage.

The right to try to convert others may be somewhat restricted because it falls within the ambit of the *forum externum*, but many states excessively restrict this right through broad anti-conversion laws that fail to meet International Covenant on Civil and Political Rights standards. For example many states allow law enforcement agents to confiscate and destroy religious teaching materials such as books and videos.

The rights of children and their parents to each of these freedoms deserve special attention because children are often subject to state or sociological restraints on conversion rights. "The Special Rapporteur is deeply concerned by reports of repressive measures targeting children, since they occur in a considerable number of countries." Some states, for example, have mandatory religious curriculum in public schools. This threatens human rights because "the parents or, as the case may be, the legal guardians of the child have the right to organize the life within the family in accordance with the religion or belief and bearing in mind the moral education in which they believe the child should be brought up." [Quoting Article 18(4) of the International Covenant on Civil and Political Rights].

State violations of these rights are often attributable to widespread misunderstanding of them. Most fundamentally, many states view broad religious freedom as a threat to social peace and interreligious harmony. Some states, for example, intentionally restrict conversion rights because they believe that a pluralistic concept of religious morality will undermine social order and morality. The moral fabric of society will unravel and contentions will arise, some believe, because conversion efforts undermine society's predominant social and moral traditions. These concerns, however, rest upon a concept of "peace" based on authoritarian control rather than respect for human dignity. In the UN's view, "a peace based on respect for dignity and freedom of all human beings goes deeper and has a better chance of stability than any societal order organized around such ideas as hegemony, customs, or mere authority." Thus countries may be more willing to expand conversion rights and other religious freedoms if they alter their fundamental understanding of "peace."

Another common misunderstanding is that the concept of free "choice" is not legitimate in the area of religion; religion is not merely a commodity you "choose." However, the language of choice theory is not intended to "commodify" religion. Rather, "by establishing legal safeguards against different forms of coercion, human rights norms can arguably even contribute to the achievement of higher degrees of sincerity, earnestness, authenticity, profoundness, loyalty, and commitment in question of religion or belief."

IV. Conclusions and recommendations

The General Assembly has repeatedly and by consensus urged States to ensure that their constitutional and legislative systems provide adequate and effective guarantees of freedom of thought, conscience and religion or belief to all without distinction, inter alia, by providing access to justice and effective remedies in cases where the right to freedom of thought, conscience and religion or belief or the right to freely practise one's religion, including the right to change one's religion or belief, is violated ....

In his daily work, however, the Special Rapporteur receives numerous reports of grave violations of the right to freedom of religion or belief in the broad area of conversion. In the present report, he has discussed this topic, distinguishing four subcategories that deserve systematic attention: (a) the right to conversion (in the sense of changing one's own religion or belief); (b) the right not to be forced to convert; (c) the right to try to convert others by means of non-coercive persuasion; and (d) the rights of the child and of his or her parents in this context.

A. Right to conversion

In addition to being exposed to manifestations of social pressure, public contempt and systematic discrimination, converts often face insurmountable administrative obstacles when trying to live in conformity with their convictions. Moreover, in a number of countries, they run the risk of losing jobs and educational opportunities, having their marriage nullified, being excluded from the right to inheritance or even losing custody of their children. In some States, converts may also face criminal prosecution, at times even including the death penalty, for such offences as "apostasy", "heresy", "blasphemy" or "insult" in respect of a religion or the country's dominant tradition and values. When seeking asylum, they may find that the genuineness of their conversion is questioned and may be deported back to their countries of origin where they may be confronted with aggravated risks to their life, freedom, well-being and security.

B. Right not to be forced to convert

Serious violations also occur in respect of the right not to be forced to convert against one's will. While some members of religious or belief minorities experience pressure to join a religion or belief deemed more "acceptable" in society, converts are often exposed to pressure to reconverting to their previous religion. Such pressure can be undertaken both by Government agencies and by non-State actors, including by directly linking humanitarian aid to expectation of conversion. The Special Rapporteur is particularly concerned about pressure or threats experienced by women, sometimes in the context of marriage or marriage negotiations, to convert to the religion of their (prospective) husband.

C. Right to try to convert others by means of non-coercive persuasion

In addition, many States impose tight legislative or administrative restrictions on communicative outreach activities. This may unduly limit the right to try to convert others by means of non-coercive persuasion, which itself constitutes an inextricable part of freedom of religion or belief. Moreover, many such restrictions are conceptualized and implemented in a flagrantly discriminatory manner, for instance, in the interest of further strengthening the position of the official religion or dominant religion of the country while further marginalizing the situation of minorities. Members of religious communities that have a reputation of being generally engaged in missionary activities may also face societal prejudices that can escalate into paranoia, sometimes even leading to acts of mob violence and killings.

D. Rights of the child and of his or her parents

The Special Rapporteur has also received reports of repressive measures targeting children of converts or members of religious minorities, including with the purpose of exercising pressure on them and their parents to reconvert to their previous religion or to coerce members of minorities to convert to more socially "accepted" religions or beliefs. Such repressive activities may violate the child's freedom of religion or belief and/or the parents' right to ensure an education for their children in conformity with their own convictions and in a manner consistent with the evolving capacities of the child.

4. Religious Voices in Defense of Religious Freedom

BEIRUT DECLARATION ON "FAITH FOR RIGHTS"

"There are as many paths to God as there are souls on Earth." (Rumi)

We, faith-based and civil society actors working in the field of human rights and gathered in Beirut ... express our deep conviction that our respective religions and beliefs share a common commitment to upholding the dignity and the equal worth of all human beings. Shared human values and equal dignity are therefore common roots of our cultures. Faith and rights should be mutually reinforcing spheres. Individual and communal expression of religions or beliefs thrive and flourish in environments where human rights, based on the equal worth of all individuals, are protected. Similarly, human rights can benefit from deeply rooted ethical and spiritual foundations provided by religion or beliefs.

We understand our respective religious or belief convictions as a source for the protection of the whole spectrum of inalienable human entitlements – from the preservation of the gift of life, the freedoms of thought, conscience, religion, belief, opinion and expression to the freedoms from want and fear, including from violence in all its forms.

"Whoever preserves one life, is considered by Scripture as if one has preserved the whole world." (Talmud, Sanhedrin, 37, a)

"Someone who saves a person's life is equal to someone who saves the life of all." (Quran 5:32)

"You shall love the Lord your God with all your heart, all your soul, all your strength, and with your entire mind; and your neighbour as yourself." (Luke 10:27)

Let them worship the Lord of this House who saved them from hunger and saved them from fear." (Sourat Quraish, verses 3, 4)

"A single person was created in the world, to teach that if anyone causes a single person to perish, he has destroyed the entire world; and if anyone saves a single soul, he has saved the entire world." (Mishna Sanhedrin 4:5)

"Let us stand together, make statements collectively and may our thoughts be one." (Rigveda 10:191:2)

"Just as I protect myself from unpleasant things however small, in the same way I should act towards others with a compassionate and caring mind." (Shantideva, A Guide to the Bodhisattva's Way of Life)

"Let us put our minds together to see what life we can make for our children." (Chief Sitting Bull, Lakota)

Based on the above, among many other sources of faith, we are convinced that our religious or belief convictions are one of the fundamental sources of protection for human dignity and freedoms of all individuals and communities with no distinction on any ground whatsoever. Religious, ethical and philosophical texts preceded international law in upholding the oneness of humankind, the sacredness of the right to life and the corresponding individual and collective duties that are grounded in the hearts of believers.

We pledge to disseminate the common human values that unite us. While we differ on some theological questions, we undertake to combat any form of exploitation of such differences to advocate violence, discrimination and religious hatred. . . .

We believe that freedom of religion or belief does not exist without the freedom of thought and conscience which precede all freedoms for they are linked to human essence and his/her rights of choice and to freedom of religion or belief. A person as a whole is the basis of every faith and he/she grows through love, forgiveness and respect. . . .

We are . . . convinced that religious actors should be enabled, both nationally and internationally, to assume their responsibilities in defending our shared humanity against incitement to hatred, those who benefit from estabilizing societies and the manipulators of fear to the detriment of equal and inalienable human dignity. . . .

To achieve the above goal, we pledge as believers (whether theistic, non-theistic, atheistic or other) to fully adhere to five fundamental principles:

a) Transcending traditional inter-faith dialogues into concrete action-oriented Faith for Rights (F4R) projects at the local level. While dialogue is important, it is not an end in itself. Good intentions are of limited value without corresponding action. Change on the ground is the goal and concerted action is its logical means. "Faith is grounded in the heart when it is demonstrated by deeds." (Hadith)

b) Avoiding theological and doctrinal divides in order to act on areas of shared inter-faith and intra-faith vision as defined in the present F4R declaration. This declaration is not conceived to be a tool for dialogue among religions but rather a joint platform for common action in defence of human dignity for all. . . .

c) Introspectiveness is a virtue we cherish. We will all speak up and act first and foremost on our own weaknesses and challenges within our respective communities. We will address more global issues collectively and consistently, after internal and inclusive deliberation that preserves our most precious strength, i.e. integrity.

d) Speaking with one voice, particularly against any advocacy of hatred that amounts to inciting violence, discrimination or any other violation of the equal dignity that all human beings enjoy regardless of their religion, belief, gender, political or other opinion, national or social origin, or any other status. . . . We have a duty to redress hate speech by remedial compassion and solidarity that heals hearts and societies alike. Our words of redress should transcend religious or belief boundaries. Such boundaries should thus no longer remain a free land for manipulators, xenophobes, populists and violent extremists.

e) We are resolved to act in a fully independent manner, abiding only by our conscience, while seeking partnerships with religious and secular authorities, relevant governmental bodies and non-State actors wherever Faith for Rights (F4R) coalitions are freely established in conformity with the present declaration.

Our main tool and asset is reaching out to hundreds of millions of believers in a preventive structured manner to convey our shared convictions enshrined in this F4R declaration. Speaking up in one voice in defence of equal dignity of all on issues of common challenges to humanity equally serves the cause of faith and rights. Human beings are entitled to full and equal respect, rather than mere tolerance, regardless of what they may believe or not believe. . . .

IV. CONFLICTS BETWEEN FREEDOM OF RELIGION AND FREEDOM OF EXPRESSION

Freedom of speech and freedom of religion are closely interconnected. At times, however, conflicts arise between religion and speech. Such conflicts take two primary forms. On the one hand, religiously motivated speech sometimes offends or causes harm to others. For example, religiously motivated speakers may speak out in condemnation of homosexuals or abortion. On the other hand, speakers may also offend or cause harm to religious believers or perhaps even to a religion itself.

For example, some speakers ridicule all religious belief, while others target particular religions through blasphemous or otherwise offensive speech. While blasphemy laws often seem anachronistic in contemporary settings, one can easily imagine how a range of communities might wish to seek the protections of anti-blasphemy legislation. This part of the chapter introduces some of the challenges that arise in trying to strike a balance between religious freedom rights and other rights and values.

A. RELIGIOUSLY MOTIVATED SPEECH THAT OFFENDS

1. Religiously Motivated Speech Condemning Homosexuality

THE PASTOR GREEN CASE

Supreme Court of Sweden, Csae No. B 1050-05 (29 November 2005)

[Åke Green, a protestant pastor, gave a sermon on 20 July 2003 in Borgholm, Sweden, that quoted numerous biblical passages that facially condemn homosexuality. While calling on those listening to show love for homosexuals, the sermon also included the following statements:

"Legalising partnerships between two men or two women will clearly create unparalleled catastrophes."

"The Bible discusses and teaches us about these abnormalities. And sexual abnormalities are a serious cancerous growth on the body of a society." "The Lord knows that sexually perverse people will even force themselves upon animals."

"Those who lie with boys are the perverted people the Bible speaks of. However, I would like to emphasize that not all homosexuals are pedophiles. Being faithful in a homosexual relationship is no better than changing your partner on an everyday basis."

"Homosexuality is a sickness, i.e., a wholesome and pure thought being replaced by a tainted thought, a wholesome heart being replaced by a sick heart."

Pastor Green was convicted of "agitation against a national or ethnic group *et al.*," and his conviction was affirmed by an intermediate court. The Supreme Court indicated that "[t]hrough the sections of his sermon set out above, viewed in their context, Åke Green has disseminated statements showing contempt for homosexuals with reference to their sexual orientation. The intention of Åke Green was to spread his beliefs in a manner that would attract significant attention."]

Reasoning of the Court

Chapter 16, Section 8 of the Criminal Code provides that a person becomes guilty of agitation against a group by making a statement or otherwise spread[ing] a message that threatens or expresses contempt for an ethnic group or any other group of people with reference to their race, skin colour, nationality or ethnic origin, religious belief or sexual orientation. On 1 January 2003, an amendment of the Act criminalized incitement against homosexuals as a group. The *travaux préparatoires* specified that homosexuals are a vulnerable group in society, and are often victims of crimes as a result of their sexual orientation.

In conjunction with the amendment of the Act, there was a discussion regarding "expressing contempt," which is an element of the crime. However, not every statement of a demeaning or degrading nature is included in this concept. Statements that are not considered to go beyond the limits of objective criticism of certain groups are not liable to punishment. Naturally, the principles of freedom of speech and the right to criticize may not be used to protect statements expressing contempt for a group of people, for example, because they are of a certain nationality and hence are inferior. However, the purview of criminal behaviour may not extend to an objective discussion about, or criticism against, homosexuality. Criminalization must not be used to restrict freedom of speech or to threaten free public debate. In addition, the freedom of science shall be maintained. This also means that these kinds of statements, which are best contested or corrected in a free and open debate, shall not be criminalized.

Naturally, a certain allowance must be made for criticism and similar expressions that are not criminalized. The determining factor is how the message appears when objectively examined. In addition, the context must clearly demonstrate that the intent of the perpetrator was to spread a message that constitutes a threat against, or expresses contempt for, the group in question.

. . . Merely citing and discussing religious scriptures, for example, does not fall within the purview of criminalized behaviour pursuant to this proposal. However, it should not be permissible to use this kind of material to threaten, or to express contempt for, homosexuals as a group, any more than it would be permissible to use religious texts to threaten, or express contempt for, Muslims or Christians.

The statements in question cannot be considered to be direct expressions of Biblical verses referred to by Åke Green, and must be seen as insulting judgments about the group in general. These statements can clearly be deemed to have overstepped the limits of an objective and responsible discourse regarding homosexuals as a group. Åke Green has intentionally spread these statements in this sermon before the congregation, with the awareness that they could be perceived as insulting. . . .

The issue, however, is whether consideration to freedom of religion and freedom of expression should favour giving the word "contempt" a more restrictive interpretation than what a direct reading of the statutory text and its legislative history would. The 2003 amendment was intended to satisfy the requirements regarding the limitation of freedom of speech, based on our constitutional protection of this right, as well as the European Convention on Human Rights and Fundamental Freedoms.

The Supreme Court, however, must now determine whether Chapter 16, Section 8 of the Criminal Code should not be applied, because such an application would violate the Constitution or the European Convention on Human Rights.

Chapter 2, §1, sub-section 1, point 6 of the Instrument of Government Act defines freedom of religion as the freedom to practice one's religion alone or with others. This freedom may not be restricted. Its definition is narrow, and such aspects that fall within other freedoms such as freedom of speech, may be limited in the same way as these freedoms. An act that is generally criminalized is not protected merely because it occurs in a religious context, as the constitutional protection means a prohibition against provisions that expressly target a certain religious practice, or which, despite a more general wording, apparently are intended to hinder a certain religious direction.

Chapter 2, §1, sub-section 1, point 6 of the Instrument of Government Act provides that freedom of speech may be limited to a certain extent by statute. Generally, this kind of restriction may be done only for achieving a purpose that is acceptable in a democratic society, and may never exceed that which is necessary in light of the purpose for which it is created, and may not go so far as to constitute a threat against the free exchange of opinions, which is one of the foundations of democracy, and may not be done only on the grounds of political, religious, cultural or other such philosophy. In addition, §13, first subsection, lists a number of special interests for which freedom of speech may be restricted. To this list may be added the principle that this freedom may otherwise be limited if especially important reasons justify this. The second sub-section of this section indicates that in considering which restrictions may be imposed pursuant to the first sub-section, the importance of having the broadest possible freedom of speech in political, religious, labour, scientific and cultural matters shall be considered.

The constitutional protection of freedom of speech does not appear to constitute a reason not to convict Åke Green according to the indictment.

The assessment to be made now is the extent to which the European Convention on Human Rights affects the criminal liability of Åke Green.

Freedom of religion pursuant to Article 9 includes the freedom to practice one's religion or belief alone or together with others, in public or in private, through religious services, study, customs and rituals. Freedom of speech pursuant to Article 10 includes the freedom to receive and disseminate information and thoughts without the interference from government authorities. The Criminal Code provision regarding incitement against a group fits within the limits set forth by the European Convention on Human Rights.

The question, however, is whether applying these provisions in Åke Green's case would be a violation against the commitments of Sweden under the Convention.

The determining factor appears to be whether the restriction of Åke Green's freedom to preach is necessary in a democratic society. This means that it must be assessed whether the restriction is proportionate to the protected interest.

It should also be noted that Article 10 protects not only the content of opinions and information, but also the way these are disseminated.

When the European Court determines whether an alleged restriction is necessary in a democratic society, the court considers whether the restriction meets a pressing social need, whether it is proportionate to the legitimate purpose to be achieved, and whether the reasons asserted by the national authorities to justify it are relevant and sufficient.

In a comprehensive assessment of the circumstances of Åke Green's case, in light of the case law of the European Court, it is at first clear that there is no question there of the kind of hateful statements known as "hate speech."

Under these circumstances, it is likely that the European Court, in a determination of the restriction of Åke Green's right to preach his Biblically-based opinion that a judgment of conviction would constitute, would find that this restriction is not proportionate, and would therefore be a violation of the European Convention on Human Rights.

The expression "contempt" in the provision regarding incitement against a group cannot be considered to have such a fixed meaning so as to lead to an actual conflict of law between the European Convention on Human Rights and the Criminal Code. As stated immediately above, such an application that conforms to the Convention would not permit a judgment of conviction against Åke Green, given the present circumstances of this case. In light of what is stated above, the indictment of Åke Green shall be dismissed.

COMMENTS AND QUESTIONS

1. According to the Swedish Supreme Court's opinion, criminalization of Pastor Green's speech does not violate Swedish constitutional norms. However, his conviction must be reversed not because the law itself is inconsistent with European Convention standards per se, but only because the application of the law in his case violated them (apparently because his sermon didn't really amount to hate speech). Is the Swedish Court correct in its interpretation of European standards?
2. Karl Marx wrote,

> Religious distress is at one and the same time the expression of real distress and also the protest against real distress. Religion is the sigh of the oppressed creature, the heart of a heartless world, just as it is the spirit of spiritless conditions. It is the opium of the people. To abolish religion as the illusory happiness of the people is to demand their real happiness. The demand to give up illusions about the existing state of affairs is the demand to give up a state of affairs which needs illusions. The criticism of religion is therefore in embryo the criticism of that vale of tears, the halo of which is religion.[30]

Under Swedish law, as interpreted in the Pastor Green case, would Marx be guilty of "agitation against a group by making a statement or otherwise spread[ing] a message that threatens or expresses contempt for [a] . . . group of people with reference to their . . . religious belief . . ."? Are protections for religious and anti-religious speech symmetrical? How robust can criticism be?

NOTE ON *VEJDELAND* v. *SWEDEN*

European Court of Human Rights, App. No. 1813/07 (9 February 2012)

In December 2004, applicants placed approximately 100 leaflets on the lockers of students in an upper secondary Swedish school. The leaflets described homosexuality as a "deviant sexual proclivity" that "has a morally destructive effect on the substance of society." It further alleged that HIV and AIDS were a modern-day plague caused by homosexuals and that homosexual lobby organizations attempted "to play down peadophilia." The applicants were thereafter charged with agitation against a national or ethnic group. In July 2006, the Swedish Supreme Court rejected the Court of Appeals decision and affirmed the District Court's conviction, holding that the applicants violated Chapter 16, Article 8 of the Penal Code which states that:

30. Karl Marx, Contribution to the Critique of Hegel's Philosophy of Law, in 3 *Karl Marx & Frederick Engels: Collected Works* 175–176 (Velta Pospelova et al., eds., Jack Cohen et al., trans., Int'l Publishers 1975) (1844).

> a person who, in a disseminated statement or communication, threatens or expresses contempt for a national, ethnic or other such group of persons with allusion to race, colour, national or ethnic origin, religion beliefs or sexual orientation, should be convicted of agitation against a nation or ethnic group.

The applicants filed a complaint with the European Court of Human Rights (ECtHR), alleging that the ruling violated their freedom of expression as outlined in Article 10 § 1 of the European Convention on Human Rights.

> 2. The exercise of these freedoms, since it carries with it duties and responsibilities, may be subject to such formalities, conditions, restrictions or penalties as are prescribed by law and are necessary in a democratic society, . . . for the protection of the reputation or rights of others, ...

The ECtHR therefore considered whether the interference with the applicant's freedom of expression served a legitimate aim and whether it was necessary to achieve that aim in a democratic society. First, the ECtHR determined that the goal of the Government to protect "the reputation and rights of others" was a legitimate aim outlined in Article 10 § 2 of the Convention. Second, the test used to determine necessity required the Court to consider whether there was a "pressing social need."

In making this determination, the ECtHR considered the case as a whole, including the content of the leaflets and the context in which the applicant's distributed them. The ECtHR explained that while freedom of expression includes ideas that offend, shock, or disturb, it is subject to exceptions. While, the ECtHR concluded that the purpose of the leaflets to spawn a debate about the lack of objectivity in the Swedish education system on homosexuality was acceptable, the applicants also had the obligation to avoid unwarrantably offensive statements that constitute an "assault on the rights of others." The ECtHR therefore examined the text of the leaflets and determined that those statements were unnecessarily offensive because the applicants could have achieved their goal and brought into question the objectivity of Swedish schools without making prejudicial allegations against homosexuals.

The ECtHR further reasoned that the leaflets were imposed, without any opportunity to reject them, on students of an impressionable age in a school in which the applicants were not given free access. Therefore, the ECtHR unanimously held that there was no violation of Article 10 because the Government's interference with the applicants' freedom of expression could be reasonably considered necessary in a democratic society for the legitimate aim of protecting the reputation and rights of others.

COMMENTS AND QUESTIONS

1. In light of the European Court of Human Rights holding in *Vejdeland*, do you think the Swedish Supreme Court was correct in its assessment of the requirements of the European Convention in the Pastor Green case?
2. The penalties imposed are an important factor in considering whether government interference with the freedom of expression was proportional. In *Vejdeland*, three of the applicants were given fines, ranging from EUR 200 to EUR 2,000, and the fourth was sentenced to probation. The ECtHR did not find these penalties to be excessive. Do you agree? The applicants were not

sentenced to imprisonment, but could have been sentenced to two years imprisonment for the crime for which they were convicted. Would your answer be the same if they were given any prison time? What if they were sentenced to two years?

NOTE ON *SNYDER v. PHELPS*

Supreme Court of the United States, 131 S.Ct. 1201 (2011)

Members of the Westboro Baptist Church traveled to Maryland to picket the funeral of Marine Lance Corporal Matthew Snyder. They began picketing 30 minutes before the funeral, approximately 1,000 feet from the church and on public land. The picketers displayed the following signs: "Thank God for Dead Soldiers," "Fags Doom Nations," "America is Doomed," "Priests Rape Boys" and "You're Going to Hell". Westboro members picket military funerals to demonstrate their opposition to the military's tolerance of homosexuality and their condemnation of the Catholic Church and its clergy involved in sexual scandals.

The deceased's father filed suit against Westboro, alleging the intentional infliction of emotional distress, among other claims. In order to prove this state tort claim, the defendant must have "intentionally or recklessly engaged in extreme and outrageous conduct that caused [...] severe emotional distress." However, speech expressing matters of public concern are entitled to special protection over those expressing matters of private concern. Therefore, the First Amendment may be used as a defense against state tort claims.

The Fourth Circuit Court of Appeals reversed the District Court of Maryland's holding that Westboro was liable for the intentional infliction of emotional distress. Upon appeal, the Supreme Court of the United States analyzed the question of whether Westboro's speech was of public or private concern in order to determine whether Westboro could be held liable. The Supreme Court previously determined that speech is considered a matter of public concern when it is a "subject of general interest and [...] value to the public", or relates to "any matter of political, social, or other concern to the community". The Court explained that it is necessary to examine the "content, form, and context," of Westboro's speech independently in order to determine whether it falls into this category.

The Court found that the "content" of Westboro's speech was of public concern because the dominant theme of the signs referenced broad national political and moral issues dealing with the military and Catholic Church and were designed to reach a large public audience. The Court explained that the "context" of the speech, where and when Westboro chose to voice its opinion, is "subject to reasonable, time, place, or manner restrictions." However, Maryland did not have a law restricting funeral picketing at the time of the funeral. The Court concluded that because the speech did not disrupt the funeral, picketing at the funeral, though hurtful, did not change the fact that the speech was of public concern. The Supreme Court therefore held that because "Westboro addressed matters of public import on public property, in a peaceful manner, in full compliance with the guidance of local officials," Westboro was protected against state tort claims by the Free Speech Clause of the First Amendment.

COMMENTS AND QUESTIONS

1. The Supreme Court in *Snyder v. Phelps* focused mainly on the question of the nature of the speech. Would the Court still hold that Westboro's speech was protected if the church instead called the father of the deceased before and after the funeral service, expressing the same messages that were on the signs?
2. In the case of *Frisby v. Schultz*, 487 U.S. 474 (1988), defendants who strongly opposed abortion picketed on public ground outside the home of a doctor who performed abortions. Anti-abortion messages are also considered speech that is on a matter of public concern. However, the Supreme Court found that because the speech was "inherently and offensively intru[sive]" on someone's residential privacy, the government has the right to place a restriction on that speech.

2. Religious Motivation and Hate Speech

NOTE ON HATE SPEECH LEGISLATION IN THE UNITED STATES

Brandenburg v. Ohio, 395 U.S. 444 (1969)

Freedom of speech is one of the most jealously protected liberties in the United States. While free speech is not an absolute right, the standard for protecting speech is probably higher in the United States than in most other countries. While the US Supreme Court has not specifically addressed religiously motivated hate speech, its standard for what speech may be regulated is set out in *Brandenburg v. Ohio*.

Clarence Brandenburg, a member of the Ku Klux Klan, was convicted of violating the Ohio Criminal Syndicalism statute in relation to speeches he made at a Klan rally in Hamilton County, Ohio. The statute prohibited "'advocating . . . the duty, necessity, or propriety of crime, sabotage, violence, or unlawful methods of terrorism as a means of accomplishing industrial or political reform' and 'voluntarily assembl(ing) with any society, group, or assemblage of persons formed to teach or advocate the doctrines of criminal syndicalism.' Ohio Rev. Code Ann. §2923.13."[31] Brandenburg appealed his conviction to the US Supreme Court, claiming that the Ohio statute violated the First and Fourteenth Amendments to the US Constitution. The Court agreed, holding that the state may prohibit speech only "where such advocacy is directed to inciting or producing imminent lawless action and is likely to incite or produce such action."[32] Since the Ohio statute did not distinguish between mere advocacy of violence and incitement to violence, the Court concluded that it violated the constitutional guarantee of freedom of speech.

NOTE ON UNIVERSITY HATE SPEECH CODES

An interesting issue in the contemporary American academic setting is the development of "hate speech" codes at universities. These codes are designed to place restrictions on offensive comments by students and faculty members. Such

31. *Brandenburg v. Ohio*, 395 U.S. 444, 444–445 (1969).
32. *Id.* at 447.

codes have been invoked to prohibit, for instance, comments that "demean the race, sex, religion, color, creed, disability, sexual orientation, national origin, ancestry or age of the individual or individuals" and "create an intimidating, hostile or demeaning environment for education, university-related work, or other university-authorized activity."[33] However, despite the attempts of universities to enforce these codes, courts have largely held that "the expanse of the suppression of speech made possible by [these policies] is as remarkable as it is illegal."[34] The Supreme Court has noted that, while school officials have authority to prescribe conduct in schools, this authority is circumscribed by constitutional safeguards.[35] Thus, while a college may regulate the time, place, and manner in which "hate speech" may be invoked, the Court has ruled that the First Amendment prohibits state schools from regulating in any way the content of such speech.[36]

Despite these rulings, some state universities are now facing questions regarding whether speech that demeans disfavored groups should be allowed on campus. In late 2016, faculty members at Washington State University asserted in an Open Letter: "a campus culture that hides behind 'tolerance' and discourses of free speech undeviatingly creates a campus that is especially disempowering to marginalized students."[37] Violent protests interrupting a peaceful demonstration at the University of California Berkeley in February 2017 led to the cancellation of a speech by "alt-right" commentator Milo Yiannopoulos, notorious for testing the limits of free speech with language seen as racist and sexist. School officials removed Yiannopoulos from campus, they said, out of concern for public safety, because "it was impossible to maintain order given the level of threat, disruption and organized violence."[38]

COMMENTS AND QUESTIONS

1. Is hate speech legislation made legitimate by adding safe harbor provisions, such as the UK's Racial and Religious Hatred Act? (See discussion on the following page.)
2. How should we think about situations such as the one at UC Berkeley, where outside demonstrators apparently disrupted a peaceful protest with unexpected violence? Can we find practical definitions of "safety" on college campuses and hold reasonable opinions about them when "does not allow" might become "cannot guarantee"?
3. College students in both the United States and the United Kingdom have begun to demand "safe spaces" on campus.

> At the heart of the new wave of censorship on British campuses is the "safe space" policy. Its origin can be traced to US protests against military recruiters on campus in the 70s. From there sprung the no-platform agenda, which then morphed over

33. *UWM Post, Inc. v. Board of Regents*, 774 F. Supp. 1163, 1165 (E.D. Wis. 1991).
34. *Dambrot v. University of Michigan*, 839 F. Supp. 477, 484 (E.D. Mich. 1993).
35. *Healy v. James*, 408 U.S. 169, 180–181 (1972).
36. *Papish v. Board of Curators*, 410 U.S. 667, 670 (1973).
37. The letter, dated 27 November 2016, is no longer available at its original source. Published by WSU faculty member David Leonard on 5 December 2017, the letter may be read in its entirety at https://medium.com/@drdavidjleonard/washington-university-campus-climate-92f3f1d2d36e.
38. David Iaconangelo Controversy Stirred after UC Berkeley Cancels Milo Yiannopoulos Speech, *Christian Science Monitor*, 2 February 2017.

> the last few years into this latest incarnation. The idea behind safe space is that people of all identities are entitled to a tolerant environment to express who they are. It sounds commendable, but the implications are startling.[39]

Flemming Rose, who published the cartoons that sparked the "Danish cartoon controversy" (see discussion on page 218) has asserted that "ideological safe spaces make those on the left and the right more extreme." Rose supports this view with observations by Van Jones, an American political and civil rights activist, controversial in his own right, and former adviser to former President Barack Obama. Jones identifies two ideas about safe spaces: a "very good one" (of providing places for "being physically safe on campus, not being subjected to sexual harassment and physical abuse") and a "terrible one" (the demand to be safe ideologically and emotionally: "I just need to feel good all the time. And if someone else says something that I don't like, that is a problem for everyone else, including the administration."[40]

4. Like their counterparts in the United States, students in the UK have protested the appearance on campus of speakers they find offensive, including Milo Yiannopoulos. Somewhat ironically, one person who was caught up in such a protest was Australian feminist icon Germaine Greer, who was scheduled to give a lecture on women and power at Cardiff University in November 2015. Students called for cancellation of her appearance on grounds that an opinion she had expressed was "transphobic" and an expression of "misogynistic views towards trans women." What these students were saying, said Greer, "is that because I don't think surgery will turn a man into a woman I should not be allowed to speak anywhere. . . . I do not know why universities cannot hear unpopular views and think about what they mean."[41]
5. In *The Silencing: How the Left is Killing Free Speech*, Kirsten Powers argues that we are witnessing the emergence of patterns of "repressive tolerance" that delegitimizes dissent.[42] Should campus culture be allowed to silence unpopular speakers? When is this appropriate? Who should judge?

NOTE ON THE HATE SPEECH PARADOX

Although hate speech codes (whether at the university level or as a matter of general law) are designed to protect minorities, they may end up protecting the majority. Commentators have observed this paradox at work in the United States and Europe, particularly in the context of racist speech. Martha Minow, for example, acknowledges that opponents of hate speech regulations present a difficult and disturbing question: "Is it not a real risk that administrators and others in authority positions will notice and seek to restrict minority speech even more than speech directed against them?"[43] As evidence of this bias, she points to the

39. Ian Dunt, Safe Space or Free Speech? The Crisis around Debate at UK Universities, *The Guardian*, 6 February 2015.
40. Flemming Rose, Safe Spaces on College Campuses Are Creating Intolerant Students, *The World Post*, 30 March 2017, updated 12 June 2017.
41. Dunt, *supra* note 44.
42. Kirsten Powers, *The Silencing: How the Left is Killing Free Speech* (Regenery 2015).
43. Martha Minow, Regulating Hatred: Whose Speech, Whose Crimes, Whose Power?—An Essay for Kenneth Karst, 47 *UCLA L. Rev.* 1253, 1264 (2000).

opposite results in two leading US Supreme Court cases involving hate speech regulations:

> In . . . *R.A.V. v. City of St. Paul*, the Court struck down as unconstitutional a hate crime statute in a case in which several white adolescents burned a cross on the property of an African American couple. But the very next year, in *Wisconsin v. Mitchell*, the Court upheld a hate crime statute used to impose an enhanced penalty on an African American youth who led his friends in beating up a white teen after discussing a movie depiction of white Ku Klux Klan violence against a praying African American child.[44]

While admitting that "many factors helped to distinguish the two cases," Minow suggests that "it is not beyond imagination that a primarily white Court could better identify with a white victim than with a black one."[45] Assuming such a bias in the enforcement authority is real, selective enforcement of hate speech regulations may result in a "disparate impact on the weakest and the most minority members of society."[46]

In Britain, selective enforcement of the Race Relations Act (of 1965) gave rise to a similar concern that "racist speech by a member of a historically victimized minority may be silenced because of its potentially explosive consequences, while racist expression by a member of a dominant, historically powerful group could be overlooked as little more than a harmless irritation."[47] A survey of cases also "suggest[ed] that outsiders [were] disproportionately prosecuted and convicted while dominant group members [were] acquitted."[48]

The problem is not simply that majority groups will tend to get favored treatment. All too often, those who are supposed to benefit from such legislation will fear to invoke its protection, because as a practical matter, doing so will act as a lightning rod to attract additional hateful conduct, either against the individual who might otherwise seek protection, against family members, or against other random members of the group. Those in the majority, or in dominant groups, are likely to feel no such inhibitions.

One can easily imagine analogous situations in the context of religiously motivated hate speech. Ultimately, hate speech regulations based on concerns for the protection of racial, ethnic, or religious minority groups must face and resolve this paradox.

B. SPEECH THAT OFFENDS RELIGIOUS SENSITIVITIES

JOSEPH BURSTYN, INC. V. WILSON

Supreme Court of the United States, 343 U.S. 495 (1952)

Mr. JUSTICE CLARK delivered the opinion of the Court.

The issue here is the constitutionality, under the First and Fourteenth Amendments, of a New York statute which permits the banning of motion picture

44. *Id.* at 1264–1265.

45. *Id.* at 1265.

46. *Id.* at 1266.

47. Michael A. G. Korengold, Note, Lessons in Confronting Racist Speech: Good Intentions, Bad Results, and Article 4(a) of the Convention on the Elimination of All Forms of Racial Discrimination, 77 *Minn. L. Rev.* 719, 729 (1993).

48. *Id.* at 730.

films on the ground that they are "sacrilegious." That statute makes it unlawful "to exhibit, or to sell, lease or lend for exhibition at any place of amusement for pay or in connection with any business in the state of New York, any motion picture film or reel (with specified exceptions not relevant here), unless there is at the time in full force and effect a valid license or permit therefor of the education department."

The statute further provides:

> The director of the (motion picture) division (of the education department) or, when authorized by the regents, the officers of a local office or bureau shall cause to be promptly examined every motion picture film submitted to them as herein required, and unless such film or a part thereof is obscene, indecent, immoral, inhuman, sacrilegious, or is of such a character that its exhibition would tend to corrupt morals or incite to crime, shall issue a license therefor. If such director or, when so authorized, such officer shall not license any film submitted, he shall furnish to the applicant therefor a written report of the reasons for his refusal and a description of each rejected part of a film not rejected in toto.

[Appellant was a motion picture distributer that obtained a license authorizing exhibition of an Italian film entitled *The Miracle*, which was part of a trilogy called "Ways of Love." It ran for about eight weeks, during which time the New York State Board of Regents, which by statute is head of the department of education, received hundreds of communications protesting and defending the exhibition. On February 16, 1951, the Regents, after viewing *The Miracle*, determined that it was "sacrilegious" and for that reason ordered the Commissioner of Education to rescind appellant's license to exhibit the film. The Commissioner did so. The appellant appealed this decision through the New York courts to the US Supreme Court.]

As we view the case we need consider only appellant's contention that the New York statute is an unconstitutional abridgment of free speech and a free press.

The present case is the first to present squarely to us the question whether motion pictures are within the ambit of protection which the First Amendment, through the Fourteenth, secures to any form of "speech" or "the press." . . . [Noting that "motion pictures are a significant medium for the communication of ideas, the Court concluded that] expression by means of motion pictures is included within the free speech and free press guaranty of the First and Fourteenth Amendments. . . .

To hold that liberty of expression by means of motion pictures is guaranteed by the First and Fourteenth Amendments, however, is not the end of our problem. It does not follow that the Constitution requires absolute freedom to exhibit every motion picture of every kind at all times and all places. That much is evident from the series of decisions of this Court with respect to other media of communication of ideas.

The statute involved here does not seek to punish, as a past offense, speech or writing falling within the permissible scope of subsequent punishment. On the contrary, New York requires that permission to communicate ideas be obtained in advance from state officials who judge the content of the words and pictures sought to be communicated. This Court recognized many years ago that such a previous restraint is a form of infringement upon freedom of expression to be especially condemned. *Near v. State of Minnesota ex rel. Olson*, 283 U.S. 697 (1931). The Court there recounted the history which indicates that a major purpose of the First

Amendment guaranty of a free press was to prevent prior restraints upon publication, although it was carefully pointed out that the liberty of the press is not limited to that protection. It was further stated that "the protection even as to previous restraint is not absolutely unlimited. But the limitation has been recognized only in exceptional cases."

New York's highest court says there is "nothing mysterious" about the statutory provision applied in this case: "It is simply this: that no religion, as that word is understood by the ordinary, reasonable person, shall be treated with contempt, mockery, scorn and ridicule." This is far from the kind of narrow exception to freedom of expression which a state may carve out to satisfy the adverse demands of other interests of society. In seeking to apply the broad and all-inclusive definition of "sacrilegious" given by the New York courts, the censor is set adrift upon a boundless sea amid a myriad of conflicting currents of religious views, with no charts but those provided by the most vocal and powerful orthodoxies. New York cannot vest such unlimited restraining control over motion pictures in a censor. Under such a standard the most careful and tolerant censor would find it virtually impossible to avoid favoring one religion over another, and he would be subject to an inevitable tendency to ban the expression of unpopular sentiments sacred to a religious minority. Application of the "sacrilegious" test, in these or other respects, might raise substantial questions under the First Amendment's guaranty of separate church and state . . . with freedom of worship for all. However, from the standpoint of freedom of speech and the press, it is enough to point out that the state has no legitimate interest in protecting . . . religions from views distasteful to them which is sufficient to justify prior restraints upon the expression of those views. It is not the business of government . . . to suppress real or imagined attacks upon a particular religious doctrine, whether they appear in publications, speeches, or motion pictures. . . .

Reversed.

OTTO-PREMINGER-INSTITUT V. AUSTRIA

European Court of Human Rights, App. No.13470/87, 20 September 1994

[The applicant, Otto-Preminger-Institut für audiovisuelle Mediengestaltung (OPI), is an Austrian private association that promotes creativity, communication, and entertainment through the audiovisual media. In May 1985, OPI announced a series of screenings of the film *Das Liebsekonzil* (Council in Heaven) by Werner Schroeter. The Innsbruck diocese of the Roman Catholic Church requested that the public prosecutor charge OPI's manager, Mr. Dietmar Zingl, with the crime of "disparaging religious doctrines." Mr. Zingl was subsequently convicted, all public showings were prevented, and a case aimed at suppression of the film resulted in an order of forfeiture.]

II. The Film "Das Liebeskonzil" ["Council in Heaven"] . . .

22. The film portrays the God of the Jewish religion, the Christian religion and the Islamic religion as an apparently senile old man prostrating himself before the Devil with whom he exchanges a deep kiss and calling the Devil his friend. He is also portrayed as swearing by the Devil. Other scenes show the Virgin Mary permitting an obscene story to be read to her and the manifestation of a degree of

erotic tension between the Virgin Mary and the Devil. The adult Jesus Christ is portrayed as a low grade mental defective and in one scene is shown lasciviously attempting to fondle and kiss his mother's breasts, which she is shown as permitting. God, the Virgin Mary and Christ are shown in the film applauding the Devil. . . .

I. Alleged Violation of Article 10

42. The applicant association submitted that the seizure and subsequent forfeiture of the film Das Liebeskonzil gave rise to violations of its right to freedom of expression as guaranteed by Article 10 of the Convention.

A. Whether there have been "interferences" with . . . freedom of expression

43. [It was conceded] before the Court [that] . . . both the seizure and the forfeiture constituted such interferences. Such interferences will [not] entail violation of Article 10 if they were "prescribed by law", pursued an aim that was legitimate and were "necessary in a democratic society" for the achievement of that aim.

B. Whether the interferences were "prescribed by law"

[The Court concluded that the interferences were "prescribed by law" and that Austrian law had been correctly applied.]

C. Whether the interferences had a "legitimate aim"

46. The Government maintained that the seizure and forfeiture of the film were aimed at "the protection of the rights of others," particularly the right to respect for one's religious feelings, and at "the prevention of disorder."

47. As the Court pointed out in . . . *Kokkinakis v. Greece*, freedom of thought, conscience and religion . . . is one of the most vital elements [in] the identity of believers and their conception of life.

Those who choose to exercise the freedom to manifest their religion, irrespective of whether they do so as members of a religious majority or a minority, cannot reasonably expect to be exempt from all criticism. They must tolerate and accept the denial by others of their religious beliefs and even the propagation by others of doctrines hostile to their faith. However, the manner in which religious beliefs and doctrines are opposed or denied is a matter which may engage the responsibility of the State, notably its responsibility to ensure the peaceful enjoyment of the right guaranteed under Article 9 to the holders of those beliefs and doctrines. Indeed, in extreme cases the effect of particular methods of opposing or denying religious beliefs can be such as to inhibit those who hold such beliefs from exercising their freedom to hold and express them.

In the *Kokkinakis* judgment the Court held, in the context of Article 9, that a State may legitimately consider it necessary to take measures aimed at repressing certain forms of conduct, including the imparting of information and ideas, judged incompatible with the respect for the freedom of thought, conscience and religion of others. The respect for the religious feelings of believers as guaranteed in Article 9 can legitimately be thought to have been violated by provocative portrayals of objects of religious veneration; and such portrayals can be regarded as malicious violation of the spirit of tolerance, which must also be a feature of democratic society.

48. The measures complained of were based on section 188 of the Austrian Penal Code, which is intended to suppress behaviour directed against objects of religious veneration that is likely to cause "justified indignation." It follows that their purpose was to protect the right of citizens not to be insulted in their religious feelings by the public expression of views of other persons. The Court accepts that the impugned measures pursued a legitimate aim under Article 10, namely "the protection of the rights of others."

4. Whether the Seizure and the Forfeiture were "Necessary in a Democratic Society"

49. As the Court has consistently held, freedom of expression constitutes one of the essential foundations of a democratic society, one of the basic conditions for its progress and for the development of everyone, applicable not only to "information" or "ideas" that are favourably received or regarded as inoffensive or as a matter of indifference, but also to those that shock, offend or disturb. Such are the demands of that pluralism, tolerance and broadmindedness without which there is no "democratic society".

However, whoever exercises [this freedom] undertakes "duties and responsibilities". Amongst them—in the context of religious opinions and beliefs—may legitimately be included an obligation to avoid as far as possible expressions that are gratuitously offensive to others and thus an infringement of their rights, and which therefore do not contribute to any form of public debate capable of furthering progress in human affairs.

[Thus,] it may be considered necessary in certain democratic societies to sanction or even prevent improper attacks on objects of religious veneration.

50. As in the case of "morals" it is not possible to discern throughout Europe a uniform conception of the significance of religion in society. For that reason it is not possible to arrive at a comprehensive definition of what constitutes a permissible interference with the exercise of the right to freedom of expression. A certain margin of appreciation is therefore to be left to the national authorities in assessing the existence and extent of the necessity of such interference.

The authorities' margin of appreciation, however, is not unlimited. The necessity for any restriction must be convincingly established. . . .

52. The Government defended the seizure of the film in view of its character as an attack on the Christian religion, especially Roman Catholicism.

53. The applicant association claimed to have acted in a responsible way aimed at preventing unwarranted offence. It noted that it had planned to show the film in its cinema, which was accessible to members of the public only after a fee had been paid; furthermore, its public consisted on the whole of persons with an interest in progressive culture. Finally, pursuant to the relevant Tyrolean legislation in force, persons under seventeen years of age were not to be admitted to the film. There was therefore no real danger of anyone being exposed to objectionable material against their wishes.

54. The Court notes first of all that although access to the cinema to see the film itself was subject to payment of an admission fee and an age-limit, the film was widely advertised. There was sufficient public knowledge to give a clear

indication of its nature; for these reasons, the proposed screening of the film must be considered to have been an expression sufficiently "public" to cause offence.

55. The issue before the Court involves weighing up the conflicting interests of the exercise of two fundamental freedoms guaranteed under the Convention, namely [the interests of free expression and religious freedom.] In so doing, regard must be had to the margin of appreciation left to the national authorities, whose duty it is in a democratic society also to consider the interests of society as a whole.

56. The Austrian courts, ordering the seizure and subsequently the forfeiture of the film, held it to be an abusive attack on the Roman Catholic religion according to the conception of the Tyrolean public.

The Court cannot disregard the fact that the Roman Catholic religion is the religion of the overwhelming majority of Tyroleans. In seizing the film, the Austrian authorities acted to ensure religious peace in that region and to prevent that some people should feel the object of attacks on their religious beliefs in an unwarranted and offensive manner. It is in the first place for the national authorities, who are better placed than the international judge, to assess the need for such a measure.

No violation of Article 10 can therefore be found as far as the seizure is concerned.

FOR THESE REASONS, THE COURT

Holds, by six votes to three, that there has been no violation of Article 10 of the Convention as regards either the seizure or the forfeiture of the film.

Joint Dissenting Opinion of Judges PALM, PEKKANEN, and MAKARCZYK

. . .

3. There is no point in guaranteeing [freedom of expression] only as long as it is used in accordance with accepted opinion.

4. The necessity of a particular interference for achieving a legitimate aim must be convincingly established[, especially] in cases such as the present, where the interference . . . takes the form of prior restraint. There is a danger that if applied to protect the perceived interests of a powerful group in society, such prior restraint could be detrimental to that tolerance on which pluralist democracy depends. . . .

6. The Convention does not guarantee a right to protection of religious feelings. More particularly, such a right cannot be derived from the right to freedom of religion, which in effect includes a right to express views critical of the religious opinions of others.

Nevertheless, it may be "necessary in a democratic society" to set limits to the public expression of criticism or abuse. To this extent we can agree with the majority.

7. The duty and the responsibility of a person seeking to avail himself of his freedom of expression should be to limit, as far as he can reasonably be expected to, the offence that his statement may cause to others. Only if he fails to take necessary action, or if such action is shown to be insufficient, may the State step in.

Even if the need for repressive action is demonstrated, the measures concerned must be "proportionate to the legitimate aim pursued".

The need for repressive action amounting to complete prevention of the exercise of freedom of expression can only be accepted if the behaviour concerned reaches so high a level of abuse, and comes so close to a denial of the freedom of religion of others, as to forfeit for itself the right to be tolerated by society.

9. The film was to have been shown to a paying audience in an "art cinema" which catered for a relatively small public with a taste for experimental films. It is therefore unlikely that the audience would have included persons not specifically interested in the film. This audience, moreover, had sufficient opportunity of being warned beforehand about the nature of the film. Unlike the majority, we consider that the announcement put out by the applicant association was intended to provide information about the critical way in which the film dealt with the Roman Catholic religion; in fact it did so sufficiently clearly to enable the religiously sensitive to make an informed decision to stay away.

We therefore conclude that the applicant association acted responsibly in such a way as to limit the possible harmful effects of showing the film. . . .

11. We do not deny that the showing of the film might have offended the religious feelings of certain segments of the population in Tyrol. However, taking into account the measures actually taken by the applicant association in order to protect those who might be offended and the protection offered by Austrian legislation to those under seventeen years of age, we are, on balance, of the opinion that the seizure and forfeiture of the film in question were not proportionate to the legitimate aim pursued.

COMMENTS AND QUESTIONS

1. A number of subsequent European Court of Human Rights cases have involved expressions offensive to religious sensitivities. *See, e.g.*, *Wingrove v. United Kingdom*, App. No. 17419/90 (25 November 1996) (upholding refusal to license video work depicting St. Teresa of Avila's ecstatic visions in a pornographic setting fell within permissible limitations on freedom of expression); *Paturel v. France*, App. No. 54968/00 (22 December 2005) (upholding conviction for publication attacking private anti-sect movements in receipt of public funding violated ECHR Article 10); *Giniewski v. France*, App. No. 64016/00 (31 January 2006) (imposition of a fine for publication of an article critiquing a Catholic encyclical violated ECHR Article 10).

   In 2005 and 2006, the Court issued judgment in two cases resulting from defamation convictions in Turkey. Though involving similar facts and both brought under the free expression provisions of Article 10, the court ruled differently in each case. In *İA. v. Turkey*, App. No. 42571/98 (13 September 2005), the applicant published a novel titled *The Forbidden Phrases*, which contained passages referring to the imaginary nature of God, the irrationality of Muslim beliefs, and the poor reasoning skills of imams. Only 2,000 copies of the book were printed before the author was charged with and convicted of "blasphemy against God, Religion, the Prophet and the Holy Book." The Court held 4–3 that the conviction did not violate Article 10, citing principles set forth in *Otto-Preminger-Institut.* Eight months later, however, in *Aydin Tatlav v. Turkey*, App. No. 50692/99 (2 May 2006), the Court held unanimously that a conviction for profaning Islam did violate freedom of expression. In that case, the historical text *The Reality of Islam* had gone through five editions by the time its author was prosecuted for the book's concededly atheistic orientation, which was sharply critical of Islam at various points. The Court noted that where there is no European consensus in a matter, granting a wide margin of appreciation to the respondent country is appropriate. This should not be interpreted as conferring on religious people a right to be exempted from any criticism; religions must accept that others have the right to spread doctrines that reject and are even hostile to their beliefs. The Court referred to the *İA* decision, but only to distinguish the case in a conclusory way. Acknowledging that Muslims reading the book's "caustic comments on their religion" could certainly feel offended, the Court "did not observe in the incriminating passages an insulting tone aimed directly to believers, or an abusive attack against [Islamic] sacred symbols." Thus there was no evidence of a "pressing social need" to restrict the applicant's freedom of expression.

2. In *E.S. v. Austria*, App. No. 38450/12 (25 October 2018), the Court returned to the reasoning of *Otto-Preminger-Institut* to support finding that a criminal conviction for "calling Muhammad a paedophile" did not breach Article 10, as the conviction was pursuant to the legitimate aims of maintaining order (religious peach) and protecting the rights (religious feelings) of others against such "malicious violation of the spirit of tolerance, which was one of the bases of a democratic society." §53. The applicant asserted that the remarks she had made, characterized by the courts as mere value judgments, were historically proven facts that contributed to the public debate and did not imminently incite violence, so were permissible under Article 10. Read more about this highly controversial case on the Web Supplement.

NOTE ON *ALEKHINA AND OTHERS V. RUSSIA* (the Pussy Riot Case)

In February 2012, the feminist rock group known as Pussy Riot attempted to perform their song *Punk Prayer—Virgin Mary, Drive Putin Away* in the Russian Orthodox Cathedral of Christ the Savior in Moscow. The song was meant as a protest against the 2012 re-election of Vladimir Putin and a condemnation of growing ties between the Russian Orthodox Church and the Russian State. The group criticized Kirill I, Patriarch of the Orthodox Russian Church in Moscow, for having openly supported Putin's campaign, calling Putin a miracle from God, and criticized the Church, as a "weapon in a dirty election campaign."[49] Three of the group's members were arrested, denied bail, and charged with hooliganism motivated by religious hatred. They were convicted to two years in prison for inciting hatred and hostility against the Orthodox Church. While the conviction motivated protests and acts of vandalism against religious sites across the country, the "vast majority" of Russians disapproved of Pussy Riot's actions. "According to surveys during the trial, 86% of Russians thought its members should be punished. Most favoured a large fine or forced labour."[50]

In June 2012, the women lodged a complaint with the European Court of Human Rights, alleging violations of their liberty, security, and expression rights

49. Marc Bennetts, In Putin's Russia, Little Separation between Church and State, *The Washington Times*, 12 August 2012.

50. Alec Luhn, Pussy Riot members take Kremlin to European Court of Human Rights, *The Guardian*, 28 July 2014.

under the European Convention, in the harsh, degrading, unlawful treatment they suffered during pre-trail detention and unjust trial proceedings, and from "gross, unjustifiable and disproportionate interference with their freedom of expression."[51]

One of the women in the band was given a suspended sentence in October 2012. The other two served 21 months in harsh conditions in remote prisons. On 2 December 2013, the Russian government received from the European Court of Human Rights a 17-page "Statement of Facts and Questions to the Parties." The women were released later that month "in what was largely viewed as a gesture of goodwill by the Kremlin before the Sochi Olympics."[52]

In June 2015, the Russian government delivered to the Court a 35-page response to this "obviously unfounded" complaint, asserting that the women's "imprisonment was a 'side-effect' of its desire to protect Russian Orthodox worshippers' freedom of belief" and that "deliberately provocative behavior in a place that is dedicated to the spiritual needs of believers and is a symbol of the Russian Orthodox community clearly undermines tolerance and cannot be seen as a normal, sincere exercise of the rights of the [European Convention on Human Rights]."[53] On 17 July 2018, the ECtHR delivered judgment in the case, ruling on all counts in favor of the young women. The Court accepted that "a reaction to breaching the rules of conduct in a place of religious worship might have been warranted," but sentencing them to imprisonment for simply for their behavior, without analyzing the lyrics of their song or the context of their performance, had been "exceptionally severe." In essence, the domestic courts 'had merely endorsed the overall findings of [reports] without making their own analysis."

Could the Pussy Riot protest be defined as an actionable instance of religious hatred? Can blasphemy against religion exist in a secular state like Russia?

NOTE ON THE UK's RACIAL AND RELIGIOUS HATRED ACT 2006

While blasphemous libel is no longer an offense in the United Kingdom, the Racial and Religious Hatred Act of 2006 prohibits certain acts that would have previously constituted blasphemy, and it applies equally to all religions—not just Christianity. The law criminalizes acts intended to stir up religious hatred. According to Section 29B(1) of the Act, "A person who uses threatening words or behaviour, or displays any written material which is threatening, is guilty of an offense if he intends thereby to stir up religious hatred." Religious hatred is defined as "hatred against a group of persons defined by reference to religious belief or lack of religious belief." The scope of the act, however, is circumscribed by Section 29J, which protects freedom of expression:

> Nothing in this Part shall be read or given effect in a way which prohibits or restricts discussion, criticism or expressions of antipathy, dislike, ridicule, insult or abuse of particular religions or the beliefs or practices of their adherents, or of any other belief system or the beliefs or practices of its adherents, or proselytising or urging adherents

---

51. *Alekhina and Others v. Russia*, Statement of Facts and Questions to the Parties, App. No. 38004/12 (ECtHR, communicated to the Russian Government 19 June 2013; judgment 17 July 2018).

52. Luhn, *supra* note 32.

53. *Id. See* also Dmitry Uzlaner, The Pussy Riot Case and the Peculiarities of Russian Post-Secularism, 1 *State, Religion and Church*, 23–58 (2014).

of a different religion or belief system to cease practising their religion or belief system.

Some critics of the Religious Hatred Act responded by arguing that, taken literally, the Act would make major religious works such as the Bible or Qur'an illegal. However, given the protection afforded by Section 29J, it seems that these criticisms may be unfounded since all but the most threatening speech is protected.

In July 2009, Ben and Sharon Vogelenzang were charged with violating the Racial and Religious Hatred Act for comments made to a Muslim guest at the Bounty House Hotel in Liverpool, which they operate. While many of the facts presented at the trial are in dispute, the couple apparently referred to the Prophet Mohammed as a "warlord," likened the Muslim headscarf to bondage, referenced Saddam Hussein and Hitler in the discussion, and reported that the Muslim guest considered Jesus Christ to be only a minor prophet and claimed that the Bible was not true. The judge dismissed the case after two days, finding that the evidence from witnesses present was inconsistent.[54]

Similarly dismissed was a case arising from a video that emerged on the Internet showing seven hooded young men in a car park in the northern England town of Gateshead in September 2010, pouring petrol on two books, assumed to be copies of the Qur'an, and setting them on fire. The Crown Prosecution Service chose not to prosecute the case due to insufficient evidence because they could not confirm who recorded or posted the video, there was no evidence of threatening behavior, and there was no evidence that any one present at the burning was upset or offended by what they saw.[55]

COMMENTS AND QUESTIONS

Is religious hate speech legislation, broadened to protect all religions and narrowed to focus on threats and incitement rather than insult, the modern heir of blasphemy laws? Would the British Racial and Religious Hatred Act pass muster under US constitutional requirements?

NOTE ON THE "CARTOON CONTROVERSIES"

The episodes known as the "Danish cartoon controversy" began after 12 editorial cartoons, most of which depicted the Prophet Muhammad, were published in the Danish newspaper *Jyllands-Posten* on 30 September 2005. The newspaper said it was publishing the cartoons in an attempt to contribute to the debate about Islam and self-censorship. Many European newspapers republished the pictures, claiming they were defending freedom of expression.

Danish Muslim organizations objected to the depictions and responded with a series of public protests. There is evidence that the flames of the controversy were fanned by Muslim leaders in the Middle East. The controversy spread across Europe as well as to predominantly Muslim countries. This led to another escalating round of protests and violence. Many Muslim leaders called for peaceful protests, but some others issued death threats. Numerous people (mostly Muslims) lost their lives as a result of the violent protests that were sparked. Iran announced

54. Christian hoteliers cleared in Muslim woman abuse row, *BBC News*, 9 December 2009.
55. No prosecution over Gateshead car park Koran burning, *BBC News*, 21 January 2011.

it was halting trade with Denmark and protestors bombed the Danish embassy in Iran; Norway's embassy in Syria was set on fire; there was a general strike in Kashmir that closed shops and businesses; Afghan President Hamid Karzai called on Western nations to take "a strong measure" to ensure that such cartoons do not appear again; and there was a general uproar across the globe.

The Danish controversy helped sensitize the rest of the world to the fact that for a variety of reasons, including religiously grounded taboos on pictorial depictions of the Prophet Mohammed, Muslims have much higher sensitivities regarding offensive speech and insults concerning their religion. The deadly attack on the satirical publisher Charlie Hebdo by Islamist extremists in Paris in January 2015 brought this issue again into sharp international focus. While condemnation of the violence and destruction of life was swift, from Muslims and non-Muslims alike, the public debate over the balance between freedom of expression and limitations to protect religious sensitivities intensified. While many observers worldwide proclaimed support for unfettered freedom of expression, others noted important exceptions in the laws of many nations, and Muslim scholars renewed calls for the United Nations to make "contempt of religions" illegal.[56]

However, broad defamation laws, particularly criminal ones, have come under extreme criticism from a wide array of UN and regional human rights leaders. For example, in December 2008, the four freedom of expression rapporteurs of the UN, the Organization for Security and Co-operation in Europe (OSCE), the Organization of the American States (OAS), and the African Commission on Human and Peoples' Rights (ACHPR) issued a joint statement urging international organizations to stop supporting the idea of defamation of religions because "it does not accord with international standards accepted by pluralistic and free societies. . . . Restrictions on freedom of expression to prevent intolerance should be limited in scope to advocacy of national, racial or religious hatred that constitutes incitement to discrimination, hostility or violence."[57]

COMMENTS AND QUESTIONS

1. Flemming Rose, publisher of the Danish cartoons, explained that by satirizing the Muslim religion in the same way he would satirize any other religion, he was sending an important message of acceptance and inclusion in Danish society; a message of recognition and respect rather than disrespect.[58] Are devout Muslims likely to accept that argument? In the fall of 2009, Yale University Press decided against republishing the cartoons in Jytte Klausen's book on the subject, *The Cartoons That Shook the World.* The publisher did not want to be responsible for another round of violence. What is the most

---

56. *See* Javier Martínez-Torrón and W. Cole Durham, Jr., General Report 58, in *Religion and the Secular State: National Reports* Issued for the Occasion of the 18th Congress of the International Academy of Comparative Law (Universidad Complutense de Madrid 2015).

57. Joint Declaration on Defamation of Religions and Anti-Terrorism and Anti-Extremism Legislation, Frank La Rue, UN Special Rapporteur on Freedom of Opinion and Expression, Miklos Haraszti, OSCE Representative on Freedom of the Media, Catalina Botero, OAS Special Rapporteur on Freedom of Expression, and Faith Pansy Tlakula, ACHPR Special Rapporteur on Freedom of Expression, 2 (10 December 2008), http://www.osce.org/documents/rfm/2008/12/35705_en.pdf.

58. Flemming Rose, Editorial, Why I Published the Muhammad Cartoons, *New York Times*, 31 May 2006.

responsible way to address heightened Muslim sensitivity to disrespectful pictorial treatment of the Prophet Mohammed? How thick-skinned should free speech doctrines require sensitive minorities to be? How great is the gap between what is legally and what is morally or ethically permissible here?

2. A number of European jurisdictions make denial of the Holocaust an actionable offense. The tragic historical background and problems of continuing anti-Semitism affect sensitivities in this area. Does restricting expression with respect to Holocaust denial in fact receive distinctive treatment? Should it?

Additional Web Resources:	Additional information on the Danish cartoon, Charlie Hebdo, and related controversies. (We don't republish the cartoons or images, but we do provide cultural background on why publication of such material was more dangerous than expected.)

Report of Special Rapporteurs on Incitement to Racial and Religious Hatred and the Promotion of Intolerance

A/HRC/2/3, 20 September 2006

23. In the context of her activities, the Special Rapporteur on freedom of religion or belief has been made aware of numerous situations in which religious communities or beliefs have been the target of critical analysis from a merely theological point of view to the most extreme forms of incitement to violence or hatred against members of a religious group. Between these two extremes, one can find all sorts of expressions, including stereotyping, ridicule, derogatory comments and insults.

24. The Special Rapporteur has noted that these forms of expression target either the content of religious beliefs themselves or members of religious or belief communities because of the beliefs they hold. She has further noted that these forms of expression are directed towards many religious and belief communities, whether they are old or new, big or small. In this regard, the Special Rapporteur has been able to note that, while criticism of major religions attracts a lot of attention, numerous cases of criticism of smaller religions can go relatively unnoticed.

25. Regarding the authors of these forms of expression, the Special Rapporteur notes that they are not necessarily secularists, but also members of religious communities. Religious groups and communities are therefore not only the target of critical forms of expression, but also in many cases the origin. . . .

36. As such, the right to freedom of religion or belief, as enshrined in relevant international legal standards, does not include the right to have a religion or belief that is free from criticism or ridicule. Moreover, the internal obligations that may exist within a religious community according to the faith of their members (for example, prohibitions on representing religious figures) do not of themselves constitute binding obligations of general application and are therefore not applicable to persons who are not members of the particular religious group or

community, unless their content corresponds to rights that are protected by human rights law.

37. The right to freedom of expression can legitimately be restricted for advocacy that incites to acts of violence or discrimination against individuals on the basis of their religion. Defamation of religions may offend people and hurt their religious feelings but it does not necessarily or at least directly result in a violation of their rights, including their right to freedom of religion. Freedom of religion primarily confers a right to act in accordance with one's religion but does not bestow a right for believers to have their religion itself protected from all adverse comment. . . .

42. In a number of States, in all regions of the world and with different religious backgrounds, some forms of defamation of religion constitute a criminal offence. While the different responses to such defamations depend on various factors, including historical and political factors, criminalizing defamation of religion can be counterproductive. The rigorous protection of religions as such may create an atmosphere of intolerance and can give rise to fear and may even provoke the chances of a backlash. There are numerous examples of persecution of religious minorities as a result of excessive legislation on religious offences or overzealous application of laws that are fairly neutral. As a limit to freedom of expression and information, it can also limit scholarship on religious issues and may asphyxiate honest debate or research.

43. Criminalizing speech that defames religions, whilst not amounting to forms of expression prohibited by international law, can limit discussion of practices within religions that may impinge upon other human rights. In such a context, criticism of practices—in some cases adopted in the form of a law—appearing to be in violation of human rights but that are sanctioned by religion or perceived to be sanctioned by religion would also come within the ambit of defamation of religion. The dilemma deepens, as independent research on the impact of such laws may not be possible, as a critical analysis of the law may by itself, in certain situations, be considered as defaming the religion itself. . . .

[Article 20(2) of the ICCPR provides: "Any advocacy of national, racial or religious hatred that constitutes incitement to discrimination, hostility or violence shall be prohibited by law."]

47. The Special Rapporteur notes that article 20 of the Covenant was drafted against the historical background of the horrors committed by the Nazi regime during the Second World War. The threshold of the acts that are referred to in article 20 is relatively high because they have to constitute advocacy of national, racial or religious hatred. Accordingly, the Special Rapporteur is of the opinion that expressions should only be prohibited under article 20 if they constitute incitement to imminent acts of violence or discrimination against a specific individual or group.

NOTE ON THE UNITED NATIONS HUMAN RIGHTS COMMITTEE'S CONDEMNATION OF BLASPHEMY LEGISLATION

In July 2011, the UN Human Rights Committee adopted its General Comment 34, which elaborated upon and clarified the rights set forth in ICCPR Article 19. Although this General Comment focused on freedom of expression, including freedoms of speech, press, and media, it included the following strong paragraph aimed at curtailing blasphemy legislation:

> 48. Prohibitions of displays of lack of respect for a religion or other belief system, including blasphemy laws, are incompatible with the Covenant, except in the specific circumstances envisaged in article 20, paragraph 2, of the Covenant. Such prohibitions must also comply with the strict requirements of article 19, paragraph 3, as well as such articles as 2, 5, 17, 18 and 26. Thus, for instance, it would be impermissible for any such laws to discriminate in favour of or against one or certain religions or belief systems, or their adherents over another, or religious believers over non-believers. Nor would it be permissible for such prohibitions to be used to prevent or punish criticism of religious leaders or commentary on religious doctrine and tenets of faith.

Article 20 (2): "Any advocacy of national, racial or religious hatred that constitutes incitement to discrimination, hostility or violence shall be punished by law." In effect, paragraph 48 indicates that blasphemy legislation is only permissible in the narrowly circumscribed situations in which hate speech is proscribed.

COMMENTS AND QUESTIONS

1. In 1965, Indonesian President Sukarno passed Decree No 1/PNPS/1965, commonly referred to as the "Blasphemy Law," which was created to protect the orthodox teachings of Indonesia's official religions. Basuki Tjahaja Purnama, ("Ahok") was the first Christian Governor of Jakarta, Indonesia since 1964. In 2017, following a speech in which he claimed that the Qur'an does not forbid Muslims from voting for a non-Muslim, Ahok was accused of criticizing the Qur'an and subsequently was charged with blasphemy, convicted and sentenced to two years' imprisonment. Ahok is Christian and ethnically Chinese. The 2017 report of the US International Commission on International Religious Freedom (USCIRF) on Indonesia highlights Ahok's political stature, religion, and ethnicity as possible reasons behind his prosecution. In March 2018 the Indonesia Supreme Court announced it would prioritize review of the case due to "widespread public attention". Does selective enforcement of blasphemy laws create the prospect of discrimination? Why or why not?
2. In the aftermath of the 2015 Charlie Hebdo attacks, the worldwide public debate over the balance between freedom of expression and limitations to protect religious sensitivities sharpened. While many observers proclaimed support for unfettered freedom of expression, others noted important exceptions in the laws of many nations,[59] and Muslim scholars renewed calls for the United Nations to make "contempt of religions" illegal.[60] Can you make reasonable arguments on both sides of this question, or do you see only one justifiable position?

---

59. For example, Pope Francis observed that while killing in the name of God was "an aberration," there were limits to freedom of expression when it "insults or ridicules someone's faith." *See, e.g.,* Gerard O'Connell, Full text in English of the Pope's Press Conference on Flight from Colombo to Manila, *America: Jesuit Review*, 15 January 2015. Mr. Iyad Madani, secretary-general of the Organization of Islamic Cooperation, summarized the issue in this way: "Freedom of speech must not become a hate-speech and it must not offend others. No sane person, regardless of doctrine, religion or faith, accepts his beliefs being ridiculed." Muslim World Questions Logic behind Charlie antics, *Arab News*, 15 January 2015.

60. Muslim Scholars Urge UN to Outlaw 'Contempt' of Religions, *Arab News*, 21 January 2015.

3. Global concerns earlier addressed under the rubric "defamation of religions" have been addressed in more productive ways through the "Rabat Plan of Action on the prohibition of advocacy of national, racial or religious hatred that constitutes incitement to discrimination, hostility of violence." The Rabat Plan contains the conclusions and recommendations of experts from four regional workshops organized by the UN Office of the High Commissioner for Human Rights, adopted in Rabat, Morocco, on 5 October 2012.[61]

Additional Web Resources:	For further discussion of this topic *see* Brett G. Scharffs, International Law and the Defamation of Religion, *The Review of Faith & International Affairs* (2013), 11:1, 66–75, and related items on the Web Supplement.

NOTE ON BLASPHEMY LAWS IN PAKISTAN

Apostasy and blasphemy laws are still being applied in dozens of countries around the world,[62] perhaps most notoriously in Pakistan. Four of Pakistan's nine existing laws concerning offense against religion are based on laws introduced in 1860 under colonial rule in India, for the stated purpose of maintaining law and order in a multi-cultural country. These included prohibitions against intentional damage or defilement of a place or object of worship, disturbing religious ceremonies or gatherings, trespassing on places of burial, and intentionally insulting an individual's religious feelings. Upon independence in 1947, Pakistan retained the penal code inherited from the British, and over the next 30 years there were only ten reported judgments relating to offenses against religion.[63]

In 1974, the Pakistan constitution was amended to define "a Muslim" in a way that specifically excluded members of the Ahmadiyya community, and between 1980 and 1986 five provisions relating specifically to Islam and Muslim beliefs were added to the Pakistan Penal Code. It is reported that between 1987 and 2014 633 Muslims, 494 Ahmadis, 187 Christians, and 21 Hindus were tried under the Pakistan's blasphemy laws,[64] and a sentence of death is mandatory for certain forms of blasphemy. New death sentences for blasphemy were issued by an anti-terrorism court in Gujranwala, Punjab Province in June 2016, to Christians, Anjum Naz Sindhu and Javed Naz, and a Muslim, Jaffar Ali.[65] In June 2017, the anti-terrorism court of Bahawalpur in Lahore sentenced 30-year-old Taimoor Raza, a member of a minority Shia community, to death for playing blasphemous and hate speech material on his phone at a bus stop.

61. Report of the United Nations High Commissioner for Human Rights on the expert workshops on the prohibition of incitement to national, racial or religious hatred, A/HRC/22/15/Add.4, 11 January 2013. *See also* OHCHR, Between Free Speech and Hate Speech: The Rabat Plan of Action, a practical tool to combat incitement to hatred, 21 February 2013.

62. See Angelina E. Theodorou, Which Countries Still Outlaw Apostasy and Blasphemy? *Pew Research Center Fact Tank*, 29 July 20116.

63. *See* International Commission of Jurists, *On Trial: The Implementation of Pakistan's Blasphemy Laws*, November 2015, https://www.icj.org/wp-content/uploads/2015/12/Pakistan-On-Trial-Blasphemy-Laws-Publications-Thematic-Reports-2015-ENG.pdf.

64. *See* Human Rights Commission of Pakistan, State of Human Rights, 2014, 46-51.

65. US Department of State, International Religious Freedom Report 2017: Pakistan, 62.

Though no death sentence for blasphemy has been carried out, acts of violence, including extrajudicial lynching, of those accused of blasphemy has shown an alarming rise in recent years. While 40 people are on death row or serving life imprisonment for blasphemy charges (5 have died in custody), more than 70 people accused of blasphemy have been killed by vigilantes in Pakistan since 1990.[66] To mention only three egregious examples: In July 2014, a mob attack on the Ahmadiyya community in Gujranwala killed sisters aged 8 months and 7 years along with their 54-year-old grandmother. Also in 2014, several hundred Muslim men in Punjab bludgeoned a Christian man and his pregnant wife to death and threw their bodies into a burning brick kiln after the couple was accused desecrating the Qur'an. In April 2017, a Muslim university student was stripped, beaten, shot, and thrown from a second-floor dormitory window by a mob who falsely accused him of blasphemy after a debate about religion. "The brutality of the attack, which was recorded on mobile phone cameras and posted online, stunned the public and led to widespread condemnation—including from prominent Islamic clerics."[67] The shooter was sentenced to death, 25 others were given three-year sentences, and 26 accused were acquitted.

An extensive 2016 report by Amnesty International asserts that once a person is accused of blasphemy in Pakistan, "they become ensnared in a system that offers them few protections, presumes them guilty, and fails to safeguard them against people willing to use violence."[68] Indeed, in its 2015 judgment in *Malik Muhammad Mumtaz Qadri v. the State*, the Supreme Court of Pakistan itself noted that the "majority of blasphemy cases are based on false accusations stemming from property issues or other personal or family vendettas rather than genuine instances of blasphemy and they inevitably lead to mob violence against the entire community" (para. 17).

Such violence has followed the blasphemy conviction of Asia Naurīn Bibi, a Catholic mother of five, sentenced to death by hanging in Lahore in 2010. In this most notorious of Pakistan's blasphemy cases a fruit picker was accused by Muslim co-workers of insulting the Prophet Muhammad during an altercation over drinking water the others said she had no right to share with them. From the beginning Bibi insisted she is innocent, and that her accusers were acting on a personal grudge.

Bibi first appealed her sentence to the Lahore High Court, which found no reason to discredit the witnesses and rejected the appeal in November 2014. However, in response to an observation by Bibi's counsel as to the requirement under Islamic law that a *hudud* offense (for which the only sentence provided is death, see Section III.B.2, above), requires witnesses (and by extension examiners) to be "truthful persons and abstain from major sins," the Lahore Court ordered a copy of its decision to be sent to the Pakistan Government for consideration of an "amendment in procedural law for testing credibility of a witness at such a higher

---

66. *See* F.M. Shakil, Infamous Blasphemy Law May Be Amended to Rein in False Claims, *Asia Times,* 12 March 2018.

67. Mashal Khan: Death Sentence for Pakistan Blasphemy Murder, *BBC*, 7 November 2018.

68. "As Good as Dead": The Impact of Blasphemy Laws in Pakistan, *Amnesty International* 2016.

standard."[69] Some observers saw this as an attempt by the Court to find a way around what they seemed to feel was an inevitable judgment.

In March 2018, with Asia Bibi still in prison following a series of postponed re-hearings, a Special Committee on Human Rights in the Pakistan Senate proposed to amend the law so that complainants making baseless accusations of blasphemy would be subject to the same punishments as those convicted of blasphemy, apparently following up on a similar suggestion made a year earlier, in March 2017, by the Islamabad High Court. At the same time, the Islamabad Court directed the Pakistan Telecommunication Authority to create a firewall to block unwanted and sacrilegious content from reaching Pakistan, which gave some to wonder whether the impetus is towards deterring the occasion for blasphemy, or an accusation of blasphemy, rather than to change the blasphemy law itself.

In January 2011, Salman Taseer, governor of Punjab, shortly after visiting Asia Bibi in prison was shot dead by his own Elite Force guard, Malik Mumtaz Hussein Qadri, who claimed it was his religious duty to kill someone who opposed the blasphemy laws.[70] Taseer's funeral saw large-scale protests against him and in favor of his killing. Three months later Shahbaz Bhatti, the only Christian minister in the Pakistan government, was assassinated for opposing the blasphemy law and expressing sympathy for Bibi. Qadri's 2016 conviction and execution for the murder of Taseer sparked yet more violence. "Kill Asia Bibi [was chanted] in the city's streets [and there was] a $10,000 bounty for whoever [would kill] her."[71]

The case of Asia Bibi and the violence that followed upon it sparked international outrage. Nearly 700,000 people from more than 200 nations and territories signed a petition circulated ACLJ demanding her freedom. In September 2017, she was nominated for the European Parliament's Sakharov Prize for Freedom of Thought. In January 2018, Ján Figeľ, the European Union's special envoy for the promotion of international religious freedom, announced that future favorable economic relations between Pakistan and the European Union "will be directly linked to the positive outcome of Asia Bibi's blasphemy case."[72] At the same time the US State Department, following repeated recommendations of the United States Commission on International Religious Freedom (USCIRF) that pointed to continuing oppressive application of blasphemy laws, placed Pakistan on a watch list for "severe violations" of religious freedom.[73]

In July 2015, the Pakistan Supreme Court suspended Bibi's death sentence during the pendency of her appeals. In early 2018, appeal was once more delayed when one Supreme Court judge recused himself as ineligible to sit on the grounds he was part of the bench in the Qadri murder trial. On 19 April, the Chief Justice of Pakistan, Mian Saqib Nisar, announced that he would hear the case himself, soon. By the end of September 2018, visitors reported that Bibi's mental health was in decline. A month later, on 30 October 2018—as demonstrations demanding

69. *See* Donlu Thayer, Case Note, Mst Asia Bibi v The State, 4 *Ox. J. L. & Relig.* (1) 147–149 (2015).

70. Salman Taseer Murder: Pakistan Hangs Mumtaz Qadri, *BBC News Asia*, 29 February 2016.

71. Claire Giangravè, Family of Pakistani Woman Condemned for Blasphemy Urges Pope's Help, *Crux: Taking the Catholic Pulse*, 24 February 2016.

72. The EU Remembers Asia Bibi, *European Union Cooperation in Pakistan*, 1 February 2018.

73. Maria Abi-Habib and Salman Masood, Pakistan's Shields Suddenly Step Aside, Placing it on Terrorism Listing, *The New York Times*, 1 March 2018.

Bibi's execution continued and in the face of a pledge by the newly elected Pakistani Prime Minister Imran Khan to revive the UN campaign for global blasphemy laws—a three-judge panel of the Supreme Court of Pakistan announced that Asia Bibi, the first female non-Muslim to have been accused of blasphemy in Pakistan, had been acquitted. In his ruling, Chief Justice Nisar cited the Quran, in support of the notion that tolerance is the basic principle of Islam, and the religion condemns injustice and oppression.[74] As human rights advocates hailed "a landmark ruling for religious freedom," demonstrations against the ruling intensified in Pakistan, and the fate of Asia Bibi remained unclear.

The UN Special Rapporteur on the Independence of Judges and Lawyers, following a mission to Pakistan in 2012, found that Pakistan's blasphemy laws "serve the vested interests of extremist religious groups and are not only contrary to the Constitution of Pakistan, but also to international human rights norms, in particular those relating to non-discrimination and freedom of expression and opinion" (UN Doc. A/HRC/23/43/Add.2).

Given that for a great many people it is not misuse of blasphemy laws but the fact that such laws exist at all that is the problem, how it is possible to engage in productive dialogue in this matter?

V. IS THE RIGHT TO FREEDOM OF RELIGION OR BELIEF REDUNDANT?

Thus far in this chapter we have focused primarily on cases where religious expression is coerced, or where rights to freedom of religion and freedom of expression come into tension with each other. In this final section, we raise the theoretical question whether a suitably broad version of freedom of expression rights might supplant and obviate the need for a separate right to freedom of religion. Indeed, after the United States Supreme Court's downgrading of free exercise protections in the 1990 *Smith* case, so that virtually any neutral and general law can trump religious liberty claims,[75] it has been suggested that freedom of expression might provide even stronger protection than classical religious freedom norms. The better view is that freedom of religion claims should receive protection at least as strong as that provided by freedom of speech, freedom of association, and equal protection norms,[76] but so long as those norms are available, the argument runs, an additional right to freedom of religion is unnecessary.

This contention is an example of a broader line of argumentation that can be characterized as religious freedom reductionism. Such arguments contend that religious freedom is a redundant right, and that reducing the constellation of human and constitutional rights by eliminating it would not result in any functional loss of protection.

For example, Professor Mark Tushnet asks, "Suppose the Free Exercise Clause were simply ripped out of the Constitution. What would change in contemporary

74. Shehab Kahn, Asia Bibi: Pakistan Releases Christian Woman Who Spent Eight Years on Death Row for Blasphemy after Drinking from the Wrong Cup, *The Independent*, 31 October 2018.

75. *Employment Division v. Smith*, 494 U.S. 872 (1990).

76. *See, e.g.*, Frederick Mark Gedicks, Towards a Defensible Free Exercise Doctrine, 68 *Geo. Wash. L. Rev.* (2001).

constitutional law?"[77] His response: Not much. Rather, "other constitutional doctrines protect a wide range of actions in which religious believers engage." These include direct protection of speech; bans on coerced speech; symbolic speech (i.e., expressive conduct that is intended to communicate and is so understood by others); and free speech doctrines that proscribe viewpoint discrimination, require equal access to public resources, or proscribe disparate regulatory impacts. Also significant are rights of expressive association, which can help explain legal doctrines such as the ministerial exception to legislation forbidding employment discrimination (religious groups can engage in preferential hiring of their own members) and more generally, the right of religious communities to autonomy in their own affairs.

The same basic argument can be made at the level of international norms. Thus, Professor James Nickel has argued that freedom of religion is adequately covered by a constellation of nine basic liberties that are widely recognized in international law: (1) freedom of belief, thought and inquiry; (2) freedom of communication and expression; (3) freedom of association; (4) freedom of peaceful assembly; (5) freedom of political participation; (6) freedom of movement; (7) economic liberties; (8) privacy and autonomy in the areas of home, family, sexuality, and reproduction; and (9) freedom to follow an ethic, plan of life, lifestyle, or traditional way of living.[78] In his view, once this full set of basic liberties is in place, no separate mention of freedom of religion is necessary to protect the interests traditionally covered by freedom of religion. In his view, this has at least four advantages. First, it clarifies that no special religious reasons need to be given for grounding religious freedom; it has the same general grounding as other basic liberties. Second, it provides a "broad and ecumenical scope for freedom of religion that extends into areas such as association, movement, politics, and business," further underscoring the multifaceted character of religious freedom. Third, this approach transcends a clause-bound approach to religious freedom that sees its contours as defined by the happenstance of the wording of constitutional and international documents. And fourth, it resists "exaggerating the priority of religious freedom," setting it on a more equal footing with other rights.

Neither Tushnet nor Nickel questions the significance of the underlying right. Moreover, both recognize that the other rights may need to be stretched somewhat to provide the necessary coverage. For example, Nickel acknowledges that symbolic speech may not be sufficient to cover certain activities motivated by religious belief, because while they are "intended to communicate . . . belief, [they] are not generally understood to be communications."[79] Similarly, expressive association cases may not provide full protection to church-related employment cases, because American law respects the autonomy of religion with respect to all employment decisions, not merely those in which direct religious expression activities are involved.[80] But in general, he concludes that "[c]ontemporary constitutional doctrine may render the Free Exercise Clause redundant."[81]

---

77. Mark Tushnet, The Redundant Free Exercise Clause?, 33 *Loy. U. Chi. L.J.* 71 (2001).

78. James W. Nickel, Who Needs Freedom of Religion?, 76 *U. Colo. L. Rev.* 941, 943 (2005).

79. *Id.* at 76–77.

80. *See* Tushnet, *supra* note 78, at 86, *citing* Michael W. McConnell, The Problem of Singling Out Religion, 50 *DePaul L. Rev.* 1, 20 (2000).

81. Tushnet, *supra* note 78, at 73.

As Cole Durham has noted,[82] the redundancy arguments are "virtually always made in support of a secularist agenda, and they typically foster secularism as opposed to secularity. That is, the concern is to advance secularism as an ideology and end in itself, as opposed to secularity conceive as a neutral framework welcoming a wide range of world views." Such arguments "have growing force in our equalitarian environment."[83]

COMMENTS AND QUESTIONS

1. Durham believes that the redundancy arguments "pose a genuine threat to religious freedom. We are witnessing a paradigm shift from freedom to equality norms as the deep structure of human rights, and key dimensions of freedom of religion or belief disappear or suffer de-emphasis as a result of this shift." [84] Is anything lost if freedom of religion is eliminated as a special type of right to be protected? Can we expect protection of freedom of expression, association, assembly, press, and so forth to provide sufficient protection for freedom of conscience and belief?
2. Tushnet and Nickel, says Durham, "recognize that the freedom of religion right—the legitimacy of which none of them questions—can only be covered by other rights if some stretching of the other rights is allowed." Durham has identified some potential "coverage shortfalls." Might such a shortfall arise when, for example, the European Court of Human Rights analyzes headscarf cases in terms of secular priorities, giving little weight to religious concerns? (See Chapter 3.) In the freedom of association area, one thinks of the "Bahá'í Case" (see Chapter 11)—one of the key German precedents in the domain of religious autonomy and the law of registration of religious associations. Under German association law applied as normally interpreted, the distinctive Bahá'í religious structure could not have been approved. With respect to the core freedom of "thought, conscience and belief," should secular thought be the core, and religion the penumbra, or vice versa, or should both be regarded as equally important?

82. W. Cole Durham, Jr., *Against Free Exercise Reductionism, Presentation for the Religious Freedom Discussion Series*, International Center for Law and Religion Studies, J. Reuben Clark Law School, 22 March 2013.

83. *Id.* In this regard, *see also* Brett G. Scharffs, Four Views of the Citadel: The Consequential Distinction between Secularity and Secularism, 16 *Rel. & Hum. Rts.* 109–126 (2011).

84. Durham, *supra* note 83.

224-256

CHAPTER 6

LIMITATIONS ON RELIGIOUS ACTIONS AND MANIFESTATIONS

I. INTRODUCTION

In the autumn of 2008, the world watched in horror as news broke that Al-Shabaab, a radical Islamic militant group that was struggling to gain control of war-torn Somalia, had publicly executed Aisha Ibrahim Duhulow on charges of adultery. The execution, by stoning, took place in a public stadium as more than a thousand people watched, some of whom were shot by armed guards while attempting to intervene in Duhulow's behalf. Duhulow was only 13 years old, and her sole crime was attempting to report that she had been raped by a group of armed men.

This incident was rightly condemned by human rights groups such as Amnesty International, and it generated a great deal of publicity in the Western news media, drawing attention to topics such as Shari'a law, honor killings, victims' rights, and the dangers of religious extremism.

An equally gruesome incident of religious extremism occurred less than two years earlier, also on the African continent, when Chukwuemeka Ezeugo, a self-proclaimed Christian pastor, doused six of his parishioners with gasoline and lit them on fire for the sin of fornication. One woman died. Ezeugo, who insisted on being called "The Most Holiness Dr. Reverend King," had a long history of tyrannical behavior towards his followers, including large fines assessed for even the most minor infractions, severe beatings performed personally or by his associates, and keeping young women as sex slaves.

Like Duhulow's stoning, Ezeugo's crime (for which he is still, more than ten years later, awaiting execution in a Nigerian prison) was an exceptionally atrocious example of self-styled justice carried out in the name of religion. Unlike these graphic examples of the abuse of religion, the most difficult issue in the vast majority of religious freedom cases is determining whether particular religious freedom claims should be protected, or whether countervailing interests justify a limitation of the right. Stated differently, the question is where the permissible boundaries of religious freedom lie and how they are determined. Under any theory of religious freedom, some limitations must exist. If all religious beliefs were protected without limitation, those who kill in the name of religion, or someone who asserted that their beliefs call for the enslavement of others would be entitled to absolute protection, which would clearly infringe on the rights and freedoms of others, including their own religious liberty claims. Precisely where the limitations should be drawn is a different issue, but that there must be some limitations is clear. Even the absolute protections of the internal forum apply only within the internal forum.

Determining what does and does not count as a religious manifestation is not always easy. Some religiously-motivated actions are familiar, such as attending religious services, observing holidays, rules, and rituals attending marriage and divorce, burial, and evangelizing. But other manifestations of religion may be less familiar (at least to some of us in some places), such as certain prayer observances, dietary restrictions, restrictions on appearance (such as beards or shaving one's head), or attire (such as headscarves or sacred underclothing).

The central constitutional drama in the law and religion field relates to the evolution of the standards of review applicable to claims of freedom of religion or belief. In the United States, this drama has taken the form of constitutional battles over whether burdens on religious liberty must be justified by a narrowly tailored compelling state interest (a "strict scrutiny" approach), or whether neutral, generally applicable laws should suffice to override most religious freedom claims. The European Court of Human Rights in Strasbourg, in comparison, assesses whether interferences with freedom of religion or belief are "prescribed by law," serve to further one of a circumscribed set of legitimating aims (public safety, order, health or morals, or the rights and freedoms of others), and, most importantly, are "necessary in a democratic society" to further one or more of the legitimating aims. The "necessity" test has been held to require the Contracting States to justify any restrictions with convincing and weighty reasons demonstrating that there is a "pressing social need" that is "proportionate to the legitimate aim pursued." As in the United States, however, there are pressures on the Strasbourg court to narrow the scope of protections by broadening the legitimating aims, by adopting a broad "margin of appreciation" that defers to states, and by adjusting the rigor of the proportionality test.

Interestingly, in both the United States and Europe (and in many other systems as well) the critical operative aspects of the applicable standards are judicial constructs that emerge as much from the internal logic of applying the underlying norms and from evolving judicial craft as from the literal words of constitutional and treaty texts. Viewing cases through the slightly different conceptual filters posed by the various tests contributes not only to a richer understanding of the range of questions needing resolution, but also to deeper comparative insight into differing judicial methodologies.

II. THE UNITED STATES

The protection of religious freedom in the United States has been a circuitous journey. A widespread consensus exists among scholars in the United States that the current doctrinal framework for analyzing religious liberty claims is far less protective of constitutional free exercise today than it was a generation ago. In this section, we trace the decline and partial resurgence of heightened standards of protection, including the abandonment of the "compelling state interest" test by the Supreme Court and the resilience of that standard in a variety of other settings. George Washington, who was always conscious that his actions as the first President of the United States could establish precedent, was eager to demonstrate that America would be a religiously tolerant nation. On at least two occasions prior to the adoption of the Bill of Rights, he wrote letters to members of religious minority communities to reassure them that their ability to worship would be respected.

For example, in spite of his personal disagreement with their views on military service, he expressed his great admiration for Quakers:

> I assure you very explicitly, that in my opinion the conscientious scruples of all men should be treated with great delicacy and tenderness; and it is my wish and desire, that the laws may always be as extensively accommodated to them, as a due regard to the protection and essential interests of the nation may justify and permit.[1]

Washington proved to be prescient, recognizing the complexity of balancing the "protection and essential interests of the nation" with accommodation of religious conscience broadly and magnanimously, "with great delicacy and tenderness." Note the early indication of the components of a balancing test to weigh the states' interests against those of a religion claiming the need for an accommodation of religious conscience under the law.

A short time later, he wrote to members of the Jewish community, a group that had suffered centuries of persecution in Europe and America, informing them that adherents of no religion would be made second-class citizens due to their beliefs:

> It is now no more that toleration is spoken of as if it were the indulgence of one class of people that another enjoyed the exercise of their inherent natural rights, for, happily, the Government of the United States, which gives to bigotry no sanction, to persecution no assistance, requires only that they who live under its protection should . . . as good citizens [give] it on all occasions their effectual support. . . . May the Children of the Stock of Abraham, who dwell in this land, continue to merit and enjoy the good will of the other Inhabitants; while every one shall sit in safety under his own vine and figtree, and there shall be none to make him afraid. May the father of all mercies scatter light and not darkness in our paths, and make us all in our several vocations useful here, and in his own due time and way everlastingly happy.[2]

Washington hoped that, in contrast to Europe, America would be a land where no religion was merely "tolerated" like an unwanted house guest, but one in which all would be given protection, a place where all could rest peaceably under their own "vine and figtree."[3] For Washington, then, the purpose of protecting religious freedom is not just a matter of vindicating rights, it is to allow every person to have a safe place, a place to live without fear.[4]

---

1. Letter from Washington to the Society of Quakers, in 4 *The Papers of George Washington: Presidential Series* 266 (W.W. Abbot et al. eds., 1993).

2. Letter from Washington to the Hebrew Congregation in Newport, Rhode Island, in 6 *The Papers of George Washington: Presidential Series* 285 (W.W. Abbot et. al. eds., 1993).

3. *See* Micah 4:4, "But they shall sit every man under his vine and under his fig tree; and none shall make them afraid: for the mouth of the Lord of hosts hath spoken it."

4. *See* Brett G. Scharffs, Our Fractured Attitude Towards Corporate Conscience, *Wheatley*

A. THE NINETEENTH-CENTURY BACKGROUND

In its first hundred years, the Supreme Court of the United States evinced relatively little concern for the free exercise interests of religious minorities. In large part, this was a result of its holding in *Barron v. City of Baltimore*, 32 U.S. (7 Pet.) 243 (1833) that the protections embodied in the Bill of Rights, including freedom of religion, constrained only the federal government and did not apply to the individual states.

However, because Utah was a territory and not a state from shortly after its initial settlement in 1847 until statehood in 1896, the federal Congress was its lawgiver during the federal anti-polygamy campaign in the late nineteenth century.[5] Accordingly, members of The Church of Jesus Christ of Latter-day Saints (Mormons) living in Utah could invoke the First Amendment language providing that "*Congress* shall make no law respecting an establishment of religion or prohibiting the free exercise thereof."[6] [emphasis added] The free exercise claim that arose concerning the church's right to practice polygamy ultimately reached the Supreme Court in the case of *Reynolds v. United States*, 98 U.S. 145 (1878).

In *Reynolds*, the defendant was accused of practicing polygamy, that is, taking multiple wives, all concurrently living. Among other issues, the court examined whether a statute prohibiting polygamy was an unconstitutional abrogation of the free exercise of religion if polygamy constituted an integral part of a valid religious belief. The Mormons' free exercise challenge to the federal government's crusade against polygamy proved unavailing. The result in *Reynolds* was clear: Free exercise was not a defense to a bigamy charge. But the logic in the decision could be interpreted in various ways. At one level, the Court justified its decision in terms of what has come to be known as the "belief/action" distinction, according to which there is an absolute ban on regulation of belief, but less constraint on the state's authority to regulate conduct. Specifically, the Court sustained criminalization of bigamy on the basis that "laws are made for the government of actions, and while they cannot interfere with mere religious belief and opinions, they may with practices."[7] But it was not clear whether the Court was saying that any law could override religious liberty claims, or whether the law in question had to be a "general and neutral law" or a particularly significant law, such as long-standing criminal legislation. Moreover, there was very strong language in the opinion to the effect that the state interest behind the

---

Institute Religious Liberty Lecture Series, 12 March 2014.

5. The polygamy issue is far too complex to address in detail here. For excellent treatments of both the social phenomena and the related legal issues, *see* Kathryn M. Daynes, *More Wives Than One: Transformation of the Mormon Marriage System, 1840–1910* (2001); Edwin Brown Firmage and R. Collin Mangrum, *Zion in the Courts: A Legal History of The Church of Jesus Christ of Latter-day Saints, 1830–1900* (1988); Sarah Barringer Gordon, *The Mormon Question: Polygamy and Constitutional Conflict in Nineteenth-Century America* (2002); Richard S. Van Wagoner, *Mormon Polygamy: A History* (2d ed. 1989); Orma Linford, The Mormons and the Law: The Polygamy Cases, Part II, 9 *Utah L. Rev*. 543, 543–591 (1965); Orma Linford, The Mormons and the Law: The Polygamy Cases, Part I, 9 *Utah L. Rev*. 308, 308–370 (1964).

6. U.S. Const. amend. I (emphasis added).

7. *Reynolds*, 98 U.S. at 166.

anti-bigamy legislation was to protect marriage, "this most important feature of social life . . . [upon which] society may be said to be built."[8] Thus, depending on which of these rationales is thought to be most crucial to the Court's decision, the case can be read either as a "belief/action" case, as an antecedent of the *Smith* decision (excerpted below), or as a forerunner of the compelling state interest test.

A very broad reading of the belief/action dichotomy that would prohibit only the regulation of belief and permit all regulation of religiously motivated action would appear to be inconsistent with the Constitution's protection of the free "exercise" of religion, which connotes the protection of action and not just belief or expression. The *Reynolds* Court's reading may reflect Protestant sensibilities about the centrality of belief to salvation, whereas many religious traditions require adherents to *do* as well as to *believe* certain things. In any event, the belief/action reading of *Reynolds* suggests a very broad field of permissible government regulation of religiously motivated conduct.

To grasp the significance of the interpretation that allows virtually any regulation of conduct, it is helpful to consider legislation rolled out during what two leading scholars of the period have called "the war against Mormon society,"[9] running from the mid-1850s until the early 1890s. During this period, federal officials launched a series of measures aimed not just at polygamy, but at Mormon society in general. Little if any conduct was necessary to serve as a rationale for state-imposed sanctions. In *Davis v. Beason*, 133 U.S. 333 (1890), for example, the Supreme Court held that mere membership in a religious organization that believed in plural marriage was sufficient grounds for denial of voting rights. In addition to laws aimed at plural marriage,[10] ostensibly neutral legislation was passed that excluded past or present polygamists from juries and from voting.[11] The federal judiciary was effectively placed in non-Mormon hands and given preeminence over territorial courts.[12] Women, who had been given the right to vote by Utah's territorial legislature in 1870,[13] were deprived of that right by Congress in 1887.[14] The common law protection of spousal immunity was abolished in the Utah Territory.[15] Mormons were excluded from holding public office, both as a result of disenfranchisement and by law.[16] A territorial law allowing wives and children of polygamous marriages to inherit on the same terms as heirs of monogamous marriages was annulled, and "illegitimate" children were not allowed to inherit, whether by will or intestate succession.[17] The Perpetual Emigration Fund, which had been established to help foster migration of poor Mormon converts from abroad, was dissolved and its assets

---

8. *Id.* at 164–166.

9. Firmage and Mangrum, *supra* note 5, at 210–260.

10. Morrill Act, 12 Stat. 501 (1862); Edmunds Act, 22 Stat. 30 (1882) (amended 1887); Edmunds-Tucker Act, 24 Stat. 635 (1887) (amending Edmunds Act, 22 Stat. 30 (1882)).

11. Edmunds Act, §§5, 8 (1882).

12. Poland Act, 18 Stat. 253 (1874); *see* Firmage and Mangrum at 219.

13. Firmage and Mangrum *supra* note, at 235.

14. Edmunds-Tucker Act, §20

15. Firmage and Mangrum, *supra* note 5, at 206.

16. *Id.* at 236.

17. Edmunds-Tucker Act, §11.

seized.[18] Administrative and diplomatic efforts were aimed at deterring Mormons from immigrating.[19]

The ultimate blow came with legislative dissolution of the Church and confiscation of Church property in excess of $50,000, including the Salt Lake City Temple,[20] the constitutionality of which was affirmed by the United States Supreme Court in a case with a name that previewed its holding, *The Late Corporation of The Church of Jesus Christ of Latter-day Saints v. United States*, 136 U.S. 1 (1890).

Faced with these pressures, Wilford Woodruff, the president of the The Church of Jesus Christ of Latter-day Saints at the time, issued the 1890 "Manifesto,"[21] which ultimately led to the termination of the practice of plural marriage within the Church. The Church's property was restored, and Utah was admitted as a state, with the express requirement that it prohibit polygamy. Today individuals who practice polygamy are excommunicated from the main body of the Church, which has no interest in revisiting the nineteenth-century anti-polygamy decisions. But there can be no doubt that ending polygamy was a significant redirection, and a number of small groups split off from the main body of the Church as a result, and continue to practice plural marriage even today.[22] The polygamy cases illustrate dramatically how even laws that are ostensibly "neutral and general" can still target particular religious practices.

B. THE EMERGENCE OF THE COMPELLING STATE INTEREST TEST

The Court's approach to free-exercise challenges began to shift in the middle of the twentieth century. As we saw in Chapter 1, in *Cantwell v. Connecticut*, 310 U.S. 296 (1940), the Supreme Court held that the Free Exercise Clause applied to states as well as to the federal government, and reversed a conviction of Jehovah's Witnesses who had solicited religious contributions without first obtaining a license required by state law. Three years later, in two other cases involving Jehovah's Witness, which are addressed in Chapter 5, the protection of free exercise was further strengthened. In *Murdock v. Pennsylvania*, 319 U.S.

---

18. *Id.* at §15.

19. Firmage and Mangrum, *supra* note 5, at 241–244.

20. Edmunds-Tucker Act, 24 Stat. 637, §13. The Act provided limited exceptions for "[p]roperty used exclusively for purposes of worship, parsonages, and burial grounds." Firmage and Mangrum at 252. The impact of the legislation was reduced as a result of a variety of transfers made in anticipation of passage of the Edmunds-Tucker Act, so that property would be in friendly hands, beyond the reach of federal expropriators.

21. Doctrine & Covenants, Official Declaration I (1890).

22. The best estimates indicate 30,000 to 35,000 people in families adhering to offshoot groups that still practice polygamy—a fairly small number compared with more than 16,000,000 members of the Church (2017). *See* Daynes, *supra* note 5, at 210.

105 (1943), the Court held that a license tax applied to street preachers was unconstitutional, and in *West Virginia State Board of Education v. Barnette*, 319 U.S. 624 (1943), the Court invalidated compulsory flag salute legislation. The latter case was significant in part because it reversed *Minersville School District v. Gobitis*, 310 U.S. 586 (1940), which only three years earlier had held that an ostensibly neutral and general law requiring participation in flag salute ceremonies overrode free exercise claims.

In denying a religiously based exemption from saluting the flag in *Gobitis*, the Court had stated that "the mere possession of religious convictions which contradict the relevant concerns of a political society does not relieve the citizens from the discharge of political responsibilities." *Id.* at 594–595. Yet in *Barnette*, the Court explicitly overturned its earlier decision and sided with individual liberty in creating an exemption based on religious scruples. This marked the beginning of the evolution toward a strict scrutiny standard. Although the Court in *Barnette* continued to rely more explicitly upon the Free Speech Clause than the Free Exercise Clause, the fact that the students were Jehovah's Witnesses and objected to saluting the flag on religious grounds affirmed the principle that religious conduct can sometimes be protected under the First Amendment against conflicting statutory mandates.

As one might expect, the trend toward expanding the protection of religious minorities was not uninterrupted. In *Braunfeld v. Brown*, 366 U.S. 599 (1961), the Supreme Court considered a challenge by an Orthodox Jewish store owner of a law requiring stores to be closed on Sunday. Such laws impose significant burdens on Saturday Sabbatarians, since it results in their businesses being closed all weekend, which is the most important time of the week for retail sales. The Supreme Court gave short shrift to this burden and held that the Sunday closing law did not violate the Free Exercise Clause, since there was a legitimate secular purpose for the law (having a uniform day of rest) and because the law imposed only "indirect" as opposed to "direct" burdens on religious practice.

Just three years later, in *Sherbert v. Verner*, however, the Supreme Court for the first time explicitly applied a compelling state interest test to a free exercise claim.

SHERBERT V. VERNER

Supreme Court of the United States, 374 U.S. 398 (1963)

Mr. Justice BRENNAN delivered the opinion of the Court.

Appellant [Adell Sherbert], a member of the Seventh-day Adventist Church, was discharged by her South Carolina employer because she would not work on Saturday, the Sabbath Day of her faith. When she was unable to obtain other employment because from conscientious scruples she would not take Saturday work, she filed a claim for unemployment compensation benefits under the South Carolina Unemployment Compensation Act. That law provides that, to be eligible for benefits, a claimant must be "able to work and . . . available for work"; and, further, that a claimant is ineligible for benefits "if . . . he has failed, without good cause . . . to accept available suitable work when offered him by the employment office or the employer. . . ." The appellee Employment Security

Commission, in administrative proceedings under the statute, found that appellant's restriction upon her availability for Saturday work brought her within the provision disqualifying for benefits insured workers who fail, without good cause, to accept "suitable work when offered . . . by the employment office or the employer."

The Commission's finding was sustained by the Court of Common Pleas for Spartanburg County. That court's judgment was in turn affirmed by the South Carolina Supreme Court, which rejected appellant's contention that, as applied to her, the disqualifying provisions of the South Carolina statute abridged her right to the free exercise of her religion secured under the Free Exercise Clause of the First Amendment through the Fourteenth Amendment. The State Supreme Court held specifically that appellant's ineligibility statute "places no restriction upon the appellant's freedom of religion nor does it in any way prevent her in the exercise of her right and freedom to observe her religious beliefs in accordance with the dictates of her conscience." We noted probable jurisdiction of appellant's appeal. We reverse the judgment of the South Carolina Supreme Court and remand for further proceedings not inconsistent with this opinion.

I

The door of the Free Exercise Clause stands tightly closed against any governmental regulation of religious *beliefs* as such. Government may neither compel affirmation of a repugnant belief; nor penalize or discriminate against individuals or groups because they hold religious views abhorrent to the authorities; nor employ the taxing power to inhibit the dissemination of particular religious views. On the other hand, the Court has rejected challenges under the Free Exercise Clause to governmental regulation of certain overt acts prompted by religious beliefs or principles, for "even when the action is in accord with one's religious convictions, [it] is not totally free from legislative restrictions." The conduct or actions so regulated have invariably posed some substantial threat to public safety, peace or order.

Plainly enough, appellant's conscientious objection to Saturday work constitutes no conduct prompted by religious principles of a kind within the reach of state legislation. If, therefore, the decision of the South Carolina Supreme Court is to withstand appellant's constitutional challenge, it must be either because her disqualification as a beneficiary represents no infringement by the State of her constitutional rights of free exercise, or because any incidental burden on the free exercise of appellant's religion may be justified by a "compelling state interest in the regulation of a subject within the State's constitutional power to regulate. . . ." *NAACP v. Button*, 371 U.S. 415, 438. . . .

II

We turn first to the question whether the disqualification for benefits imposes any burden on the free exercise of appellant's religion. We think it is clear that it does. . . . For "[i]f the purpose or effect of a law is to impede the observance of one or all religions or is to discriminate invidiously between religions, that law is constitutionally invalid even though the burden may be characterized as being only indirect." Here not only is it apparent that appellant's declared ineligibility for benefits derives solely from the practice of her religion, but the pressure upon her to forgo that practice is unmistakable. The ruling forces her to choose between following the precepts of her religion and forfeiting benefits, on the one hand, and abandoning one of the precepts of her religion in order to accept work, on the other hand. Governmental imposition of such a choice puts the same kind of burden upon the free exercise of religion as would a fine imposed against appellant for her Saturday worship. . . .

Significantly South Carolina expressly saves the Sunday worshipper from having to make the kind of choice which we here hold infringes the Sabbatarian's religious liberty. When in times of "national emergency" the textile plants are authorized by the State Commissioner of Labor to operate on Sunday, "no employee shall be required to work on Sunday . . . who is conscientiously opposed to Sunday work; and if any employee should refuse to work on Sunday on account of conscientious . . . objections he or she shall not jeopardize his or her seniority by such refusal or be discriminated against in any other manner." No question of the disqualification of a Sunday worshipper for benefits is likely to arise, since we cannot suppose that an employer will discharge him in violation of this statute. The unconstitutionality of the disqualification of the Sabbatarian is thus compounded by the religious discrimination which South Carolina's general statutory scheme necessarily effects.

III

We must next consider whether some compelling state interest enforced in the eligibility provisions of the South Carolina statute justifies the substantial infringement of appellant's First Amendment right. In this highly sensitive constitutional area, "[o]nly the gravest abuses, endangering paramount interests, give occasion for permissible limitation," *Thomas v. Collins*, 323 U.S. 516, 530. No such abuse or danger has been advanced in the present case. The appellees suggest no more than a possibility that the filing of fraudulent claims by unscrupulous claimants feigning religious objections to Saturday work might not only dilute the unemployment compensation fund but also hinder the scheduling by employers of necessary Saturday work. . . . There is no proof whatever to warrant such fears of malingering or deceit as those which the respondents now advance. . . . For even if the possibility of spurious claims did threaten to dilute the fund and disrupt the scheduling of work, it would plainly be incumbent upon the appellees to demonstrate that no alternative forms of regulation would combat such abuses without infringing First Amendment rights. . . .

In these respects, then, the state interest asserted in the present case is wholly dissimilar to the interests which were found to justify the less direct burden upon religious practices in *Braunfeld v. Brown*. The Court recognized that the Sunday closing law which that decision sustained undoubtedly served "to make the practice of (the Orthodox Jewish merchants') religious beliefs more expensive." But the statute was nevertheless saved by a countervailing factor which finds no equivalent in the instant case–a strong state interest in providing one uniform day of rest for all workers. That secular objective could be achieved, the Court found, only by declaring Sunday to be that day of rest. Requiring exemptions for

Sabbatarians, while theoretically possible, appeared to present an administrative problem of such magnitude, or to afford the exempted class so great a competitive advantage, that such a requirement would have rendered the entire statutory scheme unworkable. In the present case no such justifications underlie the determination of the state court that appellant's religion makes her ineligible to receive benefits.

IV

In holding as we do, plainly we are not fostering the "establishment" of the Seventh-day Adventist religion in South Carolina, for the extension of unemployment benefits to Sabbatarians in common with Sunday worshippers reflects nothing more than the governmental obligation of neutrality in the face of religious differences, and does not represent that involvement of religious with secular institutions which it is the object of the Establishment Clause to forestall. . . .

The judgment of the South Carolina Supreme Court is reversed . . .

Mr. Justice DOUGLAS, concurring. . . .

Religious scruples of Moslems require them to attend a mosque on Friday and to pray five times daily. Religious scruples of a Sikh require him to carry a regular or a symbolic sword. Religious scruples of a Jehovah's Witness teach him to be a colporteur, going from door to door, from town to town, distributing his religious pamphlets. Religious scruples of a Quaker compel him to refrain from swearing and to affirm instead. Religious scruples of a Buddhist may require him to refrain from partaking of any flesh, even of fish.

The examples could be multiplied, including those of the Seventh-day Adventist whose Sabbath is Saturday and who is advised not to eat some meats. . . . These suffice, however, to show that many people hold beliefs alien to the majority of our society–beliefs that are protected by the First Amendment but which could easily be trod upon under the guise of "police" or "health" regulations reflecting the majority's views.

Some have thought that a majority of a community can, through state action, compel a minority to observe their particular religious scruples so long as the majority's rule can be said to perform some valid secular function. That was the essence of the Court's decision in the Sunday Blue Law Cases, . . . a ruling from which I then dissented . . . and still dissent.

[South Carolina] asks us to hold that when it comes to a day of rest a Sabbatarian must conform with the scruples of the majority in order to obtain unemployment benefits.

The result turns not on the degree of injury, which may indeed be nonexistent by ordinary standards. The harm is the interference with the individual's scruples or conscience–an important area of privacy which the First Amendment fences off from government. . . .

Mr. Justice HARLAN, whom Mr. Justice WHITE joins, dissenting. . . .

South Carolina's Unemployment Compensation Law was enacted in 1936 in response to the grave social and economic problems that arose during the depression of that period.

Thus the purpose of the legislature was to tide people over, and to avoid social and economic chaos, during periods when *work was unavailable*. But at the same time there was clearly no intent to provide relief for those who for purely personal reasons were or became *unavailable for work*. In accordance with this design, the legislature provided, in § 68–113, that "[a]n unemployed insured worker shall be eligible to receive benefits with respect to any week *only* if the Commission finds that . . . [h]e is able to work and is available for work (emphasis added), but no claimant shall be considered available for work if engaged in self employment of such nature as to return or promise remuneration in excess of the weekly benefit amounts he would have received if otherwise unemployed over such period of time. . . ."

The South Carolina Supreme Court has . . . consistently held that one is not "available for work" if his unemployment has resulted not from the inability of industry to provide a job but rather from personal circumstances, no matter how compelling. . . .

In the present case all that the state court has done is to apply these accepted principles. Since virtually all of the mills in the Spartanburg area were operating on a six-day week, the appellant was "unavailable for work," and thus ineligible for benefits, when personal considerations prevented her from accepting employment on a full-time basis in the industry and locality in which she had worked. The fact that these personal considerations sprang from her religious convictions was wholly without relevance to the state court's application of the law. . . .

. . . What the Court is holding is that if the State chooses to condition unemployment compensation on the applicant's availability for work, it is constitutionally compelled to *carve out an exception* – and to provide benefits – for those whose unavailability is due to their religious convictions. Such a holding has particular significance in two respects.

First, despite the Court's protestations to the contrary, the decision necessarily overrules *Braunfeld v. Brown*, which held that it did not offend the "Free Exercise" Clause of the Constitution for a State to forbid a Sabbatarian to do business on Sunday. The secular purpose of the statute before us today is even clearer than that involved in *Braunfeld*. And just as in *Braunfeld* – where exceptions to the Sunday closing laws for Sabbatarians would have been inconsistent with the purpose to achieve a uniform day of rest and would have required case-by-case inquiry into religious beliefs – so here, an exception to the rules of eligibility based on religious convictions would necessitate judicial examination of those convictions and would be at odds with the limited purpose of the statute to smooth out the economy during periods of industrial instability. . . .

Second, the implications of the present decision are far more troublesome than its apparently narrow dimensions would indicate at first glance. The meaning of today's holding, as already noted, is that the State must furnish unemployment benefits to one who is unavailable for work if the unavailability stems from the exercise of religious convictions. The State, in other words, must *single out* for financial assistance those whose behavior is religiously motivated, even though it denies such assistance to others whose identical behavior . . . is not religiously motivated.

COMMENTS AND QUESTIONS

1. Under the reasoning of the majority, what are the limits on religious claims for an exemption? Under the reasoning of the dissenting justices?
2. Are the dissenting justices correct that this case constitutes a tacit reversal of *Braunfeld v. Brown*?
3. Who has the better argument about financial assistance: the dissenters, who argue that the holding singles out religious believers for financial assistance that it denies to others, or Justice Douglas, who argues that this is not a case about what an individual can demand of government, but solely a case about what government may not do to an individual in violation of his religious scruples?
4. The *Sherbert* court notes at one point that even if a compelling state interest is present, the state cannot show that a burden on free exercise is justified unless it also shows that no alternative forms of regulation would solve the problem. As a practical matter, how important is this aspect of the strict scrutiny test?
5. Who more accurately describes the situation, the majority which sees this as a case requiring non-discrimination, or the dissent that sees this as a case of carving out a special exception for religion?

WISCONSIN V. YODER

Supreme Court of the United States, 406 U.S. 205

[Members of the Old Order Amish religion and the Conservative Amish Mennonite Church found themselves in violation of Wisconsin's compulsory school attendance law, which requires attending school until age 16, when they declined to send their children to school after the eighth grade. On complaint of the school district administrator for the public schools, the three respondents were charged, tried, and convicted in County Court, and were fined the sum of $5 each. The Wisconsin Supreme Court sustained the parents' claim that this violated their free exercise rights. The US Supreme Court granted a writ of certiorari to review the state Supreme Court's decision.]

Mr. Chief Justice BURGER delivered the opinion of the Court. . . .

[F]or Wisconsin to compel school attendance beyond the eighth grade [when opposed on Free Exercise Clause grounds], it must appear either that the State does not deny the free exercise of religious belief by its requirement, or that there is a state interest of sufficient magnitude to override the interest claiming protection under the Free Exercise Clause. . . .

The respondents freely concede, and indeed assert as an article of faith, that their religious beliefs and what we would today call "life style" have not altered in fundamentals for centuries. Their way of life in a church-oriented community, separated from the outside world and "worldly" influences, their attachment to nature and the soil, is a way inherently simple and uncomplicated, albeit difficult to preserve against the pressure to conform. Their rejection of telephones, automobiles, radios, and television, their mode of dress, of speech, their habits of manual work do indeed set them apart from much of contemporary society. . . .

The impact of the compulsory attendance law on respondents' practice of the Amish religion is not only severe, but inescapable, for the Wisconsin law affirmatively compels them, under threat of criminal sanction, to perform acts undeniably at odds with fundamental tenets of their religious beliefs. . . . Nor is the impact of the law confined to grave interference with important Amish religious tenets from a subjective point of view. It carries with it precisely the kind of objective danger to the free exercise of religion that the First Amendment was designed to prevent. As the record shows, compulsory school attendance to age 16 for Amish children carries with it a very real threat of undermining the Amish community and religious practice as they exist today; they must either abandon belief and be assimilated into society at large, or be forced to migrate to some other and more tolerant region. . . .

[T]he unchallenged testimony of acknowledged experts in education and religious history, almost 300 years of consistent practice, and strong evidence of a sustained faith pervading and regulating respondents' entire mode of life support the claim that enforcement of the State's requirement of compulsory formal education after the eighth grade would gravely endanger if not destroy the free exercise of respondents' religious beliefs.

[Wisconsin did not challenge the trial court's findings or the nature of the Amish faith, but the State argued that its interest in compulsory education "is so great that it is paramount to the undisputed claims of respondents that their mode of preparing their youth for Amish life . . . is an essential part of their religious belief and practice."]

Wisconsin concedes that under the Religion Clauses religious beliefs are absolutely free from the State's control, but it argues that "actions," even though religiously grounded, are outside the protection of the First Amendment. But our decisions have rejected the idea that religiously grounded conduct is always outside the protection of the Free Exercise Clause. It is true that activities of individuals, even when religiously based, are often subject to regulation by the States in the exercise of their undoubted power to promote the health, safety, and general welfare, or the Federal Government in the exercise of its delegated powers. . . . But to agree that religiously grounded conduct must often be subject to the broad police power of the State is not to deny that there are areas of conduct protected by the Free Exercise Clause of the First Amendment and thus beyond the power of the State to control, even under regulations of general applicability. [Citations omitted.] This case, therefore, does not become easier because respondents were convicted for their "actions" in refusing to send their children to the public high school; in this context belief and action cannot be neatly confined in logic-tight compartments. . . .

Nor can this case be disposed of on the grounds that Wisconsin's requirement for school attendance to age 16 applies uniformly to all citizens of the State and does not, on its face, discriminate against religions or a particular religion, or that it is motivated by legitimate secular concerns. A regulation neutral on its face may, in its application, nonetheless offend the constitutional requirement for governmental neutrality if it unduly burdens the free exercise of religion. . . .

We turn, then, to the State's broader contention that its interest in its system of compulsory education is so compelling that even the established religious practices of the Amish must give way. Where fundamental claims of religious freedom are at stake, however, we cannot accept such a sweeping claim; despite its admitted validity in the generality of cases, we must searchingly examine the interests that the State seeks to promote by its requirement for compulsory education to age 16, and the impediment to those objectives that would flow from recognizing the claimed Amish exemption. . . .

The State advances two primary arguments in support of its system of compulsory education. It notes, as Thomas Jefferson pointed out early in our history, that some degree of education is necessary to prepare citizens to participate effectively and intelligently in our open political system if we are to preserve freedom and independence. Further, education prepares individuals to be self-reliant and self-sufficient participants in society. We accept these propositions.

. . . [T]he effect that an additional one or two years of formal high school for Amish children in place of their long-established program of informal vocational education would do little to serve those interests. . . . It is one thing to say that compulsory education for a year or two beyond the eighth grade may be necessary when its goal is the preparation of the child for life in modern society as the majority live, but it is quite another if the goal of education be viewed as the preparation of the child for life in the separated agrarian community that is the keystone of the Amish faith. . . .

Indeed, the Amish communities singularly parallel and reflect many of the virtues of Jefferson's ideal of the "sturdy yeoman" who would form the basis of what he considered as the ideal of a democratic society. Even their idiosyncratic separateness exemplifies the diversity we profess to admire and encourage.

We hold, with the Supreme Court of Wisconsin, that the First and Fourteenth Amendments prevent the State from compelling respondents to cause their children to attend formal high school to age 16.

Beyond [an established history of self-sufficient success and sincere religious beliefs], they have carried the even more difficult burden of demonstrating the adequacy of their alternative mode of continuing informal vocational education in terms of precisely those overall interests that the State advances in support of its program of compulsory high school education. In light of this convincing showing, one that probably few other religious groups or sects could make, and weighing the minimal difference between what the State would require and what the Amish already accept, it was incumbent on the State to show with more particularity how its admittedly strong interest in compulsory education would be adversely affected by granting an exemption to the Amish. . . .

Mr. Justice WHITE, with whom Mr. Justice BRENNAN and Mr. Justice STEWART join, concurring.

Cases such as this one inevitably call for a delicate balancing of important but conflicting interests. I join the opinion and judgment of the Court because I cannot say that the State's interest in requiring . . . compulsory education in the ninth and tenth grades outweighs the importance of the concededly sincere Amish religious practice to the survival of that sect.

This would be a very different case for me if respondents' claim were that their religion forbade their children from attending any school at any time and from complying in any way with the educational standards set by the State. Since the Amish children are permitted to acquire the basic tools of literacy to survive in modern society by attending grades one through eight and since the deviation from the State's compulsory-education law is relatively slight, I conclude that respondents' claim must prevail, largely because "religious freedom–the freedom to believe and to practice strange and, it may be, foreign creeds–has classically been one of the highest values of our society." *Braunfeld v. Brown.*

Mr. Justice DOUGLAS, dissenting in part.

. . . [N]o analysis of religious-liberty claims can take place in a vacuum. If the parents in this case are allowed a religious exemption, the inevitable effect is to impose the parents' notions of religious duty upon their children. . . . As the child has no other effective forum, it is in this litigation that his rights should be considered. And, if an Amish child desires to attend high school, and is mature enough to have that desire respected, the State may well be able to override the parents' religiously motivated objections. . . .

It is the future of the student, not the future of the parents, that is imperiled by today's decision. If a parent keeps his child out of school beyond the grade school, then the child will be forever barred from entry into the new and amazing world of diversity that we have today. The child may decide that that is the preferred course, or he may rebel. It is the student's judgment, not his parents', that is essential if we are to give full meaning to what we have said about the Bill of Rights and of the right of students to be masters of their own destiny. If he is harnessed to the Amish way of life by those in authority over him and if his education is truncated, his entire life may be stunted and deformed. The child, therefore, should be given an opportunity to be heard before the State gives the exemption which we honor today. . . .

COMMENTS AND QUESTIONS

1. How important is it to the Amish that the two years of extra education not be mandatory? Does this importance affect the court's analysis?
2. Chief Justice Burger's opinion contains language that seems to characterize the Amish religion as a quaint, aesthetically pleasing one. How important was this characterization to his decision? Might the outcome have been different if the religion at issue were less appealing?
3. Should the rights of the child be given preference over the rights of the parents (and the community) as Justice Douglas maintains?
4. In assessing a free exercise claim, whose beliefs should count: those of the individual or those of the community? *See Thomas v. Review Board*, 450 U.S. 707 (1981) (sustaining the free exercise claim of a Jehovah's Witness who held stricter views on whether he could work in a munitions plant than did many other co-religionists).

C. THE PARTIAL ABANDONMENT OF THE COMPELLING STATE INTEREST TEST

In the years after *Yoder*, the compelling state interest test was eroded in a number of decisions of the Supreme Court. The Court ruled in *Goldman v. Weinberger*, 475 U.S. 503 (1986) and *O'Lone v. Shabazz*, 482 U.S. 342 (1987), that a more lenient standard should apply in military settings and prisons respectively because of special regulatory considerations. In *Lyng v. Northwest Indian Cemetery Protective Association*, 485 U.S. 439 (1988) the Court declined to apply the compelling interest test in managing its own lands rather than to impose general social regulations, and in *United States v. Lee*, 455 U.S. 252 (1982), the Court chose not to apply the test in the context of tax restrictions. In other cases, the Court held, perhaps too readily, that the compelling state interest test had been satisfied.[23]

In *Employment Division v. Smith*, 494 U.S. 872 (1990), the Court went considerably further, repudiating the compelling state interest test in all but limited set of free exercise cases.

EMPLOYMENT DIVISION, DEPARTMENT OF HUMAN RESOURCES OF OREGON V. SMITH

Supreme Court of the United States, 494 U.S. 872 (1990)

Justice SCALIA delivered the opinion of the Court.

This case requires us to decide whether the Free Exercise Clause of the First Amendment permits the State of Oregon to include religiously inspired peyote use within the reach of its general criminal prohibition on use of that drug, and thus permits the State to deny unemployment benefits to persons dismissed from their jobs because of such religiously inspired use. . . . [The religious claimants in the case were fired from their jobs with a private drug rehabilitation organization because they used peyote for sacramental purposes at a ceremony of the Native American Church. Peyote is a hallucinogenic but by no means recreational drug, often causing nausea and similar discomfort. The Native American Church is a bona fide religion with a well-documented and lengthy history. There was no question of the sincerity of the claims being asserted in the case.]

The Free Exercise Clause of the First Amendment, which has been made applicable to the States by incorporation into the Fourteenth Amendment, provides that "Congress shall make no law respecting an establishment of religion, or *prohibiting the free exercise thereof*. . . . "The free exercise of religion means, first and foremost, the right to believe and profess whatever religious doctrine one desires. Thus, the First Amendment obviously excludes all "governmental regulation of religious *beliefs* as such." The government may not

---

23. *See, e.g., Austin v. Michigan Chamber of Commerce*, 494 U.S. 652, 655 (1990); *Boos v. Barry*, 485 U.S. 312, 334 (1988) (plurality); *see also Burson v. Freeman*, 504 U.S. 191, 198 (1992) (plurality); *Board of Airport Comm'rs v. Jews for Jesus, Inc.*, 482 U.S. 569, 573 (1987); *Cornelius v. NAACP Legal Defense and Educ. Fund, Inc.*, 473 U.S. 788, 800 (1985); *United States v. Grace*, 461 U.S. 171, 177 (1983); *Perry Educ. Ass'n v. Perry Local Educators' Ass'n*, 460 U.S. 37, 45 (1983).

compel affirmation of religious belief, punish the expression of religious doctrines it believes to be false, impose special disabilities on the basis of religious views or religious status, or lend its power to one or the other side in controversies over religious authority or dogma. [Citations omitted.]

But the "exercise of religion" often involves not only belief and profession but the performance of (or abstention from) physical acts. . . . It would be true, we think (though no case of ours has involved the point), that a State would be "prohibiting the free exercise [of religion]" if it sought to ban such acts or abstentions only when they are engaged in for religious reasons, or only because of the religious belief that they display. It would doubtless be unconstitutional, for example, to ban the casting of "statues that are to be used for worship purposes," or to prohibit bowing down before a golden calf.

Respondents in the present case, however, seek to carry the meaning of "prohibiting the free exercise [of religion]" one large step further. They contend that their religious motivation for using peyote places them beyond the reach of a criminal law that is not specifically directed at their religious practice, and that is concededly constitutional as applied to those who use the drug for other reasons. They assert, in other words, that "prohibiting the free exercise [of religion]" includes requiring any individual to observe a generally applicable law that requires (or forbids) the performance of an act that his religious belief forbids (or requires). As a textual matter, we do not think the words must be given that meaning. . . .

We have never held that an individual's religious beliefs excuse him from compliance with an otherwise valid law prohibiting conduct that the State is free to regulate. On the contrary, the record of more than a century of our free exercise jurisprudence contradicts that proposition. As described succinctly by Justice Frankfurter in *Minersville School Dist. Bd. of Educ. v. Gobitis*: "Conscientious scruples have not, in the course of the long struggle for religious toleration, relieved the individual from obedience to a general law not aimed at the promotion or restriction of religious beliefs. The mere possession of religious convictions which contradict the relevant concerns of a political society does not relieve the citizen from the discharge of political responsibilities."

. . . We first had occasion to assert that principle in *Reynolds v. United States*, [where] we rejected the claim that criminal laws against polygamy could not be constitutionally applied to those whose religion commanded the practice. "[W]hile [laws] cannot interfere with mere religious belief and opinions, they may with practices. . . . Can a man excuse his practices to the contrary because of his religious belief? To permit this would be to make the professed doctrines of religious belief superior to the law of the land, and in effect to permit every citizen to become a law unto himself."

Subsequent decisions have consistently held that the right of free exercise does not relieve an individual of the obligation to comply with a valid and neutral law of general applicability on the ground that the law proscribes (or prescribes) conduct that his religion prescribes (or proscribes). . . .

The only decisions in which we have held that the First Amendment bars application of a neutral, generally applicable law to religiously motivated action have involved not the Free Exercise Clause alone, but the Free Exercise Clause in conjunction with other constitutional protections, such as freedom of speech and of the press, or the right of parents to direct the education of their children. [*E.g.*, *Cantwell* and *Yoder*.] . . .

The present case does not present such a hybrid situation. . . . Respondents urge us to hold, quite simply, that when otherwise prohibitable conduct is accompanied by religious convictions, not only the convictions but the conduct itself must be free from governmental regulation. We have never held that, and decline to do so now. . . .

Respondents argue that even though exemption from generally applicable criminal laws need not automatically be extended to religiously motivated actors, at least the claim for a religious exemption must be evaluated under the balancing test set forth in *Sherbert v. Verner*. Under the *Sherbert* test, governmental actions that substantially burden a religious practice must be justified by a compelling governmental interest. We have never invalidated any governmental action on the basis of the *Sherbert* test except the denial of unemployment compensation. Although we have sometimes purported to apply the *Sherbert* test in contexts other than that, we have always found the test satisfied. In recent years we have abstained from applying the *Sherbert* test (outside the unemployment compensation field) at all.

Even if we were inclined to breathe into *Sherbert* some life beyond the unemployment compensation field, we would not apply it to require exemptions from a generally applicable criminal law. The *Sherbert* test, it must be recalled, was developed in a [non-criminal unemployment compensation] context that lent itself to individualized governmental assessment of the reasons for the relevant conduct. . . . We conclude today that the sounder approach, and the approach in accord with the vast majority of our precedents, is to hold the test inapplicable to [general criminal prohibitions of conduct]. To make an individual's obligation to obey such a law contingent upon the law's coincidence with his religious beliefs, except where the State's interest is "compelling"–permitting him, by virtue of his beliefs, "to become a law unto himself,"–contradicts both constitutional tradition and common sense.

The "compelling government interest" requirement seems benign, because it is familiar from other fields. But using it as the standard that must be met before the government may accord different treatment on the basis of race, or before the government may regulate the content of speech, is not remotely comparable to using it for the purpose asserted here. What it produces in those other fields–equality of treatment and an unrestricted flow of contending speech–are constitutional norms; what it would produce here–a private right to ignore generally applicable laws–is a constitutional anomaly.

Nor is it possible to limit the impact of respondents' proposal by requiring a "compelling state interest" only when the conduct prohibited is "central" to the individual's religion. . . . It is no more appropriate for judges to determine the "centrality" of religious beliefs before applying a "compelling interest" test in the free exercise field, than it would be for them to determine the "importance" of ideas before applying the "compelling interest" test in the free speech field. What principle of law or logic can be brought to bear to contradict a believer's assertion that a particular act is "central" to his personal faith? Judging the centrality of different religious practices is akin to the unacceptable "business of evaluating the relative merits of differing religious claims.". . . As we reaffirmed only last

Term, "[i]t is not within the judicial ken to question the centrality of particular beliefs or practices to a faith, or the validity of particular litigants' interpretations of those creeds." . . . Repeatedly and in many different contexts, we have warned that courts must not presume to determine the place of a particular belief in a religion or the plausibility of a religious claim. [fn 4: There is no way out of the difficulty that, if general laws are to be subjected to a "religious practice" exception, both the importance of the law at issue and the centrality of the practice at issue must reasonably be considered.]

If the "compelling interest" test is to be applied at all, then, it must be applied across the board, to all actions thought to be religiously commanded. Moreover, if "compelling interest" really means what it says . . . , many laws will not meet the test. Any society adopting such a system would be courting anarchy, but that danger increases in direct proportion to the society's diversity of religious beliefs, and its determination to coerce or suppress none of them. Precisely because "we are a cosmopolitan nation made up of people of almost every conceivable religious preference," and precisely because we value and protect that religious divergence, we cannot afford the luxury of deeming *presumptively invalid*, as applied to the religious objector, every regulation of conduct that does not protect an interest of the highest order. The rule respondents favor would open the prospect of constitutionally required religious exemptions from civic obligations of almost every conceivable kind. . . . The First Amendment's protection of religious liberty does not require this. [fn 5 . . .[I]t is horrible to contemplate that federal judges will regularly balance against the importance of general laws the significance of religious practice.]

Values that are protected against government interference through enshrinement in the Bill of Rights are not thereby banished from the political process. . . . It is therefore not surprising that a number of States have made an exception to their drug laws for sacramental peyote use. But to say that a nondiscriminatory religious-practice exemption is permitted, or even that it is desirable, is not to say that it is constitutionally required, and that the appropriate occasions for its creation can be discerned by the courts. It may fairly be said that leaving accommodation to the political process will place at a relative disadvantage those religious practices that are not widely engaged in; but that unavoidable consequence of democratic government must be preferred to a system in which each conscience is a law unto itself or in which judges weigh the social importance of all laws against the centrality of all religious beliefs.

Because respondents' ingestion of peyote was prohibited under Oregon law, and because that prohibition is constitutional, Oregon may, consistent with the Free Exercise Clause, deny respondents unemployment compensation when their dismissal results from use of the drug.

The decision of the Oregon Supreme Court is accordingly reversed. It is so ordered.

Justice O'CONNOR concurring in the judgment. [Justices BRENNAN, MARSHALL, and BLACKMUN joined those parts of Justice O'Connor's opinion calling for retention of the compelling state interest test.]

Although I agree with the result the Court reaches in this case, I cannot join its opinion. In my view, today's holding dramatically departs from well-settled

First Amendment jurisprudence and is incompatible with our Nation's fundamental commitment to individual religious liberty. . . .

The Court today extracts from our long history of free exercise precedents the single categorical rule that "if prohibiting the exercise of religion . . . is . . . merely the incidental effect of a generally applicable and otherwise valid provision, the First Amendment has not been offended." . . . To reach this sweeping result, however, the Court must . . . disregard our consistent application of free exercise doctrine to cases involving generally applicable regulations that burden religious conduct.

The Court endeavors to escape from our [decision in] *Yoder* by labeling [it a] "hybrid" decision, but there is no denying that [*Yoder*] expressly relied on the Free Exercise Clause [and has been consistently regarded as part] of the mainstream of our free exercise jurisprudence. . . .

A State that makes criminal an individual's religiously motivated conduct burdens that individual's free exercise of religion in the severest manner possible, for it results in the choice to the individual of either abandoning his religious principle or facing criminal prosecution. . . .

To me, the sounder approach . . . is to apply [a "compelling state interest"] test in each case to determine whether the burden on the specific plaintiffs before us is constitutionally significant and whether the particular criminal interest asserted by the State before us is compelling. . . .

[Justice O'Connor proceeds to apply the test by identifying the governmental interest in Oregon's prohibiting the use of peyote and other dangerous substances as one of protecting the people and preventing trafficking of controlled substances.]

For these reasons, I believe that granting a selective exemption in this case would seriously impair Oregon's compelling interest in prohibiting possession of peyote by its citizens. Under such circumstances, the Free Exercise Clause does not require the State to accommodate respondents' religiously motivated conduct. Accordingly, I concur in the judgment of the Court.

Justice BLACKMUN, with whom Justice BRENNAN and Justice MARSHALL join, dissenting.

[The majority's] distorted view of our precedents leads [to their conclusion] that strict scrutiny of a state law burdening the free exercise of religion is a "luxury" that a well-ordered society cannot afford, and that the repression of minority religions is an "unavoidable consequence of democratic government." I do not believe the Founders thought their dearly bought freedom from religious persecution a "luxury," but an essential element of liberty–and they could not have thought religious intolerance "unavoidable," for they drafted the Religion Clauses precisely in order to avoid that intolerance.

For these reasons, I agree with Justice O'Connor's analysis of the applicable free exercise doctrine, [though I disagree] with her specific answer to that question. . . .

I

In [using the "compelling interest" test], it is important to articulate in precise terms the state interest involved. It is not the State's broad interest in fighting the critical "war on drugs" that must be weighed against respondents' claim, but the State's narrow interest in refusing to make an exception for the religious, ceremonial use of peyote.

[The dissent points out that the State has not offered evidence that peyote is harmful and has failed to prosecute users of peyote. It seeks to withhold unemployment benefits only as a symbolic gesture. The dissent rejects a symbolic gesture as a compelling state interest.]

II

. . . Respondents believe, and their sincerity has *never* been at issue, that the peyote plant embodies their deity, and eating it is an act of worship and communion, [an essential religious ritual]. If Oregon can constitutionally prosecute them for this act of worship, they, like the Amish, may be "forced to migrate to some other and more tolerant region."

For these reasons, I conclude that Oregon's interest in enforcing its drug laws against religious use of peyote is not sufficiently compelling to outweigh respondents' right to the free exercise of their religion. . . . The State of Oregon cannot, consistently with the Free Exercise Clause, deny respondents unemployment benefits.

I dissent.

COMMENTS AND QUESTIONS

1. Is the *Smith* case much ado about nothing? After all, Justice Scalia, who jettisons the compelling state interest test, and Justice O'Connor, who applies it, reach the same result.
2. Why does it matter whether the compelling state interest test is used or not? What is the likely impact on initial negotiations between a religious claimant and a government official opposing an exemption if there is a compelling state interest test? If there is not? For a detailed discussion of the impact of the Smith decision and the significant resurgence of the compelling state interest test, discussed below, see W. Cole Durham, Jr., Robert T. Smith, and William W. Bassett, *Religious Organization and the Law* §1:6 (2nd ed., Thompson Reuters/West 2017).)
3. Would granting an exemption result in allowing every person to become a law unto himself as Justice Scalia repeatedly warns?
4. In his majority opinion Justice Scalia went to great lengths to suggest he was not overruling precedent. For example, he cited *Gobitis*, not mentioning the crucial fact that it was overruled three years later. He distinguishes *Sherbert* on the ground that it didn't include criminal law. He distinguishes *Yoder* on the ground that it involved hybrid rights! Which of these distinctions is the most credible?
5. Under what circumstances will a strict scrutiny standard be applied to a free exercise claim after *Smith*? Should strict scrutiny still be used in analyzing a free exercise challenge to a statutory regime that does not explicitly target a particular religion but has numerous individualized exceptions so that only one or a few religions are burdened? *See, e.g.*, *Church of the Lukumi Babalu Aye v. City of Hialeah*, 508 U.S. 520 (1993) (city regulations forbidding ritual

slaughter of animals subjected to strict scrutiny because analysis of exception scheme showed targeting of Santeria religion).

6. Is there any need for freedom of religion rights in domains where they function because of the presence of a hybrid right? What does freedom of religion add in these contexts? Are there any contexts in which religious rights cannot be linked with at least one other right?
7. Compare the *Hosanna-Tabor* case discussed in Chapter 10 with *Smith*. Are the two cases consistent?

D. THE RESILIENCE OF THE COMPELLING STATE INTEREST TEST

1. The Congressional Response to *Employment Division v. Smith*: The Religious Freedom Restoration Act of 1993 (RFRA)

The public reaction to *Employment Division v. Smith* was predominantly negative. A broad coalition of religious and civil liberty groups, both conservative and liberal, pressed Congress to enact a statute reinstating the compelling state interest test. Congress responded by overwhelmingly passing the Religious Freedom Restoration Act of 1993 (RFRA). The House vote was unanimous, and in the Senate only three senators voted against passage, and President Bill Clinton signed the bill. In pertinent part RFRA, 42 USCA §2000bb provided that:

> [T]the compelling interest test as set forth in set forth in prior Federal court rulings is a workable test for striking sensible balances between religious liberty and competing prior governmental interests. . . . The purposes of this chapter are—(1) to restore the compelling interest test as set forth in *Sherbert v. Verner* . . . and *Wisconsin v. Yoder* . . . and to guarantee its application in all cases where free exercise of religion is substantially burdened; and (2) to provide a claim or defense to persons whose religious exercise is substantially burdened by government. (a) In general, Government shall not substantially burden a person's exercise of religion even if the burden results from a rule of general applicability, [except] (b) Government may substantially burden a person's exercise of religion only if it demonstrates that application of the burden to the person—(1) is in furtherance of a compelling governmental interest; and (2) is the least restrictive means of furthering that compelling governmental interest. (c) A person whose religious exercise has been burdened in violation of this section may assert that violation as a claim or defense in a judicial proceeding and obtain appropriate relief against a government.

RFRA's award of attorneys' fees for the successful claimant increased the incentives and practical ability to pursue claims, and created incentives for government officials to find satisfactory accommodations.

2. The Supreme Court's Response to RFRA and Its Aftermath: The Unconstitutionality of RFRA as Applied to the States and Subsequent Legislation

The purpose of RFRA was in effect to repeal *Smith* and reinstate the compelling state interest test of *Sherbert*. The idea of Congress attempting to reverse a constitutional decision might seem counterintuitive, except that in many cases Congress (and the individual states) can impose requirements that are higher than the constitutional threshold. The constitutionality of RFRA was hotly debated. The key issue turned out to be whether Congress, with its limited enumerated powers, was authorized to pass RFRA.

The Court addressed that question in *City of Boerne v. Flores*, 521 U.S. 507 (1997). When church filed an application for a building permit to construct the expansion was denied because the renovations were inconsistent with requirements established by a local historic landmark ordinance. The denial was eventually appealed to the Supreme Court. The Court held that the power that Congress had relied on to pass RFRA—Section 5 of the Fourteenth Amendment —did not give Congress the power to impose RFRA on the states. The Court did not, however, hold RFRA unconstitutional with respect to federal law:

> Congress' power under §5 . . . extends only to "enforc[ing]" the provisions of the Fourteenth Amendment. The Court has described this power as "remedial." The design of the Amendment and the text of §5 are inconsistent with the suggestion that Congress has the power to decree the substance of the Fourteenth Amendment's restrictions on the States. Legislation which alters the meaning of the Free Exercise Clause cannot be said to be enforcing the Clause. Congress does not enforce a constitutional right by changing what the right is. It has been given the power "to enforce," not the power to determine what constitutes a constitutional violation. Were it not so, what Congress would be enforcing would no longer be, in any meaningful sense, the "provisions of [the Fourteenth Amendment]." . . . When the political branches of the Government act against the background of a judicial interpretation of the Constitution already issued, it must be understood that in later cases and controversies the Court will treat its precedents with the respect due them under settled principles, including *stare decisis*, and contrary expectations must be disappointed. RFRA was designed to control cases and controversies, such as the one before us; but as the provisions of the federal statute here invoked are beyond congressional authority, it is this Court's precedent, not RFRA, which must control. (501 US 519, 536)

Justice O'Connor, joined by Justice Breyer, wrote in dissent:

> . . . I agree with the Court that the issue before us is whether the Religious Freedom Restoration Act of 1993 (RFRA) is a proper exercise of Congress' power to enforce the Fourteenth Amendment. But as a yardstick for measuring the constitutionality of RFRA, the Court uses its holding in *Employment Div., Dept. of Human Resources of Ore. v. Smith*, 494 U.S. 872 (1990), the decision that prompted Congress to enact RFRA as a means of more rigorously enforcing the Free Exercise Clause. I remain of the view that *Smith* was wrongly decided, and I would use this case to reexamine the Court's holding there. Therefore, I would direct the parties to brief the question whether *Smith* represents the correct understanding of the Free Exercise Clause and set the case for reargument. If the Court were to correct the misinterpretation of the Free Exercise Clause set forth in *Smith* it would simultaneously put our First Amendment jurisprudence back on course and allay the legitimate concerns of a majority in Congress who believed that *Smith* improperly restricted religious liberty. We would then be in a position to review RFRA in light of a proper interpretation of the Free Exercise Clause. (544)

3. The Resilience of Free Exercise: Developments Since *Boerne*

Following *Boerne*, Congress went back to the drawing board and adopted legislation in a number of specific, more limited areas where it was confident it did have constitutional power to enact religious freedom legislation. The American Indian Religious Freedom Act Amendment of 1994[24] (AIRFAA) was enacted shortly after RFRA to legalize religious use of peyote by Native Americans. Pursuant to its bankruptcy power, it passed the Religious Liberty and Charitable Donation Protection Act of 1998,[25] which prevented bankruptcy trustees from recapturing donations made to religious organizations within three months prior to a declaration of bankruptcy. The Religious Land Use and Institutionalized Persons Act (RLUIPA) of 2000, 42 USC §§2000cc et seq. is probably the post-*Boerne* enactment that has had the broadest impact. As its name suggests, it imposes heightened religious freedom protections in settings involving land use and institutional settings (primarily prisons and mental hospitals). As noted above, RLUIPA was upheld against an Establishment Clause challenge in *Cutter v. Wilkinson*, 544 U.S. 709 (2005).

NOTE ON THE STATUS OF "FEDERAL" RFRA: *Gonzales v. O Centro Espirita Beneficente Uniao Do Vegetal*

Supreme Court of the United States, 546 U.S. 418 (2006)

RFRA was declared unconstitutional with respect to state and local government action in *City of Boerne*. As yet, the Supreme Court has assumed that the "federal RFRA" is constitutional without squarely confronting the issue. However, in *Cutter v. Wilkinson*, 544 U.S. 709 (2005), the Court held that RLUIPA did not violate the Establishment Clause. RLUIPA is much more narrowly drafted than RFRA, but the basic rationale of the case, according to which increasing the level of protection of a prisoner's religious freedom rights does not violate the Establishment Clause, would seem to apply in the federal RFRA setting.

Moreover, although the issue of the of federal RFRA's constitutionality was not formally before the Court in *Gonzales v. O Centro Espirita Beneficente Uniao Do Vegetal*, 546 U.S. 418 (2006), the fact that the Supreme Court applied RFRA in a manner that allowed religious adherents claiming an exemption from federal drug laws to prevail with no intimation that there might be a constitutional problem that had to be considered on remand suggests that the Supreme Court is not likely to strike down RFRA's federal reach.

---

24. Pub. L. No. 103–344, 108 Stat. 3125 (1994) (codified at 42 USC §1996a (2007)). Prior to amendment, the American Indian Religious Freedom Act, Pub. L. No. 95–341, 92 Stat. 469 (1978) (codified at 42 USC §1996 (2007)), was treated by the Supreme Court as a "sense of Congress joint resolution" that "has no teeth in it." *Lyng v. Northwest Indian Cemetery Protective Ass'n*, 485 U.S. 439, 455 (quoting Congressman Udall, the sponsor of the legislation). "Nowhere in the [AIRFA] law is there so much as a hint of any intent to create a cause of action or any judicially enforceable individual rights." *Lyng*, 485 U.S. at 455.

25. Pub. L. No. 105–183, 112 Stat. 517 (1998) (amending 11 USC §§544, 546, 548, 707, 1325 (1994)).

The *O Centro* case involved a Christian spiritist sect based in Brazil, with an American branch of approximately 130 individuals, that "receives communion by drinking a sacramental tea, brewed from plants unique to the region, that contains a hallucinogen regulated under the Controlled Substances Act by the Federal Government." (546 U.S. 423) The government conceded that this practice is a sincere exercise of religion, but nevertheless sought to prohibit use of the drug by members of the Church in the United States on the ground that it violated the Controlled Substances Act. The religious group responded by arguing that RFRA applied to this case and that it prohibited the federal government from substantially burdening a person's exercise of religion unless the government "demonstrates that application of the burden to the person" (413) and that the burden imposed represents the least restrictive means of advancing a compelling state interest.

The government argued that it had a compelling state interest in the uniform application of the drug laws and that no exception to the ban on hallucinogenic drugs could be made to accommodate the sect's sincere religious practice. The Supreme Court applied RFRA and concluded that the government failed to carry its burden of proving that it had a compelling state interest in barring the Church's sacramental use of hoasca tea.

> RFRA, and the strict scrutiny test it adopted, contemplate an inquiry more focused than the Government's categorical approach. RFRA requires the Government to demonstrate that the compelling interest test is satisfied through application of the challenged law "to the person"—the particular claimant whose sincere exercise of religion is being substantially burdened. RFRA expressly adopted the compelling interest test "as set forth in *South*, and *Wisconsin v. Yoder*." In each of those cases, this Court looked beyond broadly formulated interests justifying the general applicability of government mandates and scrutinized the asserted harm of granting specific exemptions to particular religious claimants. (430-431)
>
> Under the more focused inquiry required by RFRA and the compelling interest test, the Government's mere invocation of the general characteristics of Schedule I substances, as set forth in the Controlled Substances Act, cannot carry the day. It is true, of course, that Schedule I substances such as DMT [the hallucinogenic component of hoasca tea] are exceptionally dangerous. Nevertheless, there is no indication that Congress, in classifying DMT, considered the harms posed by the particular use at issue here–the circumscribed, sacramental use of hoasca by the UDV [Church]. Congress' determination that DMT should be listed under Schedule I simply does not provide a categorical answer that relieves the Government of the obligation to shoulder its burden under RFRA. (432)

The Court also rejected the government's sweeping claim that it had a compelling interest based on its obligation to comply with the 1971 United Nations Convention on Psychotropic Substances, a treaty signed by the United States that calls upon signatories to prohibit the use of hallucinogens, including DMT.

> The fact that hoasca is covered by the Convention, however, does not automatically mean that the Government has demonstrated a compelling interest in applying the Controlled Substances Act, which implements the Convention, to the UDV's sacramental use of the tea. At the present stage, it suffices to observe that the Government did not even submit evidence addressing the international consequences of granting an exemption for the UDV. The Government simply submitted two affidavits by State Department officials attesting to the general importance of honoring international obligations and of maintaining the leadership position of the

> United States in the international war on drugs. We do not doubt the validity of these interests, any more than we doubt the general interest in promoting public health and safety by enforcing the Controlled Substances Act, but under RFRA invocation of such general interests, standing alone, is not enough. (438)

In conclusion, the Court noted that even though the balancing required by RFRA is difficult, it is what Congress has mandated the courts to do in this case.

> The Government repeatedly invokes Congress' findings and purposes underlying the Controlled Substances Act, but Congress had a reason for enacting RFRA, too. Congress recognized that "laws 'neutral' toward religion may burden religious exercise as surely as laws intended to interfere with religious exercise," and legislated "the compelling interest test" as the means for the courts to "strik[e] sensible balances between religious liberty and competing prior governmental interests." We have no cause to pretend that the task assigned by Congress to the courts under RFRA is an easy one. Indeed, the very sort of difficulties highlighted by the Government here were cited by this Court in deciding that the approach later mandated by Congress under RFRA was not required as a matter of constitutional law under the Free Exercise Clause. See *Smith*. But Congress has determined that courts should strike sensible balances, pursuant to a compelling interest test that requires the Government to address the particular practice at issue. Applying that test, we conclude that the courts below did not err in determining that the Government failed to demonstrate, at the preliminary injunction state, a compelling interest in barring the UDV's sacramental use of hoasca. (439)

Because the case came before the Court on an appeal from the grant of a preliminary injunction, it was remanded to lower courts for adjudication on the merits. As indicated above, however, the Court's opinion contains no hint that the statutory language of RFRA, which was carefully applied by the Court, suffers from any constitutional defects in the federal setting. Subsequently, in *Burwell v. Hobby Lobby*, 134 S.Ct. 2761 (2014) the Court indicated that there is no lack of congressional power to act where RFRA is regulating federal agency action because the same enumerated power that supports the particular agency's work also supports the applicability of RFRA in that domain.

As a practical matter, both religious claimants and federal officials are unlikely to challenge federal RFRA—the claimants because they seek the most favorable possible protection, and federal officials because, although federal prosecutors might be interested in asserting such a challenge, the top-level federal officials charged with making such decisions (the Attorney General and the Solicitor General) have a duty to defend rather than attack federal legislation, and they are particularly unlikely to attack legislation that is as politically popular as RFRA.

Some of the most significant RFRA developments have occurred at the state level. In contrast to Congress, which *Boerne* held lacked power to raise free exercise standards vis-à-vis the individual states, there is no impediment to the states holding themselves to a higher standard than required by *Smith*.

By the end of 2017, 21 states—Alabama, Arizona, Arkansas, Connecticut, Florida*, Idaho, Illinois, Indiana*, Kansas, Kentucky*, Louisiana, Mississippi*, Missouri, New Mexico*, Oklahoma*, Pennsylvania, Rhode Island, South Carolina*, Tennessee*, Texas, and Virginia—had adopted "state RFRAs", either by state legislation or constitutional amendment (*eight of these were considering amendments), and courts in 14 states have ruled that their state's constitution provides a similar level of protection.)[26] Ten states—Alaska, Hawaii, Indiana, Maine, Massachusetts, Michigan, Minnesota, New York, Washington, and Wisconsin—have interpreted their state constitutions' free exercise and religious liberty provisions to require strict scrutiny or some other form of heightened scrutiny more rigorous than *Smith* requires. Only three state high courts—those of Maryland, New Jersey, and Wyoming—have explicitly followed the *Smith* line of reasoning in interpreting their state constitutions. Of eight other states that have addressed free exercise claims, four—California, Colorado, Utah, and Vermont – have expressly deferred the decision as to which standard to apply to future decisions. Four others—Iowa, Montana, Nebraska, and Nevada—have applied *Smith* principles, though without making it clear whether they were applying state or federal law. The high courts of another nine states—Arkansas, Delaware, Georgia, New Hampshire, North Carolina, North Dakota, Oregon, South Dakota, and West Virginia—have not yet had the opportunity to decide whether to reject or follow *Smith*. However, many of these states have high court decisions antedating *Smith* that applied strict scrutiny standards, and it is likely that at least some of these will not abandon the heightened protections.

RFRA bills proposed in other states in 2016 and 2017—Colorado, Georgia, Iowa, Michigan, North Carolina, West Virginia—were stalled, postponed in committee, vetoed, awaiting governor's action, essentially because of concerns over nondiscrimination provisions or the necessity of a state RFRA.

It seems likely that a majority of jurisdictions will ultimately maintain strict scrutiny protections. Coupled with the residual vitality of federal RFRA and other major federal legislation on the topic, this suggests that a high percentage of religious liberty claims will continue to receive strict scrutiny protection in coming years.[27]

The landscape for passage of state RFRAs has been transformed by concerns that religious freedom protections, particularly if extended to corporate persons, may serve as a mask for invidious discrimination. Such concerns manifested, for example, in a media blitz in Arizona in early 2015 opposing proposed amendments to the state's RFRA. Under such pressure, Governor Jan Brewer vetoed the bill, which would have extended religious freedom rights to corporations, would have permitted a RFRA defense even if the government were a party to the proceedings, and would have codified the compelling state interest test of *O Centro*.[28] LGBT groups and a number of large corporations asserted that the bill would permit businesses to use religious beliefs to deny services to LGBT people. (Ironically, in Arizona, sexual orientation is not among the protected classes under public accommodation laws in the first place.)

Other state RFRA actions attempted or passed during this period of intense activity nationwide regarding LBGT rights resulted in potentially economy-

---

26. Baptist Joint Committee, *State RFRA Bill Tracker*.

27. *See* updating discussion in W. Cole Durham, Jr., Robert T. Smith, and William Basset, *Religious Organizations and the Law* §§ 3: 26-29 and 19.2 (Thomson Reuters/West, 2nd ed. 2017), available on Westlaw, and Becket Law's RFRA Info Central. *See also*, from the point of view of the LRBT community, *Protect Thy Neighbor, 2017 State Legislation Tracker*.

28. *See* Durham, Smith, and Basset, § 3:29.

crushing boycotts. Indiana's proposed RFRA was amended within a week of passage in March 2015 to add sexual orientation and gender identity to the list of factors protected from denial of service by businesses, but the economic effects of the reactionary boycott were severe: "cancellations of planned events and business expansions, travel bans and denunciations from across the spectrum: companies including Salesforce, Apple, Eli Lilly and Angie's List; sports leagues including the NCAA, NBA and WNBA; states and municipalities coast to coast; rock concerts; comedy shows and church groups" did damage to the state's economy costing Indianapolis alone approximately $60 million in lost revenue.[29]

At about the same time, there was a much different result in Mississippi, where a bill also characterized as anti-gay and in substance very similar to the legislation that failed in Arizona, passed almost unanimously.

Obviously, the notion of appropriate free exercise protections varies considerably from state to state. At the opposite extreme to RFRAs and similar laws, in 2017, the California legislature passed Assembly Bill No. 1887, Prohibition on State-Funded and State-Sponsored Travel to States with Discriminatory Laws, which mandates that "California must take action to avoid supporting or financing discrimination against lesbian, gay, bisexual, and transgender people." The states on the banned list as of June 2018 were Alabama, Kansas, Kentucky, Mississippi, North Carolina, South Carolina, Tennessee, Texas, and Oklahoma.

COMMENTS AND QUESTIONS

1. A frequent feature of free exercise litigation is the need to compare the state interests at stake with the nature of the interest being asserted by the free exercise claimant. If, as the government attempted to do in *O Centro*, the state's interest is characterized in the abstract as the need to enforce national drug policy and to comply with international interests, whereas the individual's interest is characterized as an isolated individual's need for exceptional (and implicitly unequal) treatment, the balance of interests is strongly skewed in favor of the government. For that reason, the US Supreme Court has been careful to insist that the individual's interest be compared with the marginal cost to the government of making the accommodation requested for the particular claimant. (See, for example, *O Centro*, 546 U.S. at 430–33, 438 and *Hobby Lobby*, 134 S.Ct. at 2779.) The recurring risk is that legal analysis can be distorted by manipulating characterizations of the interests at stake in limitations contexts. What judicial techniques are available to minimize this risk? Does classifying rights claims into categories that do or do not warrant strict scrutiny avoid this problem?
2. Are religious freedom claims inevitably a cloak for bigotry? How does one distinguish legitimate religious freedom claims from claims that in fact abuse religious freedom rights?

---

29. Andrew Bender, Indiana's Religious Freedom Act Cost Indianapolis $60 Million in Lost Revenue, *Forbes*, 21 January 2016.

III. THE EUROPEAN AND INTERNATIONAL APPROACH TO LIMITATIONS

As is evident in European cases discussed in earlier chapters, the European Court of Human Rights has applied a proportionality test that typically starts an inquiry into religious freedom claims by ascertaining whether there has been an "interference" with Article 9 rights. Assuming there has been, the question then becomes whether the interference is a permissible limitation. As noted in Chapter 5, limitations may be imposed only on "manifestations" of religion; the *forum internum* is not subject to limitation. Where a "manifestation" of religion is involved, the basic touchstone for assessing the limitations is set forth in the "limitation clause" of Article 9 of the Convention:

> 2. Freedom to manifest one's religion or beliefs shall be subject only to such limitations as are prescribed by law and are necessary in a democratic society in the interests of public safety, for the protection of public order, health or morals, or for the protection of the rights and freedoms of others.

Article 9(2) thus establishes three criteria that must be met to justify an interference. First, limitations can be imposed only by law, and in particular, by laws that comport with the rule-of-law ideal. As summarized in *Svyato-Mykhaylivska Parafiya v. Ukraine*,[30] this requirement has a formal and a qualitative dimension:

> [T]he impugned measures must not only have some basis in domestic law, but also refer to the quality of the law in question, which must be sufficiently accessible and foreseeable as to its effects, that is formulated with sufficient precision to enable the individual–if need be with appropriate advice–to regulate his conduct.

As a general matter, this requirement is usually fairly easily met, although there have been cases where statutory language is vague or where government officials have ignored orders from their own judiciary, such that violation of the rule-of-law constraint has been enough on its own to result in a violation of Article 9.[31]

Second, limitations must further one of a narrowly circumscribed set of legitimating social interests or grounds. Thus, limitations are permissible only if they further public safety, public order, health or morals, or the rights and freedoms of others. Significantly, as the UN Human Rights Committee's General Comment on the parallel language of Article 18(3) of the ICCPR points out, the language of the limitations clause is to be strictly interpreted:

> Restrictions are not allowed on grounds not specified there, even if they would be allowed as restrictions to other rights protected in the Covenant, such as national security. Limitations may be applied only for those purposes for which they were prescribed and must be directly related and proportionate to the specific need on which they are predicated. Restrictions may not be imposed for discriminatory purposes or applied in a discriminatory manner.[32]

---

30. *Svyato-Mykhaylivska Parafiya v. Ukraine*, App. No. 77703/01 (ECtHR, 14 September 2007), §115 (citing earlier cases).

31. *See, e.g.*, *Hasan and Chaush v. Bulgaria*, App. No. 30985/96 (26 October 2000).

32. General Comment No. 22 (48) on Article 18, adopted by the United Nations Human Rights Committee on 20 July 1993, UN Doc. CCPR/C/21/Rev.1/Add.4 (1993), reprinted in UN

Originally, the idea of "public order" as a legitimating ground was understood narrowly as referring to the prevention of public disturbances or similar disorder that threatened concrete harm, as opposed to a more generalized sense of respecting general public policies. This seemed clear from both the French and English variants of the original ICCPR language. Significantly, the term for "public order" in the French version of the ICCPR is not *ordre public*, which is often used in French public and administrative law to refer to the general policies of the community, but rather *la protection de l'ordre*,[33] terminology suggesting concrete public disturbance and disorder. Like the rule-of-law requirement, the Court generally does not have difficulty finding a legitimating ground for challenged state action, though again, there are interesting exceptions.

Third, even if a particular limitation on freedom of religion or belief passes all the foregoing tests, it is permissible as a matter of international human rights law only if it is genuinely necessary. In most European Court cases, the outcome turns on analysis of what is "necessary in a democratic society." Insistence that limitations be genuinely and strictly necessary puts crucial brakes on state action that would otherwise impose excessive limitations on manifestations of religion. The necessity test places limits on limitations.

As the European Court has framed the issue, an interference with religion is necessary only when there is a "pressing social need" that is "proportionate to the legitimate aim pursued."[34] Clearly, when analyzed in these terms, the issue of necessity must be assessed on a case-by-case basis. Assessment takes place along a sliding scale, rather than a following a categorical approach emphasizing differences in the degree of scrutiny given to government actions. However, certain general conclusions have emerged. First, in assessing which limitations are "proportionate," it is vital to remember that "freedom of thought, conscience and religion is one of the foundations of a 'democratic society.'"[35] State interests must be weighty indeed to justify abrogating a right that is this significant. Second, limitations cannot pass the necessity test if they reflect state conduct that is not neutral and impartial,[36] or that imposes arbitrary constraints on the right to manifest religion.[37] Discriminatory and arbitrary government conduct is not "necessary"—especially in a democratic society. In particular, state regulations that impose excessive and arbitrary burdens on the right to associate and worship

---

Doc. HRI/GEN/1/Rev.1 at 35 (1994), para. 8.

33. Carolyn Evans, *Freedom of Religion Under the European Convention of Human Rights* 150 (Oxford Univ. Press 2001); Manfred Nowak and Tanja Vospernik, Permissible Restrictions on Freedom of Religion or Belief, in *Facilitating Freedom of Religion or Belief: A Deskbook* 152–153, n.23, Tore Lindholm, W. Cole Durham, Jr., and Bahia G. Tahzib-Lie, eds. (Martinus Nijhoff 2004).

34. *See, e.g.*, *Kokkinakis v. Greece*, App. No. 14307/88 (25 May 1993), para. 49; *Wingrove v. United Kingdom*, App. No. 17419/90 (22 October 1996), para. 53; *Manoussakis and Others v. Greece*, App. No. 18748/91 (26 September 1996), paras. 43–53; *Serif v. Greece*, App. No. 38178/97 (14 December 1999), para. 49; *Metropolitan Church of Bessarabia v. Moldova*, App. No. 45701/99 (13 December 2001), para. 119.

35. *Metropolitan Church of Bessarabia* at para. 114.

36. *Id.*, para. 116.

37. *Id.*, para. 118; *Manoussakis and Others v. Greece*, at paras. 43–53.

in community with others—such as burdensome registration requirements—are impermissible.[38] In general, where religious groups can point to alternative ways in which a particular state objective can be achieved that would be less burdensome for the religious group and would substantially accomplish the state's objective, it is difficult to claim that the more burdensome alternative is genuinely necessary.

Just as the words "compelling state interest" do not appear in the First Amendment, the words "proportionality" or "proportionate" do not appear the text of Article 9. Nevertheless, the proportionality analysis that lies at the core of Court decisions setting European limitations analysis has become

> an overarching principle of constitutional adjudication. . . . From German origins, [it] has spread across Europe, including to the post-Communist states in Central and Eastern Europe, and into Israel. It has been absorbed into Commonwealth systems–Canada, South Africa, New Zealand, and via European law, the U.K.–and it is presently making inroads into Central and South America. By the end of the 1990s, virtually every effective system of constitutional justice in the world, with the partial exception of the United States, had embraced the main tenets of [proportionality analysis]. Strikingly, proportionality has also migrated to the three treaty-based regimes that have serious claims to be considered "constitutional" in some meaningful sense: the European Union (EU), the European Convention on Human Rights (ECHR), and the World Trade Organization.[39]

As you read the materials that follow, you should reflect on what has made this approach so attractive, and also on the ways in which it differs from the various standards of review that have emerged in the United States.

A. INTERFERENCE WITH FREEDOM OF RELIGION OR BELIEF

JEWISH LITURGICAL ASSOCIATION CHA'ARE SHALOM VE TSEDEK V. FRANCE

ECtHR, App. No. 27417/95 (Grand Chamber, 27 June 2000)

2\. . . . The applicant association alleged a violation of Article 9 of the Convention on account of the French authorities' refusal to grant it the approval necessary for access to slaughterhouses with a view to performing ritual slaughter in accordance with the ultra-orthodox religious prescriptions of its members. . . .

16\. The Torah (Lev. Vii, 26 and 27; xvii, 10–14) prohibits consumption of the blood of 259rganizati mammals and birds, and slaughter must be carried out "as the [Lord has] commanded" (Deut. Xii, 21). It is forbidden to eat meat from animals that have died of natural causes or have been killed by other animals (Deut. Xiv, 21). It is likewise forbidden to eat meat from an animal showing signs of disease or blemishes at the time of slaughter (Num. xi, 22). Meat and other products of permitted animals (such as milk, cream or butter) must be eaten

38\. *Metropolitan Church of Bessarabia* at para. 118.

39\. Alec Stone Sweet and Jud Mathews, Proportionality Balancing and Global Constitutionalism, *Colum. J. Transnat'l L.* 73–74 (2008).

and prepared separately, in and with separate utensils, because the Torah prohibits the cooking of a kid in its mother's milk (Exod. Xxii; Deut. Xiv, 21).

17. With a view to ensuring compliance with all the prohibitions laid down in the Torah, later commentators established very detailed rules concerning, in particular, the approved method of slaughter, initially by handing down the oral tradition but later by compiling an encyclopedic collection of commentaries–the Talmud.

18. Observance of the above rules on the eating of meat necessitates special slaughter processes. . . .

[The Court then recounts the details of such slaughter, including the draining of blood by certain procedures and the examination for any signs of disease or abnormalities.]

22. On 1 July 1982 the approval necessary for power to 260rganizat slaughterers was granted to the Joint Rabbinical Committee alone. The Joint Rabbinical Committee is part of the Jewish Consistorial Association of Paris [ACIP], which is an offshoot of the Central Consistory, the institution set up by Napoleon I by means of the Imperial Decree of 17 March 1808 to administer Jewish worship in France. . . .

24. The Consistory includes congregations representing most of the main denominations within Judaism, with the exception of the liberals, who believe that the Torah should be interpreted in the light of present-day living conditions, and the ultra-orthodox, who advocate, on the contrary, a strict interpretation of the Torah. . . .

27. The liturgical association Cha'are Shalom Ve Tsedek is an association declared on 16 June 1986 with its registered office in the rue Amelot, Paris. . . .

30. Originally the applicant association came into being as a minority movement which split away from the Jewish Central Consistory of Paris. Its members are determined to 260rganiza their religion in the strictest orthodoxy. In particular, the applicant association wishes to perform ritual slaughter according to stricter rules than those followed by the slaughterers 260rganizati by the Paris Central Consistory as regards examination of slaughtered animals for any signs of disease or anomalies.

31. [Meat meeting this standard] is referred to by the Yiddish word "*glatt*", meaning "smooth".

32. For meat to qualify as "*glatt*", the slaughtered animal must not have any impurity, or in other words any trace of a previous illness, especially in the lungs. . . . [A]ccording to the applicant association, the ritual slaughterers under the authority of . . . the Central Consistory are selling meat which has not been adequately inspected and which its members consider impure and therefore unfit for consumption.

33. The applicant association submitted that it was therefore obliged, in order to be able to make "*glatt*" kosher meat available to its adherents, to slaughter illegally and to obtain supplies from Belgium. . . .

58. The applicant association, whose arguments were endorsed by the Commission, submitted that by refusing it the approval necessary for it to 260rganizat its own ritual slaughterers to perform ritual slaughter, in accordance

with the religious prescriptions of its members, and by granting such approval to the ACIP alone, the French authorities had infringed in a discriminatory way its right to manifest its religion through observance of the rites of the Jewish religion. . . .

61. The applicant association submitted that the refusal to approve it could not be justified by any of the legitimate aims set out in Article 9 § 2 of the Convention and that it was disproportionate . . . for the purposes of . . . the Convention. It 261rganizati that it was not contested that the ritual slaughterers it employed were just as scrupulous as those of the ACIP in complying with the hygiene regulations in force in slaughterhouses and that the Government could not therefore seriously maintain that the refusal to approve the association pursued the legitimate aim of "protection of public health". . . .

67. In the Government's submission, there had been, in the final analysis, no interference with the right to freedom of religion, since in the present case the only impact of the refusal to approve the applicant association lay in the fact that it was impossible for Jews, given meat of equal quality, to choose meat from animals slaughtered by the applicant association, which differed from the meat offered for sale by the ACIP only in its price, since the slaughter tax levied by the applicant was lower by half than the tax levied by the ACIP. In the Government's view, this freedom of choice was an economic, not religious freedom. That was evidenced by the fact that, according to the ACIP, the applicant had at one time tried to obtain a kind of delegated authority from the ACIP allowing it to perform ritual slaughter itself, under cover of the approval granted to the ACIP, but that approach had come to nothing for lack of agreement on the financial terms of the contract.

68. Even supposing that there had been interference with the applicant association's right to manifest its religion, the Government maintained that such interference was prescribed by law, namely the 1980 decree regulating slaughterhouse practice, and that it pursued a legitimate aim, that of protecting order and public health. In that connection, the Government argued that ritual slaughter derogated very markedly from the principles underpinning the domestic and international legal rules applicable to the protection of animals and public hygiene. The written law in force prohibited ill-treatment of animals and required them to be stunned before slaughter to spare them any suffering. . . .

75. The Court will first consider whether, as the Government submitted, the facts of the case disclose no interference with the exercise of one of the rights and freedoms guaranteed by the Convention. . . .

77. [T]he fact that the exceptional rules designed to regulate the practice of ritual slaughter permit only ritual slaughterers 261rganizati by approved religious bodies to engage in it does not in itself lead to the conclusion that there has been an interference with the freedom to manifest one's religion. The Court considers, like the Government, that it is in the general interest to avoid unregulated slaughter, carried out in conditions of doubtful hygiene, and that it is therefore preferable, if there is to be ritual slaughter, for it to be performed in slaughterhouses supervised by the public authorities. Accordingly, when in 1982 the State granted approval to the ACIP, an offshoot of the Central Consistory, which is the body most representative of the Jewish communities of France, it did not in any way infringe the freedom to manifest one's religion.

78. However, when another religious body professing the same religion later lodges an application for approval in order to be able to perform ritual slaughter, it must be ascertained whether or not the method of slaughter it seeks to employ constitutes exercise of the freedom to manifest one's religion guaranteed by Article 9 of the Convention.

79. The Court notes that the method of slaughter employed by the ritual slaughterers of the applicant association is exactly the same as that employed by the ACIP's ritual slaughterers, and that the only difference lies in the thoroughness of the examination of the slaughtered animal's lungs after death. It is essential for the applicant association to be able to certify meat not only as kosher but also as "*glatt*" in order to comply with its interpretation of the dietary laws, whereas the great majority of practising Jews accept the kosher certification made under the aegis of the ACIP.

80. In the Court's opinion, there would be interference with the freedom to manifest one's religion only if the illegality of performing ritual slaughter made it impossible for ultra-orthodox Jews to eat meat from animals slaughtered in accordance with the religious prescriptions they considered applicable.

81. But that is not the case. It is not contested that the applicant association can easily obtain supplies of "*glatt*" meat in Belgium. Furthermore, it is apparent from the written depositions and bailiffs' official reports produced by the interveners that a number of butcher's shops operating under the control of the ACIP make meat certified "*glatt*" by the Beth Din available to Jews.

82. It emerges from the case file as a whole, and from the oral submissions at the hearing that Jews who belong to the association can thus obtain "*glatt*" meat. . . . Admittedly, the applicant association argued that it did not trust the ritual slaughterers authorised by the ACIP as regards the thoroughness of the examination of the lungs of slaughtered animals after death. But the Court takes the view that the right to freedom of religion guaranteed by Article 9 of the Convention cannot extend to the right to take part in person in the performance of ritual slaughter and the subsequent certification process, given that, as pointed out above, the applicant association and its members are not in practice deprived of the possibility of obtaining and eating meat considered by them to be more compatible with religious prescriptions.

83. Since it has not been established that Jews belonging to the applicant association cannot obtain "*glatt*" meat, or that the applicant could not supply them with it by reaching an agreement with the ACIP, in order to be able to engage in ritual slaughter under cover of the approval granted to the ACIP, the Court considers that the refusal of approval complained of did not constitute an interference with the association's right to the freedom to manifest its religion.

That finding absolves the Court from the task of ruling on the compatibility of the restriction challenged by the applicant with the requirements laid down in the second paragraph of Article 9 of the Convention. However, even supposing that this restriction could be considered an interference with the right to freedom to manifest one's religion, the Court observes that the measure complained of, which is prescribed by law, pursues a legitimate aim, namely protection of public health and public order, in so far as organisation by the State of the exercise of worship is conducive to religious harmony and tolerance. Furthermore, regard being had to the margin of appreciation left to Contracting States . . . , particularly with regard to establishment of the delicate relations between the State and religions, it cannot be considered excessive or disproportionate. In other words, it is compatible with Article 9 § 2 of the Convention.

COMMENTS AND QUESTIONS

1. Is requiring people to buy meat shipped from Belgium to obtain meat processed in accordance with their religious tenets better characterized as an inconvenience or as an interference with religious interests?
2. What do you think of the Court's assertion in paragraph 80 that an interference with the freedom to manifest one's religion would only exist if the illegality of performing ritual slaughter made it impossible for ultra-orthodox Jews to obtain meat that conformed with their religious strictures?
3. How does the Court's finding of non-interference here compare with the "incidental burden" imposed by Sunday closing laws on an observant Jew in *Braunfeld*? Is it always the case that monetary burdens do not constitute burdens on or interferences with religious rights?
4. Who should determine whether a burden is substantial, courts or claimants? If a court determines a burden is insubstantial, what are the effects on religious liberty? If a claimant decides that a burden is substantial, what are the effects on the rule of law? Are there ways to limit the discretion that courts or claimants have in this inquiry? [40]
5. Does the focus on "interference" with a manifestation of religion differ in any significant way from "burden" or "substantial burden" on free exercise in setting the threshold for cognizable religious freedom claims?
6. The Polish Constitutional Court found unconstitutional the exception to slaughterhouse stunning requirements for Jewish *kosher* and Muslim *halal* slaughter, as legislation used to justify the regulatory exception was outside the regulatory power of the Ministry granting the exception. This "unusual approach to statutory interpretation [treated] 'ritual slaughter and animal welfare as irreconcilable'."[41] Is it important to such a finding that "[f]or many small communities, it can be either uneconomical or impractical to perform ritual slaughter themselves. . ."?[42] (Case summary in Chapter 9.)
7. Denmark's ministry of agriculture sees the clash as between human religious rights and animal rights: "Animal welfare takes precedence over religion."[43] Should this argument be taken seriously?
8. Suppose that state administrators refused to register a particular Christian denomination, reasoning that other Christian denominations could adequately

40. For a summary of debates on this matter, *see* Frederick Mark Gedicks, Substantial" Burdens: How Courts May (and Why They Must) Judge Burdens on Religion Under RFRA, *85 Geo. Wash. L. Rev. 94* (2015)

41. Joel Silver, Case Comment *Zgodnie z Obyczajami Religijnymi* (According to Religious Rights): A Dissenting Opinion on the Polish Slaughter Case, 3 *Oxford J. L. & Relig.* 2, 347–353 (2014).

42. *Id.* at 353.

43. Andrew Brown, Denmark's Ritual Slaughter Ban Says More about Human Hypocrisy than Animal Welfare, *The Guardian*, 20 February 2014.

provide baptism services. Would this be an interference of religion? Is the ritual slaughter case distinguishable?

B. LEGITIMATING AIMS: DOES NATIONAL SECURITY QUALIFY?

NOLAN AND K V. RUSSIA

European Court of Human Rights, App. No. 2512/04 (12 Feb. 2009)

[The Unification Church (sometimes referred to as the Moonies) is a new religious movement with beliefs derived from the Christian Bible that was founded in South Korea by Sun Myung Moon in 1954.] Patrick Nolan, a US citizen, joined the Unification Church in 1988 and had been working as a missionary for an affiliate of the Unification Church in Rostov-on-Don in southern Russia since 1994. The Unification Church was officially registered in Russia in 1991, and Nolan's work permits were routinely extended. In 2000 the acting president of the Russian Federation amended "Decree no 24, the Concept of National Security of the Russian Federation." The relevant paragraph of Chapter IV, "Ensuring the National Security of the Russian Federation," was amended to read:

> Ensuring the national security of the Russian Federation also includes the protection of its . . . spiritual and moral heritage . . . the forming of a State policy in the field of spiritual and moral education of the population . . . and also includes opposing the negative influence of foreign religious organizations and missionaries . . ." (para. 12).

In May 2002 Nolan traveled to Cyprus, leaving his infant son (for whom he was the legal guardian) with his nanny. When Nolan returned to Russia, he was detained, and eventually deported. His visa was annulled and he was denied entry into Russia. He was eventually reunited with his son in the Ukraine, when his nanny brought him there. He brought suit in Russian courts challenging the administrative decision to deny his return to Russia, but he lost on the ground that he posed a threat to national security. The Moscow Regional Court that dismissed his complaint stated, "In the opinion of Russian Federal Security Service experts participating in the preparation of the report, the [applicant's] activities in our country are of a destructive nature and pose a threat to the security of the Russian Federation. The representative . . . emphasized that the threat to State security is created by the activities, not the religious beliefs, of [the applicant]" (§37). After exhausting his appeals in Russia, Nolan filed a claim with the European Court of Human Rights alleging, among other things, that his Article 9 rights had been violated. The reasoning of the Court follows. Despite requests from the European Court, the Russian authorities refused to present the Federal Security Service report that provided the basis for the finding that Nolan was a national security risk.]

Existence of an Interference with the Applicant's Right
to Freedom of Religion

61. While religious freedom is primarily a matter of individual conscience, it also implies, *inter alia,* freedom to "manifest [one's] religion". Bearing witness in words and deeds is bound up with the existence of religious convictions. The Court has held on many occasions that the imposition of administrative or criminal sanctions for manifestation of religious belief or exercise of the right to freedom of religion was an interference with the rights guaranteed under Article 9 §1 of the Convention. . . .

62. The gist of the applicant's complaint was not that he was not allowed to stay or live in Russia but rather that his religious beliefs and/or activities had prompted the Russian authorities to ban his re-entry. The Court reiterates in this connection that, whereas the right of a foreigner to enter or remain in a country is not as such guaranteed by the Convention, immigration controls have to be exercised consistently with Convention obligations. . . . As regards specifically Article 9, it emphasises that "deportation does not . . . as such constitute an interference with the rights guaranteed by Article 9, unless it can be established that the measure was designed to repress the exercise of such rights and stifle the spreading of the religion or philosophy of the followers" see *Divine Light Zentrum v. Swizerland*, ECmHR 1981). More recently the Court has examined cases against [Bulgaria (see *Al-Nashif v. Bulgaria* 2001 and *Lotter v. Bulgaria* 1997) and Latvia (*Perry v. Latvia* 2007)]. . . . It follows that, in so far as the measure relating to the continuation of the applicant's residence in a given State was imposed in connection with the exercise of the right to freedom of religion, such measure may disclose an interference with that right.

63. Accordingly, the Court's task in the present case is to establish whether the applicant's exclusion from Russia was connected with his exercise of the right to freedom of religion. The Court observes that the applicant came to Russia in 1994 on an invitation of the Unification Church, a religious association officially registered in Russia. He was granted leave to stay which was subsequently extended on an annual basis through invitation from the Unification Church and an associated non-denominational organisation in St Petersburg. In 1999 he moved to Rostov-on-Don to work for the Rostov branch of the Unification Church. There is no indication in the case-file, and it was not claimed by the Government, that the Unification Church or its branches had engaged in activities other than spreading of their doctrine and guiding their followers in the precepts of Rev. Moon's spiritual movement. . . .

64. Furthermore, nothing indicates that the applicant held any employment or position outside the Unification Church and its organisations or that he had exercised any activities other than religious and social work as a missionary of the Unification Church. The Government consistently maintained that the threat to national security had been posed by the applicant's "activities" rather than "religious beliefs". However, at no point in the proceedings before the Court did they indicate the nature or character of any non-religious activities which the applicant allegedly may have undertaken. Whereas they vaguely mentioned certain "findings" of the operational and search measures relating to the applicant's "activities", they forfeited the opportunity to substantiate that claim

by failing to submit a copy of the report by the Federal Security Service which was repeatedly requested by the Court.

65. Finally, the Court cannot overlook the applicant's submission that the Concept of National Security of the Russian Federation, as amended in January 2000, declared that the national security of Russia should be ensured in particular through opposing "the negative influence of foreign religious organisations and missionaries". The unqualified description of any activities of foreign religious missionaries as harmful to the national security lends support to his argument that his religious beliefs, combined with his status as a foreign missionary of a foreign religious organisation, may have been at the heart of the Russian authorities' decision to prevent him from returning to Russia.

66. On the strength of the parties' submissions and the information emerging from the case-file, the Court finds that the applicant's activities in Russia were primarily of a religious nature and amounted therefore to the exercise of his right to freedom of religion. [The] Court thus considers it established that the applicant's banning from Russia was designed to repress the exercise of his right to freedom of religion and stifle the spreading of the teaching of the Unification Church. There has therefore been an interference with the applicant's rights guaranteed under Article 9 of the Convention. . . .

67. In order to determine whether that interference entailed a breach of the Convention, the Court must decide whether it satisfied the requirements of Article 9 §2, that is, whether it was "prescribed by law", pursued a legitimate aim for the purposes of that provision and was "necessary in a democratic society."

Justification for the Interference

. . .

70. The justification for the interference offered by the Government in the present case was confined to the assertion that the applicant's activities had posed a threat to national security. Obviously, given the sensitive nature of the information, solely the respondent Government, and not the applicant, had access to material which would be capable of substantiating that claim. However, the Government did not submit any such material or offer an explanation as to why it was not possible to produce evidence supporting their allegation. Moreover, they consistently refused to provide the report of 18 February 2002 which had apparently been at the heart of the Russian authorities' decision to exclude the applicant from Russia on the grounds of national security, or at least to make a summary of its contents.

71. The Court further observes that no evidence corroborating the necessity to ban the applicant from entering Russia was produced or examined in the domestic proceedings. It reiterates that even where national security is at stake, the concepts of lawfulness and the rule of law in a democratic society require that measures affecting fundamental human rights must be subject to some form of adversarial proceedings before an independent body competent to review the reasons for the decision and relevant evidence, if need be with appropriate procedural limitations on the use of classified information. The individual must be able to challenge the executive's assertion that national security is at stake. While the executive's assessment of what poses a threat to national security will naturally be of significant weight, the independent authority must be able to react

in cases where invoking that concept has no reasonable basis in the facts or reveals an interpretation of "national security" that is unlawful or contrary to common sense and arbitrary. . . .

72. In the instant case, counsel acting for the Federal Security Service in the domestic proceedings referred to the report of 18 February 2002 but did not make specific submissions on the factual circumstances underlying its findings or the nature of allegations of unlawful conduct on the part of the applicant, if such were indeed contained in the report. . . . In these circumstances, the Court is unable to discern in the domestic decisions any concrete findings of fact corroborating the Government's argument that the applicant's religious activity posed a threat to national security.

73. Furthermore, in so far as the Government relied on the protection of national security as the main legitimate aim of the impugned measure, the Court reiterates that the exceptions to freedom of religion listed in Article 9 §2 must be narrowly interpreted, for their enumeration is strictly exhaustive and their definition is necessarily restrictive. . . . Legitimate aims mentioned in this provision include: the interests of public safety, the protection of public order, health or morals, and the protection of the rights and freedoms of others. . . . However, unlike the second paragraphs of Articles 8, 10, and 11, paragraph 2 of Article 9 of the Convention does not allow restrictions on the ground of national security. Far from being an accidental omission, the non-inclusion of that particular ground for limitations in Article 9 reflects the primordial importance of religious pluralism as "one of the foundations of a 'democratic society' within the meaning of the Convention" and the fact that a State cannot dictate what a person believes or take coercive steps to make him change his beliefs. . . . It follows that the interests of national security could not serve as a justification for the measures taken by the Russian authorities against the applicant. . . .

75. . . . [T]he Court finds that the Government did not put forward a plausible legal and factual justification for the applicant's exclusion from Russia on account of his religious activities. There has therefore been a violation of Article 9 of the Convention.

NOTE ON NATIONAL SECURITY

National security is specified as a ground for limitation of ICCPR rights with respect to liberty of movement (Article 12), expulsion (Article 13), fair trial (Article 14), freedom of expression (Article 19), peaceful assembly (Article 21), and freedom of association (Article 22), but not freedom of religion or belief (Article 18). In part, this may simply be because the various articles "were drafted, revised and adopted at different times and were consequently couched in varying terms."[44] Several delegations urged that "these clauses should be drawn up in a uniform manner, except where a difference in substance was intended, in order that no serious issues of interpretation and application would arise in the future. However, no action on this matter was taken."[45] The Siracusa Principles

44. UN Secretary General, Draft International Covenants on Human Rights Annotation, A/2929, Chapter VI, para. 112 (1 July 1955).

45. *Id. See* Heiner Bielefeldt, Nazila Ghanea, and Michael *Wiener, Freedom of Religion or*

of 1984 provide that "the scope of limitation referred to in the Covenant shall not be interpreted so as to jeopardize the essence of the right concerned"[46] and "[a]ll limitation clauses shall be interpreted strictly and in favour of the rights at issue."[47] This is understood to mean among other things that limitations are restricted to "those contained in the ICCPR, according to the scope outlined . . ."[48] The UN Human Rights Committee's General Comment on Article 18 explicitly states that "paragraph 3 of article 18 [i.e., the limitations clause] is to be strictly interpreted: Restrictions are not allowed on grounds not specified there, even if they would be allowed as restrictions to other rights protected in the Covenant, *such as national security.*"[49] The special treatment of freedom of religion or belief with respect to national security limitations parallels the distinctive non-derogability of freedom of religion or belief.[50]

COMMENTS AND QUESTIONS

1. Was the Court correct in concluding there had been an interference with Mr. Nolan's religious freedom rights even though the European Convention does not guarantee the right of a foreigner to enter or remain in a country?
2. What is the significance of the Court's conclusion that national security is not a legitimate basis for restricting religious freedom rights? Are there other bases for limitations in paragraph 2 of Article 9 that Russian authorities could have successfully invoked in this case? What could they invoke when genuine national security threats are at stake?
3. Deportation of a foreigner is not itself a violation of the European Convention, so what is a violation?
4. What is the significance of the Court's assertion in paragraph 69 that "the burden of proof lies upon him who affirms, not upon him who denies"?
5. Article 8 (privacy and family life), Article 10 (freedom of expression), and Article 11 (freedom of peaceful assembly and association) all explicitly provide for limitations based on national security. Is it significant that the drafters of the Convention conspicuously omitted national security as a legitimate basis for limiting rights of thought, conscience, and religion?

Additional Web Resources:	Materials from the European Court and other jurisdictions addressing circumstances when health, safety, order, morals, and the rights of others may justify limiting freedom of religion or belief

Belief: An International Commentary 554 (Oxford Univ. Press 2016).

46. Siracusa Principles on the Limitation and Derogation Provisions in the International Covenant on Civil and Political Rights, E/CN.4/1985/4, annex, para. 2.

47. *Id.*, para. 3.

48. Bielefeldt, Ghanea, and Wiener at 554.

49. UN Human Rights Committee, General Comment 22 (48), adopted on 20 July 1993, UN Doc. CCPR/C/21/Rev.l/Add.4 (1993), reprinted in UN Doc. HRI/GEN/1/Rev.1 at 35 (1994).

50. See ICCPR, article 4(2); Bielefeldt, Ghanea, and Wiener at 544–545.

C. NECESSITY AND PROPORTIONALITY

1. Europe

For examples of the European Court of Human Rights' treatment of necessity and proportionality issues, see *Metropolitan Church of Bessarabia v. Moldova* and *Church of Scientology Moscow v. Russia*, excerpted in Chapter 11, and *Svyato-Mykhaylivska Parafiya v. Ukraine* in Chapter 10.

2. Canada

MULTANI V. COMMISSION SCOLAIRE MARGUERITE-BOURGEOYS AND ATTORNEY GENERAL OF QUEBEC

Supreme Court of Canada, 1 S.C.R. 256, 2006 SCC 6 (2006)

[A Canadian Sikh youth Gurbaj Singh Multani, and his father brought suit against the Commission Scolaire Marguerite-Bourgeoys ("CSMB") to challenge a ban on bringing dangerous objects to school, which they claimed interfered with concededly sincere beliefs requiring a metal kirpan to be worn at all times. A kirpan, which resembles a dagger, is an important religious symbol for orthodox Sikhs. An accommodation initially proposed by school board personnel and acceptable to the plaintiffs allowed the boy to wear a kirpan if it was sealed and sewn inside his clothing. Ultimately, however, the local school board's council of commissioners rejected this solution.]

Infringement of Freedom of Religion

32. This Court has on numerous occasions stressed the importance of freedom of religion. [The Court reproduced the following statement from *Big M Drug Mart*, explaining that under the *Canadian Charter of Rights and Freedoms*, all Canadians have the right to decide what their "religious obligations, if any, should be and it is not for the state to dictate otherwise"]:

> The essence of the concept of freedom of religion is the right to entertain such religious beliefs as a person chooses, the right to declare religious beliefs openly and without fear of hindrance or reprisal, and the right to manifest religious belief by worship and practice or by teaching and dissemination. But the concept means more than that. . . . Freedom means that, subject to such limitations as are necessary to protect public safety, order, health, or morals or the fundamental rights and freedoms of others, no one is to be forced to act in a way contrary to his beliefs or his conscience.

[The Court cited *Amselem*, in which it held that claimants must demonstrate (1) that they sincerely believe in a practice or belief that has a nexus with religion, and (2) that the third-party conduct interferes with their "ability to act in accordance with that practice or belief" in a nontrivial manner. It explained in *Amselem* that freedom of religion is "the freedom to undertake practices and harbour beliefs, having a nexus with religion, in which an individual demonstrates he or she *sincerely* believes or is *sincerely* undertaking in order to connect with the divine or as a function of his or her spiritual faith. . . . [Emphasis added.] This freedom is not required to conform to an "official religious dogma or . . . the position of religious officials."]

35. . . . What an individual must do is show that he or she sincerely believes that a certain belief or practice is required by his or her religion. The religious belief must be asserted in good faith and must not be fictitious, capricious or an artifice. [There was no genuine doubt that Gurbaj Singh sincerely believed he was required to wear a metal kirpan at all times.] . . .

[The Court held that the prohibition "deprived [Gurbaj Singh] of his right to attend a public school," holding that "the interference with [his] freedom of religion," which required him to leave school "to follow his religious convictions," was "neither trivial nor insignificant."]

41. Thus, there can be no doubt that the council of commissioners' decision prohibiting Gurbaj Singh from wearing his kirpan to Sainte-Catherine-Labouré school infringes his freedom of religion. This limit must therefore be justified under s. 1 of the *Canadian Charter*.

Section 1 of the *Canadian Charter*

42. [T]he council of commissioners made its decision pursuant to . . . the *Education Act*. [Prohibiting kirpans at school] constitutes a limit prescribed by a rule of law within the meaning of s. 1 of the *Canadian Charter* and must accordingly be justified in accordance with [section 1]:

> 1. The *Canadian Charter of Rights and Freedoms* guarantees the rights and freedoms set out in it subject only to such reasonable limits prescribed by law as can be demonstrably justified in a free and democratic society.

43. The onus is on the respondents to prove that, on a balance of probabilities, the infringement is reasonable and can be demonstrably justified in a free and democratic society. To this end, two requirements must be met. First, the legislative objective being pursued must be sufficiently important to warrant limiting a constitutional right. Next, the means chosen by the state authority must be proportional to the objective in question: Oakes; *R. v. Edwards Books and Art Ltd.*, [1986] 2 S.C.R. 713.

Importance of the Objective

44. As stated by the Court of Appeal, the council of commissioners' decision [translation] "was motivated by [a pressing and substantial] objective, namely, to ensure an environment conducive to the development and learning of the students. This requires [the CSMB] to ensure the safety of the students and the staff. This duty is at the core of the mandate entrusted to educational institutions." The appellant concedes that this objective is laudable and that it passes the first stage of the test. The respondents also submitted fairly detailed evidence . . . explaining the importance of safety in schools and the upsurge in [weapons-related school violence].

45. Clearly, the objective of ensuring safety in schools is sufficiently important to warrant overriding a constitutionally protected right or freedom. It remains to be determined what level of safety the governing board was seeking to achieve by prohibiting the carrying of weapons and dangerous objects, and what degree of risk would accordingly be tolerated. . . . [T]he possibilities range from a desire to ensure absolute safety to a total lack of concern for safety. Between these two extremes lies a concern to ensure a reasonable level of safety. [The

Court accepted the intervener Canadian Human Rights Commission's proposed level of safety sought by the school board as "reasonable safety, not absolute safety."]

Proportionality

Rational Connection

49. The first stage of the proportionality analysis consists in determining whether the council of commissioners' decision was rendered in furtherance of the objective. The decision must have a rational connection with the objective. . . . [P]rohibiting Gurbaj Singh from wearing his kirpan to school was intended to further this objective. Despite the profound religious significance of the kirpan for Gurbaj Singh, it also has the characteristics of a bladed weapon and could therefore cause injury. The council of commissioners' decision therefore has a rational connection with the objective of ensuring a reasonable level of safety in schools. . . .

Minimal Impairment

50. The second stage of the proportionality analysis is often central to the debate as to whether the infringement of a right protected by the Canadian Charter can be justified. The limit, which must minimally impair the right or freedom that has been infringed, need not necessarily be the least intrusive solution. In *RJR-MacDonald Inc. v. Canada* (Attorney General), [1995] 3 S.C.R. 199, at para. 160, this Court defined the test as follows:

> The impairment must be "minimal", that is, the law must be carefully tailored so that rights are impaired no more than necessary. . . . If the law falls within a range of reasonable alternatives, the courts will not find it overbroad merely because they can conceive of an alternative which might better tailor objective to infringement. . . .

[The Court framed the issue as whether the respondents demonstrated that an absolute prohibition, which they claim is necessary for school safety, is justified. The Court notes, however, that Gurbaj Singh is willing to wear his kirpan under the court-imposed conditions.]

Safety in Schools

[The respondents contended that kirpans at school "create a risk that they will be used for violent purposes," whether by their possessor or other students who acquire them by force. The Court dismissed this argument, pointing out that Gurbaj Singh had no behavioral problems or incidents of violence at school. Furthermore, the Court labeled the risk of Gurbaj Singh "us[ing] his kirpan for violent purposes . . . highly unlikely." Similarly, the Court called the risk of another student taking the kirpan away from him "quite low" since the student would "have to physically restrain him, then search through his clothes, remove the sheath from his guthra, and try to unstitch or tear open the cloth enclosing the sheath in order to get to the kirpan." Such students, the Court suggests, "could find another way to obtain a weapon." It also pointed out that many harmless and more accessible objects could be weapons of choice, including scissors, pencils, and bats.]

63. . . . [S]afety is just as important in schools as it is on airplanes and in courts. However, it is important to remember that the specific context must

always be borne in mind. . . . In *Nijjar*, Mr. Nijjar's complaint that he had been denied the right to wear his kirpan aboard a Canada 3000 Airlines aircraft was dismissed because, *inter alia*, he had failed to demonstrate that wearing a kirpan in a manner consistent with Canada 3000's policies would be contrary to his religious beliefs. . . . While it concluded that Mr. Nijjar had not been discriminated against on the basis of his religion, the [Tribunal] did nevertheless consider the issue of reasonable accommodation. . . .

65. . . . The school environment is a unique one that permits relationships to develop among students and staff. These relationships make it possible to better control the different types of situations that arise in schools. . . .

66. . . . [E]ach environment is a special case with its own unique characteristics that justify a different level of safety, depending on the circumstances. [The Court rejected an absolute prohibition, dismissing the argument that kirpans are inherently dangerous.]

Proliferation of Weapons in Schools

[The Court rejected the argument that permitting "Singh to wear his kirpan to school could have a ripple effect" that would lead "students who learn that orthodox Sikhs may wear kirpans [to desire to bear arms to] defend themselves. . . ." The Court recognized that this argument is based on the [argument] that "kirpans in school pose a safety risk to other students, forcing them to arm themselves." Notwithstanding, the Court called this argument "purely speculative" and noted that the "evidence does not support this argument . . . and cannot be accepted. . . ."]

Negative Impact on the School Environment

[The Court also rejected the argument that "kirpans in schools will contribute to poisoning of the school environment" because it is a "symbol of violence" and "sends the message that using force is the way to assert rights and resolve conflict." In contrast, it held,] "Not only is this assertion contradicted by the evidence regarding the symbolic nature of the kirpan, it is also disrespectful to [Sikh] believers . . . and does not take into account Canadian values based on multiculturalism. . . . [I]t is incumbent on the schools to discharge their obligation to instill in their students this value that is . . . at the very foundation of our democracy."

The Court accordingly concluded, "A total prohibition against wearing a kirpan to school undermines the value of this religious symbol and sends students the message that some religious practices do not merit the same protection as others. On the other hand, accommodating . . . [the wearing of the] kirpan under certain conditions demonstrates the importance that our society attaches to protecting freedom of religion and to showing respect for its minorities. The deleterious effects of a total prohibition thus outweigh its salutary effects."

COMMENTS AND QUESTIONS

1. *Multani* focused on a balancing test between rights of religious minorities and public safety. While there were no incidences of violence in *Multani* that justified prohibiting the kirpan, there have been recent cases where the kirpan

was used to inflict violence. In 2010, a 52-year old Sikh man was charged with attempted murder and aggravated assault when he beat and used his kirpan to stab the president of the Sikh Lehar Centre in Brampton, Ontario, in the abdomen, legs, thighs, and forehead.[51] In another case, a 13-year-old student threatened two other students with his kirpan, although he was later acquitted of all charges except those relating to threatening violence with a hairpin used to secure his turban. These cases brought the kirpan back into the forefront of the national debate in Canada, as there were renewed concerns over public safety.[52]

In April 2014 Canadian Minister of Foreign Affairs, noting that "Canada's diversity is one of our greatest strengths, and freedom of religion is a fundamental Canadian value, "announced a new policy regarding the kirpan in Canadian diplomatic missions worldwide, noting that: "Visitors to Canadian missions who declare themselves to be Sikhs will be permitted to retain their kirpans when entering the missions, provided their kirpans are secured within a sheath, attached to a fabric belt and worn under clothing across the torso."[53]

2. How does the "minimal impairment" test articulated in *Multani* paragraph 50 compare with the proportionality analysis of the European Court and the least restrictive means test in the United States?
3. In *Tagore v. United States*, 735 F.3d 324 (5th Cir. 2013), a member of the Sikh faith was refused permission to wear a kirpan inside the federal building where she worked for the Internal Revenue Service (IRS). When Tagore failed to receive an appropriate waiver, she lost her job. Her kirpan blade was 3 inches, and federal law stipulates that anything over 2.5 inches is a dangerous weapon. The Fifth Circuit affirmed the summary judgment in favor of Tagore's Title VII claim because the government had tried to accommodate her, suggesting she carry a smaller blade or request a waiver if the longer blade was desired, both of which she chose not to do. However, when it came to her RFRA claim, the Court held that "further development of evidence concerning the government's compelling interest in enforcing against this plaintiff the statutory ban on weapons with blades exceeding 2.5 inches" was required. Furthermore, the court below was instructed to determine if it is truly "a matter of fact whether Tagore holds a sincere religious belief in wearing a kirpan with a blade exceeding the federally prescribed maximum and, if so, whether the government has proven that application of the 2.5 in rule to Tagore furthers a compelling government interest with the least restrictive means. In 2014, the parties settled, allowing Tagore and other Sikhs to enter federal buildings with a kirpan.[54]

---

51. Raveena Aulakh, Prominent Sikh lawyer injured in brawl outside temple, *The Toronto Star* (3 April 2010).

52. *See, e.g.*, Kirpan Debate Rages On after Stabbing Outside Sikh Temple, *City News Toronto* (7 April 2010).

53. *New Policy Accommodating Sikh Kirpan at Canadian Missions Abroad.*

54. *See* Donlu Thayer, Case Note: Tagore v. United States, 3 *Oxford. J. L. & Relig.* (1) 176–178 (2014).

COMMENTS AND QUESTIONS

How would you decide the question of Tagore's "sincerely held religious belief" that her blade must be longer than 2.5 inches? Couldn't she just carry a smaller kirpan and avoid this entire situation?

Now consider the following information: In December 2012, as a result of this case, but before a judgment had been issued, the US Department of Homeland Security's Federal Protective Service released the "Prohibited Items Program" Directive (Directive Number 15.9.3.1).[55] According to the Directive, "There is no prescribed blade length for the Kirpan; its size varies based on personal choice. The majority of Kirpan blades range in size from 3 to 6 inches, but blades may be as small as 2 inches." Does this change your analysis? Why or why not?

3. South Africa

The current Constitution of the Republic of South Africa was drawn up by the first post-apartheid South African Parliament, elected in 1994 in the first non-racial elections. Promulgated by President Nelson Mandela, the Constitution came into effect in February 1997. It is widely viewed as a model of a contemporary human rights-based constitution. The jurisprudence of the South African Constitutional Court has also become very influential, across the continent of Africa and beyond. Compare the South African Constitutional Court's consideration of a religious freedom-based argument for an exemption from a general and neutral drug law to the reasoning of the US Supreme Court in the *Employment Division v. Smith* case.

PRINCE V. PRESIDENT, CAPE LAW SOCIETY

South Africa Constitutional Court (2002)

[The appellant, Garreth Prince, was a practicing member of the Rastafarian religion, which uses cannabis in its worship practices. He brought a lawsuit against the Law Society of the Cape of Good Hope when it refused to register his contract for community service necessary for him to become an attorney. Even though Prince had satisfied all of the academic requirements to be admitted as an attorney, the Law Society refused to register his contract on the grounds that his stated intention to continue breaking the law made him unfit to be admitted. In a 5-to-4 decision, the constitutional court ruled in favor of the Law Society, affirming lower court decisions. Note that the first opinion presented by the Court is by one of the dissenting judges, Ngcobo J, followed by the judges writing for the majority: Chaskalson CJ, Ackermann and Kriegler JJ. A second dissenting opinion, by Sachs J is included at the end.]

---

55. For discussion *see* The Sikh Coalition, *New Federal Kirpan Policy: What YOU Need to Know*, 13 February 2013, and *Know Your Rights: Wearing a Kirpan into a Federal Building*, August 2013.

NGCOBO J, dissenting[56]:

[37] The right to freedom of religion is contained in section 15(1) of the Constitution which provides: "Everyone has the right to freedom of conscience, religion, thought, belief and opinion" and in section 31(1)(a) which provides: "Persons belonging to a cultural, religious or linguistic community may not be denied the right, with other members of that community . . . to enjoy their culture, practise their religion and use their language."

[38] This Court has on two occasions considered the contents of the right to freedom of religion. On each occasion, it has accepted that the right to freedom of religion at least comprehends: (a) the right to entertain the religious beliefs that one chooses to entertain; (b) the right to announce one's religious beliefs publicly and without fear of reprisal; and (c) the right to manifest such beliefs by worship and practice, teaching and dissemination. Implicit in the right to freedom of religion is the "absence of coercion or restraint." Thus "freedom of religion may be impaired by measures that force people to act or refrain from acting in a manner contrary to their religious beliefs."

[39] Seen in this context, sections 15(1) and 31(1)(a) complement one another. Section 31(1)(a) emphasises and protects the associational nature of cultural, religious and language rights. In the context of religion, it emphasises the protection to be given to members of communities united by religion to practice their religion. . . .

[42] . . . [T]he Court should not be concerned with questions whether, as a matter of religious doctrine, a particular practice is central to the religion. Religion is a matter of faith and belief. The [fact that] beliefs are bizarre, illogical or irrational to others or are incapable of scientific proof, does not detract from the fact that these are religious beliefs for the purposes of enjoying the protection guaranteed by the right to freedom of religion. . . .

[45] To pass constitutional muster, the limitation on the constitutional rights must be justifiable in terms of section 36(1) of the Constitution. The limitation analysis requires an enquiry into whether the limitation is reasonable and justifiable in an open and democratic society based on human dignity, equality and freedom. . . . The limitation analysis thus involves the weighing up of competing values and ultimately an assessment based on proportionality.

[46] . . . [T]he weighing-up and evaluation process must measure the three elements of the government interest, namely, the importance of the limitation; the relationship between the limitation and the underlying purpose of the limitation; and the impact that an exemption for religious reasons would have on the overall purpose of the limitation. The government interest must be balanced against the appellant's claim to the right to freedom of religion which also encompasses three elements: the nature and importance of that right in an open and democratic society based on human dignity, equality and freedom; the importance of the use of cannabis in the Rastafari religion; and the impact of the limitation on the right to practice the religion. In particular, in this case, the proportionality exercise

56. Justice Zakeria Yacoob, one of the judges on the South Africa Constitutional Court that decided this case, explained to the authors of this casebook that the placement of the dissent first was nothing more than a clerical error.

must relate to: ". . . whether the failure to accommodate the appellant's religious belief and practice by means of the exemption . . . can be accepted as reasonable and justifiable in an open and democratic society based on human dignity, freedom and equality". . . .

[48] The right to freedom of religion is probably one of the most important of all human rights. Religious issues are matters of the heart and faith. Religion forms the basis of a relationship between the believer and God or Creator and informs such relationship. . . . In *Christian Education* and in *Prince 1*, we observed:

> The right to believe or not to believe, and to act or not to act according to his or her beliefs or non-beliefs, is one of the key ingredients of any person's dignity. Yet freedom of religion goes beyond protecting the inviolability of the individual conscience. For many believers, their relationship with God or creation is central to all their activities. It concerns their capacity to relate in an intensely meaningful fashion to their sense of themselves, their community and their universe. For millions in all walks of life, religion provides support and nurture and a framework for individual and social stability and growth. Religious belief has the capacity to awake[n] concepts of self-worth and human dignity which form the cornerstone of human rights. It affects the believer's view of society and founds the distinction between right and wrong. It expresses itself in the affirmation and continuity of powerful traditions that frequently have an ancient character transcending historical epochs and national boundaries.

[49] The right to freedom of religion is especially important for our constitutional democracy which is based on human dignity, equality and freedom. . . . The protection of diversity is the hallmark of a free and open society. It is the recognition of the inherent dignity of all human beings. Freedom is an indispensable ingredient of human dignity. . . .

[52] Yet, there can be little doubt about the importance of the limitation in the war on drugs. That war serves an important pressing social purpose: the prevention of harm caused by the abuse of dependence-producing drugs and the suppression of trafficking in those drugs. The abuse of drugs is harmful to those who abuse them and therefore to society. The government thus has a clear interest in prohibiting the abuse of harmful drugs. Our international obligations too require us to fight that war subject to our Constitution.

[54] The government does not contend that the achievement of its goals requires it to impose an absolute ban on the use or possession of drugs. . . . The use and possession of cannabis for research or analytical purposes under the control of the government can hardly be said to be harmful, let alone an abuse of cannabis. Similarly, the use of cannabis for medicinal purpose under the care and supervision of a medical doctor cannot be said to be harmful. This is so because a medical doctor will control the dosage taken and thus ensure that its use does not cause harm. These uses of cannabis are exempted because they do not undermine the purpose of the prohibition. It follows therefore that if the use of cannabis by the Rastafari is not inherently harmful or if its use can effectively be controlled by the government to prevent harm and trafficking in cannabis, refusal to allow for a religious exemption in these circumstances can hardly be said to be reasonable and justifiable. But, is it so? . . .

[62] Cannabis is smoked in a chalice or burnt as incense at Nyahbinghis, which are religious ceremonies. There are very few of these ceremonies in the

Rastafari ritual calendar. . . . It is smoked at religious gatherings or ceremonies presided over either by a priest, an assistant priest or an elderly. Whether smoking cannabis in a chalice on these few occasions can be described as a "prolonged heavy use or use of a more potent preparation" is not easy to say on the record. However, even if it is, there is no suggestion that its consumption at these few and isolated religious ceremonies cannot be controlled effectively and limited to the consumption of the amount that poses no risk of harm. . . .

[69] The suppression of illicit drugs does not require a blanket ban on the sacramental use of cannabis when such use does not pose a risk of harm. What is required is the regulation of such use in the same manner as the government regulates the exempted uses of drugs. . . .

[72] . . . [Under the] relevant international instruments . . . the criminalisation of the listed forms of conduct must take place subject to each Party's "constitutional limitations". Thus, if under our Constitution an exemption for the religious use of cannabis is required, such an exemption would not fall foul of the [instruments]. . . .

[77] In weighing the competing interests and in the evaluation of proportionality, it is necessary to examine closely the relation between the complete ban on the sacramental use or possession of cannabis by the Rastafari and the purpose of the limitation as well as the existence of the less restrictive means to achieve this purpose. The prohibition is ostensibly aimed at the abuse of harmful drugs and trafficking in those drugs. . . . Yet a sacramental use of cannabis that has not been demonstrated to be harmful, such as the burning of cannabis as an incense, is proscribed. The ban on religious use is so complete that a religious practice that requires followers to bow before a cannabis plant and pray, is hit by the prohibition. That such use of cannabis is not harmful to the health of the followers matters not. . . .

[79] In a constitutional democracy like ours that recognises and tolerates diverse religious faiths, tolerance of diversity must be demonstrated by accommodating the practices of all faiths, if this can be done without undermining the legitimate government interest. Thus when Parliament is faced with a religious practice that involves some conduct that runs counter to its objectives, the proper approach under our Constitution is not to proscribe the entire practice but to target only that conduct that runs counter to its objectives, if this can be done without undermining its objectives. This approach is consistent with the constitutional commitment to tolerance and accommodation of different religious faiths implicit in our Constitution. The requirement that less restrictive means must be used in the limitation of constitutional rights is indeed a manifestation of this commitment. . . .

[81] I accept that the goal of the impugned provisions is to prevent the abuse of dependence-producing drugs and trafficking in those drugs. I also accept that it is a legitimate goal. The question is whether the means employed to achieve that goal are reasonable. In my view, they are not. The fundamental reason why they are not is because they are overbroad. They are ostensibly aimed at the use of dependence-producing drugs that are inherently harmful and trafficking in those drugs. But they are unreasonable in that they also target uses that have not been shown to pose a risk of harm or to be incapable of being subjected to strict regulation and control. . . . On that score they are unreasonable and they fall at

the first hurdle. This renders it unnecessary to consider whether they are justifiable.

[82] It follows, therefore, that the prohibition contained in the impugned provisions is constitutionally bad because it proscribes the religious use of cannabis even when such use does not threaten the government interest. But it is bad to that extent, and only that extent. In view of this conclusion, it not necessary to consider other constitutional challenges.

[85] . . . [T]he appropriate remedy is to declare the provisions of section 4(b) of the Drugs Act and section 22A(10) of the Medicines Act invalid to the extent that they do not allow for an exemption for the religious use, possession and transportation of cannabis by bona fide Rastafari. . . .

[86] However, a declaration of invalidity that takes immediate effect poses a real danger to society. It would result in an uncontrolled use of cannabis and this will undermine the admittedly legitimate governmental goal of preventing the harmful effects of dependence-producing drugs and trafficking in those drugs. Parliament must therefore be afforded the opportunity to remedy the defects in these two statutes. The declaration of invalidity should therefore be suspended for a period of twelve months for that purpose.

(MOKGORO and SACHS JJ and MADLANGA AJ concurred in the judgment of Ngcobo J.)

By CHASKALSON CJ, ACKERMANN and KRIEGLER JJ (for the majority):

[111] We agree with Ngcobo J that the legislation criminalising the use and possession of cannabis limits the religious rights of Rastafari under the Constitution, and that what has to be decided in this case is, whether that limitation is justifiable under section 36 of the Constitution. It is in regard to this question that the respective views of Ngcobo J and ourselves diverge. For the reasons that follow, we do not believe that it is incumbent on the State to devise some form of exception to the general prohibition against the possession or use of cannabis in order to cater for the religious rights of Rastafarians. . . .

[114] In the proportionality analysis required by section 36 of the Constitution, there can be no doubt that the right to freedom of religion and to practise religion are important rights in an open and democratic society based on human dignity, equality and freedom, and that the disputed legislation places a substantial limitation on the religious practices of Rastafari. It must also be accepted that the legislation serves an important governmental purpose in the war against drugs. In substance, the appellant contends that the legislation, though legitimate in its purpose and application to the general public, is overbroad because it has been formulated in a way that brings within its purview the use of cannabis by Rastafari that is legitimate and ought not to be prohibited. A challenge to the constitutionality of legislation on the grounds that it is overbroad is in essence a challenge based on the contention that the legitimate government purpose served by the legislation could be achieved by less restrictive means. . . .

[116] The unchallenged general prohibition in the disputed legislation against the possession or use of harmful drugs is directed in the first instance to cutting off the supply of such drugs to potential users. It seeks to address the harm caused by the drug problem by denying all possession of prohibited substances (other than for medical and research purposes) and not by seeking to penalise

only the harmful use of such substances. This facilitates the enforcement of the legislation. . . . This method of control is actually prescribed by the 1961 Single Convention on Narcotic Drugs to which South Africa is a party.

[117] The State was not called upon to justify this method of controlling the use of harmful drugs. The validity of the general prohibition against both possession and use was accepted. The case the State was called upon to meet in this Court was that in addition to the medical and research exemptions contained in the legislation, provision should also have been made for the use of cannabis for religious purposes by members of the Rastafari religion.

[118] We are accordingly unable to agree with the significance attached by Ngcobo J to the fact that certain of the uses to which cannabis is put by Rastafari are not harmful. Subject to the limits of self-discipline, the use may or may not be harmful, but that holds also for non-Rastafarians who are prohibited from using or possessing cannabis, even if they use it sparingly and without harming themselves. . . .

[119] In the United States of America similar contentions to that raised by the appellant have been rejected by . . . the United States Supreme Court in [*Employment Division v. Smith*, 494 U.S. 872 (1990)]. [In that case, which involved criminal prohibition of sacrament use of peyote, the majority of the Court held that free exercise of religion]

> does not relieve an individual of the obligation to comply with a 'valid and neutral law of general applicability on the ground that the law proscribes (or prescribes) conduct that his or her religion prescribes (or proscribes)'. [494 U.S. 880]

To allow this, the majority held,

> would open the prospect of constitutionally required religious exemptions from civic obligations of almost every conceivable kind - ranging from compulsory military service . . . to the payment of taxes . . . to health and safety regulations such as manslaughter and child neglect laws, . . . compulsory vaccination laws, . . . drug laws, . . . and traffic laws; . . . to social welfare legislation such as minimum wage laws, . . . child labour laws, . . . animal cruelty laws, . . . environmental protection laws, . . . and laws providing for equality of opportunity for the races . . . . The First Amendment's protection of religious liberty does not require this. [494 U.S. 888-889]

[122] The minority [in *Smith*], in an approach that is more consistent with the requirements of our Constitution, took a different view. They agreed that the First Amendment insofar as it applies to the practice of religion, as distinct from belief, is not absolute. It could be subordinated to a general governmental interest in the regulation of conduct, but only if the government were able to justify that "by a compelling state interest and by means narrowly tailored to achieve that interest". . . .

[128] [A]s Sachs J pointed out in the *Christian Education* case, our Constitution in dealing with the limitation of rights does not call for the use of different levels of scrutiny, but "expressly contemplates the use of a nuanced and context- sensitive form of balancing" in the section 36 proportionality analysis.

[129] Nevertheless the *Smith* case does demonstrate the difficulty confronting a litigant seeking to be exempted for religious reasons from the provisions of a criminal law of general application. There can be little doubt that

even on the strict scrutiny test adopted by the minority in that case, a prohibition of the use of a drug such as cannabis, in the way that Rastafari use it, would not have been permitted. Cannabis, unlike peyote, is a drug in which there is a substantial illicit trade which exists within South Africa and internationally. Moreover, the use to which cannabis is put by Rastafari is not simply the sacramental or symbolic consumption of a small quantity at a religious ceremony. It is used communally and privately, during religious ceremonies when two or more Rastafari come together, and at other times and places. According to his own evidence, the appellant uses cannabis regularly at his home and elsewhere. . . .

[130] There is no objective way in which a law enforcement official could distinguish between the use of cannabis for religious purposes and the use of cannabis for recreation. It would be even more difficult, if not impossible, to distinguish objectively between the possession of cannabis for the one or the other of the above purposes. Nor is there any objective way in which a law enforcement official could determine whether a person found in possession of cannabis, who says that it is possessed for religious purposes, is genuine or not. Indeed, in the absence of a carefully controlled chain of permitted supply, it is difficult to imagine how the island of legitimate acquisition and use by Rastafari for the purpose of practising their religion could be distinguished from the surrounding ocean of illicit trafficking and use. . . .

[132] . . . If an exemption in general terms for the possession and use of harmful drugs by persons who do so for religious purposes were to be permitted, the State's ability to enforce its drug legislation would be substantially impaired.

[133] The appellant, appreciating this difficulty, suggested that a permit system be introduced allowing bona fide Rastafari to possess cannabis for religious purposes. In support of this contention he sought an analogy in the provisions of the legislation permitting the use of harmful drugs for medical purposes. The analogy is unsound, however. Permitted use of a prohibited substance for medical purposes is dependent upon a written prescription being issued by a medical practitioner which must limit the use of the drug to particular quantities for a limited period of time, and is subject to ongoing control by the doctor. . . .

[134] There would be practical difficulties in enforcing a permit system. . . . They include the financial and administrative problems associated with setting up and implementing any such system, and the difficulties in policing that would follow if permits were issued sanctioning the possession of cannabis for religious purposes. . . .

The appeal is dismissed.

(GOLDSTONE and YACOOB JJ concurred in the judgment of CHASKALSON CJ, ACKERMANN and KRIEGLER JJ.)

Sachs J (dissenting):

[145] Intolerance may come in many forms. At its most spectacular and destructive it involves the use of power to crush beliefs and practices considered alien and threatening. At its more benign it may operate through a set of rigid mainstream norms which do not permit the possibility of alternative

forms of conduct. The case before us by no means raises questions of aggressive targeting. The laws criminalising the use of dagga were not directed at the Rastafari nor were they intended expressly to interfere with their religious observance. Although they appear to be neutral statutes of general application they impact severely, though incidentally, on Rastafari religious practices. Their effect is accordingly said to be the same as if central Rastafari practices were singled out for prohibition. The Rastafari claim that as a religious community they are subject to suppression by the implacable reach of the measures, and as individual believers they are driven to a constitutionally intolerable choice between their faith and the law. Through a test case brought by Mr Prince, law graduate, aspirant attorney and appellant in this matter, a number of them approach this Court for relief. . . .

[147] By concluding that the granting even of a limited exemption in favour of the Rastafari would interfere materially with the ability of the State to enforce anti-drug legislation, I believe that the majority judgment effectively, and in my view unnecessarily, subjects the Rastafari community to a choice between their faith and respect for the law. Exemptions from general laws always impose some cost on the State, yet practical inconvenience and disturbance of established majoritarian mind-sets are the price that constitutionalism exacts from government. In my view the majority judgment puts a thumb on the scales in favour of ease of law enforcement, and gives insufficient weight to the impact the measure will have, not only on the fundamental rights of the appellant and his religious community, but on the basic notion of tolerance and respect for diversity that our Constitution demands for and from all in our society.

[148] In my opinion, the judgment of Ngcobo J convincingly shows that appropriate balancing and application of the principle of reasonable accommodation would allow for protection to be given to core sacramental aspects of Rastafari belief and practice without unduly impacting upon the broader campaign against harmful drugs. The most useful approach would appear to involve developing an imaginary continuum, starting with easily-controllable and manifestly-religious use at the one end, and ending with difficult-to-police utilisation that is barely distinguishable from ordinary recreational use, at the other. The example given by Ngcobo J of officially recognised Rastafari dignitaries receiving dagga from State officials for the burning of incense at tabernacles on sacramental occasions, would be at the easily-controllable and manifestly-religious starting point. Such a narrow and closely defined exemption would be subject to manageable State supervision, and would be understood publicly as being intensely and directly related to religious use. One step further along would be to allow designated priests to receive dagga for sacramental use, including smoking of a handed-round chalice, at designated places on designated occasions. This too could be easily supervised and be readily appreciated by the public as being analogous to religion as widely practised; indeed, I cannot imagine that any reasonable balancing of the respective interests of the Rastafari and of the State could provide for less. At the other end of the continuum would be the granting of everything that the appellant asks for, including the free use of dagga in the privacy of Rastafari homes. Such use would be extremely difficult to police and would completely blur the distinction in the public mind between smoking for purposes of religion and recreational smoking. It would be for

Parliament to work out the best means of securing the operational exemption to which the Rastafari are constitutionally entitled. The result might fall far short of what the Rastafari initially claimed, but at least would cast a flicker of constitutional light into the murky moral catacombs in which they exist and secure to them a modest but meaningful measure of dignity and recognition. The fact that they cannot be given all that they ask for is not a reason for giving them nothing at all. . . .

[155] Limitations analysis under our Constitution is based not on formal or categorical reasoning but on processes of balancing and proportionality as required by section 36. This Court has accordingly rejected the view of the majority in the United States Supreme Court that it is an inevitable outcome of democracy that in a multi-faith society minority religions may find themselves without remedy against burdens imposed upon them by formally neutral laws. Equally, on the other hand, it would not accept as an inevitable outcome of constitutionalism that each and every statutory restriction on religious practice must be invalidated. On the contrary, limitations analysis under section 36 is antithetical to extreme positions which end up setting the irresistible force of democracy and general law enforcement, against the immovable object of constitutionalism and protection of fundamental rights. What it requires is the maximum harmonisation of all the competing considerations, on a principled yet nuanced and flexible case-by-case basis, located in South African reality yet guided by international experience, articulated with appropriate candour and accomplished without losing sight of the ultimate values highlighted by our Constitution. In achieving this balance, this Court may frequently find itself faced with complex problems as to what properly belongs to the discretionary sphere which the Constitution allocates to the legislature and the executive, and what falls squarely to be determined by the judiciary.

[156] The search for an appropriate accommodation in this frontier legal territory accordingly imposes a particularly heavy responsibility on the courts to be sensitive to considerations of institutional competence and the separation of powers. Undue judicial adventurism can be as damaging as excessive judicial timidity. On the one hand, there is the temptation to proffer an overvaliant lance in defence of an under-protected group without paying regard to the real difficulties facing law-enforcement agencies. On the other, there is the tendency somnambulistically to sustain the existing system of administration of justice and the mind-set that goes with it, simply because, like Everest, it is there; in the words of Burger CJ, it is necessary to be aware of "requirements of contemporary society exerting a hydraulic insistence on conformity to majoritarian standards." *Wisconsin v. Yoder*, 406 U.S. 205 at 217 (1972). Both extremes need to be avoided.

[157] The hydraulic insistence on conformity could have a particularly negative impact on the Rastafari, who are easily identifiable, subject to prejudice and politically powerless, indeed, precisely the kind of discrete and insular minority whose interests courts abroad and in this country have come jealously to protect. . . .

[170] In conclusion I wish to say that this case illustrates why the principle of reasonable accommodation is so important. The appellant has shown himself to be a person of principle, willing to sacrifice his career and material interests in

pursuance of his beliefs. An inflexible application of the law that compels him to choose between his conscience and his career threatens to impoverish not only himself but all of South Africa and to dilute its burgeoning vision of an open democracy. Given our dictatorial past in which those in power sought incessantly to command the behaviour, beliefs and taste of all in society, it is no accident that the right to be different has emerged as one of the most treasured aspects of our new constitutional order. Some problems might by their very nature contain intractable elements. Thus, no amount of formal constitutional analysis can in itself resolve the problem of balancing matters of faith against matters of public interest. Yet faith and public interest overlap and intertwine in the need to protect tolerance as a constitutional virtue and respect for diversity and openness as a constitutional principle. Religious tolerance is accordingly not only important to those individuals who are saved from having to make excruciating choices between their beliefs and the law. It is deeply meaningful to all of us because religion and belief matter, and because living in an open society matters.

[171] The central issue in this case has accordingly not been whether or not we approve or disapprove of the use of dagga, or whether we are believers or non-believers, or followers of this particular denomination or that. Indeed, in the present case the clarion call of tolerance could resonate with particular force for those of us who may in fact be quite puritan about the use of dagga and who, though respectful of all faiths, might not be adherents of any religion at all, let alone sympathetic to the tenets of Rastafari belief and practice. The call echoes for all who see reasonable accommodation of difference not simply as a matter of astute jurisprudential technique which facilitates settlement of disputes, but as a question of principle central to the whole constitutional enterprise. In *Christian Education* this Court held that a number of provisions in the Constitution affirmed "[t]he right of people to be who they [were] without being forced to subordinate themselves to the cultural and religious norms of others, and highlight the importance of individuals and communities being able to enjoy what has been called the 'right to be different'. In each case, space [had] been found for members of communities to depart from a general norm. These provisions collectively and separately acknowledged the rich tapestry constituted by civil society, indicating in particular that language, culture and religion constitute a strong weave in the overall pattern."

COMMENTS AND QUESTIONS

1. Which do you think provides the more appropriate approach to resolving issues of freedom of religion or belief: the approach of the US Supreme Court in *Smith*, the Canadian approach, or the South African approach? Do the latter two give excessive power to the judiciary?
2. Professor Gerald Neuman has compared American-style compelling state interest analysis with European (and implicitly also Canadian and South African) proportionality analysis.

> To be sure, the right to manifest one's religious beliefs is not absolute, and the criteria for justification of limitations on the right are not identical to the compelling interest test of United States constitutional law. Article 18(3) lists specific interests that might justify the limitation of the right, and because rights under Article 18(3) are nonderogable, this list cannot be supplemented by

> assertion of emergency powers. The listed interests–public safety, order, health and morals, and the fundamental rights and freedoms of others–is probably broad enough to include any interest that would be recognized as compelling in US law, as well as some non-compelling interests. The standard "necessary to protect [those interests]," as generally interpreted in the CCPR and comparable human rights treaties, incorporates a principle of proportionality. "Limitations may be applied only for those purposes for which they were prescribed and must be directly related and proportionate to the specific need on which they are predicated." The requirement of proportionality may entail that only compelling interests would justify severe interferences with the right to manifest beliefs in practice, while imposing a more relaxed burden of justification on less severe interferences.[57]

Are there additional ways in which the alternative approaches differ?

3. According to Professor Robert Alexy, one of the leading theorists supporting European-style proportionality analysis, the proportionality test (balancing in the broad sense) has four prongs: "Two prongs—suitability and necessity—focus on empirical concerns, demanding that principles be realized to the greatest extent that is factually possible. The other two—legitimate ends and balancing [in the narrow sense] —are normative, requiring that principles be realized to the greatest extent possible in light of countervailing norms."[58] Professor Julian Rivers, who has translated Professor Alexy's key work from German into English, summarizes Alexy's approach to proportionality as in this way:

   > The theory of principles entails the "principle" [really a set of rules] of proportionality. . . . Alexy argues that necessity is to be understood as the requirement to optimize the relevant principles in the light of what is empirically, or factually, possible, and that the test of proportionality in the narrow sense is to be understood as the requirement to optimize the relevant principles in the light of what is legally possible. Necessity asks whether any less intrusive means would achieve the same end, which is essentially an empirical question of prognosis and causation, and proportionality asks whether the end is worth pursuing, given what it necessarily costs. It is important to see that necessity and proportionality (in the narrow sense) are different tests: a measure may be the least intrusive means to achieve a certain end, and yet even the least intrusion necessary may be too high a price to pay in terms of the interference with other legally recognized interests.[59]

   How does Alexy's proportionality analysis as described by Professors Kumm and Rivers compare with strict scrutiny analysis in the United States?

4. According to Prof. Mattias Kumm, a measure is necessary under proportionality analysis

---

57. Gerald L. Neuman, The Global Dimension of RFRA, 14 *Const. Comment.* 33, 45–46 (Spring 1997) (internal citations omitted).

58. Mattias Kumm, Constitutional Rights as Principles: On the Structure and Domain of Constitutional Justice. A review essay on *A Theory of Constitutional Rights*, 2 *Int'l J. Const. L.* 574, 579 (2004).

59. Julian Rivers, Translator's Introduction, in *Robert Alexy, A Theory of Constitutional Rights* xxxi–xxxii (Julian Rivers, trans., Oxford Univ. Press 2002).

> only if there is no less restrictive but equally effective measure available to achieve the intended policy goal. This test incorporates but exceeds the requirement, known to US constitutional lawyers, that a measure has to be "narrowly tailored" to its policy goal. The "necessity" requirement incorporates the "narrowly tailored" requirement, because any measure that falls short of being narrowly tailored also falls short of being necessary. At the same time, it goes beyond the "narrowly tailored" requirement, because it allows for the consideration of alternative means rather than insisting on refining the means already chosen to address the problem. [60]

Which approach to assessing means-ends fit and to assessing alternatives seems preferable?

5. Which seems most apt: conceptualizing religious freedom rights as trumps,[61] as shields against state intervention,[62] or as a principle that demands optimization within the bounds of what is factually and legally possible, as Alexy's theory of proportionality would suggest?

60. Kumm, Constitutional Rights as Principles at 580.
61. Ronald Dworkin, *Taking Rights Seriously* 24, 26 (Harvard Univ. Press 1977).
62. Frederick Schauer, Prescriptions in Three Dimensions, 82 *Iowa L. Rev.* 911–922 (1997).

CHAPTER 7

RELIGIOUS RIGHTS IN SPECIALIZED REGULATORY CONTEXTS

I. INTRODUCTION

Having explored the analytic tools available in different systems for determining the limits on the protection of freedom of religion or belief in Chapter 6, we now turn to applications of these tools in a variety of practical domains. In this chapter we focus on three regulatory contexts: land use regulations, specialized institutional settings such as prisons and mental health institutions, and the unique context of military life. While these areas have taken on special significance in the United States, the first two corresponding to the two halves of the Religious Land Use and Institutionalized Persons Act (RLUIPA), they are also significant in a global context. Every society encounters the "not in my backyard" problem: Essentially everyone is in favor of religion and religious freedom until an unfamiliar (or familiar) religion acquires property and wants to move in next door. Similarly, every country faces problems of how to deal with religious claims of institutionalized persons, and every society needs to think about how to accommodate religious rights in the military.

The areas covered by this chapter are helpful for thinking about how the bureaucratic state views religious freedom. Typical of these settings is that important community values encompass complicated areas addressed by correspondingly complex legislation. The regulatory objectives often have broad social significance that touch religious concerns only incidentally.

The bureaucrats involved generally assume that they are dealing with neutral laws of general applicability that are not necessarily designed with issues of religious accommodation in mind. These officials tend to be vested with substantial discretion in the administration of their programs. They can mask religious discrimination by justifying their decisions in any number of ways. For example, there are often neutral, or neutral-sounding, reasons that planning commissions and city councils invoke when they make land use decisions that burden or constrain religious groups. The problems in prisons and mental hospitals are even more acute, since what happens in these settings quite literally takes place behind locked doors. Thus, the issues in this chapter are representative of the challenges of protecting religious freedom within the day-to-day regulatory contexts of the bureaucratic state.

These issues frequently are significant for religious worship, teaching, practice, and observance. In addition, they are also representative of a broad array of situations involving the interface of freedom of religion or belief with state regulatory apparatus. Other related spheres exist as well, including broadcasting, education, labor law, health regulations, intellectual property, taxation, and countless others. Many of these are dealt with in other chapters or on the Web Supplement.

II. LAND USE AND ZONING

A. LAND USE PROCESSES: ZONING, PERMITS, COMPATIBILITY OF USES

Both because typical land use regulations are complex, and because the decisions in this area are typically made by lower-level governmental officials subject to a variety of political and social pressures, land use decisions can easily result in seemingly justified state conduct that instead masks religious discrimination. A number of studies have documented this reality in the United States, and similar problems are encountered virtually everywhere. What the empirical evidence shows is that less popular religious groups have disproportionately greater difficulty acquiring sites for worship, acquiring general land use approvals, getting necessary building and occupancy permits, and so forth.[1] These problems can arise in a broad range of ways, ranging from delegating state power to powerful majority religious groups to make land use decisions, to drafting specific laws on approval of "house of worship" permits, to regulating historical landmarks and matters of cultural heritage.

1. The United States

LARKIN V. GRENDEL'S DEN INC.

Supreme Court of the United States, 459 U.S. 116 (1982)

[In 1977, a Massachusetts License Commission denied an application to serve alcohol from operators of the Grendel's Den restaurant, citing an objection from the nearby Holy Cross Armenian Catholic Parish. A Massachusetts statute (16C) provided that churches and schools could object to liquor license applications for businesses within 500 feet of their facilities.]

Burger, C.J., delivered the opinion of the Court.

---

1. *See* Douglas Laycock, State RFRAS and Land Use Regulation, 32 *U.C. Davis L. Rev.* 755 (1999).

The purposes of the First Amendment guarantees relating to religion were twofold: to foreclose state interference with the practice of religious faiths, and to foreclose the establishment of a state religion familiar in other eighteenth century systems. Religion and government, each insulated from the other, could then coexist. Jefferson's idea of a "wall," . . . was a useful figurative illustration to emphasize the concept of separateness. Some limited and incidental entanglement between church and state authority is inevitable in a complex modern society [*see, e.g.*, *Lemon v. Kurtzman*], but the concept of a "wall" of separation is a useful signpost. Here that "wall" is substantially breached by vesting discretionary governmental powers in religious bodies.

This Court has consistently held that a statute must satisfy three criteria to pass muster under the Establishment Clause:

> First, the statute must have a secular legislative purpose; second, its principal or primary effect must be one that neither advances nor inhibits religion . . . ; finally, the statute must not foster 'an excessive government entanglement with religion'. [*Lemon v. Kurtzman*]

Independent of the first of those criteria, the statute, by delegating a governmental power to religious institutions, inescapably implicates the Establishment Clause.

The purpose of §16C, as described by the District Court, is to "protec[t] spiritual, cultural, and educational centers from the 'hurly-burly' associated with liquor outlets." There can be little doubt that this embraces valid secular legislative purposes. However, these valid secular objectives can be readily accomplished by other means—either through an absolute legislative ban on liquor outlets within reasonable prescribed distances from churches, schools, hospitals and like institutions, or by ensuring a hearing for the views of affected institutions at licensing proceedings where, without question, such views would be entitled to substantial weight.

Appellants argue that §16C has only a remote and incidental effect on the advancement of religion. The highest court in Massachusetts, however, has construed the statute as conferring upon churches a veto power over governmental licensing authority. Section 16C gives churches the right to determine whether a particular applicant will be granted a liquor license, or even which one of several competing applicants will receive a license.

The churches' power under the statute is standardless, calling for no reasons, findings, or reasoned conclusions. That power may therefore be used by churches to promote goals beyond insulating the church from undesirable neighbors. . . . In addition, the mere appearance of a joint exercise of legislative authority by Church and State provides a significant symbolic benefit to religion in the minds of some by reason of the power conferred. It does not strain our prior holdings to say that the statute can be seen as having a "primary" and "principal" effect of advancing religion.

Turning to the third phase of the inquiry called for by *Lemon v. Kurtzman*, we see that we have not previously had occasion to consider the entanglement implications of a statute vesting significant governmental authority in churches. This statute enmeshes churches in the exercise of substantial governmental powers contrary to our consistent interpretation of the Establishment Clause;

"[t]he objective is to prevent, as far as possible, the intrusion of either [Church or State] into the precincts of the other." *Lemon*. . . . [T]he core rationale underlying the Establishment Clause is preventing "a fusion of governmental and religious functions," *Abington School District v. Schempp*. The Framers did not set up a system of government in which important, discretionary governmental powers would be delegated to or shared with religious institutions.

Section 16C substitutes the unilateral and absolute power of a church for the reasoned decision making of a public legislative body acting on evidence and guided by standards, on issues with significant economic and political implications. The challenged statute thus enmeshes churches in the processes of government and creates the danger of "[p]olitical fragmentation and divisiveness on religious lines," *Lemon*. Ordinary human experience and a long line of cases teach that few entanglements could be more offensive to the spirit of the Constitution.

The judgment of the Court of Appeals is affirmed.

***

In his dissenting opinion, Justice Rehnquist argued that the Massachusetts zoning law served as an appropriate and efficient means for keeping alcohol distribution away from incompatible areas such as schools and churches. For Rehnquist, the statute should have been upheld as less restrictive regulation compared with an absolute ban on liquor sales close to schools, churches, and similar institutions, which the Court recognized would be valid.

Rehnquist also argued that "by its frequent reference to the statutory provision as a 'veto,' the Court indicates a belief that §16C effectively constitutes churches as third houses of the Massachusetts legislature,"[2] without providing sufficient support for this view. Failing to discover how the statute advanced religion, Rehnquist explained that the statute

> does not sponsor or subsidize any religious group or activity. It does not encourage, much less compel, anyone to participate in religious activities or to support religious institutions. To say that it "advances" religion is to strain at the meaning of that word. . . . The state does not, in my opinion, "advance" religion by making provision for those who wish to engage in religious activities, as well as those who wish to engage in educational activities, to be unmolested by activities at a neighboring bar or tavern that have historically been thought incompatible.

Finally, Rehnquist argued that the Court's fear that a church's ability to block a liquor license could be abused did not justify a finding that the statute violated the Establishment Clause because the case at hand did not involve any such abuse. Concluding his dissent, Rehnquist contended, "The heavy First Amendment artillery that the Court fires at this sensible and unobjectionable Massachusetts statute is both unnecessary and unavailing. I would reverse the judgment of the Court of Appeals."

---

2. *Larkin v. Grendel's Den, Inc.*, 459 U.S. 116, 129 (1982) (Rehnquist, J., dissenting).

COMMENTS AND QUESTIONS

1. Would an absolute ban on alcohol distribution within a certain proximity of churches be constitutional? Would it be religiously neutral?[3]
2. Imagine two other, alternative versions of a new law similar to that in question in *Grendel's Den*. Would either of these be constitutional? Why or why not?
   a. A total ban on liquor within 500 feet of a church or school, without any option for veto or waiver on the part of churches or schools.
   b. A total ban on liquor, but with the option for all churches in the 500-foot radius to unanimously waive the protection.
3. The Court mentions the possibility that a statute might provide for "a hearing for the views of affected institutions at licensing proceedings where, without question, such views would be entitled to substantial weight." How different is ensuring a right to a hearing from granting a veto? What if the church has very strong political support in the community? What if it is relatively weak? Unpopular? At what point does state delegation of *any* power become impermissible?

RELIGIOUS LAND USE AND INSTITUTIONALIZED PERSONS ACT (RLUIPA)

42 USCA §2000cc (Land Use Provisions)

The key land use provisions of RLUIPA relevant to the two cases that follow are:
Section 2. Protection of Land Use as Religious Exercise.
(A) Substantial Burdens—

(1) General Rule—No government shall impose or implement a land use regulation in a manner that imposes a substantial burden on the religious exercise of a person, including a religious assembly or institution, unless the government demonstrates that imposition of the burden on that person, assembly, or institution—

(a) is in furtherance of a compelling governmental interest; and

(b) is the least restrictive means of furthering that compelling governmental interest.

(B) Discrimination and Exclusion—

(1) Equal Terms—No government shall impose or implement a land use regulation in a manner that treats a religious assembly or institution on less than equal terms with a nonreligious assembly or institution.

(2) Nondiscrimination—No government shall impose or implement a land use regulation that discriminates against any assembly or institution on the basis of religion or religious denomination.

(3) Exclusions and Limits—No government shall impose or implement a land use regulation that—

(a) totally excludes religious assemblies from a jurisdiction; or

---

3. For one view on the issue, *see* Cynthia A. Krebs, Note, The Establishment Clause and Liquor Sales: The Supreme Court Rushes in Where Angels Fear to Tread—Larkin v. Grendel's Den, 103 S.Ct. 505 (1982), 59 *Wash. L. Rev.* 87 (1983).

(b) unreasonably limits religious assemblies, institutions, or structures within a jurisdiction.

ST. JOHN'S UNITED CHURCH OF CHRIST V. THE CITY OF CHICAGO

United States Court of Appeals, Seventh Circuit, 502 F.3d 616 (7th Cir. 2007)

[After the Supreme Court held in *City of Boerne v. Flores* that the Religious Freedom Restoration Act was unconstitutional, many states, including Illinois, responded by enacting State RFRAs, which reinstituted the compelling state interest test with respect to government actions that substantially burden religious freedom. These laws were designed to afford greater protection to religious activity under state law than is required by the federal constitution as construed by *Employment Division v. Smith.* Following the passage of the Illinois RFRA (IRFRA), in order to facilitate the expansion of the O'Hare Airport (one of the three largest airports in the United States), the Illinois legislature adopted the O'Hare Modernization Act (OMA) in 2003. The OMA amended IRFRA to prevent strict scrutiny of OMA activities that would have an impact on religious land uses – in particular, on cemeteries that stood in the way of airport expansion. This was done by adding a new Section to IRFRA, which stated that nothing in IRFRA limited the City under the OMA from relocating cemeteries and graves. St. John's Church sued, arguing that the amendment to IRFRA violated its Free Exercise rights under the standard articulated in *Smith*, because the amendment was not neutral and specifically targeted religion. In addition, St. John's argued that the amendment violated RLUIPA's land use provisions, which also mandate a compelling state interest test with respect to land use issues.]

IV

. . . The first question is whether St. John's is entitled, as a matter of state law, to the protection afforded by the Illinois Religious Freedom Restoration Act. Before the district court, St. John's argued that the OMA's amendment of IRFRA violated the Free Exercise Clause of the First Amendment. The Free Exercise Clause prohibits the government from "plac[ing] a substantial burden on the observation of a central religious belief or practice" without first demonstrating that a "compelling governmental interest justifies the burden." *Hernandez v. C.I.R.* (1989). In *Employment Division v. Smith*, however, the Supreme Court held that neutral laws of general applicability do not run afoul of the Free Exercise Clause, even if these laws have the incidental effect of burdening a religious practice. In order to determine whether a law is neutral, as the Court used the term in *Smith*, we must examine the object of the law. A law is not neutral if "the object of the law is to infringe upon or restrict practices because of their religious motivation." *Lukumi.* The related principle of "general applicability" forbids the government from "impos[ing] burdens only on conduct motivated by religious belief" in a "selective manner." . . .

According to St. John's, a major tenet of its religious beliefs is that the remains of those buried at the St. Johannes Cemetery must not be disturbed until Jesus Christ raises these remains on the day of Resurrection. . . . We accept those representations. St. John's continues with a claim that the OMA impermissibly targets the religious cemeteries adjacent to O'Hare. . . . [The district court] decided, however, that this was the wrong perspective: it saw no discrimination or targeting of religious institutions because *any* property, religious or otherwise, within the area designated for O'Hare expansion is subject to the extraordinary powers conferred in the OMA . . . .

We conclude there is nothing inherently religious about cemeteries or graves, and the act of relocating them thus does not on its face infringe upon a religious practice, as *Lukumi* uses that term.

Even if a law passes the test of facial neutrality, it is still necessary to ask whether it embodies a more subtle or masked hostility to religion. To answer that question, we must look at . . . the law's object, including the effect of the law as it is designed to operate, [its] historical background . . . , and the [act's] legislative or administrative history. . . .

Although St. John's alleges in its complaint that the City targeted its religious rights when the City asked the Illinois General Assembly to amend IRFRA as part of the OMA . . . [t]here are simply no facts in the voluminous record on appeal that support any such claim of targeting religious institutions or practices. According to its stated purpose, the OMA was enacted, in part, to insure that "legal impediments to the completion of the [O'Hare] project be eliminated." As we noted earlier, most of the OMA's provisions have absolutely nothing to do with religion, cemeteries, or IRFRA. . . .

St. John's makes the obvious point that, as matters have developed, it is now the only cemetery in the State of Illinois affected by the new [section] of IRFRA. That is true, but an "adverse impact will not always lead to a finding of impermissible targeting." *Lukumi*. In fact, if this point matters at all, it may cut in favor of the City. . . . The fact that the legislation leaves other religious cemeteries untouched reinforces the proposition that the legislature had the nondiscriminatory purpose of clearing all land needed for O'Hare's proposed expansion. . . . We conclude that the OMA, including the portion that amends IRFRA, is a neutral law of general applicability. The Illinois legislature was entitled to restore Illinois law to the regime governed by *Smith* in order to facilitate the airport project.

[Although it was unnecessary to address the issue, the court concluded that the City employed the least restrictive means of furthering a governmental interest. The court addressed the magnitude of the government's interest in addressing the problems of O'Hare Airport's inadequacies, and concluded that the proposed expansion was the least restrictive means of addressing this interest.]

VI

Last, St. John's invokes the Religious Land Use and Institutionalized Persons Act (RLUIPA). . . . The question before us is whether the "land use" part of RLUIPA applies here. . . . We must decide whether the City's plan to condemn the St. Johannes Cemetery is a "land use regulation" within the meaning of RLUIPA. We agree with the district court's conclusion that it is not. . . .

The term "land use regulation" is defined by RLUIPA as follows:

> [A] zoning or landmarking law, or the application of such a law, that limits or restricts a claimant's use or development of land (including a structure affixed to land), if the claimant has an ownership, leasehold, easement, servitude, or other property interest in the regulated land or a contract or option to acquire such an interest.

St. John's have not objected, however, to any plan on the City's part to zone their property in an unfavorable way or to impose restrictions on it under a landmarking law. St. John's claims instead that the OMA is a "zoning-type law" because it changes the permitted use of its land from a religious cemetery to land designated as "airport property." . . . As Illinois courts have long recognized, the "police power [zoning] and eminent domain are distinct powers of government." *Sanitary Dist. of Chi. v. Chi. & Alton R.R. Co.* Because zoning and eminent domain are "two distinct concepts" that involve land "in very different ways," we reject the argument that the City's plan to condemn the St. Johannes Cemetery under the OMA is an act of zoning. . . .

Because this case does not involve a "land use regulation," there is no need for us to address RLUIPA's other element – whether the City's proposed actions will substantially burden Plaintiffs' religious exercise. . . .

Accordingly, we affirm the judgment of the district court.

RIPPLE, Circuit Judge, concurring in part and dissenting in part.

I join my colleagues in affirming the judgment of the district court with respect to the claims by Rest Haven and the municipal defendants. However, I believe that the amendments to the Illinois RFRA made in OMA violate the Free Exercise Clause and, for that reason, must be subject to strict scrutiny. I further believe that there remain factual questions regarding whether the City of Chicago ("City") has shown that the proposed modernization and expansion plan of O'Hare Airport is narrowly tailored to meet the compelling interest the City claims . . . Therefore, I respectfully dissent. . . .

The OMA's amendment to the Illinois RFRA is not facially neutral. . . . The *only* cemeteries affected by OMA's amendment to the Illinois RFRA are those *religious* cemeteries that the City may seek to relocate. The OMA amendment to the Illinois RFRA offends the Free Exercise Clause by penalizing those individuals whose religious observance is affected by the expansion project by denying them "an equal share of the rights, benefits, and privileges enjoyed by other citizens." *Lyng v. Northwest Indian Cemetery Protective Ass'n* (1988). . . . Thus, the OMA's amendment to the Illinois RFRA both burdens the free exercise of religion and lacks facial neutrality, and, therefore, strict scrutiny must be applied to the amendment.

However, even if the amendment to the OMA was facially neutral, it would still be subject to strict scrutiny because it imposes a substantial burden on religion. As the Supreme Court said in *Church of the Lukumi Babalu Aye, Inc. v. City of Hialeah* (1993): "Facial neutrality is not determinative. The Free Exercise Clause, like the Establishment Clause, extends beyond facial discrimination. The Clause 'forbids subtle departures from neutrality,' *Gillette v. United States*. . . . Official action that targets religious conduct for distinctive treatment cannot be shielded by mere compliance with the requirement of facial neutrality."

We have held that a burden on the free exercise of religion rises to the level of a constitutional injury when the law places significant pressure on the adherent to forgo its religious precepts. . . . The relocation of St. Johannes would force St. John's to forgo its religious precepts regarding the burial of its members. This burden goes further than placing pressure on St. John's to forgo its religious precepts. By relocating St. Johannes Cemetery, St. John's would be "coerced by the Government's action into violating [its] religious beliefs." *Lyng*.

Because the amendments to the Illinois RFRA offend the Free Exercise Clause, the law must survive strict scrutiny under both the First Amendment and the Equal Protection Clause of the Fourteenth Amendment. Under strict scrutiny review, the Government bears the burden of proving both that the act in question advances a compelling state interest and that the means chosen to pursue that interest are narrowly tailored to that end. . . . At this stage in the litigation, there has been none of the factual development necessary to determine whether the means chosen by the City are narrowly tailored to meet the compelling interest asserted here.

Therefore, I would remand the case for further proceedings to allow factual development. For these reasons, I respectfully dissent from the portion of the panel's opinion that rejects St. John's claim. I am pleased to join the opinion in all other respects.

NOTE ON MOSQUES

The terrorist attacks of 11 September 2001—by 19 radicals trained by the Islamist extremist group Al-Qaeda flying hijacked airplanes into the two tallest buildings in the largest city in the United States and into the military headquarters in the nation's capital—had an incalculable effect on the nation's political, financial, social, and religious institutions. Three thousand people died at attack time, including 372 non-US citizens and 11 unborn babies. Three hundred people were killed on the ground by burning debris and falling bodies. Millions of Americans and others worldwide watched the events unfold as they were broadcast live. By 11 September 2013, an additional 2,500 people who had been among rescue workers, responders, and others at "Ground Zero" in New York City had died or had been diagnosed with cancers, and many more still carry carbon nanotubes in their lungs from the smoke and dust from the site.

For most Americans, this was the most terrifying collective national experience they had ever known. Not surprisingly, this event and the self-identification of the terrorists as "Islamist" had significant bearing when, in 2009, a Muslim developer proposed building an Islamic center two blocks from Ground Zero. The backlash to the proposal, including reactions from relatives of victims of the 2001 attacks, became an issue of such importance that it impacted the 2010 mayoral elections. New York City's Mayor Michael Bloomberg insisted that "The government should never, never be in the business of telling people how they should pray, or where they can pray. We want to make sure that everybody from around the world feels comfortable coming here, living here, and praying the way they want to pray."[4] But others pointed to the perceived affront of

4. Javier C. Hernandez, Planned Sign of Tolerance Bringing Division Instead, *New York*

building a mosque so close to the site of destruction created by people purporting to be connected to Islam. Eventually the center was renamed, and a modest renovation of the existing building was completed.

Nine hundred miles away, in a small town in Tennessee, plans for the Murfeesboro Mosque met similar controversy. Initial plans for expansion of the mosque, approved by the county planning commission, were opposed by people expressing fears of Islamist takeovers and imposition of Shari'a law, and, more concretely, asserting that the commission gave inadequate notice of the meeting in which the plans were announced. Many people in the town and nationwide supported the mosque, but the mosque's opponents sued, asserting that the First Amendment's religion clauses did not apply to the mosque because Islam is not a religion, and because the mosque was a threat to the community. The District Court issued a temporary restraining order under RLUIPA, opening the mosque in July 2012.[5] The case ended in June 2014, when the US Supreme Court declined to hear the appeals of the mosque's opponents.

COMMENTS AND QUESTIONS

1. What types of land use does RLUIPA protect? Do you agree with the majority in the St. John's cemetery case that a state exercise of eminent domain power does not apply a "zoning or landmarking law . . . that limits or restricts a claimant's use or development of land" under RLUIPA? Should state eminent domain power automatically trump religious freedom concerns?
2. State RFRAs are inherently weaker than the federal RFRA would have been (but for *Boerne*) because they do not have the benefit of the federal Supremacy Clause. The federal RFRA would have overridden any state constitutional or statutory provisions, including those adopted after RFRA itself. When state RFRAs were being passed, it was generally assumed that they had an inherent structural weakness in that under normal principles of legislation, they can be repealed or amended expressly or impliedly by subsequent legislation. The *St. John's* dissent raises the possibility that state RFRAs may be stronger than originally thought in that once a state RFRA is passed, any effort to retract it will be aimed at restricting a prior grant of religious freedom, and thus will invoke the residual free exercise protections available when government actions specifically target religious activity. Do you agree with the majority or the dissent on this issue?
3. Can a religious symbol have a secular purpose? Why or why not?

Additional Web Resources:	Analysis by Professor Douglas Laycock of empirical evidence underscoring the need for RLUIPA protections in the land use area

Times, 14 July 2010, A22.

5. *United States v. Rutherford Cnty., Tenn.*, 3:12-0737, 2012 WL 2930076 (M.D. Tenn 18 July 2012).

2. Europe

Manoussakis and Others v. Greece

European Court of Human Rights, App. No. 18748/91 (26 September 1996)

[In 1983, Mr. Manoussakis rented a room in Heraklion (Crete) "for all kinds of meetings, weddings, etc. of Jehovah's Witnesses." On several occasions he filed complaints with the local police because the windows of the room were broken. In June 1983, Mr. Manoussakis applied with the Minister of Education and Religious Affairs for authorization to use the room as a place of worship. The local Orthodox Church complained to police that the room was being used as an unauthorized place of worship by the Jehovah's Witnesses and informed the police about the applications made to the Minister. The Orthodox Church authorities "asked the police to carry out an inspection of the premises, to take punitive measures against those responsible and above all to prohibit any further meetings until the Minister had granted the authorization in question." Over the next 13 months, the applicants received a series of five letters from the Ministry informing them that it was not yet in a position to make a decision concerning their application because it had not received all the necessary information from the other departments concerned. In March 1986, the Heraklion public prosecutor's office instituted criminal proceedings against applicants on the ground that they were operating a place of worship without proper authorization. At trial they were acquitted, but an appeals court sentenced each of the accused to three months' imprisonment convertible into a pecuniary penalty of 400 drachmas per day of detention, and fined them 20,000 drachmas each. After exhausting remedies in Greece, applicants appealed their case to the European Court of Human Rights, alleging violations of the freedom of religion provisions of Article 9 of the Convention.]

[The Court found that the applicants' conviction was an "interference" with their Article 9 rights and found it unnecessary to address the question of whether the inference was "prescribed by law," since it was incompatible with Article 9 on other grounds.]

2. Legitimate Aim

39. According to the Government, the penalty imposed on the applicants served to protect public order and the rights and freedoms of others. . . . In Greece virtually the entire population was of the Christian Orthodox faith, which was closely associated with important moments in the history of the Greek nation. The Orthodox Church had kept alive the national conscience and Greek patriotism during the periods of foreign occupation. [Further, this] intervention of the State to regulate this area with a view to protecting those whose rights and freedoms were affected by the activities of socially dangerous sects was indispensable to maintain public order on Greek territory.

40. Like the applicants, the Court recognises that the States are entitled to verify whether a movement or association carries on, ostensibly in pursuit of religious aims, activities which are harmful to the population. . . . [The] Court considers that the impugned measure pursued a legitimate aim for the purposes of

Article 9 para. 2 of the Convention (art. 9-2), namely the protection of public order.

3. "Necessary in a Democratic Society"

41. The main thrust of the applicants' complaint is that the restrictions imposed on Jehovah's Witnesses by the Greek Government effectively prevent them from exercising their right to freedom of religion. In terms of the legislation and administrative practice, their religion did not, so they claimed, enjoy in Greece the safeguards guaranteed to it in all the other member States of the Council of Europe. The "pluralism, tolerance and broadmindedness without which there is no democratic society" were therefore seriously jeopardised in Greece. . . . The apparently innocent requirement of an authorisation to operate a place of worship had been transformed from a mere formality into a lethal weapon against the right to freedom of religion. The term "dilatory" used by the Commission to describe the conduct of the Minister of Education and Religious Affairs in relation to their application for an authorisation was euphemistic. The struggle for survival by certain religious communities outside the Eastern Orthodox Church, and specifically by Jehovah's Witnesses, was carried on in a climate of interference and oppression by the State and the dominant church as a result of which Article 9 of the Convention had become a dead letter. That Article was the object of frequent and blatant violations aimed at eliminating freedom of religion. . . .

42. According to the Government, in order to resolve the question of the necessity of the applicants' conviction, the Court should first examine the necessity of the requirement of prior authorisation, which owed its existence to historical considerations. . . . There were essential public-order grounds to justify making the setting up of a place of worship subject to approval by the State. In Greece this control applied to all faiths; otherwise it would be both unconstitutional and contrary to the Convention. Jehovah's Witnesses were not exempt from the requirements of legislation which concerned the whole population. The setting up of a church or a place of worship in Greece was, so the Government affirmed, often used as a means of proselytism, in particular by Jehovah's Witnesses who engaged in intensive proselytism, thereby infringing the law that the Court had itself found to be in conformity with the Convention (see the above-mentioned *Kokkinakis* judgment). . . .

45. The Court notes in the first place that Law no. 1363/1938 and the decree of 20 May/2 June 1939 . . . allow far-reaching interference by the political, administrative and ecclesiastical authorities with the exercise of religious freedom. In addition to the numerous formal conditions prescribed in the decree, some of which confer a very wide discretion on the police, mayor or chairman of the district council, there exists in practice the possibility for the Minister of Education and Religious Affairs to defer his reply indefinitely—the decree does not lay down any time-limit—or to refuse his authorisation without explanation or without giving a valid reason. In this respect, the Court observes that the decree empowers the Minister . . . to assess whether there is a "real need" for the religious community in question to set up a church.

46. The Government maintained that the power of the Minister of Education and Religious Affairs to grant or refuse the authorisation requested was not discretionary. . . .47. The Court observes that, in reviewing the lawfulness of refusals to grant the authorisation, the Supreme Administrative Court has developed case-law limiting the Minister's power in this matter and according the local ecclesiastical authority a purely consultative role. The right to freedom of religion as guaranteed under the Convention excludes any discretion on the part of the State to determine whether religious beliefs or the means used to express such beliefs are legitimate. Accordingly, the Court takes the view that the authorisation requirement under Law no. 1363/1938 and the decree of 20 May/2 June 1939 is consistent with Article 9 of the Convention (art. 9) only in so far as it is intended to allow the Minister to verify whether the formal conditions laid down in those enactments are satisfied.

48. It appears from the evidence and from the numerous other cases cited by the applicants and not contested by the Government that the State has tended to use the possibilities afforded by the above-mentioned provisions to impose rigid, or indeed prohibitive, conditions on practice of religious beliefs by certain non-Orthodox movements, in particular Jehovah's Witnesses. . . . [T]he extensive case-law in this field seems to show a clear tendency on the part of the administrative and ecclesiastical authorities to use these provisions to restrict the activities of faiths outside the Orthodox Church.

49. In the instant case the applicants were prosecuted and convicted for having operated a place of worship without first obtaining the authorisations required by law. . . .

51. The Court notes . . . that both the Heraklion public prosecutor's office, when it was bringing proceedings against the applicants, and the Heraklion Criminal Court sitting on appeal, in its judgment of 15 February 1990, relied expressly on the lack of the bishop's authorisation as well as the lack of an authorisation from the Minister of Education and Religious Affairs. The latter, in response to five requests made by the applicants between 25 October 1983 and 10 December 1984, replied that he was examining their file. To date, as far as the Court is aware, the applicants have not received an express decision. Moreover, at the hearing a representative of the Government himself described the Minister's conduct as unfair and attributed it to the difficulty that the latter might have had in giving legally valid reasons for an express decision refusing the authorisation or to his fear that he might provide the applicants with grounds for appealing to the Supreme Administrative Court to challenge an express administrative decision.

52. In these circumstances the Court considers that the Government cannot rely on the applicants' failure to comply with a legal formality to justify their conviction. The degree of severity of the sanction is immaterial.

53. Like the Commission, the Court is of the opinion that the impugned conviction had such a direct effect on the applicants' freedom of religion that it cannot be regarded as proportionate to the legitimate aim pursued, nor, accordingly, as necessary in a democratic society.

In conclusion, there has been a violation of Article 9 (art. 9).

CONCURRING OPINION OF JUDGE MARTENS

1. I completely share the views expressed in the Court's judgment, but I would have preferred to decide the merits on the basis of the "prescribed by law" requirement, that is to decide the issue which the Court leaves open.

2. The substance of the "necessary in a democratic society" requirement is a balancing exercise of the elements of the individual case. However, as follows from paragraph 38 of the Court's judgment, the very essence of the applicants' complaints is not one of individual, but one of general injustice: what they complain of is not so much the harassment they have been subjected to, but, basically, the obstruction to setting up a Jehovah's Witnesses chapel in general. The "prescribed by law" requirement is therefore more suitable to do justice to what . . . is the essential thesis of the applicants, viz. that the Law of Necessity no. 1363/1938 is incompatible with Article 9, either per se or in any event as consistently applied by the competent authorities.

3. I suggest that this approach, although perhaps a little innovatory, is in line with the Court's doctrine that part of its task under the "prescribed by law" requirement is to assess the quality of the law invoked as a justification for the interference under examination.

4. Turning now to the applicants' thesis that the Law of Necessity no. 1363/1938 is incompatible with Article 9, I agree with counsel for the Government that the first question to be discussed is whether under Article 9 there is room at all for "prior restraint" in the form of making the construction or operation of a place of worship conditional on a prior governmental authorisation and of making such construction or operation without such authorisation a criminal offence.

5. As in the province of Article 10, I am opposed to answering this question outright in the negative. It is conceivable that the operation—and a fortiori the construction—of a place of worship in a particular area may raise serious public-order questions and that possibility, in my mind, justifies not wholly excluding the acceptability of making such operation or construction depend on a prior governmental authorisation.

6. Nevertheless, I think that here, where freedom of religion is at stake—even more than in the province of Article 10—the question is very delicate, for public-order arguments may easily disguise intolerance. It is all the more sensitive where there is an official State religion. In such cases it should be absolutely clear both from the wording of, and from the practice under the law in question that the requirement of a prior authorisation in no way whatsoever purports to enable the authorities to "evaluate" the tenets of the applicant community; as a matter of principle the requested authorisation should always be given, unless very exceptional, objective and insuperable grounds of public order make that impossible.

7. The Government have tried to convince us that the Law of Necessity no. 1363/1938 meets these admittedly strict requirements, but in vain. Counsel for the Government has alleged that under that Law there is no room for discretion, but he has at the same time made it clear that it required the authorities to scrutinise whether the application arose from genuine religious needs or as a

means of proselytising and, moreover, whether the tenets of the applicant community were acceptable. And indeed, the requirement that there should be at least fifty families from more or less the same neighbourhood illustrates not only that there is ample room for discretion but also that the Law of Necessity no. 1363/1938 goes much further than is permissible in respect of prior restraint of freedom of religion. On top of this there is the involvement of the clerical authorities of the dominant religion in the authorisation procedure which—even if they were confined to a strictly advisory role (which I doubt)—implies in itself that the Law in question does not meet the above-mentioned strict requirements and is incompatible with Article 9.

8. In sum, I find that the applicants rightly say that the Law of Necessity no. 1363/1938 is per se incompatible with Article 9.

Additional Web Resources:	*Kuznetsov and Others v. Russia*, ECtHR (2007) (Russian case holding that disruption of a religious service ostensibly for lack of appropriate papers violated Article 9 of the ECHR)

B. LANDMARK STATUS

Having your church designated as a landmark might seem like an honor or recognition of the importance of the religious building to the community. In some jurisdictions, landmark status qualifies properties for receiving public monies for upkeep or restoration. But landmark status can also have the effect of prioritizing the historical value of a place of worship over its religious function. Consider the case of St. Bartholomew's Church.

1. The United States

ST. BARTHOLOMEW'S CHURCH V. CITY OF NEW YORK

United States Court of Appeals, Second Circuit, 914 F.2d 348 (2d Cir. 1990)

[An Episcopal church located on Park Avenue, St. Bartholomew's Church was designed in a Venetian adaptation of Byzantine architecture. In 1967 the Landmarks Preservation Commission designated the Church and the adjacent Community House as "landmarks," thus prohibiting any alteration or demolition without government approval. At the time, the church did not object to the landmarking of its property. However, beginning in 1983, the church submitted several applications to the Commission with the intent to replace the Community House with a large office tower. All requests were denied by the Commission as inappropriate alterations. The church asserted that this constituted imposition of an impermissible burden on its free exercise of religion and excessive entanglement in violation of the Establishment Clause. It also asserted that the Landmarks Law violated the Equal Protection and Due Process Clauses of the Fourteenth Amendment and was a taking of property without just compensation.]

1. The Free Exercise Claim

The Church argues that the Landmarks Law substantially burdens religion in violation of the First Amendment as applied to the states through the Fourteenth Amendment. In particular, the Church contends that by denying its application to erect a commercial office tower on its property, the City of New York and the Landmarks Commission (collectively, "the City") have impaired the Church's ability to carry on and expand the ministerial and charitable activities that are central to its religious mission. It argues that the Community House is no longer a sufficient facility for its activities, and that the Church's financial base has eroded. The construction of an office tower similar to those that now surround St. Bartholomew's in midtown Manhattan, the Church asserts, is a means to provide better space for some of the Church's programs and income to support and expand its various ministerial and community activities. The Church thus argues that even if the proposed office tower will not house all of the Church's programs, the revenue generated by renting commercial office space will enable the Church to move some of its programs—such as sheltering the homeless—off-site. The Church concludes that the Landmarks Law unconstitutionally denies it the opportunity to exploit this means of carrying out its religious mission. Although the Landmarks Law substantially limits the options of the Church to raise revenue for purposes of expanding religious charitable activities, we believe the Church's claims are precluded by Supreme Court precedent.

As the Court recently stated in *Employment Division v. Smith*, the free exercise clause prohibits above all "governmental regulation of religious *beliefs* as such." No one seriously contends that the Landmarks Law interferes with substantive religious views. However, apart from impinging on religious beliefs, governmental regulation may affect conduct or behavior associated with those beliefs. Supreme Court decisions indicate that while the government may not coerce an individual to adopt a certain belief or punish him for his religious views, it may restrict certain activities associated with the practice of religion pursuant to its general regulatory powers . . . .

The synthesis of this case law has been stated as follows [in *Smith*]: "[T]he right of free exercise does not relieve an individual of the obligation to comply with a 'valid and neutral law of general applicability on the ground that the law proscribes (or prescribes) conduct that his religion prescribes (or proscribes).'" The critical distinction is thus between a neutral, generally applicable law that happens to bear on religiously motivated action, and a regulation that restricts certain conduct because it is religiously oriented.

The Landmarks Law is a facially neutral regulation of general applicability within the meaning of Supreme Court decisions. . . .

It is true that the Landmarks Law affects many religious buildings. The Church thus asserts that of the six hundred landmarked sites, over fifteen percent are religious properties and over five percent are Episcopal churches. Nevertheless, we do not understand those facts to demonstrate a lack of neutrality or general applicability. Because of the importance of religion, and of particular churches, in our social and cultural history, and because many churches are designed to be architecturally attractive, many religious structures are likely to fall within the neutral criteria – having "special character or special historical or aesthetic interest or value"– set forth by the Landmarks Law. This, however, is not evidence of an intent to discriminate against, or impinge on, religious belief in the designation of landmark sites.

. . . [A]bsent proof of the discriminatory exercise of discretion, [the exercise of discretion in the landmarking process has] no constitutional relevance . . . .

It is obvious that the Landmarks Law has drastically restricted the Church's ability to raise revenues to carry out its various charitable and ministerial programs. In this particular case, the revenues involved are very large because the Community House is on land that would be extremely valuable if put to commercial uses. Nevertheless, we understand Supreme Court decisions to indicate that neutral regulations that diminish the income of a religious organization do not implicate the free exercise clause. . . .

We agree with the district court that no First Amendment violation has occurred absent a showing of discriminatory motive, coercion in religious practice or the Church's inability to carry out its religious mission in its existing facilities. . . . In sum, the Landmarks Law is a valid, neutral regulation of general applicability, and as explained below, we agree with the district court that the Church has failed to prove that it cannot continue its religious practice in its existing facilities.[6]

2. The Takings Claim

[The court holds the takings claim invalid under *Penn Central*, in which the Supreme Court determined that the application of New York's Landmarks Law did not constitute a taking.]

3. Findings of the District Court

The principal factual finding of the district court–one central to its rejection of the Church's free exercise and takings claims–was that the Church "failed to show by a preponderance of the evidence that it can no longer conduct its charitable activities or carry out its religious mission in its existing facilities." . . .

Fatal, however, to the Church's claim is the absence of any showing that the space deficiency in the Community House cannot be remedied by a reconfiguration or expansion that is consistent with the purposes of the Landmarks Law. . . . In fact, the building has a modern, light steel frame structure and was designed so that two additional floors could easily be added.

---

6. The Church also argues that the Landmarks Law involves an excessive degree of entanglement between church and state in violation of the Establishment Clause. The district court dismissed this argument as irrelevant in the present context, reasoning that the entanglement doctrine applies only to instances of government funding of religious organizations. However, in *Jimmy Swaggart Ministries v. Board of Equalization of California*, 493 U.S. 378 (1990), the Supreme Court considered an entanglement claim in the context of government taxation of the sale of religious materials by a religious organization. The Court found no constitutional violation, as the regulation imposed only routine administrative and recordkeeping obligations, involved no continuing surveillance of the organization, and did not inquire into the religious doctrine or motives of the organization. These same factors are of course largely true of the Landmarks Law. The only scrutiny of the Church occurred in the proceedings for a certificate of appropriateness, and the matters scrutinized were exclusively financial and architectural. This degree of interaction does not rise to the level of unconstitutional entanglement.

Moreover, the Commission has indicated that it would be receptive to a proposal from the Church for such an addition. While expanding the amount of available space in the Community House may not provide ideal facilities for the Church's expanded programs, it does offer a means of continuing those programs in the existing building. Certainly the intermediate option of limited expansion must be thoroughly explored before jumping to replacement with a [large] office building.

b. Cost of Repair and Rehabilitation

The Church also argues that the necessary repairs to the physically deteriorating Church building and Community House would be prohibitively expensive. [The Church's expert estimated that repairs would cost approximately $11 million. The District Court rejected these estimates, indicating that they were biased in favor of replacement and were contradicted by other estimates of neutral consultants and those opposed to the development.] . . .

As our discussion in the next section indicates, even if the potential cost of repairs totaled $4.5 million, the Church has not adequately demonstrated that it is unable to meet this expense. . . .

c. The Church's Finances

As a corollary to its claim that repair and rehabilitation of the Church building and Community House would be too costly, the Church argues that its financial condition does not allow it to make the necessary improvements and also continue its other programs. The district court, however, found that appellant had failed adequately to prove this assertion, a finding that is not clearly erroneous. . . .

The Church's principal argument is that a major improvement expenditure of the type required to repair and renovate the Church building and Community House would severely damage [the] "precarious" balance of [its] revenues and expenses. . . .

While a reduced principal will yield less investment income, the Church has not demonstrated that its budget cannot withstand building improvement expenditures under a reasonable financing procedure. For example . . . withdrawals from the endowment might be made gradually to minimize lost investment income, or the Church might borrow against its endowment, and repay the loan over an extended period of time. Appellant has offered no financial projections or cash flow analyses to prove that these financing methods are not feasible. Without such data, the district court's finding that the Church failed to prove prospective financial hardship is not clearly erroneous.

We also cannot ignore the paucity of evidence offered by the Church to show that other forms of revenue are not available. Its claim that a capital fundraising drive already has been exhausted as a financing possibility is undercut by evidence that longtime members of the congregation cannot recall any such drive. Also, evidence before the Commission indicated that the transferrable development rights for the airspace above the Church property are, contrary to the Church's claim, not worthless.

Finally, the Church argues that even if its endowment could withstand a building project, it is not at liberty to withdraw large sums for that purpose because of legal restrictions on the use of its investment funds. In particular, it urges that prohibits the Church from expending the sums necessary to undergo a building project. That provision, however, does no more than impose upon the Church a fiduciary duty of care to manage the congregation's money in a prudent and responsible fashion, and would be implicated only if the expenditures in question would unacceptably impair the Church's financial condition. . . .

COMMENTS AND QUESTIONS

1. The court engages in detailed second-guessing about the church's financial capacity. Is this a constitutionally permissible inquiry for a court to make? Or is it an impermissible entanglement of church and state?
2. Even in France, which has one of the most separationist regimes of Europe, public funds are available to support the maintenance costs of religious structures that constitute historical landmarks.[7] Non–Establishment Clause principles in the United States would presumably forbid similar subsidies to help with costs on a structure such as St. Bartholomew's Church. The *Penn Central* case, 438 U.S. 104 (1978), holds that the landmarking statute constitutes an exercise of regulatory authority rather than a taking that would give rise to just compensation claims. Should the state have some obligation (and ability) to compensate churches for the costs of maintaining landmarks?
3. To what extent are the limitations imposed by landmarking legislation permissible under the ICCPR and the ECHR? What legitimizes the legislation–public safety, health, order, morals, or the rights of third parties? Note that other forms of building regulations such as safety codes, sanitary codes, environmental laws, and the like tend to be rooted in health and safety concerns. Landmarking statutes, in contrast, are concerned more with aesthetics and historical sensitivities. Do the latter fit among the permissible legitimating grounds for limiting manifestations of religion under international standards? To what extent should aesthetic and historic preservation values outweigh religious freedom rights?[8]
4. What if a landmark authority seeks to block changes in interior design (such as placement of an altar) that are relevant to liturgical practice? *See, e.g., Society of Jesus of New England v. Boston Land Marks Comm'n*, 564 N.E.2d 571 (Mass. 1990) (striking down landmarking regulations that would have prevented changed placement of altar to accord with Catholic teachings on the basis of state constitutional provision). Should changes called for by liturgy receive greater deference than changes motivated by considerations of church finance?

7. *See* Norman Doe, *Law and Religion in Europe: A Comparative Introduction* 180–181 (Oxford Univ. Press 2011).

8. *See* Angela C. Carmella, Landmark Preservation of Church Property, 34 *Cath. Law.* 41 (1991).

III. RELIGIOUS FREEDOM IN SPECIALIZED INSTITUTIONAL SETTINGS

A. PRISONS AND GOVERNMENT SUPERVISION

1. The United States

Three years prior to jettisoning the compelling state interest test in *Employment Division v. Smith*, the United State Supreme Court in *O'Lone v. Shabazz*, 483 U.S. 342 (1987), articulated a constitutional test for free exercise claims in prison contexts that was substantially less demanding than the compelling state interest test. The case was brought by Muslim prisoners who claimed that their prison's policy of not allowing them to gather for Friday prayers violated their free exercise rights. The Supreme Court rejected their claim, holding that "when a prison regulation impinges on inmates' constitutional rights, the regulation is valid if it is reasonably related to legitimate penological interests." Essentially, the Court took the position that because of the distinctive requirements of prison environments, which assume substantial narrowing of inmate rights, greater deference should be given to legitimate penological concerns in determining the extent of prisoner rights. If anything, *Smith* further relaxed constitutional standards in the prison setting, holding that any general or neutral law (or policy) would override religious freedom claims.

In the years since the *Smith* decision was handed down in 1990, the appropriate standard for prison cases has been a controversial issue. Some initial opposition to the passage of Religious Freedom Restoration Act of 1993[9] (RFRA) came from prison administrators, who feared that religious claims would complicate prison administration. Similarly, after the Supreme Court struck down RFRA as it applied to the states, similar opposition was frequently raised when state RFRAs were being passed. Nonetheless, as indicated in Chapter 6, the majority of US jurisdictions passed state RFRAs, and Congress adopted the Religious Land Use and Institutionalized Persons Act of 2000[10] (RLUIPA), Section 3 of which provides: "No government shall impose a substantial burden on the religious exercise of a person residing in or confined to an institution . . . even if the burden results from a rule of general applicability, unless the government demonstrates that imposition of the burden on that person (1) is in furtherance of a compelling governmental interest; and (2) is the least restrictive means of furthering that compelling governmental interest." Thus, RLUIPA reasserted the pre-*Smith* compelling state interest test for prison settings. Because RLUIPA was passed by exercising enumerated Congressional powers not subject to the challenge brought against RFRA in *Boerne*, the strict scrutiny of religious claims commanded by RLUIPA is binding throughout the nation in prison contexts. Not surprisingly, however, this does not mean prisoners automatically prevail on their claims.

---

9. 107 Stat. 1488, 42 USC § 2000bb *et seq.*
10. 114 Stat. 803, 42 USC § 2000cc *et seq.*

HOLT V. HOBBS

Supreme Court of the United States, 135 S.Ct. 853 (2015)

Justice ALITO delivered the opinion of the Court.

[Gregory Holt (aka Abdul Maalik Muhammad), an inmate in custody of the Arkansas Department of Correction, objected on religious grounds to the Department's grooming policy, which provides that "[n]o inmates will be permitted to wear facial hair other than a neatly trimmed mustache that does not extend beyond the corner of the mouth or over the lip." The policy makes an exception for medical conditions, but not for religious needs.]

. . . Petitioner sought permission to grow a beard and, although he believes that his faith requires him not to trim his beard at all, he proposed a "compromise" under which he would grow only a 1/2-inch beard. Prison officials denied his request, and the warden told him: "[Y]ou will abide by [Arkansas Department of Correction] policies and if you choose to disobey, you can suffer the consequences." . . .

[At an evidentiary hearing on the matter, witnesses] expressed the belief that inmates could hide contraband in even a 1/2-inch beard, but neither pointed to any instances in which this had been done in Arkansas or elsewhere. Both witnesses also acknowledged that inmates could hide items in many other places, such as in the hair on their heads or their clothing. In addition, one of the witnesses—Gaylon Lay, the warden of petitioner's prison—testified that a prisoner who escaped could change his appearance by shaving his beard, and that a prisoner could shave his beard to disguise himself and enter a restricted area of the prison. Neither witness, however, was able to explain why these problems could not be addressed by taking a photograph of an inmate without a beard, a practice followed in other prison systems. Lay voiced concern that the Department would be unable to monitor the length of a prisoner's beard to ensure that it did not exceed one-half inch, but he acknowledged that the Department kept track of the length of the beards of those inmates who are allowed to wear a 1/4-inch beard for medical reasons.

. . . [The] Magistrate Judge recommended that the preliminary injunction be vacated and that petitioner's complaint be dismissed for failure to state a claim on which relief can be granted[, emphasizing] that "the prison officials are entitled to deference," *id.*, at 168, and that the grooming policy allowed petitioner to exercise his religion in other ways, such as by praying on a prayer rug, maintaining the diet required by his faith, and observing religious holidays.

The District Court adopted the Magistrate Judge's recommendation in full, and the Court of Appeals for the Eighth Circuit affirmed in a brief *per curiam* opinion, holding that the Department had satisfied its burden of showing that the grooming policy was the least restrictive means of furthering its compelling security interests. The Court of Appeals stated that "courts should ordinarily defer to [prison officials'] expert judgment" in security matters unless there is substantial evidence that a prison's response is exaggerated. . . .

We [subsequently] granted certiorari . . . .

The Department argues that its grooming policy represents the least restrictive means of furthering a "broadly formulated interes[t]," namely, the Department's compelling interest in prison safety and security. But RLUIPA, like RFRA, contemplates a "a more focused " inquiry and "requires the Government to demonstrate that the compelling interest test is satisfied through application of the challenged law 'to the person'—the particular claimant whose sincere exercise of religion is being substantially burdened." . . .

The Department contends that enforcing this prohibition is the least restrictive means of furthering prison safety and security in two specific ways.

. . . The Department first claims that the no-beard policy prevents prisoners from hiding contraband. The Department worries that prisoners may use their beards to conceal all manner of prohibited items, including razors, needles, drugs, and cellular phone subscriber identity module (SIM) cards.

We readily agree that the Department has a compelling interest in staunching the flow of contraband into and within its facilities, but the argument that this interest would be seriously compromised by allowing an inmate to grow a ½-inch beard is hard to take seriously. As noted, the Magistrate Judge observed that it was "almost preposterous to think that [petitioner] could hide contraband" in the short beard he had grown at the time of the evidentiary hearing. . . . Since the Department does not demand that inmates have shaved heads or short crew cuts, it is hard to see why an inmate would seek to hide contraband in a ½-inch beard rather than in the longer hair on his head . . . .

[T]he Department cannot show that forbidding very short beards is the least restrictive means of preventing the concealment of contraband. "The least-restrictive-means standard is exceptionally demanding," and it requires the government to "sho[w] that it lacks other means of achieving its desired goal without imposing a substantial burden on the exercise of religion by the objecting part[y]." *Hobby Lobby*. "[I]f a less restrictive means is available for the Government to achieve its goals, the Government must use it." *United States* v. *Playboy Entertainment Group, Inc.*, 529 U.S. 803, 815 (2000).

The Department failed to establish that it could not satisfy its security concerns by simply searching petitioner's beard. The Department already searches prisoners' hair and clothing, and it presumably examines the ¼-inch beards of inmates with dermatological conditions. It has offered no sound reason why hair, clothing, and ¼-inch beards can be searched but ½-inch beards cannot. . . .

The Department contends that its grooming policy is necessary to further an additional compelling interest, *i.e.*, preventing prisoners from disguising their identities. The Department tells us that the no-beard policy allows security officers to identify prisoners quickly and accurately. It claims that bearded inmates could shave their beards and change their appearance in order to enter restricted areas within the prison, to escape, and to evade apprehension after escaping.

We agree that prisons have a compelling interest in the quick and reliable identification of prisoners, and we acknowledge that any alteration in a prisoner's appearance, such as by shaving a beard, might, in the absence of effective countermeasures, have at least some effect on the ability of guards or others to make a quick identification. But even if we assume for present purposes that the Department's grooming policy sufficiently furthers its interest in the identification of prisoners, that policy still violates RLUIPA as applied in the circumstances present here. The Department contends that a prisoner who has a beard when he is photographed for identification purposes might confuse guards by shaving his beard. But as petitioner has argued, the Department could largely solve this problem by requiring that all inmates be photographed without beards when first admitted to the facility and, if necessary, periodically thereafter. . . . In fact, the Department . . . already has a policy of photographing a prisoner both when he enters an institution and when his "appearance changes at any time during [his] incarceration." Arkansas Department of Correction, Inmate Handbook 3–4 (rev. Jan. 2013). . . .

We are unpersuaded by these arguments for at least two reasons. First, the Department failed to show, in the face of petitioner's evidence, that its prison system is so different from the many institutions that allow facial hair that the dual-photo method cannot be employed at its institutions. Second, the Department failed to establish why the risk that a prisoner will shave a 1⁄2-inch beard to disguise himself is so great that 1⁄2-inch beards cannot be allowed, even though prisoners are allowed to grow mustaches, head hair, or 1⁄4-inch beards for medical reasons. All of these could also be shaved off at a moment's notice, but the Department apparently does not think that this possibility raises a serious security concern. . . .

In addition to its failure to prove that petitioner's proposed alternatives would not sufficiently serve its security interests, the Department has not provided an adequate response to two additional arguments that implicate the RLUIPA analysis.

First, the Department has not adequately demonstrated why its grooming policy is substantially underinclusive in at least two respects. Although the Department denied petitioner's request to grow a 1⁄2-inch beard, it permits prisoners with a dermatological condition to grow 1⁄4-inch beards. The Department does this even though both beards pose similar risks. And the Department permits inmates to grow more than a 1⁄2-inch of hair on their heads. . . . Hair on the head is a more plausible place to hide contraband than a 1⁄2-inch beard–and the same is true of an inmate's clothing and shoes. Nevertheless, the Department does not require inmates to go about bald, barefoot, or naked. Although the Department's proclaimed objectives are to stop the flow of contraband and to facilitate prisoner identification, "[t]he proffered objectives are not pursued with respect to analogous nonreligious conduct," which suggests that "those interests could be achieved by narrower ordinances that burdened religion to a far lesser degree."

In [comparison with] 1⁄2-inch beard is longer than the 1⁄4-inch beard allowed for medical reasons . . . the Department has failed to establish . . . that a 1⁄4-inch difference in beard length poses a meaningful increase in security risk. The Department also asserts that few inmates require beards for medical reasons while many may request beards for religious reasons. But the Department has not argued that denying petitioner an exemption is necessary to further a compelling interest in cost control or program administration. At bottom, this argument is but another formulation of the "classic rejoinder of bureaucrats throughout history: If

I make an exception for you, I'll have to make one for everybody, so no exceptions." . . .

[T]he Department [also] failed to show . . . why the vast majority of States and the Federal Government permit inmates to grow 1/2-inch beards, either for any reason or for religious reasons, but it cannot. . . .

We do not suggest that RLUIPA requires a prison to grant a particular religious exemption as soon as a few other jurisdictions do so. But when so many prisons offer an accommodation, a prison must, at a minimum, offer persuasive reasons why it believes that it must take a different course . . . . Despite this, the courts below deferred to these prison officials' mere say-so that they could not accommodate petitioner's request. RLUIPA, however, demands much more. Courts must hold prisons to their statutory burden, and they must not "assume a plausible, less restrictive alternative would be ineffective."

We emphasize that although RLUIPA provides substantial protection for the religious exercise of institutionalized persons, it also affords prison officials ample ability to maintain security. We highlight three ways in which this is so. First, in applying RLUIPA's statutory standard, courts should not blind themselves to the fact that the analysis is conducted in the prison setting. Second, if an institution suspects that an inmate is using religious activity to cloak illicit conduct, "prison officials may appropriately question whether a prisoner's religiosity, asserted as the basis for a requested accommodation, is authentic." Third, even if a claimant's religious belief is sincere,, an institution might be entitled to withdraw an accommodation if the claimant abuses the exemption in a manner that undermines the prison's compelling interests. . . .

In sum, we hold that the Department's grooming policy violates RLUIPA insofar as it prevents petitioner from growing a 1/2-inch beard in accordance with his religious beliefs. The judgment of the United States Court of Appeals for the Eighth Circuit is reversed, and the case is remanded for further proceedings consistent with this opinion.

COMMENTS AND QUESTIONS

1. Would *Holt* have come out the same way under *O'Lone v. Shabazz*? Under *Smith*? How would *O'Lone* have come out under RLUIPA?
2. The Supreme Court applied RLUIPA standards in *Sossamon v. Texas*, 563 U.S. 277 (2011), when an inmate sought monetary and injunctive relief for two alleged RLUIPA violations by a state prison. First, Sossamon claimed that the prison violated his right to practice Christianity when it barred all prisoners' use of the Christian prison chapel for worship services. Prisoners were allowed access to the chapel for non-religious purposes and could hold worship services in a multi-purpose room that lacked religious symbols, but prisoners could not use the chapel for worship services because the wardens believed that congregational meetings in the chapel posed unique security risks. Second, Sossamon challenged a prison policy prohibiting "cell-restricted inmates," inmates whose privileges were limited as a result of disciplinary violations, from attending church services even though cell-restricted inmates were allowed to leave to participate in secular activities

such as educational classes. Instead of considering the case's substantive merits, the Court invoked sovereign immunity to affirm the dismissal of Sossamon's claims. Specifically, the Court held that RLUIPA's authorization of private causes of action did not waive state sovereign immunity to monetary damages. Thus, Sossamon could only seek injunctive relief. This decision limits RLUIPA's scope, at least with respect to private suits. As the dissent noted, "By depriving prisoners of a damages remedy for violations of their statutory rights, the majority ensures that plaintiffs suing state defendants under RLUIPA will be forced to seek enforcement of those rights with one hand tied behind their backs. . . . [T]he unavailability of monetary relief will effectively shield unlawful policies and practices from judicial review in many cases." 563 U.S. at 303-305.

3. In *Cutter v. Wilkinson*, 544 U.S. 709 (205) the Sixth Circuit that held that RLUIPA violated the Establishment Clause because it afforded special benefits to religious prisoners that aren't awarded to non-religious prisoners. The Supreme Court reversed that decision and unanimously held that RLUIPA is permissible under the Constitution to protect the religious freedoms of prisoners because RLUIPA "alleviates exceptional government-created burdens on private religious exercise." (720, 726).

2. Europe

In its 57-year history, the European Court of Human Rights (ECtHR) and its predecessor institution the European Commission of Human Rights (ECmHR), have rendered decisions in more than 60 cases in which an incarcerated person claimed violation of rights protected by Article 9 (freedom of religion or belief) of the European Convention of Human Rights (ECHR). Reaching the Court after "domestic remedies" have been unsatisfactorily exhausted, these claims, "among other subject matters, have concerned prison chapel visits and church service attendance, access to members of the clergy, possession and use of religious items, compliance with religious dietary requirements, and the observance of other religious rituals."[11] Only one of them, *X v. Austria*, App. No. 1753/63 (ECmHR, 15 February 1965), included an "appearance" issue, involving, like *Holt v. Hobbs*, an inmate's desire for exemption from prison rules so that he could wear a beard as mandated by religious beliefs.

In the excerpt that follows, Netherlands scholar Jeroen Temperman asserts that "there are there are strong penological and societal interests to taking the rights, including freedom of religion or belief, of prisoners seriously." Indeed,

> *not* taking religious freedom of prisoners seriously may come at great costs. Notably, fostering religious liberties, a marketplace of free religious discourse, and the freest possible (obviously within the confines of prison security) 'space' for or accommodation of religious practises, all contribute to religious pluralism. It is by promoting such pluralism—rather than by suppressing religion from the prison regime—that the risk of radicalization of prisoners may be minimized.
>
> [F]rom a civil rights perspective the protection of freedom of religion is an end in itself [and] even if there is no chance that one will ever return to society the

11. Jeroen Temperman, Freedom of Religion or Belief in Prison: A Critical Analysis of the European Court of Human Rights' Jurisprudence, 6 *Oxford J. L. & Relig.* (1) 48, 53 (2017).

protection of the prisoner's freedom of religion or belief remains crucial. It is in that particular vein that international legal or soft-law benchmarks underscore the importance of respecting freedom of religion or belief in prisons.[12]

JEROEN TEMPERMAN, FREEDOM OF RELIGION OR BELIEF IN PRISON: A CRITICAL ANALYSIS OF THE EUROPEAN COURT OF HUMAN RIGHTS' JURISPRUDENCE

6 *Oxford J. L. & Relig.* (1) 48, 53 (2017)

Both at the regional European (the European Prison Rules) and at the universal level (the [2015] UN Nelson Mandela Rules) soft-law benchmarks exist on the rights of prisoners, including their freedom of religion or belief. . . .

. . . [To be sure, these rules are not binding.] They have not been adopted in form of a treaty to be signed and ratified by states. They are based on best penological practices; yet since they have been politically adopted by consensus they do carry some authoritative weight. What makes them so pertinent for prison managements, law makers, judges, practitioners, and academics alike, is that these rules flesh out what freedom of religion or belief clauses in international human rights treaties cannot possibly flesh out in any detail–the extent to which public authorities must ensure respect to prisoners' religious rights. Indeed, Article 9 of the European Convention on Human Rights and Article 18 of the International Covenant on Civil and Political Rights do not say anything about prisoners' right to freedom of religion or belief.

The proliferation of these soft-law prison benchmarks and their respective updates, at the universal and the regional levels, raise the question of possible fragmentation of these norms. While the European Prison Rules formally 'bear in mind' their UN counterpart, . . . there are a number of interesting differences between the respective sets of rules on the point of ensuring respect to freedom of religion or belief of prisoners. . . .

[B]oth the Nelson Mandela Rules and the European Prison Rules are realistic enough to acknowledge that the prison regime may make unencumbered religious freedom rather problematic at times. . . . Yet it goes without saying that precisely what is and what is not 'practicable' in prisons is debatable and prisoners may indeed mobilize the law, including international human rights law, to shift the boundaries of acceptable religious observation and practice.

[Member States of the Council of Europe] have agreed, in the form of international human rights treaties, to protect the right to freedom of religion or belief. Convicted prisoners are not stripped of their citizenship. Thus, they remain the right-holders of fundamental rights, including the right to freedom of religion or belief. While the prison regime may imply that some of those rights become [more or less curtailed, . . .] prisoners in principle *have* those rights, and . . . any restrictions on those rights must be justified. . . .]

International prison benchmarks are silent on the question whether prisoners have a religious right to maintain a certain, religiously motivated, appearance. Notably, while the European Prison Rules avoid the word 'beard' altogether, the

12. *Id.* at 49.

Nelson Mandela Rules discuss beards and shaving under the heading of personal hygiene, indicating that prisoners must be in a position to 'maintain a good appearance compatible with their self-respect' and that therefore 'facilities shall be provided for the proper care of the hair and beard, and men shall be able to shave regularly'. This is not a definitive answer to the question if prisoners ought to be permitted to grow a beard if they wish so for religious reasons.

This very question has been put to the European Commission of Human Rights (and other monitoring bodies and courts . . .). The applicant in [X] *v Austria* (1965), serving a sentence of 20 years' imprisonment for murder, was of Jewish origin, but had converted to Buddhism. The Austrian prison did not allow him to grow a short chin beard, something X claimed to be prescribed by his Buddhist beliefs. Before the European Commission of Human Rights the Austrian Government submitted that X was denied this 'for identification purposes', . . .underscoring the fact that X did not have a beard prior to his arrest and conviction. The Commission [agreed] that this limitation on X's rights was justified in the interest of the protection of public order.

The Commission at no point seeks to deconstruct and closely evaluate the arguments advanced by the respondent state. Does a chin beard truly impede the possibility of identification? Presumably, upon imprisonment photographs of the prisoner were made. Could not new pictures be taken, updating the prisoner's file with the prisoner's new appearance? In other words, it is not at all clear whether the limitation–the outright refusal–was truly necessary in a democratic society.

. . . [T]his issue has not recurred before the ECtHR . . . [but on] two occasions the UN Human Rights Committee has been presented with a prisoner's-right-to-wear-a-beard case. The first time the Committee could not rule on the merits of the complaint brought by a convicted murderer [because he] had not exhausted domestic remedies on this point. In the second case, again brought by a practising Muslim . . . against Trinidad and Tobago, [the applicant,] Mr Boodoo[,] alleged that the respondent state on two different occasions, first upon having his photograph taken after his conviction (after which event he sought and received permission to grow it back), and later during a search of his cell, forcibly shaved his beard. In finding a violation of Article 18 of the ICCPR . . . , the Committee 'reaffirms that the freedom to manifest religion or belief in worship, observance, practice and teaching encompasses a broad range of acts and that the concept of worship extends to ritual and ceremonial acts giving expression to belief, as well as various practices integral to such acts'. A decade before this decision, the Committee had already ruled that prisoners continue enjoying their right to freedom of religion or belief. Taken together, these considerations mean that it was Trinidad and Tobago that faced the burden of proving the necessity of the ostensible interferences with Boodoo's religious rights. Failing to come up with any such substantiation, the Committee declares a breach of the Covenant.

By way of further comparison it may be interesting to briefly compare the rather non-accommodative approach taken by the European Commission of Human Rights with a recent decision of the Supreme Court of the United States, which in *Holt v Hobbs* (2015) essentially ruled that prisoners have a right to wear a (small) beard if they so desire for religious reasons. . . . The judicial approach taken by the US Court strikingly differs from that of the [ECmHR]. Notably, these highest federal judges went out of their way so as to underscore the importance and status of the right to freedom of religion or belief in prison. . . .

4. CONCLUSION: REVISITING A SYSTEMIC INEQUALITY

In numerous cases, the European Court of Human Rights declares complaints inadmissible because it cannot fathom the precise nature of the case. Thus when the respondent government and applicant present differing versions of the facts of the case, the Court typically sides with [grants a wide "margin of appreciation" to] the government. The result is that the complaint is deemed inadmissible for being 'manifestly ill-founded'. This practice raises questions as to the adequate burden and standard of proof in this type of case, especially considering a basic and significant inequality—prison authority versus incarcerated person.

[When] facts presented by prisoners lack sufficient coherence and cogency to engage the Convention, or the respondent state can prove the complaint to be patently false . . . it is obvious what the Strasbourg Court must do. . . . [But] in the light of what can be perceived as a systemic inequality, taking religious rights of prisoners seriously means that monitoring bodies must better recognize those factors and circumstances that warrant a shift of the burden of proof to prison authorities. In addition to the burden of proof, the required standards of proof also must be critically considered by monitoring bodies. Some recognized grounds for limiting freedom of religion are on their face very relevant in the context of prisons. Yet it is all too easy to make 'safety', 'public order', 'health', or 'rights of others' arguments in the abstract. Monitoring bodies must duly cross-examine states to ascertain the necessity and proportionality of imposed interferences with prisoners' religious rights.

[T]he rationale of many restrictions can be hidden under the cloak of 'prison discipline'. However . . . not every administrative burden, inconvenience, or nuisance has the force of a public order argument. Taking religious rights seriously means accommodating diversity. This only works if it is understood and accepted that even the shackles of prison life can be loosened if and when human rights are at stake.

COMMENTS AND QUESTIONS

1. Temperman compares a 1995 decision of the European Commission of Human Rights (which at the time handled a substantial portion of the caseload of the European Court of Human Rights) with a 2015 decision by the ultimate appeals court of the United States. How should courts or other tribunals best take the unique context of prison life into account in assessing the religious freedom claims of prisoners? Are there bright line rules or presumptions that can protect prisoner rights without requiring time-intensive case-by-case analysis of each claim? To what extent does the fact of criminal conviction and incarceration justify substantive narrowing of religious freedom claims?
2. There is considerable evidence that engagement of prisoners with religious ministries in prisons may result in improved prison discipline and reduced

recidivism rates.[13] This may be attributable to voluntary self-selection patterns for engagement, to internalization of religious ideals by prisoners, to the building of social ties which help provide a bridge to a new set of social relations once a prisoner is released, or to other similar factors. Against such positive benefits it is necessary to consider whether allowing prison ministries may constitute an impermissible breach of non-establishment or state neutrality norms, or whether such ministries need to be accommodated because otherwise free exercise rights of prisoners would suffer. There are also risks that to the extent benefits are linked to religious engagement, there may be undue influence to participate in religious programs. In addition, there are questions about whether contacts with prisoners holding radical religious views can contribute to further radicalization of other prisoners, or whether, for example, Islamic outreach in prisons contributes to peace within prisons and long-term rehabilitation.[14] How should prison officials address these conflicting concerns?"

B. THE MILITARY

The military is another context in which religious freedom protections may vary somewhat from what is guaranteed in civilian contexts. In the United States, the existence of the chaplaincy in the military has been defended against non-establishment challenges on the ground that in light of the more coercive environment of the military, if the chaplaincy were not allowed, the free exercise rights of soldiers would suffer. On the other hand, there are various ways in which religious freedom protections give way to the demands of military life.

1. The United States

GOLDMAN V. WEINBERGER

Supreme Court of the United States, 475 U.S. 503 (1986)

[Goldman was an Orthodox Jew and ordained rabbi serving in the Air Force as a clinical psychologist at the mental health clinic of an air base in California. Seeking to protect his right to wear a yarmulke, he brought suit challenging Air Force Regulation (AFR) 35-10, which provided that "[h]eadgear will not be worn . . . [w]hile indoors . . .".]

Our review of military regulations challenged on First Amendment grounds is far more deferential than constitutional review of similar laws or regulations designed for civilian society. The military need not encourage debate or tolerate protest to the extent that such tolerance is required of the civilian state by the First Amendment; to accomplish its mission the military must foster instinctive obedience, unity, commitment, and esprit de corps. The essence of military

13. *See* Alexander Volokh, Do Faith-Based Prisons Work?, 63 *Alabama L. Rev.* 43 (2011).

14. *See e.g.*, SpearIt, Religion as Rehabilitation? Reflections on Islam in the Correctional Setting, 34 *Whittier L. Rev.* 29 (2012).

service "is the subordination of the desires and interests of the individual to the needs of the service."

These aspects of military life do not, of course, render entirely nugatory in the military context the guarantees of the First Amendment. But "within the military community there is simply not the same [individual] autonomy as there is in the larger civilian community." . . .

The considered professional judgment of the Air Force is that the traditional outfitting of personnel in standardized uniforms encourages the subordination of personal preferences and identities in favor of the overall group mission. Uniforms encourage a sense of hierarchical unity by tending to eliminate outward individual distinctions except for those of rank. The Air Force considers them as vital during peacetime as during war because its personnel must be ready to provide an effective defense on a moment's notice; the necessary habits of discipline and unity must be developed in advance of trouble. We have acknowledged that "[t]he inescapable demands of military discipline and obedience to orders cannot be taught on battlefields; the habit of immediate compliance with military procedures and orders must be virtually reflex with no time for debate or reflection." . . .

Goldman contends that the Free Exercise Clause of the First Amendment requires the Air Force to make an exception to its uniform dress requirements for religious apparel unless the accouterments create a "clear danger" of undermining discipline and esprit de corps. He asserts that in general, visible but "unobtrusive" apparel will not create such a danger and must therefore be accommodated. He argues that the Air Force failed to prove that a specific exception for his practice of wearing an unobtrusive yarmulke would threaten discipline. He contends that the Air Force's assertion to the contrary is mere ipse dixit, with no support from actual experience or a scientific study in the record, and is contradicted by expert testimony that religious exceptions to AFR 35-10 are in fact desirable and will increase morale by making the Air Force a more humane place.

But whether or not expert witnesses may feel that religious exceptions to AFR 35-10 are desirable is quite beside the point. The desirability of dress regulations in the military is decided by the appropriate military officials, and they are under no constitutional mandate to abandon their considered professional judgment. Quite obviously, to the extent the regulations do not permit the wearing of religious apparel such as a yarmulke, a practice described by petitioner as silent devotion akin to prayer, military life may be more objectionable for petitioner and probably others. But the First Amendment does not require the military to accommodate such practices in the face of its view that they would detract from the uniformity sought by the dress regulations. The Air Force has drawn the line essentially between religious apparel that is visible and that which is not, and we hold that those portions of the regulations challenged here reasonably and evenhandedly regulate dress in the interest of the military's perceived need for uniformity. The First Amendment therefore does not prohibit them from being applied to petitioner even though their effect is to restrict the wearing of the headgear required by his religious beliefs.

COMMENTS AND QUESTIONS

One year after the Supreme Court decided *Goldman*, the United States Congress passed a law allowing the wearing of religious articles of clothing such as yarmulkes in the military in most circumstances. What does the passage of this law say about the malleability of "public order" as a basis for limiting religious manifestations? Is this another example of Congress being more respectful of the religious freedom interests of a minority group than the Supreme Court is?

2. Europe

KALAÇ V. TURKEY

European Court of Human Rights, App. No. 20704/92 (1 July 1997)

[Kalaç was a judge advocate in the Turkish air force. He was found to have adopted "unlawful fundamentalist opinions" contrary to the Turkish regulations on the assessment of officers and noncommissioned officers, and his compulsory retirement was ordered by the Supreme Military Council in August 1990. Kalaç was a practicing Muslim who prayed five times a day and observed the Ramadan fast. These practices were permitted within the confines of the armed services. However, the Turkish government contended that he was a member of the fundamentalist Suleyman sect and had accordingly demonstrated a lack of loyalty to the principle of secularism on which the Turkish nation was founded and which it was the duty of the armed forces to guarantee. Kalaç applied to the Supreme Administrative Court to set aside the compulsory retirement order, but his application was dismissed. After exhausting remedies in Turkey, Kalaç took the case to Strasbourg.]

27. The Court reiterates that while religious freedom is primarily a matter of individual conscience, it also implies, inter alia, freedom to manifest one's religion not only in community with others, in public and within the circle of those whose faith one shares, but also alone and in private . . . . Article 9 lists a number of forms which manifestation of one's religion or belief may take, namely worship, teaching, practice and observance. Nevertheless, Article 9 does not protect every act motivated or inspired by a religion or belief. Moreover, in exercising his freedom to manifest his religion, an individual may need to take his specific situation into account.

28. In choosing to pursue a military career Mr. Kalaç was accepting of his own accord a system of military discipline that by its very nature implied the possibility of placing on certain of the rights and freedoms of members of the armed forces limitations incapable of being imposed on civilians. . . . States may adopt for their armies disciplinary regulations forbidding this or that type of conduct, in particular an attitude inimical to an established order reflecting the requirements of military service.

29. It is not contested that the applicant, within the limits imposed by the requirements of military life, was able to fulfil the obligations which constitute the normal forms through which a Muslim practises his religion. For example, he was in particular permitted to pray five times a day and to perform his other

religious duties, such as keeping the fast of Ramadan and attending Friday prayers at the mosque.

30. The Supreme Military Council's order was, moreover, not based on Group Captain Kalaç's religious opinions and beliefs or the way he had performed his religious duties but on his conduct and attitude. . . . According to the Turkish authorities, this conduct breached military discipline and infringed the principle of secularism.

31. The Court accordingly concludes that the applicant's compulsory retirement did not amount to an interference with the right guaranteed by Article 9 since it was not prompted by the way the applicant manifested his religion.

There has therefore been no breach of Article 9.

COMMENTS AND QUESTIONS

1. If there was no interference with Kalaç's Article 9 rights because his compulsory retirement "was not prompted by the way the applicant manifested his religion," doesn't it follow that the compulsory retirement was prompted by his inner beliefs (i.e., his alleged adherence to the Suleyman sect and his insufficient belief in secularism), and thus should be entitled to the arguably greater absolute protections of the internal forum?
2. Which gives greater deference to the special needs of the military, the *Goldman* or the *Kalaç* court?

3. Conscientious Objection and Alternative Military Service

Conscientious objection to military service appears to be shifting from a contested to an accepted right. The UN Human Rights Committee has noted, "The [ICCPR] does not explicitly refer to a right of conscientious objection, but the Committee believes that such a right can be derived from article 18, inasmuch as the obligation to use lethal force may seriously conflict with the freedom of conscience and the right to manifest one's religion or belief."[15]

Because the United States currently has an all-volunteer army, the core question of a conscientious right to be exempted from mandatory military service is less likely to occur, although some interesting cases have arisen where individuals who have joined the military subsequently experience a change of religious beliefs that lead them to become conscientious objectors while in the military. Not surprisingly, perhaps, these cases tend to have arisen at times when there is a shift from peacetime to wartime mobilization.

A right to substitute alternative service for service in the ordinary military has become standard in many systems that continue to have conscription systems. In a number of countries, this is now anchored in constitutional provisions. For example, Article 4(3) of the German Basic Law provides, "No one may be compelled against his conscience to render military service involving the use of arms." Further, Article 12a(2) states, "A person who refuses, on grounds of conscience, to render war service involving the use of arms may be required to

15. UN Human Rights Committee, General Comment No. 22 (48), 20 July 1993, UN Doc. CCPR/C/21/Rev.1/Add.4 (1993), reprinted in UN Doc. HRI/GEN/1/ Rev.1 at 35 (1994).

render a substitute service. The duration of such substitute service shall not exceed the duration of military service." Judicial interpretation has held that there can also be conscientious objection to the use of arms in times of peace. Also, the notion that substitute service cannot be longer than regular service has been stretched so that the regular alternative service can be as long as the combination of basic training and reserve service for normal conscripts. There are substantial variations in the ways that countries address alternative service. These are addressed on the Web Supplement.

BAYATYAN V. ARMENIA

European Court of Human Rights, App. No. 23459/03 (Grand Chamber 7 July 2011)

[Vahan Bayatan is an Armenian national. A Jehovah's Witness convert in 1996, he sought to be excluded from the draft in Armenia on the basis of his religious belief. Following his non-compliance, the Erebunis District Prosecutor brought criminal proceedings against him.]

. . . 110. In this respect, the Court notes that Article 9 does not explicitly refer to a right to conscientious objection. However, it considers that opposition to military service, where it is motivated by a serious and insurmountable conflict between the obligation to serve in the army and a person's conscience or his deeply and genuinely held religious or other beliefs, constitutes a conviction or belief of sufficient cogency, seriousness, cohesion and importance to attract the guarantees of Article 9. Whether and to what extent objection to military service falls within the ambit of that provision must be assessed in the light of the particular circumstances of the case. . . .

111. The applicant in the present case is a member of Jehovah's Witnesses, a religious group whose beliefs include the conviction that service, even unarmed, within the military is to be opposed. The Court therefore has no reason to doubt that the applicant's objection to military service was motivated by his religious beliefs, which were genuinely held and were in serious and insurmountable conflict with his obligation to perform military service. In this sense, and contrary to the Government's claim[], the applicant's situation must be distinguished from a situation that concerns an obligation which has no specific conscientious implications in itself, such as a general tax obligation. . . .

(a) Whether there was an interference

112. The Court considers that the applicant's failure to report for military service was a manifestation of his religious beliefs. His conviction for draft evasion therefore amounted to an interference with his freedom to manifest his religion as guaranteed by Article 9 § 1. Such interference will be contrary to Article 9 unless it is "prescribed by law", pursues one or more of the legitimate aims set out in paragraph 2 and is "necessary in a democratic society". . . .

(b) Whether the interference was justified

(i) Prescribed by law

113. The Court reiterates its settled case-law that the expression "prescribed by law" requires firstly that the impugned measure should have a basis in domestic law. It also refers to the quality of the law in question, requiring that it be accessible to the persons concerned and formulated with sufficient precision to enable them—if need be, with appropriate advice—to foresee, to a degree that is reasonable in the circumstances, the consequences which a given action may entail and to regulate their conduct.

114. The Court observes that the applicant's conviction was based on Article 75 of the then Criminal Code, which prescribed the penalty for draft evasion. It further observes that at the time of the applicant's conviction there was no law on alternative service and both the Armenian Constitution and the Military Liability Act required all male citizens aged between 18 and 27, unless found to be physically unfit, to perform military service. The Court considers that these provisions, which it is undisputed were accessible, were couched in sufficiently clear terms. . . .

[In view of its finding regarding necessity, the Court elected not to give formal resolution to the prescribed by law question.]

(ii) Legitimate aim

117. The Government referred to the need to protect public order and, implicitly, the rights of others. The Court, however, does not find the Government's reference to these aims to be convincing in the circumstances of the case, especially taking into account that at the time of the applicant's conviction the Armenian authorities had already pledged to introduce alternative civilian service and, implicitly, to refrain from convicting new conscientious objectors. It, nevertheless, considers it unnecessary to determine conclusively whether the aims referred to by the Government were legitimate within the meaning of Article 9 § 2, since, even assuming that they were, the interference was in any event incompatible with that provision for the reasons set out below.

(iii) Necessary in a democratic society

118. . . . [R]eligion is one of the foundations of a "democratic society" within the meaning of the Convention. This freedom is, in its religious dimension, one of the most vital elements that go to make up the identity of believers and their conception of life, but it is also a precious asset for atheists, agnostics, sceptics and the unconcerned. The pluralism indissociable from a democratic society, which has been dearly won over the centuries, depends on it. That freedom entails, *inter alia*, freedom to hold or not to hold religious beliefs and to practise or not to practise a religion

119. While religious freedom is primarily a matter of individual conscience, it also implies, *inter alia*, freedom to manifest one's religion, alone and in private, or in community with others, in public and within the circle of those whose faith one shares. . . .

120. The Court has frequently emphasised the State's role as the neutral and impartial organiser of the exercise of various religions, faiths and beliefs, and stated that this role is conducive to public order, religious harmony and tolerance in a democratic society. The State's duty of neutrality and impartiality is incompatible with any power on the State's part to assess the legitimacy of religious beliefs or the ways in which those beliefs are expressed.

121. According to its settled case-law, the Court leaves to States party to the Convention a certain margin of appreciation in deciding whether and to what extent an interference is necessary. This margin of appreciation goes hand in hand with European supervision embracing both the law and the decisions applying it. The Court's task is to determine whether the measures taken at national level were justified in principle and proportionate . . . .

122. In order to determine the scope of the margin of appreciation in the present case the Court must take into account what is at stake, namely the need to maintain true religious pluralism, which is vital to the survival of a democratic society (see *Manoussakis and Others* and *Metropolitan Church of Bessarabia and Others*). The Court may also have regard to any consensus and common values emerging from the practices of the States parties to the Convention . . . .

123. The Court has already pointed out above that almost all the member States of the Council of Europe which ever had or still have compulsory military service have introduced alternatives to such service in order to reconcile the possible conflict between individual conscience and military obligations. Accordingly, a State which has not done so enjoys only a limited margin of appreciation and must advance convincing and compelling reasons to justify any interference. In particular, it must demonstrate that the interference corresponds to a "pressing social need". . . .

124. The Court cannot overlook the fact that, in the present case, the applicant, as a member of Jehovah's Witnesses, sought to be exempted from military service not for reasons of personal benefit or convenience but on the ground of his genuinely held religious convictions. Since no alternative civilian service was available in Armenia at the material time, the applicant had no choice but to refuse to be drafted into the army if he was to stay faithful to his convictions and, by doing so, to risk criminal sanctions. Thus, the system existing at the material time imposed on citizens an obligation which had potentially serious implications for conscientious objectors while failing to allow any conscience-based exceptions and penalising those who, like the applicant, refused to perform military service. In the Court's opinion, such a system failed to strike a fair balance between the interests of society as a whole and those of the applicant. It therefore considers that the imposition of a penalty on the applicant, in circumstances where no allowances were made for the exigencies of his conscience and beliefs, could not be considered a measure necessary in a democratic society. Still less can it be seen as necessary taking into account that there existed viable and effective alternatives capable of accommodating the competing interests, as demonstrated by the experience of the overwhelming majority of the European States.

125. The Court admits that any system of compulsory military service imposes a heavy burden on citizens. It will be acceptable if it is shared in an equitable manner and if exemptions from this duty are based on solid and

convincing grounds. The Court has already found that the applicant had solid and convincing reasons justifying his exemption from military service. It further notes that the applicant never refused to comply with his civic obligations in general. On the contrary, he explicitly requested the authorities to provide him with the opportunity to perform alternative civilian service. Thus, the applicant was prepared, for convincing reasons, to share the societal burden equally with his compatriots engaged in compulsory military service by performing alternative service. In the absence of such an opportunity, the applicant had to serve a prison sentence instead.

COMMENTS AND QUESTIONS

1. The international instruments adopted shortly after World War II did not explicitly recognize a right to conscientious objection to military service. Has such a right emerged in the meantime? How does this type of process occur?
2. How broad should the right to conscientious objection be? Does it extend beyond traditional religious views to secular *Weltanschauungen*? *See Welsh v. United States*, 398 U.S. 333 (1970). To personalized religious views? *Cf. Thomas v. Review Board*, 450 U.S. 707 (1981) (sustaining claim of Jehovah's Witness whose views were stricter than some of his co-religionists)? To selective conscientious objection? *See Gilette v. United States*, 401 U.S. 437 (1971).
3. How accommodating must alternative service be? Can states require that those choosing the alternative service option serve longer than those accepting the risks of normal military life? Has an adequate alternative been provided if the alternative service options are all under the military control and direction of the military?
4. On 3 June 2014, the European Court of Human Rights in *Buldu and Others v. Turkey* (App. No. 14017/08) unanimously concluded that Turkey had violated the European Convention when it convicted four Jehovah's Witnesseses in Turkey for their conscientious objection because of deeply held religious beliefs to military service: "The measures taken against the applicants . . . are an interference that was not necessary in a democratic society within the meaning of Article 9 of the Convention."

Additional Web Resources:	Additional cases and materials on conscientious objection and an overview of differing approaches to alternative military service

CHAPTER 8

RESPONDING TO RELIGIOUS EXTREMISM

I. INTRODUCTION

While legal protection of religion is clearly essential in modern societies, tension can arise between protecting religious rights and protecting society from harms that can emanate from religious groups. Are some groups so problematic that their functioning ought to be restricted in the public interest? The answer in the twenty-first century is without a doubt yes. Systematic persecution, violence perpetrated against individuals and religious minorities, acts of terrorism, mass kidnappings, even genocide, undertaken by groups self-identified as religious or as acting from religious motives, have had an incalculable impact upon global society.

Yet it is not easy to decide when or under what circumstances such groups should be restricted or stopped, for the greater good of all humanity. Such a decision may be prefaced with a caution: No one should use religion as a pretext for harm, or perpetrate violence in the name of religion. On the other hand, the fundamental right of religious freedom may be jeopardized when a self-described religious group is classified as sufficiently dangerous to justify the withdrawal of religious freedom protections. In egregious cases of harm or violation of rights and human dignity, it seems clear that society must act to attempt to curb unfettered "manifestations" of religious belief. But care is needed to avoid the impact of prejudices that are all too often involved when new or unfamiliar religious groups are labeled as dangerous simply because they are new or unfamiliar. There is also a risk that societal concerns about security can be overbroad and can place unnecessary and even counterproductive restrictions on freedom, including religious freedom.

Harmful misunderstandings can arise simply from terminology. The very act of labeling may constitute persecution, or may be used by others as a justification for it. For example, the term "extremist religion" is loaded with pejorative normative content. One person's extremism may be another person's orthodoxy. For some people the term "fundamentalist" carries connotations of being extreme and dangerous, while for others it implies true, basic belief. In this area, as in so many others, the use of language and labels carries significant implications, including fundamental misunderstanding. Consider for example the English words *cult* and *sect*. In the United States the term "cult" is generally viewed as having far more negative, even sinister connotations, compared with "sect," which might connote merely a harmless offshoot or other small belief group. In countries with Latin-based languages, however, *culte* or *culto* comes closer to meaning simply "religion" or "worship," while *secte, setto, secta* tend to be pejorative, carrying many of the same negative connotations as "cult" does for English-speakers.

Before the proliferation of international terrorism in the twenty-first century, considerable attention was paid to policy issues surrounding new ethical, spiritual, or religious groups, referred to as new religious movements (NRMs) to avoid the pejorative connotations of the terms "cult" or "sect." Professor Eileen Barker, a leading sociologist in this field, has raised fundamental questions: What is it about new religious movements that make them peculiarly susceptible to such discrimination? Is there is something intrinsic to an NRM that invites others to feel the need to treat them as deserving a special kind of control? On the other hand, is there something about societies that encourages them to place restrictions on the freedom of new religions?[1]

Barker sees shared characteristics among NRMs: An "atypical" (young), "first-generation" membership under the influence of a charismatic leader teaching a set of clear, if dichotomous beliefs, which might lead both to withdrawal from mainstream society and to active rebellion against it. A proliferation of new religious movements in the 1970s led to fears that young people were being "brainwashed." Such brainwashing, it was thought, might be undone by "deprogramming" to "cure" people of their "crazy" beliefs.[2]

Societal concern to protect or reclaim misguided youth can be both caring and self-interested. Of critical urgency in the terrorism age are concerns about how to prevent or cure radicalization of people—many of them young, disenfranchised, idealistic, angry—who will strap bombs to their chests or drive vehicles into crowds, apparently without fear of death themselves, while invoking the name of their God and citing holy texts to motivate their killing of innocent people. How do we counter extremism when the extremists see their behavior as righteous zeal?

This chapter explores the boundaries of legitimate limitations on manifestations of religion or belief in the context of "extreme" or even "dangerous" religious groups. How do the limitation provisions discussed in Chapter 6 apply? Are the standard limitations adequate for the problems posed by these distinctive groups? When might an extremist group with avowed religious motives justifiably be considered beyond the protections societies offer for those motivated by religious belief?

---

1. *See,* Eileen Barker, Why the Cults? New Religious Movements and Freedom of Religion or Belief, in *Facilitating Freedom of Religion or Belief: A Deskbook* 571, 571–580 (Tore Lindholm, W. Cole Durham, Jr., & Bahia G. Tahzib-Lie, eds., Martinus Nijhoff 2004).

2. *Id.*

II. TARGETING "DANGEROUS" SECTS AND CULTS

A. THE UNITED STATES

EXPERIENCE WITH THE (OLD) CULT AWARENESS NETWORK

The Cult Awareness Network (CAN) was founded shortly after the high-profile deaths of more than 900 members of the Peoples Temple of the Disciples of Christ Agricultural Project (led by Marxist and self-styled Methodist pastor Jim Jones) in the "utopian" community of Jonestown, Guyana in 1978.[3] The "Jonestown massacre"—mostly leader-induced suicides (the origin of the expression "drink the kool-aid") but also related murders (including of more than 300 children, a US congressman, and three members of the media)—raised serious concerns about the potential dangers of influential new religious movements. (Peoples Temple was a tax-exempt religious organization in the United States.)

CAN was founded shortly after the Jonestown tragedy with the stated purpose of providing information about "dangerous cults"—groups that were accused of using mind control and brainwashing to unduly influence their followers. In reality, CAN was heavily involved in connecting people who disapproved of the religious beliefs of a loved one with "deprogrammers."

Eventually, given the unsavory reputations of many practitioners, deprogrammers adopted new euphemisms for their roles, such as "interventionists" and "exit counselors." Such terms may legitimately apply to voluntary discussions among NRM members and their families guided by a trained counselor, or they may represent a linguistic dodge used by coercive deprogrammers. But whatever the terminology, the purpose of the activity is to "exit" members from their associations in non-approved religions, often by forceful means.[4] "To equate dramatic religious conversions with brainwashing," says scholar Douglas Laycock, "is to declare war on the free exercise of religion."[5]

Even though CAN's official policy forbade involuntary deprogramming, there is evidence that CAN was aware of the violent and coercive tactics used by deprogrammers to whom they referred people.[6]

CAN used claims of brainwashing and the label of dangerous cult to profit from the efforts of these deprogrammers.[7] As CAN became more powerful, the list of organizations it kept records on expanded to include, by the mid-1990s, more than 1,500 groups, including Amish, Amway, Baha'i, Catholics, Lutherans, and *Teen* Magazine.[8] In the mid-1990s, many members of groups targeted by CAN took legal action against them. One such case was brought by an 18-year-old who had been kidnapped by deprogrammers. He eventually escaped and brought a tort

---

3. *See e.g.,* Chris Higgins, Stop Saying 'Drink the Kool-Aid', *The Atlantic*, 8 November 2012.

4. Douglas Laycock, *Religious Liberty, Volume 2: The Free Exercise Clause* 748 (W.B. Eerdmans 2010).

5. Ansen Shupe and Susan E. Darnell, CAN We Hardly Knew Ye: Sex, Drugs, Deprogrammers' Kickbacks, and Corporate Crime in the (Old) Cult Awareness Network, paper presented at the 2000 meeting of the Society for the Scientific Study of Religion.

6. *Scott v. Ross*, 140 F.3d 1275, 1282 (9th Cir. 1998).

7. Shupe and Darnell, *supra* note 5.

8. For a complete list of organizations monitored by CAN, *see id.* at Appendix B.

suit against his deprogrammer that resulted in a judgment of more than $1 million against CAN.[9] As a result of this case and many others, CAN was forced to declare bankruptcy.

The story of CAN's rise and ultimate downfall illustrates some of the problems with letting any one group dictate which religious organizations are acceptable. CAN took advantage of fears, some of them undeniably legitimate, that existed about cults and brainwashing at the time, as well as the tendency of many Americans to overreact to the use of the word "cult." Examples of the dangerous effects of this way of thinking can be seen in the case studies that follow.

COMMENTS AND QUESTIONS

1. To what extent should an organization such as CAN be protected in its activities on freedom of expression and association grounds?
2. In a number of European countries anti-cult groups receive substantial government funding. How does the picture change if the government itself establishes and funds such an organization?
3. The United States government's interaction with an apocalyptic Christian group in Texas in 1993 illustrates the tragic consequences possible when government intervention is not guided and restrained.

NOTE ON WACO AND THE BRANCH DAVIDIANS

In the early 1990s a religious group known as the Branch Davidians built a compound near Waco, Texas, to anticipate the imminent end of the world. The group's leader, Vernon Wayne Howell, who called himself David Koresh, claimed to have prophetic powers. He took "spiritual wives," including married women and some children reportedly as young as eleven. With evidence that the Davidians were stockpiling illegal firearms and suspecting that Koresh was sexually abusing children, agents of the United States Bureau of Alcohol, Tobacco, Firearms and Explosives (ATF) and the FBI obtained warrants to search the compound. ATF agents approached the compound to serve the warrants on 28 February 1993 and ultimately exchanged fire with the Davidians, who believed the agents were encroaching on their property illegally. In the firefight, four ATF agents and six Davidians were killed and 32 persons from both sides were wounded. After the fight, the Davidians refused to leave the compound, and a two-month standoff ensued. FBI hostage negotiators corresponded with Koresh, but the negotiations did not progress. Early in the negotiations, Koresh agreed to release the church members if the negotiators would broadcast a religious videotape he had made. After the videotape was broadcast, Koresh reneged on his promise and claimed that God told him not to allow the church members to leave. It is important to note that the church members likely did not see themselves as hostages but rather as righteous followers of God amidst apocalyptic doom. In an attempt to smoke the members out of the compound, an FBI hostage rescue team injected "tear gas" through windows. Upon sensing the gas, group members apparently decided to start a fire to burn the compound down. The conflagration killed at least 74 people, including 21 children and two expectant mothers.

9. *Scott*, 140 F.3d at 1280.

When briefed by the FBI on the deteriorating conditions of the siege in Waco, President Bill Clinton was concerned about insuring the safety of the children in the compound and negotiating the peaceful surrender of Koresh and his followers. But the site commander, Jeffrey Jamar, instead formulated an "emergency assault plan" to force the group from the compound. Environmentalist and civil rights lawyer Albert Bates describes the result.

ALBERT K. BATES, WHAT REALLY HAPPENED AT WACO? "CULT" OR SET-UP?

Communities Magazine (Fall 1995)

Jamar's weapon of choice was not tear gas—not even a gas at all. It was CS (O-chlorobenzalmalononitrile), a fine particulate banned from warfare by the Chemical Weapons Convention. Use for domestic law enforcement is against international law and numerous UN human rights conventions. Military branches which use CS are advised by the label that it is lethal in closed areas and should never be used indoors. Moreover, CS in methylene chloride aerosol is extremely flammable, and can be explosive in closed spaces. When burned or mixed with water, it produces a witches' brew of by-products, including hydrogen chloride, carbon monoxide, and hydrogen cyanide. . . .

FBI's behavioral scientists arrived from Washington and advised that the usual strategy—coupling negotiations with increasing tactical pressure—was inapplicable, and that this strategy could "eventually be counterproductive and could result in the loss of life. Every time his followers sense movement of tactical personnel, Koresh validates his prophetic warnings that an attack is forthcoming and they are going to have to defend themselves."

The Hostage Rescue Team (HRT) called upon two regular consultants from the FBI's National Center for the Analysis of Violent Crime to analyze Koresh. Despite having no expertise in religious charismatics, they recommended, "Since these people fear law enforcement, [FBI should] offer them the opportunity of surrendering to a neutral party of their choosing accompanied by appropriate law enforcement personnel."

Jamar rejected the advice[, instead favoring] increasing tactical pressure[and viewing] the group's religious beliefs as a convenient cover. He continued to refer to the people in the compound as hostage[s.]

Dutifully, the FBI's behavioral scientists redrew their recommendations to suggest ways of increasing the discomfort levels inside the church including interrupting water and power, moving equipment and manpower suddenly, controlling television and radio reception, and cutting off negotiations.

JAMES D. TABOR AND EUGENE V. GALLAGHER, WHY WACO? CULTS AND THE BATTLE FOR RELIGIOUS FREEDOM IN AMERICA

Univ. of California Press 1995, 3–4, 6, 10–11

On the very evening following the initial Sunday raid by the BATF, Koresh, who had been seriously wounded, spoke several times by live telephone hookup over Dallas radio station KRLD and CNN cable television. Koresh began, in those gripping interviews, the first of hundreds of hours of explanations, based on his understanding of the biblical apocalyptic significance of the situation in which he found himself. His last direct communication with anyone other than government agents was an impromptu conversation with the station manager Charlie Serafin over KRLD radio at 1:50 A.M. the next morning. In those live broadcasts Koresh offered the key to the Branch Davidians' biblical understanding of events. Unfortunately, neither the FBI agents in charge nor the myriad of advisers upon whom they relied could comprehend their perspective . . . .

Listening carefully to what Koresh said in those live interviews over KRLD and CNN, a person familiar with the biblical texts could have perceived the situation in wholly different terms from the government's "hostage rescue." For the Branch Davidians, no one was a hostage. The only "rescue" they needed was from the government itself. In their view, the federal agents represented an evil government system, referred to in the book of Revelation as "Babylon." The idea of "surrendering to proper authority," as the government demanded throughout the next seven weeks, was absolutely out of the question for these believers unless or until they became convinced it was what God willed. As they saw it, their group had been wantonly attacked and slaughtered by government agents whom they understood to be in opposition to both God and his anointed prophet David Koresh. Their fate was now in God's hands.

The Waco situation could have been handled differently and possibly resolved peacefully. This is not unfounded speculation or wishful thinking. It is the considered opinion of the lawyers who spent the most time with the Davidians during the siege and of various scholars of religion who understand biblical apocalyptic belief systems such as that of the Branch Davidians. There was a way to communicate with these biblically oriented people, but it had nothing to do with hostage rescue or counterterrorist tactics. Indeed, such a strategy was being pursued, with FBI cooperation, by Phillip Arnold of the Reunion Institute in Houston and James Tabor of the University of North Carolina at Charlotte . . . . Arnold and Tabor worked in concert with the lawyers Dick DeGuerin and Jack Zimmerman, who spent a total of twenty hours inside the Mount Carmel center between March 29 and April 4, communicating directly with Koresh and his main spokesperson, Steve Schneider. Unfortunately, [by the time these attempts] began to bear positive results, decisions had already been made in Washington to convince Attorney General Janet Reno to end the siege by force . . . . What the authorities apparently never perceived is that Koresh's preaching was to him and to his followers, the *only* matter of substance and that a "surrender" could only be worked out through dialogue within the biblical framework in which the Branch Davidians lived.

QUESTIONS

1. If you had been advising the officials in the Waco situation, are there steps you might have taken to avoid the tragedy that occurred?
2. How should free exercise principles apply in a situation such as the encounter with the Branch Davidians? Are law enforcement concerns so compelling that they override any arguable free exercise claim? To what extent are law enforcement officials obligated to consider and implement "less restrictive

alternatives"? In what ways does free exercise guide the calculus of public officials charged with responding to such situations?

B. CHINA AND THE FALUN GONG

Falun Gong, "the practice of the wheel of the Dharma," is a breathing exercise group that claims to have inherited the wisdom of Buddhism, Taoism, and Chinese qigong. Founded in 1992 by Li Hongzhi ("Master Li"), the group advances Falun Dafa (the Great Law), a spiritual movement based on the motto of "truth, benevolence, and forbearance" that aims to cultivate the practitioner's mind and body. Falun Gong's philosophy of self-improvement involves participation in five exercises; three involve physical movement and two consist of stationary meditation. Among practitioners' many beliefs is that illness is the result not of physical viruses or bacteria but of karma, and thus modern medical techniques are ineffective for either diagnosing or treating disease. Practitioners generally reject the notion that the group is a religion, cult, or sect.

ANNE S.Y. CHEUNG, IN SEARCH OF A THEORY OF CULT AND FREEDOM OF RELIGION IN CHINA: THE CASE OF FALUN GONG

13 *Pac. Rim L. & Pol'y* 1-30 (2004)

[In] July 1999, the Chinese government [PRC] . . . introduced a series of legislative reforms and judicial instructions to outlaw cult activities. Falun Gong was eventually banned in October 1999, and by the end of 2002, tens of thousands of the group's followers were reportedly detained. . . .

Human rights groups often perceive the PRC's crackdown as a serious violation of freedom of religion despite the fact that Falun Gong denies being a religious group, and that Chinese authorities consider Falun Gong a cult rather than a religion . . . .

This Article argues that the Chinese government suppresses groups like the Falun Gong in part because of the rival ideology to state power that they represent . . . . [In 1999 Falun Gong, with more than 70 million followers, exceeded the membership of the Chinese Communist Party (CCP, then at 63 million), making it the largest "religious" community in China after Chinese Buddhism.[10]] In labeling certain groups as cults, the Chinese government condemns the nature of these groups, and announces that they lead others on a wrong path, blinding their followers to impartial and sound judgment . . . .

The fundamental implication of the Chinese government's labeling of an entity as a cult is that the group's religion becomes deemed illegal or immoral. Thus, when a group is officially labeled a cult, it is indirectly and intrinsically stripped of its status as a religious entity, and therefore of its right to religious freedom . . . . The state asserts that it has the right to intervene if a religious group distorts one's rational reasoning and affects one's exercise of mind. From this perspective, when there is a conflict between the two categories of freedom, freedom of belief prevails over freedom of religion . . . .

10. Special Report: *The Battle for China's Spirit: Falun Gong* (Freedom House 2017).

Cults and the Challenges They Pose to Religious Liberties . . .

The problem of Falun Gong is only a recent instance of the ruling Chinese authority adopting an intolerant stance towards an emergent religious group. This approach can partly be attributed to patterns in Chinese history and Marxist-Communist teachings that disavow the existence of a transcendent spiritual realm. One common ambition shared by Chinese rulers, ancient and new, is to contain and control new religious groups, and if necessary, to uproot them in their early formative days. The [CCP's] response to Falun Gong is one consistent with China's experience.

Scholars have argued that the CCP's desire to gain total control over religious activity stems from a deep-rooted fear and keen awareness that religious groups, especially quasi-religious or popular religious groups, often have potentially subversive power. The danger of religious groups to the political order is particularly worrisome because spiritual leaders and religious beliefs have played powerful roles in mobilizing rebel forces. Further, protests often take the form of popular "cross-class" and "cross-territorial" campaigns. Religious groups do not merely advocate for emancipation from the material world, but also often promote an alternative order of righting wrongs in present social systems.

The perceived threat of religion within China pre-dates the Maoist era. Chinese history is replete with examples of uprisings with religious overtones that are often motivated by political concerns . . . . Since the Ming Dynasty, cults and quasi-religious sects have often been banned under Chinese criminal law.

One may wonder why the PRC . . . would allow any religious freedom. It is indeed true that from a Marxist perspective, religion is the "opiate of the masses" and that religion is antagonistic to the fundamental nature of socialist atheism. However, realizing that it is impossible to eliminate all religious beliefs, the CCP conceded that religion must be tolerated as an inevitable consequence of human civilization and of China's long historical march to a communist utopian state. Hence, boundaries of tolerance are clearly marked. Religion is allowed only if it does not disturb political stability and economic development. As early as 1982, before the problem of Falun Gong arose, the CCP announced that religion should always be in line with Marxism, Leninism, and Maoism, and subject to the approval of the CCP leadership and to registration by government officials . . . .

Given concerns about social stability and the ideological coherence of the Marxist state, the rise of Falun Gong from a seemingly benign group founded in 1992 to a well-organized and highly efficient force in 1999 alarmed the CCP leadership . . . . After seven years in existence, the Falun Gong made headlines on April 25, 1999. Ten thousand followers gathered for twelve hours outside Zhongnanhai, the Chinese leadership compound, to protest an academic journal article that warned of the dangers posed by PRC cults and the mounting pressure from the government. China's top leaders were immediately alarmed because the protest was the largest systematic gathering since the 1989 Tiananmen student movement. What was more worrying was that Falun Gong was believed to have attracted tens of millions of followers, with a network extending from the PRC to the United States, Canada, Australia and Europe. Falun Gong arguably represents the greatest internal threat that the Chinese government has faced in the post-Mao period . . . . To the authorities, it does not truly matter whether Falun Gong is a religious sect or a qigong (breathing exercise) group; in the eyes of the government, so long as Falun Gong is perceived as having subversive potential, it must be uprooted . . . .

In November 1999, the Supreme People's Court notified all Chinese courts that all judicial officers should implement the NPC interpretation regarding heretical organizations. On November 30, 1999, the first case against Falun Gong members came to trial . . . . The four defendants were sentenced to two to fourteen years imprisonment for organizing illegal gatherings and spreading Falun Gong doctrine. On December 26, 1999, harsher punishment was passed by the Beijing Intermediate Court, when the four top organizers of Falun Gong were sentenced to seven to eighteen years imprisonment. All of the defendants were CCP members and were charged with "obstructing justice, causing human deaths in the process of organizing a cult and illegally obtaining state secrets." Falun Gong estimated that between July 1999 until the end of 2001, 6000 members were sentenced without trial, 100,000 were sent to re-education camps, and several thousands were sent to mental asylums . . . .

The [CCP]'s reaction further proves that a group's doctrine is often irrelevant because the state defines a group's "evilness" according to its ability to challenge the established authority . . . . What Falun Gong challenges is not orthodox religious understanding, but the CCP leadership.

* * *

Since 2004, when Professor Cheung wrote the article excerpted above, activities of Falun Gong in China, and consequent persecution of practitioners, have not abated. See the following excerpt from a 2017 Special Report by the US watchdog organization Freedom House:

- **Survival:** Despite a 17-year Chinese Communist Party (CCP) campaign to eradicate the spiritual group, millions of people in China continue to practice Falun Gong, including many individuals who took up the discipline after the repression began. . . .
- **Ongoing large-scale persecution:** Falun Gong practitioners across China are subject to widespread surveillance, arbitrary detention, imprisonment, and torture, and they are at a high risk of extrajudicial execution. Freedom House independently verified 933 cases of Falun Gong adherents sentenced to prison terms of up to 12 years between January 1, 2013, and June 1, 2016, often for exercising their right to freedom of expression in addition to freedom of religion. This is only a portion of those sentenced, and thousands more are believed to be held at various prisons and extralegal detention centers.
- **Cracks in the crackdown:** Despite the continued campaign, repression appears to have declined in practice in some locales. . . . [T]he purge and imprisonment of former security czar Zhou Yongkang and other officials associated with the campaign as part of Xi [Jinping]'s anticorruption drive, together with Falun Gong adherents' persistent efforts to educate and discourage police from persecuting them, have had an impact.
- **Economic exploitation:** The party-state invests hundreds of millions of dollars annually in the campaign to crush Falun Gong, while

simultaneously engaging in exploitative and lucrative forms of abuse against practitioners, including extortion and prison labor. Available evidence suggests that forced extraction of organs from Falun Gong detainees for sale in transplant operations has occurred on a large scale and may be continuing.

COMMENTS AND QUESTIONS

1. From the point of view of a government such as that of China, which kind of organization poses a greater risk to society, one like Aum Shinrikyo, discussed below, or one like Falun Gong? Why?
2. There is a tendency to think of security concerns and the religious freedom of "dangerous" groups as being in inevitable tension with each other. Yet at a general level it is clear that religious freedom norms emerged at least in part to reduce risks of religious warfare and to provide a secure basis for a stable and peaceful society. When should security concerns override religious freedom protections? Are there ways that religious freedom protections can enhance religious freedom? Consider these questions as you look at the following commentary on developments in Russia beginning in 2016.

C. RUSSIA AND THE JEHOVAH'S WITNESSES

The "Religious Organization of Jehovah's Witnesses in the Soviet Union" was originally registered on 27 March 1991, and the current version of its Charter (designating the organization as "The Administrative Center of Jehovah's Witnesses in Russia") was registered by the Ministry of Justice of the Russian Federation on 29 April 1999. This Charter had been revised to comply with Russian Federal Law No. 125-FZ on the Freedom of Conscience and Religious Associations. On 2 March 2016, the Office of the Prosecutor General of the Russian Federation served a notice on the organization warning it to abstain from prohibited activities. Four months later, changes to Russia's anti-extremism law brought catastrophic consequences for Jehovah's Witnesses and others defined by the new Russian legislation as extremist.

ELIZABETH CLARK, RUSSIA'S NEW ANTI-MISSIONARY LAW IN CONTEXT

Religious Freedom Institute: *Cornerstone Blog*, 30 August 2016

As of [20 July 2016], ordinary Russian citizens and foreigners living in Russia face enormous fines for sharing their beliefs, even if they do so in their own homes. This represents a new level of repression of free speech and civil society in post-Soviet Russia. . . . [B]y imposing restrictions on what religious individuals may say, even in the confines of their own homes, Russia joins the ranks of countries like Vietnam, which similarly bans the sharing of religious beliefs outside of religious facilities. As Mikhail Odintsov, who until recently was responsible for the protection of religious rights in the Russian Federal Ombudsman's office, noted: "In religious policy, we are drawing close to the norms of the Soviet Union."

The July ["Yarovaya"] legislation . . . was styled as a series of amendments to the anti-extremism law. The religion provisions were introduced five days before the second reading and adopted without public input, despite widespread public protest. Although labeled as an anti-extremism law, it can be best understood as part of the ongoing crackdown on civil society in Russia. .... While violence from religious extremists and others is a real concern in Russia, as elsewhere, "extremism" has been a handy label for targeting unpopular groups that pose no threat of violence to the state, such as Russian Orthodox Old Believers and followers of the Turkish theologian Said Nursi.

The increasing repression of civil society combines with widespread fears of predatory foreign religions to make a toxic mix. Since the fall of the Soviet Union, some in Russia have expressed concern about the perception of well-funded foreigners coming in to build their congregations at the expense of Russian Orthodoxy, weakened by the Soviet system. After 70 years of religious persecution and religions being co-opted by the state, this is perhaps understandable. Protecting Russian Orthodoxy, however, has come to be perceived as being aligned with national strategic interests. In 2000, a Russian federal policy statement on national security stated that "[e]nsuring the national security of the Russian Federation also includes the protection of its . . . spiritual and moral heritage" and "includes opposing the negative influence of foreign religious organizations and missionaries."

The Yarovaya law stretches the concept of extremism and conflates it with "national security" protections from [proselytizing]. It is extensive—banning most forms of missionary activity, including the sharing of beliefs in private residences. Missionary activity, defined as "activity of a religious association aimed at disseminating information about its doctrine [including online information sharing] among individuals who are not participants," can only now be carried out by individuals carrying authorization from their religious association and proof of their organization's registration. Authorized representatives may only engage in missionary activities on church property, and the religious activity must be in the region that has regstered the religious organization or group. Proselytizng in residential areas is specifically forbidden, as are attempts to circumvent the law by converting residential premises to non-residential ones for religious use. Individuals who violate the law are subject to fines from 5,000 to 50,000 rubles (up to six weeks' worth of an average salary, or US $780). Organizations are liable for violations of their members and can be fined from 100,000 to 1,000,000 rubles and liquidated. Foreign missionaries are also restricted: they can only be invited into the country by a religious organization, with whom they must have a contract, and representative offices of foreign religious organizations (foreign religions that have not obtained local or national registration) cannot engage in missionary activity.

Parts of the law are vaguely worded and it is unclear how it will be interpreted. The law includes broad bans of all missionary activity that is aimed at "violation of public safety and public order; extremist activity, coercion into destroying the family," "damaging morals," and "motivation of individuals to refuse to fulfil civic duties established by law." Such broad categories leave it impossible for individuals to determine if they are complying. "Refusing to fulfil civic duties," for example, was a catchall used in the Soviet era to jail religious dissidents.

Ambiguities abound. Is it illegal missionary work if the "missionary" does not belong to a registered religious organization? What activities are "church services" or "religious ordinances and ceremonies" (that are permitted in homes) and when do those activities become illegal "missionary work"? Several individuals in various regions have already been prosecuted under the law, and the precedents suggest that the law will be interpreted broadly. A Ghanian citizen was convicted . . . for performing baptisms in a rented sanatorium swimming pool, even though he claimed we was not trying to involve new members. A US independent Baptist preacher was fined . . . for holding a worship service in his home because he allegedly advertised it on the bulletin board of nearby apartment buildings.

. . . The law clearly violates Russian constitutional protections of freedom of speech and religion, as well as Russia's international commitments to religious freedom and free speech. Russian law and international norms all give latitude for laws that would protect the state from credible threats of violence, but by the banning simple sharing of beliefs, the Yarovaya law moves clearly into the core of protected religious speech and harms otherwise law-abiding citizens. Mikhail Fedotov, the chair of the Russian Presidential Council on Civil Society Development and Human Rights, has personally protested to Putin that the law would "create unjustified and excessive restrictions on the freedom of conscience of believers of all religions, and encroach upon the fundamental constitutional principle of non-interference by the state in the internal arrangements of religious associations."

Writing in August 2016, Clark noted that constitutional challenges to the new law were in the works, and "one can still hope that the law will be struck down." A year later, however, the application of the law was in full swing.[11] In 2017, claiming that the Jehovah's Witnesses continued to engage in extremist activities after the notice of March 2016 to abstain, the Ministry of Justice applied to the Supreme Court for liquidation of the organization "on the grounds that activities of the Organization and the 365 religious organizations of Jehovah's Witnesses incorporated into the structure of the Organization are carried out in violation of the charter goals, tasks, and legislation of the Russian Federation, including the Federal Law No. 114-FZ, of 25 July 2002 on Combating Extremist Activity."

In support of this claim, the Ministry of Justice pointed to the fact that the organization and its related local organizations disseminated various materials published by the Watch Tower Bible and Tract Society of New York and various other Jehovah's Witness institutions that had been declared extremist "due to the fact that they contain information inciting religious discord, that they propagandize exclusivity, and that they promote the superiority and inferiority of citizens based on their religious affiliation." The materials held to be extremist included Russian issues of the magazines "Awake" and "The Watchtower" that are standard Jehovah's Witness publications used around the world. Jehovah's Witness websites were also registered as "extremist" under the anti-extremism law. A total of 95 publications were declared "extremist."

The Ministry of Justice also submitted information that the central organization directly participates in the funding of local units of the Jehovah's Witnesses, and noted that eight such local units had already been liquidated

11. *See* Victoria Arnold, Russia: One Year of "Anti-missionary" Punishments, 8 August 2017, and Russia: "Anti-missionary" punishments full listing, 9 August 2017, *Forum 18.*

"because of signs of threats to the security of the Russian Federation and signs of targeted extremist activity . . ." before the 2016 notice, and more continued afterwards. The Court also found that the central organization itself exhibited signs of extremist activity, in that it "coordinates and directs the activities of incorporated local religious organizations of Jehovah's Witnesses, imports into the Russian Federation literature either previously declared as extremist or declared as such afterwards, and participates in funding local religious organizations including those that are declared as extremist afterwards." While the Court catalogued a variety of such alleged offenses, it did not identify activities that were in any way different from typical missionary activities of Jehovah's Witnesses familiar in many countries around the world, nor did it provide any indications of particular dangers posed by such activities.

The defendant Jehovah's Witness Organization claimed that the identified materials had been "unfairly identified as extremist owing to their incorrect evaluation in the relevant cases," and that "it takes all reasonable measures to comply with requirements of anti-extremism legislation," and "has never funded extremist activites through the financial support of the charter activities of the local religious organizations," which are separately incorporated and "are not its regional or structural branches." The organization also "guesses that the liquidation of its incorporated branches does not comply with the Russian Federation's legislative demands and its international law obligations and that the claim should therefore be dismissed.

The Supreme Court of the Russian Federation decided to sustain the claims of the Ministry of Justice.

SUPREME COURT OF THE RUSSIAN FEDERATION CASE NO. APKI17-238[12]

20 April 2017 [appealed, rejected, and decision final 17 July 2017]

Y. G. IVANENKO, J., for the Court

. . . According to Art. 28 of the Constitution of the Russian Federation, everyone shall be guaranteed the freedom of conscience and religion, including the right to manifest individually or collectively any religion or not to manifest any religion, and freely to choose, keep and disseminate religious and other convictions and act in accordance with them.

Recognizing everyone's right of association and guaranteeing the activities of public associations (Art. 30), the Constitution of the Russian Federation prohibits establishing and operating public associations whose goals and activities are aimed at forcibly changing the foundation of the constitutional order and at violating the integrity of the Russian Federation, at undermining its security, at creating armed units, and at instigating social, racial, national and religious strife (the fifth part of Art. 13), all forms of limitations of human rights on social, racial, national, language or religious grounds (the second part of Art. 19), propaganda or agitation, which arouses social, racial, national or religious hatred and hostility, as well as propaganda of social, racial, national, religious or linguistic supremacy (the second

12. Unofficial English translation by Dmytro Vovk, used by permission.

part of Art. 29). The exercise of human and civil rights and freedoms must not violate the rights and freedoms of other people (the third part of Art. 17).

Legal relations in the field of human and civil rights to freedom of conscience and freedom of religion as well as the legal status of religious associations, including the particularities of their civil law status, are regulated by the Federal Law on Freedom of Conscience and Religious Associations, which prescribes that religious associations can be established as religious groups or religious organizations. A religious organization is a voluntary association of citizens of the Russian Federation and other persons legally residing in the Russian Federation established for the shared manifestation and dissemination of their faith and registered as a legal entity in the order prescribed by the law. A centralized religious organization is one consisting of at least three local organizations (the first paragraph of Art. 6, the first and fourth paragraphs of Art. 8). . . .

According to the Charter of the Organization, its primary activities are the coordination of preaching activities of Jehovah's Witnesses for the purpose of manifesting and disseminating the faith, including preaching in public and in homes, all necessary and possible informational, legal, consulting and other assistance to Jehovah's Witnesses, the coordination and direction of religious organizations affiliated with the Center, the representation and protection of their interests, providing them with liturgical and religious literature and religious items, assistance in building religious buildings and facilities (objects of religious significance), as well as financial, material, technical, informational, consulting, methodical and other assistance necessary for providing their religious activities, production, purchase, translation, export, import, dissemination of liturgical, religious literature, printed, audio and video materials and other religious items, and the storage and transportation of literature, materials and other religious items . . . .

The general grounds for liquidating a religious organization are prescribed by Art. 14 of the Federal Law on Freedom of Conscience and Religious Associations. In particular, one of the grounds is actions directed to extremist activities (subparagraph 3 of the second paragraph). In addition, a religious organization can be liquidated, and a religious association that does not act as a legal person can be prohibited, under the procedure and on the grounds provided in the Federal Law on Combating Extremist Activity (the seventh paragraph).

Extremist activities (extremism) is a violent transformation of the foundation of the constitutional order and a violation of the integrity of the Russian Federation; the public justification of terrorism or other terroristic activities; the incitement of social, race, national or religious strife; any propaganda of exclusivity touting the supremacy or inferiority of a person based on his or her social, race, ethnic, religious or linguistic identity or attitude towards religion; the violation of rights, freedoms and lawful interests of man and citizen based on social, race, ethnic, religious or linguistic identity or attitude towards religion; . . . the organization and preparation of the said acts, as well as incitement to committing them; financing the above acts or any other support with their organization, preparation and exercise, inter alia, by providing the following educational, printing, material and technical facilities, phone, and other types of communication or providing informational services . . . .

The aforementioned Federal Law prohibits the organization and activities of public and religious associations and other organizations, which goals or activities are aimed at carrying out extremist activities, the dissemination of extremist materials, or their production or storage for the purposes of dissemination (the first part of Art. 9, the first part of Art. 13). . . .

The fourth part of Art. 7 of the Federal Law on Combating Extremist Activity prescribes that in the event of a notice not being appealed in court under the established procedure or not being declared unlawful by a court, and where the respective public or religious association or other organization or its regional or other structural branches fails, within the time limit set in the notice, to eliminate the violations committed constituting grounds for the serving of notice, or where, within 12 months following the date on which notice was served, new facts pointing to the presence of characteristics of extremism within its activities are uncovered, the public or religious association or other organization concerned shall be liquidated under the procedure established by the present Federal Law, and the activity of the respective public or religious association that is not a legal entity shall be banned. . . .

In accordance with the second and the third parts of Art. 9 of the Federal Law on Combating Extremist Activity in the event provided for in the fourth part of Art. 7 of this Federal Law, or in the event of the carrying out by public or religious associations or other organizations or their regional or other structural branches, of extremist activity resulting in a violation of human and civil rights and freedoms, damage to an individual, to citizens' health, the environment, public order, public safety, property, or to the lawful economic interests of individuals and/or legal entities, society and the State, or creating a real threat of causing such damage, the corresponding public or religious association or other organization may be liquidated and the activity of the respective public or religious association that is not a legal entity may be banned by decision of a court on the basis of an application by the Prosecutor General of the Russian Federation or the respective prosecutor subordinate to them, or on the basis of an application by the federal state registration authority or a respective territorial authority thereof.

According to the third part of Art. 55 of the Constitution of the Russian Federation, as well as the second paragraph of Art. 22 of the International Covenant on Civil and Political Rights and the second paragraph of Article 11 of the Convention for the Protection of Human Rights and Fundamental Freedoms, restrictions of the rights of individuals and their associations must be prescribed by federal law for achieving an important public goal (i.e., the protection of the fundamental principles of the constitutional system, morality, health, the rights and lawful interests of other people, and for ensuring the defense of the country, security of the State, and public order), that appears to be necessary in a democratic society (relevant and sufficient, proportionate to an important social aim).

Liquidation of a religious association is a measure of public law liability, as applied upon the claim of a competent body or representative official in administrative judicial proceedings (paragraph 1 of the Ruling of the Plenary Session of the RF Supreme Court of 27 December 2016 No. 64 "On Certain Issues Arising during Consideration of Cases on the Suspension of Activities or

Liquidation of Non-Commercial Organizations, as well as regarding Prohibition of Activities of Public or Religious Associations that Are Not Legal Entities"[13]).

Taking into account the above facts circumstances, the Supreme Court of the Russian Federation recognizes the reasonableness of the request for the liquidation of the centralized religious organization on the basis of the Federal Law on Combating Extremist Activity and considers that the implementation of this exceptional measure will not arbitrarily interfere with and restrict in an unwarranted manner citizens' right of association and freedom of religion.

The case file shows that the facts attesting to the Organization's and its structural branches' extremist activities have been established in the manner prescribed by law annually during the last seven years.

The measures undertaken in this decision to combat extremist activities, including numerous procuratorial actions . . . , the unscheduled inspection of the defendant's activities, as well as organizational measures taken by the Organization itself . . . , did not end the activities showing signs of extremism. Thus the only way to end them is to uphold the claim on liquidating the Organization.

The grounds for this interference are set forth by the federal law to achieve an important public goal—combating extremist activity and, accordingly, protecting human and civil rights and lawful interests, and ensuring the security of the State and public order.

Contrary to the defendant's arguments, this interference is proportionate and necessary in a democratic, law-governed state, insofar as it eliminates violations of rights, freedoms, and lawful interests of an unspecified group of persons, as well as a real threat of causing damage to individuals, the health of the people, to public order, public safety, society and the state, and insofar as it is the only measure to strike a balance between the rights and lawful interests of parties in public-law relations. . . .

Upholding the claim for liquidation meets the requirement of Art. 9-11 of the Convention for the Protection of Human Rights and Fundamental Freedoms, which allows for restrictions of the freedom of association in the interests of national security and public order, in the aim of preventing riots and crimes, for protecting health and morals, or for protecting the rights of others.

The Provisions of Art. 18, 19, and the second of paragraph of Art. 29 of the Universal Declaration of Human Rights, along with Art. 19 and 20 of the International Covenant on Civil and Political Rights do not present an obstacle for an imposed by law ban on any advocacy of ethnic, race or religious hatred, which is an incitement to discrimination, hostility and violence, if it is necessary for ensuring due recognition and respect of rights and freedoms of others and of meeting the just requirements of morality, public order and the general welfare in a democratic society.

As indicated by The Constitutional Court of the Russian Federation, the Shanghai Convention on Combating Terrorism, Separatism, and Extremism (ratified on 15 July 2001) does not prevent State Parties from establishing provisions in their legislation for a wide interpretation of extremism, and obliges them to take such measures as can prove necessary, including, as appropriate, in

13. Available in English at: http://www.supcourt.ru/en/files/16425/.

the field of national legislation, in order to ensure that under no circumstances should terrorism, separatism, and extremism be subject to acquittal based upon exclusionary political, philosophical, ideological, racial, ethnic, religious or any other similar considerations, and that they should entail punishment proportionate to their gravity (the second paragraph of Art. 1, Art. 3). The necessity for the legal limitation of freedom of expression, assembly, and associations for the purpose of fighting extremism is articulated in the Resolution of the Parliamentary Assembly of the Council of Europe 1344 (2003), "Threats Posed to Democracy by Extremist Parties and Movements in Europe" (the Ruling of the RF Constitutional Court of 2 July 2013, No. 1053-O).

The State, in protecting the rights, freedoms, and legal interests of person and citizen, as well as public order and public safety, and in uncovering facts associated with activities identified as extremist, is not obligated to wait for a "cumulative negative effect" when the number of violations showing signs of extremism takes a new quality and these violations no longer result in the threat of violating rights or causing damage, but in real damage to individuals, the health of citizens, environment, public order, public safety, property, the lawful economic interests of individuals and legal entities, society and the state. . . .

In the event of liquidation of a public or a religious association by the court on the grounds provided by this federal law, an association's regional and other structural branches must also be liquidated (the fourth part of Art. 9).

[The Court provides fairly detailed reasons for this conclusion, including civil code provisions holding that centralized organizations must be regarded as a "unified subject of legal relations," that centralized religious organizations in particular have to have local organizations as part of their structure, and that while separate incorporation of local units is allowed, this does not mean that they are separate from the structure from the perspective of provisions governing liquidation.]

Objections that local religious organizations are not structurally affiliated and are therefore not subject to liquidation are based on a misunderstanding of the norm of the law. . . .

In accordance with the forth part of Art. 7, parts 1-4 of Art. 9 of the Federal Law on Combating Extremist Activity, not only facts about the activities of a ruling or coordinating body of a certain association, but also facts about illegal activities of even one of its regional or other structural branches can serve as grounds for liquidation of this association. . . .

Since the decision on liquidation of the Organization is taken on the grounds set forth in the Federal Law on Combating Extremist Activity ..., the Religious Organization "Administrative Center of Jehovah's Witnesses in Russia", including all local religious organizations integrated into its structure, is declared an extremist organization (second paragraph of Art. 1 of the aforementioned federal law) on the date this decision comes into force.

The legal consequence of finding a centralized religious organization extremist is the prohibition of its operation in the Russian Federation. . . .

In accordance with the third part of Art. 264 of the Code of Administrative Court Proceedings of the Russian Federation, in the event the claim on liquidation is upheld, the court's decision is immediately enforceable with respect to suspension of its activity and the activities of local religious organizations integrated to its structure.

On the grounds of Art. 175-180, 264 of the Code of Administrative Court Proceedings of the Russian Federation, the Supreme Court of the Russian Federation rules to uphold the claim of the Ministry of Justice of the Russian Federation and liquidate the Religious Organization "Administrative Center of Jehovah's Witnesses in Russia" and the local religious organization integrated into its structure.

The Courts' decision to uphold the claim on liquidation of the Religious Organization "Administrative Center of Jehovah's Witnesses in Russia" is immediately enforceable with respect to suspension of its activity and any activities of local religious organizations integrated into its structure.

COMMENTS AND QUESTIONS

1. The Russian Supreme Court declared Jehovah's Witnesses, who are members of a Christian denomination that rejects violence, to be an extremist organization, "banning the group from operating on Russian territory and putting its more than 170,000 Russian worshipers in the same category as Islamic State militants."[14] What consequences could derive from a high court's equating such groups? What result would you anticipate as such cases are heard at the European Court of Human Rights?
2. The Court relies on a provision in Russia's anti-extremism law that proscribes "any propaganda of exclusivity touting the supremacy or inferiority of a person based on his or her social, race, ethnic, religious or linguistic identity or attitude towards religion." The Convention on the Elimination of Racial Discrimination (CERD) contains somewhat similar language. While prohibiting claims of superiority or inferiority based on race is certainly understandable, is it reasonable to expect that religious groups will not make claims regarding the superiority of their beliefs? Is there a plausible reading of the Russian statutory provision that would allow Jehovah's Witnesses (or members of the Russian Orthodox Church) to make "exclusivity" claims without triggering extremism prohibitions?
3. The Court cites numerous administrative actions finding that Jehovah's Witness organizations have been found to violate extremism laws. (There are many more cited in the full decision.) Can the liquidation decision be justified under Article 9(2) of the European Convention for the Protection of Human Rights and Fundamental Freedoms (ECHR)? What challenges are the Jehovah's Witnesses likely to face in vindicating their claims?
4. Was the provision requiring a warning notice prior to liquidation a helpful protection? Are there reasons it was not effective protection in this case?
5. Are anti-extremism measures intrinsically likely to be overbroad in ways that allow unjustifiable state enforcement action? Are there measures that you can suggest that would reduce such risks?
6. Do you see any parallels here with the Blasphemy Law Case brought in 2010 before the Indonesian Constitutional Court, discussed in Chapter 5?

7. Could the Yarovaya constraints be justified as mere "time, place and manner" restrictions of the type allowed under US free speech law?
8. Efforts of the governments of the United Kingdom to codify a counter-extremism policy and the United States to secure its borders through immigration and travel control are examined in Section III below. Do you see similarities and differences between these efforts and those of Russia in attempts to control perceived harms of religious extremism?

D. EUROPE

COMMENTARY ON FRANCE AND BELGIUM

Although Europe enjoys a long tradition of religious liberty, some highly publicized cult-related murder-suicide events in the 1990s provided the impetus for the modern anti-cult movement, particularly in French-speaking Europe. The mass suicide and murder perpetrated by members of the Order of the Solar Temple was among the most disturbing. The Order of the Solar Temple was a small cult based primarily in France, Switzerland, and Canada. Its belief system consisted of a mixture of what some have called "neo-Templar" ideology, environmentalism, Christianity, and a variety of New Age beliefs. The members of the cult believed that death was simply an illusion, that once they had passed on they would live again on other planets, and that death by fire was a vital part of the process of their being cleansed.

Between 1995 and 1997, 74 deaths—most of them suicides, but some of them murders—occurred in connection with the group. Particularly shocking was the ritual murder of an infant the group's leader believed to be the anti-Christ. Although the many deaths associated with the group shocked the European public, the upper-middle-class social and economic status of many of the cult members was even more distressing.

The response to the cult movement in Europe has varied. The excerpt below discusses the approaches taken by the French and Belgian governments.

WILLY FAUTRÉ, THE SECT ISSUE IN FRANCE AND IN BELGIUM

In *International Perspectives on Freedom and Equality of Religious Belief*, Derek H. Davis and Gerhard Besier, eds. (J.M. Dawson Institute of Church-State Studies, Baylor Univ. 2002)

In the first half of the [1990s], the world was horrified by a series of collective suicides, homicides, and attacks perpetrated in America, Europe and Asia at the initiative of leaders of religious movements or movements claiming to be religious.

On April 19, 1993, eighty-eight Davidians died from confrontations with the police in Waco (Texas). On October 4, 1994, a mass suicide-homicide cost the lives of fifty-three members of the Order of the Solar Temple (OST) in Switzerland and Canada. On March 5, 1995, about five thousand people were injured and [twelve] killed in a gas attack perpetrated by Aum in Tokyo's subway. In December 1995, another suicide-homicide of sixteen members of the OST took place in the Vercors in France. Since then, [a] homicide-suicide claiming almost a thousand lives took place in the African state of Uganda in March 2000.

The European Union, the Council of Europe and a number of member states have expressed their concern about that phenomenon in various ways. The issue is whether a specific policy should be designed and carried out with regard to unconventional religions in order to prevent the repetition of such tragedies. The responses have been varied.

The position of eleven member states of the European Union was that "sects" do not harm the individual, the family, society or their democratic institutions to the point of necessitating to create new institutions or organizations to combat them. . . . Consequently, they did not take any political or legal measures that might have encroached on international human rights norms pertaining to freedom of religion or belief. However, four EU member states decided to take a new course of action: . . . [Austria, Germany, France, and Belgium].

Austria created an information and documentation center about sects, placing it under the authority of the Federal Ministry of the Environment, Youth and the Family. . . . [warning] principally against eleven guru-led movements of oriental origin, three psychological groups, two groups claiming to spring from new revelations, three religions of Christian origin and four other groups under the category "Various". Germany set up a parliamentary commission and published a report. Scientology was placed under surveillance but no legal [action was taken]. Various *Länder* published and distributed information brochures warning against sects . . . . [Substantially stronger reactions occurred in France and Belgium.]

Development of State Anti-Sect Policies

France

As early as 1985, following a request by the Prime Minister, former member of parliament and minister Alain Vivien wrote a report entitled: *Sects in France: Expression of Moral Freedom or Sources of Manipulation?* [describing the sect phenomenon and making] recommendations (maintain appropriate surveillance of the sect phenomenon by means of an interministerial structure; warn and inform the public in an impartial way, etc.).

On June 29, 1995, the National Assembly unanimously adopted a resolution creating an inquiry commission "to study the sect phenomenon" [which] carried out its work in strict secrecy . . . , publish[ing] a report entitled *Sects in France*[, which listed] 173 movements as . . . potentially harmful sects [and] advocated increasing information about such groups and administrative repression of sects, including small Evangelical churches. [A succession of steps were taken] . . . .

Step 1: On May 9, 1996, an Interministerial Observatory on Sects was created by means of a decree. Its mandate was to analyse the phenomenon of sects, to inform the Prime Minister of its work and to make recommendations so as to provide better tools to fight sects. The Observatory did not survive the publication of its first report of activities in 1998. . . .

Step 2: From 1996 to 1998, training and awareness programs for the police, state prosecutors, judges and teachers were initiated with the goal of reinforcing control of sects by government agencies and the state. Academics were not involved in the process.

Step 3: On November 7, 1997, [the] Minister of Interior . . . sent a circular to the police chiefs concerning the "combat against reprehensible actions of sectarian movements" [appealing] to the non-governmental organisations UNADFI and

CCMM (. . . associations for the protection of "victims of sects") for help in heightening public awareness. However, the government created no mechanism for checking the accuracy of the statements made about sects by these groups, nor was a mechanism provided that would ensure open debate on the information, interpretations and assessments presented. Additionally, the circular called for the mobilisation of all state officials against "sects," including exchanging information, heightening vigilance, and work, school and health inspections. The circular repeated that "this fight comes within the framework of an activity of national priority."

Step 4: On October 7, 1998, [as the result of intense pressure of the Study Group on Sects at the National Assembly and of the effective militancy of UNADFI and CCMM leaders] the President of the Republic and the Prime Minister signed a decree creating the *Mission interministérielle de lutte contre les sectes* (MILS–Interministerial Mission to Combat Sects) . . . .

Step 5: On December 1, 1998, The Ministry of Justice sent to the staff of the public prosecutor's office a circular to ask prosecutors and judges to make common cause with anti-sect associations . . . , "to combat attacks on persons or private property committed by groups of a sectarian nature."

Step 6: On December 15, 1998, the authorities set up a Parliamentary Commission of Inquiry into the finances, property and fiscal standing of sects, as well as their economic activities and their relations with economic and financial circles. This Commission had six months to broadly investigate and report on the financial dealings, resources and assets of groups it had classified as sects.

Step 7: On 30 May 2001, all parliamentary groups of the French National Assembly unanimously adopted . . . the About and Picard draft law meant to strengthen prevention and repression of sectarian groups liable to undermine human rights and fundamental freedom.

This law allows courts to dissolve associations condemned for damages to individuals, illegal practice of medicine or pharmaceuticals, misleading publicity or fraud. It also stipulates that banned groups which re-form under a different name can face prosecution.

A controversial clause making a crime of 'mental manipulation', a first in the world, sparked an outcry from several minority religious groups, Catholic and Protestant leaders and academics when it first went before the National Assembly in June 2000. It was eventually dropped after an official consultative human rights body [found it] questionable. However, it was replaced by a similar provision that already exists in the criminal code for other purposes and is known as abuse of someone's weakness. Despite a change in the legal basis of the law, its philosophy remained the same and the result too. The crime of "abuse of a person's state of weakness" is from now on applicable to activities of so-called cults and can be punished by a possible sentence of up to 3 years in jail and a maximum fine of up to 350,000 USD . . . . The law also allows anti-cult groups, state-recognized of public utility, to be civil parties for the victims.

Belgium

On January 10, 1996, the Justice Commission of the House of Representatives started examining a proposal . . . to set up a parliamentary enquiry commission which would work out a policy against sects and the dangers they pose to people, particularly to minors.

This enquiry commission which comprised 11 members, started its work on April 25, 1996, held 58 meetings and heard 136 witnesses, making no distinction between public and private spheres . . . . [Most] witnesses were heard behind closed doors, sometimes by only a few members of the Commission and without the others' knowledge. Sociologists of religions were not consulted. Associations suspected of being dangerous or harmful sects, including some small Evangelical churches, were not invited to participate in the hearings, but the commission sent a letter to 71 of the associations mentioned by various state agencies as potentially harmful to society or to the individual. The letter asked the groups to describe their objectives and to refute their possibly sectarian character, but they were not informed of the accusations raised against them during the public and non-public hearings. They could therefore not defend themselves. The other 118 movements that were listed did not get such an invitation and were consequently not able to present a summary of their activities or to contest any accusations.

On April 28, 1997, the parliamentary commission issued its 670-page report. A list of 189 movements was attached. In the introduction to the list, the drafters admitted that they had not been able to control the collected data. Nevertheless, unilateral accusations made against the movements were reproduced in the report without any further investigation or any cross-examination and sometimes despite strong evidence presented by the incriminated movements that criticisms voiced under oath were false. The Parliament failed to adopt the report as such and only voted to accept the conclusions and recommendations (19 pages). This reluctance, mainly expressed by the ruling Catholic political parties CVP and PSC, was certainly due to the fact that some Catholic movements such as the Opus Dei, The Work, the Opstal Community and the Charismatic Renewal were included on the list. Despite this disavowal, the government did not find inappropriate to publish the whole report, including the controversial list . . .

On June 2, 1998, the Parliament adopted the *Law regarding the establishment of an Information and Advice Center and an Administrative Coordination Agency*.

On April 29, 1999 at its last session before its dissolution, the House of Representatives appointed the 12 members and the 12 deputy members of the *Information and Advice Center on Harmful sectarian organisations* for a period of four years. The members were chosen "from eminent personalities that are known for their knowledge, experience and interest in the problems of the harmful sectarian movements" (Article 4 of the Law). . . .

Deviations of State Anti-Sect Policies from International Human Rights Norms for Freedom of Religion and Belief

As members of the United Nations, the Organisation for Security and Cooperation in Europe and the Council of Europe, France and Belgium have committed themselves to numerous international and European treaties and covenants that protect religious freedom.

The two most relevant international instruments to which the three countries are a party are the International Covenant on Civil and Political Rights ("ICCPR") and the Declaration on the Elimination of All Forms of Intolerance and of Discrimination Based on Religion or Belief ("1981 Declaration").

The state anti-sect policies developed in France and in Belgium as described are not consistent with the provisions of these international instruments to which both countries are committed.

Following publication of the parliamentary reports and the "lists of sects," many cases of intolerance and discrimination in the public and private sectors were reported in France and in Belgium. Complaints from French and Belgian individuals belonging to one of the blacklisted sects have steadily increased: libel and slander, victimisation in the neighbourhood, at the workplace and at school, damage to individuals' reputation, loss of jobs or promotions, dismissals, loss of visitation rights or child custody in divorce settlements, inability to rent facilities for religious ceremonies or for meetings, unilateral and unfounded closure of bank accounts of "sects" or of individuals affiliated with them, humanitarian agencies' refusal to accept donations from "sects," denial of access to public display boards, and police surveillance.

Conclusions and Recommendations

Anti-sect policies in France and in Belgium have triggered an up to now unknown wave of discrimination and intolerance against non-conventional religious and belief groups. They also contravene with the obligations to freedom of religion and belief that are enshrined in international and European treaties and covenants to which these countries are committed.

France's choice to combat sects stands in sharp contrast to the majority of the member states of the European Union . . . [T]he stance taken by France also reveals a political will to stand out, to affirm its cultural identity, difference and leadership within its zone of influence so that the "sect issue" has moved out of the sphere of a social phenomenon scrutinised by sociologists of religions and has become a public, political and diplomatic issue.

A number of human rights organisations and states have criticised the French government's position. Up to now, French political decision-makers have failed to take those criticisms into account and to adapt their policy to the international human rights standards.

Moreover, the Interministerial Mission for [the] Fight Against Sects [(MILS)] tries to export the French anti-sect model to other countries, especially in Central and Eastern Europe, and to make common cause with states and mainstream churches which have chosen to combat sects.

Other countries, like Belgium and Switzerland (Canton of Geneva), have also been stigmatised by the international community because they have made the same choice as France: to fight against sects instead of opening a dialogue.

***

Since its inception, the French anti-*secte* effort has changed both in its focus and its scope. In 2002, the name of the French government's anti-cult effort was changed from MILS (*Mission interministérielle de lutte contre les sectes*, or interministerial mission to fight against sects) to MIVILUDES (*Mission interministérielle de vigilance et de lutte contre les dérives sectaires*, or interministerial mission for monitoring and combating cultic deviances). The name change reflects the French government's lack of an official definition of what a sect actually is and a shift in focus for the French authorities from targeting sects as groups to targeting sect behavior.[15]

A major turning point for MIVILUDES occurred in 2005, when departing Prime Minister Jean-Pierre Raffarin issued a *circulaire* (a type of administrative directive) addressing sect activities in France. The memo reiterated the idea that maintaining lists of groups was an inefficient means of combating sect activity. Specifically, the *circulaire* encouraged MIVILUDES to pursue groups and individuals based more on their behavior and characteristics than on whether they appeared on the list of sects. Raffarin also cited the difficulty of trying to maintain any such list, due to the decentralized nature of many cults in the wake of the popularity of the Internet. In fact, the listis now considered "obsolete".[16]

The 2007 election of President Nicolas Sarkozy also contributed to a move away from punishing membership in groups to punishing behavior. Sarkozy, known for his idea of *laïcité positive,* moved MIVILUDES toward a "liberal but firm" policy, pushing to shore up previous policies to "repress" behavior that may trouble the public order while avoiding the stigmatization and arbitrary enforcement of law that often occur when lists of groups are used. Although this policy has met with some resistance, particularly from politicians such as Alain Gest, who was involved in the creation of the original list of sects, the "liberal but firm" approach has become official French policy.

On 10 April 2017, the Parliamentary Assembly of the Council of Europe (PACE) adopted Resolution 1992 on The Protection of Minors Against the Excesses of Sects.[17] In its final draft the Assembly rejected a controversial report[18] from the French Deputy Rudy Salles, Rapporteur of the Committee of Legal Affairs and Human Rights, the vote (28 for, 18 against, and 13 abstentions) falling short of the two-thirds majority required to pass.

As observed by Willy Fautré, the Salles report aimed to

> 1.1. conduct a study about the scale of the phenomenon of sects affecting minors at European level, on the basis of information provided by the member States;
>
> 1.2. set up a working group to exchange information between member States on excesses of sects affecting minors and to develop good practices for preventing the problem; and
>
> 1.3. seek to improve co-operation at European level with a view to implementing joint activities to prevent excesses of sects and protect minors against them.
>
> . . . [P]oint 6 which contained very alarming recommendations to the Member States has disappeared, in particular:
>
> 6.6. to carry out awareness-raising measures about the scale of the phenomenon of sects and excesses of sects, in particular for judges, ombudsmen's offices, the police and welfare services;

---

15. Religioscope, http://www.religioscope.info/article_138.shtml.

16. La dernière liste exhaustive des sectes en France date de 1995; Qualifié de scandaleux par Emmanuelle Mignon, ce document est jugé obsolète par le gouvernement, *Le Figaro,* 22 February 2008.

17. Text adopted by the Parliamentary Assembly of the Council of Europe 10 April 2017 (17th Sitting).

18. Rapporteur, Mr. Rudy Salles (France, EPP/CD): The protection of minors against excesses of sects, Council of Europe Parliamentary Committee on Legal Affairs and Human Rights.

> 6.7. to adopt or strengthen, if necessary, legislative provisions punishing the abuse of psychological and/or physical weakness, and enabling associations to join proceedings as parties claiming damages in criminal cases concerning excesses of sects;
>
> 6.8. to support, including in financial terms, the action of private bodies which provide support for the victims of excesses of sects and their relatives and, if necessary, encourage the establishment of such bodies . . . .
>
> So, the French "model" of policy against "sects" has not been endorsed. The adopted Resolution expresses general concern about abuses against minors, but also recommends respecting the rights of children and parents to freedom of religion or belief and freedom from discrimination. . . .
>
> The only point that remains disputable in the Resolution is:
>
> 8. The Assembly also calls on national parliaments to set up study groups on the protection of minors, in particular those belonging to religious minorities.
>
> However, this point is countered by the . . . last one:
>
> 9. The Assembly calls on member States to ensure that no discrimination is allowed on the basis of which movement is considered as a sect or not, that no distinction is made between traditional religions and non-traditional religious movements, new religious movements or "sects" when it comes to the application of civil and criminal law, and that each measure which is taken towards non-traditional religious movements, new religious movements or "sects" is aligned with human rights standards as laid down by the European Convention on Human Rights and other relevant instruments protecting the dignity inherent to all human beings and their equal and inalienable rights.

Thus failed, observed Fautré, "the French idea pushed by the anti-sect activists . . . to protect children from their parents' beliefs and deny parents the right to educate their children in conformity with their own beliefs, which is guaranteed under the European Convention on Human Rights (Protocol, Article 2) and the International Covenant on Civil and Political Rights (Article 18.4)."[19]

COMMENTS AND QUESTIONS

1. The "sect lists" in France and Belgium have been highly controversial because, although they were not formally adopted or approved, and so cannot be formally withdrawn or appealed, they have been used in ways that lead to serious discrimination. To what extent should state authorities be engaged in labeling or listing "dangerous" groups?

2. Is it permissible (or a violation of human rights) for a state institution to characterize a group using disparaging language such as "sect" or "cult"? The European Court of Human Rights case *Leela Förderkreise e.V. and Others v. Germany* (App. No. 58911/00, 6 November 2008) concerned three associations registered under German law as religious or meditation groups belonging to the Osho Movement. The associations had initiated proceedings in German domestic courts in 1984, complaining of a campaign of the German government to discredit them using terms such as "youth religion," "youth sect, "sect," "destructive religious cults," "pseudo-salvation teachings,

19. Willy Fautré, Human Rights Without Frontiers, France's Policy Against "Sects" Disavowed by the Council of Europe, ISKCON News, 11 April 2014.

"pseudo-religious," and "manipulated their members." After a series of dismissals in the lower courts, an 11-year proceedings before the Federal Constitutional Court resulted in a 2002 ruling that the government was authorized to characterize the applicant associations' movement as a "sect," "youth religion," "youth sect," and "psycho-sect" and was allowed to provide the public with adequate information about it. Other terms were barred. The ECtHR ruled that such interference did not absolutely prohibit such manifestation, and as the interference had been "prescribed by law" and had pursued the "legitimate aim" of providing information about the dangers of groups which were commonly known as sects, the interference fell within the limitations permitted by Article 9. The information campaign had aimed to settle a matter of major public concern at the relevant time by warning citizens of a phenomenon viewed as disturbing, that is to say the emergence of new religious movements and their attraction for young people. The Court therefore found that the government's statements, as delimited by the Constitutional Court, had not overstepped what a democratic State might regard as in the public interest.

III. RELIGIOUSLY MOTIVATED TERRORISM

"Confusion on the definition of 'terrorism' abounds," noted the United States Second Circuit Court of Appeals in its decision to deny an appeal of the convicted 1993 World Trade Center bomber, Ramzi Yousef, and his associates:[20] Due in no small part to the strong pejorative power of a word deriving from "terror" and the amorphous nature of the groups whose actions it is often used to describe, identifying what is and what is not terrorism is indeed the cause of much confusion among policymakers, scholars, law enforcement, and military personnel.

The United Nations, in spite of the adoption of a far-ranging Global Counter-Terrorism Strategy[21] that strongly condemns "terrorism in all its forms and manifestations," has yet to adopt a resolution as to what "terrorism" actually means.[22] Significant debate has arisen when representatives of one of the 57 member states of the Organization of Islamic Cooperation or one of the 120 members states of the Non-Aligned Movement insists that terrorism "should not be equated with the legitimate struggle of peoples under colonial or alien domination for self-determination and national liberation," urging a definition that takes into account the "root cause of terrorism," which is generally meant to be not religious hatred but poverty and other sources of disenfranchisment or

20. *United States v. Yousef*, 327 F.3d 56, 108 n.42 (2d Cir. 2003).

21. GA Res. 60/288, UN Doc. A/RES/60/288 (20 September 2006).

22. *See* The United Nations Global Counter-Terrorism Strategy Review, Reslution adopted by the General Assembly on 13 June 2014, A/RES/68/276. *See also* Oral report of the Chairman of the Working Group Mr. Rohan Perera (Sri Lanka), 7 November 2014.

marginalization.[23] But whatever its causes—poverty, anger, societal corruption and volatility[24]—most agree that terrorism involves violence or the threat of violence in order to effect a societal change. The level of violence, identity of the perpetrators, and other specifics continue to be a point of contention among scholars, policymakers, and nations.

Definitions of terrorism become only more contentious when a religious element is added to the mix. Terrorism has more often been concerned with achieving temporal political success rather than with attaining the other-worldly gains sought by the faithful. It is unsurprising, then, that religious terrorism has most often been connected with political movements, such as anti-colonial, separatist, irredentist, and other movements.

Although recent world events have brought greater attention to terrorist groups claiming Islamic roots, members of most, if not all, major religious traditions have committed acts of violence in the name of their faith. First-century CE Jewish Zealots publicly assassinated Romans and their Jewish collaborators.[25] Six hundred years later in India, the Thugs—a religious movement devoted to worshipping Kali, the Hindu goddess of terror and destruction—ritually strangled to death hundreds of travelers each year.[26] More recently, in 1984, Sikhs claiming religious justification for their actions and acting in response to the Indian government's assault on the Golden Temple, Sikhism's holiest shrine, assassinated the Prime Minister of India, Indira Gandhi. In the United States, loosely organized movements claiming Christian roots, such as Christian Identity, have been responsible for several attacks, such as the assassination of Alan Berg and possibly the 1999 attack on the Los Angeles Jewish Community Center. In 1994, Baruch Goldstein, a Jew believed to be influenced by the extremist religious teachings of Rabbi Meir Kahane, killed 29 Muslims and injured over a hundred more in an attack on a mosque. The ongoing persecution of Rohingya Muslims in Buddhist Myanmar is notorious.[27]

Perhaps most importantly, religious terrorism differs from secular terrorism in the willingness of its perpetrators to kill. As political scientist and terrorism expert Bruce Hoffman has noted:

> For the religious terrorist, violence is first and foremost a sacramental act or divine duty executed in direct response to some theological demand or imperative. Terrorism thus assumes a transcendental dimension, and its perpetrators are consequently unconstrained by the political, moral, or practical constraints that may affect other terrorists. Whereas secular terrorists rarely attempt indiscriminate killing on a massive scale because such tactics are not consonant with their political aims and therefore are regarded as counterproductive, if not immoral, religious terrorists often seek the elimination of broadly defined categories of enemies and accordingly regard such

---

23. *See* Oral Report by the Chairman of the Working Group on Measures to Eliminate International Terrorism at the UN General Assembly Sixth Committee, 6 November 2012.

24. *See e.g.*, Beenish Ahmed, What's the Real Root Cause of Terrorism: Poverty or Anger?, *ThinkProgress*, 19 February 2015.

25. Bruce Hoffman, *Inside Terrorism* 83 (Columbia Univ. Press 2006), reiterated in Measures to Eliminate International Terrorism, the November 2013 Report of the General Assembly's Sixth Committee.

26. *Id.*

27. *See, e.g.*, US Department of State, International Religious Freedom Report 2016: Burma.

large-scale violence not only as morally justified but as a necessary expedient to the attainment of their goals.[28]

In a report that focused on "violence in the name of religion," Heiner Bielefeldt, former United Nationas Special Rapporteur for Freedom of Religion or Belief, emphasized two sources of oversimplification that lead to misunderstandings in this area. On the one hand, "[t]he experience that religion is invoked in civil wars, communal violence, terrorist acts, or other violent conflicts causes some observers to use the label 'religion' broadly and loosely when analyzing those phenomena." This overlooks the need for "careful, contextualized analysis of all relevant factors" in a conflict situation, and can lead to overemphasizing the role of religion as a problem factor in such settings. On the other hand, the "instrumentalization thesis" underestimates the role of religion in conflicts, denying from the outset "that religious motives can play a genuine role in incidents of violence, and assuming instead "that perpetrators of such violence merely "instrumentalize" religion for political, economic or other mundane purposes."[29] The report goes on to provide a deeper analysis of the multifaceted challenges posed by "violence in the name of religion."

As religious terrorists are often not concerned about—or may even seek—excessive civilian casualties and collateral damage, they have perpetrated the most violent terrorist acts in recent history and have been particularly innovative in their methods. Terrorists claiming religious motivation have been the first to use weapons of mass destruction—defined as chemical, biological, radiological, or nuclear weapons—in their attacks. In 1984, members of an Oregon cult attempted to influence an important local election by contaminating a reservoir and distributing salmonella bacteria onto food served at various salad-bars throughout the city, killing none but injuring more than 700.[30] In 1995, two members of a Christian white supremacist terrorist group called the Minnesota Patriots Council produced enough ricin, a deadly toxin, to kill more than a hundred people and planned to use it on government personnel before their capture.[31] More recently, some terrorist groups in Iraq have begun including chlorine cylinders in their improvised explosive devices in an attempt to make crude chemical weapons, and it seems likely that other terrorist groups have made efforts to acquire nuclear weapons.

To date the most catastrophic use of weapons of mass destruction by a terrorist group remains the 20 March 1995 Tokyo subway attacks carried out by five members of the Japanese "cult" group Aum Shinrikyo, who released a normally highly toxic nerve agent known as sarin in five Tokyo subway cars. Although members of Aum intended to kill thousands, and used sufficient sarin to carry out their intentions, the poor quality of both the delivery system and the toxin itself limited the effectiveness of the gas. Nonetheless the attack resulted in 12 deaths and more than 5,000 injuries.[32]

---

28. Hoffman, *supra* note 25 at 88.

29. Report of the Special Rapporteur on freedom of religion or belief, Heiner Bielefeldt, to the Human Rights Council, 28th Session, UN Doc. A/HRC/28/66, paras. 12-18.

30. *Id.* at 119.

31. *Id.* at 107.

32. *Sarin*, Council on Foreign Relations, January 2006, http://www.cfr.org/publication/9553/.

A. JAPAN: AUM SHINRIKYO

BRUCE HOFFMAN, INSIDE TERRORISM

Columbia Univ. Press 2006, 119-125

The Aum Shinrikyo (Aum 'Supreme Truth' sect) arguably represents a new kind of terrorist threat, posed not by traditional secular adversaries but by a mass religious movement motivated by a mystical, almost transcendental, divinely inspired imperative. The group was founded in 1987 by Shoko Asahara [when] God sent a 'message' to him that he had been chosen to 'lead God's army' . . . .

. . . [W]ith just ten followers, Asahara opened up the first Aum office. [His] highly idiosyncratic mixture of Buddhism and Hinduism fused with notions of apocalyptic redemption exerted a powerful attraction for young, intelligent Japanese alienated by society's preoccupation with work, success, technology and making money. Hence, by the end of 1987 Aum had 1,500 members with branches in several Japanese cities; in less than a decade, it would have some 10,000 members, organized within twenty-four branches scattered throughout Japan, alongside an estimated twenty to thirty thousand followers in Russia alone, with an additional ten to twenty thousand converts in at least six other countries, and offices in New York, Germany, Australia and Sri Lanka.

From the start, Asahara preached about the inevitability of an impending apocalypse, stressing his unique messianic mission and variously describing himself as 'Today's Christ' . . . and 'the one and only person who had acquired supreme truth'. Particular emphasis was given to the Hindu god of destruction and subsequent regeneration, Shiva, whose fifteen-foot visage dominated the entrance to the Satian-7 laboratory where the group manufactured the sarin nerve gas used in the subway attack . . . . Asahara also borrowed Judeo-Christian notions of Armageddon and frequently cited Nostradamus, whose recently translated works had become best-sellers in Japan. According to Asahara the world would end–he was never sure exactly when, variously fixing 1997, 1999, 2000 and 2003 as likely times. Whatever the date, Asahara was certain that Armageddon would be caused by a Third World War. Citing his other-worldly abilities . . . , he proclaimed before an Aum conference in 1987 that nuclear war was 'sure to break out' between 1999 and 2003. This catastrophe could be averted, Asahara assured his followers, provided they worked actively to establish an Aum branch in every country in the world . . . .

From these apocalyptic predictions sprang Asahara's obsession with American enmity towards the Japanese in general and himself in particular. 'As we move toward the year 2000,' an Aum pamphlet warned, 'there will be a series of events of inexpressible ferocity and terror. The lands of Japan will be transformed into a nuclear wasteland. Between 1996 and January 1998, America and its allies will attack Japan, and only 10 percent of the population of the major cities will survive.' . . . Asahara thus deliberately fostered a climate of paranoiac expectation within the cult, driven by the same Manichean world-view embraced by other religious terrorist movements, with its conviction of the world as a battleground between good and evil. The sect's avowed enemies gradually expanded to include not only the predatory US government and its minions in the Japanese government . . ., but a mysterious international cabal of Freemasons, Jews and financiers . . . .

Asahara warned that Armageddon would be precipitated by a poisonous gas cloud dispatched from the United States that would engulf Japan. Thereafter, a cataclysmic global conflict would erupt–involving both nerve gas and nuclear weapons— . . . that would lead to a thousand years of peace, after which the appearance of a new messiah would create a 'paradise on earth'. In 1993, however, Asahara suddenly began to proclaim that the forth-coming apocalypse could be averted if Aum took proper action. 'We need a lot of weapons to prevent Armageddon,' he repeatedly told his closest aides. . . .

Thus Aum embarked on its programme to acquire an array of conventional and non-conventional weaponry that would effectively dwarf the arsenals of most established nation-states' standing forces. To achieve this goal, the group recruited scientists and technical experts from Japan, Russia . . . and other countries . . . . Moreover, with its vast financial resources (Aum's assets exceeded an estimated $1 billion . . .), the sect was able to purchase whatever additional knowledge and resources its members lacked . . . . Aum succeeded in obtaining a . . . helicopter, complete with chemical spray dispersal devices. The group had ambitious plans—and had already acquired sophisticated robotic manufacturing devices—to produce at least 1,000 . . . AK-47 assault rifles, along with one million bullets. It had also perfected the manufacture of TNT and the central component of plastic explosives, RDX.

Aum's intentions, however, went far beyond a revolution facilitated by conventional armaments alone. . . . When police raided the sect's laboratories following the nerve gas attack on the Tokyo underground, they found enough sarin to kill an estimated 4.2 million persons . . . .

Aum's most ambitious project was its attempt to develop a nuclear capability. To this end, the group had purchased a 500,000-acre sheep station . . . in a remote part of Western Australia. There, they hoped to mine uranium that was to be shipped back to Aum's laboratories in Japan, where scientists would convert it into weapons-grade nuclear material . . . .

'With the use of sarin we shall eradicate major cities,' Asahara had declared; and, on the morning of 20 March 1995, his disciples put his deadly plan into action. The date was much sooner than had been expected; but Aum informants inside the National Police Agency had warned that police were about to search the cult's compounds, and so Asahara suddenly ordered the planned attack . . . in hopes of . . . completely derailing the intensifying police investigation into Aum's activities. At approximately 8:00 a.m., in the midst of the Monday morning rush hour, selected Aum cadres placed eleven packages containing sarin nerve gas on five subway trains . . . . Almost immediately, passengers were affected by the noxious fumes: some were quickly overcome, others were afflicted with nosebleeds, oral hemorrhaging, uncontrollable coughing fits or convulsions . . . . The casualties might even have been far greater had not favourable weather conditions fortuitously combined with hastened—and therefore perhaps botched—preparations to reduce the sarin's potency.

Amazingly, this was neither the first nor the last Aum attack to employ chemical or biological warfare agents. In April 1990, the group had attempted to realize one of Asahara's dire prophecies of an impending catastrophe by staging an attack with botulinus toxin. Using an aerosol device developed by Aum's scientists to disperse the poison over a wide area, the sect targeted downtown Tokyo and specifically the Diet (parliament) building. The toxin, however, proved ineffective. Another attempt to disperse botulinus in downtown Tokyo failed in June, as did a suspected Aum plot to spread anthrax the following month. Then, in June 1994, the group had tried to kill three judges presiding over a civil suit brought against Aum in the rural resort town of Matsumoto. The plan was to spray a block of flats where the judges were sleeping with sarin. Seven persons were killed and more than 250 others were admitted to the hospital with nerve-gas-induced symptoms. Though taken seriously ill, the judges survived. . . . Finally, in a last spasm of activity designed to avert governmental onslaught in the wake of the underground attacks, members of the sect attempted to stage a chemical attack using hydrogen cyanide—more infamously known as Zyklon B . . . —on . . . the national 'Children's Day' holiday.

On 15 December 1995 the Japanese prime minister, invoking a 1952 anti-subversion law, ordered Aum disbanded and seized all its assets.

[Shortly after the dissolution order, representatives of Aum Shinrikyo challenged the prime minister's order in Japanese courts. These appeals reached the High Court of Japan, which quickly handed down an opinion on 30 January 1996 in support of the dissolution of Aum Shinrikyo's legal entity while reaffirming the rights of freedom of belief and association of former members of the defunct group.]

THE SUPREME COURT OF JAPAN DECISION IN THE AUM SHINRIKYO CASE

30 January 1996

The Law purports to grant legal capability to religious organisations in order for these organisations to own and manage installations for rituals and other assets and provides that organisations may be granted juridical personality. Thus, the regulation on religious organisations by the Law solely addresses the eclectic aspect of religious organisations and does not [extend] to its spiritual or religious aspects. The Law does not intend to interfere with the freedom of religion such as the conduct of religious rituals by the believers. The Dissolution Order addressed to religious organisations as provided by the Law is designed to enable the compulsory dissolution of religious organisations [if the organization harms the public] since in such cases, it is inappropriate or unnecessary to leave the religious organisation with legal capability. This is similar to the order to dissolve companies.

Therefore, even if a religious organisation is dissolved as a result of a dissolution order, believers are not prevented from continuing a religious organisation without juridical personality or from creating such an organisation anew, nor are they prevented from conducting religious acts or from procuring new installations or equipment for the exercise of such acts. The Dissolution Order does not accompany any legal effect which prohibits or limits religious acts by the believers. Admittedly, when a dissolution order takes effect, a liquidation procedure follows, and as a result, the assets of the religious organisation used for religious acts will be disposed of. . . . Although legal regulations on religious organisations do not accompany the effect of legally restricting the religious acts of the believers, if there is a possibility of some disruption to them, in light of the significance of religious freedom which is one of the spiritual freedoms guaranteed by the Constitution, whether the Constitution allows such restrictions should be examined carefully.

If one looks at the present case from the above viewpoint, the system of the dissolution order of religious organisations is solely for an eclectic purpose, and does not intend to interfere with the spiritual and religious aspects of religious organisations or the believers, and thus, the goal of the system is reasonable. According to the facts established by the original instance court, the representative officer of the appellant, and many cadres of the organisation under [his] instruction, plotted to produce sarin, which is a poisonous gas, for the purpose of mass murder and produced it systematically in an organised manner by mobilising many believers, using the installations and financial resources of the appellant. It is evident that the appellant has acted against the law and committed an act which is substantially against public welfare and has substantially exceeded the goal of a religious organisation. In order to deal with such an act by the appellant, it is necessary and appropriate to dissolve the appellant and to deprive it of its juridical personality. The Dissolution Order, even when considering the effect it may have on the spiritual and religious aspects of Aum Shinrikyo as a religious organisation and its believers, can be regarded as a necessary and unavoidable legal regulation in order to deal with the acts of the appellant.

It goes without saying that the freedom of religious acts should be respected to the maximum degree possible, but it is not absolutely limitless.

***

The Japanese Supreme Court sentenced Shoko Ashara and eleven other members of Aum Shinrikyo to death, while five other members received life sentences. In 2012, three notorious Aum fugitives were apprehended, and in June 2014 one of them, Naoko Kikuchi, was sentenced to five years in prison for her role in the 1995 attacks.

Japan's surveillance law allows the Public Security Investigation Agency to supervise any organization that has committed indiscriminate mass murder in the past and enables the authorities to raid the facilities of such organizations without a police warrant. The law also allows officials to place restrictions on cult activities and requires dangerous organizations to identify their members. In January 2015 the Public Security Examination Commission extended the surveillance of Aum successor cults in Japan for three more years. In early 2016, it was reported Aum Shinrikyo was surfacing in Europe, with members coming mostly from countries that were once part of the Soviet Union. In March, 58 members of the cult were expelled from Montenegro. A handful of this group were from Japan, Belarus, Ukraine, and Uzbekistan, but 43 were from Russia.[33] The cult, with an estimated 30,000 members in 2017, is illegal in Russia and, as in Canada, the United States, and many other countries, is a designated terrorist organization.

In July 2018, Shoko Ashara and all other condemned Aum members were executed by hanging in Japan.

33. Aum Shinrikyo: The Japanese Cult Surfacing in Europe, *BBC News Asia*, 6 April 2016.

B. TERRORISM AND ISLAM

A number of terrorist groups have attempted to associate themselves with Islam through their words and other propaganda efforts. Such groups often justify their violent actions by citations to the same holy works that the overwhelming majority of Muslims use, and frequently refer to themselves as "Islamic" or "jihadi." The SITE Intelligence Group lists a total of 227 past or present jihadi/Islamist groups worldwide, with 55 "popular jihadist groups" in active operation, and a similar number of "past" popular jihadist/insurgent groups.[34]

The association of the name of any group with the word "terrorism" is bound to cause controversy. This has been particularly true in the case of Islam, especially since the 11 September 2001 attacks in the United States by the terrorist group al-Qaeda, and ongoing violence throughout the Middle East and Afghanistan that thrust the issue of terrorists claiming to act in the name of Islam into worldwide consciousness. The perception intensified with the atrocities of the group calling itself "Islamic State," whose avowed objective was, by eliminating all obstacles—including Christians, Jews, Yazidis, "apostate" Muslisms—to re-create the original Islamic caliphate and to rule, under the banner of the Prophet Muhammed, the entire Muslim world.

Many world religious and political leaders, including of course many Muslim leaders, have declared all acts of terrorism to be outside of Islam (or any other religion) and have encouraged the media and others to cease associating terrorism with Islam entirely. However, faced with groups who claim inspiration from Islam and its prophet, who cite the Qu'ran to justify their violent campaigns, and shout the name of Allah as they attack, Western scholars, media, and policymakers have struggled to create a name to describe these terrorists. Some have turned to the use of terms such as "radical Islamic terrorism" and "Islamist extremism." Others have taken the approach of using more neutral terms, such as "militants." Still others have chosen to use the Arabic names some of these groups have called themselves, such as "mujahideen" (holy warriors) or a "jihad" movement, or in the case of Islamic State choosing an acronym, ISIS (Islamic State of Iraq and Syria), ISIL (Islamic State of Iraq and the Levant), or Da'esh, acronym for the Arabic phrase al-Dawla al-Islamiya al-Iraq al-Sham (equivalent to ISIL and for a number of reasons greatly disfavored by the group to which it referred[35]).

Whatever such groups are called, it is good to remember this:

> Terrorism is a tactic, not a religion, and it has been employed in the past 150 years by Muslims, Jews, anarchists, communists, Christians and Buddhists, all of whom were to some extent motivated by their beliefs. Yet there is a persistent belief in the west today that Islam has some unique and visceral connection to violence and intolerance that no other faith approaches. This is wrong in theory and untruthful as to the facts. It tends also to conceal the real damage that some interpretations of Islam can do to the lives of believers, and of unbelievers too.[36]

---

34. Jihadist Groups, *SITE Intelligence Group*, https://ent.siteintelgroup.com/jihadist-groups-2.html, consulted 30 August 2017.

35. Colin Randall, Why Does a Simple Word Like Daesh Disturb Extremists so Much? *The National*, 18 October 2014.

36. Editorial, The Guardian View on Fear of Islam: Terrorism is not a Religion, *The Guardian*, 30 January 2017.

Each of the authors of the following excerpts adopts a different posture toward Muslims who engage in terrorist activity. How might each evaluate the behavior of such groups as Islamic State? Why, do you think, it seems to be so difficult for the majority of Muslims, whose views are represented by these writers, to influence extremist groups?

Benazir Bhutto, Reconciliation: Islam, Democracy, and the West

HarperCollins 2008, 20–22, 27

[Benazir Bhutto held the position of prime minister of Pakistan and was the first woman to lead a majority Muslim state in modern history. Educated in the United States and the United Kingdom, Bhutto was often seen as a bridge between the Western and Muslim worlds. Although both of her administrations faced numerous controversial charges of corruption, she remained very popular among her compatriots and, after receiving amnesty from the contested corruption charges, she returned to her homeland in 2007 to campaign for her party and to encourage a more democratic Pakistan. On 27 December 2007, she was assassinated as she left a campaign rally. Shortly before her death Bhutto had completed the manuscript for her book *Reconciliation: Islam, Democracy, and the West*, published by HarperCollins in 2008.

In this work she describes a "great confusion" she saw worldwide, driven by a generalized misunderstanding of the term "jihad"—a word co-opted by terrorists to describe their murderous actions. Bhutto calls for an immediate dispelling of the notion that Islam calls for holy war against the rest of humanity, that Islamic belief sanctions violence. Citing the work of Islamic scholar Asma Afsaruddin, Bhutto stresses that the Quranic meaning of "jihad" (literally, "to struggle"), the meaning she learned as a child, is to struggle in the path of God, to follow the right path, the "basic endeavor of enjoining what is right and forbidding what is wrong."

The passages excerpted below begin with Bhutto's description of efforts in Afghanistan during the 1980s by a "small, violent minority of Muslims" to mobilize an "offensive 'holy' army," first against Russia and then against the United States and its allies, and involving terrorist attacks against Muslim and non-Muslim civilians with the ostensible purpose of liberating Muslims worldwide from "the yoke of decadence and Western domination." This group, calling themselves the Islamic Emirate of Afghanistan (IEA) but more commonly known as the Taliban, brought the notion of violent jihad to global consciousness in the late 1900s. Enforcing a harsh tribal and cultural form of Sharia law, they gained control of up to three-quarters of Afghanistan until they were overthrown by American-led forces following the 11 September 2001 attacks on the United States Islamist extremists. In contrast to these violent notions, Bhutto describes a more correct understanding of jihad.]

In the history of Islam, there are two different constructs of the term "jihad." First there is the internal jihad, a jihad within oneself to be a better person, to resist the temptations of the soul. This is a struggle centered on eradicating character flaws such as narcissism, greed, and wickedness. This is the greater jihad. The second form of jihad is personal conduct at a time of war or conflict. The Prophet is said to have remarked when he came home from a battle, "We return from the lesser jihad to the greater jihad." This shows the importance of the constant internal struggle that we all face within ourselves. It is nonviolent struggle that makes us become better people. The greater, internal jihad is seen as more important than the lesser, external jihad . . . .

Let us look specifically at the issue of terrorism. Muslim jurists developed a specific body of laws called *siyar* that interprets and analyzes the just causes for war. Part of the law indicates that "those who unilaterally and thus illegally declare a call to war, attack unarmed civilians and recklessly destroy property are in flagrant violation of the Islamic juristic conceptions of *bellum justum*. Islamic law has a name for such rogue militants, *muharibun*. A modern definition of *muharibun* would very closely parallel the contemporary meaning of 'terrorists.' The acts that these *muharibun* commit would be called *hiraba* ('terrorism'). Thus all terrorism is wrong. There is no 'good terrorism' and 'bad terrorism.'" Osama bin Laden's creed that "the terrorism we practice is of the commendable kind" is an invented rationalization for murder and mayhem. In Islam, no terrorism—the reckless slaughter of innocents—is ever justified.

MARY HABECK, KNOWING THE ENEMY: JIHADIST IDEOLOGY AND THE WAR ON TERROR

Yale Univ. Press 2006

[I]t would be . . . wrong to conclude that the [11 September 2001] hijackers, al-Qaida, and the other radical groups have nothing to do with Islam . . . . These extremists explicitly appeal to the holy texts (the Qur'an, and *sunna*, as laid out in the *hadith*) to show that their actions are justified. They find, too, endorsement of their ideas among respected interpreters of Islam and win disciples by their piety and their sophisticated arguments about how the religion supports them. The question is *which* Islam they represent. As the religion of over a billion people, Islam does not present a united face, and it is practiced in a variety of ways: syncretistic forms in Indonesia and Africa; traditional beliefs in rural areas of central Asia, Egypt, Iran, and North Africa; secularized variants in Tunisia, Iraq, Syria and Turkey; and mystical Sufi sects, which dominate large swathes of the Muslim world. None of these versions of Islam – which encompass the vast majority of the world's Muslims – have called for a war against the United States. To blame "Islam"—full stop—for September 11 is not only wrongheaded, it is ultimately self-defeating . . . .

[. . . T]he nineteen men who attacked the United States [on 11 September 2001] and the many other groups who continue to work for its destruction—including al-Qaida – are part of a radical faction of the multifaceted Islamist belief system. This faction—generally called "jihadi" or "jihadist"—has very specific views about how to revive Islam, how to return Muslims to political power, and what needs to be done about its enemies. The main difference between jihadis and other Islamists is the extremists' commitment to the violent overthrow of the existing international system and its replacement by an all-encompassing Islamic state. To justify their resort to violence, they define "jihad" (a term that can mean an internal struggle to please God as well as an external battle to open countries to the call of Islam) as fighting alone. Only by understanding the elaborate ideology of the jihadist faction can . . . the world determine how to contain and eventually end the threat they pose to stability and peace . . . .

How do the jihadis explain their actions? They say that they are committed to the destruction of the entire secular world because they believe this is a necessary first step to create an Islamic utopia on earth. The chain of thought that leads to this conclusion uses reasoning that anyone outside the extremist camp may find hard to fathom. This, as we may expect, matters little to the jihadis. They do not care if their assertions find resonance within any community other than their own. It is also worth emphasizing that they play fast and loose with both historical fact and traditional religious interpretation in order to understand their past as they believe it must be understood. First, they argue that Islam is meant to be the only way of life for humanity. After earlier versions of the one true religion had become corrupted by willful men, God sent down to mankind the Qur'an and Muhammad to show people how to please Him and how to create the perfect society . . . . Once Muslims were given the Truth, it was now their duty to share with others the way to divine favor and the ideal society. If prevented by unrighteous rulers from doing so, they must fight (wage jihad) to open the country for the call to Islam. In addition, since Islam is a message meant to create a community of believers, jihadis argue that Muslims must live in a society that implements all the laws commanded by God . . . . Not even the least of the ordinances of God can be ignored or flouted. In their vision of history, Muslims did as they were commanded for over a thousand years . . . and in return were granted the right to rule the world, dispensing justice and calling people out of darkness into light.

Then, in the jihadist account, something went terribly wrong with this God-ordained order. Christians and Jews, followers of the corrupted religions, somehow became the new leaders of mankind and began to dictate to Muslims how they should live. The Christian Europeans even conquered and occupied Islamic territory and created Israel as a permanent bridgehead in the lands of the umma. Meanwhile, the United States, Europe, and even Japan and the other Asian states developed militarily, economically, and politically into superpowers that dominated . . . all of human life. Every day the community of true believers is publicly humiliated, reminded that it is powerless and ruled by the unbelievers rather than ruling them.

How did this terrible situation come about? Jihadist ideologues offer three basic explanations. One locates the problem in the earliest years of Islam, after the four righteous Caliphs (*al-Rashidun*) were replaced by a hereditary monarchy under the Abbasids . . . . Politically and religiously, the new monarchy gave rise to despotic rulers who created their own laws rather than implement the God-given law system of shari'a. The jihadis argue that these tyrants . . . still exist—Mubarak, Musharraf, Assad, and the Saudis are all the spiritual heirs of those first hereditary rulers—and are supported in their apostasy by the United States and other Western countries, which use them as their puppets to undermine Islam and destroy God's laws on earth . . . .

Other jihadis believe that the trouble began on 3 March 1924, when Mustafa Kemal Ataturk abolished the Ottoman Caliphate—the religious ruler seen as the only authority for all of Islam. That act, called the "mother of all crimes" by one jihadist professor, spelled an end to "true" Islam. Despite the overwhelming evidence to the contrary, jihadis assert that since the death of Muhammad there had existed only one Caliph at a time who ruled the entire community of believers . . . . Since only under a Caliph recognized by the entire Muslim nation could the shari'a be fully implemented, the abolition of the Caliphate destroyed Islam. Sayyid Qutb, the main ideologue of modern jihadist groups, argued that this crime meant that so-called Muslims had been living in sin since 1924 and that Islam was no longer being practiced anywhere in the world . . . .

Finally there are jihadis who believe that Muslims lost their dignity and honor through a deliberate assault by "unbelief" on Islam. Since the beginning of time falsehood (*batil*) and unbelief (*kufr*), envisioned as purely evil forces that take on different forms depending on the epoch, have attempted to destroy the one true faith. With the coming of the last prophet, Muhammad, the conflict between the two sharpened into outright warfare. . . . Then the latest embodiments of unbelief, Europe and America, . . . managed to weaken the umma as none other forms of unbelief had–colonizing their lands and humiliating them before the entire world . . . . The entire purpose of imperialism was, in this view, to destroy Islam and kill as many Muslims as possible.

In many ways, the course of action chosen to correct the ills that have befallen Islam and Muslim societies depends upon which of these explanations a particular jihadist group prefers.

KHALED ABOU EL FADL, THE PLACE OF TOLERANCE IN ISLAM

Joshua Cohen & Ian Lague, eds., Beacon Press 2002, 3-26

[I]slam is now living through a major shift, unlike any it has experienced in the past. The Islamic civilization has crumbled, and the traditional institutions that once sustained and propagated Islamic orthodoxy–and marginalized Islamic extremism–have been dismantled. Traditionally, Islamic epistemology tolerated and even celebrated divergent opinions and schools of thought. [The jurists' legitimacy] rested largely on their semi-independence from a decentralized political system, and their dual function of representing the interest of the state to the laity and the interests of the laity to the state.

But in Muslim countries today, the state has grown extremely powerful and meddlesome, and is centralized in ways that were inconceivable two centuries ago. In the vast majority of Muslim countries, the state now controls the private religious endowments (*awqaf*) that once sustained the juristic class. Moreover, the state has co-opted the clergy, and transformed them into its salaried employees. This transformation has reduced the clergy's legitimacy, and produced a profound vacuum in religious authority. Hence, there is a state of virtual anarchy in modern Islam: it is not clear who speaks with authority on religious issues . . . . Where religion remains central to the dynamics of public legitimacy and cultural meaning, the question of who represents the voice of God is of central significance.

Puritanism and Modern Islam

It would be wrong to say that fanatic supremacist groups such as al-Qaeda or al-Jihad organizations now fill the vacuum of authority in contemporary Islam . . . . Fanatic groups remain sociologically and intellectually marginal in Islam. Still, they are extreme manifestations of more prevalent intellectual and theological currents in modern Islam.

Fanatic groups derive their theological premises from the intolerant Puritanism of the Wahhabi and Salafi creeds. Wahhabism was founded by the eighteenth century evangelist Muhammad ibn ‘Abd al-Wahhab in the Arabian peninsula . . . . According to the Wahhabi creed, it was imperative to return to a presumed pristine, simple, straightforward Islam, which could be entirely reclaimed by literal implementation of the commands of the Prophet, and by strict adherence to correct ritual practice. Importantly, Wahhabism rejected any attempt to interpret the divine law historically or contextually, with attendant possibilities of reinterpretation under changed circumstances . . . .

[Wahhabism gained prominence after the Al-Saud family united with the movement and eventually succeeded in overthrowing Ottoman rule in the early twentieth century.] Even with the formation of the Saudi state, Wahhabism remained a creed of limited influence until the mid-1970s when the sharp rise in oil prices, together with aggressive Saudi proselytizing, dramatically contributed to its wide dissemination in the Muslim world.

Wahhabism did not propagate itself as one school of thought or a particular orientation within Islam. Rather, it asserted itself as the orthodox “straight path” of Islam . . . . Its proponents insisted that they were simply abiding by the dictates of *al-salaf al-salih* (the rightly-guided predecessors, namely the Prophet and his companions), and in doing so, Wahhabis were able to appropriate the symbolisms and categories of Salafism . . . .

By the 1970s . . . , Wahhabism had succeeded in transforming Salafism from a liberal modernist orientation to a literalist, puritan, and conservative theology. The sharp rise in oil prices in 1975 enabled Saudi Arabia, the main proponent of Wahhabism, to disseminate the Wahhabi creed under a Salafi guise, which purported to revert back to the authentic fundamentals of religion uncorrupted by the accretions of historical practice. In reality, however, Saudi Arabia projected its own fairly conservative cultural practices onto the textual sources of Islam and went on to proselytize these projections as the embodiment of Islamic orthodoxy.

Despite its intolerance and rigidity, however, Wahhabism itself does not bear primary responsibility for the existence of terrorist groups in Islam today. To be sure, Wahhabism and its militant offshoots share both attitudinal and ideological orientations . . . . But Wahhabism is distinctively inward-looking—although focused on power, it primarily asserts power over other Muslims . . . . Militant puritan groups, however, are both introverted and extroverted—they attempt to assert power against both Muslims and non-Muslims. As populist movements, they are a reaction to the disempowerment most Muslims have suffered in the modern age at the hands of harshly despotic governments, and at the hands of interventionist foreign powers . . . .

The Theology of Intolerance

Islamic puritans, whether of the Wahhabi or more militant varieties, offer a set of textual references in support of their exclusionary and intolerant theological orientation. For instance, they frequently cite the Qur’anic verse that states: “O’ you who believe, do not take the Jews and Christians as allies. They are allies of each other, and he amongst you who becomes their ally is one of them. Verily, God does not guide the unjust.” Wahhabi and militant Puritanism read this and similar Qur'anic verses literally and ahistorically, and therefore reach highly exclusionary conclusions . . . .

Islamic Puritanism also often invokes the Qur'anic verse asserting that, "whosoever follows a religion other than Islam this will not be accepted from him, and in the Hereafter he will be among the losers." This verse is invoked in arguing that the theology and rituals of Islam are the exclusive path to salvation . . . .

As to the principles that should guide the interaction between Muslims and non-Muslims, the puritan trend cites the Qur'anic verse commanding Muslims to fight the unbelievers, "until there is no more tumult or oppression, and until faith and all judgment belongs to God." Moreover, justifying an essentially supremacist view towards non-Muslims, proponents of Puritanism often quote the following Qur'anic injunction: "Fight those among the People of the Book (Jews and Christians) who do not believe in God or the Hereafter, who do not forbid what God and His Prophet have forbidden, and who do not acknowledge the religion of truth—fight them until they pay the poll tax (*jizyah*) with willing submission and feel themselves subdued."

Relying on such textual evidence, Muslim puritans assert that Muslims are the inheritors of an objectively ascertainable and realizable divine truth; while Jews and Christians may be tolerated, they cannot be befriended. Ultimately, however, they must be subdued and forced to acknowledge Muslim supremacy. . . . The puritan doctrine is not necessarily or entirely dismissive of the rights of non-Muslims, and it does not necessarily lead to the persecution of Jews and Christians. But it does assert a hierarchy of importance, and the commitment to toleration is correspondingly fragile and contingent. So it is conducive to an arrogance that can easily descend into a lack of respect or concern for the well-being or dignity of non-Muslims. When this arrogant orientation is coupled with textual sources that exhort Muslims to fight against unbelievers (*kuffar*), it can produce a radical belligerency.

COMMENTS AND QUESTIONS

1. What is the significance of El Fadl's use of the term "puritan"? What associations are usually made with the word? What are the implied comparisons? Are puritans heroic actors at the forefront of religious freedom movements, religious zealots, or historical relics? Is the term "puritan" a better term to use than "fundamentalist"?

COMMENTARY ON RAPOPORT'S "WAVES" OF TERRORISM

Political scientist David C. Rapoport, a founding figure of terrorism studies, asserts that "the distinctiveness of modern terror [can]not be understood without emphasizing the importance of time and the changing character of the international political context which gives terrorism a cyclical character."[37] In the ancient world and continuing through the late nineteenth century terrorism was a local, domestic

37. David C. Rapoport, It Is Waves, Not Strains, 28 *Terrorism and Political Violence* (2), 217. *See also* Rapoport, The Four Waves of Modern Terror: International Dimensions and Consequences, in *An International History of Terrorism: Western and Non-Western Experiences* 282–310 (Jussi M. Hanhimäki, Bernhard Blumenau, eds., Routledge 2013).

matter—the Jewish Zealots, medieval Assassins (Nizari Ismailis, a branch of Shia Islam), the Ku Klux Klan struck close to home. Modern terrorism, however, is international, and it comes in waves. In the late 1800s, communication and travel were suddenly much faster; bombs were cheap and easy to make; French and Russian revolutionary ideas could spread. In the resulting "Anarchist Wave" of terrorism, assassination was the preeminent tactic, from the killing of US President William McKinley in September 1901 through the assassination of Austro-Hungarian Archduke Franz Ferdinand in June 1914 that precipated World War I.

The second wave of modern terrorism was largely anti-colonial, focused on achieving individual rule for former colonial powers. The third wave served anarchist interests. The fourth wave—the present wave—is largely religious terrorism, centered on Islamic terrorism, but also including groups such as Aum Shinrikyo. Interestingly, Rapoport notes that each wave lasts about one generation, as parents' dreams are lost on children. Based on this, the current wave could be expected to die out by 2025, perhaps to be replaced by a different kind of terrorism.

COMMENTS AND QUESTIONS

1. Is the idea that terrorism comes in waves useful to framing today's conflicts? Is there something different about the present wave, in that its primary perpetrators claim affliation with what is projected to be, by 2050, the religion with the most members in the world?[38]
2. How should counter-terrorism programs targeting violence in the name of religion be structured in Muslim communities or in areas where Islam is the prevailing religion?

COMMENTARY ON THE UNITED KINGDOM

In early 2014, Ofsted (the UK's Office for Standards in Education, Children's Services and Skills) issued a series of reports finding that a "culture of fear and intimidation" existed in some primary and secondary schools in Birmingham, England, due to what came to be known as "Operation Trojan Horse", an alleged city-wide "Islamist plot" involving a "sustained, coordinated agenda to impose segregationist attitudes and practices of a hardline, politicised strain of Sunni Islam" in secular state schools. Left unchecked, the report asserted, such an agenda "would confine schoolchildren within an intolerant, inward-looking monoculture that would severely inhibit their participation in the life of modern Britain."[39] It was reported, moreover, that one of the parent leaders in the "hardline Muslim takeover" had "close links to alleged terrorists". [40] In response to the Ofsted reports, the British education secretary announced that the government would require all of Britain's primary and secondary schools to "promote British values,"

---

38. *See* The Future of World Religions: Population Growth Projections, 2010–2050, *Pew Reseach Center Religion & Public Life*, 2 April 2015 .

39. Patrick Wintour, Trojan Horse Inquiry: "A Coordinated Agenda to Impose Hardline Sunni Islam," *The Guardian,* 17 July 2014.

40. Andrew Gilligan, Trojan Horse "Links to Terror," *The Telegraph*, 8 June 2014.

including "the primacy of British civil and criminal law, religious tolerance and opposition to gender segregation".[41]

Clearly, this whole process involved controversy, not only over the facts but also over wider questions about how the common values of a secular society might be defined and protected without infringing upon religious rights. During a debate in Westminster Hall on 20 January 2016, on the proposed regulation of out-of-school education settings, Sir Edward Leigh (Gainsborough) asked: "[W]hy does tackling abuse and radicalisation in a very tiny number of madrassas mean that every voluntary group in England that instructs children for six or more hours a week has to register with the state? . . . Why are we requiring tens of thousands of totally innocent groups to register with the state?" [42]

The allegations of a city-wide plot in Birmingham were never substantiated, and finally were thought to have been a hoax. Nevertheless, by April 2016, Ofsted could point to "remarkable progess" at Rockwood Academy, the school at the center of the controversy, where problems had been clearly identified[43] and where students "are now experiencing a suitably broad education that ensures they are well prepared for life in modern Britain." [44]

The British government's more extensive counter-extremism policies have also met with controversy, and concern over unintended consequences.

In early summer 2016, the UK Parliament's Joint Committee on Human Rights (JCHR), anticipating that the government's proposed bill "would be likely to raise significant human rights concerns, specifically [involving] Articles 9 (freedom of religion), 10 (freedom of expression) and 11 (freedom of association)," engaged in "what was in effect a prelegislative scrutiny" into the government's proposals and issued a report identifying five key problems:[45]

- **No clear definition of extremism**—The Counter-Extremism Strategy, launched in October 2015 . . . defines extremism as the "vocal or active opposition to our fundamental values, including democracy, the rule of law, individual liberty and the mutual respect and tolerance of those of different faiths and beliefs". This is currently too vague to be workable as a legislative definition. There is neither a consensus on the meaning of "extremism" nor "British values". The extent to which a lack of mutual respect and tolerance towards different faiths and beliefs will be unlawful is likely to be particularly contentious.
- **Discrimination and religious freedom**—The difficulty here is twofold. Measures which impact on those expressing religious conservatism would either operate indiscriminately against any religious conservatism which had no intention of inciting violence (including, for example, Islam, Orthodox Judaism, Evangelical Christianity), or would operate discriminately, specifically targeting Muslims and alienating the Muslim community.

41. Richard Adams, Patrick Wintour and Steven Morris, All Schools Must Promote "British Values," says Michael Gove, *The Guardian*, 9 June 2014.

42. House of Commons Debates, Daily Hansard, Westminster Hall, 20 January 2016, Column 567WH, Out-of-school Education Settings.

43. Andrew Gilligan, Extremists and the "Trojan Horse" Approach in State Schools, 9 March 2014.

44. Richard Adams, Ofsted Hails Trojan Horse School's "Remarkable Progress," *The Guardian*, 14 April 2016.

45. Charlotte Bellamy, Counterextremism Bill, Counterproductive? *UK Human Rights Blog*, 26 July 2016.

- **The "escalator" approach**—In trying to tackle extremism by placing restrictions on religious conservatism, the Government has wrongly assumed that violent jihadism necessarily follows from religious conservatism. Yet there is no proof that the two are correlated. The focus should rather be on extremism which leads to violence. Placing restrictions on religious conservatism amounts to suppressing views with which the Government disagree.
- **Conflicting duties on universities**—Universities are under a duty to promote free speech under Section 202 of the Education Reform Act 1988, which provides that University Commissioners have a duty to ensure that academic staff have "freedom within the law to question and test received wisdom and to put forward new ideas and controversial or unpopular opinions." It is unclear how "controversial or unpopular opinions" will be differentiated from "vocal or active opposition to our fundamental values", and therefore what will count as extremism.
- **The civil order regime**—In the Queen's speech in May 2016, a "new civil order regime" was mentioned, though with little detail. There is concern that ill-defined civil orders, breach of which would be a criminal offence, should not be used by the Government to avoid having to make a criminal case to a higher standard of proof, especially where a proper definition of the prohibited behaviour is lacking. It is likely that these orders may interfere with freedom of religion, expression and association.

The Committee concluded that the Government should not legislate, least of all in areas which impinge on human rights, unless there is a clear gap in the existing legal framework for terrorism and public order offences. In their view, the Government has not been able to demonstrate that such a gap exists, and there is a danger that any new legislation would be counter-productive.

In June 2017, the UK House of Commons issued *Counter-Extremism Policy: An Overview*, with the following introduction and rationale:

> Since the terrorist attacks in New York on 11 September 2001, the UK's approach to combating terrorism has evolved from focusing on the threat posed by foreign nationals affiliated with Al-Qaida and related groups, to the threat from "home grown" terrorists. In recent years, government policy has increasingly sought to confront the underlying causes of terrorist behaviour, including extremist ideologies.
>
> The *Prevent* strategy, part of the Government's wider counter-terrorism strategy . . . , seeks to deal with those individuals and groups promoting division and hatred, and with the factors that predispose individuals or groups to respond to terrorist ideologies . . . . Under *Prevent* public sector organisations are subject to a duty to prevent people from being drawn into terrorism. This duty was recently placed on a statutory footing by the Counter-terrorism and Security Act 2015, together with guidance setting out how different sectors should play their part in implementing the strategy. . . .[46]

COMMENTS AND QUESTIONS

1. Almost simultaneously with the issuing of the government's Counter-Extremism Policy in June 2017, a sequence of terror attacks hit the UK: On 22 March a Britsh Muslim drove a car into pedestrians on Westminster Bridge,

---

46. *See* Joanna Dawson and Samantha Godec, Briefing Paper No. 7238, 23 June 2017, House of Commons Library.

injuring 50 and killing 4. On 22 May, a 22-year-old man born in Manchester to Libyan refugee parents killed at least 22 people and wounded 59 in a suicide bombing at the Manchester Arena. On 3 June, three self-proclaimed jihadis killed at least 7 people and wounded at least 48 more by driving a van into people on London Bridge and killing more in knife attacks on pedestrians. And on 19 June, Cardiff resident Darren Osborne drove a van into a crowd of worshippers at the Finsbury Park mosque in London, killing one and injuring 11, and according to witnesses shouting "I want to kill all Muslims!"[47]

2. Do you think that ideological education in schools can be an effective counter-extremism policy?
3. Given the assertion of the JCHR that a "consultation which does not provide a clear legal definition of what is meant by extremism would be futile," do you think such a definition is possible? If your answer is no, why not? If yes, upon what facts or principles would you begin to build such a definition?

COMMENTARY ON THE UNITED STATES

On 2 December 2015, Chicago-born Syed Rizwan Farook and his wife, Pakastani-born Tashfeen Malik, killed 14 people at the holiday party of the Inland Regional Center in San Bernardino, California, where Farook worked. An investigation showed that the couple were inspired by ISIS. Five days later, presidential candidate Donald Trump proposed

> a total and complete shutdown of Muslims entering the United States until our country's representatives can figure out what is going on. . . . Until we are able to determine and understand this problem and the dangerous threat it poses, our country cannot be the victim of horrendous attacks by people that believe only in Jihad, and have no sense of reason or respect for human life.

President Trump's proposal was not embraced by any of the other major party candidates, and was rejected by many leaders across the political spectrum. Indiana Governor Mike Pence, for example, tweeted, "Calls to ban Muslims from entering the US are offensive and unconstitutional."

Soon after Donald Trump became the 45th President of the United States, with Mike Pence as his vice president, he issued an executive order barring entry into the United States of citizens from seven predominantly Muslim countries—Iraq, Syria, Sudan, Iran, Somalia, Libya, and Yemen—and suspending the US refugee program. Actions to block implementation of the ban began immediately in various federal courts, and on March 6, the administration issued a new order, removing Iraq from the list and making other changes to mollify the effects of the ban; later changes included provisions for people with "close" relatives already living in the United States. The Administration then released a third travel ban, targeting six of the seven original countries, plus North Korea and Venezuela.

A series of challenges to the travel ban filed in federal courts in New York, Massachussets, Washington, Hawaii, and Maryland resulted in the Supreme Court's hearing the consolidated appeals from the Ninth Circuit as *Trump v. Hawaii*, Docket no. 17-965. The case raised four issues: whether respondents' challenge to the president's suspension of entry of aliens abroad is justiciable;

47. *See* United Kingdom: Extremism and Counterextremism, *Counter Extremism Project*.

whether the Proclamation is a lawful exercise of the president's authority to suspend entry of aliens abroad; whether the global injunction is impermissibly overbroad; and whether the Proclamation violates the Establishment Clause. In its 5-4 ruling of 26 June 2018, the Court upheld the ban on the basis of presidential authority to act in the interest of national security, rejecting contrary arguments that the ban intentionally and unfairly targeted Muslims.[48]

COMMENTS AND QUESTIONS

1. What are the policy arguments for and against responding to terror attacks by banning people based on religion? The constitutional arguments? Should such a ban be factually connected with the demonstrable likelihood that those banned will perpetrate terrorist attacks? How overinclusive or underinclusive can the ban be and retain legitimacy? Does it matter, for example, that the Trump travel ban would have had no effect on Syed Rizwan Farook, who was a native-born US citizen, and his wife, who had permanent residence status, and thus could both leave and re-enter the country at will?
2. If the object is to curb terrorism, what are the advantages and disadvanges to immigration bans based on country of origin, rather than on religion? What should be the criteria for selecting the states to be included in such a ban?
3. One reason that opponents of the actual policy implemented by President Trump claim it is unconstitutional is because of his seemingly anti-Muslim rhetoric during the campaign. Should campaign rhetoric be used to interpret the motivation of a subsequently issued executive order? Under what circumstances should hatred or animus against a group invalidate a properly issued executive order? Are national security concerns sufficient to validate the executive order even if such animus is established?
4. Can you suggest a more sensitive basis for identifying individuals who should be denied entry visas because of security risks that they pose?

Additional Web Resources:	Information about ongoing developments concerning the the topics and issues raised in this section

48. *See* Amy Howe, Opinion Analysis: Divided Court Upholds Trump Travel Ban, *SCOTUSblog*, 26 July 2018, and other analysis on the Web Supplement.

CHAPTER 9

RELIGIOUS CONFLICT AND TENSIONS BETWEEN RELIGIOUS FREEDOM AND OTHER RIGHTS

I. INTRODUCTION

This chapter addresses different types of religious conflict, ranging from the horrors of extreme persecution to more mundane (though still reprehensible) forms of discrimination. The hope is that better implementation of religious freedom norms will contribute to the reduction of tension between religious communities, thereby reducing the risks of violence stemming from interreligious intolerance, resentment, and hatred, and improving the prospects for nondiscrimination and mutual respect. Sometimes, however, it seems that protecting religious freedom simply means protecting or entrenching patterns of conduct that exacerbate tensions. Sometimes it provides an excuse for continuing discriminatory or other harmful patterns of conduct. What one community perceives as wrong may be precisely what another perceives as right. When does protecting religious and ideological differences constitute healthy pluralism, and when does it go beyond the bounds of what society can permit?

A. THE COMPLEMENTARY DIMENSIONS OF RELIGIOUS FREEDOM AND OTHER HUMAN RIGHTS

Prior to an analysis of religious conflicts, it is important to recognize the many ways in which human rights are complementary and mutually reinforcing. This is the nub of truth behind the assertion that "[a]ll human rights are universal, indivisible and interdependent and interrelated."[1] More than they conflict with other human rights, religious freedom rights are reinforced, affirmed, and given content by other human rights guarantees, which they benefit in return.

In many circumstances, religious freedom interests align or overlap with other important human rights. Moreover, there are other complementary international norms designed to deter anti-religious conduct ranging from discrimination to the

1. *See, e.g.*, Vienna Declaration and Programme of Action, adopted by the World Conference on Human Rights on 25 June 1993, I sec. 5.

most heinous of crimes, genocide. In addition, as noted in Chapter 2, social science research makes it increasingly clear that religious freedom is part of a bundled set of social goods, including economic development and education. Indeed, the way a society treats religious freedom may be an important indicator of its observance of other rights and its state of social and economic development.

B. TENSIONS BETWEEN RELIGIOUS FREEDOM AND OTHER RIGHTS

Despite their complementary relationship, there are times when religious freedom is in tension or conflict with other rights. In a general sense, this tension was encountered in Chapter 6, in the analysis of limitations on freedom of religion or belief. After all, one of the legitimating grounds for limiting manifestations of religion is "the protection of the [fundamental] rights and freedoms of others." ICCPR, Article 18(3); ECHR, Article 9(2). Moreover, other legitimating grounds for limitations (public safety, health, order, and morals) generally have sufficient priority to override religious freedom claims precisely because of their importance in safeguarding other rights. In that sense, this is not the first treatment of the general problem of conflicts with other rights in this text.

There are a number of areas where conflicts with religious freedom rights have attracted particular attention and deserve closer analysis. Because of limitations of space, this chapter focuses on tensions between religious freedom and discrimination on the basis of race, gender, and sexual orientation. Modules are available on the Web Supplement for distinctive issues that arise in connection with the rights of indigenous peoples and children.

II. RELIGION IN CONFLICT WITH NONDISCRIMINATION NORMS

US law professor Martha Nussbaum has cogently described the tensions that can arise between religious freedom and other rights. Quoting a student of law in India, Nussbaum explains, "Although all religions were initially founded with the aim of purifying men and women and helping them to lead ethical lives through prayer, it was found in some instances that blind traditions, customs and superstition often resulted in—not the cathartic effects of religion—but the spread of communalism, fanaticism, fundamentalism and discrimination."[2] Nussbaum adds:

> Modern liberal democracies typically hold that religious liberty is an extremely important value, and that its protection is among the most important functions of government. These democracies also typically defend as central a wide range of other human interests, liberties, and opportunities. Among these are the freedom of movement, the right to seek employment outside the home, the right to assemble, the right to bodily integrity, the right to education, and the right to hold and to inherit property. Sometimes, however, the religions do not support these other liberties. Sometimes, indeed, they deny such liberties to classes of people in accordance with a morally irrelevant characteristic, such as race or caste or sex. Such denials may not

2. Heera Nawaz, Towards Uniformity, in *Justice for Women: Personal Laws, Women's Rights and Law Reform* (Indira Jaising, ed., The Other India Press 1996).

> mean much in nations where the religions do not wield much legal power. But in [some] nations, where religions run large parts of the legal system, they are fundamental determinants of many lives.
>
> In this way, a dilemma is created for the liberal state. On the one hand, to interfere with the freedom of religious expression is to strike a blow against citizens in an area of intimate self-definition and basic liberty. Not to interfere, however, permits other abridgments of self-definition and liberty. It is not surprising that modern democracies should find themselves torn in this area.. . ."[3]

JOHAN D. VAN DER VYVER, THE RELATIONSHIP OF FREEDOM OF RELIGION OR BELIEF NORMS TO OTHER HUMAN RIGHTS

In *Facilitating Freedom of Religion or Belief: A Deskbook* 85 (Tore Lindholm, W. Cole Durham, Jr., and Bahia G. Tahzib-Lie, eds., Martinus Nijhoff 2004)

In 1996, the South African Parliament adopted legislation prohibiting corporal punishment "at a school to a learner."[4] The legislation followed an earlier decision of the Constitutional Court,[5] and the jurisprudence of several neighboring countries, that flogging constitutes a cruel and inhuman punishment.

The constitutionality of the South African statute was challenged, on religious freedom grounds, by an association originally established in the United States "to promote evangelical Christian education" and which controlled 196 independent Christian schools in South Africa with an enrollment of 14,500 pupils. These schools sought to maintain an active Christian ethos, of which corporal punishment allegedly constitutes an integral part. The constitutional challenge was based on a supposition that the legislative prohibition of corporal punishment in the applicant's schools violated the individual, parental, and community rights of those associated with the applicant to freely practice their religion.

In support of that position, the applicant cited several Bible texts pertinent to the need for "corporal correction":

Proverbs 22:6: "Train up a child in the way it should go and when he is old he will not depart from it."

Proverbs 22:15: "Foolishness is bound in the heart of a child, but the rod of correction shall drive it from him."

Proverbs 19:18: "Chasten thy son while there is hope and let not thy soul spare for his crying."

Proverbs 23:13-14: "Do not withhold discipline from a child, if you punish with a rod he will not die. Punish him with a rod and save his soul from death."

The constitutionality of the contested legislation was upheld in the High Court and by the Constitutional Court. The Court in both instances accepted the religious sincerity of the applicant and assumed that the need for corporal correction constituted part of the religious belief it professed. However, the Biblical texts cited in support of its submissions confined the duty to chastise a child to the

---

3. Martha Craven Nussbaum, *Women and Human Development: The Capabilities Approach* 167 (Cambridge Univ. Press 2000).

4. South African Schools Act, Act 84, sec. 10 (1996).

5. *Christian Education South Africa v. Minister of Education* (CCT4/00) [2000] ZACC 11; 2000 (4) SA 757; 2000 (10) BCLR 1051 (18 August 2000).

parents and did not provide support for the parent to delegate that responsibility to third parties, including teachers.

The significance of the judgment for purposes of the present survey is reflected in an observation of Justice Albie Sachs (in whose judgment all the other nine judges sitting in the matter concurred) noting that "a multiplicity of intersecting constitutional values and interests are involved in the present matter—some overlapping, some competing," including the right of the child to human dignity, to freedom and security of the person, and to be protected from maltreatment, neglect, abuse, or degradation. In terms of the South African Constitution, "[a] child's best interests are of paramount importance in every matter concerning the child." [6]

In almost all situations involving freedom of religion or belief similar intersecting values and concerns will inevitably arise. The interaction between freedom of religion or belief and other basic human rights touched upon in the South African case is a recurring theme: on the one hand is the need to afford meaningful protection to freedom of religion or belief by also protecting rights and freedoms that complement the free exercise of religion or belief, and on the other is a certain tension between basic rights and freedoms perceived by proponents of a particular religion or belief as violating the norms upon which their convictions are founded. Freedom of religion or belief cannot prosper on its own: it requires protection of collateral rights such as freedom of expression and of assembly. Many religions, conversely, as a matter of religious principle, advocate male dominance in the family and in ecclesiastical structures, or condemn homosexuality, and consequently find nondiscrimination decrees based on gender equality offensive to the tenets to which they subscribe. . . .

The right to self-determination of faith communities. . .do[es] not exist, and cannot be exercised, in isolation from a whole range of other basic human rights and fundamental freedoms, including the right to equal protection and nondiscrimination, freedom of expression, freedom of assembly and association, and an effective remedy to vindicate the freedom of religion or belief or for the protection of the integrity of members of the faith community. . . .

The freedom to manifest one's freedom of religion or belief is thus not an absolute freedom. It is essentially limited to an enclave of entitlements determined by the conceptual meaning of "religion or belief." It must be exercised with due regard for the rights and freedoms of others and within the confines of the *general* interest.

COMMENTS AND QUESTIONS

1. As described by Johan van der Vyver, the South African Constitutional Court did several remarkable things in analyzing this conflict. What do you think of them? For one thing, it accepted the religious sincerity of the applicants. Second, it assumed that corporal punishment was a necessary corollary of their religious beliefs. It also gave an authoritative interpretation, backed by the coercive power of the state, of the meaning of a religious text. What do you think of the Court's conclusion that the Bible verses cited by the schools

6. Republic of South Africa Const. of 1996, sec. 28(2).

applied only to parents and not to teachers? In general, parents are far more likely than teachers to injure children. Do we want secular courts to be in the business of interpreting religious texts?

2. The Court engaged in a balancing analysis, noting that the case involves a "multiplicity of constitutional values and interests," some of which overlap and some of which compete with each other. What do you think about the priority the Court affords to the best interests of the child? Are the "best interests" different from the rights of the child?
3. Justice Albie Sachs said in the opinion that "believers cannot claim an automatic right to be exempted by their beliefs from the laws of the land. At the same time, the state should, wherever reasonably possible, seek to avoid putting believers to extremely painful and intensely burdensome choices of either being true to their faith or else respectful of the law."[7] What is your response to this statement? Does it move the analysis forward in a helpful way?
4. In the United States, similar issues have been raised in conscientious objection, for religious reasons, by pharmacists to a law requiring them to distribute certain products. *Stormans v. Wiesman* (formerly *Stormans v. Selecky*) involves regulations in Washington State requiring pharmacies to stock Plan B contraception, even in the face of religious objections to being required to dispense what a person considers to be an abortion-causing drug. The trial court ruled that such regulations would place an unconstitutional burden on religious and other conscientious objectors because they bear the regulation's sole burden on religious freedom. The United States Ninth Circuit Court of Appeals, however, ruled in favor of the state (794 F.3d 1064 (2015). The issue on petition for certiori to the United States Supreme Court was "[w]hether a law prohibiting religiously motivated conduct violates the Free Exercise Clause when it exempts the same conduct when done for a host of secular reasons, has been enforced only against religious conduct, and has a history showing an intent to target religion." In a move that many observers found suprising, the Supreme Court declined to hear the case.[8] Writing in dissent, Justice Alito, joined by Chief Justice Roberts and Justice Thomas, declared the decision a "cause for concern," even "ominous."[9] Some observers thought that the Supreme Court's denial of review was justified, because it is a mistake to see for-profit companies as having religious freedom.[10] Another view is that the Ninth Circuit ruling could stand "as authority for the proposition that governments may treat religious claims for exemptions worse than others or may selectively single out religiously motivated conduct for regulation."[11] Which position seems right to you?
5. Human euthanisia (assisted suicide, assisted dying, "death with dignity") is another area where conscience may come into conflict with law. As of May

---

7. *Christian Education*, *supra* note 4.

8. *See, e.g.,* Emma Green, Even Christian Pharmacists Have to Stock Plan B, *The Atlantic*, 29 June 2016, and Alliance Defending Freedom, US Supreme Court Allows Extreme Washington State Pharmacy Policy to Stand, 28 June 2016.

9. *See Stormans v. Wiesman*, 579 U.S. ____ (2016), *cert. denied*, Alito J, dissenting.

10. *See* Michael Sean Winters, Four Challenges for the Pro-life Movement, *National Catholic Reporter*, 29 June 2016.

11. Rick Garnett, Why Storman's Is a "Cause for Concern," *Mirror of Justice*, 30 June 2016.

2018, human euthanasia was legal in the Netherlands, Belgium, Canada, Colombia, Luxembourg, India, and medically assisted suicide was legal in Switzerland, Germany, Japan, Albania, and South Korea. In the United States, Montana provided for medically assisted euthansia through court ruling and California, Oregon, Washington, Colorado, and Vermont through legislation, with 24 states considering such legistation (for updates *see* deathwithdignity.org). Protections available to conscientious objectors vary significantly among jurisdictions. The Royal Dutch Medical Association states that a physician must refer patients to another physician if the physician objects to euthanasia on religious or other grounds, while section 14 of Belgium's euthanasia act prohibits compelling anyone to perform or assist in a euthanasia procedure. Should doctors be protected from refusing even to refer patients to those who will perform euthanasia procedures? How much religious discretion should doctors be granted in providing medical services?

III. DISCRIMINATION AGAINST RACIAL MINORITIES

A. SOUTH AFRICA

Religion and Apartheid

The following excerpt from Courtney W. Howland describes the International Court of Justice (ICJ) Advisory Opinion in the Namibia apartheid case.[12] The case was heard by the court in 1971 and concerned the legality of the South African occupation of Namibia and the implementation of apartheid there. The International Court of Justice concluded that the occupation was illegal, and declared that the policy of apartheid was "a flagrant violation of the purposes and principles of the Charter of the United Nations."

> The apartheid system in South Africa (and consequently Namibia) was founded on the Afrikaners' Old Testament Christianity of Calvinist origin. Afrikaners believed that they were the chosen people with a divine mission to rule over all others, and from this followed their belief in white supremacy and a policy of racial segregation and discrimination. The ICJ refused to allow South Africa to present factual evidence to prove both South Africa's "good faith" concerning apartheid and its intention to promote the well-being and progress of the inhabitants. Instead the ICJ found as a matter of law that the government's intent and motives concerning its systematic discrimination were irrelevant and that it was not necessary to determine the effects of apartheid. Thus, it would not have been relevant if South Africa had argued any of the following: that its intent concerning apartheid was in "good faith" because it was protecting the (Afrikaner) populace's right to religious freedom; that its good intent was clear because it was fulfilling the divine plan for Afrikaners; that Afrikaners' freedom of religious belief would be deeply infringed if they were not able to assert

12. *Legal Consequences for States of the Continued Presence of South Africa in Namibia (South West Africa) notwithstanding Security Council Resolution* 276 (1970), International Court of Justice, 21 June 1971.

their divinely ordained supremacy over Africans; or that the divine plan was clear about the natural role for whites and blacks and this was reflected in the policy of apartheid. The Court found that no motive or intent, whatever the source, could justify such systematic discrimination and denial of human rights under the Charter. Furthermore, evidence that the apartheid system worked well—such as testimony by Africans that the system of apartheid promoted their well-being and progress—was also irrelevant. By refusing to hear evidence on either intent or the beneficial quality of apartheid the Court was essentially finding systematic discrimination per se illegal and without any possible justification under the Charter.

Although South Africa did not raise the religious arguments, the ICJ must have been aware of them. The Court specifically noted that the policy of apartheid, and its related laws and decrees, were a matter of public record of which the Court was cognizant. Thus, the Court did not need to be informed of the Afrikaners' religious beliefs because those beliefs were evidenced in all the past laws and decrees as a matter of public record from the early Voortrekker republics to contemporary South Africa and Namibia. Such knowledge did not persuade the Court that religious beliefs could justify apartheid policy or be evidence of "good faith" with respect to the policy.

These arguments justifying systematic racial discrimination and apartheid on the basis of religious belief are superfluous now. There is no chance that the international community would accept that religious belief justifies systematic racial discrimination. Thus, even to the extent that the Court did not have the religious justification arguments in mind in the opinion, it is clear that international law would not now accept the freedom of religious belief as justification for systematic racial discrimination. In this context of racial discrimination, the ICJ established the standard for nondiscrimination under the Charter: the Charter prohibits establishing and enforcing distinctions, exclusions, restrictions and limitations exclusively on the ground of race.[13]

COMMENTS AND QUESTIONS

Contrast the approach taken by the South African Constitutional Court to the religious justification in the corporal punishment case with that of the ICJ in the Namibian apartheid case. Although the religious justifications are rejected in both cases, the manner of the rejection is quite different. The South African Court accepted the applicant's arguments as sincere and balanced them against the best interests of the child. Here, the ICJ basically asserted that some religious arguments, even if made in good faith, are beyond the pale and do not need to be taken seriously. Which approach is preferable? Is it possible that each approach is appropriate in certain circumstances? Do you think these cases exemplify those contrasting circumstances?

B. THE UNITED STATES

NOTE ON *BOB JONES UNIVERSITY V. UNITED STATES*

Bob Jones University is a private Christian university located in Greenville, South Carolina. While the university is not specifically connected to any particular

13. Courtney W. Howland, The Challenge of Religious Fundamentalism to the Liberty and Equality Rights of Women: An Analysis Under the United Nations Charter, 35 *Colum. J. Transnat'l L.* 271, 347–349 (1997).

religious denomination or sect, it is dedicated to "teaching and propagat[ing] . . . its fundamentalist Christian religious beliefs." *Bob Jones University v. United States*, 461 U.S. 574, 580 (1983). From the time of the university's inception until many years after *Bob Jones* was decided, the university espoused the belief that the Bible prohibits interracial dating and marriage. The Court acknowledged the sincerity of this religious belief. In support of this conviction, African Americans were denied admission to the University until 1971, at which point the University began accepting applications from African Americans, but only from those individuals who had already married within the African American race. Beginning in 1975, in response to *McCrary v. Runyon*, 515 F.2d 1082 (4th Cir. 1975), *aff'd*, 427 U.S. 160 (1976), which prohibited racial exclusion from private schools, unmarried blacks were allowed to enroll, but a disciplinary rule continued to prohibit interracial dating.

Pursuant to a change in Internal Revenue Service policy in 1970, the IRS announced that it could "no longer legally justify allowing tax-exempt status [under Internal Revenue Code §501(c)(3)] to private schools which practice racial discrimination." Bob Jones University's tax exempt status was ultimately revoked. This was challenged in lower courts and its appeal ultimately reached the US Supreme Court, which reasoned that

> Charitable exemptions are justified on the basis that the exempt entity confers a public benefit—a benefit which the society or the community may not itself choose or be able to provide, or which supplements and advances the work of public institutions already supported by tax revenues. History buttresses logic to make clear that, to warrant exemption under §501(c)(3), an institution must fall within a category specified in that section and must demonstrably serve and be in harmony with the public interest. The institution's purpose must not be so at odds with the common community conscience as to undermine any public benefit that might otherwise be conferred.

Stressing that "[a]n unbroken line of cases following *Brown v. Board of Education* establishes beyond doubt this Court's view that racial discrimination in education violates a most fundamental national public policy," the Court sustained the denial of Bob Jones' tax exempt status.

In reaching this conclusion, the Court rejected the University's argument that, while the tax policy might be valid as to non-religious universities, it could not be applied to schools that discriminate because of genuine religious beliefs, because this would violate their free exercise rights. The Court had no difficulty finding that the "government interest at stake here is compelling" and "outweighs whatever burden denial of tax benefits places on petitioners' exercise of their religious beliefs." Further, "no 'less restrictive means' . . . are available to achieve the governmental interest."

Justice Powell concurred with the majority's conclusion that denial of tax exemptions to Bob Jones University does not violate the First Amendment, but "was troubled by the broader implications of the Court's opinion with respect to the authority of the [IRS and its interpretation of the key Internal Revenue Code provisions]." He reasoned as follows:

> [T]roubling to me is the element of conformity that appears to inform the Court's analysis. The Court asserts that an exempt organization must "demonstrably serve and be in harmony with the public interest," must have a purpose that comports with "the common community conscience," and must not act in a manner "affirmatively at odds

> with [the] declared position of the whole government." Taken together, these passages suggest that the primary function of a tax-exempt organization is to act on behalf of the Government in carrying out governmentally approved policies. In my opinion, such a view of §501(c)(3) ignores the important role played by tax exemptions in encouraging diverse, indeed often sharply conflicting, activities and viewpoints. As Justice BRENNAN has observed, private, nonprofit groups receive tax exemptions because "each group contributes to the diversity of association, viewpoint, and enterprise essential to a vigorous, pluralistic society.". . . Far from representing an effort to reinforce any perceived "common community conscience," the provision of tax exemptions to nonprofit groups is one indispensable means of limiting the influence of governmental orthodoxy on important areas of community life.[14]

Given the importance of our tradition of pluralism, "[t]he interest in preserving an area of untrammeled choice for private philanthropy is very great."

In dissent, Justice Rehnquist acknowledged the strong national policy against racial discrimination, but contended that the IRS lacked authority to change the requirements for §501(c)(3) status (which had been set by Congress) without explicit congressional authorization through new legislation.

Aftermath of *Bob Jones University v. United States*

In 2000, Bob Jones III, then president of the university, officially lifted the interracial dating rule. In 2008, BJU issued a "Statement about Race at BJU":

> For almost two centuries American Christianity, including BJU in its early stages, was characterized by the segregationist ethos of American culture. Consequently, for far too long, we allowed institutional policies regarding race to be shaped more directly by that ethos than by the principles and precepts of the Scriptures. We conformed to the culture rather than providing a clear Christian counterpoint to it.
>
> In so doing, we failed to accurately represent the Lord and to fulfill the commandment to love others as ourselves. For these failures we are profoundly sorry. Though no known antagonism toward minorities or expressions of racism on a personal level have ever been tolerated on our campus, we allowed institutional policies to remain in place that were racially hurtful.
>
> On national television in March 2000, Bob Jones III, who was the university's president until 2005, stated that BJU was wrong in not admitting African-American students before 1971, which sadly was a common practice of both public and private

---

14. Certainly sec. 501(c)(3) has not been applied in the manner suggested by the Court's analysis. The 1,100-page list of exempt organizations includes such organizations as American Friends Service Committee, Inc., Committee on the Present Danger, Jehovah's Witnesses in the United States, Moral Majority Foundation, Inc., Friends of the Earth Foundation, Inc., Mountain States Legal Foundation, National Right to Life Educational Foundation, Planned Parenthood Federation of America, Scientists and Engineers for Secure Energy, Inc., and Union of Concerned Scientists Fund, Inc. See Internal Revenue Service, Cumulative List of Organizations Described in Section 170(c) of the Internal Revenue Code of 1954, at 31, 221, 376, 518, 670, 677, 694, 795, 880, 1001, 1073 (Rev'd Oct. 1981). It would be difficult to argue that each of these organizations reflects the views of the "common community conscience" or "demonstrably...[is] in harmony with the public interest." Identifying these organizations, taken at random from the tens of thousands on the list, does not imply disapproval of their being exempt from taxation. Rather, they illustrate the commendable tolerance by the US government of even the most strongly held divergent views, including views that actually may be "at odds" with the position of the government, which has consistently recognized that such disparate groups are entitled to share the privilege of tax exemption. *Id.* at 609–10.

universities in the years prior to that time. On the same program, he announced the lifting of the University's policy against interracial dating.[15]

Not until 1 March 2017 did BJU fully regain tax-exempt status.

COMMENTS AND QUESTIONS

1. In footnote 30 of the opinion in *Bob Jones*, the court also addressed an Establishment Clause claim by the university:

   > Bob Jones University also contends that denial of tax exemption violates the Establishment Clause by preferring religions whose tenets do not require racial discrimination over those which believe racial intermixing is forbidden. It is well settled that neither a State nor the Federal Government may pass laws which "prefer one religion over another," but "[i]t is equally true" that a regulation does not violate the Establishment Clause merely because it "happens to coincide or harmonize with the tenets of some or all religions." The IRS policy at issue here is founded on a "neutral, secular basis," and does not violate the Establishment Clause. In addition, as the Court of Appeals noted, "the uniform application of the rule to all religiously operated schools *avoids* the necessity for a potentially entangling inquiry into whether a racially restrictive practice is the result of sincere religious belief."

   Which do you think is the stronger, the Establishment Clause claim or Free Exercise claim? Why? Does it matter that *Bob Jones* predated *Smith*? How would you defend a religious university if the IRS sought to take away its tax-exempt status because they discouraged (but did not forbid) interracial dating?
2. Does this decision infringe on the religious freedom of Bob Jones University, or does it merely make it more expensive for the university to act on its beliefs? Is this a case that balances a compelling state interest against an incidental burden to religion? What if the state had made it a crime to operate an educational institution that engaged in racial discrimination, or that disallowed interracial dating? Could such a statute survive a free exercise challenge?
3. Is the IRS the proper organ of government to encourage churches to change their doctrines and policies? Are the pluralism considerations advanced by Justice Powell sufficient to override national policies against racial discrimination?
4. What are the risks of religious backlash in response to government pressure? Are there times when autonomous change within a tradition may be healthier than government-induced change? How much patience should government policymakers have? Was the ultimate shift in Bob Jones' practices a triumph of tax policy or an example of excessive government intrusion in religious affairs? In this regard, should government policy initiatives be the same or different when it comes to discrimination on the basis of gender or sexual orientation?
5. The case of *R(E) v. Governing Body of JFS*, 2009 UKSC 15 (United Kingdom) is similar to *Bob Jones*. JFS, a prestigious Jewish school, gives priority to students who are Jewish according to the United Hebrew Congregation of the Commonwealth. Therefore, an applicant's mother must be an Orthodox Jew

15. *See* Bob Jones University, *Statement about Race at BJU*.

through the matrilineal test or by conversion. In a 5-4 decision, the court held the policy was racially discriminatory according to the Race Relations Act of 1976, which includes ethnic origins as a racial group. The court reasoned that "but for" the applicant's ethnic origins, he would have qualified to attend JFS. They concluded that a policy may be racially discriminatory even when entwined with a religious purpose. In contrast, the two concurring opinions and the dissent argued there was no direct discrimination because the admittance decisions were based on religious grounds only. However, the concurring opinion concluded that JFS was indirectly discriminatory in its policy because, while its aim to promote Orthodox Jewish principles was legitimate, JFS failed to show that the policy was proportionate.

IV. RELIGION AND GENDER

Tension between religious beliefs and women's rights exists across a broad range of issues—abortion, ordaining of women to religious offices, religious influence on the shaping of social roles for men and women, religious rules on marriage and divorce and their influence on roles within the family, and countless others. Laws about these tensions are in criminal law (abortion and rape), family law (divorce) and civil law (employment anti-discrimination laws). Feminism has brought new perspectives on the many ways such issues mold or distort not only legal institutions, but our notions of the nature of rights themselves and the methods of resolving tensions and conflicts. And, of course, there are many feminisms. There are angry critiques of patriarchy and male oppression, and yet in many and perhaps most cultures, women are more engaged in, committed to, and even protected by religion than are men. Women may seek liberation from some of the things religion has been interpreted to mean, but they do not necessarily wish to escape religion (or belief) as a source of meaning, a call of conscience, and a bond of community.

Because of the many ways to view the tensions, it is impossible to do more than touch the surface of the issues in this section.

A. CEDAW

A plausible starting point is the Convention on the Elimination of All Forms of Discrimination Against Women (CEDAW), adopted in 1979 by the UN General Assembly. CEDAW is often thought of as an international bill of rights for women. Consisting of a preamble and 30 articles, it provides a definition of what constitutes discrimination against women and establishes an agenda for national action to eliminate such discrimination.[16] The full text along with supplemental materials is provided on the Web Supplement. Following, in addition to some of the fundamental stipulations of the Convention, are provisions that potentially collide with religious freedom norms.

16. In July 2010, the United National created UN Women by consolidating the UN Division for the Advancement of Women and other UN organizations for the advancement of women.

Convention on the Elimination of All Forms of Discrimination Against Women (CEDAW)

Adopted and opened for signature, ratification and accession by General Assembly Resolution 34/180 of 18 December 1979; *entered into force* 3 September 1981

Article 1 [Discrimination]

For the purposes of the present Convention, the term "discrimination against women" shall mean any distinction, exclusion or restriction made on the basis of sex which has the effect or purpose of impairing or nullifying the recognition, enjoyment or exercise by women, irrespective of their marital status, on a basis of equality of men and women, of human rights and fundamental freedoms in the political, economic, social, cultural, civil or any other field.

Article 2 [Policy Measures]

States Parties condemn discrimination against women in all its forms, agree to pursue by all appropriate means and without delay a policy of eliminating discrimination against women and, to this end, undertake:

(a) To embody the principle of the equality of men and women in their national constitutions or other appropriate legislation if not yet incorporated therein and to ensure, through law and other appropriate means, the practical realization of this principle;

(b) To adopt appropriate legislative and other measures, including sanctions where appropriate, prohibiting all discrimination against women;

(c) To establish legal protection of the rights of women on an equal basis with men and to ensure through competent national tribunals and other public institutions the effective protection of women against any act of discrimination;

(d) To refrain from engaging in any act or practice of discrimination against women and to ensure that public authorities and institutions shall act in conformity with this obligation;

(e) To take all appropriate measures to eliminate discrimination against women by any person, organization or enterprise;

(f) To take all appropriate measures, including legislation, to modify or abolish existing laws, regulations, customs and practices which constitute discrimination against women;

(g) To repeal all national penal provisions which constitute discrimination against women. . . .

Article 5 [Sex Role Stereotyping and Prejudice]

States Parties shall take all appropriate measures:

(a) To modify the social and cultural patterns of conduct of men and women, with a view to achieving the elimination of prejudices and customary and all other practices which are based on the idea of the inferiority or the superiority of either of the sexes or on stereotyped roles for men and women;

(b) To ensure that family education includes a proper understanding of maternity as a social function and the recognition of the common responsibility of men and women in the upbringing and development of their children, it being understood that the interest of the children is the primordial consideration in all cases. . . .

Article 9 [Citizenship]

1. States Parties shall grant women equal rights with men to acquire, change or retain their nationality. They shall ensure in particular that neither marriage to an alien nor change of nationality by the husband during marriage shall automatically change the nationality of the wife, render her stateless or force upon her the nationality of the husband.

2. States Parties shall grant women equal rights with men with respect to the nationality of their children.

Article 16 [Marriage and Family Life]

1. States Parties shall take all appropriate measures to eliminate discrimination against women in all matters relating to marriage and family relations and in particular shall ensure, on a basis of equality of men and women:

(a) The same right to enter into marriage;

(b) The same right freely to choose a spouse and to enter into marriage only with their free and full consent;

(c) The same rights and responsibilities during marriage and at its dissolution;

(d) The same rights and responsibilities as parents, irrespective of their marital status, in matters relating to their children; in all cases the interests of the children shall be paramount;

(e) The same rights to decide freely and responsibly on the number and spacing of their children and to have access to the information, education and means to enable them to exercise these rights;

(f) The same rights and responsibilities with regard to guardianship, wardship, trusteeship and adoption of children, or similar institutions where these concepts exist in national legislation; in all cases the interests of the children shall be paramount;

(g) The same personal rights as husband and wife, including the right to choose a family name, a profession and an occupation;

(h) The same rights for both spouses in respect of the ownership, acquisition, management, administration, enjoyment and disposition of property, whether free of charge or for a valuable consideration.

2. The betrothal and the marriage of a child shall have no legal effect, and all necessary action, including legislation, shall be taken to specify a minimum age for marriage and to make the registration of marriages in an official registry compulsory.

COMMENTS AND QUESTIONS

1. Which of the foregoing CEDAW provisions are likely to collide with religious beliefs? For example, does a church that has only male clergy violate the Convention? Does the state have power under Article 5 to modify this?
2. How rigorous should state enforcement be? Does Article 5(a) obligate states to coerce change of religious prejudices or practices? What are "all *appropriate* measures"? Is it appropriate for states to implement measures inconsistent with religious convictions? Do state interests in eliminating

gender discrimination weigh as heavily in the balance against religious freedom claims as the comparable interests in ending racial discrimination?

3. CEDAW has been entered into with more reservations than any other major human rights convention. Several Muslim states have entered reservations to all portions of Article 16 on the ground that they conflict with Shari'a. Israel has registered similar reservations to safeguard implementation of its personal status law in the courts of its religious communities. Various other countries have also submitted reservations—some with predominantly Catholic populations, such as Ireland and Brazil, and others with Asian cultures, such as Korea and Thailand. *See* Note by the Secretary-General, Declarations, Reservations, Objections and Notifications of Withdrawal of Reservations Relating to the Convention on the Elimination of All Forms of Discrimination Against Women, UN Doc. CEDAW/SP/1992/2 (1991). Are such reservations inconsistent with core CEDAW values, or do they allow needed flexibility in a pluralistic world?
4. The United States is the world's only industrialized democracy that has not ratified CEDAW, in spite of five Senate hearings on the matter over the course of 25 years. US opponents of CEDAW insist that such human rights treaties violate American sovereignty, contravene constitutional limitations on federal power, violate freedom of religion and association, and in any event provide less concern for and protection of women's rights than are already available under US law. Proponents of CEDAW have seen such arguments as part of a narrow-minded and defiant refusal to understand that the convention actually makes global norms of American values of equality and women's rights.[17] Who is right? Why?
5. Consider the following views on religion and women's rights. Where would you position yourself on such issues?

JULIET SHEEN, BURDENS ON THE RIGHT OF WOMEN TO ASSERT FORB RIGHTS

In *Facilitating Freedom of Religion or Belief: A Deskbook* 513, 513–514 (Tore Lindholm, W. Cole Durham, Jr., and Bahia G. Tahzib-Lie, eds., Martinus Nijhoff 2004)

Of particular interest are those rights violations that arise out of the human right to enjoyment and freedom of belief. Whilst that right has been set out in detail in the 1981 UN Declaration on the Elimination of All Forms of Intolerance and of Discrimination Based on Religion and Belief, there are violations that might go unnoticed even in our gender-sensitive environment. Religion is so heavily masculinized that the tenets and extensions of religious belief are sometimes, in and of themselves, violations of women's human rights.

The manifestations and practices which are protected under the freedom of religion and belief are deeply entwined with other rights and freedoms, directly or indirectly. These include the freedom to associate and to assemble peacefully, freedom of expression and communication, freedom of movement, freedom of political and other opinion, freedom from discrimination and access to effective

---

17. *See, e.g.*, Lisa Baldez, *Defying Convention: The United States, the United Nations, and the Treaty on Women's Rights* (Cambridge University Press 2014).

remedies, freedom from arbitrary interference, freedom to marry and found a family, freedom to educate and be educated, and freedom to own property, among others. All these rights and freedoms are crucial to the maintenance and continuity of religious and other belief systems and their organizations, as is recognized in articles 5 and 6 of the 1981 UN Declaration. Yet these are the very freedoms that are at issue for women when freedom of religion is played as a trump card to justify their subordination.

Mary Ann Glendon, Women's Unfinished Journey

Position Paper, quoted in How to Treat a Woman, *Zenit*, 15 February 2005, citing *L'Osservatore Romano*, 5 January 2005

The journey of women's liberation, Pope John Paul II wrote in his 1995 World Day of Peace Message, "has been a difficult and complicated one and, at times, not without its share of mistakes. But it has been substantially a positive one, even if it is still unfinished. . . . The 25th Anniversary of [CEDAW] . . . provides an occasion to reflect on that journey. . . ."

The preparation of CEDAW in the turbulent 1960s and 1970s coincided with the emergence of a peculiar form of feminism that was characterized by negative attitudes toward men, marriage, and motherhood. The leading spokeswomen of this movement tragically underestimated the heavy burdens that sexual "liberation" would impose on women, and radically discounted the importance of biological differences between women and men. A feminism so profoundly at variance with the needs and desires of most women was destined to be a short-lived phenomenon. But it was at its height during the years when CEDAW took shape.

As a result, the document that was opened for signature in 1979 contains a number of problematic features. Along with provisions that could help to improve women's access to education, health care, and economic opportunity there is much ambiguous language that has often been construed to discourage or even ban special protections for mothers. Furthermore, the requirement of governmental intervention to promote gender equality in the private as well as public sectors creates severe tension with the fundamental human rights to freedom of association, opinion, expression, and belief.

Frances Raday, Gender and Democratic Citizenship: The Impact of CEDAW

10 *I*CON* (2), 512- 515 (2012) (notes omitted)

The central feminist claim made in criticism of CEDAW is that it is assimilationist and shackles women to the male model as the dominant norm. Much has been written about the problem of a legal agenda which requires women to claim equality with a male comparator, which thus precludes the kind of transformative change which would allow women to participate in social and political institutions on their own terms and in accordance with their own realities. A second and equally important claim is the intersectionality claim, according to which there can be no one expression of feminism which is indistinguishably applicable to women of different ethnicity, cultural or class identity. It is claimed that CEDAW largely treats women as a homogenous group. A postmodernist claim is made that the very retention of the category of womanhood in CEDAW is essentialist and neither accurate nor effective; that it has not achieved the broad transformative equality promised and cannot do so as long as "the harms it addresses focus solely on "women" as a group."

. . . [T]he development of my theme will show how that [these critiques] may be belied both by the language of CEDAW and by institutional interpretation and developments at the international and domestic levels. Indeed many of the writers who have questioned the effectiveness of the international human rights regime as a vehicle for achieving women's autonomy and their right to self-determination within the international and constitutional framework of states, have nevertheless acknowledged the potential—if challenging—of the international human rights framework and of CEDAW to be the harbingers of transformative equality. . . .

CEDAW takes an uncompromising stance on the primacy of women's right to equality which must prevail in the face of traditionalist religious or neoliberal challenges. There are considerable achievements which can be in large part attributed to CEDAW. Achievements include international recognition of women's rights as human rights, creation of national machinery for the advancement of women, collection of sex-disaggregated data by states parties, promotion of TSMs for women's political participation, and enactment of specifi c domestic violence legislation. CEDAW also addresses intersectionality, treating the differing requirements of women in cultural, social, or economic subgroups as requiring special attention and listing, amongst others, women in poverty, women belonging to minorities, women with disabilities, refugees, migrants, stateless women, lesbians, girls, and elderly women. CEDAW's tools for addressing cultural, social, and economic intersectional differences between women are offshoots of the core right to equality and are not a vehicle for the fragmentation of it. In this respect, CEDAW is consonant with a core concept of feminism rather than with a subjective and relativist collection of feminisms.

The conceptual clarity of CEDAW is not fully matched by states parties' record in implementation. . . .

Additional Web Resources:	Materials on CEDAW, with full text of the Convention, detail on reservations, official recommendations from the UN Committee on the Elimination of Discrimination Against Women, Ten-Year Review and Appraisal of Beijing Declaration and Platform for Action, and other materials

B. RELIGION IN CONFLICT WITH WOMEN'S RIGHTS

1. Divorce

a. India

In August 2017 the Supreme Court of India declared unconstitutional a mechanism by which a Muslim man was permitted to divorce a wife through "triple talaq," a practice with a thousand-year history in Islam, though not prescribed in the Qur'an, and in fact long-since outlawed in India's neighboring Muslim countries of Bangladesh, Pakistan, and Indonesia. This process of "instant divorce" involves repeating in one sitting (in person, or in modern times on the telephone, through letter via speedpost, by Skype and WhatsApp) three times the word *talaq* ("I divorce you," derived from the Arabic term for "repudiate"). After the pronouncement by the husband, a woman was "entitled to claim only the dowry, or *mehr*, that [she] had been given by the man at the time of marriage,[18] and no further maintenance. [19]

A sort of remedy for this practice, which left many Muslim women in India in desperate circumstances, was found through Section 125 of the Criminal Code,

> [which] forbids a man "of adequate means" to permit various close relatives, including (by special amendment in 1973) an ex-wife, to remain in a state of "destitution and vagrancy." Many women divorced under Muslim law had been able to win grants of maintenance under this Section; the recognition of ex-wives as relations ... was introduced specifically for this purpose (and was objected to by members of the Muslim League on grounds of religious free exercise). [20]

The inadequacy of such remedies is illustrated in the tragic case of Shah Bano Begum.

NOTE ON *MOHAMMED AHMED KHAN v. SHAH BANO BEGUM*[21]

In Madhya Pradesh in 1978, an elderly Muslim woman named Shah Bano was thrown out of her home by her husband, a prosperous lawyer, after 44 years of marriage. As required by Islamic law, he returned her marriage portion, Rs. 3000 (about $60 by [2001] exchange rates). Following what was by then a common practice, she applied for relief under Section 125. The case found its way to the Supreme Court. Deciding in Shah Bano's favor and awarding her a maintenance of Rs. 180 per month (about $4), Chief Justice Chandrachud, a Hindu, wrote a lengthy opinion, both criticizing Islamic practices and interpreting Islamic texts on his own hook to show that this grant of maintenance was consistent with Islamic norms. The rhetoric of the opinion was most unfortunate: The Chief Justice cited a British commentary on the Koran in support of the proposition that the "fatal point in Islam is the degradation of women." He also stated, "Undoubtedly, the Muslim husband enjoys the privilege of being able to discard his wife whenever he chooses to do so, for reasons good, bad, or indifferent. Indeed, for no reason at all."

The high publicity given to this contemptuous opinion produced a most unfortunate reaction. Up to this time, there was broad support in the Muslim community for sex equality and even for the goal of a Uniform Civil Code. Women had been winning grants of maintenance with no interference. . . . But now much

18. *See* Qur'an 4:4. ("And give the women [upon marriage] their [bridal] gifts graciously. But if they give up willingly to you anything of it, then take it in satisfaction and ease."), as cited in Martha Nussbaum, International Human Rights Law in Practice: India: Implementing Sex Equality Through Law 2 *Chi. J. Int'l L.* 35, 44 (2001).

19. Cited in Nussbaum, *supra* note 18.

20. *Id.*

21. *Mohammed Ahmed Khan v. Shah Bano Begum and Ors.*, 1985 SCR (3) 844 (23 April 1985). The text of this note is from Nussbaum, *supra* note 18.

of the Muslim community, feeling its honor slighted and its civic position threatened, rallied round the cause of denying women maintenance. Women were barely consulted when statements were made about what Indian Muslims wished and thought; an impression was created . . . that all Muslims disagreed with the judgment.

Meanwhile the Muslim leadership persuaded the government of Rajiv Gandhi to pass a law, the Muslim Women's (Protection after Divorce) Act of 1986, which deprives all, and only, Muslim women of the opportunity to win maintenance under the Criminal Code. The government never consulted with other segments of the community; [rather, they allowed the irate Muslim leaders to speak for all]. Muslim women expressed outrage. One activist stood on the steps of Parliament the day the 1986 law was passed and said, "If by making separate laws for Muslim women, you are trying to say that we are not citizens of this country, then why don't you tell us clearly and unequivocally that we should establish another country—not Hindustan or Pakistan but Auratstan (women's land)?" Hindu men, meanwhile, complained that the new law discriminates against Hindus, giving Muslim males "special privileges." In the aftermath of the Muslim Women's Bill, many divorced Muslim women are leading lives of poverty. Worse still, the destitution of these women has had the effect of crippling their children's education, as children who would otherwise be in school are put to work supporting their mothers. Efforts of women to challenge the new law on the ground of religious non-discrimination (by petition to the Supreme Court) have been unsuccessful: Apparently, the Court is in retreat from the controversy occasioned by its role in the *Shah Bano* judgment.

* * *

This "retreat" would last for another three decades. Meantime, Shah Bano returned to her village but became a social outcast, both within her family and among others in her village.[22]

> On November 2, 1985, Shah Bano, in the presence of four male witnesses, signed with her thumbprint an open letter to all Muslims, stating that Islamic leaders had explained to her the commands concerning divorce and maintenance, in the light of Quran and Hadith. Using legal language that she is extremely unlikely to have chosen herself or perhaps even to have understood, she renounces her claim to maintenance and demands that the Indian government withdraw the Supreme Court decision. She further states that "Article 44 of the Indian Constitution, in which there is a directive for enacting a uniform civil code for all, is quite contrary to the Quran and the hadith." She asks that the government renounce the goal of uniformity and resolve that "no interference would be ever attempted in future" with the operation of Islamic courts. "In the end," she concludes, "I thank Maulana Habib Yar Khan and Haji Abdul Ghaffar Saheb of Indore who showed me the straight path and helped me follow the Truth and thus saved me in this world and in the hereafter." [23]

---

22. From Martha Craven Nussbaum, *Women and Human Development: The Capabilities Approach* 239–240 (Cambridge Univ. Press 2000).

23. Shah Bano's Open Letter to Muslims, published in *Inquilab*, 3 November 1985, and translated into English by A. Karim Shaikh. Reprinted in Engineer, ed., 211–212. Shah Bano died in Indore in 1992, at the age of 89.

In August 2017, a Constitutional Panel of the Supreme Court of India, comprising five judges of five faiths—Christian, Hindu, Muslim, Sikh, and Zoroastrian—delivered its long-awaited judgment in *Shayara Bano v. Union of India and others*, Writ Petition (Civil), 118 of 2016, holding that the practice of "talaq-e-biddat" is unconstitutional and with immediate effect is set aside.

The similarity in the names of the petitioners is coincidental, and the two cases have apparently little in common. Shah Bano Begum's plea was for lifetime maintenance when her husband divorced her. The pleas of Shayara Bano and her co-petitioners were for the declaration that not only triple talaq but also "nikah halala" (the requirement that a divorced Muslim woman contract another marriage before she can return to her earlier husband) are illegal, unconstitutional, un-Islamic, and antithetical to Islam itself.[24] Both, however, turned on the relationship of Muslim Personal Law to the constitutional provisions in a secular state.

The Shayara Bano case created controversy across the political spectrum. At the extremes, Prime Minister Modi "lent his support to the Muslim women fighting against the practice of triple talaq," while the "All India Muslim Personal Law Board (AIMPLB) . . . warned secular authorities against interfering with religious law."[25] The ruling itself—from five judges, expressing three views, and issuing one order—was "hesitant and split": "You get a 395-page court document that includes three different judgements which contradict each other on terminological definitions (*talaq e-biddat*, triple talaq or instant talaq?), what constitutes Shariat and whether personal law can be regulated by the Constitution."[26]

The legal controversy centers on the compatibility of the Muslim Personal Law (Shariat) Application Act of 1937 with Article 25, " one of the most misinterpreted articles of the Indian Constitution."[27] Section 2 of the 1937 Act provides in relevant part: "Notwithstanding any customs or usage to the contrary, in all questions [of] . . . marriage, dissolution of marriage, including talaq . . . the rule of decision in the cases where parties are Muslims shall be the Muslim Personal Law (Shariat). Article 25 states that every individual is "equally entitled to freedom of conscience" and has the right "to profess, practice and propagate religion" of one's choice, limited by considerations affecting "public order, morality and health."

In his prevailing opinion in *Shayara Bano*, Judge Rohinton Fali Nariman (Zoroastrian), endorsed by Judge Uday Umesh Lalit (Hindu), noted that while the 1937 Act recognizes and enforces triple talaq, notwithstanding any customs or usage to the contrary, "the rule of decision does not fall within the confines of Article 25 of the Constitution." Triple talaq is manifestly arbitrary, and the 1937 Act, insofar as it recognizes the practice, is unconstitutional and is consequently struck down. The judgment of Judge Kurian Joseph (Christian) came to the same conclusion, by observing that triple talaq is against the basic tenets of the Qur'an

24. *See* Mani Shankar AIyar, Rajiv Gandhi Was Attacked for this Decision. I Believe It Was Genius, *NDTV*, 2 August 2016.

25. Gautam Bhatia, Triple Talaq and the Constitution, *The Hindu*, 11 May 2017.

26. Baijayant "Jay" Panda, Turning Point for India: Supreme Court's Triple Talaq Judgment Sets the Country on Course to a Uniform Civil Code, 30 August 2017. *See also* Aviral Virk and Vakasha Sachdev, Triple Talaq: 5 Judges, 3 Views, 1 Order, But Why No Clarity?, *The Quint*, 22 August 2017.

27. Shubhojit, Meaning of Article 25 of the Indian Constitution, *Elections.in*, 22 December 2014.

and is not an intergral part of Islam. These two judgments constitute the panel's "majority". A third judgment was given by the current Chief Justice of India, Jagdish Singh Khehar, the first Sikh to serve in this post, joined by the Muslim member, Abdul Nazeer. Justice Khedar contended that though triple talaq is not an intergral part of Islam itself, it is integral to Islam in India and is part of Muslim Personal Law (Shariat). This judgment, written before the others, enjoined Muslims from exercising triple talaq for six months and directed the Union of India to frame a law governing the matter.

In the aftermath of *Shayara Bano*, the Indian government proposed a bill criminalizing triple talaq, based on the assumption that declaraing the practice unconsitutional would not stop it. Such organizations as the All India Muslim Personal Law Board (AIMPLB) strongly opposed this move, preferring "societal correction to penal correction" for inevitable violaton this long-traditional practice, and asserting that the government's bill was itself unconstitutional and that it would "harm women's interests, as a husband may neither agree to divorce nor fulfil his responsibilities towards his wife if he were booked." [28] Claiming support from "several women's organisations," AIMPLB advocated "societal pressure" and efforts to push acceptance of Islamic marriage contracts (*nikahnama*) containing clauses binding on the groom to refrain from issuing triple talaq.

By September 2018, more than 200 triple talaq divorces had been reported by the government since the Supreme Court's ruling, and the draft bill had failed in Parliament. On 19 September President Ram Nath Kovind issued an executive order making triple talaq a criminal offense in India, an action both hailed as triumph for women in India and decried as "neither perfect nor necessary" and even as an action "against women." [29]

COMMENTS AND QUESTIONS

1. Why do you suppose Shah Bano backed down in the aftermath of this case and renounced the rights she had received from the court? What does this say about the connections between culture, the law, and the social conditions that must exist for a legal remedy to be effective?
2. While the protection of the rights of women has been repeatedly asserted in such cases as those discussed here, the "majority of those practising Islam consider the laws of the Shariat to be completely correct and so they cannot be subjected to legislative changes considering the fact that freedom of religion, practices and so on, are part of fundamental rights."[30]
3. Can you see the points of view of both the Indian government—which has come under international criticism in recent years for violating religious

---

28. AIMPLB prefers "correction" of triple talaq, *The Hindu*, 12 February 2018.

29. *See, e.g.,* two articles from *The Indian Express:* Faizan Mustafa, Why the Triple Talaq Ordinance is Neither Perfect nor Necessary, 21 September 2018, and Balaji Srinivasan and Arunava Mukherjee, Why Triple Talaq Ordinance: For Law without Justice Is Wound without Cure, 214 September. Follow ongoing reports and discussion on the Web Supplement.

30. Shariat and Muslim Personal Law: All Your Questions Answered, *The Indian Express*, 22 August 2017.

liberties of minorities amid a surge of Hindu nationalism[31]—and the AIMPLB in this matter?

b. Canada

NOTE ON SHARIA THROUGH ARBITRATION: PRIVATE JURISDICTION FORECLOSED

RAN HIRSCHL AND AYELET SHACHAR, THE NEW WALL OF SEPARATION: PERMITTING DIVERSITY, RESTRICTING COMPETITION

Excerpted from Ran Hirschl and Ayelet Shachar, The New Wall of Separation: Permitting Diversity, Restricting Competition, 30 *Cardozo L. Rev.* 2535, 2554–2556 (2009) (most citations omitted)

Consider the acrimonious controversy that erupted in 2003 in Ontario following a proposal emanating from some members of the province's large and diverse Muslim community to draw upon the provincial Arbitration Act of 1991 to establish Shari'a-based arbitration tribunals in personal status matters.[32] This proposal did not come to the fore in the usual legislative process nor did it originate from a governmental initiative or law-reform process. Instead, a small and relatively conservative nongovernmental organization, named the Canadian Society of Muslims, declared in a series of press releases its intention to establish the a "[P]rivate Islamic Court of Justice," or Shari'a tribunal, as this proposal came to be known in the ensuing debate. The envisioned tribunal, according to its proponents, would have permitted consenting parties to rely on the (then existing) Arbitration Act not only to enter a less adversarial, out-of-court dispute resolution process, but also to use the Act's choice of law provisions to apply religious norms to the resolution of family disputes, according to the "laws (fiqh) of any [Islamic] school, e.g., Shiah or Sunni (Hanafi, Shafi'i, Hambali, or Maliki)." The tribunal's advocates further argued that once the possibility to turn to binding Shari'a arbitration becomes readily available, it should represent a clear choice for Muslim Canadians: governance of oneself by the personal law of religion or governance by secular Canadian family law. This construction of the proposal had the effect of presenting it as a frontal "non-state-law-as-competition" challenge, which even tolerant, multicultural Ontario (the largest Canadian province and arguably the country's most influential common-law jurisdiction) could not accept with indifference.

A major controversy soon erupted. Opponents argued that a religious tribunal of this kind would set a dangerous precedent by allowing different communities to "carve out" certain aspects of the law and to insulate themselves from the purview of Charter provisions and other basic norms of statutory and administrative law.

---

31. See, for example, Alex Caro, What We Can Learn from Religious Liberty Battles in India, *Real Clear Religion*, 6 September 2017.

32. See Arbitration Act, S.O., ch. 17 (1991) (Ont.) ("allow[ing] the parties to choose the law applicable to their disputes. . . . It does so by allowing the parties to vary or opt out of the applicability and choice of law sections."), *see also* John D. Gregory, Anne Marie Predeko, and Juliet Nicolet, *Faith-Based Arbitration* 1 (2005).

Establishing such enclaves of unregulated "islands of privatized jurisdiction" would be detrimental to the universality of the rule of law in Canada. Feminist activists and grassroots organizations, such as the Canadian Council of Muslim Women, further emphasized that such tribunals would put undue burden on Muslim women who, for fear of being ostracized or otherwise sanctioned, would be coerced by the community to consent to such Shari'a-based arbitration processes. Others expressed the concern that these tribunals would fall prey to intra-community politics or would be dominated by community "big-men." As tensions mounted, the debate over the proposed faith-based tribunal became highly politicized and polarized. It was in this climate that Ontario Premier Dalton McGuinty decided to terminate the debate by publicly announcing that no religious or faith-based arbitration in Ontario may be based on the province's Arbitration Act. The concept of alternative dispute resolution (ADR) may be effective in reducing the burden on the court system. However, it is not meant to carve out enclaves of religious jurisdiction operating outside of the purview of the general rule of law.

The clearest statement of this governmental position was expressed by the Attorney General, the highest civil official in Ontario authorized with developing and enforcing the tenets of the civil religion [of constitutionalism]. Upon revealing the proposed legislation that amended the Arbitration Act, the Attorney General stated that "[a]ll family law arbitrations [in Ontario will be] conducted under Canadian law." [33] The answer to the non-state-law-as-competition challenge, then, was to declare officially and accordingly legislate that "resolutions based on other laws and principles—including religious principles—would have no legal effect and would amount to advice only." This change took effect in 2006 and was further elaborated with regulations published in 2007. Bringing the point home, the Attorney General reaffirmed that only those charged with securing the implementation of the civil religion have a claim to speak authoritatively on behalf of the governed, stating forcefully that "[t]here is one family law for all Ontarians and that is Canadian law." Any other sources of normativity and authority, including religious principles, are relegated to the realm of "unofficial," "unrecognized" and, indeed, "non-law" status—not at all part of the rule of law.

c. United Kingdom

BRITISH SHARI'A COUNCILS

Sahmeer Ahmed, Pluralism in British Islamic Reasoning: The Problem with Recognizing Islamic Law in the United Kingdom, 33 *Yale J. Int'l L.* 491, 492–493 (2008) (citations omitted).

One problem British Muslims have encountered is the issue of "limping" marriages, which are considered valid by one legal system, but dissolved by another. Because some Islamic scholars believe a British civil divorce is not

33. Ministry of the Att'y Gen., Ontario Passes Family Statute Law Amendment Act, *Ontario Newsroom*, 15 February 2006. These changes were implemented with the passage of the Arbitration Act, S.O. ch. 1, §1(2) (2006) (incorporated into section 2.2. of the 1991 Arbitration Act) and 2007 regulations pursuant to this legislation. See Family Arbitration, O. Reg. 134/2007.

religiously valid, many British Muslims divorce twice—civilly and Islamically. However, a problem exists when a Muslim man divorces his wife in a civil proceeding, but not according to Islamically accepted procedures. Since the couple would still be considered married under some interpretations of Islamic law, they would be in a limping marriage. Since polygyny has historically been allowed in Islamic law, under these circumstances the husband is still able to remarry both civilly and Islamically. In contrast, the wife is held hostage, unable to remarry because, in the eyes of many in the Muslim community, she is still married. Furthermore, she has no recourse to British state law because the couple is legally divorced. Some Muslim men have, therefore, been able to blackmail their wives by withholding an Islamic divorce unless their wives agree to favorable settlements on financial compensation, property, and child custody.

Since the UK legal system has very few remedies to adequately resolve the limping marriages problem, British Muslims have developed their own informal dispute settlement processes: shari'a councils. These have been established by British Muslim leaders who have recognized the need to create an unofficial Islamic family law system that would allow Muslim women to divorce their husbands "Islamically" without the risk of being blackmailed. The primary function of shari'a councils is to act as qadis (Islamic judges) and issue "Islamic divorces" to Muslim women trapped in limping marriages, allowing them to leave their former husbands without fearing religious consequences.. . .

British Islamic scholars differ over whether shari'a councils, which are currently not recognized by the British legal system, are the best way of resolving Muslims' marital disputes and implementing Islamic family law in the United Kingdom. For the most part, they have taken one of three positions on the issue: (1) the United Kingdom needs a legally enforceable Islamic family law system; (2) unofficial shari'a councils are adequate to meet the needs of British Muslims; or (3) shari'a councils are unnecessary, because Muslims can solely follow British law and still adhere to the principles of the shari'a.

d. United States

Michael Broyde, Jewish Law Courts in America: Lessons Offered to Sharia Courts by the Beth Din of America Precedent

27 *N.Y.L. Sch. L. Rev.* 287, 288–289 (2012-2013) (notes omitted)

After a lengthy trial-and-error history, Jewish law in America has found a home in a well-defined and expansive system of Jewish law courts around the country referred to as batei din. The Beth Din of America (BDA), one of the nation's most prominent rabbinic courts, was founded in 1960 to accommodate the portion of the Jewish community in America committed to living in accordance with both secular and religious law. For some time, batei din struggled to find their footing within the American legal system. Secular courts were initially uncomfortable upholding and enforcing decisions issued in accordance with what was essentially foreign law. Today, however, the BDA provides a sprawling network of Jewish law courts that function as arbitration panels (and more), offering litigants access to a religious forum marked by the characteristic expedience and affordability of the arbitration process. More significantly, the

BDA has gained widespread acceptance among America's secular courts, which, to date, have never overturned a BDA-issued decision. As the Muslim community in America embarks upon a quest to develop and refine its own religious court system, it should regard the BDA precedent as a useful navigation tool.

. . . [T]he BDA's viability came to rest on six pillars of the revised Jewish arbitration process: (1) the BDA issued and publicized detailed and standardized rules of procedure; (2) in addition to its arbitration services, the BDA developed an internal appellate process; (3) the BDA provided choice-of-law provisions to facilitate accommodation of both Jewish and secular law where possible; (4) in addition to Jewish scholars, the BDA employed, as arbitrators, skilled lawyers and professionals who could provide expertise in the areas of secular law and contemporary commercial practices; (5) to ensure the effective resolution of commercial arbitrations, the BDA gleaned and abided by common commercial customs to the extent permitted by Jewish law; and (6) the BDA accepted that an aggregate of individual arbitrations gave rise to an active role in communal governance.

These six modifications demonstrated the innovation and adaptation required of Jewish law in its pursuit of judicial acceptance. While each is ultimately consistent with Jewish law, each also represents a departure from the traditional practice thereof. Thus, it follows that the adoption of such changes for Sharia law courts—and those courts' ultimate viability—rest on Sharia law's ability to adhere to the American arbitration system and to embrace American law more generally.

. . .

[B]oth Jewish and Sharia law prescribe the process for obtaining a religious divorce. No amount of compromise in the arbitration process, however, will permit a religious divorce to serve in lieu of a couple's obtaining a civil divorce. Thus, occasionally, co-existence between religious and secular laws requires more than choice-of-law clause recognition on the part of a religious court: it encompasses also an inherent choice of forum.

This realization is especially difficult because it forces a conclusion not contemplated by both Jewish and Sharia law. In some cases, litigants will be forced to resolve their issues in secular court because it is the only forum capable of granting a civil divorce, for example. The BDA accepted this proposition as a necessity of American existence and, with respect to the above example, requires divorcing couples to obtain both a religious and civil divorce. Indeed, the document given at the conclusion of every Jewish divorce to the former couple states directly that:

> This is to certify that [name of husband] divorced his wife [name of wife] on [day of week], the [day of Hebrew month] of [Hebrew month], [Jewish year], corresponding to the [day of month of [month], [year] *c.e.* according to Orthodox Jewish law. *[Name of man/woman] is free to marry provided that s/he is also civilly divorced.*

Jewish law simply cannot grant a civil divorce and we recognize that our community is ill served without recognizing that fact and encouraging people to ensure that their civil status and religious status match when possible.

To improve their dual-system reconciliation, Sharia courts will need to follow suit in acknowledging certain areas in which religious law cannot be substituted for secular law. For the remaining areas in which the two regimes may be reconciled, Sharia courts will benefit immensely from a commitment to choice-of-law recognition and the cultivation of dual-trained arbitrators.

COMMENTS AND QUESTIONS

1. Which of the three British approaches seems preferable? Would any of them be acceptable in Canada? Could the Islamic Courts actually serve to empower women?
2. What do you think of Broyde's suggestion that American Muslims should model Shari'a courts on Beth Din?

2. Female Genital Cutting

The highly controversial practice of female genital cutting (FGC), which includes practices sometimes referred to as female circumcision or female genital mutilation (FGM), has deep cultural roots and often strong religious justifications. FGC is against the law in many countries, as it was in the United States (under USC § 116 (c)), when a federal district court in Michigan, without examining the practice itself, found that Congress lacked the power to enact such a law on a federal level (*United States v. Nagarwala et al.*, Criminal No. 17-CR-20274). The now-acquitted defendants in the Michigan case were a doctor accused of performing FGC on young girls, the owners of the clinic where the procedures were performed, and the mothers of six girls brought to the clinic for the procedure, who argued that the practice in which they engage is not harmful (no more than a very small cut, like a paper cut, which arguable is not circumcision, excision, or infibrilation, as proscribed by the statute), and is an action motivated by their sincere religious beliefs as Dawoodi Bohras.[34] The statute took no account of "the effect on the person on whom the operation is performed or of any belief on the part of that person that the operation is required as a matter of custom or ritual." As you read the following excerpt, consider whether any form of FGC, mild or severe, deserves a higher degree of protection if those performing or receiving the procedure assert religious justifications, as in the case of male circumcision among Jews and Muslims, than if performed for other reasons.

BAHIA G. TAHZIB-LIE, THE FREEDOM TO UNDERGO FEMALE GENITAL MUTILATION VS. THE PROTECTION OF PUBLIC HEALTH

In *Facilitating Freedom of Religion or Belief: A Deskbook* 455 (Tore Lindholm, W. Cole Durham, Jr., and Bahia G. Tahzib-Lie, eds., Martinus Nijhoff 2004)

FGM is practiced on females in different parts of the world, usually at an early age, for a variety of nontherapeutic reasons, including custom, tradition, religion, belief, and aesthetics. It is known to be practiced among followers of different religions and beliefs, including Christians of many denominations, Sunni and

34. A sect within the Ismā'īlī branch of Islam, with Yemeni and Indian roots, which places a high value on education of every man and woman. *See* http://www.thedawoodibohras.com/.

Shiite Muslims, Ethiopian Jews (the Falasha), and adherents of indigenous African beliefs. FGM is generally accepted as having predated a variety of monotheistic religions, including Islam and Christianity. It is widely acknowledged that FGM is not encouraged or required by any major monotheistic religion and many therefore claim that FGM has erroneously been associated with religion. Nevertheless, in some cultures women and girls consider this controversial practice to be associated with their religion or belief, including less well known, nonglobal, nontheistic or atheistic beliefs. They will argue that FGM is a religiously prescribed or religiously motivated ritual associated with certain stages of life. On that basis they will demand protection of their external freedom of religion or belief. Dissenting women who favor the practice will probably prefer to refer to it as "female circumcision," "female genital cutting," or "female genital surgery." The term "female genital mutilation" is considered by them a derogatory value judgment by outsiders, which implies insensitivity and disrespect both toward women and girls who have undergone the practice and people involved in the practice.

In a country that specifically bans any form of FGM in the interests of public health, the law of the state typically conflicts with dissenting women's outward manifestation of their religion or belief. This warrants an assessment of whether the state can justify the restriction of their external freedom on the grounds of public health. It has been established that a state may invoke the grounds of "public health" in order "to take measures dealing with a serious threat to the health of the population or individual members of the population. These measures must be specifically aimed at preventing disease or injury or providing care for the sick and injured."

To justify in the present case a restriction based on the interests of "public health," a state must distinguish between situations involving dissenting adult women and those involving dissenting girls. In the case of dissenting women, the state must demonstrate that the health effects of FGM are serious. For instance, they can produce evidence of the immediate and long-term health risks FGM entails, which vary depending on the nature and extremity of the procedure followed. The well-documented physical complications include hemorrhage, severe pain, damage to surrounding organs, urinary retention, keloids, recurrent infections, complications during childbirth, and in some cases death. Beyond physical injury, the health consequences may extend to severe shock, emotional stress, and various psychological, sexual, and reproductive disorders. Furthermore, the state may demonstrate that the strong consensus of the world community, as evidenced in numerous international forums and non-governmental organizations, has denounced FGM as a serious threat to the health of women and girls and specifically called upon states to legislate against it. Moreover, the state may submit that the restriction is not arbitrary, unfair, or based on irrational considerations. The restriction is necessary in the interest of public health and warrants overriding external freedom. The public authorities will therefore argue that they have satisfied the second and third prongs too.

In the case of dissenting girls, the state can produce the same overwhelming evidence in revealing the harmful effects of FGM. In addition, it can refer to an internationally agreed prohibition on harmful practices such as FGM which establishes that "[p]ractices of a religion or belief in which a child is brought up must not be injurious to his physical or mental health or to his full development."

This prohibition demonstrates that the restriction of external freedom is justified to preserve the health or even the life choices of the girls in question. Furthermore, the state can point out that these girls are for the most part very young and in no position to give informed consent. . . .

Dissenting women who make a cognizant, fully informed, and uncoerced choice to undergo FGM and give their informed consent may nevertheless reject the claim that the restriction is necessary to protect public health, since only their health is at risk.. . .[A]dults are allowed to make choices about their own bodies, including those that may adversely affect their health and impose a burden upon the public health system. In this connection, they can point out that the public health system is more burdened with the effects of excessive alcohol consumption and cigarette smoking than with the effects of FGM. According to this line of thinking, the adult's informed consent precludes a state from prohibiting persons to cut or carve their bodies and even injure themselves.

The state may respond by providing numerous reasons why this line of reasoning is not tenable. First, the term "public health" includes both collective and individual health interests. Second, if the woman has a sexual partner, the psychosexual and psychological effects of FGM could give rise to conflict with the partner and therefore affect his health and well-being too. Third, a sexually active woman who has contracted a blood borne disease, such as hepatitis B or human immunodeficiency virus/acquired immunodeficiency syndrome (HIV/AIDS), as a result of undergoing FGM, may transmit this disease to others and thereby put their health at risk. Fourth, FGM can lead to complications during pregnancy and childbirth, thereby endangering the health and life of the unborn child. Fifth, it seems reasonable that states have an obligation to inform the public, most notably women and girls, of the risks of FGM and its detrimental effects on health. Health information and education are crucial strategies for eliminating FGM and should not be seen as unusual. For instance, states regularly inform the public of the harmful effects of excessive alcohol consumption and cigarette smoking as matters of public health. Sixth, unlike excessive alcohol consumption and cigarette smoking, FGM is banned because it constitutes a physical intervention with immediate and long-term health risks. Any form of FGM involving partial or total removal of the external female genitalia is irreversible. Seventh, the very nature of a public health system implies that the community as a whole will bear the costs of treating complications from FGM, which often occur frequently and in a variety of forms. The financial implications for the community are therefore another reason why it is in the "public" interest to ban the practice. Moreover, various African states have pointed out that FGM constitutes "a major public health problem for health services that are already overburdened and frequently deficient." This last reason is, however, not or less relevant in some other parts of the world where, for example, the effects of over consumption of alcohol and nicotine are relatively a bigger burden to the public health system.

The state may bring to light that the second, third, and fourth reasons demonstrate that the health of others is at stake too. In addition to the public health ground, it could therefore also rely on the fundamental rights and freedoms of others ground to ban FGM, in particular by referring to the right of others to the enjoyment of the highest attainable standard of health.

The foregoing demonstrates that there are compelling reasons to recognize the ban on FGM as necessary on the grounds of public health. . . .

In this context, however, it is important to emphasize a broader governmental strategy to change individual behavior and social norms to deter people from practicing FGM. While not compromising the determination to prohibit FGM, states should be sensitive to affected women and girls and offer them assistance in finding non-harmful alternatives to the practice. For instance, in traditions in which FGM symbolizes the girl's passage to womanhood, the wearing of a special bracelet or a symbolic gift-giving may be encouraged. In this way the ceremonial traditions underlying the practice can continue without the harmful practice.

COMMENTS AND QUESTIONS

1. Should someone who sincerely but mistakenly conceives a belief to be religious be allowed to claim religious freedom protection for that belief?
2. What about male circumcision? Does it matter that this usually takes place with an infant only a few days old? Does it matter if the parent who has a child circumcised is motivated by religion, or culture, or health? Is this a decision that should be left to parents, or does the state have a sufficiently large interest that it should intervene? How does this conflict play out when circumcision is required by Muslims and Orthodox Jews? Should it be permissible to invoke public health paternalistically, that is, as a ground for intervention in the life of the person who claims a religious freedom right against the intervention?
3. Laws in the United States generally allow male circumcision, although one form, Metzitzah B'Peh, is regulated because of potential health risks. The Second Circuit has ruled that one such regulation is subject to strict scrutiny under the Free Exercise Clause.[35]
4. Male circumcision continues to be a legal controversy in northern Europe, where it technically classifies as assault in several countries. In 2012, a regional court in Cologne, Germany, heard a case filed by the public prosecutor against a doctor who had performed a circumcision on a four-year-old boy of Muslim parents, who had brought the boy, suffering from profuse bleeding, to an emergency room two days after the procedure. The court found that the procedure, though done for religious reasons (required by Islamic law), was bodily harm under the German Penal Code. Later that year, the Bundestag (Parliament) approved a law clarifying that circumcision was legal in Germany. What do you think of these arguments? What do you think of the application of the mitigating factors the courts considered?

Additional Web Resources:	Additional materials on FGC, representing a variety of viewpoints Modules on tensions between freedom of religion or belief and the rights of specific groups

35. *See Central Rabbinical Congress v. NYC Department of Health & Mental Hygiene Ruthann Robson*, 763 F.3d 183 (3d Cir. 2014), and dicussion in Second Circuit Finds NYC's MBP Circumcision Regulation Merits Strict Scrutiny, *Constitutional Law Profs Blog*, 18 August 2014.

V. RELIGIOUS FREEDOM—EMPLOYERS AND EMPLOYEES

In March 2010, the Patient Protection and Affordable Care Act and the Health Care and Education Reconciliation Act were passed and signed into law in the United States. Collectively, the acts are known as the Affordable Care Act and are often referred to informally as "Obamacare." In July 2010, the Department of Health and Humans Services (HHS), along with the Department of Treasury and the Department of Labor, published an interim final rule "the HHS Mandate" under the Affordable Care Act. The HHS Mandate required group and individual health insurance providers to cover preventive care including coverage for contraceptives for women or pay substantial penalties per employee.[36]

The HHS Mandate did provide for a narrow exemption from the contraception provision requirements for certain religious employers. The religious organization had to (1) have the purpose of inculcating religious values, (2) primarily employ persons of the same faith as the organization, (3) primarily serve persons of the same faith as the organization, (4) and be a nonprofit organization under IRS definition.[37]

The exemption, however, did not meet the needs of a great many employers with objections based on religious conviction, and these objections were expressed in more than 100 lawsuits representing some 320 plaintiffs.[38] In response, the Federal government announced a series of revisions to the Mandate, beginning in January 2012, that extended deadlines for implementation and altered rules for non-profit and for-profit employers. The eighth such revision was announced on 9 October 2014,[39] in response to the US Supreme Court's decision in *Burwell v. Hobby Lobby Stores*, the best known of the cases challenging the HHS Mandate.

BURWELL V. HOBBY LOBBY

United States Supreme Court, 134 S.Ct. 2751 (2014)

Justice ALITO delivered the opinion of the Court.

We must decide in these cases whether the Religious Freedom Restoration Act of 1993 (RFRA permits the United States Department of Health and Human Services (HHS) to demand that three closely held corporations provide health-insurance coverage for methods of contraception that violate the sincerely held religious beliefs of the companies' owners. We hold that the regulations that impose this obligation violate RFRA, which prohibits the Federal Government from taking any action that substantially burdens the exercise of religion unless that action constitutes the least restrictive means of serving a compelling government interest. . . .

At issue in these cases are HHS regulations promulgated under the . . . Affordable Care Act of 2010 (ACA). ACA generally requires employers with 50

36. 76 Fed. Reg. 46623 (3 August 2011).

37. 45 CFR § 147.130(a)(iv)(B).

38. Becket, HHS Mandate Information Central.

39. Centers for Medicare & Medicaid Services, *Women's Preventive Services Coverage and Non-Profit Religious Organizations*.

or more full-time employees to offer "a group health plan or group health insurance coverage" that provides "minimum essential coverage." Any covered employer that does not provide such coverage must pay a substantial price. Specifically, if a covered employer provides group health insurance but its plan fails to comply with ACA's group-health-plan requirements, the employer may be required to pay $100 per day for each affected "individual." . . . In August 2011, . . . the HRSA promulgated the Women's Preventive Services Guidelines. The Guidelines provide that nonexempt employers are generally required to provide "coverage, without cost sharing" for "[a]ll Food and Drug Administration [(FDA)] approved contraceptive methods, sterilization procedures, and patient education and counseling." Although many of the required, FDA-approved methods of contraception work by preventing the fertilization of an egg, four of those methods (those specifically at issue in these cases) may have the effect of preventing an already fertilized egg from developing any further by inhibiting its attachment to the uterus.

HHS also authorized the HRSA to establish exemptions from the contraceptive mandate for "religious employers." That category encompasses "churches, their integrated auxiliaries, and conventions or associations of churches," as well as "the exclusively religious activities of any religious order." In its Guidelines, HRSA exempted these organizations from the requirement to cover contraceptive services.

In addition, HHS has effectively exempted certain religious nonprofit organizations, described under HHS regulations as "eligible organizations," from the contraceptive mandate. An "eligible organization" means a nonprofit organization that "holds itself out as a religious organization" and "opposes providing coverage for some or all of any contraceptive services required to be covered . . . on account of religious objections." To qualify for this accommodation, an employer must certify that it is such an organization. When a group-health-insurance issuer receives notice that one of its clients has invoked this provision, the issuer must then exclude contraceptive coverage from the employer's plan and provide separate payments for contraceptive services for plan participants without imposing any cost-sharing requirements on the eligible organization, its insurance plan, or its employee beneficiaries. Although this procedure requires the issuer to bear the cost of these services, HHS has determined that this obligation will not impose any net expense on issuers because its cost will be less than or equal to the cost savings resulting from the services.

II

B

David and Barbara Green and their three children are Christians who own and operate two family businesses. Forty-five years ago, David Green started an arts-and-crafts store that has grown into a nationwide chain called Hobby Lobby. There are now 500 Hobby Lobby stores, and the company has more than 13,000 employees. . . . Hobby Lobby is organized as a for-profit corporation under Oklahoma law. . . .

Though these . . . businesses have expanded over the years, they remain closely held . . . .

Hobby Lobby's statement of purpose commits the Greens to "[h]onoring the Lord in all [they] do by operating the company in a manner consistent with Biblical principles." . . . Each family member has signed a pledge to run the businesses in accordance with the family's religious beliefs and to use the family assets to support Christian ministries. . . . In accordance with those commitments, Hobby Lobby . . . stores close on Sundays, even though the Greens calculate that they lose millions in sales annually by doing so. . . . The businesses refuse to engage in profitable transactions that facilitate or promote alcohol use; they contribute profits to Christian missionaries and ministries; and they buy hundreds of full-page newspaper ads inviting people to "know Jesus as Lord and Savior." . . .

[T]he Greens believe that life begins at conception and that it would violate their religion to facilitate access to contraceptive drugs or devices that operate after that point. . . .They specifically object to the same four contraceptive methods [but], they have no objection to the other 16 FDA-approved methods of birth control. . . .

The Greens [and] Hobby Lobby . . . sued HHS and other federal agencies and officials to challenge the contraceptive mandate under RFRA and the Free Exercise Clause. The District Court denied a preliminary injunction, . . . and the plaintiffs appealed, moving for initial en banc consideration. The Tenth Circuit granted that motion and reversed in a divided opinion. . . .

We granted certiorari. . . .

III

A

RFRA prohibits the "Government [from] substantially burden[ing] *a person's* exercise of religion even if the burden results from a rule of general applicability" unless the Government "demonstrates that application of the burden to *the person*—(1) is in furtherance of a compelling governmental interest; and (2) is the least restrictive means of furthering that compelling governmental interest." The first question that we must address is whether this provision applies to regulations that govern the activities of for-profit corporations like Hobby Lobby . . . .

HHS contends that neither these companies nor their owners can even be heard under RFRA. According to HHS, the companies cannot sue because they seek to make a profit for their owners, and the owners cannot be heard because the regulations, at least as a formal matter, apply only to the companies and not to the owners as individuals. HHS's argument would have dramatic consequences.

Consider this Court's decision in *Braunfeld* v. *Brown* . . . . In that case, five Orthodox Jewish merchants who ran small retail businesses in Philadelphia challenged a Pennsylvania Sunday closing law as a violation of the Free Exercise Clause. Because of their faith, these merchants closed their shops on Saturday, and they argued that requiring them to remain shut on Sunday threatened them with financial ruin. The Court entertained their claim (although it ruled against them on the merits), and if a similar claim were raised today under RFRA against a jurisdiction still subject to the Act, the merchants would be entitled to be heard. According to HHS, however, if these merchants chose to incorporate their businesses—without in any way changing the size or nature of their businesses—they would forfeit all RFRA (and free-exercise) rights. HHS would put these merchants to a difficult choice: either give up the right to seek judicial protection of their religious liberty or forgo the benefits, available to their competitors, of operating as corporations. . . .

. . . Congress provided protection for people like the Greens by employing a familiar legal fiction: It included corporations within RFRA's definition of "persons." But it is important to keep in mind that the purpose of this fiction is to provide protection for human beings. A corporation is simply a form of organization used by human beings to achieve desired ends. An established body of law specifies the rights and obligations of the *people* (including shareholders, officers, and employees) who are associated with a corporation in one way or another. When rights, whether constitutional or statutory, are extended to corporations, the purpose is to protect the rights of these people. For example, extending Fourth Amendment protection to corporations protects the privacy interests of employees and others associated with the company. Protecting corporations from government seizure of their property without just compensation protects all those who have a stake in the corporations' financial well-being. And protecting the free-exercise rights of corporations like Hobby Lobby . . . protects the religious liberty of the humans who own and control those companies. . . .

B

1

As we noted above, RFRA applies to "a person's" exercise of religion . . . and RFRA itself does not define the term "person." We therefore look to the Dictionary Act, which we must consult "[i]n determining the meaning of any Act of Congress, unless the context indicates otherwise." . . .

Under the Dictionary Act, "the wor[d] 'person' . . . include[s] corporations, companies, associations, firms, partnerships, societies, and joint stock companies, as well as individuals." . . .

2

The principal argument advanced by HHS and the principal dissent regarding RFRA protection for Hobby Lobby . . . focuses not on the statutory term "person," but on the phrase "exercise of religion." According to HHS and the dissent, these corporations are not protected by RFRA because they cannot exercise religion. Neither HHS nor the dissent, however, provides any persuasive explanation for this conclusion.

Is it because of the corporate form? The corporate form alone cannot provide the explanation because, as we have pointed out, HHS concedes that nonprofit corporations can be protected by RFRA. The dissent suggests that nonprofit corporations are special because furthering their religious "autonomy . . . often furthers individual religious freedom as well." (quoting *Corporation of Presiding Bishop of Church of Jesus Christ of Latter-day Saints* v. *Amos*), . . . But this principle applies equally to for-profit corporations: Furthering their religious freedom also "furthers individual religious freedom." . . .

If the corporate form is not enough, what about the profit-making objective? In *Braunfeld*, . . . we entertained the free-exercise claims of individuals who were attempting to make a profit as retail merchants, and the Court never even hinted that this objective precluded their claims. . . .

If, as *Braunfeld* recognized, a sole proprietorship that seeks to make a profit may assert a free-exercise claim, why can't Hobby Lobby, and Mardel do the same?

Some lower court judges have suggested that RFRA does not protect for-profit corporations because the purpose of such corporations is simply to make money. This argument flies in the face of modern corporate law. "Each American jurisdiction today either expressly or by implication authorizes corporations to be formed under its general corporation act for *any lawful purpose* or business." While it is certainly true that a central objective of for-profit corporations is to make money, modern corporate law does not require for-profit corporations to pursue profit at the expense of everything else, and many do not do so. For-profit corporations, with ownership approval, support a wide variety of charitable causes, and it is not at all uncommon for such corporations to further humanitarian and other altruistic objectives. . . .

HHS would draw a sharp line between nonprofit corporations (which, HHS concedes, are protected by RFRA) and for-profit corporations (which HHS would leave unprotected), but the actual picture is less clear-cut. Not all corporations that decline to organize as nonprofits do so in order to maximize profit. For example, organizations with religious and charitable aims might organize as for-profit corporations because of the potential advantages of that corporate form, such as the freedom to participate in lobbying for legislation or campaigning for political candidates who promote their religious or charitable goals. In fact, . . . States have increasingly adopted laws formally recognizing hybrid corporate forms. Over half of the States . . . now recognize the "benefit corporation," a dual-purpose entity that seeks to achieve both a benefit for the public and a profit for its owners. . . .

IV

Because RFRA applies in these cases, we must next ask whether the HHS contraceptive mandate "substantially burden[s]" the exercise of religion. We have little trouble concluding that it does.

As we have noted, the Greens have a sincere religious belief that life begins at conception. They therefore object on religious grounds to providing health insurance that covers methods of birth control that, as HHS acknowledges, may result in the destruction of an embryo. By requiring the Hahns and Greens and their companies to arrange for such coverage, the HHS mandate demands that they engage in conduct that seriously violates their religious beliefs.

If the Hahns and Greens and their companies do not yield to this demand, the economic consequences will be severe. If the companies continue to offer group health plans that do not cover the contraceptives at issue, they will be taxed $100 per day for each affected individual. For Hobby Lobby, the bill could amount to $1.3 million per day or about $475 million per year. [This sum is] surely substantial. . . .

In taking the position that the HHS mandate does not impose a substantial burden on the exercise of religion, HHS's main argument is basically that the connection between what the objecting parties must do (provide health-insurance coverage for four methods of contraception that may operate after the fertilization of an egg) and the end that they find to be morally wrong (destruction of an embryo) is simply too attenuated. . . .

This argument dodges the question that RFRA presents (whether the HHS mandate imposes a substantial burden on the ability of the objecting parties to conduct business in accordance with *their religious beliefs*) and instead addresses a very different question that the federal courts have no business addressing (whether the religious belief asserted in a RFRA case is reasonable). . . .

V

Since the HHS contraceptive mandate imposes a substantial burden on the exercise of religion, we must move on and decide whether HHS has shown that the mandate both "(1) is in furtherance of a compelling governmental interest; and (2) is the least restrictive means of furthering that compelling governmental interest." . . . We will assume that the interest in guaranteeing cost-free access to the four challenged contraceptive methods is compelling within the meaning of RFRA, and we will proceed to consider the final prong of the RFRA test, *i.e.*, whether HHS has shown that the contraceptive mandate is "the least restrictive means of furthering that compelling governmental interest."

B

The least-restrictive-means standard is exceptionally demanding, . . . and it is not satisfied here. HHS has not shown that it lacks other means of achieving its desired goal without imposing a substantial burden on the exercise of religion by the objecting parties in these cases. . . .

The most straightforward way of doing this would be for the Government to assume the cost of providing the four contraceptives at issue to any women who are unable to obtain them under their health-insurance policies due to their employers' religious objections. This would certainly be less restrictive of the plaintiffs' religious liberty, and HHS has not shown, that this is not a viable alternative. HHS has not provided any estimate of the average cost per employee of providing access to these contraceptives, two of which, according to the FDA, are designed primarily for emergency use. Nor has HHS provided any statistics regarding the number of employees who might be affected because they work for corporations like Hobby Lobby . . . .

HHS contends that RFRA does not permit us to take this option into account because "RFRA cannot be used to require creation of entirely new programs." But we see nothing in RFRA that supports this argument, and drawing the line between the "creation of an entirely new program" and the modification of an existing program (which RFRA surely allows) would be fraught with problems. We do not doubt that cost may be an important factor in the least-restrictive-means analysis, but both RFRA and its sister statute, RLUIPA, may in some circumstances require the Government to expend additional funds to accommodate citizens' religious beliefs.

In the end, however, we need not rely on the option of a new, government-funded program in order to conclude that the HHS regulations fail the least-restrictive-means test. HHS itself has demonstrated that it has at its disposal an approach that is less restrictive than requiring employers to fund contraceptive methods that violate their religious beliefs. As we explained above, HHS has already established an accommodation for nonprofit organizations with religious objections. . . . Under that accommodation, the organization can self-certify that it opposes providing coverage for particular contraceptive services. . . . If the organization makes such a certification, the organization's insurance issuer or third-party administrator must "[e]xpressly exclude contraceptive coverage from the group health insurance coverage provided in connection with the group health plan" and "[p]rovide separate payments for any contraceptive services required to be covered" without imposing "any cost-sharing requirements . . . on the eligible organization, the group health plan, or plan participants or beneficiaries." . . .

We do not decide today whether an approach of this type complies with RFRA for purposes of all religious claims. At a minimum, however, it does not impinge on the plaintiffs' religious belief that providing insurance coverage for the contraceptives at issue here violates their religion, and it serves HHS's stated interests equally well. . . .

C

. . . The contraceptive mandate, as applied to closely held corporations, violates RFRA. Our decision on that statutory question makes it unnecessary to reach the First Amendment claim . . . .

Justice GINSBERG, with whom Justice SOTOMAYOR joins, and with whom Justice BREYER and Justice KAGAN join as to all but Part III–C–1, dissenting.

In a decision of startling breadth, the Court holds that commercial enterprises, including corporations, along with partnerships and sole proprietorships, can opt out of any law (saving only tax laws) they judge incompatible with their sincerely held religious beliefs. . . . Compelling governmental interests in uniform compliance with the law, and disadvantages that religion-based opt-outs impose on others, hold no sway, the Court decides, at least when there is a "less restrictive alternative." And such an alternative, the Court suggests, there always will be whenever, in lieu of tolling an enterprise claiming a religion-based exemption, the government, *i.e.,* the general public, can pick up the tab. . . .

In the Court's view, RFRA demands accommodation of a for-profit corporation's religious beliefs no matter the impact that accommodation may have on third parties who do not share the corporation owners' religious faith—in these cases, thousands of women employed by Hobby Lobby and Conestoga or dependents of persons those corporations employ. Persuaded that Congress enacted RFRA to serve a far less radical purpose, and mindful of the havoc the Court's judgment can introduce, I dissent. . . .

II

Any First Amendment Free Exercise Clause claim Hobby Lobby or Conestoga[7] might assert is foreclosed by this Court's decision in *Employment Div. v. Smith,* . . . The First Amendment is not offended, *Smith* held, when "prohibiting the exercise of religion . . . is not the object of [governmental regulation] but merely the incidental effect of a generally applicable and otherwise valid provision." . . . The ACA's contraceptive coverage requirement applies generally, it is "otherwise valid," it trains on women's well being, not on the exercise of religion, and any effect it has on such exercise is incidental.

Even if *Smith* did not control, the Free Exercise Clause would not require the exemption Hobby Lobby and Conestoga seek. Accommodations to religious beliefs or observances, the Court has clarified, must not significantly impinge on the interests of third parties.

The exemption sought by Hobby Lobby and Conestoga would override significant interests of the corporations' employees and covered dependents. It would deny legions of women who do not hold their employers' beliefs access to contraceptive coverage that the ACA would otherwise secure. . . .

III

A

Lacking a tenable claim under the Free Exercise Clause, Hobby Lobby and Conestoga rely on RFRA, a statute instructing that "[g]overnment shall not substantially burden a person's exercise of religion even if the burden results from a rule of general applicability" unless the government shows that application of the burden is "the least restrictive means" to further a "compelling governmental interest." In RFRA, Congress "adopt[ed] a statutory rule comparable to the constitutional rule rejected in *Smith*." . . .

RFRA's purpose is specific and written into the statute itself. The Act was crafted to "restore the compelling interest test as set forth in *Sherbert v. Verner* and *Wisconsin v. Yoder* and to guarantee its application in all cases where free exercise of religion is substantially burdened." . . .

B

Despite these authoritative indications, the Court sees RFRA as a bold initiative departing from, rather than restoring, pre-*Smith* jurisprudence. . . . As amended by RLUIPA, RFRA's definition now includes "any exercise of religion, whether or not compelled by, or central to, a system of religious belief." That definitional change, according to the Court, reflects "an obvious effort to effect a complete separation from First Amendment case law." . . .

The Court's reading is not plausible. RLUIPA's alteration clarifies that courts should not question the centrality of a particular religious exercise. But the amendment in no way suggests that Congress meant to expand the class of entities qualified to mount religious accommodation claims, nor does it relieve courts of the obligation to inquire whether a government action substantially burdens a religious exercise. . . .

Next, the Court highlights RFRA's requirement that the government, if its action substantially burdens a person's religious observance, must demonstrate that it chose the least restrictive means for furthering a compelling interest. "[B]y imposing a least-restrictive-means test," the Court suggests, RFRA "went beyond what was required by our pre-*Smith* decisions." . . .

The Congress that passed RFRA correctly read this Court's pre-*Smith* case law as including within the "compelling interest test" a "least restrictive means" requirement. . . . And the view that the pre-*Smith* test included a "least restrictive means" requirement had been aired in testimony before the Senate Judiciary Committee by experts on religious freedom. *See, e.g.*, Hearing on S. 2969 before the Senate Committee on the Judiciary, 102d Cong., 2d Sess., 78–79 (1993) (statement of Prof. Douglas Laycock).

C . . .

1

RFRA's compelling interest test . . . applies to government actions that "substantially burden *a person's exercise of religion*." (emphasis added). This reference, the Court submits, incorporates the definition of "person" found in the Dictionary Act, which extends to "corporations, companies, associations, firms, partnerships, societies, and joint stock companies, as well as individuals." . . . The Dictionary Act's definition, however, controls only where "context" does not "indicat[e] otherwise." Here, context does so indicate. RFRA speaks of "a person's *exercise of religion*." (emphasis added). Whether a corporation qualifies as a "person" capable of exercising religion is an inquiry one cannot answer without reference to the "full body" of pre-*Smith* "free-exercise caselaw." . . . There is in that case law no support for the notion that free exercise rights pertain to for-profit corporations.

Until this litigation, no decision of this Court recognized a for-profit corporation's qualification for a religious exemption from a generally applicable law, whether under the Free Exercise Clause or RFRA. The absence of such precedent is just what one would expect, for the exercise of religion is characteristic of natural persons, not artificial legal entities. . . .

The First Amendment's free exercise protections, the Court has indeed recognized, shelter churches and other nonprofit religion-based organizations. "For many individuals, religious activity derives meaning in large measure from participation in a larger religious community," and "furtherance of the autonomy of religious organizations often furthers individual religious freedom as well." . . . The Court's "special solicitude to the rights of religious organizations," . . . however, is just that. No such solicitude is traditional for commercial organizations. Indeed, until today, religious exemptions had never been extended to any entity operating in "the commercial, profit-making world. . . .

The reason why is hardly obscure. Religious organizations exist to foster the interests of persons subscribing to the same religious faith. Not so of for-profit corporations. Workers who sustain the operations of those corporations commonly are not drawn from one religious community. Indeed, by law, no religion-based criterion can restrict the work force of for-profit corporations. . . . The distinction between a community made up of believers in the same religion and one embracing persons of diverse beliefs, clear as it is, constantly escapes the Court's attention. One can only wonder why the Court shuts this key difference from sight. . . . Reading RFRA, as the Court does, to require extension of religion-based exemptions to for-profit corporations surely is not grounded in the pre-*Smith* precedent Congress sought to preserve. Had Congress intended RFRA to initiate a change so huge, a clarion statement to that effect likely would have been made in the legislation. . . .

Citing *Braunfeld v. Brown,* the Court questions why, if "a sole proprietorship that seeks to make a profit may assert a free-exercise claim, [Hobby Lobby and Conestoga] can't . . . do the same?" . . . In a sole proprietorship, the business and its owner are one and the same. By incorporating a business, however, an individual separates herself from the entity and escapes personal responsibility for the entity's obligations. One might ask why the separation should hold only when it serves the interest of those who control the corporation. In any event, *Braunfeld* is hardly impressive authority for the entitlement Hobby Lobby and Conestoga seek. The free exercise claim asserted there was promptly rejected on the merits.

The Court's determination that RFRA extends to for-profit corporations is bound to have untoward effects. Although the Court attempts to cabin its language to closely held corporations, its logic extends to corporations of any size, public or private. Little doubt that RFRA claims will proliferate, for the Court's expansive notion of corporate personhood—combined with its other errors in construing RFRA—invites for-profit entities to seek religion-based exemptions from regulations they deem offensive to their faith.

2

[With respect to whether the ACA imposes a "substantial burden,"] I would conclude that the connection between the families' religious objections and the contraceptive coverage requirement is too attenuated to rank as substantial. The requirement carries no command that Hobby Lobby or Conestoga purchase or provide the contraceptives they find objectionable. Instead, it calls on the companies covered by the requirement to direct money into undifferentiated funds that finance a wide variety of benefits under comprehensive health plans. . . .

Importantly, the decisions whether to claim benefits under the plans are made not by Hobby Lobby or Conestoga, but by the covered employees and dependents, in consultation with their health care providers. . . . It is doubtful that Congress, when it specified that burdens must be "substantia[l]," had in mind a linkage thus interrupted by independent decisionmakers (the woman and her health counselor) standing between the challenged government action and the religious exercise claimed to be infringed. Any decision to use contraceptives made by a woman covered under Hobby Lobby's or Conestoga's plan will not be propelled by the Government, it will be the woman's autonomous choice, informed by the physician she consults. . . .

4

After assuming the existence of compelling government interests, the Court holds that the contraceptive coverage requirement fails to satisfy RFRA's least restrictive means test. But the Government has shown that there is no less restrictive, equally effective means that would both (1) satisfy the challengers' religious objections to providing insurance coverage for certain contraceptives (which they believe cause abortions); and (2) carry out the objective of the ACA's contraceptive coverage requirement, to ensure that women employees receive, at no cost to them, the preventive care needed to safeguard their health and well being. A "least restrictive means" cannot require employees to relinquish benefits accorded them by federal law in order to ensure that their commercial employers can adhere unreservedly to their religious tenets. . . .

Then let the government pay (rather than the employees who do not share their employer's faith), the Court suggests. "The most straightforward [alternative]," the Court asserts, "would be for the Government to assume the cost of providing . . . contraceptives . . . to any women who are unable to obtain them under their health-insurance policies due to their employers' religious objections." . . . The ACA, however, requires coverage of preventive services through the existing employer-based system of health insurance "so that [employees] face minimal logistical and administrative obstacles."

And where is the stopping point to the "let the government pay" alternative? Suppose an employer's sincerely held religious belief is offended by health coverage of vaccines, or paying the minimum wage, . . . or according women equal pay for substantially similar work . . . ? Does it rank as a less restrictive alternative to require the government to provide the money or benefit to which the employer has a religion-based objection? Because the Court cannot easily answer that question, it proposes something else: Extension to commercial enterprises of the accommodation already afforded to nonprofit religion-based organizations. . . . I have already discussed the "special solicitude" generally accorded nonprofit religion-based organizations that exist to serve a community of believers, solicitude never before accorded to commercial enterprises comprising employees of diverse faiths.

NOTE ON *ZUBIK v. BURWELL*, THE "LITTLE SISTERS OF THE POOR" CASE

In the days following the ruling in *Hobby Lobby*, the Supreme Court also stayed a regulation requiring a non-profit to tell their third-party insurer they object to contraceptives, thus enabling the insurer to offer contraception. The Court ruled in the case of *Wheaton College v. Burwell*, 134 S.Ct. 2806 (2014), that the government could order the third-party insurer to provide the coverage without participation from the objector. Following this, the Department of Health and Human Services modified the regulations to match the stay. This regulation still met with objections, however, because it treated religious non-profits (such as the Little Sisters of the Poor), differently than fully exempted houses of worship, a claim akin to an Establishment Clause violation. On 16 May 2016, the Supreme Court issued its judgment, *per curiam* (in the name of the Court), in the case of seven petitioners, including Little Sisters of the Poor, consolidated as *Zubik et al. v. Burwell*, 136 S.Ct. 1557 (2016).

The petitioners were primarily nonprofit organizations that provide health insurance to their employees. Unless they submitted a specified form either to their insurer or to the federal government, stating that they objected on religious grounds to providing contraceptive coverage, these organizations were required by federal regulations to cover certain contraceptives as part of their health plans. The petitioners alleged that submitting this notice substantially burdened the exercise of their religion, in violation of RFRA.

Following oral argument, the Court took the unsual step of requesting supplemental briefing from the parties, to address the issue of "whether contraceptive coverage could be provided to petitioners' employees, through petitioners' insurance companies, without any such notice from petitioners." As a result, both petitioners and the Government confirmed that such an option was feasible. In the process the petitioners clarified that their religious exercise is not infringed where they "need to do nothing more than contract for a plan that does not include coverage for some or all forms of contraception," even if their employees receive cost-free contraceptive coverage from the same insurance company. At the same time, the Government confirmed that the challenged procedures "for employers with insured plans could be modified to operate in the manner posited in the Court's order while still ensuring that the affected women receive contraceptive coverage seamlessly, together with the rest of their health coverage." In light of these reports, the Court vacated the judgments below and remanded to the Third, Fifth, Tenth, and D.C. Circuit Courts of Appeal.

Given the gravity of the dispute, said the Court, and "the substantial clarification and refinement in the positions of the parties, the parties on remand should be afforded an opportunity to arrive at an approach going forward that accommodates petitioners' religious exercise while at the same time ensuring that women covered by petitioners' health plans 'receive full and equal health coverage, including contraceptive coverage.'" The Court expressed no view on the merits of the cases. In particular, it did not decide whether the "petitioners' religious exercise ha[d] been substantially burdened, whether the Government has a compelling interest, or whether the current regulations are the least restrictive means of serving that interest."

Finally, the Court held that nothing in the opinion, or in the opinions or orders of the courts below, was to affect the ability of the Government to ensure that women covered by petitioners' health plans "obtain, without cost, the full range of FDA approved contraceptives."

COMMENTS AND QUESTIONS

1. Four workplace discrimination cases lost by Christians in UK courts were brought to the European Court of Human Rights in 2010. The applicants all "complained that domestic law failed adequately to protect their right to manifest their religion." Lillian Ladele (a registrar for the London Borough of Islington) and Gary McFarlane (a guidance counselor for the private organization RELATE) "complained specifically about sanctions taken against them by their employers as a result of their concerns about performing services which they considered to condone homosexual union," and Nadia Eweida (a Coptic Christian working as check-in staff at British Airways), and Shirley Chaplin (a nurse) "specifically about restrictions placed by their employers on their wearing of a cross visibly around their necks." The four applications were eventually heard together, and judgment was delivered on all of them in *Eweida and Others v. United Kingdom* (App. Nos. 48420/10, 59842/10, 51671/10 and 36516/10, 15 January 2013). Of the four applicants, only Ms. Eweida realized a favorable outcome, as the Court ruled that while a large crucifix posed a health risk, a small cross on a uniform did not. In the case of Ms. Ladele and Mr. McFarlane, the national courts had struck a "fair balance" in upholding the employers' actions in "pursuing a policy of nondiscrimination against service-users." Moreover, the right not to be discriminated against on the ground of sexual orientation was also protected under the Convention.
   a. The hospital's rationale for forbidding a cruxifix was health and safety; the airline's rationale was their corporate image. Should this difference control the outcome?
   b. The Court also ruled that there was no right of a counselor to not counsel same-sex couples, as he "voluntarily took on a job where he knew that

filtering of clients in accordance with his religious views was not accepted by his employer." And a registrar did not have a freedom of religion right not to hold a civil partnership ceremony. When the registrar's case was heard on first appeal in the UK, the court cited an early European Commission of Human Rights case, *C v. United Kingdom* (App. No. 10358/38, 1983): Article 9 "primarily protects the sphere of personal beliefs and religious creeds and does not always guarantee the right to behave in the public sphere in a way which is dictated by such a belief." Is this an accurate statement of current doctrine?

VI. RELIGIOUS FREEDOM AND THE SAME-SEX MARRIAGE CONTROVERSY

In many parts of the world, same-sex marriage has become a heated controversy. The first country to legalize same-sex marriage was the Netherlands, in 2000. As of December 2017, same-sex marriage was legal in all or parts of 27 countries (including some jurisdictions in Mexico).[40]

In 1996, President Bill Clinton signed the federal Defense of Marriage Act (DOMA), passed by a nearly unanimous Congress, upholding states' rights to ban same-sex marriage and prohibiting the federal government from recognzing same-sex marriage. In 1997, Hawaii became the first US state to offer same-sex couples domestic partnership, followed by California in 1999. In 2000, Vermont enacted a law permitting same-sex civil unions (and California voters approved Proposition 22, banning same-sex marriage in state law). Massachussets was the first US state to legalize same-sex marriage, pursuant to a State Supreme Court case in 2003. By June 2013, 12 other states had followed. In that month, the US Supreme Court handed down its landmark ruling in *United States v. Windsor*, 133 S.Ct. 2675 (2013), holding the relevant provisions of DOMA to be unconstitutional. Following this ruling, challenges to laws banning same-sex marriage succeeded in several state and federal courts. In January 2015, the Supreme Court agreed to hear the matter. In its decision in *Obergefell v. Hodges*, 135 S. Ct. 2584, handed down on 26 June 2015, the Court held that "the Fourteenth Amendment requires a State to license a marriage between two people of the same sex and to recognize a marriage between two people of the same sex when their marriage was lawfully licensed and performed out-of-State."

OBERGEFELL V. HODGES

Supreme Court of the United States 135 S.Ct. 2584 (2015)

Justice KENNEDY delivered the opinion of the Court.

The Constitution promises liberty to all within its reach, a liberty that includes certain specific rights that allow persons, within a lawful realm, to define and express their identity. The petitioners in these cases seek to find that liberty by

[40] *See* Gay Marriage around the World, *Pew Research Center: Religion & Public Life*, 8 August [updated 8 December] 2017.

marrying someone of the same sex and having their marriages deemed lawful on the same terms and conditions as marriages between persons of the opposite sex.

I

. . . The petitioners are 14 same-sex couples and two men whose same-sex partners are deceased. The respondents are state officials responsible for enforcing the laws in question. The petitioners claim the respondents violate the Fourteenth Amendment by denying them the right to marry or to have their marriages, lawfully performed in another State, given full recognition. . . .

II

A

From their beginning to their most recent page, the annals of human history reveal the transcendent importance of marriage. The lifelong union of a man and a woman always has promised nobility and dignity to all persons, without regard to their station in life. Marriage is sacred to those who live by their religions and offers unique fulfillment to those who find meaning in the secular realm. Its dynamic allows two people to find a life that could not be found alone, for a marriage becomes greater than just the two persons. Rising from the most basic human needs, marriage is essential to our most profound hopes and aspirations.

The centrality of marriage to the human condition makes it unsurprising that the institution has existed for millennia and across civilizations. Since the dawn of history, marriage has transformed strangers into relatives, binding families and societies together. Confucius taught that marriage lies at the foundation of government. . . . This wisdom was echoed centuries later and half a world away by Cicero, who wrote, "The first bond of society is marriage; next, children; and then the family." . . . There are untold references to the beauty of marriage in religious and philosophical texts spanning time, cultures, and faiths, as well as in art and literature in all their forms. It is fair and necessary to say these references were based on the understanding that marriage is a union between two persons of the opposite sex.

That history is the beginning of these cases. The respondents say it should be the end as well. To them, it would demean a timeless institution if the concept and lawful status of marriage were extended to two persons of the same sex. Marriage, in their view, is by its nature a gender-differentiated union of man and woman. This view long has been held—and continues to be held—in good faith by reasonable and sincere people here and throughout the world.

The petitioners acknowledge this history but contend that these cases cannot end there. Were their intent to demean the revered idea and reality of marriage, the petitioners' claims would be of a different order. But that is neither their purpose nor their submission. To the contrary, it is the enduring importance of marriage that underlies the petitioners' contentions. This, they say, is their whole point. Far from seeking to devalue marriage, the petitioners seek it for themselves because of their respect—and need—for its privileges and responsibilities. And their immutable nature dictates that same-sex marriage is their only real path to this profound commitment. . . .

B

The ancient origins of marriage confirm its centrality, but it has not stood in isolation from developments in law and society. The history of marriage is one of both continuity and change. That institution—even as confined to opposite-sex relations—has evolved over time.

For example, marriage was once viewed as an arrangement by the couple's parents based on political, religious, and financial concerns; but by the time of the Nation's founding it was understood to be a voluntary contract between a man and a woman. . . . As the role and status of women changed, the institution further evolved. Under the centuries-old doctrine of coverture, a married man and woman were treated by the State as a single, male-dominated legal entity. . . . As women gained legal, political, and property rights, and as society began to understand that women have their own equal dignity, the law of coverture was abandoned. . . . These and other developments in the institution of marriage over the past centuries were not mere superficial changes. Rather, they worked deep transformations in its structure, affecting aspects of marriage long viewed by many as essential. . . .

These new insights have strengthened, not weakened, the institution of marriage. Indeed, changed understandings of marriage are characteristic of a Nation where new dimensions of freedom become apparent to new generations, often through perspectives that begin in pleas or protests and then are considered in the political sphere and the judicial process. . . .

For much of the 20th century, moreover, homosexuality was treated as an illness. When the American Psychiatric Association published the first Diagnostic and Statistical Manual of Mental Disorders in 1952, homosexuality was classified as a mental disorder, a position adhered to until 1973. . . . Only in more recent years have psychiatrists and others recognized that sexual orientation is both a normal expression of human sexuality and immutable. . . .

In the late 20th century, following substantial cultural and political developments, same-sex couples began to lead more open and public lives and to establish families. This development was followed by a quite extensive discussion of the issue in both governmental and private sectors and by a shift in public attitudes toward greater tolerance. As a result, questions about the rights of gays and lesbians soon reached the courts, where the issue could be discussed in the formal discourse of the law.

This Court first gave detailed consideration to the legal status of homosexuals in *Bowers v. Hardwick*, . . . There it upheld the constitutionality of a Georgia law deemed to criminalize certain homosexual acts. . . . [In] 2003, the Court overruled *Bowers*, holding that laws making same-sex intimacy a crime "demea[n] the lives of homosexual persons." . . .

After years of litigation, legislation, referenda, and the discussions that attended these public acts, the States are now divided on the issue of same-sex marriage. . . .

III

Under the Due Process Clause of the Fourteenth Amendment, no State shall "deprive any person of life, liberty, or property, without due process of law." The fundamental liberties protected by this Clause include most of the rights enumerated in the Bill of Rights. . . . In addition these liberties extend to certain personal choices central to individual dignity and autonomy, including intimate choices that define personal identity and beliefs. . . .

The identification and protection of fundamental rights is an enduring part of the judicial duty to interpret the Constitution. That responsibility, however, "has not been reduced to any formula." . . . Rather, it requires courts to exercise reasoned judgment in identifying interests of the person so fundamental that the State must accord them its respect. That process is guided by many of the same considerations relevant to analysis of other constitutional provisions that set forth broad principles rather than specific requirements. History and tradition guide and discipline this inquiry but do not set its outer boundaries. . . . That method respects our history and learns from it without allowing the past alone to rule the present.

The nature of injustice is that we may not always see it in our own times. The generations that wrote and ratified the Bill of Rights and the Fourteenth Amendment did not presume to know the extent of freedom in all of its dimensions, and so they entrusted to future generations a charter protecting the right of all persons to enjoy liberty as we learn its meaning. When new insight reveals discord between the Constitution's central protections and a received legal stricture, a claim to liberty must be addressed.

Applying these established tenets, the Court has long held the right to marry is protected by the Constitution. In Loving v. Virginia . . . which invalidated bans on interracial unions, a unanimous Court held marriage is "one of the vital personal rights essential to the orderly pursuit of happiness by free men." The Court reaffirmed that holding in *Zablocki v. Redhail*, . . . which held the right to marry was burdened by a law prohibiting fathers who were behind on child support from marrying. The Court again applied this principle in *Turner v. Safley*, . . . which held the right to marry was abridged by regulations limiting the privilege of prison inmates to marry. . . .

It cannot be denied that this Court's cases describing the right to marry presumed a relationship involving opposite-sex partners. The Court, like many institutions, has made assumptions defined by the world and time of which it is a part. This was evident in *Baker v. Nelson*, . . . a one-line summary decision issued in 1972, holding the exclusion of same-sex couples from marriage did not present a substantial federal question.

Still, there are other, more instructive precedents. . . . In defining the right to marry these cases have identified essential attributes of that right based in history, tradition, and other constitutional liberties inherent in this intimate bond. . . . And in assessing whether the force and rationale of its cases apply to same-sex couples, the Court must respect the basic reasons why the right to marry has been long protected. . . .

This analysis compels the conclusion that same-sex couples may exercise the right to marry. The four principles and traditions to be discussed demonstrate that the reasons marriage is fundamental under the Constitution apply with equal force to same-sex couples.

A first premise of the Court's relevant precedents is that the right to personal choice regarding marriage is inherent in the concept of individual autonomy. This abiding connection between marriage and liberty is why *Loving* invalidated interracial marriage bans under the Due Process Clause. . . . Like choices concerning contraception, family relationships, procreation, and childrearing, all of which are protected by the Constitution, decisions concerning marriage are among the most intimate that an individual can make. . . . Indeed, the Court has noted it would be contradictory "to recognize a right of privacy with respect to other matters of family life and not with respect to the decision to enter the relationship that is the foundation of the family in our society." . . .

The nature of marriage is that, through its enduring bond, two persons together can find other freedoms, such as expression, intimacy, and spirituality. This is true for all persons, whatever their sexual orientation. . . . There is dignity in the bond between two men or two women who seek to marry and in their autonomy to make such profound choices. . . .

A second principle in this Court's jurisprudence is that the right to marry is fundamental because it supports a two-person union unlike any other in its importance to the committed individuals. . . . *Griswold* described marriage this way: "Marriage is a coming together for better or for worse, hopefully enduring, and intimate to the degree of being sacred. It is an association that promotes a way of life, not causes; a harmony in living, not political faiths; a bilateral loyalty, not commercial or social projects. Yet it is an association for as noble a purpose as any involved in our prior decisions." . . .

. . . The right to marry thus dignifies couples who "wish to define themselves by their commitment to each other." . . . Marriage responds to the universal fear that a lonely person might call out only to find no one there. It offers the hope of companionship and understanding and assurance that while both still live there will be someone to care for the other.

As this Court held in *Lawrence*, same-sex couples have the same right as opposite-sex couples to enjoy intimate association. Lawrence invalidated laws that made same-sex intimacy a criminal act. And it acknowledged that "[w]hen sexuality finds overt expression in intimate conduct with another person, the conduct can be but one element in a personal bond that is more enduring." . . . But while *Lawrence* confirmed a dimension of freedom that allows individuals to engage in intimate association without criminal liability, it does not follow that freedom stops there. Outlaw to outcast may be a step forward, but it does not achieve the full promise of liberty.

A third basis for protecting the right to marry is that it safeguards children and families and thus draws meaning from related rights of childrearing, procreation, and education. . . . By giving recognition and legal structure to their parents' relationship, marriage allows children "to understand the integrity and closeness of their own family and its concord with other families in their community and in their daily lives." . . . Marriage also affords the permanency and stability important to children's best interests. . . .

As all parties agree, many same-sex couples provide loving and nurturing homes to their children, whether biological or adopted. And hundreds of thousands of children are presently being raised by such couples. . . . Most States have allowed gays and lesbians to adopt, either as individuals or as couples, and many adopted and foster children have same-sex parents . . . This provides powerful confirmation from the law itself that gays and lesbians can create loving, supportive families.

Excluding same-sex couples from marriage thus conflicts with a central premise of the right to marry. Without the recognition, stability, and predictability marriage offers, their children suffer the stigma of knowing their families are somehow lesser. They also suffer the significant material costs of being raised by unmarried parents, relegated through no fault of their own to a more difficult and uncertain family life. The marriage laws at issue here thus harm and humiliate the children of same-sex couples.

That is not to say the right to marry is less meaningful for those who do not or cannot have children. An ability, desire, or promise to procreate is not and has not been a prerequisite for a valid marriage in any State. In light of precedent protecting the right of a married couple not to procreate, it cannot be said the Court or the States have conditioned the right to marry on the capacity or commitment to procreate. The constitutional marriage right has many aspects, of which childbearing is only one.

Fourth and finally, this Court's cases and the Nation's traditions make clear that marriage is a keystone of our social order. Alexis de Tocqueville recognized this truth on his travels through the United States almost two centuries ago:

"There is certainly no country in the world where the tie of marriage is so much respected as in America ... [W]hen the American retires from the turmoil of public life to the bosom of his family, he finds in it the image of order and of peace. . . . [H]e afterwards carries [that image] with him into public affairs."

In *Maynard v. Hill* . . . (1888), the Court echoed de Tocqueville, explaining that marriage is "the foundation of the family and of society, without which there would be neither civilization nor progress." Marriage, the *Maynard* Court said, has long been "a great public institution, giving character to our whole civil polity." . . . This idea has been reiterated even as the institution has evolved in substantial ways over time, superseding rules related to parental consent, gender, and race once thought by many to be essential.

For that reason, just as a couple vows to support each other, so does society pledge to support the couple, offering symbolic recognition and material benefits to protect and nourish the union. Indeed, while the States are in general free to vary the benefits they confer on all married couples, they have throughout our history made marriage the basis for an expanding list of governmental rights, benefits, and responsibilities. These aspects of marital status include: taxation; inheritance and property rights; rules of intestate succession; spousal privilege in the law of evidence; hospital access; medical decisionmaking authority; adoption rights; the rights and benefits of survivors; birth and death certificates; professional ethics rules; campaign finance restrictions; workers' compensation benefits; health insurance; and child custody, support, and visitation rules. . . . Valid marriage under state law is also a significant status for over a thousand provisions of federal law. . . . The States have contributed to the fundamental character of the marriage right by placing that institution at the center of so many facets of the legal and social order.

There is no difference between same- and opposite-sex couples with respect to this principle. Yet by virtue of their exclusion from that institution, same-sex couples are denied the constellation of benefits that the States have linked to marriage. This harm results in more than just material burdens. Same-sex couples are consigned to an instability many opposite-sex couples would deem intolerable in their own lives. As the State itself makes marriage all the more precious by the significance it attaches to it, exclusion from that status has the effect of teaching that gays and lesbians are unequal in important respects. It demeans gays and lesbians for the State to lock them out of a central institution of the Nation's society. Same-sex couples, too, may aspire to the transcendent purposes of marriage and seek fulfillment in its highest meaning.

The limitation of marriage to opposite-sex couples may long have seemed natural and just, but its inconsistency with the central meaning of the fundamental right to marry is now manifest. With that knowledge must come the recognition that laws excluding same-sex couples from the marriage right impose stigma and injury of the kind prohibited by our basic charter.

Objecting that this does not reflect an appropriate framing of the issue, the respondents refer to *Washington v. Glucksberg*, . . . which called for a "careful description" of fundamental rights. They assert the petitioners do not seek to exercise the right to marry but rather a new and nonexistent "right to same-sex marriage." . . . *Glucksberg* did insist that liberty under the Due Process Clause must be defined in a most circumscribed manner, with central reference to specific historical practices. Yet while that approach may have been appropriate for the asserted right there involved (physician-assisted suicide), it is inconsistent with the approach this Court has used in discussing other fundamental rights, including marriage and intimacy. *Loving* did not ask about a "right to interracial marriage"; *Turner* did not ask about a "right of inmates to marry"; and *Zablocki* did not ask about a "right of fathers with unpaid child support duties to marry." Rather, each case inquired about the right to marry in its comprehensive sense, asking if there was a sufficient justification for excluding the relevant class from the right. . . .

That principle applies here. If rights were defined by who exercised them in the past, then received practices could serve as their own continued justification and new groups could not invoke rights once denied. This Court has rejected that approach, both with respect to the right to marry and the rights of gays and lesbians.

. . .

The right to marry is fundamental as a matter of history and tradition, but rights come not from ancient sources alone. They rise, too, from a better informed understanding of how constitutional imperatives define a liberty that remains urgent in our own era. Many who deem same-sex marriage to be wrong reach that conclusion based on decent and honorable religious or philosophical premises, and neither they nor their beliefs are disparaged here. But when that sincere, personal opposition becomes enacted law and public policy, the necessary consequence is to put the imprimatur of the State itself on an exclusion that soon demeans or stigmatizes those whose own liberty is then denied. Under the Constitution, same-sex couples seek in marriage the same legal treatment as opposite-sex couples, and it would disparage their choices and diminish their personhood to deny them this right.

The right of same-sex couples to marry that is part of the liberty promised by the Fourteenth Amendment is derived, too, from that Amendment's guarantee of the equal protection of the laws. The Due Process Clause and the Equal Protection Clause are connected in a profound way, though they set forth independent principles. Rights implicit in liberty and rights secured by equal protection may rest on different precepts and are not always co-extensive, yet in some instances each may be instructive as to the meaning and reach of the other. In any particular case one Clause may be thought to capture the essence of the right in a more accurate and comprehensive way, even as the two Clauses may converge in the identification and definition of the right. . . . This interrelation of the two principles furthers our understanding of what freedom is and must become.

The Court's cases touching upon the right to marry reflect this dynamic. In *Loving* the Court invalidated a prohibition on interracial marriage under both the Equal Protection Clause and the Due Process Clause. The Court first declared the prohibition invalid because of its unequal treatment of interracial couples. It stated: "There can be no doubt that restricting the freedom to marry solely because of racial classifications violates the central meaning of the Equal Protection Clause." . . . With this link to equal protection the Court proceeded to hold the prohibition offended central precepts of liberty: "To deny this fundamental freedom on so unsupportable a basis as the racial classifications embodied in these statutes, classifications so directly subversive of the principle of equality at the heart of the Fourteenth Amendment, is surely to deprive all the State's citizens of liberty without due process of law." The reasons why marriage is a fundamental right became more clear and compelling from a full awareness and understanding of the hurt that resulted from laws barring interracial unions. . . .

This dynamic also applies to same-sex marriage. It is now clear that the challenged laws burden the liberty of same-sex couples, and it must be further acknowledged that they abridge central precepts of equality. Here the marriage laws enforced by the respondents are in essence unequal: same-sex couples are denied all the benefits afforded to opposite-sex couples and are barred from exercising a fundamental right. Especially against a long history of disapproval of their relationships, this denial to same-sex couples of the right to marry works a grave and continuing harm. The imposition of this disability on gays and lesbians serves to disrespect and subordinate them. And the Equal Protection Clause, like the Due Process Clause, prohibits this unjustified infringement of the fundamental right to marry. . . .

These considerations lead to the conclusion that the right to marry is a fundamental right inherent in the liberty of the person, and under the Due Process and Equal Protection Clauses of the Fourteenth Amendment couples of the same-sex may not be deprived of that right and that liberty. The Court now holds that same-sex couples may exercise the fundamental right to marry. No longer may this liberty be denied to them. . . .

IV

There may be an initial inclination in these cases to proceed with caution—to await further legislation, litigation, and debate. The respondents warn there has been insufficient democratic discourse before deciding an issue so basic as the definition of marriage. In its ruling on the cases now before this Court, the majority opinion for the Court of Appeals made a cogent argument that it would be appropriate for the respondents' States to await further public discussion and political measures before licensing same-sex marriages. . . .

Yet there has been far more deliberation than this argument acknowledges. There have been referenda, legislative debates, and grassroots campaigns, as well as countless studies, papers, books, and other popular and scholarly writings. There has been extensive litigation in state and federal courts. . . . This has led to an enhanced understanding of the issue—an understanding reflected in the arguments now presented for resolution as a matter of constitutional law.

Of course, the Constitution contemplates that democracy is the appropriate process for change, so long as that process does not abridge fundamental rights. . . . Indeed, it is most often through democracy that liberty is preserved and protected in our lives. But . . . [t]he dynamic of our constitutional system is that individuals need not await legislative action before asserting a fundamental right. . . .

The respondents also argue allowing same-sex couples to wed will harm marriage as an institution by leading to fewer opposite-sex marriages. This may occur, the respondents contend, because licensing same-sex marriage severs the connection between natural procreation and marriage. That argument, however, rests on a counterintuitive view of opposite-sex couple's decisionmaking processes regarding marriage and parenthood. Decisions about whether to marry and raise children are based on many personal, romantic, and practical considerations; and it is unrealistic to conclude that an opposite-sex couple would choose not to marry simply because same-sex couples may do so. . . .

Finally, it must be emphasized that religions, and those who adhere to religious doctrines, may continue to advocate with utmost, sincere conviction that, by divine precepts, same-sex marriage should not be condoned. The First Amendment ensures that religious organizations and persons are given proper protection as they seek to teach the principles that are so fulfilling and so central to their lives and faiths, and to their own deep aspirations to continue the family structure they have long revered. The same is true of those who oppose same-sex marriage for other reasons. In turn, those who believe allowing same-sex marriage is proper or indeed essential, whether as a matter of religious conviction or secular belief, may engage those who disagree with their view in an open and searching debate. The Constitution, however, does not permit the State to bar same-sex couples from marriage on the same terms as accorded to couples of the opposite sex.

V

These cases also present the question whether the Constitution requires States to recognize same-sex marriages validly performed out of State. As made clear by the case of Obergefell and Arthur, and by that of DeKoe and Kostura, the recognition bans inflict substantial and continuing harm on same-sex couples. . . . As counsel for the respondents acknowledged at argument, if States are required by the Constitution to issue marriage licenses to same-sex couples, the justifications for refusing to recognize those marriages performed elsewhere are undermined. . . . The Court, in this decision, holds same-sex couples may exercise the fundamental right to marry in all States. It follows that the Court also must hold—and it now does hold—that there is no lawful basis for a State to refuse to recognize a lawful same-sex marriage performed in another State on the ground of its same-sex character. . . .

No union is more profound than marriage, for it embodies the highest ideals of love, fidelity, devotion, sacrifice, and family. In forming a marital union, two people become something greater than once they were. As some of the petitioners in these cases demonstrate, marriage embodies a love that may endure even past death. It would misunderstand these men and women to say they disrespect the idea of marriage. Their plea is that they do respect it, respect it so deeply that they seek to find its fulfillment for themselves. Their hope is not to be condemned to live in loneliness, excluded from one of civilization's oldest institutions. They ask for equal dignity in the eyes of the law. The Constitution grants them that right. . . .

The judgment of the Court of Appeals for the Sixth Circuit is reversed. . . .

Chief Justice ROBERTS, with whom Justice SCALIA and Justice THOMAS join, dissenting.

Petitioners make strong arguments rooted in social policy and considerations of fairness. They contend that same-sex couples should be allowed to affirm their love and commitment through marriage, just like opposite-sex couples. That position has undeniable appeal; over the past six years, voters and legislators in eleven States and the District of Columbia have revised their laws to allow marriage between two people of the same sex.

But this Court is not a legislature. Whether same-sex marriage is a good idea should be of no concern to us. Under the Constitution, judges have power to say what the law is, not what it should be. The people who ratified the Constitution authorized courts to exercise "neither force nor will but merely judgment." The Federalist No. 78 . . . .

Although the policy arguments for extending marriage to same-sex couples may be compelling, the legal arguments for requiring such an extension are not. The fundamental right to marry does not include a right to make a State change its definition of marriage. And a State's decision to maintain the meaning of marriage that has persisted in every culture throughout human history can hardly be called irrational. In short, our Constitution does not enact any one theory of marriage. The people of a State are free to expand marriage to include same-sex couples, or to retain the historic definition.

Today, however, the Court takes the extraordinary step of ordering every State to license and recognize same-sex marriage. Many people will rejoice at this decision, and I begrudge none their celebration. But for those who believe in a government of laws, not of men, the majority's approach is deeply disheartening. Supporters of same-sex marriage have achieved considerable success persuading their fellow citizens—through the democratic process—to adopt their view. That ends today. Five lawyers have closed the debate and enacted their own vision of marriage as a matter of constitutional law. Stealing this issue from the people will for many cast a cloud over same-sex marriage, making a dramatic social change that much more difficult to accept.

The majority's decision is an act of will, not legal judgment. The right it announces has no basis in the Constitution or this Court's precedent. The majority expressly disclaims judicial "caution" and omits even a pretense of humility, openly relying on its desire to remake society according to its own "new insight" into the "nature of injustice." As a result, the Court invalidates the marriage laws of more than half the States and orders the transformation of a social institution that has formed the basis of human society for millennia, for the Kalahari Bushmen and the Han Chinese, the Carthaginians and the Aztecs. Just who do we think we are?

It can be tempting for judges to confuse our own preferences with the requirements of the law. But as this Court has been reminded throughout our history, the Constitution "is made for people of fundamentally differing views." *Lochner v. New York* (Holmes, J., dissenting), . . . Accordingly, "courts are not concerned with the wisdom or policy of legislation." . . . The majority today neglects that restrained conception of the judicial role. It seizes for itself a question the Constitution leaves to the people, at a time when the people are engaged in a vibrant debate on that question. And it answers that question based not on neutral principles of constitutional law, but on its own "understanding of what freedom is and must become." I have no choice but to dissent.

Understand well what this dissent is about: It is not about whether, in my judgment, the institution of marriage should be changed to include same-sex couples. It is instead about whether, in our democratic republic, that decision should rest with the people acting through their elected representatives, or with five lawyers who happen to hold commissions authorizing them to resolve legal disputes according to law. The Constitution leaves no doubt about the answer.

I

Petitioners and their amici base their arguments on the "right to marry" and the imperative of "marriage equality." There is no serious dispute that, under our precedents, the Constitution protects a right to marry and requires States to apply their marriage laws equally. The real question in these cases is what constitutes "marriage," or—more precisely—who decides what constitutes "marriage"?

The majority largely ignores these questions, relegating ages of human experience with marriage to a paragraph or two. Even if history and precedent are not "the end" of these cases, I would not "sweep away what has so long been settled" without showing greater respect for all that preceded us. . . .

A

As the majority acknowledges, marriage "has existed for millennia and across civilizations." For all those millennia, across all those civilizations, "marriage" referred to only one relationship: the union of a man and a woman. As the Court explained two Terms ago, "until recent years, ... marriage between a man and a woman no doubt had been thought of by most people as essential to the very definition of that term and to its role and function throughout the history of civilization." *United States v. Windsor*, . . .

This universal definition of marriage as the union of a man and a woman is no historical coincidence. Marriage did not come about as a result of a political movement, discovery, disease, war, religious doctrine, or any other moving force of world history—and certainly not as a result of a prehistoric decision to exclude gays and lesbians. It arose in the nature of things to meet a vital need: ensuring that children are conceived by a mother and father committed to raising them in the stable conditions of a lifelong relationship. . . .

The premises supporting this concept of marriage are so fundamental that they rarely require articulation. The human race must procreate to survive. Procreation occurs through sexual relations between a man and a woman. When sexual relations result in the conception of a child, that child's prospects are generally better if the mother and father stay together rather than going their separate ways. Therefore, for the good of children and society, sexual relations that can lead to procreation should occur only between a man and a woman committed to a lasting bond.

Society has recognized that bond as marriage. And by bestowing a respected status and material benefits on married couples, society encourages men and women to conduct sexual relations within marriage rather than without. As one prominent scholar put it, "Marriage is a socially arranged solution for the problem of getting people to stay together and care for children that the mere desire for children, and the sex that makes children possible, does not solve." J.Q. Wilson, *The Marriage Problem* 41 (2002).

This singular understanding of marriage has prevailed in the United States throughout our history. The majority accepts that at "the time of the Nation's founding [marriage] was understood to be a voluntary contract between a man and a woman." . . .

The Constitution itself says nothing about marriage, and the Framers thereby entrusted the States with "[t]he whole subject of the domestic relations of husband and wife." . . . There is no dispute that every State at the founding — and every State throughout our history until a dozen years ago — defined marriage in the traditional, biologically rooted way. . . .

This Court's precedents have repeatedly described marriage in ways that are consistent only with its traditional meaning. Early cases on the subject referred to marriage as "the union for life of one man and one woman," *Murphy v. Ramsey*, . . . which forms "the foundation of the family and of society, without which there would be neither civilization nor progress," *Maynard v. Hill*, . . . We later described marriage as "fundamental to our very existence and survival," an understanding that necessarily implies a procreative component. . . .

As the majority notes, some aspects of marriage have changed over time. Arranged marriages have largely given way to pairings based on romantic love. States have replaced coverture, the doctrine by which a married man and woman became a single legal entity, with laws that respect each participant's separate status. Racial restrictions on marriage, which "arose as an incident to slavery" to promote "White Supremacy," were repealed by many States and ultimately struck down by this Court. *Loving*, . . .

The majority observes that these developments "were not mere superficial changes" in marriage, but rather "worked deep transformations in its structure." They did not, however, work any transformation in the core structure of marriage as the union between a man and a woman. . . .

II

Petitioners first contend that the marriage laws of their States violate the Due Process Clause. . . .

The majority purports to identify four "principles and traditions" in this Court's due process precedents that support a fundamental right for same-sex couples to marry. In reality, however, the majority's approach has no basis in principle or tradition, except for the unprincipled tradition of judicial policymaking that characterized discredited decisions such as *Lochner v. New York.* Stripped of its shiny rhetorical gloss, the majority's argument is that the Due Process Clause gives same-sex couples a fundamental right to marry because it will be good for them and for society. If I were a legislator, I would certainly consider that view as a matter of social policy. But as a judge, I find the majority's position indefensible as a matter of constitutional law.

A

Petitioners' "fundamental right" claim falls into the most sensitive category of constitutional adjudication. Petitioners do not contend that their States' marriage laws violate an enumerated constitutional right, such as the freedom of speech protected by the First Amendment. There is, after all, no "Companionship and Understanding" or "Nobility and Dignity" Clause in the Constitution. They argue instead that the laws violate a right implied by the Fourteenth Amendment's requirement that "liberty" may not be deprived without "due process of law."

This Court has interpreted the Due Process Clause to include a "substantive" component that protects certain liberty interests against state deprivation "no matter what process is provided." Reno v. Flores, . . . The theory is that some liberties are "so rooted in the traditions and conscience of our people as to be ranked as fundamental," and therefore cannot be deprived without compelling justification. *Snyder v. Massachusetts*, . . .

Allowing unelected federal judges to select which unenumerated rights rank as "fundamental"—and to strike down state laws on the basis of that determination—raises obvious concerns about the judicial role. Our precedents have accordingly insisted that judges "exercise the utmost care" in identifying implied fundamental rights, "lest the liberty protected by the Due Process Clause be subtly transformed into the policy preferences of the Members of this Court." *Washington v. Glucksberg*, . . . see Kennedy, Unenumerated Rights and the Dictates of Judicial Restraint 13 (1986) (Address at Stanford) ("One can conclude that certain essential, or fundamental, rights should exist in any just society. It does not follow that each of those essential rights is one that we as judges can enforce under the written Constitution. The Due Process Clause is not a guarantee of every right that should inhere in an ideal system.").

The need for restraint in administering the strong medicine of substantive due process is a lesson this Court has learned the hard way. The Court first applied substantive due process to strike down a statute in *Dred Scott v. Sandford*, . . . (1857). There the Court invalidated the Missouri Compromise on the ground that legislation restricting the institution of slavery violated the implied rights of slaveholders. The Court relied on its own conception of liberty and property in doing so. It asserted that "an act of Congress which deprives a citizen of the United States of his liberty or property, merely because he came himself or brought his property into a particular Territory of the United States . . . could hardly be dignified with the name of due process of law." . . . In a dissent that has outlasted the majority opinion, Justice Curtis explained that when the "fixed rules which govern the interpretation of laws [are] abandoned, and the theoretical opinions of individuals are allowed to control" the Constitution's meaning, "we have no longer a Constitution; we are under the government of individual men, who for the time being have power to declare what the Constitution is, according to their own views of what it ought to mean." . . .

Dred Scott's holding was overruled on the battlefields of the Civil War and by constitutional amendment after Appomattox, but its approach to the Due Process Clause reappeared. In a series of early 20th-century cases, most prominently

Lochner v. New York, this Court invalidated state statutes that presented "meddlesome interferences with the rights of the individual," and "undue interference with liberty of person and freedom of contract." . . .

In the decades after *Lochner*, the Court struck down nearly 200 laws as violations of individual liberty, often over strong dissents contending that "[t]he criterion of constitutionality is not whether we believe the law to be for the public good." *Adkins v. Children's Hospital of D.C.*, . . By empowering judges to elevate their own policy judgments to the status of constitutionally protected "liberty," the *Lochner* line of cases left "no alternative to regarding the court as a . . . legislative chamber." L. Hand, *The Bill of Rights* 42 (1958).

Eventually, the Court recognized its error and vowed not to repeat it. "The doctrine that . . . due process authorizes courts to hold laws unconstitutional when they believe the legislature has acted unwisely," we later explained, "has long since been discarded. We have returned to the original constitutional proposition that courts do not substitute their social and economic beliefs for the judgment of legislative bodies, who are elected to pass laws." . . . Thus, it has become an accepted rule that the Court will not hold laws unconstitutional simply because we find them "unwise, improvident, or out of harmony with a particular school of thought." *Williamson v. Lee Optical of Okla., Inc.*, . . .

Rejecting *Lochner* does not require disavowing the doctrine of implied fundamental rights, and this Court has not done so. . . . Our precedents have required that implied fundamental rights be "objectively, deeply rooted in this Nation's history and tradition," and "implicit in the concept of ordered liberty, such that neither liberty nor justice would exist if they were sacrificed." [*Glucksberg*] . . . .

Proper reliance on history and tradition of course requires looking beyond the individual law being challenged, so that every restriction on liberty does not supply its own constitutional justification. The Court is right about that. But given the few "guideposts for responsible decisionmaking in this unchartered area," Collins, . . ."an approach grounded in history imposes limits on the judiciary that are more meaningful than any based on [an] abstract formula,". . . Expanding a right suddenly and dramatically is likely to require tearing it up from its roots. Even a sincere profession of "discipline" in identifying fundamental rights, does not provide a meaningful constraint on a judge, for "what he is really likely to be 'discovering,' whether or not he is fully aware of it, are his own values," J. Ely, *Democracy and Distrust* 44 (1980). The only way to ensure restraint in this delicate enterprise is "continual insistence upon respect for the teachings of history, solid recognition of the basic values that underlie our society, and wise appreciation of the great roles [of] the doctrines of federalism and separation of powers." . . .

B

The majority acknowledges none of this doctrinal background, and it is easy to see why: Its aggressive application of substantive due process breaks sharply with decades of precedent and returns the Court to the unprincipled approach of *Lochner*.

1

The majority's driving themes are that marriage is desirable and petitioners desire it. The opinion describes the "transcendent importance" of marriage and repeatedly insists that petitioners do not seek to "demean," "devalue," "denigrate," or "disrespect" the institution. . . . Nobody disputes those points. Indeed, the compelling personal accounts of petitioners and others like them are likely a primary reason why many Americans have changed their minds about whether same-sex couples should be allowed to marry. As a matter of constitutional law, however, the sincerity of petitioners' wishes is not relevant.

When the majority turns to the law, it relies primarily on precedents discussing the fundamental "right to marry." . . . These cases do not hold, of course, that anyone who wants to get married has a constitutional right to do so. They instead require a State to justify barriers to marriage as that institution has always been understood. In *Loving*, the Court held that racial restrictions on the right to marry lacked a compelling justification. In *Zablocki*, restrictions based on child support debts did not suffice. In *Turner*, restrictions based on status as a prisoner were deemed impermissible. . . .

[Justice Roberts then noted that none of the past cases questioned the core definition of marriage.]

. . . In short, the "right to marry" cases stand for the important but limited proposition that particular restrictions on access to marriage as traditionally defined violate due process. These precedents say nothing at all about a right to make a State change its definition of marriage, which is the right petitioners actually seek here. . . . Neither petitioners nor the majority cites a single case or other legal source providing any basis for such a constitutional right. None exists, and that is enough to foreclose their claim.

2

The majority suggests that "there are other, more instructive precedents" informing the right to marry. . . . Although not entirely clear, this reference seems to correspond to a line of cases discussing an implied fundamental "right of privacy." *Griswold*. . . . In the first of those cases, the Court invalidated a criminal law that banned the use of contraceptives. . . . The Court stressed the invasive nature of the ban, which threatened the intrusion of "the police to search the sacred precincts of marital bedrooms." . . . In the Court's view, such laws infringed the right to privacy in its most basic sense: the "right to be let alone." *Eisenstadt v. Baird*. . . .

The Court also invoked the right to privacy in *Lawrence v. Texas*, . . . which struck down a Texas statute criminalizing homosexual sodomy. *Lawrence* relied on the position that criminal sodomy laws, like bans on contraceptives, invaded privacy by inviting "unwarranted government intrusions" that "touc[h] upon the most private human conduct, sexual behavior . . . in the most private of places, the home." . . .

Neither *Lawrence* nor any other precedent in the privacy line of cases supports the right that petitioners assert here. Unlike criminal laws banning contraceptives and sodomy, the marriage laws at issue here involve no government intrusion. They create no crime and impose no punishment. Same-sex couples remain free to live together, to engage in intimate conduct, and to raise their families as they see fit. No one is "condemned to live in loneliness" by the laws challenged in these cases—no one. . . . At the same time, the laws in no way interfere with the "right to be let alone." . . .

In sum, the privacy cases provide no support for the majority's position, because petitioners do not seek privacy. Quite the opposite, they seek public recognition of their relationships, along with corresponding government benefits. Our cases have consistently refused to allow litigants to convert the shield provided by constitutional liberties into a sword to demand positive entitlements from the State. . . . Thus, although the right to privacy recognized by our precedents certainly plays a role in protecting the intimate conduct of same-sex couples, it provides no affirmative right to redefine marriage and no basis for striking down the laws at issue here.

3

Perhaps recognizing how little support it can derive from precedent, the majority goes out of its way to jettison the "careful" approach to implied fundamental rights taken by this Court in *Glucksberg*. . . . It is revealing that the majority's position requires it to effectively overrule *Glucksberg*, the leading modern case setting the bounds of substantive due process. At least this part of the majority opinion has the virtue of candor. Nobody could rightly accuse the majority of taking a careful approach.

Ultimately, only one precedent offers any support for the majority's methodology: *Lochner v. New York*. . . . The majority opens its opinion by announcing petitioners' right to "define and express their identity.". . . [and] later explains that "the right to personal choice regarding marriage is inherent in the concept of individual autonomy.". . . This freewheeling notion of individual autonomy echoes nothing so much as "the general right of an individual to be free in his person and in his power to contract in relation to his own labor." . . .

4

Near the end of its opinion, the majority [insists that] [e]xpanding marriage to include same-sex couples . . . would "pose no risk of harm to themselves or third parties." This argument again echoes *Lochner*, which relied on its assessment that "we think that a law like the one before us involves neither the safety, the morals nor the welfare of the public, and that the interest of the public is not in the slightest degree affected by such an act." . . .

Then and now, this assertion of the "harm principle" sounds more in philosophy than law. The elevation of the fullest individual self-realization over the constraints that society has expressed in law may or may not be attractive moral philosophy. But a Justice's commission does not confer any special moral, philosophical, or social insight sufficient to justify imposing those perceptions on fellow citizens under the pretense of "due process." There is indeed a process due the people on issues of this sort—the democratic process. Respecting that understanding requires the Court to be guided by law, not any particular school of social thought. . . .

The majority's understanding of due process lays out a tantalizing vision of the future for Members of this Court: If an unvarying social institution enduring over all of recorded history cannot inhibit judicial policymaking, what can? But this approach is dangerous for the rule of law. The purpose of insisting that implied fundamental rights have roots in the history and tradition of our people is to ensure that when unelected judges strike down democratically enacted laws, they do so based on something more than their own beliefs. The Court today not only overlooks our country's entire history and tradition but actively repudiates it, preferring to live only in the heady days of the here and now. . . .

III

In addition to their due process argument, petitioners contend that the Equal Protection Clause requires their States to license and recognize same-sex marriages. The majority does not seriously engage with this claim. Its discussion is, quite frankly, difficult to follow. The central point seems to be that there is a "synergy between" the Equal Protection Clause and the Due Process Clause, and that some precedents relying on one Clause have also relied on the other. Absent from this portion of the opinion, however, is anything resembling our usual framework for deciding equal protection cases. It is casebook doctrine that the "modern Supreme Court's treatment of equal protection claims has used a means-ends methodology in which judges ask whether the classification the government is using is sufficiently related to the goals it is pursuing.". . . The majority's approach today is different[.] . . .The majority [asserts] in conclusory fashion that the Equal Protection Clause provides an alternative basis for its holding. Yet the majority fails to provide even a single sentence explaining how the Equal Protection Clause supplies independent weight for its position, nor does it attempt to justify its gratuitous violation of the canon against unnecessarily resolving constitutional questions. . . . *Northwest Austin Municipal Util. Dist. No. One v. Holder* . . . . In any event, the marriage laws at issue here do not violate the Equal Protection Clause, because distinguishing between opposite-sex and same-sex couples is rationally related to the States' "legitimate state interest" in "preserving the traditional institution of marriage." *Lawrence*, . . . (O'Connor, J., concurring in judgment) . . . .

Justice SCALIA, with whom Justice THOMAS joins, dissenting.

I join THE CHIEF JUSTICE's opinion in full. I write separately to call attention to this Court's threat to American democracy. The substance of today's decree is not of immense personal importance to me. The law can recognize as marriage whatever sexual attachments and living arrangements it wishes, and can accord them favorable civil consequences, from tax treatment to rights of inheritance. Those civil consequences—and the public approval that conferring the name of marriage evidences—can perhaps have adverse social effects, but no more adverse than the effects of many other controversial laws. So it is not of special importance to me what the law says about marriage. It is of overwhelming importance, however, who it is that rules me. Today's decree says that my Ruler, and the Ruler of 320 million Americans coast-to-coast, is a majority of the nine lawyers on the Supreme Court. The opinion in these cases is the furthest extension in fact—and the furthest extension one can even imagine—of the Court's claimed power to create "liberties" that the Constitution and its Amendments neglect to mention.

This practice of constitutional revision by an unelected committee of nine, always accompanied (as it is today) by extravagant praise of liberty, robs the People of the most important liberty they asserted in the Declaration of Independence and won in the Revolution of 1776: the freedom to govern themselves.

I

Until the courts put a stop to it, public debate over same-sex marriage displayed American democracy at its best. Individuals on both sides of the issue passionately, but respectfully, attempted to persuade their fellow citizens to accept their views. Americans considered the arguments and put the question to a vote. The electorates of 11 States, either directly or through their representatives, chose to expand the traditional definition of marriage. Many more decided not to. Win or lose, advocates for both sides continued pressing their cases, secure in the knowledge that an electoral loss can be negated by a later electoral win. That is exactly how our system of government is supposed to work.

The Constitution places some constraints on self-rule—constraints adopted by the People themselves when they ratified the Constitution and its Amendments. Forbidden are laws "impairing the Obligation of Contracts," denying "Full Faith and Credit" to the "public Acts" of other States, prohibiting the free exercise of religion, abridging the freedom of speech, infringing the right to keep and bear arms, authorizing unreasonable searches and seizures, and so forth. Aside from these limitations, those powers "reserved to the States respectively, or to the people" can be exercised as the States or the People desire. . . .

. . . When the Fourteenth Amendment was ratified in 1868, every State limited marriage to one man and one woman, and no one doubted the constitutionality of doing so. That resolves these cases. When it comes to determining the meaning of a vague constitutional provision—such as "due process of law" or "equal protection of the laws"—it is unquestionable that the People who ratified that provision did not understand it to prohibit a practice that remained both universal and uncontroversial in the years after ratification.We have no basis for striking down a practice that is not expressly prohibited by the Fourteenth Amendment's text, and that bears the endorsement of a long tradition of open, widespread, and unchallenged use dating back to the Amendment's ratification. Since there is no doubt whatever that the People never decided to prohibit the limitation of marriage to opposite-sex couples, the public debate over same-sex marriage must be allowed to continue.

But the Court ends this debate, in an opinion lacking even a thin veneer of law. Buried beneath the mummeries and straining-to-be-memorable passages of the opinion is a candid and startling assertion: No matter what it was the People ratified, the Fourteenth Amendment protects those rights that the Judiciary, in its "reasoned judgment," thinks the Fourteenth Amendment ought to protect. That is so because "[t]he generations that wrote and ratified the Bill of Rights and the Fourteenth Amendment did not presume to know the extent of freedom in all of its dimensions . . . . " One would think that sentence would continue: ". . . and therefore they provided for a means by which the People could amend the Constitution," or perhaps ". . . and therefore they left the creation of additional liberties, such as the freedom to marry someone of the same sex, to the People, through the never-ending process of legislation." But no. What logically follows, in the majority's judge-empowering estimation, is: "and so they entrusted to future generations a charter protecting the right of all persons to enjoy liberty as we learn its meaning." The "we," needless to say, is the nine of us. "History and tradition guide and discipline [our] inquiry but do not set its outer boundaries." Thus, rather than focusing on the People's understanding of "liberty"—at the time of ratification or even today—the majority focuses on four "principles and traditions" that, in the majority's view, prohibit States from defining marriage as an institution consisting of one man and one woman.

This is a naked judicial claim to . . . super-legislative power; a claim fundamentally at odds with our system of government. Except as limited by a constitutional prohibition agreed to by the People, the States are free to adopt whatever laws they like, even those that offend the esteemed Justices' "reasoned judgment." A system of government that makes the People subordinate to a committee of nine unelected lawyers does not deserve to be called a democracy. . . .

II

But what really astounds is the hubris reflected in today's judicial Putsch. The five Justices who compose today's majority are entirely comfortable concluding that every State violated the Constitution for all of the 135 years between the Fourteenth Amendment's ratification and Massachusetts' permitting of same-sex marriages in 2003. They have discovered in the Fourteenth Amendment a "fundamental right" overlooked by every person alive at the time of ratification, and almost everyone else in the time since. They see what lesser legal minds—minds like Thomas Cooley, John Marshall Harlan, Oliver Wendell Holmes, Jr., Learned Hand, Louis Brandeis, William Howard Taft, Benjamin Cardozo, Hugo Black, Felix Frankfurter, Robert Jackson, and Henry Friendly—[] could not. They are certain that the People ratified the Fourteenth Amendment to bestow on them the power to remove questions from the democratic process when that is called for by their "reasoned judgment." These Justices know that limiting marriage to one man and one woman is contrary to reason; they know that an institution as old as government itself, and accepted by every nation in history until 15 years ago, cannot possibly be supported by anything other than ignorance or bigotry. And they are willing to say that any citizen who does not agree with that, who adheres to what was, until 15 years ago, the unanimous judgment of all generations and all societies, stands against the Constitution.

The opinion is couched in a style that is as pretentious as its content is egotistic. It is one thing for separate concurring or dissenting opinions to contain extravagances, even silly extravagances, of thought and expression; it is something else for the official opinion of the Court to do so. . . .

Hubris is sometimes defined as o'erweening pride; and pride, we know, goeth before a fall. The Judiciary is the "least dangerous" of the federal branches because it has "neither Force nor Will, but merely judgment; and must ultimately depend upon the aid of the executive arm" and the States, "even for the efficacy of its judgments." With each decision of ours that takes from the People a question properly left to them—with each decision that is unabashedly based not on law, but on the "reasoned judgment" of a bare majority of this Court—we move one step closer to being reminded of our impotence. . . .

Justice ALITO, with whom Justice SCALIA and Justice THOMAS join, dissenting.

Until the federal courts intervened, the American people were engaged in a debate about whether their States should recognize same-sex marriage.The question in these cases, however, is not what States should do about same-sex marriage but whether the Constitution answers that question for them. It does not. The Constitution leaves that question to be decided by the people of each State.

I

The Constitution says nothing about a right to same-sex marriage, but the Court holds that the term "liberty" in the Due Process Clause of the Fourteenth Amendment encompasses this right. Our Nation was founded upon the principle that every person has the unalienable right to liberty, but liberty is a term of many meanings. For classical liberals, it may include economic rights now limited by government regulation. For social democrats, it may include the right to a variety of government benefits. For today's majority, it has a distinctively postmodern meaning.

To prevent five unelected Justices from imposing their personal vision of liberty upon the American people, the Court has held that "liberty" under the Due Process Clause should be understood to protect only those rights that are "'deeply rooted in this Nation's history and tradition.'" And it is beyond dispute that the right to same-sex marriage is not among those rights. . . . Indeed:

"In this country, no State permitted same-sex marriage until the Massachusetts Supreme Judicial Court held in 2003 that limiting marriage to opposite-sex couples violated the State Constitution. Nor is the right to same-sex marriage deeply rooted in the traditions of other nations. No country allowed same-sex couples to marry until the Netherlands did so in 2000.

"What [those arguing in favor of a constitutional right to same sex marriage] seek, therefore, is not the protection of a deeply rooted right but the recognition of a very new right, and they seek this innovation not from a legislative body elected by the people, but from unelected judges. Faced with such a request, judges have cause for both caution and humility."

For today's majority, it does not matter that the right to same-sex marriage lacks deep roots or even that it is contrary to long-established tradition. The Justices in the majority claim the authority to confer constitutional protection upon that right simply because they believe that it is fundamental.". . .

Today's decision shows that decades of attempts to restrain this Court's abuse of its authority have failed. A lesson that some will take from today's decision is that preaching about the proper method of interpreting the Constitution or the virtues of judicial self-restraint and humility cannot compete with the temptation to achieve what is viewed as a noble end by any practicable means. I do not doubt that my colleagues in the majority sincerely see in the Constitution a vision of liberty that happens to coincide with their own. But this sincerity is cause for concern, not comfort. What it evidences is the deep and perhaps irremediable corruption of our legal culture's conception of constitutional interpretation.

Most Americans—understandably—will cheer or lament today's decision because of their views on the issue of same-sex marriage. But all Americans, whatever their thinking on that issue, should worry about what the majority's claim of power portends.

COMMENTS AND QUESTIONS

1. Does it matter whether same-sex marriage is legalized by the democratic process or not? Could one believe in both a fundamental right to same-sex marriage and in using the democratic process to deal with religious liberty concerns? In their amicus brief before the United States Supreme Court in *Obergefell*, major religious organizations argued that robust protections are more often afforded to religious liberty when legislative action (rather than when judicial decision) gave same-sex couples the right to marry, and they argued that the Court should keep in mind the protections necessary for religious freedom because it lacks a legislature's ability to better represent different perspectives (and protect both). Are they correct?
2. In July 2014, the European Court of Human Rights ruled that there is no right to same-sex marriage under the European Convention. In *Hämäläinen v. Finland*, App. No. 37359/09, a man who had a sex-change operation desired to have her status as a woman legally recognized by Finland without obtaining a divorce, to which she and her wife, now living together as a female same-sex couple, objected, ironically enough on religious grounds. Finland refused the request, noting that marriage was defined as between a man and a woman, and a civil partnerships was an available alternative. The Court ruled that Finland had properly balanced the competing rights and was under no obligation to change its existing marriage law. Can religious objections to homosexuality and a legal right to same-sex marriage co-exist in the same legal framework?
3. In *Minister of Home Affairs v. Fourie* [2005] ZACC 19, the South Africa Constitutional Court found that the gender-specific language of South Africa's Marriage Act conflicted with the constitution's wide scope of protected rights, especially the "right to be different" and the right of equal protection. Parliament's solution was to retain the old gender-specific Marriage Act, which provided for legally binding religious marriages, and to pass the Civil Union Act to allow for same-sex marriages under gender-neutral language. Both statues provide a route to legally recognized marriage, and civil servants may decline to perform marriages to which they have religious objections. The Civil Union Act was extremely controversial, however, and passed only because South Africa's ruling party, the African National Congress, required its members in Parliament to vote for the bill. Does this approach accommodate both sides?
4. In May 2012, a New Mexico Court of Appeals ruled in *Elane Photography v. Willock* that a photographer's refusal to photograph the "commitment ceremony" of a homosexual couple was discrimination on the basis of "sexual orientation" by a "public accommodation" (because the business advertised its services to the public) and therefore was in violation of the New Mexico Human Rights Act. The US Supreme Court declined to hear that case, but in

June 2018, the Court ruled on a similar "wedding vendor" case, *Masterpiece Cakeshop, Ltd. v. Colorado Civil Rights Commission*, 584 U.S. ___ (2018), to find by a 7-2 majority that the actions and hostile language of the Commission against the baker who refused to make cakes for same-sex weddings because of sincerely held religious beliefs was not sufficiently neutral to withstand free exercise scrutiny. The Court left unresolved the issues of the baker's freedom of expression rights. Find extensive discussion of this important case on the Web Supplement.

5. Businesses often risk closure when they assert a religious right not to provide a service because of the high cost of defending their actions in court. If such a business is not successful in court, the resulting fines only increase the likelihood it will close permanently. Assuming same-sex couples have a fundamental right to marriage, is this an appropriate penalty?
6. In March 2015, the signing into law by Governor Mike Pence of Indiana's state RFRA, which also included a private right of action, evoked intense opposition to what many perceived as a license for business to discriminate against homosexuals on religious grounds. Public demonstrations in opposition to the law proliferated, and organizations including Angie's List, Apple, and the NCAA announced intentions to boycott the state. The mayors of San Francisco and Seattle, as well as the governor of Connecticut, banned subsidized travel to Indiana. Governor Pence insisted that this response was a misunderstanding and mischaraterization of the law, which was modeled on both the Federal RFRA and the existing RFRAs of 19 other states. After all, "four federal courts of appeal and the Obama Justice Department have all taken the position that RFRA can be used as a defense in private suits involved the enforcement of laws that substantially burden free exercise of religion."[41] However, Indiana's RFRA was broader than the federal RFRA in explicitly protecting "the exercise of religion by entities as well as individuals" and in including corporations, without limiting this to closely-held companies as in *Hobby Lobby*. Indiana law could be invoked when a person's religious exercise was "likely" to be substantially burdened by government action, before such action had even occurred. And, unlike the federal RFRA, the Indiana RFRA offered religious freedom as a legitimate defense in disputes between private citizens, even if the government was not involved. Revisions to the Indiana law, banning businesses from discriminating against LGBT customers, allayed some fears, though this did not satisfy those calling for repeal of any sort of RFRA at all, and, on the other hand, some observers felt that the "gutted" law had "sacrifced religious liberty without protecting gays." Is there anything lawmakers can do to "get things right" concerning this issue? Or are these differences irreconcilable?
7. While Indiana was wrestling with its RFRA, legislators in Utah, including an openly gay Democrat senator in largely conservative state, were hammering out anti-discrminiation legislation. Eventually, all parties agreed to set aside some of the most hotly disputed issues (including the issue of public accommodation), and they brought about a "miracle" when on 12 March 2015, Governor Gary Herbert signed Senate Bill 296, "protecting LGBT people from

41. Josh Blackman, Is Indiana Protecting Discrimination?, *National Review*, 30 March 2015.

discrimination in housing and employment while also providing exemptions for religious institutions and protections for religious speech."[42] The legislation provided broader protections for LGBT groups than most "blue" (liberal) states, while providing important religious freedom protections. To what extent can similar compromises be struck elsewhere?

8. In the United Kingdom the Equality Act (Sexual Orientation) Regulations (EASOR) of 2007 make direct or unjustified indirect discrimination on the grounds of sexual orientation unlawful. Under EASOR direct discrimination exists where person A treats person B less favourably than others on the ground of B's sexual orientation; indirect discrimination exists when person A applies a general policy or practice to person B and others not of B's sexual orientation, which puts B at a particular disadvantage compared to those others, and the policy or practice is not reasonably justified by reference to matters other than B's sexual orientation. Under EASOR, civil partnership and marriage are not to be treated as materially different.

   In *Bull and another v. Hall and another* [2013] UKSC 73 (27 November 2013), Christian owners of a private hotel, who stated on their booking form that double bedrooms were available only to "heterosexual married couples," refused a room to homosexual couple who had contracted a legal civil partnership, contending their action did not constitute direct discrimination under EASOR, as their policy differentiated on the basis not of sexual orientation but of marital status, and if it did constitute indirect discrimination, EASOR should be applied in a manner compatible with their religious freedom rights under Article 9 of the European Convention on Human Rights. The UK Supreme Court agreed that EASOR engaged Article 9, but the consequent interference with the owners' rights was was a justified and proportionate restriction on those rights in the interest of protectng the rights of others.[43] What do you think of Lady Justice Rafferty's assertion that "the Appellants [do not] face any difficulty in manifesting their religious beliefs, they are merely prohibited from so doing in the commercial context they have chosen"?

9. Owen and Eunice Johns were rejected by the (UK) Derby City Council to be short-term foster parents because their views as devout Christians on homosexuality were at odds with National Minimum Standards for Fostering Services meant to ensure "value diversity and promote equality." In *Johns & Anor, R (on the application of) v. Derby City Council & Anor* [2011] EWHC 375 (Admin) (28 February 2011), the court rejected the argument that in the context of considering foster care applications, not only is the local authority entitled to weigh an applicant's religious views on homosexuality, but "equality provisions concerning sexual orientation should take precedence" over "equality provisions concerning religious discrimination," finding that the City Council would have likewise rejected non-religious applicants with similar anti-homosexual views, and therefore that the discrimination was not based on the Johns' religious beliefs; rather, only upon their views of homosexuality.

---

42. Charles Haynes, First Amendment: LGBT Rights, Religious Freedom and the Utah Miracle, *Newseum Institute*, 17 April 2015.

43. *See* Rosalind English, Supreme Court Upholds Gay Discrimination Ruling in Hotel Case, *UK Human Rights Blog*, 27 November 2013.

Additional Web Resources:	Additional materials on same-sex marriage, including developments in the United States and various European countries; module on freedom of religion or belief and the rights of children

VII. CONCLUSION

As noted at the beginning of this chapter, one should not exaggerate the conflicts that arise between religious freedom and other important human rights and human goods. Nevertheless, such conflicts do arise and need to be addressed in sensitive ways. Often the conflict is not with religious freedom itself, but between a particular religion or religious belief and some other value (perhaps a conflicting religious or secular belief). In such contexts, freedom of religion or belief protects the right of a person to hold the religion or religious belief that is a potential source of conflict. But it is not religious freedom itself that is the source of tension; the conflict is usually with a particular religion or religious belief rather than with the concept of religious freedom. It is a mistake to conflate a conflict between *a* religion and another value as a conflict of *religion* with that value, much less a conflict of *religious freedom* with that value.

In addressing such conflicts when they do arise, this counsel from the European Court of Human Rights is useful:

> [I]n the name of freedom of religion it is not authorized to apply improper pressure on others from a wish to promote one's religious convictions. . . . However, the role of the authorities in such circumstances is not to remove the cause of tension by eliminating pluralism, but to ensure that the competing groups tolerate each other. . . .[44]

It is important to remember that democratic majorities themselves are often sensitive to the rights and needs of minorities within their midst. It is also important not to be guilty of legal myopia, and to recognize that we can benefit in this area from non-juriscentric approaches to addressing these problems. Often education and attitudes, more than written law, are the key to finding solutions.

44. *Gldani Congregation of Jehovah's Witnesses v. Georgia*, App. No. 71156/01 (3 May 2007), § 132, *citing Serif v. Greece*, App. No. 38178/97 (14 December 1999), § 53.

PART III

THE RELATIONSHIP BETWEEN RELIGIOUS INSTITUTIONS AND THE STATE

In this part of the book the focus shifts to issues involving the relationship between religious institutions and the state. Whereas modern international and constitutional norms regarding freedom of religion or belief generally have broadly parallel structures (burden/interference analysis, compliance with rule of law, limited legitimating grounds for overriding religious freedom claims, and necessity/proportionality analysis), the institutional relationships between religion and the state have complex historical and cultural backgrounds, and often take quite different forms in different countries. A general framework for thinking about these differences was provided in Chapter 4. The great diversity of configurations of religion-state relationships makes comparative analysis complex but all the more interesting.

The types of issues covered in the following chapters correspond generally with the issues that arise under the provision of the First Amendment to the United States Constitution that proscribes state action "respecting an establishment of religion." Constitutional thinkers in other parts of the world often think that this "non-establishment" or separation principle is irrelevant to their situations, since most of the world's constitutions do not have non-establishment provisions. Systems involving cooperation between religion and the state are far more typical, and of course many states go even further and maintain official state religions.

In reality, however, there has been substantial convergence among differing regimes of state-religion relationships as suggested in Chapter 4. On the one hand, interpretation of the non-establishment principle in the United States in recent years has made it easier for the state and religious communities to cooperate. This has not been without controversy, as critiques of "faith-based initiatives" indicate. Nonetheless, principles of granting religious institutions "equal access" to government facilities and programs have increased the range of potential cooperation, even in areas involving certain types of state subsidies for activities carried out by religious organizations. Similarly, other countries with strong separationist traditions, such as France, channel substantial financial support to religiously affiliated institutions.

On the other hand, many of the issues that arise in the United States and are analyzed under the rubric of the Establishment Clause are paralleled by similar issues in Europe and elsewhere that are assessed under a variety of governing legal norms, including the religious freedom provisions of national constitutions, religious autonomy norms, equality norms, and provisions of various statutes and agreements governing relations with religious communities. Further, the US approach is not as unusual as some believe, since a number of countries, such as Japan, the Philippines, and Australia, have constitutional provisions that closely resemble the Establishment Clause of the United States Constitution (although these are often interpreted in quite different ways). Moreover, a considerably larger number of constitutions have provisions emphasizing the secular character of the state. What such secularism provisions require in modern legal contexts is itself a matter that deserves to be probed in depth. In short, despite greater historical and cultural variations, comparative analysis can be particularly fruitful in this area.

CHAPTER 10

RELIGIOUS AUTONOMY

I. INTRODUCTION

In common parlance, the term "autonomy" has emerged as a synonym for "liberty" or "freedom," and in that sense, religious autonomy might be viewed simply as a way to speak of the general right to freedom of religion or belief. In this chapter, however, we use the phrase "religious autonomy" in a more specialized sense to refer to the right of religious communities to independently determine their own doctrines and teachings, their missions, their organizational and communal structures (hierarchical, connectional, representational, congregational, etc.), their personnel, their internal normative and administrative structures, and in general, their own authentic natures and aspirations.

Professor Perry Dane has described "the legal problem of religious autonomy" as

> the effort by secular law to make sense of religious self-governance, particularly institutional or communal self-governance. In the United States, contexts in which religious autonomy is at issue include classic disputes over church property and personnel, in which secular courts have to gauge their deference to organs of governance within the religious community. They also include more recently developing questions over the extent to which regulatory regimes such as labor law, civil rights law, and even malpractice and defamation and contract law, can intervene in the internal relations of religious institutions and communities. . . .
>
> In the American context, many controversies arising under our "Establishment Clause"—such as cases about state sponsorship of religious practices and state financial support of religious institutions—can be understood as efforts to work out principles of separation and deference at a general or "wholesale" level, while many issues arising under our "Free Exercise Clause" can be understood as arising out of the need to adjust those principles at the "retail" level to particular religions and religious individuals. The most crucial of these "retail" questions, whose solution remains bitterly contested, is the problem of religion-based exemptions. . . .
>
> The problem of "religious autonomy" straddles the Establishment and Free Exercise Clauses, and therefore straddles the efforts at drawing "wholesale" and "retail" boundaries between religion and the state. As it sits on the "free exercise" side of the straddle, religious autonomy is a species of religious liberty. But it is a species with its own attributes. For one thing, it generally involves a well-defined institutional or communal interest, and not merely an individual one. Moreover, at least the paradigmatic claims to religious autonomy do not depend for their force on the specific norms of a particular religious community. Rather, they invoke limitations on

> government intrusion in *any* religious community. For example, the argument that secular anti-discrimination laws should not apply to the hiring of clergy is not limited to religions whose norms require them to discriminate; it applies to all religions, and rests on the general idea that the state should not interfere in any ecclesiastical appointments. In this sense, religious autonomy claims differ radically from the more purely "retail" claims to religious exemptions.[1]

In German religion-state theory, religious autonomy is linked to the "right of self-determination for churches."[2] This notion is articulated in Article 137(III) of the Weimar Constitution, as incorporated into the German Basic Law by Article 140: "Religious societies shall regulate and administer their affairs independently within the limits of the law that applies to all." This provision, including a formulaic limitations clause that has been progressively narrowed by interpretation over time,[3] ensures broad protection for religious autonomy. "Standing together with the freedom of religion and the separation of state and church, the recognition of the right to self-determination for churches is the third column of the system of state-church relations of the [German] constitution [Basic Law]."[4] The self-determination right of religious communities both overlaps with and is independent of the basic protection for freedom of religion or belief provided in Article 4 of the Basic Law.[5]

The right of independence and self-determination protects the notion of religious autonomy in its broadest form. "The constitution not only gives [religious communities] a kind of right to self-administration but acknowledges their right to self-determination, their complete freedom from supervision and tutelage through the state."[6] Its coverage extends beyond "internal" religious affairs, since in the German view religion has a public dimension and religious mandates by their nature extend into the public arena. The self-determination right covers matters

---

1. Perry Dane, The Varieties of Religious Autonomy in *Church Autonomy: A Comparative Survey* 119–120 (Gerhard Robbers, ed., Peter Lang 2001).

2. *See* Hermann von Mangoldt et al., *14 Das Bonner Grundgesetz Kommentar, Rdn.* 75, 77 (3d. rev. ed., Vahlen Verlag 1991).

3. The phrase "within the limits of the law that applies to all" dates back to the eighteenth century but has been progressively narrowed over time. In its original formulation, it was understood as a rule-of-law constraint on absolute power: the sovereign was free to pass any law, so long as it applied to all. As summarized by Prof. Gerhard Robbers:

> For some time, the Federal Constitutional Court used the formula that a law would not be contrary to the right of self-determination of religious communities when the law did not particularly affect the religious community but instead affected everyone. Subject to that, a law breaches a Church's right of self-determination when the Church itself is not affected to the same extent as everyone else, but rather, within its special qualities as a Church, its self-identity and in particular its spiritual-religious duty is subject to particular disadvantages. More adequate is another formula created by the Federal Constitutional Court whereby the right to self-determination cannot prevail against a general law that represents a provision of particular importance to the common weal.

Gerhard Robbers, State and Church in Germany, in *State and Church in the European Union* 77, 83 (2d ed., Gerhard Robbers, ed., Nomos 2005).

4. Axel Freiherr von Campenhausen, Church Autonomy in Germany, in *Church Autonomy: A Comparative Survey* 77 (Gerhard Robbers, ed., Peter Lang 2001).

5. *See id.* at 77–78.

6. *Id.*

that are the religious organization's *own*.[7] That is, they are matters that come distinctly within the religious organization's sphere, which extends beyond mere internal affairs. The mission and self-understanding of churches have great weight in determining what are their "own" affairs.[8] The Federal Constitutional Court has held that "what is meant by the Church's own affairs is determined particularly by how the Church itself views its own affairs, although the competence to take a final decision on the basis of the Basic Law is still reserved for the State Courts."[9] Significantly, the right to assert this autonomy is not restricted to the religious organization, but extends to related entities involved in carrying out its tasks. Thus, "the right of self-determination is . . . not merely attributed to a Church itself as a distinct entity, but instead it is something common to all institutions which are connected in some way or another with the Church regardless of the legal form taken by those links. This is true so long as, according to their self-identity, their goals or duties are suitably carried out and are held to be true mandates of the Church."[10]

The German insistence that religious autonomy rights are independent from, though naturally overlapping with, basic religious freedom rights corresponds with Professor Dane's notion that religious autonomy doctrine occupies an intermediate position between free exercise and non-establishment in the United States. Significantly, US religious autonomy cases were distinguished and were not overruled or limited by the jettisoning of the compelling state interest test in *Employment Division v. Smith*, 494 U.S. 872, 877, 887 (1990) (discussed in Chapter 6).

Many of the most difficult religious autonomy issues arise in contexts where there is a dispute between different factions of a religious community concerning control of physical assets, or control of religious authority and appointments to religious positions within the religious community. These problems are extremely difficult for states that are constitutionally committed to remaining neutral in religious disputes. Is the state's desiring to remain neutral when rendering any decision (including a decision not to decide) in fact likely to have the effect of favoring one side or the other? This chapter examines these challenging issues, focusing particularly on cases involving conflicts over religious property and the selection and disciplining of religious personnel.

COMMENTS AND QUESTIONS

1. How should religious autonomy rights be conceptualized? Are they derivative from individual religious free exercise rights? Are they a species of group or establishment rights? Are they subject to limitation clauses in the same way that individual religious freedom claims are? Or are they more "jurisdictional" in nature? That is, should religious autonomy rights be conceptualized as a right that should be balanced against state interests? Or is it an assertion that the state lacks power (jurisdictional competence) to intervene in particular matters?

---

7. *Id.* at 79.
8. *Id.*
9. Robbers, State and Church in Germany, *supra* note 3, at 83.
10. *Id.* (citing BVerfGE 70, 138/162).

2. Constitutions that lack establishment, separation, or secularism provisions may nonetheless protect the right to religious autonomy. What would be the functional differences, if any? Which is most likely to optimize religious freedom—explicit institutional separation, provisions on secularism, religious autonomy or equality, or a combination of the foregoing?
3. Where are religious autonomy issues most likely to arise? Consider the following comments by Mark Chopko:

> I do not find it particularly useful to speak about "the separation of church and state" but rather to speak more comprehensively and sensitively about the need to protect authentic religious beliefs and exercises against governmental encroachment, and vice versa. Certain matters in human life belong only to Religion, and are none of the business of government. At the same time there are governmental interests that belong only to Government and not to religion. Where most conflict between Religion and Government occurs [lies in . . .] interests [that] are legitimately thought of as being accomplished by both religion and government. . . . All of the discussion about church autonomy presumes that some person has an injury which that person would lay at the feet of a religious institution. The issue for the practitioner is—where is the remedy, in the church or in the civil court?[11]

II. DISPUTES REGARDING RELIGIOUS PROPERTY

A. THE UNITED STATES

1. Deference to Polity under Federal Common Law: *Watson v. Jones*

In *Watson v. Jones*, 80 U.S. (13 Wall.) 679 (1872), the United States Supreme Court rejected the traditional British "departure from doctrine" approach, which awarded property in church faction disputes to the group that retained the closest position to original church doctrines. The Court held that this standard was inconsistent with American commitments to religious freedom based on the principle of deference to the legislature.

Watson involved a post–Civil War dispute in Kentucky between factions of a church that had been divided over slavery. The question before the Court was which faction should own the Walnut Street Presbyterian Church in Louisville, Kentucky. The Presbyterian Church was run by a hierarchy of judicatories known as Church Sessions, Presbyteries, Synods, and the General Assembly. Formally, the Walnut Street property was owned by three trustees who were elected biannually by the congregation and held legal title to the church. The trustees were subject to the Session in managing the property. The Session operated the church and was composed of the pastor and ruling elders. The Session was responsible for maintaining the spiritual government of the local congregation. The elders decided issues by a majority vote but did not have the power to dispose of church property. Over time, competing groups of pro- and antislavery trustees had been elected.

11. Mark Chopko, Constitutional Protection for Church Autonomy: A Practitioner's View, in *Church Autonomy: A Comparative Survey* 95 (Gerhard Robbers, ed., Peter Lang 2001).

In May 1865, the Presbyterian Church General Assembly declared that it would support the federal government in its opposition to slavery. The local Presbytery that was in charge of the Walnut Street Church refused to comply with the order and the following September issued a pamphlet denouncing the "heretical doctrines and practices which have obtained and been propagated in the Presbyterian Church." In June 1867, the Presbyterian General Assembly, which was the highest judicatory of the church, declared that the proslavery party was excluded and disconnected from the Assembly and that the antislavery leaders were the true Presbytery and Synod of the local church. The local church was divided over the issue, and a schism developed. The proslavery group joined the Presbyterian Church of the Confederate States in 1868. *Watson v. Jones* was filed in federal court by Indiana citizens who were members of the Louisville church to determine which group should be recognized as the body entitled to hold the property in question.

In this dispute, the Court determined that "whenever the questions of discipline, or of faith, or ecclesiastical rule, custom, or law have been decided by the highest of these church judicatories to which the matter has been carried, the legal tribunals must accept such decisions as final and as binding on them." . . . (727). Since the General Assembly of the church determined that the antislavery group should have control as the new leaders, the Supreme Court ruled as follows:

> In this country the full and free right to entertain any religious belief, to practice any religious principle, and to teach any religious doctrine which does not violate the laws of morality and property, and which does not infringe personal rights, is conceded to all. The law knows no heresy, and is committed to the support of no dogma, the establishment of no sect. The right to organize voluntary religious associations to assist in the expression and dissemination of any religious doctrine, and to create tribunals for the decision of controverted questions of faith within the association, and for the ecclesiastical government of all the individual members, congregations, and officers within the general association, is unquestioned. All who unite themselves to such a body do so with an implied consent to this government, and are bound to submit to it. But it would be a vain consent and would lead to the total subversion of such religious bodies, if any one aggrieved by one of their decisions could appeal to the secular courts and have them reversed. It is of the essence of these religious unions, and of the right to establish tribunals for the decision of questions arising among themselves, that those decisions should be binding in all cases of ecclesiastical cognizance, subject only to such appeals as the organism itself provides for. (728-729)

Although *Watson v. Jones* was decided under federal common law principles long before the First Amendment had been held applicable to the states, it has remained an important precedent. The opinion radiates "a spirit of freedom for religious organizations, an independence from secular control or manipulation, in short, power to decide for themselves, free from state interference, matters of church government as well as those of faith and doctrine."[12]

12. *Kedroff v. St. Nicholas Cathedral*, 344 U.S. 94, 116 (1952).

2. Deference to Polity Under the First Amendment: *Kedroff v. St. Nicholas Cathedral*

In *Kedroff v. St. Nicholas Cathedral*, 344 U.S. 94 (1952), the Supreme Court held that a New York law that transferred control of Russian Orthodox churches in New York from the central governing hierarchy of the Russian Orthodox Church in Moscow to governing authorities of the Russian Church in America, was unconstitutional as a violation of the Free Exercise Clause. The hierarchical structure of the Russian Orthodox Church placed the control of the church in Russia. The law in question

> undertook to pass control of the New York churches of the Russian Orthodox religion from the central governing hierarchy of the Russian Orthodox Church, the Patriarch of Moscow and the Holy Synod, to the governing authorities of the Russian Church in America, a church organization limited to the diocese of North America and the Aleutian Islands. This transfer takes place by virtue of the statute. Such a law violates the Fourteenth Amendment. It prohibits in this country the free exercise of religion. Legislation that regulates church administration, the operation of the churches, the appointment of clergy, by requiring conformity to church statutes "adopted at a general convention (sobor) held in the City of New York"... prohibits the free exercise of religion. 107-108)

Cold War concerns about the extent to which the hierarchy of the Russian Orthodox Church were subject to communist influence did not constitute sufficient grounds to see the case differently. Nor did the fact that the Americans had become accustomed to self-governance and started a separationist movement make a difference. The Russian hierarchy had never relinquished its claims of control or recognized American autonomy. The Supreme Court held that the law directly prohibited the free exercise of an ecclesiastical right, the Church's choice of its hierarchy. As in *Watson v. Jones*, the Supreme Court held that civil courts must defer to the decisions of the Russian hierarchy, even though there was suspicion about the extent to which the hierarchy was genuinely autonomous given the power of communist authority in Russia.

3. Rejection of the "Departure from Doctrine" Test

PRESBYTERIAN CHURCH IN THE UNITED STATES V. MARY ELIZABETH BLUE HULL MEMORIAL PRESBYTERIAN CHURCH

Supreme Court of the United States, 393 U.S. 440 (1969)

Mr. Justice BRENNAN delivered the opinion of the Court.

This is a church property dispute which arose when two local churches withdrew from a hierarchical general church organization. Under Georgia law the right to the property previously used by the local churches was made to turn on a civil court jury decision as to whether the general church abandoned or departed from the tenets of faith and practice it held at the time the local churches affiliated with it. The question presented is whether the restraints of the First Amendment, as applied to the States through the Fourteenth Amendment, permit a civil court to award church property on the basis of the interpretation and significance the civil court assigns to aspects of church doctrine.

[In 1966, the membership of the local congregations of the Hull Memorial Presbyterian Church and Eastern Heights Presbyterian Church voted to withdraw from the general Presbyterian Church because they believed certain actions and pronouncements of the general church were violation of that organization's constitution and constituted departures from the doctrine and practice in force at the time of affiliation with the general church. After an effort at reconciliation, the general church took over control of the local church property until new local leadership could be appointed. The churches filed suits claiming that the local churches owned the property. The cases were consolidated and submitted to a jury on the theory that Georgia law implies a trust of local church property for the benefit of the general church on the sole condition that the general church adhere to its tenets of faith and practice existing at the time of affiliation of the local churches. The jury returned a verdict in favor of the local churches. The trial judge held that the implied trust had terminated and enjoined the general church from interfering with the local churches' use of the property in question. The Supreme Court of Georgia affirmed.]

It is of course true that the State has a legitimate interest in resolving property disputes, and that a civil court is a proper forum for that resolution. Special problems arise, however, when these disputes implicate controversies over church doctrine and practice. The approach of this Court in such cases was originally developed in *Watson v. Jones*. . . . The *Watson* Court refused [to decree the termination of an implied trust because of departures from doctrine by the national organization], pointing out that it was wholly inconsistent with the American concept of the relationship between church and state to permit civil courts to determine ecclesiastical questions. . . .

Later cases, however, also decided on nonconstitutional grounds, recognized that there might be some circumstances in which marginal civil court review of ecclesiastical determinations would be appropriate. The scope of this review was delineated in *Gonzalez v. Roman Catholic Archbishop of Manila*, 280 U.S. 1 (1929) when Justice Brandeis, speaking for the Court, defined the civil court role in the following words: "In the absence of fraud, collusion, or arbitrariness, the decisions of the proper church tribunals on matters purely ecclesiastical, although affecting civil rights, are accepted in litigation before the secular courts as conclusive, because the parties in interest made them so by contract or otherwise."

In *Kedroff* . . . the Court converted the principle of *Watson* as qualified by *Gonzalez* into a constitutional rule. . . .

[The *Kedroff*] holding invalidating legislative action was extended to judicial action in *Kreshik v. St. Nicholas Cathedral*, 363 U.S. 190 (1960), where the Court held that the constitutional guarantees of religious liberty required the reversal of a judgment of the New York courts which transferred control of St. Nicholas Cathedral from the central governing authority of the Russian Orthodox Church to the independent Russian Church of America.

Thus, the First Amendment severely circumscribes the role that civil courts may play in resolving church property disputes. It is obvious, however, that not every civil court decision as to property claimed by a religious organization jeopardizes values protected by the First Amendment. Civil courts do not inhibit free exercise of religion merely by opening their doors to disputes involving church property. And there are neutral principles of law, developed for use in all property disputes, which can be applied without "establishing" churches to which property is awarded. But First Amendment values are plainly jeopardized when church property litigation is made to turn on the resolution by civil courts of controversies over religious doctrine and practice. If civil courts undertake to resolve such controversies in order to adjudicate the property dispute, the hazards are ever present of inhibiting the free development of religious doctrine and of implicating secular interests in matters of purely ecclesiastical concern. Because of these hazards, the First Amendment enjoins the employment of organs of government for essentially religious purposes. . . . [T]he Amendment therefore commands civil courts to decide church property disputes without resolving underlying controversies over religious doctrine. Hence, States, religious organizations, and individuals must structure relationships involving church property so as not to require the civil courts to resolve ecclesiastical questions.

The Georgia courts have violated the command of the First Amendment. The departure-from-doctrine element of the implied trust theory which they applied requires the civil judiciary to determine whether actions of the general church constitute such a "substantial departure" from the tenets of faith and practice existing at the time of the local churches' affiliation that the trust in favor of the general church must be declared to have terminated. This determination has two parts. The civil court must first decide whether the challenged actions of the general church depart substantially from prior doctrine. In reaching such a decision, the court must of necessity make its own interpretation of the meaning of church doctrines. If the court should decide that a substantial departure has occurred, it must then go on to determine whether the issue on which the general church has departed holds a place of such importance in the traditional theology as to require that the trust be terminated. A civil court can make this determination only after assessing the relative significance to the religion of the tenets from which departure was found. Thus, the departure-from-doctrine element of the Georgia implied trust theory requires the civil court to determine matters at the very core of a religion—the interpretation of particular church doctrines and the importance of those doctrines to the religion. Plainly, the First Amendment forbids civil courts from playing such a role. . . .

The judgment of the Supreme Court of Georgia is reversed, and the case is remanded for further proceedings not inconsistent with this opinion.

4. The "Neutral Principles of Law" Test

Following the decision in the *Hull Memorial Presbyterian Church* case, the Georgia Supreme Court, in an effort to develop an alternative to the departure-from-doctrine test, applied what has come to be known as the "neutral principles of law" test. Under this approach, a court may examine deeds to properties, state statutes, and other relevant documents using secular techniques to interpret such documents, and also to see whether any express or implied trust had been created that could resolve intra-church disputes. The new approach came before the US Supreme Court in *Jones v. Wolf*, 241 Ga. 208, 243 S.E.2d 860 (1978).

The case arose from a schism within the Vineville Presbyterian Church in Macon, Georgia. A vote was held in which a majority of the members chose to break off from the main body of the Presbyterian church. A substantial minority was determined by the general church to be "the true congregation of the Vineville Presbyterian Church," and the majority faction, which had retained possession of the church building, was denied recognition. The minority faction brought suit seeking vindication of their right to exclusive possession and use of the Vineville church property as a member congregation of the Presbyterian Church of the United States (PCUS). The trial court, purporting to apply Georgia's "neutral principles of law" approach to church property disputes, granted judgment for the majority faction. The Supreme Court of Georgia, holding that the trial court had correctly stated and applied Georgia law, and rejecting the minority's challenge based on the First and Fourteenth Amendments, affirmed. Excerpts from the Court's opinion follow.

JONES V. WOLF

Supreme Court of the United States, 443 U.S. 595 (1979)

Mr. Justice BLACKMUN delivered the opinion of the Court.

This case involves a dispute over the ownership of church property following a schism in a local church affiliated with a hierarchical church organization. The question for decision is whether civil courts, consistent with the First and Fourteenth Amendments to the Constitution, may resolve the dispute on the basis of "neutral principles of law," or whether they must defer to the resolution of an authoritative tribunal of the hierarchical church. . . .

Most importantly, the First Amendment prohibits civil courts from resolving church property disputes on the basis of religious doctrine and practice. As a corollary to this commandment, the Amendment requires that civil courts defer to the resolution of issues of religious doctrine or polity by the highest court of a hierarchical church organization. . . . At least in general, we think the "neutral principles of law" approach is consistent with the foregoing constitutional principles.

The primary advantages of the neutral-principles approach are that it is completely secular in operation, and yet flexible enough to accommodate all forms of religious organization and polity. The method relies exclusively on objective, well-established concepts of trust and property law familiar to lawyers and judges.

This is not to say that the application of the neutral-principles approach is wholly free of difficulty. The neutral-principles method, at least as it has evolved in Georgia, requires a civil court to examine certain religious documents, such as a church constitution, for language of trust in favor of the general church. In undertaking such an examination, a civil court must take special care to scrutinize the document in purely secular terms, and not to rely on religious precepts in determining whether the document indicates that the parties have intended to create a trust. In addition, there may be cases where the deed, the corporate charter, or the constitution of the general church incorporates religious concepts in the provisions relating to the ownership of property. If in such a case the interpretation of the instruments of ownership would require the civil court to resolve a religious controversy, then the court must defer to the resolution of the doctrinal issue by the authoritative ecclesiastical body.

On balance, however, the promise of non-entanglement and neutrality inherent in the neutral-principles approach more than compensates for what will be occasional problems in application. These problems, in addition, should be gradually eliminated as recognition is given to the obligation of "States, religious organizations, and individuals [to] structure relationships involving church property so as not to require the civil courts to resolve ecclesiastical questions." *Presbyterian Church v. Mary Elizabeth Blue Hull Memorial Presbyterian Church*, 393 U.S. 440, 449 (1969). We therefore hold that a State is constitutionally entitled to adopt neutral principles of law as a means of adjudicating a church property dispute. . . .

It remains to be determined whether the Georgia neutral-principles analysis was constitutionally applied on the facts of this case. Although both the trial court and the Supreme Court of Georgia viewed the case as involving nothing more than an application of the principles developed in *Presbyterian Church II* and in [*Carnes v. Smith*, 236 Ga. 30, 222 S.E.2d 322, *cert. denied*, 429 U.S. 868 (1976)*,* the present case contains a significant complicating factor absent in each of those earlier cases. *Presbyterian Church II* and *Carnes* each involved a church property dispute between the general church and the entire local congregation. Here, the local congregation was itself divided between a majority of 164 members who sought to withdraw from the PCUS, and a minority of 94 members who wished to maintain the affiliation. Neither of the state courts alluded to this problem, however; each concluded without discussion or analysis that the title to the property was in the local church and that the local church was represented by the majority rather than the minority.

Petitioners earnestly submit that the question of which faction is the true representative of the Vineville church is an ecclesiastical question that cannot be answered by a civil court. At least, it is said, it cannot be answered by a civil court in a case involving a hierarchical church, like the PCUS, where a duly appointed church commission has determined which of the two factions represents the "true congregation." Respondents, in opposition, argue in effect that the Georgia courts did no more than apply the ordinary presumption that, absent some indication to the contrary, a voluntary religious association is represented by a majority of its members.

If in fact Georgia has adopted a presumptive rule of majority representation, defeasible upon a showing that the identity of the local church is to be determined by some other means, we think this would be consistent with both the neutral-principles analysis and the First Amendment. Majority rule is generally employed in the governance of religious societies. Furthermore, the majority faction generally can be identified without resolving any question of religious doctrine or polity. Certainly, there was no dispute in the present case about the identity of the duly enrolled members of the Vineville church when the dispute arose, or about the fact that a quorum was present, or about the final vote. Most importantly, any rule of majority representation can always be overcome, under the neutral-principles approach, either by providing, in the corporate charter or the constitution of the general church, that the identity of the local church is to be established in some other way, or by providing that the church property is held in trust for the general church and those who remain loyal to it. Indeed, the State may adopt any method of overcoming the majoritarian presumption, so long as the use of that method does not impair free-exercise rights or entangle the civil courts in matters of religious controversy.

Neither the trial court nor the Supreme Court of Georgia, however, explicitly stated that it was adopting a presumptive rule of majority representation. Moreover, there are at least some indications that under Georgia law the process of identifying the faction that represents the Vineville church involves considerations of religious doctrine and polity. Georgia law requires that "church property be held according to the terms of the church government," and provides that a local church affiliated with a hierarchical religious association "is part of the whole body of the general church and is subject to the higher authority of the organization and its laws and regulations." *Carnes* at 325. All this may suggest that the identity of the "Vineville Presbyterian Church" named in the deeds must be determined according to terms of the Book of Church Order, which sets out the laws and regulations of churches affiliated with the PCUS. Such a determination, however, would appear to require a civil court to pass on questions of religious doctrine, and to usurp the function of the commission appointed by the Presbytery, which already has determined that petitioners represent the "true congregation" of the Vineville church. Therefore, if Georgia law provides that the identity of the Vineville church is to be determined according to the "laws and regulations" of the PCUS, then the First Amendment requires that the Georgia courts give deference to the presbyterial commission's determination of that church's identity.

This Court, of course, does not declare what the law of Georgia is. Since the grounds for the decision that respondents represent the Vineville church remain unarticulated, the judgment of the Supreme Court of Georgia is vacated, and the case is remanded for further proceedings not inconsistent with this opinion.

COMMENTS AND QUESTIONS

1. The Cold War was in full swing during *Kedroff.* How does that impact how you view that decision?
2. Does *Jones v. Wolf* overrule *Hull Memorial Church*? That is, does *Jones require* a neutral principles approach?
3. Which affords greater protection for religious autonomy—the deference to church polity or the neutral principles approach?
4. How, if at all, does the neutral principles approach of *Jones v. Wolf* relate to the "neutral laws of general applicability" that suffice to override religious freedom claims in *Employment Division v. Smith* (see Chapter 6)?

B. EUROPE

Religious property disputes in Europe often have much deeper historical provenance than those in the United States. In this regard, Ukraine is a particularly interesting case, because it straddles the boundary between civilizations rooted in Western and Eastern Christianity. The resulting religious differences were suppressed to a considerable extent during the Soviet era, but since 1990 they have reappeared in significant ways. According to a comprehensive national survey[13] in February 2015, of Ukraine's 44.4 million people (number including Crimea, invaded and claimed by Russia in 2014), 73.7 percent self-identify as Orthodox Christian. Adherents of the Ukrainian Greek Catholic Church (UGCC), an eastern rite Church that is oriented toward Rome, constitute the country's second largest group, and the largest group in the western part of the country, with an estimated four million adherents. An estimated 8.1 percent of the population self-identifies as Greek Catholic, 0.8 percent as Roman Catholic, 0.9 percent as Protestant, and 0.7 percent as followers of "other" religious groups. Another 8.5 percent self-identify as "just a Christian" and 6.1 percent say they do not belong to any religious group. The Muslim population of Ukraine is estimated by government agencies and independent think tanks at 500,000, most of whom (300,000) are Crimean Tatars. Some Muslim leaders estimate that as many as two million Muslims live in Ukraine.[14]

Of Ukrainans identifying as Orthodox Christian, 37.9 percent identify with the Ukrainian Orthodox Church of the Kyiv Patriarchate (UOC-KP), 19.6 percent with the Ukrainian Orthodox Church (Moscow Patriarchate) (UOC-MP), 39.1 percent with neither Orthodox Church and self-identifying as "just an Orthodox believer," 1.3 percent identified with the Ukrainian Autocephalous Orthodox Church (UAOC), and 1.1 percent undecided about affiliation. .

The Kyiv Patriarchate was formed in 1992, after Ukraine withdrew from the Soviet Union. Its formation was linked to Ukrainian nationalism. The UOC-MP does not recognize the Kyiv Patriarchate and is registered as the Ukrainian Orthodox Church. Adherents of the UOC-KP, UAOC, and UGCC are concentrated more in the center and western portions of the country; UOC-MP is more strongly represented in the east. While the exact mix has changed over time, and the UOC-KP is relatively new, the basic divide between east and west has roots extending back centuries. The division within the Orthodox tradition has made for a more pluralistic setting in Ukraine, but also one that has resulted in various kinds of religious property disputes.

SVYATO-MYKHAYLIVSKA PARAFIYA V. UKRAINE (ST. MICHAEL'S PARISH V. UKRAINE)

European Court of Human Rights, Application No. 77703/01 (14 June 2007)

In April 1989 a group of 25 individuals including Volodymyr Makarchykov formed a religious association with the intention of building a church named "Svyato-Mykhaylivska Church of 1,000 years of Baptisms in the Kyivan Rus." The group was registered as a religious association of the Orthodox Church on 22 February 1990, and four days later was granted permission to build the church. On 4 March 1990 the religious association approved its statute (charter) and elected its governing bodies (the Parishioner's Assembly, the Parishioners' Council, and

13. Conducted by independent polling groups Center for Social and Marketing Research, SOCIS, Sociological Group Rating, the Kyiv International Institute of Sociology, and the Razumkov Center.

14. US Department of State, International Religious Freedom Report 2015: Ukraine.

the Supervisory Board). In accordance with fixed membership requirements that contemplated membership by only a small leadership group, the Parishioners' Assembly varied from about 20 to 27 members from the date of its creation through December 1999. Makarchykov was elected as a member of the Parishioners' Council and became its chairman. He also acted as chairman of the religious association and frequently as a secretary during the meetings of the Parishioners' Assembly.

The religious association initially was independent in its organizational, religious, and commercial activities. It was decided that it should act under the religious guidance of the Archbishop of the Finnish Orthodox Church in canonical issues. Later that year, however, the association decided to affiliate with the UOC-MP. On 19 November 1992 the Parishioners' Assembly adopted a new statute seeking its registration as a legal entity. On 8 February 1993 the representative of the president of Ukraine made a formal decision to register the revised statute of the Parish as a legal entity, and from that date onward the Parish belonged to the UOC-MP.

In 1994 and again in 1999, the Parishioners' Assembly refused to introduce changes that would have conformed its charter to the standard statutes for religious associations belonging to the UOC-MP, at least until the construction of the new church building for the use of the religious association was satisfactorily completed.

Toward the end of 1999, there was a falling out with the Moscow Patriarchate. There were charges and countercharges of financial mismanagement. The Parishioners' Assembly apparently believed Makarchykov's account, according to which there had been misdealing by the current and past priors of the church who were aligned with the UOC-MP, involving withholding of US$2,880,000 from the Parish. The Parish Assembly accordingly resolved to teminate the current prior and to proceed with criminal complaints against him and the previous prior. On 24 December 1999, the original Parishioners' Assembly, with 21 of its then 27 members present, decided to withdraw from the jurisdiction and canonical guidance of the Moscow Patriarchate and to affiliate with the Kyiv Patriarchate. The assembly authorized Makarchykov and another individual to register the amendments to the Parish's charter needed to effect this change. Archbishop Filaret formally declared the Parish a part of the Kyiv Patriarchate on 25 December 1999 and 10 January 2000.

However, before the amendments could be formally registered by state officials, 150 to 200 clerics and lay people supporting the Moscow Patriarchate occupied the building. Representatives of the Moscow Patriarchate authorized the holding of a new Parishioners' Assembly. On 2 January 2000, 309 supporters of the Moscow Patriarchate, many from different churches in Kjiv, held a meeting in which they ostensibly acted as the Parish Assembly and elected new governing bodies of the church. This new Assembly adopted the model statute for churches belonging to the UOC-MP. Both sides to the dispute sought various forms of vindication or support for their positions from political and administrative sources and engaged in mutual recriminations.

On 21 January 2000, the Kyiv City State Administration refused to register the amendments proposed by the original Parishioners' Assembly, because the documents had not been signed (as required by article 2.5 of the association's statute) by the prior (an individual the original Parishioners'Assembly had fired) or the chairman of the Parishioner's Assembly. On 21 April 2000, the Kyiv City Court rejected the claims [of the original association, holding] among other things, that the refusal to register the amendments was not unlawful because (1) they had been adopted contrary to the organization's charter and would infringe believers' rights; and (2) the original Parishioners' Assembly had actually withdrawn from the Moscow Patriarchate and affiliated with the Kyiv Patriarchate before the amendments were proposed. The Supreme Court rejected the original association's appeal, among other reasons because the fixed membership provisions of the charter did not allow the majority of the religious group to manifest their religion by participating in the administration of church affairs. It further held that because the legislation governing creation of religious organizations does not provide for fixed membership, the association's charter was unlawful. In the Supreme Court's view, the "parishioners' assembly" and the "general assembly of the religious group" are really the same, and the provisions of the original association's charter that limited members in the governing councils and thus would not recognize the meeting orchestrated by the Moscow patriatchate "led to factual obstacles for a majority of the religious community" in violation of the rights of the majority (i.e., the Moscow Patriarchate supporters who occupied the building) to manifest their religion.

Several of those associated with the original association's officers experienced substantial ongoing harassment, including Makarchykov and his sister. The case was ultimately taken to the European Court of Human Rights. The applicant association claimed that the refusal to register the amendments was in breach of Article 9 of the Convention. Excerpts from the European Court's decision follow.

A. General Principles Enshrined in the Court's Case-law

112. The Court . . . recalls that while religious freedom is primarily a matter of individual conscience, it also implies, *inter alia*, freedom to "manifest [one's] religion" alone and in private or in community with others, in public and within the circle of those whose faith one shares. . . .

113. Seen from this perspective, the right of believers to freedom of religion, which includes the right to manifest one's religion in community with others, encompasses the expectation that believers will be allowed to associate freely, without arbitrary State intervention. The State's duty of neutrality and impartiality, as defined in the Court's case-law, is incompatible with any power on the State's part to assess the legitimacy of religious beliefs. . . .

Whether There Was Interference with the Applicant Association's Rights

123. The Court . . . concludes that the refusal of the Kyiv City State Administration to register the changes and amendments the applicant association's statute, as upheld by the Kyiv City Court and the Supreme Court . . . constituted an interference with the applicant association's right to freedom of religion [since it] restricted the ability of the religious group concerned . . .to exercise the full range of religious activities and activities normally exercised by registered non-

governmental legal entities. . . . It also prevented it from joining the Kyiv Patriarchate as an independent religious group administering the affairs of a church it had built and been accustomed to worship in. . . .

2. Whether the interference was "necessary in a democratic society"

137. The Court notes at the outset that it is true that in a democratic society it may be necessary to place restrictions on freedom of religion to reconcile the interests of the various religious groups....However, the list of these restrictions, as contained in Articles 9 and 11 of the Convention, is exhaustive and they are to be construed strictly, within a limited margin of appreciation allowed for the State and only convincing and compelling reasons can justify restrictions on that freedom. Any such restriction must correspond to a "pressing social need" and must be "proportionate to the legitimate aim pursued". . . .

138. The Court's task is thus to determine whether the refusal to register changes and amendments to the statute of the applicant association were justified in principle and were proportionate to the legitimate aim pursued. [This requires determining] whether it was "proportionate to the legitimate aim pursued" and whether the reasons adduced by the national authorities to justify it are "relevant and sufficient" [and whether they are based] on an acceptable assessment of the relevant facts. . . .

139. In this relation the Court observes that the grounds given by the domestic authorities for refusing registration of the applicant association were not consistent. Although the Kyiv City State Administration initially referred to Article 2.5 of the statute, [which required documents to be signed by the prior,] this alleged defect in the documents submitted for registration was not the main ground for refusing the applicant association's re-registration in the subsequent judicial decisions. In particular, the first-instance court found that the Parishioners' Assembly held on 24 December 1999 had invalid composition as it did not comprise all the members of the Parish...and the Supreme Court further ruled that the requirements of the statute regarding fixed membership were incompatible with the Act. . . .

140. Thus, the Court considers it necessary to examine these three main reasons for refusing the applicant association's re-registration in turn and to test them against the criteria mentioned above.

i. Compliance with Article 2.5 of the statute

. . . [The Court concluded that in light of the fact that different Charter provisions governed amendments to the Charter, the contention that registration of the amendments should not be permitted because the documents had not been signed by the (terminated) prior were] were neither 'relevant nor sufficient'."

ii. The finding that the Parishioners' Assembly held on 24 December 1999 was illegitimate as it did not comprise all the members of the Parish

145. The Court observes that section 7 of the Freedom of Consciousness and Religions Act gave no clear definition of a "religious organisation". Section 8 also defined religious groups as local level religious organisations...composed of "believers of the same religion or religious cult, who voluntarily united for the

purposes of satisfying their religious needs". Contrary to the findings of the domestic courts, Sections 7 and 8 of the Act did not specify that a religious group had to be composed of all persons or all believers attending religious services of a particular church. . . .

146. Furthermore, section 8 of the Act did not place any restrictions on or prevent a religious organisation from determining at its own discretion the manner in which it would decide whether to admit new members, the criteria for membership and the procedure for electing its governing bodies. For the purposes of Article 9 of the Convention, read in the light of Article 11, these were private-law decisions, which should not be susceptible to interference by State bodies, unless they interfere with the rights of others or the restrictions specified in Articles 9 § 2 and 11 § 2 of the Convention. In other words, the State cannot oblige a legitimately existing private-law association to admit members or exclude existing members. Interference of this sort would run counter to the freedom of religious associations to regulate their conduct and to administer their affairs freely. The Court must therefore examine the regulations contained in the statute as to membership of the Parish and the factual circumstances of the case.

147. It notes at the outset that the applicant association was created in April 1989 and until January 2000 was continuously composed of some 20 to 30 members. . . . At present it is still composed of 30 members. Furthermore, under Article 1.1 of the statute, the Parish is a religious group composed of secular priests, church ministers and laymen. In other words, this Article refers to those who were generally eligible for membership of the Parish. However, under Article 2.1 the highest governing body of the Parish was the Parishioners' Assembly, composed of the founding members and those admitted after the establishment of the Parish, on the conditions specified in Article 2.12 from among those generally eligible for membership of the Parish. The Court considers, therefore, that the Parish's internal organisation was clearly defined in the statute. The domestic authorities, including the courts, disregarded this internal structure of the Parish as a private-law association, stating the religious group concerned was a mere minority of the "permanent members of the religious group" composed of some 300 people, who were not invited to attend the meeting of the Parishioners' Assembly, even though they were part of the group. . . .

149. The Court notes that both the Kyiv City Court and the Supreme Court ignored the internal regulations of the Parish, and the history of the Parish administration from 1989 to 2000 and based their findings on an unclear reference in section 8 of the Act as to what constituted a "religious group" and to arguably analogous meanings of the words "parish", "group", "general assembly" and "parishioners' assembly". It accordingly finds that the Kyiv City Court's refusal to order the registration of the changes and amendments that had been made to the statute was based on reasoning that was not "relevant or sufficient".

iii. The requirement of "fixed membership"

150. The Court reiterates that religious associations are free to determine at their own discretion the manner in which new members are admitted and existing members excluded. The internal structure of a religious organisation and the

regulations governing its membership must be seen as a means by which such organisations are able to express their beliefs and maintain their religious traditions. The Court points out that the right to freedom of religion excludes any discretion on the part of the State to determine whether the means used to express religious beliefs are legitimate....

151. The Court considers that the conclusions contained in the Supreme Court's ruling of 21 April 2000 that the requirement of "fixed membership" of a religious organisation was not laid down by legislation and that "parishioners' assembly" and "general assembly of a religious group" had analogous meanings so that the rights of the majority of the religious group and their right to exercise their religion were infringed, were neither "relevant and sufficient".

5. Overall conclusions

152. In the light of the foregoing and conclusions reached with regard to different reasons for refusal to register changes to the statute..., the Court considers that the interference with the applicant association's right to freedom of religion was not justified. It also considers that the lack of safeguards against arbitrary decisions by the registering authority were not rectified by the judicial review conducted by the domestic courts, which were clearly prevented from reaching a different finding by the lack of coherence and foreseeability of the legislation. In summary, there has therefore been a violation of Article 9 of the Convention, read in the light of Articles 6 § 1 and 11 of the Convention.

COMMENTS AND QUESTIONS

1. Does the European Court follow an approach that is closer to the "neutral principles" or the "deference to ecclesiastical polity" method used by US courts? If the latter, what is the ecclesiastical polity to which deference is owed—the legal entity created by a number of adherents or the social reality of the religious community?
2. The ouster of the original Parishioners' Assembly occurred at the beginning of 2000. The UOC-MP had controlled the church for many of the years between that time and the time of the European Court's decision. Presumably, individuals content with the UOC-MP have continued to worship at St. Michael's and the UOC-MP has incurred costs of maintenance (and likely further construction). The European Court has in effect concluded that the intervening occupation was wrongful, but how does one optimally protect the rights of those who have been using the facility in the meantime?

III. RELIGIOUS AUTONOMY AND PERSONNEL ISSUES

In the religious autonomy cases examined thus far, the focus has been on the extent to which civil courts can resolve disputes over the control of property by religious communities while remaining neutral and not getting entangled in resolving matters of religious belief. The issues become even more complex when disputes arise about religious personnel. Sometimes the resolution of claims about who should hold a particular office or position has implications for who will control property; sometimes what is at issue is who should have authority to decide who will be in particular positions. Either way, examination of these cases deepens understanding of how the interaction of state and religious normative systems should be structured.

A. AUTONOMY WITH RESPECT TO RELIGIOUS OFFICIALS

1. The United States

SERBIAN EASTERN ORTHODOX DIOCESE V. MILIVOJEVICH

Supreme Court of the United States, 426 U.S. 696 (1976)

[During the course of a protracted dispute over the control of the Serbian Eastern Orthodox Diocese for the United States and Canada, the Holy Assembly of Bishops and the Holy Synod of the Serbian Orthodox Church (Mother Church) suspended and ultimately removed and defrocked the Bishop, respondent Dionisije, and appointed petitioner Firmilian as Administrator of the Diocese, which the Mother Church then reorganized into three Dioceses. The Serbian Orthodox Church is a hierarchical church, and the sole power to appoint and remove its Bishops rests in the Holy Assembly and Holy Synod. Dionisije filed suit in the Illinois courts seeking to enjoin petitioners from interfering with Diocesan assets of respondent not-for-profit Illinois corporations and to have himself declared the true Diocesan Bishop. After a lengthy trial, the trial court resolved most of the disputed issues in favor of petitioners. The Supreme Court of Illinois affirmed in part and reversed in part, holding that Dionisije's removal and defrockment had to be set aside as "arbitrary" because the proceedings against him had not in its view been conducted in accordance with the Church's constitution and penal code, and that the Diocesan reorganization was invalid because it exceeded the scope of the Mother Church's authority to effect such changes without Diocesan approval. The US Supreme Court reversed, holding that the Illinois Supreme Court's decision constituted improper judicial interference. An excerpt of the Supreme Court's opinion follows.]

Mr. Justice BRENNAN delivered the opinion of the Court.

The fallacy fatal to the judgment of the Illinois Supreme Court is that it rests upon an impermissible rejection of the decisions of the highest ecclesiastical tribunals of this hierarchical church upon the issues in dispute, and impermissibly substitutes its own inquiry into church polity and resolutions based thereon of those disputes. For where resolution of the disputes cannot be made without extensive inquiry by civil courts into religious law and polity, the First and Fourteenth Amendments mandate that civil courts shall not disturb the decisions of the highest ecclesiastical tribunal within a church of hierarchical polity, but must accept such decisions as binding on them, in their application to the religious issues of doctrine or polity before them.

Resolution of the religious disputes at issue here affects the control of church property in addition to the structure and administration of the American-Canadian

Diocese. This is because the Diocesan Bishop controls respondent Monastery of St. Sava and is the principal officer of respondent property-holding corporations. Resolution of the religious dispute over Dionisije's defrockment therefore determines control of the property. Thus, this case essentially involves not a church property dispute, but a religious dispute the resolution of which under our cases is for ecclesiastical and not civil tribunals. Even when rival church factions seek resolution of a church property dispute in the civil courts there is substantial danger that the State will become entangled in essentially religious controversies or intervene on behalf of groups espousing particular doctrinal beliefs. Because of this danger, "the First Amendment severely circumscribes the role that civil courts may play in resolving church property disputes." *Presbyterian Church v. Hull Church*, 393 U.S. 440, 449 (1969).

Although *Watson* had left civil courts no role to play in reviewing ecclesiastical decisions during the course of resolving church property disputes, *Gonzalez* first adverted to the possibility of "marginal civil court review," *Presbyterian Church v. Hull Church*, in cases challenging decisions of ecclesiastical tribunals as products of "fraud, collusion, or arbitrariness." However, since there was "not even a suggestion that [the Archbishop] exercised his authority [in making the chaplaincy decision] arbitrarily," the suggested "fraud, collusion, or arbitrariness" exception to the *Watson* rule was dictum only. And although references to the suggested exception appear in opinions in cases decided since the *Watson* rule has been held to be mandated by the First Amendment, no decision of this Court has given concrete content to or applied the "exception." However, it was the predicate for the Illinois Supreme Court's decision in this case, and we therefore turn to the question whether reliance upon it in the circumstances of this case was consistent with the prohibition of the First and Fourteenth Amendments against rejection of the decisions of the Mother Church upon the religious disputes in issue.

The conclusion of the Illinois Supreme Court that the decisions of the Mother Church were "arbitrary" was grounded upon an inquiry that persuaded the Illinois Supreme Court that the Mother Church had not followed its own laws and procedures in arriving at those decisions. We have concluded that whether or not there is room for "marginal civil court review" under the narrow rubrics of "fraud" or "collusion" when church tribunals act in bad faith for secular purposes, no "arbitrariness" exception – in the sense of an inquiry whether the decisions of the highest ecclesiastical tribunal of a hierarchical church complied with church laws and regulations—is consistent with the constitutional mandate that civil courts are bound to accept the decisions of the highest judicatories of a religious organization of hierarchical polity on matters of discipline, faith, internal organization, or ecclesiastical rule, custom, or law. For civil courts to analyze whether the ecclesiastical actions of a church judicatory are in that sense "arbitrary" must inherently entail inquiry into the procedures that canon or ecclesiastical law supposedly requires the church judicatory to follow, or else into the substantive criteria by which they are supposedly to decide the ecclesiastical question. But this is exactly the inquiry that the First Amendment prohibits; recognition of such an exception would undermine the general rule that religious controversies are not the proper subject of civil court inquiry, and that a civil court must accept the ecclesiastical decisions of church tribunals as it finds them.

Indeed, it is the essence of religious faith that ecclesiastical decisions are reached and are to be accepted as matters of faith whether or not rational or measurable by objective criteria. Constitutional concepts of due process, involving secular notions of "fundamental fairness" or impermissible objectives, are therefore hardly relevant to such matters of ecclesiastical cognizance.

Similar considerations inform our resolution of the second question we must address—the constitutionality of the Supreme Court of Illinois' holding that the Mother Church's reorganization of the American-Canadian Diocese into three Dioceses was invalid because it was "'in clear and palpable excess of its own jurisdiction.'" Essentially, the court premised this determination on its view that the early history of the Diocese "manifested a clear intention to retain independence and autonomy in its administrative affairs while at the same time becoming ecclesiastically and judicially an organic part of the Serbian Orthodox Church," and its interpretation of the constitution of the American-Canadian Diocese as confirming this intention. It also interpreted the constitution of the Serbian Orthodox Church, which was adopted after the Diocesan constitution, in a manner consistent with this conclusion.

This conclusion was not, however, explicitly based on the "fraud, collusion, or arbitrariness" exception. Rather, the Illinois Supreme Court relied on purported "neutral principles" for resolving property disputes which would "not in any way entangle this court in the determination of theological or doctrinal matters." Nevertheless the Supreme Court of Illinois substituted its interpretation of the Diocesan and Mother Church constitutions for that of the highest ecclesiastical tribunals in which church law vests authority to make that interpretation. This the First and Fourteenth Amendments forbid.

We will not delve into the various church constitutional provisions relevant to this conclusion, for that would repeat the error of the Illinois Supreme Court. It suffices to note that the reorganization of the Diocese involves a matter of internal church government, an issue at the core of ecclesiastical affairs; Arts. 57 and 64 of the Mother Church constitution commit such questions of church polity to the final province of the Holy Assembly. The constitutional provisions of the American-Canadian Diocese were not so express that the civil courts could enforce them without engaging in a searching and therefore impermissible inquiry into church polity.

As a practical matter the effect of the reorganization is a tripling of the Diocesan representational strength in the Holy Assembly and a decentralization of hierarchical authority to permit closer attention to the needs of individual congregations within each of the new Dioceses, a result which Dionisije and Diocesan representatives had already concluded was necessary. Whether corporate bylaws or other documents governing the individual property-holding corporations may affect any desired disposition of the Diocesan property is a question not before us.

In short, the First and Fourteenth Amendments permit hierarchical religious organizations to establish their own rules and regulations for internal discipline and government, and to create tribunals for adjudicating disputes over these matters. When this choice is exercised and ecclesiastical tribunals are created to decide disputes over the government and direction of subordinate bodies, the Constitution requires that civil courts accept their decisions as binding upon them.

Reversed.

Justice REHNQUIST joined by Justice STEVENS, dissenting. . . .

Unless civil courts are to be wholly divested of authority to resolve conflicting claims to real property owned by a hierarchical church, and such claims are to be resolved by brute force, civil courts must of necessity make some factual inquiry even under the rules the Court purports to apply in this case. We are told that "a civil court must accept the ecclesiastical decisions of church tribunals as it finds them.". . . But even this rule requires that proof be made as to what these decisions are, and if proofs on that issue conflict the civil court will inevitably have to choose one over the other. In so choosing, if the choice is to be a rational one, reasons must be adduced as to why one proffered decision is to prevail over another. Such reasons will obviously be based on the canon law by which the disputants have agreed to bind themselves, but they must also represent a preference for one view of that law over another.

If civil courts, consistently with the First Amendment, may do that much, the question arises why they may not do what the Illinois courts did here regarding the defrockment of Bishop Dionisije, and conclude, on the basis of testimony from experts on the canon law at issue, that the decision of the religious tribunal involved was rendered in violation of its own stated rules of procedure. Suppose the Holy Assembly in this case had a membership of 100; its rules provided that a bishop could be defrocked by a majority vote of any session at which a quorum was present, and also provided that a quorum was not to be less than 40. Would a decision of the Holy Assembly attended by 30 members, 16 of whom voted to defrock Bishop Dionisije, be binding on civil courts in a dispute such as this? The hypothetical example is a clearer case than the one involved here, but the principle is the same. If the civil courts are to be bound by any sheet of parchment bearing the ecclesiastical seal and purporting to be a decree of a church court, they can easily be converted into handmaidens of arbitrary lawlessness. . . .

COMMENTS AND QUESTIONS

1. Much of the reasoning in the *Milivojevich* case is based on the conclusion that the "arbitrary" exception cannot be applied in church autonomy cases because it requires the civil court to evaluate church doctrine. Is this necessarily true? Do you think there are situations when a church's decision is so clearly arbitrary that it would justify civil intervention?
2. Would the decision in the *St. Michael's Parish* case be any different if the reasoning of the majority in *Milivojevich* were applied?
3. Often individuals think of personal religious rights being primary and church autonomy being of secondary importance. However, religious autonomy in some form has often emerged earlier than notions of religious rights. Does this indicate that church autonomy is of equal or greater importance than personal

religious freedom? What is the connection between the personal right and the institutional rights, and which precedes which?

2. Europe

SERIF v. GREECE

European Court of Human Rights, Application No. 38178/97 (14 December 1999)

[In 1985 one of the two Muslim religious leaders of Thrace, the Mufti of Rodopi, died. On 6 April 1990 the President of the Republic confirmed M.T. in the post of Mufti of Rodopi. However, there was a dispute concerning the validity of that appointment, and the applicant was elected as mufti following Friday prayers on 28 December 1990. Shortly before that, on December 24, a legislative decree changed the method of selecting muftis, and this decreet was retroactively validated by Law No. 1920, adopted by Parliament on 4 February 1991.]

Law no. 1920 did not change the functions of the mufti, but provided that muftis would be appointed by presidential decree following a proposal by the Minister of Education, who in turn must consult a committee composed of the local prefect and a number of Muslim dignitaries chosen by the state.

Articles 175 and 176 of the Greek criminal code provide for punishment for "[a] person who intentionally usurps the functions of a State or municipal official" or "who publicly wears the dress or the insignia" of such officials. The provisions also apply to a person who "usurps the functions of [or publicly wears the dress or insignia of] a lawyer or a minister of the Greek Orthodox Church or another known religion." The applicant, who had been elected as a mufti by unofficial means, was convicted of violation of Articles 175 and 176, although the evidence showed that at most the applicant had taken part in religious ceremonies, and none of the witnesses claimed that the applicant had purported to discharge judicial or other such functions.

Appeals were unsuccessful, and the case was taken to the European Court of Human Rights, which ultimately held in favor of the applicant. The case is best known for its last few paragraphs:

52. The Court is not oblivious of the fact that in Rodopi there existed, in addition to the applicant, an officially appointed mufti. Moreover, the Government argued that the applicant's conviction was necessary in a democratic society because his actions undermined the system put in place by the State for the organisation of the religious life of the Muslim community in the region. However, the Court recalls that there is no indication that the applicant attempted at any time to exercise the judicial and administrative functions for which the legislation on the muftis and other ministers of "known religions" makes provision. As for the rest, the Court does not consider that, in democratic societies, the State needs to take measures to ensure that religious communities remain or are brought under a unified leadership.

53. It is true that the Government argued that, in the particular circumstances of the case, the authorities had to intervene in order to avoid the creation of tension among the Muslims in Rodopi and between the Muslims and the Christians of the area as well as Greece and Turkey. Although the Court recognises that it is possible

that tension is created in situations where a religious or any other community becomes divided, it considers that this is one of the unavoidable consequences of pluralism. The role of the authorities in such circumstances is not to remove the cause of tension by eliminating pluralism, but to ensure that the competing groups tolerate each other. In this connection, the Court notes that, apart from a general reference to the creation of tension, the Government did not make any allusion to disturbances among the Muslims in Rodopi that had actually been or could have been caused by the existence of two religious leaders. Moreover, the Court considers that nothing was adduced that could warrant qualifying the risk of tension between the Muslims and Christians or between Greece and Turkey as anything more than a very remote possibility.

54. In the light of all the above, the Court considers that it has not been shown that the applicant's conviction under Articles 175 and 176 of the Criminal Code was justified in the circumstances of the case by "a pressing social need". As a result, the interference with the applicant's right, in community with others and in public, to manifest his religion in worship and teaching was not "necessary in a democratic society . . . for the protection of public order" under Article 9 § 2 of the Convention. There has, therefore, been a violation of Article 9 of the Convention. . . .

COMMENTS AND QUESTIONS

1. How significant is the fact that the position of mufti is a public office with public responsibilities? Does the state have a legitimate interest in appointing the mufti?
2. How strong is the case for a religious autonomy claim here? Is there a legitimate *religious* objection to Law no. 1920, which ended selection of the mufti by direct election?
3. What happens when a state church deals with disputes involving its clergy? Consider the following cases. (a) The applicant in *Karlsson v. Sweden*, App. No. 12356/86 (ECmHR, 8 September 1988), was a priest in the Swedish State Church who objected to the ordination of women. The Diocesan Chapter of a church to which he applied for a position determined that he was ineligible because he could "not be expected to co-operate with female colleagues." The Commission noted that churches, including a state church, are not required to "grant religious freedom to their members and servants." The Commission further noted that the priest in question was able to retain his current position and was not being subjected to any pressures to change his views. Accordingly, there was no interference with his Article 9 rights. (b) In *X v. Denmark*, App. No. 7374/76 (ECmHR, 8 March 1976), the applicant clergyman in the State Church of Denmark made it a condition for christening children that the parents attend five religious lessons. The Church Ministry thought he had no right to make such conditions, and insisted that he desist. The Commission held that Article 9(1) does not include the right of a clergyman, in his capacity of a civil servant in a state church system, to set up conditions for baptizing that are contrary to the directives of the highest administrative authority within that church (i.e., the Church Minister). (c) In *Delgado Páez v. Colombia*, No. 195/1895, CPR/C/39/D/195/1985, a Catholic teacher dissented from some

views of his church. He was told he could not teach religion any more and was assigned instead to teach manual labor and handicrafts. Despite this, he was still subject to harrasment and ultimately fled the country. The Human Rights Committee ruled that this harrassment violated Mr. Delgado's rights under the First Optional Protocol to the International Covenant on Civil and Political Rights.

B. THE SCOPE OF RELIGIOUS AUTONOMY IN EMPLOYMENT SETTINGS

1. The United States

CORPORATION OF THE PRESIDING BISHOP V. AMOS

Supreme Court of the United States, 483 U.S. 327 (1987)

[An action was brought by former employees of various church-related enterprises claiming that they had suffered discrimination on the basis of religion in violation of §703 of the Civil Rights Act of 1964. Plaintiffs originally included (a) former employees of Beehive Clothing Mills who helped manufacture garments with religious significance for members of The Church of Jesus Christ of Latter-day Saints; (b) a truck driver for Deseret Industries, a division of the Church's Welfare Services Department; and (c) a building engineer who had worked for Deseret Gymnasium, a nonprofit facility open to the public and run by the Corporation of the Presiding Bishop of The Church of Jesus Christ of Latter-day Saints (sometimes referred to as the Mormon or LDS Church). Only the claim of the building engineer proceeded to the Supreme Court. In each case, the employees lost their jobs because they were not able to provide their employers with a current "temple recommend," a document signed by their local religious leaders indicating that they were living in accordance with specified Church standards such as regular church attendance, tithing, and abstinence from coffee, tea, alcohol, and tobacco. Section 702 of the Civil Rights Act exempts religious organizations from Title VII's prohibition against discrimination on the basis of religion. The question presented was whether applying the §702 exemption to the secular nonprofit activities of religious organizations violates the Establishment Clause.]

Justice WHITE delivered the opinion of the Court. . . .

"This Court has long recognized that the government may (and sometimes must) accommodate religious practices and that it may do so without violating the Establishment Clause." *Hobbie v. Unemployment Appeals Comm'n of Fla.*, 480 U.S. 136 (1987). It is well established, too, that "[t]he limits of permissible state accommodation to religion are by no means co-extensive with the noninterference mandated by the Free Exercise Clause." *Walz v. Tax Comm'n*, 397 U.S. 664 (1970). There is ample room under the Establishment Clause for "benevolent neutrality which will permit religious exercise to exist without sponsorship and without interference." At some point, accommodation may devolve into "an unlawful fostering of religion,". . . but these are not such cases, in our view.

Lemon requires first that the law at issue serve a "secular legislative purpose." This does not mean that the law's purpose must be unrelated to religion–that would amount to a requirement "that the government show a callous indifference to religious groups,". . . and the Establishment Clause has never been so interpreted. Rather, *Lemon's* "purpose" requirement aims at preventing the relevant governmental decisionmaker—in this case, Congress—from abandoning neutrality and acting with the intent of promoting a particular point of view in religious matters.

Under the *Lemon* analysis, it is a permissible legislative purpose to alleviate significant governmental interference with the ability of religious organizations to define and carry out their religious missions. . . . After a detailed examination of the legislative history of the 1972 amendment, th e District Court concluded that Congress' purpose was to minimize governmental "interfere[ence] with the decision-making process in religions." We agree with the District Court that this purpose does not violate the Establishment Clause.

The second requirement under *Lemon* is that the law in question have "a principal or primary effect . . . that neither advances nor inhibits religion." Undoubtedly, religious organizations are better able now to advance their purposes than they were prior to the 1972 amendment to §702. But religious groups have been better able to advance their purposes on account of many laws that have passed constitutional muster: for example, the property tax exemption at issue in *Walz v. Tax Comm'n*, or the loans of schoolbooks to schoolchildren, including parochial school students, upheld in *Board of Education v. Allen*. A law is not unconstitutional simply because it *allows* churches to advance religion, which is their very purpose. For a law to have forbidden "effects" under *Lemon*, it must be fair to say that the *government itself* has advanced religion through its own activities and influence. As the Court observed in *Walz*, "for the men who wrote the Religion Clauses of the First Amendment the 'establishment' of a religion connoted sponsorship, financial support, and active involvement of the sovereign in religious activity."

The District Court appeared to fear that sustaining the exemption would permit churches with financial resources impermissibly to extend their influence and propagate their faith by entering the commercial, profit-making world. The cases before us, however, involve a nonprofit activity instituted over 75 years ago in the hope that "all who assemble here, and who come for the benefit of their health, and for physical blessings, [may] feel that they are in a house dedicated to the Lord." Dedicatory Prayer for the Gymnasium. These cases therefore do not implicate the apparent concerns of the District Court. . . . In such circumstances, we do not see how any advancement of religion achieved by the Gymnasium can be fairly attributed to the Government, as opposed to the Church.

We find unpersuasive the District Court's reliance on the fact that §702 singles out religious entities for a benefit. Although the Court has given weight to this consideration in its past decisions, it has never indicated that statutes that give special consideration to religious groups are *per se* invalid. That would run contrary to the teaching of our cases that there is ample room for accommodation of religion under the Establishment Clause. Where, as here, government acts with the proper purpose of lifting a regulation that burdens the exercise of religion, we see no reason to require that the exemption come packaged with benefits to secular entities.

Appellees argue that §702 offends equal protection principles by giving less protection to the employees of religious employers than to the employees of secular employers. Appellees rely on *Larson v. Valente*, 456 U.S. 228 (1982), for the proposition that a law drawing distinctions on religious grounds must be strictly scrutinized. But *Larson* indicates that laws discriminating *among* religions are subject to strict scrutiny, and that laws "affording a uniform benefit to *all* religions" should be analyzed under *Lemon*. In cases such as these, where a statute is neutral on its face and motivated by a permissible purpose of limiting governmental interference with the exercise of religion, we see no justification for applying strict scrutiny to a statute that passes the *Lemon* test. The proper inquiry is whether Congress has chosen a rational classification to further a legitimate end. . . .

It cannot be seriously contended that §702 impermissibly entangles church and state; the statute effectuates a more complete separation of the two and avoids the kind of intrusive inquiry into religious belief that the District Court engaged in [in] this case. The statute easily passes muster under the third part of the *Lemon* test.

The judgment of the District Court is reversed, and the cases are remanded for further proceedings consistent with this opinion.

COMMENTS AND QUESTIONS

1. The district court in *Amos* believed that religious activities of religious employers can permissibly be exempted under § 702, but not secular activities. The Supreme Court rejected that view, at least with respect to nonprofit sector jobs. Why might a religious organization think that it is important for all its employees to exemplify its teachings? Why might a labor organization want to insist that a job be religion related for it to be exempted from rules forbidding discrimination on the basis of religion?
2. To what extent does the limitation of the *Amos* rule to the nonprofit sector—a point emphasized by the concurring opinion of Brennan and Marshall—reflect an assumption that legitimate religious groups will not be engaged in for-profit activities?
3. To what extent should religiously affiliated employers be able to terminate employees who fail to live the sponsoring religion's standards? For example, there are numerous cases in which unmarried teachers who become pregnant or married teachers who are divorced are threatened with loss of their jobs.[15]

---

15. *See, e.g.*, Molly Redden and Dana Liebelson, A Montana School Just Fired a Teacher for Getting Pregnant. That Actually Happens All the Time., *Mother Jones*, 10 February 2014.

THE MINISTERIAL EXCEPTION FROM ANTI-DISCRIMINATION LAWS FOR CLERGY AND ANALOGOUS PERSONNEL

HOSANNA-TABOR EVANGELICAL LUTHERAN CHURCH AND SCHOOL V. EEOC

Supreme Court of the United States, 132 S.Ct. 694 (2012)

CHIEF JUSTICE ROBERTS delivered the opinion of the Court.

Certain employment discrimination laws authorize employees who have been wrongfully terminated to sue their employers for reinstatement and damages. The question presented is whether the Establishment and Free Exercise Clauses of the First Amendment bar such an action when the employer is a religious group and the employee is one of the group's ministers.

I.

A.

Petitioner Hosanna-Tabor Evangelical Lutheran Church and School is a member congregation of the Lutheran Church-Missouri Synod, the second largest Lutheran denomination in America. Hosanna-Tabor operated a small school in Redford, Michigan, offering a "Christ-centered education" to students in kindergarten through eighth grade.

The Synod classifies teachers into two categories: "called" and "lay." "Called" teachers are regarded as having been called to their vocation by God through a congregation. To be eligible . . . a teacher must satisfy certain academic requirements. . . . [At] at Hosanna-Tabor, a call could be rescinded only for cause and by a supermajority vote of the congregation.

"Lay" or "contract" teachers, by contrast, are not required to be trained by the Synod or even to be Lutheran. At Hosanna-Tabor, they were appointed by the school board, without a vote of the congregation, to one-year renewable terms. Although teachers at the school generally performed the same duties regardless of whether they were lay or called, lay teachers were hired only when called teachers were unavailable.

Respondent Cheryl Perich was first employed by Hosanna-Tabor as a lay teacher in 1999 [but subsequently became] a called teacher . . . and received a "diploma of vocation" designating her a commissioned minister.

Perich taught kindergarten during her first four years at Hosanna-Tabor and fourth grade during the 2003-2004 school year...She also taught a religion class four days a week, led the students in prayer and devotional exercises each day, and attended a weekly school-wide chapel service. Perich led the chapel service herself about twice a year.

Perich became ill in June 2004 with what was eventually diagnosed as narcolepsy. Symptoms included sudden and deep sleeps from which she could not be roused. Because of her illness, Perich began the 2004-2005 school year on disability leave. On January 27, 2005, however, Perich notified the school principal, Stacey Hoeft, that she would be able to report to work the following month. Hoeft responded that the school had already contracted with a lay teacher to fill Perich's position for the remainder of the school year. Hoeft also expressed concern that Perich was not yet ready to return to the classroom.

On January 30, Hosanna-Tabor held a meeting of its congregation at which school administrators stated that Perich was unlikely to be physically capable of returning to work that school year or the next. The congregation voted to offer Perich a "peaceful release" from her call, whereby the congregation would pay a portion of her health insurance premiums in exchange for her resignation as a called teacher. Perich refused to resign and produced a note from her doctor stating that she would be able to return to work on February 22. The school board urged Perich to reconsider, informing her that the school no longer had a position for her, but Perich stood by her decision not to resign.

On the morning of February 22—the first day she was medically cleared to return to work—Perich presented herself at the school. Hoeft asked her to leave but she would not do so until she obtained written documentation that she had reported to work. Later that afternoon, Hoeft called Perich at home and told her that she would likely be fired. Perich responded that she had spoken with an attorney and intended to assert her legal rights.

Following a school board meeting that evening, board chairman Scott Salo sent Perich a letter stating that Hosanna-Tabor was reviewing the process for rescinding her call in light of her "regrettable" actions. . . . As grounds for termination, the letter cited Perich's "insubordination and disruptive behavior" on February 22, as well as the damage she had done to her "working relationship" with the school by "threatening to take legal action." The congregation voted to rescind Perich's call on April 10, and Hosanna-Tabor sent her a letter of termination the next day.

B.

Perich filed a charge with the Equal Employment Opportunity Commission [under the] Americans with Disabilities Act. The ADA prohibits an employer from discriminating against a qualified individual on the basis of disability. It also prohibits an employer from retaliating . . . "because such individual made a charge, testified, assisted, or participated in any manner in an investigation, proceeding, or hearing under [the ADA]."

The EEOC brought suit against Hosanna-Tabor, alleging that Perich had been fired in retaliation for threatening to file an ADA lawsuit. Perich intervened in the litigation, claiming unlawful retaliation under both the ADA and the Michigan Persons with Disabilities Civil Rights Act. The EEOC and Perich sought Perich's reinstatement to her former position (or frontpay in lieu thereof), along with backpay, compensatory and punitive damages, attorney's fees, and other injunctive relief.

. . . Invoking what is known as the "ministerial exception," the Church argued that the suit was barred by the First Amendment because the claims at issue concerned the employment relationship between a religious institution and one of its ministers. According to the Church, Perich was a minister, and she had been fired for a religious reason--namely, that her threat to sue the Church violated the Synod's belief that Christians should resolve their disputes internally.

The District Court agreed that the suit was barred by the ministerial exception and granted summary judgment in Hosanna-Tabor's favor. The court explained that "Hosanna-Tabor treated Perich like a minister and held her out to the world as such long before this litigation began," and that the "facts surrounding Perich's employment in a religious school with a sectarian mission" supported the Church's characterization. . . .

The [Sixth Circuit] vacated and remanded, directing the District Court to proceed to the merits of Perich's retaliation claims. The Court of Appeals recognized the existence of a ministerial exception barring certain employment discrimination claims against religious institutions—an exception "rooted in the First Amendment's guarantees of religious freedom." The court concluded, however, that Perich did not qualify as a "minister" under the exception, noting in particular that her duties as a called teacher were identical to her duties as a lay teacher. . . . We granted certiorari.

II.

[The Court discusses the history that led to the adoption of the Establishment and Free Exercise Clauses of the First Amendment and affirms that both Clauses bar the government from interfering with a religious group's decision to fire one of its ministers. The Court then concludes that the Establishment Clause prevents the government from appointing ministers and the Free Exercise Clause prevents interference with a religious group's selection of its own clergy. Also, the Court emphasizes that the First Amendment permits religious organizations to establish their own rules and regulations for discipline and internal government under the Free Exercise Clause. The opinion then addresses the nature and scope of the ministerial exception.] . . .

C.

Until today, we have not had occasion to consider whether this freedom of a religious organization to select its ministers is implicated by a suit alleging discrimination in employment. The Courts of Appeals, in contrast, have had extensive experience with this issue. Since the passage of Title VII of the Civil Rights Act of 1964, and other employment discrimination laws, the Courts of Appeals have uniformly recognized the existence of a "ministerial exception," grounded in the First Amendment, that precludes application of such legislation to claims concerning the employment relationship between a religious institution and its ministers.

We agree that there is such a ministerial exception. . . . Requiring a church to accept or retain an unwanted minister, or punishing a church for failing to do so, intrudes upon more than a mere employment decision. Such action interferes with the internal governance of the church, depriving the church of control over the selection of those who will personify its beliefs. By imposing an unwanted minister, the state infringes the Free Exercise Clause, which protects a religious group's right to shape its own faith and mission through its appointments. According the state the power to determine which individuals will minister to the faithful also violates the Establishment Clause, which prohibits government involvement in such ecclesiastical decisions.

The EEOC and Perich . . . grant, for example, that it would violate the First Amendment for courts to apply such laws to compel the ordination of women by the Catholic Church or by an Orthodox Jewish seminary. According to the EEOC and Perich, religious organizations could successfully defend against employment discrimination claims in those circumstances by invoking the constitutional right to freedom of association – a right "implicit" in the First Amendment. The EEOC and Perich thus see no need—and no basis—for a special rule for ministers grounded in the Religion Clauses . . . .

We find this position untenable. The right to freedom of association is a right enjoyed by religious and secular groups alike. It follows under the EEOC's and Perich's view that the First Amendment analysis should be the same, whether the association in question is the Lutheran Church, a labor union, or a social club. That result is hard to square with the text of the First Amendment itself, which gives special solicitude to the rights of religious organizations. We cannot accept the remarkable view that the Religion Clauses have nothing to say about a religious organization's freedom to select its own ministers.

The EEOC and Perich also contend that our decision in [*Smith*] precludes recognition of a ministerial exception. In *Smith*, two members of the Native American Church were denied state unemployment benefits after it was determined that they had been fired from their jobs for ingesting peyote, a crime under Oregon law. We held that this did not violate the Free Exercise Clause, [as the law was a] "valid and neutral law of general applicability" . . . .

It is true that the ADA's prohibition on retaliation, like Oregon's prohibition on peyote use, is a valid and neutral law of general applicability. But a church's selection of its ministers is unlike an individual's ingestion of peyote. *Smith* involved government regulation of only outward physical acts. The present case, in contrast, concerns government interference with an internal church decision that affects the faith and mission of the church itself. . . . The contention that *Smith* forecloses recognition of a ministerial exception rooted in the Religion Clauses has no merit.

III.

Having concluded that there is a ministerial exception grounded in the Religion Clauses of the First Amendment, we consider whether the exception applies in this case. We hold that it does.

Every Court of Appeals to have considered the question has concluded that the ministerial exception is not limited to the head of a religious congregation, and we agree. We are reluctant, however, to adopt a rigid formula for deciding when an employee qualifies as a minister. It is enough for us to conclude, in this our first case involving the ministerial exception, that the exception covers Perich, given all the circumstances of her employment.

To begin with, Hosanna-Tabor held Perich out as a minister, with a role distinct from that of most of its members. When Hosanna-Tabor extended her a call, it issued her a "diploma of vocation" according her the title "Minister of Religion, Commissioned." She was tasked with performing that office "according to the Word of God and the confessional standards of the Evangelical Lutheran Church as drawn from the Sacred Scriptures." The congregation prayed that God "bless [her] ministrations to the glory of His holy name, [and] the building of His church." ...

Perich's title as a minister reflected a significant degree of religious training followed by a formal process of commissioning. . . . [The Court reviewed the process of obtaining a "call" previously explained in Part I.] . . .

[The Court further noted that Perich further specifically stated that she felt "called" to the ministry, even after becoming sick.] . . .

Perich's job duties reflected a role in conveying the Church's message and carrying out its mission. Hosanna-Tabor expressly charged her with "lead[ing] others toward Christian maturity" and "teach[ing] faithfully the Word of God, the Sacred Scriptures, in its truth and purity and as set forth in all the symbolical books of the Evangelical Lutheran Church." In fulfilling these responsibilities, Perich taught her students religion four days a week, and led them in prayer three times a day. Once a week, she took her students to a school-wide chapel service, and—about twice a year—she took her turn leading it, choosing the liturgy, selecting the hymns, and delivering a short message based on verses from the Bible. During her last year of teaching, Perich also led her fourth graders in a brief devotional exercise each morning. As a source of religious instruction, Perich performed an important role in transmitting the Lutheran faith to the next generation.

In light of these considerations—the formal title given Perich by the Church, the substance reflected in that title, her own use of that title, and the important religious functions she performed for the Church—we conclude that Perich was a minister covered by the ministerial exception.

In reaching a contrary conclusion, the Court of Appeals committed three errors. First, the Sixth Circuit failed to see any relevance in the fact that Perich was a commissioned minister. . . .

Second, the Sixth Circuit gave too much weight to the fact that lay teachers at the school performed the same religious duties as Perich. . . .[T]hough relevant, it cannot be dispositive that others not formally recognized as ministers by the church perform the same functions—particularly when, as here, they did so only because commissioned ministers were unavailable.

Third, the Sixth Circuit placed too much emphasis on Perich's performance of secular duties. It is true that her religious duties consumed only 45 minutes of each work day, and that the rest of her day was devoted to teaching secular subjects. The EEOC regards that as conclusive, contending that any ministerial exception "should be limited to those employees who perform exclusively religious functions." We cannot accept that view. Indeed, we are unsure whether any such employees exist. The heads of congregations themselves often have a mix of duties, including secular ones such as helping to manage the congregation's finances, supervising purely secular personnel, and overseeing the upkeep of facilities.

Although the Sixth Circuit did not adopt the extreme position pressed here by the EEOC, it did regard the relative amount of time Perich spent performing religious functions as largely determinative. The issue before us, however, is not one that can be resolved by a stopwatch. The amount of time an employee spends on particular activities is relevant in assessing that employee's status, but that factor cannot be considered in isolation, without regard to the nature of the religious functions performed and the other considerations discussed above. . . .

The case before us is an employment discrimination suit brought on behalf of a minister, challenging her church's decision to fire her. Today we hold only that the ministerial exception bars such a suit. We express no view on whether the exception bars other types of suits, including actions by employees alleging breach of contract or tortious conduct by their religious employers. There will be time enough to address the applicability of the exception to other circumstances if and when they arise.

The interest of society in the enforcement of employment discrimination statutes is undoubtedly important. But so too is the interest of religious groups in choosing who will preach their beliefs, teach their faith, and carry out their mission. When a minister who has been fired sues her church alleging that her termination was discriminatory, the First Amendment has struck the balance for us. The church must be free to choose those who will guide it on its way.

The judgment of the Court of Appeals for the Sixth Circuit is reversed.

COMMENTS AND QUESTIONS

1. In the Court of Appeals, the government didn't formally question the validity of the ministerial exception—perhaps because binding precedent in that Court confirmed the existence of the exception. Before the Supreme Court, however, the government shifted to arguing that there was no categorical exception for ministers under the Free Exercise or Establishment Clauses—only a more general freedom of association. In oral argument, Justice Scalia called the government's position "extraordinary," and Justice Kagan called the position "amazing," previewing the opinion's square holding that there are extra protections for religious groups that secular organizations don't have.
2. A second argument the government raised was that the ministerial exception, if it existed, did not apply to claims of retaliation. But if retaliation claims were an exception, petitioner argued, courts would have to weigh retaliation claims against the church's claim that the minister was a bad minister. Who is right? How did the court address the issue?
3. In *Hosanna-Tabor*, the Court stated that *both* the Free Exercise and Establishment Clauses require a ministerial exception? Which clause do you think is the stronger basis for the ministerial exception?

2. Germany

NOTE ON GERMAN RELIGIOUS EMPLOYMENT CASES

Obst v. Germany, App. no. 425/03 (23 September 2010)
Schüth v. Germany, App. no. 1620/0323 (23 September 2010)
Siebenhaar v. GermaNy, App. No. 18136/02 (2 March 2011)

European Court of Human Rights

Beginning in late 2010, the European Court of Human Rights reviewed three cases in six months concerning the lawful dismissal of church employees under German employment law.[1] The first two cases, *Obst v. Germany* and *Schüth v.*

Germany, decided on the same day, both concerned male applicants' dismissal from employment by a church because of an extra-marital relationship. The third case, *Siebenhaar v. Germany*, involved a female teacher at a Protestant kindergarten dismissed for "active involvement in another religious community."

In *Obst* and *Schüth* the Court "for the first time addressed the dismissal of Church employees on grounds of conduct falling within the sphere of their private lives." [16] Both cases dealt with the rights of religious communities to self-determination in dealing with their personnel where their employees fail to abide by standards of conduct fundamental to the communities' doctrines and beliefs.

In *Schüth*, the applicant served as organist and choirmaster in the Catholic parish of St Lambert in Essen at the time of his dismissal. In *Obst* the applicant served in a high-profile position as director of European public relations for The Church of Jesus Christ of Latter-day Saints (the Mormons), of which he had long been a member. Both applicants argued that dismissal from their employment violated Article 8.

In *Obst* the Court unanimously found no violation of Article 8 of the European Convention (right to respect for private and family life) and in *Schüth* unanimously found that a violation of Article 8 had occurred.

The Court sustained national court judgments in *Obst* because "the German labour courts had taken account of all the relevant factors and undertaken a careful and thorough balancing exercise regarding the interests involved. They had pointed out that the Mormon Church had only been able to base Mr. Obst's dismissal on his adultery because he had informed the Church of it by his own initiative. According to the German courts' findings, his dismissal amounted to a necessary measure aimed at preserving the Church's credibility, having regard in particular to the nature of his post. The courts had explained why the Church had not been obliged to inflict a less severe penalty, such as a warning, and they had underlined that the injury suffered by Mr. Obst as a result of his dismissal was limited, having regard among other things to his relatively young age.

In the case of *Schüth*, however, the German courts had not balanced the full range of interests at stake, having focused primarily on the applicant's interest in keeping his post without addressing his privacy interests. The German courts had addressed the fact that although the applicant's "functions as organist and choirmaster did not fall within the group of employees who in case of serious misconduct had to be dismissed, namely those working in counselling, in catechesis or in a leading position, his functions were nonetheless so closely connected to the Catholic Church's proclamatory mission that the parish could not continue employing him without losing all credibility." On the other hand, the Court had not adequately addressed "Mr Schüth's de facto family life," which he had established with a new partner after the separation from his wife. "The interests of the Church employer had thus not been balanced against Mr Schüth's right to respect for his private and family life, but only against his interest in keeping his post." The Court also emphasized that, given the specialized nature of his work as

16. *Dismissal of church employees for adultery: domestic courts required to balance rights of both parties and take account of specific nature of post concerned*, Press Release issued by the Registrar of the European Court of Human Rights, No. 888, 23 September 2010.

a church musician, Mr. Schüth "had only limited opportunities of finding another job."

The *Obst* judgment upholds earlier decisions by the German Federal Labor Court and the Federal Constitutional Court, which have affirmed long-standing constitutional principles under Germany's Basic Law protecting the right of religious communities to independence and autonomy in their affairs (Selbständigkeit in ihren Angelegenheiten, see Article 137 of the Weimar Constitution, incorporated into the current Basic Law of Germany by Article 140), including the right of churches to structure contractual relations with their employees in ways that are consistent with the religious beliefs of the community and that impose reasonable expectations of loyalty to these principles that are clearly understood when the employment relationship is established.

In contrast, although the Court "reiterated that the autonomy of religious communities was protected against undue interference by the State under Article 9," *Schüth* calls for a more explicit balancing of the full range of interests involved. Exactly how that balancing is likely to come out in individual cases will depend on a variety of factors mentioned in the two cases. These include: (1) voluntary assumption of obligations of loyalty to the hiring institution; (2) the range of alternative employment available to the dismissed employee; (3) the importance attached to the conduct in question by the religious community (or other belief, ideological or ethos society); (4) the nature of the employment and its place in carrying out the mission of the organization; (5) the effect of continued employment on the credibility of the religious community in affirming and living by its teaching; (6) whether less drastic measures might suffice; (7) the right of a religious community to independence in its own affairs; and (8) the family and privacy rights of the discharged individual.[17]

Ms Astrid Siebenhaar was employed as a teacher in a kindergarten run by Protestant congregation in Pforzheim, Germany. Her employment contract stated that "employees were obliged to be loyal to the Church and that they were not allowed to be members of and work for organisations whose views or activities were in contradiction to the Church's mandate." When it was found out that Ms. Siebenhaar was a member of another religious group, the Universal Church/Brotherhood of Humanity, and that she taught primary lessons for that group, she was dismissed from her position at the Protestant parish for "active involvement in another religious community."

When German Labour Courts ruled in favor of the church, Ms Siebenhaar lodged a complaint with the European Court of Human Rights, based on Article 9 of the European Convention, which guarantees freedom of religion. The fact that Ms. Siebenhaar brought her complaint under Article 9 constitutes an important distinction between the her case and the *Obst* and *Schüth* cases, which pitted the respective churches' religious rights against the applicants' rights to private life, not their rights to religious freedom.

---

17. The passages concerning *Obst* and *Schüth* are derived from an Analysis by by W. Cole Durham, Jr., and David M. Kirkham, European Court Issues Rulings in Two German Church Employment Cases, 23 September 2010, published on the website of the Strasbourg Consortium: https://www.strasbourgconsortium.org/common/document.view.php?docId=6054. Quotations in the analysis are from the Court's press release, *supra* note 16.

The Court found that the German Labour Courts had properly balanced the religious freedom interests involved and, therefore, that there had been no violation of Ms. Siebenhaar's rights. Specifically, the Court ruled that Ms. Siebenhaar's dismissal had been necessary to preserve the credibility of the church, and that when she signed the contract, she should have been aware that she would not be able to teach in a different congregation.

COMMENTS AND QUESTIONS

1. How does the reasoning in the *Schüth* and *Obst* cases differ from that of the US Supreme Court in *Hosanna-Tabor*? Which approach seems more attractive?
2. The German cases have broad implications for treatment by the European Court of Human Rights of personnel matters in religious, ideological, and ethos organizations, as well as for broader issues concerning the right to religious autonomy. The opinions in *Obst* and *Schüth* in particular indicate that countries will have a substantial margin of appreciation in assessing relevant factors in such cases. Of the eight factors listed above, do any seem to you more difficult to assess, or more likely to lead to unpredictable results?
3. Note that cases involving religious employment involve two continua: the degree of religiosity of the employer, and the degree of religiosity of the employment. The first is a range of types of employer. This continuum starts with the "constituted church" or religion, moves from there to subdivisions of the church or religion, to affiliated charities of the religious organization (schools, hospitals, humanitarian aid institutions, etc.), to for-profit businesses controlled in whole or in part by religious organizations. In addition to variations in the type of organization, there can be variations in the degree of control, from total control by the religious community to the situation where only a few shares of stock in a company are held as an investment by the religious community.

   The second continuum concerns the religious nature of the work in which personnel are involved. This continuum starts with religious leaders and other ministerial personnel, then moves to others not directly part of the clergy or religious leadership but performing similar functions (teaching, broadcasting, representing the religious community in public settings), to those engaged in the charitable work of the community, to support staff (e.g., secretaries or administrative assistants to religious leaders, bookkeepers, etc.), to those performing ordinary labor (cooks, janitors, etc.).

   How far should religious autonomy protections extend on each of these scales?
4. Does it make a difference that the applicants in *Schüth* and *Obst* brought suit not for violation of religious freedom rights but for interference with their private and family lives?
5. Judgments in two important religious autonomy cases were issued by the Grand Chamber of the European Court of Human Rights in 2013 and 2014. In *Sindicatul "Păstorul cel Bun" v. Romania* (App. no. 2330/09, 9 July 2013), the Court considered the refusal of the Romanian government to register a trade union (Păstorul cel Bun) set up by 32 Romanian Orthodox priests and 3

lay employees of the Church. The union's application to be granted legal personality and entered into the register of trade unions was opposed by the Archdiocese of Craiova, which argued that that the establishment of the union without the archbishop's consent and blessing was prohibited by the Statute ofthe Romanian Orthodox Church. The Romanian court, however, allowed the application and registered the union. The Archdiocese challenged the judgment, arguing that the provisions of domestic and international law on which it was based were not applicable to the case at hand. Relying on Article 29 of the Constitution, which guarantees religious freedom and the autonomy of religious communities, it argued that the principle of religious freedom could not be overridden by other constitutional principles such as freedom of association, including trade-union freedom. The county court permitted the appeal of the Archdiocese and ultimately revoked the trade union's registration.[18] The union brought the issue before ECtHR asserting a violation of Article 11 of the European Convention on Human Rights, the guarantee of Freedom of Assembly and Association. The Court's Third Section issued a judgment in January 2012, finding a violation of the union's rights. The Romanian government applied for review before the Grand Chamber, and in its July 2013 judgment this body found no violation of Article 11: "The County Court's refusal to register the union for failure to comply with the requirement of obtaining the archbishop's permission had been a direct consequence of the right of the religious community concerned to make its own organisational arrangements and to operate in accordance with the provisions of its Statute. Furthermore, the union had not put forward any reasons to justify its failure to seek the necessary permission from the archbishop." The Court held that in refusing to register the applicant union, the State had simply declined to become involved in the organization and operation of the Romanian Orthodox Church, thereby observing its duty of denominational neutrality under Article 9 of the European Convention.

Which body was right in your view, the Third Section or the Grand Chamber?

6. At issue in *Fernández Martinez v. Spain* (App. no. 56030/07, 12 June 2014) was the employment of José Antonio Fernández Martínez. Ordained a Catholic priest in 1961, Fernández Martínez in 1984 petitioned the Holy See for dispensation to marry. While awaiting a response, he married in 1984, fathered five children, and in 1991 began a career as a teacher of Catholic religion and morality. In November 1996, he appeared with his family on the cover of the magazine of the Movement for Optional Celibacy, of which he was a member. His dispensation from celibacy was a last granted by the Pope in August 1997. One month later, the Bishop of Cartagena informed the Ministry of Education that the teaching contract of Mr. Fernández Martínez could not be renewed because he had violated his obligation to fulfill his duties as a teacher of religion in a public school "without risking scandal," a condition of his dispensation from celibacy. Fernández Martínez was successful in his demand

18. *See Refusal to register a trade union for priests on account of the autonomy of religious communities is not unreasonable*, Press Release of the Registrar issued by the European Court of Human Rights, No. 209, 9 July 2013.

that the failure to renew his contract be deemed a dismissal, thereby opening the possibility of a finding of infringement of his rights. The Labour Court so found, and ordered his immediate reinstatement. The Superior Court reversed the decision, pointing out that religious freedom has both an individual aspect and "what might be called a communitarian aspect," under which religious communities are entitled to "appoint and train their ministers" and to "disseminate and propagate their own beliefs."

Mr. Fernández Martínez brought his case before the European Court of Human Rights alleging violation of Article 8 of the European Convention, which protects the right to respect for private and family life. In its Grand Chamber judgment of June 2014, the Court found that the interference with the applicant's Article 8 rights by the government of Spain had been, as the Spanish Constitutional Court had asserted "neither disproportionate nor unconstitutional." In respect of both the margin of appreciation afforded to the States and the autonomy of religious communities recognized by the State, the was no violation of Mr. Fernández Martínez' rights. In particular, "the State should accept the right of such communities to react, in accordance with their own rules and interests, to any dissident movements emerging within them that might pose a threat to their cohesion, image or unity. It was therefore not the task of the national authorities to act as the arbiter between religious communities and the various dissident factions that existed or might emerge within them."[19] In the light of the review exercised by the national courts, "it did not appear that the autonomy of the Church had been improperly invoked: the Bishop's decision could not be said to have contained insufficient reasoning, to have been arbitrary, or to have been taken for a purpose that was unrelated to the exercise of the Catholic Church's autonomy."[20]

How does the European Court of Human Rights notion of a "margin of appreciation" granted to States Parties affect the issue of church autonomy in these cases from Romania and Spain? Are the same issues raised under the notion of a "ministerial exception" in the US legal scheme?

IV. AUTONOMY AND ACCESS TO SACRED SPACE

We have seen how various jurisdictions have dealt with property and personnel issues when the autonomy of religious communities comes up against secular claims and institutions. Additional examples from Spain, Turkey, Israel (the "Holy Land"), and India illustrate some different countours of these issues.

A. "MOSQUE-CATHEDRAL"

The medieval city of Cordoba was famous for its historical reputation for tolerance and interfaith harmony among Christians, Muslims, and Jews. One of the city's most significant landmarks today is the "Mosque-Cathedral of Cordoba,"

19. *The decision not to renew the contract, as religious education teacher, of a married Catholic priest was legitimate and proportionate*, Press Release issued by the Registrar of the European Court of Human Rights, No. 170, 12 July 2014.

20. *Id.*

first built on the site of a Visigothic church in the eighth century, commissioned as a mosque by Abd al-Rahman I in 785, and expanded by al-Rahman's Umayyad successors. When Cordoba succumbed to Ferdinand III in 1236, the new Christian rulers converted the mosque into a cathedral, but reserved its prayer niche facing toward Mecca, as well as its famous red-and-white horseshoe arches. The structure has been a UNESCO world heritage site "of exceptional universal value" since 1984. In 2006, the diocese of Cordoba paid €30 to register ownership of what it calls the cathedral-mosque, or sometimes just the cathedral, and references to its historical status as a mosque are now frequently dropped. In 2013, hundreds of thousands of people signed a petition for the building to be managed by local government authority rather than the church to conserve its cultural heritage. In 2017, when Google ceased referring to the cite as a "mosque-cathedral," an objecting petition received 55,000 signatures in less than three days.

Another historic place of worship for both Christians and Muslims is Turkey's Hagia Sophia ("Holy Wisdom"). Built in Constantinople, the seat of the Eastern Roman (Byzantine) Empire, during 535-537, Hagia Sophia was for almost a thousand years a Christian, and for most of that time the world's largest, cathedral. In 1453 Constantinople was conquered by Ottoman forces under Sultan Mehmet II, and Hagia Sophia became for the next five hundred years (1453-1931) the Imperial Mosque of the Ottoman Empire. Establishment of the secular Republic of Turkey after World War I, under the leadership of Mustafa Kemal Pasha, known as Atatürk (Father of the Turks), led both to the expulsion of post-World War I Western occupiers and the abolition of the Sultanate, ending Ottoman rule. As the first President of (secular) Turkey, Atatürk in 1935 transformed Hagia Sophia, in the city now known as Istanbul, into a Museum. By 2014, the edifice and it surrounding complex were attracting more than three million international visitors annually.

Although use of the Hagia Sophia for religious purposes has been prohibited by the Turkish government from the beginning of the Republic, Christian and Muslim museum staff have been allowed a prayer room in the museum complex, and since 2013 a muezzin has sung the call to prayer twice daily in the afternoon. Recent calls from both Christians[21] and Muslims[22] for a restoration of the building to its "original" or "historic" functions have resulted in increasing tension, intensifying with appointment by the government of Recep Tayyip Erdoğan of a permanent imam for Hagia Sophia. In July 2016 Muslim prayers were heard in Hagia Sophia for the first time in 85 years. Well-publicized prayers, recitations, and demonstrations outside the building in spring and summer 2017 led to an international outcry against returning Hagia Sophia—"the premier monument of Byzantine civilization"[23]—back to religious purposes. "The Hagia Sophia belongs to world heritage under UNESCO," read a sharply worded statement from the

---

21. Group Unveils Initiative on Hagia Sophia, *Homeboy Media News*, 16 June 2007, reporting on international efforts to "restore the Hagia Sophia Cathedral" as a place of worship for all the world's Christians.

22. Jaccob Resneck, Turkish Leaders Want to Convert the Hagia Sophia Back into a Mosque, *Religion News Service/The Washington Post*, 4 December 2013.

23. Fergus M. Bordewich, A Monumental Struggle to Preserve Hagia Sophia, *Smithsonian Magazine*, December 2008.

Greek government. "The attempt to turn it into a mosque by way of Koran reading is an affront to the global community."[24]

COMMENTS AND QUESTIONS

1. How should ownership or management of such structures as the Mosque-Cathedral of Cordoba or Hagia Sophia be assessed? How should the interests of Chrisitans and Muslims in worshipping in such structures be balanced? How in turn should these values be balanced against public interest in the historical and symbolic value of the buildings?
2. Architecural historian Robert Ousterhout observed that Hagia Sophia "has always been treated in a symbolic way—by Christians, Muslims, and by Ataturk and his secular followers. Each group looks at Hagia Sophia and sees a totally different building."[25] To whom, then, does Hagia Sophia actually "belong"? How should a "huge international outcry" and "affront to the global community" at efforts to resume Islamic worship in Hagia Sophia be balanced with the fact that the such an effort has widespread support in Turkey, where more than 99 percent of the population is Muslim?

B. "HOLY LAND"

Perhaps the place on earth where a single space presents the greatest symbolic differences for groups "looking at" it, and thus the greatest potential for conflict, is the area on a hill in the Old City of Jerusalem, a place sacred to the "three monotheistic religious": Judaism, Christianity, and Islam.

The complex situation in this part of the world cannot be captured here. But, in brief, a Jew might see the area not only as legitimately within the borders of the State of Israel (established in 1948) but also as Judaism's holiest site, by a Divine appointment extending back 3000 years. This is Har Habayit (Mount of the House of God or Temple Mount; someimes also identified as "Mount Zion"), perhaps the location of Mount Moriah, where Abraham took his son Isaac for sacrifice, central to the Promised Land of the people Moses led out of Egypt, and identified as the location of ancient Jewish temples and of a "third temple" to be built with the coming of the Messiah. According to Jewish sacred text, this is the spot from which the world was created.

For Christians, Jerusalem, with Temple Mount at its heart, holds both its Old Testament (Hebrew) meanings and its New Testament significance in the narrative of the life and ministry of Jesus and his followers. To point to one internationally controversial episode, so important was Jerusalem both literally and metaphorically (representing the Church of Christ) to the followers of Jesus that the medieval endeavors known as the Crusades were undertaken by soldiers under solemn vow to "deliver the Holy Places from Mohammedan tyranny."[26]

For Muslims, the Mount is Al-Ḥaram Al Sharif (the Noble Sanctuary of Jerusalem), Islam's third holiest site and the place of Muhammad's ascent to heaven. Three historic buildings—al-Aqsa Mosque, the Dome of the Rock, and the

24. Kersten Knipp, Hagia Sophia: Museum or Mosque? *Deutshce Welle*, 26 June 2017.
25. In Bordewich, *supra* note 23.
26. *Crusades*, Catholic Encyclopedia.

Dome of the Chain—stand on the hill, which for more than 800 years has been controlled and managed by the Jerusalem Islamic Waqf (trust), at present funded and administered by the King of Jordan.

To many Muslims, as to many others worldwide, the establishment of a "Jewish homeland" in Palestine in 1948 was an illegitimate act. Israelis therefore are an "occupying Power" with no legitimate claim to the Holy City of Jerusalem at all. In May 2017 UNESCO announced the adoption of a resolution on "Occupied Palestine"—submittted by Algeria, Egypt, Lebanon, Morocco, Oman, Qatar, and Sudan, joined by Bangladesh, Brazil, China, Russian Federation, Iran, Malaysia, Mauritius, Nicaragua, Nigeria, Oman, Pakistan, Senegal, South Africa, Sweden, Chad, Vietnam—that served in part to "remind"

> that all legislative and administrative measures and actions taken by Israel, the occupying Power, which have altered or purport to alter the character and status of the Holy City of Jerusalem, and in particular the "basic law" on Jerusalem, are null and void and must be rescinded forthwith . . . .[27]

Germany, Greece, Italy, Lithuania, Paraguay, Netherlands, Togo, Ukraine, United Kingdom, and the United States voted against this resolution, and 23 other states abstained from voting.

Ironically, though Israel claims the territory of Temple Mount and controls primary access to the sacred space, by a 1967 agreement no Israeli flag flies on the hill, and non-Muslims have been forbidden to pray there. The stated purpose of the agreement is "not to offend the susceptibility of the Moslem population and to prevent disturbances between the religious communities."[28] Some Jewish religious leaders have noted that prayer at this "Holy of Holies" is properly forbidden; Jews instead pray at the "Western Wall," a remant of an encasement of the hill begun as part of the Second Temple of Herod the Great.

"Preventing disturbances" has been an ideal not realized, and "Israel is therefore confronted with a paradoxical situation in which not only have Jews refrained from exercising their inherent right, but the Government of Israel has even brought to justice those who have attempted to pray on the Temple Mount."[29] Following the March 2015 victory of Rabbi Yehuda Glick before the Jerusalem Magistrate's Court, support for Jewish prayer on the Mount began to widen, and conflict intensified. [30] The US State Department's International Religious Freedom Report for 2016—Israel and The Occupied Territories, issued in January 2018, contained the following passage:

> Following the continued tensions at the Temple Mount/Haram al-Sharif and violent incidents between Israelis and Palestinians, the Ambassador [David Saperstein] and embassy officers spoke with government officials and Knesset leaders about the

---

27. UNESCO Executive Board, Decision on Item 30: Occupied Palestine, 201 EX/PX/DR.30.1.

28. *See* UN Security Council Official Records 31st Year, UN Doc. S/PV.1894, 22 March 1976, para. 17.

29. *Id. See also*, for example, Behind the Headlines the Temple Mount Case, *Jewish Telegraphic Agency*, 15 March 1976, and Ban on Jewish Prayer at Temple Mount. Upheld. Special to the *New York Times*, 22 March 1976.

30. Amanda Borschel-Dan, As Support Widens for Jewish Prayer on Temple Mount, Should We Fear Apocalyptic Consequences? *The Times of Israel*, 28 April 2016. *See also* Aviel Schneider, Israel's Role in Shameful UN Temple Mount Decision, *Israel Today*, 27 October 2016.

> importance of maintaining the agreed-upon status quo [barring Jewish worship] at the Temple Mount/Haram al-Sharif and not escalating tensions through provocative actions or statements. In meetings with government officials, visiting high-level US government officials and embassy officers also stressed the importance of religious pluralism and respect for all streams of Judaism.

Aharon Barak, from 1975-1978 Attorney General of Israel, and from 1978-2006 a member of Israel's Supreme Court, the last decade as Chief Justice, has laid out the issues this way:

> The basic principle is that every Jew has the right to enter the Temple Mount, to pray there, and to have communion with his maker. This is part of the religious freedom of worship, it is part of the freedom of expression. However, as with every human right, it is not absolute, but a relative right. . . . Indeed, in a case where there is near certainty that injury may be caused to the public interest if a person's rights of religious worship and freedom of expression would be realized, it is possible to limit the rights of the person in order to uphold the public interest.[31]

In 1999, Chief Justice Barak considered the issue of religious freedom and sacred space in a different context.

SHAVIT V. THE CHEVRA KADISHA OF RISHON LE ZION

Supreme Court of Israel (Sitting as the Court of Civil Appeals), CA 6024/97 (1999)

[The local rabbi in charge of the Chevra Kadisha (hereinafter, the "Burial Society") refused a family's request to have the deceased's name inscribed on the tombstone in both Hebrew and Latin characters. Prior cases (*Gideon* and *Kestenbaum*) had sustained the right of surviving family members to engrave Latin characters and non–Jewish calendar dates on gravestones, even though Jewish burial societies handling funeral proceedings objected on the basis of leading halakhic (Jewish law) authority to the effect that foreign dates and lettering on gravestones "must be absolutely forbidden." In 1996, after decision of the earlier cases, the Right to Alternative Civil Burial Law was enacted, which gave Israelis the option of being buried in civil cemeteries. After the legislation passed, the Orthodox Burial Society refused to allow family members to inscribe both Hebrew and Latin characters on tombstones. The Society contended that since civil burials were permitted, the inscription of Latin characters was no longer required in its cemeteries. The District Court held that the changed legal situation justified overruling the prior cases. The Israeli Supreme Court, sitting as a Court of Civil Appeals, acknowledged that "a later statute may overturn an earlier law or decision," but noted that the question in such cases is "whether the later law contradicts its predecessors irreconcilably."]

Justice M. CHESHIN [majority opinion, joined by Chief Justice BARAK]: . . .

7. Under the [Alternative Burial Law], the Minister of Religious Affairs will designate places to be used as alternative civilian cemeteries, which will be located in the different regions of the country at reasonable distances from each other. . . .

---

31. *Reported in* Rivka Gonen, *Contested Holiness: Jewish, Muslim, and Christian Perspectives on the Temple Mount in Jerusalem* 154 (KTAV Publishing House 2003).

11. . . . The law is meant to pave the way for burial corporations other than Jewish burial societies and the establishment of alternative civilian cemeteries in which people may be buried, if they so choose, in ways other than according to the Orthodox Jewish tradition. . . .

15. The lower court effectively held that the Alternative Burial Law implied the rescission of the ruling of *Gideon-Kestenbaum*. We cannot agree with this conclusion. A ruling made by the Supreme Court bases itself on basic principles of the legal system in Israel – human dignity, public policy, the principles of public law—and it is so sturdy and strong, that we find it difficult to accept that it was rescinded by implication, allegedly, simply due to the passing of the Alternative Burial Law. . . .

16. . . . In *Kestenbaum*, Justice Barak said the following:

> Human dignity in Israel is not a metaphor. It is the reality, and we draw operative conclusions from it. In the matter before us, the necessary conclusion is that a government agency's general mandate to carry out certain activities—for example, the management of a cemetery—should not be interpreted to mean that this same government agency is licensed to cause serious and severe harm to the human dignity of those involved in this case. A government authority that seeks to infringe on human dignity must have explicit and clear authorization from the legislature. . . .

18. . . . The Jewish Burial Society also claims that it must bow to the Jewish legal ruling of its chief rabbi and to the orders of the chief rabbi of Rishon Lezion, and that these rulings forbid it to carve foreign letters and Gregorian dates of birth and death. This claim is not acceptable to us either. . . . [I]t is known that there is no sweeping and comprehensive Jewish law that prohibits the carving of foreign characters or Gregorian birth and death dates on a gravestone. In many cemeteries in Israel, there is no such prohibition. [The] ruling giving the local rabbi the last word in his area—the concept of the "local rabbinic authority"—is only binding among the religiously observant public or through an express law of the state. In former days, and in Jewish communities that were dispersed among the nations in many lands, this was Jewish Law, and there was no other. This is still Jewish Law in Jewish communities in the Diaspora in the present day. . . . The case is different here in Israel, as we have been gathered back to our homeland. I can find no good reason—in terms of the laws of state—to impose the ruling of the local rabbinic authority on all—on those who are religiously observant and those who are non-religious as if it were the law of the state. . . .

20. This claim of harm to the dignity of the dead and the feelings of the families is not new to us. It came up in *Kestenbaum*, and the Court dealt with it comprehensively. Justice Barak wrote the following about inscriptions on gravestones:

> Recognition of human dignity mandates giving people the freedom to inscribe gravestones in the way they see fit. The negation of this freedom and the imposition of exclusively Hebrew writing constitute a severe and serious violation of the fundamental value of human dignity.

26. . . . [With regard to Justice Englard's dissent, the question is whether the will and dignity of the individual or the local rabbinic authority should prevail.]

We must keep in mind that the State of Israel is not run according to Jewish Law. It is a state run by law. Israel is a democracy, and the law rules within her borders. Our considerations revolve around the individual, the human being, his or her wishes, interests, well-being, and welfare—all according to law of the state. . . .

Justice I. ENGLARD [dissenting]. . . .

3. . . . The judges have been dragged into this dispute, which at root is a purely ideological clash. It is known that a legal ruling has no power to solve the ongoing ideological conflict regarding the Jewish character of Israel and the relationship between religion and state in this Jewish democratic country. The carving of dates is only one aspect of this dispute. . . .

4. . . . I believe that where beliefs and opinions are concerned, there is no possibility of measuring sensibilities objectively. We face an ideological clash focused on symbols, and their importance to different people cannot be measured by any external yardstick of reason. Any ruling on the logical weight of a symbol will certainly be an expression of subjective values. Furthermore, the standing of a certain symbol in society is not fixed for any length of time. It can change according to social and political factors, which are ever dynamic. . . .

13. Everyone agrees that there is a threshold of sensitivity among the religiously observant public that should not be crossed. . . . I question if it is the role of the Court to establish the "legitimate" boundaries of the sensibilities of believers in general, and of the religiously observant public in particular. In addition, the definition of the boundaries of "reasonable" sensitivity is based largely on subjective views, as illustrated by the differences of opinions among the judges themselves.

18. The major question at issue now is the relationship between the basic freedom of religion of the Jewish burial society and the religiously observant relatives of the dead, on one hand, and, on the other hand, the basic freedom of other relatives of the dead to behave according to their ideology. . . . To my mind, we have no right to measure the emotional or essential weight of the opposing demands, using a hierarchy of values that is personal in nature. . . . The real struggle is outside the boundaries of the cemetery; behind this dispute, forces are warring for the character of Judaism and the State of Israel. This is the real issue that stands before this Court, and there is no ignoring it.

20. . . . This is the problem of true justice: in a situation where, unfortunately, it is impossible to safeguard all the legitimate interests, there is a need to give preference to one over the other. It is great in theory to talk about balancing opposing interests. I am not convinced that this metaphor accurately describes the judicial process under which we are bound, at the end of the day, to reject the right of one in favor of the right of another.

Be that as it may, I am of the opinion that in the matter at hand, the right of the relatives of the deceased to carve the gravestones as they like must retreat in the face of the right of the Jewish burial society to act in accordance with the local rabbinic authority's ruling. Why is this so? The Jewish burial society is, as its name reveals, holy. It is an institution performing a religious function that is known in the Jewish tradition as "the true kindness." The Jewish burial society must act according to Jewish law as ruled by the local rabbinic authority; this takes precedence. This is laid down in the terms of its license, this was the expectation of many of the deceased of the city, and this is demanded many of the relatives of the deceased.

21. In my opinion, this court is not authorized to force a religious body—be it public or private—to act in contravention of religious law. This coercion seriously violates freedom of religion. Such a violation is allowed only by the express order of the legislature.

Chief Justice A BARAK, concurring: . . .

6. In *Kestenbaum*, on one side of the scales of justice, weighed the value of safeguarding the Hebrew language, and on the other side weighed the value (and liberty) of human dignity. Now we must add to one side, the value of safeguarding the Hebrew language, and the value (and liberty) of freedom of religion, which to my mind is really an aspect of human dignity. Simultaneously we must add, on the other side, an additional aspect of harm to human dignity, specifically the harm which occurs when human dignity is violated for religious reasons. Actually, in my view, freedom from religion is also an aspect of human dignity. Therefore, one person enjoys freedom of religion, but another has the freedom to act according to the autonomy of his personal desires. This is the freedom of an individual not to be bound by a religious prohibition in which he or she does not believe. This is the freedom of the individual to choose his or her own path – in life and in death—according to his or her ideology. . . . [T]he Court must weigh the opposing considerations on the scales of justice. It must balance the conflicting values and principles. . . .

9. . . . [W]e cannot say that, in a conflict between freedom of religion and freedom from religion, one always has the upper hand. If we said that, we would be undermining the constitutional standing of one of these freedoms. The appropriate practice is to balance conflicting values and principles that fall within the bounds of the same liberty. In the framework of this balancing, we must aim to preserve the "core" of each of these liberties so that any damage will only affect the "shell.". . .

12. . . . It seems to me that in the present circumstances, the deceased and her relatives who wish to carve Latin lettering on the gravestone must be given the upper hand. The reasons for my approach are twofold: First, the harm to the deceased and the relatives – who are prevented from having writing in the language they choose – is direct and serious. On the other hand, the harm to the other deceased and their relatives when others are allowed non-Hebrew writing is indirect and not serious.

13. Second, the prohibition against foreign writing for religious reasons—to differentiate from the prohibition for the sake of the Hebrew language –constitutes religious coercion.... On the other hand, the harm to the religiously observant populace—harm which I acknowledge and take into consideration—in that they are not able to fulfill the ruling of the local rabbinic authority is not as serious or severe. We should recall that the issue here is "local" Jewish Law, as every local rabbinic authority makes its own rulings.

15. . . . I cannot accept [the argument that the outcome of the balancing depends on whether the balancing is conducted from a religious or secular outlook.] Balancing is neither secular nor religious. It weighs the conflict between values and principles from the appropriate perspective of the state's general values as a democratic and Jewish state. This is an integrative viewpoint, based on a synthesis between Jewish and democratic values. The Court is neither secular nor religious. The Court considers the feelings of everyone; the Court takes into the account the liberties of everyone; the Court expresses the values of everyone—Jewish values and democratic values. To the best of its ability, it balances the conflicting feelings, liberties and values.

16. . . . In [Justice Englard's] view, even if it wields public authority, a religious body that operates according to the norms of Jewish Law must be allowed—based on its freedom of religion—to follow religious directives. . . . In my colleague's view, the "balancing doctrine" does not apply to a case where the liberty in question is freedom of religion.

19. Negating the power of the Court to set appropriate boundaries to protect religious sensibilities will ultimately lead us—in a State of Israel that is not a theocracy—to fail to consider these sensibilities. Indeed, a democratic society that seeks to recognize and protect the human rights of all its citizens must acknowledge people's sensibilities and balance them by considering degrees of harm to sensibilities. Only harm that crosses the "threshold of tolerance" will warrant protection.

QUESTIONS

1. Which comes first, the religious freedom of the individual or the religious community to which he or she belongs?
2. Which do you find more persuasive, the concurrence of Chief Justice Barak or the dissent of Justice Englard?
3. In many ways, Chief Justice Barak's analysis parallels general German analysis of constitutional rights. Would he reach the same conclusion as the German Constitutional Court in the religious employment cases? How would his approach resolve the American religious autonomy cases?

C. "EQUALITY OF ENTRY" INTO SACRED SPACE: TWO CASES FROM INDIA

Court challenges in India have been bought by both Muslim and Hindu women seeking to be admitted to worship in spaces where they are prohibited by religious authorities. In both cases the women assert that the bans are customary and arbitrary, not religiously mandated, as women were in the past admitted to worship in these structures, and that the bans therefore are not protected by the religious autonomy provisions of the Indian Constitution and instead constitute unconstitutional violations of the women's equality rights.

"EQUALITY OF ENTRY": NOTE ON THE *HAJI ALI DARGAH* CASE

Dr. Noorjehan Safia Niaz and 1 Anr v. State of Maharashtra and Ors
(Bombay High Court, No. 106 of 2014, 26 August 2016)

Dr. Noorjehan Safia Niaz and 1 Anr v. State of Maharashtra and Ors concerned a ban on the entry of women into the sanctum sanctorum of the Haji Ali Dargah, a mosque and tomb (of a Muslim saint) that is, in the words of the Court, "one of the most popular religious places in Mumbai, visited by people of all religions and … one of India's most famous and prestigious landmarks" (para. 14). Petitioners, representing "a national secular autonomous mass movement of Muslim Women with over 50,000 members in 15 States", asserted that they had been visiting the mosque since childhood, and, entering the sanctum sanctorum through a special door for women, had been praying there until barred in 2012.

The President of the Haji Ali Dargah Trust, which administers the structure, asserted "that earlier they were not aware of the provisions of Shariat and had made a mistake and therefore had taken steps to rectify the same" (para. 5). The Trust asserted morever that

> (i) the entry of women in close proximity to the grave of male Muslim Saint was a grievous SIN, as per Islam; (ii) Article 26 of the Constitution of India confers upon the Trust a fundamental right to manage its own affairs in the matters of religion; (iii) it is in the interest of safety and security of women; and (iv) at no point of time women were allowed to enter the close proximity of the Tomb. (para. 22)

For the Court it was "therefore, necessary to consider what constitutes 'matters of religion' and whether the practice is essential and an integral part of Islam and whether, if women were permitted to enter the sanctum sanctorum, the very nature of its religion would change" (para. 27).

The Court ruled in favor of the women, finding that in this case the respondents were not able to show that the ban was of such a nature as to permit the Constitution's Article 26 (Freedom to manage religious affairs) to override the application to the situation of the women of Articles 14 (Equality before the law), 15 (Prohibition of discrimination on grounds of religion, race, caste, sex or place of birth), and 25 (Freedom of conscience and free profession, practice and propagation of religion).

NOTE ON THE SABARIMALA TEMPLE CASES

S. Mahendran v. Secretary, Travancore Devaswom Board
(Kerala High Court, AIR 1993 Ker 42, 5 April 1991)
Indian Young Lawyers Association & Ors v. State of Kerala & Ors
(Supreme Court of India Writ Petition No. 373 of 2006)

The Sabarimala complex, located high in the densely forested Periyar Tiger Reserve in the southwest state of Kerala, is the object of one of the world's largest pilgrimages. Some 45-50 million worshippers each year make the strenuous two-and-a-half-month journey, preceded by such efforts as a 41-day regimen of celibacy, restricted diet, teetotalism, emotional control, and good works. At the end of a steep mountain path pilgrims arrive at the temple of Ayyappa, the Hindu god of growth, and each may enter only if carrying an Irumudikkettu (sacred bundle of holy objects) on his head.[32] Women between the ages of 10 and 50 (from menarche through menopause) have, "since time immemorial" it is said, been banned from making the piligrimage and from entry into the the temple at any time of the year. Reasons given for the restriction include honoring the mission of the celebate Ayyappa and keeping him from being distracted in any way by the presence of women, and recognizing that "for physiological reasons" menstruating women could not undergo the pilgrimage, or its preparations and requirements, including fasting and purification.[33]

The ban was codified in the Kerala Hindu Places of Public Worship (Authorisation of Entry) Act 1965: "women who are not by custom and usage allowed to enter a place of public worship shall not be entitled to enter or offer worship in any place of public worship." In 1991 the Kerala High Court in *S. Mahendran v. Secretary, Travancore Devaswom Board* ruled in favor of the ban and directed the Kerala government to see that it was enforced.

The Kerala Court opinion contains inconsistent reports about females, young or old, worshipping or even appearing at Sabarimala in the distant past, but in any event notes that recent appearance of young women, including tourists and "even a newly married couple," have interfered with "the sanctity and purity of the surroundings" (para. 32). As to "whether the denial of entry of [the specified] class of woman amounts to discrimination and violative of Articles 15, 25 and 26 of the Constitution . . . and [w]hether directions can be issued by [the] Court to the Devaswom Board and the Government of Kerala to restrict the entry of such woman to the temple" (para. 12), the Court explained, pointing to Article 26:

> A religion can not only lay down a code of ethical rules, but it can also prescribe rituals, observances, ceremonies and modes of worship[, which] are also regarded as integral parts of religion. If the tenets of religion lay down that certain ceremonies are to be performed at certain times in a particular manner, those ceremonies are matters of religion and are to be enforced as a religious belief. (para. 23)

The Court concluded there was no violation of either Article 26 or of the 1965 Act, "since there is no restriction between one section and another section or between one class and another class among the Hindus in the matter of entry to a temple whereas the prohibition is only in respect of women of a particular age group and not women as a class" (para. 44).

Appeals to this ruling made slow progresss. A 2006 petition from the Indian Young Lawyers Association and Others requesting Supreme Court of India review had by April 2016 been heard by 10 judges in 10 years. In July 2016 the Supreme Court moved the case from one three-judge bench to another, and in October 2017 the Court referred the case to a five-judge Constitution bench, which commenced hearing of the case on 18 January 2018. Finally, in a 4-1 verdict handed down on 28 September 2018, the Supeme Court ruled that the Sabarimala Temple rule violated women's right to equality and right to worship, and in any event is not an essential religious practice.

Interestingly, the dissenting vote to the Sabarimala ruling came from the sole woman of the bench, Justice Indu Malhotra, who agreed that the rule violated

---

32. *See*, for example, The Pilgrimage, at sabarimalaayyappan.com/.

33. *See* Soumya Rao, The Legal Journey of the Ban on Women Entering the Sabarimala Temple, *Scroll.in*, 17 January 2018.

women's rights, but nevertheless "said that a secular polity must allow heterogeneity in religion, allow diverse forms of worship, even if irrational, insisting that courts must not enter into areas of faith."[34]

COMMENTS AND QUESTIONS

1. Lawyer Gautam Bhati observed that the Haji Ali Dargah case "was arrived at by hewing closely to the constitution, to law, and to the task of defending individual rights. It is admirable for resisting the temptation of interpretive adventurism."[35] Writing in October 2017, Bhati expressed similar hopes for the outcome of the Sabarimala case, on the same issues.[36] From the brief description given here, do you see any differences that might account for the apparent reluctance of the Supreme Court to move to judgment in the Sabarimala case?
2. What do you think about the persistance of the argument by Justice Malhotra that a ruling such as the one ultimately made in Sabarimala is not within the provence of secular courts? What do you think of the contrary assertion of the bench in Sabarimala that "it is an essential part of the Hindu religion to allow Hindu women to enter a temple as devotees"?[37]
3. Testimony in *S. Mahendran v. Secretary, Travancore Devaswom Board* given by the Thantri (Vedic head priest) of the Sabarimala Temple explained that astrologers had revealed "that the deity does not like young ladies entering the precincts of the temple" (para. 36), leading one Supreme Court justice to ask why a woman would want to go where the deity doesn't want her to be. Assuming this is a serious and not a disrespectful question, how would you answer it?
4. What weight, in a court of law, would you give to an assertion that something had been true "since time immemorial"? Could such an assertion be supported in any legally meaningful way in jurisdictions with which you are familiar?

Additional Web Resources:	Materials concerning autonomy rights with respect to determination of the mission of an organization and in determining membership in religious communities
	Materials concerning sacred spaces, uses, conflicts, including a module on the Temple Mount
	Updates on conflicts and issues raised in this chapter

34. Samanwaya Rautray, Women of All Ages Can Enter Sabarimala Temple, Rules Supreme Court, *The Economic Times*, 29 September 2018.

35. Gautam Bhatia, The Equality of Entry, *The Hindu*, updated 22 September 2016.

36. Gautam Bhatia, The Case against Customary Exclusion, *The Hindu*, 20 October 2017.

37. Rautray, *supra* note 35.

CHAPTER 11

RIGHT TO ASSOCIATION AND LEGAL PERSONALITY

I. INTRODUCTION

The focus of this chapter is the ability of a religious organization to acquire and retain legal entity status. This issue is seldom encountered as a practical issue in the United States, since access to entity status is so easy and the range of available structures so broad. As a practical matter, tax-exempt status is generally a more significant issue, but even this is virtually automatic for religious groups. In many other countries, however, issues relating to registration and recognition (what would typically be described as "incorporation" in the United States) are among the most important religious freedom issues faced by religious organizations, especially minority or new religious organizations. As a general matter, laws governing the establishment, registration, and recognition of religious communities can be used as instruments for either facilitating or hindering of religious freedom.

A country's law and practice regarding religious entities constitutes a crucial test of its performance in facilitating freedom of religion or belief. This may seem surprising. The intricacies of the law of religious associations clearly are not the most dramatic religious freedom problem. But on closer reflection, it is obvious that the law governing the creation, recognition, and registration of appropriate legal entities is vital for the life of most religious communities in a modern legal setting. While there are a small number of groups that object to being required to obtain legal entity status, most groups desire to register and obtain recognition, because only in this way can they gain the benefits of juristic personality. The precise set of rights associated with such status varies from legal system to legal system. But at a minimum, in the contemporary world it is extremely difficult for a group without entity status to engage in the most rudimentary legal acts—opening a bank account, renting or acquiring property for a place of worship or for other religious uses, entering into contracts (ranging from employment agreements with key religious personnel, to arrangements for publication of religious material or production of items needed for worship or observance, to mundane contracts for acquisition of supplies, electricity, heat, and other routine items needed in connection with religious life), to sue and be sued (i.e., to defend the rights of the organization by instituting legal actions, and to be subject to lawsuits), and so forth. These issues multiply for larger organizations that build and maintain multiple edifices for worship, develop networks of pastoral care, and establish an array of charitable and educational services—all in accordance with and rooted in sensitive patterns of conscientious belief.

Legal entity status is vital because, as a practical matter, a religious organization of appreciable magnitude cannot operate effectively and efficiently without it. In today's world, religious communities interact with the secular legal order in countless ways to carry out their affairs. Arranging such matters without legal entities is hopelessly cumbersome and exposes religious communities to liability risks and legal problems that should not be imposed on religious communities against their will. For example, if the property of a religious group is owned in the name of an individual, the interests of the group as a whole are jeopardized because of the risk that the individual may appropriate the property for his own use, or may incur unexpected liabilities in contract or tort that could be satisfied using the religious property, or he or she may die, which might result in discord between heirs and the religious group regarding ownership of the property. Moreover, a variety of additional legal issues are often linked to legal entity status. In many legal systems, registration is a necessary precondition for obtaining land use or other governmental permits; inviting foreign religious leaders, workers, and volunteers into one's country; arranging visits and ministries in hospitals, prisons, and military establishments; establishing educational institutions (whether for educating children or for training clergy); creating separate religiously motivated charitable organizations; obtaining exemption from a variety of different forms of taxation; and benefiting from the deductibility of contributions to religious organizations.

The general point is that it is extremely difficult as a practical matter to carry out the full range of a group's legitimate religious activities without access to legal entity status that carries with it the necessary corporate powers. Denial of access to such entity status thus constitutes a severe burden and limitation both on a community's right to freedom of religion and belief as a collectivity and on the rights of its individual believers.

Unduly restrictive laws in this area result in significant loss of social capital. Religious organizations play a powerful role in inculcating altruism and other personal characteristics that enhance social stability, productivity, and other forms of social capital such as increased volunteerism, social commitment, integrity, and general creativity. This impact is felt not only within religious organizations, but in the broader society as well. While religion can have negative as well as positive effects, it is socially wasteful to regulate religion in ways that unnecessarily curtail its positive potential.

For an authoritative study of international and regional norms in this area, as well as best practices, see the *Guidelines on the Legal Personality of Religious or Belief Communities* promulgated jointly the Venice Commission of the Council of Europe and by the Office for Democratic Institutions and Human Rights (ODIHR) of the Organization for Security and Co-operation in Europe (OSCE), available at http://www.osce.org/odihr/139046.

II. THE RIGHT OF RELIGIOUS COMMUNITIES TO ACQUIRE LEGAL PERSONALITY

A. THE UNITED STATES

In the United States, no permission or registration is required for a religious group to meet, organize, and worship. There may be land use or building permit obstacles to meeting at a certain location, but legal recognition of the religious community per se is not required. Thus, while government-imposed requirements for registration and recognition—along with other administrative red tape—can seriously hamper religious association in many countries, religious groups in the United States are free of such legal barriers to organization. At the same time, however, religious groups typically seek some form of legal-entity status to carry out their affairs. The various types of entities available to religious groups in the United States and their respective characteristics are summarized below.[1]

The creation of legal entities is a matter of state law in the United States, and laws vary to a considerable extent from state to state. About 15 states—typically older jurisdictions – have specific laws dealing with the organization of particular denominations.[2] This bears some analogy to the agreement system in Italy, Spain, and many other countries with strong Roman Catholic influence, except that in each of the American jurisdictions there is a "default" law for "other" religions that allows any religious group to incorporate.[3] As one would expect, these denomination-specific statutes tend to be tailored to the particular needs of the denominations involved and afford them appropriate flexibility in owning property and dealing with various other issues.

The laws of 18 states provide for trustee corporations.[4] Historically, trusteeship corporations represented the initial stage in moving from a heavy reliance on the trust form to more general use of corporate structures. In effect, the trusteeship corporation simply incorporated the trustees. Possibly because this form sometimes sets limitations on the permissible range of actions of trustees (for example, in selling property without judicial approval), it tends to be used sparingly.

Far more common today is the membership corporation, which is available in 43 jurisdictions. In 31 of these jurisdictions it is the only type of ecclesiastical corporation. The membership corporation is analogous in many ways to the business corporation, except that usually no stock certificates are issued. In effect, the members of the corporation (typically defined in the bylaws or articles

1. This excerpt is taken from W. Cole Durham, Jr., Facilitating Freedom of Religion or Belief Through Religious Association Laws, in *Facilitating Freedom of Religion or Belief: A Deskbook* 337–342 (Tore Lindholm, W. Cole Durham, Jr., and Bahia G. Tahzib-Lie, eds., Martinus Nijhoff 2004) (most footnotes omitted).

2. The states with such laws are Connecticut, Delaware, Illinois, Kansas, Louisiana, Maine, Maryland, Massachusetts, Michigan, Minnesota, New Hampshire, New Jersey, New York, Vermont, and Wisconsin. The number of denominations covered by specific statutes differs markedly from state to state. New York provides for more than 35 denominations. Most states with this type of statute cover no more than 7.

3. The "default" law could be a normal not-for-profit corporation law, or it may be a generic religious corporation law.

4. Fifteen of the 18 jurisdictions are located east of the Mississippi River.

of incorporation) are incorporated, and the members control the corporation. This form of organization is more democratic than other forms and tends to appeal to denominations that are organized in congregational fashion.

Twenty-six states provide for corporations sole. The corporation sole is a form of entity that traces its history back to the mid-fifteenth century, when it emerged as a type of entity ecclesiastical organizations could use to hold property in perpetuity. The corporation sole is a one-person corporation that incorporates a particular office, such as that of a bishop, and allows the current incumbent of the office to control the property owned by the corporation. What is distinctive about the corporation sole is that the ecclesiastical official chosen in accordance with the canons, rites, regulations, or discipline of a particular religion may be incorporated and is thereupon authorized to deal with property vested in the corporation sole in accordance with principles of church governance of the religion in question. Upon the death, resignation, or removal of the person who is the corporation sole, the successor is automatically vested with title to and power and authority over the property on the same terms as the predecessor. This significantly simplifies the problems of transition by making control of property follow the office, and not the officeholder.

In virtually all states,[5] religious groups can incorporate as simple nonprofit organizations, although they may be required to indicate (at their option) what type of nonprofit corporation they are. For instance, many states follow the example of the California Nonprofit Corporation Law and the Model Nonprofit Corporation Act, which distinguish between public benefit, mutual benefit, and religious corporations, with public benefit entities receiving the highest degree of regulation, and with religious corporations receiving a lower degree of regulation out of respect for the religious freedom rights of these organizations.

One additional source of flexibility in the United States may flow from the nature of its federal system. Along the lines suggested by business corporation laws, many states provide for the operation of corporations from other states within their borders. Generally, they allow entities from other states to perform the same acts as domestic corporations. This means that if a religious group does not find a legal structure that optimally fits its needs in one state, it may organize in a state that has the preferred legal form, and then function as a nonprofit entity in the state with the less attractive laws.

Generally speaking, most states afford religious groups multiple options so that they can find the form most suitable to their ecclesiastical polity. Because both the trust and simple not-for-profit organization forms are always available as fallbacks, practice consistently views these and other forms as devices designed to facilitate religious activity. Regardless of the form chosen, the red tape in acquiring entity status is minimal.

In the mid-1990s the DePaul Center for Church/State Studies surveyed 261 national-level religious organizations in the United States to assess what types of

---

5. The major exceptions are Virginia and West Virginia, whose constitutions, for historical reasons, prohibit the granting of incorporation to any church or religious denomination. *See* Va. Const, art. IV, §14; W.Va. Const, art. VI, §47.

legal structures these churches used to carry out their affairs.[6] The survey covered most major denominations in the United States and, of course, many minor ones as well. Despite the fact that approximately two-thirds of the respondents indicated that the nature of their religious organization was religiously or scripturally based, and a variety of other considerations suggested that the groups were quite diverse, the pattern of organization was surprisingly consistent. Respondents were asked, "Which *one* of the following would best characterize the formal legal structure of your organization?" The survey yielded the following variations in legal form:

- An unincorporated association—8%
- A religious not-for-profit corporation—87%
- A not-for-profit corporation—3%
- A charitable or religious trust—1%
- A corporation sole—1%
- A for-profit corporation—1%
- Some other type of legal structure—1%[7]

A remarkable convergence is evident in the "religious not-for-profit corporation," with 87 percent of religious communities electing to use that form. Typically, organization as a "religious" not-for-profit corporation gives some advantages over the regular nonprofit form—essentially in alleviating various reporting and other burdens out of respect for religious freedom. This form appears to be easily accessible and sufficiently flexible to meet a wide array of organizational needs. It should be noted that the foregoing survey addressed the issue of the types of entities denominations use to organize their affairs at the national level. The results might be quite different if one were trying to determine how property is held by entities at the local level.

Several things should be emphasized about the range of entity options available to religious groups in the United States. First, whatever the early history of these various options, virtually all are now easily accessible to religious groups that desire to use them. Approval of the necessary documents by state officials is generally very prompt, typically taking only a few minutes, or at most, a few days. Second, the number of founders required is small—generally less than ten. Third, to the extent that document filings are analogous to the registration process in Europe, the documents serve primarily a notice or informational function. Fourth, acquisition of entity status is, if anything, less burdensome than acquisition of normal nonprofit association status, among other reasons because religious groups are free to organize using trust or religious corporation statutes. Fifth, acquisition of entity status is typically not directly connected to state financial benefits such as tax-exempt status. This means that whether or not an entity is eligible for financial benefits in its interaction with the state, it is free to carry out the full range of its religious activities. With respect to a new organization, the ability to acquire entity status and move forward with

6. Rhys H. Williams and John Massad, Religious Diversity, Civil Law and Institutional Isomorphism, in *Religious Organizations in the United States: A Study of Legal Identity, Religious Freedom and the Law* 111, 121 (James A. Serritella, ed., Carolina Academic Press 2004).

7. *Id.*

religious activities is not delayed or obstructed because of questions about eligibility for other state benefits. Finally, it is significant to note that the various structures are not viewed as instrumentalities for controlling the religious sector. As opposed to trying to address potential problems before they occur through association law, actual problems are dealt with as they arise by ordinary laws, such as criminal, tax, or land use ordinances. This facilitates the activities of religious groups and focuses control functions on genuine problems.

COMMENTS AND QUESTIONS

1. Many countries use the registration process as a first line of defense for identifying and stopping groups that are undesirable or dangerous. Is the United States too permissive?
2. What resources does the United States have at its disposal to address the problem of dangerous or undesirable groups as an alternative to the registration system?

B. EUROPE

Silvio Ferrari, An Overview of European Systems[8]

The basic level or outer circle

1. The right of a religious association to obtain legal personality is increasingly recognized as part of the collective right of religious liberty. Decisions of the European Court of Human Rights have stated that denying legal personality can amount to a breach of religious freedom under Article 9 of the European Convention on Human Rights.

2. This right can be recognized in different ways. Contemporary legal systems are more and more complex and articulated, as they have to respond to different requests. Since the needs of religious associations are not identical to those of other associations (political parties, trade unions, etc.), many legal systems provide for a specific type of legal personality reserved exclusively for religious associations. In many cases, religious groups have the option to choose between being granted the "general" legal personality available to all associations (or large groups of them)[9] or the "specific" legal personality reserved for religious associations; in some states (e.g., in the Czech Republic) only the latter option is available.

3. Providing for a specific form of legal personality reserved for religious associations is nothing extraordinary and the same system is applied to many other associations. But this choice entails a definition of religious association: without it, it is impossible to establish whether the association requesting to make use of this specific type of personality has the right to obtain it.

---

8. This section is drawn from Silvio Ferrari, Religious Communities As Legal Persons: An Introduction to the National Reports, in *Churches and Other Organisations as Legal Persons: Proceedings of the 17th Meeting of the European Consortium for Church and State Research* 3–8 (Sweden, 17–20 November 2005) (Lars Friedner, ed., Uitgeverij Peeters 2007).

9. In some legal systems religious communities can incorporate as nonprofit organizations, foundations, and even commercial companies.

4. Being a religious association is seldom sufficient for obtaining the legal personality reserved for religious associations. Many legal systems demand further requirements such as: a minimum number of faithful; a minimum number of years during which the association must have been active in the country; a minimum number of local congregations pertaining to the applicant religious group; some guarantees of financial solidity; and so on. Sometimes these requirements are rigidly established; sometimes they are formulated in a way that leaves flexibility for discretion on the part of the state institutions (courts, government departments, etc.), which have the task of dealing with the applications from the religious association. The nature and the number of these requirements raise at least a couple of questions.

a) First of all, should they have regard only to the structure of the religious association or also to its doctrine and the corresponding behavior of its faithful? In some states, legal personality is refused if the religion's articles of faith are contrary to human rights. This condition sounds reasonable, but it could lead to far-reaching results: is equality between men and women a human right that could prevent the acquisition of legal personality if it is not respected by a religious group in its own internal organization? What about, for example, Jehovah's Witnesses' refusal of blood transfusions? Is that enough to deny that religious community the enjoyment of the form of legal personality reserved for religious associations?

b) What kind of "structural" (as opposed to "doctrinal") requirements are admissible? Some legal systems, for example, require a few hundred members as the minimum number for obtaining legal personality. Is that a form of discrimination against small religious communities, which are deprived of this ability just because they are small?

These requirements have a reduced impact on the religious community's life if the option to obtain legal personality is available to them, but if a religious community can gain legal personality only in the specific form reserved for religious associations, the requirements can amount to preventing that religious group from performing basic activities that are indispensable for its survival.

5. In some states, legal personality is automatically obtained if a time span (for example, one year) has passed since the filing of the application by the religious group and no answer has been given by the state body in charge of evaluating that request. But some legal systems do not fix any time limit within which the application from a religious association has to be dealt with. Sometimes this means that applications are left pending for a long time and the association is kept in a sort of "limbo" for a number of years. In these cases, the lack of a time frame may work as a hidden but effective way of rejecting undesired applications without having to face the consequences of an explicit rejection.

6. It is not completely clear what remedies are available to a religious association whose application for obtaining legal personality has been rejected. In some countries, it is possible to appeal to courts while, in others, the only way to appeal is through an administrative procedure. In most cases, this topic is not dealt with and one has the impression that national legal systems are not completely transparent on this point [or leave the issue to general provisions of administrative law].

7. Finally, there are religious communities that object to any form of registration or state recognition. Some legal systems give unincorporated associations the right to perform a few basic legal activities: consequently, these religious communities have the ability to organize and act, although their legal status is somewhat limited. In other cases, no such option is available. As a rule, religious activities such as gathering for prayer etc. can be performed without the need for any legal

organization; however, according to some scholars, the inability to obtain legal personality can indirectly affect religious liberty when it prevents the religious community from owning or renting a place of worship, opening a bank account, etc.

The upper level(s) or the inner circle(s)

8. Legal personality is valuable both in terms of the freedom of the religious communities and of cooperation by the State. Without legal personality, a religious community may be unable to perform acts and activities that are essential to its life; it is a matter of basic freedoms. But obtaining legal personality may also pave the way to receiving support from the State in the form of advantageous tax regimes, access to public institutions like schools, etc. It is hard to pinpoint exactly where freedom ends and cooperation starts. This position is differently located in each national legal system. But in most of them, state cooperation is not evenly distributed among religious communities—each state cooperates with some religions more than with others.

9. The selection of which religious communities will receive state support, and how this support is divided among them, frequently results from subdividing the religious communities that enjoy legal personality as religious associations into further categories, each of which has its own legal status. There is no European pattern here and each state has its own structure of legal categories and its own way of distributing religious associations within them. In Finland, three different types of legal personality can be distinguished, namely, those of the Evangelical Lutheran Church, the Finnish Orthodox Church and the registered religious associations. In Italy, there are about 30 religious groups that have the status of recognized religious associations. According to a law of 1929, six communities have concluded an agreement with the Italian State, and the Roman Catholic Church, whose legal position is defined through a concordat. In Denmark, there are five different categories of religious organization: religious groups recognized by the tax authorities; religious bodies without recognition or approval; approved religious entities; recognized religious entities; and the official Church.

10. How religious communities are placed in these different categories again depends on the national legal systems. Everywhere some conditions need to be fulfilled but they vary from state to state. Generally speaking, they are not different from the requirements to obtain legal personality as a religious association but the demand is higher: more members of the religious community; more years of presence in the country, etc., are required. In the Czech Republic, 300 members are enough for a religious community to obtain registration, but about 10,000 (0.1% of the country's population) are required to get the "special rights" reserved for some religions.[10] In Portugal, registration is available to all religious communities that have an organized presence in the country, but a presence of at least 30 years is required to obtain the higher status of "religion settled in the country".[11]

11. Also the type of state cooperation relating to each category differs according to the national legal system. In Portugal, registered religious communities enjoy tax

10. In the Czech Republic, there are two categories of religious communities with legal personality: registered religious communities and registered religious communities "with special rights."

11. In Portugal, religious communities are distributed among the following categories: unincorporated associations; private corporations; religious corporations (that is, registered religious communities); religious communities settled in the country.

exemptions, but only "settled" religious communities can receive state subsidies, conclude agreements with the State, celebrate religious marriages that have effect in the state legal system, etc. In the Czech Republic, only religious communities with "special rights" can teach religion in the schools, receive state support to pay the salaries of their ministers, have chaplains in the army and in prisons, etc.

12. Scholars are divided about the merits of this system. Some compare it with Latin American pyramids that have platforms placed at different levels—at each level the number of religious communities decreases and the amount of state support increases. Some lawyers object to this description. They prefer to depict the system in terms of inner circles, implying that the differentiation between the various categories does not reflect an intent to "hierarchize" religious groups and to give a privilege to some of them, but only to provide adequate answers to their needs, which can be different according to the size, history, and cultural roots of each group. Be that as it may, it is a fact that most European legal systems differentiate among religious communities and provide for different legal disciplines. Again, there is nothing extraordinary here. Looking at other parts of the world, it is difficult to find a legal system that does not differentiate among religious communities. Even those systems that stress equal treatment, like that of the United States, cannot avoid making distinctions between religious communities when it comes to issues like tax exemption. Once the basic freedoms are granted to any religious community, a reasonable degree of differentiation in favour of those groups that are more deeply rooted in the history and culture of a country can be defended. But not any kind of differentiation is acceptable: it must be (at least) rational and transparent.

13. These two conditions are not always respected by the European legal systems. To some observers they appear exceedingly baroque in their structure and sometimes they are based on requirements that cannot be precisely assessed. In Austria, for example, the 1998 reform created one more category of religious communities (officially registered religious communities) and established that only religious communities characterized by "a positive attitude to the society and the State" can be legally recognized.[12] The exact meaning of this requirement is open to debate: conscientious objection to military service and refusal of blood transfusions could be interpreted as signs of a negative attitude towards (respectively) the State and the society. In Belgium, religious communities can have legal personality as nonprofit associations or as recognized religions; to obtain recognition, "no formal requirements exist. All norms are unwritten. They are just informal guidelines inspiring and steering administrative praxis". A Belgian commentator affirms that "there should be 'enough' members: probably some tens of thousands" and stresses that the existence of hierarchical religious structures is "helpful" in obtaining recognition. The system may work well, but it seems to be very vaguely structured and to leave a lot of room for discretionary judgment by the public administration authority.

***

In the first decade of the twenty-first century, a major line of decisions of the European Court of Human Rights in Strasbourg held that freedom of association

---

12. In Austria, there are three categories of religious communities: a) religious communities with legal personality under private law; b) state-registered religious communities; c) legally recognised churches and religious communities.

and freedom of religion entail a right to acquire legal-entity status.[13] These cases were based upon a variety of provisions of the European Convention, with the focus being Article 9 (freedom of religion) and Article 11 (freedom of association). The right to legal-entity status is now firmly entrenched in international human rights law, particularly as interpreted by the European Court of Human Rights in Strasbourg.

The Court's insistence in this line of cases that "Article 9 must be interpreted in the light of the protection afforded by Article 11"[14] recognizes that the protections that have been worked out in the Article 11 context should be carried over to the Article 9 context and given full effect, while maintaining sensitivity to the religious context and the substance of religious freedom rights. In the setting of religious organizational issues, associational freedom protection translates into a concern for religious autonomy, which is both "indispensable for pluralism in a democratic society" and "at the very heart of the protection which Article 9 affords."[15] In effect, Article 11 concerns are absorbed into and recognized as part of Article 9 protections, where they protect both the collective and the individual dimensions of freedom of religion or belief. If the organizational issues were left unprotected, "all other aspects of the individual's freedom of religion would become vulnerable."[16] Thus, the right to entity status initially identified under Article 11 applies *a fortiori* in the Article 9 setting.

1. Germany

BAHÁ'Í CASE

German Constitutional Court, 5 February 1991

[The Spiritual Assembly of the Bahá'ís in Tübingen applied for registration as a registered association. This application was rejected by a local court on the ground that the Spiritual Assembly, which was part of a hierarchically structured religion, did not "demonstrate the necessary legal independence because its existence was dependent on the one hand on the local community, and on the other hand on the National Spiritual Assembly." The court reached this conclusion on the basis of provisions in the Statutes [charter documents] upon which the application for registration was based. These gave the National Spiritual Assembly control over exclusion from membership (Article 4.2), the

13. *See, e.g., Canea Catholic Church v. Greece*, App. No. 25528/94 (16 December 1997) (legal personality of the Roman Catholic Church protected); *United Communist Party of Turkey v. Turkey*, App. No. 19392/92 (30 January 1998); *Sidiropoulos & Others v. Greece*, App. No. 26695/95 (10 July 1998); *Freedom and Democracy Party (ÖZDEP) v. Turkey*, App. No. 23885/94 (8 December 1999); *Hasan and Chaush v. Bulgaria*, App. No. 30985/96 (26 October 2000); *Metropolitan Church of Bessarabia v. Moldova*, App. No. 45701/99 (13 December 2001); *Moscow Branch of the Salvation Army v. Russia*, App. No. 72881/01 (5 October 2006); *Church of Scientology of Moscow v. Russia*, App. No. 18147/02 (5 April 2007); *Svyato-Mykhaylivska Parafiya v. Ukraine*, App. No. 77703/01 (14 Sept. 2007).

14. *Hasan and Chaush v. Bulgaria* at para. 65.

15. *Id.*, para. 62.

16. *Id.*

right to supervise by-elections (Article 5.2), the right to decide on the jurisdiction of a local Spiritual Assembly (Article 11.1(c)), the right to approve amendments to the statutes (Article 13.2), and control over dissolution (Article 14). The complainants, by contrast, claimed that "the institutional structure of the world wide Bahá'í community was based on a divine foundation act, and that they were unable to alter it. Since in accordance with the constitutional law of the Bahá'ís all jurisdictional power lay with the elected bodies, these had to acquire legal capacity in order to be able to perform legal transactions." Appeals to higher civil courts were unsuccessful. The higher courts concurred that the Statutes violated the principle of autonomy of association].

The Bahá'í religious community, a creed originating from Shiite Islam, is represented in a large number of countries. It has a hierarchical structure and is currently led by the "Universal House of Justice," headquartered in Haifa (Israel) and consisting of nine elected members. In countries with a larger number of local communities, a nine-person National Spiritual Assembly is indirectly elected annually by the entire membership. The Assembly is established in the Federal Republic of Germany as a registered association; in other states, it uses other legal forms under the law on associations or societies in accordance with the statutes applicable there. As management bodies at local level, the Spiritual Assemblies, also consisting of nine members, which are responsible for taking care of local affairs, are elected by the faithful of the local community. . . .

The constitutional complaint particularly relates to the question of whether the complainant may be refused registration as an association, causing it to fail to acquire legal capacity, without violating its fundamental right under Article 4.1 and 4.2 of the Basic Law. The complainant alleges a violation of its freedom to practice a religion by virtue of it being made impossible, through denial of its entry in the register of associations, to organize itself in line with the obligatory internal constitution largely specified by the content of the Bahá'í faith. Hence, the area protected by the fundamental right of freedom of religion is affected. . . .

The court rulings do not do justice to the significance of the fundamental right of religious freedom of association guaranteed in Article 4.1 and 4.2 of the Basic Law in conjunction with Article 140 of the Basic Law/Article 137.2 and 137.4 of the Weimar Constitution for the interpretation (and application) of the law on associations contained in the Civil Code, and thereby violate the complainants' fundamental rights. . . .

Freedom of religion within the meaning of Article 4.1 and 4.2 of the Basic Law also encompasses religious freedom of association, as emerges from this provision in conjunction with the relevant Weimar Church Articles incorporated by Article 140 of the Basic Law. . . [Although religious freedom of association] is not explicitly named in Article 4.1 and 4.2 of the Basic Law, . . . [the] intention of the legislature which adopted the constitution after the experience of the persecution of religion by the National Socialist regime was . . . to guarantee freedom of religion not only in certain partial freedoms, but fully. At least, none of the religious freedom rights which had been recognized as a result of centuries of historical development in the Weimar Constitution should now be excluded. These religious freedom rights included freedom of faith and freedom of conscience, including freedom to profess a belief, freedom of private and public practice of religion (freedom of worship) and religious freedom of association (see Articles 135, 136 and 137.2 of the Weimar Constitution). . . .

The guarantee contained in religious freedom of association encompasses the freedom to associate and to organize on the basis of a shared faith to form a religious society. The term "religious *society*" already indicates a union founded on the state legal system, and not for instance only a purely spiritual community of worship. The possibility to form a religious society is intended to open up the path towards organization as an association of individuals to carry out their joint religious purpose, to take on a legal form and to participate in general legal transactions. This does not refer to a right to a *specific* legal form, such as that of an association with legal capacity or another form of legal person; the possibility of some form of legal existence is guaranteed, including participation in general legal transactions.

This requirement is met by Article 140 of the Basic Law in conjunction with Article 137.4 of the Weimar Constitution opening up and guaranteeing to the religious societies the possibility to acquire legal capacity according to the general provisions of civil law. The religious societies must in principle observe these provisions like anyone else. Nothing is therefore lost if a religious society or one of its sub-organizations is unable to obtain a specific legal form to which it aspires because of a faith-based special organization. Religious freedom of association, however, requires particular accommodation of the religious society's understanding of itself, insofar as it is rooted in the area of freedom of faith and freedom to profess a belief that is guaranteed as inalienable by Article 4.1 of the Basic Law, and is given concrete expression by the practice of religion protected by Article 4.2 of the Basic Law, in interpreting and applying the relevant law, in this case the law on associations contained in the Civil Code. . . .A result completely excluding one religious society as to its internal organization from participation in general legal transactions or only making this possible with difficulties which are unacceptable would be incompatible with religious freedom of association. . . .

The impugned rulings do not satisfy the regulatory content of religious freedom of association. The law on associations contained in the Civil Code permits the accommodation of particular requirements as to the internal organization emerging from the specific nature of religious associations which are sub-organizations of a religious society or are specially linked with it. . . .

It is possible, and indeed it is a constitutional requirement, in the context of the law on associations contained in the Civil Code to particularly accommodate the faith-related requirements placed on the internal organization of the local Spiritual Assembly of the Bahá'ís as a religious association and sub-organization of a religious society.

[Case-law emphasizes that the principle of autonomy of association characterizing the law on associations can be exercised in such a manner that the right of self-administration of the association is restricted by Statutes; also such a restriction constitutes an exercise of autonomy; it would hence mean a restriction on autonomy if such provisions were declared to be impermissible]. . . .

The principle of autonomy of association, as understood in the case-law and legal literature, is hence characterized as to its content by two not necessarily parallel tendencies. On the one hand, it protects autonomy regarding the formation and organizational structure of the association according to the freely formed decision of the members, which can also include insertion in a hierarchically organized community; secondly, it safeguards the self-determination of the association and of its members against a renunciation that almost brings to a standstill the expression of individual will. It does not rule out, indeed it is open to, balancing out in its interpretation and application both tendencies taking account of the concrete case, i.e., also related to the purpose and character of the association in question. Thus, it is considered to comply with autonomy of association to create tiered associations within which the sub-associations—be they with legal capacity, be they associations without legal capacity—are dependent on higher associations, but do not thereby lose their character as an association insofar as they also independently perform tasks. . . .

If the specific nature of religious associations organized as part of a religious community is considered in this context, it can be suggested as to the frequently observed faith-related hierarchical internal organization of religious societies that associations which are sub-organizations of religious societies or are specially linked with them wish to be part of the hierarchy of their religious community. This cannot necessarily be regarded as submission to third-party determination from outside which affects the core of the independence and self-administration of the association. . . .

[To the extent that] courts generally regard the influence of the National Spiritual Assembly on existence, membership and activity of the local Spiritual Assembly provided in the Statutes as impermissible third-party determination of the association from outside, they have misjudged the specific nature of religious associations which organize themselves as a sub-organization of a religious society with a hierarchy defined by their beliefs, and hence the significance of the fundamental right of religious freedom of association for the interpretation and application of the principle of autonomy of association. They have regarded the National Spiritual Assembly as an alien organization determined by other goals and interests which exercises a dominating influence, without accommodating the unity and commonality given by the connection under religious law. The same ultimately applies to the selection of the members of the local Spiritual Assembly by the faithful of the local Bahá'í community. By virtue of the connection under religious law, these are also not to be regarded as third parties subjecting the association to determination from outside, and hence removing its self-determination; rather, this type of establishment of memberships complies with the purpose of the association, as a hierarchical management body to administrate the affairs of the local Bahá'í community (Article 2.1 of the Statutes and the Preamble), and in fact serves to realize it. . . .

The above-referenced rulings hence violate the complainants' fundamental right under Article 4.1 and 4.2 of the Basic Law in conjunction with Article 140 of the Basic Law/Article 137.2 and 137.4 of the Weimar Constitution by virtue of the fact that they do not sufficiently accommodate the specific nature of the local Spiritual Assembly as a . . . sub-organisation of a religious society. . . . They are hence to be overturned . . . .

COMMENTS AND QUESTIONS

In effect, the *Bahá'í* case requires state officials to interpret the German Civil Code in a way that avoids inconsistency with Bahá'í beliefs. Can this decision be squared with the rationale of the US Supreme Court's decision in *Employment Division v. Smith*?

2. Moldova

METROPOLITAN CHURCH OF BESSARABIA AND OTHERS V. MOLDOVA

European Court of Human Rights, Application No. 45701/99 (5 December 2001)

[This case involves a subgroup within the Orthodox religious community (the Metropolitan Church of Bessarabia) that preferred to affiliate with the Romanian Orthodox Church instead of the Moscow Patriarchate of the Russian Orthodox Church. The political authorities in Moldova favored the Metropolitan Church of Moldova, which is subservient to the Moscow Patriarchate, and repeatedly refused to grant entity status to the Bessarabian Church. The full text of the opinion details numerous incidents of discrimination and outright persecution of individuals affiliated with the Bessarabian Church by public officials.]

The Court refers to its settled case-law to the effect that, as enshrined in Article 9, freedom of thought, conscience and religion is one of the foundations of a "democratic society" within the meaning of the Convention. It is, in its religious dimension, one of the most vital elements that go to make up the identity of believers and their conception of life, but it is also a precious asset for atheists, agnostics, sceptics and the unconcerned. The pluralism indissociable from a democratic society, which has been dearly won over the centuries, depends on it.

While religious freedom is primarily a matter of individual conscience, it also implies, *inter alia*, freedom to "manifest [one's] religion" alone and in private or in community with others, in public and within the circle of those whose faith one shares. Bearing witness in words and deeds is bound up with the existence of religious convictions. That freedom entails, *inter alia*, freedom to hold or not to hold religious beliefs and to practise or not to practise a religion. . . . Article 9 lists a number of forms which manifestation of one's religion or belief may take, namely worship, teaching, practice and observance. Nevertheless, Article 9 does not protect every act motivated or inspired by a religion or belief. . . .

The Court has also said that, in a democratic society, in which several religions coexist within one and the same population, it may be necessary to place restrictions on this freedom in order to reconcile the interests of the various groups and ensure that everyone's beliefs are respected. . . .

However, in exercising its regulatory power in this sphere and in its relations with the various religions, denominations and beliefs, the State has a duty to remain neutral and impartial. . . .What is at stake here is the preservation of pluralism and the proper functioning of democracy, one of the principle characteristics of which is the possibility it offers of resolving a country's problems through dialogue, without recourse to violence, even when they are irksome. Accordingly, the role of the authorities in such circumstances is not to remove the cause of tension by eliminating pluralism, but to ensure that the competing groups tolerate each other.

The Court further observes that in principle the right to freedom of religion for the purposes of the Convention excludes assessment by the State of the legitimacy of religious beliefs or the ways in which those beliefs are expressed. State measures favouring a particular leader or specific organs of a divided religious community or seeking to compel the community or part of it to place itself, against its will, under a single leadership, would also constitute an infringement of the freedom of religion. In democratic societies the State does not need to take measures to ensure that religious communities remain or are brought under a unified leadership. . . . Similarly, where the exercise of the right to freedom of religion or of one of its aspects is subject under domestic law to a system of prior authorisation, involvement in the procedure for granting authorisation of a recognised ecclesiastical authority cannot be reconciled with the requirements of paragraph 2 of Article 9. . . .

Moreover, since religious communities traditionally exist in the form of organised structures, Article 9 must be interpreted in the light of Article 11 of the Convention, which safeguards associative life against unjustified State interference. Seen in that perspective, the right of believers to freedom of religion, which includes the right to manifest one's religion in community with others, encompasses the expectation that believers will be allowed to associate freely, without arbitrary State intervention. Indeed, the autonomous existence of religious communities is indispensable for pluralism in a democratic society and is thus an issue at the very heart of the protection which Article 9 affords. . . . In addition, one of the means of exercising the right to manifest one's religion, especially for a religious community, in its collective dimension, is the possibility of ensuring judicial protection of the community, its members and its assets, so that Article 9 must be seen not only in the light of Article 11, but also in the light of Article 6. . . .

The Court's task is to ascertain whether the measures taken at national level are justified in principle and proportionate.

In order to determine the scope of the margin of appreciation in the present case the Court must take into account what is at stake, namely the need to maintain true religious pluralism, which is inherent in the concept of a democratic society. . . . Similarly, a good deal of weight must be given to that need when determining, as paragraph 2 of Article 9 requires, whether the interference corresponds to a "pressing social need" and is "proportionate to the legitimate aim pursued.". . .

(b) Application of the Above Principles

The Government submitted that the interference complained of was necessary in a democratic society. In the first place, to recognise the applicant church the State would have had to give up its position of neutrality in religious matters. . . .It was therefore in order to discharge its duty of neutrality that the Government had urged the applicant church to settle its differences with the Metropolitan Church of Moldova first.

Secondly, the refusal to recognise. . .was necessary for national security and Moldovan territorial integrity, regard being had to the fact that the applicant church engaged in political activities, working towards the reunification of Moldova with Romania. . . . [In support of these their assertions, the Government] mentioned articles in the Romanian press favourable to recognition of the applicant church by the Moldovan authorities and reunification of Moldova with Romania. Such activities endangered not only Moldova's integrity but also its peaceful relations with Ukraine, part of whose present territory had been under the canonical jurisdiction of the Metropolitan Church of Bessarabia before 1944. The Government further asserted that the applicant church was supported by openly pro-Romanian Moldovan parties, who denied the specificity of Moldova, even sometimes during debates in parliament, thus destabilizing the Moldovan State. . . .

Lastly, the Government emphasized that, although they had not recognised the Metropolitan Church of Bessarabia, the Moldovan authorities were acting in a spirit of tolerance and permitted the applicant church and its members to continue their activities without hindrance.

The applicants submitted that the refusal to recognise the Metropolitan Church of Bessarabia was not necessary in a democratic society. They asserted that all the arguments put forward by the Government were without foundation and unsubstantiated and that they did not correspond to a "pressing social need". There was nothing in the file to show that the applicants had intended or carried on or sought to carry on activities capable of undermining Moldovan territorial integrity, national security or public order.

They alleged that the Government, by refusing recognition even though they had recognised other Orthodox churches, had failed to discharge their duty of neutrality for preposterously fanciful reasons.

Non-recognition had made it impossible for the members of the applicant church to practice their religion because, under the Religious Denominations Act, the activities of a particular denomination and freedom of association for religious purposes may be exercised only by a denomination recognised by the State. Similarly, the State provided its protection only to recognised denominations and only those denominations could defend their rights in the courts. Consequently, the clergy and members of the applicant church had not been able to defend themselves against the physical attacks and persecution which they had suffered, and the applicant church had not been able to protect its assets.

The applicants denied that the State had tolerated the applicant church and its members. They alleged, on the contrary, not only that State agents had permitted acts of intimidation which members of the applicant church had suffered at the hands of other believers but also that in a number of cases State agents had participated in such acts.

(i) Arguments Put Forward in Justification of the Interference

Upholding Moldovan Law and Moldovan Constitutional Principles

The Court notes that Article 31 of the Moldovan Constitution guarantees freedom of religion and enunciates the principle of religious denominations' autonomy *vis-à-vis* the State, and that the Religious Denominations Act (the Law of 24 March 1992) lays down a procedure for the recognition of religious denominations.

The Government submitted that it was in order to comply with the above principles, including their duty of neutrality as between denominations, that the applicant church had been refused recognition and instead told first to settle its differences with the already recognised church from which it wished to split, namely the Metropolitan Church of Moldova.

The Court notes first of all that the applicant church lodged a first application for recognition on 8 October 1992 to which no reply was forthcoming, and that it was only later, on 7 February 1993, that the State recognised the Metropolitan Church of Moldova. That being so, the Court finds it difficult, at least for the period preceding recognition of the Metropolitan Church of Moldova, to understand the Government's argument that the applicant church was only a schismatic group within the Metropolitan Church of Moldova, which had been recognised.

In any event, the Court observes that the State's duty of neutrality and impartiality, as defined in its case-law, is incompatible with any power on the State's part to assess the legitimacy of religious beliefs, and requires the State to ensure that conflicting groups tolerate each other, even where they originated in the same group. In the present case, the Court considers that by taking the view that the applicant church was not a new denomination and by making its recognition depend on the will of an ecclesiastical authority that had been recognised–the Metropolitan Church of Moldova—the Government failed to discharge their duty of neutrality and impartiality. Consequently, their argument that refusing recognition was necessary in order to uphold Moldovan law and the Moldovan Constitution must be rejected.

Threat to Territorial Integrity

The Court notes in the first place that in its articles of association, in particular in the preamble thereto, the applicant church defines itself as an autonomous local church, operating within Moldovan territory in accordance with the laws of that State, and whose name is a historical one having no link with current or previous political situations. Although its activity is mainly religious, the applicant church states that it is also prepared to cooperate with the State in the fields of culture, education and social assistance. It further declares that it has no political activity.

The Court considers those principles to be clear and perfectly legitimate.

At the hearing on 2 October 2001 the Government nevertheless submitted that in reality the applicant church was engaged in political activities contrary to Moldovan public policy and that, were it to be recognised, such activities would endanger Moldovan territorial integrity.

The Court reiterates that while it cannot be ruled out that an organisation's programme might conceal objectives and intentions different from the ones it proclaims, to verify that it does not the Court must compare the content of the programme with the organisation's actions and the positions it defends. . . . In the present case it notes that there is nothing in the file which warrants the conclusion that the applicant church carries on activities other than those stated in its articles of association. . . .As for the possibility that the applicant church, once recognised, might constitute a danger to national security and territorial integrity, the Court considers that this is a mere hypothesis which, in the absence of corroboration, cannot justify a refusal to recognise it. . . .

(ii) Proportionality in Relation to the Aims Pursued

The Government submitted that although the authorities had not recognised the applicant church they acted in a spirit of tolerance and permitted it to continue its activities without hindrance. In particular, its members could meet, pray together and manage assets. As evidence, they cited the numerous activities of the applicant church.

The Court notes that, under Law no. 979-XII of 24 March 1992, only religions recognised by a Government decision may be practised in Moldova. In particular, only a recognised denomination has legal personality (section 24), may produce and sell specific liturgical objects (section 35), and engage clergy and employees (section 44). In addition, associations whose aims are wholly or partly religious are subject to the obligations arising from the legislation on religious denominations (section 21).

That being so, the Court notes that in the absence of recognition the applicant church may neither organise itself nor operate. Lacking legal personality, it cannot bring legal proceedings to protect its assets, which are indispensable for worship, while its members cannot meet to carry on religious activities without contravening the legislation on religious denominations.

As regards the tolerance allegedly shown by the Government towards the applicant church and its members, the Court cannot regard such tolerance as a substitute for recognition, since recognition alone is capable of conferring rights on those concerned.

The Court further notes that on occasion the applicants have not been able to defend themselves against acts of intimidation, since the authorities have fallen back on the excuse that only legal activities are entitled to legal protection. . . .

Lastly, it notes that when the authorities recognised other liturgical associations they did not apply the criteria which they used to refuse to recognise the applicant church and that no justification has been put forward by the Moldovan Government for this difference in treatment.

In conclusion, the Court considers that the refusal to recognise the applicant church has such consequences for the applicants' freedom of religion that it cannot be regarded as proportionate to the legitimate aim pursued or, accordingly, as necessary in a democratic society, and that there has been a violation of Article 9.

Additional Web Resources:	German and ECtHR cases on access of religious groups to "upper tier" recognition

3. Russia

NOTE ON *MOSCOW BRANCH OF SALVATION ARMY v. RUSSIA*

European Court of Human Rights, App. No. 72881/01 (5 October 2006)

Following adoption of the 1997 Russian Law on Freedom of Conscience and on Religious Organizations, the Salvation Army sought to re-register, as required by the law. Its re-registration application was denied by the Moscow Justice Department for three reasons: (1) failure to meet a ten-member minimum attendance requirement at a governing meeting; (2) failure to provide visas of foreign members or other documents establishing their lawful residence in Russian territory; and (3) the group's status as a "subordinate to a centralised religious organisation in London . . . [that] was 'most probably' a representative office of a foreign religious organisation operating on behalf and by order of the latter" (para. 14). The Salvation Army branch brought suit for violation of its rights under the European Convention.

The European Court held that dissolution of the legal entity of the Salvation Army, a well-respected Protestant religious group, violated both the freedom of association and the freedom of religion provisions of the European Convention. Citing its prior cases, the Court held that "a refusal by the domestic authorities to grant legal-entity status to an association of individuals amounts to an interference with the applicants' exercise of their right to freedom of association," and "[w]here the organisation of the religious community is at issue, a refusal to recognise it also constitutes interference with the applicants' right to freedom of religion under Article 9 of the Convention" (para. 71). Significantly, the European Court found that there was an interference with religious freedom even during the period when Russian authorities were continuing to seek dissolution after a decision of the Russian Constitutional Court, which held that the initial grounds for dissolution could not withstand a constitutional challenge. That is, even withholding registration during an appeal period violates religious freedom. The implication is that a group may not lose registered status except after a judicial determination that is made final only after all permissible appeals.

The *Moscow Branch* decision is significant in two other respects. First, the European Court rejected arguments for refusing registration that were based on the foreign status of the Moscow Branch. Specifically, even though the Russian religious associations law prohibited foreign nationals from being founders of Russian religious organizations, the Court found "no reasonable and objective justification for a difference in treatment of Russian and foreign nationals as regards their ability to exercise the right to freedom of religion through participation in the life of organized religious communities" (para. 82). Stated differently, the Court found that registration provisions precluding foreign nationals from being founders constituted impermissible discrimination in violation of religious freedom rights, since only a "reasonable" or "objective justification" would have prevented the differential treatment involved from being discriminatory. Moreover, the fact that the Salvation Army's headquarters was located abroad was not a legal ground for refusing registration (para 83-85).

Second, the Court rejected a variety of claims that the Moscow Branch had not described its religious affiliation and practices in a sufficiently precise manner. In fact, as required by the Russian religious associations law, the articles of association of the Moscow Branch indicated that it was a Christian faith, also described as Evangelical, which followed the teachings of the Salvation Army. The European Court rejected claims that this was confusing or otherwise inappropriate. Further, the Court held that there was "no apparent legal basis" for the requirement [imposed by Russian officials] to describe all "decisions, regulations and traditions" of the denomination.[17] The Court went one step further and added,

> [i]f the applicant's description of its religious affiliation was not deemed complete, it was the national courts' task to elucidate the applicable legal requirements and thus give the applicant clear notice how to prepare the documents in order to be able to obtain re-registration.[18]

The practical point of this requirement is that administrative bodies may not exploit vague language governing what is to be contained in registration documents in order to play a game of infinite delay by requiring additional details after each new submission.

On a more substantive note, the Court rejected the claims that the Salvation Army was an impermissible "paramilitary organization" on three grounds. In the first place, "the right to freedom of religion as guaranteed under the Convention excludes any discretion on the part of the State to determine whether religious beliefs or the means used to express such beliefs are legitimate" (para. 92). Thus, the fact that the Salvation Army chose to use "ranks similar to those used in the military and [wear] uniforms were particular ways of organizing the internal life of their religious community and manifesting [its] religious beliefs," (para. 92) and as such, should not be evaluated by state officials. Second, in reviewing religious beliefs and structures, state officials have a strict "duty of neutrality and impartiality vis-à-vis . . . religious communit[ies]" (para. 97). Third, the record was utterly devoid of any evidence that the Salvation Army "advocated a violent change of constitutional foundations," threatened to undermine "the integrity or security of the State," or for that matter had been engaged in unlawful conduct of any kind (para. 92; *see* paras. 92-96. Particularly in the absence of any clear evidence that a religious group poses provable dangers to society, denial of legal entity status constitutes a clear violation of religious freedom norms.

CHURCH OF SCIENTOLOGY MOSCOW V. RUSSIA

European Court of Human Rights, App. No. 18147/02 (5 April 2007)

[The Church of Scientology Moscow was officially registered on 25 January 1994 as a religious association having legal entity status under the Russian Religions Act of 25 October 1990. Following adoption of the 1997 Russian Law on Freedom of Conscience and on Religious Associations, the Church of

17. *Id.*, para. 89.
18. *Citing Tsonev v. Bulgaria*, App. No. 45963/99 (ECtHR, 13 April 2006), para 55.

Scientology Moscow repeatedly sought re-registration as contemplated by the legislation. The Moscow Justice Department had rejected applications for re-registration of the Church of Scientology on at least eleven occasions. A variety of reasons were given, but none could withstand scrutiny. In effect, the European Court recognized that lower level bureaucrats in Moscow were manipulating the 1997 Law to block re-registration of an unpopular group. Because of the number of excuses advanced in defense of this behavior, the European Court's decision in this case provides a list of types of bureaucratic action in denying entity status to religious communities that cannot be squared with the requirements of freedom of religion under the European Convention.]

The Court's Assessment

1. General Principles

[The Court reiterated a statement of principles very similar to that set forth in *Metropolitan Church of Bessarabia*, above.]

[T]he only necessity capable of justifying an interference with any of the rights enshrined in those Articles is one that may claim to spring from "democratic society". . . .

The State's power to protect its institutions and citizens from associations that might jeopardise them must be used sparingly, as exceptions to the rule of freedom of association are to be construed strictly and only convincing and compelling reasons can justify restrictions on that freedom. Any interference must correspond to a "pressing social need"; thus, the notion "necessary" does not have the flexibility of such expressions as "useful" or "desirable". . . .

2. The Applicant's Status as a "Victim" of the Alleged Violations

[T]he Court notes that the situation of the applicant is similar to that of the applicant in the case of *The Moscow Branch of the Salvation Army*. The applicant was denied re-registration required by the Religions Act and the entering of information concerning the applicant into the Unified State Register of Legal Entities was solely linked to the establishment of that register and to the shifting of registration competence from one authority to another following enactment of a new procedure for registration of legal entities. The national authorities have never acknowledged the alleged breach of the applicant's Convention rights and have not afforded any redress. The judgments by which the refusal of re-registration was upheld have not been set aside and have remained in force to date. . . .

Likewise, the Court finds unconvincing the Government's argument that the applicant may not claim to be a "victim" because it has not taken so far appropriate steps for properly applying for re-registration. Over a course of six years from 1999 to 2005 the applicant has filed no fewer than eleven applications for re-registration, attempting to remedy the defects of the submitted documents, both those that were identified by the domestic authorities and those that were supposed to exist in the instances where the Justice Department gave no indication as to their nature. . . .

Having regard to the above considerations, the Court finds that the applicant may "claim" to be a "victim" of the violations complained of. In order to ascertain whether it has actually been a victim, the merits of its contentions have to be examined.

3. Existence of Interference with the Applicant's Rights

In the light of the general principles outlined above, the ability to establish a legal entity in order to act collectively in a field of mutual interest is one of the most important aspects of freedom of association, without which that right would be deprived of any meaning. The Court has expressed the view that a refusal by the domestic authorities to grant legal-entity status to an association of individuals may amount to an interference with the applicants' exercise of their right to freedom of association. Where the organisation of the religious community is at issue, a refusal to recognise it also constitutes interference with the applicants' right to freedom of religion under Article 9 of the Convention (see *Metropolitan Church of Bessarabia*). The believers' right to freedom of religion encompasses the expectation that the community will be allowed to function peacefully, free from arbitrary State intervention.

. . .A failure to obtain "re-registration" for whatever reason before the expiry of the time-limit [specified in the 1997 Law] exposed the religious organisation to a threat of dissolution by judicial decision. . . .

Accordingly, the Court considers that there has been interference with the applicant's rights under Article 11 of the Convention read in the light of Article 9 of the Convention. It must therefore determine whether the interference satisfied the requirements of paragraph 2 of those provisions, that is whether it was "prescribed by law," pursued one or more legitimate aims, and was "necessary in a democratic society".

Justification for the Interference

(a) General Principles Applicable to the Analysis of Justification

The Court reiterates that the restriction on the rights to freedom of religion and assembly, as contained in Articles 9 and 11 of the Convention, is exhaustive. The exceptions to the rule of freedom of association are to be construed strictly and only convincing and compelling reasons can justify restrictions on that freedom. In determining whether a necessity within the meaning of paragraph 2 of these Convention provisions exists, the States have only a limited margin of appreciation, which goes hand in hand with rigorous European supervision embracing both the law and the decisions applying it, including those given by independent courts.

When the Court carries out its scrutiny, its task is not to substitute its own view for that of the relevant national authorities but rather to review the decisions they delivered in the exercise of their discretion. This does not mean that it has to confine itself to ascertaining whether the respondent State exercised its discretion reasonably, carefully and in good faith; it must look at the interference complained of in the light of the case as a whole and determine whether it was "proportionate to the legitimate aim pursued" and whether the reasons adduced by the national authorities to justify it are "relevant and sufficient". In so doing, the Court has to satisfy itself that the national authorities applied standards which were in conformity with the principles embodied in the Convention and, moreover, that they based their decisions on an acceptable assessment of the relevant facts.

(b) Arguments Put Forward in Justification of the Interference

The Court observes that the grounds for refusing re-registration of the applicant were not consistent throughout the time it attempted to secure re-registration. The first application was rejected by reference to on-going criminal proceedings against the church president and the second one for textual discrepancies between the charter and the Religions Act. The third to sixth applications were not processed for a failure to submit a complete set of documents, and that ground was also endorsed by the District and City Courts. The expiry of the time-limit for re-registration was invoked as the ground for leaving the seventh to tenth applications unexamined. After the courts determined that the refusal to examine the amended charter had had no lawful basis, the Justice Department refused the eleventh application on a new ground, notably the failure to produce a document showing the applicant's presence in Moscow for at least fifteen years.

The Court observes that the Moscow Justice Department refused to process at least four applications for re-registration, referring to the applicant's alleged failure to submit a complete set of documents. However, it did not specify why it deemed the applications incomplete. Responding to a written inquiry by the applicant's president, the Moscow Justice Department explicitly declined to indicate what information or document was considered missing, claiming that it was not competent to do so. The Court notes the inconsistent approach of the Moscow Justice Department on the one hand accepting that it was competent to determine the application incomplete but on the other hand declining its competence to give any indication as to the nature of the allegedly missing elements. Not only did that approach deprive the applicant of an opportunity to remedy the supposed defects of the applications and re-submit them, but also it ran counter to the express requirement of the domestic law that any refusal must be reasoned. By not stating clear reasons for rejecting the applications for re-registration submitted by the applicant, the Moscow Justice Department acted in an arbitrary manner. Consequently, the Court considers that that ground for refusal was not "in accordance with the law".

Examining the applicant's complaint for a second time, the District Court advanced more specific reasons for the refusal, the first of them being a failure to produce the original charter, registration certificate and the document indicating the legal address. With regard to this ground, the Court notes that the Religions Act contained an exhaustive list of documents that were to accompany an application for re-registration. That list did not require any specific form in which these documents were to be submitted, whether as originals or in copies. According to the Court's settled case-law, the expression "prescribed by law" requires that the impugned measure should have a basis in domestic law and also that the law be formulated with sufficient precision to enable the citizen to foresee the consequences which a given action may entail and to regulate his or her conduct accordingly. The requirement to submit the original documents did not follow from the text of the Religions Act and no other regulatory documents which might have set out such a requirement were referred to in the domestic proceedings. . . . In these circumstances, the Court is unable to find that the domestic law was formulated with sufficient precision enabling the applicant to foresee the adverse consequences which the submission of copies would entail. Furthermore, the Court considers that the requirement to enclose originals with each application would have been excessively burdensome, or even impossible, to fulfill in the instant case. The Justice Department was under no legal obligation to return the documents enclosed with applications it had refused to process, and it appears that it habitually kept them in the registration file. As there exists only a limited number of original documents, the requirement to submit originals with each application could have the effect of making impossible re-submission of rectified applications for re-registration because no more originals were available. This would have rendered the applicant's right to apply for re-registration as merely theoretical rather than practical and effective as required by the Convention. . . .In these circumstances, the District Court's finding that the applicant was responsible for the failure to produce these documents was devoid of both factual and legal basis.

The Nikulinskiy District Court also determined that the applicant had not produced information on the basic tenets of creed and practices of the religion. The Court has previously found that the refusal of registration for a failure to present information on the fundamental principles of a religion may be justified in the particular circumstances of the case by the necessity to determine whether the denomination seeking recognition presented any danger for a democratic society. The situation obtaining in the present case was different. It was not disputed that the applicant had submitted a book detailing the theological premises and practices of Scientology. The District Court did not explain why the book was not deemed to contain sufficient information on the basic tenets and practices of the religion required by the Religions Act. The Court reiterates that, if the information contained in the book was not considered complete, it was the national courts' task to elucidate the applicable legal requirements and thus give the applicant clear notice how to prepare the documents. This had not, however, been done. Accordingly, the Court considers that this ground for refusing re-registration has not been made out.

The Court does not consider it necessary to examine whether the refusals grounded on the expiry of the time-limit for re-registration were justified because in the subsequent proceedings the domestic courts acknowledged that the Moscow Justice Department's decision not to process an application for registration of the amended charter on that ground was unlawful. In any event, as the Court has found above, the applicant's failure to secure re-registration within the established time-limit was a direct consequence of arbitrary rejection of its earlier applications by the Moscow Justice Department.

Finally, as regards the rejection of the most recent, eleventh application on the ground that the document showing fifteen-year presence in Moscow had not been produced, the Court notes that this requirement had no lawful basis. The Constitutional Court had determined already in 2002 that no such document should be required from organisations which had existed before the entry into force of the Religions Act in 1997. The applicant had been registered as a religious organisation since 1994 and fell into that category.

It follows that the grounds invoked by the domestic authorities for refusing re-registration of the applicant had no lawful basis. A further consideration relevant for the Court's assessment of the proportionality of the interference is that by the time the re-registration requirement was introduced, the applicant had lawfully existed and operated in Moscow as an independent religious community for three years. It has not been submitted that the community as a whole or its individual members had been in breach of any domestic law or regulation governing their associative life and religious activities. In these circumstances, the Court considers that the reasons for refusing re-registration should have been particularly weighty and compelling. In the present case no such reasons have been put forward by the domestic authorities.

In view of the Court's finding above that the reasons invoked by the Moscow Justice Department and endorsed by the Moscow courts to deny re-registration of the applicant branch had no legal basis, it can be inferred that, in denying registration to the Church of Scientology of Moscow, the Moscow authorities did not act in good faith and neglected their duty of neutrality and impartiality vis-à-vis the applicant's religious community.

In the light of the foregoing, the Court considers that the interference with the applicant's right to freedom of religion and association was not justified. There has therefore been a violation of Article 11 of the Convention read in the light of Article 9.

COMMENTS AND QUESTIONS

Because of the repeated denials of registration on various grounds, the Russian *Scientology* case constitutes an extensive list of bureaucratic techniques that violate religious freedom principles. What additional types of religious freedom problems might emerge in the registration context?

Additional Web Resources:	Excerpts from the 1997 Russian Religious Associations Law Summary of Standards for Religious Association Laws under International Human Rights Law and European Court Jurisprudence

4. Hungary

MAGYAR KERESZTÉNY MENNONITA EGYHÁZ AND OTHERS V. HUNGARY

European Court of Human Rights, App. No. 70945/11 and others (8 April 2014)

[The applicants in this case were religious communities that possessed legal church status in Hungary under the 1990 Act on Freedom of Conscience and Religion and Churches (Act IV) ("the 1990 Church Act"), but lost such status following the adoption of the 2011 Hungarian Act on Right to Freedom of Conscience and Religion and the Legal Status of Church, Denominations and

Religious Communities (Act CCVI) ("the 2011 Church Act"). This new law allowed religious communities to function only as associations and required them to re-register unless listed in the Appendix as a recognized church. The applicants alleged that the de-registration and the discretionary re-registration of churches constituted a violation of their right to freedom of association and religion and was discriminatory.]

The 1990 Church Act defined churches as religious communities with membership exceeding 100 persons. In 2011, Hungary adopted a new Basic Law (Constitution) which gave the Hungarian Parliament power to identify recognized churches and provide criteria to recognize churches additionally admitted in the future. Formerly registered churches having 10 persons could be transformed into associations with continued, equal, safeguarded autonomy through registration, but were not entitled to State subsidies. To become an "incorporated church," an additionally admitted recognized church, the religious community must either prove that it has existed for 100 years internationally, or that it has functioned in Hungary in an organized manner for 20 years and has a membership equaling at least 0.1 per cent of the nation's population. Also, the religious community must prove "its intention and long-term ability to co-operate with the State for public-interest goals." (para. 94)

The Court's Assessment

In April 2014 the European Court of Human Rights issued a judgment on the merits of the cases, holding that there was an unjustifiable interference with the applicants' right to freedom of association and religion granted by Articles 9 and 11 of the Convention by the de-registration of the applicants as churches, noting previous cases where refusal of re-registration constituted such an interference (see *Moscow Branch of the Salvation Army* and *Church of Scientology Moscow v. Russia*). The Court reasoned that although the interference was "prescribed by law," namely by the 2011 Church Act, and that it presumably served a legitimate aim in seeking to eliminate religious organizations that abused State subsidies by claiming religious purpose while solely seeking financial gain, it was not "necessary in a democratic society."

Further, religious organizations have no right under Article 11 in conjunction with Article 9 to have a specific legal status. Articles 9 and 11 require only that the State "ensure that religious communities have the possibility of acquiring legal capacity as entities under the civil law; they do not require that a specific status under the public law be accorded to them. However, importantly, the Court emphasized that

> [t]he distinctions in the legal status granted to religious communities must not portray those adherents in an unfavourable light in public opinion, the latter being sensitive to the official evaluation of a religion – and of the church incarnating it – afforded by the State in public life. In the traditions of numerous countries, the denomination as a church and its State recognition are the key to social reputation, without which the religious community may be seen as a suspicious sect. In other words, the non-recognition of a religious community as a church may amplify prejudices against the adherents of such, often smaller communities, especially in case of religions with new or unusual teachings. (para. 92)

The Government did not demonstrate that less drastic solutions were not available, for example, judicial control or dissolution of churches *proven* to be of an unlawful or abusive character. Furthermore, while acknowledging that a two-tier church recognition scheme is justifiable, it was reasoned that such a scheme is normally part of "historical-constitutional traditions" and that the government neglected its duty of neutrality by establishing a "politically tainted re-registration procedure." (paras. 100, 111) For example, the duration requirement could be justified toward "newly established and unknown religious groups" (para. 111) but hardly toward familiar religious groups established just after the end of the Communist regime, barely falling short of the imposed duration. Lastly, the applicants were treated differently from other incorporated churches in relation to cooperation possibilities and the securing of faith-related benefits without any objective grounds.

The Court reaffirmed that discriminatory treatment calls for the strictest of scrutiny and that "the notion 'necessary' does not have the flexibility of such expressions as 'useful' or desirable'." (para. 79) Therefore, the Court held that this interference did not correspond to a "pressing social need" and subsequently violated Article 11 read in the light of Article 9.

[Judge Spano, joined by Judge Raimondi, wrote a dissenting opinion.]

In a subsequent ruling, in June 2016, the court ordered Just Satisfaction to the parties in varying amounts.

5. Turkey

NOTE ON *SINAN ISIK v. TURKEY*

European Court of Human Rights, App. No. 21924/05 (2 February 2010)

Turkish law required religion to be recorded on identity cards until 2006, when it became optional to leave the entry blank. The applicant, Sinan Isik, a member of the Alevi religious community, requested that his religious affiliation be listed as "Alevi" rather than "Islam." Some scholars consider the Alevi faith to be a branch of Islam while others regard it as a separate religion. The lower courts, however, found the religion to be a branch of Islam and therefore dismissed the applicant's request. The applicant alleged that being required to disclose his belief was a violation of Article 9 enshrining freedom of thought, conscience and belief, and that the present indication of "Islam" on his identity card was incorrect.

The Government argued that the indication of religion on identity cards was necessary for public purposes and did not affect freedom of religion or belief; that it was not intended to compel an individual to disclose his or her belief or to be used to discriminate. The Court found that there had been a violation of Article 9, however, and that the State had breached its duty of neutrality in assessing the applicant's faith. The Court held that the violation ultimately arose not from the refusal to indicate the applicant's faith (Alevi) on his identity card but from the fact that his identity card contained an indication of religion, regardless of whether it was voluntary or compulsory. Referencing *Sofianopoulos and Others v. Greece*, the Court reasoned that "the right to manifest one's religion or beliefs also has a negative aspect, namely an individual's right not to be obliged to disclose his or her religion or beliefs . . . ." (para. 41)

6. Austria

NOTE ON JEHOVAH'S WITNESSES AND CHURCH STATUS IN AUSTRIA

A number of countries, in addition to having rules for basic entry status of religious organizations, have rules governing a higher status. Austria for example has had since 1998 a three-tier structure, with ordinary civil associations at the base level, publicly registered religious communities at the intermediate level, and recognized religious societies at the highest level. The "recognized religious society" status was established pursuant to the Act of 20 May 1874 Concerning the Legal Recognition of Religious Societies. The intermediate "religious community" status was created in 1998 pursuant to the 1998 Act on the Legal Status of Registered Religious Communities.[19] Many believe that the 1998 Act was passed at least in part as a stalling tactic, to avoid the need for immediate recognition of the Jehovah's Witnesses. This may explain some of the impatience of the European Court with the delays in the case that follows. The case raises larger questions, however, about how equality values apply in the multi-tier structures that characterize so much of European church-state law.

The procedural background of the case is complex. The application arose as a result of obstacles and delays Jehovah's Witnesses encountered while they sought status as a recognized religious society in Austria. This status carries with it a number of benefits over and above the basic benefits of legal personality, such as military exemption for clergy, the right to run schools, and certain tax exemptions that are not available to religious communities. To become a recognized religious society, an organization must meet the criteria established in the 1998 Act on the Legal Status of Registered Religious Communities (notably, presence in Austria for at least 20 years, at least 10 years as a registered religious community, and a minimum membership of approximately 16,000 persons), as well as additional criteria set out in the 1874 Recognition Act.

The Jehovah's Witnesses first filed a request for recognition as a religious society with the Ministry for Education and Arts in 1978, under the 1874 Recognition Act. When the Ministry failed to act on their request, they filed a complaint with the Ombudsman's office. The Ombudsman issued a statement in February 1981 saying that the delay was an undesirable state of affairs, but that nothing could be done in light of an agreement of undisclosed terms reached between the Ministry and the Jehovah's Witnesses since the time their complaint was filed.

---

19. These Austrian laws are described in the full version of the case excerpted below, *Religionsgemeinschaft der Zeugen Jehovas v. Austria*, App. No. 40825/98 (ECtHR, 31 July 2008), §§ 42–54. For additional background, see Christopher J. Miner, Losing My Religion: Austria's New Religion Law in Light of International and European Standards of Religious Freedom, 1998 *BYU L. Rev.* 607. *See also* Richard Potz, Austria, in *Encyclopedia of Law and Religion* (Gerhard Robbers, W. Cole Durham, Jr., and Donlu Thayer, eds.. Brill 2016).

In June 1987 the Jehovah's Witnesses again applied to the Ministry for recognition as a religious society under the 1874 Act. After being informed by the Ministry that they had no right to a formal decision on their request, the Jehovah's Witnesses sought redress in the courts. From 1991 to 1995 they were shuttled between the Constitutional and Administrative courts, with neither court able to hear their complaint or issue a decision against the Ministry. Finally, in October 1995, the Constitutional Court issued a decision granting the Administrative Court jurisdiction over the Jehovah's Witnesses' complaint.

In December 1995 the Administrative Court issued a decision ordering the Ministry to give reasons for not granting the Jehovah's Witnesses' request for recognition. After further delays and submissions, the Ministry finally responded on 21 July 1997 by dismissing the applicants' recognition request on the basis of the group's unclear internal organization, negative attitude toward the state and its institutions, refusal to perform military service or any form of alternative service, refusal to participate in local community life and elections, and refusal to undergo certain types of medical treatment such as blood transfusions. This decision was challenged in the Austrian Constitutional Court, which communicated the case to the Minister with a request to submit the case file and any observations within eight weeks. The Minister did not respond. On 11 March 1998, the Constitutional Court quashed the Minister's decision of 21 July 1997 on the basis of the Jehovah's Witnesses' submissions.

In the meantime, the 1998 Act had come into effect. The Minister decided that the earlier request for recognition should be handled under the new act, and that the Jehovah's Witnesses had acquired legal personality as a registered religious community. Not satisfied with this intermediate-tier status, the Jehovah's Witnesses submitted a new request for recognition under the 1874 Act on 22 July 1998. The Minister dismissed it pursuant to Section 11(1) of the 1998 Act, which held that a religious community could be recognized as a religious society only after being a religious community under the 1998 Act for at least ten years. This decision was also challenged in the Austrian Constitutional Court, which now found that the ten-year waiting period requirement was in conformity with the Austrian Constitution.

Following some additional proceedings, the Jehovah's Witnesses filed a complaint in the European Court of Human Rights alleging multiple complaints, including violation of their right to religious freedom (Article 9) and association (Article 11), discriminatory treatment (Article 14 taken together with Articles 9 and 11), and an unreasonably long wait for a decision (Article 6). These allegations stemmed from the inability of the Jehovah's Witnesses to gain any recognition whatsoever, and from the difference in treatment between religious communities and the upper-tier recognized religious societies.

RELIGIONSGEMEINSCHAFT DER ZEUGEN JEHOVAS V. AUSTRIA

European Court of Human Rights, App. No. 40825/98 (31 July 2008)

66. The Court is not persuaded by [the Government's argument that there had been no interference with the applicant's Article 9 right because the religious community had eventually been granted legal personality and members of the Jehovah's Witnesses had not been hindered in practicing their religion.] . . .[T]he

period which elapsed between the submission of the request for recognition and the granting of legal personality is substantial and it is therefore questionable whether it can be treated merely as a period of waiting while an administrative request was being processed . . . . [D]uring this period the first applicant did not have legal personality, with all the consequences attached to this lack of status.

67. The fact that no instances of interference with the community life of the Jehovah's Witnesses have been reported during this period and that the first applicant's lack of legal personality may be compensated in part by running auxiliary associations, as stated by the applicants, is not decisive. The Court reiterates in this connection that the existence of a violation is conceivable even in the absence of prejudice or damage . . . .

68. The Court therefore considers that there has been an interference with the applicants' right to freedom of religion, as guaranteed by Article 9 §1 of the Convention . . . .

[The Court concluded that the interference was prescribed by law, not only in the sense that the "impugned measures have some basis in domestic law," but also in the sense that they meet the qualitative standards of the rule of law in that they are "sufficiently accessible and foreseeable as to its effects" and that they are "formulated with sufficient precision to enable the individual—if need be with appropriate advice—to regulate his conduct . . . . "§§70-73. It also found that the interference complained of furthered the legitimate aim of protection of public order and public safety.] . . .

78. [Noting the 20-year delay from 1978 to 1998 in granting legal personality, the Court] finds that such a prolonged period raises concerns under Article 9 of the Convention. In this connection the Court reiterates that the autonomous existence of religious communities is indispensable for pluralism in a democratic society and is thus an issue at the very heart of the protection which Article 9 affords . . . .

79. Given the importance of this right, the Court considers that there is an obligation on all of the State's authorities to keep the time during which an applicant waits for conferment of legal personality for the purposes of Article 9 of the Convention reasonably short. The Court appreciates that during the waiting period the first applicant's lack of legal personality could to some extent have been compensated by the creation of auxiliary associations which had legal personality, and it does not appear that the public authorities interfered with any such associations. However, since the right to an autonomous existence is at the very heart of the guarantees in Article 9 these circumstances cannot make up for the prolonged failure to grant legal personality to the first applicant.

Since the Government have not relied on any "relevant" and "sufficient" reasons justifying this failure, the above measure went beyond what would have amounted to a "necessary" restriction on the applicants' freedom of religion.

80. It follows that there has been a violation of Article 9 . . . .

83. The applicants submitted that the status of a registered religious community was inferior to that of a religious society, and that this constituted discrimination prohibited by the Convention. They relied on Article 14 read in conjunction with Article[s] 9 and 11 of the Convention . . . .

88. Having regard to the above findings under Article 9, the Court finds that there is no doubt that Article 14 of the Convention, taken in conjunction with Article 9, is applicable in the present case.

89. The applicants submitted that the status of a religious community conferred upon the first applicant [the religious community] was inferior to the status held by religious societies, as religious communities were subject to more severe State control in respect of their religious doctrine, their rules on membership and the administration of their assets pursuant to sections 3-5 and 11 of the 1998 Religious Communities Act . . . .

91. The applicants further complained of the discriminatory nature of section 11 of the 1998 Religious Communities Act. This provision amended the Recognition Act in that it introduced further requirements for recognition as a religious society. In particular, it requires the existence of the religious association for at least twenty years in Austria and for at least ten years as a registered religious community; a minimum number of two adherents per thousand members of the Austrian population (at the moment, this means about 16,000 persons); the use of income and other assets for religious purposes, including charity activities; a positive attitude towards society and the State; and no illegal interference as regards the association's relationship with recognised or other religious societies.

92. The Court observes that under Austrian law, religious societies enjoy privileged treatment in many areas. These areas include exemption from military service and civilian service, reduced tax liability or exemption from specific taxes, facilitation of the founding of schools, and membership of various boards. Given the number of these privileges and their nature, in particular in the field of taxation, the advantage obtained by religious societies is substantial and this special treatment undoubtedly facilitates a religious society's pursuance of its religious aims. In view of these substantive privileges accorded to religious societies, the obligation under Article 9 of the Convention incumbent on the State's authorities to remain neutral in the exercise of their powers in this domain requires therefore that if a State sets up a framework for conferring legal personality on religious groups to which a specific status is linked, all religious groups which so wish must have a fair opportunity to apply for this status and the criteria established must be applied in a non-discriminatory manner . . . .

95. The applicants disputed the necessity of the ten-year waiting period, as the recognition of the Coptic Orthodox Church by a specific law in 2003 proved the contrary. The Coptic Orthodox Church had only existed in Austria since 1976 and had been registered as a religious community in 1998, whereas the first applicant, which had existed in Austria for a considerably longer period, was still a religious community.

96. The Court reiterates that Article 14 does not prohibit a member State from treating groups differently in order to correct "factual inequalities" between them; indeed in certain circumstances a failure to attempt to correct inequality through different treatment may in itself give rise to a breach of that Article . . . . A difference of treatment is, however, discriminatory if it has no objective and reasonable justification; in other words, if it does not pursue a legitimate aim or if there is not a reasonable relationship of proportionality between the means employed and the aim sought to be realised. The Contracting State enjoys a

margin of appreciation in assessing whether and to what extent differences in otherwise similar situations justify a different treatment . . . .

97. The Court finds that the imposition of a waiting period before a religious association that has been granted legal personality can obtain a more consolidated status as a public-law body raises delicate questions, as the State has a duty to remain neutral and impartial in exercising its regulatory power in the sphere of religious freedom and in its relations with different religions, denominations and beliefs.... Such a waiting period therefore calls for particular scrutiny on the part of the Court.

98. The Court could accept that such a period might be necessary in exceptional circumstances such as would be in the case of newly established and unknown religious groups. But it hardly appears justified in respect of religious groups with a long-standing existence internationally which are also long established in the country and therefore familiar to the competent authorities, as is the case with the Jehovah's Witnesses . . . .

99. The Court therefore finds that the difference in treatment was not based on any "objective and reasonable justification". Accordingly, there has been a violation of Article 14 of the Convention taken in conjunction with Article 9.

QUESTIONS

Why didn't the factors relied on by the Ministry of Education in denying recognition to the Jehovah's Witnesses constitute "objective and reasonable" considerations? What factors might justify differential treatment stemming from multi-tier systems?

C. EGYPT

In contrast to the European Court of Human Rights, which determined (see the cases from Greece and Turkey, above) that recording religion on identity cards, whether voluntary or compulsory, violates principles of freedom of thought, conscience, and religion enshrined in Article 9 of the Convention, Egyptian courts sought to discern lawful ways of indicating religious affiliation on national identity cards as required by Egyptian law.

NOTE ON *HUSAM IZZAT MUSA AND RANYA ENAYAT RUSHDY v. THE MINISTRY OF THE INTERIOR*

Egyptian Administrative Court, Case No. 24044/45 (4 April 2006)

Husam Izzat Musa and Ranya Enayat Rushdy were Egyptian citizens of the Baha'i faith whose identity cards and passports were confiscated upon requesting the addition of their daughters' names to their passports. These applicants filed a lawsuit requesting that identity cards be given them, as well as birth certificates for their daughters, indicating their Baha'i faith.

Egyptian citizens are required to declare their religious affiliation on national identity cards. A great difficulty arose when Baha'is tried to list their religion, however, since Islam, Christianity and Judaism are the only formally recognized religions in Egypt. If Baha'is were permitted to declare their faith, it was not legally recognized; if they were not permitted to do so, they were forced to declare a faith other than their own, which was a lie and also constituted a violation of the law. As national identity cards are essential to the practicalities of civil and political life, this difficulty dramatically increased in 2004 when paper identity cards were replaced by computerized ones that did not provide for a "Baha'i" entry, producing a crisis that alerted officials of the violation. Thus, when the applicants' paper documentation declaring their Baha'i faith was confiscated, they found it impracticable to resume the daily necessities of life, and filed suit.[20]

The lower administrative court held that the refusal of the Administration to provide the applicants with identity cards and birth certificates indicating the Baha'i religion was unlawful. The court reasoned that the Shari'a provisions (Islamic jurisprudence) requires that every Egyptian be given an identity card and birth certificate indicating his name and religion as prescribed by the Civil Registry Act no. 143 of 1994. Rather than it being inconsistent with Islamic tenets to indicate a banned religion, the court reasoned that "these [religions] must be indicated so that the status of its bearer is known and thus he does not enjoy a legal status to which his belief does not entitle him . . . ." To illustrate, the court noted that non-Muslims have consistently lived in Muslim lands without being forced to change their beliefs, but that only religious beliefs recognized under Islamic rule were permitted for open practice under such circumstances.

Members of parliament were upset with the lower court's decision and challenged it in the Supreme Administrative Court (SAC). The SAC reversed the lower court's decision, also reversing its own 1983 decision used by the lower court, and held that the state was prohibited from entering the Baha'i faith on identity cards or birth certificates. The SAC reasoned that entering the Baha'i faith on identity cards was a violation of public order since Islamic law doesn't recognize the Baha'i faith. The SAC distinguished between the right to religious belief and the right to express that belief: "As to the freedom of practicing religious rites, this is subject to the limitation . . . of respecting the public order and public morals."[21]

The SAC's decision was controversial as it forced Baha'is to lie or abandon their faith, both of which also violated Islamic principles, by requiring them to enter Islam, Christianity, or Judaism as their affiliated religion on national identity cards. This contradiction led a human rights organization, the Egyptian Initiative on Personal Rights (EIPR), to step in on the case of another Baha'i family, the Rauf Hindi family. In a strategic move by the EPIR, it was requested that the Baha'is be given permission to leave the required field blank rather than enter their faith on the national identity cards. This request seemed satisfactory as expressed by the lower Administrative Court Justice: "In keeping with the

20. The information contained in this paragraph is adapted from Saba Mahmood and Peter Danchin, Religious Freedom in the Jurisprudence of the Egyptian and European Court of Human Rights, 13 *South Atlantic Quarterly*, 5–10 (2014).

21. *Id.* at 14–15 (quoting Supreme Administrative Court case nos. 16834 & 18971/52 (16 December 2006)) (http://info.bahai.org/pdf/EGYPTSAC_16DEC06_ENGLISH.pdf; translation modified by Mahmood for legal terms and idiomatic phrases) .

principle of not forcing any citizen to embrace a divine religion . . . issuing a national identity card with no space for religion or with a symbol indicating that he does not belong to any of the three divine religions . . . would conform with the law and reality."[22]

D. CHINA

1. Historical Background

DEVELOPMENTS REGARDING RELIGIOUS FREEDOM IN CHINA[23]

To some extent Western perceptions of the religious situation in China are stuck in a time warp, based on policies and realities that existed during the Cultural Revolution, when Mao Zedong closed all places of worship and tried to extinguish religion altogether. While there is in the United States and elsewhere in the West quite a deep understanding and appreciation for the dramatic economic changes that have taken place in China in the past four decades, there is less understanding of the ways in which laws and policies governing religion have also undergone significant transformation. For example, while there are still only five officially recognized religious groups in China (Buddhism, Daoism, Islam, Catholicism, and Protestantism), and despite ongoing concern about foreign domination of Christian denominations in China, there has been a dramatic increase in the types and levels of interaction between Christians in China and their foreign counterparts. Tensions exist between the registered and unregistered churches of a single denomination. Unregistered religious groups, sometimes labeled "evil cults," can become targets for particular government concern.

Since the 1980s there has been a dramatic growth in religious belief in China. The Chinese government estimates that there are more than 100 million religious believers in China today, a majority of whom are Buddhist. The growth has not been limited to the five officially recognized religious groups, but includes unofficial Buddhist organizations and Protestant "house churches," which meet in small groups in believers' homes. For example, after a century of missionary efforts in China from the 1840s until the establishment of the People's Republic of China in 1949, there were approximately 700,000 Protestants in China. Even with the communist government's official policy of atheism and the harsh suppression of religion during the Cultural Revolution, since 1978 there has been a quiet resurgence of Protestantism in China. Official estimates place the number of registered Protestants in China at 15 million, and some church groups estimate that there are more than 50 million unregistered Protestants. In addition to 5 million registered Catholics, the Vatican estimates that there are another 7 million unregistered Catholics. These numbers will come as a surprise to many in

22. *Id.* at 18–19 (quoting Administrative Court case no. 18354/58 (29 January 2008)).

23. Adapted from W. Cole Durham and Brett G. Scharffs, Foreword, in Kim-Kwong Chan and Eric R. Carlson, *Religious Freedom in China: Policy, Administration, and Regulation: A Research Handbook* (2005).

the West, who remain under the impression that religion is absolutely suppressed in China. . . .

In a widely distributed statement of China's policy toward religion, in 2002 Ye Xiaowen stated: "In China, the state treats all religions equally and the law protects the equal rights of all religions. While stressing the protection of the freedom to believe in religions, the law also provides for protection of the freedom not to believe in religions. All are equal before the law. Citizens enjoy the right to religious freedom." This statement would seem to be significantly different from many outsider views about the status of religious freedom in China.

There are several keys to understanding Mr. Ye's assertions. First, as noted above, there are only five "religions" recognized in China–Buddhism, Taoism, Islam, Catholicism, and Protestantism—and there is an official, recognized structure for these religions. Other churches or religions are not considered "religions" but rather "evil cults" not entitled to legal recognition or protection. Second, the five recognized "religions" are independent of their foreign counterpart organizations and subject to a degree of oversight and supervision by the Communist Party. Thus "unregistered" or "underground" churches are not considered religions at all, and equal treatment and equal rights apply only to the five officially recognized religious groups.

2. Registration Developments[24]

Not unlike the histories of religion in other regions, the history of religion in China is comprised of a patchwork of timelines of both benevolence and sordid blunders. As in Europe, many of the religious philosophies that have flourished in China are not native to China. However, to draw similar conclusions about Chinese attitudes towards religion by comparing China with other regions would be a mistake. Perhaps most influential in the development of PRC [People's Republic of China] and CPC [Communist Party of China] policy has been the history of religion in China during the 150-year period immediately preceding the ascension of the Communist Party. During this time, organized religious societies have been influential factors in civil wars, rebellions, corrupt principles, the spread of foreign influence, and the decline of Chinese traditions and culture. When these factors are combined with Communist ideology on religion, there is little wonder that the CPC's initial policies were unfavorable and intolerant of organized religious groups and, at times, even of unorganized religious practice. During its sixty-year history, PRC and CPC policy has vacillated between attempts to control religious organizations and attempts to eradicate religion from the lives of Chinese citizens. . . .

[In 1982] the PRC adopted a new constitution. Included in the new constitution was Article 36, which purports to guarantee religious freedoms for citizens of the PRC. This provision states that citizens enjoy the freedom to either believe in or not believe in religion; however, the practice of religion is limited to

24. Taken from A Broken System: Failures of the Religious Regulatory System in the People's Republic of China, 2014 *BYU L. Rev.* 733 (2014), from work of Liu Peng, Brett G. Scharffs, and Carl Hollan, http://digitalcommons.law.byu.edu/lawreview/vol2014/iss3/11 (notes generally omitted).

the practice of "normal religious activities." "Normal religious activities" are not defined in the constitution; therefore, the normalcy of religious activity has been defined by UFWD [United Front Work Department] policy and RAB [the Religious Affairs Bureau] administration. Moreover, the constitution reaffirms the ideals of the three-self movement for religious organizations.

This regulatory framework ultimately led to the development of China's current unique religious market. Scholar Fenggang Yang offers a useful model for understanding this situation,[25] describing religious organizations as belonging to one of three separate markets: the red market, which consists of religious organizations aligned with the CPC-sponsored patriotic religious associations; the black market, which consists of religious organizations that the PRC government has officially banned; and the gray market, which consists of religious organizations that are not aligned with the patriotic religious associations, but not officially banned, or religious organizations aligned with patriotic religious associations acting outside legal boundaries. . . .

While the structure of the religious regulatory system in China has seen little change since the early 1980s, the policies surrounding religion have changed dramatically. In the 1980s, following the beginning of the collapse of the Soviet Union in eastern Europe, CPC leaders became increasingly worried about "antirevolutionary activities that are undertaken under the cloak of religion," and foreigners and destabilizing groups "us[ing] religion to turn [their] young people against [them]."[26] Unfortunately for the CPC leaders who sought to tighten the controls of the UFWD and the State Administration for Religious Affairs (SARA) over these potentially subversive organizations, one of the major effects of the Cultural Revolution was that religious organizations were driven underground. In response, CPC officials vacillated between liberal allowances of religious freedom and tightened policies to gain the loyalty of underground religious groups, to appease Western demands, and to ensure control over religious groups. The UFWD and RAB also approved the creation of several new Official Religious Associations, raising the total number of Party-approved religious associations to eight.

Along with the policy reforms of the 1980s came an explosion in religious membership, particularly in Catholic and Protestant membership. The PRC estimated that there were approximately three million Catholics and three million Protestants in China in 1982. By 1994, the number of Catholics in China had increased to over twelve million, with membership split between the official Patriotic Religious Association and underground Catholic churches. Protestant church membership saw a later but steady rise in membership, increasing to six million in 1993, to ten million in 1997, and to over fourteen million in 2004. Much to the disappointment of UFWD and RAB officials, a large percentage of these new religious members joined churches led by religious clergy who had been imprisoned during the Cultural Revolution, who were released during the

25. *See* Fenggang Yang, The Red, Black, and Gray Markets of Religion in China, 47 *Soc. Q.* 93 (2006).

26. Beatrice K. F. Leung, Catholic Bridging Efforts with China, 28 *Religion, St. & Soc'y* 185, 186 (2010).

era of reform, and who ignored CPC directives and chose to operate within the "gray market".

In response to increased worries by CPC leadership about the growth of religious groups and their potential to harbor subversive elements that might undermine CPC control, restrictions on religious freedom saw a general increase throughout the early 1990s. The main thrust of these regulations was to crack down on unofficial religious organizations and to encourage the patriotic religious associations to further "adapt to the socialist regime." Official clergymen were targeted by the Party and State and were sent to RAB conferences for indoctrination seminars, while unofficial clergy were arrested. Jiang Zemin, then the CPC and PRC leader, explained to the UFWD what this adaptation to the socialist regime would entail: "This type of adaptation does not require religious adherents to abandon theism and religious beliefs. . . . [Rather,] [t]hey should alter those religious systems and doctrines which do not go along with socialism . . . ." During this same period there were periodic crackdowns against Buddhists in Tibet and Muslims in Xinjiang, which the PRC government said were instigated by "religious activities [that] threatened national security."

QUESTION

How do the religious association laws and practices of China fare in light of international standards?

CHAPTER 12

FINANCIAL RELATIONSHIPS BETWEEN RELIGION AND STATE

I. INTRODUCTION

There are significant differences around the world in approaches to state funding of religion. To some extent, the United States' constitutional prohibition on an establishment of religion and the interpretation of the Establishment Clause as erecting a wall of separation between church and state have resulted in a more stringent financial separation than in many other parts of the world. But this separation has not been as absolute as a casual observer might believe. In this chapter we will discuss both direct aid (Section II) and indirect aid (Section III) to religion by the state. Section IV is a discussion of aid to religiously affiliated social service organizations. Significant additional materials on this topic are included on the Web Supplement.

EUROPEAN AND AMERICAN APPROACHES TO STATE FINANCIAL SUPPORT FOR RELIGION [1]

While Americans and Europeans share broad consensus on the importance of the rights of individuals and groups to freedom of religion, it has generally been assumed that the separation of religion and state called for by the American Establishment Clause makes American experience largely irrelevant in the European context, where established churches continue to exist or where strong cooperation between church and state (including financial support for religious institutions) prevail. In fact, the United States has a complex and varied history of thought and opinion regarding state support of religion, and while this history imposes much stricter constraints on public financing of religion than is typical in European patterns, many of the background considerations (both at the level of

1. This reading is adapted from W. Cole Durham, Jr. and Christine G. Scott, Public Finance and the Religious Sector in the United States: Expanding Cooperation in a Separationist State, *Il Dirrito Ecclesiastico* 361–362 (2006).

theory and the level of sensitivity to equal treatment and canons of respect for human dignity in contexts where aid is permissible) have strong parallels.

American approaches to allowing religion to draw in limited degrees on the public fisc is in flux. It appears that the United States Supreme Court is tending towards a neutralist rather than strict separationist approach to the relationship between religion and the government, and to the extent this is the case, there is some convergence with cooperationist approaches in Europe. It is important to note that there is still no long-settled consensus with a judicial history of consistent application.

A few comparisons deserve mention. It is fair to say that the United States system imposes much sharper constraints on public finance flowing to religion than most European countries. Even separationist France allows substantially greater levels of government funding to flow to support of secular aspects of private education and to maintenance and operation of religious structures than would be conceivable in the United States. Nevertheless, even in the United States substantially greater public support flows to religion than typical stereotypes would lead one to believe.

This is not simply a recent development. Rather, a variety of indirect forms of support for religion have existed throughout American history, although these forms of assistance have typically taken the form of indirect assistance rather than direct subsidy. Religious property and revenues have been exempt from taxation throughout American history. From the very beginning of modern Establishment Clause law after World War II, aid going to demonstrably secular activities (such as providing transportation for students) and objects (such as textbooks) was permissible, particularly when it was clear that the aid was going to parents and children, rather than directly to religious organizations. While the precise scope of aid that is permissible may differ considerably in European countries from what is allowed in the United States, the question of the extent to which it is better to provide aid through direct or indirect channels remains an issue that both systems must address. By their nature, indirect channels allow individual citizens greater flexibility in steering the benefits in accordance with the dictates of their own conscience, and reduce the likelihood that the tax system will support believers only in preferred communities. While different church-state systems address these issues in different ways, our sense is that in the more sensitive cooperationist regimes, things are structured to maximize individual steering of support (e.g., through check-off systems) and through channeling tax contributions from the citizen to his or her religious community (e.g., German church tax channels that withhold funds to the taxpayer's church).

Another commonality is that the countries of Europe and the United States are attempting to apply Enlightenment ideals of religious freedom and equality in the context of modern welfare states, while remaining sensitive to their own historical traditions . . . . It is worth noting that the Enlightenment ideals have had rather different historical resonances in the United States and Europe. Most notably, the idea of separation of church and state was an Enlightenment solution to problems of religious intolerance and persecution, and was intended as an institutional means to promote religious freedom. However, separation took a much more hostile form in Europe, where it was part of a revolt against very powerful organized religion. In contrast, while there have been elements of French-style separation, the idea of separation in the United States has typically been understood as something that was friendly to and protective of religious communities. The ideal of separation is not implemented in as thoroughgoing a way in Europe, particularly when funding is involved, but Europe has a long tradition of understanding and respecting the significance of religious autonomy, and this is what American separationism was fundamentally about.

A final area worth highlighting is the shift to neutralist perspectives. This has been very much in evidence in recent American cases, and it is also very much at the center of the case law of the European Court of Human Rights. In the modern welfare state, our baselines for evaluating equality and neutrality have shifted. In an earlier day, when state institutions were much smaller, it was natural to assume, almost without thinking, that the easiest way to treat religious and non-religious organizations equally was to proscribe financial aid to all religious groups. In the United States, at least, from early in the 19th century, official state religions were disestablished. Aid to any particular religion automatically led to criticism and political conflict, and it was simply easier to insist on a no-aid philosophy. The baseline was absence of government activity, and any government aid seemed to lead to problems.

With the advent of the social welfare state, the situation has changed. The government carries out a host of social programs, from education to health care, to care for the elderly, and so forth. Often, such programs are carried out most effectively by private organizations. In this world, allowing any secular organization to apply for funding to carry out a secular program that the government wanted to support, while forbidding religious organizations to apply or to receive aid for identical programs, seems discriminatory. Now the baseline is not an assumption of state inaction, but an assumption that certain types of secular programs deserve state support. At least some of these—health care, provision of meals for those in need, and so forth—can be provided by religious as well as secular service providers. Here the point is that by engaging in comparative legal analysis, we are able to see our own baseline assumptions more clearly. Too often, baseline assumptions are invisible premises of our thought. Comparative analysis can sharpen our awareness of not only our express beliefs, but also of our tacit baseline assumptions.

II. DIRECT STATE FINANCIAL AID TO CHURCHES

A. THE UNITED STATES

As noted in Chapters 1 and 2, the history of state aid to religion through taxation was given much of its direction by the outcome in Virginia concerning the proposed bill for religious assessments. If Virginia had enacted the bill to provide financial support to churches, the history of church-state financial relations in the United States might be very different.

THE ESTABLISHMENT CLAUSE PROHIBITION ON DIRECT AID TO CHURCHES [2]

Debates rage over the original purpose and intent of the Framers in adopting the religion clauses. Echoing Father Thomas Curry, Professor Frederick Gedicks has noted that in the founding era, an "establishment of religion" was understood to "refer to a church which the government funded and controlled and in which it coerced participation, like the Church of England in the British Empire, or the Roman Catholic Church in southern Europe." It appears that there were three primary concerns that drove the adoption of the Establishment Clause. The first was concern about the church exercising the coercive power of government, including the power to enforce criminal laws that reflected the church's denominational and moral requirements. The second was direct financial support of the church in aid of its worship, rituals, and other denominational activities, through general tax revenue. The third was control by the state over the church, particularly in its definition of doctrine and selection of leaders.

Concern for the autonomy both of the church and of the state is at the heart of each of these three concerns. If churches perform governmental functions, the autonomy of the state is threatened; if the state funds churches, the autonomy of churches is threatened, and the autonomy of the state may be jeopardized as well if a powerful church receives all or a predominant share of state funding; and if the state controls church doctrine, the autonomy of the state is undermined. Indeed, it is scarcely an overstatement to say that the primary purpose underlying the Establishment Clause and Free Exercise Clause of the First Amendment is the preservation of autonomy—of the state, of religious institutions, and of individuals. This purpose, however, has often gone unrecognized and has been obscured by doctrinal constructions utilized by the Supreme Court. As a result, jurisprudence under the religion clauses is fragmented and inconsistent. In general, however, it is clear that the Establishment Clause prohibits the United States from having a state church, and it prohibits direct aid from government to churches.[3]

The distinction between direct and indirect aid, however, is not always clear, and as the debate about "charitable choice" illustrates, separationist and accommodationist viewpoints diverge sharply upon the permissibility of allowing religiously affiliated organizations to participate in such programs. As will be discussed in greater detail below, allowing parochial schools to benefit from tuition voucher programs, allowing church-affiliated entities to qualify for state funding grants for social service programs, and allowing scholarships to be used by students studying for the clergy are examples of state aid to religion that might be viewed as jeopardizing the independence of churches.

---

2. Adapted from Brett G. Scharffs, The Autonomy of Church and State, 2004 *BYU L. Rev.* 1217, 1231–1232, 1262 (2004).

3. *See Everson v. Board of Education*, 330 US 1, 15 (1947) ("Neither a state nor the Federal Government can set up a church. Neither can pass laws which aid one religion, aid all religions, or prefer one religion over another.").

B. EUROPE

1. Religion and State Relationships in Europe

As noted in Chapter 3, the treaties establishing the European Union contemplate the possibility of countries of the Union having a state church. Declaration 11 of the final act of the Treaty of Amsterdam (1997) states, "The European Union respects and does not prejudice the status under national law of churches and religious associations or communities in the Member States. The European Union equally respects the status of philosophical and non-confessional organizations." The principle that religion and state relationships is not a European matter is re-affirmed in Article 17 of the Treaty on the Functioning of the EU (TFEU) introduced by the Treaty of Lisbon (2009), which provides a legal basis for an open, transparent and regular dialogue between the EU institutions and churches, religious associations, and philosophical and non-confessional organizations. (See Chapter 3, Section 3B, and full text documents on the Web Supplement.)

Much like the original United States Constitution, these provisions are concerned with preventing unified establishment, not establishment by individual states. They have been underscored in the dialogue and work of ongoing high-level conferences convened by the European Parliament each year, which are open to all dialogue partners and bring to the table "topical and relevant themes connected with ongoing parliamentary work and debate in these matters."[4] During one such meeting in 2017, the EU vice president was tasked with responsibility for implementing Article 17 dialogue, assisted by the secretariat of the Bureau and other relevant services of Parliament.

2. State Funding of an Established Church

In *Darby v. Sweden*, App. No. 15581/85 (ECtHR, 23 October 1990), both the European Commission and the European Court of Human Rights confirmed that the state of Sweden could directly collect taxes for an established church without violating the European Convention. The Commission also held that in order for an individual to be exempt from such a tax, the state can require that person to notify the state that she has changed religious affiliation.

Sweden is not alone in the adoption of such an arrangement. A number of state churches receive state funding in Europe, including the Orthodox Church in Greece and Finland, the Church of England, the Lutheran Church in Denmark and Finland. According to Belgian scholar Rik Torfs,

> In general, there is a tendency to weaken the ties between the state and its official religion. Already long ago the church of Wales has been disestablished as happened to the church of Sweden in the year 2000. In any case, even if some churches do remain state churches, the consequences of that principle are less relevant today than they used to be in the past. For instance, the mere existence of an official church does not prohibit other churches from enjoying religious freedom. Conversely, quite often an official

4. *See* The European Parliament, Dialogue with religious and non-confessional organisations Article 17 TFEU, http://www.europarl.europa.eu/at-your-service/en/be-heard/religious-and-non-confessional-dialogue.

status does not lead to financial support, as is the case for the Church of England that is entitled to perform certain acts relevant in the public sphere, and finds itself paid for it. At the same time the Church of England does not receive any financial support without having delivered a concrete service.[5]

In many European countries, financial support is given to religious groups without these groups enjoying an official status as a national religion or anything comparable. This is the case in countries like Romania, Austria, Belgium, or Luxembourg. What increasingly does matter is the development of, sometimes official, sometimes informal criteria leading to church financing. Two grounds seem to be more acceptable than others, namely statistics and history. It is logical that large religious groups qualify more easily for financial state support than smaller denominations do. However, measuring exactly the statistical strength of a religious group remains hazardous, as in many countries census is not authorized. In that hypothesis, the state has to rely upon information offered by religious groups themselves as far as membership statistics are concerned. It goes without saying that errors or even some forms of manipulation are not excluded.

Next to statistics, history can be a good financing criterion. But then again, one should be nuanced in using historical roots as an instrument for possible distinction between religious groups. In the past, history led to a radical preference for the historical majorities, very often at the expense of smaller religious groups. More than once the latter were not just deprived of financial support, but also of basic religious freedom. Today, history can be helpful in the opposite way. It may become a tool in improving the legal status of minority religious groups. To put it another way, in a more modern approach, history sustains the position of the weak, more than it petrifies the privileged status of the majoritarian religious group. Two examples can illustrate this thesis.

The first is the situation of the Orthodox Church in Finland. Statistically its importance is far from being spectacular. The Orthodox Church has a membership number that can be situated around one percent of the nation's population. And yet, together with the Lutheran church, the Orthodox Church is an official state religion. Just relying upon statistics, this approach cannot be understood. So there is another reason explaining the position of the Orthodox Church. The history of Finland finds its origin in Karelia, today situated in Russia. It is a region with very strong orthodox presence. The privilege enjoyed by the Orthodox Church can be seen as a tribute to the birth and the past of the Finnish nation. History corrects the overwhelming dominance of the current Lutheran majority.

Another, very different, example is offered by the presence in the board of the official German broadcasting company of a Jewish member, next to a Catholic and a Protestant. Again, just looking at statistics, one learns that Catholics and Protestants are approximately equally strong in today's Germany, outnumbering by far the tiny Jewish minority. Yet, nobody will challenge the Jewish presence on this board, as Jews were the victims of the Nazi regime. Propaganda was a very important instrument of the Hitler regime. In that regard, the Jewish presence is highly understandable. Very similar to the Finnish case, this German dossier offers some form of positive discrimination to minority groups deeply rooted in local history.

---

5. Rik Torfs, Religion and State Relationships in Europe, address at the conference ' Religion and the Rule of Law in Southeast Asia: Continuing the Conversation' (Vietnam, November 3–4, 2007), 1 *Religious Studies Review* 4:31–41 (December 2007), 34, 36–37.

Professor Torfs goes on to identify three trends as significant in Europe:

(1) There is a clear move towards the disestablishment of the established churches. Forms of disestablishment can be found in Wales and Sweden, with clear tendencies in the same direction in Norway. At the same time, in England, more and more decision making power has been attributed to the General Synod of the Church of England.

(2) With regard to the self-determination of religious groups, there is a double tendency. On one hand religions are more autonomous than before, as they are no longer political rivals of the state. In the nineteenth century that rivalry was very explicit. On the other hand, in various countries, including France, Belgium and The Netherlands, there is a trend among secular tribunals to control more thoroughly the coping with internal ecclesiastical procedures. Moreover, a Belgian report of experts published in the fall of 2006 suggest connecting church support with the observance of the principles guiding the democratic state and the rule of law by the churches and religious groups concerned.

(3) Church financing, either direct or indirect, remains a typical feature of European religion and state relationships. However, the underpinning reasons gradually move. Three different eras can be distinguished in the European history of the last centuries. In the early nineteenth century, reasons for church financing included compensation for the nationalization of church goods by the state. At the same time, however, the historical dignity of churches was seen as an element of utmost importance. ... [A] second era started with the growth of the welfare state. Early traces of this phenomenon can be situated immediately after World War I, yet its massive development took place in the late forties of the twentieth century. The welfare state was directed towards cooperation with various players belonging to society as a whole. . . . In the third era, in which we live now, the key word is no longer cooperation, but in the aftermath of 9/11, it is increasingly security. . . . While churches are still welcome to collaborate with the State for the well being of citizens, State authorities sometimes feel some fear towards religious groups. A basis for their financing could be situated in their willingness to accept the democratic state, the rule of law, and the legal order. Churches receive money when they are respectful to the legal context in which they are operating. The evolution is clear. It leads from dignity to cooperation to security. Church financing goes on, but the political assumptions underlying it undergo transformation.[6]

Sweden and Norway have moved away from government establishment of their respective churches. The Swedish disestablishment movement began in 1957, when the Swedish government requested a removal of the church exemption to the Equal Rights Law (in order to effectually create church ordination of women). The proposal was soundly defeated by the church counsel, which viewed it as secular intrusion into a religious matter. This caused an uproar in the government and in general, and the Parliament passed the law anyway, then intimated to the church that refusal to accept the proposal would result in at least removal of the church veto power and likely in church disestablishment and the seizure of church assets by the government. The new proposal passed, albeit with a "conscience clause," which would allow bishops to avoid personally ordaining women, but the connection between church and state was shaken. As the Swedish people became more secular and as the church worked to remove those "orthodoxists" who

6. *Id.* at 39.

refused to appoint women, the government decided to disestablish the church. The church tax, which had once raised £300 million a year for the Church of Sweden, became an optional tax to be paid to any religion of choice by 2000. No doubt for several reasons, millions of members of the church of Sweden have moved to renounce their baptism.

The Norwegian split made a large step in 2012, when an amendment was passed nearly unanimously by the Norwegian Parliament. This amendment has the following results:

1. The Lutheran Church of Norway was renamed The People's Church.
2. Norway will no longer have an official national religion.
3. The government no longer participates in the appointment of bishops and deans.
4. There is no longer be a requirement for parliamentary officials to be members of the Lutheran Church.
1. The following things have not been changed: The church tax remains in place (although a per-member portion goes to humanist organizations and minority faiths).
2. A church office remains in the government, headed up by a minister.

This has been viewed as a victory for secular organizations in Norway, which has a 3 percent church attendance rate. Religiously minded people have claimed that the liberal theology of the Church in recent years is one of the main reasons that society has become so secularized.

COMMENTS AND QUESTIONS

1. Professor Torfs wrestles with a key difficulty at the heart of church-state financial relations in many European countries. How can one justify the differential financial treatment that favors some religious communities over others in many if not most European religion-state systems? He points to two key factors: statistics and history. These clearly explain what is happening, but do they provide satisfactory reasons capable of explaining why the differences do not constitute unjustifiable discrimination?
2. What is the role equality plays in the Establishment Clause?

3. Compelling Non-believers to Pay Church Taxes

In the *Kustannus* case, the European Commission held that a non-believer may be required to pay the proportion of taxes paid to a state church that the church uses for carrying out "secular functions," such as keeping records of births and deaths, performing marriages, and arranging for funerals, even if the non-believer opposes such involvement of the church in secular functions. In addition, a juridical person, such as an LLC, can be required to pay church tax.

Kustannus Oy Vapaa Ajattelija AB and Others v. Finland

European Commission of Human Rights, App. No. 20471/92 (15 April 1996)

The Facts

The first applicant (in English "Publishing Company Freethinker Ltd.") is a limited liability company registered in Helsinki. The second applicant ("The Freethinkers' Association") is the registered umbrella association for the Finnish freethinkers. The third applicant is a Finnish citizen, born in 1957 and resident in Helsinki. He is the manager of the applicant company as well as a member of one of the branches of the applicant association . . . .

A. Particular Circumstances of the Case

. . . According to the applicants, the company was founded in 1982 with the primary aim of publishing and selling books reflecting and promoting the aims of the freethinkers' movement. It was seen as useful and practical to transfer the commercial activities of the association to the company, although this arrangement did not affect the respective tax burden of the two . . . .

'The aim of the association is to promote a scientific view of the world as well as to further the activity of its member associations in their work . . . towards the separation of the two State Churches from the State and the abolition of their position in public law.' . . .

Finland recognises two State Churches, the Evangelical-Lutheran Church and the Orthodox Church of Finland. Approximately 86 per cent of the population belong to the Evangelical-Lutheran Church and about 1 per cent belong to the Orthodox Church of Finland. A physical person who is not a member of any of the two State Churches is registered in the civil population register, since the State Churches administer their own population registers. None of the applicants are members of any of the State Churches . . . .

. . . [Under Finnish law], legal persons and associations became liable to pay 25 per cent in tax on their income (later increased to 28 per cent). 0,84 per cent of these tax revenues were to be passed on to the Evangelical-Lutheran and the Orthodox parishes (0,76 and 0,08 per cent respectively).

. . . The applicant company was ordered to pay income tax [including an] amount which was to be passed on to the parishes . . . [and appealed to the Supreme Administrative Court of Finland], arguing that the part of the income tax which was to be passed on to the Church should not have been imposed [on grounds that included their lack of membership in the State Churches.] . . .

The Supreme Administrative Court . . . rejected the applicant company's appeals. It noted that the company was not a religious community, nor had it been argued that it was a public utility organisation. In the tax returns submitted by the company it had referred to its commercial activities which consisted of the publishing and printing of books. The Court recalled that the 1919 Constitution Act . . . only protected physical persons' freedom of religion. Rendering legal persons liable to pay church tax could not be considered as violating that freedom. Moreover, the levying of church tax on the applicant company neither directly nor indirectly restricted the right under Article 18 para. 1 of the International Covenant on Civil and Political Rights to freedom of thought, conscience and religion . . . .

[I]n regard to the church tax levied for 1990, the Supreme Administrative Court . . . [and] found that the freedom of thought, conscience and religion guaranteed by Article 9 para. 1 of the Convention had not been restricted . . . .

1. The Company's Obligation to Pay Church Taxes or Other Taxes Reserved for Church Activities

. . . [R]eligious freedom as guaranteed by Article 9 is, as held by the Court, primarily a matter of individual conscience (*Kokkinakis v. Greece* . . .). In the Government's view Article 9 cannot therefore be invoked by a company functioning on a commercial basis such as the present applicant company.

. . . The Government [also] submit[s] that the complaint as a whole is manifestly ill-founded, since there was no lack of respect for the right of any of the applicants to freedom of religion. The company's objections to paying the tax at issue cannot be considered as an exercise of its religious freedom. The Government furthermore recall that the Commission has not objected to a State Church system as such (*Darby v. Sweden* . . .). In Finland various tax revenues cover 75 per cent of the parishes' expenses. The parishes are responsible for carrying out many tasks which benefit the Finnish society as a whole, including persons who do not belong to a State Church. They are, for instance, responsible for the burial of practically every deceased (98 per cent). They maintain most cemeteries, keep population registers and maintain historically valuable buildings. Finally, in cooperation with volunteers the parishes also provide welfare services to any needy person, including non-members of a State Church.

In this connection the Government also recalls that under Article 1 of Protocol No. 1 the Contracting States are entitled to enforce such laws as they deem necessary to control the use of property to secure the payment of taxes. It follows that the Finnish State must be free to make use of tax income for purposes which the applicants may object to . . . .

The applicants contend that they may all claim to be victims within the meaning of Article 25 of the Convention, since the church tax levied on the applicant company violated their respective right to freedom of religion within the meaning of Article 9 para. 1. Finnish law does not require that a limited liability company should be established and run for the purpose of making a profit or that it should otherwise be of a commercial character. A corporate body may therefore also serve religious or philosophical purposes. Although the applicant company carries out certain modest economic activities, it does not aim at producing profit but at having the Church separated from the State. It was a form of organisation chosen for practical reasons, its aim being to further the ideals of the freethinkers by acting as an integral part of its Finnish movement . . . . The applicants stress that the company neither was nor could have been established in order to avoid church tax . . . .

The applicants add that the applicant association is undisputedly working for certain philosophical goals. It also constitutes the applicant company's majority shareholder and had a direct interest in the outcome of the taxation proceedings concerning the company . . . .

As regards Article 9 of the Convention in isolation, all applicants contend that their "negative freedom of religion" has been violated on account of the church tax levied on the applicant company. Although the non-believers in Finland largely outnumber the members of the second State Church, only other religious denominations and their parishes are exempted from paying church tax. Moreover, this tax is not used for the benefit of non-members of a State Church . . .[and] legal persons and associations liable to pay such tax do not make use of those services and cannot be members of the Church . . . .

[The Decision of the Commission]

(i) The Commission determines, inter alia, only the Applicant company and not the association or Mr. Sundström can claim "victim" status under Article 25 of the European Convention [because the taxes in question were levied exclusively on the applicant company] . . . .

(iii) Turning to the substance of the complaint, the Commission recalls that the first limb of Article 9 para.1 guarantees to "everyone" a general right to freedom of thought, conscience and religion which cannot be restricted (see, e.g., *Darby v. Sweden* . . .). The freedom enshrined in Article 9 is one of the foundations of a "democratic society" within the meaning of the Convention and is, among other characteristics, a precious asset for atheists, agnostics, sceptics and the unconcerned . . . .

[T]he Commission has held that a limited liability company, given the fact that it concerns a profit-making corporate body, can neither enjoy nor rely on the rights referred to in Article 9 para. 1 . . . .

The Commission has repeatedly held that a church body or an association with religious and philosophical objects is capable of possessing and exercising the right to freedom of religion, since an application by such a body is in reality lodged on behalf of its members . . . .

In the present case the Government have argued that the applicant company is neither a religious nor a philosophical community but a limited liability company which aims at generating profit for its shareholders . . . . The applicant company, for its part, has contended that it was created principally in order to publish and sell books promoting the aims of the freethinkers and not in order to produce profit. It may therefore enjoy freedom of religion within the meaning of Article 9. A finding to the contrary would effectively limit the freethinkers' possibility of organising themselves with a view to manifesting their beliefs.

. . . The Commission would . . .not exclude that the applicant association is in principle capable of possessing and exercising rights under Article 9 para. 1. However, the complaint now before the Commission merely concerns the obligation of the applicant company to pay taxes reserved for Church activities. The company form may have been a deliberate choice on the part of the applicant association and its branches for the pursuance of part of the freethinkers' activities. Nevertheless, for the purposes of domestic law this applicant was registered as a corporate body with limited liability. As such it is in principle required by domestic law to pay tax as any other corporate body, regardless of the underlying purpose of its activities on account of its links with the applicant association and its branches and irrespective of the final receiver of the tax revenues collected from it. Finally, it has not been shown that the applicant association would have been prevented from pursuing the company's commercial activities in its own name.

The Commission therefore concludes that in the circumstances of the present case the applicant company cannot rely on the rights referred to in Article 9 . . . .

For these reasons, the Commission, by a majority, *Declares the Application Inadmissible.*

C. GERMANY

THE GERMAN TAX COLLECTION SYSTEM FOR FAVORED CHURCHES [7]

As a result of repeated appropriation of church property in the past, churches in Germany now have only a small amount of property. As compensation for this secularization following the *Reichsdeputationshauptschluss* of 1803, a series of government decisions guaranteed funds for the churches. They are guaranteed by Article 138(1) WRV [Weimar Republic Constitution] in conjunction with Article 140 GG [German Basic Law]. This provision also envisages the ending of those payments which are necessarily linked to the payment of compensation; this so far has not been pursued on grounds of impracticality. In addition, other subsidies granted by the State are often related to long-standing claims of the churches; an important example is the fact that the local authorities must discharge their public duty to contribute to the maintenance of church buildings. Likewise, on the basis of contractual terms, there are some obligatory contributions to be made by the State to the church, such as subsidies to the salaries of church officials.

Approximately 80% of the entire church budget, however, is covered by the church tax; guaranteed by Article 137(6) WRV in conjunction with Article 140 GG. On the basis of the civil tax lists, in accordance with the law of the *Länder* [German States], the religious communities that are public corporations are allowed to levy taxes. The large churches have made ample use of this opportunity, but smaller religious communities with the status of public corporation, such as the Jewish communities, have also done so. Only members of the particular church authorized to levy the church tax are obliged to pay. Those desiring to be free of the tax may achieve that result by leaving the church. Withdrawal from the church is effected by de-registering with the proper State officials and simply means that one has according to the State classification, officially ended one's membership of the particular church in question.

A further important source of income for some church institutions is being part of general public funding systems. Church-run hospitals, which in some parts of Germany make up the majority of the available hospital beds, are thus part of the publicly-run financing systems for hospitals, supported mainly by money paid in medical insurance for the number of beds filled. Further, many churches receive allocations from the State for activities in the same way as other publicly funded activities: it is part of the idea of State neutrality that church activities are not to be put in a worse position than that of, say, State funded local athletic clubs.

Churches also receive a certain number of tax exemptions. The church tax and charitable donations to the church may be deducted from income tax; this applies equally to donations to non-profit organizations. Churches are also not required to pay certain taxes and duties.

---

7. Excerpted from Gerhard Robbers, State and Church in Germany, in *State and Church in the European Union* 89–90 (2d ed., Gerhard Robbers, ed., Nomos 2005).

COMMENTS AND QUESTIONS

1. How characteristic are the payments that continue to flow from the *Reichsdeputationshauptschluss*—that is, payments that constitute compensation for past takings of religious property? This is analogous to paying rent on property. In Germany, for example, the German churches owned 40 percent of German land prior to the expropriation of church property. Thus, the payments were in exchange for government use of this land. The general question is, to what extent do states owe churches compensation for past wrongs done, and how long should such compensation payments go on? One payment? Two hundred years? Forever? To what extent is this really a standard feature rather than a transitional feature of regimes? Can the persistence of "upper-tier" systems be rationalized as a kind of long-term "payment for services"?
2. Because of the income tax collected by the government for the churches in an agreement-taxation system such as Germany (where the rate is 8-9% of tax liability), voluntary personal contributions tend to be very low to supported churches in states with agreement-taxation schemes. Taxpayers seem to feel that since they have already been required to contribute to the church through tax, their duty is done and there is no need to voluntarily give more. This can make transitioning away from an agreement-taxation scheme very difficult.

   Another set of challenges arise when a state moves from a monopolistic church regime to a more tolerant pluralistic society. In attempting to equalize state support, does the state bring the funding of the dominant church down to the level of other groups, or bring the funding of other groups up to the level of the dominant church? If the latter, then smaller, more obscure churches are often left out in the cold, so to speak, because legislatures seldom care enough about those churches to stretch the funds from the 8-9 percent tax to include them in funding. Note that smaller groups may prefer a voluntary contribution system rather than a state-collected contribution, but they may also not be eligible for tax exemptions or tax deductions in a system designed with the large churches in mind.

   Finally, funding churches constitutes a tremendous expenditure for governments that do so. As a result, most states face pressures not to fund churches. The difficulty of withdrawing support, however, is that if churches have come to rely on substantial support from the government, withdrawal looks like an attack on religion even though it may not be. Dependence on existing finance schemes creates significant inertia that impedes transition toward more separationist or egalitarian structures.

   According to Robbers, The two largest churches in Germany (Roman Catholic and Evangelical) receive about 8-9 billion euros (10-12 billion dollars) per year in state funding.
3. While there are historical reasons that help explain the German church-tax system, which was created to help secularize the state, among other things, is it likely to be an appealing model for a state today? [8]

8. *See, e.g.*, David Pocklington, "Pay, Pray and Obey" meets Church and State: the Church Tax and the German Courts, *Law & Religion UK*, 26 September 2012. For how recent changes in the

D. ITALY

THE FINANCIAL RELATIONSHIP OF CHURCH AND STATE IN ITALY[9]

[In Italy], [f]or centuries the livelihood of the clergy was secured by the beneficium (benefice), an amount of property connected to the office exercised by each clergyman. This system secured a certain degree of economic independence, as each clergyman could directly administer the returns on his own beneficium; however it caused great disparities between the holders of rich and poor beneficia. If the returns of a benefice were excessively low, the State supplemented it by paying a sum of money called the "supplemento di congrua" ("supplement of adequacy," because it was meant to secure an "adequate" living by supplementing the returns of the benefice). As this money was part of the general State budget consisting of the taxes paid by all citizens, this arrangement meant that all citizens automatically contributed towards the payment of Catholic clergy, even if they were of no declared religious persuasion or belonged to another religion.

The agreement on Church entities and property reached between the Italian State and the Catholic Church in 1984 was given effect by Law No. 222 of 20 May 1985. Benefices were abolished and their property transferred to newly established bodies, the diocesan institutes for the support of the clergy. These are to provide for the financial support of the clergymen in office in each diocese. Directly afterwards a central institute for the support of the clergy was founded which is to supplement the financial resources of those diocesan institutes that cannot deal with their tasks on their own. Through this reform, the Catholic clergy has been transformed into a stipendiary clergy, according to a model already in operation in the Church of England. This is supposed to secure a substantial equalization of payment between all clergymen, even at the risk of restricting their economic freedom. The abolition of benefices has also caused the end of the *supplementi di congrua* paid by the State. In its place two systems of financing have been established, benefiting not only the Catholic Church, but also the other denominations which have signed an agreement. The first type concerns a quota of 0.8% of the revenue from IRPEF (*imposta sul reclclito dellepersone fisiche*—income tax), which is paid annually by all Italians liable to taxation who earn more than a certain minimum income. In his or her income tax declaration the person liable to taxation can, by ticking the respective box, determine who is to benefit:

a) the Italian State for extraordinary measures against famine in the world, natural disasters, aid to refugees, the conservation of cultural monuments;

b) the Catholic Church, for the worship needs of the population, the support of the clergy, welfare measures benefiting the national community or third world countries;

c) one of the denominations which have signed an agreement with the Italian State; this declaration is subject to the special conditions explained below.

German Tax Code have impacted religious believers, *see, e.g.*, Chase Gummer, In Germany, Many Believers Balk at Tweak to Church Tax, *The Wall Street Journal*, 2 September 2014.

9. Excerpt from Silvio Ferrari, State and Church in Italy, in *State and Church in the European Union* 221–224 (2d ed., Gerhard Robbers, ed., Nomos 2005).

The quota of 0.8% is distributed on the basis of the declarations [tax returns] of the persons liable to taxation. The percentage which equals the proportion of persons who have not declared their preference is distributed among the different recipients in proportion to the choice made by the rest of the population liable to income tax. The data available . . . [for 1997] show the following distribution: 40% of taxed persons have made a choice, and 81% of these (which roughly equals 32% of all persons liable to income tax) have opted in favor of the Catholic Church, whereas 15% preferred the Italian State and the remaining 4% are divided among the Seventh-day Adventists, the Assemblies of God (Pentecostals), the Valdensians, the Lutherans and the Union of Jewish Communities. Of the sums thus attributed to the Italian Conference of Bishops, 35% were used for the maintenance of the clergy, about 20% for welfare measures and the remainder (about 45%) for purposes of worship for the benefit of the population.

The second type of financing, also created by agreement for members of the Catholic Church as well as of other denominations, is the possibility of off-setting donations from taxable income up to Euro 1,032.91 to the Central Institute for the Support of the Clergy or similar institutions of other denominations.

. . . [T]he two channels of funding just described are also open to the six denominations which have signed an agreement with the Italian State. [But some churches either decline to take part in the program or donate the tax to humanitarian projects, preferring to fund themselves through voluntary contributions.]

Scattered amongst various other legal provisions are additional forms of direct or indirect funding of the denominations. For instance, the regional laws which allocate lots and parcels of land for the erection of Church buildings, and Law No. 390 of 1986, which facilitates the loan or hire of State real property to Church bodies with only minimal rental payments. In both cases it is uncertain whether these provisions apply to only the Catholic Church and the denominations with an agreement or to all denominations.

There is no doubt that the present system of financing, which follows the Spanish model, is a step forward compared with the situation in Italy before 1984. It is in certain respects preferable to the systems in other European countries, which are characterized by inflexible mechanisms that may sometimes come into conflict with fundamental rights of religious freedom. However, in addition to the distribution of the quota of IRPEF pertaining to persons who have not declared their preference, there are certain fundamental characteristics of the present provisions which may present problems, in particular, the precondition for access to the two main channels of finance (0.8% IRPEF and donation deductible from taxable income) is the setting up of a concordat or an agreement with the Italian State. This means that many denominations are excluded from all forms of state funding, either because they cannot or do not want to come to such an agreement, or because their application has been rejected by the State which, according to the most recent view of the matter, enjoys a large discretionary power freedom in the making of this decision. In the area of taxation the denominations enjoy numerous privileges. As, however, the legal provision is particularly fragmentary, only the basic principles of the system may be mentioned here. The legal basis is, as already noted, the equal treatment of the religious aims and those of worship of the Church entities with those of welfare and education. This equal treatment is provided for the Catholic Church bodies in Article 7(3) of the Agreement of Villa Madama and for the other denominations by Article 12 of the Royal Decree of 28 February 1930, which was passed for the implementation of Law No. 1159 of 1929. The same provision is contained, in more or less unaltered form, in the text of the agreements between the State and some denominations. Because of this equal treatment the Church entities enjoy numerous advantages, for instance a rebate of 50% on corporation tax (*imposta sul reddito delle persone giuridiche*, IRPEG), and exemption from inheritance and donation tax. Further exemptions concern value added tax (*imposta sul valore aggiunto*, IVA), local land transfer tax (*imposta comunale sull'incremento di valore dei beni immobili*) and other indirect taxation.

Finally it must be noted that such real property of the Holy See as is located on Italian territory (Articles 13 and 14 of the Lateran Treaty) as well as the other real property named in Articles 13 and 14 of that Treaty is exempt from any kind of tax or duty toward the State or other public entities.

COMMENTS AND QUESTIONS

1. France has had separated the institutions of church and state since 1905. This includes a prohibition on funding for religious groups. The state does, however, pay for religiously-oriented private schools (1959), the upkeep of French cathedrals, military chaplains and various projects with religious origins. France also plays a role in appointing Catholic bishops. Is this really separation, or is it government control disguised as separation?
2. Consider the European Court of Human Rights case *Association Les Témoins de Jehovah v. France,* App. No. 8916/05 (30 June 2011). The French Government attempted to impose a tax on "hand-to-hand gifts" received by one of the national governing bodies of the Jehovah's Witnesses. The Court ruled that imposing such a tax violated the European Convention, as such gifts are an important source of funding and the Association was not able to foresee, to a reasonable extent, the consequences that could result from the act of receiving contributions and submitting its accounting records to the tax authorities. Consequently the interference was not prescribed by law within the meaning of Article 9 § 2 of the European Convention.
3. Spain uses a checkoff system that is similar in many respects to Italy's. What are the advantages and disadvantages vis-à-vis the German church tax system? The original plan in Spain was for the checkoff system ultimately to replace direct state funding of the Catholic Church, but to fund the difference between past subsidies and initial yield from the checkoff system with gap-filling subsidies. In fact, the gap-filling subsidies have continued. Is this like the ongoing payments in Germany that go back to Napoleonic times? In Hungary, when a similar move to a checkoff system was being proposed, it was opposed by the Catholic Church because it meant changing allocations based on percentage of Catholic population to checkoffs, reflecting actual decisions of Catholic members to allocate their "checkoff amounts" to the Catholic Church.
4. In Norway, the government allocates religious subsidies from amounts established in national and municipal budgets to religions and other life stance communities on a per capita basis. The Church of Norway obviously receives the largest amount of support from this system, because a high percentage of Norwegian citizens still have at least nominal affiliation with that church. But

other religious or life stance communities are treated equally in the sense that they get a similar pro rata share. Secular life stance communities have to meet a higher numerical threshold than religious communities (500 as opposed to fewer than 10) to be eligible for allocations.

5. Which system—tax deduction of contributions, tax credit for contributions, church tax, checkoff allocations (with proportional allocations of those who make no checkoff in accordance with those who do, as in Italy), checkoff systems with explicit charitable alternatives, or the Norwegian per capita approach—best promotes the principle of "channeling," according to which religious support is channeled to (and only to) the religion or belief of the individual from whom revenues are appropriated?

E. JAPAN

THE YASUKUNI SHRINE CONTROVERSY

The Yasukuni Shrine is uniquely important among Shinto shrines. The Shrine is dedicated to all the Japanese war dead and provides a list of approximately 2.6 million names of individuals who have died for the Empire, in combat or otherwise. The Shrine is controversial because among those 2.6 million names are about 1,000 war criminals, including such individuals as Tojo, a Class A war criminal in World War II, convicted and executed for crimes against humanity. The practice of honoring the war dead—including war criminals—is widely condemned by nations that have been subject to Japanese invasion and rule as well as by other groups in Japan and elsewhere. Because of this controversy, the choice by Japanese prime ministers whether or not to visit the Shrine to pay homage to the war dead and attend the religious ceremonies has become politically significant. A prime minister who chooses not to visit runs the risk of being viewed as capitulating to foreign pressures.

Visits and contributions to the Shrine by government officials have also sparked controversy over the proper relationship between religion and government in Japan. Article 20 of the 1946 Japanese Constitution provides that "[f]reedom of religion is guaranteed to all. No religious organization shall receive any privileges from the State, nor exercise any political authority. No person shall be compelled to take part in any religious act, celebration, rite or practice. The State and its organs shall refrain from religious education or any other religious activity." Article 89 further provides that "[n]o public money or other property shall be expended or appropriated for the use, benefit or maintenance of any religious institution or association, or for any charitable, educational or benevolent enterprises not under the control of public authority."

In the case below, known as the *Yasukuni Shrine Case*, the Supreme Court of Japan addressed the constitutionality of financial contributions by the government to the Yasukuni Shrine and other shrines. The case describes several classifications of contributions, including *tamagushiryo*, which refers to money to purchase the sprig of a sacred tree for use in Shinto ceremonies; *kentoryo*, which is money used to purchase a votive lantern for use in such ceremonies; and *kumotsuryo*, which is a more general offering of money.

Anzai v. Shiraishi (Yasukuni Shrine Case)

Supreme Court, Grand Bench, 2 April 1997

1. The Facts and Judicial History

[Various appellees had contributed funds as *tamagushiryo*, *knetoryo*, or *kuotsuryo* to the Yasukuni and Gokoku shrines for various ceremonies they held. The District Court decided that these expenditures were unconstitutional because they must be regarded as a "religious activity," prohibited under Article 20(3) of the Constitution . . . . The High Court judgment, on the contrary, said that the expenditure in this case violated neither Article 20(3) nor Article 89 of the Constitution, because it did not support, promote or, conversely, oppose or interfere with other religions . . . . The case was then appealed to the Supreme Court.]

The ruling of the High Court cannot be accepted. The reasons are as follows:

(1) The Principle of Separation of State and Religion and the State Acts Prohibited under Articles 20(3) and 89 of the Constitution

The Constitution has several provisions, such as the latter part of Article 20(1), Article 20(3), and Article 89, that refer to what is called the principle of separation of state and religion.

Generally, the principle of separation of state and religion has been understood to mean that the state, which includes local government in this judgment, is not to interfere with religion and that it should have a secular nature and religious neutrality . . . . The present Constitution has newly provided for the unconditional freedom of religion and, in order to secure its guarantee further, established the principle of separation of state and religion. Historically, several religions have developed pluralistically in Japan. In these circumstances an unconditional guarantee of religious freedom alone has not been enough to guarantee fully the freedom of religion. So as to eliminate all ties between the state and religion, it has also been necessary to enact rules providing for the separation of state and religion. Thus, the Constitution should be interpreted as striving for a secular and religiously neutral state by regarding the total separation of state and religion as its ideal.

However, originally the provision of the separation of state and religion is only an institutional and indirect guarantee of the freedom of religion. It does not guarantee freedom of religion directly, but it attempts to guarantee it indirectly by securing a system that separates state and religion. Moreover, the state unavoidably connects with religion when the state regulates social life or implements various policies to promote or subsidize education, social welfare, or culture. Thus, an actual system of government that attempts a total separation of state and religion is virtually . . .impossible. Furthermore, to attempt total separation would inevitably lead to unreasonable situations in society. Thus, it follows that there are inevitable and natural limits to the separation of state and religion. So when the principle of separation of state and religion is actually established as a state system, a state must accept some degree of actual relationship with religion according to its own social and cultural characteristics. Therefore, under these premises, the remaining question must be to what extent such a relationship will be tolerated under the basic purpose of the principle of guaranteeing freedom of religion. From this perspective, the principle of separation of state and religion, which is the basis of the constitutional provision and becomes the guiding principle for interpretation, demands the religious neutrality of the state but does not prohibit all connection with religion. Rather, taking the purposes and effects of the given conducts into consideration, it should be interpreted as prohibiting the state's conducts that are beyond the appropriate limits in light of the social and cultural circumstances of our country.

According to such significance of the principle of separation of state and religion, "religious activity" in Article 20(3) should not be interpreted as prohibiting all religious activities that the state or state authority might be involved in. Rather, only the activities exceeding such reasonable limits, the purpose of which have some religious meaning and the effect of which is to support, promote, or, adversely, oppose or interfere with religion, should be prohibited. And in determining whether a given religious act constitutes a prohibited "religious activity" or not, not only the external aspects of the conduct but also the place of the conduct, the average person's religious understanding toward the conduct, the existence or extent of the actor's religious intention, purpose, or awareness in holding the ceremony, and the effect or influence on the average person should be considered as factors. And at that time, objective judgment based on socially accepted ideas is necessary . . . .

(2) The Illegality of the Expenditure

Then, from these standpoints, the illegality of the offerings in this case should be examined.

(a) . . . It is a judicially noted fact that holding ceremonies are the main religious activities for Shinto, that the main points of the Spring and Autumn Ceremony or Memorial Ceremony are religious rites held according to Shinto tradition, that they are among the most important traditional ceremonies held by each shrine, and that the memorial ceremony has almost the same religious rite and takes place on the largest scale among ceremonies held by Yasukuni Shrine. Moreover, it is clear that each shrine has regarded tamagushiryo, kumotsuryo, and kentoryo as having religious meanings, because tamagushiryo and kumotsuryo are offered to the Shinto god when religious rites are held at the time of the Spring and Autumn Ceremony or memorial ceremony, and because, when kentoryo is offered, lights with the contributors' names are displayed within the precincts of the shrines at the time of the Mitamasai ceremony . . . .

The appellees contended that this expenditure did not violate the Constitution, because it was just a social custom with a secular purpose to mourn for the war dead and to console the bereaved families and an administrative act intended to support the bereaved families . . . . The relationship between a local government and a specific religion cannot be allowed as not exceeding the reasonable limit that the Constitution stipulates, even if not a few local residents wish so. We consider that it is possible to mourn for the war dead and to console the bereaved families without such a special relationship with a specific religion. Moreover, as we mentioned above, we do not consider that the offering of tamagushiryo to a shrine's ceremonies has become a social courtesy . . . .

Based on the above consideration, it is reasonable to assume that these offerings by a local government to Yasukuni Shrine or Gokoku Shrine, as mentioned above, constitute prohibited religious activities under Article 20(3) of the Constitution, because the purpose of the offerings had religious significance and the effect of the offerings led to support or promotion of a specific religion, and the relationship between the local government and Yasukuni Shrine or other shrines caused by these offerings exceeded the reasonable limit under the social and cultural conditions of Japan. Thus, these disbursements were illegal because they were made to religious activities prohibited by the article. The trial court failed to interpret this article.

(2) It is clear that Yasukuni Shrine and Gokoku Shrine are religious organizations as stipulated by Article 89 of the Constitution, and, as mentioned above, it is assumed that these offerings of tamagushiryo to Yasukuni Shrine and Gokoku Shrine resulted in a special relationship between the local government and these shrines that exceeded reasonable limits under the social and cultural conditions of Japan. So the expenditure was in the category of payment of public funds prohibited by this article and illegal. Thus, the trial court also failed to interpret the law concerning this article.

[Appellees' liability to compensate damages omitted]

2. Conclusion

From the above-mentioned, the appellants' claim against appellee Shiraishi should be accepted, and the appellants' claim against the other appellees should be dismissed . . .

[The supplementary opinions of Justice Hiroshi Fukuda concerning part 2 of Section I, and the opinion of Justice Itsuo Sonobe concerning part 2 of Section I have been omitted.]

COMMENTS AND QUESTIONS

1. Twenty years earlier, in *Kakunaga v. Sekiguchi* (the *Tsu City Groundbreaking Ceremony Case*, JSCt, 1977), the Supreme Court of Japan decided a case involving the visit of the Mayor of Tsu, Kakunaga Kiyoshi, to attend the groundbreaking ceremony of a city gymnasium, where a local Shinto priest officiated. In that case, the government paid Shinto priests a little over $20.00 to pronounce a blessing on the forthcoming construction. The state was challenged under the same constitutional provisions raised in the *Yasukuni Shrine Case*. Although this might appear to be a straightforward violation of the constitutional prohibition of using public money for the benefit or maintenance of any religious institution or association, the Supreme Court dismissed the constitutional challenge. The Court maintained that the Shinto ceremony was not religious, and that in any event, based upon a "purpose and effect" test, this was essentially a secularized ritual that did not have religious meaning. These conclusions have been criticized by Japanese law professor Keiko Yamagishi:[10]

   > By defining the ceremony as non-religious, the Court moved a step toward increasing and broadening the scope of permissible ways in which religion and state may mix. Here, it was permissible for a state actor to use public funds . . .for

10. *See* Keiko Yamagishi, Freedom of Religion, Religious Political Participation, and Separation of Religion and State: Legal Considerations from Japan, 2008 *BYU L. Rev.* 919, 931–932.

what was essentially religious—a professional Shinto priest in religious robes and following specific Shinto rituals prepared a particular petition for the ceremony and used particular ceremonial equipment. Moreover, the priest who performed the service did so, one can assume, out of religious conviction and belief. Thus the argument that the ceremony was non-religious seems facially wrong, and it appears that the Supreme Court played a game of semantics in calling the ceremony non-religious.

Although the Court admitted the ceremony had religious overtones, it created a purpose and effect test to determine if the activity was prohibited 'religious activity' for purposes of constitutional analysis. The Court wrote: "Even if the ceremony is performed in the style of an existing religion, as long as it remains within the bounds of well-established and widely-practiced usage, most people would perceive it as a secularized ritual without religious meaning, a social formality that has become customary at the start of construction work."

Scholars have called this line of reasoning the "purpose and effect test." The Court summarized its argument in these terms: "'religious activity' under Article 20, paragraph 3 of the Constitution does not mean all conduct of the State and its organs that is related to religion, but conduct whose purpose has a religious significance and whose effect is to subsidize, promote, or, conversely, suppress or interfere with religion . . . .

The decision in *Kakunaga v. Sekiguchi* has not only diluted the definition by excluding from the category of prohibited state actions what are clearly religious ceremonies, but it has also allowed state support of religious institutions that were specifically targeted by the postwar Constitution."

2. At what point does something that has been religious cease to have religious significance and become wholly cultural? Where is the line that divides the two?
3. Interestingly, the Japanese Supreme Court used what looks essentially like the *Lemon* test as the standard for determining the constitutionality of contributions to the Yasukuni Shrine, reaching a separationist conclusion, while it used a "purpose and effect" test, also facially similar to the *Lemon* test in the *Tsu City Groundbreaking Ceremony Case* to reach an outcome that appears much more accommodationist. What do you make of the use of "purpose and effect" tests in these two cases? How do these cases compare with *Lynch v. Donnelly*, the Christmas crèce case discussed in Chapter 4?

F. TURKEY

The Hybrid of Separation and Control in Religion-State Relations in Turkey

Turkey is unique because, despite an explicitly secular separationist state based upon the French model of *laïcité*, there is quite a high degree of funding by the state of official Islamic organization. This includes support for mosques, Sunni-oriented religious instruction in public schools, payment of the salaries of religious officials, and even prescribing of Friday sermons by imams. According to initial assumptions in American society, any funding of religion or religious activities appears primarily to be a benefit. But funding, quite understandably, and inevitably, carries with it regulation to ensure that it is being spent in accordance with the purposes for which it is appropriated. To what extent does aid "inhibit" as well as "advance" religion? At what point does a "cooperation" regime become a "control" regime?

COMMENTS AND QUESTIONS

In theory, the right to regulate should follow public spending, but sometimes regulatory burdens extend beyond the government assistance provided. In 1984, the US Supreme Court decided *Grove City College v. Bell*, 465 U.S. 555 (1984), a case in which a small college had studiously avoided taking any government grants. In spite of the college's refusal of government funding, it was still subjected to federal Title IX regulations dealing with gender discrimination because of grants its students received from the government and the college lost the case. When a religious organization accepts government funding (and sometimes, even when it does not), it finds it very difficult to argue against the government's authority over where that money goes. To what extent does a religious organization's acceptance of public funding entitle the state to alter or redirect the mission or activities of that organization?

Additional Web Resources:	Materials describing the financial relationship of religion and the state in Turkey

III. INDIRECT STATE AID TO CHURCHES

A. THE UNITED STATES

1. Qualifying for Tax-Exempt Status in the United States (IRS Code §501(c)(3))

To qualify for tax-exempt status and to retain that qualification, religious organizations and other nonprofit organizations must meet a number of qualifications set forth in the Internal Revenue Code. Section 501(a) of the IRC provides that organizations described under §501(c)(3) "shall be exempt from taxation." Section 501(c)(3) is thus the key section defining the qualifications for tax-exempt status, and it provides as follows:

> (3) Corporations, and any community chest, fund, or foundation, organized and operated exclusively for *religious*, charitable, scientific, testing for public safety, literary, or educational purposes, . . . no part of the net earnings of which inures to the benefit of any private shareholder or individual, no substantial part of the activities of which is carrying on propaganda, or otherwise attempting, to influence legislation . . ., and which does not participate in, or intervene in (including the publishing or distributing of statements), any political campaign on behalf of (or in opposition to) any candidate for public office.

In addition to the private inurement, lobbying, and political campaigning constraints, qualification since *Bob Jones University v. United States*, 461 U.S. 574

(1983), requires that the organization's purposes and activities not be illegal or violative of fundamental public policies.

Unlike other tax-exempt organizations, churches are not required to apply for and obtain recognition of their tax-exempt status from the IRS; they are tax-exempt provided they meet the requirements of §501(c)(3). Many churches apply to the IRS for such recognition anyway, to obtain a letter that helps assure donors that their contributions will be tax-deductible. Churches and religious organizations, like other tax-exempt organizations, may engage in business or other income-producing activities unrelated to their tax-exempt purposes, so long as carrying such unrelated business is not the organization's primary purpose. However, the income thus generated is taxed as unrelated business income. To prevent improper entanglement, special procedural protections sharply limit inquiries and audits of churches by the IRS.

Additional Web Resources:	Full provisions of relevant tax law and regulations relevant to religious organizations in the US IRS Tax Guide for Churches and Religious Organizations Materials on extent to which religious organizations can engage in loggying or political campaigning, including challenges to such restraints Materials on procedures limiting audits of churches

2. Tax Exemptions and the Establishment Clause

WALZ V. TAX COMMISSIONER

Supreme Court of the United States, 397 U.S. 664 (1970)

Mr. Chief Justice BURGER delivered the opinion of the Court.

Appellant, owner of real estate in Richmond County, New York, sought an injunction in the New York courts to prevent the New York City Tax Commission from granting property tax exemptions to religious organizations for religious properties used solely for religious worship . . . . The essence of appellant's contention was that the New York City Tax Commission's grant of an exemption to church property indirectly requires the appellant to make a contribution to religious bodies and thereby violates provisions prohibiting establishment of religion under the First Amendment which under the Fourteenth Amendment is binding on the States.

Appellee's motion for summary judgment was granted and the Appellate Division of the New York Supreme Court, and the New York Court of Appeals affirmed. We noted probable jurisdiction . . . and [now] affirm.

I

. . . The Court has struggled to find a neutral course between the two Religion Clauses, both of which are cast in absolute terms, and either of which, if expanded to a logical extreme, would tend to clash with the other . . . .

The course of constitutional neutrality in this area cannot be an absolutely straight line; rigidity could well defeat the basic purpose of these provisions, which is to insure that no religion be sponsored or favored, none commanded, and none inhibited. The general principle deducible from the First Amendment and all that has been said by the Court is this: that we will not tolerate either governmentally established religion or governmental interference with religion. Short of those expressly proscribed governmental acts there is room for play in the joints productive of a benevolent neutrality which will permit religious exercise to exist without sponsorship and without interference.

Each value judgment under the Religion Clauses must therefore turn on whether particular acts in question are intended to establish or interfere with religious beliefs and practices or have the effect of doing so. Adherence to the policy of neutrality that derives from an accommodation of the Establishment and Free Exercise Clauses has prevented the kind of involvement that would tip the balance toward government control of churches or governmental restraint on religious practice . . . .

II

The legislative purpose of the property tax exemption is neither the advancement nor the inhibition of religion; it is neither sponsorship nor hostility. New York, in common with the other States, has determined that certain entities that exist in a harmonious relationship to the community at large, and that foster its "moral or mental improvement," should not be inhibited in their activities by property taxation or the hazard of loss of those properties for nonpayment of taxes. It has not singled out one particular church or religious group or even churches as such; rather, it has granted exemption to all houses of religious worship within a broad class of property owned by nonprofit, quasi-public corporations which include hospitals, libraries, playgrounds, scientific, professional, historical, and patriotic groups. The State has an affirmative policy that considers these groups as beneficial and stabilizing influences in community life and finds this classification useful, desirable, and in the public interest . . . .

Governments have not always been tolerant of religious activity, and hostility toward religion has taken many shapes and forms—economic, political, and sometimes harshly oppressive. Grants of exemption historically reflect the concern of authors of constitutions and statutes as to the latent dangers inherent in the imposition of property taxes; exemption constitutes a reasonable and balanced attempt to guard against those dangers. The limits of permissible state accommodation to religion are by no means co-extensive with the noninterference mandated by the Free Exercise Clause. To equate the two would be to deny a national heritage with roots in the Revolution itself . . . . We cannot read New York's statute as attempting to establish religion; it is simply sparing the exercise of religion from the burden of property taxation levied on private profit institutions.

We find it unnecessary to justify the tax exemption on the social welfare services or "good works" that some churches perform for parishioners and others—family counselling, aid to the elderly and the infirm, and to children . . . . To give emphasis to so variable an aspect of the work of religious bodies would introduce an element of governmental evaluation and standards as to the worth of particular social welfare programs, thus producing a kind of continuing day-to-day relationship which the policy of neutrality seeks to minimize. Hence, the use of a social welfare yardstick as a significant element to qualify for tax exemption could conceivably give rise to confrontations that could escalate to constitutional dimensions.

Determining that the legislative purpose of tax exemption is not aimed at establishing, sponsoring, or supporting religion does not end the inquiry, however. We must also be sure that the end result—the effect—is not an excessive government entanglement with religion. The test is inescapably one of degree. Either course, taxation of churches or exemption, occasions some degree of involvement with religion. Elimination of exemption would tend to expand the involvement of government by giving rise to tax valuation of church property, tax liens, tax foreclosures, and the direct confrontations and conflicts that follow in the train of those legal processes.

The grant of a tax exemption is not sponsorship since the government does not transfer part of its revenue to churches but simply abstains from demanding that the church support the state. No one has ever suggested that tax exemption has converted libraries, art galleries, or hospitals into arms of the state or put employees "on the public payroll." There is no genuine nexus between tax exemption and establishment of religion . . . . The exemption creates only a minimal and remote involvement between church and state and far less than taxation of churches. It restricts the fiscal relationship between church and state, and tends to complement and reinforce the desired separation insulating each from the other.

Separation in this context cannot mean absence of all contact; the complexities of modern life inevitably produce some contact and the fire and police protection received by houses of religious worship are no more than incidental benefits accorded all persons or institutions within a State's boundaries, along with many other exempt organizations. The appellant has not established even an arguable quantitative correlation between the payment of an ad valorem property tax and the receipt of these municipal benefits.

All of the 50 States provide for tax exemption of places of worship, most of them doing so by constitutional guarantees. For so long as federal income taxes have had any potential impact on churches—over 75 years—religious organizations have been expressly exempt from the tax. Such treatment is an "aid" to churches no more and no less in principle than the real estate tax exemption granted by States. Few concepts are more deeply embedded in the fabric of our national life, beginning with pre-Revolutionary colonial times, than for the government to exercise at the very least this kind of benevolent neutrality toward churches and religious exercise generally so long as none was favored over others and none suffered interference.

It is significant that Congress, from its earliest days, has viewed the Religion Clauses of the Constitution as authorizing statutory real estate tax exemption to religious bodies . . . . It is obviously correct that no one acquires a vested or protected right in violation of the Constitution by long use, even when that span of time covers our entire national existence and indeed predates it. Yet an unbroken practice of according the exemption to churches, openly and by affirmative state action, not covertly or by state inaction, is not something to be lightly cast aside. . . .

Nothing in this national attitude toward religious tolerance and two centuries of uninterrupted freedom from taxation has given the remotest sign of leading to an established church or religion and on the contrary it has operated affirmatively to help guarantee the free exercise of all forms of religious belief. Thus, it is hardly useful to suggest that tax exemption is but the "foot in the door" or the "nose of the camel in the tent" leading to an established church. If tax exemption can be seen as this first step toward "establishment" of religion, as Mr. Justice DOUGLAS fears, the second step has been long in coming. Any move that realistically "establishes" a church or tends to do so can be dealt with "while this Court sits." . . .

Affirmed.

Mr. Justice BRENNAN, concurring.

. . . [I]n my view, the history, purpose, and operation of real property tax exemptions for religious organizations must be examined to determine whether the Establishment Clause is breached by such exemptions.

The existence from the beginning of the Nation's life of a practice, such as tax exemptions for religious organizations, is not conclusive of its constitutionality. But such practice is a fact of considerable import in the interpretation of abstract constitutional language. On its face, the Establishment Clause is reasonably susceptible of different interpretations regarding the exemptions. This Court's interpretation of the clause, accordingly, is appropriately influenced by the reading it has received in the practices of the Nation . . . . The more longstanding and widely accepted a practice, the greater its impact upon constitutional interpretation. History is particularly compelling in the present case because of the undeviating acceptance given religious tax exemptions from our earliest days as a Nation. Rarely if ever has this Court considered the constitutionality of a practice for which the historical support is so overwhelming . . . .

Government has two basic secular purposes for granting real property tax exemptions to religious organizations. First, these organizations are exempted because they, among a range of other private, nonprofit organizations contribute to the well-being of the community in a variety of nonreligious ways, and thereby bear burdens that would otherwise either have to be met by general taxation, or be left undone, to the detriment of the community . . . .

Second, government grants exemptions to religious organizations because they uniquely contribute to the pluralism of American society by their religious activities. Government may properly include religious institutions among the variety of private, nonprofit groups that receive tax exemptions, for each group contributes to the diversity of association, viewpoint, and enterprise essential to a vigorous, pluralistic society . . . .

Finally, I do not think that the exemptions "use essentially religious means to serve governmental ends, where secular means would suffice." The means churches use to carry on their public service activities are not "essentially religious" in nature. They are the same means used by any purely secular organization—money, human time and skills, physical facilities. It is true that each church contributes to the pluralism of our society through its purely religious activities, but the state encourages these activities not because it champions religion per se but because it values religion among a variety of private, nonprofit enterprises that contribute to the diversity of the Nation. Viewed in this light, there is no nonreligious substitute for religion as an element in our societal mosaic, just as there is no nonliterary substitute for literary groups . . . .

Mr. Justice DOUGLAS, dissenting.

The question in the case . . . is whether believers—organized in church groups—can be made exempt from real estate taxes, merely because they are believers, while nonbelievers, whether organized or not, must pay the real estate taxes . . . .

In affirming this judgment the Court largely overlooks the revolution initiated by the adoption of the Fourteenth Amendment. That revolution involved the imposition of new and far-reaching constitutional restraints on the States . . . . [T]he revolution occasioned by the Fourteenth Amendment has progressed as Article after Article in the Bill of Rights has been incorporated in it and made applicable to the States.

Hence the question in the present case makes irrelevant the "two centuries of uninterrupted freedom from taxation," referred to by the Court. If history be our guide, then tax exemption of church property in this country is indeed highly suspect, as it arose in the early days when the church was an agency of the state. The question here, though, concerns the meaning of the Establishment Clause and the Free Exercise Clause made applicable to the States for only a few decades at best.

With all due respect the governing principle is not controlled by *Everson v. Board of Education* . . . . *Everson* involved the use of public funds to bus children to parochial as well as to public schools . . . . This case, however, is quite different. Education is not involved. The financial support rendered here is to the church, the place of worship. A tax exemption is a subsidy. Is my Brother BRENNAN correct in saying that we would hold that state or federal grants to churches, say, to construct the edifice itself would be unconstitutional? What is the difference between that kind of subsidy and the present subsidy?

The problem takes us back where Madison was in 1784 and 1785 when he battled the Assessment Bill in Virginia. That bill levied a tax for the support of Christian churches, leaving to each taxpayer the choice as to "what society of christians" he wanted the tax paid; and absent such designation, the tax was to go for education. Even so, Madison was unrelenting in his opposition . . . . [Madison's] Remonstrance covers some aspects of the present subsidy, including Madison's protest . . . to a requirement that any person be compelled to contribute even "three pence" to support a church . . . .

Madison's assault on the Assessment Bill was in fact an assault based on both the concepts of "free exercise" and "establishment" of religion later embodied in the First Amendment. Madison, whom we recently called "the leading architect of the religion clauses of the First Amendment," was indeed their author and chief promoter . . . .

Direct financial aid to churches or tax exemptions to the church *qua* church is not, in my view, even arguably permitted. Sectarian causes are certainly not antipublic and many would rate their own church or perhaps all churches as the highest form of welfare. The difficulty is that sectarian causes must remain in the private domain not subject to public control or subsidy . . . .

The exemptions provided here insofar as welfare projects are concerned may have the ring of neutrality. But subsidies either through direct grant or tax exemption for sectarian causes, whether carried on by church *qua* church or by church *qua* welfare agency, must be treated differently, lest we in time allow the church *qua* church to be on the public payroll, which, I fear, is imminent . . . .

I conclude that this tax exemption is unconstitutional.

COMMENTS AND QUESTIONS

1. *Walz* was decided in 1970, a year before the debut of the *Lemon* test in the 1971 case *Lemon v. Kurtzman.* Are the elements of the *Lemon* test already present in *Walz*? Consider the three prongs. Does the Court discuss secular purpose? What about advancing or inhibiting religion? Does a tax exemption advance or inhibit religion? Does it create or prevent excessive entanglement?
2. Justice Douglas's dissent equates tax exemptions with subsidies. Is this view necessarily correct? For the classic article analyzing this issue, *see* Boris Bittker, Churches, Taxes and the Constitution, 78 *Yale L.J.* 1285 (1969). Tax exemptions are viewed by many economists and by advocates of "tax expenditure theory" as the functional equivalent of a "subsidy." However, in assuming that an exemption is a subsidy (in other words, that tax revenue is being given up by the government because of the exemption), an a priori assumption is made that what is being exempted is part of the tax base (and therefore would have generated tax revenue had the exemption *not* been made). To illustrate, consider a law that imposes a tax on vehicles. Would that law apply to roller skates? A bicycle? Exempting these items from the tax base does not constitute a "subsidy" of roller skating or bicycle riding. That brings us to the question of church property. There really is no a priori way of knowing what is included in the tax base. So how do we determine whether church property should or should not be considered as part of the tax base (and therefore whether an exemption for churches does or does not constitute a subsidy)?

   One means of making such a determination might be to ask, "Who is being benefited by the taxes?" The benefits of real property taxes, typically levied at the state and local levels and typically used to pay for fire and police protection, as mentioned in *Walz*, are arguably enjoyed by the religious community as much as by anyone else. So perhaps the right approach is to define the tax base as anyone who is benefiting from the services that are paid for with the tax base. Under this definition, a tax exemption for church groups could be seen as a subsidy. On the other hand, *Walz* points out that religious groups are just part of a much broader category of nonprofit organizations that benefit society. So perhaps one way of analyzing whether the benefit is *impermissible* is to ask whether the benefit targets religious groups specifically, or whether the benefit is simply directed to a general category within which religious groups happen to fall.

Another possibility involves basic considerations of jurisdiction. Consider the phrase "Render unto Caesar the things that are Caesar's, and render unto God the things that are God's." It could be that the religious domain simply never belonged to Caesar. Stated differently, the claim that religious organizations constitute part of the tax base is an inherently statist position, one that assumes state sovereignty over all aspects of social life. Perhaps there are good reasons, going back to *Locke* and beyond, why temporal jurisdiction should be limited in ways that do not encroach on the spiritual domain as a functional matter. Two centuries of American history suggest that, for a variety of reasons, church groups have traditionally not been part of the tax base. But the divide between the two domains is much older than the American nation. Should the Supreme Court assume that tax exemptions are subsidies?

3. Justice Burger is careful not to link the justification of tax exemptions directly to the public benefit religious organizations provide. In contrast, contemporary law in the United Kingdom has attempted to forge a direct link between charitable status and public benefit provided. For example, in 2009 the Charity Commission for England and Wales promulgated a "guidance" document providing "supplementary public benefit guidance for charities whose aims include advancing religion."[11] While the guidance was not part of the law itself, it explained the charity trustees' "statutory duty to have regard to [the Commission's] guidance on public benefit where it is relevant for their charity."[12] In this document, the Charity Commission noted that there were approximately 29,000 charities on the Commission's Register with aims that include advancing religion, a number projected to increase "as those charities whose aims include advancing religion which were previously excepted from the requirement to register will shortly be required to register. Under the Charities Act 2006, "all had to demonstrate that the way in which they carry out their aims is for the public benefit, as do all other charities." What potential problems and advantages might result from following such a course?

Additional Web Resources:	Materials on the debate about when tax exemptions are a subsidy Materials on the extent to which tax-exempt status should be linked to public benefit, and how public benefit should be defined New guidance from the United Kingdom's Charity Commission on Public Benefit and the Advancement of Religion in the determination of eligibility for status such as a charity

11. *See* Charity Commission, The Advancement of Religion for the Public Benefit (2009), archived. The 2009 guidance document has been superceded by three public benefit guides published in 2013: Public benefit: the public benefit requirement (PBI1); Public benefit: running a charity (PB2); and Public benefit: reporting (PB3).

12. *Id.* at B4.

TEXAS MONTHLY V. BULLOCK

Supreme Court of the United States, 489 U.S. 1 (1989)

[From 1984 to 1987, a Texas statute exempted religious periodicals from sales tax. The publisher of a general-interest magazine not entitled to the exemption challenged its constitutionality under the Establishment Clause. A state appellate court held that the exemption complied with *Lemon*, whereupon the case was appealed to the US Supreme Court.]

. . . In proscribing all laws "respecting an establishment of religion," the Constitution prohibits, at the very least, legislation that constitutes an endorsement of one or another set of religious beliefs or of religion generally. It is part of our settled jurisprudence that "the Establishment Clause prohibits government from abandoning secular purposes in order to put an imprimatur on one religion, or on religion as such, or to favor the adherents of any sect or religious organization." The core notion animating the requirement that a statute possess "a secular legislative purpose" and that "its principal or primary effect . . . be one that neither advances nor inhibits religion," *Lemon v. Kurtzman*, 403 U.S. 602, 612, is not only that government may not be overtly hostile to religion but also that it may not place its prestige, coercive authority, or resources behind a single religious faith or behind religious belief in general, compelling nonadherents to support the practices or proselytizing of favored religious organizations and conveying the message that those who do not contribute gladly are less than full members of the community.

It does not follow, of course, that government policies with secular objectives may not incidentally benefit religion. The nonsectarian aims of government and the interests of religious groups often overlap, and this Court has never required that public authorities refrain from implementing reasonable measures to advance legitimate secular goals merely because they would thereby relieve religious groups of costs they would otherwise incur. Nor have we required that legislative categories make no explicit reference to religion. Government need not resign itself to ineffectual diffidence because of exaggerated fears of contagion of or by religion, so long as neither intrudes unduly into the affairs of the other . . . .

In all [cases so deciding] we emphasized that the benefits derived by religious organizations flowed to a large number of nonreligious groups as well. Indeed, were those benefits confined to religious organizations, they could not have appeared other than as state sponsorship of religion; if that were so, we would not have hesitated to strike them down for lacking a secular purpose and effect . . . .

Texas' sales tax exemption for periodicals published or distributed by a religious faith and consisting wholly of writings promulgating the teaching of the faith lacks sufficient breadth to pass scrutiny under the Establishment Clause. Every tax exemption constitutes a subsidy that affects nonqualifying taxpayers, forcing them to become "indirect and vicarious 'donors.'" *Bob Jones University v. United States* . . . . Insofar as that subsidy is conferred upon a wide array of nonsectarian groups as well as religious organizations in pursuit of some legitimate secular end, the fact that religious groups benefit incidentally does not deprive the subsidy of the secular purpose and primary effect mandated by the Establishment Clause. However, when government directs a subsidy exclusively to religious organizations that is not required by the Free Exercise Clause and that either burdens nonbeneficiaries markedly or cannot reasonably be seen as removing a significant state-imposed deterrent to the free exercise of religion, as Texas has done, . . . it "provide[s] unjustifiable awards of assistance to religious organizations" and cannot but "conve[y] a message of endorsement" to slighted members of the community . . . . This is particularly true where, as here, the subsidy is targeted at writings that *promulgate* the teachings of religious faiths. It is difficult to view Texas' narrow exemption as anything but state sponsorship of religious belief, regardless of whether one adopts the perspective of beneficiaries or of uncompensated contributors.

How expansive the class of exempt organizations or activities must be to withstand constitutional assault depends upon the State's secular aim in granting a tax exemption. If the State chose to subsidize, by means of a tax exemption, all groups that contributed to the community's cultural, intellectual, and moral betterment, then the exemption for religious publications could be retained, provided that the exemption swept as widely as the property tax exemption we upheld in *Walz.* By contrast, if Texas sought to promote reflection and discussion about questions of ultimate value and the contours of a good or meaningful life, then a tax exemption would have to be available to an extended range of associations whose publications were substantially devoted to such matters; the exemption could not be reserved for publications dealing solely with religious issues, let alone restricted to publications advocating rather than criticizing religious belief or activity, without signaling an endorsement of religion that is offensive to the principles informing the Establishment Clause . . . .

We conclude that Texas' sales tax exemption for religious publications violates the First Amendment . . . .

COMMENTS AND QUESTIONS

1. If a tax exemption that benefits only religious periodicals is unconstitutional, what should be said of the constitutionality of a tax that burdens only religious literature? *See Swaggart Ministries v. Board of Equalization*, 493 U.S. 378 (1990).
2. In *Arizona Christian School Tuition Organization v. Winn*, 536 U.S. 125 (2011), Arizona taxpayers sued the state alleging that tax credits for donations to School Tuition Organizations (STOs), which then used the contributions to provide scholarships for students attending private schools, including religious schools, violated the Establishment Clause. The Supreme Court ultimately distinguished *Flast v. Cohen*, 392 U.S. 83 (1968), which granted a limited exception to a constitutional rule holding that mere taxpayer status is generally not sufficient to be accorded standing to sue, holding in *Winn* that because the issue in the present case involved a tax credit and not a government expenditure, respondents lacked standing to contest the law. The dissent countered that the difference between a subsidy and a tax credit was immaterial and that by refusing standing to the taxpayers in this case, the court was inviting statutes to end-run *Flast's* guarantee of access to the judiciary, thus providing for future government support of religion through tax credits while precluding taxpayer review. What role are the tax credits in determining government influence on religion? Could it be manipulative?

3. Free Exercise Claims for Exemptions from Taxation

UNITED STATES V. LEE

Supreme Court of the United States, 455 U.S. 252 (1982)

BURGER, C.J., delivered the opinion of the Court, in which BRENNAN, WHITE, MARSHALL, BLACKMUN, POWELL, REHNQUIST, and O'CONNOR, JJ., joined. STEVENS, J., filed an opinion concurring in the judgment.

. . . Appellee, a member of the Old Order Amish, is a farmer and carpenter [who rejected his obligations in relation to social security on religious grounds.] From 1970 to 1977, appellee employed several other Amish to work on his farm and in his carpentry shop. He failed to file the quarterly social security tax returns required of employers, withhold social security tax from his employees, or pay the employer's share of social security taxes. In 1978, the Internal Revenue Service assessed appellee in excess of $27,000 for unpaid employment taxes. . . . [Appellee challenged this assessment in federal court.]

The District Court held the statutes requiring appellee to pay social security and unemployment insurance taxes unconstitutional as applied . . . . The court noted that the Amish believe it sinful not to provide for their own elderly and needy and therefore are religiously opposed to the national social security system. The court also accepted appellee's contention that the Amish religion not only prohibits the acceptance of social security benefits, but also bars all contributions by Amish to the social security system. The District Court observed that in light of their beliefs, Congress has accommodated self-employed Amish and self-employed members of other religious groups with similar beliefs by providing exemptions from social security taxes . . . . The court's holding was based on both the exemption statute for the self-employed and the First Amendment; appellee and others "who fall within the carefully circumscribed definition provided . . . are relieved from paying the employer's share of [social security taxes] as it is an unconstitutional infringement upon the free exercise of their religion." . . .

The exemption provided [in the statute] is available only to self-employed individuals and does not apply to employers or employees. Consequently, appellee and his employees are not within [the statute's express provisions.] Thus any exemption from payment of the employer's share of social security taxes must come from a constitutionally required exemption.

The preliminary inquiry in determining the existence of a constitutionally required exemption is whether the payment of social security taxes and the receipt of benefits interferes with the free exercise rights of the Amish. The Amish believe that there is a religiously based obligation to provide for their fellow members the kind of assistance contemplated by the social security system . . . . It is not within "the judicial function and judicial competence," . . . to determine whether appellee or the Government has the proper interpretation of the Amish faith; "[c]ourts are not arbiters of scriptural interpretation." We therefore accept appellee's contention that both payment and receipt of social security benefits is forbidden by the Amish faith. Because the payment of the taxes or receipt of benefits violates Amish religious beliefs, compulsory participation in the social security system interferes with their free exercise rights.

The conclusion that there is a conflict between the Amish faith and the obligations imposed by the social security system is only the beginning, however, and not the end of the inquiry. Not all burdens on religion are unconstitutional . . . . The state may justify a limitation on religious liberty by showing that it is essential to accomplish an overriding governmental interest . . . .

Because the social security system is nationwide, the governmental interest is apparent. The social security system in the United States serves the public interest by providing a comprehensive insurance system with a variety of benefits available to all participants, with costs shared by employers and employees . . . . The design of the system requires support by mandatory contributions from covered employers and employees. This mandatory participation is indispensable to the fiscal vitality of the social security system . . . . Moreover, a comprehensive national social security system providing for voluntary participation would be almost a contradiction in terms and difficult, if not impossible, to administer. Thus, the Government's interest in assuring mandatory and continuous participation in and contribution to the social security system is very high.

The remaining inquiry is whether accommodating the Amish belief will unduly interfere with fulfillment of the governmental interest. In *Braunfeld v. Brown*, 366 U.S. 599, 605 (1961), this Court noted that "to make accommodation between the religious action and an exercise of state authority is a particularly delicate task . . .because resolution in favor of the State results in the choice to the individual of either abandoning his religious principle or facing . . . prosecution." The difficulty in attempting to accommodate religious beliefs in the area of taxation is that "we are a cosmopolitan nation made up of people of almost every conceivable religious preference." *Braunfeld* . . . . To maintain an organized society that guarantees religious freedom to a great variety of faiths requires that some religious practices yield to the common good. Religious beliefs can be accommodated, . . .but there is a point at which accommodation would "radically restrict the operating latitude of the legislature." *Braunfeld* . . . .

[I]t would be difficult to accommodate the comprehensive social security system with myriad exceptions flowing from a wide variety of religious beliefs . . . . The tax system could not function if denominations were allowed to challenge the tax system because tax payments were spent in a manner that violates their religious belief . . . . Because the broad public interest in maintaining a sound tax system is of such a high order, religious belief in conflict with the payment of taxes affords no basis for resisting the tax.

. . . Congress and the courts have been sensitive to the needs flowing from the Free Exercise Clause, but every person cannot be shielded from all the burdens incident to exercising every aspect of the right to practice religious beliefs. When followers of a particular sect enter into commercial activity as a matter of choice, the limits they accept on their own conduct as a matter of conscience and faith are not to be superimposed on the statutory schemes which are binding on others in that activity. Granting an exemption from social security taxes to an employer operates to impose the employer's religious faith on the employees. Congress drew a line in . . . exempting the self-employed Amish but not all persons working for an Amish employer. The tax imposed on employers to support the social security system must be uniformly applicable to all, except as Congress provides explicitly otherwise.

Accordingly, the judgment of the District Court is reversed, and the case is remanded for proceedings consistent with this opinion.

Reversed and remanded.

Justice STEVENS, concurring in the judgment.

The clash between appellee's religious obligation and his civic obligation is irreconcilable. He must violate either an Amish belief or a federal statute. According to the Court, the religious duty must prevail unless the Government shows that enforcement of the civic duty "is essential to accomplish an overriding governmental interest." . . . That formulation of the constitutional standard suggests that the Government always bears a heavy burden of justifying the application of neutral general laws to individual conscientious objectors. In my opinion, it is the objector who must shoulder the burden of demonstrating that there is a unique reason for allowing him a special exemption from a valid law of general applicability.

Congress already has granted the Amish a limited exemption from social security taxes . . . . As a matter of administration, it would be a relatively simple matter to extend the exemption to the taxes involved in this case. As a matter of fiscal policy, an enlarged exemption probably would benefit the social security system because the nonpayment of these taxes by the Amish would be more than offset by the elimination of their right to collect benefits. In view of the fact that the Amish have demonstrated their capacity to care for their own, the social cost of eliminating this relatively small group of dedicated believers would be minimal. Thus, if we confine the analysis to the Government's interest in rejecting the particular claim to an exemption at stake in this case, the constitutional standard as formulated by the Court has not been met.

The Court rejects the particular claim of this appellee, not because it presents any special problems, but rather because of the risk that a myriad of other claims would be too difficult to process. The Court overstates the magnitude of this risk because the Amish claim applies only to a small religious community with an established welfare system of its own.

Nevertheless, I agree with the Court's conclusion that the difficulties associated with processing other claims to tax exemption on religious grounds justify a rejection of this claim. I believe, however, that this reasoning supports the adoption of a different constitutional standard than the Court purports to apply.

The Court's analysis supports a holding that there is virtually no room for a "constitutionally required exemption" on religious grounds from a valid tax law that is entirely neutral in its general application. Because I agree with that holding, I concur in the judgment.

COMMENTS AND QUESTIONS

1. As indicated in Chapter 11, European church-state systems are often much more complex than the system in the United States. Many countries have a multi-tier system with base-level entities that correspond in many ways to typical nonprofit or religious corporations in the United States, some feature intermediate levels of recommendation, and several have an "upper tier" typically populated by a small number of religions with significant historical

roots in the country. Tax and other benefits are often linked to the level within the multi-tier structure that a particular religious community has attained. Thus, it makes sense to focus here on what is involved in acquiring access to "upper tier" status. This obviously varies from country to country, depending on which religions have been dominant throughout the particular country's history and a variety of other factors.[13]

2. Can tax systems that give preferences to some religious communities but not others be squared with non-discrimination principles? Recall *Ortega-Moratilla v. Spain*, App. No. 17522/90 (ECmHR, 11 January 1992), discussed in Chapter 4. There a Protestant group was unable to obtain a tax exemption because it did not have an agreement with the state and, accordingly, did not have access to upper-tier benefits. Discrimination occurs only when like cases are treated differently, not when different situations are treated differently. But there needs to be an "objective and reasonable justification" for the differential treatment. Were there "objective and reasonable justifications" for the differential tax treatment in *Ortega-Moratilla*?

IV. AID TO RELIGIOUSLY AFFILIATED CHARITABLE ACTIVITIES

A. THE CIRCUITOUS US APPROACH TO STATE FUNDING OF RELIGIOUSLY AFFILIATED CHARITABLE ACTIVITIES

One uniquely American debate has centered on whether the government can aid religiously affiliated social service organizations. The Supreme Court initially adopted a permissive approach. In *Bradfield v. Roberts*, 175 U.S. 291 (1899), the Court addressed the question of whether federal money could be used to pay for the construction of a Catholic-affiliated hospital in the District of Columbia pursuant to an act of Congress. The plaintiff, a taxpayer, claimed that the agreement between the government and the Catholic nuns was void because it would result in Congress appropriating money to a religious society in violation of the Establishment Clause.

The Court held that by appropriating money to the hospital, Congress was merely compensating the hospital and those who ran it for tending to the needs of poor patients under a contract. In so holding, the Court noted:

> The act shows that the individuals named therein and their successors in office were incorporated under the name of "The Directors of Providence Hospital," with power to receive, hold and convey personal and real property, as provided in its first section. By the second section the corporation was granted "full power and all the rights of opening and keeping a hospital in the city of Washington for the care of such sick and invalid persons as may place themselves under the treatment and care of the said corporation." The third section gave it full power to make such by-laws, rules and

13. As noted in Chapter 3, Article 11 of the Declaration on the Status of Churches and Non-confessional Organizations, included as part of the Treaty of Amsterdam, ensures respect for these distinctive structures: "the European Union respects and does not prejudice the status under national law of churches and religious associations or communities in the Member States."

> regulations that might be necessary for the general accomplishment of the objects of the hospital, not inconsistent with the laws in force in the District of Columbia. Nothing is said about religion or about the religious faith of the incorporators of this institution in the act of incorporation. It is simply the ordinary case of the incorporation of a hospital for the purposes for which such an institution is generally conducted.

In short, the Establishment Clause does not bar paying funds for secular services rendered to a corporation with exclusively secular purposes, even if it is controlled by a religious community.

1. Social Welfare Programs

In the 1970s and 1980s the Supreme Court adopted a predominantly separationist approach under the *Lemon* test. But, as discussed in Chapter 4, the holdings of *Agostini v. Felton* in 1997 and *Mitchell v. Helms* in 2000 made significant changes in First Amendment jurisprudence. For over two decades, the *Lemon* test had reigned as the standard for determining constitutionality under the Religion Clauses. "Excessive entanglement" had operated as part of the *Lemon* test as a very strong protector of the boundaries between religion and the state. However, in *Agostini* and *Helms*, Justice O'Connor channeled the test in a different direction, reading excessive entanglement as an element of the "primary effect" prong of the *Lemon* test rather than as a prong in and of itself. This folding into the primary effect test eroded the boundary-protecting function of the excessive entanglement prong. Among other consequences, it opened the door to consideration of voucher programs such as those approved in *Zelman v. Simmons-Harris*, 536 U.S. 639 (2002), discussed in Chapter 13.

This new direction of analysis has opened the way for a far more lenient approach to the Religion Clauses—an approach that emphasizes neutrality. Other developing strands of Establishment Clause analysis strengthened the neutralist trend toward allowing religious organizations to compete on an equal footing with other groups seeking funding in state-supported programs. For example, in *Bowen v. Kendrick*, 487 U.S. 589 (1988), the question was whether religious organizations could qualify for government grants funding programs aimed at preventing teenage pregnancies. The Court's analysis focused on the primary effect of the state program, which was intended to respond to the perceived crisis in teenage pregnancies. The court said in *Bowen*:

> . . . Nothing in our previous cases prevents Congress from making such a judgment or from recognizing the important part that religion or religious organizations may play in resolving certain secular problems . . . . In addition, although the AFLA [Adolescent Family Life Act] does require potential grantees to describe how they will involve religious organizations in the provision of services under the Act, it also requires grantees to describe the involvement of "charitable organizations, voluntary associations, and other groups in the private sector." In our view, this reflects the statute's successful maintenance of "a course of neutrality among religions, and between religion and non-religion."
>
> We note in addition that this Court has never held that religious institutions are disabled by the First Amendment from participating in publicly sponsored social welfare programs . . . . Of course, even when the challenged statute appears to be neutral on its face, we have always been careful to ensure that direct government aid

> to religiously affiliated institutions does not have the primary effect of advancing religion.
>
> Indeed, the contention that there is a substantial risk of such institutions receiving direct aid is undercut by the AFLA's facially neutral grant requirements, the wide spectrum of public and private organizations which are capable of meeting the AFLA's requirements, and the fact that, of the eligible religious institutions, many will not deserve the label of "pervasively sectarian." . . .[W]e do not think the possibility that AFLA grants may go to religious institutions that can be considered "pervasively sectarian" is sufficient to conclude that no grants whatsoever can be given under the statute to religious organizations. We think that the District Court was wrong in concluding otherwise.

The combination of greater flexibility in Establishment Clause standards and a sense that religious service providers ought to be treated equally helped open the door to more extensive consideration of educational charitable choice programs.

2. Educational Programs

Consider the facts in *Witters v. Washington Department of Services for the Blind*, 474 U.S. 481 (1986), Washington gave money for vocational education to all visually impaired individuals. But when a student asked for money for his career as a pastor or other church related jobs, the state refused.

The Washington Supreme Court upheld the refusal, claiming that giving the student funds would violate the Establishment Clause. But the United States Supreme Court reversed. Noting that the Washington program is generally available to secular and religious students, not "skewed towards religion," the Court concluded unanimously that giving money to a student for him to give towards a religious school for a religious vocation does not violate the Establishment Clause.

Decades later, *Trinity Lutheran Church v. Comer*, 582 U.S. ___ (2017) arose because Missouri denied fundng to a religious school to resurface a playground to have a safer surface made of recycled tires. The Church sued, claiming that the church had a right to the funding under the Free Exercise Clause. The Supreme Court held that discrimination based on religious status is subject to strict scrutiny: "To condition the availability of benefits . . . upon [a recipient's] willingness to . . . surrender[] his religiously impelled [status] effectively penalizes the free exercise of his constitutional liberties." (citation omitted) (modifications in original). The Court ruled that the constitution requires funding be given on an equal basis to the religious and non-religious.

3. Charitable Choice and Faith-Based Initiatives: Expanding Cooperation in a Separationist State[14]

The concepts of charitable choice and faith-based initiatives have generated considerable controversy. In the United States, the idea of charitable choice first appeared in the Welfare Reform Act of 1996.[15] Resulting from the growing welfare

---

14. For history of this notion *see* W. Cole Durham, Jr., and Christine G. Scott, *supra* note 1, at 380-385 and summary on the Web Supplement.

15. 42 U.S.C. §604a (Supp. II 1996). For a concise history, *see* Carl H. Esbeck, Appendix: Charitable Choice and the Critics, in *Religious Organizations in the United States* 391 (James A.

crisis and calls for reform of the welfare system, charitable choice encourages state and local governments to partner with private charities, including faith-based organizations (FBOs), through block grants and other programs that states can use to contract with private organizations for social services.[16] Aimed at harnessing the unique power of religion to change lives, the Act relies on three principles. First, the government must not discriminate with regard to religion in determining program eligibility; the focus must be on the nature of the service, not the nature of the provider. Second, the government must not interfere with an FBOs religious autonomy, specifically the "definition, development, practice, and expression of its religious beliefs." Third, the Act requires that both the government and FBOs not abridge certain rights of the beneficiaries of the services.[17] The FBOs must not refuse beneficiaries because of their religion or their desire not to participate in a religious practice. Likewise, if a beneficiary objects to receiving services from an FBO, the government must provide services from an alternative provider.[18] Significantly, charitable choice legislation does not require an FBO to separate its secular and sectarian activities, so long as the government aid does not directly advance religion.[19]

In 2001, President Bush expanded charitable choice with his Faith-Based Initiative. Legislation in favor of charitable choice stalled, but President Bush moved the program forward by signing an executive order creating the White House Office of Faith-Based and Community Initiatives, and directing various cabinet-level departments to create similar centers within each agency. The office's purpose was to further the effort "to enlist, expand, equip, empower and enable the work of faith-based and community service groups."[20] After nearly a decade of the faith-based initiative experiment, the White House Office of Faith-Based and Community Initiatives reported for fiscal year 2005 that FBO participation in the program was progressing but not overwhelming.[21]

In 2009, the Obama administration changed the name of the Faith-Based Initiative to the White House Office of Faith-Based and Neighborhood Partnerships and created an Advisory Council including secular leaders and those who seek to protect the rights of minorities. President Obama stated an intention to change rules governing the eligibility of FBOs to participate in federally funded social service programs, eliminating exemption from the employment discrimination laws that have allowed FBOs to favor members of their church in

---

Serritella et al., eds., Carolina Academic Press 2006).

16. Susanna Dokupil, A Sunny Dome with Caves of Ice: The Illusion of Charitable Choice, 5 *Tex Rev. L. & Pol.* 149, 151 (2000).

17. Esbeck, *supra* note 15, at 391–393.

18. *Id.* at 392–393.

19. Steven Fitzgerald, Note, Expansion of Charitable Choice, the Faith-Based Initiative, and the Supreme Court's Establishment Clause Jurisprudence, 42 *Cath. Law.* 211, 212 (2002).

20. President George W. Bush, *Rallying the Armies of Compassion* (2001), available at https://archives.hud.gov/reports/rally.pdf .

21. Grants to Faith-Based Organizations, Fiscal Year 2005, White House Office of Faith-Based and Community Initiatives, 9 March 2006. For 2005, of the $19.7 billion in funding that was distributed, only 10.9% ($2.1 billion) went to FBOs, while secular nonprofit organizations (SNPs) received 64.4% ($12.7 billion). These numbers indicate an increase in FBO participation from 8.1% in 2003 and 10.3% in 2004, but hardly evidence a fundamental shift from government or secular to sectarian service providers.

hiring. However, in the end Obama administration mostly left President Bush's policies intact, instead reviewing issues on a "case by case" basis.[22]

In late 2010, President Obama issued an executive order emphasizing a commitment to respect the free exercise of religion and avoid any governmental establishment of faith, in accordance with constitutional guarantees. Faith-based organizations that receive federal funding must keep sectarian activities separate in time and location from the federally funded social services they provide, but their participation in the faith-based initiative should not impair their independence, autonomy, expression outside the programs in question, or religious character. FBOs could "use their facilities to provide social services supported with Federal financial assistance, without removing or altering religious art, icons, scriptures, or other symbols from these facilities" and "may retain religious terms in its name, select board members on a religious basis, and include religious references in organization's mission statements and other chartering or governing documents."[23] Issues remained unsettled until August 2015, when nine federal agengies issued recommendations for reforms that "would clarify rules that apply to [faith-based] partnerships and extend added protections for social service beneficiaries."[24] Regulations providing "new religious liberty protections for beneficiaries of federally funded social service programs" were published on 4 April 2016.[25]

In May 2018, the Trump Administration created a "White House Faith and Opportunity Initiative" to unify the efforts of all departments "to ensure that the faith-based and community organizations that form the bedrock of our society have strong advocates in the White House and throughout the Federal Government."[26] While some observed that the expansion would enable an effective program to "do even greater work," others asserted that it "actually weakens religious freedom."[27] Coverage of this initiative and ongoing developments is available on the Web Supplement.

The ability to challenge faith-based initiative programs appears to have been sharply limited as a result of the 2007 US Supreme Court ruling *Hein v. Freedom From Religion Foundation, Inc.*, 551 U.S. 587, holding that taxpayers do not have standing to challenge executive branch initiatives on Establishment Clause grounds. Specifically, the Court refused to extend the holding in *Flast* granting a a limited exception to the rule that mere taxpayer status is generally not sufficient to be accorded standing to sue. The exception in *Flast* allowed taxpayers standing

22. Philip C. Aka, Shaping Their Better Character: Religion in African American Politics in the Age of Obama, 16 *Rutgers J. Law & Relig.* 1, 50 (Fall 2014).

23. Executive Order—Fundamental Principles and Policymaking Criteria for Partnerships with Faith-Based and Other Neighborhood Organizations, 17 November 2010.

24. *See* Melissa Rogers, Promoting Common-Ground Reforms of Social Service Partnerships, *The White House Blog*, 5 August 2015.

25. Federal Agency Final Regulations Implementing Executive Order 13559: Fundamental Principles and Policymaking Criteria for Partnerships with Faith-Based and Other Neighborhood Organizations.

26. President Donald J. Trump Stands Up For Religious Freedom in the United States, Fact Sheet, *The White House Blog*, 3 May 2018.

27. *See, e.g.*, Kelsey Dallas, "Nothing Is More Powerful Than God": A Look at President Donald Trump's New Faith-Based Initiatives, *Deseret News*, May 2018, and Melissa Rogers, President Trump Just Unveiled a New White House "Faith" Office. It Actually Weakens Religious Freedom, *The Washington Post*, 14 May 2018.

to challenge legislative measures on Establishment Clause grounds, but the Court in *Hein* refused to extend the exception to cover similar challenges to executive measures. Standing requirements were further heightened in *Winn*.

CHAPTER 13

RELIGION AND EDUCATION

I. INTRODUCTION

One of the social contexts in which the interaction of law and religion is most controversial is in schools. Stakes are high when it comes to educating the rising generation in any society, but when the issue is the proper place of religion in schools, given the impressionability and vulnerability of children, special concern arises over issues such as indoctrination.

As the US Supreme Court noted,

> [we have] been particularly vigilant in monitoring compliance with the Establishment Clause in elementary and secondary schools. [Families] entrust public schools with the education of their children, but condition their trust on the understanding that the classroom will not purposely be used to advance religious views that may conflict with the private beliefs of the student and his or her family. Students in such institutions are impressionable and their attendance is involuntary. The state exerts great authority and coercive power through mandatory attendance requirements, and because of the students' emulation of teachers as role models and the children's susceptibility to peer pressure.[1]

Underlying the necessity articulated here for increased policing by the courts is the concern that parents are generally unable to directly monitor the content of classroom discussion, thus increasing the need for the state to play an active role. In addition to parental rights concerns, there is also the macro-level concern that, particularly where political parties and movements may be tied to specific religious (or irreligious) affiliations, the inclusion of religious content in schools may be viewed as an attempt to influence the overall balance of power by tilting the next generation toward a particular viewpoint.

This chapter is divided into three primary sections. Section II focuses on religious schools and their relationship with the state, in particular through access to funding or other state aid. Section III discusses non-discrimination norms and freedom of religion in education, and Section IV focuses on state schools and their

1. *Edwards v. Aguillard*, 482 U.S. 578 (1987).

relationship with religion, particularly efforts to include religious instruction or religious worship in state-sponsored schools.

In a sense, Section II is a natural continuation of Chapter 12, since many of the United States Supreme Court's decisions on religion and finance have involved the educational context. Section III, with its focus on discrimination, echoes some of the concerns in Chapter 9. And Section IV provides a transition to Chapter 14, which explores a number of issues concerning religion in public settings.

In a deeper sense, however, this chapter represents a crucial context for religion-state structures in every legal system. Schools are often one of the key domains in which tensions between religious freedom and other rights are worked out, as demonstrated by sensitive issues such as the right to wear headscarves in educational institutions in Chapter 3, subsidized transportation to schools in Chapter 4's treatment of *Everson*, the flag salute cases of Chapter 5, and treatment of the Amish practice of taking children out of public schools after the eighth grade in Chapter 6. It is also linked to Chapter 7, which explores the issue of religious freedom in specialized contexts. Public schools provide a particularly significant "specialized context," in that they involve a certain measure of state coercion and the complexities of the "evolving capacities of the child" (to quote a key phrase from Article 14 of the Convention on the Rights of the Child).

The links to other chapters should not be surprising, because in a general sense, the educational system is a microcosm of society, aimed at guiding new generations not only by teaching subjects but by providing experience through the modeling of societal ideals. From a comparative perspective, cases involving religion and schools offer insight into the ways different societies envision themselves and what they hope to become.

II. STATE AID TO RELIGIOUS SCHOOLS

A. THE UNITED STATES

1. The Early Accommodationist Interpretation

The same summer that the Constitution was framed, the Continental Congress, acting under the Articles of Confederation, adopted the 1787 Northwest Ordinance. Article 3 of this document provided, "Religion, morality and knowledge, being necessary to good government and the happiness of mankind, schools and the means of education shall forever be encouraged." The earliest decisions aimed at accommodating religion in education in the United States predate the post–World War II decision in *Everson v. Board of Education*, 330 U.S. 1 (1947), discussed in Chapter 4, which held the Establishment Clause applicable to the several states.

The first decision turned on the proper interpretation of a statute. In *Quick Bear v. Leupp*, 210 U.S. 50 (1908), the United States Supreme Court rejected the claim of Sioux Tribe Indians that the Commissioner of Indian Affairs should not be able to use the Sioux Treaty Fund and the Sioux Trust Fund to contract with the Bureau of Catholic Indian Missions of Washington, DC for the organization of sectarian schools for Indian children. The Sioux Tribe argued that such use of the funds violated both the Sioux Treaty of 29 April 1868, and the Indian Appropriation Acts of 1895, 1896, and 1897, which provided that the government "shall make no appropriation whatever for education in any sectarian school." The Court interpreted this provision as applying "only to the appropriations of the public moneys of the United States, raised by taxation from persons of all creeds and faiths, or none at all, and appropriated gratuitously for the purpose of education among the Indians." The Sioux Treaty Fund and Sioux Trust Fund, on the other hand, constituted "'tribal funds,' which belong to the Indians themselves" and were held by the United States as trustee. The Court held that the statutory restriction therefore did not apply.

In *Pierce v. Society of Sisters*, 268 U.S. 510 (1925), the Supreme Court held that the right to liberty under the Fourteenth Amendment protected the right of "parents and guardians to direct the upbringing and education of children under their control," and hence that a statute mandating attendance at public schools could not be enforced against parents sending their children to private schools, whether religious or secular. "The fundamental theory of liberty upon which all governments in this Union repose excludes any general power of the state to standardize its children by forcing them to accept instruction from public teachers only." The right to establish private schools protected in *Pierce* is now widely respected in other countries.

Following these decisions, the *Everson* Court, as discussed in Chapter 4, advocated a strict "wall of separation between Church and State." However, in considering whether a New Jersey township could subsidize bus transportation for children attending private religious schools, the Court took an accommodationist turn and held that the subsidy constituted a "general program" for transporting children to accredited schools "regardless of their religion" and was therefore permissible.

Two decades later, in *Board of Education v. Allen*, 392 U.S. 236 (1968), the Supreme Court addressed a controversy over lending textbooks used in New York public schools to students attending parochial schools. Following the rationale of *Everson*, the Court affirmed the decision of the New York Court of Appeals, holding that the New York law involved was not unconstitutional, because the law in question had a secular legislative purpose and a primary effect that neither advanced nor inhibited religion.

Noting that the purpose of the New York statute, as stated by the New York legislature, was to further the educational opportunities of school-aged children, and that the books were furnished to individual students upon request rather than to the parochial schools themselves, the Court held that the secular purpose of the statute neither advanced nor inhibited religion. "Perhaps free books make it more likely that some children choose to attend a sectarian school," the Court reasoned, "but that was true of the state-paid bus fares in *Everson* and does not alone demonstrate an unconstitutional degree of support for a religious institution."

Justice Harlin's concurrence is noteworthy:

> The attitude of government toward religion must, as this Court has frequently observed, be one of neutrality. Neutrality is, however, a coat of many colors. It requires that "government neither engage in nor compel religious practices, that it effect no

favoritism among sects or between religion and nonreligion, and that it work deterrence of no religious belief." Realization of these objectives entails "no simple and clear measure" by which this or any case may readily be decided, but these objectives do suggest the principles which I believe to be applicable in the present circumstances. I would hold that where the contested governmental activity is calculated to achieve nonreligious purposes otherwise within the competence of the State, and where the activity does not involve the State "so significantly and directly in the realm of the sectarian as to give rise to . . . divisive influences and inhibitions of freedom," it is not forbidden by the religious clauses of the First Amendment.

In my opinion, [the New York law] does not employ religion as its standard for action or inaction, and is not otherwise inconsistent with these principles.

2. The "No Aid" Principles and the "No Religious Uses" Doctrine

Just three years after the Supreme Court's accommodationist holding in *Board of Education v. Allen*, the Court issued *Lemon v. Kurtzman*, 411 U.S. 192 (1973). This time, in contrast to the earlier holdings of *Everson* and *Allen*, the Court invalidated state salary supplements to parochial school teachers, even though the teachers were forbidden by law from teaching religion in their classes. The case has become known for its tripartite "*Lemon* test," which provides that an action by the government (1) must have a secular purpose, (2) must not have the primary effect of either advancing or inhibiting religion, and (3) must not result in an "excessive government entanglement" with religion. Although the test announced in *Lemon* obviously built upon prior precedent, its "non-entanglement" prong set strong limits to the extent of permissible accommodation.

With very few exceptions, the series of cases that followed *Lemon* from 1971 to 1985 enforced a muscular separation between church and State in matters of government funding, especially in the educational setting. Over the next fourteen years, the Court:

- Held that the government could not make grants to religious colleges to build or repair buildings without receiving a permanent pledge that the building would not be used for religious purposes, *Committee for Public Education and Religious Liberty v. Nyquist*, 413 U.S. 756 (1973);
- Struck down a statute that reimbursed religious schools for the costs of administering and recording state-required examinations, *Levitt v. Committee for Public Education*, 413 U.S. 472 (1973);
- Struck down a law providing for the loan of instructional equipment and materials to sectarian schools and allowing auxiliary services to be provided on school premises, *Meek v. Pittenger*; 421 U.S. 349 (1975),
- Held that a law providing for reimbursement of costs for teacher-led field trips at religious schools violated the First Amendment, *Wolman v. Walter*, 433 U.S. 229 (1977);
- Invalidated a federal program that paid public school teachers to teach remedial classes to children at religious schools in poor inner-city neighborhoods, *Aguilar v. Felton*, 473 U.S. 402 (1985); and
- Struck down remedial and enrichment programs provided to classes of non-public students on the premises of religious schools, *Grand Rapids School District v. Ball*, 473 U.S. 373 (1985).

Part of the concern in these cases was that to ensure fulfillment of a secular purpose, monitoring was necessary to verify that teachers and other personnel did not stray over the line into participation in religious indoctrination. Such monitoring, however, would involve excessive entanglement. This meant that, to some degree, the *Lemon* test's structure led to a presumption of invalidity.

The *Lemon* test remains the law, and it has been vehemently criticized, questioned, and departed from both by academics and by members of the Court. Critics say that each of the three prongs of the test creates its own ambiguity, and this problem is exacerbated by their accumulation. Critics say the "secular purpose" prong, improperly focuses on the motives of those who support a government activity, regardless of its effects. The "primary effect" prong, which should address this problem, fails to set up a workable standard differentiating permissible government support of religion, such as providing police and fire protection, and favorable treatment that exceeds proper boundaries. Finally, the "excessive entanglement" prong, among other problems, leaves the question of what is excessive entirely to the discretion of individual judges. The latitude afforded to the judges by the ambiguity of the *Lemon* test, along with the dissatisfaction expressed by several members of the Supreme Court, has resulted in a string of cases that lack doctrinal coherency. Cases that applied *Lemon*—including *Meek*, *Wolman*, *Ball*, and *Aguilar* (described above)—have been overruled, yet the *Lemon* test remains.

While the Supreme Court has not overruled *Lemon*, the test has not been controlling in several education cases. It was completely ignored in *Lee v. Weisman,* 505 U.S. 577 (1992) (invalidating nonsectarian prayer at graduation ceremony; see the section on school prayer, below) in favor of Justice Kennedy's "coercion" test, according to which government activity is held to violate the Establishment Clause if it coerces individuals to participate in a religious exercise. Justice Scalia, joined by three other justices in his dissent, observed that "the Court today demonstrates the irrelevance of *Lemon* by essentially ignoring it . . . and the interment of that case may be the one happy byproduct of the Court's otherwise lamentable decision."

However, to the surprise of many, the Court returned to it that same year in deciding *Lamb's Chapel v. Center Moriches Union Free School District*, 508 U.S. 384 (1993) (upholding equal access to public school premises for religiously oriented activities where other community organizations are allowed such access is not an establishment of religion), and again a few years later in *Santa Fe Independent School District v. Doe*, 530 U.S. 290 (2000) (holding student-initiated, student-led prayer before high school football games impermissibly coercive, in violation of the Establishment Clause). The Court's on-again, off-again approach to invoking the *Lemon* test has given validity to Justice Scalia's claim in his concurrence in *Lamb's Chapel:* "Like some ghoul in a late night horror movie that repeatedly sits up in its grave and shuffles abroad, after being repeatedly killed and buried, *Lemon* stalks our Establishment Clause jurisprudence once again. . . . Such a docile and useful monster is worth keeping around, at least in a somnolent state; one never knows when one might need him" (508 U.S. 398-399).

3. Neutrality and the "Private Choice" Doctrine

In *Mueller v. Allen*, 463 U.S. 388 (1983), the Supreme Court upheld a state income tax deduction for costs of tuition, books, transportation, and other educational expenses that was neutrally available to parents of children in religious or non-religious schools. The Court emphasized that any assistance given to religious schools came only through the private choice of many individual parents:

> By channeling whatever assistance it may provide to parochial schools through individual parents, Minnesota has reduced the Establishment Clause objections to which its action is subject. It is true, of course, that financial assistance provided to parents ultimately has an economic effect comparable to that of aid given directly to the schools attended by their children. It is also true, however, that under Minnesota's arrangement public funds become available only as a result of numerous, private choices of individual parents of school-age children. Where, as here, aid to parochial schools is available only as a result of decisions of individual parents no "imprimatur of State approval" . . . can be deemed to have been conferred on any particular religion, or on religion generally.

Further, the Court rejected an argument that the law, though facially neutral, primarily benefited religious schools, even though 96 percent of the program's beneficiaries were parents of children attending parochial schools: "We would be loath to adopt a rule grounding the constitutionality of a facially neutral law on annual reports reciting the extent to which various classes of private citizens claimed benefits under the law." Thus, the Minnesota statute satisfied the second prong of *Lemon*'s test because the statute's "principal or primary effect . . . neither advance[d] nor inhibit[ed] religion."

The Court likewise found prongs 1 and 3 of the *Lemon* test satisfied. Concerning the first prong, the statute had a "secular legislative purpose" because a "state's decision to defray the cost of educational expenses incurred by parents—regardless of the type of schools their children attend—evidences a purpose that is both secular and understandable." Concerning the third prong, the Minnesota statute did not "'excessively entangle' the state in religion" because the "only plausible source of the 'comprehensive, discriminating, and continuing state surveillance' necessary to run afoul of this standard would lie in the fact that state officials must determine whether particular textbooks qualify for a deduction." Because making this decision was not significantly different from state decisions about whether a book was secular or not (previously approved in *Board of Education v. Allen*), the Court found that Minnesota's tax deduction did not affect excessive state entanglement.

a. Establishment Clause does not bar use of state scholarship by blind student at religious institution due to presence of private choice

Three years after *Mueller v. Allen*, the Court confirmed its private choice doctrine in *Witters v. Washington Department of Services for the Blind*, 474 U.S. 481 (1986). As explained in Chapter 12, the state of Washington gave scholarships to blind citizens seeking education in the "professions, business or trades." One recipient, Larry Witters, used his scholarship to "study at a religious institution to become a pastor." The Court found that such funding did not offend the

Establishment Clause because "any aid . . . that ultimately flows to religious institutions does so only as a result of the genuinely independent and private choices of aid recipients." The Court noted that, like the program in *Mueller*, the "program is made available generally without regard to the sectarian-nonsectarian, or public-nonpublic nature of the institution benefited." In separate opinions, five justices also explained that the amount of aid that reached religious institutions was irrelevant, since parental private choice had directed that aid. However, the amount of aid likely to reach religious schools in the context of *Witters* was relatively small.

b. Publicly funded interpreters for deaf students at religious schools permissible

In 1993 the Court extended its neutrality and private choice doctrine to state interpreters in private religious schools. In *Zobrest v. Catalina Foothills School District*, 509 U.S. 1 (1993), the Court held that an Arizona school district could constitutionally provide an interpreter for a student attending a parochial school. The student, James Zobrest, had been deaf since birth, and when his parents moved him from the public school system to a Roman Catholic high school, they requested that the school district provide him with an interpreter (pursuant to Arizona's counterpart statute to the Individuals with Disabilities Education Act (IDEA)). The school district declined to provide the interpreter, believing such action would violate the Establishment Clause.

The Supreme Court, however, cited both *Mueller* and *Witters* and held there was no violation of the Establishment Clause since the program was neutrally available and involved private choice. The Court noted that "the service . . . is part of a general government program that distributes benefits neutrally to any child qualifying as 'handicapped' under the IDEA, without regard to the 'sectarian-nonsectarian, or public-nonpublic nature' of the school the child attends." Further, because individual private citizens make the choice about which school to attend, not the government, the state could not be said to be unconstitutionally benefiting religion. *Zobrest* underscores the Court's willingness to approve narrow programs targeted to help students with special needs so long as the programs are neutral and give parents the opportunity to choose religious or secular schools.

4. A Shift Toward Neutrality and Increased Accommodation

In 1976, Jay Sekulow, a young Jewish man, became associated with the religious group "Jews for Jesus" while studying at Atlanta Baptist College. A few years after Sekulow graduated from Mercer University Law School, he became the general legal counsel for the national Jews for Jesus organization. In 1984, "a minster of the Gospel" for the organization was evicted from the Los Angeles International Airport for distributing religious leaflets. The case was brought to California courts arguing, as was typical for cases involving religion up until that time that the airport policy interfered with the organization's free exercise of religion. Taking the case to the Supreme Court, however, Sekulow chose to argue under the Free Speech Clause, not mentioning religion. He argued that "polite distribution of pamphlets" should be protected alongside protected obnoxious expression, such as waving picket signs and distributing obscenity. The Court had been far more "generous in extending protection to controversial speech than [it had to] intrusive religious activities" and ruled unanimously in favor of the religious organization.[2] Sekulow had represented several other religious parties under the same argument when prominent American religious leader Pat Robertson asked him to start a conservative counterpart to the ACLU, the American Center for Law and Justice (ACLJ). The ACLJ's first case dealt with the New York state law that allowed school property to be used by "social, civil, and recreational meetings." Lamb's Chapel, a small evangelical church, was prohibited from showing six films that featured lectures by a central figure in the national evangelical movement. Sekulow insisted that while religion could not be privileged, it also could not be penalized. In *Lamb's Chapel,* the Court once again ruled unanimously in favor of the church. Sekulow succeeded in his arguments in several other similar cases,[3] and by the mid-1990s, a clear movement towards religious equality had occurred. "[I]f a school, airport, or other public forum was going to open up its facilities to some individuals or groups, the authorities couldn't exclude religious speakers from the list."[4]

Twelve years after the original 1985 decisions in *Aguilar* and *Grand Rapids*, the Supreme Court was asked pursuant to Federal Rule of Civil Procedure 60(b) to reconsider the injunctions in those cases. Using this unusual procedure, the Court reopened and reversed the two earlier decisions. *Agostini v. Felton*, 521 U.S. 203 (1997). The Court concluded that intervening precedents had undermined (1) the presumption that placement of public employees in the pervasively sectarian environment of religious schools would lead to a symbolic union of government and religion and to indoctrination (in the absence of monitoring), and (2) the rule that all direct aid to religious schools is impermissible. This led to a reformulation of the *Lemon* test. In particular, the Court specified the criteria for applying *Lemon*'s "primary effect" prong by requiring a determination that government aid does not have the effect of advancing or inhibiting religion (1) through direct governmental indoctrination, (2) by defining its recipients with reference to religion in non-neutral ways, or (3) by creating an excessive entanglement of religion and the state. *Agostini* thereby marked a shift toward a more lenient judicial approach to the First Amendment, which emphasized neutrality rather than strict separation.

In *Mitchell v. Helms*, 530 U.S. 793 (2000), the Court extended the reasoning of *Agostini* to analysis of Chapter 2 of Louisiana's Education Consolidation and Improvement Act of 1981, which provided for use of federal funds for purchasing educational materials and equipment, such as textbooks and computers, that were subsequently loaned to public and private schools. The effect was to overrule much of both *Meek* and *Wolman.* While the Court failed to marshal a majority for an opinion, six justices agreed that, under *Agostini*, Chapter 2 could not be considered a violation of the Establishment Clause. In his plurality opinion joined by three

---

2. Board of Airport Commissioners v. Jews for Jesus, 482 U.S. 569 (1987).

3. *E.g.*, *United States v. Kokinda*, 497 U.S. 720 (1990), *Board of Education of Westside Schools v. Mergens*, 496 US 226 (1990), *Lee v. Int. Society for Krishna Consciousness*, 505 U.S. 831 (1992), *Bray v. Alexandria Women's Health* Clinic, 506. U.S. 263 (1993), *Schenck v. Pro-Choice Network of Western New York*, 519 U.S. 357 (1997).

4. Jeffrey Toobin, *The Nine: Inside the Secret World of the Supreme Court* 88–95 (Doubleday 2000).

other Justices, Justice Thomas argued that the "question of whether governmental aid to religious schools results in governmental indoctrination is ultimately a question of whether any religious indoctrination that occurs in those schools could reasonably be attributed to governmental action." Since the aid provided to religious schools by virtue of Chapter 2 was consistent with the principle of neutrality in that it was "offered to a broad range of groups or persons without regard to religion," any indoctrination by those schools could not be attributed to the government. Justice Thomas further supported his conclusion by appeal to the private choice doctrine. "If aid to schools, even 'direct aid,' is neutrally available and, before reaching or benefiting any religious school, first passes through the hands (literally or figuratively) of numerous private citizens who are free to direct the aid elsewhere, the government has not provided any 'support of religion.'" According to this logic, since allocation of aid is determined by enrollment, the amount of aid available to a school is directly related to the private choice of individuals who enroll there. Finally, the respondents claimed that the resources had been diverted to use for indoctrination. Justice Thomas, however, rejected the argument that the Constitution requires aid not to be divertible for religious use. Such a rule, he said, would engender hostility toward religious persons and require an invasive inquiry into the religious views of aid recipients.

Justices O'Connor and Breyer concurred in the judgment upholding Chapter 2 and overruling *Meek* and *Wolman.* However, they perceived Justice Thomas's opinion to be an unnecessary and inappropriate extension of *Agostini.* Justice O'Connor wrote separately because (1) "the plurality's treatment of neutrality comes close to assigning that factor singular importance in the future adjudication of Establishment Clause challenges to government school aid programs" and (2) "the plurality's approval of actual diversion of government aid to religious indoctrination is in tension with our precedents and, in any event, unnecessary to decide the instant case."

Justice O'Connor hesitated to endorse any program that actually approved of the diversion of aid to religious indoctrination, but found the evidence of such diversion *de minimis* in this case.

While *Mitchell* perhaps does not provide a crystal-clear holding, it entrenches the course taken in *Agostini*, focusing on the principle of neutrality in determining whether government aid to schools violates the Establishment Clause. This trend breaks from the "no aid," separationist jurisprudence established by the Court in the 1970s and 1980s and reflects a willingness on the part of the Court to recognize a relationship between government and religion in the context of education.

5. Educational Vouchers for Parochial Education

ZELMAN v. SIMMONS-HARRIS

Supreme Court of the United States, 536 U.S. 639 (2002)

Chief Justice REHNQUIST delivered the opinion of the Court.

The State of Ohio has established a pilot program designed to provide educational choices to families with children who reside in the Cleveland City School District . . . The question presented is whether this program offends the Establishment Clause of the United States Constitution. We hold that it does not.

There is no dispute that the program challenged here was enacted for the valid secular purpose of providing educational assistance to poor children in a demonstrably failing public school system. Thus, the question presented is whether the Ohio program nonetheless has the forbidden "effect" of advancing or inhibiting religion.

To answer that question, our decisions have drawn a consistent distinction between government program that provide aid directly to religious schools and programs of true private choice, in which government aid reaches religious schools only as a result of the genuine and independent choices of private individuals. . . . *Mueller, Witters*, and *Zobrest*. . .make clear that where a government aid program is neutral with respect to religion, and provides assistance directly to a broad class of citizens who, in turn, direct government aid to religious schools wholly as a result of their own genuine and independent private choice, the program is not readily subject to challenge under the Establishment Clause. The incidental advancement of a religious mission, or the perceived endorsement of a religious message, is reasonably attributable to the individual recipient, not to the government, whose role ends with the disbursement of benefits. . . . [W]e have never found a program of true private choice to offend the Establishment Clause.

We believe that the program challenged here is a program of true private choice, consistent with *Mueller, Witters*, and *Zobrest*, and thus constitutional. As was true in those cases, the Ohio program is neutral in all respects toward religion. It is part of a general and multifaceted undertaking by the State of Ohio to provide educational opportunities to the children of a failed school district. It confers educational assistance directly to a broad class of individuals defined without reference to religion, *i.e.*, any parent of a school-age child who resides in the Cleveland City School District. The program permits the participation of *all* schools within the district, religious or nonreligious. . . .

There are no "financial incentive[s]" that "skew" the program toward religious schools. . . . The program here in fact creates financial *dis*incentives for religious schools, with private schools receiving only half the government assistance given to community schools and one-third the assistance given to magnet schools. Parents that choose to participate in the scholarship program and then to enroll their children in a private school (religious or nonreligious) must copay a portion of the school's tuition. Families that choose a community school, magnet school, or traditional public school pay nothing. Although such features of the program are not necessary to its constitutionality, they clearly dispel the claim that the program "creates. . .financial incentive[s] for parents to choose a sectarian school."

Justice SOUTER speculates that because more private religious schools currently participate in the program, the program itself must somehow discourage the participation of private nonreligious schools. But Cleveland's preponderance of religiously affiliated private schools certainly did not arise as a result of the program; it is a phenomenon common to many American cities. . . .

Respondents and Justice SOUTER claim that even if we do not focus on the number of participating schools that are religious schools, we should attach constitutional significance to the fact that 96% of scholarship recipients have enrolled in religious schools. They claim that this alone proves parents lack genuine choice, even if no parent has ever said so. The constitutionality of a neutral educational aid program simply does not turn on whether and why, in a particular area, at a particular time, most private schools are run by religious organizations, or most recipients choose to use the aid at a religious school. . . .

This point is aptly illustrated here. The 96% figure upon which respondents and Justice SOUTER rely discounts entirely (1) the more than 1,900 Cleveland children enrolled in alternative community schools, (2) the more than 13,000 children enrolled in alternative magnet schools, and (3) the more than 1,400 children enrolled in traditional public schools with tutorial assistance. Including some or all of these children in the denominator of children enrolled in nontraditional schools during the 1999–2000 school year drops the percentage enrolled in religious schools from 96% to under 20%. . . .

In sum, the Ohio program is entirely neutral with respect to religion. It provides benefits directly to a wide spectrum of individuals, defined only by financial need and residence in a particular school district. It permits such individuals to exercise genuine choice among options public and private, secular and religious. The program is therefore a program of true private choice. In keeping with an unbroken line of decisions rejecting challenges to similar programs, we hold that the program does not offend the Establishment Clause.

The judgment of the Court of Appeals is reversed. *It is so ordered.*

Justice SOUTER, with whom Justice STEVENS, Justice GINSBURG, and Justice BREYER join, dissenting. . . .

How can a Court consistently leave *Everson* on the books and approve the Ohio vouchers? The answer is that it cannot. It is only by ignoring *Everson* that the majority can claim to rest on traditional law in its invocation of neutral aid provisions and private choice to sanction the Ohio law. It is, moreover, only by ignoring the meaning of neutrality and private choice themselves that the majority can even pretend to rest today's decision on those criteria.

II. A.

In order to apply the neutrality test it makes sense to focus on a category of aid that may be directed to religious as well as secular schools, and ask whether the scheme favors a religious direction. Here, one would ask whether the voucher provisions, allowing for as much as $2,250 toward private school tuition (or a grant to a public school in an adjacent district), were written in a way that skewed the scheme toward benefiting religious schools.

This, however, is not what the majority asks. The majority looks not to the provisions for tuition vouchers, . . . but to every provision for educational opportunity. The majority then finds confirmation that "participation of *all* schools" satisfies neutrality by noting that the better part of total state educational expenditure goes to public schools, thus showing there is no favor of religion.

The illogic is patent. If regular, public schools (which can get no voucher payments) "participate" in a voucher scheme with schools that can, and public expenditure is still predominantly on public schools, then the majority's reasoning would find neutrality in a scheme of vouchers available for private tuition in districts with no secular private schools at all. "Neutrality" as the majority employs the term is, literally, verbal and nothing more. . . .

B.

The majority addresses the issue of choice the same way it addresses neutrality, by asking whether recipients or potential recipients of voucher aid have a choice of public schools among secular alternatives to religious schools. Again, however, the majority asks the wrong question and misapplies the criterion. The majority has confused choice in spending scholarships with choice from the entire menu of possible educational placements, most of them open to anyone willing to attend a public school. The majority's view that all educational choices are comparable for purposes of choice ignores the whole point of the choice test: it is a criterion for deciding whether indirect aid to a religious school is legitimate because it passes through private hands that can spend or use the aid in a secular school. The question is whether the private hand is genuinely free to send the money in either a secular direction or a religious one.

Defining choice as choice in spending the money or channeling the aid is, moreover, necessary if the choice criterion is to function as a limiting principle at all. If "choice" is present whenever there is any educational alternative to the religious school to which vouchers can be endorsed, then there will always be a choice and the voucher can always be constitutional, even in a system in which there is not a single private secular school as an alternative to the religious school. And because it is unlikely that any participating private religious school will enroll more pupils than the generally available public system, it will be easy to generate numbers suggesting that aid to religion is not the significant intent or effect of the voucher scheme. . . .

If, contrary to the majority, we ask the right question about genuine choice to use the vouchers, the answer shows that . . . something is influencing choices in a way that aims the money in a religious direction: of 56 private schools in the district participating in the voucher program (only 53 of which accepted voucher students in 1999–2000), 46 of them are religious; 96.6% of all voucher recipients go to religious schools, only 3.4% to nonreligious ones. Unfortunately for the majority position, there is no explanation for this that suggests the religious direction results simply from free choices by parents.

III.

I do not dissent merely because the majority has misapplied its own law, for even if I assumed *arguendo* that the majority's formal criteria were satisfied on the facts, today's conclusion would be profoundly at odds with the Constitution. Proof of this is clear on two levels. The first is circumstantial, in the now discarded symptom of violation, the substantial dimension of the aid. The second is direct, in the defiance of every objective supposed to be served by the bar against establishment.A.

The scale of the aid to religious schools approved today is unprecedented, both in the number of dollars and in the proportion of systemic school expenditure supported. Each measure has received attention in previous cases. . . .

The Cleveland voucher program has cost Ohio taxpayers $33 million since its implementation in 1996 ($28 million in voucher payments, $5 million in administrative costs), and its cost was expected to exceed $8 million in the 2001–2002 school year. These tax-raised funds are on top of the textbooks, reading and math tutors, laboratory equipment, and the like that Ohio provides to private schools, worth roughly $600 per child.

The gross amounts of public money contributed are symptomatic of the scope of what the taxpayers' money buys for a broad class of religious-school students. In paying for practically the full amount of tuition for thousands of qualifying students, cf. *Nyquist* (state aid amounting to 50% of tuition was unconstitutional), the scholarships purchase everything that tuition purchases, be it instruction in math or indoctrination in faith. The consequences of "substantial" aid hypothesized in *Meek* are realized here: the majority makes no pretense that substantial amounts of tax money are not systematically underwriting religious practice and indoctrination.

B.

It is virtually superfluous to point out that every objective underlying the prohibition of religious establishment is betrayed by this scheme, but something has to be said about the enormity of the violation. I anticipated these objectives earlier, in discussing *Everson*, which cataloged them, the first being respect for freedom of conscience. Jefferson described it as the idea that no one "shall be compelled to . . . support any religious worship, place, or ministry whatsoever," even a "teacher of his own religious persuasion,"[5] and Madison thought it violated by any "authority which can force a citizen to contribute three pence . . . of his property for the support of any . . . establishment.' Memorial and Remonstrance ¶3. . . .

As for the second objective, to save religion from its own corruption, Madison wrote of the "experience . . . that ecclesiastical establishments, instead of maintaining the purity and efficacy of Religion, have had a contrary operation." Memorial and Remonstrance ¶7. In Madison's time, the manifestations were "pride and indolence in the Clergy; ignorance and servility in the laity, in both, superstition, bigotry and persecution." In the 21st century, the risk is one of "corrosive secularism" to religious schools, and the specific threat is to the primacy of the schools' mission to educate the children of the faithful according to the unaltered precepts of their faith. . . .

Increased voucher spending is not, however, the sole portent of growing regulation of religious practice in the school, for state mandates to moderate religious teaching may well be the most obvious response to the third concern behind the ban on establishment, its inextricable link with social conflict. As appropriations for religious subsidy rise, competition for the money will tap sectarian religion's capacity for discord.

---

5. A Bill for Establishing Religious Freedom §1, 2 (1786) (adopted by the General Assembly of Virginia on 16 January 1786; now part of Code of Virginia, §57-1).

COMMENTS AND QUESTIONS

1. Do you agree with the majority that Cleveland's pilot program gave parents "true private choice"? The answer largely depends on whether one examines the total range of educational choices available to parents in the Cleveland system (including public schools) or instead only the range of institutions where parents could spend the scholarships offered by the new program. Can you imagine a voucher program that would not survive constitutional scrutiny under the majority's analysis?
2. The majority conducted no inquiry into the amount of government money reaching religious schools. Why does Justice Souter think such an inquiry would support the underlying objectives of the First Amendment's Establishment Clause?
3. We have seen that protection for free exercise can be reduced if the Free Exercise Clause is interpreted as an equality norm (recall *Employee Division v. Smith*, and the "general and neutral law" test). Are there similar risks if the Establishment Clause is interpreted primarily as an equal treatment provision?
4. In the 2010 case *Arizona Christian School Tuition Organization v. Winn*, Arizona taxpayers sued the state alleging that tax credits for donations to School Tuition Organizations (STOs), which then used the contributions to provide scholarships for students attending private schools, including religious schools, violated the Establishment Clause.[6] The District Court dismissed the case for lack of standing; the Ninth Circuit reversed under *Flast v. Cohen*, holding that respondents had standing. The Ninth Circuit was in turn reversed by the US Supreme Court,[7] which ruled that there was not a sufficient nexus between a taxpayer and a choice by STOs to encourage attendance at private schools. The dissent in *Winn* countered that the difference between a subsidy and a tax credit was immaterial and that by refusing standing to the taxpayers in this case, the Court was inviting statutes to end-run *Flast's* guarantee of access to the judiciary, thus providing for future government support of religion through tax credits while precluding taxpayer review.[8] Is this in fact a further limitation of standing under *Flast*, extending the *Hein* decision discussed in Chapter 12?
5. For a number of reasons, voucher programs have not greatly increased since *Zelman*. First, although the voucher program in *Zelman* did overcome constitutional scrutiny at the federal level, such programs may be unconstitutional according to some state constitutions.[9] Second, voucher programs remained unpopular among the voting population and lost support, particularly from the religious right and civil rights groups. The religious right had initially supported vouchers to help fund sending their children to religious private institutions; however, with the implementation of standards in the No Child Left Behind program, many in this group feared that religious private

---

6. *Arizona Christian School Tuition Organization v. Winn*, 131 S.Ct. 1436, 1437 (U.S. 2011).

7. 131 S. Ct. at 1437.8. *Id.* at 1451.

8. *Id.* at 1451.

9. The information in this paragraph is taken from Tyler Heid, Why Have School Voucher Programs Not Expanded Very Much Since the Supreme Court's *Zelman v. Simmons-Harris* Ruling? 3 (December 2014) (unpublished manuscript on file with the authors).

institutions would be held to the federally mandated standards, which caused this sector's support of voucher programs to diminish.[10] Similarly, civil rights groups initially supported the voucher programs as an opportunity to give racial minorities more educational options by providing funding for private school attendance. Many in this group now view voucher programs as harmful to public schools.[11] Third, the dramatic increase in charter schools throughout the United States provided more educational opportunities for children, which undercut one of the main reasons for supported voucher programs: increased school choice. Finally, lower courts have narrowly interpreted *Zelman* so that voucher programs are only permissible in fact patterns similar to those presented in this case, namely where a public school is poor and failing.

6. How much difference does the form of a financial benefit make for Establishment Clause purposes? *Nyquist* invalidated a scheme that provided outright grants to low-income parents and computed benefits for higher-income parents in accordance with a formula that would yield a benefit comparable to the tuition grants of lower-income parents. (There were debates about whether the tax benefit involved was a credit, a deduction, or some more general type of tax modification (413 U.S. at 789.) The benefits, however, were provided only to those with children in non-public schools. In *Mueller*, a tax deduction for educational expenses for all parents was sustained. As just described, voucher plans have taken a variety of forms, but typically involve a financial instrument that parents can use to direct state payments to a school of their choice. Which systems will work best for low-income families?

Additional Web Resources:	Materials on voucher programs, together with empirical studies and other materials arguing in favor of or against their adoption

B. EUROPE

In contrast to the United States, many European countries allow substantial funding of at least secular components of education at religious schools. The Evangelical Church (EKD) and Catholic Church in Germany receive billions of euros every year to support church school through a combination of contributions, taxes, fees, and state subsidies. The state also provides funding to religions for activities that serve the general public, such as local athletic clubs, on the grounds that churches may not be put in a worse position than secular groups that receive public funds for providing similar activities. Additionally, instructors of religion at public schools and universities are paid by the state. The remainder of the churches' income is made up of fees for church services, such as school instruction, child care services, and third party donations.[12]

10. *Citing* James Forman, Jr., The Rise and Fall of School Vouchers: A Story of Religion, Race, and Politics, 54 *UCLA L. Rev*. 547 (2007).

11. *Citing* Nancy Kanode, Private Schools Vouchers: Bad for America, *The Constitutional Principle: Separation of Church and State*, July 1998, http://candst.tripod.com/nkanode.htm.

12. *See* Gerhard Robbers, *Religion and Law in Germany* 274, 273–276 (Roger Blanpain et al. eds., Kluwer Law International 2010).

The European Convention allows states to subsidize religious schools, but it does not impose a positive obligation on states to fund religious schools. The leading case on this issue was decided by the European Commission of Human Rights in 1978.

X. v. The United Kingdom

European Commission of Human Rights, App. No. 7782/77 (2 May 1978)

Summary of the Facts

The applicant states that he is one of a group of parents who are anxious to see the development in Northern Ireland of non-denominational schools. According to him, state schools, most of which were formerly private Protestant schools, have remained under that religious influence whereas private catholic schools are under the influence of that religion. The former, controlled by public authorities, are entirely state-maintained, whereas the latter, in which private bodies have a controlling interest, receive financial aid from the State, representing 85% of capital expenditure and 100% of their recurrent costs.

Private bodies wishing to set up a non-denominational ("integrated") school must therefore bear 15% of the capital costs themselves which in the eyes of the applicant represents an unsurmountable obstacle.

The Law

1. The applicant complains that the failure of the education authority to provide a 100% grant for a parent controlled integrated school results in his religious and philosophical beliefs, and those of other parents, not being respected, contrary to Article 2 of the First Protocol [to the ECHR]. He submits correspondence with the various authorities responsible for education in Northern Ireland as evidence of his attempt to establish an integrated primary school on the basis of a 100% Government grant.

Article 2 of the First Protocol provides as follows:

> "No person shall be denied the right to education. In the exercise of any functions which it assumes in relation to education and to teaching, the State shall respect the right of parents to ensure such education and teaching in conformity with their own religious and philosophical convictions."

It is clear from the interpretation given to Article 2 by the European Court of Human Rights in the case of *Kjeldsen, Busk Madsen and Pedersen* (the Danish Sex Education Cases) that the second sentence of Article 2 is an adjunct of the fundamental right to education and that the Article should be interpreted as a whole. In the interpretation of the first sentence of Article 2 the Court also made it clear, in the *Belgian Linguistic Case*, that there is no obligation on the State to "establish at their own expense, or to subsidise, education of any particular type or at any particular level." Accordingly, interpreting the Article as a whole, there is no positive obligation on the State, in relation to the second sentence of Article 2, to subsidise any particular form of education in order to respect the religious and philosophical beliefs of parents. It is sufficient for the State in order to comply with its obligations under Article 2 to evidence respect for the religious and philosophical beliefs of parents within the existing and developing system of education. . . .

The Commission observes that, in fact, a considerable financial subsidy (85% capital costs and 100% recurrent costs), assuming a proposed scheme to have been approved by the Department of Education, is available to parents wishing to establish a voluntary integrated school.

2. The Commission has also examined, *ex officio*, whether the difference in subsidy available to State schools on the one hand and voluntary schools on the other hand, is a breach of Article 14 of the Convention in conjunction with the second sentence of Article 2 of the First Protocol.

Article 14 provides as follows:

> The enjoyment of the rights and freedoms set forth in this Convention shall be secured without discrimination on any ground such as sex, race, colour, language, religion, political or other opinion, national or social origin, association with a national minority, property, birth or other status.
>
> . . .

[I]n the present case, when it is clear that Article 2 of the First Protocol does not give rise to an obligation to subsidise any particular type of education, Article 14 would require that the authorities do not discriminate in the provision of available financial subsidies.

However, it is established that there is a difference in the grant available to bodies who want to set up a voluntary school (85% capital costs and 100% recurrent costs) and the grant available to controlled schools (100% capital and recurrent costs). In its determination whether there is discrimination within the meaning of Article 14 in the present case, the Commission considers that it is legitimate for the State to exercise substantial control in the ownership and management of schools for which it provides a full 100% subsidy. Conversely, the Commission is of the opinion that it is reasonable for the State, in relation to bodies that seek ownership and decisive control over management policy in voluntary schools, to require some degree of financial contribution. The Commission does not consider that the requirement of a 15% contribution [in] capital costs is an unreasonable or disproportionate requirement, taking into consideration that ownership of the school would be vested in trustees representative of the body concerned and the exercise of two thirds control in the governing body.

Accordingly the Commission is of the opinion that there has been no discrimination within the meaning of Article 14. . . .

For these reasons, the Commission DECLARES THE APPLICATION INADMISSIBLE.

Additional Web Resources:	Later cases regarding the lack of a positive obligation to fund religious schools Materials on state regulation of religious schools

III. NON-DISCRIMINATION NORMS AND FREEDOM OF RELIGION IN EDUCATION

One significant conflict in many parts of the world is between non-discrimination norms and the religious freedom of religious schools.

A. UNITED STATES

With increasing frequency, religious schools in the United States are called upon to explain to legislatures and accreditation bodies why school policies with moral codes on sexuality should not serve to disqualify them from tax-exempt status, threaten their accreditation, or even call for civil fines.

In California, for example, two bills have been proposed that seek to burden religious schools that expect students or faculty to have moral codes on sexuality. The first bill, in 2016, would have cut off state loans to students at religious schools who sought exemptions from Title IX based on their religious teachings about gender and sexuality. A compromise was found that did not penalize the students, and the bill was passed with few opponents.

However, the next year another bill sought to forbid religious schools from having codes of conduct that limit what the bill calls "reproductive health care decisions," such as having an abortion or a child out of wedlock.[13] The bill also forbids firing or demoting an employee on similar grounds. Should this bill become law, discussion will appear on the Web Supplement.

In other situations, complaints are being filed with accreditation bodies against religious schools because they speak out on issues of sexuality. For example, the president of Gordon College, the only nondenominational Christian college in Massachusetts, signed a letter that encouraged enacting protection for the LGBT community through an executive order while at the same time allowing exemptions from that order—so that "an extension of protection for one group not come at the expense of faith communities."[14] The letter triggered an outcry and Gordon College's regional accreditation was called into question. While the college was eventually able to maintain its accreditation, and indeed, federal law protects religious schools' religious mission,[15] such calls for accreditation to be revoked represent a worrisome trend.

B. CANADA

Trinity Western University (TWU) is a private Christian university established in British Columbia in 1957 by the Evangelical Free Church of America. In 2012, TWU submitted a proposal to the provincial Ministry of Advanced Education and the Federation of Law Societies of Canada for offering a Juris Doctor program. The Ministry and the Federation gave approval of the program, and automatic accreditation of TWU law graduates was approved by the law societies of all provinces except those of Upper Canada (Ontario) and Nova Scotia (New

13. See California State Legislature, AB-569 Discrimination: reproductive health.
14. Letter from Joel C. Hunter, et al. to President Obama, 1 July 2014.
15. Higher Education Opportunity Act of 2008, Public Law 110-315 (2008).

Brunswick was only one vote away from refusal), majorities of whose members objected to the provision TWU's admission requirement that students sign a Community Covenant which stated, in part, "In keeping with biblical and TWU ideals, community members voluntarily abstain from . . . sexual intimacy that violates the sacredness of marriage between a man and a woman."[16] In 2014, the British Columbia Minister of Advanced Education revoked the province's approval, and some 3000 or the 13,000 members of the Law Society of British Columbia voted to reverse its decision in favor of accreditation, with the remaining 8,000 members not registering a vote.

TWU filed lawsuits against the Nova Scotia Barristers Society, the Law Society of Upper Canada, and the Law Society of British Columbia alleging that the accreditation refusals constituted violation of the law students' freedoms of religion, expression, and association. In the provincial suits, TWU prevailed only in Nova Society. TWU's victory in the latter case was affirmed, but so was its loss in the Upper Canada decision. This split was further compounded when the lower British Columbia decision was reversed. In February 2017, the Supreme Court of Canada granted leave to TWU to appeal the decision of the Ontario court. The case, heard 30 November–1 December 2017, involved an "unprecedented list of interveners [including] humanists, atheists, lawyers, Evangelicals, Sikhs, Seventh Day Adventists, Catholic bishops, secularists, teachers, charities . . ." attempting to influence the outcome of this landmark hearing.[17]

On 15 June 2018, the Supreme Court issued its decision in *Law Society of British Columbia v. Trinity Western University*, 2018 SCC 32. The 7-2 ruling upholding the rights of the law societies to refuse to admit graduates of TWU's proposed law school was seen as a "severe blow" to religious freedom in Canada and throughout the West, a decision that, in the words of the Canadian Conference of Catholic Bishops, is "a harbinger for serious disputes to come."[18]

COMMENTS AND QUESTIONS

1. Should it make a difference to the outcome of a case such as *Trinity Western* if the university were receiving direct state subsidies to carry out its programs? If students were receiving state scholarships or state-backed loans to pursue their education? If TWU were a tax-exempt organization and donors receive tax deductions for contributions made to TWU?
2. Note that nothing about the Trinity Western covenant requires its eventual graduates, when they are later practicing law, to discriminate against LGBT individuals. Should accreditation bodies be able to deny accreditation to an institution based on the possibility that some of its graduates may engage in discrimination?
3. Then Chief Justice of Canada Beverly McLachlin spoke in 2002 of a "dialectic of normative commitments":

---

16. Trinity Western University, *Community Covenant Agreement*. *See* Barry W. Bussey, Space Enough for a Christian Law School, *Oxford J. L. & Religion* 2015, 4, 303–307.

17. Ian Mulgrew, Supreme Court interveners speak for and against TWU law school, *Vancouver Sun*, 1 December 2017.

18. Celeste McGovern, Canadian Top Court Renders 'Severe Blow' to Religious Freedom in Trinity Western Case, *National Catholic Register*, 28 July 2018.

> What is good, true and just in religion will not always comport with the law's view of the matter, nor will society at large always properly respect conscientious adherence to alternate authorities and divergent normative, or ethical, commitments. Where this is so, two comprehensive worldviews collide. It is at this point that the question of law's treatment of religion becomes truly exigent. The authority of each is internally unassailable. What is more, both lay some claim to the whole of human experience. To which system should the subject adhere? How can the rule of law accommodate a worldview and ethos that asserts its own superior authority and unbounded scope? There seems to be no way in which to reconcile this clash; yet these clashes do occur in a society dedicated to protecting religion, and a liberal state must find some way of reconciling these competing commitments.

In its Reasons for Judgment in the Trinity Western case, the Court of Appeal for British Columbia quoted the above passage from Chief Justice McLachlin and noted further,

> A society that does not admit of and accommodate differences cannot be a free and democratic society—one in which its citizens are free to think, to disagree, to debate and to challenge the accepted view without fear of reprisal. This case demonstrates that a well-intentioned majority acting in the name of tolerance and liberalism, can, if unchecked, impose its views on the minority in a manner that is in itself intolerant and illiberal.

Consider these ideas in comparison with the reasoning of the Supreme Court in June 2018 ruling, where the justices found that the law society

> in this case interpreted its duty to uphold and protect the public interest as precluding the approval of TWU's proposed law school because the requirement that students sign the Covenant as a condition of admission effectively imposes inequitable barriers on entry to the school and ultimately, inequitable barriers on entry to the profession.

See extensive treatment of the *Trinity Western* case and its aftermath on the Web Supplement.

IV. RELIGION IN STATE SCHOOLS

A. THE HUMAN RIGHTS FRAMEWORK OF FREEDOM OF RELIGION AND EDUCATION

The international instruments afford nations substantial latitude in structuring educational programs at various levels in ways that can reconcile religious instruction with freedom of thought, religion, and belief. Critical issues are the degree of state action; the maturity of the individual receiving the education; and whether there is endorsement of a particular religion or religions on the one hand, and whether there is disparagement, discrimination, and exclusion on the other.

In addition to the general protections for freedom of religion or belief (e.g., ICCPR, Article 18(1)-(3) and ECHR Article 9), special protections are provided with respect to the rights of parents and guardians in the context of education. ICCPR Article 18(4) provides: "The States Parties to the present Covenant undertake to have respect for the liberty of parents and, when applicable, legal guardians to ensure the religious and moral education of their children in conformity with their own convictions." The 1981 UN Declaration on the Elimination of All Forms of Intolerance and of Discrimination Based on Religion or Belief, Art. 5.2, goes into somewhat more detail:

> 2. Every child shall enjoy the right to have access to education in the matter of religion or belief in accordance with the wishes of his parents or, as the case may be, legal guardians, and shall not be compelled to receive teaching on religion or belief against the wishes of his parents or legal guardians, the best interests of the child being the guiding principle.

In 1993 the UN Human Rights Committee issued the following statements regarding teaching religion in public schools as part of its General Comment 22(48):

> 6. The Committee is of the view that article 18(4) permits public school instruction in subjects such as the general history of religions and ethics if it is given in a neutral and objective way. The liberty of parents or legal guardians to ensure that their children receive a religious and moral education in conformity with their own convictions, set forth in article 18(4), is related to the guarantees of the freedom to teach a religion or belief stated in article 18(1). The Committee notes that public education that includes instruction in a particular religion or belief is inconsistent with article 18(4) unless provision is made for non-discriminatory exemptions or alternatives that would accommodate the wishes of parents and guardians. . . .
>
> 10. If a set of beliefs is treated as official ideology in constitutions, statutes, proclamations of the ruling parties, etc., or in actual practice, this shall not result in any impairment of the freedoms under article 18 or any other rights recognized under the Covenant nor in any discrimination against persons who do not accept the official ideology or who oppose it.[19]

If the state decides to conduct religious instruction of some form, it is vital that this be handled in as neutral and objective a way as possible. In fact, this is extremely difficult to do. Any instruction will reflect some orientation or other, if only a "secularist" orientation, which is problematic for many religious believers. At a minimum, individuals who object to such instruction should be given a right to opt out, and the opt-out procedure and actual administration of the system should be structured in a way that minimizes the likelihood that an individual will be discriminated against or stigmatized.

Under the provisions of the 1989 UN Convention on the Rights of the Child (CRC), which has been ratified by virtually every nation on earth,[20] the rights of children—"below the age of eighteen years unless under the law applicable to the child, majority is attained earlier" (Art. 1)—are guaranteed "without discrimination of any kind, irrespective of the child's or his or her parent's or legal guardian's race, colour, sex, language, religion, political or other opinion, national, ethnic or social origin, property, disability, birth or other status" (Preamble). This guarantee protects "the right of the child to freedom of thought, conscience and religion" and "the rights and duties of the parents and, when applicable, legal guardians, to provide direction to the child in the exercise of his or her right in a

---

19. General Comment No. 22(48), UNHRC, at §§6, 10 (1993).

20. UN Res. 44/55 20 November 1989, entry into force 2 September 1990. With the ratification by South Sudan and Somalia in 2015, the United States remains the only UN Member State not to have ratified the CRC.

manner consistent with the evolving capacities of the child" (Art. 14). In addition, Article 30 provides that in States where "ethnic, religious or linguistic minorities or persons of indigenous origin exist, a child belonging to such a minority or who is indigenous shall not be denied the right, in community with other members of his or her group, to enjoy his or her own culture, to profess and practise his or her own religion, or to use his or her own language."

Additional Web Resources:	UN Human Rights Committee decision in *Leirvåg v. Norway* (holding that insufficiently sensitive opt-out requirements from Christian culture course violated Article 18(4) of ICCPR)

B. THE UNITED STATES

1. School Prayer

In *Engel v. Vitale*, 370 U.S. 421 (1962), the parents of ten students in a New York school district brought suit when the district adopted the practice of requiring each class to recite a prayer at the beginning of each school day. The prayer was composed by the State Board of Regents, a government agency with authority over the state's public school system, and read: "Almighty God, we acknowledge our dependence upon Thee, and we beg Thy blessings upon us, our parents, our teachers and our Country." The parents challenged both the state law authorizing the practice and the school district's regulation ordering the practice, asserting that they violated the Establishment Clause. New York's highest court upheld the use of the prayer. The Supreme Court disagreed, holding there "could be no doubt" that a daily invocation was a religious activity, and that such a practice was "wholly inconsistent with the Establishment Clause."

The Court noted, "It is a matter of history that this very practice of establishing governmentally composed prayers for religious services was one of the reasons which caused many of our early colonists to leave England and seek religious freedom in America." (425)

In response to an argument by the Board of Education that to apply the Constitution in such a way as to prohibit the daily prayers was to "indicate a hostility toward religion or toward prayer," the Court concluded,

> Nothing, of course, could be more wrong. The history of man is inseparable from the history of religion. And perhaps it is not too much to say that since the beginning of that history many people have devoutly believed that "More things are wrought by prayer than this world dreams of." It was doubtless largely due to men who believed this that there grew up a sentiment that caused men to leave the cross-currents of officially established state religions and religious persecution in Europe and come to this country filled with the hope that they could find a place in which they could pray when they pleased to the God of their faith in the language they chose. And there were men of this same faith in the power of prayer who led the fight for adoption of our Constitution and also for our Bill of Rights with the very guarantees of religious

> freedom that forbid the sort of governmental activity which New York has attempted here. These men knew that the First Amendment, which tried to put an end to governmental control of religion and of prayer, was not written to destroy either. It is neither sacrilegious nor antireligious to say that each separate government in this country should stay out of the business of writing or sanctioning official prayers and leave that purely religious function to the people themselves and to those the people choose to look to for religious guidance. (434-435)

MOMENTS OF SILENCE

Two decades after *Engel v. Vitale*, the Court considered whether a state statute requiring a moment of silence at the beginning of each school day violated the Establishment Clause. In *Wallace v. Jaffree*, 472 U.S. 38 (1985), the plaintiffs, again parents of children in the affected public schools, brought suit to challenge the constitutionality of an Alabama statute providing for a one-minute period of silence at the beginning of each day in all public schools for the purpose of "meditation or voluntary prayer." The Supreme Court applied the "secular purpose" prong of the *Lemon* test, asking "whether the Government's actual purpose was to endorse or disapprove of religion." Based on testimony from the legislation's sponsor that the legislation was an "effort to return voluntary prayer" to public schools, and on the legislative context, the Court found that "the State did not present evidence of any secular purpose," that the legislature enacted the law "for the sole purpose of expressing the State's endorsement of prayer activities for one minute at the beginning of each school day," and that such an endorsement was "not consistent with the established principle that government must pursue a course of complete neutrality toward religion."

In her concurring opinion, Justice O'Connor applied her endorsement test to assess whether the "moment of silence" approach "sends a message to nonadherents that they are outsiders, not full members of the political community." She concluded that moment-of-silence laws are not automatically invalid and unconstitutional, though the one at issue in *Wallace v. Jaffree* was:

> A state-sponsored moment of silence in the public schools is different from state-sponsored vocal prayer or Bible reading. First, a moment of silence is not inherently religious. Silence, unlike prayer or Bible reading, need not be associated with a religious exercise. Second, a pupil who participates in a moment of silence need not compromise his or her beliefs. During a moment of silence, a student who objects to prayer is left to his or her own thoughts, and is not compelled to listen to the prayers or thoughts of others. For these simple reasons, a moment of silence statute does not stand or fall under the Establishment Clause according to how the Court regards vocal prayer or Bible reading. [72] . . .
>
> By mandating a moment of silence, a State does not necessarily endorse any activity that might occur during the period. [73] . . .
>
> If a legislature expresses a plausible secular purpose for a moment of silence statute in either the text or the legislative history, or if the statute disclaims an intent to encourage prayer over alternatives during a moment of silence, then courts should generally defer to that stated intent. [74] . . .
>
> Since there is arguably a secular pedagogical value to a moment of silence in public schools, courts should find an improper purpose behind such a statute only if the statute on its face, in its official legislative history, or in its interpretation by a

responsible administrative agency suggests it has the primary purpose of endorsing prayer. [75]

PRAYER AT PUBLIC SCHOOL GRADUATION CEREMONIES

LEE V. WEISMAN

Supreme Court of the United States, 505 U.S. 577 (1922)

Justice KENNEDY delivered the opinion of the Court.

. . . The question before us is whether including clerical members who offer prayers as part of the official school graduation ceremony is consistent with the Religion Clauses of the First Amendment. . . .

Deborah Weisman graduated from Nathan Bishop Middle School, a public school in Providence, at a formal ceremony in June 1989. She was about 14 years old. For many years it has been the policy of the Providence School Committee and the Superintendent to permit principals to invite members of the clergy to give invocations and benedictions at middle school and high school graduations. . . . Acting for himself and his daughter, Deborah's father, Daniel Weisman, objected to any prayers at Deborah's middle school graduation, but to no avail. . . .

The school board (and the United States, which supports it as *amicus curiae*) argued that these short prayers and others like them at graduation exercises are of profound meaning to many students and parents throughout this country. We assume this to be so in addressing the difficult case now before us, for the significance of the prayers lies also at the heart of Daniel and Deborah Weisman's case. . . .

These dominant facts mark and control the confines of our decision: State officials direct the performance of a formal religious exercise at promotional and graduation ceremonies for secondary schools. Even for those students who object to the religious exercise, their attendance and participation in the state-sponsored religious activity are in a fair and real sense obligatory, though the school district does not require attendance as a condition for receipt of the diploma. . . .

[T]he controlling precedents as they relate to prayer and religious exercise in primary and secondary public schools compel the holding here that the policy of the city of Providence is an unconstitutional one. . . . The government involvement with religious activity in this case is pervasive, to the point of creating a state-sponsored and state-directed religious exercise in a public school. Conducting this formal religious observance conflicts with settled rules pertaining to prayer exercises for students, and that suffices to determine the question before us.

The principle that government may accommodate the free exercise of religion does not supersede the fundamental limitations imposed by the Establishment Clause. It is beyond dispute that, at a minimum, the Constitution guarantees that government may not coerce anyone to support or participate in religion or its exercise, or otherwise act in a way which "establishes a [state] religion or religious faith, or tends to do so." The State's involvement in the school prayers challenged today violates these central principles. . . .

The State's role did not end with the decision to include a prayer and with the choice of a clergyman. Principal Lee provided Rabbi Gutterman with a copy of the

"Guidelines for Civic Occasions," and advised him that his prayers should be nonsectarian. Through these means the principal directed and controlled the content of the prayers. . . . It is a cornerstone principle of our Establishment Clause jurisprudence that "it is no part of the business of government to compose official prayers for any group of the American people to recite as a part of a religious program carried on by government," *Engel v. Vitale*, and that is what the school officials attempted to do.

Petitioners argue, and we find nothing in the case to refute it, that the directions for the content of the prayers were a good-faith attempt by the school to ensure that the sectarianism which is so often the flashpoint for religious animosity be removed from the graduation ceremony. The school's explanation, however, does not resolve the dilemma caused by its participation. The question is not the good faith of the school in attempting to make the prayer acceptable to most persons, but the legitimacy of its undertaking that enterprise at all. . . .

It is argued that our constitutional vision of a free society requires confidence in our own ability to accept or reject ideas of which we do not approve, and that prayer at a high school graduation does nothing more than offer a choice. By the time they are seniors, high school students no doubt have been required to attend classes and assemblies and to complete assignments exposing them to ideas they find distasteful or immoral or absurd or all of these. Against this background, students may consider it an odd measure of justice to be subjected during the course of their educations to ideas deemed offensive and irreligious, but to be denied a brief, formal prayer ceremony that the school offers in return. This argument cannot prevail, however. It overlooks a fundamental dynamic of the Constitution.

The First Amendment protects speech and religion by quite different mechanisms. Speech is protected by ensuring its full expression even when the government participates, for the very object of some of our most important speech is to persuade the government to adopt an idea as its own. The method for protecting freedom of worship and freedom of conscience in religious matters is quite the reverse. In religious debate or expression the government is not a prime participant, for the Framers deemed religious establishment antithetical to the freedom of all. The Free Exercise Clause embraces a freedom of conscience and worship that has close parallels in the speech provisions of the First Amendment, but the Establishment Clause is a specific prohibition on forms of state intervention in religious affairs with no precise counterpart in the speech provisions. . . .

As we have observed before, there are heightened concerns with protecting freedom of conscience from subtle coercive pressure in the elementary and secondary public schools. . . . Our decisions in *Engel v. Vitale* and *School Dist. of Abington* [the bible-reading case] recognize, among other things, that prayer exercises in public schools carry a particular risk of indirect coercion. The concern may not be limited to the context of schools, but it is most pronounced there. . . .What to most believers may seem nothing more than a reasonable request that the nonbeliever respect their religious practices, in a school context may appear to the nonbeliever or dissenter to be an attempt to employ the machinery of the State to enforce a religious orthodoxy.

We need not look beyond the circumstances of this case to see the phenomenon at work. The undeniable fact is that the school district's supervision and control of a high school graduation ceremony places public pressure, as well as peer pressure, on attending students to stand as a group or, at least, maintain respectful silence during the invocation and benediction. This pressure, though subtle and indirect, can be as real as any overt compulsion. Of course, in our culture standing or remaining silent can signify adherence to a view or simple respect for the views of others. And no doubt some persons who have no desire to join a prayer have little objection to standing as a sign of respect for those who do. But for the dissenter of high school age, who has a reasonable perception that she is being forced by the State to pray in a manner her conscience will not allow, the injury is no less real. There can be no doubt that for many, if not most, of the students at the graduation, the act of standing or remaining silent was an expression of participation in the rabbi's prayer. That was the very point of the religious exercise. It is of little comfort to a dissenter, then, to be told that for her the act of standing or remaining in silence signifies mere respect, rather than participation. What matters is that, given our social conventions, a reasonable dissenter in this milieu could believe that the group exercise signified her own participation or approval of it. . . .

It is, we concede, a brief exercise during which the individual can concentrate on joining its message, meditate on her own religion, or let her mind wander. But the embarrassment and the intrusion of the religious exercise cannot be refuted by arguing that these prayers, and similar ones to be said in the future, are of a *de minimis* character. . . .

There was a stipulation in the District Court that attendance at graduation and promotional ceremonies is voluntary. Petitioners and the United States, as *amicus*, made this a center point of the case, arguing that the option of not attending the graduation excuses any inducement or coercion in the ceremony itself. The argument lacks all persuasion. Law reaches past formalism. And to say a teenage student has a real choice not to attend her high school graduation is formalistic in the extreme. . . . Everyone knows that in our society and in our culture high school graduation is one of life's most significant occasions. . . . Attendance may not be required by official decree, yet it is apparent that a student is not free to absent herself from the graduation exercise in any real sense of the term "voluntary," for absence would require forfeiture of those intangible benefits which have motivated the student through youth and all her high school years. Graduation is a time for family and those closest to the student to celebrate success and express mutual wishes of gratitude and respect. . . .

The importance of the event is the point the school district and the United States rely upon to argue that a formal prayer ought to be permitted, but it becomes one of the principal reasons why their argument must fail. Their contention . . . is that the prayers are an essential part of these ceremonies because for many persons an occasion of this significance lacks meaning if there is no recognition, however brief, that human achievements cannot be understood apart from their spiritual essence. We think the Government's position that this interest suffices to force students to choose between compliance or forfeiture demonstrates fundamental inconsistency in its argumentation. It fails to acknowledge that what for many of Deborah's classmates and their parents was a spiritual imperative was for Daniel and Deborah Weisman religious conformance compelled by the State. The Constitution forbids the State to exact religious conformity from a student as the price of attending her own high school graduation. This is the calculus the Constitution commands. . . .

We do not hold that every state action implicating religion is invalid if one or a few citizens find it offensive. People may take offense at all manner of religious as well as nonreligious messages, but offense alone does not in every case show a violation. We know too that sometimes to endure social isolation or even anger may be the price of conscience or nonconformity. But, by any reading of our cases, the conformity required of the student in this case was too high an exaction to withstand the test of the Establishment Clause. The prayer exercises in this case are especially improper because the State has in every practical sense compelled attendance and participation in an explicit religious exercise at an event of singular importance to every student, one the objecting student had no real alternative to avoid. . . .

The sole question presented is whether a religious exercise may be conducted at a graduation ceremony in circumstances where, as we have found, young graduates who object are induced to conform. No holding by this Court suggests that a school can persuade or compel a student to participate in a religious exercise. That is being done here, and it is forbidden by the Establishment Clause of the First Amendment.

For the reasons we have stated, the judgment of the Court of Appeals is *Affirmed.*

Justice SCALIA dissented, joined by CHIEF JUSTICE REHNQUIST, Justice WHITE, and Justice THOMAS. Justice SCALIA reasoned, in part:

Three Terms ago, I joined an opinion recognizing that the Establishment Clause must be construed in light of the "government policies of accommodation, acknowledgment, and support for religion [that] are an accepted part of our political and cultural heritage." That opinion affirmed that "the meaning of the Clause is to be determined by reference to historical practices and understandings." . . . *County of Allegheny v. American Civil Liberties Union*, 492 U.S. 573, [670] (1989) (KENNEDY, J., concurring in judgment in part and dissenting in part).

These views of course prevent me from joining today's opinion, which is conspicuously bereft of any reference to history. In holding that the Establishment Clause prohibits invocations and benedictions at public-school graduation ceremonies, the Court—with nary a mention that it is doing so—lays waste a tradition that is as old as public-school graduation ceremonies themselves, and that is a component of an even more longstanding American tradition of nonsectarian prayer to God at public celebrations generally. As its instrument of destruction, the bulldozer of its social engineering, the Court invents a boundless, and boundlessly manipulable, test of psychological coercion. Today's opinion shows more forcefully than volumes of argumentation why our Nation's protection, that fortress which is our Constitution, cannot possibly rest upon the changeable philosophical predilections of the Justices of this Court, but must have deep foundations in the historic practices of our people. . . . From our Nation's origin, prayer has been a prominent part of governmental ceremonies and proclamations. The Declaration of Independence, the document marking our birth as a separate people, "appealed to the Supreme Judge of the world for the rectitude of our intentions" and avowed "a firm reliance on the protection of divine Providence." In his first inaugural address, after swearing his oath of office on a Bible, George Washington deliberately made a prayer a part of his first official act as President. . . .

In addition to this general tradition of prayer at public ceremonies, there exists a more specific tradition of invocations and benedictions at public school graduation exercises. By one account, the first public high school graduation ceremony . . . in Connecticut in . . . 1868 [contained long majestic prayers]. As the Court obliquely acknowledges in describing the "customary features" of high school graduations . . . the invocation and benediction have long been recognized to be "as traditional as any other parts of the [school] graduation program and are widely established." . . .

STUDENT-LED PRAYER AT SCHOOL FOOTBALL GAMES

In 2000, a school prayer case arose in the context of school athletics where the prayers were student led and student initiated. The policy of the Texas school district in *Santa Fe Independent School District v. Doe*, 530 U.S. 290 (2000), permitted the practice of having the student-elected "student council chaplain" deliver a prayer over the public address system at the beginning of each varsity home game. Two students, with their respective mothers, brought suit to challenge the constitutionality of this practice under the Establishment Clause of the First Amendment. To protect them from harassment, the District Court allowed them to bring the suit anonymously (hence "Doe" as the Respondent).

The District Court ordered a modification of the policy to "permit only nonsectarian, nonproselytising prayer." Both parties appealed, and the Fifth Circuit Court agreed with the Does that the policy remained a violation of the Establishment Clause, even as modified, and the school district appealed to the US Supreme Court. The Court held that the policy violated the Establishment Clause.

The school district's argument that these prayers were private, student speech rather than public speech were rejected because speech "on school property, at school-sponsored events, over the school's public address system, by a speaker representing the student body, under the supervision of school faculty, and pursuant to a school policy that explicitly and implicitly encourages public prayer" could not be characterized as private speech. The Court also rejected the school district's argument that attending extracurricular events is voluntary, much like attending a graduation ceremony as in *Lee*, and therefore the policy permitting prayer at football games did not coerce students to participate in religious practices. The Court provided, "To assert that high school students do not feel immense social pressure, or have a truly genuine desire, to be involved in the extracurricular event that is American high school football is "formalistic in the extreme."

COMMENTS AND QUESTIONS

1. From a constitutional point of view, does it make sense to read the Establishment Clause as prohibiting prayer in schools in all contexts, or does it make sense to read it as prohibiting sectarianism?

2. Are the situations in classrooms, graduation ceremonies, and football games sufficiently similar (or sufficiently different) to warrant the same (or different) treatment?
3. Are we better off as citizens listening to a wide variety of prayers, including those of traditions to which we do not belong, or should prayer be excluded from our public spaces? What problems are likely to arise if we were to pursue a policy of inclusion and taking turns?
4. In assessing secular purpose, should the issue be the actual purpose of legislators, or whether there is a legitimate (or conceivable) secular purpose? Why isn't introduction of a moment of silence a reasonable accommodation of those who do and those who do not wish to pray? What if silent prayer is not a religious option for some students?
5. Should schools provide rooms that can be used as prayer rooms for Muslims? Christians? Others?
6. In an effort to bypass the school prayer cases, some schools offer a moment of silence, providing secular reasons why quiet time at the start of the day is beneficial to students. Several circuits have upheld this practice as constitutional in primary schools. *See, e.g. Croft v. Governor of Texas*, 562 F.3d 735 (5th Cir. 2009) and *Brown v. Gilmore*, 258 F.3d 265 (4th Cir. 2001). Are they right?
7. Homeschoolers face special restrictions in some states as they seek to forge a program different from the public curriculum. What restrictions should be allowed on homeschoolers who homeschool for religious reasons? Should this be different from homeschooling generally? Why?

2. Bible Reading: The Line Between Inculcating Religion and Acknowledging Culture

A year after daily school prayer was ruled unconstitutional in *Engel v. Vitale*, the US Supreme Court, in *Abington School District v. Schempp*, 374 U.S. 203 (1963), considered the constitutionality of laws in Pennsylvania and Maryland that required the practice of beginning each school day with the reading of passages from the Bible or reciting the Lord's Prayer in the public school classrooms. Rejecting claims that the practice had nonreligious purposes, including "the promotion of moral values" and "the teaching of literature," the Court found that the readings and recitations constituted a religious ceremony and were "intended by the State to be so." The Court held that to require such a ceremony violated the states' Establishment Clause obligation to refrain from "aiding or opposing religion," invalidating both the practice and the laws requiring it.

TEACHING *ABOUT* RELIGION VERSUS TEACHING RELIGION

While Bible devotional readings have been declared unconstitutional by the Court, the study of the Bible "as an object of study, not God's received word" could likely be constitutional.[21] Indeed, Justice Robert Jackson, in the 1948 release

21. *See L.W. v. Knox County Bd. of Educ.*, 2006 WL 2583151 (E.D. Tenn.) (holding that the right to read and discuss the Bible at recess with Friends is a clearly established right under the First Amendment); *Doe v. Porter*, 370 F.3d 558 (6th Cir. 2004) (holding that teaching the Christian Bible

time case *McCollum v. Board of Education*, 333 U.S. 203 (1948), explained, "One can hardly respect the system of education that would leave the student wholly ignorant of the currents of religious thought that move the world society for . . . which he is being prepared." In *Schempp* itself, Justice Tom C. Clark agreed, saying, "nothing we have said here indicates that such study of the Bible or of religion, when presented objectively as part of a secular program of education, may not be effected consistently with the First Amendment." Concurring in *Schempp*, Justice Arthur Goldberg explained that "the teaching of religion" was impermissible, while the "teaching about religion" is constitutional.

In the early 2000s, the United States experienced something of a resurgence of interest in Bible literacy classes. In 2005, the school board in a West Texas town voted unanimously to add a Bible class to its high school curriculum. In 2006, Georgia became the first state in some time to offer funds for Bible classes. Two private entities produced Bible curricula that, by 2007, were purportedly used in some 450 school districts in 37 states. Proponents of such programs argue that the Bible is the most influential book ever written and that a person cannot be fully educated without knowing about it. Opponents argue that courses should not focus solely on the Bible, but should be comparative so as not to "ignore the faiths of millions of Americans." Indeed, the Texas Freedom Network found in 2006 that "the majority of public schools in Texas that offer Bible courses do not teach about the Bible in a historical or literary context as required under state law, but rather take a devotional and sectarian approach."

In 2008, the Program on Freedom of Religion or Belief of the American Civil Liberties Union (ACLU) was instrumental in settling lawsuits in favor of challengers to a curriculum in Texas which, they asserted, "rather than teaching about the Bible objectively in a historical or literary context [promoted] religion, as well as a particular religious viewpoint . . . not shared by Jews, Catholics, Orthodox Christians and many Protestants." [22] As T. Jeremy Gunn, Director of the ACLU Program, noted, "Parents, not public schools, should teach religious beliefs to children."[23]

The Republican Platform announced during the 2016 presidential election included the following passage: "A good understanding of the Bible being indispensable for the development of an educated citizenry, we encourage state legislatures to offer the Bible in a literature curriculum as an elective in America's high schools, encouragement of the teaching of elective courses about the Bible in public high schools." [24]

Proponents of this notion said they were not trying to inculcate schools with Christianity but to "make sure that young people are acquainted with a document that has played a significant role in shaping Western culture." [25] As the leader of

---

as religious truth in public school classes constituted an unconstitutional establishment of religion, even if the classes had a secular purpose to teach character development).

22. *See* ACLU Successfully Helps Parents Challenge Bible Classes in Texas Public Schools, *ACLU.org,* 5 March 2008, https://www.aclu.org/bible-public-schools.

23. *Id.*

24. *See* Great American Families, Education, Healthcare, and Criminal Justice, *Republican Platform 2016*, http://bit.ly/2fxksaX, 33.

25. *See* Emma Brown, GOP platform encourages teaching about the Bible in public schools, *The Washington Post*: *Education,* 14 July 2016, http://wapo.st/29Bf40f.

one advocacy group stated it, "You can't really fully understand the American form of government without some understanding of the Bible."[26] Opponents pointed to the "dangerous territory" of the possibility of a "Sunday school standpoint" or an inevitable bias creep, rather any guaranteed of an objective processes in the classroom.[27]

COMMENTS AND QUESTIONS

1. What criteria do you think the Court should use to determine if a school improperly "teaches religion" or "religious beliefs" instead of "teaching about religion"? Can the state oversee such instruction without running afoul of the prohibition on excessive entanglement of church and state?
2. Does the singing of religious music in public school choirs violate the Establishment Clause? Should choirs be allowed to sing masses? Spirituals? Christmas carols? The US national anthem (recall that its third verse contains the phrase "And this be our motto: 'In God is our trust'")? Does it matter where such music is sung? Is a shopping mall an appropriate venue? A school assembly? A performance for parents? May a school choir sing at the funeral of a classmate killed in a traffic accident? Should there be an opt-out right?

THE PLEDGE OF ALLEGIANCE

When the Pledge of Allegiance was written in 1892, and when it was codified by federal law in 1942, it did not include any reference to a deity. In 1952 the Knights of Columbus (a Catholic organization) began lobbying Congress to add the words "under God," which they took from Lincoln's Gettysburg Address. This revision was approved by Congress in 1954, with the House of Representatives affirming "the belief that the human person is important because he was created by God and endowed by Him with certain inalienable rights which no civil authority may usurp." The House also explicitly stated that adding the mention of God to the Pledge would "further acknowledge the dependence of our people and our Government upon the moral directions of the Creator" and "deny the atheistic and materialistic concepts of communism."[28] In the signing ceremony, President Eisenhower also alluded to atheist communism and declared, "We are reaffirming the transcendence of religious faith in America's heritage and future."[29]

In *Elk Grove Unified School District v. Newdow*, 542 U.S. 1 (2004), the father of a California elementary school student brought suit claiming that the school district's policy of requiring students to recite the Pledge of Allegiance daily was a violation of both the Establishment Clause and the Free Exercise Clause because the Pledge contained the phrase "under God." Newdow, an atheist, claimed that the practice constituted "religious indoctrination" of his child. The Ninth Circuit

---

26. *Id.*

27. *Id.*

28. H.R. Rep. No. 83-1693, at 1-2 (1954), reprinted in 1954 U.S.C.C.A.N. 2339, 2340. *See also* Steven B. Epstein, Rethinking the Constitutionality of Ceremonial Deism, 96 *Colum. L. Rev.* 2083, 2118–2122. For more on other historical information in this paragraph, *see* Steven G. Gey, "Under God, the Pledge of Allegiance, and Other Constitutional Trivia, 81 *N.C. L. Rev.* 1865, 1874–1880 (2003).

29. 100 Cong. Rec. 6348 (1954) (statement of Sen. Ferguson, quoting Pres. Eisenhower).

held in favor of Newdow. However, prior to the ruling by the Ninth Circuit, the child's mother, Sandra Banning, filed a motion to intervene or dismiss, claiming that a family court had granted her *sole* legal custody of the child and that Newdow had no legal right to involve the child as a party in the suit. The Supreme Court concluded that Newdow had no standing, and reversed the holding of the Ninth Circuit.

Newdow, in order to overcome the standing barrier, then joined with three unnamed families and filed a new suit. Despite the Supreme Court's decision in the first case, the district court found that it was still bound by the Ninth Circuit's decision on the merits, and thus held that the school district's Pledge of Allegiance policy violated the Establishment Clause. On appeal, however, the Ninth Circuit found no establishment of religion in the school district's policy, citing both Congress's purpose to promote the concept of inalienable rights, along with language from the Supreme Court's opinions in the original *Newdow* case stating that the Pledge of Allegiance is primarily a patriotic exercise that is not converted into a religious exercise simply by inclusion of the two words "under God." Subsequent cases in the First Circuit and the Massachusetts Supreme Court also upheld the constitutionality of the Pledge.[30]

COMMENTS AND QUESTIONS

1. Does an opt-out provision immunize the Pledge of Allegiance from First Amendment challenge? Under current law, a public school may lead the Pledge of Allegiance daily, as mandated by a state statute, so long as students can choose not to participate. A Florida law requiring written parental permission for children to opt out of the Pledge was ruled unconstitutional by a Florida district court, but the 11th Circuit Court of Appeals reversed, upholding the law as a "parental-rights statute" distinguishable from *Barnette.*[31] The phrase "under God" was added to the Pledge during the height of the Cold War as a counterpoint to the "godless communism" of the Soviet Union.[32] In 2000, Russia revised the words of its national anthem to include references to God. The new lyrics begin with "Russia—our sacred state" and later declare, "God keeps safe this native land!" Consider the irony that "under God" may be held unconstitutional in the United States, whereas references to God have been inserted into the Russian national anthem. Are the pressures to include such symbolic assertions appropriate? Avoidable? In need of restraint?
2. In determining the constitutionality of the words "under God" in the Pledge of Allegiance, should we look at the Pledge as a whole, or at the history of the inclusion of the words? If we consider the enactment history, does the addition of the words "under God" look like an "endorsement" of religion? What if the

---

30. *See Newdow v. Rio Linda Union School Dist.*, 597 F. 3d 1007 (9th Cir. 2010), *Freedom From Religion Found. v. Hanover Sch. Dist.*, 626 F.3d 1 (1st Cir. 2010), and *Doe v. Acton-Boxborough Reg'l Sch. Dist.*, 468 Mass. 64 (2014).

31. *Frazier v. Alexandre*, 434 F. Supp. 2d 1350 (S.D. Fla. 2006), *rev'd*, 535 F.3d 1279 (11th Cir. 2009).

32. Respondent's Brief on the Merits at 11–12, *Elk Grove Unified School District v. Newdow*, 542 U.S. 1 (2004) (No. 02-1624); *see also* Gey, *supra* note 27, at 81.

enactment is measured against the purpose and effects prongs of the *Lemon* test? Does it satisfy the Court's requirement of neutrality?

3. A Wisconsin high school had conducted its graduation ceremony in an Evangelical church for nearly a decade when nine students and parents sued the school district claiming that the ceremony endorsed a particular religion, violating the Establishment Clause of the First Amendment. The church's lobby contained "evangelical literature, much of which addresse[d] children and teens" and Christian banners and posters. Church members also opened religious information booths during some of the ceremonies. The ceremony was held in the sanctuary of the church where a 15- to 20- foot-tall Latin cross was attached to the wall and Bibles, hymnal books, and donation envelopes filled the pews. In 2012, the United States Court of Appeals for the Seventh Circuit held in *Doe v. Elmbrook School District* that "[t]he atmosphere of the Church, both inside and outside the sanctuary, is indisputably and emphatically Christian," providing a proselytizing environment that impermissibly endorses religion. The Supreme Court declined to hear the case, leaving it to stand as the law of the circuit.

Additional Web Resources:	Module on civil religion, including additional materials on the Pledge of Allegiance, more general materials on civil religion in the United States, the debate about whether references to Christianity should be included in a European constitution, and the question whether laïcité is the civil religion of France

3. Evolution and Creation Science

In *Epperson v. Arkansas*, 393 U.S. 97 (1968), a public high school teacher in Little Rock, Arkansas, was dismissed for violating a state statute that prohibited the teaching of evolution in any state-supported school, college, or university. The Supreme Court overturned the law as unconstitutional, holding that "[t]he State's undoubted right to prescribe the curriculum for its public schools does not carry with it the right to prohibit, on pain of criminal penalty, the teaching of a scientific theory or doctrine where that prohibition is based upon reasons that violate the First Amendment."

Nearly 20 years later, in *Edwards v. Aguillard*, 482 U.S. 578 (1987), the Supreme Court struck down a Louisiana State law—the Louisiana Balanced Treatment for Creation-Science and Evolution-Science in Public School Instruction Act—requiring that scientific creationism be taught when evolution was taught. The Act's stated purpose was to protect academic freedom, but the Court found that the Act was not designed to further that purpose and held that the Act in fact "advances a religious doctrine by requiring either the banishment of the theory of evolution from public school classrooms or the presentation of a religious viewpoint that rejects evolution in its entirety. The Act violates the Establishment Clause of the First Amendment because it seeks to employ the symbolic and financial support of government to achieve a religious purpose."

COMMENTS AND QUESTIONS

1. With respect to the question of secular purpose, the Court in *Edwards* stated that "we need not be blind in this case to the legislature's preeminent religious purpose in enacting this statute." The Court went on to find that the legislation "sought to alter the science curriculum to reflect endorsement of a religious view that is antagonistic to the theory of evolution." Does the Court's position in effect endorse a belief system that sends a message of exclusion to those holding "a particular interpretation of the Book of Genesis"?
2. After the Supreme Court issued its ruling in *Wallace v. Jaffree* (the Alabama "moment of silence" case discussed above), the case returned to the district court for an injunction to be issued against the schools' unconstitutional practices. Douglas Smith and others filed a motion to intervene, arguing that if the court enjoined Christian activity in the public schools, it should also enjoin the teaching of "the religions of secularism, humanism, evolution, materialism, agnosticism, atheism and others." The district court agreed, enjoining the use of 44 textbooks on history, social sciences, and home economics, on grounds that they "established the religion of secular humanism." How would you rule on appeal? For the actual district court and appellate decisions, see *Smith v. Board of School Comm'rs of Mobile County*, 655 F. Supp. 939 (S.D. Ala. 1987), *rev'd*, 827 F.2d 684 (11th Cir. 1987). What if the parents only sought an exception for their children and not the whole school? *Cf. Parker v. Hurley*, 514 F.3d 87 (1st Cir. 2008) (parents sought unsuccessfully to exempt their second-grade child from reading a book favoring same-sex marriage).
3. Is the aim of the secular purpose test to endorse a secular worldview? Or is it to affirm a secular system in which all or at least a broad range of viewpoints can live together? How can this best be accomplished?

Additional Web Resources:	Module on intelligent design—the latest iteration of the creationism debate—including several cases and academic commentary

4. School Facilities and Equal Access

The question of equal access by religious and non-religious groups to public facilities and opportunities highlights what has been perceived as a tension between the Establishment Clause and the Free Exercise Clause. On one hand, allowing religious groups access to state resources undoubtedly "advances" religion in the form of a benefit it would not otherwise receive. On the other hand, refusing equal access to a group simply because it is religious may manifest a hostility to religion that is not required, and may actually be impermissible discrimination forbidden by the Constitution.

The earliest significant equal access case was *Widmar v. Vincent*, 454 U.S. 263 (1981). A state university in Missouri had an "open forum" policy that provided for the use of university facilities by registered student groups for their activities. A registered student religious group called Cornerstone that had received permission to use university facilities for several years was informed in 1977 that it could no longer do so because of a university regulation prohibiting use of its facilities "for purposes of religious worship or religious teaching." Members of the religious group sued, contending that this regulation, by prohibiting equal access by religious groups to university facilities, infringed on their right to free exercise and freedom of speech. The Supreme Court held that to justify the discriminatory exclusion from the open forum, the university was required to show that it had a narrowly tailored compelling state interest to do so, because a content-based exclusion was involved. Compliance with the Establishment Clause was concededly a compelling interest, but the exclusion was not required by that Clause. The Court concluded that the secular purpose and entanglement prongs of the *Lemon* test were met without difficulty, and since there was no evidence that religious groups would dominate the university's forum, and thus would not have the primary effect of advancing religion, the test satisfied the second prong as well. An asserted interest "in achieving greater separation of church and State than is already ensured under the Establishment Clause of the Federal Constitution" was not sufficiently compelling to justify a content-based regulation of speech. Accordingly, the state university was required to allow the same access to registered religious groups as was granted to other registered student groups.

THE EQUAL ACCESS ACT

Three years later, Congress passed the Equal Access Act, which provides:

> (a) It shall be unlawful for any public secondary school which receives Federal financial assistance and which has a limited open forum to deny equal access or a fair opportunity to, or discriminate against, any students who wish to conduct a meeting within that limited open forum on the basis of the religious, political, philosophical, or other content of the speech at such meetings.
>
> (b) A public secondary school has a limited open forum whenever such school grants an offering to or opportunity for one or more non-curriculum related student groups to meet on school premises during non-instructional time.
>
> (c) School shall be deemed to offer a fair opportunity to students who wish to conduct a meeting within its limited open forum if such school uniformly provides that—the meeting is voluntary and student-initiated; there is no [public sponsorship of the meeting. . .; [public officials]. . .are present at religious meetings only in a non-participatory capacity; the meeting does not materially and substantially interfere with the orderly conduct of educational activities within the school; and non-school persons may not direct, conduct, control, or regularly attend activities of student groups.
>
> (d) Nothing in this subchapter shall be construed to authorize the United States or any state or political subdivision thereof—to influence the form or content of any prayer or other religious activity; to require any person to participate in prayer or other religious activity; to expend public funds beyond the incidental cost of providing the space for student-initiated meetings;. . .to sanction meetings that are otherwise unlawful; to limit the rights of groups of students which are not of a specified numerical size; or to abridge the constitutional rights of any person.

The constitutionality of the Equal Access Act was sustained in *Board of Education of Westwide Community Schools v. Mergens*, 496 U.S. 226 (1990). Citing the Establishment Clause, school officials denied Mergens permission to form a Christian club that would have the same privileges and meet the same requirements as other student organizations. Justice O'Connor, with Chief Justice Rehnquist, Justice White, and Justice Blackmun, held that the same *Lemon* analysis that sustained equal access policy at the state university level in *Widmar* justified its extension to secondary schools. Justices Kennedy and Scalia agreed that the Equal Access Act did not violate the Establishment Clause, but they reached this result without relying on the plurality's *Lemon* analysis. Instead, they concluded that there was no Establishment Clause violation because the accommodation required by the Act was neutral and neither benefited religion to such a degree that it in fact established a state religion nor coerced student participation in religious activity.

Another equal access case was *Lamb's Chapel v. Center Moriches School District*, 508 U.S. 384 (1993). A New York school district issued rules and regulations for the after-hours use of public school property for social, civic, and recreational purposes. An evangelical church requested permission to use the school facilities for the showing of a partially religious film series on family values and child rearing. The school district refused due to the religious nature of the group and the activity, as meetings for religious purposes were not among the purposes specified by New York Law for after-hours use of school property. The church filed suit, alleging a violation of its First Amendment right of free speech.

Because the district's rules opened the property to a fairly broad range of "social, civic, and recreational" purposes, the Court indicated that there was "considerable force" to the view that subject matter and speaker exclusions had to be justified by a narrowly tailored compelling state interest as in *Widmar*. However, the Court concluded that even if the lower courts that had considered and rejected this contention were correct, and the school property in question had remained a nonpublic forum, the school district still could limit access to the forum on the basis of subject matter or speaker identity only if the distinctions drawn met the more lenient standard of being "reasonable in light of the purpose served by the forum and [were] viewpoint neutral." This it did not do. The fact that all religious viewpoints were excluded did not make the principle of exclusion viewpoint neutral, since films on family life from a non-religious viewpoint would not be excluded from the forum. The district sought to preserve the rulings in its favor in the lower courts on the ground that permitting its property to be used for religious purposes would violate the Establishment Clause. The Supreme Court rejected this argument for the same reasons it had given in *Widmar* and *Mergens*. Applying the *Lemon* test, the Court concluded that allowing the church access to school facilities would not constitute an establishment of religion, "since the film series would not have been shown during school hours, would not have been sponsored by the school, and would have been open to the public, there would be no realistic danger that the community would think that the District was endorsing religion or any particular creed, and any benefit to religion or the Church would have been incidental." The Court also rejected the School District's asserted justification for the exclusion, that "allowing access to a 'radical' church would lead to threats of public unrest and violence."

Just two years later, in 1995, the Supreme Court prohibited the exclusion of a student newspaper with a Christian viewpoint from financial assistance available to other student organizations at a state university in *Rosenberger v. Rector of University of Virginia*, 515 U.S. 819 (1995). The student newspaper claimed that the denial of funds amounted to a violation of their right to freedom of speech—the right to express a certain viewpoint—under the First Amendment. The Fourth Circuit held for the university, concluding that the university's viewpoint on discrimination did violate the right to freedom of speech, but that the violation was necessary to abide by Establishment Clause principles.

The Supreme Court reversed, holding that, as in *Lamb's Chapel*, the speech involved was being regulated not merely on the basis of its content, but on the basis of its viewpoint. That is, the Court distinguishes between content discrimination (discrimination based on subject matter, which may be permissible) and viewpoint discrimination (discrimination based on "the speaker's specific motivating ideology, opinion, or perspective," which is impermissible). Citing *Lamb's Chapel*, the Court concluded that the university's actions here were based on impermissible viewpoint discrimination and were not justified by countervailing Establishment Clause concerns. The university sought to distinguish *Lamb's Chapel*, arguing that provision of access to facilities is different from actual provision of state funds, and refusal to pay direct subsidies for a religious activity was therefore justified. The Court rejected this distinction, noting that while content-based decisions are inevitable when the State and its representatives (here, the university) are the speaker, as when the university decides which courses it will provide, it does not follow that viewpoint-based restrictions are proper when it "expends funds to encourage a diversity of views from private speakers." In *Rosenberger*, the student newspaper was one of the university's "Contracted Independent Organizations," all of which are required to inform third parties they deal with that the university is not responsible for them, as they are independent of the university. Accordingly, the Court held that "although it may regulate the content of expression when it is the speaker or when it enlists private entities to convey its own message, the University may not discriminate based on the viewpoint of private persons whose speech it subsidizes." Also dispositive was the Court's finding that "the governmental program here is neutral toward religion. There is no suggestion that the University created it to advance religion or adopted some ingenious device with the purpose of aiding a religious cause. . . . The neutrality of the program distinguishes the student fees from a tax levied for the direct support of a church or group of churches."

In a case similar to *Lamb's Chapel*, the Good News Club, a Christian club for children, brought suit against a public school in New York when the school rejected the club's request to use the school's facilities for weekly after-school meetings. *Good News Club v. Milford Central School*, 533 U.S. 98 (2001). The school had a policy of allowing access for a variety of activities, including those "pertaining to the welfare of the community" and concerning the "development of character and morals from a religious perspective." However, the school found the club's activities of praying, memorizing scripture, and receiving lessons from the Bible "equivalent to religious instruction itself." The school acknowledged that the club taught good character and morals through these activities, such as being kind, being obedient, and overcoming jealously, but concluded that the club's primary activity and purpose was religious instruction. Because the school, on

Establishment Clause grounds, had denied access to other religious groups, the school felt it necessary to exclude the club as well. The Second Circuit agreed with the school, holding that the subject matter of the club's activities was "quintessentially religious," and its activities "[fell] outside the bounds of pure 'moral and character development.'" The Second Circuit therefore concluded that the school's actions in excluding the club's meetings were based on "constitutional subject discrimination, not unconstitutional viewpoint discrimination." The Supreme Court disagreed and held for the club. As in *Rosenberger*, the Court asked first whether the club's free speech rights were violated by the school and, second, whether that violation was justified by the necessity of complying with the Establishment Clause.

Concerning the right to free speech, the Court found that "the only apparent difference between the activity of Lamb's Chapel and the activities of the Good News Club is that the Club chooses to teach moral lessons from a Christian perspective through live storytelling and prayer, whereas Lamb's Chapel taught lessons through films," and that "this distinction is inconsequential." The Court also noted that although a school (the state) is not obligated to allow every kind of speech when it has established a limited public forum such as the after-hours access to public school property, the state's ability to restrict speech is limited by a prohibition against discrimination based on viewpoint. The Court concluded that the school failed to show a compelling justification for the viewpoint discrimination on Establishment Clause grounds for the same reasons that the school in *Lamb's Chapel* had failed.

Justice Stevens filed a dissenting opinion, contending that the fact that a limited public forum for religious speech is created does not necessarily imply that religious proselytizing or worship services are also authorized. Justice Souter also filed a dissenting opinion, joined by Justice Ginsburg, taking a position similar to that of Justice Stevens on whether it should be possible to limit the types of religious speech for which a limited public forum can be opened, and agreeing with Justice Breyer that the Court should have remanded the case for further factual resolution.

COMMENTS AND QUESTIONS

1. Do you agree with the Court's finding in *Good News Club* that "[t]he only apparent difference between the activity of Lamb's Chapel and the activities of the Good News Club is that the Club chooses to teach moral lessons from a Christian perspective through live storytelling and prayer, whereas Lamb's Chapel taught lessons through films," and that the distinction is "inconsequential"?
2. Do you agree with the Court that if the school in *Good News Club* allowed the club to hold its meetings there, there would have been "no realistic danger that the community would think that the District was endorsing religion or any particular creed"?
3. Under the *Good News Club* rubric, could a school decline a "gay-straight alliance" student club? Could a "content" restriction be imposed on clubs focusing on sexuality and sexual issues without engaging in "viewpoint"

discrimination? Or does a school that does not want to recognize such a club need to eliminate all extracurricular student groups?

NOTE ON *CHRISTIAN LEGAL SOCIETY v. MARTINEZ*

Supreme Court of the United States, 130 S. Ct. 2971 (2010)

The Christian Legal Society (CLS), a national association, requires that members and officers of all its chapters to sign a Statement of Faith. The CLS chapter at the University of California, Hastings College of the Law was unable to achieve official status as a student organization because it excluded as leaders those students who held different beliefs than those stated in the Statement of Faith, thereby violating Hastings' nondiscrimination policy. The school's policy required student organizations to hold open eligibility for membership and leadership to all students.

CLS claimed that the nondiscrimination policy violated its First Amendment rights to free speech, expressive association, and the free exercise of religion by forcing it to forgo the benefits given to official student organizations. Benefits included financial assistance, access to the official student newsletter and bulletin where announcements and advertisements could be placed, access to the Hastings' official e-mail address from which messages could be sent to the student body, and access to the Hastings' annual fair where they could recruit additional members.

The Supreme Court has allowed restrictions on the access to a limited public forum. However, those restrictions must be neutral and generally applicable. *Id.* Here, the Court reiterated previous decisions, stating that a public school violates the First Amendment when it "restrict[s] speech or association simply because it finds the views expressed by [a] group to be abhorrent."

Here, the Supreme Court affirmed the Court of Appeals ruling that the nondiscrimination policy was constitutional because it was neutral and generally applicable where it did not "target or single out religious beliefs." The Court reasoned that the policy did not "wield the stick of prohibition," but rather "dangl[ed] the carrot of subsidy."

QUESTIONS

Do you agree with the Supreme Court that CLS was seeking a preferential exemption from Hastings' policy and not equality? How will the Court likely rule on a policy that prohibits membership restrictions only on certain specified bases, for example, race, gender, religion, and sexual orientation instead of prohibiting all membership restrictions?

Additional Web Resources:	*Locke v. Davey* (an interesting twist on equal access): May divinity students be excluded from public scholarship programs? *Board of Education v. Grumet*: May accommodation problems be solved by creating new political subdivisions?

C. EUROPE

1. Homeschooling and "Respect for Family Life"

Home education has been banned in Germany since 1918 and carries criminal penalties. Dirk and Petra Wunderlich chose to educate their children, aged 7 through 14, at home because, they said, "we believe this to be the best environment for them to learn and thrive."[33] As they began their first day of homeschool classes in 2013, a group of more than 20 police officers and social workers forcefully took the four children out of the home without letting their parents say goodbye.[34]

The Wunderlichs requested permission from German authorities to leave Germany for France, where homeschooling is allowed, but were denied. Eventually their children were returned home on condition they attend a government-approved school. The family continued to homeschool without further repercussion. Their legal situation, however, "remain[ed] precarious, as the German government continue[d] to criminally punish families who homeschool with fines or even imprisonment."[35] The Wunderlichs lodged a complaint in April 2015 before the European Court of Human Rights alleging violation of their rights under Article 8 of the European Convention on Human Rights (ECHR) to respect for family and private life. *Wunderlich v. Germany,* App. No. 18925/15 was accepted by the Court and communicated to the German government on 30 August 2016. The German government submitted replies to the Court in January 2017, claiming the children's seizure was justified to force them to attend local school so they would learn how to deal with people who think differently. Previous court rulings in Germany have supported the ban on homeschooling, arguing education is a state function and the government has a compelling interest in preventing religious or ideological "parallel societies."[36]

But homeschooling supporters and some legal experts disagree.

> Children are born to parents, not governments, and Germany's homeschooling policy is completely out of step with other free democracies that allow home education as part of their free and civil societies," said Mike Donnelly, director of global outreach for the Home School Legal Defense Association, which is also defending the Wunderlich family. "Human rights experts at the UN and scholars worldwide have found that home education is a natural, fundamental, and protected human right. The court must hold Germany accountable to respect this." . . . A decision in favor of the family would have wider implications for the parental rights of 800 million Europeans subject to ECHR rulings. Supporters hope a victory will pressure Germany to align its legislation with the court ruling as well as spark public discourse to trigger change from within.[37]

As of October 2018, this case was still pending before the Court.

---

33. Press Release, German Home-schooling Case Goes before European Court of Human Rights, ADF International, http://bit.ly/2vODdez. *See also* Fact Sheet, The *Wunderlich vs. Germany* Homeschooling Case, ADF International, http://bit.ly/2wo2G21.

34. Kiley Crossland, German Family Continues Fight to Homeschool, *World*, 13 April 2017.

35. German Family Continues to Fight for Right to Homeschool, *Catholic News Agency*, 11 April 2017.

36. Crossland, *supra* note 33.

37. ADF Press Release, *supra* note 32.

2. Religious Challenge to Compulsory Sex Education

In 1976, the European Court of Human Rights decided *Kjeldsen, Busk Madsen and Pedersen v. Denmark*, App. Nos. 5095/71, 5920/72, and 5926/72 (7 December 1976), a case that laid the groundwork for decisions involving religion-based challenges to the content of public school curricula. Three couples with school-aged children objected to compulsory sex education in the state primary schools of Denmark on the ground that it offended their religious beliefs. The applicants invoked Article 2 of Protocol No. 1, which provides:

> No person shall be denied the right to education. In the exercise of any functions which it assumes in relation to education and to teaching, the State shall respect the right of parents to ensure such education and teaching in conformity with their own religious and philosophical convictions.

The Danish government contended that Article 2 of Protocol No. 1 applied only to religious instruction contrary to the beliefs of parents. The school argued that the sex education provided in the schools was not related to a religious or moral viewpoint and that, further, the State had a compelling interest in educating its younger citizens about sexual matters to prevent negative consequences such as sexually transmitted diseases or abortion. The Court concluded that "the legislation in itself in no way offends the applicants' religious and philosophical convictions to the extent forbidden by the second sentence of Article 2 of the Protocol," and noted that the Danish government made generous provisions for parents who wished to place their children in private schools because of displeasure with the curriculum of the public schools. The parents also alleged discrimination based on their religion in that students who objected to religious instruction could receive an exemption, but those who objected to sex education were not allowed an exemption. The Court held that there was a difference between religious instruction and sex education in that the latter merely imparted factual knowledge whereas the former imparted religious tenets. In holding as it did, the Court was sympathetic to the fact that if the state were mandated to accommodate too broad a scope of parental rights, practical problems would arise in regard to the state's ability to make educational decisions.

Nevertheless, the Court then went on to emphasize that a state "must take care that information or knowledge included in the curriculum is conveyed in an objective, critical and pluralistic manner. The State is forbidden to pursue an aim of indoctrination that might be considered as not respecting parents' religious and philosophical convictions. That is the limit that must not be exceeded." The Court maintained that states do have an obligation to respect the beliefs of parents within the public school system, even in areas not directly related to denominational instruction and that the state does not absolve itself of this obligation merely by allowing parents to opt out of public schooling altogether and send their children to religious schools.

3. Philosophical Challenge to Corporal Punishment in Schools

Six years after *Kjeldsen*, the European Court of Human Rights further defined the scope of Protocol No. 1, Article 2 in *Campbell and Cosans v. United Kingdom*, App. Nos. 7511/76 and 7743/76 (25 February 1982). Campbell and Cosans each had a child in a state school in Scotland and objected on philosophical grounds to the schools' use of corporal punishment. Though neither child had ever been punished corporally at school, Campbell and Cosans claimed that by refusing to exempt their children from the threat of corporal punishment, the state had violated their Article 2 right to ensure education "in conformity with their own religious and philosophical convictions." The United Kingdom argued in response that classroom discipline was a matter of internal administration not rising to the level of "education and teaching" in Article 2, which they claimed applied only to "the content of, and mode of conveying, information and knowledge." Further, the UK argued that opinions concerning school administration did not constitute "philosophical convictions" for the purposes of the Article.

Ruling for Campbell and Cosans, the European Court of Human Rights rejected the state's interpretation of Article 2. Education, it held, is the "whole process" by which adults "transmit their beliefs, culture, and other values to the young," and because corporal punishment played an "integral part" in developing the character of students, it was subject to Article 2. The Court also held that "philosophical convictions" include "such convictions as are worthy of respect in a democratic society and are not incompatible with human dignity," but not beliefs that "conflict with the fundamental right of the child to education." The Court found that views concerning corporal punishment "relate to a weighty and substantial aspect of human life and behaviour, namely the integrity of the person," and granted Campbell and Cosans the protection they sought under Article 2.

4. Ethics and Religious Culture Courses

In 1997, Norway introduced a course on "Christian Knowledge and Religious and Ethical Education." This was intended to provide a neutral and objective introduction to Christianity and to other world religions. Because officials hoped to promote dialogue among pupils from different faiths, and because they thought everyone should have at least some introduction to the religions involved, the course was mandatory. Some limited opt-out arrangements were made available, but these were not satisfactory to a group of humanist parents. They challenged the program in the Norwegian courts, and after exhausting all possible remedies, some of the parents took their claims to the UN Human Rights Committee while others proceeded to the European Court of Human Rights. The latter group held that remedies as to the children's rights had not been fully exhausted, so only the parents' rights under Article 2 of the First Protocol to the European Convention were considered in the Grand Chamber judgment that ensued, *Folgerø v. Norway*, App. No. 15472/02. (29 June 2007). Based on prior judgments, such as *Kjeldsen*, the Court assessed whether the Christian Knowledge course conveyed information and knowledge "in an objective, critical and pluralistic manner or whether it had pursued an aim of indoctrination not respecting the applicant parents' religious and philosophical convictions and thereby had transgressed the limit implied by Article 2 of Protocol No. 1." The Court ultimately concluded that there was a bias toward Christianity in the structure of the curriculum and that the rather complex procedures necessary to obtain opt-outs for the children involved were not satisfactory. Accordingly, the Court, concluded that there had been a violation of Article 2 of Protocol No. 1.

5. Right of Alevis to Exemptions from Compulsory Religious Education in Turkey

In the 2007 case of *Hasan and Eylem Zengin v. Turkey*, a father belonging to the Alevi faith (a branch of Islam that differs significantly from the Sunni form) challenged Turkey's compulsory religious education as a violation of Article 2 of Protocol No. 1 and a violation of Article 9 in that it taught the precepts of the Sunni form of Islam in a non-objective way. The Court made an in-depth analysis of the curriculum endorsed by the Turkish government to determine whether it conformed to the Convention's standards. Although the Court could have addressed the issues under Article 9 of the Convention,[38] it focused entirely on Article 2 of the First Protocol.

HASAN AND ELEYM ZENGIN V. TURKEY

European Court of Human Rights, App. No. 1448/04 (9 October 2007)

[The applicants alleged that the religious instruction classes in Turkish schools were not taught in an objective, critical, or pluralist manner, but rather taught the Sunni form of Islam. The fact that the ninth-grade textbook included information on the major figures of the Alevi faith was insufficient to remedy this shortcoming. The applicants argued that a secular state could not teach a religion to children in state schools. The government denied the allegations and argued that religious instruction required state supervision to prevent abuses, that religious instruction was necessary to protect children from myths and erroneous information that could lead to fanaticism, and that certain individuals could apply for exemption from religious instruction. The government also submitted that the preparation and content of school curricula fell within the discretionary power of the State.]

34. [A] general overview of religious education in Europe [provided by the Court in preceding paragraphs] shows that, in spite of the variety of teaching methods, almost all of the member States offer at least one route by which pupils can opt out of religious education classes (by providing an exemption mechanism or the option of attending a lesson in a substitute subject, or by giving pupils the choice of whether or not to sign up to a religious studies class). . . .

54. The Court reiterates that it has always stressed that, in a pluralist democratic society, the State's duty of impartiality and neutrality towards various religions, faiths and beliefs is incompatible with any assessment by the State of the legitimacy of religious beliefs or the ways . . . those beliefs are expressed. . . .

56. Pursuant to the Turkish Constitution, pupils in . . . [in state schools are] obliged to attend classes in "religious culture and ethics" from the fourth year of primary school.

57. In the light of the principles set out above, the Court must determine, firstly, if the content-matter of this subject is taught in an objective, critical and pluralist manner, in order to ensure that it is compatible with the principles which

38. *Cf. Angelini v. Sweden*, App. No. 10941/83 (ECmHR, 3 December1987) (holding that denying an atheist mother the right to have her daughter exempted from religious education did not violate Article 9).

emerge from the case-law concerning the second sentence of Article 2 of Protocol No. 1. Secondly, it will examine whether appropriate provisions have been introduced in the Turkish educational system to ensure that parents' convictions are respected.

Content of the Lessons

58. According to the syllabus for "religious culture and ethics" classes, the subject is to be taught in compliance with respect for the principles of secularism and freedom of thought, religion and conscience, and is intended to "foster a culture of peace and a context of tolerance". It also aims to transmit knowledge concerning all of the major religions. . . .

59. In the Court's view, the intentions set out above are clearly compatible with the principles of pluralism and objectivity enshrined in Article 2 of Protocol No. 1. . . In this regard, it notes that the principle of secularism, as guaranteed by the Turkish Constitution, prevents the State from manifesting a preference for a particular religion or belief, thereby guiding the State in its role of impartial arbiter, and necessarily entails freedom of religion and conscience. . . .

60. The Court observes, however, that, although the instruction is based on the principles set out above, the teaching programme also aims to raise awareness among pupils of "[the fact that] acts of worship, as well as being demonstrations of love, respect and gratitude towards Allah, enable the individuals in a group to bond with love and respect, to help each other, to show solidarity" and "using different examples, to explain that, far from being a myth, Islam is a rational and universal religion". . . .

63. Thus, the syllabus for teaching in primary schools and the first cycle of secondary school, and all of the textbooks, give greater priority to knowledge of Islam than they do to that of other religions and philosophies. In the Court's view, this itself cannot be viewed as a departure from the principles of pluralism and objectivity. . . .

66. As to the Alevi faith, it is not disputed between the parties that it is a religious conviction which has deep roots in Turkish society and history and that it has features which are particular to it. It is thus distinct from the Sunni understanding of Islam which is taught in schools. In consequence, the expression "religious convictions", within the meaning of the second sentence of Article 2 of Protocol No. 1, is undoubtedly applicable to this faith.

67. As the Government [has] recognised, however, in the "religious culture and morals" lessons, the religious diversity which prevails in Turkish society is not taken into account. In particular, pupils receive no teaching on the confessional or ritual specificities of the Alevi faith, although the proportion of the Turkish population belonging to [it] is very large. As to the Government's argument that certain information about the Alevis was taught in the 9th grade, the Court, like the applicants, considers that, in the absence of instruction in the basic elements of this faith in primary and secondary school, the fact that the life and philosophy of two individuals who had a major impact on its emergence are taught in the 9th grade is insufficient to compensate for the shortcomings in this teaching.

68. . . . [P]upils' parents may legitimately expect that the subject will be taught in such a way as to meet the criteria of objectivity and pluralism, and with respect for their religious or philosophical convictions.

69. In this regard, the Court considers that, in a democratic society, only pluralism in education can enable pupils to develop a critical mind with regard to religious matters in the context of freedom of thought, conscience and religion. . . .

70. In the light of the above, the Court concludes that the instruction provided in the school subject "religious culture and ethics" cannot be considered to meet the criteria of objectivity and pluralism and, more particularly in the applicants' specific case, to respect the religious and philosophical convictions of Ms Zengin's father, a follower of the Alevi faith, on the subject of which the syllabus is clearly lacking.

(b) As to whether appropriate means existed to ensure respect for parents' convictions

71. . . . Where a Contracting State includes religious instruction in the curriculum for study, it is then necessary, in so far as possible, to avoid a situation where pupils face a conflict between the religious education given by the school and the religious or philosophical convictions of their parents. In this connection, the Court notes that, with regard to religious instruction in Europe and in spite of the variety of teaching approaches, almost all of the member States offer at least one route by which pupils can opt out of religious education classes. . . .

72. The Court notes that, under Article 24 of the Turkish Constitution, "religious culture and ethics" is one of the compulsory subjects. However, . . . only children "of Turkish nationality who belong to the Christian or Jewish religion" have the option of exemption, "provided they affirm their adherence to those religions".

73. The Court considers at the outset that, whatever the category of pupils concerned, the fact that parents must make a prior declaration to schools stating that they belong to the Christian or Jewish religion in order for their children to be exempted from the classes in question may also raise a problem under Article 9 of the Convention. In this connection, it notes that, according to Article 24 of the Turkish Constitution, "no one shall be compelled. . .to reveal religious beliefs and convictions. . .".

74. In addition, the Supreme Council for Education's decision provides for the possibility of exemption to solely two categories of pupils of Turkish nationality. . . .

. . .76. In consequence, the Court considers that the exemption procedure is not an appropriate method and does not provide sufficient protection to those parents who could legitimately consider that the subject taught is likely to give rise in their children to a conflict of allegiance between the school and their own values. This is especially so where no possibility for an appropriate choice has been envisaged for the children of parents who have a religious or philosophical conviction other than that of Sunni Islam, where the procedure for exemption is likely to subject the latter to a heavy burden and to the necessity of disclosing their religious or philosophical convictions in order to have their children exempted from the lessons in religion.

COMMENTS AND QUESTIONS

1. How would you compare the religious instruction programs in Norway and Turkey? Recognizing that perfect neutrality and objectivity is impossible as a practical matter, how close to this ideal do states need to come if they want to avoid opt-out requirements?
2. How should opt-out requirements be structured? In the Norwegian case, one of the children was allowed some opt-out rights, but the implementation—sending the pupil to a room to study on her own—was identical to punishment given for other purposes. Also, one of the complications in Norway was that parents had to object on almost a day-by-day basis to particular items coming up in the teaching plan. How particularized should opt-out requirements be?
3. In *Zengin*, the Court suggested that requiring individuals to affirm their adherence to a particular religion in connection with a request for an exemption from religious instruction might violate Article 9. What happens to a student who asks for an exemption from instruction in the dominant religion? Are such situations an inevitable consequence of exemptions?
4. Some countries have allowed exemptions from religious lessons only for pupils whose religious communities could arrange alternative instruction. Is this an "objective and reasonable" basis for treating these pupils differently than others (such as atheists or very small religious communities) for whom arranging alternative instruction is not feasible? *See Bernard v. Luxembourg*, App. No. 08/09/1993 (ECmHR, 8 September 1993).
5. In Poland religious instruction is given in Catholicism, but it is fairly easy to get an exemption. Does that make the religious instruction course voluntary? What if students and teachers pressure a student to take the Catholic religious instruction class, and she capitulates? What if a pupil is worried that not having a Catholic religion class on his or transcript may result in job discrimination later on? Is religious instruction under such circumstances genuinely voluntary, and thus not an infringement of Article 9? *See C.J., J.J. and E.J. v. Poland*, App. No. 23380/94 (ECmHR, 16 January 1996). How would psychological pressures to conform compare with the pressures in *Weisman* (the United States graduation prayer case)?

6. Right to Exemptions from Compulsory Religious Education in the United Kingdom

Religious education is compulsory in all state-funded schools in the United Kingdom, the curriculum to be determined locally. Religious education must be Christian but must take into account the plurality of religions in the country in schools that are not of a specific religious character. The law, therefore, assumes that Christianity is the norm, but attempts to recognize other religious and require religious neutrality. In these schools, students may be "wholly or partially excused" from religious education, upon the request of their parents, until the parents withdraw the request. Also, no teachers can be required to teach religious education in these schools. In schools of a religious character the rules differ slightly, and religious education is in accordance with the religious denomination of the school. Parents in such schools have a right to opt out of this religious education and receive the non-denominational alternatives provided in schools that are not of a religious character. The opt-out clause in both types of schools has been criticized because many parents and children do not know about their right to opt out, are pressured into conforming, or fear isolation as a result of opting-out.

It is also compulsory for state-funded schools to hold a form of collective worship daily. Again, this is mainly of a Christian nature in schools that are not of a specific religious character, and in accordance with the denomination of the school in those that are of a religious character. Parents can remove their children from daily worship, and children are able to remove themselves once they are 16. This clause has been criticized because it "impedes schools' ability to provide good inclusive assemblies" and appears to protect the activities of proselytizing groups in schools. As in the case of religious education, many argue that parents and children do not understand their rights to opt out and further criticize the clause for limiting those under 16 from opting out themselves. More than that, however, critics argue that these students will be forced to miss out on other aspects of these assemblies, such as discussion on ethics and morals.[39]

7. School Prayer in Germany

German School Prayer Case

German Constitutional Court, 52 BVerfGE 223 (1979)

[Like the United States school prayer cases, the German case presented the question of whether prayer should be permitted in compulsory state schools over the objection of pupils or their parents. The case consolidated appeals from two lower court cases. In the first case, the Hesse Constitutional Court held that school prayer in a particular classroom could not be permitted if any pupil or his parents objected. This ruling was based on the right of "negative confessional freedom," which protects the right not to disclose one's religion. This was deemed absolute and to override the positive confessional rights of others in the class. According to the Hesse Court, a pupil could not be put in the position where the only option was not participating in the exercise.

In the second case, the Federal Administrative Court held that "negative confessional freedom" could not be granted automatic precedence over "positive religious freedom." The right to remain silent could not be interpreted in a way that prohibited others from manifesting their beliefs through school prayer. Because the German Basic Law allows the establishment of public denominationally affiliated schools, objections from parents and children could not serve as a basis for prohibiting school prayer.]

Judgment of the First Senate [of the Federal Constitutional Court]

. . . Article 6.2 sentence 1 of the Basic Law grants to the parents the right and the duty to plan the care and upbringing of their children in accordance with their own ideas freely and . . . also includes the right to educate children in religious and

39. From Alice Donald, *Religion or Belief, Equality and Human Rights in England and Wales*, Equality and Human Rights Commission Research Report 84, Summer 2012.

ideological matters. Article 4.1 and 4.2 of the Basic Law also includes the right of the parents to convey to their children the religious or ideological convictions that they regard as right.

On the other hand, Article 7.1 of the Basic Law grants to the state a constitutional educational mandate for schooling. The discretion open to the state in the school system, which is assigned to the *Länder* [individual states], includes not only the organizational structure of the school, but also the content definition of the courses and educational objectives. The state may hence in principle pursue its own educational goals in schools independently of the parents. The state educational mandate is separate and equal to the right of the parents to bring up their children; neither the parents' right nor the state educational mandate has absolute priority. . . .

2. [T]he introduction of Christian references in organising state schools is not absolutely forbidden, even if a minority of persons with parental rights who cannot avoid these schools in the education of their children do not want them to have a religious education. The school however may not be a missionary school, and may not claim exclusive truth for Christian articles of faith; it must also be open to other ideological and religious ideas and values . . . The affirmation of Christianity in the secular subjects refers primarily to its recognition as the formative cultural and educational factor which it has developed in Western history, not to its truths of faith. . . .

a) School prayer [is] an act of religious profession spoken outside religious instruction [it] is not a part of general schooling given in the framework of the state educational mandate. It is not instruction as characterized by lessons as such, it is not a passing on of knowledge to the pupils, and it is not targeted educational influence by the school and the teachers on the children, but is a religious act which as a rule is carried out together with the teacher. [The German system allows schools of different types—denominational, interdenominational, and secular. But since school prayer occurs outside the normal curriculum, and all of these public forms of education involve some coercion, the determination of school type does not automatically resolve the school prayer issue.]

b) Since school prayer is not a part of lessons within the meaning of school teaching, [and therefore] must be completely voluntary. . . . Even if school prayer is not and cannot be a part of the bindingly regulated lessons, it nevertheless remains . . . a school event to be attributed to the state. . . . The role of the state is . . . restricted to creating the organizational framework for school prayer and permitting prayer at the request of the parents or pupils or suggesting it itself. The state does not order it, it makes an offer which the school class may choose to take up. . . .

Article 4 of the Basic Law grants not only the freedom to believe, but also the external freedom to profess faith in public. . . . If the state permits school prayer in interdenominational schools, it is doing no other than exercising the right of school organization granted to it in accordance with Article 7.1 of the Basic Law such that those pupils who so wish may give witness to their religious faith—even if only in the restricted form of general and interdenominational invocation of God. The state gives scope here to the positive freedom to profess a belief in an area which it has taken care of entirely and in which religious and ideological ideas have always been relevant.

From the outset, the state must however strike a balance between this scope to exercise positive freedom to profess a belief by permitting school prayer and the negative freedom to profess a belief of other parents and pupils who reject school prayer. . . . Even if school prayer, if it is to have a purpose, presumes a faith-based truth, the school in this instance does not claim absolute truth for the Christian faith; it merely enables those who so wish to profess such a faith. . . .

II. 1. The Hesse Constitutional Court opines that school prayer must be prohibited if a pupil rejects it because the pupil must not be placed in a situation of having to express his or her religiously or ideologically motivated rejection of school prayer through non-participation. . . . By exercising the fundamental right *not* to participate, the person concerned reveals by that action that he or she does not agree with the conviction of the others. The constitution requires in this case the disclosure of conviction as a precondition for the exercise of the fundamental right to refuse. . .

This is closely linked to the legal view of the Hesse Constitutional Court, according to which negative freedom to profess a belief applies without restriction or exception, is neither restricted, nor can it be restricted, since it does not encroach on third-party legal spheres; by contrast, the positive freedom to profess a belief is alleged to be subject to the boundaries of Article 2.1 of the Basic Law. . . . In every case where conflicts occur between negative and positive freedom to profess a belief, particularly in schools, where such conflicts as to the joint education of children of widely differing ideological and faith-based leanings are ultimately unavoidable, a balance must be sought taking into consideration the precept of tolerance. By contrast, a misunderstood right to remain silent must not be given absolute priority over the practice of religion of others, as was done by the Hesse Constitutional Court. . . .

3. [Turning to the North Rhine Westphalia decision, the] objection of a dissident pupil or of the persons with parental rights could only make school prayer non-permissible if the right of the deviating pupil to decide freely, with no coercion, on his or her participation in school prayer were not guaranteed. As a rule, however, a pupil can reasonably avoid participation, so that he or she may decide in complete freedom for non-participation in prayer.

a) Possible means of avoidance are: The pupil can leave the classroom during the prayer; he or she can for instance not enter the room until after the prayer has finished, or can leave the room at the end of the lesson, before the final prayer is said. The dissident pupil can however also remain in the classroom during the prayer, but not say the prayer; in doing so, he or she may remain seated—unlike the fellow pupils praying.

b) It must be admitted that each of these possibilities for avoidance always emphasizes the conduct of the pupil in question when school prayer takes place as against the praying pupils. This applies particularly if there is only *one* dissident pupil. . . . This emphasis could be unacceptable for the person concerned if it would of necessity place him or her in the role of an outsider and discriminate against him or her with regard to the rest of the class. Indeed, the position of the pupil in a class is different and much more difficult than that of an adult citizen who reveals their different conviction in public by not participating in certain events. This applies in particular to younger school children who as yet are hardly able to assert their own position critically towards their environment; in general, the child is placed into a conflict as to the matter of school prayers not by himself or herself, but by the persons with parental rights on the one hand, and the parents of other pupils or the teachers on the other.

4. Nevertheless . . . certainly as a rule one need not fear discrimination of the pupil not participating in the prayer. . . . [Organizational steps can be taken to mitigate likely impacts, such as scheduling the prayer at a time when the dissident student(s) can come a few minutes late.]. . .

b) Over and above these external and organizational measures, discrimination of the pupils not participating in school prayer can be ruled out as a rule by teachers in line with the educational goal of the school encouraging all pupils to adhere to the principles of respect for one another's convictions. . . . [That is, teachers can take the fact of those opting out of prayer as an opportunity to help pupils learn about integration of and tolerance for differing views in society.]. . .

. . . The effort to injure as little as possible the rights and feelings of the dissenter emerging from respect for this principle by all concerned, primarily by the teachers and parents of all the pupils in a class, as well as by the pupils themselves, as a rule precludes placing a pupil who does not participate in the prayer in a marginal position.

[For these reasons, the judgment of the Hesse Constitutional Court that had held school prayer impermissible where a pupil or his or her parents objected, was held to be null and void. The decision in the North Rhine Westphalia decision was found to be constitutionally unobjectionable.]

COMMENT

Compare the notions of voluntariness involved in the German case below with the United States school prayer cases.

8. Crucifix in the Classroom

a. German "Classroom Crucifix II Case"

CLASSROOM CRUCIFIX II CASE

Federal Constitutional Court of Germany, 92 BVerfGE1 (1995)

[Section 13.1 sentence 3 of the School Regulations for Elementary Schools in Bavaria (Volksschulordnung—VSO) provided that "[t]he school shall support those having parental power in the religious upbringing of children. School prayer, school services and school worship are possibilities for such support. In every classroom a cross shall be affixed. Teachers and pupils are obliged to respect the religious feelings of all." The parents of three school-age minor children, followers of the anthroposophical philosophy of life as taught by Rudolf Steiner, objected to the crucifixes or crosses affixed in the schoolrooms attended by their children, asserting that this symbol influenced their children in a Christian direction, contrary to their wishes. A constitutional complaint was brought directly against orders from Administrative Court decisions arising from the controversy and indirectly against the Bavarian regulations calling for crosses in each classroom.]

The complainants object to infringement of their fundamental rights under Art. 4(1), Art. 6(2), Art. 2(1) and Art. 19(4) Basic Law.

1. The equipping of schoolrooms with crosses and crucifixes is said to infringe the State's duty of religious and philosophical neutrality. Children and young people especially were easily influenceable; their capacity to defend themselves against influences and form a critical judgment of their own was far less than with grownups. . . .

2. The parents' fundamental rights under Art. 6(2) Basic Law and Art. 4(1) Basic Law were infringed since they had to expose their children to a religious or philosophical influence in contradiction with their educational conceptions. . . .

Further, the affixation of crosses in public schools also infringed the religious freedom guaranteed in Art. 9(1) of the European Convention on Human Rights and Fundamental Freedoms (ECHR), and Art. 2, second sentence, of the additional protocol . . . to the Convention. . . .

. . . Freedom of religion does not however mean just the freedom to have a faith, but also the freedom to live and act in accordance with one's own religious convictions. . . . In particular, freedom of religion guarantees participation in acts of worship a faith prescribes or is expressed in. This implies, conversely, the freedom to stay away from acts of worship of a faith not shared. This freedom also applies to the symbols in which a faith or religion presents itself. . . . Admittedly, in a society that affords space to differing religious convictions, the individual has no right to be spared other manifestations of faith, acts of worship or religious symbols. But this must be distinguished from a situation created by the state in which the individual is exposed without an alternative to the influence of a particular faith, to the actions in which this manifests itself and the symbols through which it presents itself. . . .

[Article 4.1 imposes a duty on the state] to safeguard space for [individuals] to operate in which the personality can develop in the area of ideology and religion, and to protect them against attacks or obstruction by adherents of other religious tendencies or competing religious groups. . . . Article 4.1. . .implies the principle of state neutrality towards the various religions and denominations. The state, in which adherents of different or even opposing religious and ideological convictions live together, can guarantee peaceful coexistence only if it itself maintains neutrality in matters of faith. It may thus not itself endanger the religious peace in society.

Taken together with Art. 6(2) sentence 1 of the Basic Law, which guarantees parents the care and upbringing of their children as a natural right, Art. 4.1 of the Basic Law also covers the right to bring up children in religious and ideological respects. It is a matter for the parents to convey to their children the religious and ideological convictions that they regard as right. . . . This implies the right to keep the children away from religious convictions that appear to the parents to be wrong or harmful.

2. This fundamental right is infringed by §13.1 sentence 3 VSO, and by the decisions challenged, which are based on this provision.

a) §13.1 sentence 3 VSO prescribes the affixing of crosses in all classrooms of the Bavarian elementary schools. [The term "cross" was used to cover crosses with a body, i.e., a crucifix, and without.] In reviewing the statute, accordingly, both meanings are to be included. . . .

Taken together with universal compulsory schooling, crosses in schoolrooms mean that pupils are, during teaching, under state auspices and with no possibility of escape, confronted with this symbol and compelled to learn "beneath the cross". This distinguishes the affixing of crosses in classrooms from the frequent confrontation with religious symbols of the most varied religious tendencies arising in everyday life. Firstly, the latter does not proceed from the state but is a consequence of the spread of various religious convictions or religious communities in society. Secondly, it does not have the same degree of inescapability. . . .

Nor is the inescapability of the encounter with the cross in schoolrooms removed by the setting up of private schools allowed by Art. 7.4 of the Basic Law. First, the setting up of private elementary schools is tied in Art. 7.5 of the Basic Law to particularly strict conditions. Secondly, since these schools are as a rule financed by fees paid by parents, a large part of the population lacks the possibility of recourse to them. Such is also the complainants' case.

b) The cross is a symbol of a particular religious conviction and not merely an expression of the Western culture marked partly by Christianity. [The Court then details the significance of the cross and its impact on school children.] . . .

3. The fundamental right to freedom of faith is guaranteed without reservation. This does not however mean that it might not be subject to some sort of restrictions. These would, however, have to follow from the constitution itself. The setting up of limits not already laid out in the constitution is not something the legislature can do. Constitutional grounds that might have justified intervention are not . . . present here.

a) No such justification follows from Art. 7.1 of the Basic Law. Art. 7.1 . . . certainly gives the state an educational mandate. . . . It has not only to organize schooling and itself set up schools, but may also establish the goals of education and the course of training. In that, it is independent of parents. Accordingly, not only can schooling and family upbringing come into conflict. It is, rather, even inevitable that at school the differing religious and ideological convictions of pupils and their parents confront each other particularly intensively.

This sort of arrangement does not require the State totally to abandon religious or philosophical references in carrying out the educational mandate bestowed by Art. 7.1 of the Basic Law. Even a state that comprehensively guarantees freedom of faith and thereby commits itself to religious and philosophical neutrality cannot divest itself of the culturally conveyed, historically rooted values, convictions and attitudes on which the cohesion of society is based and the carrying out of its own tasks also depends. . . .

[T]he Federal Constitutional Court has drawn the conclusion that the Land legislature is not utterly barred from introducing Christian references in the organization of the state elementary schools, even if those with parental rights who cannot avoid these schools in the education of their children do not want them to have a religious education. There is a requirement, however, that this be associated with only the indispensable minimum of coercive elements. That means in particular that the school cannot treat its task in the religious and ideological area in missionary fashion, nor claim any binding validity for Christian articles of faith.

The affixing of crosses in classrooms goes beyond the boundary thereby drawn to the religious and ideological orientation of schools. As already established, the cross cannot be divested of its specific reference to the beliefs of Christianity and reduced to a general token of the Western cultural tradition. It symbolizes the essential core of the conviction of the Christian faith, which has undoubtedly shaped the Western world in particular in many ways, but is certainly not shared by all members of society, and is indeed rejected by many in the exercise of their fundamental right under Art. 4.1 of the Basic Law. Its affixation in state compulsory schools is accordingly incompatible with Art. 4.1 of the Basic Law insofar as these are not Christian denominational schools.

b) The affixation of the cross cannot be justified from the positive freedom of faith of parents and pupils of the Christian faith either. Positive religious freedom is due to all parents and pupils equally, not just the Christian ones. The conflict arising cannot be resolved according to the majority principle, for the fundamental right to freedom of faith specifically is aimed in a special degree at protecting minorities. . . . Insofar as the school, in harmony with the constitution, allows scope for . . . [the right to exercise their religious convictions in the context of state institutions], as with religious instruction, school prayers and other religious manifestations, these must be marked by the principle of being voluntary and allow the other-minded acceptable, nondiscriminatory possibilities of avoiding them. With affixation of crosses in classrooms, the presence and demands of which the other-minded cannot escape, this is not true. Finally, it would not be compatible with the principle of practical concordance for the feelings of the other-minded to be completely suppressed in order that pupils of the Christian faith might be able, over and above religious instruction and voluntary devotions, to learn the secular subjects too beneath the symbol of their faith. . . .

Accordingly, the provision of §13.1 sentence 3. . .that underlies the dispute is incompatible with the fundamental rights mentioned and is to be pronounced null and void. The decisions in the proceedings for provisional protection of rights challenged are to be overturned. Since the proceedings in the main case are now pending before the Bavarian Higher Administrative Court, the case is referred back to it. . . .

Judges: HENSCHEL, SEIDL, GRIMM, SÖLLNER, KÜHLING, SEIBERT, JAEGER, HAAS.

[Dissenting opinion of Judges SEIDL, SÖLLNER, and HAAS omitted.]

NOTE ON THE IMPACT OF THE *CRUCIFIX II CASE*[40]

The *Crucifix II Case* triggered a storm of protest throughout Germany. Chancellor Helmut Kohl called the decision “incomprehensible.” Conservative newspapers bashed the Constitutional Court for overriding the popular will. Numerous religious leaders condemned the decision, calling it a threat to

---

40. Adapted from Donald P. Kommers, *The Constitutional Jurisprudence of the Federal Republic of Germany* 482–483 (2d ed., Duke Univ. Press 1997).

Germany's Christian culture. Many constitutional lawyers, including a former president of the Constitutional Court, chastised the justices for their infirm reasoning. The decision produced the strongest denunciation in Bavaria. Holding crucifixes aloft, demonstrators in Munich and other communities marched in defiance of the Karlsruhe court as their political leaders called on state officials not to enforce the decision. It was the most negative reaction to a judicial decision in the history of the Federal Republic and the only instance of clear and open defiance of a ruling by the Federal Constitutional Court.

The duration and intensity of the protest worried Germany's judicial establishment. The German Judges' Association warned that the rule of law was at stake and that any refusal to obey the *Crucifix* ruling would endanger the Federal Republic's constitutional democracy. Justice Dieter Grimm, one of the five justices in the *Crucifix* majority, was prompted to answer the court's critics in the *Frankfurter Allgemeine Zeitung*, Germany's newspaper of record. Grimm's prominently displayed letter was published under the caption "Why a Judicial Ruling Merits Respect." [In his essay, Justice Grimm stated, "Not everyone will be satisfied with the court's decision, but that is in the nature of the judicial resolution of conflicts; and, at times, the majority will be the disappointed party. This is what constitutionalism is all about; its purpose is to safeguard the rights of minorities against encroachment by the majority."]. . .

Much of the early critical reaction to *Classroom Crucifix II* was in response to the headnotes that accompanied the release of the decision. The headnotes seemed to suggest that the court was mandating the removal of all crucifixes from all elementary school classrooms. If this is what *Classroom Crucifix II* required, it would indeed be a revolutionary decision, amounting to a reversal of *Interdenominational School*. . . . Perhaps in response to the public outcry, the court appeared to back away from this interpretation, indicating in a press release that the headnotes were not fully consistent with the reasoning of the case. This was taken to mean, as Bavarian school officials had already maintained, that a crucifix would have to be removed only in the presence of students objecting to it on religious grounds. Nevertheless, the debate continued as Bavarian state officials went about preparing "corrective" legislation in defiance of the court's ruling.

COMMENTS AND QUESTIONS

1. Do you think the subsequent political discussion of the meaning of the *Crucifix II Case* accurately reflected the holding of the case? What do you think is the likelihood of students objecting to the classroom crucifixes on religious grounds?
2. To what extent is the legitimacy of the court and the tradition of constitutionalism itself put at risk by massive outcry against a controversial decision?
3. Did the *Crucifix II Case* overrule the *German School Prayer* decision, or can the cases be distinguished?
4. What does the claim that the state has flexibility in the choice of school type (Christian interdenominational, denominational, or secular) and that "[r]eligion classes form part of the ordinary curriculum in state schools, except for secular schools" (Article 7.3 of the Basic Law) say about the basic

relationship of religion and the state in Germany? How does this compare with the US approach? Does the American education system even contemplate the notion of school type? Are there nonetheless in fact places where US schools have an interdenominational Christian or Protestant cast?

b. The "Italian Crucifix Case"

In 2009, and again in 2011, the European Court of Human Right considered an important and highly controversial case originating in the complaint by the Finnish mother of children being educated in their father's native country, Italy, about the presence of the crucifix in school classrooms. The original judgment, issued unanimously by the Court's Second Section in November 2009, was in favor of the applicants in the case. The Grand Chamber's ruling issued in March 2011 was overwhelmingly, though not quite unanimously (15-2), in favor of Italy. Why did his happen? What changed?[41]

The case of *Lautsi v. Italy*, the "Italian Crucifix Case," originated in the state school, Instituto compresnsivo statale Vittorino da Feltre, where a crucifix was fixed to the wall of every classroom. On 23 July 2002, Soile Lautsi ("the first applicant") alleged infringement of the principle of secularism in the Veneto Administrative Court, filing the complaint in her own name and on behalf of her minor children, Dataico and Sami Albertin Lautsi, who remained applicants to the case ("the second and third applicants") after reaching the legal age.

The Italian Administrative Court dismissed the application, ruling that royal decrees from the 1920s concerning the issue were still in force and emphasizing that "the principle of the secular nature of the State [was] now part of the legal heritage of Europe and the western democracies." The presence of crucifixes in state school classrooms did not offend against that principle. Although the crucifix "was undeniably a religious symbol, it was a symbol of Christianity in general rather than of Catholicism alone, so that it served as a point of reference for other creeds." The crucifix in fact was a historical and cultural symbol, possessing an "identity-linked value" for the Italian people, in that it "[represented] in a way the historical and cultural development characteristic of [Italy] and in general of the whole of Europe, and [was] a good synthesis of that development." The crucifix should also be considered "a symbol of a value system underpinning the Italian Constitution."

The applicants appealed to the European Court of Human Rights, arguing that Italy's actions violated their rights to education and to religious freedom, guaranteed in Article 2 of Protocol No. 1 and Article 9 of the European Convention on Human Rights. On 3 November 2009, a unanimous seven-judge Chamber of the Second Section of the ECtHR held for the applicants. The Chamber found that crucifixes in public school classrooms constituted a violation both of the right of parents to educate their children in conformity with their own convictions and of the right of children to freedom of thought, conscience, and religion, which included the right to be free from coerced religious participation or observance.

The Grand Chamber of the ECtHR accepted Italy's request for a re-hearing of the case. More than twenty European nations publicly stated their support for Italy,

41. For links to documents related to this case, including Court documents and interventions submitted, *see* http://www.strasbourgconsortium.org/portal.case.php?pageId=10#caseId=2.

and numerous non-governmental organizations (NGOs) also became involved in the lobbying. Some third-party interveners submitted written observations to the Grand Chamber, and others were allowed to intervene collectively at the hearing in support of either party.

Lautsi and Others v. Italy

European Court of Human Rights (Grand Chamber), App. No. 30814/06 (18 March 2011)

I. Alleged Violation of Article 2 of Protocol No. 1 and Article 9 of the Convention

29. [The applicants argued the presence of crucifixes in State-school classrooms infringe on their right to education, guaranteed by Article 2 of Protocol No.1, which states:] *the State shall respect the right of parents to ensure such education and teaching in conformity with their own religious and philosophical convictions.*

[They also argued that it infringed on their right to freedom of thought, conscience and religion, guaranteed by Article 9 of the ECHR.] . . .

A. The Chamber's Judgment

30. [On] 3 November 2009 the Chamber held that there had been a violation of Article 2 of Protocol No. 1 [and] Article 9 of the ECHR.

31. [The Chamber interpreted Article 2 of Protocol No. 1 as an obligation that the State not impose beliefs], even indirectly, in places where persons were dependent on it or in places where they were particularly vulnerable, emphasizing that the schooling of children was a particularly sensitive area in that respect.

The Court went on to say that among the plurality of meanings [of] the crucifix [. . .], the religious meaning was predominant. [The Chamber] accordingly considered that the compulsory . . . presence of crucifixes in classrooms was capable not only of clashing with the secular convictions of the first applicant . . . but also of being emotionally disturbing for pupils of non-Christian religions or those who professed no religion. [The] Chamber emphasised that the "negative" freedom of religion . . . deserved special protection if it was the State which expressed a belief and dissenters were placed in a situation from which they could not extract themselves if not by making disproportionate efforts and sacrifices.

B. Arguments of the parties

1. The Government

35. [The Government argued that confessional neutrality meant that the State should refrain from promoting a particular religion, atheism, and even secularism.]

36. The Government went on to argue that it was necessary to take account of the fact that a single symbol could be interpreted differently from one person to another. That applied in particular to the sign of the cross, which could be perceived not only as a religious symbol, but also as a cultural and identity-linked symbol, the symbol of the principles and values which formed the basis of democracy and western civilisation; it appeared, for instance, on the flags of a

number of European countries. Whatever the evocative power of an "image" might be, in the Government's view, it was a "passive symbol", whose impact on individuals was not comparable with the impact of "active conduct", and no one had asserted in the present case that the content of the teaching provided in Italy was influenced by the presence of crucifixes in classrooms.

That presence was the expression of a "national particularity", characterised notably by close relations between the State, the people and Catholicism attributable to the historical, cultural and territorial development of Italy and to a deeply rooted and long-standing attachment to the values of Catholicism. Keeping crucifixes in schools was therefore a matter of preserving a centuries-old tradition. The Government argued that the right of parents to respect for their "family culture" ought not to infringe the community's right to transmit its culture or the right of children to discover it. Moreover, by contenting itself with a "potential risk" of emotional disturbance in finding a breach of the rights to education and freedom of thought, conscience and religion, the Chamber had considerably widened the scope of those provisions.

37. [Additionally, the Government contented that minority religions were very well respected and even represented in the school environment. For example, Islamic headscarves and other religious clothing were allowed, the beginning and end of Ramadan were celebrated, and Jewish students were allowed to remove themselves from examinations on Saturdays.]

2. The Applicants

41. [The applicants argued that the presence of crucifixes in the classroom interfered with their right to freedom of thought and conscience and infringed on the principle of educational pluralism. The State was thereby disregarding its obligation to give special protection to minors against propaganda or indoctrination. Also, it infringed on the right to have the children educated in conformity of secularism.] . . .

D. The Court's Assessment

1. The Case of the First Applicant

a. General principles

59. The Court reiterates that in the area of education and teaching Article 2 of Protocol No. 1 is in principle the *lex specialis* in relation to Article 9 of the Convention. That is so at least where, as in the present case, the dispute concerns the obligation laid on Contracting States by the second sentence of Article 2 to respect, when exercising the functions they assume in that area, the right of parents to ensure such education and teaching in conformity with their own religious and philosophical convictions . . . .

60. [States are responsible] for ensuring, neutrally and impartially, the exercise of various religions, faiths and beliefs. [The State's role is] to help maintain public order, religious harmony and tolerance in a democratic society. . . .

62. . . . In particular, the second sentence of Article 2 of Protocol No. 1 does not prevent States from imparting through teaching or education information or knowledge of a directly or indirectly religious or philosophical kind. It does not

even permit parents to object to the integration of such teaching or education in the school curriculum.

[However, it does require] the State . . . to take care that information or knowledge included in the curriculum is conveyed in an objective, critical and pluralistic manner, enabling pupils to develop a critical mind particularly with regard to religion in a calm atmosphere free of any proselytism. The State is forbidden to pursue an aim of indoctrination that might be considered as not respecting parents' religious and philosophical convictions. . . .

b. Assessment of the facts of the case in the light of the above principles

66. [The Court agrees that the crucifix is above all a religious symbol, but contends that there is no evidence that its display may have an influence on pupils. While it is also understandable that the first applicant might interpret the presences of the crucifixes to be a lack of respect for her right to ensure their education and teaching in conformity with her own philosophical convictions, the applicant's subjective perception is not in itself sufficient to establish a breach of Article 2 of Protocol No. 1.]

67. The Government . . . added that, beyond its religious meaning, the crucifix symbolised the principles and values which formed the foundation of democracy and western civilisation, and that its presence in classrooms was justifiable on that account.

68. The Court takes the view that the decision whether or not to perpetuate a tradition falls in principle within the margin of appreciation of the respondent State. The Court must moreover take into account the fact that Europe is marked by a great diversity between the States of which it is composed, particularly in the sphere of cultural and historical development. It emphasises, however, that the reference to a tradition cannot relieve a Contracting State of its obligation to respect the rights and freedoms enshrined in the Convention and its Protocols.

As regards the Government's opinion on the meaning of the crucifix, the Court notes that the Consiglio di Stato and the Court of Cassation have diverging views in that regard and that the Constitutional Court has not given a ruling. It is not for the Court to take a position regarding a domestic debate among domestic courts.

69. [The Court explained that because the State enjoys a margin of appreciation to reconcile its functions in relation to education and teaching with respect for the right of parents, the Court has a duty to respect the States' decisions in these matters.] . . .

72. [The Court further argues that a crucifix on a wall is a passive symbol that cannot influence pupils in a manner comparable to that of didactic speech or participation in religious activities.] . . .

75. Lastly, the Court notes that the first applicant retained in full her right as a parent to enlighten and advise her children. . . .

77. [The Court accordingly concludes that there has been no violation of Article 2 of Protocol No. 1 and that no separate issue arises under Article 9 of the ECHR . . . .]

[The concurring opinion of Judge Rozakis joined by Judge Vajić, the concurring opinion of Judge Power, and the dissenting opinion of Judge Malinverni joined by Judge Kalaydjieva have been omitted.]

CONCURRING OPINION OF JUDGE BONELLO

1.4 Until relatively recently, the "secular" State had hardly bothered with education, and, by default, had delegated that primary function to Christian institutions. Only slowly did the State start assuming its responsibilities to educate and to offer the population some alternatives to a virtual religious monopoly on education. The presence of the crucifix in Italian schools only testifies to this compelling and millennial historical reality. . . .

2.2 In parallel with freedom of religion, there has evolved . . . values . . . like secularism, pluralism, the separation of Church and State, religious neutrality, and religious tolerance. [While all of these represent superior democratic values, they are not protected by the Convention.] . . .

2.5 . . . Freedom of religion is not secularism. Freedom of religion is not the separation of Church and State. Freedom of religion is not religious equidistance. . . .

2.6 Freedom of religion [. . .] consists of the rights to profess freely any religion of the individual's choice, the right to freely change one's religion, the right not to embrace any religion at all, and the right to manifest one's religion by means of belief, worship, teaching and observance. [The Convention ends] well short of the promotion of any State secularism.

2.9 . . . [While, the] presence of a crucifix in a State classroom might conceivably be viewed as a betrayal of secularism, . . . it is for the Italian authorities, not for this Court, to enforce secularism if they believe it forms part, or should form part, of the Italian constitutional architecture.

2.10 . . . Its removal would have been a positive and aggressive espousal of agnosticism or of secularism – and consequently anything but neutral. . . .

NOTE ON THE HISTORICAL BACKGROUND OF *LAUTSI* AND THE PLEDGE OF ALLEGIANCE

In a broader sense, the Court recognized that to remove the crucifix would be to deny the essential role played by Christianity in the development of human rights in Europe. The Court cited the Veneto Administrative Court's preceding decision to illustrate this point:

> 11.1. At this stage, the Court must observe, although it is aware that it is setting out along a rough and in places slippery path, that Christianity, and its older brother Judaism—at least since Moses and certainly in the Talmudic interpretation—have placed tolerance towards others and protection of human dignity at the centre of their faith.
>
> 11.2 Looking beyond appearances makes it possible to discern a thread linking the Christian revolution of two thousand years ago to the affirmation in Europe of the right to liberty of the person and to the key elements in the Enlightenment (even though that movement, historically speaking, strongly opposed religion), namely the liberty and freedom of every person, the declaration of the rights of man, and ultimately the

modern secular State. All the historic phenomena mentioned are based to a significant extent—though certainly not exclusively—on the Christian conception of the world. It has been observed—judiciously—that the rallying call "liberty, equality, fraternity" can easily be endorsed by a Christian, albeit with a clear emphasis on the third word.

11.6 Moreover, with the benefit of hindsight, it is easy to identify in the constant central core of Christian faith, despite the inquisition, despite anti-Semitism and despite the crusades, the principles of human dignity, tolerance and freedom, including religious freedom, and therefore, in the last analysis, the foundations of the secular State.

11.9 It can therefore be contended that in the present-day social reality the crucifix should be regarded not only as a symbol of a historical and cultural development, and therefore of the identity of our people, but also as a symbol of a value system: liberty, equality, human dignity and religious toleration, and accordingly also of the secular nature of the State—principles which underpin our Constitution.

In other words, the constitutional principles of freedom have many roots, which undeniably include Christianity, in its very essence. It would therefore be something of a paradox to exclude a Christian sign from a public institution in the name of secularism, one of whose distant sources is precisely the Christian religion.

13.4 The cross, as the symbol of Christianity, can therefore not exclude anyone without denying itself; it even constitutes in a sense the universal sign of the acceptance of and respect for every human being as such, irrespective of any belief, religious or other, which he or she may hold. . . .

14.1 It is hardly necessary to add that the sign of the cross in a classroom, when correctly understood, is not concerned with the freely held convictions of anyone, excludes no one and of course does not impose or prescribe anything, but merely implies, in the heart of the aims set for education and teaching in a publicly run school, a reflection—necessarily guided by the teaching staff—on Italian history and the common values of our society legally retranscribed in the Constitution, among which the secular nature of the State has pride of place. . . .

Although the Grand Chamber placed less weight on the argument that the cross was as much a cultural and historical symbol as a religious one, choosing instead to analyze the actual impact of the cross's presence on pupils, it nevertheless recognized the validity of the Administrative Court's reasoning. To remove the crucifix would be akin to philosophical patricide; it would be a denial of the very principles espoused by the European Convention on Human Rights, since those same principles had found their embodiment in the cross for centuries.

This debate closely parallels the debate that played out in *Newdow* only a few years earlier on the American continent over the use of the phrase "under God," in the Pledge of Allegiance. Like the Administrative Court, legal scholar Thomas C. Berg argues that the recitation of "under God," in the Pledge should be viewed not as a religious exercise, but rather as an acknowledgement of the role of religion in the state's recognition of inalienable human rights. He states, "The positive rationale is that 'under God' in the pledge expresses the idea that government is a limited institution, subject to standards of authority higher than itself. 'Under God' expresses the idea that the rights of persons—the 'liberty and justice' guaranteed to all—are inalienable, stemming from a source higher than the nation or any other human authority."[42]

Berg argues that, just as the presence of the crucifix in Italian classrooms acted as an acknowledgement of the religious source of European human rights, so too was the inclusion of "under God" a recognition of the religious basis of American limited government and Constitutional rights. He continues, stating,

"The first and strongest claim is that the statement 'under God' must be constitutionally permissible because the vision it expressed—that the state is limited by human dignity and rights of transcendent status—is the only sufficient justification for the rights that the Constitution protects. Religious freedom and other human rights, the argument goes, can only be solidly grounded in a reality or authority beyond any human authority. Therefore, if the Constitution prohibited the expression of the rationale for these rights, it would undermine the very rights it protects and would contradict itself."[43]

In an argument that is analogous to the Italian government's argument in *Lautsi*, Berg concludes that removing "under God" from the Pledge would not be an act of neutrality; rather, it would be a state-sponsored promotion of secularism at the expense of Christianity. He contends that the ideal manner to protect freedom is through more freedom, not less. Rather than forcing religious individuals to abandon the use of "under God," he argues all students should be free to opt out of the Pledge or modify it as they see fit.

COMMENTS AND QUESTIONS

Under what circumstances may state neutrality be considered a legitimate ground for limiting fundamental rights? And who is supposed "to be neutral" according to human rights law—states, buildings, the "public square," civil servants, teachers, students, and/or pupils? When does a symbol "interfere" with the rights and freedoms of others or public order?

D. JAPAN

Exemption from Participating in Gym Class Swordplay: Japanese Kendo Case[44]

In this case a college student, Kunihito Kobayashi, refused to participate in a required kendo class at his public technical college, claiming it violated his religious beliefs. The student was a Jehovah's Witness and believed that the scripture in Isaiah 2:4 provided a prohibition against studying any form of martial arts, including kendo. Isaiah 2:4 reads: "They will have to beat their swords into plowshares and their spears into pruning shears. Nation will not lift up sword against nation, neither will they learn war anymore."

42. Thomas C. Berg, The Pledge of Allegiance and the Limited State, 8 *Tex. Rev. L. & Pol.* 1, 13 (2003)

43. *Id.* at 20.

44. 50 Minshu 4693, Sup. Ct., 8 March 1996.

Kobayashi requested to be allowed to participate in alternative activities, such as writing reports, but his request was denied. His refusal to participate in kendo resulted in the school first retaining him in his class another year. When he again refused to participate the following year, he was dismissed from school on the basis that he was not expected to complete his studies. On appeal to Japan's Supreme Court, the school argued that it could not make an exception for Kobayashi and provide alternative assignments both because of practical difficulties in offering alternative instruction and because Article 20, Paragraph 3 of the Constitution prohibits public schools from asking about or scrutinizing students' religious faith, or ranking religions hierarchically and treating them differently. Article 20, Paragraph 3 provides, "The State and its organs shall refrain from religious education or any other religious activity." The Court rejected this argument, stating that "the Court does not believe that, in the case of a student who is not able to participate in kendo practice for valid reasons of religious faith, the action of offering alternative activities such as requiring the relevant student to take part in alternative physical training activities, write reports and so on and evaluating the results thereof, has religious implications in its purpose, or has the effect of supporting, enhancing, or promoting a specific religion or the effect of oppressing or interfering with those believing in other religions or those with no religion. . . ." The Court further reasoned that "when a student refuses to participate in kendo practice for reasons of religious faith, the school, in order to determine the justifiability of the reasons, makes an investigation to determine whether it is an excuse for idleness, or whether there is any rational relevance between the religious teachings explained by the student in question and the refusal to participate." If a student invites investigation into his or her religious convictions by asking for accommodation for their religious beliefs, then investigation does not violate the principle of religious neutrality, and failure to make an effort to accommodate the religious beliefs of the student may violate the protection of religious freedom. The Court concluded by finding that the school "fail[ed] to take into account the matters to be considered, or obviously [fell] short of rationally evaluating the facts under consideration; hence, this Court arrives at the ruling that the Appellant handed down dispositions that are lacking in appropriateness compared with the view commonly accepted in society and that are illegal beyond the scope of discretionary authority."

COMMENTS AND QUESTIONS

1. It may be difficult for Westerners to understand the cultural significance of kendo in Japan. Kendo, which means "way of the sword," is a modern variation of traditional Japanese swordsmanship. Training in kendo, which has both mental and physical dimensions, is often a mandatory part of physical education classes in high schools in Japan. It is viewed as an important way to develop self-discipline and character, inculcating values such as discipline, courtesy, honor, sincerity, and patriotism.
2. What do you think of the Japanese Supreme Court's conclusion that examining the sincerity of the religious beliefs of the student requesting an exemption does not violate the constitutional prohibition of a school's discriminating on the basis of religion?

3. How does the Japanese approach compare with European approaches?

E. SOUTH AFRICA

National Policy on Religion and Education

In 2000, the Department of Education in South Africa began a formal process of consultation with the public, inviting all concerned parties to give input as to how to balance the place religion should have in education. The resulting policy focused on creating a values-based education system with ten core values. Religion is invited to play a role in instilling values and providing a foundation for those values so that students do not feel that rules are given without reason. However, no single religion should be preferred, as the policy also calls for *constitutional impartiality*.

In South Africa, legislative and administrative action plays a much larger role in defining the role of religion in the public sector, whereas this function is dominated by the courts in the United States.

Religious and Cultural Attire in South Africa: Nose Jewelry

Pillay v. MEC for Education, KwaZulu-Natal and Others (SAConstCt, 2005) involved a female student of South Indian descent, Sunali Pillay, who acquired a nose stud over the school holidays. When she returned to school she was told that the stud violated the dress code of the school and was directed to remove it. In 2005, when Pillay returned to school with the stud in place, the school asked her mother to write a letter explaining why Sunali should be allowed to wear the stud. Ms. Pillay explained that the nose stud had cultural significance and that insertion of the nose stud was part of a religious ritual marking her coming of age. After consulting with experts, the Governing Body of the school rejected Ms. Pillay's petition for an exemption from the school dress code. Following proceedings in the Equality Court, the High Court declared the school's decision prohibiting the wearing of nose studs by Hindu/Indian learners null and void. The school appealed to the Constitutional Court, which set aside the High Court's ruling in favor of an even stronger pronouncement against the school. It declared that the refusal to grant an exemption for Pillay to wear a nose stud discriminated unfairly against her, and it ordered the Governing Body of the school to amend its Code of Conduct "to provide for the reasonable accommodation of deviations from the Code on religious or cultural grounds and a procedure according to which such exemptions from the Code can be sought and granted."

One of the issues the Court grappled with in its decision was the distinction between cultural and religious practices. Do cultural practices warrant the same protection as religious practices and, if so, how is the legitimacy of a cultural practice to be determined? While it was accepted that "in order to determine if a practice or belief qualifies as religious a court should ask only whether the claimant professes a sincere belief," there was no consensus on whether cultural beliefs or practices should be determined objectively or subjectively. While the court did not find it necessary to resolve that issue directly, since even an objective approach appeared to confirm the cultural significance of the nose stud, it did observe that "cultural convictions or practices may be as strongly held and as important to those who hold them as religious beliefs are to those more inclined to find meaning in a higher power than in a community of people," and that "while cultures are associative, they are not monolithic. The practices and beliefs that make up an individual's cultural identity will differ from person to person within a culture." After hearing the evidence, the Court concluded that the nose stud was "not a mandatory tenet of Sunali's religion or culture. But the evidence does confirm that the nose stud is a voluntary expression of South Indian Tamil Hindu culture, a culture that is intimately intertwined with Hindu religion, and that Sunali regards it as such."

The main question, then, was whether the Equality Act and the Constitution protected voluntary religious and cultural practices. The Court observed,

> The traditional basis for invalidating laws that prohibit the exercise of an obligatory practice is that it confronts the adherents with a Hobson's choice between observance of their faith and adherence to the law. There is however more to the protection of religious and cultural practices than saving believers from hard choices. Religious and cultural practices are protected because they are central to human identity and hence to human dignity which is in turn central to equality. Are voluntary practices any less a part of a person's identity or do they affect human dignity any less seriously because they are not mandatory?

The Court, therefore, concluded that these practices were protected and that "the protection of voluntary practices applies equally to culture and religion." The school's action was thus discriminatory and had to be justified as a fair discrimination in order to be upheld.

In determining whether the discrimination was fair, the Court considered the principle of reasonable accommodation, defining it as "the notion that sometimes the community must take positive measures and possibly incur additional hardship or expense in order to allow all people to participate and enjoy all their rights equally. It ensures that we do not relegate people to the margins of society because they do not or cannot conform to certain social norms." In determining the extent of the duty to accommodate, the Court adopted a flexible standard: "Reasonable accommodation is, in a sense, an exercise in proportionality that will depend intimately on the facts." The Court held that fairness required accommodation in this case, and to determine whether an exemption was proper accommodation, it weighed the importance of the practice to Sunali against the hardship the school would endure by allowing her an exemption. On the question of the importance of the practice, the Court adopted a subjective standard, arguing that "if Sunali states that the nose stud is central to her as a South Indian Tamil Hindu, it is not for the Court to tell her that she is wrong because others do not relate to that religion or culture in the same way." After considering the evidence and arguments about the potential negative effects allowing Sunali to wear her nose stud would have on the school, the Court concluded that the hardship the school faced in allowing Sunali the exemption did not outweigh the importance of the practice to her and, therefore, that the discrimination was unfair. Since Sunali was likely not the only person who would ever require an exemption, the Court ordered the school to amend its code to provide for reasonable accommodations and to establish a procedure for obtaining them.

The Court then highlighted the important distinction between equality and uniformity by quoting Justice Sachs' concurring opinion from *National Coalition for Gay and Lesbian Equality v. Minister of Justice*,[45] which declared,

> The present case shows well that equality should not be confused with Uniformity, in fact, uniformity can be the enemy of equality. Equality means equal concern and respect across differences. It does not presuppose the elimination or suppression of differences. Respect for human rights requires the affirmation of self, not the denial of self. Equality therefore does not imply a leveling or homogenisation of behaviour but an acknowledgement and acceptance of difference. At the very least, it affirms that difference should not be the basis for exclusion, marginalization, stigma and punishment—At best, it celebrates the validity that difference brings to any society.

On another occasion, Justice Sachs reiterated the need to respect freedom of conscience:

> . . . Conscience is Number One. It comes before food, before the vote. It comes before health, education, even before freedom of speech. Conscience is what makes you a person. It's so central to your notion of yourself, your community, your sense of existence, and your future. It's deep. It's profound.[46]

Although these words were offered with respect to the issue of same-sex marriage in South Africa, they could just as easily be applied to Pillay's case.

COMMENTS AND QUESTIONS

1. Sunali Pillay's case raises interesting questions, particularly since it deals not only with free exercise of religion or culture, but also freedom of expression in school. Should the exception to school dress codes extend to other aspects of one's appearance, including style of hair? (In *Danielle Antonie v. Governing Body, The Settlers High School & Head Western Cape Education Department* the court extended the exception to hairstyle for Rastafarians.)
2. How do you think the South African courts would react to a t-shirt like that found in the now-vacated US case *Harper v. Poway Unified School District*, 445 F.3d 1166 (9th Cir. 2006) (where a religiously motivated student wore a t-shirt reading "Homosexuality Is Shameful")? The Court seemed to focus on Sunali's right to human dignity in expressing her cultural and religious identity.

Additional Web Resources:	Materials on South African approach to religion-state issues Materials on regulating religious attire of students and teachers

45. *National Coalition for Gay and Lesbian Equality v. Minister of Justice*, 1999 1 SA 6 (CC) paragraph [132].

46. Justice Albie Sachs, Ray Distinguished Lecture, The Sacred and the Secular: South Africa's Constitutional Court Rules on Same-Sex Marriages, 102 *Ky. L.J.* 147, 157 (2013).

CHAPTER 14

RELIGION AND PUBLIC LIFE

I. INTRODUCTION

The appropriate role of religion in public life is one of the most interesting theoretical and most pressing practical issues in the interrelation of law and religion. This chapter introduces a broad range of issues relating to the influence of religion in politics and public life, the significance of religious symbols in public places, and ways that government invokes or tries to use religion for its own ends.

II. THE DEBATE ABOUT THE APPROPRIATE ROLE OF RELIGION IN PUBLIC LIFE

One important debate centers on the appropriateness of invoking religion and religious assumptions and beliefs in public life. The philosopher John Rawls, using terminology coined by Thomas Hobbes and employed by Immanuel Kant, developed the notion of public reason, the idea that in a liberal constitutional democracy, when citizens or officials seek publicly to justify their policies, they should rely only on reasoning accessible to all rational citizens, and should refrain from invoking reasons, such as religious justifications, that are not cogent to all rational people.

In response, Michael Perry and others articulated a defense of the concept of ecumenical dialogue and ecumenical politics, which encourages us to consider the reasons and convictions of others, even if we do not share them. They further argue against calling the views of others "irrational." As you read these excerpts, consider which position offers a better descriptive as well as normative account of justification in a liberal democracy.

A. PUBLIC REASON

JOHN RAWLS, THE IDEA OF PUBLIC REASON REVISITED

64 *U. Chi. L. Rev.* 765, 765-766 (1997)

The idea of public reason, as I understand it, belongs to a conception of a well-ordered constitutional democratic society. The form and content of this reason—the way it is understood by citizens and how it interprets their political relationship—are part of the idea of democracy itself. This is because a basic feature of democracy is the fact of a reasonable pluralism—the fact that a plurality of conflicting reasonable comprehensive doctrines, religious, philosophical, and moral, is the normal result of its culture of free institutions. Citizens realize that they cannot reach agreement or even approach mutual understanding on the basis of their irreconcilable comprehensive doctrines. In view of this, they need to consider what kinds of reasons they may reasonably give one another when fundamental political questions are at stake. I propose that in public reason comprehensive doctrines of truth or right be replaced by the idea of the politically reasonable addressed to citizens as citizens.

Central to the idea of public reason is that it neither criticizes nor attacks any comprehensive doctrine, religious or nonreligious, except insofar as that doctrine is incompatible with the essentials of public reason and a democratic polity. The basic requirement is that a reasonable doctrine accepts a constitutional democratic regime and its companion idea of legitimate law. While democracies will differ in the specific doctrines that are influential within them—as they differ in the Western democracies of Europe, the United States, Israel, and India—finding a suitable idea of public reason is a concern that faces them all.

Rawls does not argue that people should leave behind their personal commitments and beliefs, including religious ones, but rather that when engaged in political discourse in a public forum, they should translate their beliefs into terms that are genuinely accessible to everyone. Rawls's central proposal is that in public reason "comprehensive doctrines of truth or right be replaced by an idea of the politically reasonable addressed to citizens as citizens." (766) This view has been criticized for denying participants in political discourse the right to speak the truth as they understand it. To be sure, citizens may be motivated by their "comprehensive doctrines," including religious beliefs, according to Rawls, but it is unacceptable for them to appeal to those doctrines when engaging in political or legal debate.

Rawls distinguishes the idea of public reason from the ideal of public reason. "This ideal is realized," he writes, "whenever judges, legislators, chief executives, and other government officials, as well as candidates for public office, act from and follow the idea of public reason and explain to other citizens their reasons for supporting fundamental political positions in terms of the political conception of justice they regard as the most reasonable." (769) By observing this ideal, they satisfy what Rawls describes as "their duty of civility to one another and to other citizens." (769) According to Rawls, "A citizen engages in public reason. . . when he or she deliberates within a framework of what he or she sincerely regards as the most reasonable political conception of justice, a conception that expresses political values that others, as free and equal citizens might also reasonably be expected reasonably to endorse." (773)

B. ECUMENICAL DIALOGUE

MICHAEL PERRY, LOVE AND POWER: THE ROLE OF RELIGION AND MORALITY IN AMERICAN POLITICS

Oxford Univ. Press 1993, 44–45, 47, 112–114

[N]ot every kind of reliance on every kind of conviction is appropriate in a modern liberal society, least of all in one as religiously morally pluralistic as the United States. . . . The practice I defend makes room for some (but not all) kinds of reliance on some (but not all) kinds of disputed convictions.

In this [section] my principal aims are, first, to introduce the ideal of ecumenical politics, in particular, to introduce the practice of ecumenical political dialogue, which is a principal constituent of ecumenical politics; and, second, to specify several reasons for taking ecumenical politics seriously and, in particular, for taking seriously ecumenical political dialogue.

The *Oxford English Dictionary* defines "ecumenical", in relevant part, as "Belonging to the whole world; universal, general, worldwide." The adjective is often used to modify "religion" or "theology". "Ecumenical" theology aspires to discern or achieve, in a theologically pluralistic context, a common ("universal") theological ground, mainly through a dialogic or dialectical transcending of "local" or "sectarian" differences. (Dialogue is thus a principal constituent of ecumenical theology.) The effort to achieve a common ground does not presuppose that all theological differences can be overcome, or even that overcoming all such differences would be a good thing. Ecumenical theology values theological pluralism. . . . By analogy, "ecumenical" politics aspires to discern or achieve, in a religiously and morally pluralistic context, a common political ground. . . .

The principal constituents of ecumenical politics are two practices: first, a certain kind of dialogue; second, a certain kind of tolerance. . . . Ecumenical politics is, above all, both dialogic and communitarian: It is. . . a politics in which, notwithstanding our religious/moral pluralism, we continually cultivate the bonds of political community—and in which we sometimes succeed in strengthening those bonds, even, occasionally, in forging new bonds—through dialogue of a certain kind. Ecumenical politics institutionalizes a particular conception of "the place of religion in American life" and of "how we should contend with each other's deepest differences in the public sphere." The aim of ecumenical politics is, in words borrowed from *The Williamsburg Charter*, "neither a naked public square where all religion is excluded, nor a sacred public square with any religion established or semi-established." The aim, rather, "is a civil public square in which citizens of all religious faiths, or none, engage one another in continuing democratic discourse.". . .

Ecumenical political dialogue, whether justificatory or deliberative or both, aspires to discern or achieve, in a religiously/morally pluralistic context, a common ground that transcends "local" or "sectarian" differences. To the extent such dialogue is genuinely deliberative, "what is at issue . . . is not 'what should I do?' or 'how should I conduct myself?' but: 'how are we to "be" together, and what is to be the institutional setting for that being-together?'. . . It is not self-deliberation about my life, but mutual deliberation conducted between agents implicated in a common life." However, ecumenical political dialogue does not always or even often lead to agreement. Not all the important religious or moral differences "between [or among] agents implicated in a common life" can be overcome. Indeed, . . . ecumenical political dialogue should not always lead to agreement, not all the important differences should be overcome; agreement is not the true test or measure of the success of such dialogue. . . . Because common ground cannot always be achieved, another aspiration of ecumenical political dialogue is to achieve a position on a political issue that is within the range of reasonable positions on the issue, given the relevant authoritative premises. . . .

If a conception of politics is to be taken seriously as an ideal for *American* society, the conception should comport with the relevant basic features of the American constitutional tradition. A conception of politics that is in tension with, much less violates, those traditions is not an attractive ideal for American society. Ecumenical politics is, in part, a *religious* politics, in this sense: a politics in which persons with religious convictions about the good or fitting way for human beings to live their lives rely on those convictions, not only in making political choices but in publicly deliberating about and in publicly justifying such choices. Is such a politics consistent with the provision of the United States Constitution that forbids government—both the federal government and the governments of the fifty states—to make any "law respecting an establishment of religion"? Is ecumenical politics in tension with "the establishment clause"?

The establishment clause is understood (by its principal and authoritative interpreter, the United States Supreme Court) to forbid government to establish a religion—in the way, for example, the Church of England is established in England—or otherwise to act for the purpose of endorsing the institutions, theologies, or practices of one or more religions (churches, sects, denominations, communities of faith) as against the institutions, theologies, or practices of one or more other religions. More controversially, the clause is understood to forbid government to act for the purpose of endorsing religion generally—religious institutions, systems of belief, or practices—as against irreligious or nonreligious institutions, systems of belief, or practices.

Not surprisingly, the establishment clause is not understood to proscribe, as a basis for political deliberation, justification, or choice, moral beliefs: beliefs about the good or fitting way for human beings to live their lives. . . . There is no accepted interpretation of the establishment clause, nor, more important, is there any plausible interpretation of the clause (whether accepted or not), according to which citizens or their political representatives act in a constitutionally problematic way if they make political choices partly or even wholly on the basis of religious convictions about the good or fitting way for human beings to live their lives, or, much less, if they publicly deliberate about or publicly justify political choices on that basis.

The present issue, however, is more specific. The particular sort of politics—a partly religious politics—whose consistency with the establishment clause is in question is ecumenical politics. With respect to *that* issue—in particular, with respect to the question of the consistency of ecumenical political dialogue with the establishment clause . . . : The sort of reliance on religious premises about the human that is a feature of ecumenical politics is *not* sectarian or authoritarian. . . . It is difficult, in the context of a nonsectarian and nonauthoritarian approach to, and understanding of, religious morality (like that sketched by Notre Dame's James Burtchaell), to know how to administer the putative distinction between "secular" premises about the human, the dialogic role of which in politics the establishment clause certainly tolerates, and "religious" premises about the human, the dialogic role of which the clause, on some imaginable if farfetched interpretation, would proscribe.

MICHAEL PERRY, MORALITY POLITICS AND LAW

Oxford Univ. Press 1988, 183

If one can participate in politics and law—if one can use or resist power—only as a partisan of particular moral/religious conviction about the human, and if politics is and must be in part about the credibility of such convictions, then we who want to participate, whether as theorists or activists or both, must examine our own convictions self-critically. We must be willing to let our convictions be tested in ecumenical dialogue with others who do not share them. We must let ourselves be tested, in ecumenical dialogue, by convictions we do not share. We must, in short, resist the temptations of infallibilism. . . . If necessary we must revise our convictions until they are credible to ourselves, if not always or even often to our interlocutors. We must be willing to lend credibility to our convictions by being faithful to them in our lives and not merely in our polemics and our posturing. We must bring our convictions to bear as we use or as we resist power. We must resist and seek to transform a politics that represses, by marginalizing or privatizing, questions of human authenticity.

COMMENTS AND QUESTIONS

Are the underlying ideas about the purpose of dialogue different in a public reason conception of politics versus an ecumenical dialogue model of politics?

Additional Web Resources:	Readings, pro and con, on whether we should limit ourselves when engaged in political discourse to public reason

C. CREATED IN THE IMAGE OF GOD

Genesis 1:27 (KJV) reads, "So God created man in his own image, in the image of God created he him; male and female created he them." Consider whether it is appropriate for public officials, such as politicians and judges, to invoke religious concepts such as this.

JEREMY WALDRON, THE WAR ON TERROR AND THE IMAGE OF GOD[1]

Targeted Assassination

In December 2005, the Supreme Court of Israel sitting as the High Court of Justice considered the Israeli government's policy of preventative strikes aimed at killing members of terrorist organizations in the West Bank and the Gaza Strip, even when they were not actively or immediately engaged in terrorist activities.[2] The Court confronted the claim that this policy was unlawful, being "contradictory to international law, Israeli law, and basic principles of human morality" and human rights. The petitioners were an Israeli human rights organization, and it argued that the members of terrorist organizations were criminals, and so were to be dealt with by way of arrest and trial and only killed if that were strictly necessary for self-defense, or (in the alternative) that if there is a state of armed conflict between Israel and certain Palestinian organizations, the civilian members of such organizations are liable to be killed only during the time that they renounce their civilian status and take up arms and actually engage in conflict. There is no legal category of unlawful combatant liable as a civilian to attack outside the ordinary protection of the laws of war, the petitioners argued. "[A] civilian loses his immunity from attack only during such time that he is taking a direct and active part in hostilities, and only for such time that said direct participation continues . . . from the time that the civilian returns to his house, . . . even if he intends to participate again later in hostilities, he is not a legitimate target for attack, although he can be arrested and tried for [what he has already done]." That was the petitioners' contention.

In a . . . very thoughtful opinion, President (Emeritus) Aharon Barak of the Israeli Supreme Court rejected the absolutism of this contention. He argued that people who had engaged and intended to engage in terrorist activities did have the status of unlawful combatants and one couldn't rule out the right of the IDF to use force against them even while they were not actually engaged in combat: the "revolving door" phenomenon, by which each terrorist has "horns of the alt[a]r" (I Kings 1:50) to grasp or a "city of refuge" (Numbers 35:11) to flee to, to which he turns in order to rest and prepare while they grant him immunity from attack, is to be avoided.

There is no alternative, said Justice Barak, to approaching these situations on a case-by-case basis. How regular is the target's participation in terrorist attack; to what extent is his retreat back into civilian life just an opportunity for rest and preparation? Is the mandated alternative of arrest and trial available in the circumstances? And what is the likely collateral cost in terms of loss of life for civilians who are not unlawful combatants?

---

1. Jeremy Waldron, "The War on Terror and the Image of God," remarks at the Emory University Center for *the* Study of Law and Religion Conference, *From Silver to Gold: The Next 25 Years of Law and Religion* (24–26 October 2007). A revised version of this article is included in *Christianity and Human Rights: An Introduction* (John Witte Jr., and Frank S. Alexander, eds., Cambridge Univ. Press 2010).

2. *The Public Committee against Torture in Israel and Palestinian Society for the Protection of Human Rights and the Environment v. The Government of Israel and others* [2005] HCJ 769/02 (Isr.).

Image of God

I am not interested today in discussing the legality or wisdom of these conclusions. I am a great admirer of Justice Barak, and I do think the decision is a sound one. But today I am interested in something that Barak said in the course of his opinion as a sort of reminder of what was at stake. He acknowledged that "The State's fight against terrorism is the fight of the state against its enemies" and that Israel had suffered a terrible cost in the innocent lives of its own people as a result of the thousands of terrorist attacks directed against it. But he also said this:

> Needless to say, unlawful combatants are not beyond the law. They are not "outlaws". God created them as well in his image; their human dignity as well is to be honored; they as well enjoy and are entitled to protection . . . by customary international law.

God created them as well in his image. The reference is clear enough. It is biblical, a reference first of all to Genesis 1:26-7: "And God said, Let us make man in our image, after our likeness. . . . So God created man in his own image, in the image of God he created him; male and female created he them." It is a reference secondly to the Noachide laws given after the Flood, a reminder in the context of the law of homicide that "in the image of God made he man" (Genesis 9:6).

But here's my question. Why is it important to insert this specifically religious reference in this context? What is the reference to man's creation in the image of God doing here? I doubt that an American court would ever say this, in its decisions about unlawful combatant status: e.g., that the men responsible for planning and carrying out the attacks on 9/11 were created by God in his image, just as much as the victims of the attack—though there was a time when our judges did talk in these terms, a time when Justice McLean could say (in his dissent) of the petitioner in *Dred Scott v. Sandford* that "[h]e bears the impress of his Maker, . . . and he is destined to an endless existence."[3] Israeli courts are not afflicted with the Rawlsian doctrines of public reason that our philosophers put about, which are intended to limit the citation of religious considerations in public life, and which indeed take the federal courts as an exemplar of this sort of restraint. But still there's a question of what this reference is doing there and what it adds to the argument Justice Barak is making.

Reference to Dignity as an Alternative

After all, in the concurring judgment of Vice President Rivlin in the same case, a similar point is made about the terrorists, but not in the language of the image of God. Justice Rivlin said this:

> The duty to honor the lives of innocent civilians is thus the point of departure . . . but it is not the endpoint. It cannot negate the human dignity of the unlawful combatants themselves. . . . Human dignity is a principle which applies to every person, even during combat and conflict.[4]

---

3. *Dred Scott v. Sandford*, 60 U.S. 393, 550 (1856) (McLean, J., dissenting). I am grateful to Hadley Arkes for drawing this passage to my attention: *see* Hadley Arkes, *Lochner v. New York* and the Cast of Our Laws, in *Great Cases in Constitutional Law* 125 (Robert P. George, ed., Princeton Univ. Press 2000).

4. *Public Committee against Torture in Israel*, *supra* note 2, opinion of Rivlin VP, §5.

And we know that Barak could have used the apparently more secular language of dignity, too, because he did: "God created them as well in his image; *their human dignity as well is to be honored.*" So here's our question: what, if anything, does the reference to creation in the image of God add to the point about human dignity, so far as the terrorist is concerned?

I have one speculative answer and some deeper considerations to offer about the importance of religious argument in international human rights and humanitarian law.

Mishna Sanhedrin 4.5

The speculative answer to the question refers to a Jewish tradition concerning the way witnesses were admonished in advance in capital cases. Witnesses were reminded that if someone was convicted in a capital case as a result of false or equivocal testimony an evil would be done that could not be remedied.

In capital cases both the blood of the man put to death and the blood of his [potential] descendants are on the witness's head until the end of time. . . . Therefore was the first man, Adam, created alone, to teach us that whoever destroys a single life, . . . it is as if he destroyed an entire world. And whoever saves a single life, . . . it is as if he saved an entire world.

It's a bit of a stretch, but it is as though Justice Barak were repeating something like that traditional admonition, for the image of God idea is often connected in Jewish thought with the idea of God having stamped us like coins with the image of Himself that He impressed upon Adam. It is a way of reminding the court to proceed carefully in its arguments, because this was in effect like a capital case: it concerned the shedding of blood, and if the court were *wrongly* to sanction this sort of assassination, it would (like a false witness) take upon itself the grave responsibility of having provided judicially for the murder not just of a few terrorists, but of sacred human life in general and in principle.

Pulling Us Up Short

The same point may be made more directly. The reference to the image of God in paragraph 25 of Barak's judgment is intended to pull us up short. It is intended to remind us that although we are dealing with an outsider and an evil person, an enemy of the state of the Israel and the Jewish people, a threat to our lives and those of our loved ones, one who will kill and maim scores of innocent people if he gets the opportunity—although we are talking about someone who may be justly liable through his actions and intentions to deadly force—we are nevertheless not just talking about a wild beast, or an outsider to our species, or something that may be manipulated or battered or exploited as a mere tool for our own purposes (the purpose of saving the lives of members of our community). The unlawful combatant may be a threat and an outsider and an evil and dangerous man, but he is also *man-created-in-the-image-of-God* and the status associated with that characterization imposes radical limits on what may be done with him and radical constraints on how lightly we may treat the question of what may be done with him.

So a proclamation that the individual we may be targeting is created in the image of God serves as the basis of a compelling constraint, in precisely the circumstances in which we may be tempted to say that constraints no longer apply, because this man we are dealing with is not one of us, this is our enemy, this is an animal or a savage, someone who has forfeited any claim on our moral regard. It counsels us to take care and respect the holiness of the individual, even in this extremity. . . .

Human Rights

. . . Is it not sufficient to remind ourselves of certain elementary human rights? Those who believe in human rights already may not need to appeal to the idea of image of God, to persuade them that torture is absolutely wrong and that policies of targeted assassination need to be treated with the utmost caution. Won't human rights be sufficient to help us resist these inclinations?. . .

Dignity as the Ground of Rights?

Now it might be thought that it is precisely the role of human dignity to fulfill this function: it's the idea of human dignity that provides the basal underpinnings for our human rights commitments, underpinnings that may then be appealed to for the elucidation of difficult cases. And so, it might be thought, we do not need to go further than Justice Rivlin—we do not need to go as far as Justice Barak—in sounding the requisite note of caution.

I am not sure about this. Dignity is an odd and ambiguous concept. Often the idea of dignity does little more than repeat or reiterate the idea of human rights. Jacques Maritain, for example, says this about the phrase "the dignity of the human person":

> The expression means nothing if it does not signify that, by virtue of the natural law, the human person has the right to be respected, is the subject of rights, possesses rights.[5]

In this passage, as Alan Gewirth has pointed out, "The attribution of dignity adds nothing to the attribution of rights, and someone who is doubtful about the latter attribution will be equally doubtful about the former."[6]

At its best the phrase "human dignity" is a way of *expressing* something about the inherent rank or worth of the human person. Like any status term (like "citizen," for example), it may provide a ground from which further conclusions of right can be inferred; but also like any status term—in law or morality—it stands itself in need of further explication and further justification. And of course these needs for explication and justification are nowhere more compelling [than] in situations where everything in our morality militates in favor of denigrating or degrading—not to mention bestializing or instrumentalizing—those who pose the sort of threat that terrorists pose in the modern world.

I am not denying that the idea of human dignity can *convey* much of what needs to be said here, e.g., in its Kantian manifestation: in the notion of worth

---

5. Jacques Maritain, *The Rights of Man and Natural Law* 65 (D. Anson, trans., Charles Scribner's Sons 1943).

6. Alan Gewirth, *Human Rights: Essays on Justification and Applications* (Univ. of Chicago Press 1978).

beyond price, beyond trade-offs.[7] But even if the language of dignity can *convey* the Kantian point about no trade-offs, still we need a sense of the argument and justification for that point. And repeating the mantra of dignity does not by itself provide that.

Fragility of Dignity

What is needed, then, is some stronger sense of a ground for dignity that is not vulnerable to relativisation . . . some ground that can provide the basis for an objective reproach for the ways in which we are used to treating the despised among us or the outsiders and evil-doers who happen to be in our power.

Image of God as Basis of Substantive Argument

The claim about the image of God—assuming it is true . . . —does more, then, than simply *reiterate* claims about dignity in religious terms. It provides a ground and a characterization of dignity that is both substantive, objective, and compelling.

It presents itself as grounded ontologically, not in what we happen to care about or in what we happen to have committed ourselves to, but in facts about what humans are actually like, or—more accurately, what they have been made by the Creator to be like—to be like unto Himself and to command by virtue of the fact of that likeness treatment as something sacred and inviolable. We are not just clever animals, and the evil-doers among us are not just good animals gone bad: our dignity is associated with a specifically high rank in creation accorded to us by our creator and reflecting our likeness to Him. Our status even as wrongdoers is to be understood in relation to this.

The Work that *Imago Dei* does

This foundational work that *imago dei* does for dignity is, in my opinion, indispensable for generating the sort of strong moral constraint—and for motivating the positing and the observance of the sort of strong legal constraint—that we need to override what would otherwise seem like sensible and compelling strategies for dealing with outsiders, with our enemies, with terrorists, with those who can be categorized as "the worst of the worst." It is the most counterintuitive thing to say of a terrorist that he is, at some level, entitled to the same concern and respect as a human being as his innocent victims; and anything which is supposed to motivate that position, I believe, has to have this sort of power.

Our standing temptation is to build upon what might be a legitimate sense (1) that we can treat outsiders differently from the way we treat our own and (2) that we can treat the guilty in a way that is radically different from the way we treat the innocent—the standing temptation is to build upon those two perhaps legitimate starting points and head towards something much more problematic—a

7. "In the kingdom of ends everything has either a price or a dignity. What has a price can be replaced by something else as its equivalent; what, on the other hand, is raised above all price and therefore admits of no equivalent has a dignity. Whatever has reference to general human inclinations and needs has a market price; . . . but that which constitutes the condition under which alone something can be an end in itself has not merely a relative worth, that is, a price, but an inner worth, that is, dignity."

degradation of the person and a bestialization of the humanity of the evil-doer—especially when he is an evil-doer who is also an outsider, as someone or some thing to whom or to which we owe nothing in the way of rehabilitative energy, nothing in the way of civic respect. . . . That is the powerful temptation here and—accompanied as it is by the strongest feelings of moral self-righteousness and concern for ourselves and our innocents—it needs to be answered by something that goes beyond our attitudes, even beyond "our" morality, something commanded from the depths of the pre-political and pre-social foundation of the being of those we are tempted to treat in this way. . . .

But what if it is not true?

So I am not sure we can do without a concept like this. I don't want to be misunderstood. I am not saying that we should come to believe that man is created in the image of God, because it is morally efficacious to do so. . . . [W]hat we mustn't say is that religious propositions, like man's creation in the image of God, are *confirmed* or *vindicated* by the role that they can play in explaining, characterizing, grounding and motivating normative positions about human dignity and human rights. I don't want to sound too objectivist. But the religious propositions are supposed to provide reasons, and like all reasons they are vindicated in this role only if they are true.

If there is no God (or if that is believed) or if it is the case (or if it is believed) that He did not create man in His image and likeness but just as another animal—then there may be nothing to motivate the inviolability of *the* person *in extremis* and the fundamental equality of all humans. We may hope that some sense of the sacredness of the person can survive such doubt, but it cannot be anything other than a forlorn hope in the light of the experience of the last eighty years in which, as Hannah Arendt has pointed out, "the world found nothing sacred in the abstract nakedness of being human." For Arendt, dignity and rights are to be rooted in the thick substance of an existing political community and that's the ground of her famous skepticism about human rights. But I have chosen to focus on the cases in which societies have no choice but to confront the person who presents himself as *homo sacer*, as nothing but a stranger, or as just a dangerous wrongdoer, outside the bounds of all community, with nothing social or ethical to recommend him, nothing but the bare fact of his humanity. We sometimes have to decide, as the Israeli High Court had to decide, whether and in what circumstances to kill such a person, and if such a person is thrown back simply on the fact of his humanity to plead the case for restraint, he may find as Michael Ignatieff once said, echoing Arendt and Agamben, that this is the weakest claim that one person can make to another. . . .

NOTES AND COMMENTS

Aharon Barak was President of the Supreme Court of Israel from 1995 to 2006. Under his leadership, the Supreme Court broadened its power and played an active role in shaping the law surrounding some of the most contentious political issues during his tenure.[8] His influence on the legal system of Israel, which is widely held

8. Barak, Aharon (1936–), Personal History, Biographical Highlights, Personal Chronology: Influences, Contributions, Exploring, Influence on the Israeli Legal System, http://bit.ly/2Gf9OQV.

to be unparalleled, led to greater protections for Israel's Palestinian populations. Consequently, he received heated attacks by conservative Jewish writers as "an enemy of the Jews"[9] and required around-the-clock bodyguards as a result.[10]

All of this certainly makes his controversial opinion in *The Public Committee against Torture in Israel v. The Government of Israel* fascinating, but what may be the most remarkable feature of the opinion's contextual background is Judge Barak's lack of orthodoxy. His childhood experiences with the Nazi occupation in Lithuania and the Holocaust of World War II shook him from his religious faith.[11] Nonetheless, he made deliberate use of Jewish scripture in the opinion in order to speak forcefully to his audience. Perhaps recognizing that the concept of "human dignity" might not sufficiently capture the attention of some in the Israeli government, Barak reinforced the boundaries he was drawing around legitimate targeted killings by employing the deeply religious ideas of Genesis 1:26-7. He declared not only that all the citizens of Israel have "human dignity," but also that they were created "in the image of God."

Additional Web Resources:	Full text of Justice Barak's opinion in *The Public Committee against Torture in Israel and Palestinian Society for the Protection of Human Rights and the Environment v. The Government of Israel and others* (HCJ 769/02) 11 December 2005, and the full text of Jeremy Waldron's article reflecting on its significance Justice McLean's dissent in the *Dred Scott* case

III. RELIGIOUS INFLUENCE IN POLITICS

Of course, the courts are not the only place where the role of religious thought is called into question. Indeed, important questions both in the United States and around the world revolve around the relationship between religious beliefs and the expression of political views.

A. UNITED STATES

In the United States, this question emerges both in terms of religious qualifications for office and in the role of religious arguments in political campaigns, particularly in the contentious civil rights movement.

9. Joel Greenberg, Major Israeli Writer Leads Protest on Orthodox Rally, *The New York Times*, 18 February 1999, http://nyti.ms/2FdvN9V.

10. Larry Derfner, Rattling the Cage: The Jewish Tradition of Aharon Barak, *The Jerusalem Post*, 13 August 2006, http://bit.ly/2E6KSKM.

11. Barak, Aharon, *supra* note 8.

1. Religious Qualifications for Office

PROHIBITION OF RELIGIOUS TESTS

Article VI of the US Constitution prohibits religious tests for federal officeholders: It requires in relevant part that ". . . no religious Test shall ever be required as a Qualification to any Office or public Trust under the United States."

Additional Web Resources:	Cases on religious tests: *Torcaso v. Watkins*, 367 U.S. 488 (1961) (holding that requirement of a belief in God as a qualification for public office is unconstitutional); *Buscarini v. San Marino*, App. No. 24645/94 (ECtHR, 1999)

UNCONSTITUTIONALITY OF STATE PROHIBITING CLERGY FROM HOLDING ELECTIVE OFFICE

MCDANIEL V. PATY

Supreme Court of the United States, 435 U.S. 618 (1978)

[At issue in this case was a Tennessee statute barring ministers or priests from serving as delegates to the state's constitutional convention. McDaniel, an ordained minister, challenged the statute as a violation of the Free Exercise Clause. Chief Justice Berger delivered the Court's opinion.]

I.

In its first Constitution, in 1796, Tennessee disqualified ministers from serving as legislators. That disqualifying provision has continued unchanged since its adoption . . . . "

[The election of McDaniel, an ordained minister of a Baptist Church in Chattanooga, Tenn., was challenged by an opposing candidate, appellee Selma Cash Paty, who ultimately prevailed in the Tennessee Supreme Court, which held] that the disqualification of clergy imposed no burden upon "religious belief" and restricted "religious action. . . [only] in the lawmaking process of government— where religious action is absolutely prohibited by the establishment clause. . . . " The state interests in preventing the establishment of religion and in avoiding the divisiveness and tendency to channel political activity along religious lines, resulting from clergy participation in political affairs, were deemed by that court sufficiently weighty to justify the disqualification, notwithstanding the guarantee of the Free Exercise Clause. . . .

II.

A.

The disqualification of ministers from legislative office was a practice carried from England by seven of the original States; later six new States similarly excluded clergymen from some political offices. . . . The purpose of the several States in providing for disqualification was primarily to assure the success of a new political experiment, the separation of church and state. Prior to 1776, most of the 13 Colonies had some form of an established, or government-sponsored, church. Even after ratification of the First Amendment, which prohibited the Federal Government from following such a course, some States continued pro-establishment provisions. . . Massachusetts, the last State to accept disestablishment, did so in 1833.

In light of this history and a widespread awareness during that period of undue and often dominant clerical influence in public and political affairs here, in England, and on the Continent, it is not surprising that strong views were held by some that one way to assure disestablishment was to keep clergymen out of public office. Indeed, some of the foremost political philosophers and statesmen of that period held such views regarding the clergy. Earlier, John Locke argued for confining the authority of the English clergy "within the bounds of the church, nor can it in any manner be extended to civil affairs; because the church itself is a thing absolutely separate and distinct from the commonwealth." Thomas Jefferson initially advocated such a position in his 1783 draft of a constitution for Virginia. James Madison, however, disagreed and vigorously urged the position which in our view accurately reflects the spirit and purpose of the Religion Clauses of the First Amendment. Madison's response to Jefferson's position was:

> Does not the exclusion of Ministers of the Gospel as such violate a fundamental principle of liberty by punishing a religious profession with the privation of a civil right? does it [not] violate another article of the plan itself which exempts religion from the cognizance of Civil power? does it not violate justice by at once taking away a right and prohibiting a compensation for it? does it not in fine violate impartiality by shutting the door [against] the Ministers of one Religion and leaving it open for those of every other?

[Like] Madison[,] John Witherspoon, a Presbyterian minister, president of Princeton University, and the only clergyman to sign the Declaration of Independence, made a cogent protest and, with tongue in cheek, offered an amendment to a provision much like that challenged here:

> No clergyman, of any denomination, shall be capable of being elected a member of the Senate or House of Representatives . . . Provided always, and it is the true intent and meaning of this part of the constitution, that if at any time he shall be completely deprived of the clerical character . . . as by deposition for cursing and swearing, drunkenness or uncleanness, he shall then be fully restored to all the privileges of a free citizen; his offense [of being a clergyman] shall no more be remembered against him; but he may be chosen either to the Senate or House of Representatives, and shall be treated with all the respect due to his *brethren*, the other members of Assembly.

As the value of the disestablishment experiment was perceived, 11 of the 13 States disqualifying the clergy from some types of public office gradually abandoned that limitation. . . . Only Maryland and Tennessee continued their clergy-disqualification provisions into this century and, . . . [as of 1974], Tennessee remains the only State excluding ministers from certain public offices.

The essence of this aspect of our national history is that in all but a few States the selection or rejection of clergymen for public office soon came to be viewed as something safely left to the good sense and desires of the people.

B.

This brief review of the history of clergy-disqualification provisions also amply demonstrates, however, that, at least during the early segment of our national life, those provisions enjoyed the support of responsible American statesmen and were accepted as having a rational basis. Against this background we do not lightly invalidate a statute enacted pursuant to a provision of a state constitution which has been sustained by its highest court. . . .

However, the right to the free exercise of religion unquestionably encompasses the right to preach, proselyte, and perform other similar religious functions, or, in other words, to be a minister of the type McDaniel was found to be. . . . Tennessee also acknowledges the right of its adult citizens generally to seek and hold office as legislators or delegates to the state constitutional convention. . . . [I]n James Madison's words, the State is "punishing a religious profession with the privation of a civil right." In so doing, Tennessee has encroached upon McDaniel's right to the free exercise of religion. "[To] condition the availability of benefits [including access to the ballot] upon this appellant's willingness to violate a cardinal principle of [his] religious faith [by surrendering his religiously impelled ministry] effectively penalizes the free exercise of [his] constitutional liberties." *Sherbert v. Verner*, 374 U.S. 398, 406 (1963).

If the Tennessee disqualification provision were viewed as depriving the clergy of a civil right solely because of their religious beliefs, our inquiry would be at an end. The Free Exercise Clause categorically prohibits government from regulating, prohibiting, or rewarding religious beliefs as such. In *Torcaso v. Watkins*, 367 U.S. 488 (1961), the Court reviewed the Maryland constitutional requirement that all holders of "any office of profit or trust in this State" declare their belief in the existence of God. In striking down the Maryland requirement, the Court did not evaluate the interests assertedly justifying it but rather held that it violated freedom of religious belief.

In our view, however, *Torcaso* does not govern. By its terms, the Tennessee disqualification operates against McDaniel because of his *status* as a "minister" or "priest." The meaning of those words is, of course, a question of state law. And although the question has not been examined extensively in state-law sources, such authority as is available indicates that ministerial status is defined in terms of conduct and activity rather than in terms of belief. Because the Tennessee disqualification is directed primarily at status, acts, and conduct it is unlike the requirement in *Torcaso*, which focused on *belief*. Hence, the Free Exercise Clause's absolute prohibition of infringements on the "freedom to believe" is inapposite here.

This does not mean, of course, that the disqualification escapes judicial scrutiny or that McDaniel's activity does not enjoy significant First Amendment protection. The Court recently declared in *Wisconsin v. Yoder*, 406 U.S. 205, 215 (1972):

> The essence of all that has been said and written on the subject is that only those interests of the highest order and those not otherwise served can overbalance legitimate claims to the free exercise of religion.

Tennessee asserts that its interest in preventing the establishment of a state religion is consistent with the Establishment Clause and thus of the highest order. The constitutional history of the several States reveals that generally the interest in preventing establishment prompted the adoption of clergy disqualification provisions; Tennessee does not appear to be an exception to this pattern. There is no occasion to inquire whether promoting such an interest is a permissible legislative goal, however, for Tennessee has failed to demonstrate that its views of the dangers of clergy participation in the political process have not lost whatever validity they may once have enjoyed. The essence of the rationale underlying the Tennessee restriction on ministers is that if elected to public office they will necessarily exercise their powers and influence to promote the interests of one sect or thwart the interests of another, thus pitting one against the others, contrary to the anti-establishment principle with its command of neutrality. However widely that view may have been held in the 18th century by many, including enlightened statesmen of that day, the American experience provides no persuasive support for the fear that clergymen in public office will be less careful of anti-establishment interests or less faithful to their oaths of civil office than their unordained counterparts.

We hold that §4 of ch. 848 violates McDaniel's First Amendment right to the free exercise of his religion made applicable to the States by the Fourteenth Amendment. Accordingly, the judgment of the Tennessee Supreme Court is reversed, and the case is remanded to that court for further proceedings not inconsistent with this opinion.

Reversed and remanded.

NOTE ON RELIGIOUS PROHIBITIONS ON CLERGY HOLDING PUBLIC OFFICE

Some religions impose restrictions on the ability of their clergy to hold public office. For example, in 1980, Robert Drinan, a congressman from Massachusetts, was told by the Jesuit Order of the Roman Catholic Church that he must resign from Congress or step down as a priest. He resigned from Congress and remained a priest, teaching law at Georgetown University until his death in 2007.

Consider the *Bremen Evangelical Church Case*, decided by the German Constitutional Court in 1976. A provision of Bremen Evangelical Church law required any of its clergymen elected to a public office ("Bundestag [German parliament], or any other state or local legislative body") to take a leave of absence while they were in office. The Bremen Constitutional Court found that the church's rule was a violation of German constitutional law because under Article 48.2 of the German Basic Law, "persons elected to the Bundestag are protected from being dismissed from their employment because of their intention to serve in parliament." The Federal Constitutional Court, however, reversed the decision, finding that "churches bear a 'qualitatively different relationship to the state than do other large social groups'" and as such, the court should not interfere with the internal affairs of the church. The Court explained the church-state relation as an "imperfect separation" and a relationship of cooperation, not rivalry. Based on a carefully articulated delineation of the boundaries between church and state competences, and of limitations on the extent to which general laws (including constitutional provisions such as Article 43.2), the Federal Constitutional Court concluded that the church law provision requiring a leave of absence of clergy elected to public office should be sustained out of respect for church autonomy.

2. Religious Involvement in Political Issues and Major National Debates

LIMITATIONS ON POLITICAL ACTIVITIES OF CHURCHES

Recall the discussion in Chapter 12 about the limitations the IRS places on the political activities of churches in order for them to retain their tax-exempt status. In recent years, some ministers have deliberately flouted these rules to provoke the IRS into revoking their tax-exempt status, to facilitate a challenge to the constitutionality of the IRS rules.

In fact, this issue traces back to the foundation of the Republic, and in a critical way, may have been significant in the framing of the First Amendment itself. In this regard, Professor Mark Scarberry has written about the role that John Leland, a prominent Virginia Baptist, played in the role of Madison's election both to the Virginia ratifying convention in March 1788 and to the First Congress in February 1789:

> Of course, the Establishment Clause did not become a part of the Constitution until 1791; thus, Leland's actions predated its effectiveness and could perhaps, in theory, have been contrary to its purposes. Consider, however, what Madison's attitude would have been toward the Establishment Clause had its apparent meaning suggested that Leland's efforts, especially his efforts in getting Madison elected to the First Congress, were illegitimate. It is extraordinarily difficult to believe that Madison could have understood the Establishment Clause as creating a wall of separation that would prohibit (or disfavor) the very political activity that had enabled him to win election, serve in the First Congress, and argue for adoption of the Establishment Clause; that is, Leland's political activity in his role as a religious leader, political activity that had been crucial to giving Madison the opportunity to be in Congress and to propose the Bill of Rights. In fact, Leland remained a staunch Jeffersonian Republican (and, later, a Jacksonian Democrat) his entire life and continued to use his religious influence as a very popular Baptist preacher to advance that party's cause—apparently without any objection from Jefferson, Madison, Monroe, Jackson, or Van Buren—until his death in 1841. . . . Leland's role in furthering the proposal of the Bill of Rights casts doubt on any approach to the Establishment Clause that would limit or discourage participation by religious leaders and religious communities in the political arena.[12]

COMMENTS AND QUESTIONS

1. In May 2017, US President Donald Trump issued an executive order advising IRS officials not to enforce the provisions of the Johnson Amendment, a 1954 law prohibiting registered 501(c)(3) organizations—including some religious congregations—from participating in political campaigns or even endorsing political candidates, at the risk of losing their nonprofit status. Some religious organizations see this as a positive move towards persuading Congress to

12. Mark S. Scarberry, John Leland and James Madison: Religious Influence on the Ratification of the Constitution and on the Proposal of the Bill of Rights, 113 *Penn. State L. Rev.* 733, 737–738 (2009).

repeal the Amendment in the name religious freedom, including full freedom of expression by clergy. Others see value in neutrality with respect to partisan politics. It is not clear whether Trump's Executive Order would have any practical effect, because the IRS has not been actively enforcing the anti-endorsement provision anyway. More precisely, when confronted with candidate endorsements by churches, the IRS has issued letters warning that the endorsement violates applicable tax law, but also indicating that no enforcement action will be taken, so that those warned lack standing to sue to challenge the constitutionality of the non-endorsement rule.

2. To what extent *should* religious leaders be permitted to work in support of particular issues? Should they be able to work for and endorse candidates? To what extent should separation of church and state entail separation of religion and politics?

Additional Web Resources:	Information about continuing discussion of the Johnson Amendment and other religion-related tax issues in the United States

THE ROLE OF RELIGION IN THE JUSTIFICATION AND ERADICATION OF SLAVERY

JON MEACHAM, AMERICAN GOSPEL: GOD, THE FOUNDING FATHERS, AND THE MAKING OF A NATION (2006)

Random House 2006, 116-117

A Promise Kept

On Monday, September 22, 1862, in a meeting of his Cabinet on the second floor of the White House, Lincoln seemed a bit embarrassed. He was trying to explain the timing of the Emancipation Proclamation, but was not sure anyone else would understand. It had been a vicious and frightening military season; the previous Wednesday, at Antietam, in Maryland, would go down in history as the bloodiest day of the war. But the Union had won the battle, stopping the Confederate advance. Now, facing his Cabinet, Lincoln told them what he was going to do—and why. According to Treasury Secretary Salmon P. Chase's diary, Lincoln said: "When the Rebel Army was at Frederick, I determined, as soon as it should be driven out of Maryland to issue a Proclamation of Emancipation. . . . I said nothing to anyone, but I made a promise to myself, and (hesitating a little) to my Maker."

He had given his word to God, Lincoln said, and that was that. "The Rebel Army is now driven out, and I am going to fulfill that promise." Chase's account is supported by others: President Lincoln chose to emancipate the slaves at that particular moment because, he said, he had made a deal with the Almighty.

RICHARD CARWARDINE, LINCOLN: A LIFE OF PURPOSE AND POWER[13]

Random House 2006, 41-42

The Declaration of Independence . . . was for Lincoln more than a time-bound expression of political grievance. It was a near-sanctified statement of universal principles, and one that squared with essential elements of his personal faith: a belief in a God who had created all men equal and whose relations with humankind were based on the principles of justice. Lincoln found the scriptural basis for the Declaration in the book of Genesis: if humankind was created in the image of God, then "the justice of the Creator" had to be extended equally "to all His creatures, to the whole great family of man." As he told an audience in Lewistown, Illinois, the Founders had declared that "nothing stamped with the Divine image and likeness was sent into the world to be trodden on, and degraded, and imbruted by its fellows. "In setting down the Declaration's self-evident truths, they had provided a basis for resistance "in the distant future" to a "faction" or "interest" determined to argue that "none but rich men, or none but white men, were entitled to life, liberty and the pursuit of happiness." Sustain that document and you ensured that "truth, and justice, and mercy, and all the humane and Christian virtues. . . [would] not be extinguished from the land." (Emphasis added.)

THE ROLE OF RELIGION IN THE CIVIL RIGHTS MOVEMENT

The significance of religion on the Civil Rights movement can hardly be overstated. Reproduced here are excerpts from two key documents from Martin Luther King, Jr.: the "I Have a Dream" speech, delivered from the steps of the Lincoln Memorial in Washington, DC on 28 August 1963, and his "Letter from Birmingham Jail." (Biblical citations in brackets have been added to highlight some of King's references in the speech.)

MARTIN LUTHER KING, JR., "I HAVE A DREAM" (1963)

. . . Now is the time to make real the promises of democracy. Now is the time to rise from the dark and desolate valley of segregation to the sunlit path of racial justice. Now is the time to lift our nation from the quicksands of racial injustice to the solid rock of brotherhood. Now is the time to make justice a reality for all of God's children. . . . [Compare Romans 8:16]

And as we walk, we must make the pledge that we shall always march ahead. We cannot turn back. . . . No, no we are not satisfied and we will not be satisfied until justice rolls down like waters and righteousness like a mighty stream. [Amos 5:24]

I am not unmindful that some of you have come here out of great trials and tribulations. Some of you have come fresh from narrow jail cells. Some of you have come from areas where your quest for freedom left you battered by storms of persecution and staggered by the winds of police brutality. You have been the veterans of creative suffering. Continue to work with the faith that unearned suffering is redemptive. . . . [Compare Hebrews 9:12]

[13] Carwardine writes extensively of the religious influences on Abraham Lincoln the president, *for example* at 274-279 and 296-297.

Let us not wallow in the valley of despair. I say to you today my friends—so even though we face the difficulties of today and tomorrow, I still have a dream. It is a dream deeply rooted in the American dream.

I have a dream that one day this nation will rise up and live out the true meaning of its creed: "We hold these truths to be self-evident, that all men are created equal."

I have a dream that one day on the red hills of Georgia the sons of former slaves and the sons of former slave owners will be able to sit down together at the table of brotherhood.

I have a dream that one day even the state of Mississippi, a state sweltering with the heat of injustice, sweltering with the heat of oppression, will be transformed into an oasis of freedom and justice.

I have a dream that my four little children will one day live in a nation where they will not be judged by the color of their skin but by the content of their character. . . .

I have a dream today.

I have a dream that one day every valley shall be exalted, and every hill and mountain shall be made low, the rough places will be made plain, and the crooked places will be made straight, and the glory of the Lord shall be revealed and all flesh shall see it together. [Compare Isaiah 40:3-5]

This is our hope. This is the faith that I go back to the South with. With this faith we will be able to hew out of the mountain of despair a stone of hope. With this faith we will be able to transform the jangling discords of our nation into a beautiful symphony of brotherhood. With this faith we will be able to work together, to pray together, to struggle together, to go to jail together, to stand up for freedom together, knowing that we will be free one day.

This will be the day, this will be the day when all of God's children will be able to sing with new meaning "My country 'tis of thee, sweet land of liberty, of thee I sing. Land where my fathers died, land of the Pilgrim's pride, from every mountainside, let freedom ring!". . .

Let freedom ring. And when this happens, and when we allow freedom ring—when we let it ring from every village and every hamlet, from every state and every city, we will be able to speed up that day when all of God's children—black men and white men, Jews and Gentiles, Protestants and Catholics—will be able to join hands and sing in the words of the old Negro spiritual: "Free at last! Free at last! Thank God Almighty, we are free at last![14]

MARTIN LUTHER KING, JR., LETTER FROM BIRMINGHAM JAIL (1963)

. . . Oppressed people cannot remain oppressed forever. The yearning for freedom eventually manifests itself, and that is what has happened to the American Negro. Something within has reminded him of his birthright of freedom, and something without has reminded him that it can be gained. Consciously or unconsciously, he has been caught up by the Zeitgeist, and with his black brothers

14. Distribution statement: Accepted as part of the Douglass Archives of American Public Address (http://douglassarchives.org) on 16 May 1999. Prepared by D. Oetting (http://nonce.com/oetting).

of Africa and his brown and yellow brothers of Asia, South America, and the Caribbean, the United States Negro is moving with a sense of great urgency toward the promised land of racial justice. . . . The Negro has many pent-up resentments and latent frustrations, and he must release them. . . . If his repressed emotions are not released in nonviolent ways, they will seek expression through violence; this is not a threat but a fact of history. So I have not said to my people, "Get rid of your discontent." Rather, I have tried to say that this normal and healthy discontent can be channeled into the creative outlet of nonviolent direct action. And now this approach is being termed extremist.

But though I was initially disappointed at being categorized as an extremist, as I continued to think about the matter I gradually gained a measure of satisfaction from the label. Was not Jesus an extremist for love: "Love your enemies, bless them that curse you, do good to them that hate you, and pray for them which despitefully use you, and persecute you." Was not Amos an extremist for justice: "Let justice roll down like waters and righteousness like an ever-flowing stream." Was not Paul an extremist for the Christian gospel: "I bear in my body the marks of the Lord Jesus." Was not Martin Luther an extremist: "Here I stand; I cannot do otherwise, so help me God.". . . So the question is not whether we will be extremists, but what kind of extremists we will be. Will we be extremists for hate or for love? Will we be extremists for the preservation of injustice or for the extension of justice? In that dramatic scene on Calvary's hill three men were crucified. We must never forget that all three were crucified for the same crime—the crime of extremism. Two were extremists for immorality, and thus fell below their environment. The other, Jesus Christ, was an extremist for love, truth, and goodness, and thereby rose above his environment. Perhaps the South, the nation, and the world are in dire need of creative extremists. . . .

. . . In deep disappointment I have wept over the laxity of the church. But be assured that my tears have been tears of love. Yes, I love the church. How could I do otherwise? I am in the rather unique position of being the son, the grandson, and the great-grandson of preachers. Yes, I see the church as the body of Christ. But, oh! How we have blemished and scarred that body through social neglect and through fear of being nonconformists. . . .

I hope the church as a whole will meet the challenge of this decisive hour. But even if the church does not come to the aid of justice, I have no despair about the future. I have no fear about the outcome of our struggle in Birmingham, even if our motives are at present misunderstood. We will reach the goal of freedom in Birmingham and all over the nation, because the goal of America is freedom. Abuse and scorned though we may be, our destiny is tied up with America's destiny. . . . If the inexpressible cruelties of slavery could not stop us, the opposition we now face will surely fail. We will win our freedom because the sacred heritage of our nation and the eternal will of God are embodied in our echoing demands.

. . . One day the South will recognize its real heroes. . . . . . . They will be old, oppressed, battered Negro women. . . . They will be the young high school and college students, the young ministers of the gospel and a host of their elders, courageously and nonviolently sitting in at lunch counters and willingly going to jail for conscience' sake. One day the South will know that when these disinherited children of God sat down at lunch counters, they were in reality standing up for what is best in the American dream and for the most sacred values in our Judaeo-

Christian heritage, thereby bringing our nation back to those great wells of democracy which were dug deep by the founding fathers in their formulation of the Constitution and the Declaration of Independence. . . .

. . . Let us all hope that the dark clouds of racial prejudice will soon pass away and the deep fog of misunderstanding will be lifted from our fear-drenched communities, and in some not too distant tomorrow the radiant stars of love and brotherhood will shine over our great nation with all their scintillating beauty.

Yours for the cause of Peace and Brotherhood, Martin Luther King, Jr.[15]

COMMENTS AND QUESTIONS

1. Was religious involvement in the slavery and Civil Rights debates more, less, or equally appropriate compared with religious involvement in contemporary political issues such as abortion, environmental protection, and gay rights?
2. In a 1957 sermon Martin Luther King said, "Refining hate for hate multiplies hate, adding deeper darkness to a night already devoid of stars. Darkness cannot drive out darkness: only light can do that. Hate cannot drive out hate: only love can do that."[16]

Additional Web Resources:	Resources discussing religious influences on the Civil Rights movement and the anti-abortion movement

RELIGIOUS INFLUENCE ON ABORTION POLICY

HARRIS V. MCRAE

Supreme Court of the United States, 448 U.S. 297 (1980)

[A federal law denying Medicaid funds for most abortions (referred to as the Hyde Amendment) was challenged as violating the Establishment Clause because of its alignment with the religious tenets of the Roman Catholic Church. Justice Stewart wrote the majority opinion.]

III.

B.

. . . It is the appellees' view that the Hyde Amendment violates the Establishment Clause because it incorporates into law the doctrines of the Roman Catholic Church concerning the sinfulness of abortion and the time at which life commences. Moreover, insofar as a woman's decision to seek a medically necessary abortion may be a product of her religious beliefs under certain Protestant and Jewish tenets, the appellees assert that the funding limitations of the

15. Reprinted by arrangement with The Heirs to the Estate of Martin Luther King Jr., c/o Writers House as agent for the proprietor New York, NY.

16. Reproduced in Martin Luther King, Jr., *A Strength to Love* 594 (Fortress Press 2010).

Hyde Amendment impinge on the freedom of religion guaranteed by the Free Exercise Clause.

It is well settled that "a legislative enactment does not contravene the Establishment Clause if it has a secular legislative purpose, if its principal or primary effect neither advances nor inhibits religion, and if it does not foster an excessive governmental entanglement with religion." *Committee for Public Education v. Regan*, 444 U.S. 646, 653 (1973). Applying this standard, the District Court properly concluded that the Hyde Amendment does not run afoul of the Establishment Clause. Although neither a State nor the Federal Government can constitutionally "pass laws which aid one religion, aid all religions, or prefer one religion over another," (*Everson*), it does not follow that a statute violates the Establishment Clause because it "happens to coincide or harmonize with the tenets of some or all religions" (*McGowan*). That the Judaeo-Christian religions oppose stealing does not mean that a State or the Federal Government may not, consistent with the Establishment Clause, enact laws prohibiting larceny. The Hyde Amendment, as the District Court noted, is as much a reflection of "traditionalist" values towards abortion, as it is an embodiment of the views of any particular religion. In sum, we are convinced that the fact that the funding restrictions in the Hyde Amendment may coincide with the religious tenets of the Roman Catholic Church does not, without more, contravene the Establishment Clause.

We need not address the merits of the appellees' arguments concerning the Free Exercise Clause, because the appellees lack standing to raise a free exercise challenge to the Hyde Amendment. . . .

COMMENTS AND QUESTIONS

Are the arguments for or against religious influence in electoral politics different from those that arise in the Civil Rights and abortion settings?

IRISH LAW REFLECTING THE CATHOLIC CHURCH'S PROHIBITIONS CONCERNING DIVORCE

In *Johnston v. Ireland*, App. No. 9697/82 (18 December 1986) the European Court of Human Rights held that Article 9 of the European Convention was not applicable to an Irish law that did not permit divorce, even though the law reflected the social teaching and doctrine of the dominant Catholic Church. In a partly dissenting and partly concurring opinion, Judge De Meyer argued that the law was "coercive in relation to all persons, Catholics and non-Catholics, whose religious rules do not absolutely prohibit divorce in all circumstances" and "at variance with the accepted principles of religious liberty as declared at the Vatican Council and elsewhere." He added, "For so draconian a system to be legitimate, it does not suffice that it corresponds to the desire or will of a substantial majority of the population: the Court has also stated that 'although individual interests must on occasion be subordinated to those of a group, democracy does not simply mean that the views of a majority must always prevail: a balance must be achieved which ensures the fair and proper treatment of minorities and avoids any abuse of a dominant position.'" In February 1997, about a decade after this decision, the Family Law (Divorce) Act 1996 was passed, legalizing divorce in Ireland. The referendum to remove the constitutional ban on divorce was won by a margin of

0.6 percent, and the results of the referendum were contested all the way up to the Supreme Court of Ireland before the legislation finally took effect in 1997.[17]

3. Civil Religion: Religion in Public Ceremonies and Pronouncements

In many countries, the influence of background religious culture often appears in public life. In the United States, this is evident in myriad ways: in references to deity in presidential inaugural addresses, in the national motto ("In God We Trust"), in the Pledge of Allegiance (. . . one nation, under God . . .), and in the phrase "God bless America," which ends most presidential addresses. Religious figures often appear with the head of state at formal public events in Russia. Civil religion can take other forms in other countries. In France, there is an argument that secularism (*laïcité*) itself has become a civil religion. In each of these settings, there is a tension between acknowledging the role that religion has played in the history and culture of a nation, and avoiding insensitivity toward minority groups in the country who may feel excluded or resentful that such acknowledgement occurs.

NOTE ON THE NATIONAL MOTTO

During the Civil War, responding to requests for a broader recognition of religion in public life, Secretary of State (and future Chief Justice) Salmon P. Chase ordered the national mint to prepare "a motto expressing in a few words the recognition of the trust of our people in God."[18] In 1864, that motto became "In God We Trust." President Theodore Roosevelt was favorably disposed toward a new design that did not include the phrase, on grounds that such usage was more likely to encourage sacrilege than reverence, but Congress reacted by passing legislation requiring the motto to be inscribed on coinage.[19] In 1955, Congress extended this act by requiring "In God We Trust" to be printed on all paper money as well.[20] And in 1956, Congress passed a bill designating the phrase "In God We Trust" as the national motto,[21] thereby supplanting what had theretofore been the de facto (though not de jure) motto, "E Pluribus Unum" ("out of many, one"). At about the same time, in 1954, Congress added the words "under God" to the Pledge of Allegiance.[22]

William Van Alstyne has argued that the two mottos reflect very different ideals concerning the appropriate relationship of church and state in American society, "from the ideal expressed by our original Latin motto—one nation out of highly diverse but equally welcome states and people—to an increasingly pressing

---

17. Jenny Burley and Francis Regan, Divorce in Ireland: The Fear, the Floodgates and the Reality, 16 *Int'l J.L. Pol'y & Fam.* 202, 212 (2002).

18. Anson Phelps Stokes and Leo Pfeffer, *Church and State in the United States* 568 (1-vol. rev. ed., Greenwood Press 1964), *citing* Joseph Coffin, *Our American Money* (Coward-McCann 1940).

19. *Id.* at 570, *citing* U.S. Statutes at Large XX–XV, pt. I, 164 (1908).

20. *Id., citing* US Code, tit. 31, sec. 324a.

21. *Id., citing* US Code, tit. 36, sec. 186.

22. Act of June 14, 1954, 68 Stat. 249, ch. 297. *See* 4 USC §4 (for current wording of the Pledge).

enthusiasm in which government re-establishes itself under distinctly religious auspices." [23]

> The motto of the new nation, proposed in a Continental Congress committee report by Franklin, Adams, and Jefferson, and adopted for use in the Great Seal of the United States in 1782 was "E Pluribus Unum." The original legend on new coins, first in continental dollars, then on the fugio cent minted in Philadelphia, in 1787, was "Mind Your Business." The inscription on the obverse side of the Great Seal was "Novus Ordo Seclorum," A New Order of the Ages. The secular separation assured each individual that none need feel alien to this government, whatever his own religion or personal philosophy, for it was to be a temporal government not commingled with a clergy, a theism, or a church."[24]

Van Alstyne notes that given the tendency to identify religious truth with national policy, "it is scarcely surprising, given the religious antecedents of the abolitionist movement, that the Union cause in the Civil War would be mingled with the assimilation of Christian symbolism, and that Christian theology thus would itself become part of the cause."[25]

Additional Web Resources:	Module on Civil Religion, including public proclamations, debates about civil religion in various countries, the debate about whether reference to deity should be included in the European Constitution, and many other examples

B. EUROPE

Religiously Affiliated Political Parties and Democratic Order

REFAH PARTISI (WELFARE PARTY) AND OTHERS V. TURKEY

European Court of Human Rights (Grand Chamber), App. Nos. 41340/98, 41342/98, 41343/98, and 41344/98 13 (February 2003)

[The applicants alleged in particular that the dissolution of Refah Partisi (The Welfare Party) by the Turkish Constitutional Court and the suspension of certain political rights of the other applicants, who were leaders of Refah at the material time, had breached Articles 9, 10, 11, 14, 17, and 18 of the Convention and Articles 1 and 3 of Protocol No. 1. The 1995 general election made Refah the largest political party in Turkey, with a total of 158 of 450 seats in the Grand National Assembly. Not long thereafter, Refah came to power by forming a coalition government with the center-right True Path Party. In May 1997 the Principal State Counsel applied to the Turkish Constitutional Court to dissolve Refah. Charges against Refah were that its leaders advocated the wearing of

23. William Van Alstyne, Comment, Trends in the Supreme Court: Mr. Jefferson's Crumbling Wall—A Comment on *Lynch v. Donnelly*, 1984 *Duke L.J.* 770, 771 (1984). *See also* William P. Marshall, The Limits of Secularism: Public Religious Expression in Moments of National Crisis and Tragedy, 78 *Notre Dame L. Rev.* 11, 16 & n.34 (2002).

24. Van Alstyne, *supra* note 32, at 774.

25. *Id.* at 786.

Islamic headscarves in state schools (contrary to prior Constitutional Court rulings); the leader of the party, Mr. Necmettin Erbakan, had made proposals tending toward the abolition of secularism in Turkey; he had urged support for his party indicating that only his party could establish the supremacy of the Qur'an through a holy war (jihad); and he had received heads of the Islamist movements at the Prime Minister's residence. Other leaders of Refah had called for the secular political system to be replaced by a theocratic legal system. Some claimed that "blood would flow" if there was an attempt to close theological colleges. Some had indicated that they would fight until the end for the introduction of Islamic law (sharia), and called for a plural legal system that would allow believers of different religions to be governed by their preferred religious laws.

In January 1998 the Constitutional Court dissolved Refah, confiscated its assets, and held that its leaders were banned from holding office in other political parties for several years. The Constitutional Court based its opinion on the observation that secularism was one of the indispensable conditions of democracy. In Turkey the principle of secularism was safeguarded by the Constitution, on account of the country's historical experience and the specific features of Islam. In the Court's view, the rules of sharia were incompatible with the democratic regime. The principle of secularism prevented the state from manifesting a preference for a particular religion or belief and constituted the foundation of freedom of conscience and equality between citizens before the law.

Following the dissolution decision, the Refah party and a number of its leaders filed an application with the Strasbourg Court. On 31 July 2001 the Chamber [of the European Court] gave judgment, holding by four votes to three that there had been no violation of Article 11 of the Convention and unanimously agreeing that it was not necessary to examine separately the complaints under Articles 9, 10, 14, 17, and 18 of the Convention and Articles 1 and 3 of Protocol No. 1. The case was subsequently referred to the Grand Chamber.]

I. Alleged Violation of Article 11 of the Convention . . .

A. Whether there was an Interference

50. The parties accepted that Refah's dissolution and the measures which accompanied it amounted to an interference with the applicants' exercise of their right to freedom of association. The Court takes the same view.

B. Whether the Interference was Justified

51. Such an interference will constitute a breach of Article 11 unless it was "prescribed by law", pursued one or more of the legitimate aims set out in paragraph 2 of that provision and was "necessary in a democratic society" for the achievement of those aims.

1. "Prescribed by Law"...

(b) The Court's Assessment. . .

58. In the instant case the Court observes that the dispute under domestic law concerned the constitutionality of the activities of a political party and fell within the jurisdiction of the Constitutional Court. The written law most relevant to the

question whether the interference was "prescribed by law" is the Turkish Constitution.

59. The parties did not dispute that activities contrary to the principles of equality and respect for a democratic, secular republic were undoubtedly unconstitutional under Article 68 of the Constitution. Nor did they deny that the Constitutional Court had sole jurisdiction to dissolve a political party which had become a centre of activities contrary to Article 68 of the Constitution. Moreover, Article 69 of the Constitution (amended in 1995) explicitly confirms that the Constitutional Court alone is empowered to determine whether a political party constitutes a centre of anti-constitutional activities. . . .

61. It remains to be determined whether the applicants must have been aware of the possibility of a direct application of the Constitution in their case and could thus have foreseen the risks they ran through their party's anti-secular activities or through their refusal to distance themselves from that type of activity. . . .

62. . . . Refah was a large political party which had legal advisers conversant with constitutional law and the rules governing political parties. . . .

63. That being so, the Court considers that the applicants were reasonably able to foresee that they ran the risk of proceedings to dissolve Refah if the party's leaders and members engaged in anti-secular activities. . . .

64. Consequently, the interference was "prescribed by law".

2. Legitimate Aim . . .

67. . . . Taking into account the importance of the principle of secularism for the democratic system in Turkey, it considers that Refah's dissolution pursued several of the legitimate aims listed in Article 11, namely protection of national security and public safety, prevention of disorder or crime and protection of the rights and freedoms of others.

3. "Necessary in a Democratic Society". . .

(b) The Court's assessment

(i) General principles

(α) Democracy and political parties in the Convention System

86. On the question of the relationship between democracy and the Convention, the Court has already ruled . . . as follows:

> Democracy is without doubt a fundamental feature of the European public order. . . .
>
> That is apparent, firstly, from the Preamble to the Convention, which establishes a very clear connection between the Convention and democracy. . . .

89. The Court considers that there can be no democracy without pluralism. It is for that reason that freedom of expression as enshrined in Article 10 is applicable, subject to paragraph 2, not only to "information" or "ideas" that are favourably received or regarded as inoffensive or as a matter of indifference, but also to those that offend, shock or disturb. . . .

93. [In applying Convention principles regarding religion] to Turkey the Convention institutions have expressed the view that the principle of secularism is certainly one of the fundamental principles of the State which are in harmony with the rule of law and respect for human rights and democracy. . . .

(γ) The possibility of imposing restrictions, and rigorous European supervision

96. The freedoms guaranteed by Article 11, and by Articles 9 and 10 of the Convention, cannot deprive the authorities of a State in which an association, through its activities, jeopardises that State's institutions, of the right to protect those institutions. In this connection, the Court points out that it has previously held that some compromise between the requirements of defending democratic society and individual rights is inherent in the Convention system. . . .

98. . . . [T]he Court considers that a political party may promote a change in the law or the legal and constitutional structures of the State on two conditions: firstly, the means used to that end must be legal and democratic; secondly, the change proposed must itself be compatible with fundamental democratic principles. It necessarily follows that a political party whose leaders incite to violence or put forward a policy which fails to respect democracy or which is aimed at the destruction of democracy and the flouting of the rights and freedoms recognised in a democracy cannot lay claim to the Convention's protection against penalties imposed on those grounds. . . .

99. The possibility cannot be excluded that a political party, in pleading the rights enshrined in Article 11 and also in Articles 9 and 10 of the Convention, might attempt to derive therefrom the right to conduct what amounts in practice to activities intended to destroy the rights or freedoms set forth in the Convention and thus bring about the destruction of democracy. . . .

(δ) Imputability to a political party of the acts and speeches of its members

101. The Court further considers that the constitution and programme of a political party cannot be taken into account as the sole criterion for determining its objectives and intentions. The political experience of the Contracting States has shown that in the past political parties with aims contrary to the fundamental principles of democracy have not revealed such aims in their official publications until after taking power. That is why the Court has always pointed out that a party's political programme may conceal objectives and intentions different from the ones it proclaims. To verify that it does not, the content of the programme must be compared with the actions of the party's leaders and the positions they defend. . . .

(ε) The appropriate timing for dissolution

102. In addition, the Court considers that a State cannot be required to wait, before intervening, until a political party has seized power and begun to take concrete steps to implement a policy incompatible with the standards of the Convention and democracy, even though the danger of that policy for democracy is sufficiently established and imminent. . . .

(ζ) Overall examination

104. In the light of the above considerations, the Court's overall examination of the question whether the dissolution of a political party on account of a risk of democratic principles being undermined met a "pressing social need". . . must concentrate on the following points: (i) whether there was plausible evidence that the risk to democracy, supposing it had been proved to exist, was sufficiently imminent; (ii) whether the acts and speeches of the leaders and members of the political party concerned were imputable to the party as a whole; and (iii) whether the acts and speeches imputable to the political party formed a whole which gave a clear picture of a model of society conceived and advocated by the party which was incompatible with the concept of a "democratic society".

(ii) Application of the above principles to the present case . . .

(α) Pressing social need

The appropriate timing for dissolution . . .

108. [Based on the facts laid out above,] the Court considers that at the time of its dissolution Refah had the real potential to seize political power without being restricted by the compromises inherent in a coalition. If Refah had proposed a programme contrary to democratic principles, its monopoly of political power would have enabled it to establish the model of society envisaged in that programme.

109. As regards the applicants' argument that Refah was punished for speeches by its members made several years before its dissolution, the Court considers that the Turkish courts, when reviewing the constitutionality of Refah's acts, could legitimately take into consideration the progression over time of the real risk that the party's activities represented for the principles of democracy. The same applies to the review of Refah's compliance with the principles set forth in the Convention. Firstly, the programme and policies of a political party may become clear through the accumulation of acts and speeches by its members over a relatively long period. Secondly, the party concerned may, over the years, increase its chances of gaining political power and implementing its policies.

110. While it can be considered, in the present case, that Refah's policies were dangerous for the rights and freedoms guaranteed by the Convention, the real chances that Refah would implement its programme after gaining power made that danger more tangible and more immediate. That being the case, the Court cannot criticise the national courts for not acting earlier, at the risk of intervening prematurely and before the danger concerned had taken shape and become real. Nor can it criticise them for not waiting, at the risk of putting the political regime and civil peace in jeopardy, for Refah to seize power and swing into action, for example by tabling bills in Parliament, in order to implement its plans. . . .

Imputability to Refah of the acts and speeches of its members

111. The parties before the Court agreed that neither in its constitution nor in the coalition programme it had negotiated with another political party, the True Path Party (Doru Yol Partisi), had Refah proposed altering Turkey's constitutional

settlement in a way that would be contrary to the fundamental principles of democracy. Refah was dissolved on the basis of the statements made and stances adopted by its chairman and some of its members. . . .

113. The Court considers that the statements and acts of Mr. Necmettin Erbakan, in his capacity as chairman of Refah or as the Prime Minister elected on account of his position as the leader of his party, could incontestably be attributed to Refah. The role of a chairman, who is frequently a party's emblematic figure, is different in that respect from that of a simple member. Remarks on politically sensitive subjects or positions taken up by the chairman of a party are perceived by political institutions and by public opinion as acts reflecting the party's views, rather than his personal opinions, unless he declares that this is not the case. [Similarly, many other officers responsible for similar acts and statements were presented by the party soon afterwards as candidates for important posts.]. . .

The main grounds for dissolution cited by the Constitutional Court

116. The Court considers on this point that among the arguments for dissolution those cited by the Constitutional Court as grounds for its finding that Refah had become a centre of anti-constitutional activities can be classified into three main groups: (i) the arguments that Refah intended to set up a plurality of legal systems, leading to discrimination based on religious beliefs; (ii) the arguments that Refah intended to apply sharia to the internal or external relations of the Muslim community within the context of this plurality of legal systems; and (iii) the arguments based on the references made by Refah members to the possibility of recourse to force as a political method. . . .

Overall examination of "pressing social need"

132. In making an overall assessment of the points it has just listed above in connection with its examination of the question whether there was a pressing social need for the interference in issue in the present case, the Court finds that the acts and speeches of Refah's members and leaders cited by the Constitutional Court were imputable to the whole of the party, that those acts and speeches revealed Refah's long-term policy of setting up a regime based on sharia within the framework of a plurality of legal systems and that Refah did not exclude recourse to force in order to implement its policy and keep the system it envisaged in place. In view of the fact that these plans were incompatible with the concept of a "democratic society" and that the real opportunities Refah had to put them into practice made the danger to democracy more tangible and more immediate, the penalty imposed on the applicants by the Constitutional Court . . . may reasonably be considered to have met a "pressing social need".

(β) Proportionality of the measure complained of

133. After considering the parties' arguments, the Court sees no good reason to depart from the Chamber's judgment [that the dissolution of Refah was not disproportionate to the threat posed by the Party]. . . .

135. Consequently, following a rigorous review to verify that there were convincing and compelling reasons justifying Refah's dissolution and the

temporary forfeiture of certain political rights imposed on the other applicants, the Court considers that those interferences met a "pressing social need" and were "proportionate to the aims pursued". It follows that Refah's dissolution may be regarded as "necessary in a democratic society" within the meaning of Article 11 §2.

136. Accordingly, there has been no violation of Article 11 of the Convention.

. . .

137. The applicants further alleged the violation of Articles 9, 10, 14, 17 and 18 of the Convention. As their complaints concern the same facts as those examined under Article 11, the Court considers that it is not necessary to examine them separately. . . .

FOR THESE REASONS, THE COURT UNANIMOUSLY

1. *Holds* that there has been no violation of Article 11 of the Convention;
2. *Holds* that it is not necessary to examine separately the complaints under Articles 9, 10, 14, 17 and 18 of the Convention and Articles 1 and 3 of Protocol No. 1.

COMMENTS AND QUESTIONS

1. The idea that there are exceptions to or "limitations" on the codified rights of individuals and governments is clearly defined in the European Convention on Human Rights.[26] An early formulation of this idea in the United States—the notion that "the Constitution is not a suicide pact"—was employed by Thomas Jefferson to justify his approval of the purchase by his ambassadors of the Louisiana territory, even though Jefferson believed that the Constitution did not grant to the federal government the right to purchase foreign territory. Such a notion has been used to justify Abraham Lincoln's suppression of the right of *habeas corpus* during the American Civil War.
2. *Refah Partisi* was decided on the basis that it is a case reminiscent of the Nazis' rise to power by using (and then abolishing) democratic institutions. Does the Court have sound reasons for thinking the Welfare Party constituted a comparable kind of threat to democratic and constitutional institutions in Turkey?
3. The Alevi, whose religious practices (*cem*) derive from a form of Shia Islam, comprise the second largest religious group in Turkey, after Sunni Muslims. Estimated at between 10 and 20 percent of Turkey's 77 million people, the Alevi consider themselves not a religious minority but "proud former allies of Mustafa Kemal Atatürk, founder of the modern Turkish state, in his drive to implement a secular society in the war of independence that saw the end of the Ottoman Empire."[27] Turkish courts, however, have ruled that Alevism is not a full-fledged faith but a religious movement within Islam, and that Alevi meeting places (*cemevi*) are therefore not places of worship to be afforded the same sort of legal protection and subsidy as the mosques of the Sunni majority,

26. *See, e.g.*, Steven Greer, The exceptions to Articles 8 to 11 of the European Convention on Human Rights, Human Rights Files No. 15 (Council of Europe Publishing 1997).

27. Mark Hallam, Turkey Discriminates against Alevi Faith, ECHR rules, *Deutsche Welle*, 26 April 2016.

which are supported by all taxpayers in nominally secular Turkey. Failing to find redress in the Turkish courts, Alevi groups and individuals brought suits to the European Court of Human Rights.

In December 2014, the Court of found a violation of ECHR Article 14 (discrimination) taken together with Article 9 (freedom of religion) in the case of *Cumhuriyetçi Eğitim Ve Kültür Merkezi Vakfi v. Turkey*, App. No. 32093/10. The applicant members of a religious foundation that runs cemevis complained that they "had sustained a difference in treatment without any objective or reasonable justification, and that the system for granting exemptions from payment of electricity bills for places of worship under Turkish law entailed discrimination on the ground of religion." The Court agreed that the discrimination existed and, with one judge dissenting, found no reason to examine the alleged violation of the Article 9 separately. In dissent, Judge András Sajó asserted that more than granting a government subsidy for utility bills was in order, in that

> the limited status granted to cemevis by applicable law does not allow members of the Alevi community to effectively enjoy their right to freedom of religion. In these circumstances, this right appears illusory and theoretical, not practical and effective as required by the Convention . . . . The lack of recognition of the religious nature of the Alevi practices creates a feeling of inferiority among followers of that faith, which are treated as second-class citizens, in violation of state neutrality principle. The aforementioned breach cannot be remedied by the payment of electricity bills for cemevi in a spirit of non-discrimination. This solution leaves open the main issue of the status of religion and the Alevi community, and more specifically, the lack of specific and fair procedure for granting the status of place of worship. (translation from French by the editor)

4. The Turkish government refused to accept the ruling in *Cumhuriyetçi Eğitim Ve Kültür Merkezi Vakfi*. Subsequent to this decision, the Civil General Council of the Supreme Court of Appeals said that whether cemevis are places of worship cannot be decided by judicial ruling. "The individual himself/herself determines whether a place is place of worship or not."[28] Some Alevi organizations decided to stop paying the bills that continued to come, and were subsequently fined. In early December 2015, Turkey's Prime Minister, Ahmet Davutoglu, announced a series of government reforms to be implemented within the following three to six months, one of which would grant legal status to Alevi places of worship.[29] This announcement, however, proved to be premature.
5. On 26 April 2016, the ECtHR Grand Chamber delivered judgment in *İzzetin Doğan and (202) Others v. Turkey*, App. No. 62649/10. This time the Court, as a 17-member Grand Chamber which included Judge András Sajó, considered the Article 9 issue in detail (paragraphs 66-135 of the judgment), and ruled not only (by 16 votes to 1) that Alevis "were subjected to a difference

28. Top Court: It's Not Judiciary's Call to Designate Cemevi as Place of Worship or Not, *Hürriyet Daily News*, 3 December 2014.

29. *See* Turkey to grant legal status to minority Muslims' "cemevi," *FirstPost Politics*, 10 December 2015; *see also* Alev Yaman, Can Turkey deliver a landmark religious reform for the Alevi community?, *Middle East Eye*, 18 January 2016.

in treatment for which there was no objective and reasonable justification" in violation of Article 14 in connection with Article 9, but also (by 12 votes to 5) that there had been a violation of Article 9 itself. The Court "reiterated that the Convention is designed to guarantee not rights that are theoretical or illusory but rights that are practical and effective" (114) and was "not convinced that the freedom to practise its faith which the authorities leave to the Alevi community enables that community to fully exercise its rights under Article 9" (131). This ruling was greeted with optimism by Turkey's Alevi community.[30] Only three months later, however, the Alevi were seeing "dark days ahead"[31] as Turkish President Recep Tayyip Erdoğan—following an attempted coup he blamed on followers of US-based Turkish preacher and former imam (and ally of Erdoğan), Fethullah Gülen—declared an open-ended state of emergency which included an expressed intention to suspend the European Convention on Human Rights and thereby the jurisdiction of the Court. See the Web Supplement for updating information about Erdoğan's rule in Turkey.

IV. RELIGIOUS SYMBOLS

A. UNITED STATES

Constitutionality of Displays of the Ten Commandments on Public Property

In *McCreary County v. American Civil Liberties Union of Ky.*, 545 U.S. 844 (2005), and *Van Orden v. Perry*, 545 U.S. 677 (2005), a pair of cases decided by the U.S. Supreme Court in 2005, the Court drew fine distinctions between constitutionally permissible and impermissible displays of the Ten Commandments. In *McCreary*, the American Civil Liberties Union claimed that prominent displays of the Ten Commandments at two county courthouses in Kentucky violated the Establishment Clause of the First Amendment. When the district court ordered removal of the displays, the counties twice modified the displays to include other historical documents, claiming that the intent was to show the foundations of American law. The court struck down both modifications, noting that references to Christianity were the sole common element among the added historical documents, and that no other secular or historical connection existed between the Commandments and the other documents. In *Van Orden*, a Texas resident challenged a Ten Commandments display on a monument at the Texas State Capitol under the Establishment Clause. The monument was presented to the state by the Fraternal Order of Eagles, a private civic and patriotic organization, and placed on the grounds among 38 other monuments and historical markers. The lower courts held for the state of Texas, allowing the Ten Commandments display.

The US Supreme Court reached opposite conclusions in the two cases, finding the courthouse displays in *McCreary* impermissible, but the state capitol display

30. *See, e.g.,* article by Hallam, supra note 36.
31. Turkey's Alevi minority sees dark days ahead, *Free Speech Radio News*, 22 July 2016.

in *Van Orden* permissible. The difference in the holdings hinged on the purpose of the displays. The Court found that the purpose of the displays in *McCreary* was to advance religion, contrary to the professed purpose, but that the purpose of the display in *Van Orden* was to recognize the Fraternal Order of Eagles for their efforts to reduce juvenile delinquency, which constituted a valid secular purpose.

Justice Breyer's vote was the distinguishing factor in the two decisions. He joined four judges to create a majority in *McCreary* in favor of striking down the display, but voted in favor of upholding the display in *Van Orden*, writing a separate concurring opinion (joining with a plurality to reach an opposite conclusion in that case). Following is an excerpt from Justice Breyer's separate opinion in *Van Orden* that explains his reasoning in distinguishing the two cases.

VAN ORDEN V. PERRY

Supreme Court of the United States, 545 U.S. 677 (2005)

In *School Dist. of Abington Township v. Schempp*, 374 U.S. 203 (1963), Justice Goldberg, joined by Justice Harlan, wrote, in respect to the First Amendment's Religion Clauses, that there is "no simple and clear measure which by precise application can readily and invariably demark the permissible from the impermissible" (concurring opinion). One must refer instead to the basic purposes of those Clauses. They seek to "assure the fullest possible scope of religious liberty and tolerance for all." They seek to avoid that divisiveness based upon religion that promotes social conflict, sapping the strength of government and religion alike. . . . They seek to maintain that "separation of church and state" that has long been critical to the "peaceful dominion that religion exercises in [this] country," where the "spirit of religion" and the "spirit of freedom" are productively "united," "reign[ing] together" but in separate spheres "on the same soil." A. de Tocqueville, Democracy in America 282-283 (1835). . . .

The Court has made clear, as Justices Goldberg and Harlan noted, that the realization of these goals means that government must "neither engage in nor compel religious practices," that it must "effect no favoritism among sects or between religion and nonreligion," and that it must "work deterrence of no religious belief." *Schempp, supra*. . . .

But the Establishment Clause does not compel the government to purge from the public sphere all that in any way partakes of the religious. See, *e.g.*, *Marsh v. Chambers*, 463 U.S. 783 (1983). Such absolutism is not only inconsistent with our national traditions, see, *e.g.*, *Lemon v. Kurtzman*, 403 U.S. 602 (1971); *Lynch v. Donnelly*, 465 U.S. 668 (1984), but would also tend to promote the kind of social conflict the Establishment Clause seeks to avoid. . . .

If the relation between government and religion is one of separation, but not of mutual hostility and suspicion, one will inevitably find difficult borderline cases. And in such cases, I see no test-related substitute for the exercise of legal judgment. . . . That judgment is not a personal judgment. Rather, as in all constitutional cases, it must reflect and remain faithful to the underlying purposes of the Clauses, and it must take account of context and consequences measured in light of those purposes. . . .

The case before us is a borderline case. It concerns a large granite monument bearing the text of the Ten Commandments located on the grounds of the Texas State Capitol. On the one hand, the Commandments' text undeniably has a religious message, invoking, indeed emphasizing, the Deity. On the other hand, focusing on the text of the Commandments alone cannot conclusively resolve this case. Rather, to determine the message that the text here conveys, we must examine how the text is *used.* And that inquiry requires us to consider the context of the display.

In certain contexts, a display of the tablets of the Ten Commandments can convey not simply a religious message but also a secular moral message (about proper standards of social conduct). And in certain contexts, a display of the tablets can also convey a historical message (about a historic relation between those standards and the law)—a fact that helps to explain the display of those tablets in dozens of courthouses throughout the Nation, including the Supreme Court of the United States. . . .

Here the tablets have been used as part of a display that communicates not simply a religious message, but a secular message as well. The circumstances surrounding the display's placement on the capitol grounds and its physical setting suggest that the State itself intended the latter, nonreligious aspects of the tablets' message to predominate. And the monument's 40-year history on the Texas state grounds indicates that that has been its effect.

The group that donated the monument, the Fraternal Order of Eagles, a private civic (and primarily secular) organization, while interested in the religious aspect of the Ten Commandments, sought to highlight the Commandments' role in shaping civic morality as part of that organization's efforts to combat juvenile delinquency. . . . The Eagles' consultation with a committee composed of members of several faiths in order to find a nonsectarian text underscores the group's ethics-based motives. . . . The tablets, as displayed on the monument, prominently acknowledge that the Eagles donated the display, a factor which, though not sufficient, thereby further distances the State itself from the religious aspect of the Commandments' message.

The physical setting of the monument, moreover, suggests little or nothing of the sacred. . . . The setting does not readily lend itself to meditation or any other religious activity. But it does provide a context of history and moral ideals. It (together with the display's inscription about its origin) communicates to visitors that the State sought to reflect moral principles, illustrating a relation between ethics and law that the State's citizens, historically speaking, have endorsed. That is to say, the context suggests that the State intended the display's moral message—an illustrative message reflecting the historical "ideals" of Texans—to predominate.

If these factors provide a strong, but not conclusive, indication that the Commandments' text on this monument conveys a predominantly secular message, a further factor is determinative here. As far as I can tell, 40 years passed in which the presence of this monument, legally speaking, went unchallenged (until the single legal objection raised by petitioner). And I am not aware of any evidence suggesting that this was due to a climate of intimidation. Hence, those 40 years suggest more strongly than can any set of formulaic tests that few individuals, whatever their system of beliefs, are likely to have understood the monument as amounting, in any significantly detrimental way, to a government effort to favor a particular religious sect, primarily to promote religion over nonreligion, to "engage in" any "religious practic[e]," to "compel" any "religious practic[e]," or to "work deterrence" of any "religious belief." *Schempp* (Goldberg, J., concurring). Those 40 years suggest that the public visiting the capitol grounds has considered the religious aspect of the tablets' message as part of what is a broader moral and historical message reflective of a cultural heritage.

This case, moreover, is distinguishable from instances where the Court has found Ten Commandments displays impermissible. The display is not on the grounds of a public school, where, given the impressionability of the young, government must exercise particular care in separating church and state. . . . This case also differs from *McCreary County*, where the short (and stormy) history of the courthouse Commandments' displays demonstrates the substantially religious objectives of those who mounted them, and the effect of this readily apparent objective upon those who view them. . . . That history there indicates a governmental effort substantially to promote religion, not simply an effort primarily to reflect, historically, the secular impact of a religiously inspired document. And, in today's world, in a Nation of so many different religious and comparable nonreligious fundamental beliefs, a more contemporary state effort to focus attention upon a religious text is certainly likely to prove divisive in a way that this longstanding, pre-existing monument has not.

For these reasons, I believe that the Texas display—serving a mixed but primarily nonreligious purpose, not primarily "advanc[ing]" or "inhibit[ing] religion," and not creating an "excessive government entanglement with religion"—might satisfy this Court's more formal Establishment Clause tests. . . . But, as I have said, in reaching the conclusion that the Texas display falls on the permissible side of the constitutional line, I rely less upon a literal application of any particular test than upon consideration of the basic purposes of the First Amendment's Religion Clauses themselves. This display has stood apparently uncontested for nearly two generations. That experience helps us understand that as a practical matter of *degree* this display is unlikely to prove divisive. And this matter of degree is, I believe, critical in a borderline case such as this one.

At the same time, to reach a contrary conclusion here, based primarily on the religious nature of the tablets' text would, I fear, lead the law to exhibit a hostility toward religion that has no place in our Establishment Clause traditions. . . .

I recognize the danger of the slippery slope. Still, where the Establishment Clause is at issue, we must "distinguish between real threat and mere shadow." Here, we have only the shadow. . . .

I concur in the judgment of the Court.

COMMENTS AND QUESTIONS

1. How would you characterize the guidance provided by Justice Breyer's concurring opinion with respect to future cases involving religious displays on public property?
2. "The late Krister Stendahl, emeritus Lutheran Bishop of Stockholm and professor emeritus of Harvard Divinity School, established three rules for religious understanding: (1) When you are trying to understand another

religion, you should ask the adherents of that religion and not its enemies; (2) don't compare your best to their worst; and (3) leave room for 'holy envy' by finding elements in other faiths to emulate. These principles foster relationships between religions that build trust and lay the groundwork for charitable efforts."[32]

NOTE ON *PLEASANT GROVE CITY, UTAH V. SUMMUM*

Supreme Court of the United States, 555 U.S. 460 (2009)

In *Pleasant Grove City, Utah v. Summum* the Supreme Court held that a religious group was not entitled to erect a religious monument in a public park where a Ten Commandments monument already stood. The Ten Commandments monument had been donated in 1971 by the Fraternal Order of the Eagles. Other permanent displays in the public park, most of them donated, included a September 11 monument, an historic granary, and the city's first fire station. On three occasions the president of Summum, a religious organization, requested permission to erect a stone monument of "the Seven Aphorisms of SUMMUM." The city denied each request, explaining that its laws limited monuments in the park to those that "either (1) directly relate to the history of Pleasant Grove, or (2) were donated by groups with longstanding ties to the Pleasant Grove community." Summum then brought an action claiming that the city had "violated the Free Speech Clause of the First Amendment by accepting the Ten Commandments monument but rejecting the proposed Seven Aphorisms monument." The Court held that the city's decision was "best viewed as a form of government speech and . . . therefore not subject to scrutiny under the Free Speech Clause." Justice Alito, writing for the Court, explained,

> Public parks are often closely identified in the public mind with the government unit that owns the land. City parks . . . commonly play an important role in defining the identity that a city projects to its own residents and to the outside world. . . . Government decisionmakers select the monuments that portray what they view as appropriate for the place in question, taking into account such content-based factors as esthetics, history, and local culture. The monuments that are accepted, therefore, are meant to convey and have the effect of conveying a government message, and they thus constitute government speech. (474)

In addition, the Court held that public forum principles did not apply to the case:

> The forum doctrine has been applied in situations in which government-owned property or a government program was capable of accommodating a large number of public speakers without defeating the essential function of the land or the program. For example, a park can accommodate many speakers and, over time, many parades and demonstrations. . . . By contrast, public parks can accommodate only a limited number of permanent monuments. . . . If government entities must maintain viewpoint neutrality in their selection of donated monuments, they must either "brace themselves for an influx of clutter" or face the pressure to remove longstanding and cherished monuments. . . . The obvious truth of the matter is that if public parks were considered to be traditional public forums for the purpose of erecting privately donated

---

32. Respect for Diversity of Faiths, *Mormon Newsroom*, 18 April 2008, at http://www.mormonnewsroom.org/ article/respect-for-diversity-of-faiths.

monuments, most parks would have little choice but to refuse all such donations. And where the application of forum analysis would lead almost inexorably to closing of the forum, it is obvious that forum analysis is out of place. (478-480)

B. EUROPE

NOTE ON THE SWISS MINARET BAN

A minaret is tall, slender architectural feature attached or proximate to a mosque, traditionally providing one or more projecting galleries from which a muezzin could issue the five-times-daily Muslim calls to prayer. In modern times this call has been amplified by loudspeakers to be heard clearly over distances. The minaret was not a part of the earliest mosques, but it has over many centuries become a symbolic as much as a practical structure.

The Swiss Constitution can be amended by federal popular initiative, and in 2009, a popular referendum resulted in Article 72, paragraph 3: "The building of minarets is prohibited." The Swiss government opposed the ban as being out of harmony with constitutional principles, but it could not override the will of 57.5% of the participating voters. Swiss courts rejected the argument that the amendment was unlawful, and Muslim individuals and groups brought the matter to the European Court of Human Rights. In *Ouardiri v. Switzerland,* App. No. 65840/09 (28 April 2011) and *Ligue des Musulmans de Suisse and Others v. Switzerland,* App. No. 66274/09 (28 April 2011), the Court ruled that petitions challenging the mosque were inadmissible for the parties' lack of standing: only those who were actively planning to build a minaret could challenge the law.

NOTE ON THE PUBLIC DISPLAY OF CROSSES IN BAVARIA

In a highly controversial move that took effect on 1 June 2018, Markus Söder, the premier of the southern German state of Bavaria, unveiled a new regulation providing that "a clearly visible cross must be placed in the entrance area of every service building to serve as a reminder of the historical and cultural influence of Bavaria."[33] The "directive applies only to buildings housing agencies of the state of Bavaria—not to local district buildings or federal buildings, over which his government has no authority—though it does apply to all school classrooms and courts."[34]

Most observers understood this move and its support as pushback against the 2015 influx of some one million immigrants into Germany, most of them Muslim, and most entering through Bavaria. Söder defended the move as "clear signal that people have a desire to stress their identity,"[35] and insisted that the cross was a

33. Germany: Bavaria's Controversial Cross Rule Goes into Effect, *Deutsche Welle,* 31 May 2018).

34. *See* German State Orders Crosses Mounted in Government Buildings, *Deutsche Welle*, 25 April 2018.

35. *See* Kate Connolly, Bavarians Wary of New Law Requiring Crosses in All Public Buildings, *The Guardian*, 31 May 2018.

"clear avowal of our Bavarian identity and Christian values"[36]—a cultural not religious identity—in a state where some 50 percent of the population (down from 70 percent in the 1970s) identify as Catholic and Christian symbols are traditionally prominent in public places. An early poll showed that though only 29 percent of citizens across Germany supported the ruling, 56 percent of Bavarians supported it. Söder, himself a Protestant, claimed support from the Vatican,[37] but many Christian leaders, Catholic and Protestant, opposed the move, insisting for example that it effectively reduces a sacred symbol to a "folkloric object and regional custom."[38] Cardinal Reinhard Marx, head of the German Bishops' Conference, objected to "expropriating the cross in the name of the state." [39]

Insisting the cross is not a sign of religion but of identity and culture, Mr. Söder sees its display as no violation of the principle of neutrality by state authorities. His argument echoes the controversial ruling by the European Court of Human Rights in 2011 in *Lautsi v. Italy* [see discussion in Chapter 13], which found that a publicly displayed cross was "a passive symbol," not a form of "indoctrination," and thus something European countries could allow according to their history and tradition.

Germany, after a high court ruling in 1995, has generally followed a rule that crosses can be displayed, unless someone is offended enough to challenge their presence. That rarely happens.[40]

COMMENTS AND QUESTIONS

1. What do you think is the rule regarding public displays such as the Ten Commandments after the *McCreary County* and *Van Orden* cases? Justice Breyer was the swing vote in these cases. Does his concurring opinion help answer this question? Does Justice Breyer's analysis protect only established majoritarian monuments? Is it likely that a smaller group such as Summum would push for a monument without religious or ideological intent?
2. In a country such as Italy, is there a difference between contexts—schools, hospitals, courtrooms—that leads to the possibility of different answers to the question whether the crucifix should be permitted? Does it make sense to interpret the crucifix as a symbol of national unity, or does this sacrifice too much of the religious meaning of that icon?
3. Consider various places where a cross or crucifix might be located in public space: parks, public cemeteries, courtrooms, classrooms, and so on. How would you describe the principle(s) that would govern where such symbols should or should not be permitted in public space?

---

36. *See* Germany: Catholic Cardinal Rebukes Bavaria for Ordering Crosses in State Buildings, *Deutsche Welle*, 4 April 2018.

37. *See*, for example, Jane Dalton, Vatican 'Supports' Compulsory Crosses in Bavarian Public Buildings, State's Prime Minister Says, *Independent*, 2 June 2018.

38. Connolly, *supra* note 35.

39. *See* Catholic Cardinal Rebukes Barvaria, *supra* note 36.

40. Katrin Bennhold, Crosses Go Up in Public Offices. It's Culture, Bavaria Says, Not Religion, *The New York Times*, 30 May 2018.

4. Compare and contrast the approaches to public religious symbols in the United States, Italy, Germany, and France. Which of these, if any, represents the best available option?

V. CONCLUSION

The tensions and the synergies created by the intersection of law and religion pervade every area of life, from the inner sanctum of the *forum internum* through the myriad forms of manifestation of religion, on through an array of possible social settings and institutional configurations, and extending finally into symbolic interactions in public and private space. Contrary to the predictions of those who once proclaimed the inevitability of the withering away of religion, the early years of the twenty-first century are already witness to the significant and growing role of religious life in an increasingly pluralistic world. The challenge is to find optimal protections for the fragile yet adamantine dignity of conscience, in all its forms and with all that it adds to human life, and at the same time to guard against the indignities too often perpetrated in its name. This challenge does not yield to simple or simplistic solutions, but calls for determined mining, refining, and enhancing of the often less than perfect solutions that have filled the pages of this book. Only in the fruits of such striving can we hope to attain enduring solutions and to see what a modern Madison might have called "the luster" of our countries.

TABLE OF CASES

Principal cases are in italics. Non-US cases are indicated with country of origin or court in parentheses. Case names in brackets are full names of cases referenced in a short form only in the text. Note that in jurisdictions where cases are identified by numbers rather than by names of parties, a descriptive case name is used. A page number followed by an "n" and a second number (e.g. 427n11) indicates a footnote on the given page.

INDEX

Note: Page numbers followed by an "n" and a second number refer to a designated note on the indicated page. For example, "427n11" is a reference to note 11 on page 427.